After the Storm

Produced in cooperation with the
Royal United Services Institute for Defence Studies

The Royal United Services Institute for Defence Studies (RUSI) is a professional and independent body, based in London, dedicated to the study, analysis, and debate of issues affecting international security.

Founded in 1831 by the Duke of Wellington, the RUSI is one of the most senior institutes of its kind in the world that, throughout its history, has been at the forefront of contemporary political-military thinking through debates, public and private seminars, studies and briefings, conferences, lectures, and a wide range of publications.

After the Storm

The Changing Military Balance
in the Middle East

Anthony H. Cordesman

Westview Press

BOULDER AND SAN FRANCISCO

LONDON

MANSELL

Copyright © 1993 by Anthony H. Cordesman

Published in 1993 in the United States of America by Westview Press, Inc., 5500 Central Avenue, Boulder, Colorado 80301-2877

Published in 1993 in Great Britain by Mansell Publishing Limited, *A Cassell Imprint*, Villiers House, 41-47 Strand, London WC2N 5JE, England

Library of Congress Cataloging-in-Publication Data
Cordesman, Anthony H.
  After the storm : the changing military balance in the Middle East
/ Anthony H. Cordesman.
    p. cm.
  Includes bibliographical references and index.
  ISBN 0-8133-1692-8
  1. Middle East—Armed Forces. I. Title.
UA832.C66 1993
355'.033056—dc20   92-39744
                                                                CIP

A CIP catalogue record for this book is available from the British Library.
ISBN 0-7201-2157-4

Printed and bound in the United States of America

 The paper used in this publication meets the requirements
of the American National Standard for Permanence of Paper
for Printed Library Materials Z39.48-1984.

10 9 8 7 6 5 4 3 2 1

To Peter Jennings, Ted Koppel,
David Brinkley, and Roone Arledge,
for the most unexpected career change of a lifetime

Contents

Tables and Maps

Maps

Acronyms

AA	anti-aircraft
AC&W	air control and warning
ACDA	Arms Control and Disarmament Agency
ADOC	air defense operations center
AEW	airborne early warning
AIFV	armored infantry fighting vehicle
ALN	Armée de Libération Nationale
AMRAAM	advanced medium range air-to-air missile
ANP	National Popular Army
AOI	Arab Organization for Industry
APC	armored personnel carrier
ASW	anti-submarine warfare
ATBM	anti-tactical ballistic missile
ATGM	anti-tank guided missile launcher
BM	battle management
BVR	beyond visual range
C^3I	command, control, communications, and intelligence
CENTO	Central Treaty Organization
CEP	circular error probable
CIA	Central Intelligence Agency
CIS	Commonwealth of Independent States
COC	command operations center
COIN	counterinsurgency
COMINT	communications intelligence
CRC	control and reporting center
CRS	Congressional Research Service
DFLP	Democratic Front for the Liberation of Palestine
DIA	Defense Intelligence Agency
DLF	Dhofar Liberation Front
DPIK	Democratic Party of Iranian Kurdistan
EDF	Eritrean Democratic Front
ELF	Eritrean Liberation Front
ELINT	electronic intelligence
EMIS	electro-magnetic isotope separation

EPDM	Ethiopian People's Democratic Movement
EPLF	Eritrean People's Liberation Front
EPRDF	Ethiopian People's Revolutionary Democratic Front
EPRP	Ethiopian People's Revolutionary Party
ESM	electronic support measures

FAC	fast attack craft
FAE	fuel-air explosive
FAN	Conseil des Forces Armées du Nord
FFC	Field Forces Command
FGA	fighter–ground attack
FIS	Islamic Salvation Front
FLIR	forward looking infrared
FLN	Front de Libération Nationale
FLOSY	Front for the Liberation of Occupied South Yemen
FMS	foreign military sales
FRC	Fatah Revolutionary Council
FROLINT	Front de Libération Nationale de Tchad
FRUD	Front for the Restoration of Unity and Democracy

GCC	Gulf Cooperation Council
GDP	gross domestic product
GNP	gross national product
GPS	global positioning system
GRPA	Provisional Government of the Algerian Republic

HE	high explosive
HMMWV	high mobility multipurpose wheeled vehicle
HMX	high melting point explosive

IAEA	International Atomic Energy Agency
IAF	Israeli Air Force
IAI	Israeli Aircraft Industries
ICBM	intercontinental ballistic missile
IDF	Israeli Defense Forces
IDS	interdictor-strike
IFF	identification of friend or foe
IISS	International Institute of Strategic Studies
IMF	International Monetary Fund
INS	inertial navigation system
IOC	intercept operations center
IR	infrared
IRA	Irish Republican Army
IRBM	intermediate range ballistic missile
IRGC	Iranian Revolutionary Guard Corps
IUM	Islamic Unification Movement

| JTIDS | joint tactical information distribution system |

KDP	Kurdish Democratic Party
LAV	light armored vehicle
LAW	light anti-tank weapons
LCP	landing craft–personnel
LCT	landing craft–tank
LDC	less developed country
LIS	laser isotope separation
LSL	landing ship logistic
LSM	landing ship medium
MAP	Military Assistance Program
MCMV	mine countermeasure vessel
MLRS	multiple launch rocket system
MNF	multinational force
MOU	memorandums of understanding
MRL	multiple rocket launcher
MSIP	multistage improvement program
MTCR	Missile Technology Control Regime
NADGE	NATO Air Defense Ground Environment
NATO	North Atlantic Treaty Organization
NBC	nuclear-biological-chemical
NCO	noncommissioned officer
NDF	National Democratic Front
NLA	National Liberation Army
NLF	National Liberation Front
NPT	nonproliferation treaty
O&M	operations and maintenance
OAFV	other armored fighting vehicle
OAS	Secret Army Organization
OAU	Organization of African Unity
OAV	other armored vehicle
OLF	Oromo Liberation Front
OPDO	Oromo People's Democratic Organization
PCG	patrol-chaser guided missile
PDRY	People's Democratic Republic of Yemen
PFLOAG	Popular Front for the Liberation of Oman
PFLP	Popular Front for the Liberation of Palestine
PFLP-GC	PFLP–General Command
PGC	People's General Conference
PGG	patrol gunboat guided missile
PHOTINT	photo intelligence
PKK	Partiya Kartkeen Kurdistan

PLA	Palestine Liberation Army
PLF	Popular Liberation Front
PLO	Palestine Liberation Organization
PNC	Palestine National Council *
PSF	Palestine Struggle Front

RAF	Royal Air Force
RCC	Revolutionary Command Council
RCD	Constitutional Democratic Rally
RDX	rapid detonation explosive
RGFC	Republican Guard Forces Command
RPV	remotely piloted vehicle

SADR	Sahraoui Arab Democratic Republic
SAM	surface-to-air missile
SAMA	Saudi Arabian Monetary Authority
SANU	Sudan African National Union
SAS	Special Air Service
SCC	sector command center
SDI	Strategic Defense Initiative
SIGINT	signals intelligence
SIPRI	Stockholm International Peace Research Institute
SIRI	Supreme Islamic Revolution in Iraq
SLA	South Lebanon Army
SLAR	side looking aircraft radar
SNM	Somali National Movement
SOC	sector operations center
SPLA	Sudanese People's Liberation Army
SPM	Somali Patriotic Movement
SSDF	Somali Salvation Democratic Front

TACOM	U.S. Army Tank Automotive Command
TEL	transporter-erector-launcher
THAAD	theater high-altitude area defense
TPLF	Tigre People's Liberation Front

UAV	unmanned airborne vehicle
UNIFIL	UN Interim Forces in Lebanon
UNOSOM	UN Operation in Somalia
UNRWA	UN Relief and Works Agency
USAF	U.S. Air Force
USC	United Somali Congress
USCENTCOM	U.S. Central Command

YAR	Yemen Arab Republic
YSP	Yemen Socialist Party

1

Weighing the Military Balance in the Middle East

The Middle East, like much of the Third World, has been the scene of nearly constant conflict since the end of World War II. Some of these conflicts have been brief and intense. Others have been long and agonizing. All have been tragic in the sense that they have wasted human lives and resources that the region desperately needs for its economic development. The grim history of these conflicts is both a memento mori and a warning of what may happen in the future.

The Gulf War has dramatized these risks to nations outside the region, showing that local struggles can rapidly escalate to involve most of the world, that risks are inherent in massive transfers of modern arms, and that the risks of long range missile attacks and the use of weapons of mass destruction can escalate to involve the West. It has left no doubts that future conflicts in the Middle East can be even bloodier and more dangerous to both the region and the rest of the world.

The Gulf War has not, however, reinvented history. Like all the other wars in the region, it has left a strategic aftermath similar to the situation that preceded it. The key security problems in the Gulf are still shaped by the Iranian-Iraqi rivalry, the threat Iran and Iraq pose to the weaker oil rich nations in the southern Gulf, and the risk that the race for arms and weapons of mass destruction will explode into a new war that threatens the world's oil imports and populations inside and outside of the Gulf. The Gulf War has not catalyzed the Arab-Israeli confrontation states to resolve their conflict or stop their arms race, and it has not affected the tensions and conflicts in the Maghreb or the Red Sea.

In fact, there was never any real prospect that the Gulf War would lead to a new order in the Middle East, much less the world. The Middle East is not shaped by one conflict and cannot be treated as a homogeneous region that sweeps from "Marrakech to Bangladesh." It is a mixture of many different regions and nations. Though many of these nations share a common religion and language, they have very different interests and needs, and most are ethnically divided. A Jewish Israel and Persian Iran are the only exceptions to the cultural disunity of the Middle East. Islam divides as well as unifies, and the word "Arab" does not describe a common race, a common set of political attitudes, or a common set of needs.

These differences are reflected in the conflicts that shape the region from Morocco to the Indian Ocean.[1] Virtually every nation in this region has been involved in some form of enduring internal and external conflict:

- Morocco, Mauritania, and Algeria have been involved in border wars and the complex political struggle for control over the destiny of the Spanish Sahara, which has lasted well over a decade. In spite of various peace efforts, Morocco remains at war with the Polisario—a movement which claims to represent the citizens of the Spanish Sahara.
- The ambitions of Libya's leader, Col. Muammar Qadhafi, have sustained an arms race throughout the Maghreb that has affected many nations outside it. Libya has played a spoiler role in most of the conflicts in the Middle East, has fought a series of wars with various factions in Chad, and has attempted to intervene in several other sub-Saharan nations.
- Egypt has become the "hinge" of the Middle East. It must live with sustained tension with Libya and continue to maintain its defenses against Israel. Egypt also played a significant role in the Gulf War and has become increasingly involved in the problems of the Sudan and other Red Sea and African neighbors.
- The Arab-Israeli conflict is now largely a struggle among Israel, Syria, and the Palestinians, but it also forces Jordan and Lebanon to play the role of frontline states and involves other Arab states in its politics. Although peace negotiations have begun, it is not clear that these can succeed in ending the Palestinian uprising on the West Bank and Gaza. The impact of Jordan and the alignment of the Palestine Liberation Organization (PLO) with Iraq during the Gulf War must still be overcome. A new round of fighting between Israel and Syria or a war of attrition between Israeli Jews and the Arabs in the occupied territories is as likely as a stable peace.
- There are splits within the PLO and other Palestinian factions outside the occupied territories, splits within the factions inside the West Bank and Gaza, and divisions between those Palestinians who support the secular PLO and those who support the fundamentalists.
- Lebanon seems to be slowly emerging from nearly two decades of civil war between various Christian, Druze, Sunni, and Shi'ite factions. Although much of the country has come under central government control since Syria's defeat of General Michel Aoun in the fall of 1990, some elements of the Lebanese civil war continue. Lebanon is still occupied by Syrian forces, and an Israeli backed enclave has virtual autonomy in the south.
- Syria continues to expand its forces in spite of massive economic problems and the loss of much of its Soviet support. In addition to its conflict with Israel, it has been a constant rival of Iraq, an occasional rival of Jordan, and has supported outside movements such as the Kurdish independence movement in Turkey.
- Iraq is still under the control of Saddam Hussein and the Ba'ath Party, but many Shi'ites in the south and most Kurds in the north do support the

central government. Iraq is backing anti-Turkish Kurdish groups and anti-Iranian forces like the People's Mujahideen. At the same time, it is clear that Saddam Hussein is seeking to break out of the isolation enforced by the UN embargo and that Iraq may lapse into revanchism against the nations that defeated it in the Gulf War, even if Saddam Hussein does fall from power.

- Iran is rearming and continuing to acquire weapons of mass destruction. Its government seems far more pragmatic under President Ali Akbar Hashemi Rafsanjani and the Ayatollah Khameni than it did under Khomeini, but this is far from saying that it can live in stability with its southern Gulf neighbors and the West. Iran's Islamic fundamentalists are still active in Lebanon and are playing a growing role in the Sudan and other Arab countries. At the same time, Iran is playing its own game with Iraq's Kurds and is backing anti-Baath Shi'ites in southern Iraq.
- While neither Iran nor Iraq now poses an immediate threat to its southern Gulf neighbors, both continue to seek arms and weapons of mass destruction and may well go back to war with each other.
- The southern Gulf states have created a regional alliance called the Gulf Cooperation Council (GCC) and have attempted to strengthen their armed forces. However, the apparent unity of the GCC disguises rivalries between Bahrain and Qatar, between Saudi Arabia and Oman, between the key sheiks of the UAE, and between Saudi Arabia and Yemen. The GCC states have also failed to work out effective collective or individual arrangements with the U.S., Egypt, and/or Syria that provide for power projection forces that can defend them in an emergency.
- North and South Yemen have unified, ending decades of mutual rivalry. The new Yemen, however, is involved in a simmering conflict over the demarcation of its borders with Saudi Arabia and Oman. There are continuing border clashes between Yemen and Saudi Arabia, and Yemen and Oman still deploy much of their military strength along their common border.
- The Sudan is involved in a protracted civil war between the Muslim north and the Christian and animist south, a war in which Egypt, Iran, Libya, and several Gulf nations play an indirect role.
- The long civil war in Ethiopia between the regime of Mengistu Haile-Mariam in the south and Arab-backed Muslim groups in the north ended in 1991. The country is now governed by the Ethiopian People's Revolutionary Democratic Front (EPRDF), the Eritrean People's Liberation Front (EPLF), the Oromo People's Democratic Organization, and other smaller groups. It is far from clear, however, that the result will be order and stability, and new civil conflicts may soon arise. Ethiopia remains involved in a low level struggle with Somalia for control of their common border area.
- The civil war in Somalia between its northern and central tribal factions ended with the defeat of the Siad Barre government in 1991, but Somalia is now divided between regions controlled by the Somali National Movement in the north and the United Somali Congress in the south. It no longer has unified armed forces, and a state of civil war exists in much of the country.

Any understanding of the military balance in the Middle East, of arms transfers, of proliferation, and of outside security interests must be founded upon an understanding of the diversity of the forces at work. There are broad patterns in the military forces in the Middle East, but the differences between sub-regions and nations are often more important than the similarities. Any efforts to resolve the conflicts in the region, to develop effective forms of arms control, and/or to create a more stable military balance must be founded on an understanding that the Middle East is composed of sovereign nations with sovereign interests and that the military relations among these individual nations shape the prospects for future peace or future conflict.

The Casualty Effect

Table 1.1 provides more tangible evidence of the national character of the military balance in the Middle East and of the impact of the resulting conflicts. It shows that there have been shooting wars somewhere in the Middle East since 1945. Many have been small border wars or minor clashes which have gone virtually unrecorded. The present border war between Saudi Arabia and Yemen is a case in point. Some have been very intense high technology conflicts like the 1967, 1973, and 1982 Arab-Israeli conflicts; the Iran-Iraq War of 1980–1988; and the Gulf War of 1990–1991. Others have involved protracted low technology conflicts, for independence or between ethnic groups like those in North Africa and the Red Sea area—many of which have been extraordinarily bloody.

A close reading of Table 1.1 provides several other insights into the problem of arms sales to the Middle East:

- *The pattern of conflicts within given nations and sub-regions varies sharply over time, and low level conflicts often shift without warning into major struggles.* It is almost a cliché to say that war is not predictable in terms of its timing, duration, and intensity. Table 1.1 is, however, a warning regarding the illusion of new world orders. The events immediately following the Gulf War can scarcely be characterized as peaceful and tranquil, but they do reflect a pause in some aspects of the Middle East arms race. The military forces of Iran and Iraq have been decimated by the Iran-Iraq War and Gulf War, and the southern Gulf states are limited in their arms purchases by the cost of purchases made during 1990 and 1991 and aid to the UN coalition. The Red Sea states are financially exhausted by civil war, and many have lost most of their regular forces to rebel groups; the Arab-Israeli arms race has been tempered by the economic problems of the major confrontation states; and the arms race in North Africa has enjoyed a temporary hiatus. These shifts, however, are the result of coincidence, not of fundamental shifts in history, and a new escalation of the region's arms races is all too possible.
- *There has been only a limited correlation between the volume of arms imports and cost of given conflicts.* Casualties are more the product of political conditions

TABLE 1.1 Military Conflicts in the Middle East: A Post–World War II Summary[a]

Country and Conflict		War Related Deaths[b]		
		Civilian	Military	Total
North Africa and Maghreb				
Mauritania				
1974	Western Sahara war with Polisario		1,000	1,000
Algeria				
1954–1962	Independence war with France	82,000	17,100	99,100
1962	Tindouf clash with Morocco			
1963	Internal civil conflict	1,000	1,000	2,000
1963	War with Morocco over Hassi-Beida and Tindouf		100	100
Morocco				
1948	Tetuan demonstration against Spain			
1948	Oujda anti-Jewish riots	5		5
1953–1956	Civil conflict with France and Spain	3,000	0	3,000
1962	Tindouf clash with Algeria			
1963	War with Algeria over Hassi-Beida and Tindouf		100	100
1974–1991	Western Sahara war with Polisario	5,000	14,000	19,000
Chad				
1966	Wadi rebellion (north-south conflict)	400	10	410
1968–1972	Civil war	1,500	100	1,600
1978–1982	Civil war	1,000	700	1,700
1982	Lake Chad skirmishes with Nigeria			
1983–1987	Libyan-Chadian war	500	700	1,200
1988–1991	Low level civil conflict	300	200	500
Libya				
1945	Anti-Jewish riots in Tripoli	100		100
1948	Anti-Jewish riots in Tripoli	10		10
1949	Riots against U.S. air bases	15		15
1977	Border clash with Egypt		30	30
1983–1987	Libyan-Chadian war	500	2,000	2,500
1984	Clash over Tunisian based rebels		50	50
1986	U.S. raids on Libya	10	90	100
Tunisia				
1952–1956	Ben Youssef conflict with France	3,000		3,000
1984	Clash with Libya over Tunisian-based rebels	100		100
1985	Israeli Bori Cedra raid on PLO	3	50	53
North Africa Subtotal		98,443	35,430	135,673
Arab-Israeli Conflicts				
Egypt				
1948	War with Israel		2,000	2,000
1953	Suez riots with Britain	100	20	120
1956	Suez conflict with Israel, Britain, and France	1,000	3,000	4,000
1961–1967	North Yemen civil war and clashes with Saudi Arabia		1,000	1,000
1967	Six-day War	200	8,500	8,700
1967–1970	Canal war/war of attrition with Israel	50	2,000	2,050
1973	War with Israel	50	5,000	5,050
1977	Border clash with Libya		50	50
1991	War to liberate Kuwait		9	9

(continues)

TABLE 1.1 (*continued*)

Country and Conflict		War Related Deaths[b]		
		Civilian	Military	Total
Israel				
1945–1949	War with Arabs	2,500	10,200	12,700
1950	Rafah incident in Gaza	3		3
1951	Tel Mutillah clash with Syria near Galilee		30	30
1954–1955	Lake Kinneret conflict with Syria		6	6
1956	Qalqilya raid and border clashes with Jordan		40	40
1956	War with Egypt		230	230
1957–1958	Border clashes with Syria			
1962	Second Lake Kinneret clash with Syria		5	5
1965	Raids on Huleh and Meiss al Jabal/PLO raids on Israel	5	5	10
1967	War with Egypt, Jordan, Syria		800	800
1967–1970	Canal war/war of attrition with Egypt		500	500
1972–1973	Golan clashes with Syria			
1973	War with Egypt, Syria, and Iraq	5	3,000	3,005
1975–1981	Intervention in Lebanese civil war		50	50
1981	Osiraq raid on Iraq			
1982–1984	Lebanese war with Syria and PLO		800	800
1988–1991	Palestinian uprising			
1991	Iraqi Scud attacks on Israel	13		13
Syria				
1948	War with Israel		1,000	1,000
1951	Tel Mutillah clash with Israel near Galilee		50	50
1954–1955	Lake Kinneret conflict with Israel		25	25
1957–1958	Border clashes with Israel			
1959	UAR clashes with Jordan			
1962	Second Lake Kinneret clash with Israel		30	30
1963	UAR coup, clash with Lebanon		30	30
1967	War with Israel	20	700	720
1970	Clash with Jordan over PLO		200	200
1972–1973	Golan clashes with Israel		20	20
1973	War with Israel		3,000	3,000
1975–1981	Intervention in Lebanese civil war		2,000	2,000
1982	Lebanese war with Israel		1,000	1,000
1982	Government vs. Islamic movements	20,000	200	20,200
Jordan				
1948	War with Israel	200	1,000	1,200
1956	Qalqilya raid and border clashes with Israel		100	100
1959	UAR clashes with Syria			
1967	War with Israel	250	2,000	2,250
1967–1970	War of attrition with Israel		200	200
1973	War with Israel, but outside Jordan		28	28
1970–1971	Government vs. PLO	2,000	100	2,100
Lebanon				
1948	War with Israel		2,000	2,000
1949	Saadeh's rebellion	100	20	120
1958	Civil war and U.S. intervention	1,000	300	1,300
1963	UAR coup in Syria, clash with Lebanon		5	5
1965	Israeli raids on Huleh and Meiss al Jabal/PLO raids on Israel	20	30	50
1968–1975	Low level civil war, entry of PLO	2,000	250	2,250
1975–1981	Civil war and Syrian intervention	60,000	15,000	75,000
1982–1991	Israeli invasion, U.S. intervention, civil war, Syrian intervention	20,000	8,000	28,000
Arab-Israeli Subtotal		109,516	74,533	184,249

(continues)

TABLE 1.1 (*continued*)

Country and Conflict		Civilian	Military	Total
		\multicolumn{3}{c}{War Related Deaths[b]}		

Country and Conflict	Civilian	Military	Total
Gulf Region			
Iran			
1945–1946 Azerbaijani succession, UK vs. USSR confrontation	500		500
1948 War with Israel		200	200
1971 Tunb Island seizure from UAE			
1972–1975 Shatt al Arab conflict with Iraq	1,000	100	1,100
1978–1989 Upheavals leading to shah's fall, civil and ethnic conflict	70,000	18,000	88,000
1980–1988 War with Iraq	80,000	220,000	300,000
Iraq			
1959 Civil war between Shammar tribe and government (Mosul rebellion)	1,000	1,000	2,000
1961–1975 Kurds vs. government	70,000	6,000	76,000
1973 Sametah seizure of part of Kuwait		2	2
1973 War with Israel		218	218
1980–1988 War against Iran	15,000	125,000	140,000
1981 Osirak raid by Israel	10		10
1983–1987 Turkish raids on Kurds in Iraq	300	500	800
1988–1989 Kurds vs. government	9,000	1,000	10,000
1990–1991 War against UN coalition	3,000	30,000	33,000
1991 Kurds and Shiites vs. government	14,500	1,000	15,500
Bahrain			
1986 Clash with Qatar over Al-Dibal reef			
1991 War with Iraq to liberate Kuwait			
1991 Clash with Qatar over Al-Dibal reef			
Kuwait			
1973 Iraq seizes Sametah post in border area			
1990–1991 Iraqi invasion and liberation	3,000	600	3,600
1991 Internal struggles with Palestinians	300		300
Oman			
1955 Burami Oasis crisis with Saudis	2	5	7
1957–1959 Imam's rebellion	200	450	650
1961–1967 Omani civil war and clashes with South Yemen			
1970–1977 Dhofar rebellion, clashes with Yemen	2,500	1,000	3,500
1991 War with Iraq to liberate Kuwait			
Qatar			
1986 Clash with Bahrain over Al-Dibal reef			
1991 War with Iraq to liberate Kuwait			
1991 Clash with Bahrain over Al-Dibal reef			
Saudi Arabia			
1955 Burami Oasis crisis with Oman		5	5
1961–1967 North Yemen civil war and clashes with South Yemen, Saudi Arabia		1,000	1,000
1967–1970 Najran air raids in support of Royalists			
1973 Al-Wadiah border clash with South Yemen			
1988–1991 Border clashes with Yemens		300	300
1991 War with Iraq to liberate Kuwait		44	44
United Arab Emirates			
1955 Burami Oasis crisis with Saudi Arabia			
1991 War with Iraq to liberate Kuwait		8	8
Gulf Subtotal	270,312	406,432	676,744

(*continues*)

TABLE 1.1 (*continued*)

Country and Conflict		War Related Deaths[b]		
		Civilian	Military	Total
Red Sea Area				
Yemens				
1947	Aden riots	122		122
1947–1950	Independence clashes with UK	150	5	155
1953–1959	South Arabian revolt	250	80	330
1961–1967	North Yemen civil war and clashes with Egypt, South Yemen, Saudi Arabia	50,000		50,000
1967–1970	Saudi Najran air raids in support of Royalists			
1973	Al-Wadiah border clash with Saudi Arabia			
1970–1977	Dhofar rebellion, clashes with Oman	50	100	150
1979	Border clash between North and South Yemen	30	40	70
1988–1991	Border clashes with Saudi Arabia		300	300
Djibouti				
1966–1967	Somali riots	5		5
1976–1977	Pro-Somali Issa vs. Afari clashes	25		25
Ethiopia				
1950	Eritrean violence, British action	50		50
1960–1961	Ogaden conflict with Somalia		20	20
1963–1964	Ogaden conflict with Somalia		35	35
1967–1968	Eritrean war near Sudan	500	40	540
1976–1980	Eritrean war and clashes with Sudan	50,000	500	50,500
1977–1985	Ogaden war with Somalia	30,000	11,500	41,500
1987	Todghere border clashes with Somalia			
1987–1991	Civil war and famine	300,000	70,000	370,000
1976–1983	War with Somalia, Cuban intervention	15,000	24,000	39,000
Somalia				
1948	Mogadishu riots against Italy	90	10	100
1960–1961	Ogaden conflict with Ethiopia	50	100	150
1963–1964	Ogaden conflict with Ethiopia		50	50
1977–1985	Ogaden war with Ethiopia	20,000	8,000	28,000
1987	Todghere border clashes with Ethiopia	100	25	125
1988–1991	Civil war	75,000	15,000	90,000
Sudan				
1963–1972	Arab vs. black, English intervention	275,000	250,000	525,000
1984–1991	Black vs. Arab	150,000	8,000	158,000
Red Sea Total		966,422	387,805	1,354,227
North Africa Total		98,443	35,430	135,673
Gulf Total		270,312	406,432	666,744
Arab-Israeli Total		109,516	74,533	184,249
Total Middle East		1,444,693	904,200	2,340,893

[a]Casualty estimates are very uncertain and those shown have been sharply cut from many estimates in other sources. Time periods are often arbitrary, since wars or conflicts are undeclared.

[b]The term "war related deaths" includes large numbers of cases killed in accidents, paramilitary and guerrilla forces, civilians killed in war, associated famines and dislocations, and foreign military serving the forces allied with the country shown. Distinctions between civilian and military are often extremely uncertain and may reflect differences between the opposition and government side in some conflicts. Estimates are rounded. The reader should be aware that in most cases there are no reliable statistics of any kind.

SOURCES: Ruth Leger Sivard, *World Military and Social Expenditures*, Washington, World Priorities, 1991; Herbert K. Tillema, *International Armed Conflict Since 1945*, Boulder, Westview, 1991; various works by Trevor Dupuy; various editions of the SIPRI *Yearbook*, various editions of the IISS *Military Balance*, Anthony H. Cordesman, *The Lessons of Modern War*, Boulder, Westview, 1990; and various editions of John Laffin's *The World in Conflict: War Annual*, London, Brassey's.

than the volume of weapons. Civil wars, or conflicts involving civil strife, tend to be far bloodier than direct conflicts between states. Static wars, involving guerrilla conflict, trench warfare, or tactical conditions that prevent battles from reaching clear decisions, tend to be far bloodier than wars of maneuver.

- *Perhaps more importantly, in terms of some of the trends to be discussed later, there has so far been little correlation between the volume of high technology arms imports and high casualties*—in fact, high technology conflicts have tended to be quick and decisive and to produce far fewer casualties than long civil conflicts or prolonged conflicts between military forces with only moderate capability. This pattern has, of course, been dependent on two critical restraints in past conflicts: the failure to make large scale and/or effective use of weapons of mass destruction, and the fact that high technology conflicts have not generally attacked population centers and have been restricted largely to counterforce attacks by opposing military forces.

The Burden of Military Expenditures

There are inevitable interactions among the conflict, military expenditures, and size of military forces. Table 1.2 shows the trends in defense expenditure by country and major area within the Middle East over a ten year period. These trends are shown in current dollars because the available attempts to create constant dollar comparisons fail to cope with the problem of solving the complex currency conversion and deflator factors necessary to produce accurate estimates. This makes it difficult to establish direct statistical correlations among conflict, arms imports, and military expenditure, although such a correlation is obvious when Table 1.2 is compared with the other tables in this book and allowances are made for the fact that periods of conflict do not directly coincide with military expenditures and arms transfers.[2]

Table 1.2 also reflects five additional factors that shape the military balance in the Middle East:

- *The virtual institutionalization of most conflicts and tensions in the region.* Expenditures tend to peak during the periods before, during, and after actual conflict, but each successive military encounter generally fails to resolve the political problems that led to war. The resulting peace settlements and cease-fires tend to be limited or temporary. Major victories are rare and are often fleeting when they do occur. Changes in regime and political system rarely produce any meaningful lasting change in external relations. The end result is that the factors that lead to military spending and larger military forces rarely change over time.
- *The catalyst effect.* Major fighting in any given conflict tends to trigger an acceleration of the arms race throughout a broad part of the region. The Arab-Israel conflicts of 1967, 1973, and 1982 are obvious cases in point. So are the Iran-Iraq War and the Gulf War. The conflict between Morocco and the Polisario and between Libya and Chad have had more contained

TABLE 1.2 Trends in Military Expenditure Impacting on the Gulf and Near East (in current $ millions)

	1979	1980	1981	1982	1983	1984	1985	1986	1987	1988	1989	1990	1991
Middle East	36100	43600	51700	61100	68100	68800	67500	60800	56900	53800	53200	—	—
North Africa													
Mauritania	61	65	55	50	48	50	52	48	35	40	40	45	40
Morocco	520	763	830	1089	1074	1000	1000	1078	1102	1102	1203	1340	1400
Algeria	846	940	1383	1426	1137	1242	1040	1271	1264	1595	2313	1500	1100
Libya	3342	3092	3650	3376	4255	5047	5000	4000	2774	1595	3309	2510	2700
Chad	16	18	13	10	7	9	14	29	34	39	79	58	59
Tunisia	219	196	159	251	320	230	277	282	269	238	273	401	468
Egypt	3227	2923	3154	6192	6072	6844	6785	6460	6664	5559	3499	3820	4600
Total	8231	7997	9244	12394	12913	14422	14168	13168	12142	10168	10716	9674	10367
Levant													
Israel	5734	6654	6160	6026	6924	7869	7027	6431	5829	5585	5745	6160	6800
Syria	1463	1936	1959	2289	3340	3462	3627	2911	1801	1801	2234	2620	2800
Jordan	417	421	445	485	544	555	602	633	666	640	548	571	587
Lebanon	331	380	345	320	459	432	430	400	370	300	160	140	200
Total	7945	9391	8909	9120	11267	12318	11686	10375	8666	8326	8687	9491	10387
Gulf													
Iran	16620	14700	16210	18260	15940	22240	24770	17000	15000	12000	3900	3180	3770
Iraq	11350	19810	24610	25070	25260	25940	18970	16500	17500	16500	12870	8610	8000
Subtotal	27970	34510	40820	43330	41200	48180	43740	33500	32500	28500	16770	11790	11770
Saudi Arabia	12390	14990	18410	22040	24800	20400	21340	17290	16210	13600	14690	13860	26810
Kuwait	766	892	858	1120	1399	1430	1525	1300	1263	1273	1964	1504	11140
Bahrain	143	157	215	281	166	148	151	161	160	187	196	250	300
Qatar	475	604	720	948	1790	1213	2308	1800	1800	1800	1450	1900	1900
UAE	1197	1724	2090	1980	1973	1932	1901	1580	1590	1587	1471	2590	4900
Oman	700	1059	1357	1512	1744	1894	1937	1731	1518	1350	1552	1390	1440
Subtotal	15671	19426	23650	27881	31872	27017	29162	23862	22541	19797	21323	21494	46490
Total	43641	53936	64470	71211	73072	75197	72902	57362	55041	48297	38093	33284	58260

Red Sea													
North Yemen[a]	320	278	393	537	551	434	379	368	379	641	618	1000	1006
South Yemen[a]	87	101	135	156	171	197	198	211	207	217			
Djibouti											36	26	36
Sudan	279	302	317	442	230	236	220	201	313	286	339	320	340
Ethiopia	254	321	331	357	363	389	382	388	432	440	763	536	500
Somalia	38	23	30	31	31	25	39	31	60	60	39	19	21
Red Sea Total	978	1025	1206	1523	1346	1281	1218	1199	1391	1644	1795	1901	1903
Africa Total	8231	7997	9244	12394	12913	14422	14168	13168	12142	10168	10716	9674	10367
Levant Total	7945	9391	8909	9120	11267	12318	11686	10375	8666	8326	8687	9491	10387
Gulf Total	43641	53936	64470	71211	73072	75197	72902	57362	55041	48297	38093	33284	58260
Total region	60795	72349	83829	94248	98598	103218	99974	82104	77240	68435	59291	54350	80917
Other related													
Turkey	1390	1635	1945	2315	2317	2322	2552	3010	2980	2826	3150	2629	3405
India	3192	3608	4311	5092	5683	6272	6662	7302	8275	8377	8174	9000	8960
Pakistan	645	777	938	1113	1454	1495	1748	1937	2098	2309	2488	2850	3190
Afghanistan	157	167	157	147	202	279	311	340	360	520	286	320	400

[a]Now united into one country.

Source: Author's estimate based on computer data provided by the U.S. Arms Control and Disarmament Agency (ACDA) for the period up to 1989, and from the annual editions of the International Institute for Strategic Studies (IISS), *The Military Balance* for 1990 and 1991. Estimates are provided where gaps exist in original ACDA and IISS data. Figures represent current dollar value of costs of regular forces and not of most paramilitary forces. Cost of various rebel and insurgent forces are not included. Estimates are often based on U.S. intelligence estimates of the dollar cost of defense activities and not on national defense budgets. This generally understates the full cost of military expenditures by Iraq, Iran, Libya, Syria, and the PDRY because of conservative cost factors used in estimating Soviet supplied equipment costs. Djibouti is excluded because ACDA does not list this country. The total for the Middle East is an ACDA total excluding countries in Africa. Data for Kuwait and Saudi Arabia in 1990–1991 include military aid to other coalition countries. Data for Syria in 1990 include aid to pay for forces deployed in Saudi Arabia.

effects but have indirectly impacted on the entire Maghreb and most of the Red Sea countries. Even major out of area conflicts like the Falklands War usually trigger new spending on advanced technology and new forms of force structure.

- *The impact of technology.* The Middle Eastern states are increasingly seeking to obtain and operate the most advanced tactical systems available to countries of the North Atlantic Treaty Organization (NATO) and the Warsaw Pact. Even when Middle Eastern nations lack the capability to absorb advanced technology effectively, they still tend to buy the most advanced weapons available. Virtually all the regional arms races between given countries or groups of countries are also races to obtain the most advanced weapons and military technology available.

- *Increasing real cost per weapon or force element.* The acquisition of more sophisticated weapons and technology has produced sharp rises in real cost per weapon, or type of weapons, during the last decade. These increases in cost have been particularly severe since 1986 because of a more rapid rise in the real cost of weapons platforms and the resulting need for more training and use of foreign technicians, the need for new military facilities and operations and maintenance (O&M) and other support capabilities, and the need for more expensive munitions and military electronics. Further, most arms importing states have found it far harder to get easy credit terms since the early 1980s. The U.S. has sharply reduced aid to all states except Israel and Egypt, and the USSR has largely abolished both aid and barter transactions and long term credits.

- *The importance of oil.* While the real oil incomes of Middle Eastern states have fluctuated sharply since the massive oil boom following 1973, oil wealth has fueled the arms race throughout the region. It was the massive rise in oil prices after 1974, for example, that drove much of the arms race that followed. The collapse of oil prices in the mid-1980s led to the dip in spending shown for many countries during the late 1980s—although recent rises in oil prices have eased this trend in some countries. At other times, the increase in military forces has been shaped by military assistance and sales from nations outside the region. Examples include U.S. military sales and assistance to Egypt and Israel and Soviet-bloc sales to Algeria, Ethiopia, Iraq, Libya, Syria, and Yemen.

Table 1.2 again reveals that levels of military effort vary by sub-region within the Middle East. The arms race in the Maghreb is limited in scale by the standards of the Gulf and the Arab-Israel conflict, although all the Maghreb states still spend enough to seriously damage their economies and long term prospects for development. For example, Morocco's long war with the Polisario and tensions with Algeria have been particularly damaging. Libya's spoiler role throughout the region has consumed much of that nation's vast oil wealth and has forced its neighbors into high levels of defense expenditure. Egypt has suffered from being caught in a triangle of tension with Libya, instability in the Red Sea, and the failure to reach a comprehensive Arab-Israeli peace settlement. These external threats and pressures have deprived Egypt of much of the benefit of the Camp David accords.

The states involved in the Arab-Israeli conflict rank second in terms of expenditure and first in terms of military manpower. The Arab-Israeli arms race has, however, undergone some significant structural changes over time. Egypt can no longer be regarded as a confrontation state. The Camp David accords of 1978 produced the only major movement toward peace in the area, with the possible exception of the accords between Oman and the People's Democratic Republic of Yemen (PDRY) in the mid-1980s. Jordan has also shifted from being a leading military power to a sideshow caught in the arms race involving Israel, Syria, and Iraq. Jordan's forces are still highly professional, but Jordan lacks the manpower and money to compete with its larger neighbors. The continuing disintegration of Lebanon has largely removed Lebanon from the regional arms race as an active state, but it remains a killing ground for its warring ethnic groups and is the scene of recurrent military intervention by Israel and Syria.

Israel remains far more capable of absorbing and operating advanced military technology than any other Middle Eastern state, but it has experienced serious problems in funding its forces in spite of massive U.S. aid. Syria and Egypt made significant progress in improving their training and readiness between 1982 and 1987 but have since suffered from serious financing problems and have seen a significant overall decline in readiness and the ability to absorb and operate advanced military technology.

The most costly sub-region in terms of military expenditure and arms imports is that of the Gulf states. Table 1.2 shows that the Gulf states are able to afford large military expenditures and arms sales for states their size, although the southern Gulf states—Bahrain, Kuwait, Oman, Qatar, Saudi Arabia, and the United Arab Emirates—are severely constrained in manpower.

All the Gulf states are limited in terms of their indigenous ability to fully absorb advanced military technology. Iran and Iraq should be most able to make effective use of their defense expenditures, but both face problems of self-inflicted wounds. In spite of considerable oil wealth, the Iran-Iraq War has placed an immense financial burden on Iran and Iraq, costing well over $70 billion in arms imports alone. Iran has not been able to recover from the mix of revolution and the loss of most of its military equipment due to a Western arms embargo and defeats in May–August, 1988 that cost it nearly 40% of the equipment in its land forces. Iraq's debt burden is one factor that led it to invade Kuwait, and its war with the UN coalition has cost it hundreds of billions of dollars worth of military equipment.

Bahrain, Kuwait, Oman, Qatar, Saudi Arabia, and the United Arab Emirates all lack the pool of trained manpower to develop large high technology forces, and all have imported more equipment than they can effectively use. In spite of the creation of the Gulf Cooperation Council during the Iran-Iraq War, military cooperation exists largely in name only. Little is standardized. The small Gulf states each develop their forces in relative isolation and face massive diseconomies of scale that rob their military expenditures of much

of their effectiveness. Only Oman and Saudi Arabia can use native manpower, and they have serious problems in terms of both quality and quantity. The Saudi air force is the only force in the southern Gulf that is moderately effective by Western terms.

The Red Sea region spends less on military forces than the other three
major sub-regions within the Middle East, but it may well suffer the most
from actual fighting. The PDRY has wasted much of its national wealth in a
civil war and in competing with Oman. The Yemen Arab Republic (YAR)
has fought a low level civil war with Saudi Arabia. While the PDRY (formerly South Yemen) and YAR (formerly North Yemen) have merged, it is far
too soon to determine what this union really means.

The southern edge of the Red Sea region has been a politico-military
disaster area. Ethiopia has been caught in a brutal civil war for more than a
decade and in low level border conflicts with Somalia and the Sudan. Somalia has plunged from tribal feuding and conflict with Ethiopia to its own civil
war. The Sudan collapsed into a lasting civil war in the early 1980s and
shows no signs of recovery. In combination with famine and gross mismanagement of the economy, these tensions and conflicts have killed at least
several million human beings since 1980. While Ethiopia has recently
emerged from its civil war with something approaching a democratic government and an independent Eritrea, it is far from clear that it will not
splinter into ethnic enclaves or return to civil war.

What virtually all Middle Eastern states have in common is that regional
pressures have driven their military spending to levels far beyond what
developing states can afford. Every nation in the Middle East is now spending so much on military forces that the resulting expenditures seriously limit
economic growth and the provision of key services ranging from education
to improvements in infrastructure. These pressures are particularly severe in
the case of the non–oil exporting states and nations like Egypt, Israel, and
Syria. Even rich oil exporting states like Saudi Arabia, however, are spending far too much on defense, and this is often driving them into debt or
seriously distorting their economies by funneling too much of the nations'
best manpower into military forces.

The pattern of defense spending in the Middle East also raises serious
questions about the future. Most Middle Eastern states already have a severe
military debt because of past arms purchases. In many cases—particularly
those of Egypt, Israel, Jordan, Morocco, and Syria—they cannot properly
service this debt. Yet the constant pace of improvement in military technology quickly makes the inventory of Middle Eastern states obsolete.

The end effect is that few Middle Eastern states can afford to maintain
their present level of capability, and most cannot possibly afford to modernize their current force structure. This leaves them with a number of unpleas-
ant choices: (1) losing readiness and capability relative to their rivals; (2)
making major cuts in force size to fund a smaller and more capable force; (3)
going even deeper into debt with no real prospect of ever fully repaying that
debt; or (4) turning to weapons of mass destruction as a "cheap" way of
trying to get equivalent military capability.

Trends in Military Manpower

The military expenditures in the Middle East have been matched by the growth in manpower strength summarized in Table 1.3. Military manpower in the region nearly doubled during the 1980s—although civil wars in Ethiopia, Somalia, and the Sudan, the unification of the Yemens, and the defeat of Iran and Iraq in recent wars altered this trend during 1988–1991.[3]

In the process, many countries have increased their military manning levels beyond the levels they can equip and sustain. Roughly 16 people out of every 1,000 in the population are in uniform, more than three times the average in the developing world. The current levels of military manpower in most Middle Eastern states impose a severe strain on their national budgets and the manpower pool they need for development.

Some aspects of this rise in military manpower have been driven by necessity. Morocco's conflict with the Polisario, Libya's tensions with its neighbors, the arms race between Israel and Syria, the Iran-Iraq War and Gulf War, and the various conflicts and tensions in the Horn have all driven the manpower patterns shown in Table 1.3.

Something of the same ratchet effect has also driven military expenditures and arms imports. While a detailed review of Table 1.3 shows that manpower levels do rise and fall with levels of conflict, few countries cut their military manpower back to its previous level once a conflict becomes less serious. The rise in force levels tends to become institutionalized, and cuts do not occur even when nations desperately need the financial resources for military equipment modernization, economic development, or civil purposes.

This emphasis on sheer manpower has, however, done little to provide additional military capability. Military spending and arms imports have increased more rapidly than manpower. There are also comparatively few countries in the Middle East that can bring their military spending, manpower numbers, equipment numbers, and force quality into balance.

Morocco, Algeria, Egypt, Syria, Iran, Iraq, North Yemen, South Yemen, the Sudan, Ethiopia, and Somalia have all maintained far more military manpower than they can afford to properly equip, train, and support. Some of these countries try to solve their quality problem by concentrating their most modern equipment and support funds in elite units. Others simply deploy so many men that they actually weaken their force structure by dispersing scarce equipment, training, and support funds into too many units and into far too large a pool of manpower.

Only three countries in the four sub-regions shown in Table 1.3 strike a reasonably effective overall balance between manpower numbers, equipment strength, and the other aspects of force quality and make a cost-effective use of defense resources. These countries are Israel, Jordan, and Oman. Israel funds a surprisingly large total force structure by concentrating its funds on force quality and relying on mobilization to provide the bulk of its manpower. Jordan solves its funding problems by limiting its total force numbers as well as its active manpower and by limiting its equipment purchases to systems it can effectively man and support. Oman preserves

TABLE 1.3 Trends in Regular Military Manpower in the Middle East (in thousands)

	1967	1973	1975	1977	1979	1981	1983	1985	1987	1989	1991
North Africa											
Mauritania	2	3	3	17	8	12	16	20	16	16	12
Morocco	65	65	75	85	98	120	135	165	200	200	196
Algeria	75	80	80	75	88	101	130	170	170	195	126
Libya	20	20	25	30	51	55	68	91	91	91	86
Chad	5	10	11	9	5	3	4	16	30	33	17
Tunisia	25	20	20	20	24	29	28	38	38	40	35
Egypt	220	390	400	350	447	447	447	466	450	450	420
Total	412	588	614	586	721	767	768	967	995	1025	892
Levant											
Israel	75	130	172	179	181	201	205	195	180	191	141
Syria	80	115	230	250	220	270	400	402	400	400	404
Jordan	60	70	60	70	67	66	72	81	100	100	101
Lebanon	19	20	24	9	18	20	20	21	37	37	18
Total	234	335	486	508	486	557	697	699	717	728	664
Gulf											
Iran	210	285	385	350	415	660	640	745	700	604	528
Iraq	90	105	155	140	444	392	434	788	1000	1000	750
Subtotal	300	390	540	490	859	1052	1074	1533	1700	1604	1278
Saudi Arabia	50	75	75	75	79	79	80	96	95	95	112
Kuwait	8	14	25	10	11	12	13	16	20	20	8
Bahrain	2	2	2	2	2	2	2	3	4	5	7
Qatar	1	3	5	5	6	6	6	7	11	7	8
UAE	4	11	21	25	25	44	44	44	44	43	48
Oman	3	8	12	12	13	15	20	25	27	29	30
Subtotal	68	113	140	129	136	158	165	191	201	205	213
Total	368	503	680	619	995	1210	1404	1724	1701	2008	1704
Red Sea											
North Yemen[a]	10	31	42	40	36	30	22	28	43	62	65
South Yemen[a]	10	12	19	20	20	23	25	27	40	88	
Sudan	20	35	50	50	65	87	86	65	59	65	72
Ethiopia	45	50	144	228	250	240	240	240	300	250	65
Djibouti	1	2	2	2	3	3	3	3	4	5	3
Somalia	16	25	30	53	54	54	48	43	50	47	8
Total	102	155	287	393	428	487	424	406	486	517	426
Total region	1116	1581	2067	2106	2630	3071	3293	3796	3899	4278	3686
Other related											
Turkey	530	545	584	771	698	741	824	814	879	780	579
India	1420	1620	1670	1270	1286	1104	250	1515	1502	1257	1265
Pakistan	351	466	502	588	544	549	584	644	572	520	565
Afghanistan	95	91	130	143	89	45	75	55	55	55	45

[a]Now united into one country.

SOURCE: Author's estimate based on computer data provided by the ACDA and various editions of the IISS, *Military Balance*. The data for 1975–1989 are primarily from ACDA. The data for 1991 are based primarily on the relevant annual edition of the IISS, *Military Balance*. Estimates are provided where gaps exist in original data. Figures generally represent manpower in regular forces only, and not in most paramilitary forces—but ACDA normally counts more paramilitary elements than does the IISS. Manpower in mobilized reserves, revolutionary guards of various types, and various rebel and insurgent forces is not included. The true total of regular, paramilitary, and insurgent manpower is close to twice the total for regular uniformed manpower. Djibouti is partially excluded because ACDA does not list this country.

a relatively high overall level of effectiveness in its army by avoiding overambitious investments in armor, aircraft, and other expensive equipment.

It is more difficult to measure the changes taking place in the force structure of Middle Eastern states. Comparisons of unit numbers are largely meaningless. There is little standardization in defining division, brigade, or regiment, even within a given nation. The titles of formations are often misleading—"armored" often means little more than motorized infantry—and in some countries some brigades are larger than certain divisions. Units are often heavily politicized, and unit quality varies sharply. There is nothing approaching a comparable order of battle within most countries, and comparisons of unit numbers are virtually meaningless.

The Gulf countries present an additional set of problems in making force comparisons. Iran has recently been forced to mix regular and revolutionary forces with an awkward seasonal mobilization. It also has been unable to obtain the high technology weapons it wants or spare parts and advanced munitions for much of the Western equipment it bought under the shah. Since the early 1980s, Iraq has depended on "reserves" for nearly half its manpower. It has the money to provide them with good equipment, but its overall training levels have been very low and it has been highly dependent on a limited number of elite units.

With the exception of Oman, the southern Gulf states all lack the total manpower and skilled manpower to create effective forces, in spite of their vast oil wealth. Most have ended up throwing money at the problem without creating the necessary training base, infrastructure, and support forces. The Saudi air force and some elements of the Saudi navy and army are partial exceptions to this generalization.

Equipment Numbers: The Issue of Quantity

The equipment trends shown in Table 1.4 provide what may be the best simple measure of both the trends in arms sales and the trends in military capability. While the equipment counted in Table 1.4 varies sharply in quality, as does the capacity of individual nations to use it effectively, it is clear that most countries have increased equipment numbers steadily over the last decade and are likely to continue to do so in the future.

Table 1.4 shows the trends in two key measures of force strength by country. To put these tank and aircraft numbers into perspective, the Middle East now has some 23,000 main battle tanks and 3,800 combat aircraft—totals which have dropped sharply since 1990 because of the Gulf War and the disintegration of the regular armed forces of Ethiopia and Somalia. In contrast, the total active strength of all the main battle tanks in the NATO central region is around 8,000, while the total number of combat aircraft is around 1,400.

Yet even NATO's most developed nations have trouble providing enough manpower, support, and sustainability to make these forces fully effective, although they have a far more capable manpower and technology base than any Middle Eastern state with the exception of Israel. Given the total num-

TABLE 1.4 Major Weapons in Middle Eastern Forces

Country	Main Battle Tanks							Combat Aircraft						
	1973	1979	1982	1984	1988	1990	1992	1973	1979	1982	1984	1988	1990	1992
North Africa														
Mauritania	0	0	0	0	0	0	0	0	13	7	9	5	5	7
Morocco	120	140	135	120	224	284	284	48	72	97	106	109	93	90
Algeria	400	500	630	700	910	900	960	206	260	306	330	299	257	241
Libya	221	2000	2000	2000	1980	2300	2150	44	201	555	535	515	513	409
Chad	0	0	0	0	0	0	10	0	5	0	0	2	4	4
Tunisia	0	0	14	14	68	98	84	12	14	8	8	43	50	53
Egypt	1880	1600	2100	1750	2425	2410	3190	620	563	429	504	517	475	495
Total	2621	4240	4879	4584	5067	5992	6678	930	1128	1402	1492	1490	1397	1299
Levant														
Jordan	420	500	569	750	1131	1131	1130	52	73	94	103	111	104	110
Israel	1700	3050	3600	3600	3794	4288	4490	488	576	634	555	676	553	575
Lebanon	60	0	0	142	105	200	250	18	16	8	3	6	3	3
Syria	1170	2600	3990	4100	4050	4000	4350	326	389	450	503	499	558	650
Total	3350	6150	8159	8592	9080	9619	10220	884	1054	1186	1164	1292	1218	1338
Gulf														
Iran	920	1735	1110	1000	900	500	700	159	447	90	95	70	78	190
Iraq	990	1800	2300	4820	5500	5600	2300	224	339	330	580	513	730	260
Subtotal	1910	3535	3410	5820	6400	6100	3000	383	786	420	675	583	808	450
Bahrain	0	0	0	0	54	54	80	0	0	0	0	12	12	24
Kuwait	100	280	240	240	275	245	250	34	50	49	49	36	35	42
Oman	0	0	18	18	39	39	80	12	35	37	52	63	57	60
Qatar	0	12	24	24	24	24	30	4	4	9	11	13	19	20
Saudi Arabia	85	350	450	450	550	550	700	70	178	191	203	179	189	250
UAE	0	0	118	118	136	131	130	12	52	52	43	65	91	100
Subtotal	185	642	850	850	1078	1043	1270	132	319	338	358	368	403	496
Total	2095	4177	4260	6670	7478	7143	4,270	515	1105	758	1033	951	1211	946

Red Sea													
North Yemen[a]	30	232	714	664	664	715	1270	28	11	75	76	83	87	100
South Yemen[a]	50	260	470	450	480	480	—	20	109	114	103	114	94	—
Djibouti	0	0	0	0	0	0	20	0	0	0	0	0	0	4
Ethiopia	50	624	790	1020	750	1300	300	37	100	113	160	143	120	68
Sudan	130	150	190	173	175	215	215	50	36	30	34	45	53	50
Somalia	150	80	140	240	293	290	270	100	25	55	64	63	56	50
Total	410	1346	2304	2447	2362	3000	2075	235	281	387	437	448	410	272
Total region	8476	15913	19602	22293	23987	25754	23243	2564	3568	3733	4126	4181	4236	3855
Other related													
Turkey	1400	3500	3550	3532	3714	3700	3783	288	303	402	458	476	477	530
India	1700	1850	2050	2900	3150	3150	3100	541	620	635	920	836	726	630
Pakistan	850	1000	1285	1321	1750	1850	1980	248	256	219	314	451	420	375
Afghanistan	200	800	850	450	620	620	800	112	169	117	150	193	188	253

[a]Now united into one country.

Sources: Numbers are generally adapted from the editions of the IISS, *Military Balance*; JCSS, *Middle East Military Balance*; and SIPRI *Year Book* for the appropriate year. Aircraft totals generally do not include aircraft in storage as there are no comparable counts of operational aircraft: Libya is an exception, as data are not available on aircraft in storage. All estimates for 1992 are made by the author.

bers of equipment in many Middle Eastern states, it is obvious that many countries confuse sheer mass with military capability and the glitter factor inherent in being able to buy the latest equipment with the ability to operate it effectively.

The force structures of the North African and Red Sea states are particularly poorly balanced in terms of overall ability to operate total national equipment holdings. Only Algeria, Morocco, and Egypt rise to even the lower levels of mediocrity, and most of the nations in the region have low overall military capability. Libya's capabilities to use its military equipment are probably the worst of any major arms buyer in the world—nearly one-third of Libya's equipment holdings are in storage or inoperable.

Israel and Jordan do set relatively high standards. Iraq improved significantly under the pressure of the Iran-Iraq War but partially demobilized after the war and never recovered its effectiveness before its forces were shattered in the Gulf conflict. Syria improved during the period from 1982–1987 but then began to suffer from serious financial problems. As for the southern Gulf states, Bahrain, Kuwait, Qatar, and the UAE are all heavily dependent on foreign mercenaries and have more modern equipment than they can use effectively in combat. Oman lacks large numbers of heavy weapons. Saudi Arabia is able to operate most of its air equipment with reasonable effectiveness by the standards of the Gulf region but can use only about half to two-thirds of its army equipment.

Qualitative Factors Affecting the Middle Eastern Military Balance

During the last decade, many Middle Eastern states have shifted from an emphasis on mass, or force quantity, to an emphasis on force quality. This shift has been driven in large part by Israel's success in its 1967, 1970, 1973, and 1982 wars with its Arab neighbors. In each war, Israel demonstrated that its edge in technology more than overcame any Arab advantage in numbers. The Iran-Iraq War and the Gulf War have had a similar effect. Iraq used technology during the Iran-Iraq War to offset Iran's advantage in manpower and ideological motivation. The Gulf War provided a stunning example of how the technology, readiness, and superior training and organization of Western forces could smash what many believed to be the largest and most effective military forces in the Arab world.

Outside conflicts and arms races have also had a powerful influence on this shift from increasing quantity to increasing quality. The dependence of regional states on East and West, and particularly on the U.S. and Soviet Union, inevitably led them to mirror image the growing emphasis on technology in their supplier states. The U.S. use of technology in Vietnam and Soviet use of technology in Afghanistan demonstrated the potential value of new weapons and technologies—although each superpower decisively lost its respective conflict.

The resulting trends are shown in Table 1.5. Virtually all of these systems can increase military effectiveness, yet most also present growing problems for almost every Middle East country.

- *Rising real cost.* While no precise statistics are available, it is clear that the cost of new military equipment is rising far more quickly in real terms than either central government revenues or defense budgets. This rise in cost is made worse because new major weapons systems require far more costly munitions or missiles and must be integrated into highly complex sensor and command, control, communications, and intelligence (C^3I) systems. The average cost of most items of major military equipment rose by at least 50% in constant dollars during the period between 1982 and 1990 and continues to rise at this rate.

- *Rising foreign debt.* As was touched upon earlier, most Middle Eastern states already have a military debt for past equipment purchases which they cannot properly service. They cannot afford to maintain their present force structure and to continue to modernize their equipment.

- *Growing problems with absorption of more sophisticated technologies.* Further, the problems that Middle Eastern states face in acquiring and absorbing such technology and in dealing with such transfers to unfriendly states, are also accelerating. A decade ago, there was usually a lag of five to ten years between the initial deployment of major new weapons systems in U.S., NATO, Soviet, and Warsaw Pact forces and any large scale sale of such arms to the developing world. That lag is now being eliminated. Western Europe is selling aircraft, armor, and ships to developing nations at the same time it introduces such systems to its own armed forces. The USSR is not only selling its new MiG-29 fighters to India, Iraq, and Syria, it is selling coproduction rights to India. Soviet SS-21 missiles appeared in Syrian forces almost at the same time they became fully operational in Soviet forces in East Germany.

- *Need for highly sophisticated associated systems.* In most cases, the effective use of advanced weapons requires sophisticated intelligence, warning, command and control, communications, targeting, and battle damage assessment systems. These complex systems are extremely difficult for developing nations to create, maintain, and operate. They also add a major new dimension to force costs—sometimes doubling the cost of maintaining a national air force and increasing the cost of land forces by 25–33%. Further, such systems are vulnerable to countermeasures and technical change—creating new uncertainties and modernization costs.

- *Force cuts or force ineffectiveness.* These pressures have led to force cuts in some countries like Israel and awkward and ineffective compromises between force quantity and force quality in most other states in the region. All the larger Arab states have tried to maintain force size while radically altering the technology mix of their forces. This has often led the nations involved to buy high cost weapons or systems they lack the resources and skills to properly operate, leaving them to buy only the facade of capability without the mix of associated weapons, munitions, command and control

TABLE 1.5 Key Near Term Trends in the Technology of Arms Sales to the Middle East, 1988–1995

Weapon/Technology	Impact
Challenger, AMX-40, M-1A2, T-80, M-1A1, Leclerc	Advanced tanks with 3rd and 4th generation fire control systems, spaced and other advanced armor, and advanced 120mm guns. Will be matched by advanced types of other armored fighting vehicles.
TOW-2, IHOT, Dragon 2 Hellfire, Milan, AT-8, AT-6, AT-7	Advanced anti-tank missiles with full automatic tracking or fire and forget capability.
MLRS, BM-24, BM-25, Astros, ATACMS	Western and Soviet multiple rocket launchers capable of firing advanced submunitions and smart minelets at ranges beyond 30 km.
Night vision devices, thermal imaging sights, night targeting systems	Widespread use of night vision devices. "Twenty-four hour" infantry, helicopter, and armored combat.
Secure, switched, automated advanced communications	Conversion to advanced secure communications with tactical message traffic and battle management capabilities.
SA-10, Patriot, Improved Hawk, SA-12	Advanced surface-to-air missiles which cannot easily be suppressed with current weapons and electronic warfare means. Many will be netted with advanced sensor and battle management systems and linked to advanced short range systems.
SHORADS: SA-14, Stinger-POST, etc.	Next generation short range crew and man portable surface-to-air missiles and radar guided AA guns with far better tracking and kill capability and greater ranges. Many will be netted into an integrated battlefield and point defense system.
E-3A (Imp), E-2C (I), IL-76, SUAWACS	Airborne warning and control aircraft capable of managing large scale air wars using radar and electronic support measures (ESM) equivalent to NATO level capabilities.
F-15E, MiG-29, SU-27, Lavi, F-16C, F-20A, Mirage 2000, Tornado, MiG-31	Next generation air combat and attack fighters with far more accuracy and up to twice the range payload of existing fighters.
Aim 9L/M, Phoenix, Mica, AA-8, AA-X10, AA-X-P2, Super 530, Python III, AMRAAM	Advanced short and long range multi-aspect air-to-air missiles which greatly improve the air-to-air combat capability of all modern fighters.
Durandal, Paveway ERAM, ACM, SUU-65, WASP, J-233	Advanced air-to-surface munitions including runway suppression, anti-armor, anti-hard point, anti-personnel, anti-radar, and other special mission point and area weapons with far more lethality than current systems. Many will use stand off weapons like glide bombs or advanced dispensers for low altitude single pass penetrations under radar.
RPVs, IMohawk, MiG-25 (I), E-3A, JSTARS	Improved airborne sensor and reconnaissance platforms which can provide advanced targeting, intelligence, and battle management data.
PAH-2, AH-64, Mi-24	Next generation attack helicopters with much longer ranges, improved air-to-air missiles, third or fourth generation launch and leave anti-tank guided missiles, and air defense countermeasures. Will be supported by steadily improved troop lift helicopters with improved protection and firepower.

(continues)

TABLE 1.5 *(continued)*

Weapon/Technology	Impact
Peace Shield, Project Lambda, Lion's Dawn and C^{3}I/BM systems	Air sensor and battle management systems equivalent to NATO Air Defense Ground Environment (NADGE) level systems for integrating fighter and SAM defenses. Many with advanced attack mission control capabilities.
Maritime patrol aircraft	More advanced versions of E-2C-type aircraft armed with ASW weapons and air-to-surface missiles.
Silkworm and other land based anti-ship missiles	New, longer range, and more accurate land based anti-ship missiles with improved sensors and target finding capability and ranges capable of covering the entire Gulf.
FAC(M), missile frigates: Saar 5, Lupo, F-2000, etc.	Next generation missile patrol boats and corvettes with Improved Harpoon and other moderate range advanced ship-to-ship missiles.
Sea Skua, Harpoon II, Exocet II, Gabriel III/IV, AS-4, AS-6, AS-7	Advanced ship, shore, and air launched anti-ship missiles with advanced sensors and electronics, and far more lethal payloads. Can kill war ships and tankers far more effectively than today.
Coastal submarines	Advanced diesel submarines with excellent silencing, moderate cruise ranges, and smart torpedoes.
SS-22, SS-23, CSS-2, Jericho 2, Scud C, Al-Abbas, Al-Hussein	Advanced surface-to-surface missiles with ranges up to 1,500 miles.
Nerve gas, mustard gas, biological weapons, toxins, cyanide agents	Widespread stocking of single or binary nerve gas agents and limited CBW defense capabilities. Growing BW capabilities.
Nuclear weapons	Wider proliferation adding nuclear weapons capability to Iraq, Iran, and possibly other regional states.

systems, training aid, maintenance facilities and other military capabilities necessary to make them effective.

• *The further complication of uncertain financing.* These problems have been further compounded by the erratic delivery of military aid and shifts in oil prices—often forcing nations into debt to buy new technologies while still leaving them without the resources to make what they have bought effective. Further, the internal politics of many states prevents them from eliminating units, military functions, and bases which no longer are effective to save resources for the forces they need. This produces bloated and inefficient structures at every level and often leaves major amounts of equipment in storage or in hollow units that are little more than military parking lots.

• *Hollow forces.* As a result, most Middle Eastern forces often appear to be far more threatening in terms of force strength and weapons numbers than they are in terms of actual military capability. Only a small fraction of the major combat units in most countries are really effective, and the overall mix of command and control, sensor and communications, and support and logistic systems necessary to make even these units fully effective are lacking. Shortages of skilled manpower are endemic, often compounded by wretched personnel policies and management and poor pay for other ranks and junior officers.

At the same time, the pace of technological change and/or increase in weapons strength has additional important side effects.

- *First, it keeps all Middle Eastern states, except Israel, highly dependent on outside technical support and limits the value of most local efforts to develop a national arms industry.* In spite of claims to the contrary, most Middle Eastern states remain dependent on outside resupply and technical advice. Further, almost all advanced weapons production in the Middle East—with the exception of some production in Israel and Iraq—consists of coproduction or the assembly of imported parts. This does not increase independence. Such plants do not transfer real production or industrialization capability. Further, the net cost of coproduced equipment is virtually always far higher in real terms than buying fully assembled equipment that is produced efficiently and as part of longer production runs.
- *Second, it keeps most Middle Eastern forces in a constant state of military flux and prevents effective training and organization.* Far too large a percentage of the force structure of most Middle Eastern states is receiving new equipment and has to be retrained and reorganized. Coupled with force expansion, the result is almost continuous turbulence. Officers, noncommissioned officers (NCOs), and technicians are constantly being rotated and retrained. Units are constantly changing in structure. In many cases this turbulence has gone on for over a decade, and many units have never enjoyed enough stability to operate as coherent forces.
- *Finally, this pace of change makes effective manpower management virtually impossible.* The constant need to train or retrain while expanding the base of trained manpower leads to nearly chaotic conditions for career and skilled personnel with technical specialties. The basic problems of changes in force structure and equipment are compounded by generally low administrative standards. Personnel are often trained without adequate language skills or education. Trained personnel are misassigned. Insufficient career incentives are provided for trained personnel. Traditional discipline cannot adjust to the creation of highly skilled NCOs and junior officers and the need for highly skilled enlisted men.

At the same time, no Middle Eastern nation can ignore the need for modernization. The local threats in the region are generally all too real. States in the Middle East, and the outside states with capability to project power into the region, face a massive problem in terms of conventional proliferation. They not only must match potential threats in terms of equipment numbers, they must also match the new weapons technologies that will be present in the forces of hostile nations.

This complex mix of trends may benefit a few of the wealthier Gulf nations that can afford to use technology to partially compensate for their limited ground strength. At the same time, it is unlikely that even these states will achieve enough of a technical edge over the equipment in the forces of potential threat states to compensate for their superior mass.

The rest of the states in the region are likely to face serious financial constraints on funding anything approaching an effective balance of manpower and equipment strength, manpower and equipment quality, and the necessary infrastructure and support capability. Given past trends, many are likely to spend most of their money on major weapons systems and fail to fund the rest of the investment necessary to make their forces effective.

The trend towards high technology has put great pressure on Jordan and Oman, which have relatively effective forces but are particularly hard put to keep up with the race in military technology. Iran also now faces the problem of rebuilding an obsolete and low grade mix of equipment and the manpower, training, and support base necessary to use advanced weaponry. Even Israel may find much of its qualitative edge diminishing—at least in terms of pure technology. Israel is likely to retain or even increase its qualitative advantage in actually being able to use its advanced military equipment since all of the surrounding Arab states face serious—if not crippling—fiscal problems in funding a high technology force mix.

Force Quality and Continuing Weaknesses in Middle Eastern Forces

Far more is involved in shaping the regional military balance, however, than technology and weapons numbers. As the Gulf War showed, war planning and an effective concept of operations is a force multiplier as important as numbers and weapons quality. So is the ability to conduct combined arms and combined operations. A force that can fight twenty-four hours a day, and as effectively or more effectively at night, has a tremendous advantage over one that cannot. A force that can combine maneuver capability, firepower, and sustainability—rather than rely on initial numbers and attrition—acquires additional force multipliers.

Realistic training involving entire divisions and corps and land-air operations under demanding tactical conditions offers immense advantages over a force that trains at the small unit level in set-piece exercises. True military professionalism and effective chains of command offer great advantages over forces where political alignments are more important to promotion than military skill and where rivalries among units, branches, and services divide the military effort. A force with the sensors, intelligence assets, and command system to understand the battlefield deep into the enemy's territory and to target the enemy's forces beyond visual range in near real time has the advantage of fighting an enemy that is blind.

Traditional efforts to assess the military balance in the Middle East, analyses that compare equipment and manpower numbers or orders of battle, ignore these differences and treat all military forces as if they were alike. In fact, the qualitative differences between forces in most contingencies in the Middle East will be at least as important as the quantitative differences, and they make such numerical comparisons little more than misleading nonsense unless they are fully analyzed.

Further, most Middle Eastern nations do not preserve any internal consistency of force quality from unit to unit in a given service. All of the major Arab military powers and Iran have elite divisions and squadrons of relatively high quality and a mass of mediocre to low quality troops. There are no standard combat units in either the quantitative or qualitative sense. Divisions and squadrons vary sharply in terms of manpower, equipment holdings, training, and every other aspect of military capability within a given country, and even within a given type of division or squadron. Some commanders are professional, many are political, and a few succeed in being both. Command, control, intelligence, battle management, targeting, and damage assessment capabilities differ widely within given countries and given services. The ability to repair, maintain, supply, and replace the equipment in given units is equally variable.

The net impact of these qualitative problems will differ from country to country, but it is likely to produce continuing weaknesses and vulnerabilities in the forces of virtually every Middle Eastern military power. An understanding of these weaknesses and vulnerabilities is not only as critical to comprehending the Middle Eastern military balance as is an understanding of force numbers and equipment types, it is absolutely critical to any effort to shape power projection and arms control policy.

In the cases of aggressor states, these weaknesses can be exploited for peacekeeping purposes or to repel aggression. In the case of friends and allies, they must be taken into account in power projection and in arms sales and advisory efforts. They also must be considered in any assessment of the orders of battle and equipment numbers in individual Middle Eastern armies, air forces, and navies. The military balance will never be shaped by numbers alone, and in many cases the continuing qualitative weaknesses in Middle Eastern forces will be *the* key factor shaping any given military balance within the region.

These continuing weaknesses will involve the follow specific problems:

- *Training and readiness.* In virtually every case, order of battle or force strength intelligence will be a completely misleading picture of military capability. There will be critical weaknesses in training, particularly in terms of maneuver, large scale offensive operations, integration of high technology systems, and combined arms and combined operations. At the same time, there will be gaps in readiness in addition to gaps in training, imposed by a wide range of factors. These qualitative weaknesses will make threat force far less capable than a Western force of similar size, and create windows of opportunity better trained and more ready forces can exploit.
- *Intelligence, reconnaissance, and damage assessment capabilities.* Most Middle

Eastern military forces will lack satellite and advanced intelligence, reconnaissance, and damage assessment capabilities. In most cases, the assets they do have will be vulnerable to attacks, air defenses, or countermeasures. A technically superior attacker will often be able to partly blind the enemy.

- *Beyond visual range.* For similar reasons, most Middle Eastern military forces will have only limited ability to match Western forces in beyond visual range (BVR) air-to-air combat, counterbattery, and artillery targeting capability. Even in some areas where direct line of sight target acquisition is possible, Western forces may be able to acquire targets at longer ranges, particularly at night.
- *C³I/battle management/targeting.* Middle Eastern military forces lack high technology battle management, communications, intelligence, and targeting systems. In many cases, at least individual elements of potential Middle Eastern military forces will have critical shortfalls in C³I capabilities and/or critical vulnerabilities. This will restrict many aspects of maneuver, limiting the tempo and intensity of operations.
- *Air control and warning and air defense.* Middle Eastern military forces may have an air control and warning (AC&W)/air defense "system," but it will almost certainly be sharply inferior to Western levels of technology. Key weaknesses will include electronic warfare, electronic and other countermeasures, layering of different defenses, survivable sensors and command centers, area coverage, independence of action by individual aircraft (raid assessment, BVR, and multi-aspect radar/fire control/weaponry). Counterstealth, counter–unmanned airborne vehicle (UAV), and anti-missile defenses are likely to be particularly weak.
- *All-weather/night warfare.* Middle Eastern military forces are likely to have severe limitations in maneuver, firepower, and sustainability in poor weather or night operations. These problems are likely to grow steadily worse as the tempo and intensity of Western operations are increased and as threat operations are required to make effective use of combined arms or combined operations. The West has the intelligence and targeting assets to detect the key problems limiting enemy all-weather or night operations in near real time.
- *Flexibility.* In broad terms, most Middle Eastern military forces will have organization, tactical, and equipment driven rigidities that can be exploited by the West. This will be particularly true of forces under tight central authoritarian control and those separated by religious, ideological, and ethnic rivalries.
- *Precision kill/smart munitions/lethal area munitions.* Middle Eastern military forces are likely to lag significantly behind the West in virtually every aspect of munitions lethality. Even when they possess the actual weapons and munitions, they will generally lack the ability to integrate them into an overall force mix matching Western military capabilities.
- *Maneuver.* For similar reasons, Middle Eastern military forces will lack speed of maneuver and the ability to match the intensity of operations of

the better Western forces, with the possible exception of built-up areas and forested terrain.

- *Sustainability.* Middle Eastern military forces will often lack the capability to maintain equipment, recover it, conduct field or depot combat repairs, or allocate ammunition and spares. Sortie and operational availability rates will often be low or be dependent on a few vulnerable facilities.
- *Hard target killing.* Middle Eastern military forces are unlikely to have the technology mix necessary to kill defended hard targets and may often be highly dependent on hardened command and control facilities.
- *Loiter sensors/UAV killers.* Middle Eastern military forces are likely to improve their use of UAVs and long endurance sensors and kill platforms with time, but they should generally be far behind high technology Western forces in these areas.
- *Soft strategic attacks.* In most cases involving hostile countries or regular military forces, the West will be able to attack a wide range of soft strategic targets with near impunity. These include power plants, water facilities, bridges and tunnels, phone and radio facilities, etc.
- *Countermeasures.* Middle Eastern military forces are unlikely to match the West in countermeasures at virtually any level, ranging from electronic warfare to infrared. Where threat forces have parity in individual areas, they are unlikely to have them on a broad basis.
- *Strategic mobility.* Most Middle Eastern military forces will find it difficult to conduct major redeployments as distinguished from maneuver. Most will be severely constrained in intra-theater lift and mobility. When they can move units, they often will lack the ability to move support and maintenance capability.
- *Vulnerable rear areas/logistics.* Middle Eastern military forces will also find it difficult to protect rear areas and key logistic facilities. Many will be overconcentrated or overspecialized in a few narrow areas.
- *Armor/anti-armor.* While Middle Eastern military forces may have parity with the West in a few aspects of armor and anti-armor capability, they are unlikely to have broad parity relative to fully deployed Western mechanized and armored divisions. Many will lack a balanced mix of tanks and other armor; others will lack advanced armor or fire control/sensor systems.

Each of these vulnerabilities sets priorities for the states in the region, both in terms of correcting weaknesses in their own forces and in exploiting the vulnerabilities of potential threats. At the same time, the West must consider how to reduce the weaknesses of friendly states and exploit the weaknesses of radical and anti-Western states. Reducing such vulnerabilities will be difficult for all the states in the Middle East. They cannot be corrected by acquiring "magic bullets," weapons systems, and technologies. Modern military effectiveness depends upon the ability of combat ready forces to exploit a wide mix of technologies, employ them with effective operational concepts and training, and use technology to produce superior force-on-force capabilities.

Scenario and Contingency Analysis
in Middle Eastern Forces

The final factor that must be considered in analyzing the post–Gulf War military balance in the Middle East is that it is all too easy to predict that future wars will occur and virtually impossible to predict the exact form they will take. The obvious candidates for a future war are Israel and Syria, Iran and Iraq. A war between Israel and Syria, however, will take on a radically different form if it escalates to weapons of mass destruction, involves a deliberate surprise attack or carefully planned preemption, is fought for limited objectives, occurs before or after Israeli mobilization, lasts for a few days or weeks, expands to include other Arab states, is fought on the Golan or in Lebanon, and/or does or does not involve rapid intervention by outside powers.

A war between Iran and Iraq may also involve conventional warfare or weapons of mass destruction, deliberate surprise, lengthy preparation on both sides, or be crisis driven. Its course will be heavily dependent on the loyalty of the armed forces and popularity of a given regime and on access to arms and funds from other countries. A united Iraq will be a very different opponent from one divided with active Kurdish and Shi'ite opposition movements. A border war will be very different from a war intended to overthrow an opposition regime or take control of a substantial amount of enemy territory. The degree of mobilization on each side will be critical to shaping the outcome of the conflict.

At the same time, many other wars are likely to take place in the Middle East that may begin as ethnic or civil conflicts, limited wars, or tests of will but then suddenly explode into very intense conflicts. The civil wars in Somalia and the Sudan are cases in point. They have lasted in some form for decades and have often involved battles that are little more than military chaos, but each has probably already killed more people than all the Arab-Israeli wars together or the Iran-Iraq War and Gulf War combined.

Any assessment of the Middle East military balance must begin, therefore, with the understanding that there is no single military balance. The analysis of a single or worst case scenario for the Arab-Israeli situation is likely to do far more to create a grossly exaggerated or unrealistic picture of Arab forces than shed any light on the very real risks in such a conflict. The same is true of comparisons which focus solely on wars that pit all Iranian forces against all Iraqi forces, or either Iran or Iraq against all the forces of all the countries in the Middle East. Some problems really are complicated and unpredictable, and meaningful analysis of the military forces of the Middle East must depend on an understanding of all the forces that may be involved in a given conflict, and then examine the many different forms such a conflict can take.

Notes

1. The reader should be aware that the author is defining the Middle East to include all of the Arab states, plus Israel, Iran, and Ethiopia. Mauritania is defined as an Arab state. The statistical information on the region is highly uncertain, and major differences exist between

virtually all sources. Few countries in the region report any statistical information on their military forces or defense spending, and when they do it is heavily politicized and often inaccurate. The UN data on the arms race in the region is notoriously poor, and even the most authoritative sources are uncertain. Unless otherwise specified, the economic and manpower statistics used in this chapter are taken from the CIA data presented in the Arms Control and Disarmament Agency (ACDA), *World Military Expenditures and Arms Transfers, 1987*, Washington, GPO, 1988; Central Intelligence Agency (CIA), *The World Factbook, 1987*, CPAS-WF-87-001, Washington, GPO, 1987; and CIA, *Handbook of Economic Statistics, 1987*, CPAS-87-10001, September, 1987. The data on military forces are estimated by the author based on personal knowledge and background but are adapted from two primary sources: The International Institute for Strategic Studies (IISS), *The Military Balance, 1988–1989*, London, IISS, 1988; and the Jaffee Center for Strategic Studies (JCSS), *The Middle East Military Balance, 1987*, Boulder, Westview, 1988.

2. Middle Eastern military expenditures account for roughly 6–10% of the world total and roughly one-third of all military spending in the Third World. It is important to note that these trends are shown in current dollars. U.S. estimates of expenditures in constant dollars show that there has not been any significant increase in average annual military spending since 1984 and that the annual trend in real spending dropped during 1986–1989. Such trends, however, are highly unstable and can be radically altered by major regional conflicts. For example, if one measures the trends in military expenditure to coincide with the peak of the Iran-Iraq War, the Middle East had the highest growth rate of any region in the world during 1978–1988.

Military expenditures in the Middle East place a massive burden on the regional economy. Military expenditures as a percent of gross national product (GNP) ranged from 12 to 15% in 1984–1987, although they dropped to 8.8% in 1988. Nine of the countries in the Middle East normally spend more than 10% of their GNP on military forces. Roughly one-third of all central government expenditures in the Middle East goes to regular military forces, and a significant additional portion goes to paramilitary forces and the production of conventional weapons and weapons of mass destruction.

The Middle East also devotes more of its manpower to military forces than any other region in the world. It has more than 16 men in its regular armed forces per every 1,000 in the population. This compares with an average of 4.5 men for the developing world, 9.1 for NATO countries, and 13.2 for Warsaw Pact countries. The next ranking region in the developing world is East Asia, with 4.7 men in uniform per 1,000 in the population—about one-third the ratio of the Middle East. The Middle East also leads other developing regions in terms of military expenditure per capita, with $345 for the Middle East, versus $328 for Latin America—the next highest region—and $420 for the developing world as a whole.

Even these statistics, however, understate the true size of the military effort in the region. Many countries received major amounts of foreign military aid and/or loans, and these figures are often reflected only in part, if at all. Many nations devote an additional 10–20% of their central government expenditures to military bases and infrastructure and to military industry, which they report as part of their civil budget. Most importantly, none of the statistics on military expenditures or manpower include various paramilitary forces, special reserves, or armed opposition to the government. This would increase the total military effort in most nations by 20–35%. If these figures could be accurately taken into account, it would become clear that arms not only dominate government spending throughout the region, they are its largest single profession except for agriculture.

Such figures also do not reflect the relative ability of a given economy and society to provide for such expenditures. The oil exporting nations may be developing nations, but they are comparatively rich, and their military spending reflects this. The non–oil exporting nations have far less ability to pay for military forces without reducing development activities. This is particularly true of the nations in North Africa, the Horn, and Yemen.

In all too many cases, the search for national security has become the enemy of economic development and social hope. Military forces consume far too much of the disposable income available to the governments of nations that desperately need development funds. Surplus capital goes to arms and military forces in states that are already overpopulated or whose birthrates ensure a declining per capita income in the future. Scarce resources of trained personnel are concentrated in the military forces or their support. Key financial institutions that should manage debt and foreign borrowing are subverted by hidden military accounts and debts. Already grossly overburdened urban and industrial infrastructures are strained by military construction and needs, and a host of unproductive and often useless military production facilities consume resources needed by civil industry.

In most cases, the military fails to provide meaningful support to the national economy in terms of construction and development activity. Even the record of military forces in training skilled personnel is erratic. Many Middle Eastern states rely on foreign technicians for the skills with the most potential benefit to the economy; others virtually demand enlistment for life, allowing skilled personnel to leave the service only when they are in their early to mid-forties or fifties.

3. Readers unfamiliar with statistics on the Middle East should be aware that total military manning is at best a rough indication of actual force strength, and that even the best unclassified data available are highly uncertain. The ACDA data used for most of the entries for 1975–1985 are not standardized in definition and differ sharply from the data issued by the IISS and sources like the UN. This is shown in part by the differences between the data for 1975–1985 and the data for 1986–1989, which are adapted from the data issued by the IISS. The data issued by individual countries are also highly unreliable and usually heavily politicized.

2

Arms Transfers to the Middle East

The expansion of Middle Eastern military forces has been dependent on massive arms transfers from outside the region. Some have encouraged conflict and some have helped to prevent it. These transfers have also created a complex matrix of political and economic relationships between buyer and supplier, often tying conflicts in the Middle East to the tensions between the superpowers or the politics of other regional conflicts.

Both from a regional security and arms control perspective, it would be desirable if many of these arms transfers could be halted and others could be sharply reduced. The problem, however, is not simple. As the tables in chapter 1 have shown, Middle Eastern states are already so well armed that even a total embargo on arms would not halt regional conflicts and might well create local imbalances in military capability that would encourage such conflicts.

Any attempt to limit arms transfers also relates to the problem that supplier states have different motivations. The end of the Cold War has sharply reduced U.S. and Soviet tendencies to turn every regional competition into an extension of their rivalry, but the economic problems created for Western and Eastern defense industries and the need Third World suppliers have for export income, may well replace the Cold War as an incentive to sell.

Like the other aspects of the Middle East arms race, any broad efforts at arms control must take realistic account of the different needs of both buyer and supplier nations. The same is true of efforts to build up regional deterrents to war and aggression. The issue of when and what to sell cannot be resolved with ideology or slogans. It must be dealt with on the basis of a clear understanding of the issues involved.

The Problem of Data

This understanding is not easy to come by. There are only three major sources of data on the overall patterns in the arms trade: The United Nations, the Stockholm International Peace Research Institute (SIPRI) and the declassified portion of the U.S. intelligence community data base that is reported in part in CIA handbooks, in the Arms Control and Disarmament Agency's (ACDA) annual *World Military Expenditures and Arms Transfers,* and in Richard F. Grimmett's annual study for the Congressional Research Service (CRS), "Trends in Conventional Arms Transfers to the Third World by Major Supplier."

Individual aspects of the work done on arms transfers by the United Nations and the Stockholm International Peace Research Institute are excellent, but neither the UN nor SIPRI is capable of producing independent estimates of the broad patterns in arms transfers that can hope to be particularly accurate. The United Nations has no intelligence collection capability and no real capacity to assess the reports provided by member states and outside research groups. The Stockholm International Peace Research Institute has very limited collection assets and must rely largely on press reports. It can provide educated guesstimates but little more.

The U.S. intelligence community has the resources and collection capability to make considerably better estimates, and its input to the ACDA's *World Military Expenditures and Arms Transfers* is unquestionably the best source available on the overall patterns by individual nation and region. Similarly, Grimmett's annual study draws on declassified data to provide the most up-to-date estimate in terms of overall transfers, although it does not provide anything like the detail of the ACDA document. Even these two sources, however, suffer from the following problems:

- They do not reflect many expenditures relating to the proliferation of biological, chemical, and nuclear weapons, and most research and development relating to missiles and other long range delivery systems.
- The data for many countries receive only erratic updating, often at long intervals.
- The costs shown for advisory and support services seem to be estimated in different ways for given countries and regions, and many support services are not included.
- Civil items imported for military use seem to be counted for some countries but not for others; as a result, imports of military technology are sharply understated for nations like Israel. The estimate of the cost of such items seems to be erratic. For example, all trucks and engineering equipment imported from military suppliers seem to be counted as arms, but similar equipment imported for military use from civil suppliers is not.
- Conversions into current and constant dollars, particularly those concerned with transfers to and from nations with state managed economies (including most Communist states), are extremely uncertain. All conversions into constant dollars from foreign currencies are somewhat suspect as to timeliness and updating.
- Price estimates of non-U.S. military equipment often seem to be guesstimates of the actual price.
- Transfers involving aid, loans, offsets, and barterlike arrangements—

which increasingly dominate all arms transfers—are erratic and often speculative.

- Data on agreements often fail to report actual or expected agreements that fall through. Data on deliveries often confuse partial deliveries with total deliveries and may report initial deliveries in a given year as total deliveries for that year.
- The release of data is delayed by six months to over two years for security reasons, making the timely analysis of current trends virtually impossible.
- No comparable data is provided on foreign technicians and military advisors, and the limited data on weapons transfer by type and number are grouped into broad regional totals with little analytic value.

Most important of all, data on the total cost of arms by buyer and supplier country tell almost nothing about the actual impact of the transfer on the military balance. The U.S., for example, often scores very high in terms of the total value of transfers but has never been a significant arms supplier to destabilizing countries like Iran, Iraq, Libya, and Syria. U.S. arms transfers have also never been a driving factor in the bloodiest civil wars in the region—which include the civil wars in Ethiopia, Lebanon, the PDRY, Somalia, and the Sudan.

The dollar value of transfers to buyer countries is also misleading and often irrelevant. There is little correlation between such dollar values and the number of key weapons systems like tanks and jet aircraft actually entering service in given buyer countries. Saudi Arabia, for example, has one of the highest ratios of dollars spent per major weapon entering active service in the world, Syria one of the lowest. In fact, it is hard to avoid the conclusion that many analysts focus on dollar data not because they lead to valid comparisons but because they lead to easy ones that do not require an understanding of military forces. But dollars do not kill people; weapons do.

Total Regional Arms Transfers Through 1990

In spite of these problems, the most recently released U.S. data on arms transfers to the Middle East do provide a broad picture of some of the trends in arms transfers. The latest data from the Arms Control and Disarmament Agency indicate that Middle Eastern countries spent some $180 billion on arms imports during 1978–1989, with $85 billion of this total being spent during 1985–1989.[1] The major states in the region consumed some 30–33% of the world's arms imports, versus 9–10% for NATO, 8–11% for the Warsaw Pact, 7–13% for East Asia, 11–12% for Africa, 10% for South Asia and Oceania, and 7–8% for Latin America.[2]

If the ACDA percentages showing arms transfers to the Middle East included Libya, Algeria, Tunisia, and Morocco as part of the Middle East, the recent annual percentage of world arms imports would always have exceeded 40%.[3] Six of the ten largest arms importers in the world are in the Middle East: They are Iraq, Saudi Arabia, Iran, Libya, Syria, and Egypt.

More recent data analyzed by Grimmett cover the period from 1983 to 1990.[4] Unlike the ACDA data, the CRS data do not show the trends in individual countries, and do not cover Mauritania, Chad, and the southern Red Sea states. They do, however, provide a good picture of the latest trends in the Maghreb, Arab-Israeli confrontation states, and the Gulf.[5]

These data, summarized in Table 2.1, indicate that the Middle East remains the largest arms market in the Third World. In 1983–1986 the Middle East accounted for over 61% of the total value of all Third World arms transfer agreements. During 1987–1990 the region accounted for 55.7% of all such agreements. The Middle East has also had the largest value of arms deliveries received by the Third World. In 1983–1986 it accounted for 62.5% of the total value of all Third World arms deliveries. During 1987–1990 it accounted for 50.8% of all such deliveries.

The data in Table 2.1 also illustrate several important facts about Middle East arms imports that would be equally consistent if virtually any other time period were chosen from 1960 onwards:

- *There are major differences in the pattern of new agreements and deliveries.* Deliveries lag agreements by up to half a decade and often involve substantial changes in the agreement.
- *The lag between agreements and deliveries often makes it difficult to relate weapons deliveries and the buildup of Middle Eastern forces to the cause of the original arms order.* In general, however, most orders are driven by local conflicts within the region. Belligerents tend to rush orders during the conflict. Surrounding states place precautionary orders that often lag several years more.
- *There is a great deal of volatility in the total size of orders and deliveries in any given period.* For example, 1983–1986 reflects the peak of the Iran-Iraq War, the aftermath of Israel's invasion of Lebanon, and a period of fairly extreme tension in the Maghreb. The period from 1987 to 1988 reflects a cease-fire in the Iran-Iraq War and a Gulf War where major imports could not be delivered to Middle East states in the UN coalition in time to affect the totals, where Iraq faced an arms embargo, when military tensions between Israel and Syria were comparatively limited, and when the Maghreb states exhibited less tension and faced serious internal economic problems.
- *The role of given supplier states varies sharply over time.* U.S. and Soviet flows have previously tended to vary according to the alignment of each nation with given states in the region, while European suppliers have experienced boom and bust sales patterns as they compete for major sales. More recently, developing country suppliers like China and North Korea have come to play a major role, while the Soviet Union and Eastern Europe have substituted concern for hard currency for concern for ideology.

The Total Flow of Arms
to Individual Middle Eastern Countries

The detailed patterns in Middle East arms imports by importing nation are shown in Table 2.2. This table provides both a history of arms imports by

TABLE 2.1 Regional Patterns in Arms Transfers to the Middle East, 1983–1990

New Arms Transfer Agreements

Supplier Nation	Total Arms Agreements		Percentage of Total Supplier Agreements with the Developing World		Percentage of All Agreements with the Middle East	
	1983–1986	*1987–1990*	*1983–1986*	*1987–1990*	*1983–1986*	*1987–1990*
United States	14,776	30,708	64.8	76.3	16.4	35.7
Soviet Union	28,610	17,500	46.2	28.4	31.8	20.4
France	9,090	10,110	82.6	83.2	10.1	11.8
United Kingdom	9,595	7,075	86.3	73.6	10.7	8.2
China	3,925	7,055	89.6	66.4	4.4	8.2
Germany	605	1,045	29.8	52.6	.7	1.2
Italy	2,530	180	67.4	22.2	2.8	.2
All other European	14,305	6,835	73.3	82.0	15.9	8.0
All others	6,480	5,460	60.3	61.0	7.2	6.4
Major West European[a]	21,820	18,410	78.2	75.0	24.3	21.4
Total	89,916	85,968	61.1	55.7	100	100

New Arms Deliveries

Supplier Nation	Total Arms Deliveries		Percentage of Total Supplier Deliveries to the Developing World		Percentage of All Deliveries to the Middle East	
	1983–1986	*1987–1990*	*1983–1986*	*1987–1990*	*1983–1986*	*1987–1990*
United States	20,101	13,336	77.8	67.9	21.0	19.5
Soviet Union	28,970	21,360	46.1	31.2	30.2	31.3
France	14,160	6,320	83.4	80.8	14.8	9.25
United Kingdom	4,670	8,255	72.7	89.9	4.9	12.1
China	4,965	6,395	89.8	83.5	5.2	9.4
Germany	1,450	485	30.2	27.6	1.5	0.7
Italy	2,560	170	62.5	24.6	2.7	0.3
All other European	13,175	7,245	75.8	73.0	13.7	10.6
All others	5,860	4,760	63.6	50.9	6.1	6.9
Major West European[a]	22,840	15,230	70.2	78.3	23.8	22.3
Total	95,911	68,306	62.5	50.8	100	100

[a]Sub-total of France, Britain, Germany, and Italy

Source: Adapted by the author from various tables in Richard F. Grimmett, *Conventional Arms Transfers to the Third World, 1983–1990*, Washington, Congressional Research Service, CRS 91-578 F, August 2, 1991.

country and a projection of current trends. While it is not possible to discuss these data in detail, they again reveal the broad impact of arms sales on the conflicts and tensions in given parts of the Middle East.

The data for 1982–1989 are historical and are based on various ACDA reports. They reveal both the growth in total arms imports over time and different countries' reactions to periods of tension and conflict. The projections shown for 1990–1994 in Table 2.2 are rough estimates and assume that

TABLE 2.2 Near Term Annual Trends in Arms Imports Impacting on the Gulf and Near East (in current $ millions)

	1972	1974	1976	1978	1980	1982	1984	1986	1988	1990	1992	1994
North Africa												
Mauritania	2	3	20	30	3	10	20	5	10	15	15	15
Morocco	5	20	210	440	350	270	210	90	130	130	130	110
Algeria	10	20	320	800	725	1200	775	625	850	720	740	760
Libya	160	330	1000	2300	2600	3200	2100	1200	600	1100	1000	1000
Chad	1	2	10	5	1	3	40	40	50	65	70	75
Tunisia	10	10	10	10	140	60	130	90	20	40	50	50
Egypt	550	230	150	400	550	2100	1700	1200	775	1500	1700	1700
Total	738	615	1720	3985	4369	6843	4975	3250	2435	3570	3705	3710
Levant												
Israel	300	950	975	900	800	925	775	500	2000	1400	1550	1600
Syria	280	825	625	1200	3300	2600	2200	1200	1300	1800	1500	1500
Jordan	30	70	140	170	260	850	230	450	450	150	450	460
Lebanon	20	10	10	20	40	50	240	10	10	20	20	30
Total	630	1855	1750	2290	4400	4425	3445	2160	3760	3370	3520	3590
Gulf												
Iran	525	1000	2000	2200	410	1600	2700	2600	2000	2300	2300	2300
Iraq	140	625	1000	2400	2400	7000	9100	5700	4900	900	200	1500
Subtotal	665	1625	3000	4600	2810	8600	11800	8300	6900	3200	2500	3800
Saudi Arabia	100	340	440	1500	1600	2800	3300	5500	2700	5500	5500	5500
Kuwait	5	10	80	320	40	110	600	140	210	600	1100	1400
Bahrain	2	2	4	6	40	5	40	50	30	70	70	75
Qatar	3	2	5	20	90	270	210	80	30	180	140	160
UAE	10	50	100	60	170	50	190	150	60	850	120	70
Oman	5	10	10	270	100	130	310	110	30	130	130	150
Subtotal	125	414	639	2176	2040	3365	4650	6030	3060	7330	7060	7355
Total	790	2039	3639	6776	4850	11965	16450	14330	9960	10530	9560	11155
Red Sea												
North Yemen[a]	10	10	20	110	575	420	80	280	430	400	400	400
South Yemen[a]	20	40	40	350	700	250	330	110	380			
Sudan	20	30	50	120	100	240	110	50	90	70	80	90
Ethiopia	10	10	50	1500	725	575	1200	330	700	840	570	470
Somalia	20	90	100	240	200	130	90	20	30	70	60	60
Total	80	180	260	2320	2300	1615	1810	790	1630	1380	1110	1020
Total region	2238	4689	7369	15371	15919	24848	26680	20530	17785	18850	17895	19475
Other related												
Turkey	150	150	320	220	310	470	500	626	975	730	650	680
India	210	190	490	360	875	2800	1300	3200	3400	3400	3400	3600
Pakistan	110	100	190	210	450	550	625	310	420	480	400	530
Afghanistan	20	80	90	130	500	700	650	1300	2600	730	650	650

[a]Now united into one country

SOURCE: Author's estimate based on computer data provided by the ACDA. Data are historical through 1989; estimates are provided from 1990 on. Figures represent current dollar value of actual deliveries. Djibouti is excluded because ACDA does not list this country.

many current political and military trends will continue for the near term but taper off at least slightly, without a new major conflict. The actual trends may be far less smooth.

Nevertheless, such projections are almost certainly correct in reflecting the fact that once most Middle Eastern nations initiate high levels of arms imports, they create a force structure that requires constant modernization and upgrading of foreign support. Nations become caught in a trap where they must respond to the changes in the military technology in neighboring states and can only maintain their existing equipment strength if they are willing to pay for massive real increases in the cost of the necessary military hardware, munitions, and military related imports.

The Role of Arms Suppliers

If the military balance in the Middle East has been shaped by local conflicts and the flow of arms imports into the region, it has also been shaped by competition among various arms sellers. The high levels of arms imports to the Middle East reflect both the past competition between the superpowers and NATO and the Warsaw Pact and the new competition between seller nations in the West, Communist bloc, and Third World. There is an inevitable interaction between the conflicts and tensions in the region and the role of key supplier states.

The most recent patterns in the role given major suppliers play in providing arms to the Middle East have already been shown in Table 2.1. If one looks at these patterns in more depth, one discovers several interesting things about the part suppliers play:

- *The data provide a strong caution against assuming that the figures for any given period reflect a broad trend.* As has been cited earlier, the ebb and flow of political tensions in the region and the lag between agreements and deliveries make it difficult to generalize. This is reflected in the fact that total arms deliveries fell from $95.9 billion during 1983–1986 to $68.3 billion during 1981–1990, a drop of 39%. However, new agreements went from $89.9 billion to $86.0 billion, a drop of only 4.3%.[6] This difference in the trends for deliveries and agreements came about because deliveries dropped in the late 1980s because Iran and Iraq lost the money to place new orders at their past volume in the mid-1980s and other regional conflicts also declined in intensity, while the Gulf War created a massive new round of orders in 1990.[7]
- *The United States, the Soviet Union, and Europe have consistently been the region's largest suppliers, although the PRC, North Korea, Latin America, and other Asian countries are playing a more important role.* The total share of the PRC and other developing states is now over 15% of both new deliveries and agreements, although it was less than 10% in the 1970s and early 1980s. The PRC alone has increased from 5% of deliveries to 12%, and 4% of agreements to 8%, although such figures obviously mean that the PRC will lose market share in the future.

- *The end of the Cold War and the turmoil within the Soviet Union has begun to affect its arms supplies to the Middle East.* While Soviet deliveries declined only from $29.0 billion to $21.4 billion if one compares the periods 1983–1986 and 1987–1990, new agreements shrank from $28.6 billion to $17.5 billion. In terms of total market share, Soviet deliveries actually increased as a percentage of total deliveries to the region—from 30.2% to 31.3%, because of the drop in total deliveries between the two periods. New Soviet arms agreements, however, fell from 31.8% during 1983–1986 to 20.4% during 1987–1990.
- *In contrast, the U.S. increased its market share.* While deliveries dropped from 21.0% of the regional total during 1983–1986 to 10.5% during 1987–1990—reflecting a major reduction in new orders from the southern Gulf states early in the 1990s, the U.S. share of new agreements rose from 16.4% to 35.7%. These increases in orders were stimulated largely by the increase in orders from southern Gulf states at the end of the Iran-Iraq War and again after Iraq's invasion of Kuwait.
- *The patterns for European orders reflect the general volatility in supplier market share that has long affected the smaller arms exporters.* Italy, for example, declined from about 3% of regional deliveries and agreements to less than 0.5%—which meant sales to the Middle East dropped from over 60% of Italy's agreements and deliveries to the developing world to around 20–25%. France declined from about 15% of new deliveries to less than 10%, although its percentage of agreements increased slightly from 10% to 12%. Britain declined from about 11% of new deliveries to 9%, although its percentage of agreements increased sharply from 5% to 9%, reflecting a massive aircraft sale to Saudi Arabia. Germany declined from about 2% of new deliveries to less than 1%, although its percentage of agreements increased from 0.7% to 1.2%. Other European sales dropped from 14% to 11% of the region's deliveries but dropped from 16% to 8% of new agreements.
- *It is important to note, however, that the Middle East is as important to arms suppliers as arms suppliers are to the Middle East.* During 1983–1986 the United States concluded 64.8% of its Third World arms transfer agreements with the Middle East and 76.3% of its arms agreements during 1987–1990. During 1983–1986 the Soviet Union concluded 46.2% of its Third World arms transfer agreements with the Near East region, although this figure dropped to 28.4% during 1987–1990. During 1983–1986 the four major West European suppliers collectively made 78.2% of their arms transfer agreements with Middle Eastern states, and the figure was about 75% in 1987–1990. During 1983–1986 China concluded 89.6% of its Third World arms transfer agreements with nations in the Near East region, and it concluded 66.4% of its agreements there during 1987–1990.[8]
- *Such arms exports are a significant share of total exports in many major exporting countries and a critical source of hard currency to many Communist countries.* Total arms sales to all regions—which were dominated by sales to the Middle East—accounted for 3–6% of all U.S. annual exports, 19–22% of

Soviet exports, 2–5% of French exports, 1–3% of British exports, 4–8% of Chinese exports, 2–5% of Bulgarian exports, 3–8% of Czech exports, 2–7% of Polish exports, and 20–36% of North Korean exports.[9]

- *The importance of the Middle Eastern market to arms exports and total exports do not necessarily mean that suppliers will not show restraint, but they do reflect a strong motive to keep selling arms.* This is particularly true because all of the Western nations shown will see at least a 25% drop in their domestic defense markets during the period between 1991 and 1996. The Soviet Union and Eastern European states are already desperate for hard currency earnings and have large surplus stocks of arms. Developing states like China and North Korea find it difficult to export finished high technology consumer goods and also have a major need for hard currency.

Arms Costs Versus Flows of Weapons

The data in Table 2.3, divided into two parts, show the sheer volume of weapons transfers into the region between 1983 and 1990. The trends in arms imports that have driven these transfers have been explained earlier, and it is clear that they are having a massive impact on the forces in the region. Several patterns in this table are of particular importance:

- *If one looks carefully at the patterns in weapons transfers, there is a sharp cut in the number of major weapons delivered between the periods 1983–1986 and 1987–1990.* This reflects the end of the Iran-Iraq War and a cut in Soviet deliveries to states like Ethiopia, Libya, Syria, and the Yemens.
- *It also, however, reflects a growing shift away from a focus on quantity to one on quality.* There is less interest in major new weapons platforms and more interest in upgrades, sophisticated munitions, and transfers that do not always show up in the form of assembled weapons systems.
- *The flow of arms often does not track with the flow of dollars.* While dollars are used as the most common measure of arms transfers, they often exaggerate the volume of U.S. transfers and understate Communist ones because the pricing used for Communist equipment is not comparable to that used for the U.S. and because so many U.S. sales are openly recorded sales that encompass services, munitions, and spares not included in the totals for other countries.
- *The dollar-weapons number gap is particularly important in the case of the former Soviet Union.* The Soviet Union provided only 31.3% of the total arms deliveries to the Middle East in 1987–1990 if measured in dollar terms. However, it provided 47% of all tanks, 8% of all artillery, 35% of all other armored vehicles, 65% of all combat aircraft, 79% of all helicopters, and 71% of all surface-to-air missiles (SAMs).
- *The dollar-weapons number gap is also important in the case of the U.S., but for exactly the opposite reasons.* The U.S. provided 19.5% of the total arms deliveries to the Middle East in 1987–1990 if measured in dollar terms. However, it provided only 15% of all tanks, 1% of all artillery, 13% of all

TABLE 2.3 Numbers of Weapons Delivered by Major Suppliers to the Middle East (Part 1)

Weapons Category	Total	U.S.	USSR	China	Major Western Europeanª	All Other European	All Others
1983–1986							
Tanks and self-propelled guns	4627	1052	1115	1440	320	430	270
Artillery	10507	1247	1475	1330	410	5380	665
APCs and armored cars	7044	369	2855	1190	810	1245	575
Major surface combatants	35	0	15	2	15	3	0
Minor surface combatants	153	4	16	8	20	90	15
Guided missile boats	26	0	8	6	12	0	0
Submarine	7	0	5	2	0	0	0
Supersonic combat aircraft	768	77	475	90	125	0	1
Subsonic combat aircraft	115	0	75	5	30	0	5
Other aircraft	417	22	100	0	65	185	45
Helicopters	433	23	215	0	135	15	45
Surface-to-air missiles	15624	1374	7605	150	1490	5005	0
Surface-to-surface missiles	24323	4373	7255	1010	3735	7890	60
Anti-shipping missiles	1258	18	300	115	825	0	0
1987–1990							
Tanks and self-propelled guns	1757	272	820	35	0	515	115
Artillery	5614	64	740	1465	2660	245	440
APCs and armored cars	2880	380	1020	25	15	1260	180
Major surface combatants	14	8	2	0	4	0	0
Minor surface combatants	205	0	10	5	80	5	105
Guided missile boats	2	0	0	0	2	0	0
Submarines	3	0	2	0	0	0	1
Supersonic combat aircraft	537	41	370	10	115	1	0
Subsonic combat aircraft	61	0	20	1	40	0	0
Other aircraft	265	0	20	0	20	145	80
Helicopters	375	0	295	0	40	35	5
Surface-to-air missiles	4235	520	3025	385	75	110	1200
Surface-to-surface missiles	8084	4734	270	105	0	2720	255
Anti-shipping missiles	495	0	170	215	100	0	10

TABLE 2.3 Numbers of Weapons Delivered by Major Suppliers to the Middle East (Part 2)

Weapons Category	Total	U.S.	USSR	China	Major Western Europeanª	All Other European	All Others
1983–1990ᵇ							
Tanks and self-propelled guns	6384	1324	1935	1475	320	945	385
Artillery	15761	1311	2215	2795	3070	5265	1105
APCs and armored cars	9724	749	3675	1215	825	2505	755
Major surface combatants	47	6	17	2	19	3	0
Minor surface combatants	357	4	25	13	100	95	120
Guided missile boats	28	0	8	6	14	0	0
Submarines	10	0	7	2	0	0	1
Supersonic combat aircraft	1305	118	845	100	240	1	1
Subsonic combat aircraft	176	0	95	6	70	0	5
Other aircraft	682	22	120	0	85	330	125
Helicopters	808	23	510	0	175	50	50
Surf ace-to-air missiles	20909	1894	10630	505	1565	5115	1200
Surface-to-surface missiles	32407	9107	7525	1115	3735	10610	315
Anti-shipping missiles	1753	18	470	330	925	0	10

ªMajor Western European includes France, United Kingdom, Germany, and Italy as an aggregate figure.
ᵇAll data are for calendar years given.
SOURCE: U.S. Government and Richard F. Grimmett, *Conventional Arms Transfers to the Third World, 1983–1990*, Washington, Congressional Research Service, CRS 91-578F, August 2, 1991, p. CRS-76.

other armored vehicles, 7% of all combat aircraft, 0% of all helicopters, and 12% of all surface-to-air missiles.

- *Given supplier nations have a major impact on given weapons categories.* For example, the PRC provided 26% of all artillery during 1987–1990, and major Western European states provided 47%. Other European nations provided 44% of all other armored vehicles. Major Western European suppliers provided 26% of all combat aircraft. Other European countries provided 34% of all surface-to-surface missiles, and China provided 43% of all anti-shipping missiles.
- *Important as the supplier nations (U.S., former USSR, UK, France, and PRC) have been to the supply of the Middle East, they are not the only source of supply.* During 1987–1990, other nations provided 630 tanks, 685 artillery weapons, 1,440 other armored vehicles, 110 minor surface combatants, 1,320 surface-to-air missiles, and 2,975 surface-to-surface missiles to the region. At the same time, they played virtually no role in selling combat aircraft.
- *This gap between dollar and weapons numbers measures makes many efforts to rank suppliers by arms sales largely meaningless.* There is little or no statistical correlation between estimates of total sales in dollars and the impact of these sales on the regional military balance.
- *More important, it exaggerates the importance of U.S. restraint.* The U.S. certainly is a major arms seller, but it plays a far less dominant role in the Middle East than dollar based comparisons show.

Supplier Relationships with Individual Middle Eastern States

Table 2.4 provides the most recent data available on the volume of sales to individual Middle Eastern states by major supplier. It is broken into two parts because the Arms Control and Disarmament Agency changed its method of reporting in 1992, and the two parts provide a more detailed basis for comparing recent patterns by supplier. While the totals shown in Table 2.4 reveal roughly the same patterns for each supplier as those in Table 2.1, they also show several other aspects of the arms race in the Middle East

- *The East-West conflict used to play a critical role in polarizing supplier relationships.* Since the breakup of the Soviet Union and Warsaw Pact, Middle Eastern states increasingly buy from a broad world market, and developing states now sell about $1–2 billion in arms per year to the Middle East out of an annual total of $20–30 billion.[10]
- *Total arms sales provide a misleading picture of the impact of given suppliers on regional conflicts.* Although the U.S. ranks second in arms sales to the region, it did not provide any significant arms transfers affecting the Iran-Iraq War, did not dominate arms transfers to the Morocco-Polisario conflict, and did not provide the arms sales that shaped civil war in Ethiopia, Somalia, the Sudan, and the Yemens.
- *Arms sales to radical and aggressor states have generally come from the Soviet bloc, PRC, and Third World nations.* Recent arms sales to Libya, Iraq, and Iran have been dominated by the Soviet bloc, with an increasing number of transfers coming from the PRC and North Korea.

TABLE 2.4 Arms Imports Impacting on the Gulf and Near East by Major Supplier, 1984–1988 (Part 1) (in current $ millions)

	Total	USSR	U.S.	France	China	UK	Germany	Czechoslovakia	Poland	Italy	Bulgaria	Others
North Africa												
Mauritania	30	0	0	0	0	0	0	0	0	0	0	30
Morocco	890	280	250	20	0	0	0	0	0	0	0	340
Algeria	3270	2500	100	50	0	140	0	410	5	40	5	20
Libya	6315	3600	0	60	10	0	30	925	30	430	130	1100
Chad	230	0	40	160	—	—	—	—	—	—	—	30
Tunisia	570	0	400	160	0	0	0	0	0	0	0	5
Egypt	6425	460	2800	825	450	170	50	0	0	270	0	1400
Total	17730	6840	3590	1275	460	310	80	1335	35	740	135	2925
Levant												
Israel	6100	0	6100	0	0	0	0	0	0	0	0	0
Syria	8255	6900	0	20	20	0	10	625	330	0	20	330
Jordan	1730	875	480	120	0	110	5	0	0	0	0	140
Lebanon	295	0	230	60	0	0	0	0	0	0	0	5
Total	16380	7775	6810	200	20	110	15	625	330	0	20	475
Gulf												
Iran	10520	5	10	100	2500	100	10	70	20	200	800	6705
Iraq	29650	15400	0	3100	2800	30	675	675	750	370	650	5200
Subtotal	40160	15405	10	3200	5300	130	685	745	770	570	1450	11905
Saudi Arabia	19530	0	5800	7500	2500	2100	0	0	0	30	0	1600
Kuwait	1325	180	210	535	0	110	150	0	0	0	0	150
Bahrain	505	0	250	60	0	5	180	0	0	0	0	10
Qatar	360	0	10	300	0	0	0	0	0	0	0	30
UAE	610	20	320	0	220	20	0	0	0	20	0	30
Oman	670	0	30	20	0	330	280	0	0	0	0	10
Subtotal	23000	200	6620	8415	2720	2565	610	0	0	50	0	1830
Total	63160	15600	6630	11615	8020	2695	7460	745	770	620	1450	13735

Red Sea												
North Yemen[a]	1420	1300	30	0	0	5	0	0	0	0	0	90
South Yemen[a]	1510	1500	0	0	0	0	0	0	0	0	0	10
Sudan	350	0	120	30	30	10	0	0	0	0	0	160
Ethiopia	4100	3900	0	0	20	0	0	20	0	30	0	130
Somalia	200	0	60	10	10	0	0	0	0	20	0	100
Total	7580	6700	210	40	60	15	0	20	0	50	0	490
Total region	105490	37615	17240	13130	8510	3125	7600	2705	1155	1440	1605	17535
Other related												
Turkey	3320	0	3300	0	0	0	0	0	0	0	0	20
India	10990	7600	130	1900	410	400	0	320	10	60	10	150
Pakistan	1920	0	1300	0	0	0	270	0	20	40	0	290
Afghanistan	4070	4000	0	0	0	0	0	0	50	0	20	0

[a]Now united into one country.

Source: Author's estimates based on data from the 1990 edition of ACDA, *World Military Expenditures and Arms Transfers*. Estimates are provided where ACDA data are not available. Figures represent current dollar value of actual deliveries of major arms and do not include substantial amounts of military related equipment or most of the arms going to paramilitary or various rebel and insurgent factions. The data used to estimate Soviet bloc, PRC, and Third World arms supplies are based on estimates of the comparable dollar cost to produce such equipment and usually sharply underestimate the true cost to the importing country. Djibouti is excluded because ACDA does not list this country.

TABLE 2.4 Arms Imports Impacting on the Gulf and Near East by Major Supplier, 1985–1989 (Part 2) (in current $ millions)

	Total	USSR	U.S.	France	UK	China	Germany	Other Warsaw Pact	Other European	Middle East	Other East Asian	Latin America
North Africa												
Mauritania	40	0	0	5	0	0	0	0	0	30	0	0
Morocco	770	0	240	150	0	20	0	20	330	0	10	0
Algeria	3260	2700	50	20	40	0	0	430	0	0	0	0
Libya	5080	3200	0	0	0	30	10	1200	550	30	70	20
Chad	210	0	40	140	0	0	0	0	0	0	0	0
Tunisia	465	0	300	160	0	0	5	0	0	0	0	0
Egypt	5800	575	2900	677	170	190	40	320	575	0	10	340
Total	15625	6475	3530	1152	210	240	55	1970	1455	60	90	360
Levant												
Israel	6100	0	6100	0	0	0	0	0	0	0	0	0
Syria	7160	6100	0	20	0	10	0	975	30	20	5	0
Jordan	2070	1200	460	110	40	0	10	60	100	50	0	20
Lebanon	70	0	70	0	0	0	0	0	0	0	0	0
Total	15400	7300	6630	130	40	10	10	1035	130	70	5	20
Gulf												
Iran	10250	0	10	75	100	2800	50	1400	3345	40	2000	210
Iraq	22750	13000	0	1700	20	1600	90	2900	1500	420	20	1300
Subtotal	33000	13000	10	1775	120	4400	140	4300	4845	460	2020	1510
Saudi Arabia	23040	0	5000	7000	7700	2500	40	0	250	0	140	390
Kuwait	1345	180	150	450	110	0	0	5	20	430	0	0
Bahrain	515	0	260	50	5	0	200	0	0	0	0	0
Qatar	160	0	10	100	20	0	0	0	0	0	0	30
UAE	1495	20	340	725	40	0	0	0	280	0	80	10
Oman	445	0	30	0	200	0	210	0	5	0	0	0
Subtotal	27000	200	5790	8325	8075	2500	450	5	555	430	220	430
Total	60000	13200	5800	10100	8195	6900	590	4305	5400	890	2240	1940

Red Sea												
North Yemen[a]	1765	1600	20	0	0	0	5	40	0	40	20	0
South Yemen[a]	1400	1400	0	0	0	0	0	0	0	0	0	0
Sudan	330	0	100	0	0	50	0	20	20	70	0	0
Ethiopia	3805	3600	0	0	0	20	0	60	10	0	110	0
Somalia	160	0	5	0	0	0	30	0	0	150	0	0
Total	7460	6600	125	0	0	70	35	120	30	260	130	0
Total region	98485	33575	16085	11382	8445	7220	690	7430	7015	1280	2465	2320
Other related												
Turkey	3970	0	2500	20	360	0	1000	0	70	0	0	0
India	16080	11800	210	1900	650	0	470	480	480	0	80	0
Pakistan	200	5	925	80	40	410	20	60	390	0	50	10
Afghanistan	9730	9700	0	0	0	0	0	30	0	0	0	0

[a]Now united into one country.

Source: Author's estimates based on data from the 1990 edition of ACDA, *World Military Expenditures and Arms Transfers*. Estimates are provided where ACDA data are not available. Figures represent current dollar value of actual deliveries of major arms and do not include substantial amounts of military related equipment or most of the arms going to paramilitary or various rebel and insurgent factions. The data used to estimate Soviet bloc, PRC, and third world arms supplies are based on estimates of the comparable dollar cost to produce such equipment and usually sharply underestimate the true cost to the importing country. Djibouti is excluded because ACDA does not list this country.

- *Several key supplier groups tend to be disguised by data that focus on the U.S. and USSR.* The second part of Table 2.4 shows that Britain and France collectively sell more arms to the Middle East than the U.S. ($19.8 billion versus $16.1 billion). It shows that the PRC is rising in importance, that other Warsaw Pact states collectively sold $7.4 billion worth of arms during 1985–1989, and that other European states sold $7.015 billion.
- *Similarly, given blocs of Third World suppliers play an increasingly important role in arms sales to the Middle East.* Sales and resales by Middle Eastern states totaled $1.28 billion, other East Asian states (dominated by North Korea) sold $2.465 billion, and Latin America sold $2.32 billion.

The Role of Military Advisors

The reliance of given importers on given suppliers has also closely paralleled their dependence on foreign advisors—although Egypt , Iran, and Israel have carried out much of their own support and technology transfer activities. For example, before glasnost led to major cuts in the Soviet advisory effort in the Middle East, Algeria had some 875 Soviet bloc advisors in 1988, Libya 2,300, Syria 2,830, Iran 100, Iraq 1,305, the YAR 405, and the PDRY 1,075.[11] These numbers reflected each country's dependence on Soviet bloc suppliers.

Dependence on a given nation for arms imports did not, however, imply political dependence—even during the period before the upheavals that broke up the Soviet Union and Warsaw Pact began to erode the past alignments with East and West. For example, six nations—Algeria, Ethiopia, Libya, the PDRY, Syria, and the YAR—have all been heavily dependent on arms imports from the USSR. Algeria and the YAR, however, are relatively free from Soviet influence, and Libya and Syria have scarcely been Soviet satellites or strong supporters of Soviet diplomacy. The PDRY is the only state in which Soviet military advisors played a key role in policy during most of the 1980s, and Ethiopia and the PDRY were the only states in the region which claimed to be Marxist states.

The U.S. has played a dominant role in the arms imports of six Middle Eastern nations. The U.S. is Israel's only major source of arms imports. The U.S. is also a critical arms supplier to Morocco, Chad, Tunisia, Egypt, and Saudi Arabia. U.S. ties to Israel, European competition, and the Iranian revolution have steadily cut the overall impact of U.S. arms sales, however, and the U.S. advisory effort has shrunk in relative importance as France and Britain have increased their share of arms sales to the region. France and Britain now support more modern equipment in the southern Gulf than does the U.S., and France was the only Western country whose advisors played a major role in the Iran-Iraq War. The PRC has also played a growing role in providing support to the region, although most countries buying PRC-made equipment can train and operate without a significant Chinese advisory effort.

Economic and Political Forces Driving Arms Sales

A number of economic forces have driven the efforts of seller nations. The increases that have taken place in European sales since the mid-1970s have been driven by a mounting need to export to maintain the viability of national arms industries—a pressure that is likely to grow sharply as NATO countries cut their defense investment in reaction to glasnost. The Middle East market averages well over $20 billion a year and is immensely lucrative. Like other countries, European sellers have been able to capitalize on the U.S. loss of sales to Arab states because of U.S. ties to Israel, and European arms sales have also enabled their industries to increase their production runs and make their military production and research and development activities efficient.

The hard currency benefits of arms sales have had an increasing impact on Communist states. Ironically, the end of the Cold War has had a mixed impact on the USSR. Since 1988 the USSR has been far less willing to help fund the arms imports of states like Libya, Syria, Iraq, Ethiopia, and the Yemens simply to confront the West. However, the USSR has shown greater willingness to sell to all buyers and has increasingly insisted on cash payment. Arms sales have become the Soviet Union's second largest export after oil and have provided important sources of hard currency to Eastern Europe. Similar trends have emerged in several East European states, particularly Czechoslovakia, Romania, and Yugoslavia.

As has been touched upon earlier, arms sales have increasingly attracted the PRC, North Korea, and other Third World nations, particularly Latin American nations like Argentina and Brazil. The volume of PRC and other Third World arms sales has nearly doubled since 1986, and the PRC, North Korea, and Brazil are now far more important arms suppliers to the region than the Eastern European states.

A number of Middle Eastern states have taken advantage of the growing number of suppliers to diversify their sources of arms supply. These states have included Iraq, Jordan, Kuwait, and Saudi Arabia. During 1977–1990 Iraq increasingly sought advanced technology from the West that it could not obtain from the USSR. Jordan attempted to play East against West to obtain the volume of arms it needed. Kuwait tried unsuccessfully to balance East against West to obtain added security against its neighbors. Saudi Arabia sought to find more reliable and less politically constrained arms vendors than the U.S.

Table 2.4 also indicates, however, that many nations with very limited technology transfer capability—such as the southern Gulf states—have far too many suppliers for countries which are heavily dependent on foreign technical support. The excessive use of multiple suppliers leads to a lack of standardization and interoperability within their force structures, additional serious diseconomies of scale in training and creating effective military facilities, and significant additional costs.

Notes

1. Totals are based upon Arms Control and Disarmament Agency (ACDA), *World Military Expenditures and Arms Transfers, 1990*, Washington, GPO, 1992, Table III. The totals for the "Middle East" include data on Bahrain, Cyprus, Egypt, Iran, Iraq, Israel, Jordan, Kuwait, Lebanon, Oman, Qatar, Saudi Arabia, Syria, UAE, YAR, and PDRY. For historical reasons, ACDA totals for the Middle East do not include Algeria, Ethiopia, Libya, Mauritania, Morocco, Somalia, Sudan, and Tunisia.

2. These percentages on arms imports are taken from various editions of the Arms Control and Disarmament Agency (ACDA), *World Military Expenditures and Arms Transfers*, Washington, GPO. The source data do not permit adjustment of the percentages.

3. For the statistical rationale for this statement, see the arms import tables in ACDA, *World Military Expenditures and Arms Transfers, 1989*, Washington, GPO, 1990; and *World Military Expenditures and Arms Transfers, 1990*, Washington, GPO, 1990.

4. Richard F. Grimmett, *Conventional Arms Transfers to the Third World, 1983–1990*, Washington, Congressional Research Service, CRS-9 1-578F, August 2, 1991.

5. The states in the CRS totals include Algeria, Bahrain, Egypt, Iran, Iraq, Israel, Jordan, Kuwait, Lebanon, Libya, Morocco, Oman, Qatar, Saudi Arabia, Syria, Tunisia, UAE, and Yemen.

6. All of the data in this section are taken from various parts of Richard F. Grimmett, *Conventional Arms Transfers to the Third World, 1983–1990*, Washington, Congressional Research Service, CRS-9 1-578F, August 2, 1991.

7. For example, Saudi Arabia placed $18.6 billion in new orders, Afghanistan placed $3.7 billion, Iran placed $2.9 billion, Iraq placed $1.4 billion before the embargo, and Egypt placed $1.1 billion. Accurate data on Syrian and Israeli orders are not available.

8. Richard F. Grimmett, *Conventional Arms Transfers to the Third World, 1983–1990*, Washington, Congressional Research Service, CRS-9 1-578F, August 2, 1991, pp. 21–22.

9. Arms Control and Disarmament Agency (ACDA), *World Military Expenditures and Arms Transfers, 1989*, Washington, GPO, 1990, Table II.

10. Arms Control and Disarmament Agency (ACDA), *World Military Expenditures and Arms Transfers, 1989*, Washington, GPO, 1990, p. 117.

11. Based on the counts in CIA, *Handbook of Economic Statistics*, Washington, CIA, CPAS 89-0002, September, 1989, pp. 184–185.

3

Trends in the Proliferation of Weapons of Mass Destruction

Given the previous patterns in the various arms races in the Middle East and the strains inherent in paying for imports of conventional arms, it is hardly surprising that many of the major military powers in the region are already involved in some aspect of proliferation. The wide range of interactive incentives for proliferation have had a powerful effect, and the search for weapons of mass destruction is scarcely new to the region. Israel first began examining nuclear options in the 1950s, and Egypt used poison gas against the Royalists during the Yemeni civil war in the 1960s. Israel acquired a significant stockpile of nuclear weapons by 1967. Egypt and Libya sought both nuclear weapons and long range delivery systems, and Egypt and Syria were heavily equipped with chemical defense gear when they attacked Israel in 1973.

Nevertheless, recent politico-military developments have interacted with the patterns shaping the conventional arms race to accelerate the regional search for weapons of mass destruction:

- The rising cost of conventional weapons, and the need for a cheaper "force multiplier."
- The availability of systems, key parts and equipment, and technical advice from a steadily widening number of European, Latin American, and Asian suppliers.
- Iraq and Iran's use of poison gas in their war and Iraq's use of poison gas against its rebellious Kurds.
- Revelations of the size of Iraq's nuclear, chemical, and biological weapons and long range delivery system effort, and about Iran's nuclear, chemical, and biological efforts and purchases of long range missiles from North Korea.
- A series of revelations about the size of the Israeli nuclear effort and the possibility that Israel may be developing intermediate range ballistic missiles (IRBMs).
- Syria's response to Israel in the form of the development of a capability to produce and deliver nerve gas and other chemical weapons.

- Possible Soviet use of chemical weapons in Afghanistan.
- India and Pakistan's development of nuclear and chemical weapons and long range missiles.
- Libya's possible use of poison gas during the final phases of its war in Chad and its creation of a massive facility for the production of weapons of mass destruction.
- Algeria's acquisition of a nuclear reactor that seems useful largely for nuclear weapons development purposes.

The end result is that virtually every Middle Eastern nation with a major technology base or large amounts of oil money has begun some form of effort to develop or acquire weapons of mass destruction and suitable delivery systems—although many of these efforts remain at the precautionary or contingency stage. This race to proliferate has interacted with similar arms races in other regions, for example, with efforts like those of Argentina and Brazil to develop long range missiles and make nuclear weapons, with similar efforts at proliferation in Asia, with South Africa's nuclear weapons and long range missile effort, and with the attempts of various Western European firms and the PRC to enter the market for missiles, nuclear components, and the equipment needed for chemical and biological weapons.

Current Acquisition Efforts in the Middle East

It is true that most countries in the Middle East have not openly deployed weapons of mass destruction and that many of the efforts in those nations seeking to proliferate are still in their early stages. It is also true that past estimates of the probable rate of proliferation of weapons of mass destruction have been notoriously overpessimistic, and estimates of the effects of the use of such weapons—particularly chemical and biological agents—also tend to be exaggerated. Nevertheless, Table 3.1 shows that this new aspect of the regional arms race is all too real.

The Impact of Long Range Missile Systems

In order to understand why so many nations have sought weapons of mass destruction, it is necessary to understand something of the technology and military effectiveness of the key systems involved. These include the use of long range missiles as delivery system and the advantages and disadvantages of using chemical, biological, and nuclear weapons.

Table 3.2 shows an estimate of the range and lethality of a wide sampling of the current surface-to-surface systems that affect the problem of proliferation in the Middle East. The range of many of these systems is impressive, but Table 3.2 also shows that missiles can deliver far less range-payload capability than most Third World fighter bombers.[1] A missile payload is also generally less effective than a bomb because more weight must be taken up to provide space for aerodynamic performance, fusing, and sometimes guidance systems. The higher speed of the warhead also often means the missile

TABLE 3.1 The Race for Weapons of Mass Destruction

NORTH AFRICA

Mauritania
- No resources of its own and no signs of any development activity.

Morocco
- No indications of any organized activity.
- No advanced long range delivery systems.
- Holdings of CS gas.

Algeria
Delivery Systems
- SS-N-2 and SSC-3 cruise missiles.
- 18 Su-20 Fitter C fighter ground attack.
- 60 MiG-23BM fighter ground attack.
- Multiple rocket launchers and artillery.

Chemical Weapons
- Basic technology and industrial infrastructure for production of nerve, mustard, and cyanide gas present in country.
- No indications of any organized activity.

Biological Weapons
- Moderate research capability.
- No indications of any organized activity.

Nuclear Weapons
- Limited research capability.
- Nuclear reactor delivery without any applications to electric power indicates active nuclear weapons development effort may be underway.

Libya
Delivery Systems
- Possible purchase of PRC-made M-9 missile with 200–600 kilometer range, or alternative system with MRBM/IRBM range.
- Al-Fatih missile with 300–450 mile range reported to be under development with aid of German technical experts.
- 48 FROG-7 rocket launchers with 40 kilometer range.
- 80 Scud B launchers with 190 mile range. In service since 1976.
- SS-N-2C and SSC-3 cruise missiles.
- Several active missile development programs. One is a West German design with a 500 kilometer range.
- Considering Brazilian Orbita MB/EE missile with 600 kilometer range?
- Considering Otrag missile?
- 6 Tu-22 bombers.
- Su-24 long range strike fighters with limited refueling capability using C-130s. Seeking higher capability jet tanker.
- 58 Mirage 5 fighter ground attack.
- 14 Mirage F-1D fighter ground attack.
- 44 MiG-23BM Flogger F and 14 MiG-23U fighter ground attack.
- 90 Su-20 and Su-22 Fitter E, J, F fighter ground attack.
- Tube artillery and multiple rocket launchers.

Chemical Weapons
- May have used mustard gas delivered in bombs by AN-26 aircraft in final phases of war against Chad in September, 1987.
- Nerve and mustard gas production facilities in an industrial park at world's biggest chemical weapons plant at Rabta. This plant can produce both the poison gas and the bombs, shells, and warheads to contain it. Its ultimate capacity is in excess of 1.2 tons per day. Plant built beginning in January, 1985, with some Japanese corporate assistance. Are probably two other research/batch production facilities. Plant seems to have started test runs in mid-1988.
- Additional chemical weapons plant may be in construction south of Tripoli.

(continues)

TABLE 3.1 (*continued*)

- Stocks of chemical bombs and rockets with mustard and perhaps nonpersistent nerve gas.
- Unconfirmed reports of shipments of chemical weapons to Syria and Iran do not seem valid.

Biological Weapons
- Some early research activity.
- No evidence of production capability.

Nuclear Weapons
- Has actively sought to create a development and production capability but no evidence of any real progress or success.

Chad
- No resources of its own. Libya may have used poison gas in Chad during final phases of fighting in 1987.

Tunisia
- No indications of any activity.

Egypt
Delivery Systems
- Possible cooperation with Iraq in paying for development and production of Badar 2000 missile with a 750–1,000 kilometer range. This is reported to be a version of the Argentine Condor II or Vector missile. Ranges have been reported at 820–980 kilometers, with the possible use of an FAE warhead. Egyptian officers were arrested for trying to smuggle carbon materials for a missile out of the U.S. in June, 1988.
- Possible cooperation with Iraq and North Korea in developing the Saqr-80 missile, with ranges of 80 kilometers.
- Reports of development of a capability to produce an improved version of the Scud B, possibly with North Korean cooperation. This would be an extended range missile.
- 9 Scud B launch units with approximately 100 missiles with 300 kilometer range.
- 12 FROG 7 rocket launch units with 40 kilometer range.
- 9 Tu-16 bombers.
- AS-15, SS-N-2, and CSS-N-1 cruise missiles.
- 32 F-4E fighter ground attack.
- 54 Mirage 5 fighter ground attack.
- 14 Mirage 2000EM fighter ground attack.
- Saqr-80 rocket with 50 kilometer range, and other multiple rocket launcher weapons.
- Tube artillery.

Chemical Weapons
- Produced and used extensive amounts of mustard gas in Yemeni civil war in 1960s, but agents may have been stocks British abandoned in Egypt after World War II. Effort was tightly controlled by Nasser and was unknown to many Egyptian military serving in Yemen.
- Completed research and designs for production of nerve and cyanide gas before 1973.
- Seems to have several production facilities for mustard and nerve gas. May have limited stocks of bombs, rockets, and shells.
- Unconfirmed reports of recent efforts to acquire feed stocks for nerve gas. Some efforts to obtain feed stocks from Canada. May now be building feed stock plants in Egypt.
- Industrial infrastructure present for rapid production of cyanide gas.

Biological Weapons
- Major laboratory and technical base.
- No evidence of major organized research activity.

Nuclear Weapons
- Low level research effort. No evidence of more than basic research since the 1960s.

LEVANT

Israel
Delivery Systems
- New IRBM/ICBM range high payload booster in development with South Africa. Status unknown.
- Up to 50 Jericho I missiles deployed in shelters on mobile launchers with up to 400 mile range with a 2,200 pound payload, and with possible nuclear warhead storage nearby. Unverified claims that up to 100 missiles are deployed west of Jerusalem.

(continues)

TABLE 3.1 (*continued*)

- Jericho II follow-on missiles are under development. These seem to include a single stage follow-on to the Jericho I and a multistage longer range missile. The latter missile seems to have a range of up to 900 miles with a 2,200 pound payload, and may be a cooperative development with South Africa (extensive reporting of such cooperation in press during October 25 and 26, 1989).
- A major missile test took place on September 14, 1989. It was either a missile test or failure of Ofeq-2 satellite.
- The Shavit I launched Israel's first satellite on September 19, 1989. It used a three stage booster system capable of launching a 4,000 pound payload over 1,200 miles or a 2,000 pound payload over 1,800 miles.
- Work on development of TERCOM type smart warheads. Possible cruise missile guidance developments using GPS navigation systems.
- F-15, F-16, and F-4E fighter bombers capable of long range refueling and carrying nuclear and chemical bombs.
- 160 Lance missiles with 130 kilometer range.
- MAR-290 rocket with 30 kilometer range believed to be deployed.
- MAR-350 surface-to-surface missile with range of 56 miles and 735 pound payload believed to have completed development or to be in early deployment.
- Arrow ATBM with slant ranges of up to 40 kilometers, speeds of up to Mach 9, plus Rafale AB-10 close-in defense missile with ranges of 10–20 kilometers and speeds of up to Mach 4.5. Tadiran BM/C^3I system.
- Israel seeking super computers for Technion Institute (designing ballistic missile RVs), Hebrew University (may be engaged in hydrogen bomb research), and Israeli Military Industries (maker of Jericho II and Shavit booster).

Chemical Weapons

- Mustard and nerve gas production facility established in 1982 in the restricted area in the Sinai near Dimona. May have additional facilities. May have capacity to produce other gases. Probable stocks of bombs, rockets, and artillery.
- Extensive laboratory research into gas warfare and defense.
- Development of defensive systems includes Shalon Chemical Industries protection gear, Elbit Computer gas detectors, and Bezal R&D air crew protection system.
- Extensive field exercises in chemical defense.
- Gas masks stockpiled, some distributed to population on test basis.
- Warhead delivery capability for bombs, rockets, and missiles, but none believed to have been equipped with chemical gas.

Biological Weapons

- Extensive research into weapons and defense.
- Ready to quickly produce biological weapons, but no reports of active production effort.

Nuclear Weapons

- Estimates differ sharply.
- At least a small stockpile of plutonium weapons. May have well over 100 nuclear weapons assemblies, with some weapons with yields over 100 kilotons and some with possible enhanced radiation (ER) variants or variable yields. Stockpile of up to 200–300 weapons is possible.
- Director of CIA indicated in May, 1989 that Israel may be seeking to construct a thermonuclear weapon.

Syria

Delivery Systems

- 20–30 new long range North Korean Scud Cs, probably with nerve gas warheads, now being deployed.
- May be converting some long range surface-to-air and naval cruise missiles to use chemical warheads.
- 36 SS-21s with 80–100 kilometer range. May be developing chemical warheads.
- 18 Scud Bs with 310 kilometer range. Believed to have chemical warheads.
- Short range M-1B missiles (up to 60 miles range) seem to be in delivery from PRC.
- SS-N-2, SS-N-3, and SSC-1b cruise missiles.
- 18–28 Su-24 long range strike fighters.

(*continues*)

TABLE 3.1 (*continued*)

- 50 MiG-23BM Flogger F fighter ground attack.
- 19 Su-20 fighter ground attack.
- 28 Su-17 fighter ground attack.
- 24 FROG-7 rockets.
- Negotiations for PRC-made M-9 missile (185–375 mile range) in August, 1989.
- Multiple rocket launchers and tube artillery.

Chemical Weapons
- Major nerve gas, and possible other chemical agent production facilities north of Damascus. Two to three plants.
- Unconfirmed reports of sheltered Scud missiles with sarin or tabun nerve gas warheads.
- Shells, bombs, and nerve gas warheads for multiple rocket launchers.
- FROG warheads under development.
- Reports of SS-21 capability to deliver chemical weapons are not believed by U.S. or Israeli experts.
- Israeli sources believe Syria has binary weapons and cluster bomb technology suitable for delivering chemical weapons.

Biological Weapons
- Extensive research effort.
- Probable production of botulism and other agents.

Nuclear Weapons
- Ongoing research effort.
- No evidence of major progress in development effort.

Jordan

Delivery Systems
- 32 Mirage F-1D fighter ground attack.
- May be buying Tornado or Mirage 2000 fighters with long range strike capability.

Chemical Weapons
- Technology base is present, but no signs of development activity.

Biological Weapons
- Technology base is present, but no signs of development activity.

Nuclear Weapons
- No indications of any effort.

Lebanon
- No confirmed indications of proliferation.
- No advanced air strike systems. Iraq seems to have sent FROG-7 missiles to Maronite forces.
- Maronite Christians began exploring possible purchase of poison gas in 1984.
- Hizbollah may have tried to produce an agent called "metallic nitrogen" (probably nitrogen mustard gas) at a laboratory in West Beirut.

GULF

Iran

Delivery Systems
- 15–30 new long range North Korean Scuds, with ranges near 500 kilometers. Future missiles may be manufactured in Iran, possibly as cooperative effort with Syria.
- 60–80 CSS-8 surface-to-surface missiles from China with ranges of 130–150 kilometers.
- Has acquired SU-24 and Mirage F-1 fighters from Iraq, may not return them. New Soviet aircraft may be on order.
- Scud B (R-17E) missiles with 230–310 kilometer range. Missiles provided by Libya and North Korea.
- Possible order for PRC-made M-9 missile (280–620 kilometer range).
- Iranian made Iran-130 missile with 150+ kilometer range.
- Iranian Oghab (Eagle) rocket with 40+ kilometer range.
- New SSM with 125 mile range may be in production, but could be modified FROG.
- F-4D/E fighter bombers.
- HY-2 Silkworm missiles.
- Multiple rocket launchers and tube artillery.

(*continues*)

TABLE 3.1 (*continued*)

Chemical Weapons
- At least two research and production facilities.
- Stockpiles of cyanide (cyanogen chloride), phosgene, and mustard gas weapons. Include bombs and artillery.
- Production of nerve gas seems to have started.

Biological Weapons
- Extensive laboratory and research capability.
- May be involved in active production.

Nuclear Weapons
- Has revived nuclear weapons production plant begun under shah.
- Significant German and Argentine corporate support in some aspects of nuclear weapons effort.
- Centrifuge technology from PRC, possibly Pakistan.
- Stockpiles of uranium.
- Facilities heavily damaged by Iraq in final months before cease-fire.

Iraq
- Massive purchasing effort in Europe. Up to $1 billion in unauthorized loans arranged through Georgia branch of Banca Nazionale del Lavro.

Delivery Systems
- Extensive delivery systems before war. Long range strike aircraft with refueling capability and several hundred Scud missiles. Many improved longer range systems, some with chemical warheads.
- Lost most Tu-16 and Tu-22 bombers to Gulf War.
- Some MiG-29 fighters.
- Still some Mirage F-1, MiG-23BM, and Su-22 fighter attack aircraft.
- Still some Su-24 long range attack aircraft.
- Gulf War and UN cease-fire terms will largely deprive Iraq of long range missiles. However, before the Gulf War had:
  - Extensive deployment of extended range Scuds called Al-Hussein (600 kilometer range).
  - Deployed Al-Abbas missile (900 kilometer range) at three fixed sites in northern, western, and southern Iraq. At least 12 missiles deployed. Can hit targets in Iran, Gulf, Israel, Turkey, and Cyprus.
  - Begun development of the Tamuz liquid fueled missile with a range of over 2,000 kilometers, and a solid fueled missile with similar range. Clear evidence at least one design was to have nuclear warhead.
- HY-2, SS-N-2, and C-601 cruise missiles not affected by UN cease-fire terms.
- FROG 7 rockets with 40 kilometer range.
- Multiple rocket launchers and tube artillery. Included long range super guns with ranges up to 600 kilometers.
- Iraq may have sought a long range missile test site in Mauritania.

Chemical Weapons
- Had massive production facilities and stockpiles of mustard, and tabun and sarin nerve gas. Gulf War and UN inspection may largely destroy.
- Technology for toxins, dusty mustard, persistent nerve gas agents, and other advanced agents.
- Warheads for Scud missiles, rockets, bombs, and shells. Have spray dispersal systems.
- At least three major research and production facilities at Salman Pak, Samara, and Habbiniyah.
- Extensive stocks of defensive equipment.

Biological Weapons
- Major research effort before Gulf War and UN cease-fire terms prohibited.
- Production had probably begun of at least one highly lethal agent. Degree of weaponization unknown.
- Laboratory capability to make anthrax, botulism, tularemia, and other biological agents.
- Possible bombs and missile warheads.

Nuclear Weapons
- Osirak reactor was designed for weapons production.
- Have since used Calutron, centrifuges, plutonium processing, chemical defusion and foreign purchases to create new production capability after Israel destroyed most of Osiraq. UN team has found new stockpiles of illegal enriched material.

(*continues*)

TABLE 3.1 (*continued*)

- Calutron enrichment equipment and technology.
- Experiments with chemical separation technology.
- Plutonium processing technology. Very limited amounts of Pu-239.
- U.S. blocked some shipments of centrifuge technology in 1989, but Iraq may have obtained magnets from PRC and some additional technology from Netherlands. Significant technology from URENCO.
- U.S. and UK intercepted shipment of high voltage military specification capacitors designed solely for use in triggering nuclear weapons in March, 1990.

Saudi Arabia
  Delivery Systems
- PRC-made CSS-2 (DF-3A modified) surface-to-surface missiles with IRBM ranges (2,500–2,800 kilometers).
- 34 Tornado strike fighters.
  Chemical Weapons
- Low level research effort began in 1984. No evidence of efforts to acquire actual agents.
- Plastics plants and oil facilities provide much of the equipment needed for production of chemical weapons.
  Biological Weapons
- No indications of organized effort.
- Laboratory capability to make simple biological agents.
  Nuclear Weapons
- Slight indications of financial ties to the Pakistani nuclear weapons effort, but no serious evidence of such ties.

Kuwait
- Invaded and seized by Iraq in July, 1990.
- Acquiring A/F-18 with medium range strike capability.
- No indications of any interest in weapons of mass destruction.

Bahrain
- No indications of any interest in weapons of mass destruction.

Qatar
- No indications of any interest in weapons of mass destruction.

UAE
- No indications of any interest in weapons of mass destruction.
- Has recently acquired Scud missiles.

Oman
- No indications of any interest in weapons of mass destruction.

RED SEA

"North" Yemen
  Delivery Systems
- 15 Su-22 fighter ground attack.
- SS-21 missiles.
- SS-N-2B cruise missiles.
- 65 BM-21 multiple rocket launchers.
- Tube artillery
  Chemical Weapons
- May have limited stockpiles of mustard gas captured from Egypt in the 1960s.
  Biological Weapons
- No indications of organized effort.
  Nuclear Weapons
- No indications of organized effort.

"South" Yemen
  Delivery Systems
- FROG-7.
- Scud B.

(*continues*)

TABLE 3.1 (*continued*)

- SS-N-2 and SSC-3 cruise missiles.
- 15 Su-20/Su-22 fighter ground attack.

Chemical Weapons
- No indications of organized effort.

Biological Weapons
- No indications of organized effort.

Nuclear Weapons
- No indications of organized effort.

Sudan
- Reports of imports of chemical weapons from Iraq in 1990. (Ten plane loads are reported to have been delivered. *The Manchester Guardian*, August 13, 1990, p. 4.)

Ethiopia

Delivery Systems
- 40 MiG-23 fighter ground attack.
- 78 MiG-21 fighter ground attack.
- SS-N-2 cruise missiles.
- BM-21 122mm multiple rocket launchers, and tube artillery.

Chemical Weapons
- Possible limited use of chemical weapons supplied by Soviets or Cuba against EPLF in Eritrea in early 1980s.

Biological Weapons
- Reports of use of mycotoxins or other toxins supplied by Soviets or Cuba seem to be untrue.

Nuclear Weapons
- No indications of organized effort.

Djibouti
- Nature of French stockpiles, if any, are unknown.
- No local effort or capability.

Somalia
- No local effort or capability.
- SS-N-2B cruise missiles.

OTHER RELATED

Turkey

Delivery Systems
- 95 F-4E fighter ground attack.
- 100+ F-104 fighter ground attack.
- Tube artillery.

Chemical Weapons
- Fully capable in terms of technology and industrial infrastructure.
- No indications of organized effort.

Biological Weapons
- Fully capable in terms of technology and industrial infrastructure.
- No indications of organized effort.

Nuclear Weapons
- No indications of organized effort.

India

Delivery Systems
- 40 Mirage 2000H fighter ground attack.
- 44 MiG-29 fighter ground attack.
- 95 MiG-23BN Flogger H fighter ground attack.
- 24 MiG-27 Flogger D/J fighter ground attack.
- 120 BM-21 122mm multiple rocket launchers.
- Tube artillery.

(*continues*)

TABLE 3.1 (*continued*)

- Prithvi and longer range missiles under development. The Prithvi is a 150 kilometer range missile with a 500+ kg warhead and inertial navigation. It is scheduled to be ready by 1993, and orders for production were placed in September, 1989. A successor system is now in early development.
- SLV-3 space vehicle could be adapted into long range surface-to-surface missile with 1,640–2,540 kilometer range. Longer range ASLV and PSLV boost vehicles are in development. Four-stage Polar Satellite Launch Vehicle was successfully tested in October, 1989. Can lift 420–600 pound satellites into polar orbit.
- Agni system is under development with ranges of 1,500–2,500 kilometers. Can lift 500+ kilogram warhead. Tested successfully at 625 mile range with 1 ton payload on May 22, 1989. Was tested again on September 27, 1989.

Chemical Weapons
- Research complete on production of nerve, mustard, and cyanide gas.
- No evidence of production or stockpiling.
- Possible rapid production and stockpiling capability for cyanide gas.
- Status of nerve and mustard gas production capability unknown, but all basic industrial infrastructure is present.

Biological Weapons
- Research effort. Laboratories actively involved in development of biological agents. No evidence of production.

Nuclear Weapons
- Tested nuclear device in 1974.
- Active nuclear weapons development and production effort in spite of denials. Research into fusion weapons, but initial production is likely to be fission weapons in the 100 kiloton range and possibly enhanced radiation weapons.
- Known stockpiles capable of rapidly producing at least 20–35 weapons. Some experts believe has produced enough plutonium to build up to 100 bombs. Seems to have greatly accelerated production of fissile material in late 1980s.
- In May, 1989 director of CIA reported indications that India is working on a hydrogen bomb.
- Currently arguing with U.S. that two reactors India imported from U.S. and constructed at Tarapur do not involve restrictions on their plutonium production.
- Seeking super computers from U.S. for use at Indian Institute of Science and Indian Institute of Technology. Both deeply involved in missile efforts. Inspection and use restrictions seem likely to be ineffective.

Pakistan
Delivery Systems
- 39 F-16 fighter ground attack.
- 16 Mirage IIIEP fighter ground attack.
- 50 Mirage 5PA3 fighter ground attack.
- BM-21 122mm multiple rocket launchers.
- PRC supplied M-11 missiles with 5–10 TELs and 30–45 missiles. The M-11 is reported to have a range of 60–300 kilometers, and a CEP of about 300–500 meters.
- HATF 1 (King Hawk) missile with ranges up to 80 kilometers in development. The CEP may be 1,000–4,000 meters and the payload approximately 500 kilograms. Tested on February 11, 1989.
- HATF 2 (King Hawk) missile with ranges up to 300 kilometers in development. The CEP may be 1,000–4,000 meters and the payload approximately 500 kilograms. Tested on February 11, 1989.
- A new HATF III missile program with ranges in excess of 60–290 kilometers was announced on October 14, 1989. The desired CEP may be 70–300 meters and the payload approximately 500 kilograms.
- Tube artillery.

Chemical Weapons
- No evidence of stockpiling.
- Research complete on production of nerve, mustard, and cyanide gas.
- Status of production capability unknown, but all basic industrial infrastructure is present.

Biological Weapons
- Research effort. Laboratories may be involved in development of biological agents. No evidence of production.

(*continues*)

TABLE 3.1 (*continued*)

Nuclear Weapons
- Seems to have acquired enough fissile material for one device in 1985. Centrifuge production of highly enriched uranium seems to have started in this year.
- Active nuclear weapons development and production effort.
- Research into enhanced radiation and fusion weapons, but initial production is likely to be fission weapons in the 20–50 kiloton range.
- Can probably rapidly assemble 2–11 uranium fueled weapons.

Afghanistan
- No local effort or capability to develop nuclear, biological, or chemical weapons.
- Extensive stocks of Scud missiles, long range air attack capability.
- USSR may have used lethal chemical weapons, and there are highly uncertain reports of the use of biological agents.
- Long range delivery systems are reported to have included artillery, helicopters, fighter bombers, and bombers.

SOURCES: Data are estimates based on press reports and other unclassified sources and do not represent official positions of the U.S. government. Sample sources include the work of Leonard Spector for the Carnegie Endowment; Seth Carus for the CSIS and Washington Institute; unclassified testimony in 1992 by the directors of DNI and CIA, Martin S. Navias, "Ballistic Missile Proliferation in the Middle East," *Survival*, May/June, 1989, pp. 225–240; John S. McCain, "Proliferation in the 1990s," *Strategic Review*, Summer, 1989, pp. 9–20; *New York Times*, July 3, 1988, p. 3; *Christian Science Monitor*, July 15, 1988, p. 1; "A Deadly New Missile Game," *Time*, July 4, 1988, p. 38; *Washington Post*, March 27, 1988, p. C-1, and April 5, 1988, p. A-1; Giovanni A. Snilde, "United States Efforts in Curbing Chemical Weapons Proliferation," in *World Military Expenditures and Arms Transfers, 1990*, Washington, ACDA, 1990, pp. 21–24; "Ballistic Missile Proliferation in the Developing World," in *World Military Expenditures and Arms Transfers, 1988*, Washington, ACDA, 1989, pp. 17–20; and "Ballistic Missile Proliferation Potential of Non-Military Powers," CRS-87-654 SPR, August 6, 1987, and working updates by the CRS.

hits in a way that directs more of its explosive power upwards and reduces its impact on ground targets.

It is also clear from Table 3.2 that the long range missiles now available to Third World states lack the combination of accuracy and payload to be highly lethal as long as they use high explosive warheads. This is especially true because the velocity and vector of most such missiles produce less damage than an explosion by a similar amount of conventional high explosive in a regular free-fall bomb.

Conventionally armed ballistic missiles without terminal homing guided systems cannot damage military targets as large as airfields except through sheer luck, since they have so little probability of hitting a meaningful target. They have less than a 0.3 probability of kill (pk) per round against a building-sized target when fired into a crowded city. Such missiles may have technical glamour, but they are no substitute for aircraft, multiple rocket launchers, and artillery in inflicting damage.

This situation seems certain to change once user countries acquire chemical or biological warheads, or cruise missiles with advanced guidance systems reach the Third World. Even missiles with chemical and biological warheads, however, may often be more weapons of terror than true weapons of mass destruction. While critical military targets like air bases, assembly areas, headquarters and communications sites, and key supply and production sites will be highly vulnerable, dispersed military forces will be hard to attack with such weapons.

TABLE 3.2 Comparative Range and Lethality of Surface-to-Surface Missiles

Source Country	Type	Initial Operational Capability	Range (km)	Warhead Payload (kg)	Nominal CEP[a] at Range (meters)		Warhead Types
					Engineering	Operational	
USSR	SS-1B Scud A	1957	130	900	900	1800	HE, N, CB[b]
USSR	SS-1C Scud B	1965	290	1000	900	1600	HE, N, CB
USSR	Scud C	?	450	550	900	2200	HE, N, CB
USSR	FROG-7	1965	70	400–600	400	900	HE, N, CB
USSR	SS-21	1978	70	200–300	450–500	900	HE, N, CB
USSR	SS-23	1980	500	350	350	900	HE, N, CB
USSR	SS-12	1969	800	300	750	3000	N
USSR	SS-22	1979	900	300	300	700	N
USSR	Sepal SSC-1B	1962	150–225	—	—	900	N
U.S.	BGM-109G GLCM	1983	2,500	—	20	100	N
U.S.	MGM-31A/B Pershing 1A	1962	160–720	350	400	800	N
U.S.	Pershing II	1984	160–1770	—	40	180	N
U.S.	MGM-52 Lance	1972	110	250	150–400	400–900	HE, N
France	Pluton	1974	10–120	—	150–300	300–500	N
Argentina	Condor I Alacran/	?	100	—	600	900	?
	Condor II	?	820–980	600–1000	600	1200	?
Egypt	Imp. Scud Vector/	?	450–600	500	1200	2000	?
	Condor II	?	820–980	600–1000	600	1200	?
PRC	CSS-2 DF-3	1970	2700–3050	1800	800	2000	HE, N
PRC	CSS-2 DF-3A (Saudi)	1987	2400–3000	2200	800	2000	HE, N
PRC	CSS-1 DF-2	1970	1,200	1100	700	1800	HE, N
PRC	M-9	198?	600	500	500	700	N, CB
PRC	M-11	1988	650–850	500–1000	—	—	HE, C, B?
North Korea	Scud C	1990	600	500	600	900	HE, C, B?
Iran	Iran-130	1987	130–200	—	—	—	HE
Iran	Scud R-300/R-17E	1985	290–320	—	—	—	HE, C, B?
Iraq	Scud B/C/D/ R-300/R-17E Variant	1979					
	Al-Hussein Scud C/D Variant/	1987	615	135–500	1600	3200	HE, C, B?
	Al-Abbas	1989	920	390–500	3200	4800	HE, C, B?
	Solid fuel?	1990	350	1000	500	1000	?
	Tamuz	1990	2000	600–1000	600	1200	HE, CW, B?
	Solid fuel?	1990	1800	1000	600	1200	HE, CW, B

(continues)

TABLE 3.2 *(continued)*

Country	Source Type	Initial Operational Capability	Range (km)	Warhead Payload (kg)	Nominal CEP[a] at Range (meters)		Warhead Types
					Engineering	Operational	
Israel	Jericho I	?	200–480	250	1000	1800	HE, N
	Jericho Follow-on	?	490–750	450–680	1600	3200	N
	Jericho Follow-on	?	800–1480	750	2000	2700	N
India	Prithvi	?	150	600–800	1600	3200	?
	Agni	?	1700–2400	1000	3200	4800	?
Pakistan	HATF 1- King Hawk		80	600–800	600	900+	?
	HATF 2- King Hawk		300–350	800–1000	2000	4000	?
Saudi Arabia	CSS-2 (DF-3A)	1987	2500	2000	1200	2000	HE
USSR	BM-21 122mm MRL	1964	20.5	40	—	900	HE, CW
USSR	M-1972 122mm MRL	1972	20.5	40	—	900	HE, CW
USSR	BM-14/16 140mm MRL	1952	9.8	40	—	800	HE, CW
PRC	T-63 107mm MRL		8.1	12	—	600	HE
PRC	140mm MRL		10	19	—	1200	HE
U.S.	MLRS 115mm MRL	1981	30+	12	—	200	HE
Iran	Oghab	1986	40	—	—	—	HE
Iran	Shahin 2	1988	70	180	—	—	HE
USSR	M-46 130mm gun	1954	27.2	74	—	—	HE, CW
USSR	2S5 152mm gun	1980	27	96	—	—	HE,CW
U.S.	M-107 175mm gun	1962	32.7	147	70	150	HE, CW
U.S.	M-109A1 155mm how	1966	18–30	95	70	120	N, HE, CW
U.S.	M-110 203mm how	1962	21.3	170	70	120	N, HE, CW

[a]CEP stands for circular error probable and is an indication of a missile's accuracy. The figure represents the radius of a circle in which half the warheads are expected to fall. It should be noted, however, that the theoretical figure applies only to missiles that operate perfectly up to the point which the missile has left the launcher and at least its first booster and guidance system are operating perfectly. Operational CEPs can only be guesstimated but will be much lower. Missiles generally do not have fail-safe warheads, so a substantial number will have partial failures and deliver their warheads far from their intended targets.

[b]HE = high explosive; N = nuclear; CB = chemical-biological.

SOURCES: Estimated by the author using a number of sources, including various editions of the IISS, *Military Balance, Jane's Weapons Systems*, Shuey, Lenhart, Snyder, Donnelly, Mielke, and Moteff, *Missile Proliferation: Survey of Emerging Missile Forces*, Washington, D.C., Congressional Research Service, Report 88-642F, February 9, 1989; Fred Donovan, "Mideast Missile Flexing," *Arms Control Today*, May, 1990, p. 31; Duncan Lennox, "The Global Proliferation of Ballistic Missiles," *Jane's Defence Weekly*, December 25, 1989, pp. 1384–1385; working papers by General Dynamics, ACDA, and CRS data. The data shown are deliberately kept consistent with the sources shown, and the reader should consult the text for alternative estimates.

It takes tons of even the most lethal gas agents to produce large numbers of casualties under most military conditions. To put this into perspective, under optimal weather and delivery conditions, to achieve 50% lethality over a 1 square kilometer area, it takes about 21 tons of phosgene, 4 tons of mustard gas, 2 tons of tabun, 0.5 tons of sarin, or 0.25 tons of VX.[2] Under most real-world conditions, far larger amounts are required or the actual number of deaths will be far smaller. Some U.S. studies estimate that the densities of nerve gas called for in Soviet manuals could produce casualties as low as 5%, although even this percentage would have a significant inhibiting effect on military operations.[3]

Another way of looking at lethality is to examine the VX chemical warhead used on the Soviet version of the Scud missile. This is an 884mm warhead weighing 2,170 pounds, of which 1,200 pounds is actual chemical agent. A variable time fuse is fitted and the agent is dispersed by a bursting charge located along the center axis of the warhead. Assuming a burst altitude of 4,000 feet and a ground wind speed of 3 feet per second, the contaminated area would cover a band about 0.33 miles wide and 2.5 miles long that began about .5 mile from the burst. Assuming a flat plain and no protection, up to 50% of the exposed personnel would be killed. This is impressively lethal, and the agent would remain lethal for several days to several weeks. It is important to note, however, that this assumes exposed personnel, a flat plain, and optimal delivery conditions. Real lethality may be only 5–20% as high.[4]

Biological warheads can be far more lethal than chemical warheads. Botulinum toxin is about 3 million times more potent than a nerve agent like sarin. A Scud missile warhead capable of optimal distribution of its full payload of botulinum could contaminate an area of 3,700 square kilometers, or sixteen times the theoretical area that could be covered with the same payload of sarin. It is also important to note that by the time any symptoms appear, treatment for botulinum has little chance of success. Rapid field detection methods do not exist for biological agents, but botulinum can debilitate in a few hours and kill in as little as twelve. In contrast, anthrax can cover an even larger area. It is less lethal and takes two to four days to kill but is also much more persistent.[5]

At the same time, chemical and biological warheads are extremely difficult to engineer and require well planned testing efforts to produce predictable and effective results. Such design and testing are currently beyond the skills of most states in the Middle East. Iraq, for example, had only crude and relatively ineffective chemical warheads for its Scud missiles at the time of the Gulf War in spite of a major investment. Its chemical bombs and shells were moderately effective but were far less lethal than their U.S. and Soviet counterparts. The lethality of Syria's warheads for its chemically armed Scuds and new long range North Korean missiles will be highly dependent on whether Syria has acquired actual chemical warheads from the Soviet Union and North Korea or full designs. Syria has very little independent missile design capability.

Biological warhead, bomb, rocket, and shell designs are even more complex than those for chemical weapons. Dispersing biological agents efficiently requires great design skill and very demanding testing and simulation. Minor errors in dispersal, altitude of burst, and a host of other factors can deprive a warhead of much of its effectiveness. Unless such warheads use toxins, they also tend to have delayed effects and are better suited for attacks on rear areas and population centers than military targets in the area of operations.

This situation could change once cruise missiles and missiles with terminal command guidance become available to the Third World. While there is little indication that such systems will be deployed during the next few years, they are much cheaper to build than ballistic missiles, do not present the problem of high reentry velocities, and can strike a specific target within 10–20 meters. Cruise missiles with highly advanced terminal guidance are also the only missile systems sufficiently accurate to be lethal with conventional warheads against specific strategic targets at long ranges. Cruise missile systems with terminal homing require mapping and targeting capabilities beyond the reach of most Third World nations, however, and they are unlikely to enter the world arms market before the late 1990s.

In the interim, long range surface-to-surface missiles with conventional warheads will be able to do a great deal of damage to area targets but are not the best way of delivering conventional ordnance and may not even be the best way of delivering "poor man's nuclear weapons."[6] In most cases, high payload, long range fighter bombers with advanced avionics will continue to offer a far more predictable and effective way to deliver the large payloads required under the highly specialized delivery conditions necessary to be effective. Until Third World states acquire either effective biological warheads for their missiles or actual nuclear weapons, the effectiveness of missiles is likely to depend more on their political impact than their actual ability to inflict casualties or physical damage.

It should be noted, however, that there is a danger in focusing too much on the difficulties that most Middle Eastern states face in using missiles to delivery weapons of mass destruction. First, even crude and inefficient missiles armed with biological and chemical weapons are capable of producing terror and highly unpredictable political and military reactions. They can deter, but they can just as easily lead to uncontrolled escalation. Second, most Middle Eastern states already have modern strike aircraft—many refuelable—that can hit any city or target in neighboring countries. If such aircraft face a higher probability of intercept in a few countries like Israel, they can carry far higher payloads—often as much as eight to ten times the payload per aircraft of an extended range Scud. They also fly at speeds and altitudes that make the delivery of biological and chemical weapons far easier than the high reentry speeds of missiles. A single-minded focus on missile systems—overlooking aircraft and shorter range tactical systems— ignores an existing and potentially more lethal threat.

The Impact of Chemical Weapons

Chemical weapons have so far proven to be the easiest route to proliferation and they offer Middle Eastern states a wide variety of options. As Table

3.3 indicates, there are eight major categories of chemical weapons, five of which include lethal agents. The main categories are:

- *Nerve gases.* Colorless, odorless, tasteless chemicals closely related to organophosphorous insecticides. They poison the nervous system and disrupt the vital bodily functions. They kill quickly and are more lethal than any other chemical weapons except toxins.
- *Blister agents or vesicants.* Oily liquids which burn and blister the skin within hours after exposure and have general toxic effects. Mustard gas is the best known example.
- *Choking agents.* Highly volatile liquids which irritate and severely injure the lungs when breathed and cause death from choking. They are much less lethal than nerve gas.
- *Blood agents.* Chemicals that enter the body through the respiratory tract. They produce death by interfering with the tissue's use of oxygen and are much less lethal than nerve agents.
- *Toxins.* Biologically produced chemical substances which are highly toxic and can act by ingestion or inhalation. They can be more lethal than nerve gas and are sometimes categorized as biological weapons.
- *Control, tear, and harassing gases.* Nonlethal sensory irritants that cause temporary flow of tears, irritation or burning of the skin and respiratory tract, and/or nausea and vomiting. They are used in riot and population control as well as in war.[7]
- *Psycho-chemicals.* The equivalent of drugs which cause temporary mental disturbances.[8]
- *Herbicides and defoliants.* These agents poison or desiccate the leaves of plants, causing them to die. They can be used to attack food crops or clear large areas. Many have at least limited short and long term toxic effects against humans and animals.

These agents can be delivered using a wide range of means, including grenades, shells, rockets, missile warheads, bombs, dispensers, emplaced munitions, mines, and gas generators. Most small weapons and mines simply explode the gas agent over a limited area, although ripples of rockets from weapons like multiple rocket launchers can cover a wide area. Larger weapons can carry submunitions which are dispensed over the target area by the parent munition and explode independently. Alternatively, warheads filled with several hundred kilograms of an agent of low vapor pressure will cover large areas with droplets when they are exploded. Generators manufacture a gas from an area upwind of the target.

Chemical weapons rarely, however, achieve anything approaching their theoretical lethality. Wind, temperature, humidity, dust, and other climatic factors make the distribution of chemical agents unpredictable, and it is extremely difficult to build a warhead or bomb that distributes an agent evenly at the right altitude. While defense and decontamination gear is cumbersome, time-limited, and retains large amounts of body heat, they are relatively effective in most tactical situations. In spite of its very real problems, defense and decontamination gear can reduce the casualties from even intense amounts of nerve gas from 80–95% to about 5% light casualties. The quality of detection is also improving.

The operational limits of chemical weapons are indicated by the fact that only 1 ounce of mustard gas can kill a man if it is inhaled directly into the lungs, but more than 60 pounds of mustard gas were used during World War I for every man killed or wounded and only 2% of those affected by mustard gas died. Similarly, Iran claimed that 27,571 Iranians had been victims of chemical warfare by April 8, 1987, but that only 262 had died—less than 1%. It should be noted, however, that a small amount of VX nerve gas killed nearly 6,000 sheep grazing over an area of 200 square miles 30 miles away from a spraying aircraft.[9]

Large amounts of chemicals must be distributed even under optimal delivery conditions, although this varies by agent. Used on the ground (in an exposed flat area of one square kilometer), it takes 19 tons of mustard gas, 14 tons of tabun, and 2 tons of VX.[10] To put this into perspective, Libya is currently estimated to have total stocks of 100 tons of chemical weapons. The critical facilities on a single air base occupies an area of at least 5 square kilometers, and a single division may be spread over an area of 15–30 square kilometers, even when concentrated and deployed for battle.

At the same time, it is difficult to control the proliferation of such weapons. It is virtually impossible to prevent and/or detect laboratory batch production of pure mustard and nerve gases once the technology is developed, and several tons of such material are adequate to arm enough missile warheads and bombs to act as terror weapons. No currently proposed inspection regime would deny a country the capability for such production in a crisis, and the current inspection methods proposed for the Chemical Weapons Convention would allow most countries to easily conceal tons of binary agents.

The Australia Group lists fifty chemicals as precursor chemicals, of which the U.S. controls forty. This includes a core list of ten chemicals and a warning list of forty others. The ten most threatening chemicals are dimethyl methylphosphonate, dimethyl phosphite, methyl phosphonyl dichloride, methyl phosphonyl difluoride, phosphorous oxychloride, phosphorous trichloride, thiodiglycol, thionyl chloride, and trimethyl phosphite. While the most threatening chemicals are under export controls in most producing countries, controls on third party transfers are limited—particularly for amounts suitable for industrial processes.[11] Some of these chemicals are widely available from industrial countries throughout the world, although the only country in the Middle East that manufactures large amounts of such precursors for industrial purposes is Israel, which produces sodium fluoride and sodium sulfide.

The Impact of Biological Weapons

While 110 states signed a treaty prohibiting the production and stockpiling of biological weapons and toxins in 1972, this has not prevented a num-

TABLE 3.3 Major Chemical Agents That Seem Likely to Affect the Future Military Balance in the Middle East

NERVE AGENTS: Agents that quickly disrupt the nervous system by binding to enzymes critical to nerve functions, causing convulsions and/or paralysis. Must be ingested, inhaled, and absorbed through the skin. Very low doses cause a running nose, contraction of the pupil of the eye, and difficulty in visual coordination. Moderate doses constrict the bronchi, cause a feeling of pressure in the chest, weaken the skeletal muscles, and cause fibrillation. Large doses cause death by respiratory or heart failure. Can be absorbed through inhalation or skin contact. Reaction normally occurs in 1–2 minutes. Death from lethal doses occurs within minutes, but artificial respiration can help, and atropine and the oximes act as antidotes. The most toxic nerve agents kill with a dosage of only 10 milligrams per minute per cubic meter, versus 400 for less lethal gases. Recovery is normally quick, if it occurs at all, but permanent brain damage can occur:

Tabun (GA)

Sarin (GB)—nearly as volatile as water and delivered by air. A dose of 5 mg/min/m^3 produces casualties; a respiratory dose of 100 mg/min/m3 is lethal. Lethality lasts 1–2 days.

Soman (GD)

GF

VR-55 (Improved Soman)—a thick oily substance which persists for some time.

VK/VX—a persistent agent roughly as heavy as fuel oil. A dose of 0.5 mg/min/m^3 produces casualties; a respiratory dose of 10 mg/min/m^3 is lethal. Lethality lasts 1–16 weeks.

BLISTER AGENTS: Cell poisons that destroy skin and tissue, cause blindness upon contact with the eyes, and which can result in fatal respiratory damage. Can be colorless or black oily droplets. Can be absorbed through inhalation or skin contact. Serious internal damage if inhaled. Penetrates ordinary clothing. Some have delayed and some have immediate action. Actual blistering normally takes hours to days, but effects on the eyes are much more rapid. Mustard gas is a typical blister agent and exposure of concentrations of a few milligrams per meter over several hours generally at least causes blisters and swollen eyes. When the liquid falls onto the skin or eyes it has the effect of second or third degree burns. It can blind and cause damage to the lungs leading to pneumonia. Severe exposure causes general intoxication similar to radiation sickness. HD and HN persist up to 12 hours. L, HL, and CX persist for 1–2 hours. Short of prevention of exposure, the only treatment is to wash the eyes, decontaminate the skin, and treat the resulting damage like burns:

Sulfur mustard (H or HD)—a dose of 100 mg/min/m^3 produces casualties; a dose of 1,500 mg/min/m^3 is lethal. Residual lethality lasts up to 2–8 weeks.

Distilled mustard (DM)

Nitrogen mustard (HN)

Lewisite (L)

Phosgene oxime (CX)

Mustard Lewisite (HL)

CHOKING AGENTS: Agents that cause the blood vessels in the lungs to hemorrhage and fluid to build up until the victim chokes or drowns in his or her own fluids (pulmonary edema). Provide quick warning through smell or lung irritation. Can be absorbed through inhalation. Immediate to delayed action The only treatment is inhalation of oxygen and rest. Symptoms emerge in periods after exposure of seconds up to 3 hours:

Phosgene (CG)

Diphosgene (DP)

PS chloropicrin

Chlorine gas

BLOOD AGENTS: Kill through inhalation. Provide little warning except for headache, nausea, and vertigo. Interfere with use of oxygen at the cellular level. CK also irritates the lungs and eyes. Rapid action and exposure either kills by inhibiting cell respiration or it does not—casualties will either die within seconds to minutes of exposure or recover in fresh air. Most gas masks have severe problems in providing effective protection against blood agents:

Hydrogen cyanide (AC)—a dose of 2,000 mg/min/m^3 produces casualties, a respiratory dose of 5,000 mg/min/m^3 is lethal. Lethality lasts 1–4 hours.

(continues)

TABLE 3.3 *(continued)*

Cyanogen chloride (CK)—a dose of 7,000 mg/min/m^3 produces casualties, a respiratory dose of 11,000 mg/min/m^3 is lethal. Lethality lasts 15 minutes to 1 hour .

TOXINS : Biological poisons causing neuromuscular paralysis after exposure of hours or days. Formed in food or cultures by the bacterium *Clostridium botulinum*. Produces highly fatal poisoning characterized by general weakness, headache, dizziness, double vision and dilation of the pupils, paralysis of muscles, and problems in speech. Death is usually by respiratory failure. Antitoxin therapy has limited value, but treatment is mainly supportive:

Botulin toxin (A)—six distinct types, of which four are known to be fatal to humans. An oral dose of 0.001 mg is lethal. A respiratory dose of 0.02 mg/min/m^3 is also lethal.

DEVELOPMENTAL WEAPONS: A new generation of chemical weapons is under development. The only publicized agent is perfluoroisobutene (PFIB), which is an extremely toxic, odorless, and invisible substance produced when PFIB (Teflon) is subjected to extreme heat under special conditions. It causes pulmonary edema or dry-land drowning when the lungs fill with fluid. Short exposure disables, and small concentrations cause delayed death. Activated charcoal and most existing protection equipment offers no defense. Some sources refer to third and fourth generation nerve gases, but no technical literature seems to be available.

CONTROL AGENTS: Agents which produce temporary irritating or disabling effects when they come in contact with the eyes or are inhaled. They can cause serious illness or death when used in confined spaces. CS is the least toxic gas, followed by CN and DM. Symptoms can be treated by washing of the eyes and/or removal from the area. Exposure to CS, CN, and DM produces immediate symptoms. Staphylococcus produces symptoms in 30 minutes to 4 hours, and recovery takes 24–48 hours. Treatment of staphylococcus is largely supportive:

Tear: Cause flow of tears and irritation of upper respiratory tract and skin. Can cause nausea and
vomiting:
Chlororacetophenone (CN)
O-Chlorobenzyl-malononitrile (CS)
Vomiting: Cause irritation, coughing, severe headache, tightness in chest, nausea, vomiting:
Adamsite (DM)
Staphylococcus

INCAPACITATING AGENTS: Agents which normally cause short term illness, psycho-active effects (delirium and hallucinations). Can be absorbed through inhalation or skin contact. The psycho-active gases and drugs produce unpredictable effects, particularly in the sick, small children, elderly, and individuals who are already mentally ill. In rare cases they kill. In others, they produce a permanent psychotic condition. Many produce dry skin, irregular heartbeat, urinary retention, constipation, drowsiness, and a rise in body temperature, plus occasional maniacal behavior. A single dose of 0.1 to 0.2 milligrams of LSD-25 will produce profound mental disturbance within a half hour that lasts 10 hours. The lethal dose is 100 to 200 milligrams:

BZ
LSD
LSD based BZ
Mescaline
Psilocybin
Benzilates

SOURCES: Adapted from Matthew Meselson and Julian Perry Robinson, "Chemical Warfare and Chemical Disarmament," *Scientific American*, Vol. 242, No. 4, April, 1980, pp. 38–47; "Chemical Warfare: Extending the Range of Destruction," *Jane's Defence Weekly*, August 25, 1990, p. 267; Dick Palowski, *Changes in Threat Air Combat Doctrine and Force Structure*, 24th edition, Fort Worth, General Dynamics DWIC-91, February, 1992, pp. II-335 to II-339; U.S. Marine Corps, *Individual Guide for NBC Defense*, Field Manual OH-11-1A, August, 1990; and unpublished testimony to the Special Investigations Subcommittee of the Government Operations Committee, U.S. Senate, by David Goldberg, Foreign Science and Technology Center, U.S. Army Intelligence Center on February 9, 1989.

ber of Middle Eastern states from developing the capability to produce and deliver such weapons. States with at least some biological weapons capability include Iran, Iraq, and Syria. Libya has worked actively on such agents but so far does not seem to have a successful large scale effort. Israel and Egypt have conducted extensive research efforts that could quickly be turned into weapons efforts, and Algeria, too, has probably done much research.[12]

Biological weapons offer proliferating states many potential advantages. Most biological weapons are only effective during a brief period of direct exposure to the biological agent in the weapon and lend themselves to covert delivery as much as delivery by bomb or missile warhead. Biological weapons are also ideal terror weapons when they are targeted against civilian or rear area targets relatively deep in enemy territory.

As Table 3.4 shows, there are a wide range of biological weapons that Middle Eastern nations can choose from, and this table does not include biological weapons which can be used against food supplies and agriculture. Such weapons include weapons that can be used against livestock, such as anthrax and foot and mouth disease. They also include weapons that can be used against key crops, such as cereal rust (*Puccina graminis*), which produces 80% losses of wheat crops, and rice blast (*Pyricularia oryzae*), which produces 70% losses of rice crops.[13]

Biological weapons can be grouped into four main categories, although in theory protozoa and parasitic worms could be used as biological weapons:[14]

- The first category is the virus, which is the smallest form of life. Most viruses can only be seen with an electronic microscope and must be grown on living tissue like tissue cultures or fertile eggs. A virus can be altered by genetic engineering of the entire virus or its nucleic acid.
- The second category is the rickettsiae, which are intermediate between viruses and bacteria and also grow only on living tissue. Rickettsiae weapons received less attention than viruses or bacteria until the early 1970s but seem to have received more attention in the years that have followed.
- The third category is bacteria, which are larger than viruses and range in size from 0.3 to several microns. They are easy to grow in large scale using equipment and processes similar to those in the fermentation industry, but it requires special skills and experience to grow them in quantity and with high lethality. Although most bacteria are vulnerable to antibiotic drugs, many can be relatively easily bred in highly resistant strains, as well as in strains that resist sunlight and drying. Like viruses, their behavior can be altered by genetic engineering.
- The fourth category is fungi, but only a few species like coccidioidomycosis have much application to biological warfare, and they are not normally highly lethal.

Many biological weapons can be developed from local strains of a disease, and the cultures or sources of virtually all biological weapons can be

TABLE 3.4 Key Biological Weapons Likely to Be Used in the Third World

Disease	Infectivity	Transmissibility	Incubation Period	Mortality	Vaccination/ Antibiotic Therapy
Viral					
Chikungunya fever	high?	none	2–6 days	very low (–1%)	none
Dengue fever	high	none	2–5 days	very low (–1%)	none
Eastern equine encephalitis	high	none	5–10 days	high (+60%)	developmental
Tick borne encephalitis	high	none	1–2 weeks	up to 30%	developmental
Venezuelan equine encephalitis	high	none	2–5 days	low (–1%)	developmental
Hepatitis A	—	—	15–40 days	—	—
Hepatitis B	—	—	40–150 days	—	—
Influenza	high	none	1–3 days	usually low	available
Yellow fever	high	none	3–6 days	up to 40%	available
Smallpox (Variola)	high	high	7–16 days	up to 30%	available
Rickettsial					
Coxiella burnetii (Q fever)	high	negligible	10–21 days	low (–1%)	antibiotic
Mooseri	—	—	6–14 days	—	—
Prowazeki	—	—	6–15 days	—	—
Psittacosis	high	moderate-high	4–15 days	Mod-high	antibiotic
Rickettsi (Rocky Mountain spotted fever)	high	none	3–10 days	up to 80%	antibiotic
Tsutsugamushi	—	—	—	—	—
Epidemic typhus	high	none	6–15 days	up to 70%	antibiotic/vaccine
Bacterial					
Anthrax (pulmonary)	moderate-high	negligible	1–5 days	usually fatal	antibiotic/vaccine
Brucellosis	high	none	1–3 days	–25%	antibiotic
Cholera	low	high	1–5 days	up to 80%	antibiotic/vaccine
Glanders	high	none	1–2 days	usually fatal	poor antibiotic
Meloidosis	high	none	1–5 days	usually fatal	moderate antibiotic
Plague (pneumonic)	high	high	2–5 days	usually fatal	antibiotic/vaccine
Tularemia	high	negligible	1–10 days	low to 60%	antibiotic/vaccine
Typhoid fever	moderate-high	moderate-high	7–21 days	up to 10%	antibiotic/vaccine
Dysentery	high	high	1–4 days	low to high	antibiotic/vaccine
Fungal					
Coccidioidomycosis	high	none	1–3 days	low	none
Coccidiodes immitis	high	none	10–21 days	low	none
Histoplasma Capsulatum	—	—	15–18 days	—	—
Norcardia asteroides	—	—	—	—	—
Toxins[a]					
Botulinum toxin	high	none	12–72 hours	high neuro-muscular paralysis	vaccine
Mycotoxin	high	none	hours or days	low to high	?
Staphylococcus	moderate	none	24–48 hours	incapacitating	?

[a]Many sources classify as chemical weapons because toxins are chemical poisons.

SOURCES: Adapted from Report of the Secretary General, Department of Political and Security Affairs, *Chemical and Bacteriological (Biological) Weapons and the Effects of Their Possible Use*, New York, United Nations, 1969, pp. 26, 29, 37–52, 116–117; *Jane's NBC Protection Equipment*, 1991–1992; James Smith, "Biological Warfare Developments," *Jane's Intelligence Review*, November, 1991, pp. 483–487.

obtained from international centers which maintain such strains and cultures for health research. This makes it difficult to be sure how the range of agents shown in Table 3.4 can actually be developed and used.

The biological agents known to have been weaponized in the past include botulinum toxin, staphylococcus enterotoxin B, *Yersinia pestis* (plague), *Bacillus anthracis* (anthrax), *Francisella tularensis* (tularemia), *Coxiella burnetii* (Q fever), Venezuelan equine encephalomyelitis virus, *Puccinia graminis* (black stem rust of cereals), and *Pyricularia oryzae* (rice blast).

At least twenty-one other agents, however, are considered to be suitable for weaponization and could be used by countries in the Middle East. These include undulant fever, Rocky Mountain spotted fever, Rift Valley fever virus, African swine fever virus, histoplasma capsulatum, coccidiodies immitis, cholera, typhoid, dysentery, Legionnaires' disease, eastern equine encephalomyelitis, western equine encephalomyelitis, dengue fever, hepatitis A, abrin toxin, saxitoxin, Staphylococcus enterotoxin, tetrodotoxin, and trichothecene mycotoxins. Agents for use against animals include pleuropneumonia, heartwater, foot and mouth disease, and trypansoma vivax. Agents for use against agriculture include corn smut, Stewart's wilt of corn, late blight of potato, and southern bean mosaic virus.[15]

While the complex genetic engineering of such diseases by Third World nations is probably only a mid to long term risk, most of the larger countries in the Middle East have the technical capability necessary for selective breeding of the strains shown in Table 3.4. Such breeding can vary infectivity and lethality and lead to strains with improved duration and survivability. It also allows the tailoring of many other aspects of a given agent's performance.[16]

There are limits on what developing countries can do. The development of sophisticated and gene-altered biological agents requires specialized and very expensive equipment as well as highly qualified personnel. Little of the specific technology involved in creating such agents is available in the open literature. In spite of a great deal of writing about genetic engineering, the number of agents that can be radically increased in lethality by two to three orders of magnitude currently seems to be limited. For example, in the case of toxins, such activity seems likely to be limited to the bioregulatory peptides rather than the neurotoxins. Such an effort requires large scale peptide synthesizers, chemical reagents for synthesis, and chromatographic equipment for purification. It also may require purchase of kilogram quantities of existing biologically active peptides.[17]

Less advanced agents, however, are relatively easy to produce and the facilities necessary to develop biological weapons can be relatively small. They are hard to distinguish from ordinary biological research facilities and can be located in the midst of larger secure facilities used for other purposes. No precursor chemicals are required, and virtually any modest pharmaceutical industry or fermentation plant can be adapted to mass produce the agents for biological weapons. The same techniques used to manufacture vaccines and penicillin can also be used to make an infectious virus or toxin.[18]

Small batch production facilities may be impossible to distinguish from a research laboratory, and even continuous production facilities can be located underground and in relatively small sheltered facilities. Biological weapons research facilities and production facilities differ visibly from ordinary biological research and production plants only to the extent they require exceptional security. Any nation can thus retain considerable credibility in denying it has such facilities, and only intrusive surprise inspection can hope to confirm or deny that nature of the activity in any facilities that are located.

Nations that choose covert proliferation can deny that they have biological weapons with far less chance of detection than nations involved in manufacturing chemical and nuclear weapons. This, in turn, increases the risk to any nation that avoids developing weapons of mass destruction on the assumption a potential enemy does not have them or one that complies with an arms control regime that only affects chemical and/or nuclear weapons.

Biological weapons offer a wide range of possible incubation periods and effects, and most present little or no risk of infection outside the targeted area. Different biological weapons can be selected to produce either large scale incapacity or death and to produce symptoms over a very wide range of time periods. This makes it almost impossible to prove the covert use of such weapons or to detect the precise agent used until symptoms appear. Many weapons also become more effective if they are used over the target area at night, since they lose effectiveness at high temperatures and/or when exposed to ultraviolet light or sunlight.

The main problems that acquiring biological weapons present to developing states are ensurance of proper safety during manufacture and weapons handling, the inability of refrigeration or freeze-drying to extend the storage life of some weapons beyond a relatively limited time period, and the need for sophisticated weapons delivery and targeting technology. Small variations in sunlight, temperature, wind, humidity, altitude, rate of dissemination, and other factors can often sharply effect the lethal impact of a given agent. Relatively large amounts of the agent must often be sprayed or introduced into local water and food supplies with considerable precision.

Biological weapons can, however, be loaded into the same type of munitions as chemical weapons and be delivered in artillery shells, rockets, bombs, missile warheads, and covert devices. Large amounts would normally be delivered at relatively long ranges to avoid a risk of infection of friendly forces. Aircraft, cruise missiles, and drones can drop bomblets from high altitudes or spray them from low altitudes. Because small amounts of such weapons can cover large areas, they can best be delivered in bombs or warheads that scatter bomblets with 1 kilogram or less of agent over a wide area.

The airborne spraying, cluster and napalm bomb, and missile warhead technology required to develop weapons to deliver biological weapons is now becoming available in the Third World. Spraying devices are comparatively simple, and cluster bomb technology that can be adapted for such a purpose has been sold to a number of countries—including Iraq—by firms in Chile and Spain. Limited improvements in the engineering of cluster bombs allow a nation to produce dual use weapons that load either chemical or biological bomblets, although biological bomblets would normally be smaller and be released at higher altitudes than chemical weapons and would use pressure release through nozzles rather than explosive distribution of the agent.

An aircraft, including a civil airliner, can be adapted to spray a line of agent which would travel downwind and reach the ground as a "vast, elongated ineffective cloud."[19] The effectiveness of such a weapon, like all biological weapons, would be highly dependent on weather conditions, and a large weather front could be exploited to cover a much wider area. The main risk posed by such delivery is that biological weapons that are released in sprays or at high altitudes and/or into large weather fronts can produce "skip effects" where some or all of the agent can unpredictably be carried long distances before reaching the ground.

Missile warhead technology would be much more complex. The warhead would have to explosively disseminate the agent at exactly the right altitude in such a way that it would have wide area coverage. This technology is not radically different from chemical missile warhead technology but is beyond the present capabilities of many Middle Eastern countries. It would require the design or adaptation of a missile warhead that would have different weight and reentry characteristics and would mean extensive operational and simulation testing before a developing country could be sure of its performance. The technology involved was, however, well developed by the mid-1960s, and is scarcely impossible for Middle Eastern states to acquire.

Regardless of the method of delivery, the material in a biological weapon will normally be distributed as an aerosol or particles that will be breathed or absorbed through the skin. The particles will need to be small in order to remain aloft for some time; particles of 0.3 microns or larger tend to fall to the ground. This deprives ordinary hygienic measures of their effectiveness.

While the lethality of biological and chemical weapons varies sharply according to the specific weapon, delivery method and conditions, and nature of the target, it is interesting to note that biological weapons can be as lethal as nuclear weapons *under worst case assumptions* and that some offer more attractive damage characteristics to any power seeking to occupy a large area of enemy territory. In many cases, urban areas and economic facilities could be captured intact, and the same could be true of military equipment.

A study by the United Nations compared the delivery of 10 tons of highly lethal biological agent, 15 tons of chemical nerve agent, and a 1 megaton nuclear bomb. It found that the biological agents could cover an optimal area of up to 100,000 square kilometers, the chemical agent could cover up to 60 square kilometers, and the nuclear weapon could cover up to 300 square kilometers. The time before the onset of weapons effects was days for biological agents, minutes for chemical agents, and seconds for the nuclear weapon. The maximum effect on humans for biological agents was 50% morbidity and 25% deaths without medical intervention, 50% deaths for chemical agents, and 90% deaths for the nuclear weapon. The biological and chemical weapons did not destroy property, but the nuclear weapon damaged structures over an area of 100 square kilometers.[20]

The secondary effects of the biological weapon used in the UN comparison included a possible epidemic or creation of a new foci of disease, but the UN study concluded that the use of such a weapon would normally allow free use of the impacted area after the expiration of the weapon's initial incubation period. The secondary effects of the chemical weapon included contamination of the area for several days to weeks depending upon the weapon, with ability to use the area once the period of contamination was over. The secondary effects of using the nuclear weapon depended on the height of burst but could include radioactive contamination of an area of up to 2,500 square kilometers for three to six months, with safe constant use of the area no earlier than three to six months after the explosion.[21]

Studies by the World Health Organization in 1970 indicated that optimal airborne delivery of a highly lethal anthrax agent sprayed over an undefended city of 5 million could result in 100,000 deaths and incapacitate 150,000 more, even in a developed country. This assumes that antibiotics or other treatment would reduce casualties by 50%. In some of the developing countries in the Middle East, such treatment might reduce casualties by only 5%. The same study estimated that if clostridium botulin (CB) toxin were introduced into the water supply of a city of 50,000, it would kill approximately 28,000 residents.[22]

It should be noted, however, that a number of scientists feel such studies are highly theoretical and exaggerate the lethality of such agents. For example, a comparison of biological weapons with an air burst from a 200 kiloton thermonuclear weapon, which can produce high casualties over an area of 100 square kilometers, indicates it would require very different throweight (the ability to send a given payload over a given distance) for biological agents. The nuclear warhead would weigh 0.5 tons. Practical, highly infectious biological agents would require about 5 tons of material. Existing toxins would require 300 tons of material, assuming they could be stabilized. A nerve agent like sarin would require 800 tons of material.[23]

The Impact of Nuclear Weapons

Nuclear weapons remain both the most desirable goal for proliferating states and the most difficult goal to achieve. The basic problem in nuclear proliferation is not the acquisition of some or most of the materials and technology involved but rather the ability to acquire all the materials and technologies involved and to manage the complex task of integrating them into an effective weapons systems development effort.

The basic technology of nuclear weapons is now more than forty-five years old and can easily be acquired by any nation seeking to acquire nuclear weapons. Nevertheless, the practical problems in actually making nuclear weapons are far greater than those in acquiring or manufacturing chemical and biological weapons. A proliferating nation must obtain either highly enriched uranium 235 or relatively pure plutonium 239. It must develop the highly sophisticated explosive charges and triggering devices necessary to achieve a critical mass of either material and generally needs a neutron initiator to help speed the resulting chain reaction. The design parameters require an incredible amount of computing skill, and the resulting weapon must then be both reliably armed and fused and virtually accident proof.[24]

Much of the post–World War II history of nuclear weapons development has consisted of dealing with these problems, and creating the high degree of compression necessary to increase the reaction rates in fissile material by pushing its atoms together and as long as possible resisting the outward forces that tear the resulting core apart.

There are three basic design concepts for the kind of nuclear weapons most likely to be built in the Third World. One approach is to use a "gun" device that creates critical mass by "shooting" the additional U-235 at the core of the rest of the material down a tube. This design, however, does not compress the fissile material and is extremely wasteful of material. The Little Boy weapon that the U.S. dropped on Hiroshima on August 6, 1945, had a total fuel mass of 60 kilograms but only fissioned about 700 grams worth of material, for an efficiency rate of only 1.2%.

The gun type of weapon offers some significant advantages and major disadvantages: It is technically simpler, it is easier to achieve a high probability of success in a short time, and it is easier to conceal the design phase of the weapon; the diameter of the weapon can be smaller; and it can be used in hardened or penetrating weapons. Yet gun type weapons require considerably more fissile material and are generally of higher weight. They also cannot use plutonium because even relatively pure plutonium contains plutonium 240, which has very high spontaneous neutron emission, and predetonates the weapon before the mass assembly velocity can bring the fissile material into optimal critical mass.

Implosion weapons use less material and can be boosted in yield using lithium 6. The implosion of high explosive surrounding the fissile core squeezes a subcritical mass using lenses of high explosive that are specially shaped to focus their explosive power to produce an inwardly directed shock wave that rapidly increases the density of the fissile material, liquefies the material before it explodes, and forces the mass to become supercritical. The Fat Man weapons detonated over Nagasaki on August 9, 1945, used 6.2 kilograms of plutonium and fissioned about 1.3 kilograms. It had an efficiency of 21%, or about eighteen times higher than that of the Little Boy.

In practice, implosion weapons can produce two to three times more nuclear weapons with the same amount of fissile material. Implosion weapons, too, however, differ in design sophistication and in the amount of material used. Advanced weapons implode the critical material together by using spherical wedges. Intermediate implosion weapons use two hemispheric charges that compress the critical material together in a sphere. The intermediate implosion weapon is more likely to be used in the developing world, but the advanced implosion weapon is becoming technically feasible.

In all types of weapons, the conventional high explosive necessary to compress the radioactive material into critical mass must be triggered in such a way that it explodes with nanosecond timing. It must also be formed and controlled in ways that ensure that all the explosive detonates at once and that it exerts exactly the required force on the critical mass. Designing such explosives and the other components of a weapon necessary to make efficient use of the critical mass requires an immense amount of calculation. This is particularly true in the case of the more sophisticated implosion device, where the conventional explosive must be formed to parts that make up a hollow sphere around the critical mass and core of the weapons. Special high speed electronics and energy storage devices (capacitors) are required that few of the less developed countries (LDCs) can manufacture on their own.

It is at this point that additional neutrons must simultaneously be inserted into the critical mass by a neutron initiator in order to start the chain reaction and sustain it at a sufficiently high rate to consume as much fissionable material as possible. The neutron initiator is one of the most important aspects of the weapon. It requires nanosecond timing, and must release the high energy at precisely the time required, before the mechanism is destroyed by the high explosive or following fission of the critical mass. Typical initiators require the use of a small radioactive beryllium-polonium sphere or an external high voltage neutron initiator, and it is difficult both to acquire precisely the right kind of material and design such devices.[25]

A modern implosion nuclear weapon is very different from the kind of bomb-in-the-basement device that virtually any good physicist can design but that could never be built efficiently or reliably. It consists of concentric shells with a metal outermost casing, a following layer of high explosive lenses weighing up to 100 pounds and involving 40–50 lenses, each with its own detonator. The next inner layer is a combination tamper-reflector of uranium, gold, or beryllium, which reflects neutrons back into the weapon's core and briefly contains the explosion. There is an air gap to permit the tamper-reflector to gather momentum before it slams into the fissile core and then the core, which sits on an aluminum or steel cone. It can vary in diameter between a tennis ball and a soccer ball and can use uranium, plutonium, or both. The neutron initiator is external to this core.

The third type of fission weapon is probably too sophisticated for any Middle Eastern country except possibly Israel. It consists of uranium 238, or tuballoy, which normally is not fissionable and has no critical mass but which can be fissioned if it is bombarded with large numbers of high energy neutrons. This fission process can be made much more efficient if the U-238 is compressed in the process, pushing the atoms together and giving the material an inward direction that delays its explosive disintegration.

A sophisticated fission weapon can be boosted by creating a small fusion reaction in a hollow pit inside the fissile core. The energy in the core of detonating fission weapon reaches pressures and temperatures that cause fusion in some materials and radiates a much larger number of high energy neutrons back through the remaining fissile material than would otherwise be the case. This greatly increases the efficiency of the weapon in using the fissile material, often raising the yield to several hundred kilotons, although a boosted weapon could theoretically reach a yield of 1 megaton.

Lithium 6 deuteride is one possible fuel for such fusion, but it absorbs some fission neutrons. Liquid deuterium and liquid tritium are far superior but much more difficult to use. They also present problems in placing the neutron initiator. The U.S. and Soviet Union solved this through a complex gas boosting method that injected gas after the neutron initiation, but it is unclear that any developing nation can do this.

Thermonuclear or fusion weapons are even more complex and require the use of a fission weapon (normally boosted) to explode a secondary (and sometimes tertiary) fission weapon, often a tuballoy type, that then creates fusion in lithium, deuterium, or tritium. Most modern thermonuclear weapons use lithium deuteride and lithium hydride around the primary and secondary. The chief function of the primary is to make the secondary act as a kind of spark plug by irradiating it with high energy neutrons and X-rays and causing it to fission. This heats the compressed lithium deuteride and lithium hydride and breeds tritium through lithium transformation. The tritium and deuterium fuse and release high energy neutrons. They reflect off of the compressed tuballoy or oralloy jacket around the secondary and cause more fission reaction which in turn accelerates the process of fusion, a fission-fusion sequence taking place in 5–10 microseconds. This produces the fusion of the bulk of the lithium deuteride and lithium hydride material.

While the basic design features of fusion weapons are now well known and have been discussed at length in the open literature, it is important to note that they remain extremely complex, and it is doubtful that any developing nation would attempt to produce thermonuclear as distinguished from boosted weapons. There is also no practical way of knowing the performance of such a weapon without at least some fission testing, and even then the yield of any weapon that was not fully tested could be unpredictable.

A number of different materials may be used to enhance the explosion, reduce the amount of fissile material required, focus the radiation inside the weapon, or emphasize radiation over blast. The simplest uranium weapons require roughly 25 kilograms of U-235 enriched to 90–95%. The simplest plutonium weapons require 8 kilograms of Pu-239. Advanced weapons, however, require substantially less material and/or mix the use of U-235 and Pu-239.

U-235 is very difficult to create in a pure form. Natural uranium is a mix of U-235 and U-239, in which U-235 makes up only 0.7% of the total. In order to "enrich" U-235 to the proper percentage, a nation must use highly sophisticated technology and one of four production methods.

The first such production method, which is most commonly used in the West and USSR, is gaseous diffusion. This technique pushes a uranium rich gas like uranium hexafluoride (UF-6) through a long series of membranes or barriers (called cascades), each of which allows the smaller particles of U-235 to pass through more easily. While this method sounds conceptually simple, it is an extremely costly brute force method requiring large numbers of cascades, excellent design, extremely careful quality control, and complex processing and support systems. Most developing nations have found the cascade method to be too costly and complex. LIS requires extremely sophisticated technology and is still experimental even in the U.S. and USSR. This has led most Third World states to focus on either using the centrifuge method or obtaining plutonium.

A gas centrifuge is a large device, typically a cylinder about 20 feet high. Weapons grade uranium is produced by passing uranium in gaseous form through the centrifuge many times until the proper level of enrichment is obtained. The centrifuge spins at extremely high speeds, and spins the heavier 238 atoms of uranium closer to the outer wall of the device. The streams of heavier and lighter atoms are separated further by heating the gas and using convection currents. The enriched uranium is then taken off at the top, and the depleted uranium is taken off at the bottom. Under optimal conditions, a line or cascade of 2,000 centrifuges can produce 40 to 50 pounds of highly enriched uranium a year, or about enough to produce one bomb. The centrifuge, however, is a difficult path to enrichment, and few developing countries are likely to get anything approaching this level of output.[26]

The third method is laser isotope separation (LIS), which uses laser technology to separate out the particles of different weights of metallic uranium. While theoretically more efficient than the previous methods, it is an unproved technology which is extremely complex. There is no evidence that the U.S. or Soviet Union has succeeded with this technology beyond the demonstration level, although the U.S. once planned to build an LIS facility. Both Iran and Iraq have examined LIS technology but have evidently concluded that it is far beyond their current technical capabilities.

The fourth method is the Calutron method that Iraq successfully concealed from Western intelligence sources for several wars before International Atomic Energy Agency (IAEA) inspectors discovered it after the Gulf War. This method is discussed in more depth in the section on Iraq in Chapter 6. It is technically relatively simple, but it is a brute force method requiring a massive capital investment, massive methods of power, and constant operation at very high levels of efficiency.

Plutonium exists in nature only in extremely small quantities and is made by exposing U-238 to neutrons in a reactor in order to transmute some U-238 into Pu-239. This process, however, also creates Pu-240, which is far less suitable for weapons use. Since weapons grade material should contain only about 7% Pu-240, the uranium being irradiated in a reactor should be irradiated for a much shorter time than is normal in a power plant cycle, since the amount of Pu-240 grows in proportion to the length of time U-238 is irradiated.[27] The Pu-239 then has to be "reprocessed" or separated from the U-238 by chopping it up, dissolving it in acids, and chemically separating the Pu-239 from the uranium. As a result, the production of Pu-239 requires a supply of ore and ore processing facilities or of metallic U-238, nuclear reactors, and a processing plant.

The Technology and Practice of Proliferation

The central message of this chapter is that proliferation is both extremely dangerous and extremely unpredictable. A focus on one type of proliferation is unrealistic, particularly when this focus is placed on nuclear weapons—the most difficult form of proliferation of mass destruction. Similarly, accepting one view of the lethality of any given type of weapons ignores the reality that the practical effects can easily vary by one order of magnitude under real-world conditions, with equally radical military and political effects.

As will be shown in the following chapters, it is also naive to the point of absurdity to generalize about proliferation in the Middle East. Each country that is already involved in proliferation is pursuing a different path. Each is using sufficiently different mixes of weapons and delivery systems so that no one approach to arms control can be equitable or effective, and the same is true of approaches to inspection and verification. Unless great care is exercised in arms control and verification efforts, they also can have the effect of penalizing moderate states relative to aggressor states or driving states to shift toward the least verifiable form of proliferation, which will often be biological weapons.

These difficulties in arms control are scarcely an argument against existing arms control efforts or attempts to institute more demanding controls and inspection arrangements. At the same time, good intentions devoid of ruthless objectivity and demanding analysis may pave the road to hell.

Notes

1. Sources differ sharply over virtually all of the data on Table 3.1.

2. W. Seth Carus, "Chemical Weapons in the Middle East," *Policy Focus*, Number Nine, Washington Institute for Near East Policy, December, 1988, p. 7.

3. Some 60 pounds of mustard gas were required in World War I per casualty. Only 2% of the casualties died.

4. Shuey, Lenhart, Snyder, Donnelly, Mielke, and Moteff, *Missile Proliferation: Survey of Emerging Missile Forces*, Washington, D.C., Congressional Research Service, Report 88-642F, February 9, 1989, pp. 34–35; *Jane's Defence Weekly*, February 27, 1988, pp. 370–371; Defense Intelligence Agency, *Soviet Chemical Weapons Threat*, DST-1620F-051-85, 1985, p. 8.

5. Department of Defense, *Conduct of the Persian Gulf War: Final Report*, Department of Defense, April, 1992, pp. 16–18

6. Most biological agents require extremely demanding dispersal conditions in terms of altitude, light and temperature conditions, wind patterns, and dispersal into some form of reentry. This requires the ability to deliver hundreds of liters of biological agents, and specialized bombs and extremely specialized missile warheads to allow proper delivery at the extreme velocities involved.

7. *Nonlethal* is a relative term. Virtually all these gases will kill especially sensitive individuals, small children, and the elderly and become far more lethal in enclosed areas. Many can terminate pregnancies or damage the fetus. In contrast, lethal gases other than nerve agents and toxins often produce large numbers of wounded and incapacitated rather than simply deaths.

8. Some especially sensitive individuals will suffer lasting mental health problems.

9. Hearing of the Committee on Foreign Relations, "Chemical and Biological Warfare," United States Senate, Ninety-First Congress, April 30, 1986, p. 6; W. Seth Carus, "Chemical Weapons in the Middle East," *Policy Focus*, Number Nine, Washington Institute for Near East Policy, December, 1988, p. 7.

10. W. Seth Carus, "Chemical Weapons in the Middle East," *Policy Focus*, Number Nine, Washington Institute for Near East Policy, December, 1988, p. 7.

11. Letter from Robert A. Mosbacher, Secretary of Commerce, to Thomas A. Foley, Speaker of the House of Representatives, December 12, 1989.

12. James Smith, "Biological Warfare Developments," *Jane's Intelligence Review*, November, 1991, pp. 483–487; *Jane's Defence Weekly*, October 12, 1991, p. 651.

13. There are approximately sixteen major weapons that can be used against livestock and thirteen major weapons that can be used against plants. See Report of the Secretary General, Department of Political and Security Affairs, *Chemical and Bacteriological (Biological) Weapons and the Effects of Their Possible Use*, New York, United Nations, 1969, pp. 45–48.

14. Adapted from Report of the Secretary General, Department of Political and Security Affairs, *Chemical and Bacteriological (Biological) Weapons and the Effects of Their Possible Use*, New York, United Nations, 1969, pp. 26, 37–52, 94.

15. "Report of American Scientists Working Group on Biological and Toxin Weapons Verification," Federation of American Scientists, Washington, D.C., Revised October, 1990, Appendix A.

16. Much of the technology involved is in the open literature. See "Genetic Engineering and Biological Weapons," National Defense Research Institute, Umea, Sweden, November, 1987. For a discussion of the Soviet capability, see Defense Intelligence Agency, "Soviet Biological Warfare Threat," Washington, DIA DST-1610F-057-86, 1986, pp. 9–15.

17. Government of Canada working paper, "Novel Toxins and Bioregulators: The Emerging Scientific and Technical Issues Relating to Verification and the Biological and Toxin Weapons Convention," September, 1991.

18. The author sees little point in providing a precise "road map" for some of the production techniques involved. For a general description of biological warfare agent production, see Defense Intelligence Agency, "Soviet Biological Warfare Threat," Washington, DIA DST-1610F-057-86, 1986, pp. 2–4.

19. Adapted from Report of the Secretary General, Department of Political and Security Affairs, *Chemical and Bacteriological (Biological) Weapons and the Effects of Their Possible Use*, New York, United Nations, 1969, p. 18.

20. If the theoretical area coverage data shown here seems surprising, a field trial using zinc cadmium particles 2 microns in diameter from a ship traveling 16 kilometers offshore disseminated about 200 kilograms while the ship traveled a distance of 260 kilometers parallel to the coastline. The resulting aerosol traveled at least 750 kilometers and covered an area of over 75,000 square kilometers. Tests using 200 kilograms of simulated biological aerosols spraying from an airplane covered maximum areas of 5,000 to 20,000 square kilometers. In contrast, a similar amount of the most lethal nerve agent would require about 0.8 kilograms per kilometer and only cover 50 to 150 square kilometers. Similarly, in the 1960s, 500 liters of harmless bacteria were dispersed in aerosol form off of a ship traveling 150 miles down the coasts of the U.S. They covered an area of 55,000 square miles and the affected population inhaled 15 to 15,000 particles depending on wind and weather conditions. Dr. Terence White and Dr. Kathleen White, "Biological Weapons: How Big a Threat?" *International Defense Review*, 8/1990, pp. 843–846; "Defenses Against Biological Warfare," Pugwash Study Group on Biological Warfare, Marianske Lazne, Czechoslovakia, May 13–20, 1967.

21. Adapted from Report of the Secretary General, Department of Political and Security Affairs, *Chemical and Bacteriological (Biological) Weapons and the Effects of Their Possible Use*, New York, United Nations, 1969, pp. 44–45.

22. James Smith, "Biological Warfare Developments," *Jane's Intelligence Review*, November, 1991, pp. 483–487.

23. Matthew Meselson, Martin K. Kaplan, and Mark A. Mokulsky, "Verification of Biological and Toxin Weapons Disarmament, *Science and Global Security*, 1991, Vol., 2, pp. 235–252; *Health Aspects of Chemical and Biological Weapons*, World Health Organization, Geneva, 1970.

24. Space limits the technical discussion in this section. For an excellent summary of the technologies involved, see Chuck Hansen, *U.S. Nuclear Weapons: A Secret History*, New York, Orion Books, 1988; and Thomas B. Cochran, William M. Arkin, Robert S. Norris, and Jeffrey I. Sands, *Nuclear Weapons Databook*, Volume I, *U.S. Nuclear Forces and Capabilities*, New York, Ballinger, 1984, pp. 22–37, and Volume IV, *Soviet Nuclear Weapons*, New York, Ballinger, 1989, pp. 68–97.

25. Gannett News Service, September 25, 1991.

26. For a detailed description of this complex technology and explanation of how Iraq developed its effort, see David Albright and Mark Hibbs, "Iraq's Shop-Till-You Drop Nuclear Program," *Bulletin of the Atomic Scientists*, April, 1992, pp. 27–37.

27. This assumes that a proliferator wants a relatively clean weapon with a predictable yield. Most experts agree that much dirtier plutonium (higher concentrations of Pu-240 in the Pu-239) will still produce a nuclear explosion, although the yield will be less predictable and it will trade added fallout for reduced blast. Shuey, Lenhart, Snyder, Donnelly, Mielke, and Moteff, *Missile Proliferation: Survey of Emerging Missile Forces*, Washington, D.C., Congressional Research Service, Report 88-642F, February 9, 1989, pp. 26–27.

4

Trends in the Military Balance and Arms Sales in North Africa

The arms race in the Maghreb currently seems unlikely to lead to a major conflict or the emergence of some dominant hostile power. The USSR no longer shows any serious interest in power projection in this region. Mauritania's only recent military significance has been reports it might offer a missile test range on its territory to Iraq. The long war between Morocco and the Polisario seems to be winding to a close. Algeria's military buildup has not led to any significant acts of aggression. Qadhafi has little real military capability, and Tunisia lacks the military power to threaten anyone. The Maghreb does suffer from severe political and economic instability, but no nation in the Maghreb currently poses a serious military challenge to another.

The main problems that the Maghreb nations face in terms of military forces are the cost of maintaining them and the impact they have on politics and economic development. Mauritania is currently spending about 5–7% of its central government expenditures on military forces. Morocco is spending 7–9%, Algeria 8–9%, Libya over 11%, and Tunisia about 4%. While these percentages are not high by the standards of some other Middle Eastern and developing countries, they are far too high for the poorer countries in the Maghreb, and even Algeria and Libya are spending more than they can really afford.[1]

The Arms Buildup in the Maghreb

The broad patterns in the defense budgets and arms transfers shaping the military buildup in the Maghreb and North Africa are shown in Table 4.1. It is important to note that "Maghreb" has limited meaning as a geographic definition of the political forces impacting on the development of local military forces.[2] Mauritania's military forces are shaped by its poverty, its internal race problems, and its tensions with Senegal. Morocco shapes its forces to fight with the Polisario and deter the now low level risk of a confrontation with Algeria. Algeria's military forces are currently shaped more by the dominant role of its military in its internal politics than by the risk of a

Map 4.1 North Africa. Source: U.S. Government

conflict with Morocco or the military buildup in Libya. Tunisia's military efforts have been driven largely by its need to deter Libya but are increasingly shaped by its internal problems with Islamic fundamentalism. Libya has regional ambitions, but its military history is one of confrontation with Egypt and broader ambitions in sub-Saharan and East Africa and the Arab world.

The Maghreb is a mosaic of conflicting national ambitions and internal tensions whose individual strategic rationales are generally subordinated to internal politics. There have been no recent wars between Maghreb states and little more than superficial political and economic cooperation. The Maghreb states trade largely with Europe and other states outside the region and import their arms from outside the region. None of the Maghreb states played a major role in East-West competition in the days of the Cold War, and their potential strategic importance in affecting control of the Mediterranean has not been a recent factor in world politics. To the extent they "threaten" the West, this threat currently consists of tensions over emigration from states like Algeria to France, Qadhafi's acts of terrorism and political extremism, low level concerns over the stability of oil and gas exports from Algeria and Libya, and the rising tide of Islamic fundamentalism within Algeria, Morocco, and Tunisia.

The statistical trends in the military forces in the Maghreb are summarized in Table 4.2. Several key patterns have emerged in the military buildup during the period between 1972 and 1992:

- The Maghreb states followed the general pattern of rapid force buildup that characterized virtually all states in the Near East and Southwest Asia. Their military forces increased sharply after 1972, and all of the Maghreb states made massive increases in their defense budgets, arms imports, and major military equipment.
- Morocco's tensions with Algeria and Mauritania and its fifteen year long war with the Polisario were key factors shaping regional force trends. It is interesting to note, however, that many of Morocco's arms purchases were not particularly well suited to dealing with a low level guerrilla threat until 1982–1983. Even in 1992, Morocco's combat engineering efforts reflected a sounder pattern of purchases to deal with the Polisario than its weapons buys. These problems were partly the result of the fact that the Moroccan army had to be structured to deal with a possible confrontation with Algeria.
- Libya's adventures in trying to influence events in other states and its disastrous military intervention in Chad involved comparatively little actual use of Libya's total forces. Libya did, however, have a powerful catalytic affect on the military buildup of other states in the region. Bad as Libya's military forces were, no neighbor could ignore the buildup of a vast pool of military equipment and Libya's large numbers of Soviet bloc advisors.
- By the late 1980s, all the Maghreb states, with the exception of Tunisia, had expanded their force structures to the point where their economies no

TABLE 4.1 The Military Buildup in the Maghreb: Trends in Military Spending and Arms Imports

Trends in Military Expenditure (in Current $ Millions)

	1979	1980	1981	1982	1983	1984	1985	1986	1987	1988	1989	1990	1991
Middle East	36100	43600	51700	61100	68100	68800	67500	60800	56900	53800	53200	—	—
North Africa													
Mauritania	61	65	55	50	48	50	52	48	35	40	40	45	40
Morocco	520	763	830	1089	1074	1000	1000	1078	1102	1102	1203	1340	1400
Algeria	846	940	1383	1426	1137	1242	1040	1271	1264	1595	2313	1500	1100
Libya	3342	3092	3650	3376	4255	5047	5000	4000	2774	1595	3309	2510	2700
Chad	16	18	13	10	7	9	14	29	34	39	79	58	59
Tunisia	219	196	159	251	320	230	277	282	269	238	273	401	468
Egypt	3227	2923	3154	6192	6072	6844	6785	6460	6664	5559	3499	3820	4600
Africa Total	8231	7997	9244	12394	12913	14422	14168	13168	12142	10168	10716	9674	10367

Trends in Arms Imports (in Current $ Millions)

	1972	1974	1976	1978	1980	1982	1984	1986	1988	1990	1992	1994
North Africa												
Mauritania	2	3	20	30	3	10	20	5	10	15	20	20
Morocco	5	20	210	440	350	270	200	80	90	130	130	110
Algeria	10	20	320	800	725	1200	775	600	825	720	740	760
Libya	160	330	1000	2300	2500	3100	2100	1200	575	1100	1000	1000
Chad	1	2	10	5	1	3	40	10	80	65	70	75
Tunisia	10	10	10	10	140	60	130	30	20	40	50	50
Egypt	550	230	150	400	550	2100	1700	1300	725	1500	1700	1700
Subtotal	738	615	1720	3985	4269	6743	4965	3225	2325	3570	3710	3715

Source of Arms Imports by Major Supplier During 1985–1989 (in Current $ Millions)

	Total	USSR	U.S.	France	UK	PRC	Germany	Other Warsaw Pact	Other Europe	Middle East	Other East Asia	Latin America	Others
North Africa													
Mauritania	40	0	0	5	0	0	0	0	0	30	0	0	0
Morocco	770	0	240	150	0	20	0	20	330	0	10	0	0
Algeria	3260	2700	50	20	40	0	0	430	0	0	0	0	20
Libya	5080	3200	0	0	0	30	10	1200	550	0	70	20	0
Chad	210	0	40	140	0	0	0	0	0	30	0	0	0
Tunisia	465	0	300	160	0	0	5	0	0	0	0	0	0
Egypt	5800	575	2900	677	170	190	40	320	575	0	10	340	5
Africa Total	15625	6475	3530	1152	210	240	55	1970	1455	60	90	360	25

SOURCE: Estimated by the author using various editions of the ISS, *Military Balance*; and ACDA, *World Military Expenditures and Arms Transfers*.

TABLE 4.2 The Military Buildup in the Maghreb: Trends in Military Forces

Trends in Military Manpower

	1967	1973	1975	1977	1979	1981	1983	1985	1987	1989	1991
North Africa											
Mauritania	2	3	3	17	8	12	16	20	16	16	12
Morocco	65	65	75	85	98	120	135	165	200	200	196
Algeria	75	80	80	75	88	101	130	170	170	195	126
Libya	20	20	25	30	51	55	68	91	91	91	86
Chad	5	10	11	9	5	3	4	16	30	33	17
Tunisia	25	20	20	20	24	29	28	38	38	40	35
Egypt	220	390	400	350	447	447	447	466	450	450	420
Total	412	588	614	586	721	767	768	967	995	1025	892

Trends in Military Equipment

Main Battle Tanks

	1973	1979	1982	1984	1988	1990	1992
North Africa							
Mauritania	0	0	0	0	0	0	0
Morocco	120	140	135	120	224	284	284
Algeria	400	500	630	700	910	900	960
Libya	221	2000	2000	2000	1980	2300	2150
Chad	0	0	0	0	0	0	10
Tunisia	0	0	14	14	68	98	84
Egypt	1880	1600	2100	1750	2425	2410	3190
Total	2621	4240	4879	4584	5067	5992	6678

Combat Aircraft

	1973	1979	1982	1984	1988	1990	1992
North Africa							
Mauritania	0	13	7	9	5	5	7
Morocco	48	72	97	106	109	93	90
Algeria	206	260	306	330	299	257	241
Libya	44	201	555	535	515	513	409
Chad	0	5	0	0	2	4	4
Tunisia	12	14	8	8	43	50	53
Egypt	620	563	429	504	517	475	495
Total	930	1128	1402	1492	1490	1397	1299

SOURCE: Estimated by the author using various editions of the IISS, *Military Balance*, and ACDA, *World Military Expenditures and Arms Transfers*.

longer could provide the funding necessary to provide the equipment, manpower, training, logistics, infrastructure, and sustainability necessary to make these force structures effective. This overexpansion of the total force structure was particularly severe in the case of Libya, which sized its forces on its peak oil revenues in 1981–1982. Libya was never able to find the resources or manpower to use more than half of the equipment it bought, although it spent 13–20% of its GNP on military forces.

- If one includes paramilitary forces, Algeria, Mauritania, and Morocco raised their total military expenditures to at least 8–10% of their GNPs beginning in the early 1980s (including the cost of foreign borrowing and deals not reflected in formal trade and GNP statistics). While Mauritania has since lowered its military expenditures to about 4% of GNP, Morocco and Algeria are still spending at levels well above 6% of their GNPs.[3]
- Tunisia, in contrast, kept its defense spending levels at about 5–6% of its GNP during the early 1980s and has recently spent only about 3% of its GNP. As a rough rule of thumb, a less developed country with serious economic and demographic problems cannot hope to sustain military spending levels of more than 5% (including all foreign borrowing) without a major impact on economic development.
- All of the Maghreb states except Tunisia bought more military equipment than they could adequately support. The Maghreb states followed the general pattern of less developed countries in confusing weapons numbers and the glitter factor of buying advanced weapons technology with military effectiveness. They effectively saturated their military forces with weaponry between 1972 and 1985 without buying proper support and C^3I equipment, thus creating teeth-to-tail ratios about two to three times the proper ratio for military effectiveness.
- Most of the Maghreb countries overborrowed to build up their military forces. They had exceptional ability to expand their foreign loan base during 1974–1982 and make deals which did not show up on their official trade balances. With the exception of Tunisia, they planned and budgeted military expenditures using large off-budget accounts which were not fully reflected in their civil budget, ordinary trade, and foreign debt statistics and disguised the true strain of defense spending. Algeria and Libya have since made steady additional arms purchases which seem to have required additional major loans in spite of the cuts in oil prices, and Morocco has been forced to find external financing to help pay for its war against the Polisario.
- These problems were particularly severe in the case of Algeria, Libya, and Morocco. This allowed each country to buy more equipment than it could sustain. To help fund its struggle with the Polisario, Morocco, for example, created a debt of nearly $13 billion—nearly 85% of the nation's annual gross domestic product (GDP). Its debt service, prior to a rescheduling in January, 1985, was equal to only about 20% of its exports at the end of 1978 and was equal to 48% by the end of 1983. Morocco has had to reschedule its debt since that time and is almost certain to have to reschedule again in the future.

- Like most LDCs, the Maghreb states underfunded advanced training and investment in other aspects of manpower quality. None of the Maghreb states maintained average military expenditures per man in uniform high enough to buy effective manpower quality and retain technically trained manpower. All had serious problems in adapting their military organizations and discipline to take account of the need for far more skilled junior officers and NCOs, and all had poor management of military personnel and career structures. Morocco maintained a higher real average of spending per man in its career forces than did the other Maghreb states, but underfunded and undertrained its conscripts and enlisted men. Libya invested in equipment and facilities rather than a sound manpower, infrastructure, and support base, and its poorly trained conscripts and "volunteers" suffered a decisive defeat in Chad at the hands of lightly armed Chadian forces. Algeria funded heavy armor and advanced aircraft while funding its manpower and support base as if it were only a poorly equipped "popular army." Mauritania could not properly fund the expansion of its forces following its brief attempt to fight the Polisario. Tunisia provided reasonable wages for its career officers but did little to make its many twelve month conscripts into effective soldiers.
- The expansion of military manpower also served as a politically useful form of disguised unemployment and complemented similar waste on the expansion of national civil services. This, however, meant diminished long term growth and further reduced the quality of the manpower pool.
- The Maghreb states revealed very different levels of skill in force planning:

  - Libya's military equipment purchases were chaotic. They involved incredible waste and overexpenditure on equipment relative to manpower and support forces and failed to reveal any clear concept of air force development or combined arms. Libya has to keep approximately 1,200 of its tanks in storage. Its other army equipment purchases greatly outstrip the ability of its small active army and low quality reserves to absorb them. It is also forced to keep many of its aircraft in storage. Its overall ratio of weapons to manpower is militarily absurd, and Libya has compounded its problems by buying a wide diversity of equipment types that make it impossible to create an effective training and support base.
  - Algeria has showed relatively good balance in buying armor, but it has spent too much on artillery numbers and too little on mobility and quality. It has bought a poor mix of relatively low quality anti-tank weapons and air defense systems. The Algerian air force lacks modern air defense fighters and has bought only very limited numbers of modern attack aircraft.
  - Morocco spent much of its money on maintaining a force of 100,000–150,000 men in the Spanish Sahara. In 1992 its major equipment totals were much smaller than its total manning would normally indicate. Morocco has also bought so many different types of major land weapons

that it finds it difficult keep its support costs to reasonable levels, provide proper training, and provide suitable C^{3}I battle management capability. The Moroccan air force had a better balance. Nevertheless, Morocco's purchase of both French and U.S. combat aircraft have increased its training and support problems.
- Tunisia began to acquire modern armor and fighter aircraft in 1985 but still had only limited numbers in 1992. It has done a reasonably good job of expanding its army and air force, but its force size and equipment holdings are inadequate for combat with either of its larger neighbors and included far too many types to allow effective organization and support.

- The military forces of the Maghreb—particularly those of Algeria and Libya—are not designed for prolonged combat or the proper use of combined arms, and they have been developed without the proper balance of support and infrastructure capabilities. They were procured with a heavy emphasis on buying the largest possible amount of major modern military weapons with the greatest possible prestige. This kind of purchasing forces the buyer state to make very substantial cuts in the life cycle of its aircraft and weapons—since they are not properly maintained, supported, or upgraded—and to use major weapons as combat reserves or to compensate for poor serviceability rates. This, in turn, forces more rapid and larger buys of new major weapons. Newly formed military forces can defer many of their support costs for 3–5 years after the purchase of major equipment because whole new sets of equipment do not have high initial spare parts and support costs. They can then continue to defer such spending without visible loss of most of their equipment, but it will steadily decline in real-world military capability—often to the point of virtual inoperability.
- All of the Maghreb states have had to structure their military development to enhance internal security and ensure their military forces were suitably politicized. This need to politicize the armed forces and give higher priority to loyalty than professionalism was particularly characteristic of Libya and Morocco. In general such politicization compounded the effectiveness problems created by the failure to properly fund manpower quality and training and to develop effective systems for manpower management.

The future patterns in Maghreb military development are harder to estimate. It is, however, possible to make several assumptions about future military developments in the area:

- The Maghreb states will continue some expansion of their forces, or at least modernize their major weapons, in spite of diminished military requirements. This seems likely to be the result of continuing political tension, bureaucratic momentum, and demographic pressure, regardless of the outcome of the struggle in the Western Sahara. Once the expansion of military forces takes place in a less developed country, it has a powerful ratchet effect that has nothing to do with local threats or military requirements. The lack of alternative employment and career paths, coupled with the role of the military in a nation's power structure and the sheer momentum of global military expansion and technological change, leads to military expansion almost regardless of local political conditions.

- Morocco will be able to contain or limit the Polisario threat to militarily, politically, and economically acceptable levels and maintain good enough relations with Algeria to allow both states to avoid accelerating their present arms race. There is no guarantee that this will happen, and it is still impossible to rule out an accelerated arms race, or even conflict, between Algeria and Morocco.

- Libya will continue to expand its military forces, albeit at a slower rate, and seek weapons of mass destruction. This will force the other states in the region to maintain high levels of military spending, regardless of constant shifts in political alliances and Libya's military ineffectiveness.

- In spite of ongoing arms purchases, Libya and Algeria will experience growing problems during the 1990s. Much of their equipment is becoming obsolete and hard to support. The result will be a steady decline in the operational readiness of older types of equipment and growing problems in supporting the overall force mix in combat. Given Algeria and Libya's limited revenues, both states are likely to drop in net military effectiveness even though they may acquire enough equipment to have an apparent increase in force strength.

- The internal tensions within each country's military forces will make military politics more important than the use of military force. In Algeria the army suspended elections in 1992 to deny Islamic fundamentalists political control. Morocco's war with the Polisario now ties its military down but has led to significant economic strains, and the military is politicized enough so that no one can totally dismiss the possibility of a coup. A civil regime has taken over power from Habib Bourguiba in Tunisia, but the incompetence and profiteering of the civil authorities may lay the groundwork for an eventual military or radical Islamic takeover. The Libyan military seem to be largely loyal to Qadhafi, but the military is virtually the only body that could replace him.

- No radical shifts will take place in political alignments in favor of Qadhafi, and the end of the Cold War has effectively ended the threat of communism and Soviet penetration into the region's military forces. The Islamic fundamentalist movements that seem to be the new tide of political action in the region are now the rivals of the secular and regular military forces in Algeria, Tunisia, and Egypt and are unlikely to favor strong regular military forces or direct military action if they come to power.

- Proliferation is likely to be a growing problem. Algeria and Libya already seem to be competing to develop weapons of mass destruction, and at least Morocco seems likely to follow if the Algerian and Libyan efforts are not checked in the near future.

Patterns in Arms Imports
and Military Advisory Efforts

During the 1980s and early 1990s, the trends in arms imports in North Africa were driven by three key trends: the war in the former Spanish Sahara, the rivalry between Libya and its neighbors, and the failure to reach a broader Arab-Israeli peace settlement, which has forced Egypt to maintain large forces despite its own peace with Israel.

As is the case with the other sub-regions of the Middle East, the pace of the arms race has been driven by a relatively small number of actors—in this case Algeria and Libya. Egypt's actions have been almost solely defensive since the Camp David accords, and Tunisia has played a defensive role ever since independence. Mauritania is too poor to be a player, and Morocco both faces a potential threat from Algeria and Libya and already has sufficient arms to complete its conquest of the former Spanish Sahara.

Supplier relationships have been equally important. The Soviet Union has dominated the postwar transfer of arms to Algeria and Libya and shaped the buildup of Egypt's military forces through 1974. The U.S. and the West have shaped the forces of Morocco and Tunisia.

The end of the Cold War has not had a major impact on the tensions among the Arab states in North Africa, but it may change some past supplier relationships. The USSR and Eastern Europe no longer are likely to provide Algeria or Libya with arms out of ideological reasons, and the West has less reason to provide arms to Morocco and Tunisia. At the same time, however, the Maghreb is still an attractive market. If ideology is less of an incentive, hard currency is far more attractive to the USSR and East Europe and may make them equally willing to sell.

The military future of the Maghreb states will be heavily dependent on the extent to which their future arms imports can be brought into better balance with the size of the forces in each country. As of 1992, the Maghreb countries were still buying too much of the wrong equipment, and they often compound their problems by buying this equipment in far too small lots and from far too many suppliers. As a result, the needs for future standardization and efficient purchases in terms of scale are almost as important as cutting total equipment purchases back to the level that each country's forces can actually absorb.

There seems little chance that any group of supplier states will encourage more realism in Maghreb arms purchases unless the buyer states force this to happen. The countries dependent on Western suppliers have found themselves dependent on wildly different levels of national and contractor support, ranging from excellent to fraudulent. The competition among seller countries and firms has made any cohesive modernization effort difficult, and this has been compounded in the case of Morocco and Egypt by corruption, a tendency to exploit favorable credit terms, and a desire for the most advanced or glamorous weapons and technologies. Coupled to a nationalist tendency to resist adopting foreign standards, the result has often been poor readiness, poor training, poor maintenance and stocks of spare parts, inadequate facilities, and a general lack of systems integration, cohesive C^3I systems and operational concepts, and interoperability.

The nations dependent on Soviet bloc weapons have fared no better. The USSR was the dominant seller of arms to Algeria and Libya. It sold Algeria some $2,500 million worth of arms between 1983 and 1987, and sold $3,900 million worth to Libya.[4] It found arms sales to these states provide a considerable amount of hard currency, and before the collapse of the Soviet Union there was a significant increase in Soviet willingness to sell advanced weapons systems which were less "stripped down" for export.

Recent Russian arms agreements with Iran and Syria indicate that the Russian republic is willing to provide better avionics, munitions, C3I/BM gear, and surface-to-surface missiles. Examples of such Soviet and Russian republic deliveries include SA-5 and SA-13 surface-to-air missiles, improved T-72 tanks, AA-7 and AA-8 air-to-air missiles, and versions of the MiG-94 and Su-24 with improved avionics and radars.

What is less clear about future arms sales to the Maghreb—and other countries in the Middle East—is whether any exporter will provide the level of technology transfer its customers desire and improve the quality of its military advisory efforts.

The nations dependent on support from the former Soviet Union face special problems. Not only has the Soviet Union broken up, it provided only limited offensive training to Algerian and Libyan land forces before its breakup and relied on the relatively simple concepts of mass it used in training other LDCs, rather than the new tactics it began to evolve for its own and Warsaw Pact forces in the late 1970s.

Soviet air training and support was surprisingly poor, and there is little evidence that Algeria or Libya have received the advanced air training the Soviet Union provided to its own senior pilots. The Soviet Union did not transfer the kind of support skills necessary to carry out major service and overhauls with native personnel but provided a great deal of not terribly sophisticated C3I equipment without the kind of integration and netting necessary to make Algerian and Libyan fighter and SAM air defense forces fully effective.

This did not stop the Soviet Union from making a profit. It sold Libya about $15 billion worth of arms between the first Soviet sales in 1970 and 1990, and roughly $10 billion worth of this equipment was delivered as of early 1985. The Soviets also earned money training about 1,800 Libyan officers and technicians a year in the USSR (870 annually) and Eastern Europe (930 annually).

Nevertheless, Libya remained unable to operate most of what it had received. In 1990 roughly 2,300 Soviet personnel were still required to help maintain and train Libyan forces, although Libyan forces were only able to operate about 30–50% of their major combat equipment.[5] Soviet and East European advisors often manned Libya's control towers, trained its pilots, and performed or supervised most major maintenance on Libyan ships and armor. Soviet or other foreign personnel fly many MiG-23, MiG-25, Su-22, Mi-24, and Tu-22 missions. They assisted in many MiG-21 missions and even in transport missions by IL-76 and AN-26 aircraft. At least some of these problems, however, were Libyan. Qadhafi's problems with his military led him constantly to shift his commanders, break up units and command centers, and otherwise disrupt his military organization to prevent a coup.

The Soviets also acted as Algeria's major military supplier. As late as 1990 there were roughly 875 Soviet and East European military advisors in the country, roughly half of whom worked at Algerian training academies and service schools, the rest being assigned to individual combat units and equipment repair installations. About 110 Algerian officers and technicians a year receive advanced training in the Soviet bloc.[6] The Soviets sold Algeria over $5.4 billion in arms and delivered over $5 billion of this total by 1990. Soviet bloc advisors were responsible for heavy maintenance and major training activity for Algeria's T-62 and T-72 tank units; its SA-2, SA-3, and SA-6 missiles; and its MiG-21, MiG-23, and MiG-25 aircraft.

The Soviet support of Algeria's and Libya's MiG-21s is a good example of the problems in the advisory efforts available to Soviet supplied countries before the break up of the USSR. The MiG-21 is not a particularly sophisticated fighter by modern standards, and it has been deployed in less developed countries for nearly two decades. Roughly 95 of Algeria's 241 combat aircraft were MiG-21MF/Fs in 1992, and Algeria has had more experience with this fighter than any of its other first line combat aircraft.

Many of these MiG-21s, however, had at least some avionics or subsystems that were not operational or that the Algerian air force felt required major rebuilding to be competitive and effective in combat. Some older MiG-21s may well be beyond return to full service. Only fifty of Libya's 409 combat aircraft were MiG-21s in 1992, but most seem to be experiencing the same operational problems as Algeria's. Libya has also had to place many of its other aircraft in storage.

More generally, the Soviet basic air training program in Algeria emphasized Korean War–vintage basic training and tactics. Algeria now requires new tactics and training, advanced trainers, and a far more sophisticated training program if it is to make its air force effective. It also badly needs more advanced AC&W capability and air-to-air missiles. The Algerian surface-to-air missile training effort also contributed to problems in the performance of virtually all Algerian SAM units. The Soviet-developed training and operations program produces only two real periods of fully manning and alert a year—both during peak semi-annual training. Even then, only one of these training periods involves serious exercises and live firings, and although Algerian units have weeks to prepare for set-piece firings, their performance is still poor.

Mauritania

	Manpower (1,000s)	Tanks	Aircraft	Defense Spending ($ millions)	Arms Imports ($ millions)	Arms Exports ($ millions)
1967	2	–	–	3	–	–
1973	3	–	–	7	1	–
1982	16	–	7	52	5	0
1988	16	–	5	37	10	0
1991	12	–	7	45	–	–

The trends in Maghreb military forces become clearer when they are examined on a case-by-case basis.[7] The Islamic Republic of Mauritania is an extremely poor nation on the western rim of the Middle East. It is comparatively large in territory, with a total area of 1,030,700 square kilometers, or about three times the size of New Mexico. It is, however, a desert country, only 1% of which is arable; its GDP is only $942 million, its income per capita only $500, and chronic unemployment reaches over 20%.

Mauritania's subsistence agriculture is so fragile that repeated famines occurred in the 1970s and 1980s. Its only major resource is iron ore, which accounts for 50% of its exports, but this ore has long been in oversupply and depressed in price. Major fishing grounds exist off its coast, but these have been overexploited by foreign fisheries. Its economy has been seriously mismanaged in the past, although it has recently carried out some stages of an International Monetary Fund (IMF) reform plan. Its external debt was in excess of $2 billion in 1990.

Mauritania has a 754 kilometer coastline on the Atlantic and 5,074 kilometers of land boundaries. These include a 463 kilometer border with Algeria, a 2,237 kilometer border with Mali, an uncertain 1,561 kilometer boundary area with the Western Sahara (Morocco), and an 813 kilometer boundary with Senegal. The boundary with Senegal is disputed, and there has been a low level border war for some years. This war has often taken on a tribal, racist, and religious character.[8]

Military Developments in Mauritania

France created Mauritania as a colonial entity out of a largely nomadic Berber-Arab population in the northern and central part of the colony and an agricultural black population in the south. Mauritania achieved independence from France on November 28, 1960. At this time, France left power in the hands of the Arab population, who represented about 70% of the people. The Arabs aligned Mauritania with the Arab world and favored Arabicization of the language and educational system. Since much of the population was black and did not speak Arabic, this policy divided the country and led to black student strikes and riots in the south when Arabic was made the official language of the country in 1966. It led to new conflicts in 1979, when the standards for the baccalaureate, the key examination necessary to gain admittance to secondary school, were altered to favor Arabic speakers.

This split between Arab and black Mauritania has led to charges of racial discrimination and violence ever since. At the same time, the persistent droughts of the 1970s destroyed much of the nomadic economy, cutting the number of cattle by 90% and cutting camel herds by nearly 50%. These droughts helped reduce Arab population growth while the birthrate among the black population rose. As a result, Mauritania became about 50% black, and this demographic shift created new pressure for black rights.

Mauritania is critically dependent on the Senegal River for its water, and this led the Arab Mauritanians that drought drove out of the Sharel to seek black Mauritanian lands in the south, often with government encouragement. The resulting Arab-black tensions were made worse by the government's nationalization of land in 1983, which it often used to dispossess black communities, and by the creation of two major dams on the river during the 1980s. The Arabs often acquired the new agricultural lands created by these dams, although the original population was black.[9] The only other major resources in the country, the Akjoujt copper mines and Zouerate iron mines, are also under ethnic Arab control.

Changes in the government of Mauritania have also affected internal and regional stability. Mauritania was originally a single party government elected shortly after independence and headed by Ould Daddah, the leader of the Parti du Peuple Mauritanien. This party was Arab socialist, with ties to the Marxist Kadihine Party. It also became increasingly nationalist. Daddah terminated Mauritania's defense treaty with France in 1972, left the French currency bloc in 1973, and nationalized all French property.

Daddah aligned Mauritania with Algeria throughout the 1960s and during the early 1970s in an effort to check any threat of expansion from Morocco. He reversed this alignment in October, 1974, however, when he reached a secret agreement to partition the Spanish Sahara with King Hassan of Morocco. In doing so, he abandoned the local independence movement, the Frente Polisario, which had been allowed to operate on Mauritanian soil. As will be discussed in detail in the following section on Morocco, this led in 1975 to a Spanish agreement to partition the Spanish Sahara between Mauritania and Morocco, and Morocco and Mauritania occupied a divided Western Sahara in 1976. Daddah claimed that the people in the part given to Mauritania fully supported this occupation on the basis of local elections held in August, 1976, although no referendum was ever held to approve the occupation.

By mid-1976 it became clear that Algeria was willing to arm and train Polisario forces based in the Tindouf section of Algeria and that the Polisario strategy was to strike first at Mauritania, which was by far the weaker of the two countries occupying the Spanish Sahara. This led to two years of war as the small Mauritanian gendarmerie left by France tried to expand into an army. Mauritania spent some 50% of the national budget on this military expansion and fighting the Polisario, but it could not stop Polisario raids from Algeria or protect Mauritania's iron ore—its chief source of exports.

Morocco established a joint command with Mauritania in May, 1977 and sent troops into Mauritania. The Moroccan forces, however, were not large enough to secure Mauritania's border with the Western Sahara. Mauritania's situation improved slightly when France sent combat aircraft to bases in Senegal in December, 1977 and provided reconnaissance and bombing missions in support of the Mauritanian army, but this help did not halt Polisario operations. Even though Morocco had 10,000 troops in the country and France sent 300 troops as advisors, Mauritania continued to lose the war. Further, many Mauritanians in the north sympathized with the Polisario.

Daddah attempted to keep power by seeking more Moroccan and French support and by constantly altering military command positions to prevent a coup. The war, however, divided Daddah from the armed forces, and he was overthrown by Lt. Col. Mustpha Ould Mohammed, the army chief of staff, in a bloodless coup on July 10, 1978. Lt. Col. Mustpha Ould Mohammed then formed a conservative Military Council of National Salvation with eighteen officers, appointed a sixteen man cabinet with eight military members, and suspended the national assembly. The government has been a military dictatorship ever since, and no national elections have been held since 1978. The current "president" is Col. Maaouiya Ould Sid Ahmed, who came to power in December 12, 1984, and the government is still headed by the Military Council of National Salvation.[10]

The Polisario responded to the coup by declaring a unilateral cease-fire only with Mauritania, because it knew that Mauritania's new government could not formally reverse its position until it could reduce the presence of some 10,000 Moroccan troops and Moroccan garrisons in many cities. The Military Council of National Salvation began covert peace talks with the Polisario, however, and eventually persuaded Morocco to leave Mauritanian soil in return for Mauritanian willingness to give Morocco control over Mauritania's share of the Spanish Sahara. Mauritania signed a treaty with Morocco in 1979, renouncing its rights to the Western Sahara. It has stayed out of the Western Sahara conflict ever since and recognized the Sahraoui republic (Polisario government-in-exile) in 1984.

There has, however, been continuing tension between Mauritania and Senegal. The two countries are separated by the Senegal River and have often feuded over riverine rights, trading rights, and racial issues. Senegal made claims to Mauritanian territory in 1974–1976 when Mauritania experienced serious military problems in trying to annex part of the Western Sahara.

Until 1989, some 30,000 Senegalese workers used to do seasonal work in Mauritania, and up to 200,000 Mauritanians worked in Senegal, many as traders. On April 9, 1989, Mauritanian border guards shot two Senegalese in a dispute over grazing rights, and this triggered violence and riots. Many Senegalese attacked Mauritanian traders as exploiters, and up to twenty-five Mauritanians were killed when their shops and businesses were attacked during riots in Dakar, the capital of Senegal. Riots then followed in Nouakchott, the capital of Mauritania, where up to 500 people died, many of them black Mauritanians or Senegalese.[11]

Mauritania's Military Spending and Arms Imports

The data on Mauritanian military spending are contradictory but do not seem to include paramilitary forces. ACDA estimates that Mauritania's military budget was $66 million in 1978, $61 million in 1979, $65 million in 1980, $55 million in 1981 and 1982, $50 million in 1983, unknown in 1984, $52 million in 1985, $48 million in 1986, $35 million in 1987, $38 million in 1988, and $40 million in 1989.[12] These estimates are highly uncertain, and no useful estimates exist for military spending after 1989. Mauritania seems to have spent about 7–15% of its GDP on defense in recent years, and 25–30% of its central government expenditures.[13]

Mauritania has imported very few arms by the standards of other Middle

Eastern countries. ACDA estimates that Mauritania's arms exports were $30 million in 1978, $10 million in 1979, unknown in 1980, $5 million in 1981, $10 million in 1982, $10 million in 1983, $20 million in 1984, unknown in 1985, $5 million in 1986, $1 million in 1987, $10 million in 1988, and $20 million in 1989.[14]

France was Mauritania's major military supplier until the mid-1980s. ACDA estimates that Mauritania took delivery on $20 million worth of arms during 1979–1983. This included $10 million from France and $10 million from other countries.[15] Mauritania shifted towards Third World arms suppliers in the late 1980s and early 1990s. It took delivery on $30 million worth of arms during 1984–1988, all of it from countries outside the West and Soviet bloc.[16] ACDA changed its way of reporting arms sales by source in 1992, but this reporting indicates that Mauritania imported a total of $40 million worth of arms during 1985–1989, with only $5 million from France, $5 million from other developing countries, and $30 million from other Middle Eastern countries.[17]

Mauritania's Military Manpower

Mauritania had a total active military strength of roughly 11,000 in 1992, of which most manpower was volunteer, although conscription of up to two years was authorized. CIA estimates put the total population of Mauritania in mid-1991 at 2 million and the total labor force at over 465,000. This population was about 40% mixed Mauritanian and black, 30% Mauritanian, and 30% black African. Virtually all of the population was Muslim.[18]

This ethnic mix presents major problems because Mauritania was about 70% Mauritanian or "Moor" in 1960. The black population has had a far higher birthrate, particularly along the right bank of the Senegal River. While racial clashes have eased somewhat within Mauritania in recent years, there have been repeated clashes with Senegal in the border area.

The CIA estimated that there were 424,000 males in the age group from 15 to 49, and 207,000 males fit for military service.[19] The IISS estimated in late 1991 that there were a total of about 106,000 men and 103,000 women in the age group from 13 to 17 years, 91,000 men and 89,000 women in the age group from 18 to 22 years, and 126,000 men and 131,000 women in the age group from 23 to 32 years.[20]

Mauritania's Armed Forces

The Mauritanian armed forces have effectively controlled the country ever since the overthrow of President Ould Daddah in 1978. However, Mauritania has lacked the money to equip and support modern military forces that can compete with those of other Maghreb states.

Mauritania's army began converting from an internal security force to a regular army in 1975, but it still had only 10,400 men in 1992, or less than the manpower of one brigade slice in the West. Its major formations consisted of two infantry battalions, one paratroop battalion, one artillery battalion, a camel corps, three armed reconnaissance squadrons, four anti-aircraft batteries, and an engineer company. These forces, however, were dispersed over six military regions, and two independent sectors.

In 1992, the army still had no main battle tanks. Its major combat equipment consisted of eighty armored cars (fifteen EBR-75s, thirty-nine AML-60s, fourteen AML-90s, and twelve M-3A1s). The army also had forty M-3 half-tracks. Its artillery consisted of fifty-eight towed artillery pieces (eighteen LH-105 and ten M-101A1/HM-2 105mm weapons, and twelve D-74 and eighteen D-30 122mm weapons). It also had some thirty 120mm mortars, four Milan anti-tank guided missile launchers (ATGMs), a number of 57mm to 106mm recoilless rifles, and twelve D-44 85mm anti-tank guns. Its air defenses consisted largely of anti-aircraft machine guns and SA-7s, although it has fifty Z-23-2s and twenty-five 37mm and twelve 100mm AA guns. This mix of manpower, formations, and equipment was at best adequate for internal security functions or a low level border war with Senegal. Overall training and readiness was poor.

Mauritania's tiny 480 man navy was based at its one deep water port at Nouadhibou. It had ten small patrol boats. These were all inshore patrol craft based at Nouadhibou, and only four of the boats were large enough for extended duty. They included one 218-ton Neustadt-class patrol boat armed with two Bofors 40mm guns; one 148-ton Patra-class patrol boat with a 40mm and a 20mm gun; three 139-ton Lurssen FBP-36 class patrol boats with a 40mm and a 20mm gun; a 1,285-ton Jura-class fishery protection ship; and four small patrol craft. It also had two Piper Cheyenne II light aircraft with radars and cameras used for coastal surveillance. The navy was seeking two French landing craft–tanks (LCTs) or a French mine sweeper but had not been able to finance the sale.

Mauritania's 250 man air force had five light BN-2 Defender COIN aircraft as combat aircraft. Its only other aircraft were two Cheyenne II maritime reconnaissance aircraft, a Gulfstream II, a DHC-5D, two Skyvans, and an F-337.

Mauritania's paramilitary forces included 2,200 men in the six companies which made up its gendarmerie, plus a 2,800 man national guard, a 100 man border guard, and 1,000 men assigned as auxiliaries to the Interior Ministry.

Mauritania and Weapons of Mass Destruction

Mauritania has made no indigenous efforts to acquire weapons of mass destruction. Reports did surface during 1990 and 1991, however, that it had agreed to allow Iraq to create a long range missile range on its territory. There is no current evidence that such a range is under construction or functional.

Strategic Interests and Arms Control

Mauritania faces few threats and has given up all its claims to the former Spanish Sahara. Mauritania may, however, have increasing problems with Senegal. These problems come about largely because Mauritanian traders work in Senegal and are often accused of being "Arabs" who exploit the "black" Senegalese. It was this friction that led to border clashes in April, 1989 and to riots in Dakar and Nouakchott. There have also been continuing clashes over the arable land created by two new dams on the Senegal River.[21]

Mauritania may make token purchases of medium tanks and modern fighter aircraft during the next decade, but Mauritania's small military forces are likely to remain little more than a heavily armed internal security force. There is little indication that outside arms transfers or strategic ties to non–Middle Eastern states or arms control efforts are likely to have much near term impact on Mauritania. Restrictions on arms sales tied to a settlement of the Mauritania-Senegal conflict might conceivably help stabilize the relations between these two countries. At the same time, formal efforts to limit outside arms transfers to Mauritania without settlement between Mauritania and Senegal might do little more than arbitrarily tilt a racial and ethnic conflict, or lead other Middle Eastern states to provide the arms transfers other nations would not.

Morocco

	Manpower (1,000s)	Tanks	Aircraft	Defense Spending ($ millions)	Arms Imports ($ millions)	Arms Exports ($ millions)
1967	65	40	24	67	26	–
1973	65	120	48	223	6	–
1982	125	135	97	1,044	270	–
1988	195	224	93	1,138	90	–
1991	196	284	90	1,340	–	–

Morocco is a significant military power by Maghreb standards, although Table 4.3 makes it clear that Morocco's forces are far smaller than those of Algeria.[22] It has been involved in several limited conflicts with its neighbors and in a lasting conflict with the Polisario over control of the Western Sahara.

Morocco has a total area of 446,550 square kilometers. It has 2,002 kilometers of land boundaries: 1,559 kilometers with Algeria and 443 kilometers with the Western Sahara. Morocco has 1,835 kilometers of coastline, divided between the Atlantic and Mediterranean.[23] It has an important strategic position because of its potential value as a point for collecting intelligence on Africa, as a staging point for strategic airlift from the U.S., and as the southern gateway to the Mediterranean. However, it has few natural resources other than phosphates. It has only about 2,139,000 barrels of proved oil reserves and 70 billion cubic feet of gas.[24]

Military Developments in Morocco

Modern Morocco began to form when France returned Sultan Mohammed V to the country in 1955, after exiling him in 1943 and trying to substitute another ruler. Shortly before his return, a rebel military force called the Armeé de Libération Nationale (ALN) emerged. By 1956 the ALN's military

TABLE 4.3 Military Forces in the Maghreb in Early 1992

	Mauritania	Polisario	Morocco	Algeria	Tunisia	Libya
Military budget (millions of $ in 1991)	40[a]	15	1,300	660	467	1,510
Total Manpower						
Regular	11,700	4,000	195,500	125,500	35,000	85,000
(Conscripts)	?	—	?	(70,000)	(26,400)	?
Reserve	—	—	100,000	150,000	—	40,000
Paramilitary	5,700	11,000	40,000	23,000	13,500	15,000
Army						
Manpower	11,000	4,000	175,000	107,000	27,000	55,000
Main battle tanks	—	12-24	284	960[b]	84	2,150[c]
OAFVs/APCs[d]	79	55-80	1,372	1,495	347	2,120
Artillery[e]	40	20-35	326	743	145	1,740
Air Force						
Manpower	250	—	13,500	12,000	3,500	22,000[f]
Combat aircraft	7	—	90	241	30 F-5E/F[a]	409[f]
	5 Def		29 Mir F-1	57 MiG-23	11 Mark 326	5 Tu-22
	2 COIN		18 F-5E/F	6 Su-24		24 Mir F-1
	2 Cheyenne		23 Alphajet	17 MiG-25		140 MiG-23
			23 CM-170	95 MiG-21		65 MiG-25
			1 Falcon 20	30 MiG-17		45 Su-20/22
			4 OV-10	2 B-200T MR		50 MiG-21
			2 C-130H			28 Mir-5/R
						6 Su-24
						10 J-1 COIN
Armed helicopters	—	—	24 SA-342	38 Mi-24	—	35 Mi-24
				20 Mi-8/17		10 Mi-35
Major SAMs	—	—	37 M-54 SP	18 SA-6	—	108 SA-2
				30 SA-2		108 SA-3
				21 SA-3		72 SA-6/8/9/13
						36 SA-5

Navy					
Manpower	350	7,000	6,500	4,500	8,000
Submarines	—	—	2	—	6
Destroyer/frigates	—	1	3	1	3
Corvettes	—	—	3	—	7
Missile craft	—	4	11	6	24
Other patrol and mine	8	23	7	14	22
Amphibious/support	—	6	3	—	9

[a] Additional F-5s may be on order.
[b] Includes 113 T-34s in storage.
[c] Includes 1,200 in storage.
[d] Includes light tanks.
[e] Includes MRLs but not mortars.
[f] Although the air force has some Syrian pilots and Soviet, Pakistani, and North Korean instructors, many aircraft are in storage.

Sources: Adapted from *Middle East Military Balance, 1988–1989, and 1990*, Jaffee Center, Tel Aviv: IISS, *Military Balance, 1989–1990*, IISS, London, 1989, and IISS, *Military Balance, 1991–1992*, IISS, London, 1991. This table relies on these sources for the purposes of statistical consistency and often differs with the author's best estimates based on interviews and a mix of sources.

success forced France to give Morocco independence. The sultan's son, Moulay Hassan, was appointed chief of staff of the armed forces in 1957 and became king after the death of his father in 1971.

King Hassan has been ruler of Morocco ever since, although his control over the military has sometimes been uncertain, and he has been the target of several assassination attempts. One particularly bloody coup attempt occurred when a general led 1,400 military cadets in a strike on the king's palace in Rabat in July, 1971, during his birthday celebration. More than 100 of his guests were killed, but the king escaped by hiding until loyal troops could counterattack. In August, 1972 the king was almost shot down when three Moroccan air force jets attacked his plane and only broke off when the king disguised his voice and announced over the radio, "Stop firing, the tyrant is dead."[25]

The resulting purges of the military led to the execution of a number of generals in the Moroccan army, and similar purges occurred after a lesser coup attempt in 1972. The king experienced other political problems with his armed forces until at least 1975 and did not really give army and air force commanders any real authority or independence until defeats by the Polisario in the late 1970s made it clear that this was necessary to allow effective military operations.

King Hassan has, however, proved to be one of the most skillful politicians in the Arab world and Africa, and he has used his military to build support from other Arab regimes and several black African states. He provided small military contingents to Egypt and Syria during the 1973 war and has often provided "peacekeeping" troops to nations like Zaire (often for a considerable price). He has kept close ties to the West and exploited them to obtain arms and aid. He has also sought the conservative mainstream of Arab politics. He broke with Egypt over the Camp David accords but was one of the first Arab leaders to restore relations. He has protected the Jews in Morocco and shown far more interest in a peace settlement with Israel than have other Arab leaders.

This political juggling act has not protected Morocco from involvement in several military conflicts. The first was a rebellion in the Rif area of the Atlas Mountains in 1957–1958. Morocco invaded part of the Spanish Sahara in 1957 and claimed both the Western Sahara and part of Mauritania. This fighting ended in a cease-fire in April, 1958. Morocco also fought a series of border wars with Algeria from 1962 to 1964 over Moroccan claims to part of western Algeria.

The first such war with Algeria was a struggle for mineral rich areas in the Tindouf area along Morocco's southern border. This border area was never defined until 1962, when France awarded the Tindouf and neighboring Bechar areas to Algeria in granting it independence. Morocco had claimed the area since 1956. In 1961 it had traded its support for a rival of the Front de Libération National (FLN) called the Provisional Government of the Algerian Republic (GRPA) for the GPRA's agreement to cede Morocco the Tindouf. When the GPRA collapsed in early 1962 and the FLN took power, Morocco established police posts in the Tindouf and attempted to seize control of the territory. It also supported rivals of the FLN's leader, Ahmed Ben Bella. Once Algeria achieved independence on July 3, 1962, however, Ben Bella sent troops into the region and attacked several Moroccan border posts. Not ready to engage FLN forces that had grown to considerable size during their fight with the French, Morocco withdrew.

Moroccan troops again reentered the Tindouf, as well as Hassi-Beida, in September, 1963. Algeria sent in regular troops and expelled Morocco's light forces, but this time Morocco responded by deploying regular forces. This led to about two weeks of fighting along the border during October, 1963. The combat experienced Algerian forces won most of these engagements and then began to receive reinforcement from Cuban troops and armor. This tilted the balance decisively in favor of Algeria, and a cease-fire was agreed to on November 4, 1963, after Ethiopian mediation.[26]

The Struggle for the Western Sahara

Morocco's main military struggle has stemmed from King Hassan's renewed efforts to claim the Spanish Sahara. Although Spain peacefully ceded Ifni to Morocco in 1969, King Hassan began actively to seek control over the entire Western Sahara in 1974. He did so in open competition with Algeria, and despite an investigative report by the UN, dated October 15, 1975, that indicated that the majority of the inhabitants of the Spanish Sahara wanted independence. King Hassan responded by moving some 350,000 unarmed Moroccans into the frontier area and having them march across the border. With its government divided and Gen. Francisco Franco dying, Spain responded to the Moroccan march by announcing that it would withdraw from the Spanish Sahara, and Morocco reached a secret agreement with Mauritania to occupy the region. The Moroccan army occupied the northern two-thirds of the Western Sahara in December, 1975, and Mauritania occupied the southern third shortly thereafter.

The Western Sahara is a desert area of roughly 266,000 square kilometers, slightly smaller than the state of Colorado. It has 2,046 kilometers of land boundaries: Morocco 443 kilometers, Algeria 42 kilometers, and Mauritania 443 kilometers. It also has 1,110 kilometers of Atlantic coastline. The native population is virtually all Arab and Berber and nearly 100% Muslim. The Western Sahara's economy was then based on fishing and agriculture. While the region was extremely poor even by Third World standards and had almost no arable land, it was clear that it had very large phosphate deposits.[27]

By March, 1976, a Western Saharan government-in-exile was formed in Algeria, and in April Morocco and Mauritania formally laid claim to their respective portions of the region. This led to the formation of military forces by what came to be called the Popular Front for the Liberation of the Saguia el Hamra and Rio de Oro (Polisario). This movement, which was recognized by the Organization of African Unity (OAU) in 1984, soon launched a guerrilla war against Morocco and Mauritania.

By concentrating on Mauritania, which lacked effective military forces, the Polisario was able to score major victories with limited raids. Morocco had to deploy troops to the Mauritanian portion of the Western Sahara and even to Mauritania itself. The result came close to breaking up Mauritania, which could not afford any kind of war and faced serious tensions within its Arab and black populations. As a result, Mauritania renounced all claims to the region in August, 1979.

Morocco immediately occupied the territory vacated by Mauritania, leading to more intense fighting between Morocco and the Polisario. The occupation also created a crisis between Morocco and Algeria. Algeria backed the Polisario and gave the Polisario refugee camps and military bases in Algeria near the border of the disputed territory. These tensions led to a near state of war and eventually to a break in diplomatic relations between Algeria and Morocco that was not restored until 1987. Libya supported the Polisario with funds and arms, and both Algeria and Libya helped catalyze the OAU into recognizing the Polisario as an independent government. As a result, Morocco left the OAU.

Morocco's heavily politicized forces were not ready to deal with a guerrilla conflict and performed poorly during the initial fighting for control of the Western Sahara. After 1979, however, Morocco had begun to reorganize its forces, and King Hassan gave his commanders increasing authority to manage the conflict. Morocco also expanded and reequipped its forces and began to deploy them along a series of steadily expanding perimeter defenses.

In contrast, the Polisario forces increasingly suffered from a lack of heavy weapons and external support. Their total strength reached just 10,000, and only 4,000 were regulars. These forces were poorly equipped in comparison with the Moroccan army. While they scored a number of victories, they could not counter Morocco's defenses with cross country vehicles and light to medium weapons. They did, however, declare the creation of the Sahraoui Arab Democratic Republic (SADR) in 1976. In skillful political maneuvering, they received OAU recognition in 1982, obtained broad African recognition in 1984, and were recognized by some seventy countries in 1987.

By 1988 Morocco built up its forces in the Western Sahara to around 110,000 men. It also succeeded in expanding its defense zone to the point where it had reasonably effective defenses near the eastern border of the Western Sahara, These defenses consisted of an 1,800–2,400 kilometer long series of "Hassan walls."[28] These walls consisted of 2 meter high berms or earth mounds, embedded with sensors, covered in barbed wire, and defended with mines. The army was deployed in over 300 strong points on and behind the wall and equipped with night vision systems and radars that could detect moving vehicles. A "sixth wall" defended the lower part of the Western Sahara south of Dakhla. The Moroccan troops in the various strong points along and behind the wall were protected by a series of mobile desert strike units, fire bases, attack helicopters and air support forces, and twenty ground surveillance radar bases and other sensors.

In contrast, the Polisario forces had a maximum strength of 25,000, and more realistic estimates gave them a strength of about 4,000 regulars and

6,000 part time forces. Their only heavy weapons consist of some Algerian-supplied T-55s, BMP-1s, twenty to thirty EE-9 Cascavals, captured Moroccan AML-90s and Eland AFVs, captured Ratel 20s, captured Panhard APCs, M-1931 and M-1937 122mm howitzers, a few captured Steyr SK-105 105mm self-propelled anti-tank weapons, some 122mm multiple rocket launchers, 120mm and 160mm mortars, AT-4 anti-tank guided missiles, and SA-7 surface-to-air missiles. Regardless of some continuing successes against Moroccan troops in hit-and-run raids, the Polisario rarely could deploy more than 1,500–2,000 troops in the field. This allowed Morocco to field a nearly 20:1 superiority in southern Morocco and the Western Sahara.

This superiority gave Morocco an effective victory over the Polisario by 1988–1989, although the Polisario continued to fight and occupy military bases in Algeria. The Moroccan forces also were not able to eliminate several problems. The Moroccan army's tactics remain somewhat static and defensive in dealing with the Polisario, command level reaction times were often slow, and army units did not use artillery quickly and effectively enough, although its purchases of self-propelled guns and howitzers steadily improved this aspect of its military performance.

Morocco's air force made steadily better use of its helicopters, sensors, COIN aircraft, and F-5 fighters in reacting to Polisario raids, but its air effectiveness was limited because it lacked the air strength to risk any additional losses. Morocco lost more F-5 and F-1 aircraft than it should have to SA-6 and SA-7B missiles and unguided AA guns, although it slowly improved its air tactics and countermeasure performance. Morocco did provide its forces in the Sahara with good support and with modern sensors and munitions.

The wall of earthen berms that extends from Bou Craa to Amalga was virtually completed by 1990, but it required constant maintenance and sophisticated sensor coverage to detect forces crossing the barrier. It was also expensive to man and maintain, although it was the only way Morocco could continue to deprive Polisario forces of the ability to use armor, trucks, and Land Rovers for lightning "camel" raids. Even so, the Polisario can still achieve some temporary successes. As a result, the war no longer cost Morocco anything like the $1.9 billion annually it cost at its peak, but it still cost around $300 million per year. This spending remained a drain on a weak economy, with its high levels of unemployment, and helped lead growing unrest over prices and the decline in personal income. It also contributed to growing Islamic fundamentalist opposition in spite of the king's nominal title of spiritual ruler and his construction of an immense $360 million mosque in Casablanca.

Morocco's problems, however, were relatively minor compared to the growing weakness of Polisario forces. Morocco controlled 80% of the disputed territory and all its cities. Further, Morocco benefited from improving relations with Libya and Algeria. Qadhafi's adventures with his neighbors and the West created enough problems to force him to negotiate a modus vivendi with King Hassan. Algeria developed a serious interest in building a gas pipeline to Spain through Morocco and recognized that its support of the Polisario was becoming more and more futile. This helped lead Algeria to resume relations with Morocco and to push for negotiations between Morocco and the Polisario, even though it realized there was little chance the Polisario could benefit.

The result was talks between Morocco and the Polisario. Announcements that the war had come to an end in early 1989 quickly proved false when King Hassan and the Polisario could not agree on terms for a plebiscite.[29] The fighting during 1989–1991 was largely a history of repeated Moroccan victories, however, and Moroccan forces seem to have taken the Polisario's provisional capital of Bir Lahlo during the fighting in August, 1991. When Morocco and the Polisario finally did agree to a UN-mediated cease-fire on September 6, 1991, Morocco did so from a position of strength.[30]

Morocco agreed to a UN-run referendum, to a reduction of its troops to a maximum of 65,000 men, and to a 2,800 man UN peacekeeping force. It was clear that Morocco could control the outcome of the vote and enforce its victory almost regardless of the actions of the twenty-five nation UN peacekeeping force being sent to the region. It did not reduce its forces in the area as the agreement called for, and it delayed the entry of the UN peacekeeping force and its deployment.[31]

The vote scheduled for January 6, 1992, was delayed, and no new date is apparent. Both Morocco and the Polisario have attempted to alter the outcome of any vote. There were only about 80,000 residents of the Western Sahara when the last prewar census was taken in 1974. The CIA estimated in mid-1991 that the population was around 197,000, with a labor force of only 12,000, although any such estimate is highly controversial.[32]

Morocco, however, has taken no chances that the resulting mix of original residents and Moroccans will determine the outcome of any plebiscite. In 1991 it began to move residents "back" into the Western Sahara so they could vote. It provided them with tents, subsidies, and tax benefits, and submitted 120,000 new names of residents to the UN. The Polisario, in turn, claimed that it had 165,000 Sahraou refugees living in Algeria, although it had recruited nomads and other Bedouin who never were real residents of the Spanish Sahara before independence. This helps explain the delays in the plebiscite; Morocco will not allow a vote until it is certain it can win. It is equally unclear that the Polisario will accept any outcome other than victory, and Moroccan and Algerian relations have not improved to the point where Algeria has ceased arming the Polisario.[33]

Morocco's political position has improved steadily since 1990. It gained the support of Saudi Arabia, Kuwait, the UAE, and the West by being the only Maghreb state to send troops to support the UN coalition in 1990. King Hassan had considerable public support when he delayed the parliamentary elections from September, 1990 to 1992, because he claimed this would allow elections to be held after the Western Sahara had voted to join Morocco. He has freed some political prisoners and closed the prison at Tazmamart—a notoriously harsh detention center for political prisoners.

Morocco's victory over the Polisario has not prevented it from having increasing problems with its economy and Islamic fundamentalism. Morocco has been slow to improve the management of its economy and eliminate the problems that led to major riots in 1981 and 1984. While the war with the Polisario has been relatively popular in recent years, it also has put a continuing strain on Morocco's economy. In spite of considerable U.S. and Saudi aid and a $1 billion IMF bailout, Morocco has had trouble paying its bills for key military equipment deliveries like those required to support its Mirage F-1 aircraft. Saudi aid has also dropped from peak levels of nearly $1 billion annually to under $100 million. Morocco's foreign debt increased to $22,300 million in 1990, which is far too high for the nation's economy to sustain. Morocco's real per capita GNP remains at only about $1,000, and unemployment remains high.

King Hassan has dealt with these problems by both strengthening his internal security operations and offering a revised constitution that takes some steps towards increased democracy. On September 4, the Moroccan people approved a constitution that gives the king authority to name the prime minister but allows the prime minister to name his own ministers. It gives the assembly the power to conduct investigations, call for votes of no confidence, and enact laws the king must act upon in 30 days. It sets up a new constitutional council that has functions similar to those of the French supreme court, with oversight powers over all legislation. The king will choose five of its nine members. At the same time the king announced municipal elections for October and elections for the national assembly in November.

While some Moroccan political parties boycotted the elections, voter turnout was relatively high. Further, the referendum on the constitution marked the third time that the residents of the Western Sahara had voted in Moroccan elections. The vote reflected that tax and other incentives had steadily increased the number of Moroccans in the area. While King Hassan assured the UN he was still prepared to hold a referendum on control of the Sahara, the fact remained that 12 representatives from the region already sat in the Moroccan national assembly, and King Hassan was clearly committed to including the region in Morocco.[34]

Morocco's Defense Spending and Arms Imports

The key factor that has driven the trends in Morocco's defense expenditures and the military contribution to its debt has been the cost of the war with the Polisario. Estimates of Morocco's military spending after 1982 are difficult to arrive at because of the uncertainty of official data and the failure to count outside aid transfers and loans in available estimates. ACDA estimates that Morocco spent $467 million in current dollars in 1978, $520 million in 1979, $763 million in 1980, $830 million in 1981, $1,089 million in 1982, $1,074 million in 1983, $1,078 million in 1986, $1,102 million in 1987, $1,102 million in 1988, and $1,203 million in 1989. Data are not available for 1984 and 1985.

These estimates would put Moroccan military spending at about 7–10% of the GNP, and 25–35% of central government expenditures, with at least one-third going to the direct expenses of the war with the Polisario. The IISS estimates tend to confirm the ACDA totals. They put Moroccan defense spending at $860 million in 1987, $1,136 million in 1988, $1,216 million in 1989, and $1,340 million in 1990.

Morocco has imported about $900 million worth of arms since 1987, and the U.S., France, and other developing nations have been its major suppliers. ACDA estimates that Morocco imported $440 million worth of arms in 1978, $470 million in 1979, $350 million in 1980, $340 million in 1981, $270 million in 1982, $320 million in 1983, $210 million in 1984, $110 million in 1985, $90 million in 1986, $410 million in 1987, $130 million in 1988, and $40 million in 1989.[35] These estimates almost certainly undercount the actual volume of expenditures.

ACDA estimates that Morocco took delivery on a total of $1,785 million worth of arms during 1979–1983. This included $430 million worth of arms from the U.S., $950 million from France, $5 million from West Germany, $50 million from Italy, $50 million from Poland, and $1,900 million from other countries, with France acting as Morocco's single largest supplier.[36] Morocco took delivery on $890 million worth of arms during 1984–1988. This total reflected the dropping cost of the war with the Polisario and improved Moroccan relations with Algeria. It also reflected reduced Moroccan dependence on France. The total included $280 million worth of arms from the U.S., $250 million from France, $20 million from the PRC, and $340 million from other countries.[37] While these arms imports are not large by Maghreb standards, they have played a role in shaping Morocco's international debt of $21.4 billion, which is roughly equal to its GDP of $25.4 billion.[38]

As mentioned earlier, ACDA changed its way of reporting arms sales by source in 1992. According to this reporting, Morocco imported a total of $770 million worth of arms during 1985–1989. This total again reflected the reduced costs of Morocco's war with the Polisario, and the U.S. became Morocco's largest supplier for the first time. The $770 million included $240 million from the U.S., $150 million from France, $20 million from the PRC, $20 million from Warsaw Pact countries, $330 million from other European countries, and $10 million from East Asian states.[39]

Moroccan Military Manpower

The size of Moroccan military forces is constrained by money and equipment resources, rather than manpower. Morocco had a total active military strength of about 195,500 men in 1992, with some eighteen month conscripts. Its organized reserves seem to total about 100,000. This is a relatively limited burden on Morocco's labor force. The CIA puts the total population of Morocco at 26.1 million, the birthrate at 2.1%, and the total labor force at 7,400,000. The population is about 99.1% Arab and Berber, with 0.7% non-Moroccan, and 0.2% Jewish. The population in 98.7% Muslim, 1.1% Christian, and 0.2% Jewish.

The CIA estimates that there are 6,437,000 males in the age group from 15 to 49, that 4,092,000 are fit for military service, and that 300,000 males fit for military service reach the age of 18 each year. The IISS estimates that there are a total of about 1,448,000 men and 1,395,000 women in the age group from 13 to 17 years, about 1,359,000 men and 1,310,000 women in the age group from 18 to 22 years, and about 2,111,000 men and 1,390,000 women in the age group from 23 to 32 years.[40]

The Moroccan Army

The 175,000 man Moroccan army is the only force in the Maghreb that has recently had to train and organize for actual combat, although this combat has consisted largely of guerrilla warfare. The army is organized into four major commands: south, northwest, Atlas, and border. It has three mechanized infantry brigade headquarters, two paratroop brigades, and eleven mechanized infantry regiments. It also has an exceptionally large number of small independent units. These include nine armored squadron groups, thirty-seven infantry battalions, three motorized (camel corps) battalions, one mountain battalion, three cavalry battalions, ten artillery groups, one air defense group, and four engineering battalions. There is also a 1,500 man royal guard with one battalion and one cavalry squadron.

The Moroccan army has a significant number of conscripts but emphasizes regulars. Morocco's large population and low per capita income leads many poor Moroccans to make the army a career. Pay and benefits are adequate, and living conditions are acceptable, even in the camps and strong points in the south. Training, however, is still erratic, and much of it is conducted in units. This leads to very different levels of effectiveness, depending upon the particular unit involved.

A 50,000 to 100,000 man reserve exists on paper but serves little real purpose. There is little reserve training, except for specialists and skills the army would need in war. The only combat effective reserves would be men called back to units they had recently left. The Force Auxiliaire, a 30,000 man force designed to reinforce the army in a campaign against Algeria, is probably more effective and would provide service support and rear area security. It also includes a 5,000 man mobile intervention force fully equipped with light armored vehicles and Land Rovers and with automatic and crew served weapons. The Force Auxiliaire has also been used successfully in rear area security operations against the Polisario.

The army is deployed to concentrate Morocco's armored forces in the north and to deploy a large anti-guerrilla force in the south. This reflects its long standing emphasis on deterring Algeria while fighting the Polisario. There is one royal guard battalion, a mountain battalion, an armored squadron, a mechanized squadron, a cavalry squadron, and an artillery group in the northwest Atlas. The border is defended by two mechanized infantry regiments, three infantry battalions, one camel corps battalion, two armored squadrons, and one artillery group.

There are three mechanized infantry brigades, nine mechanized infantry regiments, twenty-five infantry battalions, two paratroop battalions, two camel corps battalions, four armored squadrons with UR-416 armored personnel carriers (APCs), and seven artillery groups in the south. Morocco also plays a significant peacekeeping role. One additional Moroccan battalion with 360 men is deployed in Equatorial Guinea, Moroccan troops are with the UN force in Angola, and Morocco deployed 5,000 men in the UAE during the Gulf War, including a 700 man paratroop unit.

Morocco's purchases of 224 M-48A5 and 60 M-60A1 tanks have given the army more heavy armor but still leave it with far less armor than Algeria. Morocco does, however, have 98 AMX-13 light tanks, 8 SU-100 self-propelled anti-tank guns, 30 M-56 90mm anti-tank guns, and Steyr SK-105 Kuerassier self-propelled anti-tank guns, giving it a total of 284 tanks and 164 light tanks. Overall levels of tank training are adequate, but Morocco conducts limited maneuver and large unit training.

Reports differ as to the strength and types of other fighting vehicles in Moroccan forces, but its armored reconnaissance strength in 1992 seems to have included 16 EBR-75, 80 AMX-10Cs, 190 AML-90s, 38 AML-60-7s, and 40 Elands with 90mm guns. It also has 30 Ratel 20, 30 AML-90, and 45 VAB-VCIs employed as AIFVS; and 420 M-113s and 320 VAB-VTTs employed as APCs. It may also have forty-five OT-62 and OT-64 APCs. This diverse mix of armored fighting vehicles and APCs is often of mediocre quality and lacks effective standardization. Morocco's unusual emphasis on armored infantry fighting vehicles and armored personnel carriers does, however, reflect a response to the special needs imposed by its terrain and its experience in fighting the Polisario. While Algeria poses the threat of armored warfare, Morocco has fought the Polisario largely by using mechanized infantry.

Morocco is better equipped with artillery. In 1992 it had 146 towed weapons. These included thirty-five L-118, twenty M-101, and thirty-eight HM-2 105mm weapons, eighteen M-46 122mm weapons, and thirty-six FH-70 and twenty M-114 155mm weapons. It had 132 self-propelled weapons: 98 AMX-F3, 20 M-44, 44 M-109/109A1 155mm howitzers. It also had 40 BM-21 122mm multiple rocket launchers and some 1,100 mortars. Roughly 680 of the mortars were 120mm weapons, 20 of which were mounted on VAB armored vehicles. This artillery strength again does not match that of Algeria, but it includes a large number of modern self-propelled weapons. Morocco seems to be able to operate most of its artillery weapons effectively but has problems with combined arms, artillery maneuver, and beyond visual range targeting.

Moroccan army anti-tank weapons include HOT, 440 M-47 Dragon, 80 Milan, 152 BGM-71A TOW and some AT-3 anti-tank guided missile launchers. Many of the TOWs were mounted on armored vehicles. Its other anti-tank weapons include the LAW, RPG-7 M-20, and STRIM 89 3.5" rocket launchers. The army also had some 260 M-20 75mm, 30 M-67 90mm, and 350 M-40 106mm recoilless rifles. Morocco has some 427 anti-aircraft guns, including 90 ZU-23-2s and 40 Vulcan 20mm towed guns, and 60 M-163 20mm Vulcan self-propelled anti-aircraft guns. It also has thirty-seven M-54 Chaparral self-propelled surface-to-air missile launchers, and large numbers of SA-7s.

While Morocco has some outstanding battalion sized elements, most of its heavy armor lacks proper support equipment, technical manpower, and spares. Morocco does not conduct serious large unit armored maneuver training and lacks the service support and sustaining capability it needs to fight a prolonged conflict with Algeria. Logistic support, however, is adequate, and Morocco has shown that it can maintain an adequate supply line over considerable distances.

Morocco's paramilitary forces total 40,000 men, most of which can act as land forces. These include 10,000 men in the royal guard, which is organized into one brigade, two mobile groups, an air squadron, and a coast guard unit. The gendarmerie has eighteen patrol boats, two light aircraft, and twenty-two helicopters.

The Moroccan Navy

The 7,000 man Moroccan navy is a relatively large force by local standards. It includes one frigate, four missile patrol boats, two fast attack craft, eleven large patrol craft, six coastal patrol craft, four landing craft, twenty-seven customs and coast guard vessels, three service ships, and 1,500 men in a marine naval infantry battalion. It is capable of patrolling local waters but has limited ability to operate in the Atlantic, and training is said to be mediocre. It would not be capable of successfully engaging Spanish naval forces and would experience serious problems in any engagement with Algeria. The navy is based in Casablanca, Safi, Agadier, Al Hoceima, and Dakhla. Casablanca is the key port. Dakhla and Agadier are the main secondary bases on the Atlantic, and Al Hoceima is the key secondary base on the Mediterranean.

In 1992 the navy had one 1,480-ton guided missile frigate with 4 MM-38 Exocet launchers (sea-skimming missiles with semi-active radar guidance, a range of 42 kilometers, and a 165 kilogram warhead), an octuple Aspide launcher (semi-active radar homing to 13 kilometers at Mach 2.5), one 76mm gun, six 324mm torpedo tubes, and anti-submarine mortars. It also had four 425-ton guided missile patrol craft—all of which were equipped with four MM-38 Exocets and one 76mm gun. The missile ships were generally considerably better manned and equipped than Morocco's other vessels. Individual officer training for these ships ranged from adequate to good, and crew training from mediocre to adequate. Its ability to fight an entire missile ship effectively in combat against a force equipped with modern sensors and countermeasures was uncertain, as was the ability to operate in unison as a fleet.

The navy had two 445-ton fast attack craft with one 76mm gun; six 425-ton Cormorant-class large patrol craft with 40mm and 20mm guns; four 475-ton Osprey Mark II–class large patrol craft with one 40mm and two 20mm guns; and one 374-ton large patrol craft with two Bofors 40mm guns. There also were three 1,409-ton LSMs, with the capacity to carry 140 troops or 7 tanks, one 670-ton LCT, and up to 26 LCMs. Support craft included two small 1,500-ton transports and one Ro-Ro Ferry converted to be a troop transport ship.

The navy has shown it can operate these fast attack craft, patrol craft, transport, and amphibious ships reasonably well. However, Morocco has little repair or at-sea replenishment capability, and most ships have limited endurance. It is scarcely the possessor of a "blue water" navy that can play a role in the Atlantic or in controlling the entrance to the Mediterranean, but the Moroccan navy is adequate for coastal defense and represents the largest force Morocco can support—given its limited defense budget and need to concentrate on the defense of the western border and south.

The customs and coast guard had four P-32 coastal patrol craft, eighteen Arcor 46-class coastal patrol craft, and five Arcor 17–class inshore patrol craft.

The Moroccan Air Force

In 1992 the 13,500 man Moroccan air force had about ninety combat aircraft and twenty-four armed helicopters. These forces included two attack squadrons of 1/21 F-5E/F-II and 1/14 Mirage F-1CHs; one air defense squadron with fifteen Mirage F-1CHs; two COIN squadrons with 1/23 Alphajet and 1/23 CM-170 Fouga Magisters, and a Recce squadron with four OV-10s and two CH-130s with side looking radars. It had five to six main operating bases in Morocco and three to four operating bases in the south.

The Moroccan air force experienced considerable political instability in the early 1970s and then had problems in the war with the Polisario. It lost a considerable number of aircraft to Polisario SA-6s and SA-7s in the early and mid-1980s, and often aborted missions or dropped bombs where they had limited effect. Since that time, however, it has gradually corrected some of the training, maintenance, and leadership problems that limited it in the past. It has achieved a reasonable level of proficiency in using its F-5E/Fs and twenty-three Alphajets.

It is also effective in using its four OV-10 COIN and reconnaissance aircraft, and its CH-130s with side looking aircraft radar (SLAR) have proved to be of considerable value in locating and targeting Polisario movements with vehicles. It seems able to make effective use of its one C-130 and one Falcon 20 electronic intelligence (ELINT) aircraft and is one of the few regional air forces with such an electronic intelligence capability. It acquired a Westinghouse air defense system in the early 1980s and has moderately effective warning and combat air control capability.

The air force's main limitations are its lack of advanced or airborne sensors and AC&W capability, its lack of advanced combat training capability, continuing maintenance problems and dependence on foreign technicians, and its limited C3I battle management capability in the event of a major Algerian attack. Some of these problems may be solved over the next few years, since Morocco signed a contract with Westinghouse to modernize its communications, entire air defense system, and air traffic system in September, 1991.[41]

The air force also cannot properly support and operate all of its Mirage F-1 fighters, which constitute twenty-nine aircraft out of a total combat strength of ninety. There are fourteen Mirage F-1EHs in the attack role and fifteen Mirage F-1CHs assigned to the air defense role. It is unclear whether Morocco's problems in operating the Mirage F-1 stem from problems in maintaining the aircraft or from a failure or inability to fund the spare parts and equipment it needs.

Morocco has relatively modern air munitions, including some AIM-9Js, R-530s, R-550 Magics, and 125 AGM-65B Mavericks—which can be fired by its F-5Es. Morocco will, however, need to fund more modern fighters during the next decade, including a modern Recce fighter.

Morocco also has twenty-four SA-342 armed helicopters, twelve with HOT anti-guided missiles and twelve with cannon. It has seven CH-47 heavy transport helicopters, fifty-four medium transport helicopters, and twenty-three light helicopters. Helicopter mobility and readiness are very good by regional standards. It has one Boeing 707-320, eleven C-130H transports, and three KC-130 tankers. There are eleven light transports and twenty-six training aircraft. Morocco makes extensive use of air transport and supply in its operations against the Polisario.

Strategic Interests and Arms Control

Morocco has generally supported Western and moderate Arab positions throughout the Middle East. This support has helped the U.S. in dealing with Lebanon, the Gulf War, and the Middle East peace process. Morocco also signed a transit and access agreement with the U.S. in 1982 that allows the U.S. potential use of Sidi Slimane Air Base and Mohammed V Airport.[42]

While Morocco's war with the Polisario has destablized the Maghreb, some of this destablization has also come from Algeria's efforts to use the Polisario against Morocco and from Libya's support of the Polisario. There are no clear wrongs and rights in this conflict. It does seem likely, however, that most of the residents of the Western Sahara will ultimately obtain more economic benefits as part of Morocco than as part of yet another African mini-state. The gradual end of Morocco's conflict with the Polisario, and improvements in Algerian and Moroccan relations seem to have reduced the risk of Moroccan conflicts with its neighbors while leaving Morocco's strategic value intact.

As for arms sales, Algeria does not pose a current political threat to Morocco, and Morocco does not need major new imports for its security. It will, however, need to upgrade its air force at some point in the 1990s because of the age of its primary fighters, and there are many systems in its army which will need modern replacements over the next years—particularly air defenses and other armored vehicles.

Similarly, any attempt to place stringent controls on arms sales to Morocco because of its fighting with the Polisario would be too late to affect the war for the Western Sahara and could do nothing except extend a war that produces needless suffering. What seems called for is moderate restraint in arms transfers, allowing Morocco to replace selected systems but not sharply increase its numbers. It should be noted that there would be no practical difference between shipments of "offensive" and "defensive" weapons to Morocco. Defensive weapons like AA guns and anti-tank missiles would be usable as offensive weapons against the Polisario, and maneuver weapons are its only effective defense against Algeria.

It should also be noted, however, that King Hassan has an uncertain record on human rights and economic reform and shows few signs of fully complying with the terms of the UN cease-fire agreement.[43] Further, Morocco claims the two small Spanish controlled enclaves of Ceuta and Melilla in the northern coastal area along the Mediterranean, and the Spanish-held islands of Peñon de Alhucemas, Peñon de Velez de la Gomera, and Islas Chafarinas. While Spain has tried to improve its relations with Morocco, Spain has also indicated that it intends to defend these territories and has actively organized its forces and improved its power projection capabilities to support their defense. This at least presents the possibility of some kind of struggle over vestiges of European colonialism in Africa.

Algeria

	Manpower (1,000s)	Tanks	Aircraft	Defense Spending ($ millions)	Arms Imports ($ millions)	Arms Exports ($ millions)
1967	75	240	21	106	41	5
1973	80	400	44	132	24	–
1982	120	630	306	1,772	1,200	–
1988	126	910	299	1,784	825	–
1991	126	960	241	904	–	–

Algeria's strategic importance lies in its petroleum resources, its position on the Mediterranean, and its large military forces.[44] As of January 1, 1992, Algeria had estimated proved oil reserves of 9.2 billion barrels and gas reserves of 116,500 billion cubic feet. It had about 1.2% of the world's total oil reserves and produced at a rate of about 800,000 barrels per day in 1990 and 1991.[45]

Algeria has a total area of around 2,382,000 square kilometers. It has 6,343 kilometers of land boundaries: 982 kilometers with Libya, 1,376 kilometers with Mali, 463 kilometers with Mauritania, 1,559 kilometers with Morocco, 956 kilometers with Niger, 965 kilometers with Tunisia, and 42 kilometers with the Western Sahara. Algeria has 998 kilometers of coastline on the Mediterranean.

Military Developments in Algeria

Algeria's military forces evolved out of the prolonged military struggle for independence from France which took place during 1954–1962. It was originally the Armée de Libération Nationale, which was the military arm of the Front de Libération National led by Ahmed Ben Bella. The ALN was created almost immediately after the struggle against France began and received formal recognition by much of the Arab world when the FLN set up a government-in-exile in Cairo in 1958.[46]

The war with France was the bloodiest and most bitter war for independence of any postwar struggle in the Middle East. It was fought as a guerrilla war in both rural and urban areas against a French army determined to revenge itself for its defeat in Vietnam, and a French government determined to maintain Algeria as part of metropolitan France. The FLN forces established sanctuaries in Morocco and Tunisia, and France replied by establishing barrier defenses and electrified fences to cover the border. At the same time, a struggle took place along the Libyan border to stop movement of supplies from Egypt to the FLN. Torture and terrorism were used extensively on both sides, along with an often murderous struggle using informers and execution squads to try to control the populace.

France succeeded at the military level. The FLN forces never developed to the point where they could successfully fight French forces in regular warfare, and they lost virtually every direct engagement. The political situation was very different. The war's casualties, cost, and brutality eventually made the war so unpopular in France that it brought down the Fourth Republic in 1958. Charles de Gaulle became president of the Fifth Republic and began discussions of a settlement with the FLN in 1959. This led to a near mutiny among the French forces and settlers in Algeria and the creation in Algeria of the Secret Army Organization (OAS). For three years, de Gaulle and metropolitan France struggled to bring the OAS under control while he continued negotiating with the FLN. The OAS added a new note of terrorism to the struggle for control of the Algerian populace and in 1961 launched a coup attempt against de Gaulle. De Gaulle suppressed the attempt and organized his own secret intelligence forces to attack the OAS, triggering a new wave of assassinations and counter-assassinations.

France's negotiations with the FLN finally led to a cease-fire in March, 1962, after bitter fighting with the OAS. France then granted Algeria independence in June, 1962, and all military operations ceased. By this time, some 15,000 French troops and tens of thousands of Algerians were dead. Most French settlers and many Algerians loyal to France left Algeria for France. Many of the leading entrepreneurs left with them, and Algeria became a socialist regime led by a revolutionary movement with no experience in government of any kind. At the same time, the FLN had often fought with Algeria's more conservative Islamic leaders, and this left an enduring legacy of tension between Algeria's new leaders and Islamic conservatives.

The military branch of the FLN has been the key source of power in Algeria ever since Algeria achieved independence, and most of the power struggles in Algeria have been coups or attempted coups. Algeria's first president, Ahmed Ben Bella was overthrown by his minister of defense, Houari Boumedienne, in 1965. Boumedienne put aside Algeria's constitution and governed through a revolutionary council that included virtually all the leaders of the armed forces. This set the precedent for struggles within the FLN, the outcomes often determined in large part by who controlled the military forces. He also instituted a centrally planned form of Arab socialism that slowly crippled the nation's economy, depriving it of most incentives, creating massive distribution bottlenecks, and creating high structural unemployment and major housing shortages.

Aside from its struggle with Morocco over the Western Sahara, Algeria did not play a military role in the region after independence. It did provide military support for the Polisario, however, and a number of border clashes and incidents took place with Morocco, the most significant of which occurred in 1976. This time, unlike in 1962 and 1963, Algerian land and air forces did not do well against Morocco.

While a major war with Morocco never really seemed imminent, Algeria responded by beginning a major military buildup that continued through the 1980s. Algeria was also forced to keep Libya at a distance and occasionally to pressure Libya not to threaten Tunisia. It signed a treaty in 1983 that obligated it to protect Tunisia through military intervention.

The relations between Algeria and its two major neighbors grew still worse in 1984, when Morocco signed an accord of "union" with Libya in Oujda that seemed to raise the risk of a two front conflict, and Algeria put considerable pressure on Libya in 1985, when Qadhafi expelled some 30,000 Tunisian workers from Libya. Qadhafi's volatile political alignments then shifted again, however, and Morocco exploited its union with Libya as a negotiating tactic with Algeria. Morocco ended its agreement with Libya in 1986, and Morocco and Algeria restored relations in 1988. They began negotiations that sharply reduced the military tensions between them and led Algeria to reduce its support for the Polisario. Algeria accepted a UN referendum proposal that it must have realized could give Morocco control of most of the Western Sahara, although it continues to provide arms and bases for the Polisario.

In contrast, Algeria's internal problems have become steadily more significant. Boumedienne died in December, 1978. After some jockeying among senior military officers, Col. Chadli Benjedid became "president." Benjedid proved to be a more pragmatic ruler than Boumedienne. He attempted to shift the country back towards capitalism and played a key role in negotiating the release of U.S. embassy hostages in Tehran in 1982. He did not, however, have Boumedienne's political skills, eloquence, or charisma. Where Boumedienne could dominate the party and armed forces and go directly to the people, Benjedid was a poor speaker who worked through technocrats, lacked the authority to act on his own, and had to balance an FLN divided between socialist extremists and more pragmatic technocrats.

In spite of Benjedid's efforts and some limited economic reforms, Algeria continued with the quasi-socialist economic policies the FLN had instituted after 1962, and the economy continued to degenerate as the population increased. While GNP per capita rose on paper, practical living standards declined, as did many basic services. Disguised unemployment became the rule rather than the exception, and every sector of the economy experienced growing problems. Ironically, socialism also failed to prevent elitism. By 1988 only 5% of the population had 45% of the national income, and unemployment reached 20%. Agriculture declined to the point where 95% of Algeria's export income came from gas and oil, but debt repayments absorbed $7 billion of export earnings of $11 billion and left little for domestic needs. At the same time, population growth exceeded 3%, and more than half of the population was under twenty-one.[47]

These pressures fed Islamic fundamentalism as the only remaining ideological alternative to the failure of nationalism, socialism, and Westernism. Islamic opposition had first become a significant force after the government passed reforms in 1982 that gave new rights to women and established secular laws opposed by many Islamic fundamentalists. In 1985 scattered Islamic extremist attacks took place on the government, and while the army largely suppressed such attacks during 1987 and 1988, they left a lasting legacy of opposition to the government.

In 1988 a combination of declining oil and gas revenues and economic mismanagement forced the government into austerity measures that led to massive riots and 500–700 dead. Benjedid responded by launching a political and economic reform program in 1989 and by moving towards a more democratic form of government. He announced a new constitution and attempted to reform the FLN. By this time, however, population growth and urbanization made any economic reform program extremely difficult, and secular institutions were discredited among much of Algeria's population. More than 65% of Algeria's growing population was now under twenty-five and had little reason to remember the FLN's struggle against France—and constant reason to remember its failure to govern in ways that benefited their day-to-day life.

Benjedid did try to purge both the party and the military forces, and he made further efforts to open up Algeria's economy to reform and capitalism. However, the gross incompetence and corruption of the FLN at every level from the community to the national leadership could not be easily reversed and helped make Islamic fundamentalism the most popular activist political force in Algeria. Further, the FLN splintered into at least four major factions, while the 35,000 full time party cadres paid by the government did little more than attempt to protect their jobs.

Liberalization also allowed Islamic parties to compete in elections for the first time. Several moderate parties emerged, but the key party rapidly turned out to be the Islamic Salvation Front (FIS). The FIS received national attention when it rushed relief to the victims of an October, 1989 earthquake while the government remained paralyzed by bureaucratic inertia. It also dominated the first free popular municipal elections of June 12, 1990, winning 853 of 1,589 municipal councils and taking control of every major city except one.[48]

The government initially treated this victory as something of an electoral fluke. Although 65% of the electorate voted, the parties were so divided that the FIS achieved its victory with only 15% of the vote. The leader of the FIS, Sheik Abassi Madani, also took a relatively moderate postelection position, although his deputy, Ali Belhadj, attacked democracy as a Judeo-Christian concept. The government took the FIS increasingly more seriously, however, as national elections approached and the economy continued to deteriorate. Inflation rose another 15% and the dinar lost 76% of its value relative to the dollar. As a result, the FLN instituted a welfare program worth several billion dollars to attempt to win popular support, and it carried out programs like raising child support payments by 300%.

In December, 1990 President Chadli Benjedid announced that early national elections would take place on June 27, 1991. He also announced that only 70 FLN representatives of the 296 seat national assembly would run for office in the new 430 seat assembly. Benjedid seems to have calculated that his election budget would offset the impact of what he still regarded as the FIS's "fluke" victory.

Benjedid's maneuvering led to increasing tension with the FIS, and Madani responded by calling for a general strike beginning on May 25, to protest changes in the electoral law and other government efforts to reduce the chances of the FIS. This strike failed initially because so much of the FIS's support was already unemployed, and Madani shifted to mass marches. These produced major riots and a considerable amount of violence. When the election campaign began on June 1, 1991, the FIS also began to bus supporters into the capital, resulting in some looting.

This led Benjedid to declare a four month state of siege on June 5, 1990, and to delay the national elections. The FIS responded with new calls for popular opposition, while the army began to play an active role in preventing demonstrations and political meetings and removing posters and Islamic slogans from public display. Meanwhile, Benjedid and his newly appointed prime minister, Sid Ahmed Ghozali, attempted to defuse the situation by compromising with the FIS and pushing for economic reform.

The rest of 1991 was spent in a struggle for popular support for elections rescheduled for two rounds of voting that were to begin on December 26, 1991. To the shock of the government, the FIS won 188 of the 232 seats open in the first round, which meant that it only needed 28 seats in the second round—scheduled to take place on January 16, 1992—to have a majority of the 430 seat assembly.[49]

On January 11, 1992, the army carried out a coup that suspended the results of the elections and deprived the Islamic Salvation Front of any chance of coming to power. Benjedid, who had sought to work out an agreement with the Islamic Salvation Front, resigned, and the army appointed a new government in which Mohammed Boudaif became president and Ghozali became prime minister. The seventy-two-year-old Boudaif had been living in exile for twenty-seven years after a death sentence for his prior political opposition, but he was brought back as the last living symbol of the FLN's struggle for independence. In fact, Defense Minister Khaled Nezzar and Chief of Staff Abdelmalek Guenaizia played a key role in shaping the new government, and it was clear that the army was set on confrontation rather than compromise with the FIS. Much of the new government's policy was shaped by a higher security council that included Ghozali, Nezzar, Interior Minister Larbi Belkhair, and others.[50]

By April, 1992, the government's effort to suppress the FIS had reached the point where 70–150 fundamentalists and 40 military and police officers had been killed in the various struggles over the coup. More than 30,000 FIS supporters had been detained at some point, 7,000–10,000 had been arrested under martial law, and five massive detention camps had been set up to hold them. The government had also decided to dissolve all of the 850 local assemblies led by the FIS.[51]

France and several other European governments responded by attempting to boost the secular regime with aid. France provided $550 million in aid to help Algeria import food, and a Western consortium provided $1.45 billion in credits to allow Algeria to roll over the most burdensome part of its massive $25 billion foreign debt—a debt burden equivalent to 90% of its annual revenues from gas and oil exports. This aid was partly a response to a fear that an Islamic government would create broad regional instability, but it was also a response to the existence of a large émigré population of Algerians in France.

The new Algerian government, however, became increasingly divided during 1992. Tensions between President Boudaif and Prime Minister Ghozali virtually paralyzed any economic initiatives and many of the government's other efforts to come to grips with the problems that had given the FIS a majority in the 1990 elections. The economy had degenerated to the point where Algeria was spending 70% of its oil and gas income on food imports, urban unemployment often reached 50%, the typical Algerian city dweller earned only $100 a month, and corruption in the military forces was receiving almost as much attention as corruption in the government. The former chief of staff, Gen. Mustpha Belloucif was in house arrest, pending trial for accusations that he had embezzled nearly $7 million during his period in office.

This situation exploded into new violence on June 29, 1992, when a gunman dressed in a riot squad trooper's uniform gunned down Boudaif. While fundamentalists were immediately accused of the crime and the army launched a new crackdown on the FIS, the exact responsibility for the assassination remained unclear. Rumors began to surface of disaffection among the lower ranks of the armed forces and security services, and the appointment of Ali Kafi—a senior veteran of the war of independence—as the new president did little to stabilize the situation or improve the economy. On July 8, Prime Minister Ghozali was forced to resign because of the continuing decline of the economy and political stability; he was replaced by Belaid Abdesalam. Abdesalam was clearly the choice of the armed forces, but his calls for a "war economy" did little to bring him immediate popular support.[52]

Algerian Arms Sales and Military Expenditures

Algeria's military forces are a privileged caste in terms of access to government resources, although Algeria has never spent as much of its GNP and central government expenditures on military forces as have some developing nations. Algeria's political leaders had cut real military spending in recent years, but only with the tactical support of the armed forces. No secular government can make major changes in Algerian military spending and arms imports without consulting the leaders of the armed forces.

As is the case with all Maghreb countries, estimates of military spending are uncertain. ACDA estimates that Algeria's military budget was $647 million in 1978, $846 million in 1979, $940 million in 1980, $1,383 million in 1981, $1,426 million in 1982, $1,137 million in 1983, $1,242 million in 1984, $1,040 million in 1985, $1,271 million in 1986, $1,264 million in 1987, $1,595 million in 1988, and $2,313 million in 1989.[53] The IISS and other sources estimate Algerian defense spending at $860 million in 1987, $1,050 million in 1988, $949.5 million in 1989, $904 million in 1990, and $857 million in 1991.[54]

These estimates seem sharply to understate Algerian expenditures on arms imports, but they still indicate that Algeria spent about 5% of its GNP and 10% of its central government expenditures on military forces during most of the 1980s. Most sources indicate that Algeria cut back on its military spending and arms imports after 1989, but Algeria's actual spending is very unclear. It seems unlikely that Algeria has imposed any real austerity on the armed forces, and actual military spending is likely to be substantially higher than Algerian government reporting indicates.

Algeria has long been a major arms importer, beginning to import arms from the Soviet bloc in 1963, shortly after it received independence. It has also imported arms from a number of other countries, although postindependence arms imports from the USSR alone may now exceed $10 billion. ACDA estimates that Algeria imported $800 million worth of arms in 1978, $550 million in 1979, $725 million in 1980, $1,400 million in 1981, $1,200 million in 1982, $675 million in 1983, $775 million in 1984, $480 million in 1985, $625 million in 1986, $700 million in 1987, $850 million in 1988, and $575 million in 1989.[55]

Although Algeria continued to rely on Soviet bloc suppliers during the 1980s, it imported an increasing amount of arms from the West. Algeria took delivery on $3,660 million worth of arms during 1979–1983. This included $3,200 million worth of arms from the USSR, no arms from the U.S., $30 million from France, $50 million from the UK, $300 million from West Germany, and $80 million from other countries.[56] It took delivery on $3,230 million worth of arms during 1984–1988. This included $2,500 million worth of arms from the USSR, $100 million from the U.S., $50 million from France, none from the PRC, $140 million from the UK, $125 million from West Germany, $40 million from Italy, $410 million from Czechoslovakia, $5 million from Poland, $5 million from Bulgaria, and $20 million from other countries.[57]

According to the ACDA's new methods of reporting, Algeria imported a total of $3,260 million worth of arms during 1985–1989, including $2,700 million from the former Soviet Union, $50 million from the U.S., $20 million from France, $40 million from the UK, $430 million from Warsaw Pact countries, and $20 million from other developing countries.[58]

Algerian arms imports have steadily improved its land and air strength in recent years. It took delivery on 200 more T-72s, 80 122mm 2S1 self-propelled guns, 25 152mm self-propelled guns, and 50 BM-14/16 multiple rocket launchers. These deliveries are correcting qualitative problems in its armor and artillery, and it already has 915 relatively modern Soviet BMP-1/2 armored fighting vehicles.

Algeria's military expenditures and arms imports have contributed significantly to its debt of over $26 billion, which is a little over half of its GDP. They have also contributed to its low income per capita of about $2,130, low

economic growth, and high unemployment, although the Algerian government has continuously mismanaged the economy since achieving independence.

Algerian Military Manpower

With the largest population of any state in the Maghreb, Algeria can draw
on very large manpower resources by regional standards. It has a total population of 26 million, with a growth rate of at least 2.5%. The population is
virtually 100% Arab and Berber, with less than 1% European. It is 99% Muslim, with less than 1% Jewish and Christian. The labor force is approximately
3,700,000.[59]

The CIA estimated in late 1991 that 294,000 males fit for military service
reach the age of 19 each year. It estimated that there were 6,142,000 males in
the age group from 15 to 49, and 3,780,000 were fit for military service. The
IISS estimated in mid-1991 that there were a total of about 1,580,000 males
and 1,492,000 females in the age group from 13 to 17 years, 1,366,700 men
and 1,291,500 women in the age group from 18 to 22 years, and about
2,087,000 men and 1,979,900 women in the age group from 23 to 32 years.[60]

Algerian military manning has risen by about 70% since 1980. Algeria had
a total active military strength of about 138,500 in early 1990, roughly 70,000
of whom were eighteen month conscripts. It is difficult to put this military
strength into perspective, because many conscripts serve only six months in
the army and then spend twelve months in civil works projects. Current
organized reserves are estimated to total about 150,000 men. These reserves
all serve in the army and have an obligation to serve until age fifty.

Even before the collapse of the Soviet Union, Algeria improved the training of its manpower to the point where officers no longer were trained in
massive numbers in the USSR. The army had an academy at Blida and the
air force at Taframouine. Algeria was, however, still heavily dependent on
Soviet, East German, Cuban, and French military advisors at the time the
Warsaw Pact began to collapse, and it still seems to have a substantial number of Russian advisors. Educational standards for officers are acceptable,
but training of other ranks is comparatively poor.[61]

The Algerian Army

The military wing of the FLN is called the National Popular Army (ANP).
The Algerian army is by far the largest element of the ANP and is currently
organized into six military regions. Like Morocco and Libya, Algeria has
gradually built up a network of roads and facilities in its border areas designed to allow its forces to deploy and fight against either Morocco or
Libya. Many of its units are not deployed in the border area, however, and
the Algerian army is scarcely on a wartime footing.

In 1992 the army had about 107,000 full time actives, about 70,000 of
whom were conscripts. Conscripts serve for 6 to 18 months and generally
receive inadequate basic training, unit training, and field training. Algeria
has a large reserve on paper, but it has little real structure and only limited

and highly selective call-up training. It would take weeks to retrain most reserves to serve basic military functions and months to create effective reserve units.

The army was organized into a total of three armored brigades, eight mechanized brigades, nine motorized infantry brigades, and one special forces brigade. The armored brigades have three tank, one mechanized, one engineering, and one logistic battalion, and one anti-tank and reconnaissance company each. The mechanized brigades have three mechanized, one tank, one artillery, one engineering reconnaissance, one anti-tank, and one logistic battalion each. The motorized infantry brigades have three infantry, one tank, one artillery, and one engineering brigade each. The army also has thirty-one independent infantry battalions, four paratroop battalions, seven artillery battalions, five air defense battalions, four engineer battalions, and twelve companies of desert troops.

In 1992 the Algerian army had roughly 960 tanks, excluding 113 T-34s in storage. It had 330 T-54/55s, 330 T-62s, and 300 T-72s. It had 880 120 BDRM-2 reconnaissance vehicles and 915 armored infantry fighting vehicles, including 690 BMP-1s and 225 BMP-2s. It had some 460 BTR-50 and BTR-60 armored personnel carriers. This was the most effective armored force in the Maghreb, with a high degree of standardization. Overall readiness was still limited, however, with significant maintenance problems, little large unit training, and poor to mediocre training in rapid maneuver, support and logistics, and offensive combat.

The army had 415 major towed artillery weapons, including 15 D-72, 100 M-1931/37, 40 M-30, and 190 D-30 122mm weapons, 10 M-46 130mm weapons, and 60 M-1937 152mm weapons. It also had 200 self-propelled artillery weapons, including 150 122mm 2S1s and 25 ISU-152 and 25 2S3 152mm weapons. Its multiple rocket launcher strength included forty-eight 122mm BM-21s, fifty 140mm BM-14 and BM-16s, and thirty BM-24 240mm weapons. It also had 330 120mm mortars. This artillery strength included far more self-propelled weapons than Algeria had in the mid-1980s, and the army had good capabilities for mass fire against static targets. It had little training in artillery maneuver, however, and poor capabilities for combined arms, counterbattery fire, switching fire, and beyond visual range targeting.

The Algerian army had 296 anti-tank guns, including fifty Su-100 100mm self-propelled weapons. Other anti-tank weapons included 40 AT-3 Sagger and Milan ATGMs, and 178 recoilless rifles. Some of the Saggers were mounted on BRDM-2s. About 156 of the towed anti-tank guns were obsolete 57mm weapons, and 80 more were obsolete 85mm D-44 with limited anti-armor capability against modern tanks. Few crews of any anti-tank weapon had realistic combat training in killing tanks or other armor.

The army had some 855 air defense guns, including 210 self-propelled, radar guided ZSU-23-4s. It also had large numbers of SA-7s, and twenty SA-8 and twenty SA-9 light surface-to-air missile launchers. While most of its air defense weapons had limited lethality and most crews limited training, Algeria had enough modern weapons and sheer weapons strength to provide a considerable curtain fire capability against low flying aircraft.

These weapons holdings show that Algeria is relatively well equipped for a 107,000 man army. However, much of Algeria's equipment is ten to twenty years old, and some is no longer fully operational. This includes many BTR combat vehicles and a few of Algeria's towed artillery weapons. Algeria needs more self-propelled artillery weapons, more modern short range air defenses, and third generation anti-tank guided missiles like the French-made Milans that it already has in inventory. It also needs modern artillery counterbattery radars and fire control equipment, plus improved command, control, and communications systems. It would have to be extensively reequipped for effective night combat and beyond visual range targeting.

The Algerian army has not had any real combat experience since its border clashes with Morocco in 1963, and it is heavily politicized. Training is often done strictly by the book, and combined arms, combined operations, and maneuver training are normally poor. Leadership is weak at every level, there is considerable corruption and favoritism in promotion and command assignments, and the army has serious organizational, training, logistic, and combat and service support problems. Technical training and maintenance standards are particularly weak, and the army has often bought new equipment far more quickly than it could effectively absorb it, then failed to follow up with effective training, maintenance, and logistic subsystems.

The army has added Syrian, Pakistani, and Palestinian advisors to supplement its Soviet advisors. It did reorganize into something approaching a modern brigade structure in the mid-1980s, added armored forces, and attempted to modernize its command structure. In some ways, however, it has never really converted its army from a popular or revolutionary force to one which is fully capable of modern armored and maneuver combat. Many units lack adequate manning and readiness, and large scale exercise training is poor. Algeria's lack of money and the high degree of politicization and bureaucratization of its forces may well make it impossible to change this situation during the next decade.

There is a paramilitary force of 23,000 men in the gendarmerie. This force is assigned to the Ministry of the Interior and has forty-four AML-60 and M-3 armored vehicles and twenty-eight Mi-2 helicopters. It is reasonably well trained, organized along military lines, and has played a major role in the government's efforts to assert control over the FIS. It is likely to play a key role in any further armed clashes between the government and Islamic fundamentalists.

The Algerian Air Force

Algeria's 12,000 man air force is the result of steady expansion since the clashes between Algeria and Morocco in the mid-1970s. It now has 241 combat aircraft and 58 armed helicopters. It is organized along Soviet lines, although Pakistan has provided advisors and pilots and Egypt provides air training. Its main missions are the defense of Algerian cities and the ability to conduct air defense and attack operations in the event of a conflict with Morocco or Libya. It reportedly is well based and has alternative basing capability near the Moroccan and Libyan borders.

The Algerian air force is organized into three fighter ground-attack squadrons with 1/30 MiG-17s, 1/17 MiG-23BN/MFs and ten Su-7s and 1/10-15 Su-24s. It has ten interceptor squadrons with 6/95 MiG-21 MF/bis, 2/40 MiG-23B/Es, and 1/14 MiG-25s. It has one reconnaissance squadron with three MiG-25Bs and seems to have two COIN squadrons with twenty-one CM-170s. There is a maritime reconnaissance squadron with two Super King Air B-200Ts, but it is unclear that both aircraft are operational. Algeria has a very large number of training units, and they have extensive combat strength, including twenty-five MiG-17s, three MiG-21Us, five MiG-23Us, and three MiG-25Us.

There are four attack helicopter squadrons with a total of forty Mi-24s, and one with thirty-five Mi-8s and Mi-17s. It has one heavy transport helicopter squadron with ten Mi-4s, Mi-6s, and Mi-8s, and one medium transport helicopter squadron with seven Mi-6s and Mi-8s. Algeria has extensive numbers of fixed wing transport and VIP aircraft. They include six AN-12s, ten C-130Hs, four C-130H-30s, three SE-210s, one Aero Commander 680, one Il-18, two Falcon 20s, three Gulfstream IIIs, two Super King Air 200s, four IL-76s, and three F-27s.

Its surface-to-air missile forces are organized into three surface-to-air missile regiments, one with a total of thirty to thirty-five SA-2 launchers, and two with a total of thirty to thirty-five SA-3 and fifty to sixty SA-6 launchers. It has three brigades of air defense artillery units with unguided 85mm, 100mm, and 130mm weapons. The Algerian air defense C^3I, air defense and warning system, and radar sensor net has been improved over the years, although it is scarcely a modern system.

This is a reasonable mix of medium performance aircraft and missiles. However, the air force has no real combat experience, and training is outdated and poorly organized for large scale attack or air defense operations. Reconnaissance, electronic warfare, and countermeasure capabilities range from poor to mediocre. The air force lacks modern air-to-air and air-to-ground weapons and has little operation look-down/shoot-down and modern aircraft radar capability. Maintenance standards are poor, and some aircraft are virtually in storage because of a lack of trained manpower and support capability.

The Algerian air force also suffers from massive problems in its air control and warning capability and limited and obsolete C^3I/BM capability. Its SA-2, SA-3, and SA-6 units and its air defense brigades have low readiness and operational capability and poor aircraft and munitions operability and technology. Algeria seems to have poor to mediocre electronic warfare and countermeasure capability and does not seem to have received the level of technical support and upgrading that the USSR provided to Libya.

Algeria also faces long term modernization problems. Algeria has no Soviet aircraft in operation with modern air defense or attack avionics. Many U.S. and French experts also seriously question the merit of past Algerian attempts to try to reconfigure some of these Soviet systems to use Western technology. They feel the life-cycle costs of reengining Soviet fighters and of trying to upgrade Soviet electronics and avionics would raise the life-cycle cost of such equipment above the cost of new equipment from the West.

The Algerian Navy

The 6,500 man Algerian navy is based at Mers el Kebir, Algiers, and Annaba. It has two submarines, three frigates, four corvettes, eleven missile fast attack craft, nine regular fast attack craft, one ocean going mine sweeper, one coastal patrol craft, two LSLs and one LCT, and eighteen small ships and support vessels. It has two corvettes and six regular fast attack craft in construction. The small 550 man coast guard has twenty-four small ships and two under construction.

The Algerian navy has two 2,500-ton Kilo-class submarines with six 533mm torpedo tubes and with pattern active/passive homing torpedoes and mines. These submarines have limited operational capability. Algeria had two Romeo-class submarines, but these left the fleet in 1989 and are now restricted to training. As a result, Algeria is seeking to acquire up to two more Kilos. The purpose of this submarine force is unclear. Algerian operating standards are as low as those of most Third World navies, it could not use them effectively against a modern Western navy, and it is unclear how Algeria would use them against Libya or Morocco.

Its major surface ships consist of three 1,900-ton ASW frigates (ex-Soviet Koni-class), armed with four 76mm and four 30mm guns, twin launcher SA-N-4 surface-to-air missiles, ASW rocket launchers, and depth charges. Three 850-ton missile corvettes (ex-Soviet Nanuchka-class) are armed with SS-N-2Cs (active radar or IR homing to 46 kilometers), twin launcher SA-N-4 surface-to-air missiles, and two 57mm guns. There is one 540-ton corvette with one 76mm gun. The navy also has nine obsolete Osa I and Osa II 210–245-ton missile patrol boats, armed with four SS-N-2s and four 30mm guns. It is unclear whether all these ships and their weapons systems are fully operational.

Its smaller craft include nine 200-ton Kebir-class patrol boats with 76mm guns, three of which are finishing construction and entering service. The one 590-ton mine sweeper has limited mission capability. There is one Soviet T-43 coastal mine vessel. The navy's amphibious strength is relatively large and gives Algeria a potential capability to conduct landings against Morocco or Libya. It includes two British-made 2,450-ton LSTs (240 troops, 10 tanks, 1 helicopter) and one 800-ton Polnocny B-class LSM (100 troops, 5 tanks).

The navy also operates two support ships, three survey ships, one tug, twelve fishery protection craft, SSC-3 coastal defense missiles, and two Beechcraft Super Knight 200T aircraft with weather radars. These aircraft are capable only of visual reconnaissance. The 550 man coast guard is under navy command and has seven inshore patrol craft, sixteen small patrol boats, and three PRC-made search and rescue craft.

The Algerian navy has a reasonable ship strength, but its ships are obsolete and poorly equipped in terms of their sensors and weaponry. Training and readiness are limited, and it is more a coastal patrol force than a navy.

The navy has poor overall readiness and equipment quality, and it has little prospect of improving unless it can obtain more modern vessels, weapons systems, and support.

Algerian Problems with Technology Transfer

While Algerian forces are reasonably effective by the standards of other powers in the Maghreb, the military buildup that Algeria has conducted since the early 1980s has only been partially successful. Many elements of Algeria's force structure cannot be properly manned with trained manpower, and overall training is only mediocre. Command and control capabilities are relatively limited and inflexible, and overall support and logistic capabilities are often poor—particularly when forces must move a substantial distance from their normal peacetime locations.

Algerian military planners seem to be increasingly aware that they have bought too much relatively low grade equipment and that they will have problems in trying to make that equipment effective. Much of Algeria's Soviet supplied equipment consists of stripped down export versions of this equipment with relatively low technical quality. These problems are compounded in the case of the air force, where Algeria has never provided the amount of skilled manpower necessary to operate so large a force. Algeria has experienced difficulties in operating its MiG-23s and Su-20s.

Algerian officials have made it clear since the mid-1980s that they were unsatisfied with the quality of support and technology transfer from the USSR and were actively seeking U.S. and West European military technology. There are some indications that Algerian officers have discussed the conversion and upgrading of Soviet equipment with both Syrian and Egyptian officers. There is no question that they have contacted many of the same British, French, and Italian firms regarding conversion equipment as has Syria.

Algeria tried to solve these problems by turning to the West. It bought three Brooke Marine 37 meter combat ships from Britain and thirteen C-130s and Hughes 269A helicopters from the U.S. Algeria also negotiated for Hawk light attack aircraft and trainers. It also negotiated for radars and combat aircraft from France and for a wide range of military electronics from Italy. Algeria has never made a major buy of Western weapons, however, and it is doubtful that it will use the West to solve its problems. Algeria has undergone a major economic crisis in recent years, forcing reorganization of the government in late 1988. Algeria must give added priority to civil spending in the near term and is far too heavily committed to a Soviet-supplied force structure and system of operations to allow easy conversion to Western weapons systems.

Algeria and Weapons of Mass Destruction

Algeria has at least conducted research into chemical and biological weapons and seems to have stepped up its chemical weapons research effort significantly since 1988. Reports of major surface-to-surface missile procurement efforts have not been confirmed, and it does not have such weapons now.

The most disturbing recent actions by Algeria are its creation of a secure nuclear research compound with a PRC-supplied reactor at Ain Ouserra about 150 kilometers south of Algiers. Up till now, Algeria has only had a 1 megawatt working reactor that it acquired from Argentina in April, 1989. The new reactor—which Algeria has named El Salam—was started in 1986 and is scheduled to be finished in 1992. The reactor is located in a defended military compound, with an SA-5 surface-to-air missile unit nearby and is rated at 15 megawatts, which compares with over 300 megawatts for an efficient power reactor.[62] A 15 megawatt reactor would take about three years of full time operation to produce enough material for one weapon and is too small to produce significant amounts of plutonium. This rating, however, is uncertain. A few experts feel that the oversized cooling towers indicate that the reactor can grow to capacities as large as 45–60 megawatts.

Some senior Western experts feel that Algeria is reacting to its tensions with Libya—and actions like Israel's 1985 raid on Tunis and the U.S. raids on Libya in 1981 and 1986—to develop nuclear weapons. Algeria, however, has denied any intention of building nuclear weapons and has allowed limited inspection of its nuclear facilities by the IAEA. There is no confirmation of reports that Iraq has provided any technical support or enriched material to Algeria.[63]

Strategic Interests and Arms Control

Algeria's 1984 treaty of union with Morocco defused some of the tension on Algeria's western border, but there is no question that Algeria built up its forces during the early and mid-1980s to be able to deal with both a Moroccan and Libyan threat. At the same time, Algerian nationalists strongly attacked the U.S. clashes with Libya in 1981 and 1986 and Israel's raid on Tunis in 1985. This has inspired Algeria to expand its navy and air defenses and its role as a regional power.

Even so, serious conflict between Algeria and Morocco has become increasingly less likely. Not only have Algerian-Moroccan relations been relatively friendly since the two nations began to negotiate a settlement to their differences over the Polisario in 1988, both nations are now actively seeking to expand their economic cooperation and joined together in the new Arab Maghreb Union in February, 1989. This union includes Mauritania, Libya, and Tunisia, as well as Algeria and Morocco, but it is the latter two states that seem most likely to develop serious economic cooperation.[64]

If Algeria ever did attack Morocco, it would experience more problems in invading Morocco than the ratio between the military forces of the two countries would imply. Both sides would suddenly find themselves facing wartime requirements they are not trained or properly equipped to meet. As in the Iran-Iraq conflict, they would have to improvise under pressure, and the results would be very unpredictable.

One side might win a catalytic victory over the other simply because of the collapse of a key unit or command element on the other side. What is more likely, however, is that Algeria would be unable to follow up even a major victory at the border because of inadequate preparation or support. Both nations might lock themselves into a war of attrition at virtually any level of conflict from sporadic clashes to prolonged infantry combat. The final outcome of the fighting might then depend more on the internal political stability of each regime and its ability to survive a limited or major defeat than on the other side's overall military performance. This would tend to make Morocco's monarchy more vulnerable than Algeria's nationalist government, but it seems unlikely that either government would readily take the risk of such a conflict.

More broadly, Algeria has not played an aggressive military role in the region but has been caught up in the struggle for regional influence. It remains a natural rival of Morocco and Libya. While Algeria has backed various revolutionary movements politically and economically, it has generally done so openly and with moderation. It has not made any attempts to expand its territory or sponsored any coup attempts or terrorist movements.

The great uncertainty affecting Algeria's strategic position is the outcome of the ongoing struggle between the FLN and Islamic movements like the FIS. If Islamic fundamentalism should win, it is unclear that Algeria would become more aggressive militarily. An Islamic government would face massive internal challenges and might well choose to concentrate on internal social issues and economic reform. At the same time, such an Islamic government might provide money and arms to other Islamic movements in Tunisia, Morocco, and Egypt. It is also impossible to dismiss the idea of some form of alliance of convenience between such a government and Qadhafi.

Algeria's current arms imports are not threatening to other states, but they do help destabilize Algeria's economy. Limits on land weapons imports would promote regional stability, but Algeria can legitimately point to a need to trade its aging combat aircraft for more modern types—a trade that would expand its offensive as well as defensive capabilities. The issue of weapons of mass destruction is far less uncertain. Like Libya, Algeria has no legitimate need for nuclear research capabilities, and existing arms control agreements fail to limit its nuclear, chemical, and biological weapons efforts and interest in long range strike aircraft and surface-to-surface missiles. Algeria is a case where selective controls on conventional arms transfers and tight controls on imports contributing to proliferation would significantly improve regional stability.

Libya

	Manpower (1,000s)	Tanks	Aircraft	Defense Spending ($ millions)	Arms Imports ($ millions)	Arms Exports ($ millions)
1967	20	54	17	55	8	–
1973	20	221	44	201	189	–
1982	55	2,000	555	3,738	3,200	290
1988	86	1,980	515	3,000	575	50
1991	85	2,300	409	2,510	–	–

Libya is a classic example of a destabilizing state.[65] It is governed by Col. Muammar Qadhafi, who overthrew the former monarchy in a bloodless coup in 1969.[66] Qadhafi is one of the most erratic military dictators in the world. He has challenged the West, Israel, and his neighbors at unpredictable intervals. He has tried to build up a major military machine, and Libya's arms imports have vastly exceeded its defensive needs and the forces it can properly man and support. It has contributed to terrorism throughout the world, provided endless regional clashes and tensions, invaded Chad, and has recently begun shipping tanks and other armor to Lebanon.

Libya's strategic importance consists largely of its oil resources and its strategic position along the Mediterranean and as a "bridge" to other nations in Africa. Libya had produced about 17.4 billion barrels of oil by the end of 1990 and had a moderate reserve:production ratio of 46:1.[67] As of January 1, 1992, it had estimated proved oil reserves of up to 22.8 billion barrels and gas reserves of 43,000 billion cubic feet. It had about 3% of the world's total oil reserves and produced at a rate of about 1.3 to 1.5 million barrels per day during 1990 and 1991.[68] Libya has the largest oil reserves in Africa, although its gas reserves are only about 25% of those of Algeria.

Libya is located south of Italy, divides the Maghreb, and has common border with the Mediterranean and sub-Saharan Africa. It has a total land area of 1,760,000 square kilometers, slightly larger than Alaska. It has 4,383 kilometers of land boundaries: 982 kilometers with Algeria, 1,055 kilometers with Chad, 1,150 kilometers with Egypt, 354 kilometers with Niger, 383 kilometers with the Sudan, and 459 kilometers with Tunisia.

Libya is involved in numerous territorial disputes. It claims the Gulf of Sidra to 30°, 30' north, which includes a large amount of international waters. It claims the Aozou strip in northern Chad. It has a maritime boundary dispute with Tunisia and claims about 19,000 square kilometers in Niger and about 19,400 square kilometers in southeastern Algeria.

Libya's Military Development and War with Chad

Libya has been one of the most aggressive states in the Maghreb, although most of this aggression has taken the form of threats, military clashes, and terrorism rather than significant military action. Libya's only real war has been its struggle with Chad for control of the Aozou Strip that divides the two countries and for political influence over Chad. The Aozou Strip is about 111,000 square kilometers and runs roughly 1,000 kilometers from east to west along the northern border of Chad. It is about 100 kilometers deep. It is reported to have uranium ore, although this is not confirmed.

The controversy over the Aozou Strip dates back to 1935, when France ceded the strip to Italy in a treaty intended to create a demarcated border in the Sahara between the French and Italian provinces. Italy never ratified this treaty and repudiated it in 1938, leaving the border undemarcated. Even before Qadhafi seized power, Libya provoked border incidents over the Aozou.

When Qadhafi seized power in 1969, however, he began actively to intervene in the Chadian civil war, which had begun in 1965, when Muslims in northern Chad broke with President François Tombolbaye and the black politicians ruling the country. Qadhafi backed the Muslim forces that were part of the Front de Libération Nationale de Tchad (FROLINT). He supported them in a coup attempt against Tombolbaye in August, 1971 and recognized FROLINT as the government of Chad in September. To defend himself, Tombolbaye reached an accommodation with Qadhafi and ceded the Aozou Strip to Libya in November, 1972. Libya occupied the strip in 1973 and formally annexed it in 1975.

The Chadian armed forces overthrew Tombolbaye in 1975 and set up a new government under Félix Malloum. The Malloum government protested Libyan occupation of the Aozou and demanded its return. Qadhafi then helped fund and arm a coup attempt against Malloum in April, 1976 and encouraged the FROLINT to resume its attacks on the government in the south. Malloum responded by persuading Hissein Habre, one of the leaders of FROLINT, to join him in a unified government. Another FROLINT leader, Goukouni Ouddei, who commanded the FROLINT forces in the north called the Conseil des Forces Armées du Nord (FAN), then started a new civil war.

France attempted to resolve this issue by dividing the country into spheres of influence at the fourteenth parallel and by staying out of the fighting. Ouddei proved a far more effective military leader than the Malloum-Habre combination, however, and seized the capital of Chad in March, 1979. The Organization for African Unity attempted to mediate the situation and helped set up a government with Ouddei as head of state and Habre as defense minister, but the new coalition government quickly proved unstable.

Libya took advantage of this continued instability to send 2,000 troops to attack Faya Largeau in the north. From November, 1979 to December, 1980, the fighting shifted back and forth between Ouddei and Habre, with Libya backing one side and France another. Ouddei increasingly turned to Libya for support, however, and initially seemed the victor. Libyan forces helped drive the Habre forces out of Chad and then pursued them into the Sudan.

Libya went too far, however, when it bombed Sudanese villages believed to be holding Habre's forces in September and October, 1981. The reaction from the OAU and the increasing cost of the war then led Qadhafi to pull back many of his forces to Libya. This allowed Habre's forces to regroup. They recaptured the capital, and Habre made himself president in June, 1982.

Qadhafi reorganized his forces and continued to support Ouddei. In June, 1983, forces favoring Ouddei attacked Faya Largeau. Libya backed them with air strikes in July and then sent in Libyan troops in August. France responded by sending in 1,500 troops to the south and started to help Habre fortify the fourteenth parallel. This seemed to persuade Qadhafi to reach a settlement, and in September, 1984, France and Libya agreed to remove their troops from the country. While France did withdraw, Libya quietly left many of its troops behind.

Qadhafi sent more troops into Chad in 1985, and France responded by supporting the Habre government in the south with air strikes, while the

U.S. provided a major covert aid program. This same year, the Aozou Strip issue was brought to the United Nations. A proposal was made for binding arbitration, but Libya rejected arbitration and any authority of the World Court.

A series of battles took place between the Ouddei and Habre factions in 1985 and through most of 1986, and the Ouddei forces gradually conquered all of the north. This seemed to position Qadhafi to control both the Aozou and northern Chad, but for reasons that are not fully clear, Ouddei suddenly turned on Qadhafi and began to attack his former Libyan ally in October, 1986. France immediately provided Ouddei with arms and advisors, which it airlifted in from the south. This allowed the Chadian forces to go on the offensive and to recapture the towns of Zouar and Fada in the north.

Beginning in January, 1987, the Habre forces in the south also began to attack the Libyan forces in Chad. France provided both the Habre and Ouddei forces with air support and continued to carry out a well organized effort to train and organize Chadian forces. These Chadian forces showed considerable aptitude for mobile desert warfare, and although they were lightly armed and used light Toyota trucks rather than armor, they proved far more mobile than the slow reacting Libyan troops and were often able to concentrate and attack without warning.

Chadian forces conducted a series of successful ambushes of Libyan troops in the desert, attacking a key Libyan position at Wadi Doum on March 23, 1987. This base consisted of a 3.2 kilometer long aluminum runway surrounded by troops, barbed wire, and mine fields, with a 4,000 man garrison. The Libyan forces under the command of Col. Khalifa Belkacem Mouftar allowed the Chadian forces to infiltrate their positions, however, and then failed to organize any effective defense as they were overrun. Libya lost twenty aircraft, one Mi-24, 200 tanks, numerous tank transporters, and several batteries of SA-6s—weapons worth several hundred million dollars.

Libya was forced to abandon its last military stronghold in Chad at Faya Largeau on March 27, 1987, and the 2,500 man garrison retreated to Libya. As a result, the Sudanese government refused to allow Libya to continue to operate from bases on its territory, and it forced the 2,000 men in the main Libyan camp to leave within the week following April 4, 1987.

Some 7,000-8,000 Chadian irregulars then attacked the 6,000–7,000 Libyan regulars deployed in well supplied and fortified positions in the Aozou Strip. Although France ceased providing air support when the Chadian forces crossed into the strip, the Libyan forces could not respond effectively. Chad retook the town of Aozou on August 8, 1987.

Six major battles took place by September, 1987—at Fada, Bir Kona, Wadi Doum, Aozou Village in the Aozou Strip, and the Maatan-al-Sarra air base. In five of these battles, well equipped Libyan armored and air forces were routed by lightly armored Chadian forces with little equipment heavier than four-wheel-drive trucks. Further, Chad invaded Libya at the southern end of the Aozou Strip on September 5, 1987, and launched a night attack on Libya's main air base at Maatan-al-Sarra, nearly 100 kilometers inside Libya. Some 1,700 Libyans died in this attack, and Libya lost twenty-two aircraft, seventy tanks, thirty APCs, twenty-two multiple rocket launchers, and a large number of tactical vehicles and supplies. As a result, Qadhafi had to withdraw Libyan forces from both Chad and the Aozou and sign a cease-fire on September 11, 1987.[69]

Libya lost 2,000 to 4,100 to less than 1,000 Chadians. It also lost 180 tanks and large numbers of armored cars, APC, artillery, rocket launchers, and SA-13 and SA-16 missiles. The attacking Chadian forces captured at least 1,300 Libyan prisoners and twenty-three Libyan aircraft and destroyed another twenty-eight aircraft. Even according to conservative estimates, Libya lost close to $1 billion worth of equipment in Chad in one year.[70] This led Qadhafi to offer to recognize Hissein Habre's government of Chad in May, 1988.

Although this Chadian victory seemed to end the war, the constant state of civil war in Chad—which has gone on since 1970—led to new fighting in 1990. Idriss Deby, one of the best young officers in the Chadian air force, rebelled against Habre, who led Chad during the fighting against Libya in the mid-1980s.[71] Deby's forces took over the capital at N'Djamena in December, 1990, and Habre was forced to flee to Cameroon. Deby returned some 600 Libyan prisoners of war, and his relations with Qadhafi became close enough to raise continuing concerns about Libya's future role in Chad and surrounding states.[72]

Libyan Clashes with U.S. Forces

Libya has been involved in five major clashes with U.S. forces—largely over Libyan claims to the Gulf of Sidra, Libya not abiding by the 12 nautical mile limit normally recognized in international law. The first clash occurred on March 21, 1973, when two Libyan Mirage fighters fired on a USAF C-130 reconnaissance aircraft patrolling a mission about 105 miles north of the Libyan coast. The C-130 turned away without damage.

The second clash occurred on August 19, 1981, when one of two Libyan Su-22s fired an AA-2 missile at carrier based U.S. navy F-14s that were demonstrating U.S. claims to freedom of navigation in the Gulf of Sidra. Both Su-22s were shot down. The third clash occurred on March, 22, 1986, when an SA-5 unit located at Surt fired three SA-5 missiles at U.S. aircraft involved in similar freedom-of-the-seas exercises. U.S. aircraft later destroyed the SA-5 radars using HARM missiles, as well as a Combattante-class patrol boat and a Nanuchka-class guided missile patrol boat.

The fourth and most serious incident occurred on April, 15, 1986. U.S. F-111s based in the United Kingdom and U.S. carrier based aircraft launched air raids in retaliation for an attack by Libyan terrorists on the La Belle discotheque in West Germany on April 5, 1986. The U.S. aircraft bombed the command center at the Al Azizyah barracks and airfields in Benina and Tripoli. A number of Libyan IL-76 and MiG-23 aircraft were destroyed, and one F-111 crashed at sea. The most recent incident occurred on January 4, 1989, when two U.S. Navy F-14s operating off the northeastern coast of Libya detected Libyan MiG-23s tracking them with their radars. Both MiG-23s were shot down by the F-14s using Sparrow and Sidewinder missiles.[73]

These U.S. raids and victories in air-to-air combat led Qadhafi to a policy of partial conciliation with the West, but they also led to new acts of terrorism. On December 21, 1988, Libya planted explosives on an Air Malta flight connecting with Pan Am Flight 103 from Frankfurt, Germany, to the U.S. The plane blew up over Lockerbie, Scotland, killing 280 persons. Libya also planted a bomb on a French UTA airliner, Flight 772, in 1989—perhaps in retaliation for France's support of Chad. The airliner blew up over the Sahara and killed another 170 people.

While Iran and Syria initially came under suspicion for the Pan Am 103 bombing, work by British, French, and German investigators eventually disclosed that it was far more likely that two senior Libyan intelligence officials, Ali Basset al-Megrahi and Lamen Khalifa Fhimah, had been responsible. The chain of evidence showed they had conducted the operation, stealing the Air Malta tags, that the bomb used detonators and microchips identical to ones Libya had used in Senegal in 1988, and that the Semtex explosive was identical to explosive Libya had purchased in bulk from Czechoslovakia. Similar evidence established that four other Libyan officials had been responsible for the bombing of the French airliner.

When Libya refused to extradite the intelligence officials involved, the UN first voted on January 21, 1992, for Libya to, "provide a full and effective response" to U.S. and British demands and threatened Libya with sanctions. While Qadhafi attempted to delay punishment by appealing to the World Court, using various delaying tactics, and launching a new effort to appear a moderate, the UN then voted in March, 1992 to go ahead and apply sanctions.[74] These sanctions included a prohibition on any flights from Libya landing in foreign countries except humanitarian flights, a ban on aircraft parts shipments, a prohibition on all arms sales and sales of paramilitary equipment, and significant reductions in the number of Libyan diplomats serving in any foreign country.[75]

Even before the UN voted for sanctions, Qadhafi put his troops on alert and attempted to mobilize the Libyan people to repel an invasion. When the sanctions went into effect in April, he gouged out huge trenches along the coast to try to repel any landing, set up machine gun nests around key government buildings, and put sand bagged positions for anti-aircraft (AA) guns on the roofs of various buildings. This seemed to be more a matter of political posturing than any real fear of invasion, but it was clear that Qadhafi was unwilling to make concessions and that his "moderation" was largely a matter of temporary convenience.

No evidence of any invasion surfaced in the months that followed, but Qadhafi countered with his usual shifts in tactics. In June he allowed the Libyan press to appear to attack him for defending the Arabs when the Arab states only betrayed Libya. This provided an excuse for both Libyan political attacks on the Arab states that supported the UN embargo and for an offer to the UN to turn over to a neutral court the intelligence officers the West was attempting to extradite. Qadhafi adopted a posture of seeming moderation, but he simultaneously carried on with his attempts to expand Libyan influence in Chad and improve his relations with Islamic fundamentalists in the Sudan.[76]

Other Clashes and Quarrels

Qadhafi has also provoked several quarrels with Tunisia. In 1980 Libya backed an attempt by anti-Bourguiba Tunisians to seize the border village of Gafsa in an effort to create a general uprising. Libya sent armed infiltration teams into Tunisia in 1981–1982 and sabotaged a Tunisian pipeline near the border in 1984. When anti-Qadhafi forces attacked barracks in Tripoli on May 4, 1984, Qadhafi blamed President Bourguiba for allowing the forces to organize and train on Libyan soil. Libyan troops entered Tunisia and seized three border guards that evening; a series of small border incidents followed.

In 1985 Libya and Tunisia broke relations after Libya sent letter bombs to a large number of Tunisian journalists. Qadhafi expelled all Tunisian workers from Libya and put sufficient pressure on Tunisia so that Algeria intervened to warn Qadhafi to moderate his position. Ironically, Qadhafi restored relations with Tunisia in December, 1987, after paying compensation to the Tunisian workers he had expelled. This was part of a broad effort to end his isolation and to appear more moderate after the U.S. raids on Libya in 1986. Qadhafi also promised to dismantle his garrisons along the Tunisian border but never did so.[77]

Libyan relations with Egypt have often been equally tense. Libya provided political support and money to groups who opposed Sadat's peace initiatives in 1977, and Egypt responded by providing aid to anti-Qadhafi Libyans. At the same time both countries deployed small forces near their undemarcated border. In April Egyptian and Libyan demonstrators attacked the other state's embassies, and border clashes started in July. On July 16, 1977, Libyan forces attacked Egypt's border positions. Egypt responded on July 21 by sending armor into Libya and using aircraft to attack Libyan air bases and villages in the border area. Egypt temporarily occupied part of the Libyan border and successfully bombed Libyan airfields at Gamal Abdel Nasser and Kufrah. Fighting continued until July 25, when a cease-fire encouraged by Yasser Arafat took place. Small clashes continued until both sides disengaged troops from the border on September 10, 1977. Roughly fifty troops died on each side during the fighting.[78]

Qadhafi broke relations with Egypt following Anwar Sadat's visit to Jerusalem. He violently opposed the Camp David accords and effectively broke diplomatic relations in 1979. He praised the assassins of Sadat in 1981 and called for a general revolt. In 1984 he covertly mined the Red Sea approaches to the Suez Canal and expelled Egyptian workers. In 1985 he sponsored terrorists acts in Egypt, possibly including the hijacking of an Egypt Air aircraft in Athens. While Qadhafi moderated his conduct in 1987, he has not stopped supporting Islamic extremists and other groups opposing President Hosni Mubarak in Egypt. As was the case with Tunisia, he also failed to make good on a promise to dismantle his garrisons along the Egyptian border.

Other Qadhafi adventures include the support of factions in Uganda, the Sudan, Polisario, Ethiopia, Chad, and numerous other countries. Qadhafi has also continued to play politics with his military. In 1989, as part of the celebration of the twentieth anniversary of the coup that brought him to power, Qadhafi renamed the armed forces the "armed people." He also replaced his general command staff with a general defense committee—which included the chief of each service, the inspector general, and the heads of operations and training, intelligence, and reconnaissance—and changed the title of the chief of staff to secretary of the general defense committee.[79] More significantly Qadhafi continues to change command assignments to reduce the risk of a coup and to provide overlapping surveillance of the military using different branches of the intelligence and security services.[80]

Libyan Military Spending and Arms Transfers

The development of modern Libyan military forces began shortly after Qadhafi overthrew the monarchy in 1969. Libya has since spent far more on its military buildup than any other Maghreb state. ACDA estimates that Libya's military budget was $3,144 million in 1978, $3,342 million in 1979, $3,092 million in 1980, $3,400 million in 1981, $3,576 million in 1982, $4,255 million in 1983, $5,047 million in 1984, $2,774 million in 1987, $2,900 million in 1988, and $3,309 million in 1989.[81] These expenditure levels would put military spending at about 15–18% of the GNP, and at 32–40% of central government expenditures. The IISS estimates military spending at $1,390 million in 1987, $1,420 million in 1988, and $1,510 billion in 1989, but these figures seem to exclude procurement and arms imports.[82]

Libya has long been a major arms importer. It imported $2,300 million worth of arms in 1978, $2,900 million in 1979, $2,600 million in 1980, $3,200 million in 1981, $3,200 million in 1982, $2,200 million in 1983, $2,100 million in 1984, $1,600 million in 1985, $1,200 million in 1986, $625 million in 1987, $600 million in 1988, and $575 million in 1989.[83]

Libya's primary sources of arms have been the Soviet bloc, but it has bought advanced arms from Western Europe when it could get them. Libya took delivery on $12,095 million worth of arms during 1979–1983. This included $5,800 million worth of arms from the USSR, $850 billion from France, $40 million from the UK, $380 million from West Germany, $700 million from Italy, $575 million from Czechoslovakia, $310 million from the PRC, $310 million from Romania, $230 million from Poland, and $2,900 million from other countries.[84]

Libya imported some $6.3 billion worth of arms during 1984–1988, of which $3.6 billion—or nearly 50%—came from the USSR. Over $1 billion more came from Eastern Europe, principally from Czechoslovakia. Imports from nations outside NATO and the former Soviet bloc added $1.1 billion more. Libya ranked as the fifth largest arms importer during 1983–1986, with arms imports of $7.1 billion.[85]

In 1992, by the ACDA's revised reporting methods, Libya imported a total of $5,080 million worth of arms during 1985–1989, with $3,200 million—or well over 50%— coming from the Soviet Union, $1,200 million from other Warsaw Pact countries, $10 million from West Germany, $550 million from other European countries, $30 million from the PRC, $70 million from other East Asian states, and $20 million from Latin America.[86]

These dollar figures, however, do not provide any real picture of the incredible amount of weapons Libya acquired during this period. Libya's major weapons imports include:[87]

- 2,200 T-54, T-55, T-62, T-64, T-72 tanks (USSR: 1970–1984)
- 1,000 BMP-1 AFVs (USSR: 1972–1985)
- 280 BDRM-2 AFVs (USSR)
- 380 EE-9 Cascaval APCs (Brazil)
- 850 BTR-50P, BTR-60P APCs (USSR: 1978–1987)
- 90 OT-62, OT-64 APCs (Czechoslovakia: 1978–1980)
- 100 EE-11 Urutu APCs (Brazil)
- 40 M-113 APCs (Italy: 1972–1973)
- 660 M-46 130mm, D-30 and D-74 122mm towed artillery weapons (USSR: 1980–1987)
- 190 2S1 122mm, 2S3 152mm self-propelled artillery weapons (USSR: 1980–1988)
- 160 Palmaria self-propelled howitzers (Italy: 1982–1985)
- 30 Dana 152mm self-propelled artillery weapons (Czechoslovakia: 1983–1984)
- 20 M-109 self-propelled artillery weapons (U.S.)
- 650 Type 63, BM-21, BM-11 multiple rocket launchers (USSR and PRC)
- 3,000 Vigilant, Milan, AT-3, AT-4 anti-tank missile launchers (UK, France, USSR)
- 144 mobile SA-2, SA-3, SA-5, SA-6, SA-8 surface-to-air missile launchers
- 14 SA-13 surface-to-air missile launchers on BDRM-2 vehicles (USSR: 1979–1985)
- 24 Crotale surface-to-air missile launchers (France: 1974–1980)
- 600 Zu-23, ZSU-23-4, etc. anti-aircraft guns (USSR)
- 120 Scud-BL, FROG-7 surface-to-surface missile launchers (USSR: 1976–1982)
- 24 Blinder-A Tu-22 bombers (USSR: 1979)
- 249 MiG-23, MiG-23BN, MiG-25, Su-22 Fitter J fighters (USSR: 1976–1982)
- 131 Mirage F-1A, Mirage F-1C, Mirage IIIE, Mirage 5 fighters (France: 1971–1990)
- 50 MiG-21 fighters (USSR)
- 15 Su-24 Fencer strike attack aircraft (USSR: 1989)
- 1 IL-76 Candid air refueling transport (USSR: 1989)
- 14 King Air, C-130H, Jetstar-2, L-100-30 transports (U.S.: 1975–1986)
- 50 Mi-8, Mi-14 helicopters (USSR: 1976–1983.)
- 6 Foxtrot submarines (USSR: 1976–1983)
- 1 Vosper Mk-7 frigate (UK: 1973)
- 2 Soviet Koni-class missile frigates (USSR)
- 27 Osa-2, Polnocny, Natya, Nanuchka combat ships, boats, and craft (USSR: 1976–1985)
- 9 Combattante II missile craft (France: 1982–1984)
- 12 SA-321 naval helicopters (France)

Libya has cut back on its military spending and imports of conventional weapons since 1988 because of a drop in oil prices and the resulting loss of oil revenues. Recent Libyan arms imports have also been restricted by its failure to pay all its debts. This may help explain why Libya received only $2.62 billion worth of arms during 1987–1990, versus $7,120 billion worth of arms during 1983–1986. Nevertheless, Libya has recently made major improvements to its air defenses and some aspects of its naval capabilities. It also was still one of the top ten arms importers in terms of new agreements during 1983–1986, with $5.03 billion worth of agreements, although it did not rank among the top ten in 1987–1990.[88]

Libyan Military Manpower

Much of Libya's military spending and efforts to acquire foreign arms have been wasted because Libya has never fielded the manpower necessary to make it effective. Libya's total population is 4,350,000, with a growth rate of 3.0%. It is about 97% Berber and Arab, with some Greeks, Maltese, Italians, Egyptians, Pakistanis, Turks, Indians, and Tunisians. It is about 97% Sunni Muslim. The labor force, however, is only about 1,000,000, and some 280,000 of this force—including many of its most skilled workers, are foreign.[89]

The CIA estimated in late 1991 that only about 52,000 males fit for military service reach the age of 17 each year. It estimates that there are 1,023,000 males in the age group from 15 to 49, and that 604,000 are fit for military service.[90] The IISS estimated in late 1991 that there were a total of about 271,400 men and 262,000 women in the age group from 13 to 17 years, 225,200 men and 214,1,00 women in the age group from 18 to 22 years, and 170,400 men and 319,000 women in the age group from 23 to 32 years.[91] This is still a fairly substantial manpower pool, but military service is unpopular and skilled manpower scarce.

Libya's forces have expanded from 6,500 men at the time Qadhafi came to power to 85,000 men in 1992. Even 85,000 men, however, represent far too low a force to operate Libya's massive arms imports. Further, Libya has only reached this total by conscripting low grade manpower and by employing some 3,000 to 5,000 foreign advisors and technicians. The Libyan conscription law passed in 1976 allowed Libya to make some increases in its military manpower, but conscription remains unpopular, and many of its newly formed units remain ineffective. The Libyan military training program is only adequate through basic training, although infantry and some artillery training seem adequate. Many of Libya's military displays require extraordinary rehearsal or actual operation of equipment by foreign advisors. Libya's total current organized reserves consist only of a 40,000 man people's militia.[92]

Qadhafi has compounded Libya's manpower problems by arbitrary recruitment and manpower management policies, creating a range of different militias and popular forces that compete with the regular military for manpower. There have been constant turbulence and instability in military career patterns and little attempt to create effective reserves. Qadhafi has not granted his officers or commanders the kind of recognition or security of tenure necessary to make him popular and has instead relied on constant shifts in command positions to keep the military from being able to plot against him.

This has led to problems within the Libyan military. Although experts differ sharply on the credibility of such reports, Qadhafi seems to have encountered active resistance from within the Libyan military in 1980, 1981, 1984, 1985, and 1987. The importance of opposition groups like the Libyan National Salvation Front have almost certainly exaggerated such reports, but Qadhafi's treatment of his military personnel, erratic shifts in command, and occasional efforts to replace the military with popular forces have created very real disaffection.

The Libyan Army

According to Israeli sources, the Libyan army is organized into four military districts: western, central, eastern, and southern. The western district covers the border with Tunisia, part of the border with Algeria, and the northwest coast. It has a tank unit and some mechanized elements; naval bases at Zuwarah, Tripoli, Al Khums, and Misratah; and airfields at Ouqba Ibn Nafa, Umm Aitiqah, and Misratah. The southern district covers the rest of the border with Algeria, the border with Niger, and the western half of the border with Chad. It has a mechanized division equivalent, and air bases at Brach, Sabha, Al Wigh, and Aozou City.

The central military district covers the central part of the coast and most of the eastern half of the country, along with much of the border with Egypt and about 60% of the border with Chad. It has another tank division, and airfields at Al Girdabiyah, Kufrah, and Maatan-al-Sarra. About 2,000 men and two tank and two mechanized brigades are deployed in the Aozou Strip. The eastern military district covers the northeast coast and the critical northern border area with Egypt and has about half of the Libyan army. It has naval bases at Benghazi, Derna, and Tobruk, and air bases at Benina, Al Bumbah, and Gamal Abdel Nasser.

Recent trends in Libyan forces are shown in Table 4.4. The Libyan army has a total active strength of only 55,000 men, but some reports indicate it is organized into two to three tank divisions, two to four mechanized infantry divisions, two independent tank brigades, two independent mechanized brigades, three independent tank battalions, eight mechanized infantry battalions, a republican guard brigade, twelve to thirteen paracommando battalions, seven surface-to-surface missile brigades, three surface-to-air missile brigades, forty-one artillery battalions, and two AA gun battalions.[93] Other reports indicate that it is organized into twenty-eight separate brigades, with eleven armored brigades, eleven mechanized brigades, five infantry brigades, and one national guard brigade. According to this report, it also has forty-eight tank battalions, forty-eight mechanized infantry battalions, nineteen paratroop and commando battalions, fifty-three artillery battalions, fourteen air defense artillery battalions, and seven surface-to-surface missile brigades.[94] It is clear that Qadhafi has at least one full brigade as a special presidential guard and may well have one division.

Regardless of which report is correct, such forces would require at least 150,000 to 200,000 men to be fully effective. Libya only has about 25–33% of the manpower needed to man its paper strength of combat units. Its divisions have only about 5,000 to 7,500 men, and its brigades are about the size of reinforced regiments. Even its best combat units are understrength and have severe training and leadership problems. These manpower strength problems are compounded by tight political control, promotion based on political favoritism, and training which is often limited to erratic small unit training. Qadhafi also rotates officers to prevent coup attempts and restricts many forms of training because he regards it as a threat to his security.

While the Libyan army does seem to have some 40,000 men in its people's militia, this force is more a symbol of Qadhafi's ever changing ideology than a serious force. The Libyan army seems to lack anything approaching an effective and well trained reserve system.

In 1992 the Libyan army had some 2,300 Soviet tanks, including 310 T-72s, 350 T-62s, and 1,600 T-54s and T-55s. Some 1,200 of these tanks, however, were in storage, and many of the rest had significant maintenance problems. There were 650 armored reconnaissance vehicles, including 280 BDRMs and 380 EE-9 Cascavals. There were 1,000 BMP-1 and BMP-2 armored infantry fighting vehicles and about 850 APCs, including 750 BTR-50s and BTR-60s, 90 OT-62s and OT-64s, 40 M-113s, and 100 EE-11 Urutus. Many of Libya's other armored vehicles were in storage or had serious maintenance problems. More generally, only a few battalion sized elements of Libyan armor were effective in offensive and maneuver operations.

Libya's artillery strength included some 730 major towed artillery weapons, 400 self-propelled artillery weapons, and 650 multiple rocket launchers. The towed weapons included 60 105mm M-101s, 270 D-30 and 60 D-74 130mm weapons, 330 130mm M-46 weapons, and 40 152mm weapons. The self-propelled artillery included 130 2S1 122mm weapons, 160 Palmaria and 18 M-109 155mm weapons, and 100 2S3/M-1943 152mm weapons. Libya's multiple rocket launchers included Type 63 107mm weapons and 500–700 BM-11, BM-21, and RM-70 122mm weapons. Libya also had large numbers of 82mm and 120mm mortars, some M-43 160mm mortars, and some 240mm mortars.

This artillery strength was impressive, but much of it was in storage or not operational, and Libya had poor standardization in terms of weapon and ammunition types. It also lacked the training, organization, and sensors and C^3 equipment to conduct combined arms operations, maneuver effectively, switch fires rapidly, target beyond visual range, and conduct efficient counterbattery operations. Libya also had some 40 FROG-7 and 80 Scud B surface-to-surface missile fire units.

Libya's anti-tank weapons include roughly 3,000 ATGM launchers, with Vigilants, Milans, AT-3 Saggers (some mounted on BDRMs), and AT-4 Spigots. The Vigilants are obsolete. The other anti-tank guided missiles are effective, and Libya does not normally provide effective live fire training under realistic conditions. The army also had at least 220 M-40A1 106mm recoilless rifles and large numbers of anti-tank rocket launchers.

Anything approaching an accurate count of Libya's light air defense weapons is unavailable. Some estimates indicate the army had about 600 air defense guns, including large numbers of radar guided ZSU-23-4s, ZU-23s, M-53 and M-59 30mm weapons, L/70 40mm weapons, and ninety-two S-60 57mm weapons. Libya also has large numbers of SA-7, SA-9, SA-13, and Crotale light surface-to-air missiles. Many of these weapons are also stored or have limited operational readiness. The overall air defense training of Libyan army forces is poor. The army has O1-E liaison aircraft and thirty-one transport and liaison helicopters. These include eighteen CH-47s, five AB-206s, and eleven SA-316s.

Libya also has a number of paramilitary forces that largely perform land force roles. They act as a means of controlling the power of the regular military and providing Qadhafi with security. There is a 3,000 man revolutionary guard corps (Liwa Haris al-Jamahirya) to guard Qadhafi with T-54/55/62 tanks, armored cars, APCs, multiple rocket launchers, and ZSU-23-4s and SA-8s, which are taken from the army inventory. There are 2,500 men in the Islamic Pan African Legion, which may have one armored, one infantry, and one paracommando brigade—although its total manpower strength could man only less than one brigade slice.[95] The Islamic Pan African Legion has at least 75 T-54s and T-55s and some EE-9 MICVs. Roughly 700–1,000 men from the legion were believed to be in the Sudan in 1988, but current deployments are unknown. There is also a people's cavalry force which acts largely as a parade unit, and a people's militia with a nominal strength of about 40,000 men.

In broad terms, both Libya's army and its paramilitary forces have only limited military effectiveness. While a few regular army brigades and some small unit elements may have moderate effectiveness, Libya can do comparatively little to make use of its massive inventory of land weapons. Training and readiness are very poor. Libya's erratic equipment purchases make logistics, support, and maintenance a military nightmare, and some purchases seem to be made with no regard to whether the equipment will have any military utility or can be absorbed into Libya's force structure. Nearly half the army's equipment is in storage or has limited operational availability, and overall leadership and organization are poor. Even Libya's better units would have difficulty fighting anything other than static defensive battles.

The combat support, service support, and logistic units and system are capable of little more than peacetime garrison operations and occasional set-piece exercises. They would break down quickly in the event of war. The army seems to have no real training using support and logistic capabilities at even the major combat unit level.

The Libyan Navy

Libya's 8,000 man navy and coast guard has some impressive ships but little real-world military capability for anything more than surprise or hit-

and-run missions. Maintenance and manpower readiness are poor. It has little ability to operate outside of coastal waters, and at-sea training and patrol activity are far below the level needed for high military proficiency. It cannot count on significant air support in an encounter with a Western navy and has negligible offensive capability to do anything more than launch a few missiles.

Some differences exist between Jane's and the IISS over where the navy is based. Jane's reports naval bases at Al Khums and Tobruk, a submarine base at Ras Hilal, a naval air station at Al Girdabiyah, a naval infantry battalion at Sidi Bilal, and working ports at Tripoli, Derna, and Benghazi. The IISS reports main naval bases at Tarabulus, Benghazi, Tobruk, Sidi Bilal, and Al Khums.

In 1992 the Libyan navy's main combat forces consisted of six fleet submarines with six small submarines, three frigates, seven missile corvettes, eight ocean mine sweepers, twenty-four missile fast attack craft, and fourteen large patrol craft. Libya also had five landing ships, two LCTs, one support ship, one MRC, seven tugs, one diving ship, one training ship, one salvage ship, and two floating docks.

Libya had six 1,950-ton ex-Soviet Foxtrot submarines delivered between 1976 and 1983. These were export versions of the submarine from a reactivated production line, and one returned to Leningrad for a refit in 1989. They are armed with ten 533mm torpedo tubes and have Soviet Type 53 active/passive homing torpedoes. The crews were trained in the Soviet Union, and almost all major maintenance has been done by Soviet technicians. The operational status of several of these submarines was doubtful, and Libya was seeking to overhaul and modernize them, although they evidently could operate in training missions. Libya also had six 1.4-ton Yugoslav R-2 Malal-class miniature submarines, transferred between 1977 and 1982. These are small free flood submarines for covert missions.

Libya had three missile frigates. One was an aging 1,780-ton ex-British Vosper Mark 7 frigate delivered in 1973. It was armed with four Otomat II Teso missiles (180 kilometer range), one 4.5" gun, two twin 35mm guns, and two 20mm guns. It has six 324mm torpedo tubes. The frigate was modernized in Italy during 1979–1983 but required major engine repairs in 1984–1985 and was out of service in 1989–1990. Its current readiness is uncertain. The other two frigates were 1,900-ton ex-Soviet Koni-class vessels delivered in 1986 and 1987. Each was armed with four SS-N-2C missiles (95 kilometer range), four 76mm guns, four twin 30mm guns, SA-N-4 Gecko surface-to-air missile launchers, and four 406mm torpedo tubes. They could fire Soviet Type 40 active/passive anti-submarine torpedoes. These two frigates lack some of the sensors and electronics on Soviet ships but are relatively modern. Libyan capability to fully operate such ships is uncertain.

Libya also had seven corvettes: Four were 670-ton Italian Assad-class vessels, armed with four Otomat IIs (80–160 kilometers), one 76mm gun, two twin 35mm guns, and six 324mm torpedo tubes using Whitehead Motofides A-244 homing ASW torpedoes. The others were three 850-ton Soviet Nanuchka II–class vessels with four SS-N-2C missiles (95 kilometer range),

SA-N-4 Gecko surface-to-air missile launchers, and two twin 57mm guns.

The twenty-four missile patrol craft included nine 311 ton Combattante IIG-class missile patrol boats with four Otomat Mark I/II launchers (60–80 kilometers) and twelve 76mm guns each, delivered in 1982–1983; twelve 245-ton Osa-II class boats with four SS-N-2C/D launchers (95 kilometers), and two twin 30mm guns, delivered during 1976–1980; and three 114-ton Susa-class patrol boats with eight wire-guided SS-12M missile launchers (5.5 kilometers), delivered during 1977 and refitted during 1983–1984. While some of these ships had limited operational capability, most could fire their missiles effectively.

The large patrol craft include four 159-ton Garian-class vessels with one Bofors 40mm gun, delivered in 1970, refitted in 1984. Libya also had three 100-ton Thorneycroft large patrol boats with one 20mm gun, one 100-ton Soviet Poluchat-class large patrol craft, six Yugoslav 90 ton large patrol craft with one 40mm gun, and fourteen inshore patrol craft. All were used for coast guard duties

The Libyan navy had eight 790-ton Soviet Natya-class ocean going mine sweepers and five amphibious ships, including two 2,800-ton PS-700 class landing ship-tanks (240 troops, 6 tanks, and 1 helicopter each), and three 1,150-ton ex-Soviet Polnocny D–class medium landing ships (180 troops and 6 tanks each). Libya also had four major support ships and sixteen small LCTs. It had seven coastal tugs. The navy had two squadrons of thirty-one armed helicopters, including twenty-five Mi-14 Haze ASW helicopters and twelve SA-321 Super Frelon ASW and SAR helicopters. The air force provided support in the naval reconnaissance and surface support roles.

The navy had several shore batteries, including some with Otomat and SSC-3 and SS-N-2D missiles (95 kilometers). Libya also has some kind of coastal radar and surveillance system and may be using part of its popular militia in a coast watch mission.[96]

The navy's overall training levels evidently improved between 1987 and 1990 but seem to have declined between 1991 and 1992—possibly because of less effective support. Libya remains heavily dependent on Soviet and other foreign technicians. Some individual ship crews have moderate capability but overall training, readiness, and command standards are low, and Libya cannot operate as an effective fleet. Maintenance seems to be as badly organized as most aspects of Libyan military activity, and Libya generally relies on foreign support in maintenance and training activity.

The Libyan Air Force

In 1992 Libya's 22,000 man air force and air defense command had approximately 410 combat aircraft and 45 armed helicopters. These aircraft included some of the most advanced aircraft types of any air force in the Maghreb, but the Libyan air force is still relatively ineffective. After nearly twenty years of effort, there are still severe shortages of competent pilots; training levels and quality are poor. Maintenance is mediocre, and an overcentralized and politicized command structure limits air defense proficiency and makes it difficult effectively to allocate attack aircraft and sorties.

Up to half of Libya's aircraft were in storage in 1992, and it relied heavily on Syrian pilots and Soviet, North Korean, and Pakistani "instructors" who flew actual missions.

The Libyan air force had one bomber squadron with six Tu-22 Blinders. The USSR transferred twelve long range Tu-22 bombers in April, 1979, and five to six are still operational.[97] These aircraft are obsolete medium altitude bombers that are very vulnerable to both air-to-air and surface-to-air missile defenses.

The Soviet transfer of six to ten Su-24Ds to Libya in 1989 has given it a more serious long range strike fighter which is one of the most advanced aircraft in Soviet inventory. The Su-24 is a twin seat swing wing aircraft that in terms of weight is roughly equivalent to the F-111, although it has nearly twice the thrust loading and about one-third more wing loading. It is deployed in five variants. Although it is not clear what variant has gone to Libya, it seems likely to be the Su-24D, which includes a sophisticated radar warning receiver, an improved electronic warfare suite, an improved terrain avoidance radar, satellite communications, and an aerial refueling probe and which can deliver electro-optical, laser, and radar guided bombs and missiles.[98]

Unlike many strike/attack aircraft the USSR delivered to the Third World, the Su-24 can carry the latest Soviet munitions. These include up to three AS-7 Kerry radio command guided missile (5 kilometer range), one AS-9 Kyle anti-radiation missile with passive radar guidance and an active radar fuse (90 kilometer range), three AS-10 Karen passive laser guided missiles with an active laser fuse (10 kilometer range), three AS-11 Kilter anti-radiation missiles with passive radar guidance and an active radar fuse (50 kilometer range), three AS-12 Kegler anti-radiation missiles with passive radar guidance and an active radar fuse (35 kilometer range), three AS-13 Kingposts, and three AS-14 Kedge semi-active laser guided missile with an active laser fuse (12 kilometer range). It also can carry demolition bombs, retarded bombs, cluster bombs, fuel air bombs, and chemical bombs. The Soviet KhAB-500 R-10 chemical bomb has been deployed on the aircraft in the Soviet air force.[99]

The Su-24 can carry payloads of nearly 25,000 pounds and operate on missions with a 1,300 kilometer radius when carrying 6,600 pounds of fuel. With a more typical 8,818 pound (4,000 kilogram) combat load, it has a mission radius of about 790 kilometers in the LO-LO-LO profiles, and 1,600 kilometers in the LO-HI-LO profile. With extended range fuel tanks and airborne refueling, the Su-24 can reach Italy, Egypt, Chad, and even Israel—although the latter mission would be demanding, would have to be flown out of an eastern base like Benghazi, and would allow only limited time over the target.[100]

Libya also acquired a long range refueling capability to ease many of the problems it would face in conducting such strikes. While Libya did not get the modified IL-76 to refuel its Su-24s it originally sought from the USSR, or additional deliveries of Su-24s, it got the technology it needed to convert one of its C-130s into a tanker for airborne refueling from West German firms.[101]

Libya has experimentally refueled one of its Mirage F-1s and is seeking a modifiable cargo jet so that it will be able to refuel at higher speeds and without the maneuver problems inherent in trying to refuel a jet fighter from a propeller aircraft.

Libya had seven additional fighter ground attack squadrons in 1992, with a total of 22 Mirage 5D/DD/DEs, 18 Mirage F-1ADs, 20 MiG-23BNs, 8 MiG-23Us, and 45 Su-20/22s. There was also a COIN squadron with 30 J-1 Jastrebs. Libyan aircraft performed poorly in close air support and interdiction missions in Chad, however, and there are no reports that Libya has since developed effective training systems and facilities or that the Libyan air force has practiced in meaningful exercises in low altitude combat, air defense evasion, countermeasure penetration, and combined arms with the Libyan army. Libya does, however, have a limited air refueling capability, which it acquired from West Germany, and modern Soviet air-to-surface and anti-radiation missiles.[102]

The Libyan air force had 9 fighter squadrons equipped with a total of 18 Mirage F-1ED/BDs, 50 MiG-21s, 112 MiG-23 Flogger Es, 55 MiG-25s, and 3 MiG-25Us. These air defense fighters were relatively advanced aircraft—with advanced air-to-air missiles like the AA-6 Acrid, AA-7 Apex, AA-8 Aphid, R-530, and R-550 Magic—but only the Mirage F-1s and some MiG-25s had long range intercept, or look-down/shoot-down capabilities approaching those of modern Western fighters.

Libya had a reconnaissance squadron with six Mirage-5DRs and seven MiG-25Rs and could use its bombers in visual long range surveillance missions. If the MiG-25R is similar to Soviet versions, it has infrared, side looking radar and electronic support measures (ESM) capabilities. Libya also has some remotely piloted vehicles. This gives Libyan aircraft a relatively advanced mix of attack avionics and reconnaissance capabilities, but it seems doubtful that it is organized to use them effectively. It may well rely on the slow daylight photography system of most Third World nations.[103]

Although Soviet and other foreign pilots have evidently improved Libyan air-to-air tactics since 1986, they remain far inferior to those of U.S. pilots or well trained Middle Eastern pilots like those of Egypt and Saudi Arabia. Libya still seems to have a serious shortage of even mediocre combat pilots and is dependent on Soviet and other foreign officers and technicians for effective ground controlled intercepts. It still does not seem to be able to conduct effective electronic warfare.

The overall readiness of Libyan aircraft is poor, and the air force seems to be dependent on foreign technicians for training, maintenance, and sometimes even combat missions. The operational readiness of most aircraft is limited, and most bases can evidently only support given types of aircraft. Overhaul and combat repair capability is probably very limited, and combat sustainability is likely to be poor. Libya does, however, have ten to fourteen modern bases and seems to have good stocks of munitions, including modern Soviet guided missiles, laser guided bombs, napalm, and anti-radiation missiles.

There were two attack helicopter squadrons with thirty-five Mi-24s and ten Mi-35s. Some of these helicopter forces seem to be relatively well trained and are equipped with AT-2 Swatter air-to-ground missiles.

Other air units include two transport squadrons and seven more helicopter squadrons, plus four training squadrons. The two transport squadrons have eleven An-26s, seven CH-130s, two L-100-20s, two L-100-30s, twenty G-222s, sixteen IL-76s, and fifteen L-410s. There is a heavy transport squadron with eighteen CH-47s, a medium transport squadron with seven Mi-8s and fifty Mi-4s, and a light unit with ten Mi-2s and four SA-316s. The transport forces seem to be the most effective element of the Libyan air force.

In 1992 Libya's air defense forces included four SA-5 brigades, each with two battalions of six launchers (forty-eight total), four air defense gun batteries, and a radar company. According to some reports, these SA-5 units were manned by some 2,000 Russian personnel. There were three other regional surface-to-air missile commands, each with two brigades with eighteen to thirty-six SA-2 launchers each (160–180 launchers total); two to three brigades with twelve SA-3 launchers each (100 to 110 launchers total); and three brigades which each had twenty to twenty-four SA-6s (130–150 launchers) and some SA-8s.[104] These missile units were loosely integrated by Libya's Senezh air defense and command system. Both the SAM units and command system of the air defense command were heavily dependent on expatriate support personnel, who sometimes seem to act as operators. Overall capability is low except for those forces with direct foreign "supervision."[105]

All of Libya's major surface-to-air missile forces are in an air defense command that was merged and reorganized in the late 1980s after the U.S. air strikes on Libya. This command is still effectively a separate force, however, and has been since it was formed in 1973—the year of the October War. It seems to be somewhat more effective than the air force. It is now well deployed with overlapping coverage by a range of different missiles along the coastal areas. The network of radars has been improved and modernized, as have electronic warfare and command and control assets.

If British reports are correct, it is commanded by the same kind of central command center and regional sector operations centers that the Soviet Union has used in Algeria, Syria, Iraq, and many other countries. The system has, however, been upgraded more than that of Algeria, and possibly more than that of Syria. Soviet high capacity communications systems have been installed, and extensive use is made of buried land lines to reduce the electronic and physical vulnerability of the system. The air defense command also seems to have been upgraded with relatively modern early warning radars and electronic warfare equipment.

Operator training and proficiency, however, is low. The system is overcentralized. Overall alert rates are poor to mediocre, and Libyan operators have not fully adapted to the use of Soviet automated systems. It is also unlikely that Libya's electronic warfare assets give it much protection against the level of jamming and countermeasure technology the U.S. deployed in operation Desert Storm.

The World's Largest Military Parking Lot

The result of Libya's military buildup has often been to transform Libya into the world's largest and noisiest military parking lot, and its military capabilities are unlikely to evolve much beyond the parking lot stage in the immediate future.

This parking lot syndrome has also led to problems between Qadhafi and his military. The Libyan military originally seems to have supported the move into Chad, but this situation changed in the early 1980s.[106] Qadhafi's posturing over Chad, ill chosen command decisions, and public claims that the armed forces were not even in Chad cost him considerable military support. Libya's defeat by Chadian government forces using Toyota trucks and rocket launchers in 1987 then made both Qadhafi and the Libyan military an international joke and worsened Qadhafi's relations with his military. Col. Khalifa Belkacem Mouftar, who once commanded the Libyan forces in Chad, came to oppose what he called the "terrorist, barbaric, and arbitrary regime" of Tripoli.

It is unclear, however, that there is any widespread or effective military opposition to Qadhafi today. The popular forces seem relatively loyal to Qadhafi, and Qadhafi stated in mid-1988 that the regular military and police were being converted into a "people's army" to be supervised by popular defense committees in geographic areas throughout the country. This rhetoric seems to have resulted in a new layer of political supervision over the police and the armed forces. At the same time, Qadhafi courted popular support by promising to cut most conscript service to from two to one years and to compensate such conscripts for their loss of earnings.[107]

Libya's neighbors also cannot count on the parking lot syndrome and ignore the sheer mass of Libya's arms buildup or its slow development of combat capability. Libya now seems to have nearly 2,000 men in the Aouzou Strip and a force of two armored and two mechanized battalions. This force is equipped with T-55 tanks, BMP-1s, artillery and multiple rocket launchers, air defense weapons, and Mi-24 attack helicopters.

Libya can provide costly and prolonged confrontations and clashes in the border area with its other neighbors, and while it has little hope of successfully invading Egypt or Algeria, it can create costly and politically troublesome conflicts. Algeria's oil and gas facilities might also be vulnerable to Libyan infiltration or air attack. Egypt and Algeria would also be confronted with the option of having to conduct an all-out invasion to suppress Libyan forces, an option neither is likely to initiate casually.

Libya would have more capability against Tunisia. Tunisia lacks the firepower, armor, and military training to deal with a major Libyan invasion and would probably be forced to seek U.S. or Algerian aid. This could be a serious problem in any succession crisis after Bourguiba's death, though the Tunisian army already has deployment plans to provide internal and external security in this event. Libya would, however, have to occupy Tunis to achieve any firm political control, and this might give Tunisia, Algeria, or the U.S. time to react.

Libya could also deploy large numbers of mechanized infantry by sub-Saharan standards and can play a massive spoiler role by delivering military equipment to other radical states. This could be particularly dangerous in any Libyan alliance with a radicalized Sudan—which would directly threaten Egypt and the Red Sea—although such an alliance now seems unlikely.

Intelligence and Terrorist Activities

Libya has some moderately effective intelligence and security services, although they are organized largely for internal security purposes rather than overseas or terrorist operations. Its large military intelligence service is virtually a parallel command structure throughout the Libyan armed forces, acting to ensure that no coup attempt takes place against Qadhafi. There are special deterrent battalions within the armed forces commanded by officers with kinship or other ties to Qadhafi and deployed throughout the armed forces in positions where they can prevent coups. There are also a large number of revolutionary committees that were established in 1978 to act both as the equivalent of party ideologue seeking to ensure Qadhafi's policies are carried out and as a security service that permeates Libyan society. The committees are backed by revolutionary tribunals that enforce Qadhafi's policies.

The conversion of Libya's embassies overseas to Libyan people's bureaus in 1979 involved a large expansion of Libya's intelligence and security activities overseas. In 1980 an office of external security was created to put the surveillance of foreigners and Libyans with foreign contacts under professional intelligence surveillance. These intelligence groups play an active and sometimes violent role in suppressing anti-Qadhafi groups like the National Front for the Salvation of Libya.

Qadhafi has achieved considerable success in using these intelligence and internal security forces in combination with political pressure on his neighbors. For example, the National Front for the Salvation of Libya had some effectiveness when it had bases in the Arab world and could broadcast from countries near Libya. Its only military operation, however, took place in 1984, when the front launched a small raid on Libya's military barracks at Azizyah, which Qadhafi sometimes used as a residence; the front's forces suffered a serious defeat, fifteen members being killed or executed. The shifting political currents in the Arab world, overt pressure from Qadhafi, and Libyan intelligence operations forced the front to move its headquarters from Morocco to the Sudan and finally out of the Arab world. Similarly, it moved its radio station from the Sudan to Egypt and then had to close it down.

The front was able to recruit several hundred Libyan prisoners of war taken during the fighting in Chad during the late 1980s, and the Habre government allowed it to train them as a military force. The collapse of the Habre government and Libyan pressure and intelligence operations led Chad to expel the front's force in 1990, however, and its 350 men were flown to the U.S. and allowed to settle in twenty-five different states. The front's leader, an ex-Libyan officer and diplomat named Ibrahim Sahad, is now forced to operate out of his home in Arlington, Virginia.[108]

Terrorism is, however, a very real problem. If Libya seems incapable of subverting any of its neighbors' armed forces or creating any kind of revolutionary warfare, it is all too capable of arming and supporting indigenous movements, acts of violence against civilian populations, and assassinations. Libya makes extensive use of various liberation and terrorist movements and front groups like the Association for the Propagation of Islam operating in black Africa. It uses its commercial ties, oil company ties, and Libyan airlines as fronts for both intelligence and the purchase of weapons and military technology. It has long backed extremist Irish Republican Army (IRA) and Palestinian elements like Abu Nidal and used its funds, arms, and training camps both to sponsor such movements and lever them into supporting Libyan policy and overseas adventures. Libya routinely manipulates extremist movements by giving them support or expelling them from Libya, and it alters the profile of its ties to such groups according to its need for ties with moderate states. It has continuously operated at least five major training camps since the late 1970s and has recently established ties to other camps in the Sudan. While it sometimes closes major camps, it inevitably opens others.[109]

Libya and Weapons of Mass Destruction

Libya has played a role in proliferation, although many of Qadhafi's efforts have had more publicity than success. Libya has made sporadic attempts to fund a nuclear weapon or "Islamic bomb" ever since the mid-1970s. Most of these efforts have done little more than enrich a few foreign advisors, suppliers, and outright con men. In spite of more than fifteen years of effort, Libya does not seem to have any serious nuclear weapons program.[110]

There are reports that Libya provided the financing for a substantial part of Pakistan's nuclear weapons effort in return for help in acquiring nuclear weapons material or weapons. These reports appear to be exaggerated, but Libya did sign some form of nuclear accord with Pakistan in 1973 and seems to have sought help in obtaining hot cell technology and training in order to acquire a capability to extract plutonium from uranium that was irradiated in a reactor. Libya also may have supplied Pakistan with substantial quantities of processed uranium ore, or yellow cake, between 1976 and 1980, some of which seems to have come from Niger. Further, while Libya reached a formal safeguard arrangement with the IAEA in 1980, it may not have declared all of its stocks to the IAEA. Even so, there are no convincing reports that Pakistan has given Libya serious assistance in its nuclear weapons effort.[111]

Libyan nuclear cooperation with the USSR is better documented, although it seems to have been no more productive. Libya and the USSR signed an agreement in 1975 that called for the USSR to build a small research reactor in Libya and help set up some form of research center. This agreement resulted in the USSR's building a small reactor near Tripoli at Tajoura, which began operating in 1981 or 1982.[112] Two years later, the USSR agreed to build two 440 megawatt reactors. The USSR has never, however, provided any follow-up to the agreement. The same is true of a French agreement in 1976 to build a 660 megawatt reactor: Construction has never started.[113]

Libya does seem to have begun to develop its own uranium deposits and sought to acquire the capability to produce uranium tetrafluoride. As of 1992, however, most private experts and U.S. government experts alike felt Libya was almost as far away from a nuclear weapons capability as it was in the early 1970s. Further, Libya allowed the IAEA to conduct a limited inspection of its nuclear research center at Tajoura. While Qadhafi is scarcely the most reliable witness on his own intentions, he has also declared that he was not interested in nuclear weapons, and there were no indications confirming reports that he had hired Russian scientists to work on a nuclear weapons effort as of 1992.[114]

In contrast, Libyan efforts to obtain chemical weapons have had some significant successes. The exact point at which Libya first began to acquire chemical weapons is unclear. While evidence on the source is unclear—it could have been Egypt, the USSR, a third nation, or limited laboratory scale production—Libya seems to have had a small stock of mustard gas and possibly nerve gas by the late 1970s.[115]

Libya intensified its efforts to acquire chemical weapons in 1983–1984, as a reaction to Iraq's use of chemical weapons in the Iran-Iraq War and Israel's invasion of Lebanon. It is possible that it obtained East German and Cuban assistance in such efforts, and there are reports that it used an Iraqi citizen, Ihsan Barboutti, to purchase equipment and technology for the production of chemical weapons in early 1984.[116]

Libya established a chemical and biological research center in the Sabha area during 1984–1985 and conducted field tests of gas weapons in the Libyan desert. During this period Qadhafi seems to have taken a decision to purchase a pilot plant for mustard and nerve gas production and to buy a much larger full scale production plant during mid-1985. Some sources indicate that this pilot plant is located near Tripoli and began production in late 1987, and one report indicates that it is operated by North Koreans with some support by Iranian technicians.[117]

Some U.S. government experts believe that Libya made limited—if ineffective—use of poison gas in Chad on several different occasions during 1986–1987. While some sources indicate that Libya used Sarin nerve gas, most experts seem to believe that it used mustard gas. On at least one occasion, this gas seems to have been blown back over Libyan troops.[118]

Libya then began construction of a massive chemical warfare complex that included weapons assembly and loading plants as well as plants to produce chemical weapons. This plant, located at Rabta (40 miles south of Tripoli) was called Pharma 150. This effort moved forward on a crash basis; with the aid of a wide range of European, Japanese, and other suppliers, Libya created a chemical warfare complex at Rabta which now has around thirty buildings, including a technical center for basic research, equipped with a large entrance, reinforced steel floor, and mobile cranes, and a production building stocked with advanced machine tools. The assembly line bears no relation to pharmaceutical facilities in other countries. There are sheltered underground storage facilities near the main production centers at Rabta, and the plant is defended by surface-to-air missiles and Libyan troops. Its research staff and personnel operate under tight security controls, and all of its activities are classified. The dimensions of the support roads and certain nearby facilities seem to be linked with Libya's efforts to acquire surface-to-surface missiles.[119]

While protests from the outside world have forced Libya to alter Rabta to look more like a civilian pharmaceutical plant, U.S. experts feel it still has the potential to become the largest integrated single chemical weapons plant in the Third World and the largest chemical warfare plant outside the Commonwealth of Independent States (CIS). Some experts believe it can eventually produce up to 40–45 metric tons a day of mustard gas, tabun, and sarin. The plant is also designed to manufacture chemical warheads and munitions, as well as chemical agents, and seems capable of producing binary weapons. There are also some indications that it will produce napalm.[120] Libya acquired extensive amounts of key feed stocks like thiodiglycol and the equipment and technology to produce poison gas from firms like Imhausen-Chemie in Germany, and it seemed capable of large scale production of mustard gas without additional foreign supply. It has equally large stocks of the precursor chemicals to produce nerve gases like sarin.[121]

Libya has had start-up problems since the initial production testing of Rabta in the summer of 1988 to late 1989 and experienced further problems in operating its plant in early 1990. Then, in March, 1990 the plant was swept by a devastating fire of unknown origin. This left Libya with small stocks of chemical weapons but without any way to produce the massive numbers it once planned upon.[122] Its main source of poison gas still seems to be the 9,000 pounds a day of poison gas that it is producing at its prototype facility. It seems to have produced a maximum of 30–50 tons of mustard gas by March, 1990, and U.S. experts testified in 1992 that it has produced only about 100 tons to date.[123]

Since 1990 Libya has carried out major new construction efforts that may be associated with its efforts to acquire missiles and aircraft that can use weapons of mass destruction. These projects include a major underground command site and a new site near the ancient ruins at Sabha, some 460 miles south of Tripoli. Once again reports differ sharply as to exactly what is happening, and Libya has denied such construction is under way.[124] Some reports indicate that Libya has a second chemical weapons plant under construction in underground or sheltered facilities near Libya's Otrag missile plant whose primary purpose is the production of nerve gas, and that air defenses are being set up in the area.[125] Other sources indicate these reports are exaggerated or untrue or that the plant at Sabha actually produces napalm.[126]

Finally, Libya has at least some interest in biological warfare. During the late 1980s, Libya funded some research into biological weapons and may acquire the capacity to produce limited amounts of such agents using the batch mode at some point during the next few years.[127] It is doubtful that Libya will make rapid progress in the mass production of such agents or the production of effective warheads and bombs, but Libyan chemical weapons production may eventually be joined by the production of biological weapons. Batch production of weapons using forms of anthrax and botulism should be within Libya's technical capabilities by the mid-1990s.[128]

Libya's delivery system capabilities are less advanced, but Libya does have enough operational aircraft and pilots to deliver chemical or other weapons of mass destruction against other African states using its Tu-22s or Su-24s. Libya's missile capabilities are more limited. The USSR transferred 25 Scud B missiles to Libya by 1976. It now has at least 40 FROG launchers and 80 Scud missile launchers. Its total holdings of FROG rockets and Scud missiles are unknown. Libya has, however, obtained enough Scud missiles to sell or transfer some to Iran during the Iran-Iraq War.[129]

Libya has sought longer range missiles for at least the last decade, and Libya has sponsored missile development projects with a number of Warsaw Pact, European, and Third World states. Recent ACDA reporting indicates that it may have the SS-21 and that a long range missile project with German support may be reaching the advanced development stage.

While sources differ, it seems likely that a West German firm called Otrag began satellite launcher testing in the Libyan desert in the late 1970s and early 1980s. When the German government forced Otrag to leave Libya because of fears that it might be involved in ballistic missile development efforts, elements of the original Otrag group stayed behind until the mid-1980s. These reports indicate that the German team was working at a desert camp about 60 miles from Sabha on a missile with a 500–700 kilometer range and that there may have been a test in 1987.[130]

Another West German company called Technical Oil Productions may then have been set up to work on a missile project. This missile may have been called the Al-Fatih. Various sources report the missile had a range of at least 300 miles (490 kilometers), a range approximately 110 miles further than the range of the Scud B, and might have had a range of up to 640 miles (1,000 kilometers). Globesat, another West German firm, was later fined by the Munich prosecutor for shipping rocket valves to Libya.[131]

Other reports cover a number of other potential suppliers. Some sources indicate that Libya is interested in the Chinese M-9 missile with a range of 600 kilometers, or the CSS-2.[132] There are reports of Libyan cooperation with Brazil in developing long range missiles, and in the Brazilian MB/EE, Sonda V, and SS-300 missile programs. The MB/EE seems to be the most likely of the latter two candidates and has a range of up to 620 miles (1,000 kilometers).

Still other reports indicate that Libya has obtained French missile technology and is trying to develop a short range missile. These missiles are said to include the Ittisallat, with a range of 50 miles, and the Al-Fatih, which these reports give a range of over 200 miles. British reporters indicate that Libya

TABLE 4.4 Libya's Uncertain Military Potential

Land Forces

1976		1980		1986		1992	
4	Combat units	4	Bde[a] headquarters	3	Division headquarters	3–5	Division commands
9	Infantry/mechanized infantry bns[b]	16	Infantry/mechanized infantry bns	12	Bde headquarters	18	Bde commands
		11	Tank bns	54	Infantry/mechanized infantry bns	1	Tank division
						2	Mech divisions
				38	Tank bns	38	Tank bns
				1	National guard bde	54	Mech. infantry bns
				14	Paracommando bns	12	Special forces bns
				41	Any bns	191	National guard bde
				2	AA bns	24	Field artillery bns
				6	SSM bdes	8	Reconnaissance bns
				3	SAM bdes	3	Surface-to-air missile bdes
						2	ATGW regiments
						7	SSM bdes
1,028	Tanks	2,750	Tanks	2,360	Tanks	2,150	Tanks
						(950)	"active")
1,267	APCs	2,300	APCs	2,150	APCs	2,130	APCs
						(1,200)	"active")
110	Artillery pieces	450	Artillery pieces	1,368	Artillery pieces	1,740	Artillery pieces
						(1,000)	"active")
		450	Tank transporters	450	Tank transporters	1,000	Tank transporters
						1,900	ATGW
		54	Surface-to-surface rocket/missile launchers	54	Surface-to-surface rocket/missile launchers	252	Surface-to-surface rocket/missile launchers

Navy Forces

1976		1980		1986		1992	
2	Frigates	2	Frigates	2	Frigates	3	Frigates
7	Missile boats			7	Corvettes	7	Corvettes
		19	Missile boats	24	Missile boats	24	Missile boats
		3	Submarines	6	Submarines	6	Submarines
				8	Patrol craft	14	Patrol craft
		5	Landing craft	5	Landing craft	5	Landing craft
				20	Small landing craft	2	? Small landing craft
		2	Mine sweepers	7	Mine sweepers	8	Mine sweepers

3 Support ships	3 Support ships	1 ? Support ships	4 Support ships
			2 Electronic warfare
			1,000 Zodiac boats
132 Combat aircraft	379 Combat aircraft	*Air Force*	
16 Helicopters	63 Helicopters	489 Combat aircraft	409 Combat aircraft
		138 Helicopters	134 Helicopters
		93 Transport aircraft	74 Transport aircraft
			125 Transport aircraft
			13 Reconnaissance A/C
			50 Pilotless reconnaissance A/C
20 SA-2/SA-3 bns	32 SA-2/SA-3 bns	*Air Defense Forces*	
8 SA-6 bns		45 SA-2/SA-3 bns	26 SA-2 bns
9 Crotale btys[c]	24 SA-6 bns	6 SA-5 bns	33 SA-3 bns
	9 Crotale btys	32 SA-6 bns	6 SA-5 bns
	3 SA-9 bns	? Crotale btys	26 SA-6 bns
	5 Chelika bns	? SA-9 bns	3 SA-8 bns
	3 SA-8 bns	? Chelika bns	5 SA-9 bns
		3 SA-8 bns	6 SA-13 bns
			7 Crotale btys
			1,060 SA-7 launchers
			18 Chelika bns
			29 AA arty bns
			84 Radar and alarm sites
		Electronic Warfare	
			4 Radio reconnaissance bns
			2 Surface-to-surface wireless jamming bns
			2 Electronic warfare ships
			2 Electronic reconnaissance aircraft
			2 Electronic reconnaissance helicopters

Sources: Adapted from data provided by the JCSS, IISS, and regional governments. Data are not adjusted to the updated 1992 strength estimates provided in the text in order to keep the trends consistent by source.

has a missile range or facility at Al-Qarait and in Tauwlwa and possible missile production facilities. These reports indicate a substantial Libyan effort is under way, but no details are available and there are no reports that Libya has tested a missile with ranges or performance better than that of the Scud.[133]

Strategic Interests and Arms Control

While it is easy to exaggerate Qadhafi's willingness to take risks, there is no question that Libya has one of the most unstable leaders in the Third World. Libya has stimulated a regional arms race throughout the Maghreb and has wasted billions and billions of dollars of its own resources while forcing other poorer nations to do the same. There is also no practical prospect that Libya will change as long as Qadhafi is in power. He reacts only to sustained threats and containment.

Libyan arms imports and military adventures have had an important impact on arms purchases in Morocco, Chad, and Egypt. Libya was a key source of financing for the Polisario in its battles with Morocco. Chad's arms imports were shaped by its conflict with Libya. Egypt claimed that its expenditures were heavily affected by the Libyan threat, although they were also driven by the need to keep technological parity with an accelerating Arab-Israeli arms race and by growing instability in the Sudan and Red Sea area.

Libya has been a threat in other ways. Its selective arms transfers to various governments and factions in the region have helped sustain a number of conflicts and civil wars, including those in the Sudan, Chad, and Lebanon. Libya was also one of the few Arab states to allow the Soviet Union to deploy its military reconnaissance aircraft. The USSR regularly deployed IL-38 naval reconnaissance aircraft to Libya from 1981 onwards, and Soviet surface vessels began regular port calls in the early 1980s.

There also is no question that Libya is acting as a powerful catalyst to push other Middle Eastern states towards proliferation. Libya has created a significant pressure on Egypt and Algeria to at least match Libya's efforts at proliferation, and it poses a major problem for the West. Libya also presents a very real threat that terrorist and covert groups will be given chemical and/or biological agents and that Qadhafi might introduce chemical weapons into third party conflicts or launch limited strikes to aid another nation in some conflict where he believed this would be to his advantage. This presents at least some risk that Libya could act as a catalyst that would lead to major escalation in an Arab-Israeli conflict where even the most limited Libyan strikes against Israel could create major pressures to escalate on the part of Israel, Syria, and possibly Iraq.

In short, Libya is a classic case for a targeted embargo on both arms and all technologies relating to arms and the means to manufacture and deliver weapons of mass destruction. Its history is solely one of acting as a threat rather than as a nation that is threatened. It is already overarmed by at least 50% and has no pressing needs in terms of new weapons and technologies. A sustained cut-off of arms and technology would also inevitably benefit the people of Libya by freeing resources for economic development.

Tunisia

	Manpower (1,000s)	Tanks	Aircraft	Defense Spending ($ millions)	Arms Imports ($ millions)	Arms Exports ($ millions)
1967	25	–	7		1	–
1973	20	–	12		4	–
1982	32	14	8	270	60	–
1988	40	68	43	255	20	–
1991	35	84	53	477	–	–

Tunisia is a small pro-Western state with a territory of only 163,610 square kilometers.[134] It shares a 965 kilometer boundary with Algeria and a 459 kilometer boundary with Libya. It has a 1,148 kilometer coastline on the Mediterranean and is 144 kilometers from Italy, across the Straits of Sicily. Tunisia's position between two strong and heavily militarized neighbors makes it naturally vulnerable, although historically it has only had problems with Libya. These threats have led it to maintain close military relations with the West ever since it won independence from France.

Tunisia is not a wealthy oil state by Middle East standards, but it does have about 1.7 billion barrels worth of petroleum reserves and 3 trillion cubic feet of gas.[135] Its only other major economic activities are agriculture, phosphates, tourism, and the export of light manufactures. It has an annual GDP of about $10 billion and a per capita income of $1,300 per year.

Tunisian Military Developments

Tunisia owes its independence to a struggle that began in the mid-1930s, when Habib Bourguiba formed what came to be called the Neo-Destour (Constitutionalist) Party. By 1952 the Neo-Destour Party was able to deploy sufficient military forces to challenge French control, which was exercised through the bey of Tunis. In spite of the efforts of the Foreign Legion, a guerrilla war continued from 1954 to 1956 that France could not sustain because of the pressure of trying to win its struggle to keep control of Algeria. This forced France to give Tunisia independence in February, 1956, and Bourguiba became president—a title he held along with nearly absolute power until late 1987. France kept its major naval base at Bizerte after Tunisia gained independence, but continuing military clashes forced it to evacuate Bizerte in 1961.

From 1956 to 1987, Bourguiba ruled Tunisia with great political skill, building his power base around a small political elite from his Destourian Socialist Party (now called the Constitutional Democratic Rally, or RCD). While he did not tolerate active political opposition, Bourguiba created a relatively modern secular state with considerable free market activity. He also allowed considerable political debate and media discussion.

Over the years, however, Bourguiba encountered a series of threats from Qadhafi. In 1960 a Libyan trained force of Tunisians crossed the border with Qadhafi's support and had to be suppressed by force. Qadhafi made a similar, but less successful, effort in 1982. In 1984 Libya seems to have aided in the sabotage of the pipeline between Algeria and Tunisia. In 1985 Qadhafi put pressure on Tunisia by expelling some 25,000–30,000 Tunisians working in Libya. Qadhafi also provided funds to labor and Islamic groups that opposed Bourguiba, training and arming some of the most extreme Islamic groups. Tunisia severed diplomatic relations with Libya over this action until late 1987. It has continued to have problems with Libya, however, and has also had growing problems with Iran because of its support of Islamic extremists.

Tunisia had growing internal problems in the 1980s. Bourguiba's rule grew more idiosyncratic and authoritarian by the early 1980s, and mismanagement of Tunisia's economy became an increasingly serious problem. So did the rise of Islamic fundamentalism, triggered in part by population growth and the decline in the economy. This situation came to a head in 1987, when Islamic extremists in the Islamic Tendency Movement started a series of bombings, targeted at the tourist trade. Bourguiba mismanaged the ensuing crackdown and became involved in a political dispute with Prime Minister Zine Abidine Ben Ali, who had once headed the secret police. As a result, Bourguiba was declared senile and deposed from power on November 7, 1987; Ben Ali became president after Bourguiba was declared incompetent to act.

While Ben Ali restored some degree of democracy and freed many political prisoners, he rigged the April, 1989 general election so that his party took every seat in the 141 seat parliament. He also did not permit Islamic parties. Further, he proved unable to suppress the forces of Islamic fundamentalism. Between 1987 and 1992, Tunisia was forced to adopt stricter and stricter measures to control its Islamic extremists and faced a growing political challenge from Islamic fundamentalists.

In spite of widespread arrests, abuses of human rights, and the closing of most Islamic newspapers, however, the popularity of Islamic parties continued to grow. The key Islamic party is now al-Nahda, or Renaissance Party, a hard-line Islamic party led by Rachid Ghannouchi which has committed a number of acts of terrorism and burned to death one member of the ruling party. Several close supporters of Bourguiba back al-Nahda. These include Ahmed Ben Salah, who administered part of the government's efforts at collectivism in the 1960s, and former premier Mohammed Mzali.

By 1992, the resulting struggle between the fundamentalists and the government had reached the point where the government was accusing the fundamentalists of coup attempts and assassination plots, and the fundamentalists were accusing the government of widespread torture. In July, 1992 the Tunisian government began to prosecute 300 fundamentalists for treason. The defendants were all said to be members of al-Nahda, and they were accused of planning a coup and attempting to assassinate Tunisia's president. Forty-eight of the prisoners faced the death penalty, thirty-nine for the coup attempt and nine for the assassination attempt.

It is important to note, however, that Islamic fundamentalism should not be identified with extremism. Other, more moderate Islamic leaders, like Abdelfattah Mourou, have also gained steadily in support, though some have split with Mourou over his siding with Saddam Hussein in the Gulf War and have supported Ben Ali in backing Kuwait. Ben Ali has permitted these leaders more activity, along with the five secular parties that are allowed to play a public role in politics, such as the Democratic Socialist Movement. He has not, however, given such parties any real chance at power.[136]

Ben Ali had mixed success with economic reform. Tunisia suffered from serious economic mismanagement during the last years of Bourguiba. A disastrous grain harvest in 1985 and a further drought and the collapse of oil prices in 1986 caused massive unemployment and balance-of-payments problems from which Tunisia began to recover only in 1990. Since that time, the economy has also made a partial recovery as a result of better harvests, export growth, and higher domestic investment.

The economic growth is partly the result of political change. Tunisia has carried out some of the major reforms called for by the IMF and has improved the efficiency and effectiveness of many government activities, including defense. Tunisia has reformed part of its personal and business tax system and has replaced its archaic mix of turnover and excise levies with a value added tax. Real GNP growth went from 1.5% in 1988 to 3.5% in 1989 and 6.5% in 1990, and real investment expanded by 8% in 1989 and 22% in 1990. Tunisia's economy was continuing to strengthen in 1992, in spite of some loss of economic activity in 1990 and 1991 due to the Gulf War. The government has not, however, been able to revitalize the economy to the point where adequate jobs are available for Tunisia's rapidly growing population, although the country is conducting other reforms as part of a program developed with the IMF.[137] Tunisia also still has external debt of over $7 billion.[138]

Tunisian Military Expenditures and Arms Transfers

Tunisia spent only about $50–60 million a year on defense until 1979. In 1979 it suddenly raised its defense budget to $219 million, and its budgets have remained relatively high ever since. ACDA estimates that Tunisia spent $196 million on military forces in 1980, $159 million in 1981, $251 million in 1982, $320 million in 1983, $230 million in 1984, $277 million in 1985, $282 million in 1986, $269 million in 1987, $238 million in 1988, and $273 million in 1991.[139] The IISS estimates Tunisian military spending at $860 million in 1987, $545 million in 1988, $401 million in 1990, and $469 million in 1991.[140] This put military spending during the 1980s at about 3–5% of the GNP, and 7.5–11% of central government expenditures.

While Tunisian military manpower showed limited increases between 1979 and 1983 and rose from 24,000 to 28,000 men, Tunisia's force expansion did not match its increase in military spending. Tunisia also acquired relatively little major combat equipment per dollar. It is almost impossible to determine where most of the rise in Tunisian military spending went until the mid-1980s, when Tunisia suddenly raised its military manpower from 28,000 to over 35,000 men and began to make major equipment purchases.[141]

Tunisia's arms imports peaked during the mid-1980s, when it faced an active threat from Libya. ACDA estimates that Tunisia imported $10 million worth of arms in 1978, $90 million in 1979, $140 million in 1980, $60 million in 1981, $60 million in 1982, $40 million in 1983, $130 million in 1984, $300 million in 1985, $90 million in 1986, $50 million in 1987, $20 million in 1988, and $20 million in 1989.[142]

Tunisia relies on a mix of Western military suppliers. ACDA estimates that Tunisia took delivery on $385 million worth of arms during 1979–1983. This included $110 million worth of arms from the U.S., $130 million from France, $5 million from the UK, $20 million from West Germany, $70 million from Italy, $10 million from the PRC, and $1,900 million from other countries.[143] It took delivery on $550 million worth of arms during 1984–1988. This included $5.8 million worth of arms from the U.S., $7.5 million from France, $5 million from Germany, and $5 million from other countries.

The ACDA's new method of reporting showed that Tunisia imported a total of $465 million worth of arms during 1985–1989, including $300 million from the U.S., $160 million from France, and $5 million from West Germany.[144]

It is interesting to see how limited the resulting major arms transfers are in comparison with the list provided earlier for Libya:[145]

- 54 M-60-A3s (U.S.: 1984)
- 90 M-113, M-113A1s (U.S.: 1973–1981)
- 100 T-6614 APCs (Italy: 1980)
- 86 M-101A1, M-109 A2, M-198 howitzers (U.S.: 1981–1989)
- 10 M-54 towed SAM system (U.S.: 1980)
- 14 F-5E/F Tiger-2 fighters (U.S.: 1984–1989)
- 18 SF-260/260C COIN trainers (Italy: 1975–1978)
- C-130 transports (U.S.: 1985)
- 6 UH-1N helicopters (U.S.: 1980)
- 18 AB-205 helicopters (Italy: 1979–1980)
- 4 SA-330 Puma, 318C, AS-365N helicopters (France: 1974–1984)
- 6 Tiger point defense radars (France: 1986–1988)
- 1 Edsall-class frigate (U.S.: 1973)
- 6 P-48 (Type C), Adjutant-class MSC, Combattante-III FAC warships (France: 1975–1984).
- 2 Shanghai-class patrol ships (PRC: 1977)
- 2 Tazarka-class patrol ships (UK: 1977)

Tunisian Armed Forces and Military Manpower

Tunisia has never made any pretensions of being a major regional military power but has modernized and expanded its forces reluctantly and in response to its neighbors. In 1992 Tunisia had only modest military capabilities. It had only about a brigade's worth of tanks in its entire army, seven major combat ships, and fifty-three combat aircraft.

The Tunisian military forces are one of the few Arab military forces that have not played a constant role in politics, seized power, or threatened the regime. They are also one of the few military forces that have played a significant role in peacetime development projects. The officer corps is well educated and reasonably well trained for a small and financially constrained force. There are, however, reports of corruption, nepotism, and favoritism at higher levels of command. Tunisia also seems to be experiencing at least some problems with Islamic fundamentalism among its junior officers, NCOs, and enlisted men.

Tunisia had total active military strength of about 35,000 in 1992, but roughly 26,400 of this total were conscripts that serve only eighteen months. While some more developed countries have been able to train and use soldiers effectively with only eighteen months of service, Tunisia has not. It also underpays conscripts and does not provide adequate incentives to make lower ranks stay on as regulars or to keep some of its junior officers. A great deal of training is done at the branch or specialized function level and combined arms training is poor. In-unit training varies from poor to good, and there is little realistic field training.

Some of these problems seem to be driven by fiscal and political considerations. Tunisia does not have a large manpower base, but it is adequate to support more effective manpower policies—particularly given Tunisia's high unemployment. The CIA estimated in late 1991 that Tunisia's population was about 8.3 million, with a growth rate of 2.1% and a labor force of 2.3 million. Tunisia is 98% Arab, 1% European, and less than 1% Jewish. It is about 98% Muslim, 1% Christian, and less than 1% Jewish.[146]

The CIA estimated that there were 2,052,000 males in the age group from 15 to 49 and that 1,181,000 were fit for military service. Roughly 90,200 males a year reached the military age of 20. The IISS estimated in late 1991 that there were a total of about 467,000 males and 438,300 females in the age group from 13 to 17, 435,000 men and 405,000 women in the age group from 18 to 22 years, and about 717,000 men and 695,000 women in the age group from 23 to 32 years.[147]

The Tunisian Army

Tunisia's 27,000 man army has more than 25,000 conscripts. It is organized into two mechanized brigades (each with one armored and two mechanized infantry battalions), one reinforced Sahara brigade, one paracommando brigade, one armored reconnaissance regiment, one antitank regiment, three field artillery regiments, an air defense brigade with two regiments, and one engineer regiment. These formations are relatively small. A Tunisian brigade generally has only about 5,000 men, and a regiment 1,000 to 1,500.

Lacking the active forces and equipment resources to deploy significant strength on either border in peacetime, Tunisia keeps most of its units near urban casernes. It does, however, have special units in the Sahara brigade that cover the border and provide a light screen of security forces. The total current strength of Tunisia's organized reserves is unknown. There is little indication that they are well trained or organized, or would be combat effective without months of reorganization and training.

The Tunisian army has slowly expanded to eighty-four main battle tanks (thirty M-60A1s and fifty-four M-60As). It has forty obsolete AMX-13s and ten obsolete M-41s which are in storage or withdrawn from active service, and fifty-four relatively modern Steyr SK-105 Kuerassiers. Only the Steyr SK-105 Kuerassiers currently seem to be in active service. It has fifty-nine relatively low grade armored reconnaissance vehicles, including twenty-four Saladins, twelve AML-245s, and thirty-five AML-90s. It has about 270 APCs, including 140 M-113 A-1/2s, 18 EE-11 Urutus, and 110 Fiat F-6614s.

Tunisia is learning how to use modern armor but is at best capable of largely static defense in the event of a major attack by Libya or Algeria. Its armor is poorly standardized, and many items are aging or obsolete. Overall, Tunisian armored forces have continuing maintenance and standardization problems. They are trained enough for light defensive operations but have limited maneuver and offensive capability.

The army has also made improvements in its artillery strength in recent years, and most Tunisian artillery battalions now seem to have their full complement of weapons. Total strength has risen from 80 artillery pieces in 1988 to about 145 weapons in 1992. Tunisia had forty-eight M-101A1/A2 105mm towed weapons, twelve M-114A1 155mm towed weapons, and fifty-seven M-198 155mm towed weapons in 1992. It had ten M-108 105mm and eighteen M-109 self-propelled artillery weapons. It also had twelve M-106A2 self-propelled, eighteen 120mm and 4.2" mortars, forty 107mm mortars, and ninety-five 81mm mortars. It was able to employ these weapons defensively in small batteries but had limited maneuver, command and control, counterbattery, and beyond visual range targeting capability.

The anti-tank weapons strength of the Tunisian army was limited, although it included some modern types like Milan and TOW. It had a mix of SS-11, 500 Milan, and 65 MGM-71A TOW anti-tank guided missile launchers, including 35 TOWs on its M-113s. It had 140 57mm M-18 recoilless rifles and 70 M-40A1 106mm recoilless rifles. It also had 30 M-20 3.5" and 300 LRAC 89mm anti-tank rocket launchers. Few anti-tank crews had high readiness or realistic training against mobile armor.

The air defense weapons of the Tunisian army included forty-eight RBS-70 and twenty-six MIM-72 Chaparral surface-to-air missile fire units, and twenty-six M-163 Vulcan self-propelled anti-aircraft guns. Tunisia also had 100 M-55 20mm and 20 M-1939/Type 55 37mm AA guns. These weapons were capable of providing limited low altitude point defense, but there were no heavy surface-to-air missile systems in either the army or air force.

Tunisia will not be able to build up to an effective strength of more than 100 main battle tanks before the mid-1990s. It is only beginning to acquire the elements of modern armored warfare training and faces massive problems in rationalizing its diverse inventory—which now consists of far too many erratic small buys of incompatible or hard-to-support equipment. The Tunisian army badly needs to improve its manpower management, emphasis on professionalism and career incentives, and support and logistic capabilities. At present, most units cannot operate effectively for any length of time unless they are near their peacetime depots and casernes, and even then the logistic and service support system will not be particularly effective.

Tunisia's paramilitary forces include a public order brigade with 3,500 men in the Ministry of the Interior. This force is army trained, has a strength of three battalions, and is equipped with EBR-75 armored fighting vehicles and V-150 Commando APCs. There is also a 10,000 man national guard. The national guard has a naval element with some thirteen patrol craft.

The Tunisian Navy

The 4,500 man Tunisian navy is based at Bizerte, Sfax, La Goulette, and Keliba. It has nearly 700 conscripts, but ship crews tend to be relatively professional. Its strength includes one frigate, three missile fast attack craft, two regular fast attack craft, five large patrol craft, twenty-four coastal patrol craft, and one tug. Two more regular fast attack craft are on order. This force is only capable of patrolling Tunisian waters and asserting control over infiltrating ships or commercial vessels. It is not strong enough to survive an attack by the Libyan or Algerian navies. Overall logistic and maintenance capabilities seem to be poor, and while Tunisia is able to operate its individual ships, it does not seem to be organized for any kind of fleet operation or combined arms operation.

In 1992 its strength consisted of one aging 1,490-ton ex-U.S. frigate laid down in 1943. It was armed with two 76mm guns and six 324mm torpedo tubes. Tunisia also had three Combattante II-class 425-ton missile guided fast attack craft with two quad MM-40 Exocet launchers, one 76mm gun, and two twin 40mm Breda guns.

Its other combat ships included two 131-ton ex-PRC fast attack craft with two twin 37mm and two twin 20mm guns, two 125-ton Vosper Thornycroft fast attack craft with two 20mm guns, four 80-ton coastal patrol craft with two 20mm guns, and six 38-ton coastal patrol craft with 20mm guns. The remaining vessels included ten 32-ton patrol craft operated by customs and a 860-ton tug.

The Tunisian Air Force

The 3,500 man Tunisian air force also has some 700 conscripts. It has slowly developed relatively effective manpower policies and is gradually developing the capability to train and retain competent pilots and air crews. It is expanding steadily and had fifty-three combat aircraft and eighteen attack helicopters in 1992.

The air force has done a good job of absorbing and operating its thirty F-5E/Fs in the fighter ground attack role and has gradually developed a reasonable capability for daytime air-to-air combat. It is unclear whether Tunisia still suffers from a shortage of trained F-5 pilots. It also has eleven MB-326s in the counterinsurgency (COIN) role that are reasonably effective in attack missions against troops without modern, manportable or short range guided missiles—a limitation that may present serious problems if the Tunisian air force must deal with regular Libyan or Syrian forces

Tunisian air power includes five SA-341 helicopters in the attack role and eight AB-205 and five AB-205A-1 helicopters in the assault role. None of its combat aircraft has advanced air defense or attack capabilities, however, and

Tunisia needs an additional twelve to fourteen modern combat aircraft during the next five to eight years. Given potential threats, it needs a modern all-weather air defense fighter with beyond visual range air-to-air intercept capabilities.

The air force also has two C-130Hs and two S-208M liaison aircraft, and a training wing with some combat capable SF-260s and eight M-326s. It has a wing with forty-two helicopters. These helicopters include six SA-313s, five SA-316s, eighteen AB-205s, six UH-1s, thirteen AB-205s, six AS-350Bs, and one AS-365F, giving Tunisia's armed forces considerable tactical air mobility for a force their size.

In broad terms, Tunisia has a primitive air control and warning system and limited sensor coverage of Tunisian air space. It is not organized to fight at the air force, as distinguished from the formation or squadron, level. It has the same problems as does the army in terms of retaining and training good personnel and is heavily reliant on foreign contractors for logistics and maintenance. Some effort has been made to give the Tunisian air force a combined operations capability based on U.S. doctrine and training concepts, but success is evidently still very limited.

Strategic Interests and Arms Control

Tunisia can at best hope to forge a limited deterrent during the next five to ten years. Its success will be almost totally dependent on Tunisia's ability to buy more armor and more advanced combat aircraft and to develop a better balance of overall effectiveness in all three of its military services. In the interim, Tunisia's military security will continue to be dependent on Algeria and Libya's counterbalancing each other and on reinforcement by Western forces.

Tunisia must deal with both the threat from its larger neighbors and the rising force of Islamic fundamentalism. Its forces need to be supplied with modern equipment at the modest rate that Tunisia has sought in the past, although Tunisia has a far more pressing need to be supported in continuing down the path of economic reform that it has followed since President Ben Ali and Prime Minister Hamed Karoui came to power. While Tunisia does not play a critical strategic role in the Middle East, the presence of a friendly and relatively progressive state in the Maghreb serves Western strategic interests, and its government has done a steadily better job of serving its citizens.

The Military Tragedy in the Maghreb

Barring some radical political shift, the military balance in the Maghreb is likely to move towards a kind of quasi stability. Political tensions will continue, and each nation will buy more weapons, but each will do so with little immediate prospect of major conflict. While leaders may change and alliances may shift, the Maghreb seems to have modified the classic Arab proverb that "the enemy of my enemy is my friend" into "the neighbor of my neighbor is my friend." Rather than any nation's achieving dominance, the

Maghreb powers seem likely to readjust their positions to ensure that no nation becomes too strong.

There is little current prospect that any Maghreb military force will emerge as an effective force by Western (or even Arab-Israeli) standards over the next decade, although the number of high quality small units will improve. This lack of effectiveness, moreover, does not preclude the ability to fight long and bloody wars. The irony behind the current arms race in the Maghreb is that there is so little real political or economic rationale for the forces involved or the expenditures that have taken place. Further, it is far from clear that this waste of scarce national resources will cease in the future, and the impact of military spending on development may actually increase.

The most likely prospect for the military forces of the Maghreb is one of immense waste, coupled with the steady "structural conversion" of the societies involved to maintaining large and highly expensive military forces. The longer large armed forces exist in a nation, the more they create institutional, political, and budgetary relationships that make them difficult or impossible to reduce. This structural conversion is also fed by the inevitable military buildup in neighboring states and by shifts in foreign borrowing and trade to make arms a major import. The standing military forces of the Maghreb will continue to drain scarce trained manpower and investment resources while contributing nothing to national development other than disguised unemployment.

True military expenditures will probably have consumed 5–8% of the gross national product and cost about $22 billion in foreign arms purchases between 1988 and 1992. This expenditure will aggravate the problems all Maghreb nations face because of population growth and mismanagement of their agriculture and the rest of their economies. While the leaders of the various Maghreb states have improved their political and economic cooperation in recent years, there is little immediate prospect that they can cooperate on arms control or show sufficient maturity to realize that their military expansion is mortgaging much of their future.

Notes

1. Arms Control and Disarmament Agency (ACDA), *World Military Expenditures and Arms Transfers, 1988,* Washington, GPO, 1989.

2. In theory, the Maghreb is a geographic entity based on the Berber peoples, who have heavily intermarried with Arabs since the seventh century. In practice, it has come to include Mauritania, Morocco, Algeria, Libya, and Tunisia. For a summary of political and economic trends since 1945, see Paul Balta, "Oranges, Olives, Oil—The Maghreb in Transition," *NATO's Sixteen Nations,* April, 1990, pp. 20, 23–24.

3. Most sources, such as the countries involved, CIA, and ACDA, show much lower percentages of GNP. These figures ignore the true cost of arms imports because they are "debts."

4. Arms Control and Disarmament Agency (ACDA), *World Military Expenditures and Arms Transfers, 1988,* Washington, GPO, 1989, p. 111.

5. Based on the counts in CIA, *Handbook of Economic Statistics,* Washington, CIA, CPAS 89-0002, September, 1989, pp. 184–187.

6. CIA, *Handbook of Economic Statistics*, Washington, CIA, CPAS 89-0002, September, 1989, pp. 186–187.

7. The military manpower, force strength, and equipment estimates in this section are made by the author using a wide range of sources, including computerized data bases, interviews, and press clipping services. Most are impossible to reference in ways of use to the reader. The force strength statistics are generally taken from the latest edition of the International Institute for Strategic Studies *Military Balance* (IISS, London), in this case the 1991–1992 edition. Extensive use has also been made of the annual editions of the Jaffee Center for Strategic Studies, *The Military Balance in the Middle East* (JCSS, Tel Aviv), especially the 1990–1991 edition and working materials from the coming edition. Material has also been drawn from computer print outs from NEXIS, the United States Naval Institute data base, and from the DMS/FI Market Intelligence Reports data base. Other sources include the *Military Technology* "World Defense Almanac for 1991–1992," published in 1992; country reports of the Economist Intelligence Unit (EIU); Foreign Affairs Division, "Middle East Arms Control and Related Issues," Washington, Congressional Research Service, 91-384F, May 1, 1991; and *Middle East Economic Digest*, "MEED Special Report: Defense," Volume 35, December 13, 1991.

Weapons data are taken from many sources, including computerized material available in NEXIS, and various editions of *Jane's Fighting Ships* (Jane's Publishing); *Jane's Naval Weapons Systems* (Jane's Publishing); *Jane's Armour and Artillery* (Jane's Publishing); *Jane's Infantry Weapons* (Jane's Publishing); *Jane's Military Vehicles and Logistics* (Jane's Publishing); *Jane's Land-Based Air Defense* (Jane's Publishing); *Jane's All the World's Aircraft* (Jane's Publishing); *Jane's Battlefield Surveillance Systems* (Jane's Publishing); *Jane's Radar and Electronic Warfare Systems* (Jane's Publishing), *Jane's C^3I Systems* (Jane's Publishing); *Jane's Air-Launched Weapons Systems* (Jane's Publishing); *Jane's Defence Appointments & Procurement Handbook (Middle East Edition)* (Jane's Publishing); *Tanks of the World* (Bernard and Grafe); *Weyer's Warships* (Bernard and Grafe); and *Warplanes of the World* (Bernard and Grafe).

Other military background, effectiveness, strength, organizational, and history data are taken from the relevant country or war sections of Herbert K. Tillema, *International Conflict Since 1945*, Boulder, Westview, 1991; Anthony H. Cordesman, "The Military Forces of the Maghreb," *RUSI and Brassey's Defense Yearbook*, London, Brassey's, 1986; Ravma Omaar and Janet Fleischman, "Arab vs. African," *Africa Report*, July/August, 1991, pp. 34–38; Department of Defense and Department of State, *Congressional Presentation for Security Assistance Programs, Fiscal Year 1993*, Washington, Department of State, 1992; Canadian Director, General Intelligence, *Recognition Handbook—Western Sahara Region*, CIS/2600.0000W7-F/WI/01/91/16353, Ottawa, July 29, 1991; various annual editions of John Laffin's *The World in Conflict* or *War Annual*, London, Brassey's; and John Keegan, *World Armies*, London, Macmillan, 1983.

8. The statistical data are taken largely from the CIA, *World Factbook, 1991*, pp. 200–201.

9. Ravma Omaar and Janet Fleischman, "Arab vs. African," *Africa Report*, July/August, 1991, pp. 34–38; *Armed Forces*, July, 1989, pp. 300–301.

10. Mauritania did publish a new provisional constitution on December 17, 1980, but abandoned it in 1981. A new constitutional charter was published on February 27, 1985, but has little real meaning. The country uses Islamic law.

11. *Armed Forces*, July, 1989, pp. 300–301.

12. Arms Control and Disarmament Agency (ACDA), *World Military Expenditures and Arms Transfers, 1989*, Washington, GPO, 1990, p. 60.

13. Arms Control and Disarmament Agency (ACDA), *World Military Expenditures and Arms Transfers, 1989*, Washington, GPO, 1990, p. 60.

14. Arms Control and Disarmament Agency (ACDA), *World Military Expenditures and Arms Transfers, 1989*, Washington, GPO, 1990, Table II.

15. Arms Control and Disarmament Agency (ACDA), *World Military Expenditures and Arms Transfers, 1985*, Washington, GPO, 1985, pp. 133–134.

16. Arms Control and Disarmament Agency (ACDA), *World Military Expenditures and Arms Transfers, 1989,* Washington, GPO, 1990, pp. 117–118.

17. Arms Control and Disarmament Agency (ACDA), *World Military Expenditures and Arms Transfers, 1990,* Washington, GPO, 1990, pp. 133–134.

18. CIA, *The World Factbook,* 1991, pp. 200–201.

19. CIA, *The World Factbook,* 1991, pp. 200–201.

20. IISS, *Military Balance, 1991–1992.*

21. See Edgar O'Ballance, "Mauritania-Senegal," *Armed Forces,* July, 1989, pp. 300–301.

22. The military manpower, force strength, and equipment estimates in this section are made by the author using a wide range of sources, including computerized data bases, interviews, and press clipping services. Most are impossible to reference in ways of use to the reader. The force strength statistics are generally taken from the latest edition of the International Institute for Strategic Studies *Military Balance* (IISS, London), in this case the 1991–1992 edition. Extensive use has also been made of the annual editions of the Jaffee Center for Strategic Studies, *The Military Balance in the Middle East* (JCSS, Tel Aviv), especially the 1990–1991 edition and working materials from the coming edition. Material has also been drawn from computer print outs from NEXIS, the United States Naval Institute data base, and from the DMS/FI Market Intelligence Reports data base. Other sources include the *Military Technology* "World Defense Almanac for 1991–1992," published in 1992; country reports of the Economist Intelligence Unit (EIU); Foreign Affairs Division, "Middle East Arms Control and Related Issues," Washington, Congressional Research Service, 91-384F, May 1, 1991; and *Middle East Economic Digest,* "MEED Special Report: Defense," Volume 35, December 13, 1991.

Weapons data are taken from many sources, including computerized material available in NEXIS, and various editions of *Jane's Fighting Ships* (Jane's Publishing); *Jane's Naval Weapons Systems* (Jane's Publishing); *Jane's Armour and Artillery* (Jane's Publishing); *Jane's Infantry Weapons* (Jane's Publishing); *Jane's Military Vehicles and Logistics* (Jane's Publishing); *Jane's Land-Based Air Defence* (Jane's Publishing); *Jane's All the World's Aircraft* (Jane's Publishing); *Jane's Battlefield Surveillance Systems* (Jane's Publishing); *Jane's Radar and Electronic Warfare Systems* (Jane's Publishing), *Jane's C³I Systems* (Jane's Publishing); *Jane's Air-Launched Weapons Systems* (Jane's Publishing); *Jane's Defence Appointments & Procurement Handbook (Middle East Edition)* (Jane's Publishing); *Tanks of the World* (Bernard and Grafe); *Weyer's Warships* (Bernard and Grafe); and *Warplanes of the World* (Bernard and Grafe).

Other military background, effectiveness, strength, organizational, and history data are taken from Penny Gibbens, "Morocco: Immobile Autocracy," *The Middle East,* February, 1991, pp. 23–24; Brigitte Robineault, "Polisario and Western Sahara," *International Perspectives,* March/April 1988, pp. 14–16; Allison Perry, "War over a Desert Wilderness," *The Middle East,* July 1988, pp. 24–31; the relevant country or war sections of Herbert K. Tillema, *International Conflict Since 1945,* Boulder, Westview, 1991; Anthony H. Cordesman, "The Military Forces of the Maghrib," *RUSI and Brassey's Defense Yearbook,* London, Brassey's, 1986; Department of Defense and Department of State, *Congressional Presentation for Security Assistance Programs, Fiscal Year 1993,* Washington, Department of State, 1992; Canadian Director, General Intelligence, *Recognition Handbook—Western Sahara Region,* CIS/2600.0000W7-F/WI/01/91/16353, Ottawa, July 29, 1991; various annual editions of John Laffin's *The World in Conflict* or *War Annual,* London, Brassey's; and John Keegan, *World Armies,* London, Macmillan, 1983.

23. CIA, *World Factbook, 1991,* pp. 212–213.

24. *OJJ Special, Oil and Gas Journal,* December 30, 1991, pp. 43–49; also see Joseph P. Riva, Jr., of the Congressional Research Service, writing in the *Oil and Gas Journal,* September 23, 1991, p. 62.

25. *Los Angeles Times,* April 16, 1991, p. H-2.

26. See Herbert K. Tillema, *International Conflict Since 1945,* Boulder, Westview, 1991, pp. 136–138.

27. CIA, *World Factbook, 1991*, p. 338.

28. Many maps of these defenses show a single wall and others several. Sources do not agree about the length of the walls. This description is based on *Jane's Defence Weekly*, February 4, 1989, p. 182.

29. *The Middle East*, April, 1989, p. 21; *New York Times*, January 15, 1989, p. 4; *Washington Times*, January 13, 1989, p. A-9; *Economist*, October 14, 1989, p. 52.

30. *Jane's Defence Weekly*, September 14, 1991, p. 450; Peter Hiett, "Peace Plan Falling Apart," *MEI*, August 30, 1991, p. 10; *Africa Report*, November-December, 1991, pp. 5–6; *The Middle East*, August, 1991, pp. 26–28.

31. *Washington Post*, March 14, 1992, p. A-15; *Jane's Defence Weekly*, September 21, 1991, p. 509; *Financial Times*, November 6, 1991, p. 4; *New York Times*, January 1, 1992, p. 2; *Africa News*, August 26, 1991, pp. 6–7.

32. CIA, *World Factbook, 1991*, p. 338.

33. *New York Times*, February 28, 1992, p. A-3; *Washington Post*, March 14, 1992, p. A-15; *The Middle East*, December, 1991, p. 18.

34. Department of Defense and Department of State, *Congressional Presentation for Security Assistance Programs, Fiscal Year 1993*, Washington, Department of State, 1992, pp. 245–247; *Washington Post*, September 5, 1992, p. A-16.

35. Arms Control and Disarmament Agency (ACDA), *World Military Expenditures and Arms Transfers, 1990*, Washington, GPO, 1990, Table II.

36. Arms Control and Disarmament Agency (ACDA), *World Military Expenditures and Arms Transfers, 1985*, Washington, GPO, 1985, pp. 133–134.

37. Arms Control and Disarmament Agency (ACDA), *World Military Expenditures and Arms Transfers, 1989*, Washington, GPO, 1990, pp. 117–118.

38. CIA, *The World Factbook*, 1991, pp. 200–201.

39. Arms Control and Disarmament Agency (ACDA), *World Military Expenditures and Arms Transfers, 1990*, Washington, GPO, 1990, pp. 133–134.

40. Based on the country sections in the IISS, *Military Balance, 1991–1992*; and the country section in CIA, *World Factbook, 1991*.

41. *Baltimore Sun*, September 28, 1991, p. 15B.

42. Department of Defense and Department of State, *Congressional Presentation for Security Assistance Programs, Fiscal Year 1993*, Washington, Department of State, 1992, pp. 245–247.

43. *The Middle East*, February, 1991, pp. 23–24; *Manchester Guardian Weekly*, November 3, 1991, p. 8; *Christian Science Monitor*, May 22, 1991, p. 3, September 26, 1991, p. 4.

44. The military manpower, force strength, and equipment estimates in this section are made by the author using a wide range of sources, including computerized data bases, interviews, and press clipping services. Most are impossible to reference in ways of use to the reader. The force strength statistics are generally taken from the latest edition of the International Institute for Strategic Studies *Military Balance* (IISS, London), in this case the 1991–1992 edition. Extensive use has also been made of the annual editions of the Jaffee Center for Strategic Studies, *The Military Balance in the Middle East* (JCSS, Tel Aviv), especially the 1990–1991 edition and working materials from the coming edition. Material has also been drawn from computer print outs from NEXIS, the United States Naval Institute data base, and from the DMS/FI Market Intelligence Reports data base. Other sources include the *Military Technology* "World Defense Almanac for 1991–1992," published in 1992; country reports of the Economist Intelligence Unit (EIU); Foreign Affairs Division, "Middle East Arms Control and Related Issues," Washington, Congressional Research Service, 91-384F, May 1, 1991; and *Middle East Economic Digest*, "MEED Special Report: Defense," Volume 35, December 13, 1991.

Weapons data are taken from many sources, including computerized material available in NEXIS, and various editions of *Jane's Fighting Ships* (Jane's Publishing); *Jane's Naval Weapons Systems* (Jane's Publishing); *Jane's Armour and Artillery* (Jane's Publishing); *Jane's Infantry*

Weapons (Jane's Publishing); *Jane's Military Vehicles and Logistics* (Jane's Publishing); *Jane's Land-Based Air Defence* (Jane's Publishing); *Jane's All the World's Aircraft* (Jane's Publishing); *Jane's Battlefield Surveillance Systems* (Jane's Publishing); *Jane's Radar and Electronic Warfare Systems* (Jane's Publishing), *Jane's C³I Systems* (Jane's Publishing); *Jane's Air-Launched Weapons Systems* (Jane's Publishing); *Jane's Defence Appointments & Procurement Handbook (Middle East Edition)* (Jane's Publishing); *Tanks of the World* (Bernard and Grafe); *Weyer's Warships* (Bernard and Grafe); and *Warplanes of the World* (Bernard and Grafe).

Other military background, effectiveness, strength, organizational, and history data are taken from Marko Milivojevic, "Algeria's National Popular Army," *Armed Forces*, April, 1989, pp. 158–163; Carol Migdalovitz, "Algeria in Crisis: Democracy, Islamism, and Implications for U.S. Policy," Congressional Research Service 91-591F, August 5, 1991; the relevant country or war sections of Herbert K. Tillema, *International Conflict Since 1945*, Boulder, Westview, 1991; Anthony H. Cordesman, "The Military Forces of the Maghrib," *RUSI and Brassey's Defense Yearbook*, London, Brassey's, 1986; Department of Defense and Department of State, *Congressional Presentation for Security Assistance Programs, Fiscal Year 1993*, Washington, Department of State, 1992; Canadian Director, General Intelligence, *Recognition Handbook—Western Sahara Region*, CIS/2600.0000W7-F/WI/01/91/16353, Ottawa, July 29, 1991; various annual editions of John Laffin's *The World in Conflict* or *War Annual*, London, Brassey's; and John Keegan, *World Armies*, London, Macmillan, 1983.

45. *OJJ Special, Oil and Gas Journal*, December 30, 1991, pp. 43–49. Other estimates indicate that it has 9.2 billion barrels of proven reserves and 2 billion barrels of probable reserves. See Joseph P. Riva, Jr., of the Congressional Research Service, writing in the *Oil and Gas Journal*, September 23, 1991, p. 62.

46. Some sources refer exclusively to the party as the FLN, creating clear distinctions between it and the armed forces, or ALN. Some sources use the name "FLN/ALN." Still other sources refer to the army as the entire armed forces, and use the name National Popular Army, or ANP. For simplicity's sake, the history in this section refers to the FLN as both the party and the armed forces.

47. Carol Migdalovitz, "Algeria in Crisis: Democracy, Islamism, and Implications for U.S. Policy," Congressional Research Service 91-591F, August 5, 1991.

48. David Butter, "Algeria Stares into the Abyss," *Middle East Economic Digest*, January 24, 1992, pp. 4–5; Carol Migdalovitz, "Algeria in Crisis: Democracy, Islamism, and Implications for U.S. Policy," Congressional Research Service 91-591F, August 5, 1991.

49. *Economist*, January 14, 1992, pp. 34–35; David Butter, "Algeria Stares into the Abyss," *Middle East Economic Digest*, January 24, 1992, pp. 4–5; Boutheina Cheriet, "The Resilience of Algerian Populism," *Middle East Report*, January-February, 1992, pp. 9–11.

50. David Butter, "Algeria Stares into the Abyss," *Middle East Economic Digest*, January 24, 1992, pp. 4–5; *New York Times*, February 17, 1992, p. A-2; *Financial Times*, January 17, 1992, p. A-9; *Christian Science Monitor*, January 14, 1992, p. 3.

51. *New York Times*, March 31, 1992, p. A-8; *Washington Times*, February 25, 1992, p. A-7; *Financial Times*, January 30, 1992, p. 4.

52. *Christian Science Monitor*, March 3, 1992, p. 6; *New York Times*, March 31, 1992, p. A-8; June 30, 1992, p. A-8; July 6, 1992, p. A-2; July 9, 1992, p. A-6; *Washington Times*, February 25, 1992, p. A-7; May 11, 1992, p. A-1; May 12, 1992, p. A-8; May 25, 1992, p. A-2; *Washington Post*, June 30, 1992, p. A-14; July 1, 1992, p. A-25; July 2, 1992, p. A-32; July 3, 1992, p. A-20; June 28, 1992, p. A-22; *Baltimore Sun*, May 5, 1992, p. 5A.

53. Arms Control and Disarmament Agency (ACDA), *World Military Expenditures and Arms Transfers, 1990*, Washington, GPO, 1990, Table I.

54. IISS, *Military Balance*, 1990–1991 and 1991–1992 editions.

55. Arms Control and Disarmament Agency (ACDA), *World Military Expenditures and Arms Transfers, 1990*, Washington, GPO, 1990, Table II.

56. Arms Control and Disarmament Agency (ACDA), *World Military Expenditures and Arms Transfers, 1985*, Washington, GPO, 1985, pp. 133–134.

57. Arms Control and Disarmament Agency (ACDA), *World Military Expenditures and Arms Transfers, 1989*, Washington, GPO, 1990, pp. 117–118.

58. Arms Control and Disarmament Agency (ACDA), *World Military Expenditures and Arms Transfers, 1990*, Washington, GPO, 1990, pp. 133–134.

59. CIA, *World Factbook, 1991*, pp. 4–5.

60. Based on the country sections in the IISS, *Military Balance, 1991–1992*; and CIA, *World Factbook, 1991*, pp. 4–5.

61. *Armed Forces*, April, 1989, p. 161.

62. Statement of the Director of Central Intelligence before the Senate Armed Services Committee, January 27, 1991, and testimony before Senator Glenn's Governmental Affairs Committee, January 15, 1992; *Economist*, January 11, 1992, p. 38; *Washington Times*, April 11, 1991, p. 3.

63. *Washington Post*, May 2, 1991, p. A-36; *New York Times*, January 8, 1992, p. A-10; *London Times*, January 6, 1992; *Sunday Times*, January 5, 1992; Algiers Radio, January 19, 1992, 2300 GMT; Agence France Presse, January 20, 1992; January 7, 1992; January 6, 1992.

64. *Washington Post*, February 25, 1989, p. A-18; *Economist*, February 25, 1989, pp. 38–41.

65. The military manpower, force strength, and equipment estimates in this section are made by the author using a wide range of sources, including computerized data bases, interviews, and press clipping services. Most are impossible to reference in ways of use to the reader. The force strength statistics are generally taken from the latest edition of the International Institute for Strategic Studies *Military Balance* (IISS, London), in this case the 1991–1992 edition. Extensive use has also been made of the annual editions of the Jaffee Center for Strategic Studies, *The Military Balance in the Middle East* (JCSS, Tel Aviv), especially the 1990–1991 edition and working materials from the coming edition. Material has also been drawn from computer print outs from NEXIS, the United States Naval Institute data base, and from the DMS/FI Market Intelligence Reports data base. Other sources include the *Military Technology* "World Defense Almanac for 1991–1992," published in 1992; country reports of the Economist Intelligence Unit (EIU); Foreign Affairs Division, "Middle East Arms Control and Related Issues," Washington, Congressional Research Service, 91-384F, May 1, 1991; and *Middle East Economic Digest*, "MEED Special Report: Defense," Volume 35, December 13, 1991.

Weapons data are taken from many sources, including computerized material available in NEXIS, and various editions of *Jane's Fighting Ships* (Jane's Publishing); *Jane's Naval Weapons Systems* (Jane's Publishing); *Jane's Armour and Artillery* (Jane's Publishing); *Jane's Infantry Weapons* (Jane's Publishing); *Jane's Military Vehicles and Logistics* (Jane's Publishing); *Jane's Land-Based Air Defence* (Jane's Publishing); *Jane's All the World's Aircraft* (Jane's Publishing); *Jane's Battlefield Surveillance Systems* (Jane's Publishing); *Jane's Radar and Electronic Warfare Systems* (Jane's Publishing), *Jane's C³I Systems* (Jane's Publishing); *Jane's Air-Launched Weapons Systems* (Jane's Publishing); *Jane's Defence Appointments & Procurement Handbook (Middle East Edition)* (Jane's Publishing); *Tanks of the World* (Bernard and Grafe); *Weyer's Warships* (Bernard and Grafe); and *Warplanes of the World* (Bernard and Grafe).

Other military background, effectiveness, strength, organizational, and history data are taken from Andrew Rathmell, "Libya's Intelligence and Security Services," *International Defense Review*, 7, 1991, pp. 695–697; Clyde R. Mark, "Libya: U.S. Relations," Congressional Research Service IBB6040, May 26, 1987; Al J. Verner, "Stalemate in the Sahara," *International Defense Review*, 12/1988, pp. 1571–1572; Anthony R. Tucker, "Libya May End Involvement in Chad," *Jane's Defence Weekly*, September 24, 1989, pp. 724–725; Thalif Deen, "Libya Moves to End a War it Cannot Win," *Jane's Defence Weekly*, October 7, 1989, pp. 710–711; Bob Woodward, *Veil: The Secret Wars of the CIA, 1981–1987*, New York, Simon and Schuster, 1987; the relevant country or war sections of Herbert K. Tillema, *International Conflict Since 1945*, Boulder, Westview, 1991; Anthony H. Cordesman, "The Military Forces of the Maghrib," *RUSI and Brassey's Defense Yearbook*, London, Brassey's, 1986; Department of Defense and Department of State, *Congressional Presentation for Security Assistance Programs, Fiscal Year 1993*, Washington, Department of State, 1992; Canadian Director, General Intelligence, *Recognition Handbook—Western Sahara Region*, CIS/2600.0000W7-F/WI/01/91/16353, Ottawa, July 29, 1991; various annual editions of John Laffin's *The World in Conflict* or *War Annual*, London, Brassey's; and John Keegan, *World Armies*, London, Macmillan, 1983.

66. In theory, Libya is governed by the Socialist People's Libyan Arab Jamahirya (state of the masses). It has a constitution, a unicameral general people's congress, and a general people's committee (cabinet).

67. *Oil and Gas Journal*, September 23, 1991, p. 62.

68. *OJJ Special, Oil and Gas Journal*, December 30, 1991, pp. 43–49. Other estimates indicate that it has 22.8 billion barrels of proven reserves and 8 billion barrels of probable reserves. See Joseph P. Riva, Jr., of the Congressional Research Service, writing in the *Oil and Gas Journal*, September 23, 1991, p. 62.

69. Al J. Verner, "Stalemate in the Sahara," *International Defense Review*, 12/1988, pp. 1571–1572; Anthony R. Tucker, "Libya May End Involvement in Chad," *Jane's Defence Weekly*, September 24, 1989, pp. 724–725; Thalif Deen, "Libya Moves to End a War it Cannot Win," *Jane's Defence Weekly*, October 7, 1989, pp. 710–711; Bob Woodward, *Veil: The Secret Wars of the CIA, 1981–1987*, New York, Simon and Schuster, 1987.

70. Some U.S. experts also feel that Libya suffered this defeat despite its use of mustard gas in the last of these battles. They indicate that Libyan military transports dropped 500 pound bombs that Qadhafi had obtained from Iran.

71. Habre had originally been backed by Libya in 1973, but Libya shifted to support the Forces Armées Populaires.

72. John Laffin, *The World in Conflict, 1991*, Brassey's, London, 1991, pp. 59–60.

73. Dick Palowski, *Changes in Threat Air Combat Doctrine and Force Structure*, 24th edition, General Dynamics DWIC-91, Fort Worth Division, February, 1992, pp. I-65 and II-62 to II-69; Herbert K. Tillema, *International Conflict Since 1945*, Boulder, Westview, 1991, p. 141.

74. Qadhafi also promised to end terrorism and claimed to appoint a new intelligence chief, Youssef Abdelkadr Dobri, to crack down on terrorists.

75. Libya bought 1,000 tons of Semtex plastic explosive from Czechoslovakia, but 200 grams would have been sufficient to blow up Pan Am 103. *New York Times*, November 15, 1991, p. A-8; November 17, 1991, p. E-7; November 27, 1991, p. A-6; February 19, 1992, p. A-9; March 3, 1992, p. A-10; April 1, 1992, p. 12; *Washington Times*, March 3, 1992, p. A-7; *Financial Times*, November 15, 1991, p. 10; *Washington Post*, March 23, 1990, p. A-15; *Time*, April 2, 1990, p. 29; November 15, 1991, p. 20; November 17, 1992, p. C-2; January, 26, 1992, p. 21; February 3, 1992, p. A-1; *The Middle East*, January, 1990, p. 29; April, 1990, p. 23.

76. *Washington Times*, February 12, 1992, p. A-1; February 21, 1992, p. 9; *Daily Telegraph*, December 1, 1991, p. 1; *New York Times*, November 27, 1991, p. A-6; February 19, 1992, p. A-9; April 15, 1992, p. 1; *Washington Post*, June 11, 1992, p. A-18; June 24, 1992, p. A-24; *Christian Science Monitor*, June 24, 1992, p. C-11; *London Financial Times*, April 14, 1992, p. 5; *Economist*, April 17, 1992, p. 42; *Time*, April 6, 1992, p. 29.

77. Herbert K. Tillema, *International Conflict Since 1945*, Boulder, Westview, 1991, p. 141.

78. Herbert K. Tillema, *International Conflict Since 1945*, Boulder, Westview, 1991, p. 140.

79. *Philadelphia Inquirer*, September 2, 1989, p. 9D.

80. *International Defense Review*, No. 7, 1991, p. 695; *Washington Post*, April 18, 1992, p. A-15.

81. Estimates are not available for some years. Arms Control and Disarmament Agency (ACDA), *World Military Expenditures and Arms Transfers, 1990*, Washington, GPO, 1992, Table I.

82. Some of these estimates may only direct operating costs, without some investment and infrastructure expenditures. IISS, *Military Balance*, 1990–1991 and 1991–1992 editions.

83. Arms Control and Disarmament Agency (ACDA), *World Military Expenditures and Arms Transfers, 1990*, Washington, GPO, 1990, Table II.

84. Arms Control and Disarmament Agency (ACDA), *World Military Expenditures and Arms Transfers, 1988*, Washington, GPO, 1990, pp. 113 and 131.

85. Richard F. Grimmett, *Conventional Arms Transfers to the Third World, 1983–1990*, Washington, Congressional Research Service, CRS 91-578F, August 2, 1991, p. 69.

86. Arms Control and Disarmament Agency (ACDA), *World Military Expenditures and Arms Transfers, 1990*, Washington, GPO, 1990, pp. 133–134.

87. Adapted from various issues of the IISS, *Military Balance*, and work by the Foreign Affairs Division of the Congressional Research Service in *Middle East Arms Control and Related Issues*, CRS 91-384F, May 1, 1992, and for Senator John McCain. Robert Shuey, Richard F. Grimmett, Theodor Galdi, Steven Hildreth, Todd Masses, Alfred Prados, and Shirley Kahn were the principal authors of the CRS work.

88. Richard F. Grimmett, *Conventional Arms Transfers to the Third World, 1983–1990*, Congressional Research Service, CRS 91-578F, August 2, 1991, pp. 56 and 69.

89. CIA, *World Factbook, 1991*, p. 1982.

90. CIA, *The World Factbook*, 1991, pp. 200–201.

91. IISS, *Military Balance, 1991–1992*.

92. Based on the country sections in the IISS, *Military Balance, 1988–1989* and *1989–1990*; and the country section in CIA CPAS WF89-001 (U).

93. JCSS, *The Middle East Military Balance, 1989–1990*, p. 276.

94. IISS, *Military Balance, 1991–1992*, pp. 112–114.

95. IISS, *Military Balance, 1991–1992*, pp. 112–114.

96. This is a report from one source, and the creation of a coast watch seems erratic even for Libya.

97. Reports that Libya acquired twelve Soviet SS-12M (SS–22) missiles between mid-1980 and mid-1981 do not seem accurate. Yoseff Bodansky and Vaughn Forrest, "Chemical Weapons in the Third World, Libya's Chemical-Biological Warfare Capabilities," Task Force on Terrorism and Unconventional Warfare, House Republican Research Committee, U.S. House of Representatives, Washington, D.C., June 12, 1990, p. 3; M. Sicker, *The Making of a Pariah State*, New York, Praeger, 1987, pp. 104–105; John K. Colley, *Libyan Sandstorm*, New York, Holt, Rinehart, and Winston, 1982, pp. 248–251.

98. The Su-24 has a wing area of 575 square feet, an empty weight of 41,845 pounds, carries 3,385 gallons or 22,000 pounds of fuel, has a takeoff weight of 871,570 pounds with bombs and two external fuel tanks, carries 2,800 gallons or 18,200 pounds of external fuel, has a combat thrust: weight ratio of 1.02, a combat wing loading of 96 pounds per square foot, and a maximum load factor of 7.5G. *Jane's Soviet Intelligence Review*, July, 1990, pp. 298–300; *Jane's Defence Weekly*, June 25, 1985, pp. 1226–1227; and Dick Palowski, *Changes in Threat Air Combat Doctrine and Force Structure*, 24th edition, General Dynamics DWIC-91, Fort Worth Division, February, 1992, pp. I-65 and I-110 to I-117; *New York Times*, March 29, 1990, p. A-6; *Aviation Week*, April 10, 1989, p. 19.

99. Dick Palowski, *Changes in Threat Air Combat Doctrine and Force Structure*, 24th edition, General Dynamics DWIC-91, Fort Worth Division, February, 1992, pp. I-65 and I-110 to 1-117.

100. *Aviation Week and Space Technology*, April 10, 1989, pp. 19–20; *New York Times*, April 5, 1989; September 7, 1989; *Washington Times*, January 16, 1989; *FBIS/NES*, April 10, 1989.

101. One such firm was Technical Trade und Logistik, GmbH. *Washington Post*, January 23, 1989, p. 12. Also see *New York Times*, January 18, 1989, p. 11, and March 29, 1990, p. 15.

102. See Dick Palowski, *Changes in Threat Air Combat Doctrine and Force Structure*, 24th edition, General Dynamics DWIC-91, Fort Worth Division, February, 1992.

103. Foreign technicians could provide effective support in the use of radar reconnaissance

data. The basic problems with daylight reconnaissance photography are that it is not as discriminating as radar or electro-optics, cannot be processed until the aircraft lands, then takes several hours to process and requires expert interpretation. This is adequate against static targets, but even infantry units often move too quickly to use such data for targeting purposes.

104. These total launcher estimates are based on multiplying Soviet unit holdings by the number of units in country, adjusting them for a range of launchers where the USSR is known to have provided fewer launchers to export units. As is the case throughout this book, no reliable data are available on the actual launcher holdings and related electronic order of battle, although IISS counts of such weapons seem to be more accurate than the counts in other sources.

105. Unit strength estimates are the author's estimate based on IISS, *Military Balance, 1991–1992*, pp. 112–114. JCSS, *The Middle East Military Balance, 1989–1990*, pp. 276–280.

106. Libya first occupied the Aozou Strip in 1973, possibly because of its potential oil and uranium resources, although neither resource has ever been confirmed. The border is also very uncertain. The 1935 border negotiated between France and Libya seemed to grant the Aozou to Libya, but the treaty involved was never ratified by the French assembly. The 1955 border negotiated between France and the kingdom of Libya gave the area to France. There are no traditional tribal boundaries.

107. *Washington Post*, September 1, 1988.

108. *Washington Post*, April 18, 1992, p. A-25.

109. Andrew Rathmell, "Libya's Intelligence and Security Services," *International Defense Review*, 7/1991, pp. 695–697; *Washington Post*, February 27, 1992, p. A-32.

110. Many of the conclusions and facts in this section are based on working papers made available by Leonard Spector of the Carnegie Endowment.

111. Steve Weissman and Herbert Krosney, *The Islamic Bomb*, New York, Times Books, 1981, pp. 60 and 211–212; *Washington Star*, April 14, 1981.

112. The reactor is subject to IAEA inspection. Libya ratified the nonproliferation treaty (NPT) in 1975.

113. *Bulletin of the Atomic Scientists*, August-September, 1981, p. 14; *The Middle East*, February, 1982, p. 47; *New York Times*, March 23, 1976; *Washington Post*, December 12, 1977; *Nuclear Engineering International*, April, 1986, p. 6; *Nucleonics Week*, March 31, 1983, p. 11; September 27, 1984, p. 1.

114. Agence France Presse, February 10, 1992; BBC, February 4, 1992, ME 1295A1; *Washington Post*, February 4, 1992, p. A-11; AP AM cycle, January 25, 1992; Reuters, January 25, 1992, BC cycle.

115. Yoseff Bodansky and Vaughn Forrest, "Chemical Weapons in the Third World, Libya's Chemical-Biological Warfare Capabilities," Task Force on Terrorism and Unconventional Warfare, House Republican Research Committee, U.S. House of Representatives, Washington, D.C., June 12, 1990, p. 3; El-Hussini Mohrez, *Soviet Egyptian Relations*, New York, St. Martin's Press, 1987, p. 187.

116. *Time*, February 27, 1989; Yoseff Bodansky and Vaughn Forrest, "Chemical Weapons in the Third World, Libya's Chemical-Biological Warfare Capabilities," Task Force on Terrorism and Unconventional Warfare, House Republican Research Committee, U.S. House of Representatives, Washington, D.C., June 12, 1990, pp. 4 and 8.

117. *Washington Times*, January 20, 1989; *Al-Dustur*, December 25, 1988; *Ha'aretz*, December 27, 1988.

118. Yoseff Bodansky and Vaughn Forrest, "Chemical Weapons in the Third World, Libya's Chemical-Biological Warfare Capabilities," Task Force on Terrorism and Unconventional Warfare, House Republican Research Committee, U.S. House of Representatives, Washington, D.C., June 12, 1990, pp. 2–4; *Moscow News*, July 6, 1986; *Ha'aretz*, August 14, 1986; December 23, 1989; December 25, 1988.

119. *Focus on Libya*, DoD *Current News*, "Special Edition: Chemical Weapons," February,

1990, pp. 36–37; *London Sunday Times*, April 5, 1992, pp. 1 and 26.

120. Yoseff Bodansky and Vaughn Forrest, "Chemical Weapons in the Third World, Libya's Chemical-Biological Warfare Capabilities," Task Force on Terrorism and Unconventional Warfare, House Republican Research Committee, U.S. House of Representatives, Washington, D.C., June 12, 1990, pp. 4 and 5; *Ha'aretz*, December 27, 1988; *New York Times*, January 1, 1989; *Washington Times*, May 21, 1990.

121. *Wall Street Journal*, March 23, 1990, p. A-12.

122. *Washington Post*, December 19, 1988, p. A-1; January 4, 1989, p. 12; January 8, 1989, p. C-4; January 23, 1989, p. 12; January 19, 1989, p. A-1; January 24, 1989, p. 18; March 15, 1990, p. A-1; March 31, 1990, p. A-28; April 7, 1990, p. A-11; *New York Times*, January 4, 1989, p. 1; January 14, 1989, pp. 1 and 5; January 18, 1989, p. 7; March 31, 1990, p. A-3; *Wall Street Journal*, January 16, 1989, p. 5; January 17, 1989, p. 17; March 23, 1990, p. A-12; *Newsweek*, March 19, 1990, p. 33; March 26, 1990, p. 27.

123. Statement of the Director of Central Intelligence before the Senate Armed Services Committee, January 27, 1991, and testimony before Senator Glenn's Governmental Affairs Committee, January 15, 1992, p. 10. *Washington Post*, December 19, 1988, p. A-1; January 4, 1989, p. 12; January 8, 1989, p. C-4; January 23, 1989, p. 12; January 19, 1989, p. A-1; January 24, 1989, p. 18; March 8, 1990, p. A-26; *New York Times*, January 4, 1989, p. 1; January 14, 1989, pp. 1 and 5; January 18, 1989, p. 7; March 7, 1990, pp. A-1 and A-5; June 7, 1990, p. A-14; June 19, 1990, p. A-8; *Wall Street Journal*, January 16, 1989, p. 5; January 17, 1989, p. 17; *Washington Times*, May 21, 1990, p. A-3.

124. *Washington Times*, May 7, 1990, p. A-2; *New York Times*, January 22, 1992, p. A-1.

125. Statement of the Director of Central Intelligence before the Senate Armed Services Committee, January 27, 1991, and testimony before Senator Glenn's Governmental Affairs Committee, January 15, 1992.

126. *Washington Post*, March 16, 1990, pp. A-1 and A-38; March 31, 1990, p. A-28; April 7, 1990, p. A-11; May 3, 1990, pp. A-33 and A-36; June 19, 1990; *Christian Science Monitor*, March 16, 1990, p. 3; March 22, 1990, p. 20; *Washington Times*, May 21, 1990, p. A-3; June 18, 1990, p. 1; June 19, 1990, p. 3; July 12, 1990, p. 6; *Newsweek*, March 19, 1990, p. 33; March 26, 1990, p. 27; April 9, 1990, p. A-3; *Wall Street Journal*, March 8, 1990, p. A16; *New York Times*, March 31, 1990, p. 3; *Ha'aretz*, May 6, 1990; *Der Spiegel*, May 7, 1990; *Insight*, June 11, 1990; *Washington Post*, June 28, 1990, p. A-33.

127. There are reports that Libya used biological agents like the mycotoxins in Chad and even tested them against political prisoners. There are also claims that Libya received the necessary technology from the USSR, Cuba, and East Germany. These reports seem dubious, and many of the symptoms described are characteristic of poor medical discipline in the field and poor medical treatment of prisoners. *Washington Times*, January 20, 1989; R. Harris and J. Paxman, *A Higher Form of Killing*, New York, Hill and Wang, 1982, p. 220. Yoseff Bodansky and Vaughn Forrest, "Chemical Weapons in the Third World, Libya's Chemical-Biological Warfare Capabilities," Task Force on Terrorism and Unconventional Warfare, House Republican Research Committee, U.S. House of Representatives, Washington, D.C., June 12, 1990, p. 4 and 5.

128. Statement of the Director of Central Intelligence before the Senate Armed Services Committee, January 27, 1991, and testimony before Senator Glenn's Governmental Affairs Committee, January 15, 1992. *Washington Post*, December 19, 1988, p. A-1; January 4, 1989, p. 12; January 8, 1989, p. C-4; January 23, 1989, p. 12; January 19, 1989, p. A-1; January 24, 1989, p. 18; March 8, 1990, p. A-26; *New York Times*, January 4, 1989, p. 1; January 14, 1989, pp. 1 and 5; January 18, 1989, p. 7; March 7, 1990, pp. A-1 and A-5; June 7, 1990, p. A-14; *Wall Street Journal*, January 16, 1989, p. 5; January 17, 1989, p. 17; *Washington Times*, May 21, 1990, p. A-3.

129. Estimates based on the *IISS Military Balance, 1991–1992*; ACDA, *World Military Expenditures and Arms Transfers, 1988*, Washington, GPO, March, 1988, p. 22.

130. Lora Lumpe, Lisbeth Gronlund, and David C. Wright, "Third World Missiles Fall Short," *The Bulletin of the Atomic Scientists*, March, 1992, pp. 30–36.

131. ACDA, *World Military Expenditures and Arms Transfers, 1988*, Washington, GPO, March, 1988, p. 18; *Washington Times*, October 9, 1989, p. A-2; ABC Network News, April 28, 1988; *Stern*, No. 1/1987; *Bulletin of Atomic Scientists*, June, 1988, p. 15; Shuey, Lenhart, Snyder, Donnelly, Mielke, and Moteff, *Missile Proliferation: Survey of Emerging Missile Forces*, Washington, D.C., Congressional Research Service, Report 88-642F, February 9, 1989, pp. 61–63; Fred Donovan, "Mideast Missile Flexing," *Arms Control Today*, May, 1990, p. 31; Duncan Lennox, "The Global Proliferation of Ballistic Missiles," *Jane's Defence Weekly*, December 25, 1989, pp. 1384–1385; Lora Lumpe, Lisbeth Gronlund, and David C. Wright, "Third World Missiles Fall Short," *The Bulletin of the Atomic Scientists*, March, 1992, pp. 30–36.

132. *Flight International*, May 23–29, 1990, p. 18.

133. Sources include working material provided by Leonard Specter of the Carnegie Endowment; discussions with reporter from an independent British television network; *Jane's Defence Weekly*, December 23, 1989, pp. 1384–1385; *Washington Post*, January 28, 1988; *New York Times*, March 13, 1981; *Aviation Week and Space Technology*, April 10, 1989, pp. 19–20; *Christian Science Monitor*, July 3, 1990, p. 19; *Washington Times*, July 18, 1989, p. A-1.

134. The military manpower, force strength, and equipment estimates in this section are made by the author using a wide range of sources, including computerized data bases, interviews, and press clipping services. Most are impossible to reference in ways of use to the reader. The force strength statistics are generally taken from the latest edition of the International Institute for Strategic Studies *Military Balance* (IISS, London), in this case the 1991–1992 edition. Extensive use has also been made of the annual editions of the Jaffee Center for Strategic Studies, *The Military Balance in the Middle East* (JCSS, Tel Aviv), especially the 1990–1991 edition and working materials from the coming edition. Material has also been drawn from computer print outs from NEXIS, the United States Naval Institute data base, and from the DMS/FI Market Intelligence Reports data base. Other sources include the *Military Technology* "World Defense Almanac for 1991–1992," published in 1992; country reports of the Economist Intelligence Unit (EIU); Foreign Affairs Division, "Middle East Arms Control and Related Issues," Washington, Congressional Research Service, 91-384F, May 1, 1991; and *Middle East Economic Digest*, "MEED Special Report: Defense," Volume 35, December 13, 1991.

Weapons data are taken from many sources, including computerized material available in NEXIS, and various editions of *Jane's Fighting Ships* (Jane's Publishing); *Jane's Naval Weapons Systems* (Jane's Publishing); *Jane's Armour and Artillery* (Jane's Publishing); *Jane's Infantry Weapons* (Jane's Publishing); *Jane's Military Vehicles and Logistics* (Jane's Publishing); *Jane's Land-Based Air Defence* (Jane's Publishing); *Jane's All the World's Aircraft* (Jane's Publishing); *Jane's Battlefield Surveillance Systems* (Jane's Publishing); *Jane's Radar and Electronic Warfare Systems* (Jane's Publishing), *Jane's C^{3}I Systems* (Jane's Publishing); *Jane's Air-Launched Weapons Systems* (Jane's Publishing); *Jane's Defence Appointments & Procurement Handbook (Middle East Edition)* (Jane's Publishing); *Tanks of the World* (Bernard and Grafe); *Weyer's Warships* (Bernard and Grafe); and *Warplanes of the World* (Bernard and Grafe).

Other military background, effectiveness, strength, organizational, and history data are taken from the relevant country or war sections of Herbert K. Tillema, *International Conflict Since 1945*, Boulder, Westview, 1991; Anthony H. Cordesman, "The Military Forces of the Maghrib," *RUSI and Brassey's Defense Yearbook*, London, Brassey's, 1986; Department of Defense and Department of State, *Congressional Presentation for Security Assistance Programs, Fiscal Year 1993*, Washington, Department of State, 1992; Canadian Director, General Intelligence, *Recognition Handbook—Western Sahara Region*, CIS/2600.0000W7-F/WI/01/91/16353, Ottawa, July 29, 1991; various annual editions of John Laffin's *The World in Conflict* or *War Annual*, London, Brassey's; and John Keegan, *World Armies*, London, Macmillan, 1983.

135. *OJJ Special, Oil and Gas Journal*, December 30, 1991, pp. 43–49. Other estimates indicate

that it has 1.7 billion barrels of proven reserves and 4 billion barrels of probable reserves. See Joseph P. Riva, Jr., of the Congressional Research Service, writing in the *Oil and Gas Journal*, September 23, 1991, p. 62.

136. *Washington Post,* January 11, 1992, p. A-14; *New York Times,* January 20, 1992; *Economist,* May 18, 1991, pp. 47–48; *The Middle East,* September, 1991, p. 18; *Washington Times,* May 4, 1992, p. A-1, July 10, 1992, p. A-2.

137. *IMF Survey,* June 18, 1990, p. 178; August 12, 1992, pp. 242–244.

138. CIA, *World Factbook, 1991,* pp. 313–315.

139. Arms Control and Disarmament Agency (ACDA), *World Military Expenditures and Arms Transfers, 1990,* Washington, GPO, 1990, Table I.

140. IISS, *Military Balance,* 1989–1990 and 1991–1992 country sections on Tunisia.

141. The manpower data are drawn from Arms Control and Disarmament Agency (ACDA), *World Military Expenditures and Arms Transfers, 1990,* Washington, GPO, 1992, Table II. The judgments on equipment strength are based on the trends revealed in the tables on Tunisia in the country sections of the annual editions of the IISS, *Military Balance.*

142. Arms Control and Disarmament Agency (ACDA), *World Military Expenditures and Arms Transfers, 1989,* Washington, GPO, 1990, Table II.

143. Arms Control and Disarmament Agency (ACDA), *World Military Expenditures and Arms Transfers, 1985,* Washington, GPO, 1985, pp. 133–134.

144. Arms Control and Disarmament Agency (ACDA), *World Military Expenditures and Arms Transfers, 1990,* Washington, GPO, 1990, pp. 133–134.

145. Adapted from various issues of the IISS, *Military Balance,* and work by the Foreign Affairs Division of the Congressional Research Service in *Middle East Arms Control and Related Issues,* CRS 91-384F, May 1, 1992, and for Senator John McCain. Robert Shuey, Richard F. Grimmett, Theodor Galdi, Steven Hildreth, Todd Masses, Alfred Prados, and Shirley Kahn were the principal authors of the CRS work.

146. CIA, *World Factbook, 1991,* pp. 313–315.

147. Based on the country sections in the IISS, *Military Balance, 1991–1992,* p. 121; and the country section in CIA, *World Factbook, 1991.*

5

Trends in the Military Balance and Arms Sales in the Arab-Israeli Confrontation States

The myth of the frog and the scorpion has been applied to many parts of the world and to many parts of the Middle East. There is no aspect of the military balance to which it is more appropriate than the Arab-Israeli confrontation states. The arms race between Israel and its Arab neighbors is still the best known arms race in the Middle East—overshadowing the arms races in the Gulf, North Africa, and the Horn. It is also the most intense arms race in terms of the absorption of new weapons and technologies and one that tends to set precedents for the rest of the Third World. India and Pakistan may lead the Third World in terms of a nuclear arms race, and Iran and Iraq may lead in terms of chemical weapons and missiles, but it is the Arab-Israeli arms race that sets the pace for armor, air combat, and a host of other technologies.

The Arab-Israeli arms race has also changed radically with time. In the period between the formation of modern Palestine and the UN partition of Palestine on November 29, 1947, it was largely an internal struggle between the Jewish and Arab residents of Palestine. On May 14, 1948, however, Israel declared statehood, and on May 15, 1948, the Arab residents of Palestine and the Arab nations surrounding it declared war on the Jews. By the time the war ended, thousands of Arab Palestinians had fled to other countries, Israel controlled some 8,000 square miles of Palestine, and the remaining Arabs occupied some 2,000 square miles controlled by Jordan.

From 1948 to 1967, the Arab-Israeli arms race was between Israel and Egypt, Syria, and Jordan, and the main stake was Israel's survival. Israel's sweeping military victory in June, 1967 reversed this situation after roughly a week of combat. The June War gave Israel control over Jerusalem and the rest of Palestine, the Gaza and Sinai in Egypt, and the Golan Heights in Syria. It effectively converted Jordan to the status of a defensive military power. At the same time it laid the groundwork for the rise of the Palestine Liberation Organization.

In the six years that followed, Jordan increasingly stood aside from the

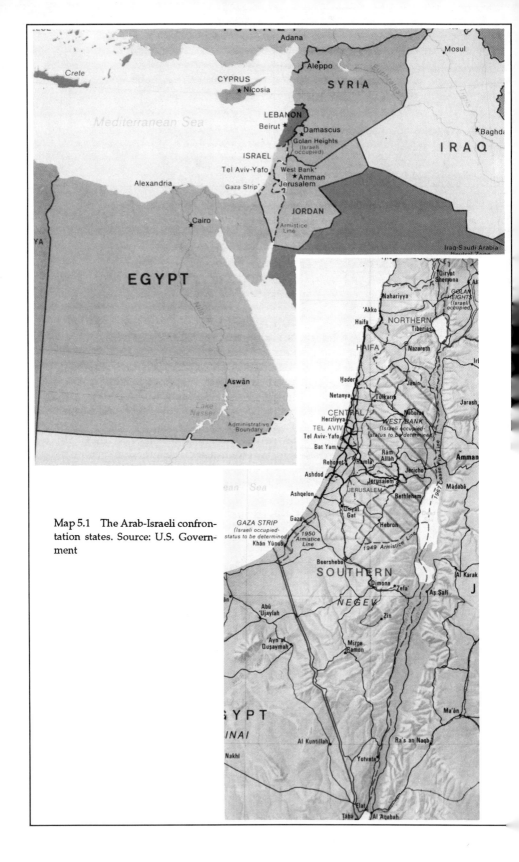

Map 5.1   The Arab-Israeli confrontation states. Source: U.S. Government

Arab-Israeli arms race and was threatened as much by the PLO and Syria as it was by Israel. In 1969–1970, Jordan was forced to fight both the PLO and Syria to retain its independence. Egypt and Syria rebuilt their military forces and virtually doubled their strength. Israel expanded its forces as well but failed to recognize Egypt and Syria's willingness to go on the offensive. The end result was that in October, 1973, Egypt and Syria were able to launch a surprise attack on Israel which briefly threatened Israel's control of the Sinai and the Golan and even the security of northern Israel. The 1973 war ended in a major Israeli military victory, but it still gave Egypt sufficient status to seek a separate peace settlement with Israel. As a result, in 1978 Egypt traded the return of all captured Egyptian territory for peace.

The Camp David accords transformed Syria from Egypt's partner in the arms race to a nation that had to struggle alone for military parity with Israel. Jordan could not afford to compete with Israel and Syria in terms of weapons numbers and military technology and became steadily more defensive. At the same time, long standing rivalries increased between Christians and Muslims in Lebanon, and the PLO created a virtual mini-state inside the country. Lebanon collapsed into civil war, and the PLO built up significant forces in Beirut, along the Lebanese coast, and in southern Lebanon along the border with Israel.

By the early 1980s, the growth of PLO military forces in southern Lebanon had led to a growing number of clashes between the PLO forces and Israel. The civil war in Lebanon created a power vacuum that led Israel and Syria to create their own security zones inside Lebanon and occasionally to use it as a killing ground to settle their rivalries. This convinced Ariel Sharon and several other Israeli leaders that Israel could create a stable and friendly Lebanon, and deal Syria and the PLO a devastating blow, by attacking Syrian and PLO forces in Lebanon and placing Lebanon under the control of a Maronite Christian government.

The result was a new Israeli-Syrian conflict which took place in 1982. Israel achieved a notable string of military victories, pushed the PLO forces out of Lebanon, and defeated Syria's air force, ground based air defenses, and ground forces in Lebanon. Israel could not, however, transform these tactical victories into any credible hope of creating a stable or friendly Lebanon or the kind of defeat of Syria that would force it to halt its search for parity. Israel thus achieved a military victory but suffered a strategic defeat.

Since 1982, Israel and Syria have continued their conventional arms race, although both have placed increasing emphasis on force quality relative to force quantity. This has strained their economies to the breaking point without materially changing the military balance. Both Israel and Syria seem to have exceeded the practical limits of the force structure they can properly man, modernize, and sustain. In the case of Israel, the arms race has made the country increasingly dependent on U.S. aid and forced it into compromises in military modernization which have limited the effectiveness of some elements of its forces. In the case of Syria, it has created a force structure much larger than Syria can effectively man, train, modernize, and supply. Both Israel and Syria, however, have also built up strong missile delivery capabilities, with Israel focusing on nuclear weapons and Syria on chemical and biological weapons.

The arms race between Syria and Israel has had broader regional impacts. It has forced Jordan into a defensive arms race that it cannot afford. It has left Lebanon divided between Syrian and Israeli zones of influence. While Egypt has remained at peace, the Syrian-Israeli arms race, tensions with Libya, and the Iran-Iraq War have pushed it into maintaining far larger military forces than it can really afford.

All four of the major participants in the original Arab-Israel arms race— Egypt, Israel, Jordan, and Syria—are now trying to maintain levels of military effort that seriously threaten their economies, their long term ability to maintain living standards in the face of population growth and/or social change, and at least some aspects of their political stability. In each case, the sheer scale of military effort is becoming almost as much of a threat to the nation as a means of protection. The PLO began to rebuild some of the elements of military power in Lebanon it had lost during the 1982 fighting, but it lost most of its new capabilities when Syria backed the Lebanese army in regaining control over most of the country in 1991. At the same time, the Palestinian uprising, or *intifada,* that began in the Gaza and West Bank in 1987 has created a major new internal security threat to the occupying Israeli forces and may yet create a Palestinian movement independent of the present leadership of the PLO.

The Historical Trends in Military Forces

Table 5.1 shows the statistical trends in the military buildup in the region. While this table is complex and some of the dynamics involved will be clear only to regional experts and military historians, it does obviously show that a steady buildup in force strength has taken place over more than half a century. Although this increase in force numbers has been limited during the last decade by the search for force quality, it is clear that quantitative build-ups have scarcely ceased.

At the same time, it is important to note that while the Syrian-Israeli balance is now the focus of any Arab-Israeli comparisons, there is no single or stable way to define the Arab-Israeli balance. Force totals are not a measure of probable war fighting forces. The Arab nations that have actually committed their forces to past wars have shifted according to the conflict, and many conflicts—such as the 1982 war—involved only a limited portion of the total forces of the nations engaged.

Table 5.1 must also be analyzed with the understanding that a fundamental shift occurred in the regional balance after the Camp David accords. The Egyptian-Israeli peace treaty effectively took Egypt out of the Arab-Israeli balance, and the arms race in this sub-region has since been driven largely by Syria and Israel. This shift has essentially eliminated the risk of a catastrophic conventional war, since no credible combination of other Arab states can hope to threaten Israel directly—particularly after Iraq's shattering defeat in the Gulf War.

Ironically, much of this security is dependent on U.S. military and economic aid to Egypt. Egyptian political and economic stability would degenerate sharply, if not collapse, without such aid. As a result, one portion of the arms transfers to the region is essential to its security. It is also important to note that the arms transfer data for Israel shown earlier sharply understate the true scale of Israel's arms imports because they do not include many of the sub-systems Israel buys for its growing arms industry. In fact, Israel imported well over $1 billion worth of military equipment per year from the U.S. during the 1980s.

More broadly, comparisons of total forces of the kind shown in Table 5.1 can be very misleading. None of the nations shown in the table can commit and sustain all their forces in war, and many would commit only a limited portion of their more capable and elite forces. It is also impossible to predict what Arab countries should be included in the Arab side of the balance with any certainty, or which elements of Arab and Israeli forces would become involved in a given contingency. There is no one or "right" Arab-Israeli balance. There are many possible balances, and any realistic assessment of war fighting capability, arms transfers, or the prospects for arms control must be founded on this fact.

The shifts in the military balance since the 1982 war are particularly important in revealing the current nature of the Arab-Israeli arms race. The Israeli-Syrian struggle—with Israel seeking to preserve its edge and Syria trying to achieve "parity"—has come to dominate the military balance in the sub-region. Egypt's firm commitment to peace and Jordan's focus on defense have not eliminated the broader Arab threat to Israel, but they have changed its character significantly. These changes are reflected in Table 5.2.

The Economic, Demographic, and Military Forces Affecting the Arab-Israeli Balance

The economic, arms import, demographic, and weapons data which currently affect Israel and the Arab states around it are summarized in Table 5.3. The trends in this table reflect several key patterns:

- Israel is able to make far more efficient use of its military expenditures and manpower than its Arab neighbors. This superiority has several causes. Israel has long had a superior technology base and finds it far easier to transfer advanced technologies into its military forces. It has developed relatively efficient defense industries and needs to import only major weapons systems and parts rather than most of its weapons systems and substantial support services. Israel's military forces are largely apolitical and can be efficiently structured. Israel relies heavily on mass mobilization to supplement its active forces (Israel has active military forces of roughly 141,000 uniformed personnel, but it can mobilize up to 504,000 additional reserves within 48 to 72 hours. It uses the savings in manpower to fund readiness and equipment).[1] Israel not only has long had access to U.S. military technology and equipment, it has received billions of dollars in

TABLE 5.1 Combat Forces Engaged in Arab-Israeli Wars, 1948–1991

Country	Manpower Total	Army	Tanks	OAVs	Artillery	Combat Aircraft
1948 (war to establish Israel; peak level of total forces)						
Egypt	55,000	20,000	80–135	80–139	60–90	30–35
Syria	8,000	5,000	20–30	20–30	30–40	?
Jordan	10,000	6,000	—	6–12	10–20	—
Lebanon	3,500	2,000	12–18	10–20	10–15	—
Iraq and others	18,000	12,000	12	30	30	—
Total Arab	94,500	45,000	124–206	146–231	140–195	?
Israel	45,000–70,000	34,400	40–55	155–220	60–90	40
1956 (Suez invasion: Israel invades Sinai; Egypt is only Arab force engaged. Total forces shown)						
Egypt	150,000	88,000	430–530	315–400	275–500	275–340
Israel	100,000	60,000	305–360	245–450	78–150	150–155
Britain	13,500	—	—	—	—	70
France	8,500	—	—	—	—	45
(Jordan	14,000	—	40	190	60–90	20)
(Syria	45,000	35,000	90	110	120	80)
(Iraq	63,000	55,000	200	250	180	65–90)
1967 (Six-Days' War; all Arab forces shown, except Lebanon, engaged. Total mobilized forces shown)						
Egypt	211,000	160,000	630–890	950–1,250	575–750	400–431
Syria	65,000	55,000	400–500	400–585	270–315	78–127
Jordan	55,000	48,000	200–288	210	263	18–28
Other Arab	8,000	5,000	—	—	—	45
Total Arab	339,000	268,000	1,230–1,678	1560–2,045	1108–1328	541–631
Israel	275,000	265,000	900–1,050	1,000–1,500	160–200	286–290
(Lebanon	11,000	10,000	45	80	70–90	8)
(Iraqi total	82,000	70,000	400–535	200–250	180–250	215)
1970 (canal war; only Israel and Egypt directly engaged. Total active forces shown)						
Syria	86,570	75,000	980	700	400	210
Jordan	60,250	58,000	310	630	110	38
Lebanon	16,250	15,000	80	200	40	24
Iraq	94,500	85,000	645	400	250–300	229
Egypt	288,000	250,000	1,240	1,220	1,040	415
Israel	75,000	61,500	1,050	1,515	370	330
1973 (Yom Kippur/Ramadan War)						
Egypt	—	315,000	2,200	2,400	1,280	598
Syria	—	140,000	1,820	1,300	675	275
Jordan (committed)	—	5,000	150	200	36	—
Iraq (committed)	—	20,000	300	300	54	73
Total Arab committed	—	480,000	4,470	4,200	2,045	946
Other Arab (many did not deploy)	—	25,000	371	120	100	92
Total Arab	—	505,000	4,841	4,320	2,145	1,038
Israel	—	310,000	2,000	4,000	570	360

(continues)

TABLE 5.1 *(continued)*

| Country | Manpower | | Tanks | OAVs | Artillery | Combat Aircraft |
	Total	Army				
1982 (only Syria, PLO, and Israel at war.)						
Forces Engaged						
Syria	22,000	22,000	352	300	300	450
PLO	15,000	15,000	300	150	350	—
Israel	76,000	76,000	800	1,500	220	634
Total Forces						
Egypt	452,000	320,000	2,100	3,330	1,812	429
Jordan	72,800	65,000	579	1,022	225	94
Lebanon	23,750	22,250	13	232	46	8
Iraq	342,250	300,000	2,300	3,100	800	330
Syria	222,500	170,000	3,200	3,990	2,660	450
Israel	174,000	135,000	3,600	4,000	758–850	634
1988 (last year of Iran-Iraq War; current force totals shown)						
Egypt	445,000	320,000	2,425	3,695	1,560	441
Jordan	82,250	74,000	979	1,340	248	114
Lebanon	16,300	15,000	90	430	69	5
Iraq	1,000,000	955,000	5,500	4,500	2,800	800
Syria	404,000	300,000	4,050	4,150	2,450	448
Israel	141,000	104,000	3,850	6,300	1,361	577
1991 (in summer, after Iraq's defeat by UN coalition—no war; current force totals shown)						
Egypt	420,000	290,000	3,190	3,640	1,458	495
Jordan	101,300	90,000	1,131	1,434	462	113
Lebanon	18,800	17,500	245	342	97	3
Iraq	650,000	350,000	2,000–2,300	3,000–3,500	1,000–1,300	330–360
Syria	404,000	300,000	4,350	4,250	2,466	651
Israel	141,000	104,000	4,488	6,300	1,420	591

Note: Totals vary sharply because of estimates of active versus total force strength and conflicting sources, and because wartime estimates do not track with the end-of-year data used in other tables. Estimates for 1948 and 1956 are particularly uncertain and include large numbers of conversions and semi-operable equipment. Israeli forces had virtually no heavy equipment and aircraft at the start of the 1948 war, and equipment counts include deliveries—some of which proved inoperable and most of which trickled in after the conflict began. Tank counts for 1948 and 1956 include light tanks. These are counted as other armored vehicles in later years. The reader should be aware that the lower range of equipment estimates are generally more correct. The figures shown in this table are often lower than those used in other sources because they add in postwar deliveries or used the end-of-year strength.

Sources: Adapted by the author from Anthony H. Cordesman and Abraham K. Wagner, *The Lessons of Modern War*, Volume 1, Boulder, Westview, 1990; Trevor Dupuy, *Elusive Victory*, New York, Harper and Row, 1978; Nadav Safran, *From War to War*, New York, Pegasus, 1969; Chaim Herzog, *The Arab-Israeli Wars*, New York, Random House, 1982; and various annual editions of the International Institute for Strategic Studies, *Military Balance*; Arms Control and Disarmament Agency, *World Military Expenditures and Arms Transfers*; and the Jaffee Center for Strategic Studies, *Middle East Military Balance*.

TABLE 5.2 The Evolution of Arab and Israeli Forces, 1982–1991

	Israel		Syria		Jordan		Egypt	
	1982	1991	1982	1991	1982	1991	1982	1991
Total								
Defense spending ($ billions)	6.1	6.5	2.4	1.92	0.4	0.6	2.1	1.7
Manpower (1,000s)								
Active	174.0	141.0	222.5	404.0	72.8	101.3	452.0	420.0
Conscript	120.3	110.0	120.0	180.0	—	—	255.0	252.0
Mobilizable	500.0	504.0	345.0	404.0	35.0	35.0	787.0	604.0
Army								
Manpower (1,000s)								
Active	135.0	104.0	170.0	300.0	65.0	90.0	320.0	290.0
Conscript	110.0	88.0	120.0	130.0	—	—	180.0	180.0
Mobilizable	450.0	494.0	270.0	392.0	—	30.0	620.0	500.0
Main battle tanks	3,600	4,488	3,990	4,350	569	1,131	2,100	3,190
OAFVs	8,000	6,500	1,600	4,250	1,022	1,334	3,030	3,660
Artillery/MRLs	960	1,620	2,100	2,466	274	462	2,000	1,458
Air Force and Air Defense Forces								
Manpower (1,000s)								
Active	30.0	28.0	50.0	100.0	7.5	11.0	113.0	120.0
Conscript	7.0	19.0	—	—	—	—	60.0	60.0
Mobilizable	35.0	37.0	—	—	—	—	133.0	90.0
Total combat								
Aircraft	634	577	450	651	94	113	429	495
Bombers	0	0	0	0	0	0	14	0
Attack/intelligence	432	403	0	172	0	62	0	123
Attack	174	121	205	0	29	0	218	0
Interceptors	28	0	244	312	45	32	152	272
Recce/EWs	28	24	0	16	0	0	45	35
OCU/Armed trainers	—	48	—	161	—	19	—	48
Armed helicopters	42	80	16	100	0	24	24	74
Major SAM bns/Bty/Sites	15	15	75	95	5	23	151	196
Navy								
Active manpower	9.0	9.0	2.5	4.0	0.3	0.3	20.0	20.0
Conscript	3.3	3.0	—	—	—	—	15.0	12.0
Mobilizable	1.0	1.0	5.0	8.0	—	—	15.0	14.0
Submarines	3	3	0	3	0	0	12	5
Guided missiles	27	20	18	16	0	0	19	21
Destroyer/Escort/ Frigate/Corvette	2	2	2	2	0	0	8	5
Small combat	44	43	12	18	9	1	56	30
Amphibious and support	7	9	?	3	0	0	20	24

Note: These figures do not show equipment in storage, use estimates which often do not reflect actual readiness of manpower and equipment, and use dated material. For example, the IISS data for Israel reflect virtually no updating between 1982 and 1986 and grossly exaggerate the size of Egypt's operational forces and equipment holdings in both 1982 and 1991. In fact, virtually no Soviet-supplied equipment in Egyptian forces is fully combat operational, and the effective strength of Egyptian forces is less than one-third the totals shown. These figures are deliberately presented as a contrast to the trend curves shown earlier, which reflect more substantial adjustments by the author. The IISS data for aircraft are also sometimes not comparable from year to year, and the data for 1991 seem to have been adjusted to delete equipment in storage. This sometimes leads to a lack of direct comparability with the data for 1982.

SOURCE: Adapted from various editions of IISS, *Military Balance*, and JCSS, *Middle East Military Balance*.

loans and grants. Unlike the U.S. aid to Arab states, U.S. aid to Israel has been consistent and predictable.

- Syria's search for parity with Israel has been partially successful in quantitative terms but has been crippled by several factors. Syria must rely largely on active forces and lacks the cadres of trained manpower necessary to cope with the rapid expansion of its forces. Syria has been heavily dependent on the Soviet bloc for arms, has received relatively poor technical advice and support, and has often received low grade export versions of Soviet equipment which are inherently inferior to the U.S. equipment used by Israeli forces. The Syrian air force still consists largely of relatively low grade export versions of Soviet fighters and fighter bombers, although Syria does have some MiG-29s and may soon acquire Su-24s. Syria's armed forces are highly politicized, and the priority given to internal security measures and loyalty to the regime has interfered with the growth of their military effectiveness. Syria's military finances have depended heavily on Saudi, Kuwaiti, and other external Arab aid, and the flow and size of this aid has been far more erratic than the promises of donor states have implied.
- Egypt still sizes its forces in ways that reflect the absence of a general Arab-Israeli peace settlement and also maintains oversized military forces to avoid political controversy over cutbacks in its armed forces and to help deal with its massive employment problems. Egypt maintains regular active armed forces of over 400,000 men, has nearly 380,000 more men in paramilitary forces, and has a reserve structure of over 600,000 men. Even if one counts only active and reserve regular manpower, this would still produce nearly twice the force structure Egypt can afford to equip effectively, in part because massive U.S. aid is offset by Egypt's need to phase out aging Soviet equipment. Maintaining its force structure is also so costly that Egypt cannot afford to replace and modernize bases and infrastructure that are often obsolete, inefficient, badly deployed, and unsuited to high technology forces.
- Jordan has suffered badly from a lack of funds and access to modern Western arms. Like Syria, it has often been promised far more Arab aid than it has actually received. While its forces remain professional, it has not been able to get many of the arms it has sought from the U.S. because of U.S. ties to Israel and Jordanian support of Iraq during the Gulf War. Its active force structure and reserves have been kept limited in size both to preserve their professionalism and to ensure they have a recruiting and manpower base that will help maintain loyalty to the regime.
- Lebanon's forces are almost impossible to count accurately. Lebanon has not had national armed forces since full scale civil war began in the mid-1970s. Its regular forces had effective training and financing during the brief period of U.S. intervention following Israel's 1982 invasion of Lebanon, and then divided into ethnic factions. The new government forces created by Syria's overthrow of the Aoun regime in 1990 are undertrained and underequipped and are largely defensive infantry and internal security forces. The navy and air force are divided into ethnic factions, lack modern equipment, and have merely token operational strength. Although the

TABLE 5.3 The Economic, Demographic, and Military Forces Affecting the Arab-Israeli Balance

Trends in Military Expenditure (in $ Current Millions)

	1979	1980	1981	1982	1983	1984	1985	1986	1987	1988	1989	1990	1991
Israel	5734	6654	6160	6026	6924	7869	7027	6431	5829	5585	5745	6160	6800
Syria	1463	1936	1959	2289	3340	3462	3627	2911	1801	1801	2234	2620	2800
Jordan	417	421	445	485	544	555	602	633	666	640	548	571	587
Lebanon	331	380	345	320	459	432	430	400	370	300	160	140	200
Total	7945	9391	8909	9120	11267	12318	11686	10375	8666	8326	8687	9491	10387

Trends in Arms Imports (in $ Current Millions)

	1972	1974	1976	1978	1980	1982	1984	1986	1988	1990	1992	1994
Israel	300	950	975	900	800	925	775	470	1900	1400	1550	1600
Syria	280	825	625	1200	3200	2600	2200	1200	1300	1800	1500	1500
Jordan	30	70	140	170	260	1100	230	260	320	450	450	460
Lebanon	20	10	10	20	40	50	240	10	10	20	20	30
Total	630	1855	1750	2290	4300	4675	3445	1940	3530	3670	3520	3590

Arms Imports By Supplier During 1985–1989 (in $ Current Millions)

	Total	USSR	U.S.	France	UK	PRC	FRG	Other Warsaw Pact	Other Europe	Middle East	Other East Asia	Latin America	Others
Israel	6100	0	6100	0	0	0	0	0	0	0	0	0	0
Syria	7160	6100	0	20	0	10	0	975	30	20	5	0	0
Jordan	2070	1200	460	110	40	0	10	60	100	50	0	20	20
Lebanon	70	0	70	0	0	0	0	0	0	0	5	0	0
Total	15400	7300	6630	130	40	10	10	1035	130	70	5	20	20

Trends in Military Manpower

	1967	1973	1975	1977	1979	1981	1983	1985	1987	1989	1991
Israel	75	130	172	179	181	201	205	195	180	191	141
Syria	80	115	230	250	220	270	400	402	400	400	404
Jordan	60	70	60	70	67	66	72	81	100	100	101
Lebanon	19	20	24	9	18	20	20	21	37	37	18
Total	234	335	486	508	486	557	697	699	717	728	664

Trends in Military Equipment

Main Battle Tanks

	1973	1979	1982	1984	1988	1990	1992
Jordan	420	500	569	750	1131	1131	1130
Israel	1700	3050	3600	3600	3794	4288	4490
Lebanon	60	0	0	142	105	200	250
Syria	1170	2600	3990	4100	4050	4000	4350
Total	3350	6150	8159	8592	9080	9619	10220

Combat Aircraft

	1973	1979	1982	1984	1988	1990	1992
Jordan	52	73	94	103	111	104	110
Israel	488	576	634	555	676	553	575
Lebanon	18	16	8	3	6	3	3
Syria	326	389	450	503	499	558	650
Total	884	1054	1186	1164	1292	1218	1338

SOURCE: Estimated by the author using various editions of IISS, Military Balance, and ACDA, World Military Expenditures and Arms Transfers.

bulk of the military forces of ethnic and religious groups have been disarmed, they remain a significant military element, and major problems continue to exist in the south. There is still an Israeli-supported enclave in the border area, and the Shi'ite Hizbollah, more secular Shi'ite Amal, and PLO forces continue to threaten Israel.

Table 5.3 does not show the potential reinforcements that could be provided by other Arab forces. By and large, such reinforcements seem to have only marginal military and political credibility. It is, however, impossible to dismiss the fact that Arab forces outside the region are improving in military capability. Iraq, for example, still retains significant forces in spite of its defeat in the Gulf War. Libya is beginning to acquire weapons of mass destruction and long range strike systems and illustrates the growing long term risk posed both by strike fighters and missiles that can reach Israel from a wide range of Arab states as well as by the growing number of Arab states that are becoming involved in efforts to develop and/or stockpile nuclear, chemical, and biological weapons.

Israel

	Manpower (1,000s)	Tanks	Aircraft	Defense Spending ($ millions)	Arms Imports ($ millions)	Arms Exports ($ millions)
1967	75	900	290	644	23	1
1973	130	1,700	488	3,740	1,710	22
1982	205	3,600	634	6,329	925	390
1988	191	3,794	676	6,001	1,900	140
1991	141	3,190	575	6,160	—	—

Israel is a unique Middle Eastern power in many ways. It has few natural resources and estimated reserves of only 1.289 million barrels of oil and 10 billion cubic feet of gas.[2] It has about 1.9 cubic kilometers of internal renewable water resources, which amounts to only about 447 cubic meters per person, or roughly one-fifth of the annual total for a citizen of the U.S.[3] Yet Israel is by far the most sophisticated Middle Eastern state in terms of technology and the ability to organize, command, train, and support military forces. It relies on mobilization rather than a standing army. Its air force plays a role of equal importance to its army. It has stressed quality over quantity since the period between the 1956 and 1967 wars, and it has selectively reduced its forces to improve its overall military effectiveness. Finally, Israel is the Middle East's only nuclear power.

At the same time, Israel is the most threatened state in the Middle East in spite of these strengths. It is the only nation in the Middle East whose very existence is threatened by its neighbors. It is dependent on the U.S. for the external aid necessary to maintain its military capabilities and sustain its economy. There are sharp demographic and territorial limits on its ability to expand its forces, and it lacks air space and strategic depth. Israel cannot easily retain its social and political viability and take high casualties. Like many Middle Eastern countries, it is also dependent on the survival of a few key urban areas and is highly vulnerable to the successful use of a weapon of mass destruction.

If one excludes the occupied territories, Israel has a total area of only about 20,770 square kilometers. This is slightly larger than the state of New Jersey. While Israel shares a comparatively secure 255 kilometer border with Egypt, its boundaries with Jordan are 238 kilometers, 79 kilometers with Syria, and 79 kilometers with Lebanon. It has a 307 kilometer border with the West Bank and a 51 kilometer border with the Gaza. Its coastline is 273 kilometers long. The occupied territory in the Gaza Strip adds another 380 square kilometers with a 40 kilometer coastline and an 11 kilometer border with Egypt. The West Bank has 5,680 square kilometers, roughly the area of Delaware. It has a 97 kilometer boundary with Jordan.[4]

A Continuous State of War

Israel has been in a constant state of war throughout its history, not only as a nation but during much of the period that shaped its emergence as a state.[5] The key Arab-Israeli conflicts are an all too familiar part of the history of the Middle East, and nothing approaching a stable peace has existed between major conflicts.

Jewish conflict with the Arabs began in the 1880s and first became serious shortly after the second major wave of Jewish settlers arrived in Palestine in 1919. World War I laid the basis for institutionalizing the Arab-Israeli conflict. Britain entered into three contradictory commitments, promising the Middle East to three different owners. During 1915–1916, the Hussein-McMahon correspondence promised the Arabs independence. During 1917, Balfour promised the Jews a homeland in Palestine. At the same time, the Sykes-Picot agreement promised the partition of the Middle East into French and British zones of influence.

The Treaty of Versailles and the League of Nations made this situation worse. The unequal peace between the Allies and Germany indirectly laid the groundwork for political turmoil in Germany and the rise of Hitler. The mandate for Palestine that the League of Nations awarded Britain in 1922 was followed by the partition of the region along the Dead Sea–Jordan River–Wadi Arabah line. This created Transjordan to the east of the line and a mixed Jewish-Arab Palestine to the west of the line. While Arab resentment initially focused on Britain and France, ongoing Jewish immigration helped lead to serious fighting and riots in 1929. When another major wave of Jewish settlers escaped Nazi persecution during the 1930s, riots turned into what came to be called the Arab revolt. A de facto state of war between Jew and Arab began in 1936 and has never ended.

These early struggles helped trigger the formation of Jewish military and militia groups like the Hashomer, Jewish Settlement Police, Fosh, the Haganah and the Irgun Zvai Leumi, and Palmach. Jewish cooperation with British forces during World War II also created a cadre of trained Jewish troops and a Jewish brigade with real military experience. In contrast, the Arab residents of Palestine tended to remain unorganized and to rely on help from Arab states like Egypt, Lebanon, Syria, and Transjordan.

When Britain surrendered its mandate over Palestine after World War II, it turned the Arab-Israeli problem over to the new United Nations. On November 29, 1947, the United Nations voted to "recommend" the partition of Palestine into three different entities: an international zone in Jerusalem with 100,000 Jews and 105,000 Arabs, a 5,500 square mile Jewish state with about 498,000 Jews and 497,000 Arabs, and a 4,500 square mile Arab state with 10,000 Jews and 725,000 Arabs.

The Zionist movement accepted the UN recommendation and declared its independence on May 14, 1948. The Arabs did not and declared war on May 15, 1948—the day Britain began its withdrawal from Palestine. The fighting for Israel's independence, however, had actually begun in November, 1947, during the UN debate over the partition of Palestine. It lasted until 1949 and was the most bitter of all the Arab-Israeli conflicts. It produced the most casualties both in absolute terms and as a percentage of the populations engaged.

Israel was forced to turn its militias into regular forces while under attack by the combined forces of Egypt, Syria, Iraq, Jordan, and Lebanon.[6] Israel was saved only because it proved able to improvise an army and air force, because the Soviet bloc sent Israel arms in an effort to disrupt British influence in the Middle East, because the Arab armies had deliberately been kept weak and ineffective by their former colonial masters, and because the king of Transjordan was willing to accept an arrangement that gave him control over much of the Arab portion of Palestine and created modern Jordan. Even then, the series of truces that began with Egypt on January 6, 1949, and culminated with one with Syria on April 13, 1949, left all the participants in a legal state of war.

The two truces left Israel with sovereignty over about 8,000 square miles of Palestine and the Arabs with 2,000 square miles. The Arab portion included the 140 square mile Gaza Strip, which was administered and occupied by Egypt, and the West Bank, which was occupied by Transjordan. Israel claimed the western half of Jerusalem and Jordan the eastern half, which included most of the old city. In 1950 Jordan annexed the West Bank and its half of Jerusalem, although only Britain and Pakistan recognized this annexation.

Equally important, Arab leaders had encouraged the Arab population to flee the Jewish-occupied portions of Palestine during the attack by Arab armies. This created a population of 500,000 to 1 million Arab refugees out of a total of 1.3 million Arabs before partition. Roughly 130,000 Arabs remained in Israeli-administered territory, including 50,000 refugees.[7]

From 1949 to 1954, the continuing state of war between Israel and its neighbors led to a long series of clashes between Israel and Jordan along their new border. Raids and reprisals began in March, 1950 and led to serious clashes at Qibya in October, 1953; Beit Liqya in September, 1954; and Battir in November, 1954. These clashes involved bloody attacks on civilians and terrorism on the part of both sides, although Israeli and Jordanian officials often attempted to halt such fighting. Similarly, incidents took place along the Gaza Strip, like the one at Rafah in June, 1950, and with Syria. The most serious clashes between Israel and Syria took place at Tel Mutillah in the Galilee in April and May, 1951 and briefly threatened to escalate into a major battle.

The rise to power of Nasser in Egypt in 1952 changed the character of these clashes to one of a conflict between Israel and a new form of Arab socialism at a time that Egypt was also attacking the last vestiges of British rule in Egypt and British control over the Suez Canal. After August, 1953, raids and artillery exchanges became common along the border between Israel and the Gaza, and both sides began to prepare for another major war. This conflict began on October 29, 1956, when Israeli forces launched a surprise attack on Gaza and the Suez and rapidly swept south with only limited resistance from disorganized Egyptian forces. On October 31, 1956, French and British forces attacked Egyptian positions at Suez. While Israel's forces were successful and occupied Gaza and the Sinai Peninsula, the French and British forces did not land until November 5, 1956, and could not prevent Nasser from blocking the Suez Canal or achieve a meaningful military victory. The U.S. then intervened and forced the withdrawal of British, French, and Israeli forces. Israel withdrew to its prewar positions in March, 1957.

Israel also continued to fight with Syria and Jordan. A series of clashes took place over control of Lake Tiberias (Yam Kinneret) that began when Syrian fisherman used the lake and led to both Syrian artillery fire on Israel and Israeli attacks on Syrian artillery positions. These clashes became particularly serious in 1955 and 1957. Another series of armed clashes took place along the Syrian border between July, 1957 and December, 1958 and intensified after an Israeli commando raid on the Syrian village of Tawafiq in January, 1960. New battles were again triggered by Syrian fishing on Lake Tiberias and artillery shelling of Israeli settlements in March, 1962. In June, 1963 Syria began to shell Israeli settlements regularly until 1967. Israel replied with artillery and air attacks, and this may in some ways be regarded as the beginning of what culminated in a full scale war between Israel and Egypt, Jordan, and Syria in June, 1967.

While relations with Jordan were somewhat more peaceful, Palestinian infiltration attempts continued to lead to clashes; serious raids and counterraids by Israeli and Jordanian troops took place from July to October, 1956, culminating in fighting over an Israeli raid on Qalqilya. Similar incidents took place over Israeli control over the Mount Scopus area in Jerusalem in 1957 and 1958, and less serious incidents occurred until 1967. Lebanon also gradually became involved as PLO forces slowly built up the ability to launch raids out of southern Lebanon. These PLO raids triggered Israeli attacks on the Lebanese villages of Houle and Meiss al Jabal in October, 1965, and started a process of raid and reprisal that continues to this day.

In the spring of 1967, the clashes between Syria and Israel moved towards war, and a major Syrian-Israeli air battle took place in April, 1967. By this time, Syria and Egypt were closely cooperating, and Nasser had forced Jordan to accept a "united Arab" command under an Egyptian general. On May 14, 1967, Egypt and Syria declared a state of emergency, claiming that Israel was mobilizing to attack Syria, and Egypt began full deployment of its army into the Sinai. Nasser called for withdrawal of the UN observers that had helped keep peace in the area since 1957, and they left on May 18. Nasser then shut off Israel's access to the Red Sea by closing the Straits of Tiran on May 23, 1967.

On June 5, 1967, Israel responded by launching a series of air strikes on the airfields of Egypt, Syria, Jordan, and Iraq that effectively destroyed Arab air power. Israel invaded the Sinai the same day and then Jordan after Jordanian forces moved into a neutral zone and began to shell Israeli air bases. Israel rapidly secured control of the Sinai, Gaza, Jerusalem, and the West Bank. On June 10, regrouped Israeli forces attacked Syria and seized the Golan Heights. Israel's brilliant use of air power and armor culminated in a cease-fire late on June 10, 1967. At the end of the war, Israel occupied all of Jerusalem, the West Bank, Gaza, and the Golan Heights along the border with Syria. Israel annexed Jerusalem in 1967.

The 1967 war created roughly 300,000 new Arab refugees from the West Bank, some 175,000 of whom had previously fled to the West Bank from Israel. Another 100,000 refugees were displaced by the Israeli occupation of the Golan; about 18,000 of these had also been refugees from the previous war. Israel offered the 70,000 Arabs in East Jerusalem citizenship after 1967, but only 300 accepted the offer.[8]

The cease-fire, however, proved to be a prelude to further fighting and to what later came to be called the canal war or war of attrition. This conflict lasted from 1967 to 1970. Egypt and Israel started artillery exchanges across the Suez on July 14, 1967—less than a week after the cease-fire—and similar artillery exchanges began with Jordan in November. In October, 1968 Egypt began commando raids across the canal. Israel replied with air strikes and raids of its own and in December, 1968 launched commando raids against Jordan. Jordan, in turn, allowed Iraqi artillery into Jordan which provided fire support for Palestinian raids on Israel until the end of 1969.

On September 9, 1969, Israel launched a major raid across the canal to try to destroy Egyptian artillery positions. When this proved to have only a limited and temporary impact, Israel began air strikes on Egyptian positions. By 1970 the war across the Suez Canal had taken on major proportions as a long series of artillery exchanges and commando raids took place. The USSR rushed in new air defense systems and technicians and allowed Soviet pilots to fly air defense combat missions in Egyptian aircraft. When the fighting escalated, the U.S. and USSR intervened, and Israel and Egypt signed a cease-fire mediated by the U.S. on August 7, 1970. This cease-fire did not, however, fully end the fighting. Egypt launched an artillery attack on Israeli positions on March 29, 1971, and Israel attacked Egyptian positions on September 18, 1971.

At the same time, Israel's growing struggle with the Palestine Liberation Organization had a mounting impact on the internal politics of Jordan, Lebanon, and Syria. The PLO emerged as a major political force that led an increasing number of raids from bases in Jordan into Israel. By early 1970, these raids threatened Jordan with a full scale Israeli invasion, while the PLO became an active rival to King Hussein. Israeli armored forces attacked Jordanian border positions in reprisal on January 20, 1970, and crossed into Jordan and destroyed PLO positions near Karameh on March 21, triggering a brief round of fighting between Israeli and Jordanian forces. This led King Hussein to try to bring the PLO raids under control in the spring and summer of 1970, and the PLO retaliated with an assassination attempt on the king on September 1. King Hussein demanded that the PLO surrender its arms on September 16, and PLO leader Yasser Arafat retaliated by calling for the overthrow of King Hussein.

The Jordanian legion attacked PLO positions near Amman on September 17, triggering a civil war between PLO forces and Jordanian forces that Jordan soon won. On September 19, however, Syria severed relations with Jordan, and three brigades of Syrian troops attacked across Jordan's northern border. Jordanian troops crossed the Syrian border the next day and were able to stop the Syrian forces for several reasons. Israel threatened retaliation against Syria if it continued its advance, and the Syrian minister of defense, Hafaz Assad, refused to provide air support for the Syrian land forces. The Syrian troops lacked logistic support and reinforcements, and the Iraqi troops in Jordan remained neutral. As a result, the Syrian forces withdrew on September 23, having set off a series of events that brought Assad to power as president of Syria. The PLO forces collapsed on September 27, and Arafat agreed to withdraw Palestinian forces from urban areas in Jordan.

The PLO soon began sporadic attacks on Jordanian forces, however, particularly in northern Jordan. As a result, Jordanian forces attacked the remaining PLO forces in the north in July, and all PLO military forces were driven into Syria by July 19, 1971. When the PLO attempted to attack Jordan from Syria, Jordan responded with artillery attacks and cross-border raids. Assad then took action to bring the PLO forces under control, and in September Jordan and Syria restored diplomatic relations with the help of Egypt.

These events created a state of relative calm along the Israeli-Jordanian border that has endured ever since. What the Palestinians came to call "Black September" did, however, have a major impact on Lebanon. Although Israel and Lebanon had been at relative peace from 1950 to 1965, the growing Palestinian buildup in southern Lebanon created a new enemy operating from Lebanese territory. These PLO forces were under considerable Lebanese restraint until 1968, but the PLO had then grown to the point where the Lebanese army no longer was willing to challenge Palestinian forces in the south. The resulting Palestinian raids on Israel led to Israeli shelling of their positions in Lebanon in May, 1968, and then to a devastating Israeli commando raid on the Beirut airport on December 28, 1968, in retaliation for a PLO strike on aircraft at Athens airport on December 26.

From 1969 to the present, Israel has regularly launched air, armored, and commando strikes against anti-Israeli forces in Lebanon. It launched armored sweeps through the Palestinian positions in southern Lebanon in

May, 1970 and February, 1972. Lebanon's weak and divided forces did not resist these actions, except for limited artillery barrages in January, 1969 and May, 1975.

Israel also continued to fight with Syria. Israeli aircraft began to launch retaliatory air strikes on Syria in February, 1969 after PLO raids from Syria. Syria began to shell Israel in December, 1969, and Israel launched commando raids in March, 1970 and then seized additional Syrian territory in April. Syrian forces attempted to recover the Golan but were repulsed, and the fighting died down by June.

During late 1970 and throughout 1971, however, PLO raids took place from Syria into Israel, and Israel retaliated with air strikes. Syria attempted to counter by launching a major series of air strikes on Israel in early March, 1972, but Israel quickly drove Syria out of the air. By September, 1972, the conflict had established a pattern: Syria regularly shelled Israel, and Israel retaliated with air strikes. This continued until the October War began in 1973.

Given this background, the Arab-Israeli conflict that began on October 6, 1973, may seem more an inevitability than a surprise. Nevertheless, the sudden advance of Egyptian forces across the Suez Canal and Syrian attack on the Golan achieved tactical and strategic surprise. Israel took days to mobilize and deploy its ground forces, and Egypt and Syria scored major initial successes. An overconfident Israeli air force also experienced major problems in adjusting to Egypt and Syria's improved air defenses and to the new reconnaissance and attack tactics needed to hit Arab ground forces effectively and survive their air defenses.

Israel succeeded in holding Egyptian and Syrian forces while it mobilized, however, and counterattacked Syria on the Golan. Israeli forces not only drove Syria out of Israel and the Golan but even took new territory in Syria by October 11. The arrival of Iraqi forces and limited forces from Jordan, Morocco, and Saudi Arabia did nothing to alter the outcome.

The fighting on the Sinai front was more complex. Israel's initial counterattack failed, partly because of poor command at the front level and weak coordination between feuding Israeli combat unit commanders, and partly because of Israeli overconfidence in attacking well entrenched Egyptian defenders equipped with anti-tank guided missiles and excellent air defenses. On October 14, however, Egyptian forces advanced outside their defensive positions and the cover of their air defense missiles in an attempt to relieve the pressure on Syria. They also divided their forces. When Israel launched a new set of counterattacks on October 16, it still encountered serious problems but was able to cross the Suez Canal and establish secure and well reinforced positions on the other bank by October 20.

In spite of limited reinforcements by Kuwait, Algeria, and Tunisia, the Egyptian forces on the West Bank were effectively cut off from resupply by October 21. This reinforced pressure from the U.S. and Soviet Union to halt the fighting, and Israel and Egypt agreed to a cease-fire on October 22. Nevertheless, Israel, Egypt, and Syria attempted to consolidate or improve their positions. The fighting on the Egyptian front did not end until October 28, and the fighting on the Syrian front did not end until October 24.

The October War was an Arab military defeat, but it was also a partial Arab political and strategic victory, particularly for Egypt. It showed that Egyptian forces could carry out a successful major attack and resist Israel's best forces until they moved out of their planned positions to aid Syria. At the same time, it became clear to Anwar Sadat that further fighting was extremely unlikely to have a more successful outcome, would almost certainly trigger superpower intervention, and might lead Israel to use its nuclear deterrent if Israel's existence should ever be threatened.

Egypt continued to engage in post-cease-fire maneuvers, but only until a disengagement agreement was reached in February, 1974. Sadat reached an expanded disengagement agreement in September, 1974 and then gradually started on the path that led to visits to Jerusalem and Camp David, to Egypt's recovery of the Sinai, and to a peace between Egypt and Israel that has lasted nearly two decades—one of the few brilliant and courageous efforts at reaching peace in the long history of the Middle East.

The war continued on Israel's other borders. While King Hussein of Jordan almost certainly wanted peace, he also wanted the return of the West Bank and Jerusalem, and any settlement with Israel was possible only if it was acceptable to Jordan's Palestinian population. In spite of fourteen years of political maneuvering after 1973, he saw the Arab League recognize the PLO as the sole, legitimate representative of the Palestinian people in 1974. Israel and Syria reached a disengagement agreement in May, 1974, and Israeli troops withdrew from Syria to their 1967 positions in June. Syria, however, took the opposite path from Egypt. It reacted to the first steps in what became Egypt's slow move towards peace by breaking relations with Egypt and then committing itself to a massive military buildup in the effort to achieve military parity with Israel. At the same time, Syria built up a force of missiles with chemical warheads.

For reasons largely unconnected with the Arab-Israeli conflict, Lebanon drifted into ethnic civil war. This reached the crisis point in April, 1975, when Christian Phalange forces attacked Palestinian positions in Beirut. The attack triggered ethnic and factional fighting throughout the country and led to divisions within the Lebanese army. Muslim army officers attempted to overthrow the Christian president, Suleiman Franjiah, in March, 1976, and Franjiah, who had good relations with Assad, asked for the intervention of Syrian forces.

Syria had intervened in Lebanon before, in 1949 and 1963, and had left, but this time it committed the equivalent of a corps size force, occupying the Bekaa Valley, other parts of eastern Lebanon, and much of Beirut. While Libya, the Sudan, and Saudi Arabia sent small contingents to other parts of Lebanon, Syria became a virtual occupying force and put down most Palestinian and other radical resistance to the Franjiah government by June. In October, 1976 a formal cease-fire was arranged, and the various Arab forces were converted into what became called the Arab Deterrent Force. While the other elements of this force slowly withdrew between November, 1976 and early 1979, Syria stayed and steadily became more deeply enmeshed in Lebanese and Palestinian politics.

Syria also did relatively little to control the PLO activities against Israel in the south, and these continued to escalate during 1975–1978. The PLO actions provoked an Israeli invasion in March, 1978, and Israeli forces moved as far north as the Litani River. Israel also created a so-called Christian army that eventually came to be called the South Lebanon Army (SLA) under Saad Haddad. The Haddad forces were trained, equipped, and financed by Israel and effectively partitioned the country between Syrian-occupied territory around Beirut and in the Bekaa and Israeli-occupied territory in the southern border region.

The UN attempted to deal with this situation by condemning the Israeli invasion on March 19, 1978, and, more importantly, by deploying a peace-keeping force called the UN Interim Forces in Lebanon (UNIFIL). The force did play an important role in separating Palestinian, other Lebanese, and Israeli forces but was not capable of keeping the peace by force. It also could do little to deal with the PLO as it steadily built up its forces and capitalized on the civil war in Lebanon to build up major military bases in or near its cities and in the south.

Israeli armored forces entered Lebanon again in April, 1980, but it became clear that they could not achieve any lasting suppression of the PLO as long as PLO forces could act without interference from Lebanese forces and controlled major bases in urban areas and outside southern Lebanon. This gradually led Israel to plan a major invasion of Lebanon designed to rapidly encircle and destroy the PLO forces in the south. Israel's minister of defense, Ariel Sharon, however, broadened the plan to include a major attack on Syrian positions in the Bekaa and Lebanon and a drive along the coast to seize Beirut, create a new Maronite-dominated government, and drive the PLO out of Lebanon. He did so without the permission of Prime Minister Menachem Begin and the Israeli cabinet.

In June 1982, this led to yet another major Arab-Israeli conflict, and Israeli forces invaded Lebanon. Israel achieved its original objectives in about 48 hours and drove north along the coast and into the Bekaa. This provoked serious fighting with Syria and led to a major air battle in which Israel first destroyed most of the Syrian land based air defenses in the Bekaa and then destroyed much of the Syrian air force when it attempted a massive air-to-air engagement of Israeli fighters. Israel achieved a major military victory but soon learned that the Maronites were too weak and divided to create a strong central government even with Israeli support. They also made enemies of many of the Shi'ite and Druze ethnic factions that had previously tacitly supported or ignored Israel.

Although the Israeli forces drove the PLO out of Lebanon, they became implicated in Maronite massacres in Palestinian refugee camps and in the Lebanese civil war. This came to a head shortly after the U.S., France, and Italy deployed a multinational force (MNF) to oversee the evacuation of PLO and Syrian troops in August, 1982. When the MNF left Lebanon in September, Israeli troops failed to prevent Maronite attacks on Palestinian civilians in refugee camps at Sabra and Shatila.

Shortly thereafter, the one strong Christian leader, Bashir Gemayel, was assassinated in a bombing, and Lebanon began to revert to ethnic civil war. The MNF then redeployed to Lebanon and tried to build a strong central government and army and to separate the Israeli forces from hostile Lebanese forces; the MNF soon became seen as pro-Israeli and pro-Maronite. This led to the suicide bombing of French and U.S. barracks on October 23, 1983, killing 240 U.S. and 50 French troops. While U.S. forces attempted to retaliate, it soon became apparent that no outside force could prevent a civil conflict. The last U.S. elements of the MNF left Lebanon in March, 1984.

Israel remained in Lebanon until June, 1985, but its military victory had turned into a political defeat. Rather than suppress the PLO and create a pro-Israeli Lebanon, it had created a new set of Shi'ite enemies discussed later in this chapter. Syria reasserted itself in Lebanese affairs and rebuilt its military forces in Lebanon, and PLO forces gradually returned to the country. Between 1985 and 1990, the situation in Lebanon degenerated to much the same state of affairs that had existed before Israel's 1982 invasion. The main differences were that civil war now devastated most of the country, and Shi'ite guerrillas rather than PLO forces dominated the attacks on the South Lebanon Army and Israel. A major Syrian intervention in the Lebanese civil war ended much of the civil conflict in 1991, and Lebanese armed forces units disarmed part of the PLO, but Israel was still fighting PLO and Shi'ite forces in Lebanon in summer 1992 and confronting Syria across the Golan.

The troubled situation in the West Bank and Jordan also continued. A major Arab uprising began in the West Bank and Gaza in December, 1987. This *intifada* helped lead King Hussein of Jordan to declare that he no longer would seek to negotiate for control of the occupied territories and would leave the issue of peace negotiations to the PLO. Some 90 nations recognized the PLO as the head of a Palestinian state when it was declared on November 15, 1988—although the new state had no territory or government. The U.S. entered into a dialogue with the PLO on December 16, 1988, after the PLO committed itself to seeking a peaceful solution with Israel. This dialogue lasted only until June 20, 1990, however, broken off because of a PLO refusal to condemn terrorist attacks on Israel.

Saddam Hussein's invasion of Kuwait created new dangers for Israel. Both Jordan and the PLO tilted towards Saddam Hussein after Iraq's invasion of Kuwait. This not only created new barriers to a peace process but made it clear that many Palestinians and Jordanians hoped that Saddam Hussein would be victorious and that his victory might be the first step in the destruction of Israel. Long before Saddam's invasion, he had threatened Israel with missile and chemical attacks. When the Gulf War actually began in early 1991, Israel found itself on the sidelines of a war that threatened to involve it but under intense pressure from the U.S. to avoid any action that might divide the UN coalition and Arab opposition to Saddam Hussein.

The sweeping victory of UN coalition air forces in the first days of the war confronted Saddam Hussein with the fact he had no real hope of winning unless he could broaden the war or divide the UN coalition. His response was to launch a series of Scud attacks on Israel and Saudi Arabia, confronting Israel with the threat that these attacks might escalate to the use of chemical weapons at any time. Largely at U.S. urging, Israel abandoned its strategy of retaliation and did not strike back at Iraq. Instead, it rushed into service two Patriot missile batteries that it had bought in September, 1990 and worked with the U.S. to deploy additional Patriot batteries. This rapidly improvised anti-theater ballistic missile defense system could not protect Tel Aviv from damage but intercepted enough Iraqi missiles to restore Israeli confidence and persuade it to ride out Israel's first "one-way" war. At the same time, Israel provided the U.S. with intelligence on the Iraqi threat, technical support, and targeting data.

The end of the Gulf War did little to aid Israel other than to weaken Iraq. The Arab security structure that had linked Egypt and Syria to the southern Gulf states collapsed in a matter of months—leaving the prospect that Iraq might reemerge as a threat the moment it was free of UN restrictions. Iran emerged from the Gulf War as a reviving military power, with far fewer restrictions on arms transfers and playing an active role in a new wave of Islamic fundamentalist movements in the Arab world. Syria had driven out the remnants of Maronite power in Lebanon and for its support of the UN coalition obtained billions of dollars in aid which it promptly used to buy new arms. The Gulf War also severely damaged tourism and other aspects of Israel's economy.

In the aftermath of the Gulf War Israel confronted new problems in its relations with the U.S. The Bush administration saw the end of the war, the weakened state of the PLO, Egyptian and Syrian cooperation during the war, and the collapse of Soviet support for the military buildup in states like Syria as a unique set of conditions in which to begin a new Arab-Israeli peace initiative. In contrast, Israel was faced with the prospect of absorbing hundreds of thousands of Jews from the former Soviet Union, and its government was deeply committed to trying to preserve Israeli control over the Golan, West Bank, and East Jerusalem.

The result was a progressive increase in tension between the U.S. and Israel from mid-1991 onwards, as the Bush Administration pushed forward with its peace initiative and brought Israel and its Arab neighbors to the conference table. While the peace talks offered Israel potential security, they also threatened Israel's economic security and challenged its ability to continue constructing settlements in the occupied territories. These settlements have grown from 50 in 1977 to 250 by 1992. The total Jewish population grew to around 250,000, with over 100,000 Jews on the West Bank, 140,000 in East Jerusalem, 3,300–5,000 in the Gaza, and 10,000–12,000 in the Golan Heights. This was equivalent to about 13% of the total population of the occupied territories. The resulting tensions between the U.S. and Israel also led to the deferment of $10 billion in loan guarantees to help Israel absorb the former Soviet Jews, new debates over aid to Israel, and bitter debates over possible Israeli transfer of secret U.S. technology to the PRC and the effectiveness of the Patriots during the Gulf War.

This situation changed, however, with the Israeli election of June 23, 1992. After a hotly contested race fought over both domestic economic issues and the issue of the peace talks and U.S.-Israeli relations, Yitzak Rabin and the

Labor Party won enough seats to allow them to form a coalition government without the participation of the Likud. Yitzak Shamir, the former prime minister, and senior Likud officials like Moshe Arens, the former minister of defense, went into retirement.

While Rabin was forced to create a coalition with left wing, orthodox, and Arab parties—some members of which opposed trading territory for peace— the new Israeli government rapidly shifted towards a more moderate position. It halted the construction of new settlements and the building of some 3,000–3,500 new houses in existing settlements, although it took a more ambiguous stand on the 16,000 housing units already under construction in the occupied territories. It eased restrictions on the Palestinians and tightened the rules of engagement in confrontations between the Israeli Defense Forces (IDF) and Palestinian youth.

The new Rabin government also made it clear that it was willing to play a much more aggressive role in the peace talks and move towards a higher and more rapid degree of Palestinian autonomy in the occupied territories. Rabin met with Secretary of State James Baker on July 19, 1992, and went to Cairo to visit President Mubarak on July 21. This was the first Egyptian-Israeli summit meeting since September, 1986, and it was rapidly followed by a round of visits by Baker to Egypt, Israel, Lebanon, and Syria. While Rabin did not make any new offers regarding the Golan, the negotiating climate had changed: Rabin encountered a very different state of U.S.-Israeli relations during a visit to Washington in early August, President Bush announcing his support for immediate action in providing Israel with $10 billion in loan guarantees.

The Challenge of Israeli Defense Planning

Challenges are not new to Israel. It has faced them since it came into existence as a state, and no nation in the world has been more successful in using its resources to create an effective mix of military forces. They have also caused Israel's military planning to be shaped by five central criteria.

- First, Israel cannot afford wars that involve long struggles of attrition or that produce high casualties if these can possibly be avoided: Israel cannot sustain either the economic drain of long conflicts or personnel losses that threaten its social and political cohesion.
- Second, Israel must maintain a decisive qualitative edge over the most likely threats both to deter conflict and ensure that any war can be won quickly and decisively.
- Third, Israel's security cannot ultimately rest in the hands of another state, and no potential threat can ever be allowed to operate in an environment where it can destroy Israel and survive—a doctrine that has led Israel to develop both a powerful nuclear force and long range missiles to deliver it.
- Fourth, Israel must be able to achieve decisive results in a major struggle before outside powers can intervene and confront Israel with a status quo

that amounts to at least a limited defeat: This has led to continuing tension with the U.S. as well as with the former Soviet Union.

• Finally, Israel must plan and organize to defeat the most likely threats but can never ignore the risk of broader combinations of Arab forces.

Outsiders may question these criteria and Israel's view of how to achieve them, but any assessment of the Arab-Israeli balance that does not take them into account is unrealistic, as is any analysis of Israeli military forces. Israeli planning is not founded on the force ratios shown in the previous tables or on some tenuous ability to win one war. It is founded on a concept of national survival that essentially boils down to one simple fact: Israel is the only nation in the Arab-Israeli balance that cannot afford to lose a single serious conflict.

At the same time, it is easy to overestimate Israel's success and the ease with which its has forged its military capabilities. Throughout its history, Israel's military buildup has placed a severe strain on its economic resources and limited manpower. Israel has always had to make hard trade-offs in choosing its force mix and force improvement programs, and these have been the subject of constant debate within the IDF and within Israeli society.

Although the U.S. has provided an increasing flow of grant aid and technology, this has eased the resource problem, not solved it. Israel must maintain a force structure with roughly the same technological sophistication as the U.S. with defense expenditures of only $5–6 billion a year, including all direct and indirect aid. To put this into perspective, Israel maintains a force structure of about 4,500 tanks and 600 combat aircraft. Germany, which in some ways has less sophisticated forces, spends over $34 billion annually for a force structure with about 7,000 tanks and 640 combat aircraft; France spends over $35 billion on a force structure with fewer than 1,400 tanks and 1,000 naval and air force combat aircraft; and Britain spends over $35 billion on a force structure with 1,300 tanks and 600 naval and air force combat aircraft. While such comparisons involve gross oversimplification, they are valid as a rough indication of the resource pressure that Israel not only faces today but has faced throughout its existence.

Israel is also a democracy and perhaps the only nation in the Middle East that allows open and free debate over virtually every aspect of its military development. The result is a force structure that evolves through contention and competition, not out of the will of a single leader, a military elite, and some central consensus or master plan. The Israeli Defense Forces are also a relatively democratic organization—at least to the extent they allow open debate among peers. At any given time, there are major struggles for resources between services and branches of a given service, debates over strategy and tactics, and arguments over organization and command. These debates are interwoven with the broader debates in Israeli society: Debates over trading territory for peace or preserving control of the occupied territory, debates over the *intifada* and relations with the Palestinians, debates over civil versus military spending, debates over economic reform, and debates over Israel's relations with the U.S. and its dependence on the U.S. for aid.

In recent years Israel has been divided by a number of more technical military issues. These cannot be addressed in detail in an overview of Israel's role in the Middle East military balance, but it is important that they be understood in judging Israel's current forces:

- The extent to which Israel's land forces should be capable of decisive sudden offensive action against Syria—or any combination of Syria, Lebanon, and Jordan—as distinguished from being capable of defending Israeli territory by halting any invasion.
- The specific contingencies Israel should plan for and the capability Syria, or Syria in combination with other Arab states, has to carry out a surprise attack on Israel across the Golan or through Lebanon and/or Jordan.
- The level of readiness Israel needs within its land and air forces to deal with a surprise or limited warning attack.
- The ability of the Israeli Air Force (IAF) and advanced conventional technology to inflict a decisive series of strikes on the Syrian military and Syrian economy within a few days using conventional weapons and without a major land offensive, or to inflict similar damage on any other neighbor.
- The level and type of force that should be used to control the *intifada* and Palestinian activity within the occupied territories, and ultimately the level of compromise or relations with the PLO that will preserve Israeli security.
- The amount of territory that might be traded for peace, and the conditions under which such a trade might take place.
- The level of forces and other resources that Israel should commit to the defense of south Lebanon.
- The extent to which Israel needs a "blue water" navy that is capable of securing its lines of communication and long range strike capability, as distinguished from securing its coasts and immediate waters.
- The level of anti-tactical ballistic missile defense that can be provided, and the level of defense Israel can provide its soldiers and population against biological, chemical, and nuclear weapons.
- The extent to which Israel should reveal or publicize its nuclear and missile capabilities.
- The extent to which the Israeli defense industry should be encouraged both to reduce dependence on the U.S. and to create a technology base for advanced exports overseas.
- The level of resources that should go to defense versus absorbing the Russian Jews and economic development.

Israel has also had no immunity to the kind of defense reform debate that challenges the effectiveness of current military plans and capabilities. These debates take place at every professional level within the IDF. Perhaps the most serious public critique of Israeli capabilities, however, has been written by Col. Emanuel Wald. In a report originally written for Israel's then Chief of Staff Moshe Levi, Wald argued that the IDF had evolved into a slow moving and feuding bureaucracy that lost the 1982 war through its inability to manage combined arms and combined operations and to take effective decisions at the command level.[9]

Further, Wald argued that the IDF had lost its professionalism at the command and combat unit level, had fragmented along branch and service lines and promoted according to bureaucratic performance, no longer realistically trained and selected its officers for combat, could not effectively coordinate or manage operations at the corps level, could not sustain a high tempo of continuous operations, wasted resources on a large and unproductive staff and support structure, inflated its number of high ranking officers, could not effectively maneuver to engage all of its forces with the enemy, had limited night combat capability, had uncertain ability to use its intelligence collection in effective battle management, and lacked the ability to set realistic politico-military objectives for battle and pursue them to a meaningful conclusion.

There is no way an outsider can put Wald's charges into perspective. All are probably true to some extent because they make up a list of weaknesses that can be found to some degree in every modern military force in the world. They are true to some extent of the military forces of every country in NATO and every former member of the Warsaw Pact. They were true to some extent of the U.S. forces that lost in Vietnam and the U.S. forces that won in Desert Storm.

Yet it is striking that Israel is now in the process of eliminating 3,000 career officer and 1,000 civilian positions from the IDF over the next four years and is phasing out a number of IDF corps, including the Training Branch, Women's Corps, Education Corps, and Gadna Youth Corps. These changes were instituted as part of broader reforms that began when Lt. Gen. Ehud Barak was appointed chief of staff of the IDF on April 1, 1992.

Barak immediately summoned 3,000 officers to a meeting where he issued a message that the IDF had become too fat and over-staffed, lacked sufficient rigor and training, needed to tighten discipline, had to focus on arming and training for the high technology battlefield of the 1990s, and had to plan to live within its tighter resources. Barak then proceeded to slash headquarters and rear area support functions by 10–20%, cut paperwork and abolish some 30 out of 32 IDF publications, remove officers who failed in command exercises or did not react quickly to terrorism, and cut reserve service and training to provide added funds for high technology modernization. Barak's changes came very close to many of those Wald had recommended.[10]

The key point is that there is much to praise in judging the efficiency of Israel's military forces, and in the trade-offs Israel has made in organizing and equipping these forces. No military force, however, is free of weakness, inefficiency, resource limitations, internal politics and debates, and risks. Military forces inevitably tend to adapt to the needs and politics of peace when they are not totally committed to major conflicts, reflect their society's values and politics, and rely on a mixture of past customs and norms and unproved concepts of organization, tactics, training, and technology. The relative ranking of any military force is not determined by its degree of perfection but by the degree to which it succeeds rather than fails.

Israeli Military Expenditures

This brief outline of the conflicts and pressures affecting Israel also helps explain why Israel has put so many of its resources into defense.[11] It is difficult, however, to put the size of Israeli military spending and the strain it has imposed upon the economy into an accurate perspective. There is no doubt that Israel's survival has depended on a massive military effort and increasingly on U.S. military assistance. At the same time, Israel has failed to modernize and reform its economy—preserving many elements of a failed mix of socialism and special interest economics. At least part of the military burden on Israel's economy is a self-inflicted wound.

This lack of reform is reflected in the fact the Israeli economy recovered very slowly from the direct and indirect costs of the 1982 fighting in spite of massive U.S. grant aid. During 1982 to 1985, Israel's GDP actually dropped from $23.2 to $22.0 billion, total debt rose from $18.3 to $23.9 billion, and the debt service ratio rose from 26% to 33%. The resulting economic crisis unquestionably slowed the modernization of Israeli forces, forced serious cuts in Israeli manpower and readiness, and meant Israel has had to draw on war reserves for routine training and operations.

Israeli immigration dropped 41% between 1984 and 1985 and reached its lowest level since 1948 during 1986–1988. These problems created major difficulties for the IDF. In FY1987–88, for example, the IDF was forced to take a $700 million military budget cut, at least $200–300 million of which had to come in the form of further cuts in readiness and training, and to reduce its domestic military expenditures from a planned level of $3.2 billion to $2.53 billion.[12]

The *intifada* then imposed new burdens. Israeli government sources indicate that the uprising raised Israel's security costs by $221.5 million (400 million shekels) in 1988 (April 1988–March 1989), helped cut income from tourism by 20%, and cut trade from the West Bank by $750 million.[13] Added to other economic pressures, this forced Israel to cut back on domestic economic development as well as military spending. There was little GNP growth in 1988, versus 5.2% in 1987 and 2.0% in 1986. Real wages outstripped productivity gains in 1988, and exports remained constant after growing 11% in 1987. The current account balance remained in serious deficit in both 1987 and 1988, versus a surplus of $1.4 billion in 1986. Even with the cuts in Israeli government spending, the budget deficit was likely to reach $1 billion for 1988–1989, versus $750 million in 1987–1988, and a near balance in 1986–1987.[14]

These problems remained serious in 1989. Israel was forced to devalue the shekel by 13% in January, 1989. Israel also had to cut its FY1990–91 military budget significantly in January, 1989, as part of cuts in its national budget which totaled $550 million in direct expenditures and $220 million in government price subsidies. These cuts in military spending seem to have reached at least $165 million—the equivalent in Israel of 3,000 to 4,000 jobs.[15]

The Gulf War, the sudden flood of Russian immigrants resulting from the breakup of the Soviet Union, and Israel's failure to carry out structural economic reform made this situation far worse in 1990 and 1991. Israeli estimated its costs for the Gulf War as $1 billion in lost tourist revenue, $1 billion in lost economic activity, $400 million in extra military expenditures, $30 million in damage from Iraqi missiles, $100 million in transport services losses, and $250 million in lost exports.[16] Israel's external debt and trade imbalance continued to rise, as did unemployment, and Israel was forced to ask the U.S. for $10 billion in loan guarantees to help it absorb the flow of Russian Jews, restructure its economy, and improve its infrastructure—loan guarantees the U.S. had not provided as of May, 1992.

Estimates of Israel's total military spending vary sharply because of the uncertainty of Israel's official data and the difficulty in determining how to count U.S. grant aid transfers as part of Israeli expenditures. ACDA estimates that Israel spent $5,734 million on military forces in 1979, $6,654 million in 1980, $6,160 million in 1981, $6,026 million in 1982, $6,924 million in 1983, $7,869 million in 1984, $7,027 million in 1985, $6,431 million in 1986, $5.14 billion in 1987, $5.71 billion in 1988, $6.37 billion in 1989, $6.16 billion in 1990, and $5.3 billion in 1991.[17] These ACDA estimates put total Israeli military spending during the 1980s at 14–29% of GNP and 23–37% of central government expenditures, although the rise in Israel's GNP meant these percentages declined as the decade progressed.[18]

The IISS estimates Israeli military spending at $5.6 billion in 1986, $5.1 billion in 1987, $5.71 billion in 1988, $6.37 billion in 1989, and $6.16 billion in 1990. The CIA estimates that Israel was spending roughly $5.3 billion on the military in 1991, including $1.8 billion in U.S. grant aid. The CIA estimates this was 13.9% of Israel's GNP.[19]

Israeli government estimates have put direct annual domestic military spending at $3.2 billion in FY1982–83 and FY1983–84, $2.7 billion in FY1984–85, $2.6 billion in FY1985–86, and $2.5 billion in FY1986–87 and FY1987–88. While Israeli dollar conversions are not available, they indicate that Israel spent 11,085 million shekels on defense in the fiscal year between April 1, 1989, and March 31, 1990, and 13,593 million shekels in the fiscal year between April 1, 1990, and March 31, 1991.[20]

The true total domestic cost of Israeli military expenditures is difficult to estimate because of the problems in deciding how to allocate Israel's past military debts. For example, the U.S. embassy in Tel Aviv estimates the total cost of Israeli domestic military spending as being about 30–35% of the national budget in recent years, of which 12.5–15.7% was interest payments.[21] Senior Israeli officials, however, put the cost of all past war debts plus military aid and loans at 50% of the annual budget. Total military spending—including U.S. aid—was equivalent to 18% of the GNP.[22]

The Israeli government estimates that military expenditures consumed 20.9% of the GDP in 1985, 15.7% in 1986, 19.1% in 1987, 16.2% in 1988, 13.6% in 1989, 13.6% in 1990, and 13.7% in 1991. These figures include the U.S. aid and Israeli funds spent on arms and other military imports. Israel estimates that domestic consumption as a percentage of GDP reached 12.4% in 1985, 10.8% in 1986, 10.7% in 1987, 10.5% in 1988, 10.3% in 1989, 10.0% in 1990, and 9.2% in 1991.[23]

While military spending dropped as a percentage of GNP and central government expenditures between 1985 and 1991, this situation was reversed in 1991. In spite of bitter debates within the government—focusing on the need for economic development and aid to Russian Jews—Israel increased its spending for defense. Spending rose by $215 million to roughly $4.5 billion or 15.8 billion shekels, and a 3% reduction was made in the budget for civil ministries.[24]

Israel faces serious problems in maintaining its current level of domestic military effort. Its economy is badly in need of structural reform to free it of many forms of state control and intervention. It has cut new housing units back from 60,000 per year to 15,000. It also must deal with the risk that the Palestinian uprising could raise its military expenditures again if the current peace negotiations fail.

Israeli Dependence on Continuing
U.S. Military Aid and Arms Transfers

Israel's current military expenditures and force structure have been made possible only through U.S. aid.[25] Israel received some $77 billion, or about $47.8 billion constant 1991 dollars, in all forms of U.S. aid between 1967 and 1991, and about three-quarters of this aid came in the form of grants.[26] It received $7.9 billion in U.S. military financing between FY1950 and FY1978. It received $3.5 billion in FMS grant aid and loans in FY1979 as compensation for the loss of its bases and facilities in the Sinai. It received $1.0 billion in FMS in FY1980, $1.4 billion in FY1981, $1.4 billion in FY1982, $1.7 billion in FY1983, and $1.7 billion in FY1984.

Israel began to receive U.S. FMS assistance on a continuing all-grant basis in FY1985, however, when Israel received $1.4 billion worth of aid. It has since received grant aid of $1.723 billion in FY1986 and $1.8 billion annually in FY1987 through FY1992. Since FY1987, this military aid has been part of a $3 billion annual package of military and economic grant aid, although most of the $1.2 billion worth of nonmilitary aid in this package simply goes from the U.S. Treasury to U.S. banks to service Israel's foreign debt. Israel also received $700 million worth of surplus military equipment from U.S. forces in Europe in October, 1990 and a Gulf War emergency economic support fund supplemental of $650 million in March, 1991. U.S. aid has also been made larger in impact and more flexible through cash flow financing, FMS loan payment waivers, FMS offsets, special research and development payments, creation of a $500 million stockpile of U.S. military equipment in Israel, early transfers, third country payments using FMS funds to buy equipment in Israel, and by allowing Israel to spend the money on goods and services obtained in Israel.[27]

Large as this amount of aid is, it still is not enough to meet all of Israel's needs. Israeli officials have quietly sought a rise of nearly 40%, or $700 million, in the present level of $1.8 billion in annual military aid.[28] The size of U.S. aid must also be kept in careful perspective. It now has far less value in current dollars than it did when it was established in FY1987. Israel still must repay past loans at high interest rates whose ultimate impact on repayment costs is compounded by long periods of deferred payment during which interest has accrued. Israel must service the debt on some $12.2 billion in past loans and pay roughly $1.2 billion a year in principal and interest. This means that the net value of U.S. aid is considerably smaller than the current level of annual grants might otherwise imply.[29] Total external debt service also adds up to 37% of all exports of goods and services and continues to put heavy pressure on the Israeli economy. Further, Israel's dependence on U.S. aid is being increased by the need to absorb over 2 million Russian Jews— which will force Israel to spend more on immigration than it does on its military forces during the next decade.

Israel's economic problems and the limits on U.S. aid have left some important gaps in Israel's forces. It has been able to produce its Merkava main battle tank at about 30–50% of the rate its forces desire. (There are about 660 Merkavas of all types out of a tank force of 4,500.) It has been able to fund only a fraction of the attack helicopter force it wants, and it is heavily reliant on about 8,000 other armored vehicles, a large portion of which are obsolete and the rest of which at best consist of M-113 conversions that are scarcely the weapon that Israeli armored experts desire. Israel is short about 40–60% of the self-propelled artillery necessary to modernize key aspects of its force structure, and it needs a significant increase in modern anti-tank guided weapons launchers. It has had to make severe compromises in the sizing and modernization of its navy, and even its air force has some readiness problems. While international sources credit it with about 591 combat aircraft, approximately 102 of these aircraft are currently in reserve status and some are in storage.

Further, it should be noted that some of the quantitative advantages that Israel gained after Camp David have been eroded by the steady increase in Syria's force strength. If one looks at the trend in comparative force strength since 1973 (Table 5.3), it is clear that Syria has moved from about one-third of Israel's land weapons strength to parity. While Syria has a low level of overall military effectiveness, mass does tell, and Israel can scarcely ignore the growth of Syria's forces.

No military force ever meets all the force goals of its military planners. These resource problems, however, illustrate the difficulty of any arms control arrangements that shut off the flow of weapons, technology, and military aid to Israel. An arms freeze might be somewhat different if it could limit enough Arab countries to prevent some combination of Arab states from forming a dramatically increased threat, but this would have to involve substantial upgrade capabilities and one-for-one trades to allow the modernization of Israeli forces. For example, about 216 of Israel's active combat aircraft are aging RF-4Es (14), Kfirs (95), A-4s (121), and F-4Es which Israel currently lacks the funds to convert to the Phantom 2000 (62).[30]

Israel is dependent upon the United States for arms transfers as well as military assistance. ACDA estimates that Israel imported $480 million worth of arms in 1979, $800 million in 1980, $1,200 million in 1981, $925 million in 1982, $500 million in 1983, $775 million in 1984, $1,000 million in 1985, $500 million in 1986, $1,800 million in 1987, $2,000 million in 1988, and $725 million in 1989.[31]

ACDA estimates virtually all of these deliveries came from the U.S. According to ACDA, Israel took delivery on $3,805 million worth of arms during 1979–1983, and $3,800 million came from the U.S., with $5 million from other countries. It imported $6,100 million worth of arms during 1984–1988, and all $6,100 million came from the U.S.[32] Israel has had no other major supplier since de Gaulle cut off the flow of French arms to Israel in the mid-1970s. ACDA changed its way of reporting arms sales by source in 1992; according to this new style of reporting, Israel imported a total of $6,100 million worth of arms during 1985–1989, and again all $6,100 million came from the U.S.[33]

If these figures are correct, Israel imported well over $12 billion worth of arms from the United States during the 1980s. If they included U.S. components for Israeli-made military equipment, they would be much higher, and the figure would be over $20 billion worth of arms, technology, and military parts and components.[34]

The importance of Israel's ability to import technology and parts versus finished weapons is illustrated by the fact that U.S. military assistance aid to Israel in FY1990 totaled $1.792 billion, but Israel signed only $355 million worth of FMS sales agreements.[35] Although Israel has a large military industry, something like 40–60% of the technology and components that go into its major land weapons comes from the United States, and Israel cannot produce the modern high performance combat aircraft that are a key to its military success.

The role of U.S. arms in shaping Israel's military capability can be illustrated by listing some of its major imports from the U.S.:[36]

- 1,715 M-48, M-60, M-60A1, M-60A3 main battle tanks
- 1,656 M-113 armored personnel carriers
- 450 M-101A1, M-109A1, M-110 artillery weapons
- 578 F-4E, A-4E/N, F-16A/B/C/D, F-15A (1969–1988)
- 75 F-16 C/D on order (1991)
- 25 F-15A/B on order (1991)
- 167 U.S. military helicopters (1972–1989)
- 10 AH-64 (1991)
- 4 E-2C early warning aircraft (1977–1978)
- 12 Lance surface-to-surface missile launchers (1976)
- 6 mobile Hawk SAM units (1980–1984)
- 3 MIM-104 PAC-2 Patriot Fire Units, 2 on order (1991)
- 16 small warships (1972–1982)
- 5 Saar 5–class missile corvettes (1989)
- 2 Dolphin-class submarines on order (from Germany with U.S aid, 1989–1991)

Israel's dependence on the U.S. is also indicated by its having physically received $212.3 million worth of U.S. FMS deliveries between August 1,

1990, and April 7, 1992, and by a short list of its major orders during the Gulf War. These orders included:[37]

- Two Patriot missile batteries with 10 launchers and 64 missiles (September 1990: $117 million)
- 14 used F-15A and F-15B fighters (September 1990: $67.3 million)
- 10 CH-53A cargo helicopters (October 1990: $13.6 million)
- One Patriot battery with 8 launchers and 57 missiles (March 1991: $105 million)
- 10 used F-15A and F-15B fighters (May 1991: $61 million)

In addition to such major equipment imports, Israel imports critical parts for its own Merkava tanks and Lavi aircraft and is dependent on U.S. aid and technology for its Arrow anti-ballistic missile defense system. Many of the key components and technologies for its electronic warfare and command and control systems are designed or made in the U.S. These high technology imports give Israel a degree of qualitative superiority, an edge critical to its ability to both deter any attack and quickly terminate a war with limited casualties. While Israel could survive for a few years without U.S. aid, it could not do so for more than two to three years.

Israeli Defense Industries

Israel's defense industries have played a critical role in giving Israel its qualitative edge and in allowing Israel to be one of the most modern military forces in the world. They not only have produced major weapons systems like the Merkava tank, they have produced the electronics that tie together virtually every aspect of Israeli C^{3}I and battle management and have modified virtually every major weapons system that Israel has imported from the U.S. to meet Israel's special operating needs and reflect its unique combat experience.

At the same time, the debates over the use of Israeli resources have led to bitter arguments over how Israel should shape its defense industries and military production. The most serious of these arguments has been over Israel's investment in combat aircraft production and in its military industries. Israel spent 60–70% of its investment funds in its air force and military electronics during 1984–1986, and did so even though its economic problems forced it to put 90 of its combat aircraft in storage, cut its active ground force strength by over 10%, delay the production of Merkava tanks and other modern armor, and cut naval modernization to the bone.[38]

Many Israelis thought from the start that Israel could not finance all the improvements in its forces necessary to respond to the operational lessons of the 1982 fighting unless it abandoned the search to use military industry as a high technology base upon which to build both civilian development and a major export industry. They believed that senior officials like Israel's Defense Minister Arens were putting far too much of Israel's money in the wrong place.

Others, like Arens, felt that Israel could only mix an economic approach to defense with the growth of high technology industry by concentrating on advanced weapons. They pointed out that Israel's arms industry had built up to a peak of nearly 80,000 workers and had become the sixth largest arms exporter in the world. According to some estimates, the arms industry impacted directly and indirectly on some 20–25% of the population, and no one could ignore the fact that Israel's military exports rose from $850 million in 1983 to about $1.3 billion in 1986, becoming Israel's largest category of exports.

Israel's new fighter, the Lavi, became the most visible symbol of this debate, and one that ended in disaster. The Lavi started out in 1980 as a low cost replacement for the IAF's aging A-4s and Kfirs. By 1982, however, the decision was taken to power it with the advanced Pratt and Whitney PW1120 engine and turn it into a multirole fighter that was supposed to be able to outperform the F-16C/D. This decision was taken in part because the IAF concluded that an A-4/Kfir replacement as a ground attack aircraft would not be a cost-effective investment. It felt such an aircraft would be too expensive to deploy for its mission benefits and that the IAF would be far better off investing in a smaller number of high performance dual capability aircraft.

Israel, however, had little practical experience with large scale systems integration or with the development and production of an aircraft that had to lead the world in many aspects of fighter performance. It constantly modified the aircraft design to use advanced technology features without realistically estimating the costs. It ran into both design and manufacturing problems and had to turn to the U.S. for permission to obtain large amounts of advanced U.S. technology at little or no R&D cost and for the right to use a large part of its FMS aid on the Lavi project. Even so, the program's problems accelerated. The design features of the Lavi were allowed to "grow" to reflect the desires of Israel's pilots with little real regard to the marginal cost benefit.

The management of the project also became more politicized. As a result, Israel and the U.S. became involved in a major debate over aircraft cost. U.S. defense experts estimated that the Lavi's development cost would be at least $300 million more than Israel budgeted and that peak production costs might be equal to 5% of Israel's GNP. They estimated that its individual unit cost was escalating to $22 million per plane including nonconcurrent spares—or about 45–65% higher than the advocates of the Lavi in Israel were willing to admit. The U.S. was particularly concerned because by the time these cost estimates were made, Israel was getting 90% of the funding for the Lavi project from U.S. military aid, and only 40% of the development cost was going back to U.S. manufacturers.[39]

Israel attempted to deal with these issues by putting a cap of $550 million per year on spending on the Lavi. This cap proved to be impractical. The project cost of the Lavi rose to $9.99 billion, or a flyaway cost of $17.36 million each, at production runs of 300 aircraft—a figure which involved the export of more than two-thirds of the total production run of 300 aircraft, although Israel had no foreign customer for the plane. This program cost compared with a program cost of $4.67 billion if Israel bought the same number of F-16C/Ds from the U.S. or $5.84 billion if it bought the F-16C/D with Israel's Peace Marble 2 design features. Israel also found it could not cost effectively produce a combat aircraft as complex and sophisticated as the Lavi. Instead of being an Israeli-manufactured plane, the changes in design reached the point where they required Israel to import 60% of the parts and equipment from the U.S. This also gradually drove the total buy of the Lavi that Israel could afford for its own forces down from 400 aircraft to 300, to 150, and then less than 100 aircraft. These problems finally forced Israel to cancel the Lavi project on August 31, 1987.[40]

Another factor that led to the cancellation of the Lavi was that the project faced virtually uniform opposition by the senior officers of the IDF and had only limited support among the senior officers of the IAF. Israel's chief of staff, Dan Shomron; Deputy Chief of Staff Major General Barak; and the commander of the IAF, Maj. Gen. Avihu Ben Nun all opposed the project as being far too expensive and a misguided exercise in economic development that did not meet Israel's military needs. In fact, all three did their best in the spring of 1988 to kill the effort to go on with the Lavi's B-3 avionics because they felt they were far too expensive and were only being continued to avoid the political costs of further cuts in the Israeli Aircraft Industries (IAI). They failed largely because Israel's new defense minister, Rabin, felt that he could not afford the political cost of such an action.[41]

The cancellation came at a point when the U.S. and Israel had already invested over $1.5 billion in the fighter and Israel still faced additional costs of $1.2–1.4 billion, with $200–300 million for the avionics alone. The investment in the Lavi program had seriously undercut the modernization of every other aspect of Israel's forces. The terms of the cancellation agreement with the U.S. did make some $476 million available for either wind-up costs or new projects. Israel, however, was forced to use almost $400 million of the money for project cancellation and wind-up costs. Even so, Israel's defense industries had to lay off large number of workers at a time a general fall in world arms sales was hurting Israel's export markets, and it was suffering further from ending its arms sales to South Africa.

Between 1985 and 1987, Israel cut the number of employees in its defense industries from roughly 80,000 to 60,000. It was able to ease this situation only by expanding its sale of advanced technology systems to the PRC and turning to the U.S. for additional help in selling arms to the U.S. Even so, Israel laid off another 1,500–2,000 defense workers in 1989, and the defense labor force dropped to around 45,000.[42] The Israeli Aircraft Industries' chief executive referred to its problems as "competing in a climate of total insecurity."[43]

These developments were countered by some significant improvements in Israeli military capability. The IDF ground forces corps was able to allocate some 47% of its budget to modernization and 40% to training in 1987. Training programs increased by 30% in comparison with the "Lavi years." The ground forces were also able to sharply increase their budget for tanks, other combined arms equipment, night combat devices, and field intelligence equipment. The changes also had a major impact in improving the quality of the intake of Israeli regular officers and NCOs. The dropout rate for officers was reduced from 40% to 34%, and from 21% to 16% for other ranks. These improvements in the regular forces seem to be continuing, although the Palestinian uprising has had a serious disruptive effect on the reserves.[44]

In February, 1988 Israel replaced the Lavi with an order of 75 more F-16C/Ds with associate support equipment, IIR target pods, IIR GBU-15 weapons systems, technical assistance, spare parts, training, and coproduction equipment. The total cost of this package was roughly $2 billion, with $1.4 billion going to the combat aircraft and major defense equipment. The deal involved an $800 million offset in U.S. purchases from Israel. Israel's defense exports also recovered to 59% of all Israeli military sales in 1989, and aggressive overseas marketing helped Israel's defense industries recover. IAI succeeded in returning to profitability in 1989 and saw its export sales rise to $1.3 billion in 1991.[45] Many other Israeli military firms made significant profits.

Israel still faces hard choices, however, in funding its high technology weapons systems, force modernization, and defense industrial base. Some industries, like Israeli Military Industries and Tadiran, still face serious losses. More significantly, Israel has embarked on an ambitious anti-tactical ballistic defense program that may also lead to major cost escalation. Israel has never succeeded in developing a high volume capability to produce the Merkava tank, has recently had to cancel a major self-propelled artillery project that threatens its future industrial base for artillery production, and still has major problems in funding the armor and attack helicopters the IDF wants as high priorities.

Some Israeli critics say that Israel cannot afford to sustain its present mix of military industries and high technology strike forces and that this effort is so costly that it is still undercutting IDF readiness and war fighting capability. These critics point out the slow rate of modernization in the IDF's armor, cutbacks in exercise activity, a loss in the readiness of reserve forces, the failure to improve the helicopter force, and other financial compromises and trade-offs that they think mean Israel is losing its operational skills at the price of technology. Regardless of whether these immediate concerns are valid, Israel does face major long term uncertainties as to what mix of defense industry and force structure it can actually afford.

Finally, Israel is not immune to the problems that affect other defense industries all over the world. It faces problems with corruption, and problems with the U.S. over reported Israeli transfers of technology to third parties. The former head of the Israeli Air Force procurement branch, Brig. Gen. Rami Dotan, was convicted of taking $7.85 million to influence his decision on buying jet engines and services as part of a $40 million fraud scheme with General Electric in 1992. The Dotan case led to a broad investigation of potential corruption in Israeli Air Force defense procurement, as well as possible corruption by other U.S. firms.[46]

What is more troublesome is that the United States and Israel became involved in a major investigation of the possible Israeli transfer of Patriot missile technology to the PRC in 1992. Israel had long been involved in technology exchanges with the PRC. For example, it has licensed the PRC to build L7 105mm tank guns and the Python 3 air-to-air missile in Hunan under the name of the PL-9.[47] In March, 1992, however, a copy of a report by the inspector general of the State Department was leaked to the U.S. press, and charges appeared that Israel had transferred a Patriot missile or the technology for the missile to the PRC. At the same time, charges were made that Israel had reexported U.S. TOW missile technology by selling the Mapatz anti-tank guided missile, air-to-surface missile technology by selling the Popeye, and Sidewinder missile technology by selling the Python, and had sold U.S. military electronic systems without U.S. permission.

A U.S. team that visited Israel found no evidence of a leak of Patriot technology. The U.S. did not issue a formal statement refuting the rest of the rumors and the inspector general's reports seemed to implicate Israel in other transfers when it was issued on April 1. However, the Mapatz has a laser guidance system totally different from the TOW guidance system, the Python 3 sold in export only used Israeli components, and the Popeye is an all-Israeli-designed system with no U.S. stealth or guidance components.[48] Similar issues would almost certainly have emerged if the U.S. had investigated the technology transfer activities of virtually all of its NATO allies, and the incident dramatized the dependence of Israel's forces and military industry on U.S. technology, and the problems Israel military forces and industries would face without continued access to U.S. support.[49]

Israeli Military Manpower

If Israel faces major resource problems, it faces equal problems in terms of manpower. In July, 1991 Israel's total population was 4,477,105, with an annual indigenous growth rate of 1.5%. This total includes 90,000 Jewish settlers in the West Bank, 13,000 in the Golan Heights, 2,500 in the Gaza, and 120,000 in East Jerusalem—but not the Arab population of the occupied territories. The population was 83% Jewish and 17% non-Jewish. Religious groups were 82% Jewish, 14% Muslim (mostly Sunni), 2% Christian, and 2% Druze and other.[50] The Gaza had an additional population of 642,253, virtually all of which was Muslim Arab, largely Sunni. The West Bank had an additional population of 1,086,081, and there were 13,000 Jewish settlers and 12,000 Druze in the Israeli-occupied portion of the Golan Heights. If one includes Jewish settlers in the West Bank and East Jerusalem, the total population was 12% Jewish and 88% Arab, with 9% of the Arab population Christian and 91% Muslim.[51]

The CIA puts the total Israeli labor force at 1,400,000. It estimates that there are 2,213,308 people in the age group from 15 to 49; that out of 1,117,733 males, 920,449 are fit for military service; and that out of 1,096,075 females, 899,022 are fit for military service. The IISS estimates that there are a total of about 221,600 men and 210,300 women in the age group from 18 to

22 years, and about 377,700 males and 356,600 women in the age group from 22 to 32 years.[52]

While Russian immigration may eventually change this situation, Israel must now keep its active military manpower to the lowest level its security permits. As a result, Israel is one of the few Middle Eastern countries to have cut its active military manpower. It had a total active military strength of about 141,000 in late 1991 versus 173,000 in 1982. About 110,000 out of the total of 141,000 were male and female conscripts. About 41,000 males and 39,000 females fit for military service reach the age of 18 each year. Officers serve for 48 months, other ranks for 36 months, and women for 24 months, although Israel's parliament voted in July, 1991 to cut conscription from 36 months to 30 months.[53] The key source of this manpower is the Jewish part of the population, although some Druze and Christian Arabs volunteer.[54]

Israel instead relies on a large pool of exceptionally well trained reserves and a system that can provide extremely rapid mobilization in an emergency. In spite of its comparatively small population, it has been able to develop a large mobilization pool. This pool totaled 504,000 in 1991, with 494,000 for the army, 1,000 for the navy, and 9,000 for the air force. Most of these reservists serve at least one month a year: two weeks in training and two weeks on active duty. Male conscripts and volunteers serve in the reserves until age 51; women serve to 34 or marriage. Reservists serve in both the regular military and as home guards.

There are roughly 370,000 reservists in the force Israel would use to bring its combat forces up to strength during the first critical hours and days of mobilization. Key reservists serve up to 60 days a year in active duty. Each combat and combat support reserve unit normally receives three weeks of field training, with officers and NCOs receiving an extra week of training. A high percentage of all combined arms training is conducted at night. Some specialists receive up to 12 additional days of individual skill training. Assembly areas provide all equipment and have stocks already loaded. Israel uses full time maintenance and support personnel to keep these centers and their equipment ready, and claims that more than 95% of IDF equipment is ready for use. Controlled dry storage is now used for most equipment and stocks.

Call-up is by code name over the radio, and mobilization can be accomplished by a public or concealed call. Each reservist is part of a neighborhood group with 10 to 15 members, with a leader and two assistants who are responsible for notifying the rest of the group. There are nine regional centers for mobilization. These centers have depots where reservists draw their prepacked personal gear, weapons, and some ammunition. They are then transported to an emergency store unit, with one unit per brigade and three per division, where they link up with their heavy equipment. Mobilization plans are exercised twice a year—once in an announced exercise and once in an unannounced exercise.[55]

The Nahal (Pioneer Youth Militia) also has a heavy reserve element. This emphasis on mobilization versus active strength allows Israel to spend an exceptionally large part of its military budget on equipment and to keep its labor force at work except during times of crisis.

Israeli Force Changes Since 1982

The most important changes in Israeli forces in recent years respond to this combination of resource and manpower pressures, and such additional needs as responding to technological change in spite of budget constraints, maintaining Israel's edge in the air, improving Israel's overall battle management capabilities, and improving Israel's mix of armor and anti-armor capabilities. While Israel is still debating how best to tailor its forces to a lower level of resources, it has made or is making the following changes in its forces:[56]

- *Mobilization and reserve capabilities.* Israel still relies on its mobilization capabilities and reserve forces and could take up to a week to fully mobilize, but it is now capable of much more effective action during the first hours of mobilization. The reserve system now allows for different levels of alert, allowing Israel to alert key cadres without paralyzing Israel's society and economy. Call-up timings and deployment schedules are more realistic, and Israel can mobilize a fighting capability in 24 to 48 hours.

- *Strategy, tactics, and battle management.* Israel continues to examine how it can use land and air offensives to quickly destroy the Syrian and Jordanian armies in offensive action before the U.S. and/or Soviet Union can intervene at a political level. It has also developed plans to use a combination of air, conventional missile, and naval power to launch a crippling sequence of blows to suppress Syrian air defenses and use conventional munitions to so devastate the advanced elements of Syria's economy and infrastructure as to deprive Syria of recovery capability for several years. This air, missile, and naval capability is deliberately a "stand-alone" capability which would allow Israel's land forces to stand still at its defensive positions and launch a rapidly escalating series of air, naval, and missile attacks to force Syria or Jordan out of a war while minimizing any casualties.

- *Long before similar systems played a key role in the Gulf War, Israel was steadily improving its reconnaissance, targeting, C³I/battle management, and damage assessment technology.* Its goal has been to speed up the tempo of operations, give them all-weather and 24-hour capability, and tighten coordination between combined arms and the air and ground forces. Israel's goal is to shorten the action-reaction cycle of firepower and maneuver to cut the time between intelligence gather and targeting and maneuver and attack to a minimum. Israel seeks to operate in near real time so that the ground combat leader is given continuous information from the rear and can draw on immediate air and artillery support without delay or fear of "friendly" fire.

- *Another key objective of Israeli battle management is to give combat elements freedom of action while maintaining a clear understanding at each echelon of what is going on at the others.* Combined arms operations have been extended down to the company level, and combined arms training at every level stresses both initiative and coordination. Israeli commanders generally lead from the front and can exercise immediate authority over the direction of the battle. This gives them the fluidity necessary rapidly to mix and recombine force elements to meet a tactical situation without regard to rigid unit integrity and rapidly to commit helicopter, reserve, or combat engineer forces to bypass enemy positions, find alternative approaches to maintaining offensive momentum, and aid units when they face superior numbers or an ambush.

• *Israel is developing its own intelligence satellite and reconnaissance program, at the same time it constantly strengthens tactical intelligence and targeting capability at every level.* It is clear that Israel wants photo intelligence (PHOTINT) and signals intelligence (SIGINT) capabilities and the ability to use satellites for both warning and targeting purposes. Senior Israeli officers have sharply criticized the amount of satellite intelligence they received from the U.S. in the 1973 and 1982 wars, and Israel believes it can no longer count on flying reconnaissance aircraft in deep penetration missions over Arab territory. It is likely that Israel will soon deploy several intelligence satellites to cover the Arab world, although the level of coverage of communications and electronic emissions is difficult to predict, as is the level of imaging capability.[57]

The Israeli Army

Israel has made some important improvements in its land forces command structure since the 1982 war.[58] It formed a new Field Forces Command (FFC) in 1984. This command has the mission of building fully integrated combined arms forces. The armored corps, which dominated IDF ground forces for two decades, has now become a subordinated command.[59] According to some reports, Israel also created a Ground Force Command in 1983, in order to coordinate its northern, central, and southern commands.

The northern, central, and southern commands remain the key operational commands in the IDF, however, and are being strengthened to give Israel the equivalent of cohesive regional corps level or army group commands. The northern command has obvious priority, because it would face Syria, but Israel has not rejected the concept of a thrust through Lebanon or even northern Jordan. The northern command covers the Lebanese border, the Golan, and the Galilee. It is difficult to get an accurate estimate of how many Israeli forces are part of this command, but they seem to include a full active armored division and a mechanized brigade, three to four reserve divisions, four to five reserve mechanized and infantry brigades, and four to five territorial infantry brigades.[60]

Israel has continued to strengthen the fixed defenses in the Golan, and this both allows Israel to free forces to counterattack from the Golan and improves the ability of its territorial reserves to hold positions on the Golan while Israel's armored and helicopter forces strike across other lines of attack. The active Israeli combat unit in the Golan is the Golani brigade.

Israel has a security zone along its border with Lebanon, with forts or observation points near the border backed by stronger positions in the rear. It cooperates closely with the South Lebanon Army to help deal with the return of PLO combat units to the border area and the buildup of anti-Israeli Amal and Hizbollah Shi'ite forces. This rise in tension forced the Golani brigade to form a 100 man long range patrol unit for operations in the Bekaa in late 1988, as part of the brigade's reconnaissance battalion. Israel reinforced its active deployment in the zone by 500 men and 50 tanks in November, 1990.

The central command includes the defense of most of Israel, Jerusalem, the West Bank, and operations along the Jordanian border—covering the possible Syrian or Jordanian route of attack through the Arava Valley. It is divided into three sub-commands, with headquarters at Benjamin, Hebron, and Nablus. The *intifada* has led Israel to strengthen its troops and impose strict security measures in the area. There are specialized infantry brigades and anti-infiltration forces in both the West Bank and the Gaza. Its strength may include one active and two to three armored and mechanized divisions, one active and several reserve parachute and infantry brigades, and five to six territorial brigades.

The southern command forces defend southern Israel, the Gaza, and the Egyptian border. Like Israel's other commands, its forces consist of a limited number of combat ready units, and reserve units are manned largely by cadre forces with a rapid mobilization capability. Its forces include a partially active armored or mechanized division, an active armored or mechanized brigade, two to three reserve infantry brigades, and several territorial brigades.

Recent reports disagree about the Israeli order of battle. The IISS indicates there are three active armored divisions (each with two armored brigades, one artillery brigade, and one mechanized infantry or armored brigade on mobilization) and five active mechanized infantry brigades (including one paratroop trained brigade, one brigade based on the NCO school, and one Nahal brigade). It reports three active regional infantry divisions, one Lance battalion, and three M-110 203mm self-propelled howitzer battalions. The IISS also reports that Israel's reserve forces include nine armored divisions (two to three armored brigades, one mechanized infantry brigade, and one artillery brigade each), one air mobile/mechanized division (three brigades with paratroop trained reservists), ten regional infantry brigades—each with its own sector of the border—and four independent artillery brigades.[61] The Jaffee Center indicates Israel's total active and reserve forces include twelve armored divisions, four mechanized/infantry/territorial divisions and eight independent brigades, and five independent air border brigades.[62]

The distinction between active and reserve forces is sometimes difficult to make because Israel's active armored divisions generally have a reserve mechanized infantry brigade. Even the active armored brigades also have at least some reserve elements and seem to have become slightly more dependent on such elements in recent years. Israel also has a very flexible reserve system, calling up most units by battalion and training them within active brigades or divisions. This exposes reserve units to realistic command training. It is less clear, however, how Israel ensures that its higher level reserve commanders have the experience needed to fight a complex combined arms war at the brigade or division level, particularly now that it has been more than ten years since Israel conducted a major military operation and nearly twenty years since it last faced a major armored attack.

Key Israeli combat and service support forces include one Lance surface-to-surface battalion with twelve launchers, and three active 203mm self-propelled howitzer battalions.[63] According to some dated estimates, this provides a total maneuver unit strength of 110 tank battalions, 40 mechanized infantry battalions, 15 paratroop battalions, 30 infantry battalions, and 125 artillery battalions. This is an incredibly large mix of combined arms elements for a country the size of Israel, even allowing its ability to rapidly mobilize around 20% of its Jewish and Druze population.[64]

Israel now has a first line strength of roughly 4,450 active main battle tanks, including some 1,180 upgraded Centurions, 550 M-48A5s, 1,100 M-60s and M-60A1s, 210 M-60 A3s and 150 upgraded M-60/Magach 7s, 430 T-54/T-55s and upgraded Soviet tanks, 110–115 T-62s, and 650–700 Merkavas. About 900 of the upgraded Centurions and 200–400 regular and upgraded T-54s and T-55s may be in reserve inventory. Israel also seems to retain some of its Mark 1, Mark 50, and Mark 51 Shermans in reserve and storage.[65]

Virtually all of Israel's tanks have had some form of conversion. The most important conversions are those affecting the Centurions and M-60s. The original Centurions had Meteor petrol engines that left them with very poor power-to-weight ratios. They have since been upgraded with the Teledyne Continental AVDS-1790-2A diesel engine, which is also used in the M-48A5, and an Allison CD-850-6 transmission. This gives the Centurion a speed of 43 km/h and about twice the cruising range of the unmodified Centurion. The rear deck has been modified, and fuel capacity has been expanded, a new fire extinguishing system has been added, ammunition has been raised to 72 rounds, and some have been fitted with heavier 12.7mm machine guns for urban warfare. Some Centurions have also been fitted with Blazer explosive reactive armor, which is also fitted to Israeli M-48s and M-60s. Some have been equipped with launch containers on each side of the tank that can conceal the tank in smoke.

The M-60s have been steadily upgraded. Thermal sleeves have been added to their guns, explosive reactive armor has been added, launch containers for smoke screening have been added, and new Urdan cupolas have been fitted with two roof mounted 7.62mm machine guns. In addition, a more recent conversion adds passive armor to the glacis, nose, turret front and sides, and forward part of the roof. Armored skirts provide improved lateral protection, and a new engine and tracks have been added to maintain mobility in spite of the added weight of armor. The Magach-7 conversion has an even more powerful engine. The Matador computerized fire control system is also being added, and laser range finders are fitted to the M-60s and M-60A1s. This system, developed by Elbit and ELOP, has a laser range finder and a digital ballistic computer and uses a meteorological mast on the rear of the turret to sense wind speed and direction, air pressure, and outside temperature. An improved penetration APSDSD-T M-413 Israeli round is standard with all of Israel's tanks using the 105mm M-68 gun. Some sources believe Israel has deployed both 105mm and 120mm depleted uranium penetrator rounds.[66]

The Merkava is the only tank that has been designed and built in the Middle East specifically for the war fighting conditions in the region. Israel has sought to build up its Merkava tank force as much as possible, but this buildup has been delayed by a lack of funds, particularly during the time Israel was attempting to implement the Lavi project. Israel did, however, have about 660–700 Merkava I/II tanks in 1992 versus 200 in 1982.

The Merkava first entered service in 1979, after nearly ten years of development and an expenditure of nearly $100 million. It has a cast and welded armor hull with the turret and fighting compartment at the rear of the vehicle rather than the front. Extensive use is made of space armor. The Mark 1 uses a 900 HP Teledyne Continental AVDS-1790-6A diesel engine and a semi-automatic Allison CD-850-6BX transmission. It weighs about 63,000 kilograms, uses a wedge shaped turret with 105mm gun, and 62 rounds stored in a fire resistant compartment. The crew, including the driver, can exit through the rear of the tank because the engine is in front, and there is a rear storage area that can be used for ammunition, infantry personnel, or special missions. It has a first generation suspension system, an electro-hydraulic turret control system, nuclear-biological-chemical (NBC) overpressure, heat protection for armor survivability, and an electronic computer fire control system with a laser range finder and night vision equipment.

The 1982 war proved the value of the Merkava I. Israel found that a massive tank could still be of great advantage in mountain and urban warfare and in ambush conditions. The Merkava I proved virtually immune to frontal fire during 1982, had higher crew survivability rates, and was more agile over rough ground than the M-60. Israel concluded, however, that the Merkava needed added firepower and fire control. This led to the development of the Merkava II in 1983. It added special armor on the front and sides of the turret, special armor on the hull roof, a 60mm mortar that can be fired within the turret, special armor to the steel skirts that protect the transmission, an advanced laser range finder and a better computer, and more advanced night vision systems. The 900 HP engine is retained, but a new automatic, electronic control transmission and second generation suspension give greater acceleration and 25% more range.[67]

The Merkava III entered service in 1989. Like the Merkava I and II, the engine and transmission are in front. The Merkava III, however, has a 120mm smoothbore gun with 50 rounds stored in an area that is both heat resistant and prevents chain detonation. It uses modular special armor and improved side skirts, is powered by a 1,200 HP engine, and has a greatly improved suspension system for greater mobility. It has a new electronic computer, a new laser range finder, third generation night vision equipment, vertical and horizontal line of sight stabilization, and an electric/electronic turret drive system. The NBC system still relies on overpressure but is filtered and air conditioned. A very advanced threat warning system is provided with readouts at the commander's station. Many of the advances in the Merkava III are being fitted to the Merkava I and II, but they are believed to retain the 105mm gun.[68]

Fiscal pressures still limit Israel's procurement of the Merkava to around 100 per year. This is a problem because the IDF will have difficulty keeping its Centurions, upgrade T-54s and T-55s, and M-48s competitive with Syrian and other first line Arab armor beyond the year 2000.

Israel is steadily increasing its number of tank transporters and has found them to be an important way of both increasing the speed of armored movements and ensuring that the maximum number of armored vehicles reach the front in fully operational condition. Israel also has a wide range of special purpose tanks, armored engineering vehicles, and armored recovery vehicles, giving it one of the most advanced armored recovery, mine plowing, ambulance, command, artillery observation, and field repair capabilities of any armored force in the world.

Israel has found that regular APCs cannot survive combat against well positioned infantry and defending forces. It has found the Merkava's ability to carry a small infantry squad in the rear of the tank to be vital in bringing troops into close combat and in providing armor with infantry support. It cannot afford to fully modernize its force with other armored fighting vehicles, but it is doing everything possible to modify the M-113 to reduce its vulnerability and the effect of successful hits and to improve its firepower. The full nature of these improvements is unclear but seems to include the extensive use of passive armor.

Israel now has about 400 armored reconnaissance vehicles—including 100 Ramta RBY M-1s (light 4 x 4 armored vehicles), 200 Shoet M-2 and M-3s, and about 100 modernized captured Soviet BDRMs—and has Re'em armored fighting vehicles on order. Israel also has about 5,900 M-113 armored personnel carriers, most of which have been improved in armor and fire power, and 80 Nagmashots (converted Centurions). It has over 100 additional armored command vehicles and 700–800 M-125 81mm mortar carriers. It also has some 40–70 BTR-50Ps, OT-62s and BMPs, and roughly 4,400 aging M-2 and M-3 half-tracks—many of which are in storage or in reserve units. These include large numbers of mortar carriers.

Israel's total operational other armored vehicle (OAV) strength is probably around 7,500–8,500. It also has 400–500 Israeli-built armored recovery vehicles and over 400 U.S.-built M-578s, although it is unclear how many of the latter are operational. It is well equipped with armored bridging vehicles.

Israel is trying to retrain and reequip its infantry to free them from overdependence on armored vehicles. It is giving them more lethal light-infantry weaponry for urban and mountain warfare and is examining new rifle and submachine gun sights, like the "red dot" system, that aid in instinctive shooting.[69] It is also steadily improving their anti-armored warfare capability by giving them more BGM-71 and TOW and M-47 Dragon anti-tank guided weapons, and by either modifying these systems or procuring more advanced versions from the U.S. Israel has roughly 300 TOW launchers, some on M-113s, and 400 Dragon launchers.[70]

Israel also continues to use the Milan in limited numbers. It has 250 106mm anti-armor rocket launchers, many mounted on jeeps. It also has several thousand 3.5" anti-tank rocket launchers, thousands of light anti-tank weapons (LAWs) and RPG-7s, B-300 82mm rocket launchers, and 250 M-40A1 106mm rocket launchers.

Israel is reported to have deployed its own Pickett and Togger ATGMs. It has recently started to produce the Mapatz laser guided anti-tank weapons system. The Mapatz has an effective range of 4.5 kilometers, and its warhead is said to penetrate 800mm of 300 Brinnel armor. The Mapatz is visually identical to the TOW and is aimed by keeping the crosshairs of a sight linked to laser on the target. The missile tracks the laser beam through sensors in the rear of the missile. Israel believes that this guidance method corrects problems it experienced in 1982 with firing wire guided missiles like the TOW over water and through brush.[71]

Israel now has about 555–625 towed tube artillery weapons, 1,000–1,100 self-propelled tube artillery weapons, and 120 operational multiple rocket launchers. It is trying to improve the mobility and lethality of its artillery rather than increase its numbers of weapons. It is increasing its ability to provide supply for off-road surge fire and is keeping its stocks at a relatively high "30 days" (1.5 wars' worth of munitions reserves). In spite of budget problems Israel is putting heavy emphasis on improved C^3I/BM and on rocket launchers with smart or guided warheads which can extend range and improve cross-reinforcement of fire, reaction time, accuracy, lethality, and volume of fire.

Israel has 85 M-46 130mm towed guns and around 140–240 M-107 self-propelled 175mm guns. It has found these long range guns to be highly effective against targets in the rear of Arab forces. Its other towed weapons include 70 M-101 105mm towed howitzers; 100–170 D-30 122mm towed howitzers, and 300 Soltam M-68, M-71, M-839P and M-845P towed 155mm howitzers. Its other self-propelled weapons include 35 M-7 105mm howitzers, 170–190 L-33 155mm howitzers, 100–110 M-50 155mm howitzers, 530 M-109A1 and M-109A2 self-propelled 155mm howitzers, and 36 M-110 203mm howitzers.[72]

Several Israeli commanders maintain that Israel still does not have enough tube artillery and that it needs more artillery mobility and surge fire power capability. Some would like to see Israel acquire the U.S. multiple launch rocket system (MLRS) and assault breaker rockets that proved so successful during Desert Storm. Israel, however, again faces severe resource constraints that have forced the IDF to cancel a new 155mm cannon design called the Slammer that used a Merkava chassis to provide mobility. It was to carry 75 rounds and charges and have a maximum range of 40 kilometers using EFRB-BB projectiles. A computerized loading and firing system was to provide a maximum rate of fire of 9 rounds per minute and train and elevate the gun. This cancellation threatens its industrial base. Soltam, the only major artillery firm in Israel and the manufacturer of a number of advanced towed artillery weapons designs, faces closure if it cannot increase its exports to compensate for the cancellation.[73]

Although it does not have the MLRS, Israel has acquired seven Lance MGM-52 missile launchers that fire missiles with advanced conventional warheads. Israel has large numbers of conventional multiple rocket launchers and 50–70 BM-21 122mm and 30–40 BM-24 240mm multiple rocket launchers captured from Arab forces in service.

Israel has developed its own long range LAR-160 160mm, MAR-290mm, and MAR-350mm multiple rocket launchers. The LAR-160 is fired from a pod of 4–18 launchers on an AMX-13 chassis and has a maximum range of 30 kilometers with a 40 kilogram HE-COFRAM warhead. The MAR-290 is fired from a pod of 4 launchers on an AMX-13 or Centurion chassis, has a maximum range of 25–40 kilometers and a 320 kilogram warhead that can carry advanced submunitions. The MAR-350 may be developmental but has a range of 30–80 kilometers, a 300 kilogram warhead, and uses either a HE-COFRAM warhead or a cluster warhead with 770 bomblets. In 1991 Israel announced an advanced laser guided missile system called the Nimrod. It has a range of 26 kilometers and can engage several different targets at once using coded laser illuminators. The system has high explosive anti-tank warheads.[74]

Israel places more emphasis on maneuver, accuracy, and rapid shifts in fire in using its multiple rocket launchers than Arab forces, which tend to emphasize massed fire. Israel claims that its own multiple rocket launcher systems are considerably more accurate and easy to target than Soviet-designed systems. It is unclear how many Israeli-built systems are in service, but they may total between 50 and 100 launchers.

Israel has some 1,200 81mm, 120mm, and 160mm mortars, including the self-propelled weapons listed earlier. These mortars provide substantial short range fire support for Israeli armor and artillery, and Israel now places more emphasis on the use of mortars and fire support to aid battlefield maneuver than it did in 1967 and 1973.

Israel has widely deployed the Hughes TPQ-37 weapon locating radar system, and its own Elta EL/M 2320 artillery radar system. It used both of these systems in the 1982 fighting and similar systems proved very effective during the Gulf War. The Elta system is a mobile, long range fire adjustment radar which is mounted on a tracked vehicle. It is designed for use with all of Israel's artillery, and has day/night and over-the-horizon targeting capability. Israel claims that target locating radars can improve the effectiveness per round by 100–200% and greatly reduce the time necessary for target acquisition. This claim tracks with the similar test experience of other armies, which have found that artillery radars are critical in targeting today's highly mobilized artillery units and in allowing the rapid independent operation of artillery weapons.[75]

Israel is unique in the Middle East in integrating a mix of mobile battlefield surveillance radars, field portable electronic and intelligence systems, unmanned airborne vehicles that can be used at any echelon of ground forces operations, tactical intelligence, and battlefield management systems. This unique ability to fight on an "electronic battlefield" seems to give the IDF a major force multiplier, but the details are classified.

Israel relies heavily on its fighters for air defense and has not modernized its land based air defenses at the same rate as the other elements of its land forces. Many of its anti-aircraft guns and all of its surface-to-air missiles are operated by the Israeli Air Force. Israel does, however, have some 850 20mm air defense cannon. It has two active air defense brigades with 48 M-163 Vulcan and 48 M-48 Chaparral gun missile systems; some ZU-23-2 towed, and 50 rebuilt ZSU-23-4 self-propelled radar guided AA guns; and roughly 1,000 37mm and 40mm L-70 AA guns. Its extensive stocks of obsolete MIM-42A Redeye manportable surface-to-air missiles are being replaced with FIM-92A Stingers.

Israel has made several modifications to its air defense artillery. It has improved the D-7 search-and-fire radar system for its 40mm 7-70 guns which it modified from the Fledermaus system and first deployed in 1964. The new Eagle Eye, or Kapuz, radar system allows six AA weapons to be linked to a common guidance system to produce a guided equivalent of "curtain fire." It also has an electro-optical system with a laser range finder. Israel found this system to be useful in 1982 in improving the visual identification of friendly and hostile aircraft and giving battery commanders a visual image of their target.[76]

Israel has steadily built up its combat engineering forces as a key combat arm for penetrating rapidly through mountain routes, repairing or replacing bridges, crossing barriers, and dealing with urban defense points. It has bought CUCV 4 x 4s to replace its jeeps and large numbers of Subaru and Suzuki tenders to improve light logistic support in base areas.[77] Israel has a very wide range of mine clearing systems, bridging systems, logistic vehicles, and protection systems. Unlike most Middle Eastern armies, it maintains high readiness and training levels for service support and logistic functions.

More broadly, Israel is the only army in the Middle East that is fully capable of combined arms and combined operations, that is fully maneuver as well as firepower oriented, and which sees service support, maintenance, and logistics as having equal priority with the creation of combat units. In spite of its resource constraints, Israel maintains the large reserves of ammunition and spare parts it built up when it was threatened with running out of some critical supplies during the October War. It has enough stocks to fight any realistic combination of Arab opponents to exhaustion and to ride out a limited embargo before achieving resupply.

Israel has developed so many improved night vision, electro-optical and other targeting systems, electronic intelligence, battlefield surveillance, tactical intelligence, combat communications and automatic communications systems that it is impossible to summarize the key systems involved. Israel has also integrated, or netted, many of these systems with its air force and with a wide range of unmanned airborne vehicles.

This integration reinforces the IDF's ability to use the electronic battlefield to maintain intense and fluid combat operations in all-weathers and on a 24-hour basis, and to kill enemy targets well beyond visual range with systems that are not vulnerable to air defenses. This gives the IDF a very different character from armies like Syria's and a wide range of force multipliers lacking in armies that have not mastered the electronic battlefield.[78]

Israel has, however, had to compromise in some areas of readiness. It still maintains high overall readiness levels, training standards, and maintenance standards but has faced growing fiscal constraints in funding training and maintenance over the last five years. While it has been able to adjust to the new demands of the *intifada*, it has had to cut back on large scale training exercises, some aspect of maintenance and logistic activity, and the manning levels in active and reserve units. A growing number of active units have reserve components, and reserve units now seem to have lower peacetime manning cadres.

The Operational Capabilities and Limitations of the Israeli Air Force

The IAF is the most effective air force in the Middle East and one of the most effective air forces in the world. It destroyed many of its opponent's aircraft on the ground in the 1967 war and then scored 72 air-to-air kills over the rest. It destroyed 113 Egyptian and Syrian aircraft in air-to-air combat during the war of attrition and killed 452 Egyptian, Syrian, Iraqi, and Jordanian aircraft during the October War in 1973. It killed at least 23 Syrian aircraft between 1973 and 1982 and killed 71 fixed wing aircraft during the fighting in 1982. It shot down 3 Syrian fighters between 1982 and 1992. While it has lost 247 aircraft in combat since the beginning of the 1948 war, only 18 have been lost in air-to-air combat. In contrast, Arab forces have lost at least 1,428 fixed wing and rotary wing aircraft in combat and 817 in air-to-air combat.[79]

Two Arab air forces—those of Egypt and Saudi Arabia—have high training standards, modern combat aircraft, and advanced battle management systems like the E-3A and E-2C. Israel is the only air force, however, that combines all of the elements of modern air power into an efficient and integrated whole. Israel has advanced combat, electronic warfare, intelligence and targeting, and battle management aircraft. These are supported by a host of advanced and special purpose weapons systems, combat electronics, unmanned airborne vehicles, night and all-weather combat systems, and command and control facilities.

Israeli pilot and air crew selection and training standards are the highest in the Middle East and some of the highest in the world. Nearly 90% of those selected as possible pilots do not make the grade as fighter pilots. Israel has a ruthless selection process to keep its pilots at a high standard, and it promotes on the basis of performance rather than seniority. High quality pilots and air crews now serve in a reserve capacity after leaving active service, which gives Israel a significant ability to expand its combat air strength in wartime—particularly with attack aircraft. El Al, the national airline, can be mobilized immediately for transport and resupply missions and to provide added technical personnel, as can skilled workers in Israel's defense industries.

The Israeli Air Force has about 2.5 pilots per combat aircraft versus less than 1 in most Arab air forces. It is equipped with first line aircraft like the F-15 and F-16, continues to emphasize training, has one of the most advanced combat training systems in the world, and takes advantage of U.S. training centers. The IAF's excellence in pilots is supported by excellence in the human dimension at all levels. If some Arab air forces have excellent pilots, the IAF not only has the most demanding pilot training and performance standards of any air force in the Middle East, it has equally demanding standards for maintenance, logistics, command and control, intelligence and targeting, and all of the other functions necessary to maintain effective air operations.

In addition, Israeli has developed a reserve system that requires exceptional performance from its air force reservists. There are no reserve squadrons in the IAF, and all squadrons can operate without mobilization. However, about one-third of the air crew in each squadron are reservists. Reserve air crews train 55–60 days a year and fly operational missions with the squadron to which they are assigned. In the event of a call-up, the reserve air crews and operations support personnel report first, and then support personnel for sustained operations. About 60% of the IAF reserves are in air and ground defense units.

In contrast, other Middle Eastern forces are weakened by their failure to enforce rigorous selection procedures for assignments other than combat pilot and by their failure to create a highly professional class of noncommissioned officers who are paid, trained, and given the status necessary to maintain fully effective combat operations. In most cases, these problems are compounded by poor overall manpower policies and promotion for political and personal loyalty. Other Middle Eastern air forces also tend to be weakened by a failure to see command and control, intelligence and targeting, high intensity combat operations, and sustainability as being equal in importance to weapons numbers and quality. While Egypt, Iraq, and Saudi Arabia have moved towards the idea of forcewide excellence in supporting an overall concept of operations, they still have a long way to go before approaching Israel's level of capability.

While the Israeli air defense system is scarcely leak proof—a fact demonstrated when a defecting Syrian pilot flew undetected deep into Israeli air space—a fully alert Israeli air defense is capable of coordinating its sensors, fighters, and land based defenses with a level of effectiveness that no other Middle Eastern air force can approach.[80] Israel has a better overall mix of systems, better trained personnel, and a far better ability to integrate all its assets with its own technology and software than any other Middle Eastern air force.

Israel's advantages in strategic and long range offensive operations are even greater. The IAF is the only air force in the Middle East that is seriously organized for strategic attacks on its neighbors. Other Middle Eastern air forces may have long range strike aircraft, effective munitions, and even a limited refueling capacity. They are, however, essentially amateurs in using their assets to inflict strategic damage on an enemy nation or conduct effective long range strategic strikes.

Ever since 1973, the IDF has organized its targeting, battle management, and strike plans for both conventional and nuclear strategic strikes on key potential enemies. Israel gives high priority to destroying and suppressing the enemy's air and land based air defense capability during the initial stages of the battle. The sheer scale of Israel's success in suppressing Syrian air defenses is indicated by the fact that during the 1982 war, Israel essentially broke the back of the Syrian surface-to-air missile network in the Bekaa Valley in one day, June 9. Israel shot down over 80 Syrian fighters and lost only 1 A-4 in flying a total of over 1,000 combat sorties—including the sorties delivered against Syrian ground based air defenses in the Bekaa. Israel was also able to devote an extraordinary percentage of its total sorties to the attack mission, although it should be noted that even in the 1973 war some 75% of all IAF sorties were attack sorties.[81]

Today the IAF is organized and equipped so that it could probably use a combination of electronic intelligence aircraft, jammers, stand-off munitions, land based strike systems, UAVs, and other countermeasures to suppress both Syrian and Jordanian air defenses in 24–48 hours. It could then maintain air supremacy over much of Syria and all of Jordan.

The IAF has learned from its mistakes in the 1973 and 1982 wars. It has steadily improved its coordination with the land forces in both combined operations and at the strategic level, when coordinating the air-land battle goes beyond tactical operations to the strategic purpose of conflict. This coordination may lack all the sophisticated technology and techniques used by U.S. forces, but it is tailored to a unique area and set of missions and allows given assets to be used with great effectiveness.

Israel has sufficient long range precision munitions, land based missile and rocket systems, and UAVs to use conventional weapons to cripple the power, water, refining, key communications and command centers, and critical industrial facilities of either or both confrontation states before the U.S. or outside powers could intervene. If Israel were to launch such attacks on a surprise or preemptive basis, or do so before Syrian and/or Jordanian air forces were fully alert and dispersed, it would achieve nearly certain success. It would have a very high probability of success even against fully alert Syrian and Jordanian forces.

Israel has the ability to strike deep into the Arab world and has greatly improved its long range strike capability since its attacks on Osiraq in 1981 and on Tunisia in 1985.[82] It has greatly improved refueling capability, targeting capability, standoff precision munitions, and electronic warfare capability. Israel could probably surgically strike a limited number of key targets in virtually any Arab country within 1,500 nautical miles of Israel and could sustain operations against western Iraq. It would, however, probably be forced to use nuclear weapons to achieve significant strategic impact on more than a few Iraqi facilities or if it had to engage Syrian and Iraqi forces simultaneously.

This does not mean that the IAF does not have performance problems or limitations. It has had some recent scandals and incidents involving senior commanders.[83] Many aspects of the IAF involve the same resource compromises as the Israeli land and naval forces, and the IAF has experienced severe financial pressures in recent years, in part because of the massive costs of the now canceled Lavi program. These resources compromises have led to reductions in procurement and supply, the mothballing of some units, cuts in training levels and flight hours, a loss of operational tempo, and early grounding for a number of qualified pilots.

Like many nations in the West, Israel has been unable to strike an efficient balance of defense industry, modernization, and operational readiness. Israel does not have the kind of satellite and long range targeting and intelligence assets available to the U.S., although its UAVs are a limited substitute. Any large scale battle with Syria or Syria and some combination of other Arab allies would force Israel to engage with a wide range of tactics, weapons, and C^3I/BM systems and techniques that are experimental and subject to failure or problems.

There is also nothing racial or magical about the IAF's superiority. As was demonstrated during the canal war in 1970 and on many other occasions, individual Arab pilots are certainly as good as their Israeli counterparts. The IAF is vulnerable to a saturation attack, particularly if this were achieved at a time of strategic surprise, when the IAF either was not fully ready or failed to react properly. Carefully planned raids, with or without weapons of mass destruction, might well reach an urban target like Haifa or Tel Aviv.

The IAF also faces certain basic operational constraints. It can contribute to the land battle, but Syria's forces near the Golan are too close to the border and too large for any combination of interdiction bombing and close air support to substitute for the IDF's land forces. Israel's ability to win rapid air supremacy and conduct strategic attacks would be radically different if it confronted both a hostile Syria and a hostile Egypt.

It confronts the same limitations as all air forces in limited wars and low level battles of attrition in conducting precision bombing in urban warfare and locating and killing guerrilla forces. The IAF cannot destroy the dispersed land forces of a major enemy like Syria within a short period, although it might be decisive in cooperation with the IDF in an air-land offensive.

Any effort to achieve a decisive blow against Syria would also lead to operational requirements that present serious political problems. Any effort to minimize IAF losses and inflict maximum damage requires strategic surprise—either through preemption or deception and rapid massive escalation. It also involves unilateral action under conditions where U.S. and outside pressure to limit IAF military action would be kept as limited as possible and deferred as long as possible.

As Israel learned in 1982, it does not make sense to reveal its air defense suppression capabilities in limited attacks with limited objectives, giving an enemy time to improve its defense and develop countermeasures. The most effective uses of Israeli air power involve preemptive and total war, risking

Syrian escalation to biological and chemical weapons and/or a level of Israeli commitment to success that could force Israel to escalate to weapons of mass destruction if conventional IAF attacks failed.

On the one hand, the IAF operates under conditions that deter large scale action. On the other hand, the IAF operates under conditions that lead it towards sudden and massive escalation. This is particularly true if Israel should seek any decisive victory over Syria or Iraq. It is unclear whether Israel believes that any land victory over Syria or Iraq would be sufficient to force Syria to accept a peace or so weaken it that it could not recover as a threat in a few years.

At least some Israeli planners have argued since 1973, reinforced by Israel's experience in 1982, that Israel must either fight very limited military actions or strategically decisive ones. While Israel's political leadership has no current intention or desire to fight a strategically decisive war, it remains a very real military possibility. It is also unclear how well the leaders of Syria or Iraq or most Western policymakers understand these military risks and realities.

Israeli Air Force Assets and Capabilities

The IAF conducts air-to-air operations, air-to-ground operations, provides naval and ground aviation support, and deploys most of Israel's major land based air defenses. It now has an active strength of roughly 28,000 men and women versus 30,000 in 1982.[84] It has roughly 19,000 conscripts, most of whom are in air defense. It has some 591 combat aircraft, with up to 102 more in storage, as well as 94 combat helicopters. This compares with about 634 combat aircraft in 1982, up to 270 of which were in storage. It is roughly the size of the British Royal Air Force.

The IAF is now organized into sixteen dual capable attack/air defense squadrons, four fighter attack squadrons, a reconnaissance force, an airborne early warning (AEW) unit, an ECM unit, a transport wing, a liaison wing, training units, seven helicopter squadrons, and an air defense force with fifteen surface-to-air Improved Hawk battalions with MIM-23B Improved Hawk missiles and four MIM-104 Patriot surface-to-air/ATBM batteries. It has some twenty air bases, with key bases at Bir Hamma, Bir Hasanah, Bir Jifjifah, Dov-Hose, Ekron, El Arish, El Bassa, Hatzor, Mahanayim, Ramat David, Sedom, and Yafo.

The attack-interceptor squadrons in the IAF had 2/28 F-15C/Ds and 2/40 F-15A/Bs in mid-1992 versus 40 F-15A/Bs in 1982, with 6 F-15As, 4 F-15Bs, and 3 F-15Ds in delivery.[85] There were 3/54 F-16A/Bs and 75 F-16C/Ds versus a total of 72 F-16A/Bs in 1982, with 21 additional F-16C/Ds in delivery. There were 4/130 F-4E-IIs versus 138 F-4Es in 1982. Approximately 30 of these F-4E-IIs have been converted to Phantom 2000s. There are 4/150 Kfir C2/C7s versus 160 Kfir C1/C2s.[86]

Israel's four FGA squadrons had a total of 121 operational A-4H/N Skyhawks, out of total holdings of around 100, versus 174 active A-4s in 1982.[87] The above totals included IDF training units which are dual capable in combat missions and use at least 16 F-4Es, 5 Kfirs, and 27 TA-4H/J

Skyhawks out of the above totals. The IISS reports that an additional 13 of the F-4E-IIs, 75 of the Kfirs, and 14 of the A-4s in the above totals were in storage, but some may be in reserve. An additional 80 CM-170 Magisters/ Tzugits evidently were no longer organized for a dual role in combat.[88]

These aircraft numbers are impressive, but they are not an adequate measure of Israeli strength. Like Israeli ground forces, the IAF has such a complex mix of capabilities and equipment that it cannot be judged by conventional order of battle standards or by comparing its manpower and aircraft strength to that of Arab forces. It is supported by many qualitative force multipliers, many of which are classified or whose performance is deliberately misreported in Israeli literature.

Israel has modified and tailored its technology at every level. Its F-15A/ Bs are the current MSIP version of the aircraft and have electronics largely identical to those in the F-15C/D, although they cannot carry the additional 2,000 pounds of fuel in the F-15C/D, and the IAF could not fund all of the USAF and Israeli modifications it wanted.[89] They use the AN/ALR-56A radar warning receiver and have U.S. or Israeli radar jammers, threat warning receivers, and chaff dispensers.[90] There have also been reports that some IAF F-15s have been upgraded with the electronic warfare package that the Israeli firm Elisra originally designed for the Lavi. This package was rejected for Israel's F-16s because it was too expensive, but the advantages inherent in superior electronic warfare capability are another of the lessons Israel learned from the 1982 war and will go into Israel's first line air defense fighter.[91] Israel used its F-15s to score 11–12 kills during 1974–1982, 37–43 kills during the 1982 fighting, and 3 more between 1982 and 1992.[92]

All Israeli F-15s routinely use a mix of Python 3 heat seeking missiles and AIM-7M radar guided missiles in air-to-air combat. The Python 3 entered service with the IAF in 1982, and some sources credit it with about 50 kills in the 1982 fighting. It is somewhat similar to the AIM-9, but is a third generation Israeli-made successor to the Shamir 2. It is 75 pounds heavier than the AIM-9, carries a larger warhead, uses an improved passive infrared homing seeker, and has an all-aspect engagement capability and a maximum range of a little more than 3 miles.[93]

The IAF's F-16A/Bs have been upgraded to match the improving capability of USAF F-16C/D aircraft. They have also been modified with Israeli avionics, including RADA data transfer systems, Elisra/Loral electronic warfare suites, Orbit airborne communications systems, Elta advanced airborne radio systems, Elbit ACE-5 mission computers, electronics and software to use the Python 3, and refueling modifications.[94] Israel is considering the possibilities of establishing an F-16 production line in Israel and modifying the aircraft to install engine vectoring nozzles to improve maneuver and short field landing capability.[95] Like the F-15s, the F-16s have an excellent air-to-air combat record. The IAF has fought 25 engagements with F-16s and scored 52 kills, with 45 of them during the 1982 fighting with Syria. One source indicates that 43 of these kills have been with the Aim-9L, three with the Aim-9P, and six with guns.[96] These figures may, however, include some Python 3 kills. The Python 3 has been fully integrated with the IAF's F-16s since 1989.[97]

Israel got its first batch of 75 F-16A/Bs in 1980–1981 and got 75 F-16C/Ds during 1986–1988. It was still receiving its third batch of 30 F-16C/Ds during 1991–1992. Financial pressures have meant that just 13 of these new F-16C/Ds could be equipped with Lantirn for night attack missions, and even these have only Lantirn for night targeting rather than night navigation capability. Israel does, however, regard developing a 24-hour or night attack capability a major priority and a key lesson from the 1973 and 1982 wars—where many interdiction targets moved and were vulnerable only at night.

Israel is examining the option of buying 60 new multirole U.S. fighters for the late 1990s and beyond. It is considering both the advanced Block 50 version of the F-16C/D and an improved version of the F-18C/D. Both aircraft would be modified to use a substantial amount of Israeli electronics, including more advanced air-to-air engagement capabilities and night vision devices. The F-18C/D would have a more powerful GE F-404/GE-402 engine with 10% more thrust. The cost of this purchase could reach $3 billion and might force the IAF to buy only 48 aircraft if it opted for the more expensive F-18. Israel is, however, seeking substantial offsets. Similar arrangements have already brought it $460 million in offsets by General Dynamics for past F-16 purchases, and $300 million in offsets from McDonnell Douglas for past F-15, AH-64, and contract services purchases. Israel is also upgrading USAF F-15s deployed in Europe under contract to McDonnell Douglas.[98]

Israel's F-4Es have improved avionics, engines, and some air frame modifications but have not been fully rebuilt. They use AN/ALQ–119V or locally built jamming pods. They have scored 140 air-to-air kills since 1967; 128 against fixed wing aircraft and 20 against helicopters.[99] Approximately 120 F-4s have received some form of life extension program and upgrading of their electronics and of their ability to use advanced precision guided munitions. They will remain in service well beyond the year 2000.[100]

Fifty F-4Es are being converted to the Phantom 2000 or Super Phantom, and some have already been completed. These modifications include conversion from analog to digital electronics, redundant 1553 multiplex avionics buses, new high resolution all-aspect radars, new heads-up displays with wide fields of view, new communications and navigation equipment, improved EW-ECM capability, multifunction displays, improved stores management, modern and highly simplified wiring, reinforcement of skins and fuel cells, new attachment fittings, new engine mounts, optional canards and large fuel tank attachments, reduced numbers of line replaceable units, built-in test equipment, and less vulnerable hydraulics.

The value of the Phantom 2000 upgrade has been severely reduced, however, by an ongoing failure of the Norden Company of the U.S. to deliver the multimode radar system for the aircraft and by the inability to upgrade the engine. Replacing the J-79 engine with the Pratt and Whitney 1120 also proved to be too expensive but would have produced a 21% shorter takeoff distance, tighter turns at high altitude, better maneuverability, higher penetration speed, and a payload increase (from 4,740 to 9,000 pounds, or 9 to 18 bombs, at Mach 0.89).[101]

Israel built a total of 212 Kfirs, and virtually all the remaining aircraft in service have been upgraded to the Kfir C7/TC7. The C7 is a single seat multirole with a maximum speed at sea level of about 750 knots and a ceiling of 55,000 feet. The fighter is derived from the Mirage V and has improved steadily over time. The C7 version has greatly improved avionics—including updated electronic warfare equipment, the WDNS-341 weapons delivery and navigation system, Elbit System 82 computerized stores management and release system, video sub-systems, and smart weapons delivery capability—and increased engine thrust. It has a hands-on throttle and stick control, and two additional stores stations in comparison with the initial Kfir C2. The Kfir C7 has Elisra SPS-200 or 2000 radar warning receivers and can carry jamming pods or chaff. It can also carry four infrared air-to-air missiles. The Kfir C7 still seems to be limited to a ranging radar but can mount the EL/M-2021 advanced pulse Doppler fire control radar. This adds both a modern look-down, air-to-air combat capability and mapping, terrain avoidance, and all-weather munitions delivery capability.[102]

Israel's A-4N Skyhawks are aging attack fighters and are vulnerable to short range and medium range air defenses and modern air-to-air fighters, but they have had major air frame improvements. These include life extension, overhaul, provision of dual disc brakes on the wheels, a steerable nose wheel, an extension of the tail pipe to reduce infrared emission, and the addition of a brake chute. Other improvements have taken place. Two hard points have been added, the cannon have been increased in caliber from 20mm to 30mm, flares and chaff dispensers have been added, changes have been made in the avionics, and the nose has been extended and the hump behind the cockpit modified to hold more electronics—including some form of electronic warfare protection.[103] While the IAF would like to replace the A-4 with a more modern aircraft, it will remain in service for some years. Israel's Magisters (Tzugits) were heavily modified and rebuilt during the 1980s to act as trainers. They are aging, however, and the IAF needs a new trainer for the 1990s.

Israel has modified its concept of combat aircraft improvement in recent years as a result of its problems with the Lavi. In the period between 1982 and 1987, Israel stressed giving its aircraft the features most desired by its pilots. The resulting cost, however, led to studies that revealed that many pilot suggestions were tailoring the aircraft to provide features that demanded more and more specialized pilot skills and which were of only marginal benefit in terms of mission capability. Israel is now much more careful to analyze mission benefits and is designing its avionics to emphasize operability for all its pilots, not just the top ranking ones.[104]

Israel is steadily improving its ability to use advanced air-to-air missiles, smart air munitions, and ground launched rocket and missiles against aircraft, SAM sites, and air bases. It sees smart and/or highly lethal munitions, linked to sophisticated targeting systems with near real-time data transmittal capabilities, as a critically important way of multiplying the effectiveness of its air units.

The IAF now has AIM-9L, AIM-7E/F/M, R-530, Shafrir II, and Python 3 air-to-air missiles in inventory. The Shafrir II air-to-air missile is still in service and is the predecessor of the Python. It is a rear hemisphere, engagement only, infrared guided missile similar to the AIM-9 B.

Israel also has Luz, AGM-65 Maverick, AGM-45 Shrike, AGM-62A Walleye, AGM-12 Bullpup, AGM-78 Standard ARM, Walleye, Rockeye, and Gabriel III air-to-surface weapons, and large numbers of cluster bombs—including its own TAL designs. It may have fuel-air explosive weapons. Israel has developed and deployed large numbers of Griffin laser guidance kits for the Mark 82, Mark 83, and Mark 84 bombs, with a range of up to 10 kilometers and a circular error probable (CEP) of 8 meters. It is developing a new laser guidance weapon called Guillotine with a range of about 30 kilometers and a CEP of 2 meters. It also has a homing bomb system called Opher with an IR seeker that can be added to Mark 82 and Mark 83 bombs as a fire and forget weapon. A TV guided bomb called Pyramid is in development.

Israel has developed a large number of guided offensive weapons. These include a large rocket boosted glide bomb called Popeye which the U.S. used as the AGM-142 or "Have Nap" on B-52s flown in Desert Storm. It is a TV guided missile which uses a Mark 84 bomb as a warhead and has a large 895 kilogram warhead, inertial guidance with TV or imaging IR homing, a digital data link, and a maximum range of about 80 kilometers. It can be launched by the Kfir, F-15, and F-16.[105] Israel also has an air launched version of the Gabriel anti-ship missile with a range of 35 kilometers, sea skimming capabilities, and a 150 kilogram semi-armor piercing warhead. A medium range laser guided air-to-surface missile called the Nimrod is in development. It has a range of 25 kilometers and a 15 kilogram warhead suited for anti-armor or small point target killing.[106]

Israel has continued to make improvements in its ability to use aircraft to support ground forces. It is steadily improving its air-to-ground munitions lethality and range—with an emphasis on high volumes of accurate delivery of dumb but more lethal munitions in low vulnerability attack profiles. It has rejected reliance on the smart munitions and point kill for broad use in close support and interdiction missions, although it is improving its ability to use such systems for shock and critical time-sensitive kill missions.

Israeli Air Force Command, Reconnaissance, and Intelligence Aircraft and Systems

Israel has one of the few Middle Eastern air forces capable of providing a full range of defensive countermeasures for its aircraft, and it has heavily modified these countermeasures to suit local combat conditions or introduced designs of its own. It regularly deploys on-board chaff and flare dispensers as well as radar homing and warning receivers. It has its own and U.S. internally active countermeasure systems and ECM pods.[107] Pilots receive excellent training in these systems, and they normally have high standards of maintenance and operational readiness.

IAF reconnaissance, electronic warfare, and C^3I/battle management units have continued to be strengthened as a result of the lessons of the 1982 and other recent conflicts. The IAF now has 14 RF-4Es and 5 Kfir RC-12s—

roughly the same strength as in 1982—but with major improvements in their equipment. Its AEW units have four updated and Israeli-modified E-2Cs fitted with AN/APS-125/138 surveillance radars and AN/ALR-73 passive detection systems.[108]

The IAF's electronic intelligence and ECM squadrons include a number of specially modified aircraft and RPVs, including 6 E-707s, 1 C-130H, 2 EV-1E ECM, 4 IAI 201 ELINT, 5 RC-12D and 6 RC-21D ELINT, and 3 RU-21A aircraft. The E-707s seem to use Elta EL/L-8300 equipment for electronic intelligence, communications intelligence, and command analysis. They cover a 360° area and transmitters up to 450 kilometers away from the aircraft. They provide a continuously updated electronic display at COMINT and ELINT consoles and have a secure air-ground data link. Some may have special naval electronic support measure or ELINT systems. The IAI 201, RU-21A, and RC-12D are configured for tactical signals intelligence missions. The IAI-201s carry ELINT and SIGINT equipment. The RU-21As are fitted for airborne direction finding against hostile communications nets. The RC-12Ds are fitted with the U.S. Guardrail V target location and identification system.[109] There are 20 Bell 206 and Bell 212 ECM and SAR helicopters. Some of these aircraft have airborne command functions.[110]

The E-2Cs play a critical role in large scale air combat. They provide vectoring for Israeli fighters, although this can sometimes be done by regional control centers on the ground. They perform electronic intelligence missions, help reduce the IFF problem, and manage overall IAF fighter deployments according to the need of the battle. Israel also, however, uses the long range radars on its F-15s so that an F-15 in the rear can help direct forward deployed Israeli fighters into combat without having to risk direct engagement. The E-2Cs also provide Israeli with excellent low altitude radar coverage, filling in the gaps left by land based radars. This allows Israeli fighters to take advantage of their excellent low altitude combat training. The IAF is one of the few forces in the Middle East capable of training and controlling its fighter forces for low altitude combat.

Israel has designed a new variant of its B-707s called the Falcon, which combines Israeli-designed early warning and command and control equipment with improved radars, equipment for identification of friend or foe (IFF), ELINT equipment, electronic warfare systems, and a variety of display systems. If this system is successful, it will be the first AWACS-type aircraft to eliminate the radar dome above the aircraft. It uses an Elta EL/M-2075 phased array radar of about 800 transmit/receive modules in six antenna arrays molded to conform with the aircraft fuselage. This allows 360° operation without interference from the wings, engines, or tail. It is claimed to be able to detect a 5m^2 target out to 350 kilometers, ships out to 500 kilometers, and cruise missiles out to 230 kilometers. It also allows all of the arrays to be concentrated in one area, provides tracking within 4 seconds versus 20–40 seconds for a rotating dome radar, and is supposed to be more sensitive to slow moving and hovering helicopters.[111]

Israel also has 24 Wild Weasel F-4Es which are specially equipped to carry the U.S. AGM-78B Standard anti-radiation missile. These aircraft were used extensively in the Bekaa Valley operations in 1982 and reflect one of the key lessons that Israel drew from the 1973 fighting: the need for effective anti-radar missiles as a key air defense suppression weapon.

The Wild Weasel F-4Es can carry four AGM-78Bs each. They have special J79-17B engines, AN/APQ-120(V)4 radars, and TISEO long range optical visual identification systems. There are special displays and provision for the launch of AGM-65 missiles. The aircraft do not have emitter location equipment separate from the missile, and Israel put its own improved Purple Heart seeker on the AGM-78Bs as a result of the lessons it learned in 1982. Israel is believed to be modifying other aircraft to use this anti-radiation missile (ARM) system.[112]

Israel continues to expand its use of unmanned airborne vehicles or remotely piloted vehicles (RPVs). It currently operates hundreds of the Mastiff, Scout, Teledyne Ryan 124R, MQM-74C Chukar I, Chukar II, Samson, Pioneer, Searcher, and Delilah (decoy) UAVs. These systems perform a wide range of targeting and intelligence functions and use photo, IR, ELINT, and possibly small radar sensors. Israel is the world's first major user of RPVs, and its Mastiffs and Scouts had logged some 10,000 flight hours and over 1,000 sorties by the mid-1980s, including the several hundred sorties they flew in 1982. Israel is believed to have some RPVs modified for attack purposes, including some designed to home on radar emitters.

Israel has deployed third and fourth generation UAVs such as the Pioneer. The Pioneer has a payload of 45 kilograms versus 38 for the Scout, and an endurance of eight to nine hours versus four to six hours for Israel's older RPVs. Its speed is increased from 60 to 70 nautical miles per hour, and its air frame is made from composite materials rather than metal to reduce its radar signature. Like previous Israeli RPVs, the Pioneer is very quiet and normally hard to see. It has a ceiling of 15,000 feet and a video transmission range of up to 200 kilometers.

The equipment on the Pioneer includes a TV camera, thermal imager, electronic warfare equipment, and a laser range finder or designator. It will be deployed in field units with four Pioneers each and can be launched with a pneumatic catapult and rocket booster or on any 250 meter long stretch of road. It can land in 70 meters with a net. The Pioneer has a greatly improved down link and display system and can be turned over to remote forward deployed control stations. The normal range of the down link is 30 to 40 kilometers.[113] It gives Israel an even greater advantage in tactical reconnaissance and surveillance capability than it had in 1982 and allows the IDF to carry out such missions without exposing personnel.[114]

Israel has more advanced systems in deployment and development. These include a twin engine system with about twice the range payload of the Pioneer. This system is called the Impact and can operate at ranges from 150 to 300 kilometers beyond Israel's front lines. It is designed to have a much lower radar cross-section than previous RPVs, has a 150 pound payload, an endurance of 12 hours, a maximum speed of 120 knots, a loiter speed of 60 knots, and a multimission stabilized TV/FLIR sensor payload. It can be deployed as a containerized unit in the back of a pickup truck.[115]

Several Israeli UAVs have been developed for air defense suppression. The Delilah is a modular system that can either be used with an active payload to simulate the presence of an attack aircraft—and draw enemy fighters, surface-to-air missiles, and anti-aircraft fire away from real attack aircraft—or with a passive payload to saturate an area with chaff to blind enemy air defense radars. It uses active elements in the A, C, and L radar bands to simulate aircraft as well as a passive Luneberg lens reflector to expand its apparent size to enemy radars. It weighs only 180 kilograms and can be carried by an attack fighter like the F-4. It can fly at speeds of Mach 0.4 to 0.8, has a range of up to 400 kilometers, and can simulate fighter maneuvers in the target area with a positioning accuracy of better than 91 meters.

Israel has also developed a remotely piloted vehicle or drone called the Harpee or STAR-1. This would be able to loiter for extended periods over the battlefield and then home in immediately on any radar that started to operate in the area, even if it only emitted for very short periods of time.[116] The Harpee is similar in concept to the U.S. Seek Spinner and Tactic Rainbow missiles. While the details are classified, the system evidently can loiter for several hours waiting for a threat radar to emit and then home in on it and kill it. This would allow it to replace the much more costly, aging, and vulnerable F-4E Wild Weasels. It seems to have been tested in simulated missions where it did home in and hit military radars. Such a system would give Israel a greatly improved ability to destroy Arab air defense systems without exposing high cost aircraft and would mean an Arab force could never predict when its air defense systems would be attacked.[117]

All of these various airborne or flying assets are linked to very sophisticated battle management and fusion centers and to field mobile C^3I/BM systems that can directly support the land forces. It is important to note that the IDF's integration of land and air intelligence, sensor, and battle management systems gives it a further advantage in the air-land battle. They are backed by a wide range of active and passive electronic warfare systems. Israel has succeeded in improving its edge over Syria in every aspect of electronic warfare. Israel has also greatly increased the sophistication of its ground based forward electronic warfare and targeting efforts, although the details remain classified.

Israeli Air Force Helicopter Forces

The Israeli Air Force is continuing to improve its attack and assault helicopter numbers and its tactics for using these helicopters. Israel found during the 1982 war that its initial operational concept for using helicopters was wrong. The IAF had planned to use helicopters to fly close support. In practice, it found it had firepower saturation in the forward area, had major IFF problems in not firing on its own helicopters, and could not spare the time to try to vector helicopters in against known targets. The IAF's attack helicopters rapidly changed behavior and began to fly search-and-kill missions behind the lines in an interdiction role. In spite of worries about power and survivability in mountain terrain, the IAF found that the helicopter could achieve surprise and considerable survivability by picking the right points of attack and that ground forces have more serious problems in detecting helicopters in mountain terrain than on the plains. Army units moving in mountain areas are noisier and have problems adjusting to the closed-in terrain which is much harder to scout from the land than the air. They also have far more predictable movements.

The IAF now has a total of 75 armed helicopters versus 42 in 1982. These include three squadrons with about 40 AH-1G/S Cobra and 35 Hughes MD-500 Defender attack helicopters, both armed with TOW anti-tank guided missiles. Israel began to build its attack helicopter force in the mid-1970s when it bought 6 AH-1G/Q Cobras and 20 of the lighter and less expensive Defender attack helicopters.

During its 1982 invasion of Lebanon, Israel formed its attack helicopters into a light anti-tank battlegroup called the Koach Peled. It used the helicopters in combination with paratroops in M-113s and jeeps equipped with TOW missiles. The attack helicopters saw extensive service in the Bekaa Valley and Shuf Mountains against Syrian tanks. They scored a significant number of tank kills, although two Cobras were lost. It was also impressed by the performance of Syrian Mi-24 attack helicopters against Israeli armor.

This combat experience led Israel to more than double its attack helicopter strength and modernize its Defenders and Cobras. Israel found during the 1982 fighting that even light attack helicopters like the Hughes 500D Defender could survive and be effective against hard targets with TOW and soft targets with rockets if pilots took advantage of their high agility, low sound levels, and terrain masking. The 500Ds repeatedly engaged enemy columns in interdiction missions. The IAF has successfully modified some 500Ds to carry four TOW anti-tank guided missiles in low drag launchers by removing the two rear seats.

The IAF has converted most of its AH-1s to the S-3 type used by the U.S., and these can carry significant firepower: up to eight TOW ATGMs, a three barreled 20mm gun, two rocket pods of 19 rockets, and/or bombs, illumination rockets, and smoke rockets. Many have been modified to improve their survivability and add firepower. The IAF is considering adding a night targeting system that integrates a television camera FLIR and an autotracker, and a new navigation and heads-up display system. According to some reports, Israel is also acting on the lessons it learned in 1982 to take advantage of such advanced U.S. technology as helmet sights and range finder readout, which are aligned to the TOW sight and a separate laser range finder, to extend the operational range at which it can hit with guns and ATGMs.

The IAF is using U.S. and Israeli systems to suppress helicopter IR emissions and U.S. radar warning receivers. It also has equipped its helicopter crews with night vision devices and regularly trains for night combat missions. It is experimenting with its own laser designated version of the TOW called the Togger and is seeking to develop a helicopter ATGM that can be fired for final target designation by an IDF soldier on the ground.[118]

Israel ordered 19 AH-64 Apache attack helicopters and 539 Hellfire missiles in April, 1990. The AH-64s are all-weather, night combat systems equipped with the AGM-114 Hellfire laser guided anti-armor missiles that proved highly effective during the Gulf War. The IAF had 1 squadron with 18 Apaches in service by 1991. The AH-64s in the IAF entered combat for the first time in November, 1991 in a night attack using Hellfires against guerrilla occupied buildings in Lebanon. The aircraft performed well and were used as part of a joint operation with AH-1Ss and Hughes 500MDs. Israel would like to buy a total of at least 24 AH-64s under its current plans and would like to order a total of 48.[119]

Because the IAF does not release data on helicopter strength, counts of its transport helicopters are uncertain. It has 32–48 variants of the heavy CH-53A/D transport helicopter, which have evidently been updated to the S-65-3 standard and given airborne refueling capability. The CH-53Ds are being further upgraded to the CH-53 2000 standard, with improved electronics, a new cockpit, a new navigation and flight instrument package, and a night vision goggle/heads-up display system, and it will be overhauled. The IAF also has 8 aging Aerospatiale SA-321K Super Frelon helicopters, 12 UH-1D medium transport helicopters, 40 Bell 206A, and 55 Bell 205 and 212 light transport helicopters. It is gradually phasing out the Super Frelons and Bell 205s.[120]

The IAF's transport wing and fixed wing support aircraft do not appear to have changed greatly since the mid- to late 1980s. They include 8 B-707s (five modified to be tankers), 2 KC-130H tankers, 24 C-130E/Hs, 10 IAI-201s, 3 IAI-1124s, and 19 C-47s. The liaison forces have 4 BN-2 Islanders, 6 Dornier Do-27s, 9 Do-28Ds, and 12 Queen Air 80s. This mix of aircraft gives Israel considerable airlift and air supply capability.

Israel's Land Based Air and Missile Defenses

The Israeli Air Force has an air defense force with Improved Hawk and Patriot surface-to-air missile defenses. As has been noted earlier, these are backed by Stinger, Redeye, and 48 Chaparral light surface-to-air missiles, and 48 Vulcan, some ZSU-23-4, and other radar-guided light anti-aircraft guns. It has numerous unguided AA guns mounted on vehicles and used as towed weapons. These include many 20mm twin towed weapons, 40mm Bofors guns, and large numbers of captured Soviet-made weapons.

In the past, Israel has relied on an outer screen of air defense fighters, a second defense line of Hawk missiles, and short range missiles and anti-aircraft guns for point defense. Missile defenses, however, have taken on steadily greater importance as a result of the proliferation of long range missiles in Arab forces and Iraq's Scud attacks on Israel during the Gulf War. While fighters remain Israel's principal air defense, it will have to rely on anti-tactical ballistic missiles (ATBMs) as a critical part of its future defenses.

Israel's major land based air defense weapons are the Improved Hawk and the Patriot. Israel has 17 battalions of Hawk surface-to-air missiles and roughly 100 launchers. While some Hawk units are manned by reservists, Israel sets far higher training, maintenance, and system readiness standards than Egypt or Syria. Further, at least two-thirds of Israel's Hawk forces are heavily modified Improved Hawks. They have radar and guidance software that allow intercepts at up to 70,000 feet. An Israeli Hawk battery in Lebanon shot down a MiG-25 at an even higher altitude and flying at Mach 2.5 on August 30, 1982.

The Israelis also added a $30,000 Supereye electro-optical detector to its Hawks in the mid-1970s to improve IFF and provide fighter detection at ranges up to 50 kilometers and identification at 30 kilometers—an addition that greatly eases the problem of deciding whether to fire at a penetrating aircraft. According to one report, there were two confirmed cases in 1982 where this system prevented Israeli units from firing on their own aircraft. Israel has steadily upgraded its Improved Hawk surface-to-air missile systems and intends to buy the new Product Improvement 3 program. It is considering modifying its Hawks to provide a limited anti-tactical ballistic missile defense capability.[121] As for Chaparral, the IDF has added an Amarit electro-optical and threat designation communication system for identification and target observation.

Israel originally had mixed feelings about the Patriot surface-to-air missile system which was extremely costly and had only limited anti-tactical missile capability. It had bought two batteries with 10 fire units before the Gulf War, but these forces were still in training when the war began.[122] Iraq's Scud attacks on Israel led the U.S. to rush the Patriot units to Israel and Israel to upgrade the anti-tactical missile training and equipment of the Israeli Patriot units on a crash basis.

These rapid deployments, problems in agreeing on method of operation and the rules of engagement, siting in inappropriate areas, and use of a point defense system in an area defense role led to operating and effectiveness problems. These difficulties were compounded by the fact that the Iraqi missiles broke up during reentry—a targeting problem that required rapid changes in the rules of engagement, operating procedures, and software.

The Patriots intercepted many Scuds over populated areas and often hit the missile body instead of the warhead. As a result, considerable physical damage still took place in the targeted areas. U.S. Army and IDF after-action studies found that the Patriots deployed in Israel affected only 40% of the incoming Scud warheads versus as many of 70% in Saudi Arabia. Nevertheless, the successful intercept of at least part of most missiles was a critical morale builder while Israel was under attack.[123]

The full range of facts surrounding the performance of the Patriot in Israel during the Gulf War remains classified, and reports attacking the performance of the missile neither accurately explain the problems that occurred nor provide an accurate picture of the missiles' success. Both U.S. and IDF experts, however, agree that the Patriot did achieve a remarkable degree of success under very demanding conditions, and that the PAC-3 improvements to the Patriot's ATBM capabilities will correct many of the problems in the system. Israel may eventually deploy six Patriot batteries.[124]

The IDF's air defense command and control system is derived from a Hughes design originally sold to Israel in the mid-1970s. Its main command centers are near Tel Aviv and in the western Negev. It once used Hughes

4118 digital computers and Westinghouse AN/TPS-43D and AN/FPS-200 radars and system, as well as a mix of other radars. It has since been updated to use Elta radars, to use data from Israel's E-2Cs and electronic intelligence assets. Communications and data processing have been vastly improved over time, as have software, computers, and displays. The operator consoles and support system has been completely modernized since the 1982 fighting.

Israel issued plans to modernize its air defense radar system in June, 1992. It is seeking two to three advanced early warning radars at a cost of $50 million. These would be sharp resolution systems with a multidirectional phased array beam. They would probably be mobile to reduce vulnerability, and one each would be deployed in the north, central, and southern parts of the country. The GE TPS-117, Westinghouse TPS-70, and a modified form of the Raytheon Pave Paws are possible candidates. They would be deployed as part of a general upgrade of Israeli communications, data processing, and ground-to-air data links and could be used to provide missile as well as aircraft warning.

The Israeli Navy

Israel is slowly modernizing its small 9,000 man navy, which performs the missions of halting seaborne infiltration, coastal defense, sea control, and support of the land forces. The Israeli navy is based at Haifa, Ashdod, and Eilat. It is very selective in choosing regular personnel and has only about 3,300 conscripts. It could grow to a strength of about 10,000 upon full mobilization, but Israel does not put heavy emphasis on calling up large reserve forces. There is a small 300 man naval commando force, and the navy maintains shore based surveillance radars and electronic warfare and intelligence equipment.

The navy has 58 vessels, including 3 patrol submarines, 20 fast attack missile ships, 12 fast attack gun ships, 3 hydrofoils, 31 coastal patrol craft, 6 LCTs, 3 LCPs, and 2 support ships. Its ships now being built or planned include 2 patrol submarines, 3 corvettes, 4 fast attack gun ships, and 2 LCTs. Most of the fleet is deployed in the Mediterranean. Only about seven Dauber-class coastal patrol boats and some smaller ships are based at Eilat.

Training and readiness levels are high, the ratio of enlisted men to officers is only about 8:1, and maintenance and logistic support is generally good. All naval combat vessels are kept ready for immediate action. The naval reserve represents about 25% of the fully mobilized navy, but an annual plan is followed to augment ship crews with reservists on a daily basis. Any given crew billet may be filled throughout the year by a continuous flow of reservists, and training is conducted on the job. There are a few specialized naval reserve units such as an emergency diving unit and a crew for one of the navy's LCTs.

Although Israel has given its navy relatively low priority because of funding problems, the 1982 war has shown that Israel should respond to the increases in Syrian long range naval strike capability. This impression was reinforced by Palestinian speed boat attacks on Israel in 1990. One basic problem that motivates Israel to modernize its navy is its dependence on resupply (some 95% of U.S. resupply in 1973 came by sea), but Israel is also reacting to Syrian orders of improved submarines and deliveries of long range anti-ship missiles from the former USSR.[125]

Israel has three 420-ton Gal-class diesel coastal submarines, which were made by Vickers nearly two decades ago. All three are equipped with the submerged launched version of Harpoon, have been modernized to use NT37E active/passive homing torpedoes, and have improved sonars. They are fully operational, and Israel has regularly overhauled and modernized them, but they are due to leave service as early as 1996.

Israel has long planned to replace its Gals with West German–made Type-206 submarines during the 1990s. This modernization effort, however, has had an uncertain history and has proved difficult to fund. Israel originally took the decision to buy two Type-206s in 1988. This decision came after a delay of nearly five years because of fiscal constraints, and Israel decided that it could only afford two Type-206s rather than the three it needed to replace the Gals. The Israeli program called for three modified West German submarines called the Dolphin class, and Israel was to construct one submarine in the FRG and assemble the others in Israel.[126]

In March, 1989 it became clear that Israel's plans to buy two submarines and three large oceangoing corvettes would cost at least $1.3 billion. This was more than Israel could afford in view of its January, 1989 budget cuts, and the navy chose to buy the corvettes and delay the submarines.[127] In July, 1989 Israel took the decision to buy the two submarines after it obtained FMS funding from the U.S. The contract called for them to be built in Germany by Howaldtswerke, with Litton as the prime contractor, and work on the hull was scheduled to begin in October, 1991.[128] In November, 1990, however, Israel ran into new funding problems because of the threat of an attack by Iraq. This forced Israel to cancel its FMS contract with the U.S., but Germany then picked up the cost of the contract as aid to Israel. The Israeli navy should get the new submarines as early as 1997, but this could leave a gap if the Gals are forced to retire earlier.

Israel is building three new Lahav-class (Saar 5) corvettes. These are 1,200-ton major surface vessels. Israel would have liked to buy a total of four such corvettes but can afford only three. The Lahav-class ships have far more range, multimission capability, and advanced electronic warfare, missile protection, and sensor gear than Israel's existing ships. The hulls will be built at the Ingalls Shipyard in Pascagoula, Mississippi, at a cost of around $300 million and be fitted in Israel. Each Lahav-class will have one Dauphin SA-366G or SH-2F helicopter or a Hellstar UAV. It will have Barak vertical launch surface-to-air/anti-missile missiles, two quad Harpoon anti-ship missile launchers, one 76mm gun, six 324mm torpedo tubes, modern electronics, and over-the-horizon attack capabilities—including an RPV. The Lahav-class ships will have very modern electronics, sensors, and electronic and IR countermeasures. The total cost of the three fully fitted ships will be around $750 million.[129] The first will be delivered in 1993 and the other two in 1994.[130]

One of the lessons that Israel has drawn from the fighting in the Falklands is that its existing vessels need better electronic and missile protection. As a result, it may operate its Lahav-class ships in task groups with its older ships. This would provide some protection for the older vessels.[131]

Israel now has twenty smaller guided missile patrol boats versus twenty-seven in 1982. These include five 488-ton Aliya/Romat-class missile patrol boats (Saar 4.5s) built between 1980 and 1990. Two have four Gabriel II/III (36 kilometer maximum range) and four Harpoon (130 kilometer maximum range) ship-to-ship missile launchers. Three have two quad Harpoon launchers and six to eight Gabriel launchers. They carry different mixes of 32 cell Barak vertical launch surface-to-air/anti-missile launch units, a 76mm gun, and Dauphin SA-366G helicopters or Hellstar RPVs for long range targeting.

There are seven 250-ton Mivtach-class (six Saar 2 and one Saar 3) fast missile attack craft. They have two or four Harpoon launchers, six Gabriel II launchers, one 76mm gun, and two or four 324mm torpedo tubes. All were built during 1968 and 1969. There are also eight 450-ton Reshef-class (Saar 4) fast missile attack craft, with four to six Gabriel II/III, and two to four Harpoon ship-to-ship missile launchers. They have one to two 76mm guns. Both the Mivtach- and Reshef-class ships have been heavily modified with Israeli electronics and countermeasure systems, and some sources indicate that Israel has modified the homing systems on its Harpoons.

The Israeli navy has a 47-ton guided missile patrol boat, the Dvora, with Gabriel missiles, built in 1977. It also has 12 Super Dvora-class fast attack craft with guns and is building four more.[132] These are 48–56 ton ships with two 20mm guns. Built in the late 1980s, these may be fitted with the Dvora missile, torpedoes, or a 130mm multiple rocket launcher. There are 31 35-ton Dabur-class coastal patrol boats, armed with two 20mm guns, torpedoes, and depth charges. They were built between 1973 and 1977 and are considered slow by current standards.

Israel has been examining the use of high speed naval assault ships like hydrofoils for missions like rapid amphibious landings since the period before the 1982 war. It has three 105-ton Shimrit (U.S. Flagstaff 2-class) hydrofoils, with two Gabriel III anti-radiation homing missiles and two Harpoon anti-ship missile launchers each. Israel has improved its amphibious and forced entry capability. It has three 750-ton Ashdod-class LCT ships with helicopter decks, three 230-ton Kishon-class LCTs, and two more LCTs planned. The LCTs can carry about 1,000 men or forty armored vehicles each and demonstrated their value during Israel's amphibious operations in Lebanon in 1982. It has three 24-ton LCPs and one 150-ton Bat Sheva–class amphibious transport. It also has a wide variety of support ships, including 1 patrol craft depot ship. Its small naval commando force has Firefish III attack craft.

The air force provides search, reconnaissance, and rescue services. It has 25 Bell 212 helicopters for use in search, reconnaissance and rescue, and coastal helicopter surveillance missions, and 3–5 IAI-1124 Seascan maritime patrol aircraft for intelligence gathering and coastal surveillance. All are equipped with Israeli electronics and modifications. Israel can use its E-2Cs for airborne early warning but generally reserves them for air force missions.

While the Israeli navy has obvious limitations in strength and strike power, it is far more sophisticated in electronic warfare, countermeasures, intelligence, warning, targeting, and missile warfare than any Arab navy—particularly Syria's. The Israeli navy no longer faces a Soviet threat and does not have to plan for a two front war against Egypt, except as a remote contingency. As a result, Israel is likely to achieve sea control against any currently likely Arab naval threat.

Israeli Paramilitary Forces

Israel makes extensive use of paramilitary forces to supplement its active forces. Its 6,000 man border guard is particularly important in halting Palestinian and Lebanese Shi'ite infiltrations and attacks. It is organized into battalions under the control of the Ministry of Interior and is equipped with 600 Walid 1, BTR-40, and BTR-152 armored personnel carriers and crew sized weapons. Recent cuts in active military forces have increased the role of the border guards, and they have become a key part of the defense of the occupied territories. The border guard is subordinated to the army in wartime.

There are 500 men in the coast guard or maritime police, which are equipped with 9 Yatush-class patrol boats and crew served weapons. This force is capable only of police operations.

The 5,000 man Nahal provides defense for the settlements and early military training and has sometimes been used to preserve civil order. It is a light infantry force, with defense cadres in most of Israel's exposed or forward settlements. It is well trained and plays a key role in dealing with infiltration by the PLO and other Palestinian forces. Members are subject to call-up to the army in war, but such call-up is selective, and key settlement forces would evidently be left intact.

Israel and Weapons of Mass Destruction

The arms control problem in Israel is further compounded by Israel's nuclear status.[133] The Vanunu disclosures have led to speculation that Israel first expanded its reactor at Dimona to 70 megawatts and then to 150 megawatts—creating special new cooling systems to disguise the expansion. Many U.S. experts believe, however, that the Dimona reactor is still at 40 megawatts and that it has not been expanded beyond 70 megawatts. This uncertainty over the expansion of the Dimona reactor creates a possible range of total Israeli production in 1985 of anywhere from 50 to 90 plutonium weapons, provided that Israel was forced to use the normal amount of plutonium in such weapons. There are no reliable reports on whether Israel has produced uranium weapons, although there are reports that it has had centrifuge separation capability since 1980 and laser isotope separation capability since 1981.[134]

These estimates of weapons numbers are complicated by other aspects of Vanunu's disclosures. In 1986 Vanunu claimed that Dimona had a production rate of about 30 kilograms of plutonium a year, which is enough for roughly 7 weapons. This production rate could have given Israel well over 100 weapons by 1985 and well over 135 weapons in 1990.[135]

Vanunu also claimed that Israel had both lithium deuteride and tritium and described the building of the required lithium isotope plant during 1982–1986 in some detail, as well as reporting the building of a pilot plant in 1977. If Vanunu is correct, such a capability would allow Israel to boost its fission weapons to yields in excess of 100 kilotons, reduce the amount of material it required per bomb, or even build a fusion weapon.[136] As a result, Israeli stockpiles may have included some highly efficient weapons by the early 1980s, as well as other enhanced yield weapons with variable yields of up to 100 kilotons or more.[137]

Some U.S. experts like Theodore Taylor speculate that Israel has the technology to build plutonium weapons using only 8.8 pounds (4 kilograms) of material versus the 16–18 pounds normally used to calculate the amount required per weapon. Other work by Frank Barnaby indicates that Israel may have at least 35 weapons with yields boosted up to 100 kilotons or more. Such high yield weapons would largely remove the need for thermonuclear weapons—since Israeli missiles almost certainly have sufficient CEPs to hit any regional target close enough to destroy it, and there are no targets hardened enough to survive such blasts.[138]

There is no way to know how advanced the Israeli nuclear effort really is. However, part of the reason that Israel smuggled some 810 high speed switches known as krytrons from the U.S. between 1981 and 1983 may have been to improve the design and yield of its nuclear weapons. The krytron greatly improves the timing of the pulses used to trigger the high explosive lenses that compress the fissile material in a nuclear bomb.[139] This kind of technology transfer also helps explain why some experts believe that Israel was producing up to ten nuclear weapons a year at its nuclear facility by the mid-1980s, had at least 100 nuclear weapons by 1981–1983, and may have had over 200 weapons by 1990.[140]

As for the current details of Israel's nuclear facilities, they are known to include major nuclear research facilities at Soreq and Negev, the 5 megawatt research reactor fueled with highly enriched uranium called the IRR-1, the so-called IRR-2 at the Negev Nuclear Research Center in Dimona, hot cell facilities at Soreq and Negev, and a pilot plant for extracting uranium from phosphates at the Negev center. The details of Israeli uranium enrichment facilities are still unknown, although Israel definitely possesses substantial centrifuge technology and is known to be experimenting with laser isotope separation.[141] Israel is not a signatory to the nonproliferation treaty, and the only facility where it permits IAEA inspection is the IRR-1.[142]

Some of the details of the development and current nature of Israel's nuclear weapons delivery systems are as uncertain as the details of its nuclear weapons. However, Israel has had long range strike fighters since it first acquired nuclear weapons, and some reports indicate that it had nuclear capable F-4 units deployed at the Tel Nof air base by the late 1960s. Israel can now deliver nuclear weapons with its F-4Es, F-16s, and F-15s, and has the technology to adapt air-to-surface missiles like the Popeye to carry nuclear warheads with ranges in excess of 30 miles—although there is no evidence that it has done so.[143] It can refuel its strike aircraft with KC-130 and B-707 tankers, giving the aircraft the range to launch missions of over 1,500 kilometers. Israel's strikes on Iraq and Tunisia have shown that it can execute long range missions with great military skill. Israel also has excellent electronic warfare capabilities and can provide excellent fighter cover using its F-15s and special purpose aircraft. A small number of Israeli attackers could probably penetrate the air defenses of virtually any nation in the region.[144]

There are convincing indications that Israel has deployed nuclear armed missiles on mobile launchers. Most outside sources call the first of these missiles the Jericho I, but Israel has never publicly named its long range missile systems. Like Israel's nuclear weapons, the basic source of Israel's missile technology is French. There is no doubt that Israel obtained the full design details of the Dassault MD620 and MD660 missiles, and Israel seems to have started work on its own adaptation of the MD620 design as early as 1963. The Israeli design seems to have used a strap-down inertial guidance system and a solid fueled propellant. Ranges have been reported of 260 to 350 miles (420–565 kilometers) and payloads of 1,000 to 2,200 pounds.[145]

The current deployment of the Jericho I force is unclear, although one source indicates they may be deployed in the Hirbat Zachariah, in the Judean Mountains southwest of Jerusalem. It does seems likely that Israel has now deployed about 50–100 of these missiles. Another source claimed in 1985 that they were deployed on mobile erector launchers in the Golan and on launchers on flatcars that could be wheeled out of sheltered cases in the Negev, but there are no reports of when such deployments took place, and other reports indicate such missiles are located at sites west of Jerusalem. The number that are on alert, command and control, and targeting arrangements and the method of giving them nuclear warheads have never been convincingly reported.

It is also possible that Israel may have deployed nuclear warheads for its MGM-55C Lance missiles. Israel has 12 Lance transporter-erector-launchers and at least 36 missiles. The Lance is a stored liquid fueled missile with inertial guidance and a range of 5–125 kilometers. It has a warhead weight of 251 kilograms and a CEP of 375 meters. It was deployed in U.S. forces with the W-70 nuclear warhead.[146]

Since the 1970s, Israel seems to have gone far beyond the Jericho I in developing long range missile systems.[147] It has developed two much longer range booster systems that outside analysts often call the Jericho II, and it has probably deployed at least one. The tests of these longer range missiles seem to have begun in the mid-1980s and may have involved both an improved single stage missile and a multistage missile. According to some reports, the new single stage missile uses strap-down inertial guidance and was first tested in mid-1986 in a launch over the Mediterranean that reached a range of 288 miles (460 kilometers). It also seems to have been tested in May, 1987. A flight across the Mediterranean reached a range of some 510 miles (820 kilometers), landing south of Crete.[148]

If it exists, the multistage missile Jericho III seems to have had its first tests in 1988.[149] A more publicized test occurred on September 14, 1989.

Israel launched a missile across the Mediterranean that landed about 250 miles north of Benghazi, Libya. The missile flew over 800 miles, and U.S. experts believed it had a maximum range of up to 900–940 miles (1,450 kilometers)—which would allow it to cover virtually all of the Arab world and even the southern USSR.[150] This same booster may have been the focus of cooperative Israeli–South African missile development and testing that was disclosed in 1989, but there are some indications that both the booster and any Israeli–South African cooperation may have focused on satellite launches.[151]

Some sources feel that 30–50 of these missiles may have already been deployed. If so, this changes the balance of power in the Middle East. While the Jericho I missile could probably only cover Syria, Jordan, Lebanon, and upper Egypt, this may mean that the first Jericho II missiles already have the range to cover all of Egypt, eastern Libya, all of Iraq, the western part of Iran, the upper Sudan, Saudi Arabia east of Riyadh, and Turkey. Arab countries would be extremely vulnerable to strikes on key cities. A single high yield weapon of 100 kilotons or more could effectively destroy a Syrian city like Damascus, Aleppo, or Homs; a Jordanian city like Amman, Irbid, or Zarqa; an Iraqi city like Baghdad, Basrah, or Mosul; a Libyan city like Tripoli or Benghazi; or most of the larger Egyptian cities of Cairo, Alexandria, or Gaza. A 20–50 kiloton weapon weapon could destroy any other city in the region, as well as any major air base.

Some experts also believe that Israel deployed large numbers of nuclear artillery rounds after the 1973 war, including rounds for its 175mm and 203mm weapons. A few experts say such rounds included enhanced radiation variants. Such capabilities are very controversial, but they would give Israel the ability to use low yield weapons against Syrian and other Arab armor and artillery formations at ranges of 18–29 kilometers and could stop massed army formations as long as they remained as much as 12 kilometers from Israeli army formations or civilians.[152]

Israel seems to have revitalized its chemical warfare facilities south of Dimona in the mid-1980s, after Syria deployed chemical weapons and Iraq began to use these weapons in the Iran-Iraq War. Israel may now have production facilities for at least two types of chemical weapons and seems to have stepped up its studies of biological weapons as well. According to one interview with an Israeli source, Israel has mustard gas, persistent and nonpersistent nerve gas, and may have at least one additional agent. Israel has at least one major biological research facility with sufficient security and capacity to produce biological weapons.[153]

Israeli Strategic Defenses

Israel's offensive capabilities cannot be divorced from the search for defense capabilities. Even before Iraq attacked Israel's population centers with the Scud, Israel changed its air strike and air defense plans to improve the IAF's capability to reduce air penetrations that might deliver chemical weapons. Israel has undertaken two major high technology development programs related to the threat of weapons of mass destruction.

One such high technology development program is a satellite program. Israel made its first test on September 19, 1988, when it became the eighth country in the world to launch a satellite. The system, called the Ofeq 1, placed a 156 kilogram Horizon satellite into orbit from a booster called the Shavit—which Israel had tested four times previously. It was launched from the Ralmachim test site south of Tel Aviv. The satellite was fired over the Mediterranean and went into a retrograde orbit (one moving from east to west, or against the direction of the earth's orbit). This orbit requires substantially more energy than a typical satellite launch, and the satellite remained in orbit for 118 days.[154]

Israel launched a 325 pound second satellite into a lower orbit during early April, 1990, although it is possible it attempted a second launch earlier and that the satellite fell back to earth and burned out.[155] The new launch was called an "experimental scientific satellite," and Israel claimed it had no reconnaissance capabilities. The timing of the launch is interesting. Israel claimed that the launch had been delayed for several weeks because of weather, but the launch came at a critical time when Israel and Iraq were exchanging threats about the potential use of long range strike systems and weapons of mass destruction.[156]

According to some reports, Israel will launch an Ofeq 3 imagery reconnaissance satellite in 1992 that will be a major advance over the Ofeq 1. It will be able to stay in space for two to three years, versus a few months, and will carry advanced digital imagery equipment with a secure real-time down link to Israel. Israel also plans to launch an Amos satellite in December, 1994; its stated purpose is communications but may include some communications intelligence (COMINT) and SIGINT functions.[157]

Such satellites will be useful for warning and tactical purposes; they will provide a way of monitoring Arab developments in producing weapons of mass destruction and the Arab deployment of missiles. They will also allow Israel to greatly improve its long range targeting capability and to strike at small military or strategic targets rather than large area targets like cities.

U.S. experts see no current indications that Israel is developing the Shavit booster it used for such satellite launches as an ICBM.[158] However, such a system would provide target coverage that the Jericho IIs cannot. It could cover virtually all of the Arab world, including Tripoli and Rabta in Libya and Tehran in eastern Iran—making it a truly regional weapon impacting on the military balance throughout the Arab world. Such a system would give Israel the ability to cover a substantial part of the southern USSR, although it is unlikely that this is a major reason for such Israeli efforts.

The second high technology development program is the creation of an anti-tactical ballistic missile system called the Arrow, with the ability to intercept short range ballistic missiles with ranges up to 330 miles. The U.S. has agreed to pay for 80% of the development cost of the Arrow as part of its Strategic Defense Initiative (SDI).

This system is currently in a state of nearly complete redesign. The missile and warhead were totally redesigned during 1991 as a result of initial test problems, three test launch failures, and the lessons of the Gulf War. Israel also realized that its initial delivery schedule was unrealistic and that it had focused on developing a missile without developing an associated radar, software, and battle management system. This forced Israel to examine either developing its own battle management radars and system or adapting the radar and technology that Raytheon had proven in the Patriot.

In late 1992 it appeared that cost factors might force Israel to work with Raytheon. According to some estimates, the total defense system seemed likely to have a price tag of $3–4 billion and consume up to 10–15% of the IDF annual budget. Other sources indicated that the U.S. had concluded that the Arrow was simply too expensive to complete as a special purpose weapons system and was trying to persuade Israel to rely on the Patriot PAC 3 or the theater high-altitude area defense (THAAD) system. These same reports indicated Rabin was reluctant to fund an Arrow program that could consume up to 15% of Israel's defense budget, and two ex-IAF commanders, Maj. Gen. Benny Peled and Avihu Ben Nun, publicly questioned the value of the system.

Cooperation between the Arrow and THAAD was difficult because the Arrow planned to use a lower frequency L-band radar while the THAAD planned to use an X-band system. The U.S. did, however, show an interest in examining the Arrow's focused charge warhead as an alternative to the hit-to-kill warhead of the THAAD.[159]

Although the revised system now cannot be deployed much before the year 2000, it could give Israel a critical defensive edge in the balance of weapons of mass destruction that none of its Arab neighbors could hope to match without massive outside aid. The concept also suits Israel's long standing effort to minimize the risk of any casualties to its small population—one of Israel's few major military and political vulnerabilities.

It should be stressed, however, that Israel may run into the same problems in funding this high technology development as it did with the Lavi. There have already been cost escalation problems. While Israeli experts initially put the development cost of the missile alone at $140 million a year for two to three years, U.S. experts put the cost at $200 million annually.

It is far from clear that Israel can fund the deployment of a layered, or even Arrow-based, system. Even though IDF planners generally believe that the Arrow is far more suited to their emphasis on deterrence, defense, and retaliatory capabilities than the Patriot PAC-3, there is no question that the Arrow competes with other force improvement priorities and is cutting into Israel's ability to maintain and modernize its conventional forces.

The Problem of the Golan

Israel faces three ongoing military challenges from its Arab neighbors: the risk of war across the Golan, tension and conflict along its border with Lebanon, and the problem of the *intifada* in the occupied territories.[160] The Golan is the only area that seems likely to produce a major conventional war, although conflict could escalate in Lebanon as well.

The Golan is one of the most critical strategic areas in the Middle East. It is a plateau that is roughly 67 kilometers long from north to south and a maximum of 25 kilometers wide from the buffer zone between Syria and Israeli-occupied territory on the Golan to Israel and Galilee. It rises to heights roughly 900 meters above the Sea of Galilee and the surrounding land below Mount Hermon, although it has a sharp north to south slope. The northern end is Mount Hermon, which reaches a height of 2,814 meters, and the southern end slopes down to heights of 350–450 meters.

Damascus can be seen from the northern heights of the Golan. It is within 20 kilometers of Israeli cities like Tiberias, and it is 60 kilometers of relatively obstacle-free terrain from Haifa and Acre. The mountainous area to the north is high enough to provide an excellent staging point for radars to cover Israel and Syria. The terrain is relatively smooth at the top but is broken up with small volcanic cones that make natural sites for defense positions and strong points. Israel occupies the key line of volcanic peaks to the west of Quneitra.

On the one hand, if Syria could regain control of the Golan, it would be an ideal platform for artillery and missile attacks on Israel, and Syria could exploit the fact that the western edge of the Golan plateau rises in steep increments of hundreds of feet in something approaching a vertical wall. This slope allows Syrian armor to descend very quickly but makes it far more difficult for the IDF to move or fight its way up the wall to the Golan Heights. It would also give Syria vastly improved sensor coverage of Israel, greatly complicating the IAF's problems in air operations and suppressing Syrian surface-to-air missiles.

On the other hand, Israeli control of the Golan provides direct line of sight and line of sensor observation of threatening movements from Lebanon and Syria. It is both an integral part of Israel's early warning system and gives Israel a springboard for attack and the ability to target movement and military positions from the Golan to Damascus. It provides an excellent platform for artillery and missile fire and for Israeli sensors and other radars that can be used in attacking Syria's land based air defenses and air force. The Golan gives Israel strategic depth to defend the Huleh and Jordan valleys. It gives Israel de facto control over the headwaters of the Jordan and Sea of Galilee and access to the critical water resources in the region. There are also some 12,000 Jews settled on the Golan in 29 settlements, and some 15,000 Druze. Syria never reoccupied its former provincial capital of Quneitra after the 1974 disengagement.

The primary Israeli concern regarding the Golan is that it is the one area where an Arab military force could attack it with enough surprise or speed to prevent it from mobilizing before Syria might take action on the ground— seizing back the Golan or even penetrating into the Galilee. The possibility of such an attack makes the issue of peacetime or fully mobilized force ratios and capabilities moot. The issue is what mix of forces each side could bring to bear in the critical 24-hour periods before the attack began and after it commenced. The character and success of any such attack would depend on Syrian ability to conduct a massive sudden move against the Golan under the cloak of weather or night, or to implement a political and military deception plan. Syria showed this all too clearly in 1973, when a Syrian force of

1,400 tanks and 28,000 other weapons and vehicles launched a surprise attack against unprepared Israeli forces on the Golan and thrust 15 kilometers into Israeli territory.

Such an attack would be extremely difficult today. Although the May 31, 1974, separation of forces agreement between Israel and Syria cost Israel about 600 square kilometers of territory on the Golan—and control over the dominant Bahta ridge line in the south and Rafid junction—Israel no longer is forced to split its forces to defend against both Egypt and Syria.

As discussed in the following section, Syria has superior active forces in the Golan area with an active strength of nearly 40,000 men. The readiness of these Syrian forces is limited, however, and the Syrian army suffers severely from a sustained lack of spare parts and outside support that has resulted from Syria's lack of funds and the breakup of the Soviet Union.

In contrast, the IDF has completely reorganized its defense of the Golan, It has deployed a wide range of all-weather sensors and can detect virtually any major Syrian movement in time to mobilize and react. It has built up major strong points in the Golan, created tailored heavy armored brigades to blunt any initial attack, improved its mining and artillery capabilities, improved its attack helicopter capabilities, and maintained the ability to achieve rapid air supremacy over Syria. While no IDF commander can dismiss worst case scenarios and the risk exists that Syria might use chemical weapons against the Golan and chemically armed missile strikes against Israeli mobilization centers, the IDF should be able to repulse any Syrian attack and inflict a devastating series of air, rocket, and missile strikes on Syria within a 12–48-hour period.

Any change in the military deployments along the Golan would significantly shift the balance between Israel and Syria, which makes it difficult to trade territory for peace. This has led to significant security differences between top IDF commanders over whether the IAF, UAVs, attack helicopters, and other Israeli military and sensor assets could compensate for withdrawal from the Golan. Some Israelis have argued for a compromise that would give back to Syria the four key Druze villages in the Golan and control of the volcanic peaks of Tel al-Aram and Tel Abu al-Nada, which overlook Quneitra. This compromise would still allow Israel to keep its settlements and some strategic depth.

The current peace talks may resolve this issue and can be based on a trade of territory for peace. Although Israel did establish administrative control over the Golan in December, 1981 and has come very close to annexation, it stopped short of total formal annexation, and some flexibility exists for negotiation. One solution being discussed in the fall of 1992 was to acknowledge Syrian sovereignty over the entire Golan but make an interim territorial compromise. This compromise would allow Syria to win its political point and Israel to preserve its security, while offering the long term option of complete return of the Golan in return for strict limits on the forces Syria could deploy in the forward area. Leading Israeli security experts pointed out that Syria had fully complied with the 1978 Golan agreement and had a proven track record of compliance with past agreements.

The Continuing Problem of Lebanon

Israel still suffers to some degree from the impact of its "Vietnam"—its 1982 invasion of Lebanon. The IDF lost over twenty times as many men after it had won its 40 kilometer security zone in Lebanon during the initial fighting in 1982 as it did in winning it. It lost some 200 men between January and August, 1983 and found itself caught up in trying to deal with some 260 attacks—all of which forced the IDF into new patterns of arrest and hostile action against Lebanese civilians.

Sharon's broadening of the war had a serious impact on public confidence in the armed forces. In 1983 and 1984, Israeli opinion polls showed that fewer than 20% of Israeli professional officers felt the Israeli public held the Israeli armed forces in high regard, and many of Israel's best officers and NCOs left the military services far sooner than in past years. The IDF recovered from these problems by the mid-1980s, but new problems arose in Lebanon.

Unlike the U.S. in Vietnam, Israel has not been able to withdraw from the scene of its problems. Various factions of Palestinian guerrillas slowly reestablished a presence in West Beirut and near Sidon and Tyre after Israeli forces pulled back from these areas in 1985. At the same time, the Israeli invasion alienated Lebanon's Shi'ites—its single largest ethnic group. In the past, many Shi'ites had tacitly supported Israel and had fought in Haddad's "Christian" forces in south Lebanon. After 1982 many saw Israel as a hostile invader that had attempted to place Lebanon under Maronite control, and they joined Shi'ite militias that called for Israel's destruction.

The resulting threat to Israel soon became as serious as the PLO threat was before the 1982 invasion. Israel had to contend with hostile elements of the Amal and Iranian-backed Shi'ites in the Hizbollah. While the Amal was often hostile to the Palestinians and showed little interest in attacking Israel—as distinguished from controlling southern Lebanon—the Hizbollah was a different story. It rejected both Israeli control of south Lebanon and Israel's right to exist. It also received substantial outside backing. With Syrian tolerance, Iran established support and training camps in the Bekaa and provided the Hizbollah with arms. The Hizbollah formed a tentative alliance with the Palestinian groups and had the declared objective of destroying Israel.

The rebirth of Palestinian activity and the creation of strong hostile Shi'ite elements out of a once largely pro-Israeli ethnic group in Lebanon forced Israel to deal with a rising number of border clashes. A total of 30 squads attempted to cross the border in 1987, and IDF forces killed well over 20 Hizbollah members and Palestinians in border incidents.

This situation continued until 1990–1991. As is discussed later in this chapter, the Syrian army intervened in Lebanon in 1990 to create a single Syrian-backed regime. This allowed the Lebanese army to reenter the south in 1991 and to partially disarm the various Palestinian forces in the area. At the same time, shifts in Iranian politics led Iran to reduce its support for the Hizbollah. This reduced the Palestinian threat but confronted Israel with a

Syrian-dominated Lebanon, and the Hizbollah was not disarmed or restrained.

Israel met this series of challenges by creating a new security zone in south Lebanon at least 10–16 kilometers wide. It also expanded its backing for the 2,500 man South Lebanon Army led by Gen. Antoine Lahd. This force is often given direct and indirect support by IDF forces and the Mossad. It is Christian-led, although there are some 180,000 Shi'ites in the zone. Israel also set up a large network of Lebanese informers and agents to cover most of the villages in the area.

At the same time, Israel strengthened its border defenses. These defenses have cordons of razor wire and anti-personnel mines. An electronically monitored wire fence and other sensors can locate any intrusion within 500 meters. A road runs behind the fence which is patrolled by command cars and new armored personnel carriers based on the hull of the Centurion tank. Each has four Israeli soldiers equipped with MAG machine guns, mortars, and rocket launchers. The area between the road and the fence is regularly plowed to show any movement and is monitored on foot by trained trackers.[161]

A line of fortresses or strong points is a few hundred meters from the border. Two out of three of these fortresses normally have 12 man squads, and the third has a company-strength force. The fortresses are surrounded by entrenchments. They are spaced at intervals of several kilometers and have lookout posts equipped with night vision devices and binoculars, backed by acoustic sensors and electronic surveillance equipment such as radars. Some of the older radars are being replaced by remotely monitored EL/M-2410 surveillance systems. There are larger compounds in the rear equipped with helicopters and light fixed wing aircraft for both search and attack missions. These now have tank units in support.

Such defenses have not stopped all incidents. There were 47 major infiltration attempts to cross the Israeli border between June, 1985 and March, 1992. Only 2 Israeli civilians died and only 1 was wounded, but 57 IDF soldiers and 91 South Lebanon Army soldiers were killed. Another 6 Israeli soldiers died in the area. There were 17 clashes between troops and guerrillas in 1991 alone: 10 IDF soldiers were killed and 14 wounded, and 35 guerrillas were killed.[162]

The combination of pressure from Palestinian and Shi'ite guerrillas has forced continuing Israeli patrol activities in southern Lebanon along virtually all of the 50 mile border, and continuing Israeli air strikes against Palestinian and Shi'ite targets. Some sources estimate that Israel has had to keep an average of 1,500 men in Lebanon or near the border to deal with defense and internal security issues in south Lebanon. The IDF has also been forced to continue sending troops into south Lebanon and to use air and commando strikes to weaken or deter the Hizbollah. The ongoing seriousness of the problem is indicated by the fact that IDF helicopter gunships killed the head of the Hizbollah, Sheik Abbas Musawi, in February, 1992. The Hizbollah fired 70 rockets into the security zone and 30 into Israel, and IDF had to launch its largest raid on Lebanon since 1982.[163]

While Israel has responded by trying to create a tacit modus vivendi with the Amal and focused on attacking the Hizbollah, it faces the near certain prospect of a continuing low level conflict in southern Lebanon. Israel cannot disengage from Lebanon but has no practical hope of dominating the country or creating a friendly regime. As a result, Israel's 1982 invasion of Lebanon may well be its last attempt at wars that try to reshape the politics of the Arab world.[164]

The Palestinian Uprising

The security problem that does most to affect day-to-day events in Israel is the Palestinian uprising, or *intifada*. The *intifada* began in the Gaza Strip in October, 1987 and grew out of a series of small unrelated incidents. Three Palestinians traded shots with Israeli soldiers in October, 1987. An Israeli merchant was stabbed and died on December 5, 1987, and an Israeli van hit two Arab vans and killed four Arabs at a Gaza Strip checkpoint on December 8, 1987. This led to rumors throughout the Gaza that the Israeli had deliberately run down the Arabs in retaliation for the stabbing.[165]

Riots and rock throwing spread all over the Gaza, West Bank, and Arab parts of Israel, and the IDF registered 1,412 separate demonstrations, tire burnings, road blockings, and barricade raisings from December, 1987 to January, 1988. In addition, there were 109 firebombings, 3 grenade attacks, 12 cases of arson, and 6 homemade bomb discoveries. At least 26 Palestinians were killed and 320 wounded by Israeli gunfire. Hundreds of Palestinians were detained and 270 were arrested.[166]

Although there had been a steady rise in the number of civil disturbances in the area during 1986 and 1987, Israel's forces, intelligence agencies, and authorities were almost totally unprepared for the sudden massive uprising. They also faced a new kind of threat. Palestinian children, teenagers, and youth blocked off streets and roads, threw stones and Molotov cocktails, and continuously challenged Israeli forces. As a result, the IDF tended to concentrate slowly and take too little action while incidents could still be controlled. In the name of moderation and restraint, IDF forces first held back and then often overreacted under pressure. Untrained forces used large amounts of tear gas and unfocused amounts of force—creating worldwide television coverage that often encouraged new uprisings and incidents.

By early 1988, the *intifada* threatened to turn into something close to civil war. As a result, Minister of Defense Rabin reacted by emphasizing a policy of decisive force. He realized that the IDF had to begin to act quickly and decisively to suppress each incident and expand its presence in the occupied territories to protect the Jewish settlements and their lines of communication. Israel committed much of its police force to dealing with the riots and deployed a massive military presence into the West Bank and Gaza. Selected Israeli defense units had their mission shifted from a focus on combined arms to a focus on training and organization to use riot control gear. Israel took delivery on rubber bullets and large amounts of tear gas dispensers, tear gas, grenades, helmets, and clubs. The IDF also made increasing use of beatings, deportations, curfews, mass arrests, destruction of homes, and detention without trial.

Several aspects of the new Israeli effort failed. Israel had shifted from too little force to untargeted force. The beatings did little more than attract worldwide attention to Israeli "brutality," and the rubber bullets proved to be ineffective at ranges beyond 15 meters. A massive IDF and police presence often stimulated as many new incidents as it prevented.

As a result, the uprising gave new visibility and power to the Palestinians in the occupied territories, although it increasingly divided them into advocates of hard-line measures and some form of peace effort. It helped persuade King Hussein to end Jordan's efforts to maintain a proxy civil service and government on the West Bank, and it both revitalized and challenged the PLO. It also gave the PLO new credibility, although large elements of the uprising remained independent and many were advocates of Islamic fundamentalism and of a much more direct form of armed struggle than that recommended by the PLO.[167]

The human costs also continued to grow. The number of Palestinians killed in clashes with Israeli security forces rose from 8 in 1985 and 22 in 1986 to 54 in 1987. By late 1988, the number was over 200.[168] In June, 1988, Israeli sources estimated the costs of the necessary security measures as being $237 million and requested a budget supplement of $156 million to meet the costs.[169] By late 1988, estimates of the cost in terms of added mobilization, military spending, and diversion of effort from the civil sector ranged from $500 million to $1 billion a year. These military efforts had a serious impact on Israeli discipline. The IDF court-martialed 66 soldiers in 1988 and 47 in 1989 for violating proper procedures and regulations in their treatment of Palestinians.[170] By early January, 1989, IDF still had to deploy three times its normal forces in Gaza and twice its force in the West Bank.

This led to further changes in the IDF's strategy that proved more successful. The Shin Bet (General Intelligence) and Aman (Military Intelligence), who had paid almost no attention to civil issues and the details of Palestinian politics before the uprising, reorganized to focus on the new threat and identify the new local leaders in each village and area. A massive network of informers and other intelligence sources was set up to identify the key individuals in the *intifada* and locate the leaders of incidents or riots.

The IDF reduced its presence in the occupied territories and shifted to carefully targeted, quicker, and stricter reprisals. IDF training created units with excellent riot control training, and sufficient force was used to quell the riots as soon as they began. Carrot and stick tactics rewarded those who did not participate in the *intifada,* and carefully targeted detentions, arrests, curfews, and deportations punished those who did. At the same time, communities were confronted with a strategy of attrition, suffering serious economic and social hardship until local incidents ceased.

Police duties in the area were transferred to the border police, an elite unit with military training, and a policy of graduated response was adopted, involving escalation from a warning through the use of tear gas, rubber bullets, water cannons, plastic bullets, and finally live ammunition aimed at the feet of demonstrators. Israel also deployed new systems of its own, including stone throwing machines (*hztatzit*), helicopters that can drop rocks, and long range rubber bullets.[171]

Restrictions on the use of force were eased as training and control improved, allowing the IDF to act with growing effectiveness and force against those actually responsible for major acts of violence, without attacking the general population. The IDF began to organize Israeli settlers in the West Bank into military squads and standby teams, and created undercover squads in civilian clothes to penetrate into Palestinian towns and areas without warning. It replaced conscripts and reservists with specially trained forces dedicated to dealing with the *intifada* and built up experienced cadres to deal with each type of incident. It used deportations, the destruction of homes, economic sanctions, and arrests with steadily greater selectivity and effectiveness. At the same time, it eased the limits on the use of deadly force against known extremists to the point where this became a major deterrent.[172]

These measures contained the Palestinian uprising, but they scarcely ended it. Incidents continued, and riots and stone throwing were replaced by ambushes and acts of violence. Israeli statistics report a total 958 firebombs thrown in the West Bank, Jerusalem, and Gaza in 1991, plus 131 shootings, 82 hand grenade throwings, 179 cases of arson, 127 bombings, and 292 stabbings and beatings.[173] Israel's estimate for January to July, 1992 was 619 firebombs, 215 shootings, 46 hand grenade throwings, 160 cases of arson, 71 bombings, and 176 stabbings.

Israel estimates that at least 250 cells of PLO opposition exist in the West Bank and Gaza, and that 53 of the shooting incidents, 45 of the bombings, and 10 of the grenade attacks during 1991 were the result of Fatah action. It blames secular groups like the Democratic Front for the Liberation of Palestine (DFLP), led by Naif Hawatmeh, and the Popular Front for the Liberation of Palestine (PFLP), led by George Habash, for additional incidents. There have also been an increasing number of guerrilla attacks from Jordan. These included 12 infiltration attempts in 1991, with 2 Israelis killed and 13 wounded, and 20 guerrillas killed.[174]

The IDF has also maintained a far tighter grip on the West Bank than on the Gaza. It reduced its presence in the Gaza by up to 40% in 1990, reduced its patrol activities, and concentrated on sealing off the border between the Gaza and Israel. While Israel continued to expand its settlements in the West Bank, it also virtually halted them in the Gaza, leaving only about 3,000–4,000 Jews among some 700,000 Arabs. About half of the 50,000–60,000 Gazans who had once commuted to Israel for work lost their jobs.

This policy of containment exhausted much of the *intifada* in Gaza and reduced the morale problems the IDF had faced with reservists and troops sent into the Gaza. At the same time, it effectively ceded control of the Gaza to hard-line Islamic fundamentalist movements like the Hamas, the Red Dragons, and the Black Panthers. These groups reject the idea of a peace settlement with Israel and cooperate with the PLO only against Israel. They have been progressively more involved in acts of violence against Israel and have killed many Palestinians they regard as pro-Israeli or as part of Israel's network of informers.

The end result is a surface calm in the *intifada*, which has in some ways become a struggle for influence between the more secular PLO and groups like Hamas, and a slow conversion to a guerrilla cell structure that could shift the *intifada* from civil rebellion to armed struggle.

Numerous Palestinians and Israelis have died or been injured. Palestinian sources estimate that 995 Palestinians died between December 8, 1987, and December 9, 1991, and that 118,000 were wounded and 15,000 were detained. They also claim that 500 Palestinian homes were demolished and 345 homes were sealed. Israeli sources claim that only 709 Palestinians were killed, 14,073 were injured, and 8,317 were detained. They report that Palestinians killed 11 Israeli soldiers and 17 Israeli civilians, wounded 3,333 Israeli soldiers and 1,418 settlers, and killed 517 other Palestinians—often because they were seen as willing to cooperate with the Israeli authorities or as informers.[175]

According to IDF sources, Israeli soldiers killed 248 Palestinians during the first year of the *intifada*, 282 Palestinians the second year, 104 the third year, 78 during 1991, and 54 during the first seven months of 1992. This is a total of 766. In contrast, Palestinians killed 2 other Arabs during the period between September 31, 1987, and December 31, 1987; 56 in 1988; 110 in 1989; 212 in 1990; 197 in 1991; and 145 in the first seven months of 1992. This is a total of 720. Killings between Hamas and Fatah became common, as did killings of suspected collaborators. As a result, the number of Arabs killed by other Arabs approached the total killed by the IDF and raised total Arab casualties to 1,486.[176] Israel estimates the number of Palestinians wounded by the IDF as 3,506 in 1988, 5,329 in 1989, 3,862 in 1990, and 1,475 in 1991. The total number of what the IDF calls violent incidents was 23,053 in 1988, 42,608 in 1989, 65,944 in 1990, and 30,948 in 1991.[177]

In contrast, Israel reports that 11 IDF soldiers and 17 Israeli civilians died because of the *intifada* during the period between 1987 and March, 1992.[178] The number of wounded Israeli soldiers totaled 781 in 1988, 918 in 1989, 1,196 in 1990, and 685 in 1991. The number of Israeli civilians wounded totaled 436 in 1988, 383 in 1989, 384 in 1990, and 238 in 1991.[179]

There is no way to predict how the Palestinian uprising will escalate into violence or what Israel's long term response will be if the current peace talks fail. Israel now has four years of experience in dealing with the *intifada* and has troops and security forces that are specially trained to deal with Palestinian resistance. It focuses its efforts on the hard core of the uprising and relies on informers, specially trained hit squads, border guards, and security detachments rather than the large scale deployment of Israeli troops. This has allowed it to reduce the number of prisoners from more than 3,000 at the height of the *intifada* to 1,500 in 1991 and fewer than 300 in 1992.

It is clear, however, that the IDF must still use substantial resources on missions that have no benefit in terms of experience in regular combat and that can thrust it into grim confrontations with Palestinian youths and demonstrators and increasingly well trained guerrilla cadres.[180] If the current peace talks and interim self-government do not meet Palestinian aspirations, the *intifada* may still pose a challenge to Israel.

Strategic Interests and Arms Control

Israel is the only state in the world whose very existence is continuously threatened by its neighbors; its survival depends both on a decisive superiority in conventional weapons and a nuclear deterrent. This superiority must be sufficient to deter or to win a war with minimal casualties, as a major loss of personnel would seriously affect Israel's economy, net balance of immigration, and ability to win a future war.

While it is possible that arms transfers to Israel could be limited, they could also be controlled to Syria and Iraq in a way that ensured Israel's security. This would have to be an extraordinary arms control arrangement, and one with absolute security guarantees. This is particularly true because the ongoing cuts in U.S. forces and the lack of any international body which could credibly enforce a peace with military force mean that Israel's security is and will be dependent on its forces in being. It cannot rely on external military guarantees because no power could deploy large amounts of land forces in time to come to Israel's aid, and there is no credible scenario under which access to operational Israeli air bases could be obtained if Israel lost the ability to operate from those bases or defend its air spaces. U.S. carrier battle groups would be the only force that could provide major and timely military reinforcements.

Ironically, it is also unclear that any peace agreement could lead to any near term reduction in Israeli arms imports. In fact, it might require an increase in such arms imports. As was the case with the withdrawal from the Sinai, any trade of territory for peace—either on the Golan or the West Bank—would require massive adjustments in Israel's military deployments and in at least some aspects of its force structure. It would also require new sensors and adjustments to Israel's maneuver and firepower to ensure that it could deal with surprise attack or some sudden increase in hostile Arab military forces.

As for Israel's weapons of mass destruction, they present the anomaly that they unquestionably stimulate other powers to import arms, but they also provide an ultimate deterrent that ensures Israel's survival. Once again, it is unclear that any near term arms control agreement can substitute for this Israeli deterrent. Further, it is unclear that some theoretical equity is required between Israel and its neighbors. It may well be that Israel can only trade major amounts of militarily sensitive territory for peace if it retains a nuclear deterrent. At the same time, the ultimate pressure on Syria and other hostile states to reach a peace agreement may be the knowledge that no military option, or success in other forms of combat, can provide a credible victory as long as Israel has a nuclear deterrent.

Syria

	Manpower (1,000s)	Tanks	Aircraft	Defense Spending ($ millions)	Arms Imports ($ millions)	Arms Exports ($ millions)
1967	80	430	150	313	58	—
1973	115	1,170	326	589	1,270	—
1982	300	3,990	450	1,907	2,600	120
1988	400	4,050	499	1,604	1,300	—
1991	404	4,350	650	3,330	—	—

Syria has been the focal point of much of the fighting in the Middle East. It has been involved in four major wars against Israel since 1945 and in numerous confrontations with neighbors like Turkey, Iraq, Jordan, and Lebanon. It also has been the scene of considerable internal unrest. While such counts are uncertain, its military forces were involved in some twenty-one coups or coup attempts before Hafaz Assad seized power, and Syria is still a de facto military dictatorship.

Part of the reason for Syria's history of conflict lies in its strategic location. It has a total territory of 185,180 square kilometers, including the 1,295 square kilometers Israel occupies on the Golan, or roughly the size of North Dakota. Its territory is a bridge between Europe and the Levant and southwest Asia. It has a 822 kilometer border with Turkey, a 605 kilometer border with Syria, a 76 kilometer border with Israel, a 375 kilometer border with Jordan, and a 375 kilometer border with Lebanon. It has a 193 kilometer coastline on the Mediterranean.

Even today, Syria has territorial, ethnic, or water disputes with most of its neighbors. Israel occupies the Golan Heights. Syria has a long standing dispute with Turkey over the Hatay question and water rights to the Tigris and Euphrates. It has had water disputes with Iraq over the Euphrates and a bitter dispute with its Baath Party and leadership. It has actively intervened in Lebanon, and its ultimate ambitions to bring Lebanon into some form of political alignment with Syria are unclear. It has divided and exploited the Palestinian movement, intervened in Palestinian politics in Jordan, and has become deeply involved in the Kurdish question by backing dissident Kurdish movements in Turkey and Iraq.

At the same time, Syria's military buildup has never reflected the kind of reckless regional ambitions that characterize the actions of Qadhafi or Saddam Hussein. Syria's leader, Assad, is one of the most skillful and sophisticated politicians in the Middle East, and his leadership deals in the practical politics of power. This has been reflected in Syria's treatment of the PLO, its support of Iran against Iraq in the Iran-Iraq War, and the recent improvements in its relations with Jordan and Egypt. It has also been reflected in Syria's support of the UN coalition against Iraq in the Gulf War, its intervention in Lebanon in 1990, and its willingness to engage in peace talks with Israel in 1991 and 1992.

The Formation of Modern Syria

The Syrian armed forces have dominated modern Syrian politics.[181] They owe their origin to the Arab army that fought against the Turks in World War I. They also, however, are the product of French efforts during 1921–1940 to create a force that would help it control Syria's Sunni majority. France recruited minority Alawite, Druze, and Circassian officers and troops in the belief it would create a colonial force that could be used for internal security purposes and would help pit one ethnic faction against another.

These French policies helped create a politically active army but did not secure French rule. The Syrian Arab forces helped the Free French and Allies seize control of Syria in 1941 but then proved impossible to bring back under full French control. They effectively won independence in 1944, and France formally granted Syria independence in 1946. They then immediately became involved in the struggle for Palestine, largely at a political level. They played only a limited and often ineffective role during the 1948 war that gave Israel full independence as a nation.

During 1948–1966, the various military elements of Syrian forces became even more politicized. Little attention was paid to military professionalism, and the military became involved in coups and politics to the point where limited increases in military equipment did little to improve military performance. This was made even worse during Syria's brief union with Egypt during 1958–1961. Although Syria obtained an increasing number of modern arms, little was done to restructure Syrian forces in ways that allowed them to make effective use of their new weapons.

This situation did not change when the Baath Party came to power in 1966. Although the USSR shipped massive amounts of arms to Syria, it suffered the same crushing defeat in 1967 as did Egypt and Jordan. It lost its positions near the Sea of Galilee and most of the Golan Heights. Nevertheless, Syria still failed to end the political divisions within its forces and to restructure its military forces to make them more professional.

These political divisions became all too clear in September, 1970, when Syria's Baath government attempted to invade Jordan in order to aid the PLO during its struggle with King Hussein. Believing that this would trigger massive Israeli intervention, Lt. Gen. Hafaz Assad—the defense minister and former commander of the air force—refused to provide air support for the Syrian brigade sent to invade Jordan. The Syrian force took serious losses and created a new series of political upheavals.

Assad exploited these upheavals to seize power in a military coup in November, 1970 and became "president" in 1971. Assad then gave senior positions to his supporters and fellow Alawites, but he also ruthlessly purged many of the more political officers in the Syrian forces. He attempted to professionalize and depoliticize the officer corps and to create a true modern army which spent its time in training rather than in politics.

While Assad had some success, Syria was not really prepared for war when it agreed to join Egypt in a surprise attack on Israel in 1973. Syria enjoyed some success during the first days of its attack on the Golan because it achieved nearly total surprise, but it experienced many problems because of its lack of effective leadership and training and was eventually driven back with heavy losses.

Assad emerged from the negotiations after the 1973 war committed to regaining the Golan and the support of the Palestinian cause. He broke with Egypt when Sadat launched his peace initiative, and Syria emerged from the Camp David accords as Israel's only major military opponent. This was a key factor that led Assad to try to expand Syria's forces to the point where they would have military parity with Israel.

He had some success. Syria's forces did achieve numerical parity with Israel in a few areas of military quantity, but this success did not extend to quality. When Israel invaded Lebanon in 1982, Syria was able to put up only limited resistance. Israel destroyed Syrian surface-to-air missile forces in the Bekaa Valley, and Syria's air forces suffered devastating losses in air-to-air combat. While some Syrian special force units and armored elements fought well, its land forces in the Bekaa and Lebanon were rapidly defeated.

Assad also encountered political problems at home. During 1979–1982, Sunni religious opposition to rule by a secular and Alawite-led government gave rise to increasing civil unrest. This led to riots in Aleppo, Homs, and Hamah in 1980 and to civil war in early 1982. Assad responded to the uprising in Hamah by attacking the city with ruthless force, killing tens of thousands of civilians. Assad fell seriously ill in late November, 1984, and his brother, Rifat, attempted to seize power. While Assad's return to health ended the crisis in early 1984, the split between Rifat and the leaders of the army threatened civil war, and Rifat was driven into virtual exile. Since this time, Assad has been careful to keep key command and intelligence positions in Alawite hands or to ensure that key second in commands are Alawites.

In the years since 1982, Syria has continued to build up its forces. Like the actions of Iran, Iraq, and Libya, Syria's military buildup has shaped the response of the states around it. In Syria's case, however, the key focus of all its military actions has been Israel. Syria has relentlessly sought parity with Israel on terms tantamount to developing a capability to fight and win another war.

The main goal of Syrian force expansion seems to have been to develop a mix of conventional war fighting capabilities and weapons of mass destruction that can overcome Israel's lead in force quality. Syria has sought both numerical parity with Israel in force quality and the ability to use technology effectively. Like Israel, Syria has sought to use technology to modernize its forces and has drawn some of the same lessons from the 1982 conflict and previous wars. Unlike Israel, Syria has lacked an external partner capable of giving it the resources and level of technology transfer it needs to achieve true parity with Israel. As a result, Syria has tended to mirror many of the force developments in the former Soviet Union and the West, but with a much lower level of technology and military effectiveness.

At the same time, Syria played one of the most sophisticated political games in the Middle East. It used ties to Khomeini's Iran to weaken Iraq and obtain oil and aid during the Iran-Iraq War, and to strengthen its position in Lebanon. It has kept these ties since the Iran-Iraq War, both to maintain pressure on Iraq and minimize any threat from Islamic fundamentalism. Iran and Syria are now cooperating in the import of long range North Korean missile systems, and they may be cooperating in establishing separate missile production facilities in each country.[182]

Syria successfully pressured Saudi Arabia and Kuwait for large amounts of aid and sided with Kuwait and the UN coalition during the Gulf War.[183] It used this support for the UN to break out of the isolation caused by its past extremism and ties to a dying Soviet Union, obtain significant additional Kuwaiti and Saudi aid, and obtain tacit permission to intervene in Lebanon and suppress the forces of General Aoun. As a result, Syria became the dominant power in Lebanon, although it signed a secret protocol to the Taif agreement that called for it to withdraw all of its troops back into the Bekaa Valley by September, 1992.

During 1991 and 1992, Assad pursued a complex mix of tactics that allowed him to keep his new ties to the West and still preserve both his options and his control over Syria. He moderated Syria's stand on Israel, allowed Syrian Jewish families to leave the country for the first time since 1948, and agreed to join in the Arab-Israeli peace talks. In March, 1992 he very publicly announced an amnesty for 3,400 political prisoners. At the same time, his representatives made it clear that Syria would refuse any compromise on the Golan and took a highly visible series of hard-line stands at the peace conference that minimized the risk of any internal or hard-line Arab backlash. Syria also continued to jail and torture dissidents and still held thousands of political prisoners.

Syria took a similarly divided stand towards the Palestinian issue. On the one hand, it strongly supported Lebanon's Army in suppressing the PLO forces in southern Lebanon. On the other hand, Syria allowed the PLO to reopen its office in Damascus in November, 1991 and continued to allow the Amal, Hizbollah, and Islamic Jihad to keep their forces in southern Lebanon and launch sporadic attacks on the South Lebanon Army and Israel. Syria has both reduced its support of terrorist and unconventional warfare activities and kept at least some ties to terrorist groups like the Popular Front for the Liberation of Palestine–General Command (PFLP-GC). It sponsors training camps in the Bekaa, and has become deeply involved in Lebanon's growing drug industry.[184]

This complex internal balancing act allows Assad to pursue a wide range of alternatives from peace to war, while playing his neighbors and the West off against each other. It also allows Assad to maintain a remarkable degree of internal stability, although much of this is enforced by Syria's overlapping layers of fifteen different intelligence and internal security forces, the loyalty of the army, and the threat of imprisonment. The great weakness in Syria's politico-military structure is that it is so dependent on one man, although Assad shows some signs of trying to make his son, Basil, into an heir apparent.[185]

Syrian Defense Expenditures and Arms Transfers

The main limitation Syria has faced in expanding its military forces are its weak economy and limited sources of outside financing. Syria's economy has been badly mismanaged since the late 1970s, and Syria has only limited oil resources: estimated proved oil reserves of about 4 billion barrels and gas reserves of 6,400 billion cubic feet. While its oil production is rising, it was only about 388,000 to 470,000 barrels per day during 1990–1991.[186] Syria has done a poor job of managing its agriculture and has only about 3.34 cubic kilometers of internal renewable water resources—449 cubic meters per person, about one-fifth the total for a citizen of the U.S.[187] Syria's economy produced only slightly more goods in 1990 than it did in 1983, although its population had grown by 20%.

Syria did somewhat better after May, 1991, when it finally adopted economic liberalization and privatization policies that were first proposed in 1974. A new investment law allowed both Syrians and foreigners to invest with seven years of exemption from Syria's tariffs and income taxes, which rapidly led to the formation of 400 new companies and $1.6 billion in investment. As a result, foreign reserves rose from only $200 just before the Gulf War to more than $1 billion in mid-1992. Although Syria was unable to make any payments on its $16 billion in foreign debt in 1991, it was able to pay $8 million a month in 1992. It also profited from cuts in Iraqi and Jordanian exports, and its fruit and vegetable exports rose from $16.8 million in 1989 to $97.1 million in 1991.[188]

Estimates of Syria's military spending vary according to source, but it is clear that Syria has often had to spend roughly 50% of its central government budget on military forces, and it has not been able to sustain increases in military spending through economic growth. Quite to the contrary, military spending has been a powerful force limiting Syria's ability to expand its civil economy, and Syria's limited economic recovery in 1992 did not begin to give it the resources it will need to make up for the Soviet aid and preferential prices that allowed it to obtain its present military equipment holdings.[189]

The U.S. estimates that Syrian military spending was $1,463 million in 1979, $1,936 million in 1980, $1,959 million in 1981, and $2,289 million in 1982. Syrian spending rose to $3,340 million in 1983, $3,462 million in 1984, and $3,627 million in 1985. It then dropped to $2,911 million in 1986, $1,801 million in 1987, $1,801 million in 1988, and then rose to $2,234 million in 1989.[190] During the 1980s, military spending ranged from 8% to 23% of the GNP and from 35% to 70% of central government expenditures.[191]

Recent estimates by the IISS present a different picture. They indicate that Syrian military spending was at $3.68 billion in 1986, $3.95 billion in 1987, $1.6 billion in 1988, $1.51 billion in 1989, and $1.62 billion in 1990. The IISS estimates seem to be far too low but reflect a legitimate drop in Syrian spending after 1985.[192] The Gulf states cut back sharply on their aid to Syria during the 1980s because of cuts in their oil revenues and in an effort to force Assad to end his support of Iran and to open Iraq's pipeline through Syria. Syria's annual growth in GDP fell from nearly 10% in 1981 to a steady decline of 1–2% in 1982–1989. Syria's balance of trade also deteriorated, and its foreign exchange reserves dropped sharply.[193]

In spite of these problems, Syria received larger arms imports than Israel. While Syria's arms imports were only 69% of Israel's during 1974–1978 ($3.3 billion versus $4.8 billion), they were 135% during 1984–1988 ($8.255 billion versus $6.1 billion).[194] It should be remembered, however, that such comparisons understate Israel's imports because of the reliance of Israel's defense industry on imported technology and components from the U.S.

The annual trends in Syrian arms imports have fluctuated significantly over time. Syria imported $1.2 billion worth of arms in 1978, $2.1 billion worth in 1979, $3.3 billion worth in 1980, $2.6 billion annually in 1981 and 1982, $3.5 billion worth in 1983, $2.2 billion worth in 1984, $1.6 billion worth in 1985, $1.2 billion worth in 1986, $2.0 billion worth in 1987, $1.3 billion worth in 1988, and $1.0 billion in 1989.[195]

The only reason Syria was able to sustain high levels of imports during the first part of the 1980s was Soviet military assistance and aid from Kuwait and Saudi Arabia. Roughly $9.2 billion out of a total of $10.53 billion worth of Syrian arms imports during 1979–1983 came from the USSR, $200 million from France, $180 million from the UK, $40 million from West Germany, $470 million from Czechoslovakia, $90 million from the PRC, $20 million from Romania, $30 million from Poland, and $300 million from other countries.[196]

Syria experienced serious credit problems in getting additional arms from the USSR after 1986, however, and had political differences with the USSR as well. Syria's total debt with the USSR rose to $15–19 billion, and Syrian policies in Lebanon, Syrian treatment of the PLO, the Soviet rapprochement with Egypt, and Soviet efforts to improve its ties with Israel increased Syrian-Soviet friction.[197]

As a result, the Soviet Union gradually denied Syria further military credits and put the supply of spare parts and ammunition on a cash payment basis. This forced Syria to reduce its arms imports and to turn to East European states like Bulgaria and Czechoslovakia, and to the PRC and North Korea, which offered Syria easier financing. During 1984–1988, Syrian arms imports totaled only $8.26 billion, with $6.9 billion from the Soviet Union, $20 million from France, $20 million from the PRC, $10 million from West Germany, $625 million from Czechoslovakia, $330 million from Poland, $20 million from Bulgaria, and $330 million from other states.[198]

Syria also faced problems in building up its offensive capabilities. Throughout the 1980s, the USSR showed more concern with Syria's defense than its search for parity in offensive capabilities. The Soviet Union did not supply the long range SS-23 missiles Syria sought and was slow to deliver long range strike aircraft like the SS-24. In March and April, 1988, the USSR sent three high level military delegations to Syria. These included delegations head by Lt. Gen. K. I. Kobets, the commander of the signal corps and deputy chief of staff; Marshal Alexandr Efimov, the commander of the Soviet air force; and Col. Gen. Vladimir Pikalov, commander of the chemical warfare forces. The thrust of these missions seems to have been that the USSR would help Syria consolidate its military modernization but not reach parity in offensive capabilities or support Syria's efforts to acquire weapons of mass destruction.[199]

Soviet transfers still brought the total value of Syria's post–World War II contracts with the USSR to over $22 billion, but Syria had to default or reduce some arms payments and was unable to pay Yugoslavia for 200 T-72s it purchased from that country according to its original payment schedule. It was often denied credit by West European and Third World arms suppliers.[200] The limits on Soviet transfers also contributed to the resentment many Syrian officers showed towards their Soviet advisors. It is common for Syrian officers to blame inadequate Soviet weapons and tactics for their defeats by Israel, to see Soviet control of arms transfers as political interference in Soviet affairs, or to see the Soviets as trying to impose concepts tailored to the needs of the Warsaw Pact on the Middle East.

The USSR was, however, more willing to modernize Syria's air defense system than its offensive capabilities. Syria had over 4,000 Soviet military technicians in the country during the period immediately after its 1982 war with Israel, including many operating its SA-5 surface-to-air missiles and C^3I/BM sites. Several thousand Soviet advisors departed Syria after 1984, and most of Syria's SA-5 sites began to be Syrian operated.[201] Even so, there were still roughly 3,000 Soviet bloc military technicians in Syria in 1988.[202] Syria was also one of the last countries to receive significant Soviet economic aid. It had over 4,700 Soviet bloc economic aid technicians in the country in 1988. It had received over $1 billion in economic aid since 1983, although it did not receive any such aid during 1986–1987. Syria also received substantial East European aid until 1986.[203]

In the late 1980s, a new problem began to affect Syria's arms imports. The breakup of the Warsaw Pact and Soviet Union led to growing problems in obtaining technical support. Nevertheless, the end of the Iran-Iraq War eased Syrian relations with Kuwait and Saudi Arabia, and Syria still ordered $5.6 billion worth of new arms and took delivery on $14.5 billion worth of arms during 1987–1990.

Over the years, Syria has received the following major arms transfers:[204]

- 4,350 T-54, T-55, T-62, T-72 tanks (USSR:1967–1989)
- 500 BDRM-2 Recce vehicles (USSR: 1980–1989)
- 2,200 BMP-1 armored fighting vehicles (USSR: 1979–1989)
- 1,500 BTR–152, 50-P, and 60 P APCs (USSR: 1969–1975)
- 500 towed 122mm and 152mm howitzers (USSR: 1973–1976)
- 10 S23 towed 180mm artillery weapons (USSR)
- 100 2S1 122mm, 36 D-30/T-24 122mm, and 50 2S3 152mm self-propelled artillery weapons (USSR: 1980–1990)
- 200 BM-21 122mm multiple rocket launchers (USSR: 1980–1989)
- 700 AT-3 and 200 AT-4 anti-tank guided missile launchers (USSR)
- 200 Milan anti-tank guided weapons launchers (France)
- 106 FROG-7, Scud C, SS-21 surface-to-surface missile systems (USSR: 1973–1985)

- 300 OT-64 APCs (Czechoslovakia: 1977–1989)
- 176 SA-3, SA-4, SA-5, SA-6, SA-8 surface-to-air missile systems (USSR: 1971–1988)
- 46 SA-13 SAMs on BRDM-2s (USSR: 1975–1986)
- 30 MiG-29 fighters (USSR: 1987–1990)
- 22 Su-24 strike fighters (USSR: 1987–1990)
- 70 Su-22 attack aircraft (USSR: 1982–1988)
- 20 Su-20 attack aircraft (USSR: 1982–1988)
- 36 MiG-25 fighters and MiG-25R Recce aircraft (USSR: 1979–1988)
- 160 MiG-23 air defense and attack fighters (USSR: 1983–1990)
- 50 Mi-25 attack helicopters (USSR)
- 126 Mi-4, Mi-6, Mi-8, Mi-24 Hind D, Ka-25 helicopters (USSR: 1971–1985)
- 66+ SA-342K/L Gazelle helicopters (50 attack) (France: 1977–1981)
- 100 L-29 and L-39 jet trainers (Czechoslovakia: 1966-1984)
- 60 SSC-1b Sepal anti-ship coastal missiles (USSR: 1986)
- 49 Komar, Natya, Osa 1/2, Petya 2, Vanya, Yevinga, Sonya-class ships (USSR: 1957–1986)
- 4 Nanuchka-class missile corvettes (USSR: 1986)
- 5 Romeo-class submarines (USSR: 1986)
- 3 Polnocny-class landing craft (Poland: 1984–1985)

The problems reducing Syrian arms imports eased in 1990. Kuwait, Saudi Arabia, the UAE, Germany, Japan, and other nations agreed to provide about \$2.5–3.2 billion in aid to Syria for its support of the UN coalition in the Gulf War.[205] This allowed Syria to import \$960 million worth of arms in 1990 alone. As a result, Syria ranked tenth in new arms orders in the developing world, and eighth in deliveries.[206] Syria received about 360 T-72s during 1986–1991 and is using the Gulf War aid it got from Kuwait and Saudi Arabia to make further arms purchases. While the exact scale of its arms orders since the Iraqi invasion of Kuwait on August 1, 1990, are uncertain, they seem to include:[207]

- 250–300 T-72M1s from Czechoslovakia, at least 80–100 of which have been delivered
- 400–600 T-72 tanks from the USSR—enough T-72 tanks to more than double its first line tank strength over the next two years
- 30–60 Improved Scud missiles from North Korea
- Self-propelled artillery from Bulgaria
- MiG-23s, MiG-29s, and Su-24s from the USSR

These transfers contribute largely to Syrian offensive capabilities. Syria already has an inventory of about 4,600 tanks, and at least 3,400 of these are deployed in active units. It continues to expand its order of battle and created yet another active division in 1990, after it sent one armored division to the Gulf. Syria does, however, face the problem that the breakup of the Soviet Union and its replacement by the CIS has created a state whose strategic interests in Syria in no way match its desire to sell arms and earn hard currency. The CIS has shown progressively less interest in providing Syria with training, support, and service activities, and the number of Soviet advisors and technicians that provided critical training and technical services in every branch of the Syrian armed forces may well have dropped below 1,000.[208]

Syrian Military Manpower

The one relatively easy part of Syria's search for parity with Israel has been its effort to increase military manpower.[209] Syria's total population was 12.7 million in July, 1991, with a growth rate of 3.8%. This total does not include 13,000 Jewish settlers and 12,000 Druze in the Israeli-occupied portion of the Golan Heights. Syria is about 90.3% Arab, and 9.7% Kurd, Armenian, and other. It is 74% Sunni Muslim; 16% Alawite, Druze, and other Muslim sects; 10% Christian; and has tiny Jewish communities in Damascus, Al Qamishli, and Aleppo.[210]

Total active Syrian military manpower rose from 222,500 in 1982, to 404,000 in 1992. To put these numbers into perspective, the CIA puts the total Syrian labor force at 2.4 million. It estimates that there are 2.825 million males in the age group from 15 to 49 and that 1.585 million are fit for military service. It estimates that 149,000 males reach military age (19) annually.[211] The IISS estimates that there are a total of about 627,800 males in the age group from 18 to 22 years, and about 986,500 males in the age group from 23 to 32 years.[212]

Syria has, however, had continuing problems in manpower quality and training. Syria has a good educational system, and its training has improved at almost every level since 1982, but its ability to make proper use of this training is often uncertain. Manpower management and the proper matching of assignments to skills are poor. There is constant turbulence and rotation in the officer corps, conscripts receive far too little training, and NCOs are poorly trained and paid.

Syria underfunds manpower quality. In spite of major increases in defense spending, Syria is spending one-third as much per man in uniform as Israel and is still underfunding its training activity, its pay and allowances for officer and NCO cadres, and its readiness and combat and service support capability. Nearly 1,000 of its tanks do not have properly trained crews, and it has substantially less than one trained pilot per combat aircraft.

Further, Syria has deployed some 12,000 to 40,000 men in Lebanon since 1982. This has disrupted training and discipline, and widespread corruption exists within the armed forces—which often have taken the lead in smuggling and bypassing Syria's strict customs regulations. Maneuver and air combat training is still relatively static and slow moving. Advanced technical training and command exercise training has improved but is still mediocre by Israeli standards.

Syrian Land Forces

In spite of Syria's funding problems, it has actively attempted to improve its war fighting capabilities against Israel. It has heavily invested in improved tanks, improved its training in the areas where Syria showed the greatest deficiencies in 1973 and 1982, improved its logistic system and road net, sought more modern anti-tank weapons and self-propelled artillery, and expanded its number of combat units and elite armored forces.

This expansion is reflected in the fact that Syrian active army manpower strength increased from 170,000 in 1982 to 250,000 in 1989 and 300,000 in 1992. Syria has a 30 month conscription period. Sources differ as to whether 130,000 or 225,000 men are currently conscripts. Syria now has total reserves of around 400,000. Army reserves have increased from 100,000 in 1982 to 270,000 in 1988 and 392,000 in 1991. These reserves, however, include all men up to age 45, and only a small portion are combat effective. Syria has only about 115,000 reserves in organized units and has established a special reserve of 50,000 men for rapid call-up. The quality of the Syrian reserve system is also highly uncertain. Reserve call-up training is poor, and Syrian attempts to mobilize in 1982 turned into a miserable failure.

Syria has steadily expanded its order of battle. It built up its total strength in division equivalents from six divisions in 1982 to nine in 1986. Syria's divisional order of battle in late 1984 included the guards, 1st, and 3rd armored divisions (largely T-72M tanks), 10th and 11th armored divisions (T-62M/K tanks), 5th and 7th mechanized infantry divisions (largely T-55 tanks), and 9th Mechanized Infantry Division (largely T-54/55 tanks). Syria raised its number of armored divisions from four to five in 1986. It also increased its mechanized divisions from two to three, and created a full special forces division. Many of Syria's older T-55s and T-54s were phased out for T-72s.[213]

Syria again expanded its forces in 1989 and 1990. In 1992 the Syrian order of battle included two corps with a total of one Presidential Guard armored division and four regular armored divisions. (These had two to three armored brigades, one mechanized brigade, one artillery regiment, one air defense regiment, one engineer battalion, one armored cavalry company, and one chemical warfare company each. Some armored divisions have one armored brigade to be mobilized in an emergency.) It had three mechanized infantry divisions (each with two armored brigades, two mechanized brigades, and one artillery brigade). Each of these divisions had one armored and one mechanized brigade at cadre strength and used a mobilization system modeled on the Israeli example. Syria also had one special forces division with three to five special forces brigades.[214]

Syria also had four independent mechanized infantry brigades and eight independent special forces regiments, and a special forces division with five paracommando regiments. Its major independent support units included two artillery brigades and three surface-to-surface missile brigades. One of these brigades was a FROG unit with two battalions, one was a Scud unit with two battalions, and one was an SS-21 unit with three battalions. Syria also had a coastal defense brigade with SC-C-1B Sepal and SS-C-3 missiles, an independent border guard brigade, and two independent anti-tank regiments.

Like Israel, Syria steadily improved the tailoring of its forces to deal with its primary threat following the 1982 war. Syria significantly increased its deployments on the Golan during the early and mid-1980s and has tailored these forces to deal with the extremely difficult military problem of the Golan. As has been discussed earlier, both Syria and Israel must plan much of their force structure to fight along an Israeli-Syrian border that is only 70 kilometers long and has only limited lines of armored advance. The average height of the Golan is 3,000 meters, with peaks of 9,300 meters in the far north. It is rough, rock-strewn terrain with many volcanic hillocks. Temperatures range from 50° Celsius in the summer to below freezing in the winter

Syria formed two new armored divisions—the 10th and 11th—in 1983–1984 out of reserve and independent active brigades. Syria then built up a strength of three divisions in the Golan area, two of which were mechanized, although these were left in garrison and were not combat deployed. The new units gave Syria a new reserve in the Golan, while freeing its 1st and 3rd armored divisions for independent action. Roughly 2,000 of Syria's main battle tanks were deployed within an 8–12-hour striking distance of Israel in early 1987, although Syria stood down some of its forces in 1988.[215]

Syria also strengthened its barrier defenses as a result of the 1982 war. Right after the fighting in 1982, Syria began to build a new defense line 10 kilometers from the Golan. It dug in and fortified large amounts of new artillery and created major new anti-tank obstacles. There are large earthworks with firing positions and obstacles to create kill zones, and very large and complex mine fields. These efforts now provide three major defense lines between the Golan and Damascus, and all are now covered by a belt of overlapping air defense systems.[216]

Syria has not, however, been able to sustain the overall training levels of its armored and maneuver forces as it has increased its manpower and forces. Overall training standards began to decline in 1985–1986 and continued to remain at inadequate levels through 1992, although Syria did improve some of its training in 1990–1991 in order to prepare for the Gulf War.[217] Syria also has not been able to keep all of its active combat units fully manned. At the same time it has expanded its number of divisions and the quality of its best units, it has had to convert at least one brigade of many units to reserve status. Most Syrian divisions now have one brigade or brigade sized elements in reserve.

Syrian commando and special forces have been kept at higher readiness. Syria concluded after 1973 that only elite forces could meet Israeli forces on anything approaching even terms. It built up its special forces units from about six battalions in 1973 (the 1st Commando Group with five battalions plus the 82nd Parachute Battalion), to at least ten battalions at the time of the 1982 fighting.[218] It has since created a special forces division and eight independent regiments, to create the equivalent of twenty-one special forces battalions. These forces also play a major internal security role and seem to be directly under the command of Assad. Assad also gradually built up two elite armored divisions under his direct control: the Assad Defense Force and Republican Guard division. The Assad Defense Force guards the president, while the Republican Guards provide control over Damascus. There is also an Assad anti-tank regiment in the capital, but its precise military and internal security functions are unclear.[219]

In 1992 the bulk of Syria's land forces remained deployed along the borders with Israel and Jordan and in Lebanon, with Syria's strongest forces in the Golan.[220] According to Israeli sources, Syria deployed two armored divisions, two mechanized divisions, and two infantry brigades in the Golan area. These forces compare with Israeli deployments of two armored brigades. The Syrian forces were placed in two defensive lines that could be shifted to offensive operations in 48 to 96 hours.

Each Syrian armored division was said to have 350 tanks, 200 APCs, 140 artillery weapons, and about 15,000 men. Each mechanized division had 300 tanks, 200 APCs, 140 artillery weapons, and about 16,000 men. Israeli sources indicated that Syria deployed all of the forces permitted in each zone of the Golan by the UN agreements made following the 1973 war. These agreements allow 6,000 troops, 75 tanks, and 35 artillery weapons within 10 kilometers of the line dividing Israeli and Syrian forces. They place no limits on personnel in the area 10 to 20 kilometers from the dividing line, but allow only 450 tanks and 163 artillery weapons. The only other constraint is that no surface-to-air missiles are allowed within 25 kilometers of the dividing line.[221]

Syria did move some 50,000 men to its eastern border during the Gulf War. While it claimed to build this force up to 100,000 men on March 28, 1991, it evidently did not actually do so. Syria also sent forces to Saudi Arabia in September, 1990, which included most of its 2nd Armored Division. This built up to a force of some 16,000 men with 300–400 T-62 tanks. This force was sharply reduced during the course of 1991. Syria activated a reserve division, or created a new division, to replace the 2nd Armored Division while it was deployed to Saudi Arabia.

While Syrian army forces only played an artillery support role during the land phase of Operation Desert Storm, they played a more significant role in Lebanon. In October, 1990 it backed a Sunni-Christian coalition in overthrowing the forces of General Aoun, giving Lebanon something approaching a viable government for the first time since 1976. Syria has since supported the Lebanese government in disarming many of its ethnic and Palestinian factions. In early 1991 Syrian artillery and fighters provided the Lebanese forces with fire and air support in suppressing PLO strongholds. There are still about 30,000–40,000 Syrian troops in Lebanon, and in August, 1991 Syria signed a mutual defense pact with Lebanon that gave it the right to intervene in Lebanon to preserve Syrian security.[222]

As for equipment, Syria acquired at least 500 new T-72/T-72M1 tanks after the end of the 1982 war and had about 1,300–1,500 T-72/T-72Ms in 1992, out of a total force of nearly 4,350–4,500 main battle tanks.[223] While experts differed sharply on the scale of Syria's orders for additional new T-72s as of 1992, the orders seemed to include 250–300 T-72M1s from Czechoslovakia and 250–300 T-72As from the former USSR. Some Israeli experts believe that Syria's recent orders of T-72s will include T-72As with advanced reactive armor and night vision devices, improved upper armor, and improved guns and fire control systems.[224] Syria still, however, retained 2,050–2,150 T-54s/T-55s, 1,000 T-62 M/Ks, and large numbers of armored recovery vehicles. This meant that nearly 50% of its tank force consisted of aging T-55s. Further, Syria could not absorb all of its tanks into its active forces. About 1,100 of its T-55s were in static positions or in storage.

Syria has emphasized purchases of the T-72 for two reasons. First, it learned from past wars that it must give priority to equipping its most effective units. It equipped its first line Assad Defense Force armored division and its Republican Guards with T-72s and self-propelled howitzers before the Gulf War. Its new T-72s allowed it to equip its 1st and 3rd armored divisions and to transfer their T-62s to its second rate armored units. This allowed it to retire some of the T-55s to storage and put others into its mechanized division.

Second, Syria bought T-72s because it concluded that any victory in a military encounter with Israel would be determined largely by the speed with which its armor could advance and maneuver, particularly in any contingency where Syria attempted a surprise attack on the Golan. Buying T-72s, particularly ones advanced enough to resist penetration by anti-tank weapons, gave Syria at least some chance to offset Israel's overall advantage in technology and weaponry.

Syria has placed less emphasis on building up a modern force of other armored vehicles. In 1992 it had 500–600 BDRM-2 reconnaissance vehicles, 350-400 BDRM anti-tank vehicles equipped with Soviet AST-3s and AT-5s, 2,250 BMP-1 and BMP-2 mechanized infantry vehicles, and 1,500 BTR-40, 50, 60, and 152 and OT-64 armored personnel carriers. This was more than twice Syria's total other armored vehicle strength in 1982, which then totaled roughly 1,600 vehicles. It gave Syrian infantry far more mobility and firepower. At the same time, however, its only modern armored infantry fighting vehicles consisted of some 400–550 BMP-2s. Syria has steadily improved the mechanization of its combat infantry, but it has never acquired the overall level of armor that Israel has acquired for its infantry and rear services elements.

Further, Syrian armored training and maintenance has lagged behind its equipment acquisitions. A great deal of Syria's armored training exercises have a set-piece character, and there is comparatively little realistic training under adverse conditions. Realistic gunnery training is limited, and so is large scale maneuver and combined arms training—particularly above the brigade level. Maintenance of armored vehicles is poor, even for the elite T-72s, and there are serious shortfalls of spare parts and repair equipment. Combat repair and recovery capability is still very limited compared to that of Israeli forces.

Syria has sought to improve its tank and anti-tank warfare capabilities in a number of other ways. It unsuccessfully sought to upgrade its Soviet-made tanks with British and other Western fire control systems, and cited its experiences in 1973 and 1982 as a reason for seeking such improvements. It also sought to buy British and French anti-tank guided weapons systems.

In practice, however, the only Western anti-tank weapons Syria has been able to acquire are 200 French Milan manportable systems. It remains dependent on Soviet-made T-12 100mm anti-tank guns, and some 700 AT-3 Sagger launchers and roughly 200 AT-4 Spigots and AT-5 launchers.[225] While a number of Syria's BDRM-2s are equipped with AT-3s, Syrian sources cite the lack of modern Western ATGMs with easy-to-operate third generation guidance systems as a major problem in equipping Syrian forces. (Soviet systems still require the operator to track both the missile and target simultaneously and guide the missile with minimal help in stabilizing the system.)

In spite of the expansion of its combat unit strength, Syria did not increase its artillery strength after the 1982 war. It instead reduced its total strength from roughly 2,600 artillery weapons in 1982 to 2,400 in 1991, eliminating lower grade systems. Syria did make significant increases in its number of self-propelled weapons. In 1992 it had 36 122mm D-30 guns on T-34 tank chassis, 200 Soviet M-1974 (2S1) 122mm guns, some ISU-152mm guns, and 50 M-1972 (2S3) 152mm howitzers, and had up to 100 more 122mm 2S1 self-propelled weapons on order from Bulgaria. While Syria put some of its older towed guns into storage, it retained about 2,000 major towed weapons, including 100 M-1931/1937 122mm weapons, 150 M-1939 122mm weapons, 500 D-30 122mm weapons, 650 M-46 130mm weapons, 50 M-1937 152mm weapons, and 10 S23 180mm weapons.[226]

Like most other Soviet-supplied armies, Syria has improved its multiple rocket launcher strength. It now has about 265–290 modern BM-21 systems, 150–200 Type-63 107mm systems, and numerous older types. Syria has over 2,000 mortars, including 82mm weapons, 400 M-1943 120mm weapons, 100 M-1943 160mm weapons, and 8–10 M-240 240mm weapons. Syria places exceptionally heavy reliance on MRLs as a way of supporting armor and suppressing Israeli defenses in the Golan. Their long range and mass fire allows Syria to attack rear positions, reinforcing units, and logistic and supply areas, and is a partial substitute for conventional air power.

Syria has improved other aspects of its artillery capabilities. It acquired a number of modern fire control and artillery radar systems. Syria also improved the training and target acquisition capabilities of its multiple rocket launcher forces and deployed more of its 120mm mortar forces in direct support. These changes have not been radical, and over 80% of Syria's artillery still consists of older towed weapons, but they have involved changes that have shifted Syrian artillery organization closer to that of Israel and the Soviet Union. While Syria is still incapable of equaling Israel in combined arms and artillery maneuver capability, it has put increasing emphasis on the rapid movement of artillery, which has given Syrian forces the ability to provide more immediate support to maneuver units.

Syria has continued to expand its anti-aircraft gun strength, partly as a response to Israel's ability to locate and kill its surface-to-air missiles during 1982. Syria now has approximately 1,785 air defense guns, including 400 ZU-23-2 towed guns, 400 ZSU-23-4 radar-guided guns, 300 M-1939 37mm towed guns, 675 S-60 57mm towed guns, 10 ZSU-57-3 57mm guns, and some M-1939 and M-1944 85mm towed guns and KS-19 100mm guns. It has consistently found the proliferation of light 23mm guns to be more effective than using limited numbers of higher caliber weapons.

Syrian service support and logistics have improved steadily since 1973 but are still seen as something of the stepchild of the Syrian army rather than as a full partner to firepower and maneuver. The Syrians try to compensate with a feed forward system modeled on the Soviet one that sends in supplies before commanders request them and helps eliminate gaps between the request and supply. This system is not particularly discriminating, however, and makes it hard to change the flow of supply to meet specific tactical needs. Syria has massive stocks of ammunition and supply, although the quality of storage is often uncertain. Syrian maintenance, repair, and recovery capabilities remain weak. There is still a strong tendency to rely on replacement rather than peacetime or combat repair.

Syria also has the same weak defense industrial base of most countries in the Middle East. It can produce conventional ammunition, but Syrian efforts to produce armor, advanced munitions, and missiles have created few tangible results. Syria has aggressively sought surface-to-surface missile production facilities in recent years, however, and may be acquiring such technology from North Korea and/or the PRC.

The Syrian Air Force

Syria increased its total air force manpower[227] from 50,000 men, including the air defense command, in 1982 to 40,000 men in the air force alone in 1988.[228] In 1992 it had 40,000 men in the air force and 60,000 men in the air defense force. Syria has a large system of air bases, secondary bases, and dispersal strips—with facilities at Abu Dubor, Aleppo, Al-Qusayer, Blay, Chiliye, Damascus, Dir e-Zor, Djirah, Dumayr, El Rasafa, Hamah, Khalkalah, Latakia, Marj Rhiyal, Mezze, Midzh, Minak, Nasseriyah, Neirals, Qatanah, Palmyra, Saigat, Sayqal, Shayarat, Suweida, and Tiyas.

The Syrian air force is organized and trained along Soviet lines. Syrian pilots have been Russian-trained in both Russia and Syria, although there are rumors Libyan pilots helped train Syrian Su-24 pilots when these planes were delivered to Syria. The Syrian air control and warning, C^3I, and air defense system are all based on Soviet equipment, although they are far less sophisticated than the Soviet system. Russia continued to modernize parts of the Syrian air defense system through 1992, in spite of Syrian payment problems and the growing upheavals in the CIS. The Syrian air force now trains the Lebanese air force.

Syria raised its combat air strength from 450 aircraft and 16 armed helicopters in 1982 to 448 combat aircraft and 110 armed helicopters in 1988 and 651 aircraft and 100 armed helicopters in 1992. These totals are somewhat misleading, however, since some aircraft are in storage.

Syria not only has replaced all the fighters it lost in 1982, it has modernized its forces. It has raised its Flogger F MiG-23BN strength from 50 to 60 aircraft and added 50 more Flogger E/G MiG-23s to its air defense force. According to some reports, it improved the MiG-25 strength of its air defense force from 25 MiG-25As to 35 MiG-25E/Us. Syria also seems to have bought 30 MiG-29s and 22 Su-24s, although only about 20 of the MiG-29s and half the Su-24s were in active service in 1992.

In 1992 Syria had a total of 10 fighter ground attack squadrons with 4/70-80 Su-22H/J/Ks, 4/60 MiG-23F(BN/M)s, 1/20 Su-20C/D/Fs, and

1/22 Su-24Ds. Syria had 18 interceptor squadrons, with 2/30 MiG-25Es, 5/80 MiG-23D/J(MF)s, and 3/22 MiG-29s. Syria also had 8/172 older MiG-21s in its air defense forces.[229] It had 6 MiG-25R reconnaissance aircraft and large numbers of armed trainers, including 90 L-39s, 50 MiG-21Us, 16 MiG-23UMs, and 5 MiG-25Us. It also has some Soviet DR-3 remotely piloted vehicles and some special purpose aircraft of unknown type and number.[230]

It is notable, however, that many of the MiG-23s delivered to Syria after 1982 were export versions that lacked all the advanced attack mission capabilities of attack fighters like the MiG-27 or air defense capabilities of the MiG-29. They had serious limitations in their radar and computer capabilities, even in medium and high altitude combat, and very limited immunity to Israeli electronic warfare capabilities.[231]

The 30 MiG-29s coming into Syrian inventory are the only fighters with a real look-down/shoot-down capacity, and Syria wants 40 to 60 more of these fighters.[232] These fighters do not have the fly-by-wire capabilities of U.S. fighters or all the advanced features of the new MiG-35. They do, however, have roughly the maneuverability of the F-16A, F-18, and Mirage 2000. They can outperform Western fighters in areas like knife edge passes and tail slides—a maneuver used to break the track of Doppler radars in air-to-air combat. They had good short takeoff capability to use damaged or unimproved runways, although their high landing speed may present problems.

The version of the MiG-29 deployed with Soviet forces is armed with a single barrel 30mm gun linked to a laser range finder. It has provision for six underwing pylons and can carry six radar guided AA-10 Alamo A air-to-air missiles or short range AA-11 Archer air-to-air missiles. The MiG-29 can also carry bombs and rockets and be used as an attack aircraft. It has a coherent pulse Doppler radar with a look-down/shoot-down capability and can detect fighter sized targets out to ranges of 100 nautical miles. This radar is backed up by an infrared search-and-track system and range finder which is linked to a helmet mounted sight which the pilot can use to track IR air-to-air missiles instead of the limited visual coverage provided by a conventional heads-up display. The aircraft has the Odd Rods IFF system and at least three electronic warfare antennas. It does, however, have a relatively large radar cross-section.[233]

The MiG-29s sent to Syria may, however, have modifications for export that remove some of the avionics and countermeasure capabilities of the Soviet version of the fighter, and have inferior electronic warfare capabilities, avionics, computers, and combat displays to Israel's F-15s and F-16s. No Syrian attack aircraft had avionics capable of the accuracy and night and all-weather performance of Israel's F-16s, and Syria had very limited reconnaissance assets.

Syria's most advanced attack aircraft in 1992 were its Su-24 strike bombers. Deliveries of these Su-24s began in 1989–1991, and Syria was seeking to deploy a total of 24 to 28 Su-24s by the end of 1992 and the eventual purchase of 24 more. There are some indications that Syria first received a small initial delivery of Su-24s as "compensation" for not receiving Soviet long range surface-to-surface missiles in 1988 and to balance Saudi and Israeli acquisition of long range strike fighters like the Tornado and F-16C.

Syria has steadily improved its flight safety and basic training procedures since 1982, but there have been only moderate overall improvements in Syrian training. Training still has a set-piece character similar to the early phases of Soviet pilot training and is heavily dependent on central control and planning. Pilots are not given realistic aggressor training in air-to-air combat or realistic training in combined operations, close air support, and penetrating to deliver munitions against land targets in heavily defended areas. There is little realistic capability for beyond visual range air combat unless Syria can somehow counter Israeli ability to jam its ground controlled intercept system and radars.

Air force maintenance and training standards are poor, partly because of the lack of spare parts and underfunding. Western observers noted a number of major maintenance problems in Syrian units in 1988–1991, with some units at only 30–70% operational availability. Syria has limited ability to support high sortie rates and sustained operations and can probably only reach about one-third to half Israel's sortie rate per aircraft, and then for just a matter of days. Combat repair capability is very limited by Israeli standards.

Syria has recognized that it must improve its air battle management and electronic warfare capabilities. It has upgraded its air and missile C^3I system, added improved low altitude acquisition and EW/GCI radars like the Soviet Big Bird, and automated much of the Vector 2 air control and warning system it received from the USSR after the 1982 war.[234]

While Syria has not made major advances relative to Israel in targeting, electronic warfare capability, or air battle management, it has aggressively sought to improve all of its assets. Its major problem has been the unavailability of the most advanced Soviet weapons and technology or similar systems from the West. It lacks any form of airborne air control and warning, long range targeting, and battle management system. It does, however, have 10 Mi-8 HIP J/K electronic warfare helicopters and large numbers of ground based jammers, and may have some fixed wing electronic warfare and jamming capability. It has received Soviet RPVs, including the UR-1, SD-3, and a new Soviet type.[235]

Syria clearly believed that its attack helicopters served it well in 1982. Some sources indicate that Syria now has as many as 220 attack and assault helicopters, although it seems likely that Syria has only about 120–140 armed helicopters in inventory and fewer than 100 of these in operational units. Syria thought its S-342K Gazelles equipped with HOT missiles performed particularly well in 1982. These were used in roving pairs against IDF tanks and armored fighting vehicles rather than as close support weapons. Although Syria took nearly 25% losses (seven shot down and two captured), it found its helicopters had a freedom of action and survivability it could not achieve with fixed wing aircraft. In 1991 Syria had built up to fifty French SA-342L Gazelles, half armed with HOT, and had increased its Mi-24 attack helicopter strength from twelve to fifty.[236]

Higher estimates of armed helicopters seem to include transport helicopters and helicopters with anti-submarine warfare (ASW) weapons or used for electronic warfare and intelligence purposes. Syria may, however, have fully armed up to 25 Mi-8s and may also have equipped 60 out of 105 Mi-8 transport helicopters, 30 out of 40 Mi-17s, and 10 out of 10 Mi-2 Hoplites with light armament. It also has 10 additional Mi-6 transport helicopters.[237]

In contrast, Syria has made only marginal improvements in its fixed wing airlift. It now has 2 squadrons with 6 An-12s, 4 An-24s, 5 An-26s, 4 IL-76s, 7 Yak-40s, and 2 Mystere-Falcon 20Fs. Its only other major air formations are training units with 90 L-39s, 10 L-29s, and 20 MB-233s.

Syrian Air Defenses and the Syrian Air Defense Command

Syria has acted on the lessons it learned in 1982 about the vulnerability of its land based air defense systems. It has increased its independent air defense command to a total strength of 60,000 men. It has some 22 air defense brigades with 95 surface-to-air missile batteries versus 50 batteries in 1982. Syria raised its medium and heavy surface-to-air missile unit strength from 23 units in 1976 to over 63 in 1986 and over 90 by 1990. Syria now has an estimated 300–340 SA-6 fire units in 11 regiments with 60 batteries. It has 300–320 SA-2 and 160–170 SA-3 launchers in 11 regiments with 60 batteries. There are some 60 SA-8 fire units for low altitude or short range defense. There seem to be 30–60 SA-9 fire units and a growing number of SA-13 units. SA-7 manportable missiles are present in Syrian forces in very large numbers, and Syria has an unknown number of the greatly improved SA-14 and SA-16.[238]

Syria has steadily improved the integration, or netting, of its air defense forces, its radars, and its electronic warfare capabilities. It now has three fully computerized air defense centers which can control both its missile units and vector air defense fighters. These computer links extend to its SA-6 and SA-8 missiles, and Syria has also steadily improved the automation, sensor, and electronic warfare capabilities of its ground based air defenses.

Syria now has one of the most advanced Soviet-supplied systems outside the Warsaw Pact, but many deficiencies remain. The level and reliability of computer controlled operation is uncertain, and the Syrians seem to have significant readiness and training problems. The Syrian system lacks many of the capabilities of current Soviet air defense control and sensor systems, and Israeli sources indicate that Syria often cannot maintain its system as an integrated net and must manually operate parts of the system.

Syria does have sophisticated Soviet electronic warfare, jamming, and intelligence assets. However, it has only limited capability to tailor Soviet-supplied systems to its specific needs, and this makes many such systems highly vulnerable to Israel's vastly superior countermeasure technology. Syrian deployments still leave many vulnerabilities to Israeli UAVs and guided weapons. While Soviet technicians have assisted Syrian units in the past and have trained Syrian units and air defense commanders, this training seems to have degraded steadily after 1988. Israel could probably "roll up" the Syrian land based air defense system within 48 hours.

Syria is expanding its missile defenses to the northeast to cover an attack by Iraq or an "end run" by Israel. However, Syria's SA-2s and SA-3s are now virtually obsolete systems, first deployed over twenty years ago and vulnerable to a wide range of countermeasures and attack capabilities. Some of Syria's SA-6 systems have been modernized but are still vulnerable to Israeli countermeasures. Israel also still has a decisive advantage in passive countermeasures to other systems and in unmanned surveillance and strike systems.

In late 1982 and early 1985, the Soviets furnished Syria with the SA-5, organized into two long range surface-to-air missile regiments (each with two battalions of two batteries each). They provided at least twenty-four launchers. Two battalions were deployed at Dumayr, some 40 kilometers east of Damascus, and two at Shansar in northern Syria southeast of Homs. The USSR agreed to provide similar systems to Libya in November, 1984 and seems to have deployed a third full SA-5 unit to Syria in the late 1980s. This has probably brought Syrian SA-5 strength to forty to fifty launchers.

These SA-5 units have received a great deal of attention, but it is unclear what variant of the SA-5 has been deployed to Syria. The SA-5 Gammon, or SA-200, dates back to 1963. It is a very large missile that is 10.6 meters long and 0.86 meters in diameter and has a top speed in excess of Mach 4. It has a minimal range of 60–80 kilometers, a nominal slant range of 250 kilometers, and a maximum ceiling of 30 kilometers. It uses the PRV-11 Side Net height finding radar and Bar Lock or Back Net early warning and acquisition radars. It also uses the Square Pair H-band fire control radar.

The SA-5 was developed to kill U.S. bombers and reconnaissance aircraft at medium to high altitudes. The first version, the SA-5a, was obsolete before it was deployed and lacked the maneuverability, electronic warfare capability, and lethality to successfully attack U.S. bombers. The SA-5b deployed around 1970 with a nuclear warhead but still lacked effective maneuverability and electronic warfare capability. The SA-5c deployed around 1975, with improved capability in every area and both conventional and nuclear warheads. It has been steadily upgraded ever since, and a version with an anti-radiation seeker was deployed in 1983, but it is still a slow maneuvering missile with sluggish controls and has never successfully caught up with Western developments in electronic warfare.[239]

Relatively small changes in model are important because the SA-5 has had a troubled development history, and the more recent versions incorporate important improvements in electronics and terminal maneuvering capabilities which are critical to successful attacks on aircraft with electronic countermeasure capability. Syria may well have older versions of the SA-5. This would allow it to harass the IDF's slow flying electronic warfare and command aircraft, but the SA-5s would probably be suppressed long before they achieved any kills.[240] This helps explain Syria's efforts to buy the Soviet SA-10 system—the most advanced system the USSR deploys except for the SA-12a and SA-12b. The SA-10 is far more resistant to countermeasures than previous Soviet systems, has a much higher rate of maneuver, and has much better guidance and reliability. The Soviets did not supply such systems—although it is unclear whether this was for political, financial, or security reasons. There are no current reports that the CIS will supply such systems in the future.

Syria has also increased the number of shorter range SA-8, SA-11, and SA-14 missiles in its army that it can use to shield its ground forces. The SA-8 has also become important to the air defense forces because it provides low altitude or close-in defense, is less vulnerable to countermeasures, and can be linked to the same data systems used for SA-5s, SA-2s, and SA-3s. SA-8 units are evidently integrated with Syria's SA-5 and some of its other long range surface-to-air missile systems.

According to some reports, the SA-13 Gopher is gradually replacing Syria's 27 batteries of SA-9s, and there are now at least 20 SA-13 fire units in Syrian forces. The SA-13 gives Syria considerably better short range ability to defend its ground forces, although the SA-13 does not have a truly advanced IR guidance system and its theoretical 10 kilometer range is actually limited to line-of-sight defense. In total, these light surface-to-air missile units give Syria the equivalent strength of 150 anti-aircraft missile batteries. Further, Syria has some 305 SA-7 platoons scattered throughout its forces.[241] There are large numbers of SA-7, SA-8, SA-9, and at least 20 SA-13 launchers in its army, many with radio links to the air defense command. Syria has moved forward its air defense net, including its SA-6 and SA-13 launchers. It also has improved its surface-to-air missile strength to a point where such air defenses virtually saturate its border areas, as well as cover all major military facilities and cities.

Syrian Naval Forces

Syria recognizes its vulnerability at sea and to amphibious operations, but it concentrates on improving its land and air forces. Syria has, however, realized that it is becoming steadily more vulnerable to an attack on its ports or shipping to and from Syria. Its main ports at Tartus and Latakia are also essential to resupply in any major war with Israel. This has led Syria to raise the readiness of its naval forces for coastal defense, while gradually trying to expand its capability for submarine, surface, and amphibious warfare. Syria built up its navy from 2,500 men in 1982 to 3,700 men in 1992, with 2,500 men in its naval reserves. It acquired three Romeo-class submarines—two in 1985 and one in 1986—and three Polnocny-class landing ship–mediums (LSMs).

The end result, however, is still an unimpressive coastal defense force. When Syria received the 1,475-ton Romeo-class submarines in June, 1985 and December, 1986, they were already obsolete. One is not operational, and the other two have limited operational capability and are used only for sea trials. Syria has actively sought to replace the Romeos with Soviet Kilo-class submarines but has lacked the money to do so.[242] The Kilos would make a difference: They are relatively silent and effective ships, with mines and eighteen torpedoes, two reloads and two spares.

Syria's major surface vessels consist of two obsolete Soviet-made 1,180-

ton Petya II–class frigates with four ASW rocket launchers, four 76mm guns, and five 533mm torpedo tubes each. The Petyas were transferred to the Syrian navy in 1975, lack effective air and missile defenses, and have little war fighting capability. The navy also has four Ka-25 and twenty-one Mi-4 ASW helicopters. These are valuable in the surface surveillance role, although the helicopter crews have limited ASW training,

Syria has 4 23–26-ton Osa-I and 10 relatively modern 31–40-ton Osa-II patrol boats. The Osa-I were delivered in the early 1970s, and the Osa-IIs in the late 1970s and early 1980s. All are equipped with aging SS-N-2A ship-to-ship missiles, which have a maximum range of 46 kilometers with active radar and IR homing, and a 513 kilogram warhead. The missiles are vulnerable to countermeasures, and both classes of Osa lack advanced radar, electronic warfare, and air defense capability. Nevertheless, they are the best trained and most combat capable units in the Syrian navy.

There are 5 Komar-class missile fast attack craft. These are 85-ton ships which have SS-N-2A missiles. They have 2 twin 25mm guns, Square Tie I-Ban surface search radars, and Drum Tile H/I-band search radars. These ships were delivered in 1974 and were laid up and refitted during 1987–1990. Their operational readiness is uncertain. Syria has had to virtually retire its remaining 4 Osa-I Komar boats. Syria has sought four Nanuchka-class missile boats from the USSR but has not received them.[243]

Syria's other ships include six 50-ton Zhuk coastal patrol craft armed with 14.5mm machine guns. There is one 790-ton Natya-class oceangoing mine vessel armed with 2 x 4 SA-N-5 surface-to-air missile launchers, two twin 30mm guns, and two twin 20mm guns. There are one 580-ton T-43 and one 450-ton Sonya-class oceangoing mine sweepers, two 280-ton Vanya-class coastal mine vessels, and five 90-ton Yevgenya-class small inshore mine vessels. It has large numbers of mines and at least some coastal mine warfare capability. The three modern Polnocny medium landing ships are relatively modern 800-ton ships, and the third Polnocny-class landing ship was delivered in 1985. Each can carry up to 100 troops and five tanks. The navy also has one Poluchat-class 100-ton degaussing ship, one 3,500-ton training ship, and three survey launches.

Syria has some small coastal defense units. It has Soviet-supplied SSC-3 and SSC-1b anti-ship missiles, and while it has limited airborne and other long range sensor and targeting capabilities, these systems give it the potential capability to attack any ships within their land based radar horizon of 26 to 30 nautical miles.

Syria also has improved its bases at Tartus, Latakia, and Minet el-Baida and has allowed the USSR to use Tartus as a support facility. Syria never, however, gave the USSR or Russia a full naval base. Tartus has long been used to repair and maintain some of the Soviet ships in the Mediterranean. The Soviet navy began to use Tartus regularly in 1969 and increased its use of the facilities in 1976, when President Sadat expelled the Soviet military from Egypt. The only evidence that Syria ever gave the Soviets a naval base is the existence of some piers and docking facilities during the late 1980s where the Syrians were allowed only limited access.[244]

Tartus did, however, become the primary facility for maintaining and replenishing Soviet and Russian submarines in the Mediterranean, and a yard oiler, water tender, and submarine tender were deployed at the port. Soviet naval aviation also expanded its deployment of reconnaissance and surface warfare aircraft during the late 1980s, and port calls increased in frequency until the breakup of the Soviet Union in 1990.[245]

Syrian Paramilitary Forces

Syria's paramilitary forces are largely oriented towards internal security. There are 15 separate intelligence and internal security services in Syria, many of which spy upon the armed forces and each other. There is a Republican Guard (Haris al-Jamahirya) brigade for protection of the president, with T-72 tanks and artillery. There is also a 1,800 man Desert Guard for the frontier, and there are "struggle companies" (*saraya al-sira*) for special operations. The Ministry of the Interior has 8,000 men in the gendarmerie, and the Baath Party has its own separate militia, or people's army.

Syria trains and equips two to three Palestinian brigades with Syrian officers and advisors. They have roughly 4,500 men; 90 T-54/55 tanks; 105mm, 122mm, and 152mm artillery weapons; multiple rocket launchers; AT-3 anti-tank guided missiles; and SA-7 light surface-to-air missiles. Part of these Palestinian units are in Lebanon.

Syria has also been one of the main causes of state-sponsored terrorism, although this activity has been kept under tighter control since 1986. Both Syrian intelligence and the Syrian air force run extensive networks of contacts with various radical factions in Lebanon and other terrorist groups. Syria obtained the assistance of Bulgaria in setting up a special training camp near Damascus in 1983 and used this camp to train various factions in the use of car bombs and explosives. It has trained and equipped some Palestinian and Lebanese Shi'ite factions to act as kidnap and assassination squads, although their targets have been restricted to Arab targets in the Arab world and Europe.

While Syria cannot be directly blamed for the bombing of the U.S. marines and embassy in Lebanon, Syrian officers worked with the Iranian-backed Shi'ite factions that carried out the April, 1983 suicide bombing of the U.S. embassy that killed sixty-three people. Similarly, the two trucks used by Shi'ite factions in the October 23, 1983, bombing that killed 241 marines seem to have been armed in the Bekaa by Syrian-trained personnel and moved along a route guarded by Syrian-backed militias.[246]

Recent Syrian Military Developments

Syria has not been able to correct many of the problems it encountered while fighting Israel in 1982. Its high command still lacks flexibility and speed of reaction and is highly politicized. Power is still overconcentrated in the hands of President Assad, officers loyal to him, members of his family, and Alawite officers. Complex dual chains of command exist to prevent a coup attempt, and Assad exerts direct control over the Syrian air force defense companies, the struggle companies, and Republican Guard. While the defense companies were drastically reduced in strength after their commander—Assad's brother, Rifat—made a grab for power during the president's illness, Syria still maintains three competing military elements simply to secure the regime.

Syria's six area commands—Damascus, northern, coastal, central, eastern, and southern—do not command combat forces but layer another level of internal security forces over the Syrian command structure. The special forces headquarters is also highly autonomous. While Syria does have a central operational command and operational commands for both the Golan and Lebanon, control of operations is still highly centralized in the rear, and the Syrian army is still organized along relatively obsolete branch lines that give its individual branches for signals, training, logistics, and so on too much authority over both the creation of effective regional military capabilities in peacetime and wartime support of any sustained operations.

Syrian military intelligence is highly compartmentalized, with relatively poor information flow to operational commanders; it is organized as part of a special staff that combines internal security and covert operations. Syrian intelligence seems biased toward peacetime political problems rather than toward the support of combat operations. The transfer of technical intelligence to operational units remains poor, although Syria has steadily improved its COMINT and SIGINT capabilities, and Syria now pays considerably more attention to the need for secure communications and careful control of its electronic emissions.

Syrian air force intelligence, and at least three other intelligence branches, also act as an internal security force which permeates the military command structure. The air force commander, Maj. Gen. Mohammed al-Khouli, devotes a considerable amount of his time to this role and directs many of Syria's activities in terrorism and covert operations. At least some of the Soviet and East European military advisors to Syria act as an additional form of internal security protection.[247]

Syria remains critically short of many spare parts, and an increasing amount of its equipment is not operational because of spare parts and maintenance problems. It has not received the modern land and air technology it needs from the USSR to give its growing force numbers real effectiveness against Israel. Syria is still largely limited to tanks without modern fire control systems, and it lacks adequate night warfare aids. It has insufficient other armored fighting vehicles and many are not sufficiently effective for their mission. Despite Syria's 2,800 artillery weapons, it badly needs more self-propelled artillery and modern all-terrain logistic vehicles.

Syria still has to rely on comparatively low grade export versions of Soviet fighters and air-to-air missiles. Even its improved ground based air defenses remain vulnerable to the kind of countermeasures the United States used in its raid over Libya and lack the C^3I/BM technology to properly engage Israeli forces.

Syria and Weapons of Mass Destruction

Since the mid-1970s Syria has made considerable progress in acquiring weapons of mass destruction.[248] Syria has never shown a serious interest in nuclear weapons, although it did seek to buy two small research reactors from the PRC in 1992—including a 24 megawatt reactor. It allowed inspection by the International Atomic Energy Agency for the first time in February, 1992.[249] It does, however, deploy sheltered missiles, armed with chemical warheads, as a means of both countering Israel's nuclear forces and maintaining its rivalry with Iraq.

Syria obtained the FROG 7 in 1972 and Scud B missile as early as 1974, but Syria does not seem to have given these missile forces a major role until Israel's invasion of Lebanon in 1982. In the ensuing fighting, Syria lost much of its air force in two brief clashes with Israeli fighters, and it saw Israel suppress its land based air defenses in Lebanon in a matter of hours. This persuaded Syria that surface-to-surface missiles were a potential means of overcoming Israel's advantage in the air and furnished a means of attacking Israel's air bases and mobilization centers. Syria also clearly saw missile forces as a means of countering Israel's nuclear weapons. While Syria has never formally declared an intention to create such forces or acknowledged the existence of any missiles armed with chemical warheads, it is clear that such weapons are an important part of Syrian military strategy.

Syria reorganized its surface-to-surface missile brigades after 1982. It obtained the SS-21, or Scarab, in 1983 and steadily improved the readiness and effectiveness of its missile units. By late 1988, Syria had created a force of more than 36 SS-21, 24 FROG-7, and 18 Scud B surface-to-surface missile fire units, plus additional Sepal SS-1B and SSC-3 coastal defense missile fire units. Syria's surface-to-surface missile forces were organized into 3 surface-to-surface missile brigades, with another brigade completing formation. The oldest unit, which was first created in 1972, was equipped with Syria's first FROG-7s. This unit had 18–24 transporter-erector-launchers (TELs) and reloaders in 1988. Another brigade had SS-1C Scud B missiles with 3 battalions and 18–24 launchers. A third brigade had 4 battalions with a total of 36 SS-21 Scarab missiles with a range of 100 kilometers, and a fourth brigade with SSC-1B Sepal medium range (200–240 kilometer) missiles was completing formation at Latakia and Tartus.[250]

Syria probably acquired limited stocks of mustard gas shortly before or after the October War in 1973. It was only after Syria's clashes with Israel in 1982, however, that Syria seems to have started a major effort in chemical and biological warfare. As was the case with missiles, Syria saw weapons of mass destruction as a way of countering Israel's advantages and as a means of maintaining its status relative to its other regional military rivals.

Syrian troops steadily increased their NBC training after 1982, and Syria began to give chemical warfare training a serious priority. More significantly, Syria started a crash effort to produce nerve gas, setting up at least two major chemical weapons plants. U.S. experts indicated in 1984 that Syria had begun manufacturing and deploying nonpersistent nerve and other gases in 1982 or 1983. By the late 1980s, Syria seems to have been operating two, and possibly three, facilities for the production of chemical weapons. One appears to have been the CERS Institute, which may also play a role in biological warfare research. Syria currently is actively stockpiling nerve gas and other chemical agents, including nonpersistent nerve gases like sarin (GB) and persistent nerve gas agents like VX.

Syria has also developed biological weapons, although it does not seem to have attempted to produce or stockpile them. It established at least one major biological warfare facility, and possibly two. One facility seems to exist near the Syrian coast and another facility may have been built underground. According to Israeli sources, Syria was able to produce botulin or ricin toxins in 1991, and probably anthrax as well.[251]

As for delivery systems and weapons, Syria seems to have modified a variant of the Soviet ZAB series incendiary bomb to deliver such chemical agents, and may have modified the PTAB-500 cluster bomb to carry chemical bomblets. Syria has probably developed chemical artillery shells and may be working on chemical rounds for its multiple rocket launchers. Syrian FROG missiles also seem to have been given chemical warheads, although there is no precise way to date when Syria acquired them.

No later than 1987, Syria modified its Scud missiles to deliver chemical weapons.[252] In fact, a number of experts believe that some Syrian surface-to-surface missiles armed with chemical weapons began to be stored in concrete shelters in the mountains near Damascus and in the Palmyra region no later than 1986, and that since that date plans have existed to deploy them forward in an emergency.[253]

Putting chemical warheads on the Scud missile gives Syria a relatively effective weapons system, and Syria has long had the Soviet designs for chemical warheads for the Scud—designs the USSR made available to a number of Third World states in the late 1970s. If Syria has successfully copied the VX chemical warhead used on the Soviet version of the Scud missile, it would have an 884 mm warhead weighing 2,170 pounds, of which 1,200 pounds would consist of a chemical agent. The warhead would be fitted with a variable time fuse, and the agent would be dispersed by a bursting charge located along the central axis of the warhead.

The resulting combination of the Scud and a modern warhead could be a highly lethal system. It would have a range of approximately 260–300 kilometers and a CEP of around 950–950 feet. Assuming a burst altitude of 4,000 feet and a ground wind speed of 3 feet per second, the contaminated area would cover a band about 0.33 miles wide and 2.5 miles long that began about .5 mile from the burst. Assuming a flat plain and no protection, up to 50% of the exposed personnel would be casualties. This is a very impressive lethal area, and a VX nerve agent would remain lethal for several days to several weeks. It is important to note, however, that this lethal area calculation assumes exposed personnel, a flat plain, and optimal delivery conditions. Real lethality might be only 5–20% as high, but this would still halt military activity in many targets.[254]

The SS-21s in Syrian hands do not have chemical warheads, and Syria would find it extremely difficult to develop such a capability without Soviet support. The problems of developing and testing an advanced missile warhead are beyond current Syrian capabilities. Given the accuracy of the SS-21, there is at least some long term risk that Syria could eventually fire nerve agents successfully at Israeli air bases, C^{3}I sites, Dimona, and mobilization centers—and seriously degrade Israeli conventional and nuclear capabilities.[255]

As a result, Syria has sought longer range missiles that will give it the range to attack any target in Israel, and particularly the reserve assembly areas for Israel's ground forces, Israel's air bases in the south, and its nuclear facility at Dimona—although the Dimona complex may be too well sheltered for attack by missiles with anything other than nuclear or advanced penetrating warheads of a kind that Syria is unlikely to acquire in the near future.[256]

From 1984 onwards, Syria tried unsuccessfully to buy more SS-21s and the SS-12 or SS-23 missile from the USSR. It was particularly interested in the SS-23, which has a 500 kilometer range and could have hit targets throughout Israel and Jordan and much of Iraq. It is clear that both President Assad and the Syrian defense minister actively sought such missiles, and they may even have asked for SS-25 ICBMs once it was clear that the USSR would agree to the INF treaty. The USSR, however, refused to provide any of these systems. Although at different times various other press reports have claimed that Syria had established an SS-23 site, had a brigade of SS-23s, and even had deployed the SS-25, none of these reports is true.[257]

In fact, the USSR seems to have consistently refused to strengthen Syrian missile forces and to have shown considerable restraint in giving Syria advanced strike fighters. In March, 1988 Col. Gen. Vladimir Pikalov, the commander of the Soviet army's chemical warfare forces, led a delegation to Syria whose main purpose seems to have been to warn Syria of the dangers of chemical warfare and possibly to warn Syria that the USSR would not support it if it used such weapons.[258]

This Soviet refusal to supply new types of missiles to Syria explains why Syria sought M-9 missiles from the PRC. Reports surfaced in August, 1989 that Syria ordered the new M-9 IRBM from China.[259] While the PRC denied this and there are no indications of any deliveries, the M-9 would meet many Syrian needs. It has a range in excess of 370 miles (600 kilometers), a projected CEP of around 600 meters, and a payload of 500 kilograms. There have also been reports that the PRC sold Syria the M-1B missile, with ranges of 50 to 60 miles, in March, 1990.[260] The PRC is developing two other long range mobile surface-to-surface missiles—the M-11 and the M-12—and Syria may have an interest in these systems as well. Syria purchased 30–90 tons of solid rocket fuel from the PRC in 1991.[261]

There is far less controversy about the fact that Syria has taken substantial deliveries of North Korean Scud C missiles. These deliveries began on March 13, 1991, when a freighter called the *Al-Yarmouk* docked in Syria. Two more deliveries took place in 1991. When the U.S. protested such shipments in February, 1992, North Korea shifted freighter movements to route them through Iran. The first such shipment took place when the North Korean freighter *Dae Hung Ho* reached Iran in March, 1992, and missile parts and manufacturing equipment were then airlifted to Syria.

Up to 50–80 missiles and 15–20 launchers were in the process of delivery as of 1992, and the first two Syrian tests of the missile took place in early August. These missiles will give Syria a weapon with an estimated range of 500–600 kilometers, a CEP of around 650–850 meters, and a payload of 450–600 kilograms. Syria has cooperated with Iran in importing these systems, and both countries seem to be interested in manufacturing the missile as well as importing it. Syria is building two missile plants near Hama, about 110 miles north of Damascus. One is for solid fueled rockets and the other is for liquid fueled systems. North Korea is evidently providing the equipment for the liquid fuel plant.[262]

While the North Korean missile is generally referred to as a Scud C, the name may be highly misleading. The original Scud A was first seen in 1953 and entered service in 1956. The improved Scud B, with a range of 300 kilometers entered service in 1965, and the Scud C, with a range of 450 kilometers, was deployed in 1968. It is likely that the North Koreans have completely resigned the now obsolete Soviet missile and have either extended the single stage liquid propelled motor or have added strap-on boosters. It is nearly certain that they have greatly improved the fusing options and strap-down inertial guidance system and the reliability of the Scud's jet vane course correction system. These improvements are likely to produce a system not only superior to the Soviet Scud C—which was being replaced by the SS-23 before the INF treaty—but one that has a higher payload, more accuracy, and more reliability than any Iraqi Scud variant.[263]

It is also likely that North Korea has made improvements over the Soviet MAZ-583 eight wheeled transporter-erector-launcher, the refueling process and ZIL-157 propellant tanker, and the command vehicle. There may also be improved position establishing and meteorological gear. If so, the set-up time for a Scud unit being moved to a new position could be cut from a minimum of 45–60 minutes to as few as 15–20 minutes. This not only would greatly reduce the probability of detection and vulnerability to attack but greatly improve operational accuracy. Commercially available global positioning gear could further improve Syria's capabilities, particularly if reports of European gear with military accuracy of 10 meters are true.

The new North Korean missile gives Syria a capability to strike at any part of Israel as well as its other neighbors. It has far better range-payload, reliability, and accuracy than the extended range Scuds that Saddam Hussein used in the Gulf War. Most experts also believe that these missiles will be armed with nerve gas warheads—joining the large number of sheltered Scud missiles with nerve gas warheads that Syria already deploys. The possibility of biological warheads cannot be dismissed, although Syria is more likely to use the latter weapons in bombs or covert delivery systems.

While any use of such missiles would risk Israeli nuclear retaliation, some Israeli experts have suggested that Syria might risk limited strikes against Israeli air bases and mobilization assembly sites as part of a surprise attack on the Golan. Such an attack would not be designed to threaten Israel's existence or to capture the Galilee but would rather attempt to establish new facts on the ground so rapidly that outside powers would force a cease-fire before Israel could counterattack and under conditions where it could not risk massive retaliation. Other Israeli experts believe that Syria will try to use its chemically armed missiles as a deterrent to Israeli strategic strikes and to allow it to attack the Golan using its armored forces without fear of massive Israeli retaliation. Such scenarios would certainly involve massive risks for Syria, but they cannot be dismissed. In fact, some Israelis argue that Syria's efforts to double its T-72 force with new purchases from the Russian republic and Czechoslovakia are designed specifically for this contingency.[264]

More generally, experts on the Syrian force raise questions about the extent to which Syrian forces would survive a conflict even after Syria deploys its North Korean missiles. Some experts maintain that Syria has a first strike or preemptive force and must use its missiles the moment it believes it is under attack. Others think it would use some of its FROGs and Scuds on Israeli air bases, command centers, and mobilization staging areas while holding others in reserve. Either tactic could be extremely destabilizing in a Syrian-Israeli conflict.

Syria may also have tried to convert some of its SA-2 surface-to-air, SSC-1B, and SS-C-3 coastal defense missiles to deliver chemical agents.[265] This illustrates a major potential problem in controlling missile technology. While the SA-2 Guideline is now an obsolete surface-to-air missile, it weighs 2,360 kilograms and is a fairly large system. The Soviet versions had nuclear warheads and a 130 kilogram high explosive warhead. The slant range of the missile in the air intercept mode is about 50 kilometers, although the system would probably be accurate to over 100 kilometers in the surface-to-surface mode. It is not an ideal system for use against surface targets by any means and would require substantial modification. It has been deployed in such large numbers, however, that Syria and many other nations might find it attractive.

The SSC-1B Sepal, a relatively modern cruise missile by Third World terms, entered Soviet service in 1970. It has a range of 450 kilometers and a warhead of up to 1,000 kilograms. While it receives little attention, it is a large, 5,400 kilogram missile with radio command midcourse guidance, a radio altimeter to control altitude, command guidance at long ranges, and terminal active radar guidance. It can fly at preset altitudes from surface skimming to 3,000–5,000 meters. It is designed for attack against ships, and the Soviet version has a 100–200 kiloton nuclear warhead. It cannot easily be modified for attacks on land targets smaller than a small town, but its large warhead lends itself to chemical use. Syria has several SSC-1B units, which normally have 16–18 missiles per battalion.

The SSC-3 is another coastal defense missile based on the Styx. It is a modern system that first deployed in Soviet forces in 1985. It has a much shorter range than the SSC-1B. Its maximum range is only 80–90 kilometers, and its warhead is unlikely to exceed 500 kilograms, although Soviet versions with yields of 1–200 kilotons have been reported. It uses inertial midcourse guidance (a programmed autopilot with precision accelerometers) and a mobile launcher based on the Soviet MAZ-543 8 x 8 all-terrain vehicle. It is specifically designed for export and has not been deployed with Soviet forces. It is normally used as a sea skimmer against naval targets but can evidently be set for a high altitude cruise phase with accuracy sufficient to hit a small town or large air base. While converting such a system to chemical warheads would not normally be cost-effective, the resulting system would be relatively mobile and easy to deploy. The possibility cannot be totally dismissed.

Further, Syria is slowly acquiring a significant long range air strike capability. It already has at least 10 Su-24 strike attack aircraft, and the former Soviet Union is in the process of delivering more. The exact performance of the export version of the Su-24 is unclear, and its avionics seem to be far less advanced than the Soviet version. Nevertheless, it is probably still a precision all-weather or night attack capable aircraft with some similarities to the F-111 or Tornado. It has a powerful pulse Doppler radar and is capable of very low altitude penetrations. It is a two seat aircraft, with a weapons/navigation officer sitting next to the pilot. It may be fitted with FLIR and electro-optical aids and has good inertial navigation capabilities. The Soviet version has a moderate to good ECM/ECCM suite and radar homing/warning. It has the range-payload to attack Israel by flying around or through Jordan, or over the Mediterranean and from the south. It is a heavy, swing wing aircraft which weighs 64,000 to 87,000 pounds loaded but can reach speeds of Mach 2.4 when clean of external munitions. Its LO-LO-LO combat radius with an 8-ton bomb load is 322 kilometers (200 miles). Its range with a 2.5-ton bomb load is 1,800 kilometers (1,115 miles). Its ferry range is about 6,400 kilometers (4,000 miles).[266]

While it is tempting to focus on missile systems, a well designed Syrian air raid on a city like Tel Aviv, saturating Israel's air defenses with other aircraft and then raiding with Syria's total inventory of Su-24s, might be able to deliver a considerable payload. Such an attack could be particularly lethal if that payload were toxins or biological weapons rather than nerve gas. At the same time, it should be noted that a ship that took advantage of favorable winds sailing off the coast of Israel could cover an area of up to several hundred square miles simply by releasing anthrax spores or some similar biological agent in a covert delivery mode.

Strategic Interests and Arms Control

An argument can be made that Syria needs strong forces to defend itself from Israel and Iraq. If so, it already has all the strength it needs. In fact, a cut-off of major new arms deliveries would still leave Syria with a significant capability to threaten Israel or any other neighbor for at least a decade. Only a total boycott on major spares, new major munitions and military electronics, and the technology to manufacture and deliver weapons of mass destruction could be effective.

This, however, presents the problem that it is almost impossible both to establish exact parity in arms control and still improve military stability in the region. A strong and secure Israel is the only Israel that can trade territory for peace. A Syria that arms for war while talking peace is a nation that Israel (and Jordan and Lebanon) may not be able to deal with. Further, Syria's interventions at the peace talks have scarcely promised peace, and its actions in Lebanon leave considerable ambiguity as to whether it is moderating its long term ambitions in the region. Some U.S. experts believe that Syria is a major source of finance for George Habash and the PFLP, and to a variety of other terrorist groups like the DFLP, Palestine Struggle Front (PSF), PFLP-GC, and Abu Nidal's bases in the Bekaa Valley in Lebanon. Syria also may be providing at least tacit aid to the Hizbollah and Islamic Jihad in their efforts to attack Israel, and has failed to aid the government of Lebanon in controlling these movements.

The acid test of Syrian behavior will be the peace talks. Syria can scarcely deny that Israel's new Labor government offers it a real chance for peace. It also can scarcely deny that arms reduction and disengagement agreements and confidence building measures would be of great value to Syria and Israel alike—both in terms of security and in terms of economic growth. The question is whether Syria and Assad will put interest before ideology and pragmatism before politics.

Jordan

	Manpower (1,000s)	Tanks	Aircraft	Defense Spending ($ millions)	Arms Imports ($ millions)	Arms Exports ($ millions)
1967	60	230	20	80	17	—
1973	70	420	53	144	47	—
1982	68	569	94	676	1,100	—
1988	100	1,131	111	882	320	40
1991	101	1,130	110	571	—	—

Jordan is in the middle of many of the strategic issues and dilemmas in the Middle East. It is a Transjordanian monarchy with a Palestinian majority, caught up in all the problems affecting the confrontation between Israel and Syria, the future of the occupied territories, and the growth of Islamic fundamentalism. It is too poor to compete in the Israeli-Syrian military buildup and too threatened not to. It has common borders with Saudi Arabia, and its economy has been heavily dependent on the Gulf, but its ties to Iraq during the Gulf War have alienated it from the southern Gulf states. It desperately needs military and economic aid but currently has no major patron to aid it.

Jordan has a total area of 91,880 square kilometers, an area somewhat smaller than Indiana. Its land boundaries are 134 kilometers with Iraq, 238 kilometers with Israel, 742 kilometers with Saudi Arabia, 375 kilometers with Syria, and 97 kilometers with the West Bank. It has a 26 kilometer coastline on the Gulf of Aqaba. Jordan has few natural resources other than phosphates. It has only about 5,000,000 barrels of proven oil reserves and 100 billion cubic feet of gas.[267] Jordan has extremely limited water resources, about 0.45 cubic kilometers of internal renewable water resources, and only

173 cubic meters per person, about one-fifteenth the total for a citizen of the U.S.[268]

The Development of Jordan's Military Forces

Jordan owes its existence as a state to Britain's need to reward the Hashemite family of the Hijaz for its support of the Arab revolt during World War I.[269] In the political maneuvering after the Treaty of Versailles, Britain split the Turkish mandate of Palestine in two and created a new entity called Transjordan. Although the Hijaz was conquered by Saudi Arabia in 1926, Britain helped the new kingdom to create military forces and used the Royal Air Force to halt advancing Saudi forces and keep them from conquering Transjordan.

The result was a small kingdom populated largely by nomadic Bedouin who had some traditional loyalty to the Hashemites as the sharifs of Mecca and because the region was part of the northern Hijaz. The Transjordanian army was founded in 1920–1921 and originally consisted of a force of five officers, 75 mounted riflemen, and 25 mounted machine gunners. The king came to use the army as a combined military force, police force, and means of paying tribute to loyal tribal leaders, and it expanded to a peak of 1,600 men. While Britain called it the Arab Legion, its name in Arabic was Al-Jaysh al-Arabi, or the Arab Army. It thus retained the name it had during the struggle against the Turks.

The Arab Legion was paid for by Britain, had British officers, and received British training. While this placed it under de facto British control, it also meant that it was one of the few Arab forces that stayed relatively apolitical and received adequate military training. In 1942 it totaled only 1,200 men, but the British built it up to 8,000 men during World War II. It fought well in support of British forces in Iraq and in liberating Syria from Vichy France. It was reduced at the end of the war but still had 6,000 men.

The Arab Legion became an independent force when Britain terminated its mandate over Transjordan in 1946, although all its British officers did not leave for some years and it kept a British commander—*glubb Pasha*—until 1956. The new country had a population of only about 500,000 Bedouin versus 3.1 million Bedouin and Palestinians today, but the Arab Legion was the only Arab force to win significant military victories during the 1948 war for independence.

Transjordan's absorption of much of Palestine in 1948 created the kingdom of Jordan and gave it a much larger population base to draw upon. It also, however, created a divided kingdom of Transjordanians and Palestinians with little natural wealth other than tourism, agriculture, and phosphates. While the Arab Legion built up to 25,000 men by 1956, nations like Egypt quickly surpassed Jordan as military powers. At the same time, the rise of Arab socialism, Nasser, and the Baath Party attracted many Palestinians and threatened Hashemite control of the country. By 1967 Jordan's forces were too small to mount a defense against Israel or Egypt and had uncertain capability against Syria.

The rise of Nasser in the early 1950s forced King Hussein into a juggling act that still continues. He was forced to accommodate Arab radicals while relying on aid and support from the West, shifting from side to side with the politics of the Arab world. This situation grew worse in 1967. Although King Hussein had tried to keep the Jordanian forces free of Palestinian and Nasserite influence, he was forced into joining an Egyptian-Jordanian-Syrian command because of his fear that Egypt would threaten his regime. The result was a military disaster: Nasser failed to tell him the truth when Israel destroyed Egypt's air force, and Jordan became involved in the fighting with Israel under conditions that rapidly led to the destruction of the Jordanian air force and a totally uncoordinated land defense of Jerusalem and the West Bank.

Jordan lost half of its economic resources in a few days of fighting, and Israel's conquest of Jerusalem and the West Bank created a massive number of refugees and led to the first organized Palestinian efforts to create major military forces since 1948.[270] At one point, these new forces, under the leadership of the Palestine Liberation Organization, threatened Hussein's control of the country. This led to a growing civil war in 1969–1970 which resulted in the expulsion of PLO forces by the Jordanian army in September, 1970.

This defeat of the PLO in the "Black September" campaign was made possible by the loyalty of the armed forces to King Hussein, Israeli threats to Syria which prevented the Syrian forces from invading Jordan, and internal political divisions in Syria which Assad exploited to come to power. During the October War in 1973, Jordan sent two armored brigades and a division headquarters to Syria, but only after the first week of the fighting. It had little choice other than to concentrate on defensive operations—although it had the potential to threaten Israel in cooperation with Syria, or with Syria and Egypt. Jordan had no meaningful air defenses and could not mount any defense against the Israeli air force. The 1982 war came at a time when Syria was at least as much a threat to Jordan as Israel, and Jordan did not play a role.

The 1973 and 1982 wars did, however, lead to important changes in Jordan's forces, accelerated in part by a Syrian-provoked border confrontation between Jordan and Syria in late 1980. Jordan reorganized its army in 1977 to create fewer but higher capability divisions. It acquired more modern fighters and Hawk surface-to-air missiles and greatly increased its armored strength. Nevertheless, Jordan lacked the resources to act on many of the lessons it learned from these two wars, and Israel and Syria stepped up their military efforts at a rate that Jordan could not match.

To put Jordan's military position into perspective, Jordan had 986 main battle tanks in late 1988, but this was only 25% of Israel's tank strength (3,900) and 25% of Syria's strength (4,000).[271] Although Jordan increased its total number of combat aircraft from 50 fighters in 1973 to 109 in 1988, it still had only 16% of Israel's combat aircraft strength (676) and 23% of Syria's (478). It also had only 5% of Israel's total mobilizable manpower strength and 5% of Syria's.

Jordan also faced growing economic and political problems. It was hurt by the drop in world oil prices and the resulting loss of aid and worker remittances from the Gulf states. Whereas other Arab states had once promised Jordan $1.25 billion for ten years for continuing the struggle against Israel, only Saudi Arabia kept up its payments, and these amounted to a mere $360 million a year.

King Hussein reacted by becoming embroiled in a new political struggle in an effort to create a new round of peace talks. His first step was to try to rebuild his relations with the PLO. In 1984 he restored the parliament that he had suspended in 1974, when the Arab League had voted that the PLO was the "sole and legitimate representative of the Palestinian people." He carefully constructed a new parliament that was designed to have a West Bank delegation and Palestinian representatives and to work out a joint Jordanian-PLO position that would have advocated a Palestinian confederation with Jordan. These efforts failed in 1986, however, and the start of the *intifada* in 1987 made the idea of Jordanian control over the West Bank and Gaza seem increasingly unrealistic. As a result, King Hussein renounced all Jordanian claims to the occupied territories and any future role in the leadership of the Palestinian cause.

In 1989 Jordan's steadily declining economy forced King Hussein to postpone many of his force modernization plans and to cancel the $875 million purchase of eight Tornado fighters from Britain.[272] These same economic problems led to the first major internal unrest since 1970. The government attempted to raise the price on fuel and several key consumer goods by 50% in order to qualify for a $250 million credit by the IMF and rescheduling of Jordan's $6.5 billion foreign debt. In April, 1989, riots broke out in towns like Maan, Karak, and Salt, the Bedouin areas normally most loyal to the king, and security forces had to be deployed to much of the country. At the same time, some 40,000 Jordanian professionals sent a letter to the king calling for the resignation of Prime Minister Zaid Rifai and for expanded democracy. King Hussein was forced to rush back from Washington, dismiss Rifai, and appoint a new government led by his cousin and former head of the army, Field Marshal Zaid Bin Shaker.[273]

The king then attempted to meet public concerns by pushing ahead with a new parliament and new elections. In November, 1989 he held elections for an eighty seat all-Jordanian parliament. The results came as something of a shock. Thirty-two of the winners were linked to the Muslim Brotherhood, an Islamic fundamentalist group, and eleven represented radical leftist sentiments. While the new members did not oppose the king, and he had no problems appointing a secular politician (Mudar Badran) to replace Bin Shaker, Jordan faced a very real prospect of moving towards an Islamic fundamentalist majority.[274]

These events left Jordan with no prospect of keeping up with Israel and Syria, and no major source of outside aid. King Hussein reacted by allying himself with Iraq and Saddam Hussein, and Jordan's economy became closely tied to that of Iraq. At the same time, the steady growth of the Palestinians relative to the number of Jordanians, intermarriage between them, the failure to establish any kind of peace process, the *intifada* in the occupied territories, and the rise of Islamic fundamentalism in Jordan continued to weaken the king's position. This was made worse by (1) the failure of Kuwait and Saudi Arabia to make good on their aid commitments; (2) low oil prices and economic problems in the Gulf; (3) the Iran-Iraq War, which had severely cut the number of jobs for expatriate Jordanian workers; and (4) continuing internal corruption and mismanagement of the Jordanian economy.

By 1990 Iraq was providing 95% of Jordan's petroleum and purchasing 23% of its imports. Further, Iraq was a significant debtor to Jordan (at least $310 million), had conducted joint military exercises with Jordan, and had even established a joint training squadron. In a nation that was 60% Palestinian, this created a situation in which King Hussein found it militarily, politically, and economically difficult not to side with Iraq in the Gulf War.

These factors help explain why Jordan tilted in favor of Iraq between August, 1990 and the end of the Gulf War and may have provided Iraq with some military support during the war.[275] Nevertheless, Iraq's defeat in the Gulf War left Jordan badly bruised and without any major source of aid in either the Gulf or the West. Further, Jordan's support of Iraq undercut years of friendly relations between Jordan and the West and raised new doubts about Jordan in Israel.

The economic costs of these events were staggering. Jordan lost at least $1.5 billion per year in income for an economy that had already been crippled by the decline in oil prices during the mid-1970s. The Gulf states canceled annual subsidies averaging $550 million, and Saudi Arabia cut off its oil supplies to Jordan.[276] At the same time, many Jordanian workers, and Palestinians with Jordanian passports, lost their jobs and savings in Iraq or were forced to leave the southern Gulf states. Kuwait alone had expelled at least 350,000 of its former total of 400,000 Palestinians by February, 1992, and 250,000–350,000 of the refugees arrived in Jordan.[277] Unemployment in Jordan rose well above 30%, and it lost some $500 million per year in annual worker remittances. Jordan also began to face a major crisis in water supplies, with shortfalls of 1.2 to 1.9 billion cubic feet out of a total national supply of 6.3 billion cubic feet.[278]

These blows reinforced the impact of a 5.7% decline in Jordan's GDP in 1989 and a 5.6% decline in 1990, led to a $1 billion deficit on current account in 1990, and increased Jordan's external debt from $6.56 billion in 1988 to $8.9 billion in 1990. This crippled Jordan's economy, in spite of its austerity program, and its ability to modernize and equip its military forces.

Jordan had only limited success in improving its position during 1991 and 1992. It did improve relations with the U.S. by agreeing to take part in the Arab-Israeli peace talks and to comply with the postwar UN sanctions on Iraq. It also rescheduled its debt in May, 1992 as part of a pact with 14 Western countries. This rescheduled up to $1.4 billion in debts originally due during 1991–1993 and laid the groundwork for rescheduling another $500 million in debt to private banks. However, the U.S. cancelled joint exercises with Jordan in June, 1992 because of claims that Jordan violated the sanctions on shipments to Iraq. While Jordan refused a U.S. request to deploy

UN monitors to see if it was obeying the sanctions, it also got into trouble with Iraq. In July Iraq seemed to accuse Jordan of supporting a potential Iraqi military plot against Iraq, and in August Iraq executed a number of leading Iraqi merchants in private trade with Jordan.

Jordan also had problems in rebuilding its political ties with moderate Arab states. While it did improve its relations with Egypt, it became involved in a growing controversy with Saudi Arabia that revived the old rivalries between the Hashemite and Saud dynasties. In April, 1992 King Hussein reacted to the cutoff of Saudi aid by asking his courtiers to address him as the "Sheif of Hejaz"—the title of his great-grandfather, the custodian of Mecca and Medina. The Saudis reacted by offering the UN aid to restore the Mosque of Al Aqsa (Dome of the Rock) in Jerusalem—challenging King Hussein's patronage over the only major Muslim shrine in Jordan and the occupied territories.[279]

Jordanian Military Expenditures and Arms Transfers

The shift in the regional balance of power is equally clear when it is measured in terms of defense spending. According to ACDA estimates, Jordan's defense expenditures increased by only 36% in constant dollars between 1972 and 1982. In contrast, Israel's expenditures increased by 92% and Syria's by an incredible 302%. If one looks at the period between 1982 and 1986, Jordan's annual expenditures in constant 1984 dollars dropped by 10% and were roughly $720 million. Israel's military expenditures shifted from about $5,270 million to $5,110 million—a drop of only 5%, leaving a level about seven times that of Jordan. Syria's military expenditures shifted from about $3,059 million to $3,680 million—a rise of 20% and a level about five times that of Jordan.[280]

It is more difficult to make comparisons of the recent trends in Jordanian military spending. ACDA estimates that Jordan's military budget was $462 million in 1978, $417 million in 1979, $421 million in 1980, $445 million in 1981, $485 million in 1982, $544 million in 1983, $555 million in 1984, $602 million in 1985, $633 million in 1986, $666 million in 1987, $640 million in 1988, and $548 million in 1989.[281] The IISS puts Jordanian military spending at $713.35 million in 1986, $745.5 million in 1987, and $762.8 million in 1988. The IISS estimates that Jordan spent $467 million in 1989, $571 million in 1990, and $587 million in 1991.[282]

If these figures are correct, Jordan's expenditure levels were about one-eighth those of Israel during the same period and one-fifth those of Syria. Jordan also spent about 14–21% of its GNP and 22–37% of its central government expenditures on military forces during the 1980s.[283]

Unlike Israel and Syria, Jordan rarely got preferential terms on arms sales. This made it highly dependent on externally funded arms sales that had to be paid at hard currency prices. Although Saudi Arabia funded some such sales in the early 1980s, this financing did not help Jordan modernize its air force, and Jordan became increasingly dependent on its own conversions of tanks to equip its land forces. It was unable to modernize its surface-to-air missile defenses and was forced to rely on vulnerable fixed Hawk sites with limited technical upgrading and an air control and warning system with limited modernization and capability.

ACDA estimates that Jordan imported $170 million worth of arms in 1978, $100 million in 1979, $260 million in 1980, $1,100 million in 1981, $850 million in 1982, $1,100 million in 1983, $230 million in 1984, $600 million in 1985, $450 million in 1986, $330 million in 1987, $450 million in 1988, and $190 million in 1989.[284]

While Jordan once depended largely on the West for its arms, reductions in U.S. aid led Jordan to turn to the Soviet bloc as well. ACDA estimates that Jordan took delivery of $3,430 million worth of arms during 1979–1983. This included $230 million worth of arms from the USSR, $975 million worth of arms from the U.S., $1,000 million from France, $1,100 million from the UK, $5 million from West Germany, $10 million from the PRC, and $110 million from other countries.[285]

During the late 1980s, the USSR replaced the U.S. as Jordan's largest arms supplier. Jordan took delivery on $1,730 million worth of arms during 1984–1988. This included $875 million from the USSR, $480 million worth of arms from the U.S., $120 million from France, $5 million from Germany, $110 million from the UK, and $140 million from other countries.[286]

According to the ACDA's new style of reporting in 1992, Jordan remained heavily dependent on the USSR. It imported a total of $2,070 million worth of arms during 1985–1989, including a total of $1,200 million from the Soviet Union, $460 million from the U.S., $110 million from France, $40 million from the UK, $10 million from West Germany, $60 million from other Warsaw Pact countries, $100 million from other European countries, $50 million from other Middle Eastern countries, $20 million from Latin America, and $20 million from other developing countries.[287]

These arms import figures do not permit direct comparisons with Israel, since Israel has to import only 30–40% of its arms as finished weapons, while Jordan and Syria must import over 90%. However, if the arms imports of each country are aggregated for the period 1984–1988 to smooth out annual variations and the Israeli figure is corrected to take account of Israel's military production capabilities, Jordan imported around $1.73 billion, Israel imported $10 billion, and Syria imported $8.26 billion. This indicates that Jordan's military investment has averaged less than one quarter of that of Israel and Syria.[288]

Jordan does not face an easy future. In the past it has received a significant amount of arms and aid from the U.S., but this aid has declined steadily over time, and the U.S. has not been willing to provide advanced combat aircraft or air defense systems since the late 1970s. This U.S. policy was a key factor in Jordan's decision to buy some $280 million worth of air defense weapons from the Soviet Union in 1981 and to buy an additional $450 million worth of air defense equipment from the USSR in 1984.

U.S. military deliveries dropped from $305 million in 1983, however, to $100 million in 1984, $139 million in 1985, and an estimated $73 million in 1986. Total U.S. Military Assistance Program (MAP) aid dropped from $39.9 million in FY1987 to $28.2 million in FY1988 and $12 million in FY1989.

Although U.S. aid rose back to $69.8 million during FY1990, it was cut to $22.2 million in FY1991 because of the Gulf War, and about $23 million in unspent FY1990 aid funds were blocked. Although the Bush administration requested $27 million in MAP aid for Jordan in FY1992, Congress held this aid back because of the belief that Jordan might have provided military assistance to Iraq.[289] Jordan owes the U.S. a total of $1.2 billion in past FMS loans, and the annual interest and principal on these loans runs about $67 to $71 million. While refinancing and the 30% devaluation of the dinar have made it hard to calculate the full impact of Jordan's debt, Jordan is scheduled to pay far more for past aid than it is likely to receive in the future.[290]

Jordan also had problems in financing non-U.S. arms sales. Non-U.S. military deliveries dropped from $921 million in 1982 to $793 million in 1983 and $153 million in 1984. They rose to $440 million in 1985, but the cuts in U.S. deliveries offset much of this rise, and the fall in oil prices in the following year severely reduced Jordan's trade and expatriate income. The rise in the growth of Jordan's GDP slowed from 10% in the early 1980s to 4% in 1986. The Gulf War proved to be a catastrophe. Jordan's GDP in 1990 was $4.6 billion, some 15% lower than in 1989. Per capita GDP has declined ever since the mid-1980s, and unemployment increased to 30% by 1992. Jordan's total debt increased to $8 billion by early 1991, and its debt service ratio rose sharply.[291]

Major Jordanian arms imports during the 1970s and 1980s included: [292]

- 382 M-48, M-60A1, M-60A2 tanks (U.S.: 1977–1985)
- ? Chieftain and ? M-60 tanks (Iraq: 1987–1990)
- 378 Centurion and Khalid (Chieftain) tanks (UK: 1973–1984)
- 322 M-52 and M-102 155mm; M-44, M-114, and M-109 A1 and A1 155mm; M-115 and M-110 203mm towed and self-propelled artillery weapons (U.S.: 1970–1985)
- 14 I-Hawk surface-to-air missile launchers (U.S.: 1977–1978)
- 14 Tigercat surface-to-air missile systems (UK: 1969–1970)
- 38 SA-8 surface-to-air missile systems (USSR: 1983–1986)
- 12 SA-13 surface-to-air missile systems on BDRMs (USSR: 1987–1988)
- 36 Mirage F-1B, F-1C fighters (France: 1982–1983)
- 104 F-104A/B, F-5E/F-5F Tiger 2 fighters (U.S.: 1969–1980)
- 12–20 Mirage 2000s (ordered, but order canceled) (France: 1988)
- 60 UH-1H, AH-1S, 500D, S-76, UH-60 helicopters (U.S.: 1976–1987)

Jordanian Military Manpower

Jordan's manpower problems are complex.[293] CIA estimates put the total population of Jordan in mid-1991 at 3,412,000, with a growth rate of 4.2% and the total labor force at over 572,000. This population was about 90% Arab, 1% Circassian, and 1% Armenian. Jordan is about 92% Muslim and 8% Christian. While any such estimates are uncertain and the distinction between Transjordanian and Palestinian is being increasingly blurred by intermarriage, about 55–60% of the total population is Palestinian.[294]

This dominant Palestinian population makes it impossible to create a massive conscript intake that is loyal to the king and has made it progressively more difficult to select officers and NCOs from loyal tribal or family groupings. Most senior Jordanian officers are of Transjordanian origin, and Jordan emphasizes recruiting from this part of the population.

The CIA estimated that there were 779,000 males in the age group from 15 to 49 and 555,000 males fit for military service, with 39,000 males coming of military age each year.[295] The IISS estimated in late 1991 that there were a total of about 268,000 men and 249,000 women in the age group from 13 to 17 years, 238,000 men and 216,000 women in the age group from 18 to 22 years, and 371,000 men and 315,000 women in the age group from 23 to 32 years.[296]

Until recently, Jordan expanded its forces in spite of the division between Transjordanian and Palestinian. Jordan had a total active military strength of about 82,500 in late 1988. This strength had risen to 101,300 men, of which a significant number were two year conscripts. Jordan's total current organized military reserves included about 35,000 men, with 30,000 in army combat units. This level of reserve strength was low, given that service in the reserves theoretically entailed an obligation up to age 40. Jordan, however, lacked the financial resources to equip and train a large reserve force, although the desire to keep a tight political control over Jordan's armed forces is also a factor.[297]

Jordan's manpower eventually peaked at about 134,000 during the Gulf War. Jordan had to cut back its total manpower to about 107,000 in early 1990, however, and to around 100,000 men in late 1991. Jordan still had about 100,000 men in its armed forces in mid-1992 but was seriously considering major cutbacks and even a possible conversion to a smaller, all-volunteer force. Reports differed over what size such a force would be but indicated that it could range from 70,000 to 100,000.[298]

The Jordanian Army

The Jordanian army sets high training standards up to the brigade level, although its ability to operate in large formations is limited and its artillery has only moderate targeting and battle management capabilities by U.S. and Israeli standards. Jordan continues to emphasize quality rather than quantity and does not expand its forces more rapidly than its training and organizational capabilities permit. It maintains a high ratio of professionals to conscripts and manages its personnel far more effectively than most other Arab forces. Junior officers and NCOs are generally of high quality.

Active army manpower strength increased from 65,000 men in 1982 to 70,000 in 1989 and was 90,000 in 1992. It now has two armored divisions (with two tank, one mechanized infantry, and one air defense brigade each), and two mechanized divisions (with one tank brigade, two mechanized, one artillery, and one air defense brigade each). There is one independent Royal Guard brigade and one special forces brigade with three airborne battalions. The major combat support formations include sixteen independent artillery battalions formed into four brigades, and four more battalions in an independent field artillery brigade assigned to the general staff. The four independent anti-aircraft battalions that used to exist in the Jordanian army are forming the core of the divisional air defense units.

Jordan normally deploys its four divisions as follows: The 4th Mechanized Division faces west from the Dead Sea to the Zarqa River north of Salt; the 12th Mechanized Division faces west and north from the Zarqa River, around Umm Qais, to Ramtha; the 5th Armored Division covers the area from Ramtha to the Iraqi border but is concentrated between Ramtha and the lava fields; and the 3rd Armored Division is in reserve, located centrally between Zarqa City and Qatrana. This means that two division equivalents are deployed opposite Israel in the western and northern parts of the country, and an armored division is deployed in the north along the Syrian border. Another armored division is located in the Zarqa area as a reserve for the other forces. One armored brigade is deployed at Qatrana to defend the access to the attack routes along the Dead Sea, and several infantry battalions defend Aqaba and Karak. The Royal Guards defend the royal family in Amman.

The Jordanian army is adequately equipped, although some of its equipment is obsolete and much of the rest is heavily modified or rebuilt to try to keep it competitive with the equipment in neighboring forces. It has 218 M-60A1s and M-60A3s, 360 Khalid variants of the British Chieftain, 280 M-47 and M-48A5 tanks (many upgunned and modernized but a significant number in storage), and 290–300 upgraded Tariq variants of the Centurion (some of which are in storage). The Tariqs have been refitted with modern range finders, fire computers, and engines at Jordan's armored workshop at Zarqa. Jordan has an adequate strength of armored recovery vehicles for both its tanks and other armored vehicles.[299]

Jordan's other armored vehicles include 19 Scorpion light tanks, 150–160 obsolete Ferret armored reconnaissance vehicles, 1,160 M-113A1/A2 APCs, 125 M-125A1 mortar carriers, 80–100 BTR-60s, and 34 Saracen armored cars. Jordan also has about 50 BMP-1 and BMP-2s that it is using as part of a new reconnaissance unit. Jordan has some 50 EE-11 Urutus from Brazil and more on order, but these are used by the Public Security Department or national police. This is not a bad mix of other armored vehicles, but the M-113s lack firepower, improved armored, and the mobility to keep up with Jordan's tanks on rough terrain.

Jordan's armored forces are well trained up to the brigade level and are unusually effective in maneuver. They do, however, have limited combined arms capability because of shortfalls in Jordan's modern artillery equipment, and they lack the kind of sophisticated simulators and training aids used in Western and some Israeli training efforts. Overall maintenance standards, repair capabilities, and battlefield repair capabilities are very good for a Third World force, but Jordan has begun to suffer from severe shortages of spare parts because of a cutoff of U.S. aid, and its readiness declined sharply in 1991 and 1992.[300]

Jordan has relatively modern anti-tank weapons and supplied large numbers of LAWs to Iraq shortly before or during the Gulf War. It has some 330 M-40A1 106mm recoilless rifles, 80 BGM-71A TOWs mounted on M-901 armored vehicles, 330 crewportable TOW anti-tank guided missile launchers, and 310 M-47 manportable Dragon anti-tank guided missile launchers. Both anti-tank guided missile systems are equipped with night sights. It also has LAW-80 94mm and APILAS 112mm rocket launchers. This is one of the most modern and effective mixes of anti-tank weapons in the Arab world, and Jordan is one of the few Arab armies that adequately trains its troops in the use of anti-tank weapons.

Jordan has significantly improved its artillery strength in recent years and acquired a significant number of self-propelled weapons. Jordan's towed artillery include 36–48 M-101A1 towed 105mm howitzers, 11 M-59 towed 155mm guns, 38 M-114 towed 155mm howitzers in reserve, and 20–30 M-115 203mm towed howitzers (many in storage). Its self-propelled weapons include 30 M-52 105mm, 230 M-109A1/A2 155mm, some M-44 155mm, and 100 M-110 203mm howitzers. It does not have multiple rocket launchers or surface-to-surface missiles. It does, however, have nearly 600 mortars, including 81mm, 107mm, and 120mm weapons.

Jordan does a good job of training and equipping its artillery forces, and they have relatively good maneuver capability. Jordan is not, however, well equipped with modern counterbattery radars, fire control systems, and targeting aids. It has experimented with a number of technical upgrades, but it is still likely to have problems in conducting demanding combined arms operations, rapidly switching fires, and beyond visual range targeting. Jordan also has begun to suffer from many of the same spare parts shortages that have affected its armor.[301]

The air defense coverage of Jordan's army is still limited but has improved in recent years. It has approximately 400 anti-aircraft guns, including 100 M-163 radar-guided 20mm Vulcan guns, 264 M-42 40mm self-propelled anti-aircraft guns, and some obsolete Bofors 40mm guns. These weapons lack range or guidance capability, however, and must rely largely on curtain fire. It has 44 self-propelled ZSU-23-4 radar guided AA guns, which are far more effective, but Israel may have countermeasures to the radar on this weapon.

Jordan also has obsolete SA-7B2 and 300 Redeye manportable surface-to-air missiles, which are largely ineffective against Israeli and Syrian fighters with countermeasures. It relies on its 50–60 SA-8s and 40–50 SA-13s mounted on vehicles, and large numbers of manportable SA-14 and SA-16 surface-to-air missiles. These latter systems are substantially less vulnerable to countermeasures. The SA-8, an improved version whose radar and IFF capability has been upgraded significantly since 1982, is supposed to be able to locate and kill hovering helicopters and even be usable against armor. Jordan has received an advanced form of the SA-14 and SA-16 with hemispheric coverage similar to that of the Stinger and improved counter-countermeasure capability. According to some reports, Jordan may have Javelins and Rapiers on order from the UK. While any immediate order seems doubtful, these weapons could significantly improve its capability.

Jordanian army logistics and support capabilities are acceptable but are one of the weaker aspects of the force. Jordan emphasizes investments in combat units and is likely to have problems in supporting its units in extended operations when they are not operating near their casernes. It has to support a wide range of aging equipment types, and this presents maintenance and repair problems under combat conditions. The lack of funds to buy added spare parts in the West has made this situation much worse since 1990.

Jordan has organized some largely symbolic paramilitary forces in the form of a 225,000 person "people's army," including men and women in the age groups 16–65 (16–45 for women). This force serves political purposes only. It does, however, have a 6,000 man Public Security Department attached to the Ministry of the Interior, with some armored vehicles. Jordan also equips and supervises a 1,200 man brigade of the Palestine Liberation Army. This force is kept under tight control and has little military effectiveness.

The Jordanian Air Force

The 9,000 man Jordanian air force has high training standards for its individual pilots and good squadron level performance in attack and daytime air-to-air combat missions. It does not have an advanced air control and warning system or anything matching Israel's airborne battle management and warning systems, electronic warfare capabilities, reconnaissance capabilities, and UAVs. It also suffers from a shortage of spare parts and operating funds. Nevertheless, it is more combat ready than the Syrian air force and is capable of more flexible operations at every level from the pilot to the high command.[302]

The air force operates Jordan's 24 armed helicopters as well as its 113 combat aircraft, and many of its ground based air defenses are devoted to the protection of air bases and fixed targets. It grew from 7,500 men and 94 combat aircraft in 1982 to 11,000 men, 114 combat aircraft, and 24 armed helicopters in 1988, but Jordan has lacked the resources to modernize and expand it since that time and has had to cut its manpower back to 8,000–9,000 men.

The air force is based at Amman, Azrak, H-4, H-5, Jaafar, and Mafraq. Jordanian main bases are sheltered, but these shelters are unlikely to survive attacks by Israeli hard target killing munitions. They also generally have one runway and are vulnerable to interdiction attacks.

The fighter–ground attack (FGA) aircraft in the Jordanian air force include four squadrons with 62 F-5Es and F-5Fs. These units are trained using U.S. techniques, modified to deal with the special problems of confronting a technically superior Israeli force. The F-5E/F aircraft can be used in both day intercept and attack missions. Their ordnance includes Belouga cluster bombs and Durandal anti-runway and hard point bombs, and Maverick missiles. The F-5Es and F-5Fs date back to May, 1975 and are equipped with the APQ-135 radar. This radar is too limited to take full advantage of modern air-to-air missiles like the AIM-9P-4. While the aircraft have been through several retrofits, they have limited attack and no electronic warfare capability and do not have self-protection systems like rear warning radars, chaff, and flare dispensers.[303]

The Jordanian air force also has two interceptor squadrons with 32 Mirage F-1s (14 CJs, 16 EJs, and 2 BJs). Its air-to-air missiles include AIM-9 Sidewinders, R-530s, and R-550 Magiques. It may have bought some British versions of the Sidewinder with anti-flare and other IR countermeasure capabilities close to the AIM-9M. The Mirage F-1s have proved to present maintenance problems and have only limited ECM and ECCM capabilities. They do not have true look-down/shoot-down capability. The only self-protection system is a radar warning receiver, and the Mirage F-1 has an inadequate electro-mechanical gunsight. Further, Jordan is heavily dependent for air defense operations on the survival of its early warning radars and on the use of ground controlled intercept systems. Both are vulnerable to jamming and attack. Jordan also has a small combat capable training unit with 15 F-5As, four F-5Bs, and 15 CasA-101s.

Jordan has sought more modern aircraft like the F-16 since the mid-1980s. Unable to obtain the agreement of the U.S. Congress to such sales before the Gulf War, Jordan sought aircraft from other sources.[304] It examined the option of buying Soviet aircraft like the MiG-29, but its main interest lay in Western aircraft like the Tornado and Mirage 2000 jet fighters.[305] Jordan believed that the lessons of the 1973 and 1982 wars demonstrated the advantages of high technology Western fighters and air munitions and that the cost of setting up an entire new logistic support and training system for a Soviet-made aircraft would offset what was reported to be a much lower purchase cost than that for any Western fighter.

The purchase of advanced aircraft became even more critical in 1987, when Syria acquired its first MiG-29s. As a result, Jordan took the risk of going into debt to buy the aircraft even though Saudi Arabia refused to finance them. Prime Minister Jacques Chirac of France announced on February 4, 1988, that Jordan had bought 12 "M" variants of the Mirage 2000, with an option for 8–20 more. Each aircraft was reported to cost roughly $23 million. Buying the "M" variant meant, however, that the aircraft would have limited air intercept avionics, no advanced EW or training edge capability, and be limited largely to a laser range finder in terms of advanced avionics. Chirac also announced that 15 of Jordan's 32 existing Mirage F-1CJ/EJs would be outfitted with modern air-to-ground and maritime attack aircraft using systems similar to the Mirage F-1CR in the French air force.[306]

In March, 1988, new reports indicated that Jordan had also bought eight Tornado interdictor-strike (IDS) aircraft with a package of weapons like the JP-233 and Skyshadow electronic warfare systems. The contract was said to be worth $860 million, and delivery was said to be scheduled in three years, with an option to buy more. Financing was said to be provided with the assistance of the British government, although the chief source of this financing seemed to be Saudi Arabia.[307] The Tornado sale was evidently intended to give Jordan a more advanced strike capability, while building up a potential standardization on the Tornado by the Jordanian, Omani, and Saudi air forces.

By March, 1989, however, Jordan's economic crisis reached the point where it had to cancel its orders for the Tornado—in large part because the FRG refused to support the UK in advancing Jordan credits on sufficiently favorable terms.[308] This situation became even worse after the Gulf War. All aid to Jordan ceased, and its economic problems grew even worse. As a result, Jordan had to cancel—or indefinitely delay—its Mirage 2000 purchases in late August, 1991.

This decision not only canceled the order for twelve Mirage 2000s and an option for eight more, it canceled the order for the modernization of fifteen of Jordan's Mirage F-1s, purchases of Durandel anti-runway bombs, and Magic 2 and Super 530 air-to-air missiles. The cancellation also confronted Jordan with significant termination costs on the $1.01 billion package of contracts. It had already missed two payments, and had only paid $168 million to date.[309]

Jordan was more successful in acquiring attack helicopters. It was impressed with the performance of helicopters in the 1982 war and other recent fighting. Its helicopter force now includes twenty-four AH-1Ss with TOW anti-tank guided missiles, which Jordan bought in 1985. The AH-1Ss are effective U.S. combat helicopter designs, and Jordan has slowly improved its tactics to make better use of them in the close air support role. Jordan maintains that armed helicopters need to operate in direct support of the army command to be most effective but has concluded that the air force is the only service that can provide cost-effective maintenance and support. Its other helicopters include five SA-316B Allouettes, ten S-76s, three S-70s, twelve SA-332Ms, four Super Pumas, and eight Hughes 500Ds.

Jordan's ground based air defenses include fourteen Improved Hawk batteries with a total of eighty-six launchers, and a major air defense command system near Amman. Jordan has PIP-II versions of the Hawk, with optical tracking systems, improved ECCM, and higher power illuminators. The launchers are supposed to be embedded in concrete in fourteen fixed sites, with fixed radars and support facilities. These sites limit their low altitude coverage and make them vulnerable to low flying attack aircraft.

Some Israeli sources believe the Hawk missile launchers have been modified to the point where they can be moved relatively quickly, but it is unclear that Jordan's Hawks have anything like the mobility to survive Israel's ability to locate them with RPVs and attack with standoff munitions. They might well be suppressed within a matter of hours. In any case, U.S. Army studies have shown that Jordan would need some forty more Hawk fire units to provide adequate coverage of the country. Jordan cannot afford these additional missiles and has little chance of U.S. authorization of the sale. In fact, Jordan's funding problems may already have created some spare parts shortages for the PIP-II configuration of the missiles, and it is unclear that Jordan can afford a badly needed $130 million upgrade to the PIP-III version of the system. Jordan also faces the problem that unless it buys this upgrade soon, its incremental cost may skyrocket and its availability may become doubtful.[310]

The Jordanian air defense net is not particularly sophisticated but has been upgraded as part of a contract with Westinghouse. Jordan has also bought two electronic warfare centers from Racal. Additional Marconi 3D radars are on order, and Westinghouse has provided a low cost system to improve the integration of the C³I/battle management links between the radars, air control centers, Jordan's fighters, and its surface-to-air defenses. There have been reports that Jordan had secure air control and warning data links to Iraq, but these have not been confirmed.

This air defense system gives Jordan reasonably good coverage of its air space near Israel and Jordan, but it is vulnerable to Israeli attack. In the past, Jordan relied on four obsolete Marconi long range early warning and height finding radars, five AN/TPS-63 and two AN-TPS-62 radars, two TPS-43 surveillance radars to provide medium to high altitude coverage of the northern and middle parts of the country, and one more TPS-43 to cover the south. There was one obsolete Marconi radar to cover the northeast. These radars had 200 kilometers of coverage at medium altitudes against a MiG or Kfir sized target but only up to 23–48 kilometers of coverage at low altitudes. They had less than 15 kilometers of coverage against several key attack sectors. The TPS-43s were relatively fixed in location and vulnerable to suppression in any major attack. Jordan had five more TPS-63 gap-filler radars, which provided 25–30 kilometers of coverage, but these are vulnerable to countermeasures and active suppression. This situation improved in the course of 1989, as Jordan took delivery on five Marconi S711 mobile radar systems, but it is still very much a poor man's system for a nation facing a potential threat from an opponent as sophisticated as Israel.[311]

The rest of Jordan's ground based air defense force that can be used for air base and point target defense consists of the lighter short range weapons obtained from the USSR that have been discussed earlier. They include 3 batteries with 30–44 SA-8 vehicle mounted surface-to-air missile fire units, 3 batteries with 25–35 SA-13 tracked vehicle mounted surface-to-air missile fire units, and 3 batteries with 36 radar guided ZSU-23-4 23mm self-propelled AA guns. There have been approximately 25 Soviet military advisors in Jordan.

The transport and support aircraft in the Jordanian air force include a transport squadron with six C-130B/Hs and three C-212As and a VIP squadron with two Boeing 727s and two Gulfstream IIIs and four S-76 helicopters. There is a force of training aircraft with sixteen Bulldogs, fifteen 101s, twelve PA-28-161s, six PA-34-200s, twelve Warrior IIs, and six Seneca IIs.

Jordanian air force maintenance used to be the best of those of any Arab state. Jordan has closely watched Israeli tactical and training developments, as well as those of the U.S., and has applied them wherever possible. It has been severely limited, however, by its lack of modern battle management, electronic warfare, and air combat systems. Further, Jordan has lacked the funds in recent years for adequate stocks of spare parts and advanced munitions. Its air capabilities would rapidly degrade after a few days of combat.[312]

The Jordanian Coast Guard and Paramilitary Forces

Jordan has a token navy or coast guard to cover its 26 kilometer coastline on the Gulf of Aqaba. It has 260 men and five small coastal patrol craft, including four 8-ton Bertram-type coastal patrol craft with 12.7mm machine guns and one 7-ton Bertram-type coastal patrol boat with 12.7mm machine guns.

Jordan has ordered three 124-ton Hawk-class fast patrol boats equipped with two twin radar controlled 30mm guns, one 20mm gun, and a 12.5mm machine gun, and chaff and other countermeasures. These ships completed trials in 1987–1991, but delivery has been delayed by payment problems and the Gulf War. Jordan also has sought three small patrol boats for the Dead Sea, but these too have been delayed because of funding problems.

The navy's only base is at Aqaba—within easy artillery range of Israel. It is not organized for combat operations, although it does have underwater demolition units and some special operations and raiding capability.

Jordan also has some 6,500 personnel in its paramilitary forces. These include a 4,000–5,000 man public security force and a civil militia or "people's army" with up to 50,000 men and women. Jordan supports a 1,500 man brigade in the Palestine Liberation Army. The public security force is little more than a national police force and has very limited paramilitary capability.

Strategic Interests and Arms Control

The tenuous financing supporting Jordan's military forces collapsed after the Gulf War. Jordan had to cancel its orders for 12–20 Mirage 2000s, although these orders were only about 25–33% of its requirements. It had to cut its army and severely cut the training and readiness of its forces. About 20–33% of its 1,131 main battle tanks are now in storage or partly inactive status, as are substantial parts of the rest of its armor. Its air force has had to reduce training levels and a sharply increased number of its 131 combat aircraft (62 F-5 E/Fs and 32 Mirage F-1s) have limited operational capability.

Jordan still has highly professional forces with considerable defensive capabilities, but it is not a match for either of its neighbors. Quite aside from its lack of major weapons, it has not been able to buy the advanced munitions and C^3I/BM systems it wants—although Jordanian planners have clearly been impressed by Israel's battle management and electronic warfare performance in 1982. Further, Jordan has not fought a major military action since 1967, while Israel has developed extremely high technology forces and has acquired a vast amount of expertise in using such systems.

While Syrian forces are generally inferior to those of Jordan on a man-for-man basis, Syria has learned a great deal from its experience in 1973 and 1982 and has some units which are almost certainly equal in quality to those of Jordan. Whatever the political and social costs of the 1982 fighting may ultimately be for Israel and Syria, it greatly strengthened both states as potential threats to Jordan.

Jordan is also vulnerable to air attack. All but one of Jordan's major population, industrial, political, and military centers are within 50 miles of the Syrian border, and all are within 50 miles—or two minutes' flying time—of Israeli air bases. The terrain in the Jordan Valley provides good terrain masking for low altitude Israeli and Syrian attacks and leaves blind spots in the coverage of Jordan's radars.[313] Israeli aircraft regularly overfly Jordan, and Israeli ground forces can rapidly thrust across the Jordan River—although they might have major problems in advancing up the heights above the East Bank without taking major casualties.

Jordan has only 1.5 active divisions to cover its entire northern border, while Syria has 2 whole corps, and at least 5 to 6 Syrian divisions are normally deployed within easy striking range of Jordan.[314] Jordanian and Syrian relations are now relatively amicable, but in 1980—when Jordan increased its contacts with Iraq and refused to strengthen its military ties to Syria—Syria accused Jordan of supporting the Muslim Brotherhood in Syria and deployed forces to the Jordanian border. These forces included 3 divisions and an air defense brigade and over 800 tanks.[315]

The practical question for the region is whether the decline in Jordan's forces can be allowed to continue. On the one hand, it can be argued that an Arab-Israeli peace settlement may have to be founded on strict limits on the military strength of Jordan and Syria, to guarantee Israel's security in the face of trades of territory for peace. On the other hand, a weak Jordan creates a situation where there is no moderate force that can credibly guarantee the ability to enforce security and stability on the West Bank, limit military or terrorist incursions across the Jordan River, or contain Syrian influence. What seems to be called for is a highly selective policy of arms transfers and military aid, coupled with a move towards a peace settlement and clear distancing of Jordan from Iraq.

Economic aid, however, is far more important than arms. No peace settlement or internal stability is possible if the Jordanian economy continues to degenerate, and King Hussein's control over the country is already uncertain. Although the king seems likely to recover from his cancer operation and the removal of a kidney in August, 1992, the state of his health inevitably has raised the succession issue. A Jordan without King Hussein might well make a peace settlement far more difficult, although Crown Prince Hassan and Field Marshal Bin Shaker offer alternative sources of leadership.

Lebanon

	Manpower (1,000s)	Tanks	Aircraft	Defense Spending ($ millions)	Arms Imports ($ millions)	Arms Exports ($ millions)
1967	19	45	8	45	—	—
1973	20	60	18	75	15	—
1982	21	—	8	295	50	—
1988	20	105	6	300	10	—
1991	18	250	3	140	—	—

Few nations in the world have had a more tragic history than Lebanon, although much of this history has been a self-inflicted wound. France created Lebanon out of the mandated territory it acquired from Turkey following World War I. It attempted to create an enclave nation with a Maronite Christian majority centered around Mount Lebanon, although the data establishing the existence of such a majority was uncertain.

Lebanon declared its independence in 1941, although French forces did not actually leave the country until 1946. The nation that emerged had a total area of 10,400 square kilometers, somewhat smaller than the state of Connecticut. It had a 225 kilometer coastline on the Mediterranean, a 79 kilometer boundary with Israel, and a 375 kilometer boundary with Syria.[316]

In 1943 the Maronites established a national pact with Lebanon's Sunnis. This pact called for a Maronite president, a Sunni prime minister, and a Shi'ite speaker of the national assembly. It also made the commander in chief of the armed forces a Maronite and established a national assembly and civil service divided on the presumed ratio of Christians to Muslims in the total population, which was claimed to be 6:5. There had been no census in Lebanon since 1932, and this ratio was almost certainly incorrect. The Sunnis were probably in the majority. In fact, a CIA estimate made in 1988 indicated that 41% of Lebanon's population was Shi'ite, 27% was Sunni, 16% was Maronite Christian, 7% was Druze, 5% was Greek Orthodox, 3% was Greek Catholic, and 1% was other Christian.[317]

Internal conflicts between leading Maronite families made the new Lebanese government an inherently unstable system. This situation was made worse, however, when Lebanon lost the few battles it fought in the 1948 conflict with Israel and was flooded with Palestinian refugees. The rise of Nasser and the aftermath of the 1956 Arab-Israeli conflict helped trigger the first Muslim attempt to gain added power in 1958 and led to a civil war that was ended only when U.S. forces landed in Lebanon.

This U.S. intervention kept the Maronites in power until 1964, and Lebanon gained enough wealth as the banking, education, trading, and entertainment center of the Arab world to give many visitors the illusion that it was a relatively modern and cosmopolitan state. By the late 1960s, however, the creation of steadily more militant Palestinian movements and the weakness of Lebanon's divided forces allowed the Palestinians to create military enclaves in southern Lebanon. They began to attack Israel in 1968 and triggered a low level border war between Israel and the PLO that lasted until April, 1975, when a new round of fighting developed between Lebanon's Maronites and its native Muslims and Druze.

This civil war involved many changes in leadership and shifting coalitions. It lasted in one form or another from 1975 to 1991, and from 1976 onwards it involved a Syrian military presence on Lebanese soil, which led to violent fighting between Syrian forces and various Christian militias in February, 1978, December, 1980, and the spring of 1981. At the same time, it led to Israeli efforts to create a pro-Israeli enclave in southern Lebanon.

Lebanon divided into armed camps, with separate Maronite, Sunni, Druze, Shi'ite, and Palestinian ethnic forces, and with divisions within each ethnic group that often led to bloody fighting among warring factions with the same ethnic background. While there were periods of peace, the cumulative result was increasingly bloody fighting and the destruction of much of Lebanon's housing and economy. At the same time, various warlords gradually built up a major narcotics industry.

Israel's invasion of Lebanon in June, 1982 made this situation far worse. Israel invaded in an effort both to drive the PLO and Syria out of Lebanon and to create a pro-Israeli Maronite government. While Israel defeated the Palestinian forces in southern Lebanon and the Syrian forces in the Bekaa Valley and forced PLO troops to leave Beirut, its effort to create a pro-Israeli Maronite government under Bashir Gemayel did little more than lead to massacres in the Palestinian refugee camps and the creation of new radical Shi'ite groups. In spite of the deployment of a multinational force in September, 1982, the situation degenerated into still bloodier ethnic fighting and the partitioning of the country into Maronite, Sunni, Druze, Shi'ite, Syrian-occupied, and Israeli-occupied armed camps.

This ethnic conflict made the mission of the multinational force impossible, and the growing radicalization of Lebanon's Shi'ites led to bombing attacks on the barracks of the U.S. and French contingents of the MNF. The loss of well over 300 American and French lives during bombing incidents in 1983 led to the MNF's withdrawal in March, 1984. This withdrawal was followed by the assassination of Gemayel a few days later.

While Gemayel's brother Amin became president, he was not able to govern the country or even maintain control over the Christian militias. He also was unable to obtain any agreement from the Lebanese parliament on a successor when his term expired on September 23, 1988. Gemayel did appoint the chief of staff of the army, Michel Aoun, as prime minister, but Aoun was a Christian, and the existing Muslim prime minister, Salem al-Huss, refused to resign. Lebanon thus was without a president for over a year but had two governments.[318]

New fighting divided the country. Israel's invasion of Lebanon had helped trigger the creation of a new radical Islamic movement among the nation's Shi'ites called the Hizbollah. This led to sporadic fighting between the Hizbollah and the older and more secular Shi'ite movement called the Amal (Hope). The fighting became more intense during January and February and was brought to an inconclusive cease-fire only after Syrian and Iranian intervention.

In mid-February, 1989, Aoun attacked the Lebanese Forces, a Maronite militia under the control of Samir Jega, in an effort to create a unified Christian force. Aoun won this fighting and brought the Lebanese Forces and most of the other Christian militias under his command. In theory, this added 6,000 regulars and 10,000 reserves to Aoun's 15,000 troops in the Lebanese armed forces. Then, on March 14, Aoun announced that he would drive the 30,000 to 40,000 man force that Syria had deployed in Lebanon out of the country.

Aoun's forces opened artillery fire against Syrian positions, and Syria, Shi'ite forces, and Syria's Druze allies counterattacked. This led to extensive fighting before a new cease-fire was declared on September 26, 1989. This cease-fire was followed by a meeting of the Lebanese national assembly in Taif, Saudi Arabia, on September 30, 1989. An agreement was then reached that preserved the Maronite presidency but expanded the national assembly to 108 seats and gave the Muslims and Druze equal representation. As a result of this agreement, the national assembly met on November 5, and Rene Muawad was elected president.[319] When Muawad was assassinated only 21 days later, Ilyas Harawi was elected president on November 24, 1989. He signed the Taif reforms into law and appointed Salem al-Huss prime minister.

Aoun refused to give up control over the Christian part of the army or his power base in East Beirut and to obey either the Taif agreement or the new president. It also became clear that Samir Jega and the Lebanese Forces were not supporting Aoun. As a result, Aoun again attacked the Lebanese Forces in February, 1990, and the fighting continued until May. Aoun may have felt that Syria would not launch an all-out attack upon him because of the fear of Western or Israeli intervention, but his posturing and the constant fighting had left him with little support.

The Gulf War also gave Syria political cover for an attack on Aoun, and in October, 1990, Syrian and Lebanese forces combined to force Aoun from power. The Syrian forces quickly defeated Aoun, and on October 13, 1990, Aoun left the presidential palace in Beirut and sought asylum in the French embassy. This not only created a single government in Lebanon, it created a government with enough Syrian power and internal popularity to partially disarm many of the militias in the regions north from Beirut to Tripoli, in the Shuf Mountains, and as far south as Sidon.

The new defense minister, Michael Murr, and the new chief of staff, Gen. Emile Lahoud, reorganized the Lebanese army. This reorganization used some 120 T-54s and T-55s provided by Syria and some additional tanks provided by Libya.[320] It also involved trimming the nominal strength of the army from 16 brigades to 10 and redeploying the brigades out of their old areas to halt the practice of having ethnic units deployed in their own ethnic areas. Brigades that were allied to one faction—such as the 6th Brigade, which had been loyal to the Amal, and the 8th Brigade, which had been loyal to Aoun—split up among other units or reconstituted as mixed ethnic units. At the same time, it was announced that the government had set the goal of expanding the Lebanese army to 60,000 men.

The reorganized Lebanese army began its effort to take back control of the country by disarming the militias in Beirut on May 1, 1991, and then sending 15,000 soldiers into the districts of Batroun, Koura, Kesrouan, and Byblos to the north and Maten, Shuf, and Aley to the south and southeast. With the backing of some 40,000 Syrian troops, teams of Lebanese army officers received much of the armor and ammunition from the eight major Christian and Muslim militias. The price of Syrian support included a treaty of brotherhood, cooperation, and coordination, which was signed on May 22, 1991. The treaty gave Syria the right to deploy troops in Lebanon to deal with any threat to its interests.

Although the militias probably hid as much as 50% of their arms, the army quickly got 70 tanks and 200 artillery weapons, along with large stocks of munitions. The 6,000 strong Lebanese Forces transferred 50 tanks, 200 artillery pieces, 5 helicopters, and control of the naval base at Juniye, 15 miles north of Beirut. The Druze and several other militias sent their arms to Syria.[321] On May 29, 1991, the government announced that it would integrate up to 20,000 Christian and Muslim militiamen into the army, beginning with an intake of 6,000.

The partial disarming of the militias, however, was only the first step in restoring Lebanon's sovereignty. It left 5,000–11,000 Palestinian troops and the Hizbollah and Amal in the south, around 2,000 Iranian revolutionary guards in the Bekaa, some 2,000–3,000 men in the South Lebanon Army, and a significant number of Israelis in support of the SLA.[322] The government's next step was to move into south Lebanon beginning on July 1, 1991. Although some scattered fighting took place between the Lebanese army and the PLO forces in the south, the army took the last PLO positions around Sidon and Tyre on July 5. It forced the PLO to move its heavy equipment away from the Israeli border and to evacuate the bases at Ain Hilwe and Mieh Mieh south of Sidon. At the same time, army forces occupied positions at Jebel al-Haleeb and Darb al-Sim, which gave them an overview of the camps and positions further to the south.[323]

A month later, General Aoun fled from the French embassy in Beirut to exile in France.[324] Equally important, on October 13, 1991, Iran announced that it would gradually withdraw all of its revolutionary guards from Lebanon.[325]

This Lebanese success, however, did not secure the border with Israel. It left Hizbollah and other Shi'ite forces in being and gave Syria de facto control of the area. Israel also was faced with the fact that there had been 33 guerrilla infiltration attempts between 1988 and July, 1991, 94 fire fights between guerrillas and Israeli troops, 202 rocket and mortar attacks on the SLA zone or Israel, and 32 Israeli soldiers, 37 SLA militiamen, and 352 Palestinian guerrillas had been killed. Israel made it clear that it would not give up the security zone, withdraw its troops and advisors, or end its support for the SLA.[326]

The seriousness of Israel's decision was made all too clear on November 1, 1991, when Israeli fighters retaliated for Hizbollah raids by launching air strikes and artillery bombardments on the Hizbollah camps in Luwayza and Nabatiye.[327] The Lebanese government did try to strengthen its position in the south. It moved into the security zone for the first time in November and even replaced some of the 5,764 man UNIFIL force in the border area in January, 1992.[328] Nevertheless, the fighting between Israelis and the Hizbollah intensified during late 1991 and 1992 and reached a new crisis on February 16, 1992, when two Israeli attack helicopters swooped down on a convoy with the head of the Hizbollah, Sheik Abbas Musawi. The helicopters killed Musawi, his wife, and six-year-old son. The attack also did little to pacify the Hizbollah. They made Sheik Hassan Nasrallah their new leader. Nineteen days later, a car bomb killed the security chief of the Israeli embassy in Ankara, and on May 17 a car bomb blasted the Israeli embassy in Buenos Aires, killing four and wounding 200. Israel conducted four major raids into southern Lebanon in May, and this pattern of sporadic raid and counterraid continued through August, 1992.[329]

Lebanon was left with weak and ill equipped armed forces and with a Syrian protector that might well not honor the Taif agreement and leave Lebanon. Indeed, the agreement was ambiguous in that it called for an initial Syrian withdrawal to the Eastern Bekaa and the approaches to the Beirut-Damascus Road by September, 1992 or until the complete restoration of Lebanese authority with Syrian assistance, if that assistance were requested. While Syria seems to have signed a secret agreement in October, 1989 that required it to leave all of Lebanon after a peace settlement, it is far from clear that Syria intends to honor this agreement. Further, the Lebanese-Syrian defense agreement, which Syria and Lebanon signed at Shataawrah on September 1, 1991, reinforced Syria's right to intervene in Lebanon in its own defense.

Much depended on the outcome of the Lebanese election that began on August 23, 1992. This was the first real election in 16 years, and the first election in which the Maronites had to compete as a clear minority. Unfortunately, the results did little to unify the country.

The election for the new 128 man assembly was scarcely fair. Some key figures like President Harawi and Druze leader Walid Jumblatt gerrymandered safe constituencies, and Lebanon's pro-Syrian minister of the interior, Gen. Sami Katib, rigged the voting lists and redistricting of Lebanon to increase the pro-Syrian vote.

At the same time, Lebanon's Christians did little to help the situation. Aoun attacked the elections from exile, while Amin Gemayel returned to participate in them as part of a campaign that owed far more to Lebanon's divided past than the realities of its present or its future needs. Most Christians eventually ended up boycotting the elections, claiming that Syria had rigged them to elect its own slate of candidates, leaving Lebanon without a representative parliament.

Similar divisions took place within the Muslim vote. Secular Muslims accused the Hizbollah of buying votes with Syrian support, and some Sunnis also boycotted the election. This helped give the Hizbollah added seats in East Beirut and the Bekaa and made Islamic fundamentalism a major force in the assembly for the first time. The more secular Shi'ites, led by Nabih Berri, contested for power with the more conservative and traditional Shi'ites, led by Kamel Assad. While there was little electoral violence, this rivalry raised at least some questions about whether the two Shi'ite factions would use force in a future power struggle.

As a result, the three rounds of voting gave Syria only an uncertain incentive to honor the Taif agreement and withdraw its troops to the Bekaa on September 21. They also did little to indicate that Lebanon would have a future government and assembly that could unite the people, reform the military, and produce sustained economy recovery.[330]

Lebanon must succeed in all three areas to establish stability and fully regain its sovereignty, and the need to build effective and unified military forces explains why President Harawi called on the U.S., Britain, and France for military aid as one of his first acts in office. He talked about introducing a new 18 month national service plan for between 15,000 and 18,000 troops beginning in the summer of 1992.[331] He discussed acquiring attack helicopters with France, and suggested that Lebanon might trade its inactive Mirage fighters for the helicopters.[332] Egypt agreed in principle to provide Lebanon with 90 M-60A1 tanks and training for 1,000 Lebanese troops, and Libya seems to have agreed to provide more T-54s, T-55s, and artillery. Lebanon had few resources, however, and received only limited aid in response to its requests. Harawi had little prospect of creating strong forces in the near future.[333]

The costs of trying to rebuild a nation without effective military forces are illustrated by the price Lebanon has already paid for its civil war. A Lebanese police report issued on March 9, 1992, indicated that 144,000 people were killed and 200,000 were wounded in the fighting between 1975 and 1990. This figure excluded 6,630 people killed and 8,000 wounded in conflicts involving Palestinians and 2,000 killed in Palestinian fighting within the refugee camps, plus 857 Palestinians killed by Maronite militiamen at the Sabra and Shatila refugee camps.[334] Further, the total excluded 3,781 Shi'ites and Muslims killed in 1985–1987 fighting between the Amal and the Palestinians.[335]

Another 17,415 people were listed as missing, including 13,968 kidnapped by Christian and Muslim militias, most of whom the Lebanese police assumed were dead. A total of 3,641 bombs were exploded during the war, killing 4,386 people and wounding 6,784. The victims included the 241 U.S. servicemen and 58 French paratroopers killed in simultaneous bombings in 1983, and 75 people killed in truck bombing attacks on the U.S. embassy in 1983 and 1984. Taken all together, around 180,000 people died during the Lebanese civil war. This compares with about 57,000 killed on all sides in all the Arab-Israeli wars, and around 30,000 to 70,000 on all sides during the Gulf War.

The economic challenge is as great as the political and military one. In addition to the human costs of the civil war, Lebanon's economy has been shattered by decades of civil war. It has no oil or gas, limited natural resources, and about 0.75 cubic kilometers of annual renewable water—which provides only 271 cubic meters per capita.[336] Lebanon lacks the resources for development and to meet its people's expectations, and it has to use much of its resources simply to support its currency. In mid-1992 Lebanon suffered from a massive budget deficit, and unemployment in excess of 30%. The Lebanese pound had also dropped from 2.5 to the dollar in 1974 to 880 in February, 1992 to well over 2,100.

These economic pressures forced Rachid Karami to resign as prime minister in May, 1992. He was peacefully replaced with Rachid Solh, a pro-Syrian member of parliament who had been prime minister some 16 years earlier and was hand-picked by Assad. It is unclear, however, that any prime minister can solve Lebanon's problems. The country has no clear source for the massive economic aid it needs and little ability to use that aid either honestly or effectively. Lebanon's large 30 man cabinet allows all ethnic groups and parties to be represented but also makes it extremely difficult to pursue any consistent economic and security policy. Its drug market creates a parallel economy that brings no revenue to the government but corrupts many officials.

Even if these electoral, military, and economic issues are favorably resolved, Lebanon's internal stability and sovereignty will remain uncertain. Syria may still occupy part of East and West Beirut, the southern suburbs of Beirut, the Bekaa Valley, and part of northern Lebanon, and it has become heavily involved in the narcotics industry in Lebanon. Israel still maintains its security zone north of the border and arms and trains the South Lebanon Army. The PLO and militias still hide a great deal of military equipment, and three Shi'ite groups—the Amal, Hizbollah, and Party of God—maintain armed forces and occasionally attack the pro-Israeli forces in the security zone.[337]

Lebanese Military Expenditures and Arms Transfers

It is almost impossible to discuss the national military forces of Lebanon in the normal sense of the term. Lebanon is only beginning to rebuild its forces after nearly two decades of intermittent civil war. At this point, it seems to be spending about only $160 million a year out of its budget on the military forces under central government control, although it is getting substantial outside aid from Syria and Libya.

The past trends in Lebanese military spending are impossible to estimate with any accuracy. ACDA indicates that Lebanon spent $203 million in 1978, $331 million in 1979, $380 million in 1980, $345 million in 1981, $320 million in 1982, $459 million in 1983, and $432 million in 1984.[338] The U.S. has not issued detailed unclassified estimates of Lebanese military spending since 1983, when the Lebanese government was credited with spending $453 million a year on defense, with having 20,000 men in the armed forces, and with spending 8.2% of the GNP and 20% of the central government budget on military forces.

This 1983 expenditure level represented about 50% more than Lebanon had made before the Israeli invasion in 1982 but was largely a response to a U.S. military aid effort, which completely collapsed after the U.S. withdrawal from Lebanon. The most recent government data on military spending date back to 1986, when military spending was said to be $100 million. Lebanon owes the U.S. and France roughly $1 billion for prior arms deliveries, a sum which is highly unlikely ever to be paid.[339]

Any estimate of arms transfers to Lebanon is misleading because it is impossible to track arms transfers to the various ethnic militias, and the burst of arms transfers that took place in 1983 and 1984 was designed to create central government forces while the MNF still occupied the country. Many of these arms fell into the hands of ethnic forces shortly after the MNF left the country. ACDA estimates that Lebanon imported $20 million worth of arms in 1978, $20 million in 1979, $40 million in 1980, $50 million in 1981,

$50 million in 1982, $230 million in 1983, $240 million in 1984, $40 million in 1985, $10 million in 1986, $10 million in 1987, $10 million in 1988, and $10 million in 1989.[340]

ACDA also estimates that Lebanon took delivery on $395 million worth of arms during 1979–1983. This included $250 million worth of arms from the U.S., $90 million from France, $10 million from the UK, $10 million from Italy, $5 million from Poland, and $30 million from other countries.[341] It estimates that the central government took delivery on $295 million worth of arms during 1984–1988, including $230 million worth of arms from the U.S., $60 million from France, and $5 million from other countries.[342] According to the ACDA's new style of reporting, Lebanon imported a total of $20 million worth of arms during 1985–1989, all of which came from the U.S.[343]

Lebanese Military Manpower

Lebanon has a population of about 3.4 million, with a low population growth rate of 1.4%.[344] This population is about 95% Arab, with 4% Armenian, and 1% other. It is deeply divided along ethnic lines, and any estimate of these ethnic divisions is highly controversial. The CIA estimates that the population is 75% Muslim and 25% Christian, with a small population of Jews.[345] There are, however, some 17 distinct sects. The Muslims are divided into Shi'ite and Sunni, with separate Alawite, Nusayri, Druze, and Ismalite sects that are normally considered Muslim. The Christians are divided into Orthodox groups (Armenian, Greek, Nestorean, and Syriac) and Uniate (Armenian, Caldean, Greek, Maronite, Protestant, Roman, and Syrian).

These divisions severely limit the ability to create unified national forces out of Lebanon's population base. The CIA estimates, however, that there are 726,000 males between the ages of 15 and 49, and that 450,000 are fit for military service. The IISS estimated in late 1991 that there were a total of about 156,000 men and 152,000 women in the age group from 13 to 17 years, 155,300 men and 154,000 women in the age group from 18 to 22 years, and 204,200 men and 239,400 women in the age group from 23 to 32 years.[346]

There currently seem to be about 30,000–35,000 men in the military forces of the central government. In the past, these military forces have been dominated by Maronite officers, and this still seems to continue. A real effort is being made, however, to create a true national army that integrates as many ethnic groups as possible.

The Lebanese Army

Repeated attempts to professionalize the army had only limited success before the civil war divided it. The army had some good individual elements, but overall quality was poor to mediocre in terms of training, leadership, support, command and control, and maintenance. The officer and NCO corps of the Lebanese forces suffered for decades from a wide variety of religious and family rivalries, competition for manpower from the various militias, and a heritage of sending ne'er-do-well sons of Maronite families into the army as a means of getting rid of them.

In 1988, when the nation divided over the successor to President
Gemayel, the regular army had a strength of only about 15,000–18,000 men,
90 M-48A/5 medium tanks, 50 AMX-30 obsolete light tanks, 225–432 operational armored personnel carriers and OAFVs, 59–70 major artillery weapons, 200 mortars and a variety of small arms, light AA weapons, and TOW,
Milan, and other anti-tank weapons.

After the split over the presidency, four largely Christian brigades—the
5th, 8th, 9th, and 10th—with roughly 15,000 men supported Aoun. This involved them in a low level war with Syria that they survived only because of
Iraqi assistance and Syria's restraint in unleashing an all-out land and air
attack. Five other brigades with some 18,000 men sided with various Muslim
groups or stayed neutral. The 3rd, 4th, and 6th brigades disintegrated or
split up. Most of the 3rd Brigade reinforced the 6th Brigade. About 1,500
Christians in the 4th Brigade moved to the Christian enclave.

These pro-Muslim forces were anything but united. The rest of the 6th
Brigade was largely Shi'ite and is aligned with the Amal in West Beirut. The
1st Brigade was based in the Bekaa Valley and aligned with pro-Syrian
Shi'ites. The 2nd Brigade was in north Lebanon and is composed of a mix of
Muslim and Maronite troops under Syrian influence. The 7th Brigade was
deployed in the Batroun region in the north, under the control of Christians
under the influence of Suleiman Franjiah, who had ties to Syria. The 11th
Brigade is largely Druze and was based in the Druze area in the Shuf.[347]

There was continued fighting between the regular forces and both Christian and Muslim factions until Aoun was driven out of East Beirut in October, 1990. One battle in February, 1989 between the army and the Christian
Lebanese Forces under Samir Jega was so intense that Aoun threatened to
wipe out the Christian forces unless they halted fighting and withdrew.[348]

Since May, 1991, efforts to create a national army have been more successful but are still uncertain. The army is nominally organized into ten full
brigades, plus two light brigades and a presidential security force, but many
Lebanese "brigades" would only be light battalions in most other countries.
Further, the government has to proceed slowly in breaking the past division
of the army into Christian, Sunni, Shi'ite, and Druze brigades and in absorbing notoriously undisciplined militia forces into the army. This still tends to
polarize the army along ethnic lines and makes effective command and control very difficult.[349]

The army now has about 28,000–33,000 men with 135–175 M-48A1/A5
and 180–220 T-54/T-55 medium tanks. Its other armored vehicles include
15–20 AMX-13 light tanks, 50 Saladin and 10 Ferret armored cars, 70 AML-
90s, 350–450 M-113 APCs, and 60–100 French VAB-VCT and AMX-VCT
APCs. The army is equipped with a limited number of TOW and Milan anti-
tank guided missile launchers, some 106mm recoilless rifles, and large numbers of anti-tank rocket launchers.

It has no self-propelled artillery weapons and a wide mix of U.S. and
Soviet bloc towed artillery weapons. These include 15 M-101A1 105mm
weapons, 18–24 M-1938/D-30 122mm weapons, some D-30 122mm howitzers, some M-46 130mm guns, and 10 Model 50, 18 M-114A1, and 36 M-198

155mm weapons. The army also has some 122mm multiple rocket launchers and 150 81mm and 30 120mm mortars. It has about 150 anti-aircraft weapons, including 15 M-42 self-propelled guns and 20mm, 23mm, and 30mm towed weapons.

The maintenance and operational readiness of much of this equipment is poor.[350] The army is having to rebuild its training and support system virtually from scratch. It also has questionable loyalty and cohesion, with much depending on Syrian authority and the politics of given factions on a given day. It has little real tactical skill or doctrine and could not successfully engage either Syrian or Israeli forces. It could experience severe problems in fighting any heavily armed ethnic militia. Manpower quality is low, and there is a tendency to engage by shelling hostile areas at a distance rather than directly advance on an enemy. Logistics and maintenance sub-systems are poor, and critical stocks are often limited.

The Lebanese Air Force

Lebanon's air force is almost nonexistent. Although it has roughly 1,000 men in service, only 3–6 obsolete Hunter F-70/T-66 light attack fighters seem to be operational. Many of its aircraft were destroyed during the fighting in 1981–1990, but the Lebanese air force has never been combat capable and never could successfully operate its 9–10 Mirage IIIs before these were put in storage during the civil war. Lebanon also has never had any sophisticated surface-to-air missiles, and its only radar and air control capabilities are two sites near Beirut International Airport.[351]

During the civil war, the "air force" was limited to one active base along the Juniye-Jubayl highway and occasional use of the airstrip at Juniye naval base. It now seems to be recovering the ability to operate out of Beirut airport, but its major fixed wing bases are at Riyaq and Kleiat and are under Syrian control. It has roughly 700–900 men, 5–6 Hawker Hunters, 3–5 armed Magister trainers, 3–5 armed Beagle Bulldog trainers, 2–7 operational SA-342 attack helicopters with SS-11/12 air-to-surface missiles, 10 medium and 5 light transport helicopters, 6 training aircraft, and 2 transport aircraft.

Pilots and ground crews have little operational readiness, and pilots have little advanced combat training. The command and support organization is weak. Spare parts and maintenance facilities are limited, and the Lebanese air force's combat aircraft, helicopters, and support aircraft have only limited operational capability.

The Lebanese Navy and Paramilitary Forces

The 500 man Lebanese navy is a largely Christian-officered coastal defense force based at Juniye. In 1992 it had three French Byblos-class 28-ton patrol boats. These were armed only with a 20mm Oerlikon gun and two Browning 12.7mm machine guns, and only one may have been fully operational. The navy also had two French Edic-class 670-ton landing craft. The customs force had two 31-ton Tracker-class coastal patrol craft, five 5.2-ton Aztec-class coastal patrol boats, and four L'Esterel 37M-class light coastal patrol boats. Some of these boats had been seized by the militias and were not operational.

The Lebanese navy has always had only token military effectiveness, even in dealing with smugglers. At present, its ships are old and less well armed than many militia and arms smuggling craft. Logistics, maintenance, and training are poor. The customs service may actually have more operational capability than the navy, although it only has light unarmed aircraft and small patrol boats.

Paramilitary forces still seem to include an internal security force in the Ministry of the Interior which has always had limited effectiveness and which has often contributed to Lebanon's problems when it has attempted to take action. It once had a strength of 8,000 men, but its current strength is unknown. In late 1991 it was equipped with small arms and 30 Chaimite APCs.

Syrian and Ethnic Forces

Although Lebanon's regular military forces are rebuilding their strength, they still have only tentative control of the country. Their ability to control the nation's militias is still uncertain and dependent on support from Syrian troops, which occupy about 65% of the country.

Syria has steadily expanded its presence in the country since it was first invited in by former President Franjiah in March, 1976. In spite of Israel's 1982 invasion and Syrian forces' remaining north of a "red line" that runs east and west across Lebanon near Rashayah, Syria is now the real military power in the country.

Syrian troop strength varies with time, but it generally keeps at least 25,000 to 30,000 troops in Lebanon and deploys them where it can control both Beirut and the Bekaa. It keeps elements of one armored brigade in Beirut, along with parts of seven special forces regiments. It has two special forces regiments and a pro-Syrian Palestine Liberation Army (PLA) element in the area around Tripoli. There are elements of one mechanized brigade in the mountains near Beirut and a corps headquarters with parts of a mechanized brigade in the Bekaa.

The treaty of brotherhood, cooperation, and coordination that Syria and Lebanon signed in May, 1991 preserves Lebanese sovereignty but gives Syria virtual free rein to intervene if any force in Lebanon should threaten Syrian security. Syrian military and intelligence officers operate freely in much of Lebanon and are key actors in its growing drug industry, particularly in the Bekaa. The Bekaa now produces between 1,000 and 1,500 tons of hashish a year and about 9–11 tons of opium, and Syrian special forces have been directly involved in a number of major drug operations. The Syrian army has also taken a major part in smuggling and black market operations that ship goods from Lebanon to Syria in ways that bypass Syria's cumbersome and excessive duties and taxes.[352]

Two other countries also play a large role in Lebanon. The 2,500 man South Lebanon Army operates in a separate enclave along the Israeli border and is little more than a mercenary force that Israel sustains to keep a security zone north of its border. The SLA was formed as an Israeli surrogate, under the command of General Lahd in 1984.[353] The SLA is nominally "Christian" but mixes pro-Israeli Christians, Shi'ites, Druze elements, and mercenaries. SLA troops receive about 10 weeks of formal military training in a course set up and run with Israeli assistance, and they have steadily improved in fighting quality over the years.

The SLA receives about $3–6 million annually in direct subsidies from Israel and is organized into paramilitary battalions, with infantry battalions covering the security zone, armored and mechanized battalions in reserve, and an additional battalion at the SLA's headquarters near Jassin. It has 40 M-4 and 30 T-54 and T-55 tanks. It has M-113 APCs, and a mix of 122mm, 130mm, and 155mm artillery weapons.[354]

The security zone the SLA covers is a strip Israel seized during the 1982 war that is about 50 miles long and 6 miles wide. It includes about 325 square miles, or 8%, of Lebanon's territory and has a population of 200,000 to 225,000. Its residents have special license plates, and about 2,000 workers in the zone have permission to work in Israel—permission that is sometimes tied to having a relative working in the SLA. Some friendly villages receive water and telephone service from Israel, and Israel has built roads, hospitals, and schools in the area.

The security zone is filled with Israeli-financed fortifications, including concrete bunkers. The SLA patrols this security zone during the day, but Israeli forces often cover the area at night, and Israeli intelligence plays a major role in securing the area. The SLA often receives Israeli artillery and air support when it operates against PLO or Hizbollah forces, and the army sometimes has the support of Israeli forces or intelligence commando units. It is difficult to get an accurate count of incidents and casualties, but about 50 SLA soldiers seem to be killed and about 150 wounded per year.

Iran also plays a role in Lebanon and once had about 1,500–3,000 revolutionary guards with the Shi'ite militias in the south, providing them with subsidies of up to $50 million per year. Most of these revolutionary guards have been withdrawn, but Iran still provides money, weapons, and political support to Lebanon's Shi'ite militias, particularly to the Islamic fundamentalist Hizbollah. The Hizbollah is affiliated with the Islamic Jihad (Islamic Amal), Revolutionary Justice Organization, and Organization of the Oppressed. It is strongly anti-Israel and anti-SLA and has launched a long series of attacks against the security zone in the south, often firing or sending small combat teams across the Israeli border.

The Hizbollah's paramilitary and guerrilla forces have about 3,500 in the standing militia plus another 15,000 men in the reserve militia. The more radical Islamic Amal has another 1,000 men. It draws its support from Shi'ite areas in the Bekaa, Beirut, and south Lebanon. Their leadership is largely radical Islamic Shi'ite clerics, and they have bases near Baalbek and in the east Bekaa. They have some APCs, large numbers of crew served weapons and anti-tank weapons, and some AA guns. The Islamic Resistance forces of the Hizbollah have been particularly active in attacking SLA and Israeli positions, and while these Hizbollah forces are relatively lightly armed, they are one of the most effective ethnic forces in Lebanon in terms of actual military action.[355]

The other main Shi'ite force is the Amal movement under the leadership of Nabih Berri.[356] The Amal has strong ties with Syria and, like the Hizbollah, is to some extent a product of Israel's 1982 invasion. The Shi'ites initially welcomed Israeli troops as liberators from the problems caused by the PLO, but Israel badly mismanaged the situation, and the Shi'ites suffered more than any other ethnic group from the Israeli occupation. As a result, Berri shifted from an anti-PLO stance to alignment with Syria. The Amal is far more secular than the Hizbollah and has launched fewer attacks on the SLA and Israel. It has about 10,200 actives and a total strength of 15,000, and has long been affiliated with the Lebanese army's 6th Brigade but transferred much of its heavy equipment to the national army in 1991. The Amal is divided, and Berri has less influence and control in the south than in the area around Beirut. Amal has also steadily lost men to the Hizbollah and has suffered from its obvious dependence on Syria.

The Druze also have links to Syria, and their Popular Liberation Army once had about 5,500–8,500 in the standing militia and 7,000 in the reserve militia. It has been affiliated with the 11th Brigade of the Lebanese army. Much of its heavy equipment has been transferred to the national army since 1990. The Druze forces are under the leadership of Jumblatt and the Progressive Socialist Party and occasionally received aid from the USSR in the 1980s, as well as more continuous aid from Syria. They were relatively well trained and disciplined before they partially disarmed in 1991 and successfully created an enclave of Druze territory before Syria intervened to oust Aoun. They drove out the Christian forces that attempted to occupy Druze territory after the 1983 Israeli invasion and control much of the Shuf, Aley, and Maten districts, and part of the Qaroun area of the south Bekaa.

The main Christian force is the Lebanese Forces Militia (including the Phalange), which had about 18,500 men operating on a part time basis and about 12,000 more men with some form of military affiliation before it partially disarmed in 1991. It has some elements of regular military organization, but it never fully recovered from the void in its leadership caused by the assassination of Bashir Gemayel in September, 1982. It was badly defeated by Druze forces when it attempted to occupy part of the Shuf in September, 1983 and suffered severely during 1984–1990 from rivalries between President Gemayel, Samir Jega, and General Aoun.[357]

The Lebanese Forces Militia had close relations with the Christian brigades in the army—including the 5th, 8th, 9th, and 10th brigades. It received some aid and military equipment from Iraq during the late 1980s, but it was in no position to seriously contest Syria's intervention in 1990. As a result, it lost much of its equipment and weaponry. The Lebanese Forces Militia still has equipment in hidden stockpiles, however, and some estimates indicate that its organized military once had as many as some 125 T-55 and M-48 tanks, 5 AMX-13s, M-113 APCs, and some 100 artillery pieces—including 60 122mm weapons and 10 155mm weapons.

There are remnants of Robert Franjiah's Marada Brigade. This unit operated in northern Lebanon and east of Tripoli in the Christian areas under the political influence of ex-president Suleiman Franjiah (Robert's father) and is a product of the ruthless fighting between Maronite families that caused the death of Robert's brother, Tony, and his family in 1978. Historically, the Marada Brigade was allied with Syria against the Lebanese Forces Militia but suffered severely when it tried to seize control of the Akura District in 1984. It did so without Syrian permission and lost much of its equipment. Elements of the Marada are still active in the north in the area around Sibil.[358]

There are also a number of highly disparate Sunni militias. Largely under Syrian control or influence, they have less ability to operate independently but are still a potential threat to central government control. These militias include the Murabitun, or Independent Nasserite Militia, under the leadership of Ibrahim Qulaylat. Based in the urban parts of the coastal area near Tripoli, this fundamentalist Sunni militia has about 200–500 men and has been affiliated with the 2nd and 12th brigades of the Lebanese army. It is loosely affiliated with the PLO and has received aid from the Hizbollah for its assistance during the Hizbollah's struggles with the Amal. Similar groups include the Union of Popular Labor Force, the Popular Nasserite Organization, and Lebanese Arab Armies.

The Islamic Unification Movement (IUM) under the leadership of Sheik Said Shaaban is another Sunni fundamentalist group based in Tripoli, with 800–1,000 men. The IUM, however, is anti-Syrian and anti-Shi'ite and has very limited influence and military capability. It was effectively defeated when it attempted to prevent Syrian forces from entering Tripoli in 1985, and while it has a loose affiliation with the PLO, it is unlikely to emerge with any real strength as long as Syria is in control of much of the country.

Finally, the Lebanese Alawites (who consider themselves to be Sunni when it is politic to do so) are organized into the Red Knights and Arab Democratic Party. These forces are headquartered in the Hirmil, Baalbek, and Tripoli areas and have received training from Rifat Assad's security forces and more recently from Syrian special forces. No recent estimates are available of their military strength, but they could include up to 1,500 men.

Syria has forced the Palestinian forces in Lebanon to hand over some of their heavy weapons, but many remain hidden and stockpiled. There are still about 10,000 men with arms in the nine major Palestinian military factions in the country.

Strategic Interests and Arms Control

Lebanon is of little strategic interest to the West, except in terms of the continued instability caused by its ethnic wars and as a cockpit for Syrian and Israeli rivalry. The human cost of civil and external conflict, however, has been great. According to recent estimates, some 180,000 people have died since 1975, over 200,000 have been wounded, 250,000 have emigrated, and nearly one-third of the population have lived as refugees.[359] There is no sign that this suffering has ended.

From an arms control viewpoint, Lebanon presents the problem that selective arms transfers may be necessary to build up a central military force strong enough to secure the country. At the same time, arms flows need to be shut off to the various local and ethnic forces, and it is far from clear that the central government of Lebanon is independent enough of Syria to ensure that significant arms transfers would not fall into Syrian hands. What is needed is a carefully tailored arms transfer policy shaped to Lebanon's specific needs and internal political situation. Any attempt to set guidelines based on some broad regional principles could make the situation worse rather than better.

Palestinian Forces

The debate over who speaks for the Palestinians and who is responsible for any given Palestinian use of force has been one of the most bitter issues since the 1948 fighting between the Arabs and Israelis. Until the formation of the new Rabin government in July, 1992, Israeli regimes consistently opposed any negotiations with the PLO, the main umbrella organization that includes most Palestinian groups, regarding it as a terrorist organization committed to the destruction of Israel.

The PLO, however, includes many different organizations with very different views and has often been in conflict with Arab governments. Different factions within the PLO have supported peace negotiations and opposed them, have fought with each other and with Arab governments, and have supported unconventional war or opposed it. At the same time, new Islamic movements have arisen within the Palestinian movement, many of which oppose the secular nature of the PLO and take a hard-line stand on any cooperation with Israel.

The Role of the PLO

The PLO was formed at the first Arab summit in Cairo in 1964, with a charter that stated that "the liberation of Palestine will destroy the Zionist and imperialist presence." It has a Palestine National Council (PNC) of 432 members that acts as its parliament and is supposed to meet once a year. There is a 93 member central council above it and an executive committee at the top which is led by Yasser Arafat. The committee has fifteen members— eight from six organizations and seven independents—elected by the PNC. The PLO taxes Palestinians throughout the world, runs businesses, and solicits aid from Arab states. It is believed to have assets of $1–5 billion.[360]

The PLO has feuded with Egypt and Syria and fought with Jordan and various factions in Lebanon as well as with Israel. Its shifting relations with Iraq, Iran, Libya, the Sudan, and Yemen have also involved some cooperation in unconventional warfare or terrorism. The PLO long delayed any effort to form a government-in-exile, but the PNC issued a unilateral declaration of independence at its meeting in Algiers on November 15, 1988. All other Arab states except Syria recognized the PLO within days, and 94 nations now recognize it as an independent state.

While the PLO traditionally opposed Israel's existence, it has gradually moved towards a willingness to engage in peace talks. During its conference of November 12–15, 1988, the PNC issued a statement indicating that the PLO accepted UN Resolutions 242 and 238 as the basis for an international peace conference and that it rejected terrorism. On December 7, 1988, Arafat signed a statement at a conference in Stockholm that again suggested the PLO was willing to engage in peace talks based on UN Resolutions 242 and 238, that the PLO accepted Israel's right to exist, and that the PLO renounced terrorism. Arafat made the same points before the UN General Assembly on December 13, 1988.

Although the Israeli government continued to state that the PLO charter still indicated that the PLO was committed to the destruction of Israel and that the PLO still engaged in terrorism and armed struggle, the U.S. began a dialogue with the Palestinians on December 16, 1988. This dialogue lasted until June 20, 1990, when President Bush suspended it because the PLO refused to denounce a May 30, 1990, Palestine Liberation Front attack on Israel.

Most Palestinians supported Saddam Hussein after his invasion of Kuwait on August 2, 1990—largely because Saddam claimed that he was acting on behalf of the Arab poor and the "Arab nation." While Arafat and the PLO leadership claimed to take a neutral position, their support was so clear that Kuwait and Saudi Arabia ended their $100–200 million a year in aid, drove most Palestinians out of their countries, and denounced Arafat. These problems were made worse when some Palestinians supported the abortive August 18, 1991, coup against Mikhail Gorbachev, and when Syrian and Lebanese forces partly disarmed many Palestinian forces during the Syrian intervention in Lebanon in 1991.

These tensions have eased since the Gulf War. Saudi Arabia slowly reestablished relations with Arafat and the PLO and renewed aid in early October, 1991.[361] On October 21, 1991, the U.S. and the Soviet Union issued invitations to the Palestinians to join Israel, Egypt, Jordan, Lebanon, and Syria in peace talks that began on October 30, 1991. While both the PLO and the Palestinian representatives at the talks took a cautious and sometimes intransigent stance between October, 1991 and May, 1992, their position eased after the formation of the new Rabin government in Israel in July, 1992. The mainstream of the Palestinian movement seemed willing to take a more flexible position on autonomy and the timing of any peace settlement, and the Rabin government tacitly allowed open contact between the PLO and Palestinian negotiators, Palestinian representatives on the West Bank, and Israeli peace activists.

The Size and Deployment of Palestinian Forces

Estimates differ over the number of Palestinians and how they should be classified. The United Nations Relief and Works Agency (UNRWA) had long registered Palestinian Arab refugees. In 1950 it registered 127,600 in Lebanon, 82,194 in Syria, 506,200 in Jordan, 198,227 in the Gaza Strip, and 45,800 in Israel: a total of 960,021 refugees. In 1991 it registered 311,000 in Lebanon, 290,000 in Syria, 960,000 in Jordan, 529,000 in the Gaza Strip, and 430,000 in the West Bank: a total of 2.5 million refugees. Some 874,000 of these lived in

61 refugee camps.[362] The CIA estimates that there were 615,575 Palestinians living in the Gaza in 1990 and 1,058,122 living in the West Bank and Jerusalem. This compares with an estimate of 2,500 Jewish settlers in the Gaza, 70,000 in the West Bank, and 110,000 in East Jerusalem. The Palestinian Academic Society for the Study of International Affairs estimated that there were about 5.5 million Palestinians, with 1.7 million in Jordan, 1.1 million in the West Bank, 730,000 in Israel, 596,000 in Gaza, 451,000 in Lebanon, 369,000 in the U.S. and Europe, 282,000 in Syria, and 23,000 in Libya. It indicates that there were 169,000 Palestinians in Saudi Arabia, 28,000 in Iraq, 378,000 in Kuwait, 62,000 in other Gulf states, and 68,000 in Egypt before the Gulf War. Many have since been forced to leave or deported.[363]

Only a small fraction of these Palestinians are involved in any kind of military organization, and an even smaller fraction of these are involved in actual military activity or unconventional warfare. These various Palestinian military groups are "freedom fighters" to most Arabs and "terrorists" to most Israelis. The rhetoric surrounding them often disguises the fact that they are so politicized that they have little military effectiveness and often consist of little more than a front to legitimize fund-raising or their use as mercenaries and proxies by governments like Iraq, Syria, and Libya.

Most of the military commanders and officers of the various Palestinian forces and militias are inexperienced and ineffective, and many are corrupt. Training, while sometimes physically active, usually lacks discipline and effective organization and is little more than a military practical joke. Palestinian forces have often fought with great courage and dedication, but their greatest successes have occurred when they have fought spontaneously and outside the formal leadership of the various military factions of the PLO and Palestinian army.

The military forces of the PLO and other Palestinian factions have suffered severely from their defeat in Lebanon in 1982 and from efforts to challenge Syrian forces when they supported the Lebanese national government in reasserting control of the country in 1990 and 1991. By its own estimates, the PLO evacuated a total of 14,300 "fighters" from Lebanon in 1982 and lost virtually all of its bases and heavy equipment. Palestinian forces slowly reentered Lebanon after 1984 and built up new bases at Sidon and elsewhere in the country. Syria, however, opposed independent Palestinian operations in Lebanon and often suppressed Palestinian forces or took control of their camps. In 1991 Syria exploited the Arab world's post–Gulf War hostility to the Palestinians to support the regular Lebanese forces in seizing control of all of the major Palestinian camps in southern Lebanon, including the major camps near Sidon and Tyre. While the Palestinian forces were able to conceal part of their equipment, they lost many of their arms and now have little capacity for independent operations.[364]

Palestinian forces have been deeply divided since the mid-1980s and have spent as much time fighting one another and other Arabs as they have preparing to fight Israel. There are now four main groups of such forces.[365] The largest is the Palestine Liberation Army, which consists of conventional forces that are totally under the control of their host states of Jordan and

Syria. These are largely showpiece forces and have only limited military effectiveness.

The second group consists of a range of guerrilla groups. The largest is Al-Fatah, which is headed by Arafat. Other mainstream PLO guerrilla groups include the Palestine Liberation Front; Al-Saiqa, which is tied to Syria; the Palestine Popular Struggle Front; and the Arab Liberation Front. There are two major guerrilla groups whose ties to the PLO have varied with time and who have often been associated with terrorism. These include the Popular Front for the Liberation of Palestine and the Democratic Front for the Liberation of Palestine. Most of the elements other than Fatah operate individually under their own leaders, and all have poor military training and equipment.

The third group consists of guerrilla forces that are not affiliated with the PLO and are sometimes hostile to it. These include the hard-line Popular Front for the Liberation of Palestine–General Command (which split off from the PFLP), the Palestine National Salvation Front (which split off from Al-Fatah in 1983), and the Fatah Revolutionary Council (FRC) led by Abu Nidal (Sabri Khalil al-Banna). The FRC and Al-Fatah have long been bitter enemies, and Abu Nidal and Arafat have frequently exchanged assassination threats.

The Fatah Revolutionary Council is one of the few Palestinian movements which can unambiguously be termed mercenary and terrorist in character.[366] It was formed in 1973 and broke away from the PLO when the PLO decided to reject terrorist attacks against Israel and the occupied territories. Operating out of Lebanon, Libya, Iraq, and the Sudan, it has blackmailed nations like Kuwait and Saudi Arabia into continuing contributions, has sold its services to various Arab leaders, and has killed over 300 people in attacks in more than 20 countries. Its camps and officials have also been the targets of numerous Israeli attacks.

The final group consists of Islamic fundamentalist groups inside the occupied territories which now are often isolated cells or small lightly armed elements of the Islamic fundamentalist movement. One key group is the Islamic Jihad, which is extremely radical and violent and has considerable strength in the Gaza. It has often attacked the PLO politically but has cooperated with it in the *intifada*. It has at least some automatic weapons and explosives. The largest movement is the Hamas, a partial acronym for al-Harakat al-Muqawwama al-Islamiyya (Islamic Resistance Movement). Hamas is an offshoot of the Muslim Brotherhood, which was founded in Egypt in 1928. Like the Islamic Jihad, it opposes any compromise or peace settlement with Israel but is less rigid about its use of violence and interpretation of Islamic law. It has great strength in the Gaza and significant strength in the West Bank.

Many believe that extremist elements in the Hamas, including the Black Panthers and Red Dragons, are responsible for the killings of so-called collaborators and Israeli reformers that have turned the *intifada* into an Arab versus Arab conflict. Finally, some experts feel that the Fatah movement in the West Bank and Gaza has increasingly become Islamic and is blurring the line between the secular PLO and a more radical religious movement. There is a considerable difference of opinion as to how well the Islamic groups in the Gaza and West Bank cooperate with the PLO.[367]

The military strength of the main factions within the Palestinian forces that are aligned with the PLO has become much more difficult to estimate since the Gulf War and the Syrian-Lebanese partial disarming of Palestinian forces in Lebanon in 1991. Probable maximum manpower strength in 1992 seems to be as follows:[368]

- Al-Fatah (pro-Arafat): 1,500 active and 7,500 semi-active reserves and 3 brigades
- Palestine Liberation Front/Abu Abbas Faction: 300 men
- Arab Liberation Front (Abd al-Rahim Ahmed): 300 men
- Palestine National Salvation Front (anti-Arafat, pro-Syrian, led by Mohammed Said Musa, or Abu Musa), or Al-Fatah Uprising: 2,500 men
- Democratic Front for the Liberation of Palestine (pro-Soviet, Hawatmeh): with 800–1,200 men and 8 battalions
- Popular Front for the Liberation of Palestine (Habash): 800–1,200 men and 6 battalions
- Popular Front for the Liberation of Palestine–General Command (Jibril): 600–800 men and 5–6 companies
- Palestine Popular Struggle Front (Bahjat Abu Gharbiyah and Samir Ghusha): 600 men
- Al-Saiqa (pro-Syrian, under Issan al-Qadi): 600–1,000 men and 5 battalions
- Palestine Communist Party: 100 men

The strength of the main factions within the Palestinian forces which are not clearly aligned with the PLO or which are actively dissident is estimated at:

- Abu Nidal Faction (Abu Nidal): 800–1,000 men
- 15th May Organization (al-Amri) with 100 men
- Popular Front for the Liberation of Palestine–Special Command (Abu Mohammed): 100 men
- FRC–Emergency Command (secessionists from Abu Nidal): 200 men
- Al-Fatah pro-Jordanian elements: 300 men

These alignments and strength estimates are highly volatile, and Palestinian forces seem likely to remain divided. Even those elements which have been consistently loyal to the PLO have limited practical allegiance to it, except through their own leaders. The Al-Fatah Uprising and Soviet-backed Democratic Front are particularly radical, although none of the present Palestinian forces have anything like the cohesion, strength, weaponry, and well established military positions they had before the 1982 invasion.

Palestinian Deployments

There are now elements of the Palestinian forces in Algeria, Egypt, Jordan, Libya, Syria, Tunisia, and Yemen, as well as Lebanon. Reports of Palestinian active military strength vary sharply, but estimates in late 1991 indicated there were about 16,500 full time actives, with 10,000–11,000 Palestinian guerrillas or three brigade equivalents in Lebanon. There were also 1,000–2,500 men or one brigade equivalent in Syria, 300–500 men in Algeria, 900–2,000 men or one brigade equivalent in Iraq, 3,000 men or one brigade equivalent in Jordan, 1,000–2,000 men in Yemen, 500 men in the Sudan, and 100 men in Tunisia. Another 10,200 men had some form of militia or paramilitary status.

There are small naval forces with 50 frogmen and 200 men in small boat units scattered in Yemen, Libya, and Algeria. Some 200 members of various PLO organizations had some kind of military flight training or experience, training in Libya, Yemen, Romania, North Korea, Pakistan, Cuba, and the USSR. Palestinian pilots have flown MiG-21 and MiG-23 aircraft and various helicopters in Libya, although none of the military elements of the PLO had an air component.[369]

The various Palestinian forces in Lebanon in 1991 deployed some 1,500 men in the Bekaa, 1,400 in the Mount Lebanon area, 800 near Tripoli and in the north, 4,000 near Beirut, and 4,000 in south Lebanon, mainly near Sidon and Tyre. Some are with the Druze near Aramun, Shueifat, Aitat, and Marrufiyehon; some in the camps in Beirut, Sidon, and Tyre; and some affiliated with Syria or the Party of God. PLO elements had again established a presence in Ain Hilwe and Mieh Mieh near Sidon.

The Future Impact of Palestinian Forces

It seems unlikely that the Palestinian forces will emerge as a serious military threat to Israel unless they can form a more stable long term coalition with the Lebanese government, Amal, Hizbollah, and/or Druze than now seems probable. The recent history of sporadic fighting between the Palestinians and the Druze, Hizbollah, and Amal raises doubts about the stability of any coalition.

For example, serious fighting between the Shi'ites in the Amal and the Palestinians in the refugee camps of Sidon, Tyre, and Beirut broke out during October, 1986 to January, 1987 and became open warfare in February, 1987. During the height of this conflict, the Amal ended in fighting their former Druze allies and the Sunnis and Palestinians. An uncertain peace was enforced only by Syrian intervention. Similarly, some Palestinian elements resisted the reestablishment of Lebanese army control over much of southern Lebanon in 1991 but found themselves without any support from the Hizbollah.

Nevertheless, a coalition of Palestinian forces and some faction like the Amal could still present a serious threat to the Israeli-backed South Lebanon Army. The PLO helped the Amal against the Hizbollah in 1988, and the Amal has been far more tolerant of the PLO military buildup in southern Lebanon. The SLA has only 2,500 relatively low grade active personnel and requires constant Israeli military backing.[370] This compares with up to 5,000 Amal and 1,000–1,500 Hizbollah troops in the area south of Sidon. The Hizbollah forces have often proved more effective than both those of Amal and the South Lebanon Army, although they have suffered from a lack of Iranian financing and support since Iran's cease-fire with Iraq in the summer of 1988.

Even without active Palestinian support of the Hizbollah, Israel has been forced to increase its support of the SLA and to improve the defenses of its security zone along the border with Lebanon. There seems little prospect that the UNIFIL forces in the area can ever provide Israel with real security, and the Lebanese government's ties to Syria make it very difficult for Israel to give up its security zone. As a result, Israel is almost certain to face continuing low level rocket or artillery attacks and infiltration attempts, and these could become far more serious if the Hizbollah or other radical elements in Lebanon should ever form a stable alliance with the Palestinians.[371] Most importantly, the number of Palestinian raids on Israel has increased since 1990, and the massive popular uprising on the West Bank and in Gaza could still revitalize the PLO's military capabilities or some other Palestinian military option if the current peace talks fail.

The PLO is also increasingly divided, and not simply along factional lines. Some Palestinians believe that elections are needed to give it unity and a more collective approach to decisionmaking; others feel that the West Bank and Gaza should play the primary role in shaping their own destiny. Conservative PLO leaders like Khalid Hassam favor elections and collective decisionmaking as a way of reducing the near paralysis caused by trying to suit all of the major factions and relying on Arafat as the sole overall authority. Key Arafat loyalists—like his deputy, Salah Khalaf; security chief, Hayel Abdel Hamud; and military chief, Khalil Wazir—have been assassinated under circumstances that raise serious questions whether other Palestinians or Israel was responsible.

Hamas, the key Islamic party on the West Bank, beat the PLO candidates in a spring, 1992 election in a traditionally liberal and secular city like Ramallah and also scored major victories in Hebron and Gaza. The majority of West Bank activists in the Intifada seem to be affiliated with Hamas, although the hard-line group called the Black Panthers is affiliated with the PLO. Hamas and the PLO became involved in bitter fighting in Gaza during June and July, 1992—although there were more beatings than killings. This fighting was caused by Hamas's objections to PLO support of the peace talks and is a further warning of what might happen if they fail.

Egypt

	Manpower (1,000s)	Tanks	Aircraft	Defense Spending ($ millions)	Arms Imports ($ millions)	Arms Exports ($ millions)
1967	220	530	400	0.3	204	1
1973	390	1,880	620	11.4	741	14
1982	447	2,100	429	7.2	1,900	360
1988	452	2,425	517	6.1	725	170
1991	420	3,190	495	5.2	—	—

Egypt has played a critical role in the Arab world throughout modern history and is one of the largest and most strategically important Middle Eastern states. It has a land area of 1,001,450 square kilometers, about three times the size of the state of New Mexico. It has an 11 kilometer border with the Gaza Strip, a 255 kilometer border with Israel, a 1,273 kilometer border with the Sudan, and a 1,150 kilometer border with Libya. It has a total of 2,450 kilometers of coastline on the Mediterranean and Red Sea. While it has only limited oil resources, it controls the Suez Canal—one of the most important trade routes in the world. It also plays a crucial role in limiting Libyan ambitions, providing security for Israel, and ensuring the security of Saudi Arabia and the pipelines carrying Saudi oil to the Red Sea.

Egypt has a relatively well developed economy for a Middle Eastern country, although it has been crippled by overpopulation, chronic misman-agement of a large and grossly inefficient state sector, and poor agricultural policies. Egypt does, however, have estimated proved oil reserves of up to 4.5 billion barrels and gas reserves of 12,400 billion cubic feet.[372] Egypt also has about 54.4 cubic kilometers of internal renewable water resources from the Nile, which is high for a Middle Eastern country. This amounts to about 1,202 cubic meters of water per person, about half the total for a citizen of the U.S.[373]

Egyptian Military Development

Unlike that of many Arab nations, Egypt's modern military history did not begin with postwar independence.[374] Egypt never lost its formal inde-pendence, and an Egyptian military officer led an uprising against British forces as early as 1882. In 1918 Egypt successfully demanded that Britain put its army under Egyptian officers. A British inspector general remained in a supervisory capacity, but his post was abolished by the Anglo-Egyptian treaty of 1936, and further withdrawals of British troops took place.

Up to this time, the Egyptian military had been officered solely by an ultraconservative upper class that played little role in Egyptian nationalism or reform but simply preserved the Turkish command system in which offic-ers were socially isolated from their men, providing little direct leadership. In 1936, however, the Egyptian Military Academy was opened to the sons of the middle class. During 1938, 1939, and 1940, a new class of Egyptian offic-ers came into service who were intensely nationalistic and anti-British. Rather than acting as a bulwark of reaction, the armed forces became a leading force for political and social change.

The new officer class often sympathized with the Axis during the fighting in North Africa because it was committed to expelling Britain from Egypt. These officers came to see King Farouk as a corrupt tool of Britain and the traditional officers around the king as a barrier to change and military effec-tiveness. Egypt's poor military performance during the conflict with Israel from May, 1948 to February, 1949 catalyzed the new officer class into action. It launched a series of anti-British and anti-monarchy movements that brought a Free Officers Movement to power in July, 1952 and forced King Farouk to abdicate.

From that point onward, the real political power in Egypt rested with the senior leadership of the armed forces. The three who have led the country since then, Nasser, Sadat, and Mubarak, have pursued very different goals and policies and have played a major political role in the Arab world.

Gamal Abdel Nasser's legacy included the struggle to remove British troops from Egyptian soil and the nationalization of the Suez Canal in 1956. These were followed by the invasion of the Sinai by Israel and the invasion of the canal zone by Britain and France. Nasser turned to the Soviet bloc for arms and built up a vastly expanded mix of Egyptian military forces. He also created a short lived unification of Egypt and Syria into the United Arab Republic from 1958 to 1961 and made a bloody attempt to dominate North Yemen that lasted until 1967. In 1967 Nasser's attempt to close the Straits of Tiran helped trigger a major new Arab-Israeli conflict that led to a sweeping Israeli victory and cost Egypt the Sinai, Jordan all of East Jerusalem and the West Bank, and Syria all of the Golan.

Egypt rebuilt its forces with massive Soviet aid, however, and its defeat in June, 1967 was followed by the canal war of 1970. Egypt used its new artillery strength, air forces, and land based air defenses to engage Israel along the Suez Canal and lock Israel into a war of attrition. While Egypt did not "win" this conflict, it did succeed in showing that it had greatly improved the effectiveness of its forces.

The 1956, 1967, and 1970 wars helped force Egypt to create a relatively modern structure of training and command and forged an Egyptian military machine equipped with Soviet bloc weapons that became the most powerful military force in the Arab world. When Anwar Sadat became president after Nasser's death in September, 1970, this military machine provided the base Sadat used to launch a shattering surprise attack on Israel in October, 1973. Acting with Syria, Egypt successfully crossed the canal, and Syria came close to seizing the Golan. Although the war ended in defeat for both Egypt and Syria, Egypt had restored its military credibility and earned Israeli respect.

Sadat then turned to negotiations with the United States and eventually to peace talks with Israel. The USSR reacted to Sadat's improving relations with the U.S. by embargoing most arms shipments and spares, and Sadat responded by ordering all Soviet military advisors to leave in 1974 and abrogating Egypt's treaty of friendship with the USSR in 1976. Soviet arms shipments to Egypt were virtually embargoed from 1975 to 1987, when Egypt negotiated a settlement of its $4 billion military debt to the Soviet Union on extremely favorable terms to Egypt.

Sadat followed his break with the USSR with a visit to Israel in November, 1977, the Camp David accords, and an Egyptian-Israeli peace treaty in March, 1979. These peace initiatives led to tension within Egypt and with Egypt's Arab neighbors. Syria and sixteen other Arab nations broke diplomatic relations with Egypt, and Egypt was expelled from many Arab organizations. Libya launched a buildup on the Egyptian border that led to border fights and near war in the summer of 1977. Egypt responded by redeploying part of its armed forces to the western border area, a redeployment it strengthened after Israeli forces withdrew from the Sinai in 1982.

In spite of Sadat's assassination on October 10, 1981, and the accession of Mubarak, the Egyptian-Israeli peace treaty has influenced the military balance of the Middle East ever since. Egypt's shift to peace with Israel effectively removed the threat of a multifront conventional attack that could overwhelm Israel's forces. Egypt's military alliance with the United States helped stabilize the Middle East and checkmate Qadhafi.

These political changes forced the Egyptian military to try to convert from Soviet-equipped to Western-equipped forces. Although the U.S. provided massive military assistance, this transformation was anything but easy. Egypt's force structure mirrored the Soviet system in emphasizing quantity over quality and attrition over sustainability. It had paid only a minor fraction of the cost of its Soviet arms and could not replace them on anything like a one-for-one basis. At the same time, Egypt suffered growing economic problems and saw other states like Iran and Iraq build up superior military forces and begin to use weapons of mass destruction like poison gas.

President Mubarak had to use the armed forces to suppress riots by conscript policemen in February, 1986. In 1987 and 1988, Egypt became involved in an attempt to smuggle missile equipment out of the U.S. in a complex operation involving front organizations like the IFAT Corporation of Zug, Switzerland. At the same time, it became apparent that Egypt was expanding its chemical weapons plant at Abu Zabaal, north of Cairo, and was smuggling in chemical weapons production equipment through firms like Krebs of Zurich. Egypt is believed to have approached Krebs in 1985, shortly after Iraq began to make large scale use of chemical weapons in the Iran-Iraq War. These events led to tensions between the U.S. and Egypt that seem to have contributed to Mubarak's decision in April, 1989 to shift the defense minister, Abu Ghazala, to a different position and replace him with Youssef Abu Taleb.[375]

Mubarak soon renewed close relations with the U.S., however, and Egypt strengthened its relations with other states. It rejoined the Arab League and mended diplomatic relations with Syria in December, 1989, after a twelve year break. This completed the restoration of relations with all of the sixteen nations that had broken with Egypt after Camp David—except for Libya.[376] Egypt took over the leadership of the Arab effort to create a broader peace with Israel and restored its ties to the Soviet Union.[377]

Mubarak played a strong and decisive role after Saddam Hussein's invasion of Kuwait. He first attempted to prevent the invasion. When this failed, he tried to mediate an Iraqi withdrawal and then took a firm line in support of the UN coalition. Approximately 36,000 Egyptian troops were deployed to Saudi Arabia and played an important part in the fighting to liberate Kuwait. After the war, Egypt took the lead within the Arab world in bringing Arab nations together for a new round of peace talks with Israel. It restored relations with Libya in August, 1991 and attempted to influence Libya to take a more pragmatic approach to politics and economics. Egypt also helped Lebanon rebuild its army, providing 90 tanks and training for some 1,000 Lebanese.[378]

Egypt was far less successful in forging a lasting security arrangement with the Gulf states after the Gulf War. Although the March, 1991 Damascus accords between the Gulf Cooperation Council states, Egypt, and Syria called for a lasting Egyptian and Syrian military presence, this had little practical follow-up. The original goal of setting up an Arab defense force with 100,000 troops, 60,000 of which would be Egyptian and Syrian, faded with the Iraqi threat.

All of Egypt's troops left Saudi Arabia by the end of July, 1991, and talk shifted to an Egyptian proposal for a force of 12,000 to 15,000 Egyptian troops and 12,000 Syrian troops. The GCC states responded with a proposal for a token Arab force where Egypt and Syria would contribute only 3,000 troops each. When the eight states met in Cairo in November, 1991, the GCC states effectively deferred any effort to create an integrated approach to Gulf security, and Kuwait and Saudi Arabia restricted their activities to providing Egypt and Syria with bilateral aid payments. Although Egypt prepared four working papers to strengthen cooperation, it was clear that progress would be slow at best. The only Gulf nation that made a real effort to secure a future Egyptian military presence was Kuwait, and other Arab states did little to encourage Egyptian efforts to create common military industries centered in Egypt.[379]

The failure of Israel, other Arab states, and the Palestinians to negotiate a broader peace has also left Egypt with a number of major security problems. Egypt has been a leader in the Arab-Israeli peace process ever since Camp David, and President Mubarak has demonstrated more consistent commitment to peace than any other leader in the Middle East. This does not, however, solve the problem Egypt faces in sizing its forces. Although few Israelis doubt Mubarak's commitment to peace, Egypt still must size its forces to take into account the possibility that another Arab-Israeli conflict might involve Egypt. At the same time, Egypt has to continue to plan to check any military threat from Libya and has had to shift its military planning to deal with the new problems posed by the instability in the Sudan and other surrounding states. While Egypt's forces may seem too large from a Western perspective, Egyptian planners feel that Egypt must size its military forces to deal with contingencies to the west, east, and south.

Egypt's domestic troubles have also mounted. Egypt began to experience growing problems with Islamic fundamentalism in the late 1980s and was faced with the choice between a massive security crackdown and a more moderate approach to internal security. President Mubarak initially chose the more moderate approach. In January, 1990, he fired his hard-line internal security chief, Interior Minister Zaki Badr, after Badr gave a speech calling for the execution of Islamic fundamentalists.[380] He replaced him with Mohammed Abdel-Halim, a professional policeman known for his skill in conciliation.

Where other governments might have become repressive, Egypt also became steadily more democratic. Mubarak was elected to a second term in 1987 by popular election, and opposition parties became active and increasingly aggressive. Egypt held regular elections for its people's assembly and *shura,* and the Muslim Brotherhood won 37 seats in the 458 seat legislature.

However, Egypt was forced to take more extreme security measures in the case of the hard-line groups like the Islamic Jihad (which seems to have played a major role in the assassination of Sadat) and the People of Shawki. The head of the People of Shawki, Shawkil Abdeltawab Tawfik, was killed by police in mid-1990 after he split from the Islamic Jihad and launched a campaign of violence. This led to reprisals, the speaker of the national assembly, Rifat Mahgoub, being gunned down as his car was driving along the Nile.

Egypt was forced to make new arrests in April, 1992, after several killings of police and military officials. Up to 5,000 paramilitary police were dispatched to control the fundamentalists in the south. While the Egyptian government reported only 78 arrests, Amnesty International reported that more than 1,000 people were rounded up by the police and that Egypt had tortured some of the fundamentalists, 46 having died. The people's assembly also approved the death penalty for "terrorist groups" in July, 1992, although it gave a amnesty to those who severed all ties with such groups during the subsequent 30 days.[381]

Unless Egypt successfully implements the economic reforms and privatization program it began in the summer of 1992, Islamic fundamentalism may well become Egypt's most serious security problem. It is already aggravating tensions between Egypt's Muslims and its Coptic Christian minority. Even when fundamentalism is nonviolent, it generally leaves little room for ultimate compromise with Egypt's current secular government. An Egyptian teacher, Hassan Banna, founded the Muslim Brotherhood, the first major Arab Islamic fundamentalist movement in 1928, setting the precedent that Islam, "admits no . . . distinction" between politics and religion.[382] This doctrine presents a very real challenge to secular rule at a time when Egypt's economy remains in decline, overpopulation continues, the public educational system is breaking down, Islamic schools that stress religion but provide little other education have more and more of an impact on youth, younger Egyptians face mounting difficulties in finding jobs and housing, and many feel that the government is corrupt and ineffective. All of these factors contribute to a degree of popular alienation that is a growing threat to Egypt's status as one of the most liberal nations in the Arab world.

Egyptian Military Expenditures

Egypt's military effort involves massive expenditures for a country whose economy is already strained by chronic mismanagement, a grossly inefficient state sector, and overpopulation. According to U.S. government estimates, Egyptian military expenditures were $4,226 million in 1978, $3,227 million in 1979, $2,923 million in 1980, $3,154 million in 1981, $6,192 million in 1982, $6,072 million in 1983, $6,844 million in 1984, $6,785 million in 1985, $6,460 million in 1986, $6,664 million in 1987, $5,559 million in 1988, and $3,499 million in 1989.[383] This puts Egypt's military spending at about 8–16% of the GNP and at 20–30% of central government expenditures. The IISS estimates that Egypt spent $5,640 million in 1989 and $6,800 million in 1990.[384]

These expenditures are extremely high for a country that began to encounter a major economic crisis in the mid-1980s as a result of falling oil prices, decreasing direct and indirect revenues, and a chronic overdependence on imports. To put this economic crisis into perspective, the fall of world oil prices in 1986 cut Egypt's oil revenues by over 50%. Other key sources of foreign exchange (tourism and worker remittances) were cut by foreign reaction to internal unrest, the loss of earnings in the Gulf that followed the fall in oil prices, and a lack of confidence in the Egyptian economy.

Driven by the collapse of oil prices, overregulation, and the inefficiencies of the public sector, Egypt's balance of payments deteriorated, and a large financing gap appeared in FY 1986–1987 that continued into 1990. Egypt's foreign civil debt rose to $37 billion, and its total military debt was well in excess of $10 billion. The Egyptian GDP dropped from an average annual growth of 9% during 1974–1982 to less than 3% in FY 1986–1987.[385]

By 1987 Egypt's heavy burden of debt service led it to begin negotiations with the IMF for balance of payments support. While Egypt reached a tentative economic reform agreement with the IMF, the resulting program meant reducing inflation, promoting economic growth, and improving Egypt's external position through measures like an austerity budget, firing surplus employees, privatizing public sector firms, and ending price surpluses. Egypt's political leaders both opposed these measures and feared a public uprising. During 1987–1992, they failed fully to comply with the IMF agreement and had to be pushed every step of the way in those areas in which they did comply. At the same time, Egypt's population grew by roughly 1 million people every seven months, an impossible rate of growth for a nation which has only 5% arable land.

These factors helped drive Egypt's civil and military external debt to $45 to $52 billion by 1990. Egypt would almost certainly have seen its total debt grow to uncontrollable levels if it had not received massive aid for its contribution to the UN coalition during the Gulf War and if the U.S. had not forgiven it past aid debts.[386] On September 14, 1990, President Bush asked Congress to forgive Egypt's $6.7 billion military debt in response to Egypt's strong support of the UN coalition in the Gulf. While this request was originally tied to a common effort at debt forgiveness, Bush successfully obtained congressional agreement to his December 27, 1990, request for unilateral debt forgiveness. In addition to easing the strain on Egypt's economy, this debt forgiveness was critical to Egyptian military modernization. Debt servicing for past FMS loans had reached a total of 50–75% of all Egyptian schedule payments to the U.S. over the subsequent five years.

In May, 1991 the International Monetary Fund approved a $372 million standby credit arrangement with Egypt. This led to the agreement by Egypt's creditors in the Paris Club to forgive 50% of Egypt's official debt and reorganize the rest. In July, 1991, international donors agreed to commit about $4 billion in economic aid to Egypt over the next two years. The UN coalition aid package amounted to a virtual bailout, rescheduling or forgiving about one-fifth of Egypt's debt and providing it with substantial additional hard currency aid for its 1990 and 1991 budgets.

Egypt also obtained very real benefits from its peace with Israel. Egypt was spending nearly 32% of its GNP on military forces in 1973–1975 but only around 8–12% of its GNP by the late 1980s. Similarly, Egypt was spending over 50% of all central government expenditures on military forces in 1973–1975 but only around 20–22% by 1986–1988.[387] While Egyptian military spending did not drop massively in real terms, the Egyptian economy grew far more quickly than military spending.

This still, however, left an economy in crisis. Egypt had a trade deficit of $7.5 billion in 1990–1991, and this situation did not seem better in 1992. In July, 1992 Egypt had an international debt in excess of $29 billion and unemployment of at least 20%—ignoring the disguised unemployment created by government jobs with no real purpose or productivity. The state sector of the economy set up under Nasser remained uncompetitive, unproductive, and corrupt but consumed nearly 40% of Egypt's domestic investment resources. Most Egyptian civil servants and teachers and many military officers worked at two or three jobs. The civil service, schools, and universities had become steadily more inefficient and corrupt. Population growth remained high, creating 400,000 new workers per year—only 50% of whom seemed likely to find any kind of job in 1992. Some 2.1 million Egyptians were working abroad, largely because of their inability to find career opportunities in Egypt.[388]

Egyptian Arms Transfers

Although Egypt has a comparatively large arms industry for a Third World state, it has always been a major arms importer. While the burden of these imports has been eased by massive U.S. military aid and by the U.S. forgiveness of all foreign military sales loans as a result of the Gulf War, Egypt has also added to its foreign debt with additional arms purchases. Unfortunately, it is difficult to obtain even halfway reasonable figures on Egypt's arms purchases from unclassified sources. Egypt normally does not disclose any details on its arms imports or their financing.

ACDA estimates that Egypt imported $350 million worth of arms in 1978, $600 million in 1979, $625 million in 1980, $900 million in 1981, $1,900 million in 1982, $1,500 million in 1983, $1,700 million in 1984, $1,500 million in 1985, $1,200 million in 1986, $1,700 million in 1987, $775 million in 1988, and $600 million in 1989.[389] It seems likely, however, that Egypt actually imported substantially more arms and that it has imported over $1,200 million a year from 1988 through 1992. This has been offset by an average of around $100 million in arms sales per year, but such sales often involve substantial use of imported components.[390]

Since Camp David, Egypt has got most of its weapons from the U.S. ACDA estimates that Egypt took delivery on $5,645 million worth of arms during 1979–1983. This included $2,400 million worth of arms from the U.S., $40 million from the USSR, $1,200 million from France, $575 million from the UK, $210 million from West Germany, $320 million from Italy, $300 million from the PRC, $50 million from Poland, and $550 million from other countries.[391]

Similarly, Egypt took delivery on $6,425 million worth of arms during 1984–1988. This included $2,800 million from the U.S., $460 million from the USSR, $825 million from France, $170 million from the UK, $50 million from West Germany, $270 million from Italy, $450 million from the PRC, and $1,400 million from other countries.[392]

In 1992 ACDA reported that Egypt imported a total of $5,800 million worth of arms during 1985–1989, including $575 million from the Soviet Union, $2,900 million from the U.S., $675 million from France, $170 million from the UK, $190 million from the PRC, $40 million from West Germany, $320 million from other Warsaw Pact countries, $575 million from other European countries, $10 million from other East Asian states, $340 million from Latin America, and $5 million from other developing countries.[393]

If Egypt has imported more arms than its economy can easily sustain, it has also faced special problems which do a great deal to explain its military development since the mid–1970s. In 1978, when the Camp David peace accords were signed, Egypt's forces were still almost totally equipped by the Soviet Union, even though Egypt had broken its military ties to the USSR some three years earlier. Much of this equipment had already begun to create major maintenance and operational readiness problems because of Egypt's inability to obtain Soviet spare parts. This problem has grown steadily worse with time. Although the U.S. has provided substantial aid and Egypt received roughly $1.3 billion in annual grants during FY1986– FY1992, Egypt still had major problems in replacing the Soviet equipment in its force structure.

A summary of Egypt's holdings of Soviet-made equipment in 1992, nearly twenty years after its break with the USSR, shows how dependent Egypt has been on obsolete and increasingly inoperable Soviet equipment.[394]

- The Soviet-made equipment still in Egypt's army included 1,640 T-54/T-55/T-62 medium tanks, 1,845 other armored vehicles, 1,108 towed artillery weapons, and 2,400 anti-tank missile launchers.
- The Soviet-made equipment in Egypt's air defense forces included 240 SA-2 launchers, 201 SA-3 launchers, 40 SA-6 launchers, at least 500 anti-aircraft guns, and at least 400 radars. The Soviet-made equipment in Egypt's air force in 1988 included 162 combat aircraft. These included 97 MiG-21s and 52 Soviet-made helicopters.
- The Soviet-made equipment still in the Egyptian navy included 9 missile patrol boats, 6 patrol boats, 4 submarines, 9 mine craft, and 3 medium landing craft.

While other Arab states have added Western equipment to a Soviet-supplied force structure, Egypt has had to reequip its force structure with supplies designed for a different training, support, logistics, and infrastructure system, and for different tactics. Although Egypt continued to obtain some critical parts from the USSR and Soviet bloc countries like Romania and

Poland and bought Chinese versions of Soviet-designed equipment, it has not been able to obtain the massive flow of supplies it needed to keep its force structure operational. The normalization of Egyptian-Soviet diplomatic relations in 1984 helped this situation but did not eliminate most of the problem.

As a result, Egypt has been forced to retire much of its major Soviet-made equipment from its first line combat units and now relegates it to low grade defensive units, reserve status, spare part uses, or sale to other nations. Egyptian efforts to manufacture entire Soviet-designed equipment items in Egypt or to obtain Western technology to convert Soviet equipment have also had limited success.

Egypt has made some progress in building light systems like the SA-7, in adapting Soviet artillery to Western chassis, and in converting Soviet equipment to Western electronics. Even these efforts, however, generally result in technically inferior equipment with only one-quarter to one-third the operational life cycle of new Western-made systems. Further, Egypt has found that performance has rarely met design expectations, and the upgraded or modified Soviet-made types that are in Egypt's forces are no longer competitive with the Soviet-made equipment in potential threat forces. Although Egypt has had more success in obtaining systems like French aircraft and light surface-to-air missiles and Spanish corvettes to supplement its purchases from the U.S., it has had very limited resources to buy such systems.

Most important, Egypt has made significant progress in its conversion to U.S. equipment. It began to get major amounts of U.S. foreign military sales aid in FY1979, when it received $1.5 billion in FMS loans. It received $550 million more FMS financing in FY1981, $900 million in FY1982, $1,325 million in FY1983, $1,365 million in FY1984, $1,175 million in FY1985, $1,244 million in FY1986, and roughly $1,300 million annually in FY1987–FY1992. Since FY1985, all of this FMS financing has been in the form of grant aid, and payments on the loans were forgiven in 1991.[395]

This aid has allowed Egypt to buy substantial amounts of U.S. military equipment. In late 1991 Egypt's army operated 1,550 U.S.-made tanks, at least 1,361 other armored vehicles, and 532 TOW launchers. Egypt's air defense forces had 72 Improved Hawk launchers and 8 TPS-63 2D radars. Egypt's air forces had 144 U.S.-made combat aircraft, including 33 F-4Es, 77 F-16s, 5 E-2Cs, 6 EW aircraft, 19 C-130H U.S.-made transport aircraft, and 14 U.S.-made CH-47C helicopters. Egypt had 101 other Western-made combat aircraft and 42 combat helicopters. The Egyptian navy had acquired two Spanish frigates but no U.S.-made ships.

Egypt was also seeking to obtain more surplus equipment from the U.S. as it cut its forces for NATO. Lt. Gen. Salah Halaby, the Egyptian chief of staff, visited Washington in July, 1992. He was seeking kits to convert Egypt's M-60A1s to M-60A3s, more TOW anti-tank missiles, M-113 armored personnel carriers, transport aircraft, and two FF-1052 Knox-class frigates. Egypt had already agreed to transfer 700 M-60A1s and 750 jeeps and light vehicles out of U.S. forces in Europe.

Egyptian Military Manpower

Egypt does not face problems in providing adequate manpower for its forces.[396] Its population is 54,451,000, making it easily the most populous Arab nation. This population is 90% Eastern Hametic, and 10% Greek, Italian, Syrian, and Lebanese. It is 94% Muslim, largely Sunni, with 6% Coptic Christian and other. The CIA puts the total Egyptian labor force at about 15 to 17 million, and much of this labor force is surplus. The official unemployment rate is around 15%, there are large numbers of artificial jobs created by the government, and about 2.5 million Egyptians worked overseas in 1988, during the peak of the Iran-Iraq War and oil boom.[397]

The CIA estimates that there were 13,333,000 males in the age group from 15 to 49 in 1991, and that 8,665,000 are fit for military service. Roughly 585,000 reach military age annually.[398] The IISS estimates that there are about 3,045,600 males and 2,886,000 females in the age group from 13 to 17, 2,623,000 men and 2,464,800 women in the age group from 18 to 22 years, and about 4,542,000 males and 4,234,000 women in the age group from 22 to 32 years.[399] This population is relatively well educated by the standards of the developing world, although population pressures and economic problems have led to the decline of educational standards since the mid-1980s.

Egypt's total military manpower now includes about 420,000–430,000 full time actives, of whom 252,000 are conscripts. Conscripts serve from two to three years. There are some 604,000 men in the reserves, with 500,000 for the army, 14,000 for the navy, 20,000 for the air force, and 70,000 for the air defense forces. Almost none of these reserves, however, receive any meaningful reserve training, and the organization of the reserve system has degenerated into near ineffectiveness since 1974.

The Egyptian Army

Reports differ on the manpower strength of the Egyptian army. Some reports indicate that Egypt's total active army manpower dropped from 313,000 in 1984 to 290,000 (180,000 conscripts) in 1992. Others show substantially higher manning, but these seem to include some paramilitary forces.[400] While the army still has a total reserve pool of nearly 500,000, its pool of trained reserves has dropped to 176,000 in 1984, and 161,000 in 1987, and to less than 150,000 in 1992.[401] At the same time, Egypt has created smaller but more advanced technology, anti-tank guided missile, and artillery forces. Egypt has also improved the mechanization of its land forces.

The Egyptian army now has two main field armies: The second and third. These two corps have a total major combat unit strength of four armored divisions (each with two armored and one mechanized brigade) and eight mechanized infantry divisions (normally with two mechanized and one armored brigade). There is also one republican guard armored brigade, one independent armored brigade, four independent mechanized brigades, three independent infantry brigades, and two air mobile and one paratroop brigade. The combat support units include fifteen artillery brigades, two heavy mortar brigades, seven commando groups, one FROG-7 surface-to-surface missile regiment, and one improved Scud B surface-to-surface missile regiment.

Egypt is one of the few Middle Eastern states that is capable of planning and conducting operations at the corps and division level, although large scale unit exercises and command exercises have declined since 1982. It also organizes and deploys its forces to deal with two main contingencies. The first is a war with Libya that is regarded a serious enough risk to keep 40,000–50,000 troops and at least two heavy divisions in the Western border area. The second is the risk of becoming involved in another Arab-Israeli conflict. Egyptian officers deny that Egypt has any offensive plans against Israel but do indicate that Egypt plans to defend the Sinai and might reinforce the brigade sized forces permitted in each zone by deploying up to two Egyptian field armies across the Suez in the event of war. The 2nd Army is located near the canal in Ismalia, and the 3rd Army in Suez City. Each army has at least one of Egypt's best armored divisions, and movements could occur relatively quickly if Egypt had a week or so of strategic warning.

In 1992 the army's major equipment included between 2,500 and 3,000 main battle tanks. They included 1,000–1,150 T-54/55, 500–600 T-62s, 700 M-60A1s, and 1,000 M-60A3s.[402] Roughly half of Egypt's tank strength consisted of modern types. Egypt upgraded several hundred of its T-54s, T-55s, and T-62s in the 1970s with German AEG/Telefunken white/infrared searchlights, and fitted some with the Iskra laser range finder. It has also fitted smoke rockets to some of its T-62s. In 1984 it began to experiment with conversions of the T-54, using separate contract efforts by U.S. Teledyne and Germany's Jung Jungenthal. These conversions involved major changes to the T-54, like fitting a Royal Ordnance 105mm L-7 gun of the kind standard in NATO and, with the M-60, adding a turbocharged diesel engine, changing the turret ring, changing the transmission and suspension, adding a SABCA Titan Mark 1 laser fire control system, adding a Cadillac Gage stabilization system, and adding new fuel tanks, fire detection and suppression gear, new communications, and new air filtration. Although the results were impressive, Egypt had not gone beyond the trial stage as of 1992 and lacked the funds to modernize a significant number of additional tanks without major cutbacks in some other aspect of its force improvement program.[403]

Egypt also experimented with upgrades to its obsolete T-34s and with upgrades to its T-62s. For example, a T-34 was modified in 1987, given a T-54 engine; modified fuel, air, and cooling systems; a modified suspension system; and a number of other improvements. Egypt claimed that the modified version had a power to weight ratio of 16.25 HP/ton and an interval between overhauls of 4,500 kilometers versus a ratio of 15HP/ton and an interval of only 150 kilometers for the regular T-34. The T-62 modification consisted largely of fitting an L-7 105mm gun to replace the regular 115mm gun. It used a kit developed by NORICUM of Austria. The kit was evidently successful, but Egypt did not use it to convert its T-62s.

The U.S. M-60A1 and M-60A3 tanks were provided to Egypt with the agreement that Egypt would phase out its older Soviet-supplied tanks as the U.S. tanks were supplied. The 1,000 M-60A3s were provided to Egypt in the

1980s. The M-60A3s are maintained by a facility at the Egyptian Army Tank Depot No.1, which was built by the Kollsman Instrument Company. The U.S. agreed to provide 700 M-60A1s from its forces in Europe in 1990, as the U.S. cut its presence in NATO. The tanks were still being absorbed into Egypt's force structure in 1992, and Egypt was seeking funds to convert them to the M-60A3 before integrating them into its units. The Gulf War had shown Egypt the vital importance of modern fire control and night vision systems, but the estimated cost of the upgrade was $280 million.[404]

In 1984 Egypt signed a $150 million contract with General Dynamics to assemble and build M-1A1 tanks in Egypt. The new plant, called Factory 200, will begin operations by overhauling M-60A3 tanks and M-88A1 armored recovery vehicles. The M-1A1 underwent trials in Egypt in 1987, and the U.S. and Egypt signed a follow-on memorandum in late 1988 that allowed Egypt to produce up to 555 M-1A1s. This production will begin with the assembly of M-1A1s, but 35–40% of the components will eventually be built in Egypt. The Egyptian version of the M-1A1 will be identical to that in the U.S. Army and will have a 120mm smooth bore gun and gas turbine engine. Egypt will not get the M-829 APFSDA round, which has a depleted uranium penetrator, but will get rounds with a Honeywell or Olin substitute. The total value of the M-1A1 contract could reach $1.2 billion over a ten year period. Egypt agreed not to export any M-1A1s without U.S. agreement.

The Egyptian army had approximately 100 PT-76 light tanks, 200 BDRM-2 reconnaissance vehicles, 300 other BDRM vehicles, 220 BMP-1 and 250 BMR-600P mechanized infantry combat vehicles, about 170 M-106A and M-125A mortar carriers, and several hundred armored command, recovery, and support vehicles in mid-1992. There were 2,700–3,100 armored personnel carriers, including about 180–200 Fahds, 1,500–1,900 BTR-40/50/152/OT-62s, and 1,000 M-113s.[405] About half of Egypt's mix of other armored vehicles was composed of obsolete or worn weapons.

The Kader Fahd armored personnel carrier is one of the few indigenous weapon designs the Arab world has produced in any quantity. Egypt built a total of about 350 Fahds for domestic use and export by 1991. An Egyptian design using a 4 x 4 drive system, it is manufactured by the Kader Factory of the Arab Organization for Industry (AOI) using a Daimler-Benz LAP-1117/32 truck body chassis with an armored body. It uses all-welded steel armor to provide enough protection to guard against 7.62mm rounds and shell splinters. It allows relatively quick entry and exit through a downward hinging rear door that forms a step. Its tire pressure can be regulated for road or desert terrain, and it can travel considerable distances with tire punctures. It can be armed with a number of turrets, including a 20mm cannon. A more advanced version, called the Fahd 30, is in development.[406]

Kader also built the Walid APC in the early 1960s. This was little more than an armored truck, with a design similar to the Soviet BTR-40. Significant numbers were manufactured. It is still in service in Algeria, Egypt, and the Sudan, and captured versions are still in service in Israel.

Egypt has sought to create modern armored units. Its exercise performance in armored maneuver and offensive warfare has improved strikingly since the mid-1970s, but only a relatively small part of its total forces has shown this improvement or had realistic maneuver training. Egyptian armored units are generally high in quality, but other mechanized units vary remarkably. The majority have poor capability. About another third are of mediocre quality, and the rest are of good to high quality—although none is a match for the best Israeli unit.

Egypt's artillery strength included around 1,100 major towed weapons, some 150 self-propelled weapons, 200 multiple rocket launchers, and over 21 surface-to-surface missile launchers. The towed artillery included 400 M-1931/1937, M-1938, and D-30 122mm weapons. It also included 440 M-46 130mm weapons and 12 M-1937 and M-20 152mm weapons. The self-propelled artillery included 150 M-109A1 155mm howitzers and an unknown number of D-30 122mm guns placed on tracked armored vehicles.

Egypt is one of the few Middle Eastern countries capable of making its own artillery weapons. Its Abu Zabaal Engineering Industries Company, also known as Factory 100, has reverse engineered the Soviet D-30 122mm towed howitzer, the PRC Type-59 130mm towed gun, and the ZU-22 towed anti-aircraft weapon. It also worked with the Royal Ordnance of the UK and BMY of the U.S. to develop competing designs for a self-propelled howitzer called the SP-122, based on the D-30 gun. Neither design had been put into production as of 1992.[407]

Egyptian holdings of multiple rocket launchers included VAP-8012 80mm weapons and 156 BM-21 and 60 al-Saqr 18 and 30 122mm weapons. They also may have included BM-14 and BM-16 140mm weapons and BM-24 240mm weapons. Egypt had 9 FROG and 9 Scud SS-1c launchers, and over 2,000 mortars—including 1,500 M-1938 and M-1943 120mm mortars, 60 M-43 160mm mortars, and 24 M-1953 240mm mortars.

The Saqr company of AOI builds three families of 122mm multiple rocket launchers in Egypt. The Saqr 36 comes with 21, 30, and 40 rails mounted on trucks. It has a maximum range of 36 kilometers and can dispense submunitions at variable altitudes. The Saqr 18 is a lighter rocket with a maximum range of 18 kilometers and can also deliver submunitions. The Saqr 10 is a very light system with 1, 3, 4, and 8 round launchers and maximum range of 10 kilometers. There is also a Saqr 80mm 12 round multiple rocket launcher, and Egypt is experimenting with a wide range of additional multiple rocket systems.

Egypt's artillery strength was adequate in terms of total numbers in 1992, and Egypt did a better job of providing training in artillery and combined arms operations than most Middle Eastern states. Nevertheless, many of its types of artillery weapons were obsolete, and Egypt had fewer than one-third of the number of self-propelled weapons needed to keep up with its armor in modern combat. Egyptian artillery training was better than that of most Middle Eastern armies, but most units are lacking in modern fire control, communications, counterbattery radars, night vision, and other targeting systems. Supply vehicles and recovery numbers are limited, and most artillery units have very slow mobility. With the exception of the best trained self-propelled artillery units, Egypt relies largely on static fire and sheer mass.

Egypt has a divided mix of anti-tank weapons. It has over 1,000 obsolete Soviet-made AT-1 Snapper and AT-2 Swatter anti-tank guided missile launchers and 1,400 obsolete AT-3 Sagger launchers—many of which are difficult to recondition. Fewer than 1,000 of these Soviet systems still seem to be in service. It has 200 British-made Swingfire launchers, but these use a first generation guidance system that is very difficult to operate. Egypt's modern anti-tank guided weapons consist of 220 French-made manportable Milan weapons and 520 TOW launchers (52 mounted on M-901 variants of the M-113). Egypt ordered 180 TOW II missile launchers, night sights, and 7,511 TOW II missiles in 1988. Egypt also has B-11 107mm recoilless rifles, some old Soviet anti-tank guns, and large numbers of rocket launchers.

Egypt does a better job of training its infantry than do many other Middle Eastern states and emphasizes the use of mechanized armored vehicles, anti-tank weapons, and automatic weapons in maneuver combat. It is well aware that one of the lessons of both the 1973 and 1982 wars is that it needs anti-tank weapons with advanced guidance systems that do not require extensive operator training, but Egypt cannot afford the systems it wants. Overall training in using anti-tank guided weapons is limited and unrealistic.

These same problems affect the army's air defense weapons. Egypt is heavily dependent on Soviet-supplied weapons or Egyptian modifications of these weapons. These include over 1,500 Soviet-made SA-7 manportable missile launchers and Egyptian-made Ayn al-Saqr variants of the SA-7. They also include 40–60 SA-9s and 26 modern M-54 self-propelled Chaparral air defense systems. Egypt's towed anti-aircraft guns include 14.5mm ZUU 2s and 4s, at least 460 ZU-23-2s, 150 M-1939 57mm guns, and 300 S-60 57mm guns. Its self-propelled weapons include 117 aging Soviet radar guided ZSU-23-4 23mm guns, 40 ZSU-57-2 57mm guns, and 45 Nile twin 23mm guns with Saqr Eye missiles.

Egypt has experimented with a number of Egyptian-built air defense systems. The Saqr Eye is an improved version of the SA-7B, which was first qualified in 1982 and went into production in 1985. The IR seeker is a U.S. design and is more sensitive than the original. The overall weapon is also more reliable. There are pedestal and vehicle mounted versions as well as the normal manportable version. Egypt also makes 23mm anti-aircraft guns and has built a Ramadan 23 or Gun King system which combines two ZU 23mm fire units with a Contraves Gun King laser/computer firing system. The system requires only one man to control it and completed trials in 1987. Egypt is deploying an M-113 mounted twin 23mm AA gun system called the Sinai. The Electronic Systems Division of Thomson CSF and Dassault developed the RA-20S E-Band radar guided system which can control several vehicles at the same time. It can also be used with optical, thermal, and radar sights. The first units entered Egyptian service in 1989.

Egypt's logistics system is partially computerized but must deal with a logistical nightmare of many different types of equipment and continued reliance on Soviet systems for which adequate spare parts are often lacking. Maintenance, repair, and combat service and recovery capabilities vary sharply in quality and effectiveness, although units with U.S. equipment are generally far better off than units with Soviet or European equipment. Munitions stocks are adequate, and Egypt is one of the few Middle Eastern countries with a major defense industry.

The Arab Organization for Industry was set up in 1975 by Egypt, Saudi Arabia, Qatar, and the UAE. It is organized into five divisions and has a work force of approximately 20,000. It assembled Egypt's Swingfire anti-tank guided weapons and has produced 134 Embraer EMB-312 Tucano trainer aircraft for Egypt and Iraq in addition to the weapons listed earlier, has assembled the Gazelle Helicopter and Alphajet, and has made components for the Super Puma and Mirage 2000. It produces many types of spare parts, an improved version of the RPG-7, several types of anti-armor and anti-personnel mines, anti-personnel mine clearing systems, artillery barrels, and small arms, tank, and artillery ammunition.[408]

The AOI has had comparatively little support from other countries, however, and there are many items Egypt cannot produce. High cost Western spares and munitions and Soviet major spares are often in short supply. The Egyptian logistic and service support force relies on many aging or obsolete vehicles and systems and receives lower priority for training and manpower quality.

The Egyptian army's forces are steadily improving as the result of the flow of U.S. aid. Egypt is acquiring U.S. combat support equipment such as TPS-37 radars and computer systems for its artillery, and TOW and radar-guided 23mm cannon conversions for its M-113s. Egypt will also coproduce up to 650 improved M-1 main battle tanks in the mid-1990s.[409] These M-1 tanks will have the new 120mm guns to enable Egypt to keep pace with the advances in first line tank technology taking place in neighboring states, and U.S. multiple rocket launchers to expand its artillery firepower. Even so, throughout the 1990s roughly 30–40% of the Egyptian army will still consist of low grade units relying primarily on Soviet equipment that is well over two decades old.

Further, Egypt lacks the domestic resources to finance the proper modernization of land forces casernes and training areas. Living conditions for troops (particularly conscripts) and NCOs are often poor. Egypt is forced to concentrate its funds on its special forces, armored divisions, and selected mechanized divisions. For many of its other combat units and support forces, it provides less far less investment in facilities than is necessary to make them combat effective. Egyptian reserve training has decayed steadily since the late 1970s, and Egypt often provides only minimal training for its less educated conscripts. Its younger officers are often well educated, but manpower management is uncertain and assignments often fail to make proper use of officer skills and the output of Egyptian army training programs.

The Egyptian Air Force

The Egyptian air force had 30,000 men in 1984. It had 28,000 men in 1992, of whom some 10,000 were conscripts. This limited cut in manpower reflected the need to respond to the far more demanding technical and maintenance requirements imposed by U.S. and European aircraft. Egypt has gone from 676 combat aircraft in 1974 to roughly 495 combat aircraft. It still has large numbers of Soviet-made aircraft, but it is being rebuilt around a smaller mix of U.S. and French-made aircraft, plus a limited number of Chinese-made fighters. Its air units are still organized into Soviet-style brigades with subordinate squadrons.

In 1992 Egypt had eight fighter ground attack squadrons with 2/31 F-4Es, 1/16 Mirage 5E2s, 1/14 Alphajets, and 4/76 J-6s. This was a relatively modest offensive strike capability, and only the aging F-4Es were capable of demanding long range attack missions. Egypt also, however, had eight brigades of air defense fighters with two squadrons per brigade. These included 2/31 F-16As, 2/39 F-16Cs, and 1/16 Mirage 2000Cs which had a high degree of dual capability in both the air defense and attack mission. They also included 2/42 Mirage 5Es, 5/83 MiG-21s, and 3/40 J-7s. The MiG-21s were modified with a Marconi HUD system to use the AIM-9P-3 air-to-air missile; the Mirage 5Es are regarded as dual capable in the air defense and attack missions and pilots are trained accordingly.[410]

There were three Mirage 2000Bs, seven F-16Bs, eight F-16Ds, five Mirage 5SDDs, thirty Alphajets, sixteen J-6s, fifty-four EMB-312 Tucanos, forty L-29s, and ten L-39s in Egypt's training forces which have dual capability as combat aircraft. Egypt had at least eighty additional MiG-21s in inventory. The Alphajets were specially modified for use in the attack mission, using the MS2 attack system.[411]

The Egyptian pilots of the U.S.-made fighters were trained according to U.S. standards, although most did not have the aggressor and simulated combat experience of U.S. pilots. The pilots of the Mirage 2000s were somewhat less advanced, and the pilots of the Soviet- and PRC-made aircraft were of much lower quality. The units with U.S. and French aircraft had reasonably good all-weather and beyond visual range combat capability, and they trained in aggressor squadron or red flag techniques. The units with Soviet- and PRC-made aircraft were limited to day and visual range operations.[412]

Egypt has stressed modern air munitions for its combat aircraft but has not been able to cost-effectively modify its Soviet aircraft to use Western missiles. Its most advanced air-to-air missiles are the Aim-9E/L/P, R-330, R-550 Magic, and Aim-7E/F/M. Its air-to-surface missiles include the AGM-65A/B/D Maverick, Exocet AM-39, AS-30 laser guided weapon, Rockeye, GBU cluster bombs, and HOT/HOT II. Its holdings of obsolete and low capability Soviet-made missiles include the AA-2 Atoll, the AS-1 Kennel, and the AS-5 Kelt. Egypt does make its own bombs and rockets, but Egyptian stocks of modern munitions are low, and some Soviet-made types are well beyond their useful shelf life.

Egyptian aircraft also have relatively modern electronic warfare assets. Its

F-16s have AN/ALR-69 radar warning systems and AN/ALE-40V chaff/ flare dispensers. They also have 40 AN/ALQ-131V third generation Westinghouse jamming pods. Its F-4Es have AN/ALR-46 digital radar warning receivers, AN/ALQ-119 dual mode jamming pods, and AN/ALE-40 chaff/ flare dispensers. Its Mirage 2000s have Thomson CSF Serval radar warning receivers and some of its Mirage 5s, MiG-21s, and F-7s have Selenia SL/ ALQ-234 dual mode jamming pods.[413]

The Egyptian air force had only limited reconnaissance assets with obsolete daytime and infrared photography assets. These were deployed in a reconnaissance brigade with one squadron of 4–6 Mirage 5SDRs and one of 6–10 MiG-21Rs. However,   Egypt also had Ryan, Banshee, and Skyeye remotely piloted vehicles. The R4E Skyeye is a small propeller driven system with a range of 100 kilometers and maximum endurance of eight hours. It uses forward looking infrared (FLIR) and electro-optical sensors and has a global positioning system to locate itself. It transmits UTM location coordinates and has a real-time infrared data transmission capability. A truck mounted system, it can be launched with little preparation. The 20 foot long Ryan Model 324 Scarab medium range RPV has a maximum range of 966 kilometers and can fly at altitudes up to 40,000 feet. It can be used as a long range reconnaissance system and is recovered using a two stage parachute system. It can be remotely piloted or programmed to fly unattended. It carries optical and infrared cameras. These RPVs make up for part of Egypt's lack of modern reconnaissance aircraft.[414]

Egypt also reacted to the lessons of the 1982 war by using its scarce resources to buy four modern E-2C Hawkeye airborne warning and control aircraft, two C-130H electronic intelligence aircraft, four Beech 1900 electronic intelligence aircraft, four Commando 2E electronic countermeasure aircraft, and at least two Beechcraft L-1900C surveillance aircraft.[415] It also has four Westland Commando 2E helicopters equipped with Selenia IHS-6 jamming equipment and electronic support measure systems. This mix of special purpose battle management, sensor, and intelligence systems gave Egypt the most modern airborne warning and control capabilities of any Middle Eastern air force except those of Israel and Saudi Arabia.[416]

Egypt had good overall proficiency in operating these airborne warning and control and electronic warfare aircraft. It was superior to Saudi Arabia in integrating such aircraft into its overall air defense system, although the E-3A is more advanced than the E-2C. It was not, however, as advanced as Israel in using such assets and proved much less successful in modifying U.S. sensors and electronics and developing systems of its own.

Egypt has steadily built up the attack strength of its helicopter force. It now has a total of 15 squadrons of helicopters. Two brigades with a total of 4 squadrons are equipped with 74 SA-342L attack helicopters: 44 of these have HOT air-to-surface missiles and 30 have 30mm guns. It also has armed 20–30 of its Mi-8 Hip helicopters. Like Israel, Egypt has opted to buy the AH-64 Apache attack helicopter. Twenty-four of these aircraft are now on order and will be delivered in 1994. The AH-64 offers Egypt an excellent long range attack platform for day-night and all-weather attacks on armor and hard targets. Egypt can rapidly deploy the AH-64 virtually anywhere in Egypt and use it with considerably more precision in close air support or armed intervention missions than is possible with any of its fixed wing attack aircraft.

Egypt hopes that its mix of advanced fighters, new helicopters, and E-2Cs can help compensate for the weakness of its navy. Nevertheless, Egypt will be forced to maintain a high-low mix of fighters. The "high" side of the mix will include the F-16 and Mirage 2000 fighters. Although Egypt has had to cut back its plans to coproduce its Mirage 2000s because of its balance of payments crisis, it has ordered a total of 153–167 F-16s. Egypt signed an order for 46 F-16C/D aircraft in April, 1991 as part of an air defense improvement program called Peace Vector IV. The aircraft may come from the Tusa production line in Turkey. This means that more than 80 additional F-16s are on order or in the process of delivery. This will eventually give Egypt one of the most advanced air forces in the Middle East.[417]

Egypt is building advanced maintenance and training facilities to maximize the operational value of the F-16, and F-16 engine and avionics repair depots. Egyptian air force planners are conscious of the training and support problems caused by the need to operate advanced fighters, and they have expanded the air force's support effort and its ability to provide depot level and other major maintenance. Nevertheless, maintenance standards remain mediocre and Egypt cannot sustain anything approaching the sortie rates of the U.S. and Israeli air forces.

The "low" side of Egypt's operational air strength will include its Alpha-jet trainer fighters, Mirage 5s, Chinese CH-6/J-6s (MiG-19 variants), 60 Chinese CH-7 (MiG-21 variants), and 33 F-4Es. These aircraft have distinctly lower training and maintenance standards than the high performance fighters, and operational readiness rates are often well below 60%. The problems posed by the original condition of the F-4Es delivered to Egypt continue to reduce the value of these aircraft. Egyptian pilots also regard the J-6 as inferior to its Soviet counterpart and as difficult to fly.[418]

Egypt also maintains large numbers of fixed and rotary wing transport and support helicopters. Its main fixed wing aircraft are two brigades (three squadrons) with 19 C-130Hs, 5 DHC-5D, and 1 Super King Air. Its rotary wing aircraft include three brigades of helicopters: 1/16 CH-47Cs, 3/40 Mi-8s (including the armed versions), 1/25 Westland Commandos, 1/20 SA-342s, 2 S-70 VIPs, 3 AS-61s, 2 UN-60s, 12 Mi-4s, and 1/17 UH-12Es.

This transport force is one of the few such forces in the Arab world that actually practices the support of land operations and is well integrated into combined arms. It has considerable theater lift capability, and this could play a major role in any operation where Egypt did not face a superior air force. It would be particularly important in any operation dealing with Libya or the Sudan. However, Egypt's airlift capability is only adequate to support Egypt's army, air force, air defense units, and navy in defensive missions on Egyptian territory. It could not support an operation in the Gulf or any other noncontiguous area without U.S. or other strategic lift support.

The Egyptian Air Defense Command

Egypt's 80,000 man land based air defenses had about 50,000 conscripts in 1992. Egypt's air defense system was one of the largest in the Middle East and one of the few systems to blend Soviet, U.S., and European technology. Nevertheless, large elements of this force had obsolete equipment and limited overall readiness.

Egypt still retains large numbers of Soviet-supplied SA-2 and SA-3 surface-to-air missiles (280–300 SA-2 launchers and 180–200 SA-3 launchers). While the SA-2s and SA-3s have evidently been improved with Yugoslav and Soviet assistance in recent years, they are still of limited effectiveness and outdated design. Israel proved in June, 1982 that a technically advanced power can counter the SA-2 and SA-3. They serve more to degrade the quality and survival of aircraft launching medium and high altitude air attacks on area targets than to be an effective means of active defense.[419]

Egypt has cut its active SA-6 force from 84 to 60 launchers and further cuts are planned, but it will have to retain most of its 60-odd SA-6 battalions beyond the late 1990s. Egypt has found these systems to be substantially more difficult to maintain and update than its SA-2s and SA-3s, although the USSR may have started modernizing some of these systems in 1987. Israel showed in 1963 that it can strike against more modern variants of the SA-6 than are deployed in Egypt, and do so with virtual impunity. Further, Libya is already acquiring aircraft with missiles that have near standoff ranges.

Egypt does, however, have 12 Improved Hawk batteries with 72 U.S.-made Improved Hawk launchers, 12 Chaparral batteries with 74 fire units, and 12 Crotale batteries with 24–36 Crotale missile launchers. The Hawk systems are being upgraded to the PIP-III version of the system.[420] Coupled to Egypt's steadily improving air defense fighters and E-2Cs, this mix of surface-to-air missiles should provide enough resources to form an adequate force to deal with any potential threat other than Israel. Some improvements have also occurred in Egypt's anti-aircraft guns. Egypt has 18 Amoun (Skyguard/RIM-7F) systems with 36 twin 35mm Skyguard guns and 36 quad surface-to-air missile launchers. These radar guided Swiss-Italian systems combine modified Aim-7F missiles and 35mm guns.

The Egyptian system began to be modernized with Western components during the early 1980s, and four AN/TPS-93 and eight Westinghouse AN/TPS-63 radars were added at a cost of about $154 million. Egypt also bought twelve AN/TSQ-143 van mounted automated operation centers for its Hawk missile batteries. These centers each have four display consoles, twelve microprocessors, and two main computers and are linked into Egypt's AN/TPS-63 radars. In 1986 Egypt decided to produce the AN/TPS-63 in Egypt and signed a contract to produce thirty-four more units at Benha Electronics of Egypt. Egypt also has British-made Plessey AR-3Ds and TSR-2100 radars. These sensors are being mixed with Soviet radars. The number of Soviet systems is not clear, although Egypt had a peak strength of 158 Soviet two dimensional radars and 48 three dimensional radars in 1975. Up to 100 Soviet radars may still be deployed.

Hughes was given a contract for overall air defense system integration in 1983. This system began in-site testing in 1987, and a follow-on improvement contract was awarded for $159 million. This system integrates fighters, missiles, ground based sensors, and the data from Egypt's E-2Cs. Egypt plans to acquire a more advanced C^3I system in the future. It has contracted with Hughes to study how it can best integrate its Improved Hawks, E-2Cs, F-16s, Mirage 2000s, and other craft into such a system. This contract builds on Project 776, which was the first phase of the Hughes effort at air defense integration. The improved program is supposed to fully net Egypt's Soviet radars into a common system with its British and U.S. radars, add data links to Egypt's surface-to-air missiles, and reduce vulnerability to some aspects of electronic countermeasures.

Egypt has a more advanced electronic warfare capability than that of many Middle Eastern countries and has modified or developed equipment of its own as well as imported U.S., European, and Soviet systems. Even so, Egypt lacks the technical resources to compete with Israel in electronic warfare and SAM-suppression technology.[421] While Libya is technically inferior to Egypt, it has made important changes in its ground based air defenses in reaction to the U.S. raid during 1986. During 1986–1990, Libya received 36 SA-5 missile launchers and at least 12 SA-13s and 8 SA-8s. It received at least 17 advanced radar systems and is installing a new Xenit C^3I system.

The Egyptian ground based air defense system is deployed in five regional divisions. The most advanced U.S. and European equipment is concentrated around Cairo and the Suez Canal. Training standards seem to be relatively high, although problems exist because of the need to support so many different types of systems and because systems integration as part of Project 776 seems to be proceeding slowly and to have encountered a number of difficulties.

The Egyptian Navy

In 1992 Egypt had a 19,500 man navy and coast guard, with some 12,000 conscripts and reserves of approximately 15,000 men. It had eight operational submarines, one destroyer, four frigates, twenty-one missile fast attack craft, two torpedo fast attack craft, eight gun fast attack craft, eight patrol fast attack craft, three landing ship–mediums, eleven landing craft–utility, seven oceangoing mine sweepers, two inshore mine sweepers, three survey craft, three Hovercraft, thirty-three miscellaneous vessels, and ninety-four small ships and craft in its coast guard. Egypt had a small coastal defense force and a small naval aviation component with five Sea King M-47 ASW and anti-ship helicopters and nine SA-342 ASW helicopters.

The Egyptian navy was based at Alexandria, Port Said, Mersa Matruh, Suez, Port Tewfig, Hurghada, Sharm al-Shaikh, and Safaga. Alexandria is the main port, with secondary ports at Suez and Safaga. The Egyptian coastal defense force is manned by the army but is under navy control. It has SM-4-1 130mm coastal guns and thirty Otomat anti-ship missiles. Older anti-ship missiles like the Samlet have been phased out of service.

Egypt's naval forces are numerically impressive, but they are often little more than a hollow shell. Four of Egypt's submarines are aging Soviet Romeos and four are PRC-made Type-033 copies of the Romeo-class. The four 1,830-ton Soviet-supplied Romeos are the survivors of six submarines that were delivered in the mid- to late 1960s. While they have had a limited update, they are effectively out of service. Only the four PRC-made vessels, which were delivered in 1982 and 1984, are to be modernized.

This modernization is being done in Egypt with PRC and U.S. assistance, and though work began in October, 1988, the submarines will not be operational until 1993. The modernized submarines are being given a Singer Librascope fire control system, Krupp passive sonars and digitizers, Loral active sonars, Ferranti data links, and a combination of updated NT37E torpedoes and Harpoon anti-ship missile launch capability.[422] The modernization will also add U.S. sonars and underwater operations equipment. Egypt has a total of about twenty-nine Harpoon missiles, including training rounds, and plans to provide U.S. variable depth sonar and guns for its sub chasers.

Egypt has also sought to buy reconditioned submarines from the UK or conventional submarines from the U.S. but has so far lacked the funds and political support in the U.S. to do so. It considered buying two ex-British 2,030-ton Porpoise- and Oberon-class, but in 1990 Egypt canceled the order because it felt that only new types would be silent enough to patrol the Red Sea and approaches to the Suez Canal as effective anti-submarine warfare systems.[423]

Egypt's major surface forces consist of one destroyer and five frigates. The destroyer, a British Z-class training ship purchased in 1955, has not been modernized since 1964. It is a 2,575-ton vessel with four 114mm guns and five 533mm torpedo tubes. Egypt's most combat effective major surface ships are two Spanish-made El Suez–class frigates with 2 x 4 Harpoons, and two PRC-made Al Zafir frigates with CSS-N-2 (HY-2) missiles. Only the 1,470-ton El Suez frigates are modern designs. They are equipped with two quad Harpoon launchers, an octuple Albatross launcher, Aspide fire control systems, and 324mm Stingray ASW torpedoes.

The two 1,702-ton PRC-made frigates—the *Najim al Zafir* and *El Nasser*—have two twin HY-2 ship-to-ship missile launchers and four twin 57mm guns. They are adequate for surface patrol purposes but lack effective air defense, resistance to countermeasures, and modern ASW capabilities. Egypt sent the *Najim al Zafir* to the UK in 1988 to see if the two ships could be fitted with modern Western equipment; this led to some upgrading of their electronics and electronic intelligence systems.[424]

There are also twenty-one guided missile patrol craft. These include six 307-ton British made Ramadan-class boats with four Otomat missile launchers and one 76mm gun; six 82-ton October-class with two Otomat missile launchers and two twin 30mm guns, six 79.2-ton PRC-made Hegu-class with two Fei Lung 2 missile launchers and two twin 23mm guns, and three aging 210-ton Soviet Osa-Is with four SS-N-2A Styx missile launchers, SA-N-5 Grail ship-to-air missiles, and two twin 30mm guns. The Hegu-class vessels are relatively limited capability designs and the Osa-Is are obsolete.

The rest of Egypt's naval strength consists of eighteen patrol boats without guided weapons, which are suitable only for coastal defense and light patrol missions. These include eight PRC-made Hainan-class 392-ton ships with two twin 57mm guns, six Shersen-class 170-ton ships with SA-N-5 missiles and two twin 30mm guns, and four PRC-made Shanghai II–class ships with two twin 37mm guns. The PRC ships were transferred in the mid-1980s, but the Soviet ships were transferred back in the 1960s.

Egypt has three 10-ton Winchester SRN-6 Hovercraft minelayers. It also has four Soviet-made 520-ton Yurka-class, three Soviet-made 580-ton 43-class, and two 180-ton T-301-class coastal mine countermeasure vessels. All of the Soviet-made ships were delivered in the 1960s and early 1970s and have the sensors and equipment to deal with modern mines. Egypt has three Soviet-made 800-ton Polnocny-class medium landing ships which can carry six tanks and 180 troops each, nine Soviet-made Vydra-class 60-ton utility landing craft with the ability to carry 200 troops or 200 tons, and two Soviet-made SMB-1-class 60-ton utility landing craft with the ability to carry 180 tons. Egypt is studying the conversion of two ships in Egypt to roll-on/roll-off status to use in moving troops and equipment to support friendly states, but funding is uncertain.

Egypt's smaller ships and support vessels include 6 ex-Soviet yard tankers, 2 ex-Soviet diving ships, two ex-Soviet torpedo recovery craft, 7 ex-Soviet tugs, and 8 Seafox underwater swimmer delivery craft. The coast guard has 12 Timsah-class 100-ton large patrol craft, 10 102-ton Swiftships large patrol craft, 2 110-ton Nisr-class large patrol craft, 26 coastal patrol craft, 6 small patrol craft, 30 DC-25 type and 4 Damen boats.

Egypt has been forced to steadily cut back on the navy's operational activity and training. While Egypt has a number of dedicated and competent naval officers, the lack of funding for the navy has had an impact on morale and retention, and the navy has suffered serious losses of trained naval cadres.

Logistics also present serious problems. The Egyptian navy does not have an effective logistic, support, or maintenance system and faces major difficulties because of the forces it must support. More than 60% of all Egyptian naval units have reached the end of their useful lives: The ex-Soviet vessels could neither be modernized nor maintained in fully operational status. The most recent deliveries of these Soviet vessels occurred in 1967–1968, and most of the weaponry and electronics on these ships are no longer operational. This includes much of the equipment on Egypt's destroyers, missile patrol boats, fast patrol boats, submarines, and sub chasers. As a result, Egyptian ships suffer large numbers of breakdowns and are forced to restrict the length of their operations.

Egypt has cheaply acquired some vessels from the People's Republic of China through a "soft" loan. These PRC-made ships, however, lack the technology for modern naval warfare and have limited combat efficiency. They serve the purpose of keeping the Egyptian navy at sea, but they do not solve its modernization problems.

The most significant recent improvement that has taken place in Egypt's naval capabilities is the acquisition of the E-2C by Egypt's air force. This will allow Egypt to use its aircraft more effectively in both air defense and maritime missions and will provide advanced maritime surveillance to the Egyptian surface fleet. Unfortunately, the E-2Cs will have to be dedicated to air-to-air operations in many contingencies. Egypt has only limited ability to patrol and provide maritime surveillance for the Gulf of Suez and the Red Sea. This is important because of the number of ships and oil rigs in the area and the vulnerability of the Suez Canal. As several incidents illustrated in July, 1984, it is comparatively easy to mine the Red Sea approaches to the canal, and sinking one large ship could block the canal for at least a limited period and deny the Egyptian navy the ability to reinforce from the Mediterranean to the Red Sea.

Egyptian Weapons of Mass Destruction

Egypt has been capable of delivering chemical weapons since the late 1950s and may have acquired British stocks of mustard gas that Britain failed to remove from inventories it deployed in the northern desert in World War II. Egypt began low level research efforts in the 1950s to develop long range guided missiles and nuclear weapons. Egypt has had the ability to produce its own mustard gas and other chemical weapons since the early 1960s, and it used poison gas in its battles against the royalist faction in North Yemen in the period before its 1967 conflict with Israel.

Although Egyptian officials have recently implied that Egypt does not have such chemical weapons, it certainly has had large stockpiles of defensive equipment since the late 1960s—much of which was captured during the fighting in October, 1973. Egypt almost certainly had stockpiles of mustard gas at the time and was probably producing limited amounts of nonpersistent nerve gas. Egypt has also been less reticent about its possession of chemical weapons in the past. The former Egyptian minister of war, Gen. Abdel Ranny Gamassay, stated in 1975, that "if Israel should decide to use a nuclear weapon in the battlefield, we shall use the weapons of mass destruction that are at our disposal."[425] In spite of the dramatic changes in its relations with Israel and careful observance of its peace treaty, Egypt seems to have continued to produce chemical agents after the Camp David accords as well as to maintain stockpiles of chemical bombs and other chemical weapons.

While Egypt does not appear to have developed the massive chemical weapons production and delivery capabilities of states like Iraq, Syria, and Libya, it does seem to have stepped up its research effort since gas began to be used extensively in the Iran-Iraq War. Egypt probably retains the ability to produce mustard gas and nonpersistent nerve gas and may well be able to produce persistent nerve gas as well.

Egypt definitely retains a long range missile capability, although it is unclear such weapons have chemical warheads. Egypt has had FROG-7 and Scud B missiles since the 1960s, and these remain operational even though former President Sadat severed military relations with the USSR in 1974.

Egypt retains two active surface-to-surface missile regiments with twelve FROG-7 free rocket launchers and has a regiment with at least nine Scud B guided missile launchers.

Egypt has developed an improved and domestically produced version of the FROG called the Saqr 80. This rocket is 6.5 meters long and 210 mm in diameter and weighs 660 kilograms. It has a maximum range of 50 miles (80 kilometers) and a 440 pound (200 kilogram) warhead. It is a TEL mounted system and can be mounted on both wheeled and tracked vehicles. Egypt uses an RPV with the system for long range targeting. A variant is being studied that would hold four rockets per vehicle instead of the usual one. Egypt reports two types of conventional warheads for the Saqr 80—one with 950 AP/AT bomblets and one with 65 anti-tank mines—and it is developing an automatic survey and fire control system for the rocket. The Saqr 80 could, however, easily be used to deliver chemical weapons.[426]

Although the Scud Bs Egypt received in 1973 would normally be inoperable because of age and lack of service, Egypt seems to have carried out a successful reverse engineering program and is attempting to mass produce its own version of the missile. Egypt has been reported to be building an improved version of the Scud B with North Korean assistance, although this has not been confirmed.[427] While the Scud B missile is normally credited with having a range of 190 miles (300 kilometers) and a 2,200 pound (1,000 kilogram warhead, some sources claim that the range and warhead size of the improved Egyptian version of the Scud may be closer to that of the Iraqi Al-Hussein, and the range may be up to twice that of a normal Scud. There are indications that Egypt stepped up its effort to develop and produce improved versions of the Scud after Israel's testing of the Jericho II missiles.[428]

While few of the details of Egypt's recent chemical weapons and missile development efforts have become public, Egypt was caught attempting to import the feedstock for nerve gas from Canada during 1988. Egypt has also placed highly specialized orders of fumigants, pesticides, arsenic, and strychnine for what seems to be use in a major poison gas production facility near or in the Ben Youssef Air Base south of Cairo.[429] As mentioned earlier, Egypt was also buying chemical weapons production equipment from such companies as Krebs. Krebs built a complex for the El Nasr Pharmaceutical Plant at Abu Zabaal to make phosphorous trichloride, a basic chemical that can be used for both insecticides and chemical weapons. Krebs was also active in designing a phosphorous pentasulfide plant for Iran that seemed to be linked to Iran's chemical weapons efforts.[430]

The U.S. also detected Egyptian efforts to build additional types of missiles. On June 23, 1988, the U.S. arrested two Egyptian military officers based at the Egyptian embassy in Washington. They were charged with conspiring with Egyptian-born rocket scientist Abdelkadr Helmy and other Egyptian agents to export 32 tons of rocket fuel chemicals, 432 pounds of carbon fiber materials for nose cones and rocket motor nozzles, propulsion hardware, telemetry tracking equipment, equipment and materials for making rocket motor casings, and missile assembly plans for the Pershing II missile. These missile plans had been obtained from Messerschmidt in the FRG and an Italian firm.[431]

In June, 1990 there were reports that Egypt had reached an agreement with the People's Republic of China to update Egypt's Saqr rocket factory to produce newer anti-aircraft missiles, the DF-4 Silkworm anti-ship missile, an improved version of the Scud, and three types of long range Saqr surface-to-surface rockets. The deal was reported to include an improved version of the DF-4, with its range extended from 50 to 90 nautical miles, and a DF-5 missile with a range of 170 miles. The regular DF-4 has a 1,000 pound warhead and can be used in a surface-to-surface as well as an anti-ship mode.[432]

Although Mubarak has categorically denied that Egypt has chemical weapons and a new long range missile development effort, there are other reasons to question such denials. Israeli sources believe that Egypt is building chemical weapons feedstock plants north of Cairo and will have a substantial capability to produce nerve and mustard gases without dependence on imports of precursor chemicals. Egypt also seems to have carried out extensive research on biological weapons and could rapidly go into production.

Many media sources reported in 1988 and 1989 that Egypt had been cooperating with Iraq in paying for development and production of the Badar 2000 long range missile since the mid-1980s. As has been discussed earlier, the Badar 2000 is reported to be based on the Argentine Condor II or Alacran missile and is said to be a solid fuel system with ranges from 480 to 1,000 kilometers and warheads of 500 to 1,000 kilograms.[433]

These media reports of Egyptian cooperation with Argentina and Iraq seem correct, but Argentina has never operationally tested the Condor II, and there is some question as to Argentina's ability to provide the proper technical skills to develop such a system. According to some reports, a major program evaluation in 1988 revealed major technical problems, and Argentina may have decided to shift its efforts to a missile with only a 200 kilometer range.

Other reports indicate that the U.S. quietly put enough pressure on Argentina and Egypt during the late 1980s to halt the project. According to such reports, this pressure succeeded in the case of Argentina once its military government fell after a disastrous defeat in the Falklands. It succeeded in the case of Egypt when Mubarak was embarrassed by the arrest of the Egyptian officers attempting to smuggle missile technology out of the U.S.[434]

There have been some rumors that Egypt is seeking to develop advanced chemical and biological warheads for its missiles systems and modern binary bombs and may be reviving its nuclear weapons research effort. If such Egyptian efforts exist, however, they are at a relatively low level of activity and largely covert. There is no significant evidence of any kind of a serious Egyptian nuclear weapons development effort.

Egyptian Paramilitary Forces

Finally, Egypt maintains paramilitary forces which may ultimately do more to threaten its stability than to help it. President Sadat originally established a large central security police to help ensure the loyalty of the regular forces. After his assassination, this force become the dumping ground for the lowest grade conscripts. They were given miserable quarters, low pay, fed two meals a day, and often retained in service long beyond the normal time of conscription.

This led to large scale riots in the force in early 1986. These riots were followed by a limited number of reforms and by a cutback from roughly 500,000 to 300,000 men. It still exists, however, and is still very poorly trained, equipped, and paid. Its only practical purpose is to provide "jobs" for Egypt's least advantaged young men.

Egypt also has a 2,000 man coast guard with 29 small inshore patrol boats, a 12,000 man frontier corps formed into 13 regiments, and a 60,000 man national guard which is slightly better off than the central security forces and which is being given Walid armored personnel carriers. These forces would have limited value in any conflict with regular military forces.

Egyptian Force Developments

Egypt's defense planners continue to face a difficult challenge: They must use U.S. aid to give Egypt an effective defense capability; find ways that Egypt can fully convert its maintenance, support, and training structure to use U.S. equipment and technology; and respond to a continuing domestic economic crisis that began with the fall of oil prices in the mid-1980s and is now driven by a serious shortfall of foreign capital and problems in industrial and agricultural output. Egypt has also had to maintain a much larger force structure than it needs as a matter of prestige, in order to ensure the political stability of the armed forces, and to help provide employment and stability for Egypt's conscript age manpower.

Egypt has sought to meet these challenges by shaping its forces according to the following principles:

- Emphasis on defensive forces and resource priority for those forces needed to deter a major attack on Egyptian soil.
- Creation of higher technology forces with fully adequate support to reduce Egypt's need for larger numbers of modern weapons (using quality as a substitute for quantity).
- Use of European and Chinese weapons systems and technologies to supplement U.S. deliveries, when these systems complement U.S.-supplied equipment and can be sustained at a reasonable cost.
  Limitation of domestic military spending to support economic reform and development.
- Retention of select Soviet equipment as long as possible as the "low" part of a "high-low" mix in Egypt's equipment. This mix frees resources to pay for more advanced Western technology and economic development.

- Modification of existing systems to support defensive missions rather than to buy large numbers of new systems overseas.
- Use of Egyptian reserves to save the cost of active manpower. This is made possible by Egypt's firm commitment to maintaining the peace and its ability to rely on defense and deterrence.
- Utilization of U.S. aid to provide key high technology systems for all services in those areas most likely to contribute to deterring war and providing territorial defense for Egypt.
- Minimal hard currency expenditures on military equipment, goods, and services.
- Minimal increases in foreign credits or loans for military imports, and maximum reliance on U.S. aid.
- Development of Egypt's domestic arms industry to provide a steadily increasing amount of support equipment, spares, munitions, and arms so that Egypt may eventually make major reductions in its need for arms imports and aid.

Egypt has faced major internal bureaucratic and political problems in achieving these objectives, and its actions reflect a continuing political need to move slowly in rationalizing and reducing its force structure and its need to make purchases of high tech military equipment for prestige purposes as well as effectiveness. Nevertheless, Egypt has succeeded in giving its defense plans a high degree of continuity and in creating reasonably well structured long term plans.

Egypt has completed implementation of both its first five year plan (1983–1987) which called for a force structure that depended on U.S. equipment, and its second plan (1988–1992). The First Defense Five Year Plan was implemented with minimal modifications that allowed Egypt to allocate enough funds to obtain an armored brigade, start a limited program in the navy, start upgrading its training centers, introduce an automated logistic system, and obtain spare parts for its land forces. While Egypt's strength in terms of fully operational equipment is far lower than what it maintained in 1973, Egypt has made impressive progress in creating a U.S.- and Western-supplied force.

Strategic Interests and Arms Transfers

Egypt has been caught in several national security dilemmas, some of which are of its own making. It has fully observed the Camp David accords, but the failure to reach a broader peace has left it with the need to maintain large forces as a contingency against some unforeseen renewal of hostilities. It has faced a long series of challenges from Libya and is largely surrounded by unstable states, many of which have been involved in major civil wars.

The external threat is, however, only part of Egypt's problems. Egypt has chosen to maintain a force structure far larger than it can actually sustain. About one-third of the Egyptian army and roughly the same portion of its air force and navy consist of low grade forces with obsolete equipment and limited to negligible modern training and combat, service, and logistic support. Egypt also has been forced to slowly phase out its Soviet-supplied arms and replace them with Western arms—largely from the U.S. This has been an incredibly expensive conversion since the Soviet bloc arms were provided at minimal cost and Egypt never before had to fund either arms or services. U.S. arms not only are far more expensive in real terms—generally by a factor of three to five—they also require completely different service, support, facilities, munitions, and logistics. As a result, Egypt cannot hope to complete its conversion to Western arms until after the year 2000.

Egypt's insistence on maintaining more forces than it can properly train, support, and equip wastes resources that would be far more effective if concentrated on fewer and higher quality units. This policy also wastes millions of dollars a year that would be far better spent on social development and economic reform. While Egypt's armed forces do have some social welfare benefits, these should not be exaggerated. Lower grade units treat their enlisted personnel so badly that they disaffect more than they unite. The token role of Egypt's forces in civil development simply distorts the economy into low pay-off projects. Egypt's military industries do have some benefits in terms of ammunition production, military supplies, and the production of small arms and artillery. Yet the country wastes large amounts of money on high technology military industries that are hollow shells that consume large amounts of hard currency and talent and are so ineffectively organized and supported with imports and material that their output and export impact is hardly worth their cost.

That said, Egypt's problems can scarcely be solved by a cutoff of arms imports. Roughly half of Egypt's armor still uses Soviet bloc systems that must be replaced. Egypt's air force is an awkward mix of U.S., Soviet, Chinese, and French aircraft. Its navy is very weak, with many obsolete or quasi-operable ships. Even a fully rationalized Egyptian force structure would require very substantial arms imports and U.S. military aid for at least the next decade to create a smaller and effective force. Further, Egypt cannot hope to play a strategic role in the Gulf without such aid. It is currently tied largely to operations near its bases and casernes and lacks the logistic and service support capability and combat support mobility needed for effective power projection. It will require massive Kuwaiti and Saudi aid and U.S. technical assistance to base forward in the Gulf to allow Egypt to fight first line Iraqi troops without U.S. control of the air.

It must also be noted that Egypt spends only 8–12% of its GDP and about 22% of its central government expenditures on military forces. This is not an unusual effort for a developing nation facing significant external threats. Further, Egypt's main political, economic, and social problems are the fault of its civil sector, not military spending. Egypt's failure to come to grips with population growth and its grindingly slow and inadequate efforts at economic reform remain major obstacles. There is no doubt that the primary threat to Egypt's national security is the civil part of its central government rather than its military or its hostile neighbors.

The situation affecting arms control is different with regard to proliferation. While Egypt has shown no recent interest in nuclear weapons, it has cooperated with Iraq in long range missile development. It has also actively pursued the modernization of its chemical weapons technology and seems to have an active—if low level—research effort in biological warfare. It is reasonable to argue that Egyptian efforts are low key and a purely defensive reaction to proliferation in Libya, Israel, Iran, and Iraq. Nevertheless, efforts to control nuclear, chemical, and biological weapons—and their means of delivery—must include Egypt as well as its neighbors.

Current Prospects for the Arab-Israeli Arms Race

The problem with the Arab-Israeli arms race is not that war is certain or even likely; it is that war is constantly possible. Further, limited conflicts can now escalate into war using weapons of mass destruction that may be directed at civilian targets. At the same time, even peace means spending vast amounts of the region's limited resources on arms and military forces and an arms race that adds to the risk of war.

It is to be hoped that the current peace negotiations will lead Israel, the Palestinians, Jordan, Syria, and Lebanon to a peace that has at least some of the stability of the Camp David accords and leads to significant reductions in military spending, the drain on skilled manpower, and the use of foreign aid for arms. It is impossible, however, to dismiss the possibility of several major risks. These include:

- A limited or major conflict between Israel and Syria that may or may not escalate to involve other states and use biological, chemical, and nuclear weapons;
- Civil war in Israel and the occupied territories, transforming the *intifada* into a guerrilla war of attrition, with or without the backing of the PLO and other Arab states;
- Civil war in Jordan, possibly involving intervention by Israel and Syria;
- Renewed civil war in Lebanon and/or wars between Syrian and Israeli forces in Lebanon or their proxies;
- Civil conflict in Egypt or Egypt's being forced into a widening Arab-Israeli conflict.

The most likely contingencies are limited border conflicts and internal conflicts. The probability that such conflicts do not escalate can also be increased by providing enough arms to Israel to maintain its edge over Syria, and willingness to show restraint, while limiting arms to Syria. If this seems a pro-Western or pro-Israeli mix of arms and arms control, it is also the mix most likely to prevent or limit war. Fueling Syria's search for parity will do nothing to support either peace or stability.

In the long run, however, only a secure and stable peace settlement can really prevent war. Every element in the Arab-Israeli struggle already has enough arms to fight, and shutting off new arms will not change this situation. Worse, the slow proliferation of weapons of mass destruction may make it tempting to try to correct any shortfalls in conventional weapons with far more lethal systems. The bad news is that the mythic frog and scorpion are still all too alive in the Middle East. The worse news is that they now have biological, chemical, and nuclear weapons.

Notes

1. Estimate based on data in the IISS, *Military Balance, 1991–1992.*

2. *Oil and Gas Journal,* September 23, 1991, p. 62.

3. *Los Angeles Times,* January 28, 1992, p. C-1.

4. CIA, *World Factbook 1991,* pp. 111, 152, 337.

5. This section draws heavily on the excellent summaries of individual conflicts provided by Herbert K. Tillema in *International Conflict Since 1945,* Boulder, Westview, 1991; Clyde R. Mark, "Palestine and the Palestinians," Congressional Research Service IB76048, January 15, 1992; work in various annual editions of John Laffin's *The World in Conflict* or *War Annual,* London, Brassey's, and by John Keegan, *World Armies,* London, Macmillan, 1983; and joint work with Abraham Wagner in *The Lessons of Modern War,* Volume 1, Boulder, Westview, 1990. For the sake of consistency, the chronology normally uses the dates in Tillema's work. The reader should be aware that many dates vary according to source or are controversial.

6. A small cadre of Saudi forces appeared briefly in October, 1948 fighting with Egyptian forces in the south.

7. There were 885,000 Arab citizens of Israel, or 18% of a total population of 4,896,000, at the end of April, 1991. The Palestinian refugee population now totals 2.4 million Arab Palestinians, including 841,860 Palestinians living in 66 UN-administered refugee camps in Lebanon, Syria, Jordan, the West Bank, and Gaza. Clyde R. Mark, "Palestine and the Palestinians," Congressional Research Service IB76048, January 15, 1992, pp. 1 and 5.

8. Clyde R. Mark, "Palestine and the Palestinians," Congressional Research Service IB76048, January 15, 1992, p. 5.

9. See Emanuel Wald, *The Wald Report: The Decline of Israeli National Security Since 1967,* Boulder, Westview Press, 1991.

10. *Jane's Defence Weekly,* July 27, 1991, p. 135; Eric Silver, "A Warrior for the Nineties," *The Jerusalem Report,* June 20, 1991, pp. 12–20.

11. The military manpower, force strength, and equipment estimates in this section are made by the author using a wide range of sources, including computerized data bases, interviews, and press clipping services. Most are impossible to reference in ways of use to the reader. The force strength statistics are generally adapted from the latest edition of the International Institute for Strategic Studies, *Military Balance* (IISS, London), in this case the 1991–1992 edition.

Extensive use has also been made of the annual editions of the Jaffee Center for Strategic Studies, *The Military Balance in the Middle East* (JCSS, Tel Aviv), especially the 1990–1991 edition and working materials from the coming edition. Material has also been drawn from computer print outs from NEXIS, the United States Naval Institute data base, and from the DMS/FI Market Intelligence Reports data base. Other sources include the *Military Technology* "World Defense Almanac for 1991–1992," published in 1992; Foreign Affairs Division, "Middle East Arms Control and Related Issues," Washington, Congressional Research Service, 91–384F, May 1, 1991; and *Middle East Economic Digest,* "MEED Special Report: Defense," Volume 35, December 13, 1991.

Weapons data are taken from many sources, including computerized material available in NEXIS, and various editions of *Jane's Fighting Ships* (Jane's Publishing); *Jane's Naval Weapons Systems* (Jane's Publishing); *Jane's Armour and Artillery* (Jane's Publishing); *Jane's Infantry Weapons* (Jane's Publishing); *Jane's Military Vehicles and Logistics* (Jane's Publishing); *Jane's Land-Based Air Defence* (Jane's Publishing); *Jane's All the World's Aircraft* (Jane's Publishing); *Jane's Battlefield Surveillance Systems* (Jane's Publishing); *Jane's Radar and Electronic Warfare Systems* (Jane's Publishing), *Jane's C³I Systems*(Jane's Publishing); *Jane's Air-Launched Weapons Systems* (Jane's Publishing); *Jane's Defence Appointments & Procurement Handbook (Middle East Edition)* (Jane's Publishing); *Tanks of the World* (Bernard and Grafe); *Weyer's Warships* (Bernard and Grafe); and *Warplanes of the World* (Bernard and Grafe).

Other military background, effectiveness, strength, organizational, and history data are taken from Tim Ripley, "Israel's Pilots Look to the Future," *International Defense Review*, 3 / 1992, pp. 261–262; Samuel M. Katz, "Israeli Airpower on the Rise," *Air Force*, November, 1991, pp. 44–51; Tony Banks, "Israel: Defense Still Top Priority," *Jane's Defence Weekly*, February 15, 1992, pp. 233–240; Emanuel Wald, *The Wald Report: The Decline of Israeli National Security Since 1967*, Boulder, Westview Press, 1991; "Rabin: Meeting the Missile Threat," *Jane's Defence Weekly*, June 10, 1989, pp. 1141–1151; Anthony H. Cordesman, *Jordanian Arms and The Middle East Balance*, Washington, Middle East Institute, 1983, *The Gulf and the Search for Strategic Stability*, Boulder, Westview, 1984; *The Gulf and the West*, Boulder, Westview, 1988; and *Weapons of Mass Destruction in the Middle East*, London, Brassey's / RUSI, 1991; Anthony H. Cordesman and Abraham Wagner, *The Lessons of Modern War*, Volume 1, Boulder, Westview, 1990.

12. See "So Much To Do, So Little Done," *Economist*, May 25, 1985, p. 69; "Israel Reports Least Immigration Since '48, Amid Worry for Future," *New York Times*, January 7, 1986, p. A-4.

13. *Jane's Defence Weekly*, February 18, 1989, p. 249.

14. Based upon data sheets provided by the U.S. embassy in Tel Aviv in January, 1989.

15. *New York Times*, January 2, 1989, p. 1; *Armed Forces Journal*, November 1988, pp. 36–37.

16. Israeli Radio, January 22, 1991; Clyde R. Mark, "Israel: U.S. Foreign Assistance Facts," Congressional Research Service IB85066, February 11, 1992, p. 14.

17. See U.S. Arms Control and Disarmament Agency, *World Military Expenditures and Arms Transfers, 1985*, Washington, GPO, 1985, p. 66; and *Defense Week*, April 16, 1986, p. 5.

18. Arms Control and Disarmament Agency (ACDA), *World Military Expenditures and Arms Transfers, 1990*, Washington, GPO, 1990, Table I.

19. CIA, *World Factbook, 1991*, p. 153.

20. Based on Israeli Ministry of Defense figures furnished to the author in February, 1992. The breakout of the spending during the fiscal year between April 1, 1989, and March 31, 1990, showed that procurement abroad cost 2,820 million shekels and domestic defense expenditures totaled 8,265 million shekels, with 3,316 million for personnel, 688 million for transfer payments, 290 million for construction, and 3,971 million for domestic procurement. The breakout of the spending during the fiscal year between April 1, 1990, and March 31, 1991, showed that procurement abroad cost 4,005 million shekels and domestic defense expenditures totaled 9,950 million shekels, with 4,310 million for personnel, 859 million for transfer payments, 356 million for construction, and 4,065 million for domestic procurement.

21. Data sheets provided by the U.S. embassy in Tel Aviv in January, 1989. This sheet showed defense spending as 21.0% of the budget in 1984 and interest payments as 14.5%; as 21.6% of the budget in 1985, and interest payments as 15.7%; as 19.8% of the budget in 1986, and interest payments as 13.4%; and as 17.2% of the budget in 1987 and interest payments as 12.5%.

22. U.S. aid is estimated to have contributed an additional $1.2 billion in FY1981, $1.4 billion in FY1982, $1.7 billion in FY1983 and FY1984, $1.4 billion in FY1985, $1.723 billion in FY1986, and $1.8 billion in FY1987–FY1992. The flow of U.S. aid does not coincide exactly with the flow of Israeli domestic expenditures because of the different months included in each country's fiscal year. Israel claims that the true value of U.S. aid is much lower than

that shown because Israel has had to repay a substantial portion in loans and because of inflation. Israel indicates that the value of U.S. aid in constant FY1977 dollars was $913 million in FY1978, $824 million in FY1979, $736 million in FY1980, $788 million in FY1981, $829 million in FY1982, $960 million in FY1983, $925 million in FY1984, $747 million in FY1985, $892 million in FY1986, $905 million in FY1987, and $873 million in FY1988.

23. Based on Israeli Ministry of Defense figures furnished to the author in February, 1992.

24. *Washington Post*, September 5, 1991, p. A-23; Associated Press, September 4, 1991, PM cycle; *The Independent*, September 5, 1991, p. 10; *London Financial Times*, March 20, 1992, p. 4; *Jane's Defence Weekly*, August 17, 1991, p. 266, September 7, 1991, p. 385; *Los Angeles Times*, July 16, 1991, p. H-1; *Philadelphia Inquirer*, September 2, 1991, p. 4A.

25. For a detailed analysis see Clyde R. Mark, "Israel: U.S. Foreign Assistance Facts," Congressional Research Service IB85066, February 11, 1992; General Accounting Office (GAO), "U.S. Assistance to the State of Israel," GAO/ID-83-51, June 24, 1983; GAO, "Security Assistance: Reporting of Program Content Changes," GAO/NSIAD-90-115, May, 1990.

26. Bank of Israel figures as quoted in the *New York Times*, September 23, 1991, p. A-10. U.S. data show a total between 1949 and 1990 of $49.3 billion in direct U.S. government aid, with $11.2 billion in military loan aid and $18.2 billion in military grant aid. See Clyde R. Mark, "Israel: U.S. Foreign Assistance Facts," Congressional Research Service IB85066, February 11, 1992, pp. 4–5.

27. As part of total aid of roughly $3 billion per year. Israel also received $1.2 billion as economic support funds, and some cooperative development and refugee aid. See Clyde R. Mark, "Israel: U.S. Foreign Assistance Facts," Congressional Research Service IB85066, February 11, 1992; Defense Security Assistance Agency, *Foreign Military Sales and Security Assistance Facts, 1987*, pp. 24–25; Clyde R. Mark, "U.S. Foreign Assistance to the Middle East and North Africa," Congressional Research Service 89-192F, March 20, 1989; Larry Q. Nowels, "Foreign Aid: Budget, Policy, and Reform," Congressional Research Service IB89014, November 12, 1991, p. 10.

28. *Defense News*, September 8, 1991, p. 4.

29. This level of debt payment will not be paid off until FY1996. By that time, Israel will have paid a total of $5.4 billion on the principal and $14.0 billion in interest.

30. IISS, *Military Balance, 1991–1992*, p. 109.

31. Arms Control and Disarmament Agency (ACDA), *World Military Expenditures and Arms Transfers, 1990*, Washington, GPO, 1990, Table II.

32. See U.S. Arms Control and Disarmament Agency, *World Military Expenditures and Arms Transfers, 1985*, Washington, GPO, 1985, p. 134; and U.S. Arms Control and Disarmament Agency, *World Military Expenditures and Arms Transfers, 1989*, Washington, GPO, 1990, p. 117.

33. Arms Control and Disarmament Agency (ACDA), *World Military Expenditures and Arms Transfers, 1990*, Washington, GPO, 1990, pp. 133–134.

34. Based on U.S. Arms Control and Disarmament Agency, *World Military Expenditures and Arms Transfers, 1985*, Washington, GPO, 1985, Table III; U.S. Arms Control and Disarmament Agency, *World Military Expenditures and Arms Transfers, 1989*, Washington, GPO, 1990, Table III; and U.S. Arms Control and Disarmament Agency, *World Military Expenditures and Arms Transfers, 1990*, Washington, GPO, 1990, Table III .

35. Department of Defense, *Defense Almanac*, Washington, Department of Defense, September/October, 1991, pp. 44–45.

36. Adapted from various issues of the IISS, *Military Balance,* and work by the Foreign Affairs Division of the Congressional Research Service in *Middle East Arms Control and Related Issues,* CRS 91-384F, May 1, 1992, and for Senator John McCain. Robert Shuey, Richard F. Grimmett, Theodor Galdi, Steven Hildreth, Todd Masses, Alfred Prados, and Shirley Kahn were the principal authors of the CRS work.

37. DSAA print out provided by DSAA/CR as of April 8, 1992; *Arms Control Today,* March, 1992, p. 34.

38. The main sources for the comments on the Lavi and debates over Israel's military industry include *Defense Week,* April 21, 1986; May 5, 1986, p. 15; and June 2, 1986, p. 13; Leonard Silk, "Military Costs an Israeli Issue," *New York Times,* June 4, 1986, p. D-2 and August 31, 1987, p. A-1; *Wall Street Journal,* August 31, 1987, p. 13 and December 17, 1987, p. 26; *Jane's Defence Weekly,* August 29, 1987, p. 361; September 12, 1987, pp. 512 and 544; October 3, 1987, p. 725; February 27, 1988, p. 356; June 11, 1988, p. 1150; June 25, 1988, p. 1295; *Armed Forces Journal,* October, 1987, p. 40; *Aviation Week,* September 7, 1987, pp. 15 and 23–25; September 14, 1987, pp. 22–23; *Washington Post,* September 1, 1987, p. A-14 and December 15, 1987, p. A-25.

39. See Thomas L. Friedman, "Skirmish Over Israel's New Jet," *New York Times,* July 20, 1986, and Friedman's reports in the editions of August 31, 1987, p. A-1; September 2, 1987, p. A-2; and September 3, 1987, p. A-10; and *Aviation Week,* September 7, 1987, p. 15.

40. *Aviation Week,* September 7, 1988, pp. 23–27.

41. *Jane's Defence Weekly,* June 11, 1988, p. 1150; June 25, 1988, p. 1295; and February 27, 1988, p. 356.

42. *Jane's Defence Weekly,* June 11, 1988, p. 1150; June 25, 1988, p. 1295; and February 27, 1988, p. 356.

43. *Jane's Defence Weekly,* March 4, 1989, pp. 374–375.

44. *Jane's Defence Weekly,* February 20, 1988, p. 301.

45. John G. Roos, "Israel's Industrial Base Fueled by International Sales Success," *Armed Forces Journal,* January 1992, p. 30; Aaron Klieman, "Israeli Military Exports," *Journal of Defense & Diplomacy,* April, 1992, pp. 24–28; Kathleen Bunten and Tony Banks, "Israeli Industry Update," *Jane's Defence Weekly,* June 8, 1991, pp. 975–982; May 9, 1992, p. 805; July 11, 1992, p. 15; August 8, 1992, p. 10; *Jerusalem Post,* June 13, 1992, p. 24.

46. *Armed Forces Journal,* April, 1992, p. 20; *Defense News,* June 15, 1992, p. 1; *Jane's Defence Weekly,* June 8, 1991, pp. 975–982, May 9, 1992, p. 805; July 11, 1992, p. 15; August 8, 1992, p. 10; *Jerusalem Post,* June 13, 1992, p. 24.

47. *International Defense Review,* 9/1991, p. 907; *Jane's Defence Weekly,* March 28, 1992, p. 504.

48. *Washington Post,* March 14, 1992, p. A-1; March 18, 1992, p. A-14; March 25, 1992, p. A-23; *New York Times,* March 20, 1992, p. A-32; *Washington Times,* March 13, 1992, p. A-8; March 14, 1992, p. A-2; March 16, 1992, p. A-1; March 20, 1992, p. A-1; March 23, 1992, p. A-1; *Wall Street Journal,* April 9, 1992, p. 7.

49. *Washington Post,* March 29, 1992, p. A-26;April 3, 1992, p. A-25; *New York Times,* April 2, 1992, p. A-7; April 3, 1992, p. 1.

50. CIA, *World Factbook, 1991,* p. 152.

51. CIA, *World Factbook, 1991,* pp. 111, 152, 337.

52. Based on the IISS, *Military Balance, 1991–1992,* pp. 101–102; CIA, *World Factbook, 1991,* pp. 152–153; and "Overseas Study of Reserve Component Issues—Switzerland and Israel," Report by the Reserve Forces Policy Board, Office of the Secretary of Defense, June 4-12, 1988.

53. The Likud Party objected. IDF officials estimated that the cut in available conscript manpower would reduce the standing army by 17%, cost the army $60 million per year in added reserve duty, and possibly force it to raise the maximum age for reservists back to 55, after cutting it to 51 in April, 1991. *Jane's Defence Review,* July 20, 1991, p. 92.

54. The U.S. embassy estimates the population of Israel as having risen from 4.2 million in 1984 to 4.3 million in 1985 and 1986, 4.4 million in 1987, and 4.5 million in 1988.

55. "Overseas Study of Reserve Component Issues—Switzerland and Israel," Report by the Reserve Forces Policy Board, Office of the Secretary of Defense, June 4-12, 1988, pp. 14–19.

56. See Trevor N. Dupuy and Paul Martell, *Flawed Victory,* Washington, Hero Books, 1985,

pp. 141–147; Richard A. Gabriel, *Operation Peace for Galilee*, New York, Hill and Wang, 1984, pp. 191–213; John Laffin, *War of Desperation*, London, Osprey, 1985, pp. 109–130; and Mark Urban, "Fire in Galilee," a three-part series in *Armed Forces*, March, April, and May, 1986.

57. *Aviation Week*, October 3, 1988, p. 28; *Jane's Defence Weekly*, October 1, 1988, p. 753 and October 15, 1988, p. 915; *Washington Post*, September 20, 1988, p. A-1; *New York Times*, September 20, 1988, p. A-1; *Washington Times*, September 20, 1988, p. A-8; *Christian Science Monitor*, November 17, 1988, p. 14.

58. The military manpower, force strength, and equipment estimates in this section are made by the author using a wide range of sources, including computerized data bases, interviews, and press clipping services. Most are impossible to reference in ways of use to the reader. The force strength statistics are generally taken from the latest edition of the International Institute for Strategic Studies, *Military Balance* (IISS, London), in this case the 1991–1992 edition. Extensive use has also been made of the annual editions of the Jaffee Center for Strategic Studies, *The Military Balance in the Middle East* (JCSS, Tel Aviv), especially the 1990–1991 edition and working materials from the coming edition. Material has also been drawn from computer print outs from the United States Naval Institute data base and from the DMS/FI Market Intelligence Reports data base. Other sources include *Military Technology*, "World Defense Almanac for 1991–1992," published in 1992; computerized material available in NEXIS, and the latest annual editions of *Jane's Fighting Ships* (Jane's Publishing), *Jane's Armour and Artillery* (Jane's Publishing), *Jane's All the World's Aircraft* (Jane's Publishing), *Tanks of the World* (Bernard and Grafe), *Weyer's Warships* (Bernard and Grafe), and *Warplanes of the World* (Bernard and Grafe).

59. "Overseas Study of Reserve Component Issues—Switzerland and Israel," Report by the Reserve Forces Policy Board, Office of the Secretary of Defense, June 4-12, 1988.

60. These strength estimates for Israeli forces in a given command come from a single Israeli source. Other Israelis give different estimates and question the existence of an Israeli field forces command separate from the corps command established in 1983.

61. IISS, *Military Balance, 1991–1992*, p. 109.

62. Aharon Levran and Zeev Eytan, *The Middle East Military Balance, 1990*, Boulder, Westview, 1991, pp. 243–244. Note that Israel tends to label infantry troops as paratroops when they have had advanced infantry training and are jump qualified. This rarely means they would be used primarily as airborne troops.

63. All air defense artillery and surface-to-air missiles are under the command of the air force, which reports to the commander of the IAF.

64. Kenneth S. Brower, "The Middle East Military Balance: Israel Versus the Rest," *International Defense Review*, 7/1986, pp. 907–913.

65. Estimates differ sharply. The figures here are adapted from interviews in Israel in January, 1992, the IISS and Jaffee Center estimates, *Jane's Armour and Artillery, 1991–1992*, and *Jane's Defence Weekly*, February 25, 1989, p. 297.

66. Based upon *Jane's Defence Weekly*, February 25, 1989, pp. 296–297, and interviews in Israel.

67. *Defense News*, July 11, 1988.

68. *Jane's Defence Weekly*, July 20, 1991, p. 85.

69. *International Defense Review*, 6/1988, p. 610.

70. It is not possible to separate reports on U.S. sales of these items to the point where it is clear that they are not over- or undercounted.

71. *International Defense Review*, 5/1988, p. 580.

72. Some estimates show 300 M-50s and L-33s. Estimates of Israeli artillery strength are highly uncertain.

73. *Financial Times*, March 5, 1990, p. 4; *Defense News*, February 17, 1992, p. 46.

74. *Jane's Defence Weekly*, July 6, 1991, p. 32.

75. *Jane's Defence Weekly*, October 15, 1988, p. 934.

76. *Jane's Defence Weekly*, October 15, 1988, p. 934.

77. *Jane's Defence Weekly*, April 30, 1988, p. 829.

78. These systems are described in detail in the various volumes of Jane's listed earlier. In addition, see Tamir Eshel, "Israel's Defense Electronic Focus: Smart and Small," *Defense Electronics*, October, 1991, pp. 87–89.

79. Dick Palowski, *Changes in Threat Air Combat Doctrine and Force Structure*, 24th Edition, Fort Worth, General Dynamics DWIC-91, February, 1992, pp. II–199 to II-227.

80. The defecting pilot was on maneuver near the Golan and suddenly turned towards Israel and flew very low and fast over the Golan and central Galilee. He landed in a remote civil strip near Megido. This led to a great deal of media comment in Israel, but such incidents are almost unavoidable. Although he flew for seven minutes without being intercepted, he flew at a time when IAF E-2Cs were not in the air and nearby aircraft were scrambled, when the IAF was in a state of low alert and flew without using any radar or communications emis-sions. He also stated later that did receive warning he was being tracked by Israeli radar. Israel later used the MiG-23ML (G) for training and test and evaluation purposes. *Washington Post*, October 13, 1989, p. A-35; October 14, 1989, p. A-18; *New York Times*, October 12, 1989, p. A-10; October 14, 1989, p. A-2; *Philadelphia Inquirer*, October 12, 1989, p. 18A; October 13, 1989, p. 17A; *Washington Times*, October 12, 1989, p. A-8; *Jane's Defence Weekly*, February 10, 1990, p. 221.

81. Kenneth S. Brower, "The Middle East Military Balance: Israel Versus the Rest," *International Defense Review*, 7/1986, pp. 910–911.

82. Samuel M. Katz, "Israeli Airpower on the Rise," *Air Force*, November, 1991, pp. 44–51.

83. *Armed Forces Journal*, October, 1991, p. 30.

84. This number may be low. If all civilian personnel performing military functions in the time of war were included, it might be 35,000–40,000.

85. Israel had taken delivery on a total of 36 F-15As, 4 F-15Bs, 18 F-15Cs, and 10 F-15Ds as of May 15, 1992. Ten were received as drawdowns from U.S. stocks (Section 599 B0 PL 101-513), and 15 were ordered at a cost of $67.3 million (FAA, September 11, 1991). See Richard F. Grimmett and Alfred B. Prados, "Near East Arms Transfers, August 2, 1990–November 1, 1991," Congressional Research Service 91-839, December 2, 1991, and DSAA computer print out dated 05/15/92: 16:16.

86. Israel had taken delivery on 67 F-16As, 8 F-16Bs, 51 F-16Cs, and 24 F-16Ds as of May 15, 1992, with an additional 21 of the 60 new F-16C/Ds in Israel and awaiting formal acceptance. Unit numbers are IISS. Aircraft numbers for the F-15 and F-16 are taken from a DSAA computer print out dated 05/15/92: 16:16. The other numbers are Israeli. The IISS reports 13 additional F-4Es and 75 Kfirs are in storage.

87. Reports on IAF holdings of the Skyhawk are contradictory and very uncertain.

88. These distinctions between combat and trainer aircraft are difficult to make in the Israeli forces, and the numbers are unusually uncertain.

89. Tamir Eshel, "Israel's Defense Electronics," *Defense Electronics*, October, 1991, pp. 87–90.

90. *Jane's Defence Weekly*, February 2, 1990, pp. 200–203.

91. *Jane's Defence Weekly*, November 19, 1988, p. 1261.

92. *International Defense Review*, 3/1992, p. 261; Dick Palowski, *Changes in Threat Air Combat Doctrine and Force Structure*, 24th Edition, Fort Worth, General Dynamics DWIC-91, February, 1992, p. II-216.

93. *Aviation Week*, June 26, 1989, p. 30.

94. Tamir Eshel, "Israel's Defense Electronics," *Defense Electronics*, October, 1991, pp. 87–90; *Aviation Week*, June 26, 1989, p. 30.

95. *Aviation Week*, March 9, 1992, p. 65.

96. Dick Palowski, *Changes in Threat Air Combat Doctrine and Force Structure*, 24th Edition, Fort Worth, General Dynamics DWIC-91, February , 1992, p. II-218. Five of these kills are debated.

97. Dick Palowski, *Changes in Threat Air Combat Doctrine and Force Structure*, 24th Edition, Fort Worth, General Dynamics DWIC-91, February , 1992, p. II-225.

98. *Defense News*, August 26, 1991, p. 34; *Jane's Defence Weekly*, May 30, 1992, pp. 946–947; *JINSA, Security Affairs*, May 1992, p. 3; *Armed Forces Journal*, June 1992, p. 19.

99. Dick Palowski, *Changes in Threat Air Combat Doctrine and Force Structure*, 24th Edition, Fort Worth, General Dynamics DWIC-91, February , 1992, p. II-212.

100. The F-4Es were originally delivered with AN/APR-36/37 or AN/ALR-46V radar homing and warning systems, and AN/ALE-40V chaff/flare dispensers. *Jane's Defence Weekly*, February 2, 1990, pp. 200–203.

101. Israel has made structural improvements in 140 of its Phantoms and improved the avionics and the radar at a cost of $5 million per aircraft. It had planned to up-engine all its F-4s with Pratt and Whitney PW-1120 engines but could not afford the cost of $10 million each. IAI brochure dated 1991; *Jane's Defence Weekly*, August 8, 1987, p. 21; June 22, 1991, p. 1083.

102. Based on Jane's reference handbooks and IAI brochures and *Jane's Defence Weekly*, February 2, 1990, pp. 200–203.

103. *Jane's Defence Weekly*, February 2, 1990, pp. 200–203.

104. *Jane's Defence Weekly*, October 3, 1987, p. 725.

105. *Jane's Defence Weekly*, November 28, 1987, p. 1239; Rafael briefing sheet, manufacturer offprint of "Rafael: Lessons of Combat" from *Military Technology*, May, 1991.

106. Tamir Eshel, "Israel's Defense Electronics," *Defense Electronics*, October, 1991, pp. 87–90.

107. Dick Palowski, *Changes in Threat Air Combat Doctrine and Force Structure*, 24th Edition, Fort Worth, General Dynamics DWIC-91, February, 1992, pp. II-199 to II-211.

108. *Jane's Defence Weekly*, February 2, 1990, pp. 200–203.

109. *Jane's Defence Weekly*, February 2, 1990, pp. 200–203; *Air Force*, November, 1991, p. 50; *Jane's Defence Weekly*, June 24, 1989, p. 1324.

110. These aircraft type counts are based on IISS data, and the number and designation of the EV-1Es, IAI 201s, RC-12Ds, RC-21Ds, and RU-21As is uncertain.

111 *Defense Electronics*, April 10, 1992, p. 14; IAI Elta Brochure; *Air Force*, November, 1991, p. 50; JINSA, *Security Affairs*, March, 1992, p. 3.

112. *Jane's Defence Weekly*, October 15, 1988, p. 959.

113. *International Defense Review*, 9/1987, p. 1204.

114. *Defense News*, April 4, 1988, p. 1; *International Defense Review*, 9/1989, pp. 1237–1238.

115. *International Defense Review*, 9/1989, pp. 1237–1238.

116. The Harpee and Star-1 may be different systems. *Defense News*, April 4, 1988, p. 1; May 11, 1992, p. 1.

117. *Defense News*, November 28, 1988, p. 17; Israeli Military Industries (IMI) manufacturer brochures.

118. "Israel's Combat Helicopter," *Defense Update*, No. 67, pp. 8–40; Tamir Eshel, "Israel's Defense Electronics," *Defense Electronics*, October, 1991, pp. 87–90.

119. The order included 14 spare Hellfire launchers, 16 spare T-700 GE engines, spare and repair parts, support equipment, tools, ammunition, integrated helmet and display systems and other spares. *Jane's Defence Weekly*, April 14, 1990, p. 691; *International Defense Review*, 3/1992, p. 262; *Wall Street Journal*, April 13, 1990, p. A-3; Tim Ripley, "Israel's Cutting Edge," *Defense Helicopter*, July-September, 1992, pp. 30–33.

120. Tamir Eshel, "Israel's Defense Electronics," *Defense Electronics*, October, 1991, pp. 87–90; Tim Ripley, "Israel's Cutting Edge," *Defense Helicopter*, July-September, 1992, pp. 30–33.

121. *Flight International*, March 14-20, 1990, pp. 31–33.

122. *Flight International*, March 6, 1990, p. 11.

123. Statement by Maj. Gen. Jay M. Garner to the Subcommittee on Legislative and National Security, Committee on Government Operations, House of Representatives, April 7, 1992.

124. These comments are based on U.S. Army and IDF briefings, and on discussions with Israeli experts appraising the Patriot's performance in Israel. The author does not believe the debate over the issue in the U.S. and Israeli press has technical merit.

125. *International Defense Intelligence*, Vol. 8, No. 28, July 14, 1986, p. 1, and *Jane's Defence Weekly*, 21 June, 1986, p. 1165; *Aviation Week*, December 2, 1991, p. 19; *Defense News*, May 13, 1991, p. 46; November 25, 1991, p. 2; December 2, 1991, p. 10.

126. Israel has sought to buy one assembled European design like the IKL 209/2000, with kits for follow-on submarines to be assembled in Israel. It has sought to obtain U.S. aid by having a U.S. contractor take the responsibility for prime contractor and then subcontracting to Israeli and European yards. The logical U.S. contractors—Bath, Ingalls, and Todd—have been reluctant to take the risk for cost escalation in deal with such a low profit margin and where they have so little real control. *Proceedings*, March, 1987, p. 53; and *Jane's Defence Weekly*, April 30, 1988, and May 14, 1988, p. 933.

127. *Defense News*, March 27, 1989, pp. 3 and 42.

128. *Jane's Defence Weekly*, June 17, 1989, p. 1209, and August 5, 1989, p. 189.

129. *Defense News*, March 27, 1989, pp. 3 and 42.

130. *International Defense Review*, 3/1990, p. 286.

131. *Jane's Defence Weekly*, April 30, 1988, and May 14, 1988, p. 933.

132. *Jane's Defence Weekly*, July 1, 1989, p. 1372.

133. For very different interpretations of the history of Israel's development of weapons of mass destruction, see Anthony H. Cordesman, *Weapons of Mass Destruction in the Middle East*, London, RUSI/Brassey's, 1991, and Seymour M. Hersh, *The Samson Option*, New York, Random House, 1991. The figures used on Israeli nuclear weapons and missile strength in this section are based on the much more conservative interpretation of Israeli strength made by the author. Hersh estimates that there are at least 300 Israeli nuclear weapons, including more than 100 nuclear artillery shells and land mines in the Golan Heights.

134. *Sunday Times*, October 5, 1986, pp. 1–3, and October 12, 1986, pp. 1 and 12; Barnaby, *The Invisible Bomb*, London, I.B. Taurus, 1989, pp. 25 and 31; *Science*, March 22, 1974, p. 15; *Washington Times*, October 6, 1986; *Boston Globe*, October 14, 1986; *New York Times*, October 27, 1986; *Washington Post*, October 31, 1986. Recent BBC and ITV reporting efforts seem to give more credibility to the idea that Israel has some form of relatively short range nuclear armed missile. Ranges of anywhere from 75 to 930 NM have been reported, with accuracy of anywhere from 1.0 km to radar correlator guidance packages capable of CEPs of 100 meters.

135. James Adams, *Engines of War*, New York, Atlantic Monthly Press, 1990, pp. 155–195.

136. *Washington Times*, November 3, 1989, p. A-6.

137. Israel acquired Meiko Scientific Supercomputers in December, 1992. These are sometimes associated with thermonuclear weapons and missile trajectory analysis. While such systems might be an aid to creating such weapons, Israel's existing mini-computers have long been adequate. There is also little incentive to use thermonuclear weapons with accurate IRBMs or in bombs because they consume added material and are more complex, and boosted weapons are adequate to destroy virtually any regional target. *New York Times*, January 9, 1992, p. D-1.

138. Based on work by Leonard Spector; *Sunday Times*, October 5, 1986, pp. 1–3, and October 12, 1986, pp. 1 and 12; *Washington Times*, October 6, 1986; *Boston Globe*, October 14, 1986; *New York Times*, October 27, 1986; and *Washington Post*, October 31, 1986.

139. Israel eventually returned some unused krytrons and claimed they were being used for research on other weapons. An American named Richard K. Smyth has been indicted for the smuggling but is living in Israel. *Washington Post*, May 14, 15, and 17, 1985;*New York Times*, May 17, 1985.

140. There are debates over whether Israel ran into production problems in the 1970s and had to go to surge production during 1977 to 1985. Based on work by Leonard Spector;

Sunday Times, October 5, 1986, pp. 1–3, and October 12, 1986, pp. 1 and 12; *Washington Times*, October 6, 1986; *Boston Globe*, October 14, 1986; *New York Times*, October 27, 1986; and *Washington Post*, October 31, 1986.

141. Warren H. Donnelly, *Israel and Nuclear Weapons*, Washington, Congressional Research Service, IB7079, May 30, 1990, p. 3; *Washington Post*, October 26, 27, 28, and 29, 1989; *New York Times*, October 27, 1989.

142. Enhanced radiation or neutron weapons maximize radiation at the expense of blast and do less physical damage, although they still produce large amounts of blast and thermal technology. Enhanced yield weapons boost a nuclear explosion to yields in excess of 100 kt and largely eliminate the need for thermonuclear weapons with highly accurate systems. Thermonuclear weapons allow explosions in excess of 25 megatons.

143. Anthony H. Cordesman and Abraham R. Wagner, *The Lessons of Modern War*, Volume 1, Boulder, Westview, 1990, pp. 244–246; *Jane's Defence Weekly*, August 8, 1987, p. 21.

144. For recent reporting on the Israeli nuclear effort, see the *Sunday Times*, October 5, 1986; *Washington Times*, October 6, 1986; *Boston Globe*, October 14, 1986; *New York Times*, October 27, 1986; and *Washington Post*, October 31, 1986.

145. Other reports indicate that the Jericho surface-to-surface missile had a range of up to 300 miles and a 1,000–1,500 pound warhead. Other reports indicate that it could reach a 400 mile range with 226 pound (100 kilogram) nuclear warhead. *Aerospace Daily*, May 1 and 7, 1985; Shuey, et al., *Missile Proliferation: Survey of Emerging Missile Forces*, p. 56; *International Defense Review*, July, 1987, p. 857; *Defense and Foreign Affairs Daily*, May 9, 1985, pp. 1–2; CIA, "Prospects for Further Proliferation of Nuclear Weapons," DCI NIO 1945/74, September 4, 1974; NBC Nightly News, July 30, 1985; *New York Times*, April 1, 1986; U.S. Arms Control and Disarmament Agency, *World Military Expenditures and Arms Transfers*, Washington, GPO, 1989, p. 18; *Jane's Defence Weekly*, November 25, 1989, p. 1143.

146. *International Defense Review*, 7/1987, p. 857; *Economist*, May 4, 1968, pp. 67–68; *New York Times*, July 22, 1987, p. A-6; *Washington Times*, July 22, 1987, p. D-4; *Defense and Foreign Affairs*, June, 1985, p. 1; *Aerospace Daily*, May 1, 1985, p. 5, and May 17, 1985, p. 100; *Aerospace Daily*, May 1 and 7, 1985; Shuey, et al., *Missile Proliferation: Survey of Emerging Missile Forces*, p. 56; CIA, "Prospects for Further Proliferation of Nuclear Weapons, " DCI NIO 1945/74, September 4, 1974; NBC Nightly News, July 30, 1985; *New York Times*, April 1, 1986; U.S. Arms Control and Disarmament Agency, *World Military Expenditures and Arms Transfers*, Washington, GPO, 1989, p. 18; Michael A. Ottenberg, "Israel and the Atom," *Americal Sentinel*, August 16, 1992, p. 1.

147. *Jane's Defence Weekly*, June 10, 1989, p. 1135.

148. Tass International, 1216 GMT, September 15, 1989; *Washington Post*, September 16, 1989; *Jane's Defence Weekly*, November 19, 1988; September 23, 1989, p. 549; *Washington Times*, July 22, 1987, p. D-4; *International Defense Review*, 7/1987, p. 857; *New York Times*, July 22, 1987, p. A-6; July 29, 1987; *Mideast Markets*, November 23, 1987, p. 11.

149. *Baltimore Sun*, November 23, 1988; *Washington Post*, September 16, 1989.

150. *Bulletin of the Atomic Scientists*, Vol. 46, Jan/Feb 1990, p. 48; *Washington Post*, September 16, 1989, p. A-17; November 15, 1989, p. A-14; *Economist*, August 1, 1987, p. 41; *Washington Times*, July 22, 1987, p. D-4; July 24, 1987, p. A-9; April 4, 1988, p. 17; *International Defense Review*, 7/1987, p. 857; *New York Times*, July 29, 1987, p. A-10. Data published by Iran after the seizure of the U.S. embassy in Tehran claimed to have found evidence that Israel was giving Iran missile technology in return for oil, and had tested new guidance systems in flights in Iran.

151. *Washington Post*, October 26, 1989, p. A-36; *Boston Globe*, October 30, 1989, p. 2; *Newsweek*, November 6, 1989, p. 52.

152. *Jane's Defence Weekly*, July 15, 1989, p. 59, and December 23, 1989, p. 1385; Johannesburg Domestic Service, 1600 GMT, July 5, 1989; *Boston Globe*, October 27, 1989; Fred Francis, NBC Nightly News, October 25 and 26, 1989; *New York Times*, October 27, 1989, p. A-1; November 15, 1989; *Newsweek*, November 6, 1989, p. 52; *Washington Times*,

June 20, 1989, p. A-1; *Washington Post*, October 27, 1989, p. A-1; October 29, 1989; Michael A. Ottenberg, "Israel and the Atom," *Americal Sentinel*, August 16, 1992, p. 1.

153. This information is unconfirmed and based on only one source. Israel does, however, have excellent research facilities; laboratory production of poison gas is essential to test protection devices as is the production of biological weapons to test countermeasures and antidotes.

154. *Washington Post*, September 20, 1988; *Financial Times*, October 18, 1988.

155. Work by Leonard Spector; *Haaretz*, October 11, 1989, p. 2; Steven E. Gery, "Israeli Missile Capabilities," Lawrence Livermore Laboratories, Z Division, October 7, 1988.

156. It is doubtful that these satellites had any significant reconnaissance capability. Some limited photo capability is possible, but it is doubtful that in early launches the systems would have more resolution than commercial earth satellites. *Jane's Defence Weekly*, April 14, 1990, p. 678; *Christian Science Monitor*, May 15, 1990, p. 13; *Daily Telegraph*, September 7, 1989, p. 14.

157. *Jerusalem Post*, February 8, 1992, p. 24; Tel Aviv IDF Radio in Hebrew, April 13, 1992, 1000 GMT.

158. See Stephen Broening, "Israel Could Build Missiles to Hit Soviets," *Baltimore Sun*, November 23, 1988, p. 1.

159. *Washington Times*, November 4, 1988, p. A-11; *Defense Electronics*, March, 1992, p. 13; *Jane's Defence Weekly*, July 4, 1992, p. 5; *Defense News*, June 1, 1992, p. 3; August 31, 1992, p. 1.

160. This discussion of the Golan is based on both Israel and Syrian background papers. For a good outside summary of the issue see Michael Collins Dunn, "The Golan Heights: A Two Edged Sword," *The Estimate*, August 29, 1991, pp. 8–11. Population data are taken from CIA, *World Factbook, 1991*, and *Washington Post*, November 5, 1991, p. A-14.

161. Interviews in Israel in 1992. The description of these defenses has been public since 1988. See *Jane's Defence Weekly*, March 12, 1988; May 14, 1988, p. 933; June 18, 1988, p. 1236.

162. Israeli Ministry of Foreign Affairs cable, March 25, 1992.

163. The IDF sent at least 36 tanks and helicopter gunships into Lebanon to seize the villages of Kafra and Yater in an attempt to reduce Hizbollah influence. *Washington Post*, February 21, 1992, p. A-1; *New York Times*, February 21, 1992, p. A-1.

164. See Dupuy, *Flawed Victory*, for an analysis of Israeli casualties. Also see Ze'ev Schiff, "The Israeli Defense Forces After Lebanon: Crisis, Change, and Uncertainty," *Middle East Insight*, Volume 4, Number 3, 1985, pp. 15–23, and William Claiborne, "Israel Studies Lessons of Lebanon War: Some See Soldier's Will to Fight Dulled," *Washington Post*, March 31, 1986, p. A-1.

165. Clyde R. Mark, "Palestine and the Palestinians," Congressional Research Service IB76048, January 15, 1992, pp. 8–9.

166. Much of the analysis of the development of the *intifada* in this section benefits from the research of Esther D. Santo, a student at Georgetown University's National Security Studies Program. Also see Ze'ev Schiff and Ehud Ya'ari, *Intifada*, New York, Simon and Schuster, 1989; Daniel Thomas, "Understanding the Palestinian Problem," *Military Intelligence*, July-September, 1991, pp. 13–16; Rex Brynen, *Echoes of the Intifada*, Boulder, Westview, 1991.

167. *Washington Post*, February 28, 1988, p. A-29, and March 7, 1988, p. A-23.

168. *Jane's Defence Weekly*, January 15, 1988, p. 80.

169. *Jane's Defence Weekly*, June 25, 1988, p. 1273.

170. Clyde R. Mark, "Palestine and the Palestinians," Congressional Research Service IB76048, January 15, 1992.

171. Ariel Levite, "New IDF Plan Prompted by Riots," *Armed Forces Journal*, February, 1988, p. 34.

172. For typical news reporting, see *Washington Post*, February 3, 1992, p. A-13; *Christian Science Monitor*, April 15, 1992, p. 1; May 26, 1992, p. 4; *New York Times*, February 2, 1992, p. A-4; *Washington Post*, May 7, 1992, p. A-37; *Chicago Tribune*, May 5, 1992, p. I-1 .

173. Israeli Ministry of Foreign Affairs cable, March 25, 1992.

174. Israeli embassy data sheet, March 17, 1992.

175. Clyde R. Mark, "Palestine and the Palestinians," Congressional Research Service IB76048, January 15, 1992, p. 9; *Davar*, December 6, 1991.

176. Israeli embassy data sheet, March 17, 1992.

177. Israeli Ministry of Foreign Affairs cable, March 25, 1992.

178. Israeli embassy data sheet, March 17, 1992; Israeli Ministry of Foreign Affairs cable, March 25, 1992.

179. Israeli embassy data sheet, March 17, 1992; Israeli Ministry of Foreign Affairs cable, March 25, 1992.

180. Israel has reported that the additional costs to the IDF of dealing with the uprising on the West Bank reached $237 million between December 1987 and June 1988. It could get only a $156 million supplement to the defense budget. The IDF stated, however, that it had saved $60 million because reserve forces had to cancel their training for duty in dealing with the uprising. *Jane's Defence Weekly*, June 25, 1988, p. 1273. Costs dropped sharply after 1988, as new security methods were introduced, but current costs are not available.

181. This section draws heavily on the excellent summaries of individual conflicts provided by Herbert K. Tillema in *International Conflict Since 1945*, Boulder, Westview, 1991; work in various annual editions of John Laffin's *The World in Conflict* or *War Annual*, London, Brassey's; and by John Keegan, *World Armies*, London, Macmillan, 1983; and joint work with Abraham Wagner in *The Lessons of Modern War*, Volume 1, Boulder, Westview, 1990. For the sake of consistency, the chronology normally uses the dates in Tillema's work. The reader should be aware that many dates vary according to source or are controversial.

182. *London Financial Times*, March 9, 1992, p. 1; *Washington Post*, August 19, 1991, p. A-11; *New York Times*, February 21, 1992, p. A-9; *Washington Times*, March 11, 1992, p. A-3; *Wall Street Journal*, July 10, 1991, p. 12.

183. Judith Miller, "Syria's Game," *New York Times Magazine*, January 26, 1992, pp. 13–17.

184. *New York Times*, November 10, 1991, p. A-15; *Washington Post*, January 26, 1992, p. C-2.

185. *Washington Post*, January 24, 1992, p. A-17.

186. *OJJ Special, Oil and Gas Journal*, December 30, 1991, pp. 43–49.

187. *Los Angeles Times*, January 28, 1992, p. C-1.

188. CIA, *World Factbook, 1991*, p. 303; *Washington Post*, August 16, 1992, pp. A-29–A-30.

189. Judith Miller, "Syria's Game," *New York Times Magazine*, January 26, 1990, pp. 13–17.

190. ACDA, *World Military Expenditures and Arms Transfers, 1990*, Washington, GPO, 1990, Table I.

191. ACDA, *World Military Expenditures and Arms Transfers, 1989*, Washington, GPO, 1990, p. 67.

192. IISS, *Military Balance, 1987–1988*, p. 113; *1989–1990*, p. 114, *1991–1992*, p. 120.

193. *Los Angeles Times*, May 26, 1986, p. I-8. Also see "A Man with Ambitions Too Big for His Country," *Economist*, May 3, 1986, pp. 37–38; and "Syrian Trade: Going West," *Economist*, June 7, 1986, pp. 84–85, for a good summary description of Assad's economic problems.

194. U.S. Arms Control and Disarmament Agency, *World Military Expenditures and Arms Transfers, 1989*, Washington, GPO, 1989, pp. 117–188; and U.S. Arms Control and Disarmament Agency, *World Military Expenditures and Arms Transfers, 1969–1978*, Washington, GPO, 1989, pp. 160–161.

195. ACDA, *World Military Expenditures and Arms Transfers, 1990*, Washington, GPO, 1990, Table II.

196. Central Intelligence Agency, *Handbook of Economic Statistics*, 1988, Washington, CIA CPAS 88-10001, September, 1988, p. 187, and ACDA, *World Military Expenditures and Arms Transfers, 1985*, Washington, GPO, 1986, p. 134.

197. *Washington Times*, July 15, 1988, p. A-8.

198. ACDA, *World Military Expenditures and Arms Transfers, 1989,* Washington, GPO, 1990, p. 118.

199. *Jane's Defence Weekly,* April 30, 1988.

200. *Washington Times,* July 15, 1988, p. A-8.

201. *RUSI Newsbrief,* February, 1986, pp. 3–4.

202. CIA, *Handbook of Economic Statistics, 1987,* Washington, GPO, CPAS 87-10001, 1987, p. 117.

203. CIA, *Handbook of Economic Statistics, 1987,* Washington, GPO, CPAS 87-10001, 1987, pp. 117–118.

204. Adapted from various issues of the IISS, *Military Balance,* and work by the Foreign Affairs Division of the Congressional Research Service in *Middle East Arms Control and Related Issues,* CRS 91-384F, May 1, 1992, and for Senator John McCain. Robert Shuey, Richard F. Grimmett, Theodor Galdi, Steven Hildreth, Todd Masses, Alfred Prados, and Shirley Kahn were the principal authors of the CRS work.

205. Any accurate breakout is very difficult to come by. Saudi Arabia probably delivered substantially less than $2 billion. Japan, Germany, and the UAE promised or delivered about $500 million each. Reports on Kuwaiti aid differ sharply, ranging from less than $250 million to over $500 million.

206. These figures are based on working papers by Richard F. Grimmett of the Congressional Research Service. ACDA published somewhat different estimates in 1992. According to this reporting, Syria imported a total of $7,160 million worth of arms during 1985–1989, with a total of $6,100 million from the Soviet Union, $20 million from France, $10 million from the PRC, $975 million from other Warsaw Pact countries, $30 million from other European countries, $20 million from other Middle Eastern countries, and $5 million from other East Asian states. ACDA, *World Military Expenditures and Arms Transfers, 1990,* Washington, GPO, 1990, Table II.

207. Reports of $2.5 billion in new orders seem to be exaggerated. Syria may have considered such purchases when it thought it would receive some $5 billion to $6 billion in aid for a much longer war and set of Syrian deployments in the Gulf than actually took place, but it only received about $2.5 billion to $3 billion in total aid, and some was for purposes other than arms transfers. The items shown are based on interviews in the U.S. and Israel and work for Senator McCain by Richard F. Grimmett and Al Prados of the Congressional Research Service in a letter dated November 18, 1991, and *Washington Post,* January 31, 1991, p. A-13; *Jane's Defence Weekly,* March 7, 1992, p. 377; October 26, 1991, p. 748; *Defense News,* July 8, 1991, p. 3; *Seattle Times,* May 12, 1990, p. 14; *London Sunday Times,* May 5, 1991, p. 14; *Washington Times,* February 29, 1992, p. A-6.

208. British Broadcasting Corporation, summary of world broadcasts, January 4, 1992.

209. The military manpower, force strength, and equipment estimates in this section are made by the author using a wide range of sources, including computerized data bases, interviews, and press clipping services. Most are impossible to reference in ways of use to the reader. The force strength statistics are generally adapted from the latest edition of the International Institute for Strategic Studies, *Military Balance* (IISS, London), in this case the 1991–1992 edition. Extensive use has also been made of the annual editions of the Jaffee Center for Strategic Studies, *The Military Balance in the Middle East* (JCSS, Tel Aviv), especially the 1990–1991 edition and working materials from the coming edition. Material has also been drawn from computer print outs from NEXIS, the United States Naval Institute data base, and from the DMS/FI Market Intelligence Reports data base. Other sources include the *Military Technology* "World Defense Almanac for 1991–1992," published in 1992; Foreign Affairs Division, "Middle East Arms Control and Related Issues," Washington, Congressional Research Service, 91-384F, May 1, 1991; and *Middle East Economic Digest,* "MEED Special Report: Defense," Volume 35, December 13, 1991.

Weapons data are taken from many sources, including computerized material available in NEXIS, and various editions of *Jane's Fighting Ships* (Jane's Publishing); *Jane's Naval*

Weapons Systems (Jane's Publishing); *Jane's Armour and Artillery* (Jane's Publishing); *Jane's Infantry Weapons* (Jane's Publishing); *Jane's Military Vehicles and Logistics* (Jane's Publishing); *Jane's Land-Based Air Defence* (Jane's Publishing); *Jane's All the World's Aircraft* (Jane's Publishing); *Jane's Battlefield Surveillance Systems* (Jane's Publishing); *Jane's Radar and Electronic Warfare Systems* (Jane's Publishing), *Jane's C³I Systems* (Jane's Publishing); *Jane's Air-Launched Weapons Systems* (Jane's Publishing); *Jane's Defence Appointments & Procurement Handbook (Middle East Edition)* (Jane's Publishing); *Tanks of the World* (Bernard and Grafe); *Weyer's Warships* (Bernard and Grafe); and *Warplanes of the World* (Bernard and Grafe).

Other military background, effectiveness, strength, organizational, and history data are taken from Martin Streetly, "Middle Eastern Airborne Electronic Warfare," *Jane's Defence Weekly*, February 3, 1990, pp. 199–203; Richard F. Grimmett and Alfred B. Prados, "Near East Arms Transfers, August 2, 1990–November 1, 1991," Congressional Research Service 91-839F, December 2, 1991; Anthony H. Cordesman, *Jordanian Arms and the Middle East Balance*, Washington, The Middle East Institute, 1983, *The Gulf and the Search for Strategic Stability*, Boulder, Westview, 1984, *The Gulf and the West*, Boulder, Westview, 1988, and *Weapons of Mass Destruction in the Middle East*, London, Brassey's/RUSI, 1991; Anthony H. Cordesman and Abraham Wagner, *The Lessons of Modern War*, Volume 1, Boulder, Westview, 1990.

210. CIA, *The World Factbook, 1991*, pp. 302–303.

211. CIA, *The World Factbook, 1987*, pp. 236–238, and CIA, *The World Factbook, 1991*, pp. 302–303.

212. IISS, *Military Balance, 1991–1992*, p. 120.

213. These estimates are based on the IISS, *Military Balance*.

214. Some of these estimates of force shifts are highly uncertain and draw heavily on Israeli sources.

215. The normal Syrian tank battalion has 31 tanks, 10 per company in platoons of 3 plus a command tank at the battalion HQ, which also has 2–3 BMP-PUs or BTR-50s. The tank battalions attached to mechanized infantry units have 40–44 tanks with three tank platoons per company. A T-72 tank battalion has 141 men and a T-55/62 battalion has 160. Soviet advisors supervise training and maintenance at the battalion level. Nevertheless, Syrian technical support remains very limited at the battalion level, and repairs are conducted at base deports at El Kisweh, Al Kuteifa, and Qatanah. There is a serious shortage of skilled Syrian technicians and maintenance personnel, and Cuban technicians have been attached to maintenance depots in the past. Syria has continued to abandon armored vehicles for service reasons that IDF units could rapidly repair in the field.

216. *New York Times*, June 6, 1986, p. 11; *Washington Post*, June 11, 1986, p. 36; and *Defense Week*, April 14, 1986, p. 5.

217. Israeli reports of improved training in 1988 differ sharply from the information of British, French, and U.S. sources.

218. While press reports of up to 30 units appeared in 1982, the Syrian order of battle seems to have had only ten airborne and special forces units.

219. Experts disagree over whether these are regular divisional formations or groups of elite units.

220. Reuter library report, August 6, 1991.

221. Israeli briefing on the Golan, January, 1992.

222. Reuter library report, September 1, 1991.

223. The following comparisons are based on the 1981–1982 and 1991–1992 editions of IISS, *Military Balance*. Estimates differ sharply in other sources. Around 900 Syrian tanks are in storage, used as reserves, or used as static defenses. Some estimates of this portion of Syria's tank force go as high as 1,200 tanks.

224. One U.S. source feels it is possible that republican guard forces may have had such upgrading. Other sources include work for Senator McCain by Richard F. Grimmett and Al Prados of the Congressional Research Service in a letter dated November 18, 1991, and

Washington Post, January 31, 1991, p. A-13; *Jane's Defence Weekly,* March 7, 1992, p. 377; October 26, 1991, p. 748; *Defense News,* July 8, 1991, p. 3; *Seattle Times,* May 12, 1990, p. 14; *London Sunday Times,* May 5, 1991, p. 14; *Washington Times,* February 29, 1992, p. A-6.

225. The AT-6 is not believed to be deployed in Syrian forces.

226. This count is based largely on the IISS, with some adaptations to reflect Israeli sources.

227. Additional sources include *Flight International,* computer data print out, November 27, 1991.

228. Maj. Gen. Avihu Ben Nun, commander of the Israeli Air Force, claimed in 1988 that Syria was spending 75% of its total defense budget on its air force and air defenses in an effort to reach strategic parity with Israel. This is highly doubtful, but this is a very high priority area of investment. *Jane's Defence Weekly,* July 30, 1988, p. 161.

229. Some estimates indicate there are over 200 MiG-21s. The use of Su-20, Su-22, Su-24, and MiG-23 type designations has been adjusted to use the types listed by Dick Palowski in *Changes in Threat Air Combat Doctrine and Force Structure,* 24th Edition, Fort Worth, General Dynamics DWIC-91, February, 1992, pp. I-30 to I-46.

230. Based on IISS and Israeli sources. Significant numbers of older Syrian combat aircraft are in storage, including up to 39 MiG-17s and 15 Su-7s.

231. Israel easily shot down two of these MiG-23s on November 19, 1985. *New York Times,* November 20, 1985, p. A-1.

232. These aircraft began to be delivered in 1987. They were originally scheduled to begin delivery in 1986, but the delivery was delayed when the Soviets insisted on prior payment. Delivery of all 24 aircraft was complete in late 1988.

233. Brigitte Sauerwein, "MiG-29 at Farnborough," *International Defense Review,* 10/1988, p. 1243.

234. There have been reports that Syria is seeking a major further upgrade of its air defense system from Russia, costing up to $1.4 billion, but these reports do not seem correct. Tony Banks, "Syria Upgrades Forces Facing Golan Heights," *Jane's Defence Weekly,* April 12, 1986, pp. 660–661; Joseph S. Bermudez, "The Syrian Missile Threat," *Marine Corps Gazette,* January, 1985, pp. 54–62; *Defense Week,* April 14, 1986, p. 5; *Washington Post,* June 11, 1985, p. 36; Department of Defense, *Soviet Military Power, 1986,* Washington, GPO, 1986, pp. 133–134; CIA, *Handbook of Economic Statistics, 1985,* Washington, GPO, CPAS-85-10001, September, 1985, pp. 118–124; and Mark Urban, "Fire in the Galilee," Parts Two and Three, *Armed Forces,* April and May, 1986.

235. Israel first shot down a Syrian RPV on June 13, 1986. *Washington Post,* May 30, 1986, p. 9; and *Jane's Defence Weekly,* August 10, 1986, pp. 260–261.

236. IISS, *Military Balance, 1987–1988;* and "Israel's Combat Helicopters," *Defense Update,* No. 67, pp. 11 and 37.

237. Based on interviews. Light armament includes optional machine guns and rocket pods without advanced fire control systems or other heavy weapons.

238. These estimates are based on Jane's, IISS, and Jordanian and Israeli sources and involve launcher counts based on extrapolation by the author.

239. *Jane's Defence Weekly,* October 12, 1985, pp. 793–794.

240. *Jane's Defence Weekly,* June 29, 1986, p. 1240.

241. See Mark Urban, "Fire in the Galilee," Parts Two and Three, *Armed Forces,* April and May, 1986.

242. *Jane's Defence Weekly,* June 29, 1986, p. 827.

243. *Proceedings,* March 1987, p. 54.

244. It is interesting to note, however, that these facilities were upgraded under the direction of Admiral Sidorov, who supervised the expansion of the Soviet facility at Cam Rahn Bay. Admiral of the Fleet V. N. Chernavin, and his deputy, Admiral Grishin, both visited the base in 1987, and the facilities now seem capable of arming and supporting relatively large ships.

245. *Jane's Defence Weekly*, May 21, 1988; *New York Times*, August 28, 1988, p. A-1.

246. *Washington Times*, September 25, 1988, p. 1A.

247. See Joseph S. Bermudez, "Syrian Command Structure," *Jane's Defence Weekly*, October 25, 1986, pp. 972–976.

248. The analysis in this section is based largely on various interviews. Also see *Jane's Defence Weekly*, July 26, 1986, p. 92; April 2, 1988, p. 613; April 30, 1988, p. 853; *Washington Post*, June 23, 1988, p. 33; September 7, 1988, p. A-25; *Los Angeles Times*, July 14, 1988, p. I-1; *Washington Times*, September 18, 1987, p. 2; *New York Times*, June 22, 1988, p. A-6.

249. Agence France Presse, computer print out, February 10, 1992; *Christian Science Monitor*, March 10, 1992, p. 1; *Washington Post*, December 7, 1991, p. A-26; February 11, 1992, p. A-16; *Daily Telegraph*, November 23, 1991, p. 10; *London Financial Times*, March 27, 1992, p. 4; *Washington Times*, November 24, 1991, p. A-17.

250. J. M. Moreaux, "The Syrian Army," *Defense Update*, No. 69, p. 31.

251. The analysis in this section is based largely on various interviews. Also see *Jane's Defence Weekly*, July 26, 1986, p. 92; April 2, 1988, p. 613; April 30, 1988, p. 853; *Washington Post*, June 23, 1988, p. 33; September 7, 1988, p. A-25; *Los Angeles Times*, July 14, 1988, p. I-1; *Washington Times*, September 18, 1987, p. 2; *New York Times*, June 22, 1988, p. A-6.

252. *London Sunday Times*, January 10, 1988, p. 1; *Washington Times*, April 8, 1988, p. 9; January 11, 1988, p. 1; *Los Angeles Times*, January 14, 1988, p. 13.

253. Syrian units deploy as close as 10 kilometers from the front line versus 20–25 kilometers for Soviet units.

254. The FROG with a VX chemical warhead carried much less agent. The Soviet version is 540 mm in diameter, and weighs about 960 pounds, of which 475 is VX agent. The FROG with a chemical warhead has a maximum range of 40 miles versus 190 miles for the Scud. Shuey, Lenhart, Snyder, Donnelly, Mielke, and Moteff, *Missile Proliferation: Survey of Emerging Missile Forces*, Washington, D.C., Congressional Research Service, Report 88-642F, February 9, 1989, pp. 34–35; *Jane's Defence Weekly*, February 27, 1988, pp. 370–371; Defense Intelligence Agency, *Soviet Chemical Weapons Threat*, DST-1620F-051-85, 1985, p. 8.

255. *New York Times*, June 6, 1986, p. 11; *Washington Post*, June 11, 1986, p. 36; and *Defense Week*, April 14, 1986, p. 5.

256. *Jane's Defence Weekly*, July 26, 1982, p. 92.

257. J. M. Moreaux, "The Syrian Army," *Defense Update*, No. 69, p. 31.

258. *Jane's Defence Weekly*, April 2, 1988, p. 614; April 30, 1988, p. 853.

259. *The Sunday Correspondent*, October 15, 1989, p. 3; *Al-Ittihad*, July 31, 1989, p. 1; Hong Kong AFP, 0629 GMT, August 7, 1989.

260. *Washington Post*, March 30, 1990, p. 1; *Washington Times*, November 22, 1989; *Defense and Foreign Affairs*, August 14–20, 1989, p. 2.

261. *Jane's Defence Weekly*, December 23, 1989, pp. 1384–1385; *Washington Post*, June 23, 1988, p. A-2; March 29, 1990, pp. A-1 and A-34; *New York Times International*, March 30, 1990, p. A-7; *New York Times*, June 22, 1988, p. 1; January 31, 1992, p. A-1.

262. *Wall Street Journal*, July 10, 1991, p. 12; *Washington Times*, March 10, 1992, p. A-3; March 11, 1992, p. A-3, July 16, 1992, p. A-3; *Time*, March 23, 1992, p. 34; *Washington Post*, February 22, 1992, p. A-15; March 11, 1992, p. A-11; March 13, 1992, p. A-18; July 14, 1992, p. A-1; *New York Times*, January 31, 1992, p. A-1; February 21, 1992, p. A-9; *Sunday Times*, December 21, 1991, p. 1.

263. *Defense News*, October 16, 1989, p. 60; *Washington Times*, June 18, 1990, p. A1; Lora Lumpe, Lisbeth Gronlund, and David C. Wright, "Third World Missiles Fall Short," *Bulletin of the Atomic Scientists*, March, 1992, pp. 30–36.

264. Interviews in Israel, January, 1992.

265. The following analysis involves considerable technical speculation by the author. It is based on various Jane's publications, and General Dynamics, *The World's Missile Systems*, Pomona, General Dynamics, 8th Edition, 1988.

266. Adapted by the author from various editions of Jane's and Ray Bonds, *Modern Soviet Weapons*, New York, ARCO, 1986, pp. 432–435.

267. *OJJ Special, Oil and Gas Journal*, December 30, 1991, pp. 43–49.

268. *Los Angeles Times*, January 28, 1992, p. C-1.

269. This section draws heavily on the excellent summaries of individual conflicts provided by Herbert K. Tillema in *International Conflict Since 1945*, Boulder, Westview, 1991; work in various annual editions of John Laffin's *The World in Conflict* or *War Annual*, London, Brassey's; and by John Keegan, *World Armies*, London, Macmillan, 1983; and joint work with Abraham Wagner in *The Lessons of Modern War*, Volume 1, Boulder, Westview, 1990. For sake of the consistency, the chronology normally uses the dates in Tillema's work. The reader should be aware that many dates vary according to source or are controversial.

270. It is still uncertain whether Jordan entered the war as the result of lies Nasser told King Hussein after Egypt's air force had already been destroyed by Israel or the actions of the Egyptian commander of a supposedly unified Arab command. Nasser had forced King Hussein to accept the Egyptian commander in 1967. It is also possible that Jordan triggered the Israeli attack by moving into neutral areas along the border and using artillery fire on Israeli air bases.

271. This includes approximately 200 relatively low quality M-47s and M-48s.

272. *Aviation Week*, April 3, 1989, p. 32; *Defense News*, March 27, 1989, p. 4.

273. *Wall Street Journal*, June 29, 1989, p. A-10; *Washington Post*, April 23, 1989, p. A-25; April 28, 1989, p. A-33; *New York Times*, April 23, 1989, p. A-9; *Boston Globe*, April 25, 1989, p. 3; April 30, 1989, p. 2.

274. *Washington Post*, November 30, 1989, p. A-1.

275. *Financial Times*, April 17, 1991, p. 1; *New York Times*, December 8, 1991, p. A-10.

276. Subsidies from the Gulf dropped from $1.25 billion during the peak year of 1981 to $550 million before Iraq's invasion of Kuwait. Stanley Reed, "Jordan and the Gulf Crisis," *Foreign Affairs*, Volume 69, Winter 1990, p. 24.

277. *Washington Post*, February 19, 1992, p. A-21.

278. Jordan's water demand rose by 10% annually although its population rose by 3.5%. *New York Times*, December 10, 1991, p. A-12.

279. *New York Times*, March 8, 1992, p. A-4, May 14, 1992, p. A-7; May 26, 1992, p. D-9, June 4, 1992, p. A-16, June 14, 1992, p. 12; *Time*, July 22, 1991, p. 42; *Washington Post*, March 13, 1992, p. A-19, June 29, 1992, p. A-20, July 7, 1992, p. A-13; *London Financial Times*, March 12, 1992, p. 5; *Christian Science Monitor*, May 29, 1992, p. 6; Washington Times, June 3, 1992, p. G-3; *Wall Street Journal*, June 9, 1992, p. 12.

280. These estimates are very uncertain. They take account of both national defense budgets and arms transfers as reflected in IISS and ACDA data, and are adjusted by the author.

281. Arms Control and Disarmament Agency (ACDA), *World Military Expenditures and Arms Transfers, 1990*, Washington, GPO, 1990, Table I.

282. IISS, *Military Balance, 1987–1988, 1988–1989, 1989–1990*, and *1991–1992*.

283. Arms Control and Disarmament Agency (ACDA), *World Military Expenditures and Arms Transfers, 1990*, Washington, GPO, 1990, Table I.

284. Arms Control and Disarmament Agency (ACDA), *World Military Expenditures and Arms Transfers, 1989*, Washington, GPO, 1990, Table II.

285. Arms Control and Disarmament Agency (ACDA), *World Military Expenditures and Arms Transfers, 1985*, Washington, GPO, 1985, pp. 133–134.

286. Arms Control and Disarmament Agency (ACDA), *World Military Expenditures and Arms Transfers, 1989*, Washington, GPO, 1990, pp. 117–118.

287. Arms Control and Disarmament Agency (ACDA), *World Military Expenditures and Arms Transfers, 1990*, Washington, GPO, 1990, pp. 133–134.

288. Author's extrapolation based on discussions with Israeli defense officials, and the data in ACDA, *World Military Expenditures and Arms Transfers*, 1989, pp. 117–118.

289. Alfred B. Prados, "Jordan: Persian Gulf Crisis and U.S. Aid," Congressional Research Service, 91-247F, March 14, 1991.

290. Congressional Presentation for Security Assistance Programs, FY1988, pp. 164–167, and information provided by the Defense Security Assistance Agency.

291. CIA, *World Factbook, 1991*, pp. 164–165.

292. Adapted from various issues of the IISS, *Military Balance*, and work by the Foreign Affairs Division of the Congressional Research Service in *Middle East Arms Control and Related Issues*, CRS 91-384F, May 1, 1992, and for Senator John McCain. Robert Shuey, Richard F. Grimmett, Theodor Galdi, Steven Hildreth, Todd Masses, Alfred Prados, and Shirley Kahn were the principal authors of the CRS work.

293. The military manpower, force strength, and equipment estimates in this section are made by the author using a wide range of sources, including computerized data bases, interviews, and press clipping services. Most are impossible to reference in ways of use to the reader. The force strength statistics are generally adapted from the latest edition of International Institute for Strategic Studies, *Military Balance* (IISS, London), in this case the 1991–1992 edition.

Extensive use has also been made of the annual editions of the Jaffee Center for Strategic Studies, *The Military Balance in the Middle East* (JCSS, Tel Aviv), especially the 1990–1991 edition and working materials from the coming edition. Material has also been drawn from computer print outs from NEXIS, the United States Naval Institute data base, and from the DMS/FI Market Intelligence Reports data base. Other sources include the *Military Technology* "World Defense Almanac for 1991–1992," published in 1992; Foreign Affairs Division, "Middle East Arms Control and Related Issues," Washington, Congressional Research Service, 91-384F, May 1, 1991; and *Middle East Economic Digest*, "MEED Special Report: Defense," Volume 35, December 13, 1991.

Weapons data are taken from many sources, including computerized material available in NEXIS, and various editions of *Jane's Fighting Ships* (Jane's Publishing); *Jane's Naval Weapons Systems* (Jane's Publishing); *Jane's Armour and Artillery* (Jane's Publishing); *Jane's Infantry Weapons* (Jane's Publishing); *Jane's Military Vehicles and Logistics* (Jane's Publishing); *Jane's Land-Based Air Defence* (Jane's Publishing); *Jane's All the World's Aircraft* (Jane's Publishing); *Jane's Battlefield Surveillance Systems* (Jane's Publishing); *Jane's Radar and Electronic Warfare Systems*(Jane's Publishing), *Jane's C³I Systems* (Jane's Publishing); *Jane's Air-Launched Weapons Systems* (Jane's Publishing); *Jane's Defence Appointments & Procurement Handbook (Middle East Edition)* (Jane's Publishing); *Tanks of the World* (Bernard and Grafe); *Weyer's Warships* (Bernard and Grafe); and *Warplanes of the World* (Bernard and Grafe).

Other military background, effectiveness, strength, organizational, and history data are taken from Ellen Laipson and Alfred B. Prados, "Jordan: Recent Developments and Implications for U.S. Interests," Congressional Research Service 90-354F, July 11, 1990; Martin Streetly, "Middle Eastern Airborne Electronic Warfare," *Jane's Defence Weekly*, February 3, 1990, pp. 199–203; Richard F. Grimmett and Alfred B. Prados, "Near East Arms Transfers, August 2, 1990–November 1, 1991," Congressional Research Service 91-839F, December 2, 1991; Anthony H. Cordesman, *Jordanian Arms and the Middle East Balance*, Washington, Middle East Institute, 1983; *Jordanian Arms and the Middle East Balance, Update*, Middle East Institute, Washington, 1985; *The Gulf and the Search for Strategic Stability*, Boulder, Westview, 1984; *The Gulf and the West*, Boulder, Westview, 1988; and *Weapons of Mass Destruction in the Middle East*, London, Brassey's/RUSI, 1991; Anthony H. Cordesman and Abraham Wagner, *The Lessons of Modern War*, Volume 1, Boulder, Westview, 1990.

294. CIA, *The World Factbook*, 1991, pp. 164–165.

295. CIA, *The World Factbook*, 1991, pp. 164–165.

296. IISS, *Military Balance, 1991–1992*.

297. Based on the IISS, *Military Balance, 1990–1991*, p. 110; and CIA, CPAS WF 87-001 (U), pp. 120–122.

298. *Defense News*, November 25, 1991, p. 1; December 23, 1991, p. 23; *Inside the Army*, April 22, 1991, p. 1; February 17, 1992, p. 3.

299. One source has reported that Jordan received 90 Chieftains, 60 M-47s, 19 British Scorpion light tanks, and 35 M-113s that Iraq captured from Iran. *Chicago Tribune*, August 18, 1988, p. I-4.

300. *Defense News*, December 23, 1991, p. 23; *Inside the Army*, April 22, 1991, p. 1; February 17, 1992, p. 3.

301. *Defense News*, November 25, 1991, p. 1; December 23, 1991, p. 23; *Inside the Army*, April 22, 1991, p. 1; February 17, 1992, p. 3.

302. Additional sources used in this section are interviews in Jordan and the U.S.; *Jane's Defence Weekly*, December 16, 1989, pp. 1329–1331; *Inside the Army*, April 22, 1991, p. 1; February 17, 1992, p. 3; *Defense News*, September 2, 1991, p. 3; November 25, 1991, p. 1; and a computer print out from *Flight International*.

303. *Jane's Defence Weekly*, December 16, 1989, pp. 1329–1331.

304. Hussein said in April, 1986, that, "we can no longer look to the United States to be our major weapons supplier. We must diversify our sources and our relations. Sensible working relations can continue between my country and the United States, but such relations will of necessity be limited in view of this . . . snub." *Jane's Defence Weekly*, April 6, 1988.

305. Jordan initially denied an interest in the MiG-29 after reports surfaced in the press. These same reports said Moscow would sell Jordan the SA-11 Gadfly and SS-23 Scarab. It later became apparent that the Soviets had made some form of offer. At this writing, Soviet sales to Jordan since the first Soviet sale in 1981 have been limited to the SA-8, AS-13, SA-14, and ZSU-23-4. *Jane's Defence Weekly*, August 8, 1987, pp. 206–207, and February 20, 1988, p. 311.

306. *Jane's Defence Weekly*, February 12, 1988, p. 239, and February 20, 1988, p. 311; *Aviation Week*, February 15, 1988, p. 21.

307. The purchase was reported at a time Jordan was ready to provide some 3,000 troops to Saudi Arabia to help compensate for its loss of Pakistani forces and provide additional security forces to deal with any potential Iranian threat to the annual hajj to Mecca. *Jane's Defence Weekly*, February 20, 1988, p. 311.

308. *Defense News*, March 27, 1989, p. 4; *Aviation Week*, April 3, 1989, p. 32; *Washington Post*, March 25, 1989, p. A-16; *Wall Street Journal*, September 13, 1988, p. 32; *Aviation Week*, March 7, 1988, p. 29.

309. *Defense News*, September 2, 1991, p. 3.

310. *Inside the Army*, February 17, 1992, p. 3.

311. *Jane's Defence Weekly*, October 15, 1988, p. 934.

312. *Defense News*, November 25, 1991, p. 1; December 23, 1991, p. 23; *Inside the Army*, April 22, 1991, p. 1; February 17, 1992, p. 3.

313. Jordan is also highly vulnerable to attack on its central water facility and a tunnel which carries virtually all of the water to its Jordan River valley farms.

314. The Syrian divisions normally include a mechanized corps with the 5th mech, 7th mech, and 9th armored divisions, and an armored corps with the 10th mech, 1st armored, and 11th armored divisions. The 3rd Armored Division could also deploy against Jordan.

315. See Anthony H. Cordesman, *Jordanian Arms and the Middle East Balance, Update,* Middle East Institute, Washington, 1985, p. 6.

316. This section draws heavily on the excellent summaries of individual conflicts provided by Herbert K. Tillema in *International Conflict Since 1945*, Boulder, Westview, 1991; work in various annual editions of John Laffin's *The World in Conflict* or *War Annual*, London, Brassey's; and by John Keegan, *World Armies*, London, Macmillan, 1983; and joint work with Abraham Wagner in *The Lessons of Modern War*, Volume 1, Boulder, Westview, 1990. For sake of consistency, the chronology normally uses the dates in Tillema's work.

The reader should be aware that many dates vary according to source or are controversial.

317. CIA, "Who's Who in Lebanon," LDA89-12142, July, 1989.

318. The following account of events draws heavily on Clyde R. Mark, "Lebanon: The Current Crisis," Congressional Research Service, IB89118, September 26, 1991.

319. *New York Times*, November 6, 1989, p. A-1.

320. Reuters, October 21, 1991, BC Cycle.

321. *New York Times*, May 1, 1991, p. A-12; *Jane's Defence Weekly*, June 15, 1991, pp. 1031–1032.

322. *New York Times*, May 1, 1991, p. A-12.

323. *New York Times*, July 6, 1991, p, A-3; *Jane's Defence Weekly*, July 13, 1991, p. 46; July 27, 1991, p. 142.

324. *Washington Post*, August 30, 1991, p. A-21.

325. *New York Times*, October 13, 1991, p. A-19.

326. *New York Times*, July 8, 1991, p. A-3; July 20, 1991, p. A-4.

327. *New York Times*, November 2, 1991, p. A-6.

328. UPI, January 29, 1992, BC Cycle; Agence France Presse, January 25, 1992; AP, AM Cycle, November 19, 1991.

329. Experts debated whether the Israeli attack was a useful strike at an irreconcilable hard-line movement or one whose interest in violence was declining and whose leader was a relative moderate loyal to Rafsanjani. Like many assassinations, the value of the attack became progressively less clear with time. *Washington Times*, February 21, 1992, p. A-7; March 24, 1992, p. 7; *New York Times*, February 23, 1992, p. E-2; May 26, 1992, p. A-10; *Christian Science Monitor*, February 19, 1992, p. 1; *Economist*, February 22, 1992, p. 31; *Washington Post*, May 22, 1992, p. A-31; *Washington Times*, May 27, 1992, p. A-7.

330. Damascus Radio, 1215 GMT, October 30, 1991; Reuters, September 1, 1991, BC Cycle; *Economist*, April 25, 1992, pp. 46–47, August 15, 1992, p. 34; *Washington Post*, August 24, 1992, p. A-10; August 31, 1992, p. A-12; *New York Times*, August 23, 1992, p. A-2; August 16, 1992, p. A-17; August 24, 1992, p. A-6; August 26, 1992, p. A-10; *Christian Science Monitor*, July 30, 1992, p. 12; *Wall Street Journal*, August 10, 1992, p. A-5.

331. *Washington Post*, September 28, 1991, p. A-15.

332. Voice of Lebanon, 1215 GMT, November 10, 1991; *Flight International*, November 27, 1991; Reuters, December 12, 1991, BC Cycle; Reuters, October 21, 1991, BC Cycle; UPI, October 1, 1991, BC Cycle; *Washington Post*, September 28, 1991, p. A-15.

333. Reuters, August 1, 1991, AM Cycle.

334. The original estimates of Palestinian dead at Sabra and Shatila were between 200 and 900.

335. These figures are taken from the *Philadelphia Inquirer*, March 10, 1992, p. B-13.

336. *Los Angeles Times*, January 28, 1992, p. C-1.

337. *Economist*, April 25, 1992, pp. 46–47; May 16, 1992, p. 56; *New York Times*, May 14, 1992, p. A-11, June 4, 1992, p. A-8; *Washington Post*, May 7, 1992, p. A-37; *Philadelphia Inquirer*, May 6, 1992, p. A-10.

338. Arms Control and Disarmament Agency (ACDA), *World Military Expenditures and Arms Transfers, 1989*, Washington, GPO, 1990, Table I.

339. IISS, *Military Balance, 1988–1989*, p. 104.

340. Arms Control and Disarmament Agency (ACDA), *World Military Expenditures and Arms Transfers, 1990*, Washington, GPO, 1990, Table II.

341. Arms Control and Disarmament Agency (ACDA), *World Military Expenditures and Arms Transfers, 1985*, Washington, GPO, 1985, pp. 133–134.

342. Arms Control and Disarmament Agency (ACDA), *World Military Expenditures and Arms Transfers, 1989*, Washington, GPO, 1990, pp. 117–118.

343. Arms Control and Disarmament Agency (ACDA), *World Military Expenditures and Arms Transfers, 1990*, Washington, GPO, 1990, pp. 133–134.

344. The military manpower, force strength, and equipment estimates in this section are

made by the author using a wide range of sources, including computerized data bases, interviews, and press clipping services. Most are impossible to reference in ways of use to the reader. The force strength statistics are generally adapted from the latest edition of International Institute for Strategic Studies, *Military Balance* (IISS, London), in this case the 1991–1992 edition.

Extensive use has also been made of the annual editions of the Jaffee Center for Strategic Studies, *The Military Balance in the Middle East*(JCSS, Tel Aviv), especially the 1990–1991 edition and working materials from the coming edition. Material has also been drawn from computer print outs from NEXIS, the United States Naval Institute data base, and from the DMS/FI Market Intelligence Reports data base. Other sources include the *Military Technology* "World Defense Almanac for 1991–1992," published in 1992; Foreign Affairs Division, "Middle East Arms Control and Related Issues," Washington, Congressional Research Service, 91-384F, May 1, 1991; and *Middle East Economic Digest*, "MEED Special Report: Defense," Volume 35, December 13, 1991.

Weapons data are taken from many sources, including computerized material available in NEXIS and various editions of *Jane's Fighting Ships* (Jane's Publishing); *Jane's Naval Weapons Systems* (Jane's Publishing); *Jane's Armour and Artillery* (Jane's Publishing); *Jane's Infantry Weapons* (Jane's Publishing); *Jane's Military Vehicles and Logistics* (Jane's Publishing); *Jane's Land-Based Air Defence* (Jane's Publishing); *Jane's All the World's Aircraft* (Jane's Publishing); *Jane's Battlefield Surveillance Systems* (Jane's Publishing); *Jane's Radar and Electronic Warfare Systems*(Jane's Publishing), *Jane's C^{3}I Systems* (Jane's Publishing); *Jane's Air-Launched Weapons Systems*(Jane's Publishing); *Jane's Defence Appointments & Procurement Handbook (Middle East Edition)*(Jane's Publishing); *Tanks of the World* (Bernard and Grafe); *Weyer's Warships* (Bernard and Grafe); and *Warplanes of the World* (Bernard and Grafe).

Other military background, effectiveness, strength, organizational, and history data are taken from Martin Streetly, "Middle Eastern Airborne Electronic Warfare," *Jane's Defence Weekly*, February 3, 1990, pp. 199–203; Richard F. Grimmett and Alfred B. Prados, "Near East Arms Transfers, August 2, 1990–November 1, 1991," Congressional Research Service 91-839F, December 2, 1991; Anthony H. Cordesman, *Jordanian Arms and the Middle East Balance*, Washington, Middle East Institute, 1983; *The Gulf and the Search for Strategic Stability*, Boulder, Westview, 1984; *The Gulf and the West*, Boulder, Westview, 1988; and *Weapons of Mass Destruction in the Middle East*, London, Brassey's/RUSI, 1991; Anthony H. Cordesman and Abraham Wagner, *The Lessons of Modern War*, Volume 1, Boulder, Westview, 1990.

345. CIA, *World Factbook 1991*, pp. 176–178.

346. IISS, *Military Balance, 1991–1992*.

347. James Bruce, "Will Geagea Push Lebanon into Partition?" *Jane's Defence Weekly*, pp. 1140–1142

348. James Bruce, "Will Geagea Push Lebanon into Partition?" *Jane's Defence Weekly*, pp. 1140–1142; *Washington Post*, October 25, 1988, p. A-19; *Philadelphia Inquirer*, February 18, 1989, p. 1.

349. *Jane's Defence Weekly*, June 15, 1991, pp. 1034–1036; July 13, 1991, p. 46; July 27, 1991, p. 142; *New York Times*, July 6, 1991, p. A-3; *Washington Post*, September 28, 1991, p. A-15; Reuters, December 12, 1991, BC Cycle.

350. These equipment estimates are extremely uncertain. They are based on interviews and press reports that provide sharply contradictory data and often assume that all recent equipment transfers and equipment taken from the militia are operational.

351. Much of this estimate is based upon *Flight International*, November 27, 1991.

352. *Economist*, October 5, 1989, p. 38.

353. Lahd's reputation is decidedly mixed. According to one rumor, he lost his unit's pay gambling in Lebanon's casino and had to go into exile.

354. *Washington Post*, October 20, 1989, p. A-33; undated working material from *Defense and Diplomacy*.

355. Undated working material from *Defense and Diplomacy*.

356. Amal is also a backwards acronym for Lebanese Opposition Brigade.

357. *Jane's Defence Weekly*, November 5, 1988, pp. 1140–1141.

358. Undated working material from *Defense and Diplomacy*.

359. Clyde R. Mark, "Lebanon: The Current Crisis," Congressional Research Service, IB89118, September 26, 1991, p. 1; *Philadelphia Inquirer*, March 10, 1992, p. B-13.

360. Clyde R. Mark, "Palestine and the Palestinians," Congressional Research Service IB76048, January 15, 1992, p. 7.

361. *Washington Times*, October 26, 1991, p. A-7.

362. Report of the Commissioner General for UNRWA, Supplement 13 (A/45/13), June 20, 1990; Supplement 13 (A/46/13), June 30, 1991.

363. Central Intelligence Agency, *The World Factbook, 1990; Los Angeles Times*, July 5, 1991, p. A-1.

364. JCSS, *Military Balance in the Middle East, 1989–1990*, pp. 300–303; *Los Angeles Times*, June 21, 1986, p. I-6; *Jane's Defence Weekly*, January 18, 1986; "Replaying a Bad Dream," *Newsweek*, October 6, 1986, p. 32; Thomas L. Friedman, "Israeli Raid: New Tactic," *New York Times*, September 26, 1986, p. A-8; "Israel Says Iranians Train Guerrillas in Lebanon," *New York Times*, September 22, 1986, p. A-4; William Drozdiak, "Shamir Accuses Syria in Attacks," *Washington Post*, September 25, 1986, p. A-28; Ihsan A. Hijazi, "Palestinian Resurgence Seen in Southern Lebanon," *New York Times*, September 25, 1986; "Israel to Use Helicopters to Back Lebanese Militia Allies," *Washington Times*, p. 8, September 22, 1986.

365. Clyde R. Mark, "Palestine and the Palestinians," Congressional Research Service IB76048, January 15, 1992, p. 7.

366. See Patrick Seale, *Abu Nidal A Gun For Hire*, New York, Random House, 1992; *Jane's Defence Review*, February 10, 1990, p. 242; *National Review*, March 30, 1992, p. 40; *Sunday Times*, November 3, 1991, p. 1; *Wall Street Journal*, August 9, 1991, p. 1; *Washington Post*, July 23, 1991, p. A-17.

367. Robert Satloff, "Islam in the Palestinian Rising," *Orbis*, Vol. 33, No. 3, Summer 1989; *Washington Post*, August 6, 1991, p. A-1; November 24, 1991, p. C-2.

368. Based on IISS and JCSS estimates, and Maxine Polack, "Seeking Unity Among the Splinters," *Insight*, October 12, 1987, pp. 36–38.

369. Based on estimates in the JCSS, *Military Balance in the Middle East, 1989–1990*, pp. 300–303, and discussions with U.S. officials.

370. There are strong indications that Iran has steadily increased its financial, training, and weapons support of the Party of God, as well as Syria, and that the Party of God has a major training camp near Baalbek. The Party of God has launched at least one four point attack against the SLA and is steadily improving in military capability.

371. *Washington Times*, September 22, 1986, p. 8; *New York Times*, September 25, 1986, p. A-11; September 26, 1986, p. A-8; October 5, 1986, p. E-3.

372. *OJJ Special, Oil and Gas Journal*, December 30, 1991, pp. 43–49.

373. *Los Angeles Times*, January 28, 1992, p. C-1.

374. This section draws heavily on the excellent summaries of individual conflicts provided by Herbert K. Tillema in *International Conflict Since 1945*, Boulder, Westview, 1991; work in various annual editions of John Laffin's *The World in Conflict* or *War Annual*, London, Brassey's; and by John Keegan, *World Armies*, London, Macmillan, 1983; and joint work with Abraham Wagner in *The Lessons of Modern War*, Volume 1, Boulder, Westview, 1990. For the sake of consistency, the chronology normally uses the dates in Tillema's work. The reader should be aware that many dates vary according to source or are controversial.

375. *Washington Post*, April 1, 1989, p. A-15; April 16, 1989, p. A-29; *Washington Times*, April 17, 1989, p. A-8; *London Financial Times*, April 18, 1989, p. 5; *Wall Street Journal*, April 4, 1989, p. A-1; *Philadelphia Inquirer*, March 11, 1989, p. 9-A; *New York Times*, March 10, 1989, p. A-1.

376. *Los Angeles Times*, December 28, 1989, p. A-1; *Baltimore Sun*, December 24, 1989, p. 2A.

377. *Philadelphia Inquirer*, December 24, 1989, p. 2-F.

378. *Washington Post*, August 12, 1991, p. A-9; Reuters, August 1, 1991, BC cycle.

379. *Chicago Tribune*, July 7, 1991, p. I-3; BBC, Summary of World Broadcasts, November 11, 1991; *Christian Science Monitor*, May 9, 1991, p. 3; *Washington Post*, May 11, 1991, p. 16; *London Financial Times*, December 2, 1991, p. 4; *The Estimate*, June 7–20, 1991, p. 1; *Defense News*, December 16, 1991, p. 1.

380. Badr's speech contained a peculiar note of moderation: "I only want to kill 1% of the population." *Washington Post*, January 13, 1990, p. A-18; *New York Times*, January 13, 1990, p. A-3.

381. *Christian Science Monitor*, April 21, 1992, p. 5; June 19, 1992, p. A-19; *Washington Times*, June 3, 1992, p. A-2; *Los Angeles Times*, August 3, 1992, p. A-1; *Washington Post*, July 18, 1992, p. A-17; July 28, 1992, p. A-15.

382. For a good summary description of contemporary Egyptian attitudes, see Caryle Murphy, "A Battle for Egyptian Souls," *Washington Post*, April 26, 1992, p. A-1, and p. A-29 of the same issue.

383. Arms Control and Disarmament Agency (ACDA), *World Military Expenditures and Arms Transfers, 1990*, Washington, GPO, 1990, Table I.

384. IISS, *Military Balance, 1987–1988, 1988–1989, 1989–1990*, and *1991–1992*. The IISS attempts to report in Egyptian fiscal years and began to quote budget and total expense data in the 1991–1992 edition that may come from Egyptian sources but are so low as to be completely unrealistic.

385. State Department, *Congressional Presentation for Security Assistance Programs, FY1988*, and *FY1989*. See country sections for Egypt.

386. CIA, *World Factbook, 1991*, pp. 89–90.

387. Estimates based on the trends in Table I of various editions of ACDA, *World Military Expenditures and Arms Transfers*.

388. For a detailed analysis, see Larry Q. Nowels, "Egyptian Military Debt Forgiveness: Costs, Implications, and the Role of Congress," Congressional Research Service, IB90137, September 25 ,1991. Also, *New York Times*, July 12, 1992, p. 6.

389. Arms Control and Disarmament Agency (ACDA), *World Military Expenditures and Arms Transfers, 1990*, Washington, GPO, 1990, Table II.

390. Arms Control and Disarmament Agency (ACDA), *World Military Expenditures and Arms Transfers, 1989*, Washington, GPO, 1990, Table II.

391. Arms Control and Disarmament Agency (ACDA), *World Military Expenditures and Arms Transfers, 1985*, Washington, GPO, 1985, pp. 133–134.

392. Arms Control and Disarmament Agency (ACDA), *World Military Expenditures and Arms Transfers, 1989*, Washington, GPO, 1990, pp. 117–118.

393. Arms Control and Disarmament Agency (ACDA), *World Military Expenditures and Arms Transfers, 1990*, Washington, GPO, 1990, pp. 133–134.

394. This estimate is based on IISS, *Military Balance, 1991–1992*, pp. 104–105. Much of this equipment is probably in storage and some may have been sold to foreign countries.

395. Material provided by the Congressional Research Service in 1992, and Defense Security Assistance Agency, *Foreign Military Sales and Security Assistance Facts,1987*, pp. 24–25.

396. The military manpower, force strength, and equipment estimates in this section are made by the author using a wide range of sources, including computerized data bases, interviews, and press clipping services. Most are impossible to reference in ways of use to the reader. The force strength statistics are generally adapted from the latest edition of International Institute for Strategic Studies, *Military Balance* (IISS, London), in this case the 1991–1992 edition.

Extensive use has also been made of the annual editions of the Jaffee Center for Strategic Studies, *The Military Balance in the Middle East* (JCSS, Tel Aviv), especially the 1990–1991 edition and working materials from the coming edition. Material has also been drawn from computer print outs from NEXIS, the United States Naval Institute data base, and from the

DMS/FI Market Intelligence Reports data base. Other sources include *Military Technology,* "World Defense Almanac for 1991–1992," published in 1992; Foreign Affairs Division, "Middle East Arms Control and Related Issues," Washington, Congressional Research Service, 91–384F, May 1, 1991; and *Middle East Economic Digest,* "MEED Special Report: Defense," Volume 35, December 13, 1991.

Weapons data are taken from many sources, including computerized material available in NEXIS, and various editions of *Jane's Fighting Ships* (Jane's Publishing); *Jane's Naval Weapons Systems* (Jane's Publishing); *Jane's Armour and Artillery* (Jane's Publishing); *Jane's Infantry Weapons* (Jane's Publishing); *Jane's Military Vehicles and Logistics* (Jane's Publishing); *Jane's Land-Based Air Defence* (Jane's Publishing); *Jane's All the World's Aircraft* (Jane's Publishing); *Jane's Battlefield Surveillance Systems* (Jane's Publishing); *Jane's Radar and Electronic Warfare Systems*(Jane's Publishing), *Jane's C³I Systems* (Jane's Publishing); *Jane's Air-Launched Weapons Systems* (Jane's Publishing); *Jane's Defence Appointments & Procurement Handbook (Middle East Edition)* (Jane's Publishing); *Tanks of the World* (Bernard and Grafe); *Weyer's Warships* (Bernard and Grafe); and *Warplanes of the World* (Bernard and Grafe).

Other military background, effectiveness, strength, organizational, and history data are taken from Martin Streetly, "Middle Eastern Airborne Electronic Warfare," *Jane's Defence Weekly,* February 3, 1990, pp. 199–203; Richard F. Grimmett and Alfred B. Prados, "Near East Arms Transfers, August 2, 1990–November 1, 1991," Congressional Research Service 91-839F, December 2, 1991; Anthony H. Cordesman, *Jordanian Arms and the Middle East Balance,* Washington, Middle East Institute, 1983; *The Gulf and the Search for Strategic Stability,* Boulder, Westview, 1984; *The Gulf and the West,* Boulder, Westview, 1988; and *Weapons of Mass Destruction in the Middle East,* London, Brassey's/RUSI, 1991; Anthony H. Cordesman and Abraham Wagner, *The Lessons of Modern War, Volume 1,* Boulder, Westview, 1990.

397. CIA, *World Factbook, 1991,* pp. 89–90.

398. CIA, *World Factbook, 1991,* pp. 89–90.

399. Based on the IISS, *Military Balance, 1991–1992,* pp. 104–105.

400. Based on interviews in Egypt.

401. The total Egyptian army reserve pool is around 500,000 men, but this simply reflects the number of men with a legal obligation to serve, not the number that are trained and would be called up in war.

402. Based on interviews in Egypt, and IISS and JCSS figures, adjusted to reflect additional U.S. deliveries shown on DSAA computer print outs.

403. The descriptions of tank modifications in this section are based upon *Jane's Armour and Artillery, 1991–1992,* pp. 16–18.

404. Tank strength and modernization estimates are adapted from the IISS, *Washington Post,* March 1, 1990, p. A-32. The transfer of U.S. tanks was part of a deal that also gave Egypt 250 jeeps, with agreement to provide 500 more in June, 1992. *Defense News,* March 30, 1992, p. 3; July 20, 1992, p. 4.

405. Based largely upon IISS, *Military Balance, 1991–1992,* pp. 104–105; interviews in Egypt; and JCSS figures, adjusted to reflect additional U.S. deliveries shown on DSAA computer print outs.

406. *Jane's Defence Weekly,* February 29, 1992, p. 350.

407. *Jane's Defence Weekly,* July 13, 1991, p. 65.

408. *Jane's Defence Weekly,* December 14, 1991, p. 1181.

409. *New York Times,* November 2, 1988, p. A-13; *Washington Times,* November 2, 1988, p. 9.

410. *International Defense Review,* 1/1988, p. 75.

411. The counts of Egyptian aircraft by type and data on organization are based on interviews in Egypt and with U.S. manufacturers, IISS and JCSS figures, and *Flight International,* November 27, 1991, computer print out, adjusted to reflect additional U.S. deliveries shown on DSAA computer print outs.

407. *Jane's Defence Weekly*, July 13, 1991, p. 65.

408. *Jane's Defence Weekly*, December 14, 1991, p. 1181.

409. *New York Times*, November 2, 1988, p. A-13; *Washington Times*, November 2, 1988, p. 9.

410. *International Defense Review*, 1/1988, p. 75.

411. The counts of Egyptian aircraft by type and data on organization are based on interviews in Egypt and with U.S. manufacturers, IISS and JCSS figures, and *Flight International*, November 27, 1991, computer print out, adjusted to reflect additional U.S. deliveries shown on DSAA computer print outs.

412. *International Defense Review*, 1/1980, pp. 63–65.

413. *Jane's Defence Weekly*, February 3, 1990, p. 199.

414. Staff article, "Employment of RPVs by the Armed Forces of Egypt," *Unmanned Systems*, Winter, 1992, pp. 13–17.

415. The L-1900Cs seem to use the Guardrail SIGINT system. *Jane's Defence Weekly*, February 3, 1990, p. 199.

416. *Jane's Defence Weekly*, February 3, 1990, p. 199.

417. Reuter Library Report, October 29, 1991, BC Cycle; *Flight International*, November 27, 1991, computer data service.

418. *International Defense Review*, 1/1990, p. 65.

419. *International Defense Review*, 1/1988, p. 75.

420. *Defense News*, January 27, 1992, p. 23.

421. *International Defense Review*, 1/1990, p. 65.

422. *International Defense Review*, 2/1990, p. 124; Michael Vlahos, "Middle Eastern Navies," *Proceedings*, March 1989, pp. 148–149.

423. *Defense News*, September 23, 1991, p. 26; *International Defense Review*, 2/1990, p. 124.

424. Michael Vlahos, "Middle Eastern Navies," *Proceedings*, March 1989, pp. 148–149.

425. *Al-Ahram*, July 25, 1975; *Al-Akhbar*, July 25, 1975.

426. *Jane's Defence Weekly*, March 12, 1988, pp. 462–463.

427. *Atlanta Constitution*, October 5, 1988, p. 17A.

428. *London Financial Times*, December 21, 1987, p. 1; June 8, 1988, p. 20.

429. The results of these orders are uncertain, and there are no confirmed reports of actual production. *Washington Post*, August 20, 1988, p. A-1; *New York Times*, June 25, 1988, p. 1.

430. *Washington Post*, April 1, 1989, p. A-15; April 16, 1989, p. A-29; *Washington Times*, April 17, 1989, p. A-8; *London Financial Times*, April 18, 1989, p. 5; *Wall Street Journal*, April 4, 1989, p. A-1; *Philadelphia Inquirer*, March 11, 1989, p. 9-A; *New York Times*, March 10, 1989, p. A-1.

431. The material was carbon-phenolic fabric which is used to make rocket nozzles and rocket heat shields. Helmy received at least $1 million from Egyptian sources to purchase the carbon fabric and other missile components. *Washington Post*, August 20, 1988, p. A-1; April 1, 1989, p. A-15; April 16, 1989, p. A-29; *New York Times*, March 10, 1989, p. A-1; June 11, 1989, p. 6; June 25, 1988, p. 1; *Los Angeles Times*, June 10, 1989, p. 10; *Washington Times*, April 17, 1989, p. A-8; *London Financial Times*, April 18, 1989, p. 5; *Wall Street Journal*, April 4, 1989, p. A-1; *Philadelphia Inquirer*, March 11, 1989, p. 9-A.

432. Abdel Darwish, "China to Update Egypt's Missiles," *The Independent* (UK), June 14, 1990, p. 2.

433. *Jane's Defence Weekly*, December 16, 1989; *Defense Electronics*, August, 1988, pp. 17 and 20; *La Nacion*, July 4, 1988; *Economist*, May 4, 1988, pp. 67–68; *Defense and Foreign Affairs*, June, 1985, p. 1; *Defense and Foreign Affairs Daily*, May 9, 1985, pp. 1–2; *International Defense Review*, July, 1987, p. 857; *New York Times*, July 22, 1987, p. A-6; *Washington Times*, July 22, 1987, p. D-4.

434. For a good summary report, see *Jane's Defence Weekly*, February 17, 1990, p. 295. Also see *Financial Times*, November 21, 1989, p. 1; *Washington Post*, September 20, 1989.

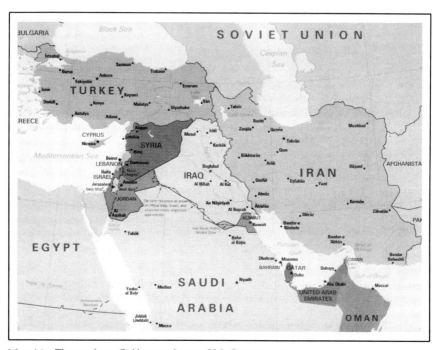

Map 6.1   The northern Gulf states. Source: U.S. Government

6

Trends in the Military Balance
and Arms Sales in the
Northern Gulf States

Iran and Iraq, the two most populous states in the Gulf, have long struggled for dominance over the Gulf region and have engaged in a massive arms race ever since the 1960s. The southern Gulf states, particularly Saudi Arabia, have responded by trying to create high technology forces that can somehow compensate for their lack of manpower. The other Arab states have sought financial aid from the oil rich states in the Gulf.

The impact of these trends on the military balance in the Gulf is reflected in Table 6.1. The patterns for Iran and Iraq reflect constant confrontation and conflict. Iran and Iraq fought a border war during the early and mid-1970s, the major Iran-Iraq War from 1979 to 1988, and Iraq then fought the Gulf War during 1990–1991. These conflicts threatened and sometimes even directly involved the southern Gulf states. At the same time, political turmoil in Iran and Iraq created new sources of instability and tension.

The Gulf War has not changed this situation. It has left Saddam Hussein in power and able to rebuild many of his military capabilities. Iran is actively rearming and has access to modern Soviet weapons. Iran and Iraq are able to pose a challenge to each other and the southern Gulf states. The southern Gulf states are forced to try to create stronger deterrent and defensive capabilities but remain dependent on Western power projection forces as the ultimate guarantee of their security.

The Dynamics of the Military Balance
in the Gulf Area

Nevertheless, the Gulf of the 1990s is scarcely going to be the Gulf of the 1970s or 1980s. Regardless of any political and economic continuities, the dynamics of the military balance in the Gulf area seem likely to shift significantly during the next decade. In fact, five key factors are already changing the threat and the way in which Gulf forces are structured:

TABLE 6.1 The Military Buildup in the Gulf

Trends in Military Expenditure (in $ Current Millions)

	1979	1980	1981	1982	1983	1984	1985	1986	1987	1988	1989	1990	1991
Iran	16620	14700	16210	18260	15940	22240	24770	17000	15000	12000	3900	3180	3770
Iraq	11350	19810	24610	25070	25260	25940	18970	16500	17500	16500	12870	8610	8000
Iran-Iraq total	27970	34510	40820	43330	41200	48180	43740	33500	32500	28500	16770	11790	11770
Saudi Arabia	12390	14990	18410	22040	24800	20400	21340	17290	16210	13600	14690	13860	26810
Kuwait	766	892	858	1120	1399	1430	1525	1300	1263	1273	1964	1504	11140
Bahrain	143	157	215	281	166	148	151	161	160	187	196	250	300
Qatar	475	604	720	948	1790	1213	2308	1800	1800	1800	1450	1900	1900
UAE	1197	1724	2090	1980	1973	1932	1901	1580	1590	1587	1471	2590	4900
Oman	700	1059	1357	1512	1744	1894	1937	1731	1518	1350	1552	1390	1440
GCC total	15671	19426	23650	27881	31872	27017	29162	23862	22541	19797	21323	21494	46490
Gulf total	43641	53936	64470	71211	73072	75197	72902	57362	55041	48297	38093	33284	58260

Trends in Arms Imports (in $ Current Millions)

	1972	1974	1976	1978	1980	1982	1984	1986	1988	1990	1992	1994
Iran	525	1000	2000	2200	410	1600	2400	2200	2000	2100	1800	2000
Iraq	140	625	1000	2400	2500	6500	9300	3800	4600	3700	4000	4100
Iran-Iraq total	665	1625	3000	4600	2910	8100	11700	6000	6600	5800	5800	6100
Saudi Arabia	100	340	440	1500	1800	3100	3100	3800	3000	5500	5500	5500
Kuwait	5	10	80	320	40	110	450	130	190	600	—	—
Bahrain	2	2	4	6	40	5	40	50	30	70	70	75
Qatar	3	2	5	20	90	270	200	80	190	230	240	260
UAE	10	50	100	60	170	50	190	30	60	130	120	70
Oman	5	10	10	270	100	130	310	10	30	130	130	150
GCC total	125	414	639	2176	2240	3665	4290	4100	3500	6660	5920	5905
Gulf total	790	2039	3639	6776	5150	11665	15990	10100	10100	12460	11420	11005

Source of Arms Imports by Major Supplier During 1985–1989 (in $ Current Millions)

	Total	USSR	U.S.	France	UK	PRC	FRG	Other Warsaw Pact	Other Europe	Middle East	Other East Asia	Latin America	Others
Iran	10250	0	10	75	100	2800	50	1400	3345	40	2000	210	220
Iraq	22750	13000	0	1700	20	1600	90	2900	1500	420	20	1300	200
Iran-Iraq total	33,000	13000	10	1775	120	4400	140	4300	4845	460	2020	1510	420

Saudi Arabia	23040	0	5000	7000	7700	2500	40	0	250	0	140	390	20
Kuwait	1345	180	150	450	110	0	0	5	20	430	0	0	0
Bahrain	515	0	260	50	5	0	200	0	0	0	0	0	0
Qatar	160	0	10	100	20	0	0	0	0	0	0	30	0
UAE	1495	20	340	725	40	0	0	0	280	0	80	0	0
Oman	445	0	30	0	200	0	210	0	5	0	0	0	20
GCC total	27000	200	5790	8325	8075	2500	450	5	555	430	220	430	440
Gulf total	60000	13200	5800	10100	8195	6900	590	4305	5400	890	2240	1940	440

Trends in Military Manpower

	1967	1973	1975	1977	1979	1981	1983	1985	1987	1989	1991
Iran	210	285	385	350	415	660	640	745	700	604	528
Iraq	90	105	155	140	444	392	434	788	1000	1000	750
Iran-Iraq Total	300	390	540	490	859	1052	1074	1533	1700	1604	1278
Saudi Arabia	50	75	75	75	79	79	80	96	95	95	112
Kuwait	8	14	25	10	11	12	13	16	20	20	8
Bahrain2	2	2	2	2	2	2	3	4	5	7	8
Qatar	1	3	5	5	6	6	6	6	11	7	
UAE	4	11	21	25	25	44	44	44	44	43	48
Oman	3	8	12	12	13	15	20	25	27	29	30
GCC total	68	113	140	129	136	158	165	191	201	205	213
Gulf total	368	503	680	619	995	1210	1404	1724	1701	2008	1704

Trends in Military Equipment

Main Battle Tanks

	1973	1979	1982	1984	1988	1990	1992
Iran	920	1735	1110	1000	900	500	700
Iraq	990	1800	2300	4820	5500	5600	2300
Iran-Iraq total	1910	3535	3410	5820	6400	6100	3000
Bahrain	0	0	0	0	54	54	80
Kuwait	100	280	240	240	275	245	250
Oman	0	0	18	18	39	39	80
Qatar	0	12	24	24	24	24	30
Saudi Arabia	85	350	450	450	550	550	700
UAE	0	0	118	118	136	131	130
GCC total	185	642	850	850	1078	1043	1270
Gulf total	2095	4177	4260	6670	7478	7143	4270

Combat Aircraft

	1973	1979	1982	1984	1988	1990	1992
Iran	159	447	90	95	70	78	190
Iraq	224	339	330	580	513	730	260
Iran-Iraq total	383	786	420	675	583	808	450
Bahrain	0	0	0	0	12	12	24
Kuwait	34	50	49	49	36	35	42
Oman	12	35	37	52	63	57	60
Qatar	4	4	9	11	13	19	20
Saudi Arabia	70	178	191	203	179	189	250
UAE	12	52	52	43	65	91	100
GCC total	132	319	338	358	368	403	496
Gulf total	515	1105	758	1033	951	1211	946

Sources: Estimated by the author using various editions of the IISS, *Military Balance*, and ACDA, *World Military Expenditures and Arms Transfers*.

- The Gulf War has gravely weakened Iraq's conventional military forces and ability to produce and deliver weapons of mass destruction. Whether Iraq once threatened to become the superpower of the Gulf, it now has far fewer offensive capabilities and far less strength relative to Iran. It has been denied any major arms imports since August, 1990 and lacks the spares and foreign technical support to properly maintain the equipment that has survived the Gulf War. Iraq does, however, remain a major regional military power. Its army has already been rebuilt to about 40% of its pre–Gulf War strength, and it is far from clear that the UN will be able to deprive Iraq of its biological and chemical weapons or of the opportunity eventually to acquire nuclear weapons.[1]

- Iran has been able to break out of the partial isolation it faced from the rise of Khomeini to the end of the Iran-Iraq War. A somewhat more moderate, or at least pragmatic and subtle, political leadership has exploited the Gulf War to reestablish a strategic dialogue with the southern Gulf states and find new sources of arms. Iran has also been able to acquire new long range missiles and strike aircraft and continue its production of chemical weapons. It almost certainly has biological weapons and is actively trying to acquire nuclear weapons. While it may be half a decade before Iran can rebuild its forces to the level of relative conventional capability they had when the shah fell from power, Iran is already a major regional power that all the Gulf states must recognize.

- The Gulf War has given new impetus to the Kurdish struggle for autonomy or independence and to the struggle of Iraq's Shi'ites for added power or autonomy. Both Iraq and Turkey are fighting low level civil wars to bring their Kurds under control. While Iraq seems to be in full military control of its Shi'ites, they remain a major source of potential internal tension and conflict.

- The southern Gulf states have failed to create any kind of significant alliance out of the Gulf War. The Gulf Cooperation Council has not been able to agree on any form of integration or cooperation that would create effective military forces to defend against Iraq or Iran. The effort to build an alliance with Egypt and Syria and Arab forces has collapsed. While Bahrain and Kuwait have reached a formal security arrangement with the U.S., no similar agreement exists with Saudi Arabia, and many of the military capabilities and prepositioning necessary to allow the West rapidly to deploy to protect the southern Gulf against Iran and Iraq are missing.

- The collapse of the Soviet Union and Warsaw Pact has largely ended superpower rivalry in the Gulf, but it has left East and West with a vast surplus of arms and military production capability. It has also created new Islamic republics that may either follow the secular development path of Turkey or turn to some variant of Iran's Islamic state. Iran is actively attempting to expand its influence over the new Islamic republics. This instability is further complicated by ethnic conflict and near civil war in Azerbaijan and Armenia and by the uncertain struggle for power in Afghanistan. While it is far too soon to tell how these conflicts will involve

Iran, the other Gulf states, and Turkey, the northern perimeter of the Gulf seems likely to be unstable for decades to come.

- The unification of the Yemens has created a state that is more moderate than the PDRY but which is involved in a complex struggle for the control of potential oil fields along its borders with Oman and Saudi Arabia. Yemen also backed Iraq during the Gulf War, and Saudi Arabia responded by halting aid and expelling many Yemeni workers in Saudi Arabia. This has created further tensions between Yemen and Saudi Arabia.
- The conflicts within and between Ethiopia, Somalia, and the Sudan also threaten to create new pressures on the Gulf states. Iran has become actively involved in supporting Islamic fundamentalist movements in these states, particularly the Sudan, and is competing with Saudi Arabia for influence over Islamic groups in Ethiopia.
- The constant increases in force quality and force numbers in Israel, Syria, and the other confrontation states in the Arab-Israeli conflict serve as a model for the arms race in the Gulf. They also reinforce the efforts of Iran and Iraq to acquire longer range strike systems and the use of chemical and nuclear weapons.
- The Iran-Iraq War, Gulf War, and Arab-Israeli arms race have led to a growing emphasis on long range air and missile strike capabilities and use of more lethal weapons such as poison gas throughout the Gulf. They have also stimulated a race to acquire the latest and most lethal conventional weapons.

The Impact of Iran and Iraq
on the Regional Military Balance

While there are many sources of tension in the Gulf region, Iran and Iraq have been the driving force behind most of the serious threats to peace and behind one of the most intense arms races in the developing world. The military trends shaping the development of Iranian and Iraqi military forces are summarized in Table 6.2, and it is clear from these statistics that Iran and Iraq have been involved in a massive arms race since the 1960s. Even a brief review of the recent history of Iran and Iraq and analysis of the arms race shown in Table 6.2 reveal a pattern of tension and conflict likely to shape the Gulf for generations to come.

In order to understand the shifts in the military balance shown in Table 6.2, it is necessary to understand the key events driving the buildup in the northern Gulf. Iran began a major military buildup in the 1960s that became a massive effort by the early 1970s. Until the fall of the shah in 1979, Iran had access to the latest and most advanced U.S. as well as British and Soviet weapons. Iraq's military buildup began after the fall of the monarchy and the collapse of the Central Treaty Organization (CENTO) and was supported largely by the Soviet bloc. Iraq lacked Iran's financial resources during the 1960s and 1970s and had a much smaller and more ethnically divided manpower base. As a result, Iran built up a decisive edge in equipment quality, air power, and manpower.

382

TABLE 6.2 The Iran-Iraq Military Balance, 1967–1991

Country	Manpower (1,000s)[a] Total	Army	Tanks	OAVs	Artillery	Combat Aircraft
1967						
Iran	221	200	225	278	120	180
Iraq	82	70	400–535	200–250	180–250	215
1973						
Iran	212	160	920	1000	380	159
Iraq	102	90	990	1330	700	224
1978 (height of shah's military buildup)						
Iran	413	280–285	1620–1775	1075–1300	782–1225	459–470
Iraq	212	180–200	1800–2450	1500–1600	956–1160	450–470
1980 (first major year of Iran-Iraq War)						
Iran	240	150	1735	1075	1000	445
Iraq	243	200	2750	2500	1240	332
1987 (last year of Iranian military superiority and occupation of part of Iraq)						
Iran	1030	605–735	1000	1060	1200	60–100
Iraq	1000	955	4500	4000	3000	500+
1988 (after August cease-fire and Iranian defeat in Iran-Iraq War)						
Iran	604	550	500–600	700–800	875	60–165[b]
Iraq	1100	1000	5500	4750	2800	500–800[b]
1990 (before Iraq invaded Kuwait)						
Iran	605	555	550–650	760–1200	800	121–180
Iraq	1000–1200	955–1100	5500–7000	6000–8800	3700–5600	513–770
1991 (in spring, operational forces after Iraq's defeat by UN coalition)						
Iran	528–600	400–430	680–750	750–850	1300–1500	180–210[b]
Iraq	500–600	300–400	2100–3100	2000–3500	1200–2000	200–300
1992 (in spring, estimated operational holdings)						
Iran	600–750	500–530	700–800	920–1000	1400–1700	200–230[b]
Iraq	600–800	400–500	2900–3100	3000–3500	2000–2600	330–360

[a]Includes Revolutionary Guards forces and Popular Army forces omitted from some estimates.
[b]Does not count any of 131 Iraqi aircraft that flew to Iran during the Gulf War. Their operational status is unknown as of this writing.
SOURCES: Adapted by the author from interviews and various annual editions of IISS, *Military Balance;* ACDA, *World Military Expenditures and Arms Transfers*; and JCSS, *Middle East Military Balance*. These sources are extremely uncertain in many areas. Even data like main battle tank counts differ radically. The range of estimates has often been adjusted by the author.

During the late 1960s through the mid- to late 1970s, Iran aligned itself with the West and supported Oman against the South Yemen–backed Dhofar rebellion on Oman's southern border. While Iran generally supported the other conservative Gulf regimes, the shah's regional ambitions grew steadily with time. Iran's forces dominated Gulf waters and seized several islands and oil fields from the UAE during the last days of British military withdrawal. Iraq, in contrast, played a radical political role in the Gulf and supported many "independence" movements in the southern Gulf. Iraq also attempted to seize Kuwait once Britain withdrew from the Gulf. If Iraq did not have the shah's military forces, its leader had the shah's ambitions.

Iran and Iraq clashed over control of key areas along the border and access to the Gulf, and they fought a border war during the early and mid-1970s. Iran used its larger and better equipped forces to win most of these clashes, and the shah also exploited an uprising by Iraq's Kurds to create a second front in the north. As a result, Iraq was forced to sign the Algiers accord of 1975. This agreement gave Iran control over most of the disputed border areas and the Shatt al Arab, the key channel that both Iran and Iraq used for access to the Gulf.

The period between the Algiers accord and the late 1970s saw some important shifts in Iraq's behavior. The rise in oil prices made Iraq wealthy, and a new Baath regime took power that shifted the country's ambitions from radical ideology to regional power. Iraq continued to build up its military power, but it simultaneously built up relatively close relations with many of the southern Gulf states. Iraq also began to import weapons and aircraft from Europe—principally from France—as well as from the Soviet bloc.

At the same time, major changes were taking place within Iran. The shah's regime gradually weakened after 1977 and then collapsed in 1979. This suddenly gave power to a radical and xenophobic Islamic government in Iran led by the Ayatollah Khomeini. Khomeini gradually forced a break with the U.S. and the West by seizing American diplomats as hostages. This hostage crisis, however, virtually cut Iran off from Western arms, munitions, and spare parts. At the same time, Iran rejected Iraq's efforts to reach a new political settlement. Khomeini aggressively encouraged Iraq's Shi'ite majority to rise up against the Baath government.

Saddam Hussein reacted by invading Iran. Exploiting the revolutionary turmoil in Iran, Iraq initially enjoyed considerable success. The shah's fall and purges of the Iranian military had crippled much of Iran's military capabilities and left it unable to make effective use of much of its air power and armor. Iraq's military machine, however, was slow moving and lacked strategic direction, and the Iraqi offensive bogged down. The pro-Arab uprising that Iraq hoped to provoke in Iran's oil rich southeast never took place, and Iraq's failure to take the key cities in the region gave Iran time to mobilize a massive popular army.

During 1981–1982, Iran's revolutionary forces gradually drove Iraq out of its conquests in Iran and placed Iraq on the defensive. Iran not only liberated its own southeast, it cut Iraq off from the Gulf and from its major oil export facilities in the Gulf. An Iranian-Syrian alliance shut down Iraq's oil export facilities through Syria, leaving Iraq only a limited export capability through Turkey. Iran also developed a new network of arms purchasing offices and was able to obtain arms from the Soviet Union, Eastern Europe, the PRC, North Korea, and many other states. Iran was never able to use this network to rebuild its armor or replace its U.S.-supplied aircraft. It was, however, able to get enough artillery and light armor to build up a force that threatened Iraq's survival from 1984 to 1987.

Iraq responded by virtually bankrupting itself buying arms to defend itself against the invading Iranian forces. Iraq became dependent on Kuwaiti and Saudi financial aid, although it was able gradually to restore much of its oil export capability by expanding its pipelines through Turkey and creating a new pipeline that joined Saudi pipelines to the Red Sea. This combination of foreign aid and restored oil revenues allowed Iraq to buy far more arms than Iran and gave it access to superior French and European military technology. However, it was only after Iraq virtually rebuilt and retrained its forces during eight years of war and Iran no longer could mobilize its superior population in the face of massive casualties that Iraq acquired a decisive military superiority over Iran. In the spring of 1988, the Iranian army was soundly defeated in a series of battles that drove Iran out of Iraq and cost Iran's army more than 40% of its major equipment. In August, 1988 Iran was forced to agree to a cease-fire.

In the period immediately following the cease-fire in the Iran-Iraq War, Iraq emerged as the dominant military power in the Gulf. It had a massive regional superiority in land and air power, surface-to-surface missiles, and chemical weapons. Yet Iraq emerged from the war as a nearly bankrupt nation, with more than $70 billion in debt. This dependence was unacceptable to Saddam Hussein. During 1988–1990, he gradually put growing pressure on the southern Gulf states to forgive Iraq's debts, to give it preferential oil quotas and prices, and to provide additional aid. At the same time, a crippled Iran slowly rebuilt its forces.

On August 1, 1990, Iraq invaded and seized Kuwait. Iraq not only attempted to annex a nation that had helped it survive the Iran-Iraq War, it did so under the flimsiest of political pretexts. Further, it moved an Iraqi corps to the Kuwaiti-Saudi border—which was defended by only one Saudi brigade. The result was immediate U.S. military intervention and UN agreement to embargo Iraq. The UN slowly created a thirty-two nation coalition to defend Saudi Arabia and liberate Kuwait. The UN then set a deadline for Iraq to withdraw from Kuwait by January, 1991 or face a UN threat to use force. When Iraq ignored this deadline, the Gulf War began. A devastating UN air campaign was followed by a brief and decisive land attack. Iraq was not only driven out of Kuwait, it lost about 40–50% of its major land weapons, saw its air force decimated and become nonoperational, and lost most of its missiles and weapons of mass destruction.

Iraq was forced to sign a cease-fire that required it to give up the rest of its missiles and weapons of mass destruction under UN supervision and that prohibited new shipments of arms. The UN victory did not, however, create a new order in the Gulf. Saddam Hussein remained in power and was able to reconstitute many of his forces. While Iraq lost many of its military capabilities, it still had the largest military forces in the Gulf. At the same time, Iran revived much of its hostility to Iraq, began to receive major shipments of conventional arms, and worked to acquire new missiles and weapons of mass destruction. The Gulf War temporarily checked aggression in the Gulf, but it did not alter the fundamental pattern of the Iranian-Iraqi arms race.

The Iranian-Iraqi Race in Arms Imports

Iranian and Iraqi arms purchases reflect the same patterns as do their competition and military buildup. Iran imported $16.1 billion worth of arms during 1984–1991, and Iraq imported $34.9 billion. Iraq was the world's second largest arms importer during 1984–1987 and the fourth largest during 1988–1991. Iran was the Third World's fourth largest arms importer during 1984–1987 and the fifth largest during 1988–1991.

Iraqi and Iranian arms imports rose by 30% annually from 1980 to 1984, when they reached a level equal to 25% of all world arms imports, 30% of all developing country imports, and 55% of all Middle Eastern imports. Iranian and Iraqi arms imports dropped by nearly 50% in 1985–1986 but rose significantly in 1987 and early 1988. During 1982–1989—the most intense period of the war—the total value of arms transfers agreements with Iran and Iraq was 39% of all arms transfers to the developing world. They rose again in 1990, although both nations faced an internal economic crisis. While Iraq was cut off from arms imports after August, 1990, Iran's imports exceeded $1.5 billion in 1991.

The patterns in the arms trade that have shaped the Iranian-Iraqi arms race since the early 1980s are shown in Table 6.3.

The Full Range of Patterns in Iranian-Iraqi Military Forces

These broad trends, however, are only part of the story. While Iran and Iraq have armed against each other, both states have been involved in a complex web of other rivalries and conflicts. Both have also developed their military forces in response to internal political pressures that have often had little to do with their mutual rivalry. As a result, the military capabilities of Iran and Iraq can best be understood by examining the separate trends in each country.

This is particularly true at the present time. Iran is trying to rebuild its political position and military forces after years of comparative isolation during the Iran-Iraq War and after a devastating series of military defeats in the last year of that conflict. Iraq is now even more isolated as a result of its invasion of Kuwait and its defeat in the Gulf War. The very different strategic positions of the two states are now as important as their mutual rivalry.

TABLE 6.3 Iranian and Iraqi Arms Transfer Agreements by Major Supplier, 1983–1991 (in current $ millions)

Iran	1983–1986	1987–1990	1983–1990	1988–1991
Soviet Union	10	2745	2755	4800
China	1845	3035	4880	4500
United States	0	0	0[a]	0
Major West European	865	145	1010	1400
All other European	3835	2090	5925	5300
All others	2385	1975	4360	3800
Total	8940	9990	18930	19800

Iraq	1983–1986	1987–1990	1983–1990	1988–1991
Soviet Union	11815	4090	15905	15800
China	1760	615	2375	2300
United States	0	0	0	0
Major West European	1005	2665	3670	4500
All other European	3990	1020	5010	4600
All others	1920	1575	3495	4600
Total	20490	9965	30455	30100

[a]Values of covert U.S. sales to Iran in 1985–1986 are not included.

Sources: U.S. Government and Richard F. Grimmett, *Conventional Arms Transfers to the Third World, 1983–1990*, Washington, Congressional Research Service, CRS-9 1-578F, August 2, 1991, and *Conventional Arms Transfers to the Third World, 1984–1991*, Washington, Congressional Research Service, CRS-9 2-577F, July 20, 1992.

Iran

	Manpower (1,000s)	Tanks	Aircraft	Defense Spending ($ millions)	Arms Imports ($ millions)	Arms Exports ($ millions)
1967	210	225	180	837	104	2
1973	285	920	159	2,990	593	2
1982	—	1,110	90	18,260	1,600	—
1988	—	900	70	12,000	2,000	—
1991	528	680–750	180–210	5,770	—	—

Iran occupies a critical strategic position along the northern Gulf and in the northern tier.[2] It has boundaries that span the distance between the former Soviet Union and the Gulf and between Southwest Asia and the Middle East. Iran has an area of approximately 1.65 million square kilometers. It has a 1,690 kilometer boundary with the USSR, a 499 kilometer boundary with Turkey, a 1,448 kilometer land boundary with Iraq, a 909 kilometer border with Pakistan, and a 936 kilometer border with Afghanistan.[3] Its access to the Gulf consists of a 3,180 kilometer coastline with a number of natural ports, although it has been forced to relocate its main ports away from the Shatt al Arab, a river whose waters it shares with Iraq.[4]

Iran is also one of the world's major oil states, although it has smaller reserves than Iraq and far smaller reserves than Saudi Arabia. Iran's oil revenues have varied sharply with world oil prices and the state of conflict in the Gulf, ranging from $7.4 billion to $22.0 billion annually during the 1980s.[5] The petroleum sector accounts for about 90% of Iran's exports. Iran had produced about 39 billion barrels of oil by the end of 1990 and had a relatively high reserve-to-production ratio of 55:1.[6]

Sources disagree over Iran's oil reserves. According to one, Iran has about 35.6 billion barrels of proven oil reserves, or about 4.4% of the world total. In contrast, this source gives Iraq at least 9% of the world's proven oil reserves and Saudi Arabia 21.1%. It does, however, give Iran some 497 trillion cubic feet of natural gas, or 12.9% of the world supply.[7] Other sources indicate that Iran had estimated proved oil reserves of up to 92.86 billion barrels as of January 1, 1992, and gas reserves of 95,000 billion cubic feet. If these totals are correct, Iran had about 12% of the world's total oil reserves and was producing at a rate of about 3.2 to 3.3 million barrels per day.[8]

Iran's most serious present problem is that its oil wealth is not sufficient to maintain high living standards for its burgeoning population, and the rest of its economy is developing at a slow rate. Iran has far less relative wealth than it did under the shah. Much of its agriculture and light industry was disrupted by the Iran-Iraq War and mismanagement by Iran's religious leadership before the death of Khomeini. Its education system is still in considerable disarray, and there are major problems with unemployment or underutilization of labor. Iran is heavily dependent on imports of food, although it has about 45.4 cubic kilometers of internal renewable water resources, which is relatively high for a Middle Eastern country.[9] Iran's post–Iran-Iraq War oil revenues have not been sufficient to cover its needs for arms imports, food imports, and imports for its civil economy.[10]

Historical Forces Shaping Iran's Military Development

Iran's political history has been shaped by shifting outside threats and pressures, a continuing struggle between a monarchy and constitutional reform, and conflict between the modernist and traditionalist elements of Iranian society. A Constitutional Movement arose in the early 1900s led by a small number of Iranian reformers who protested the backwardness, corruption, and foreign concessions of the ruling Qajar dynasty. This group forced the monarchy to grant a constitution and create a popular assembly, or Majlis, in October, 1906.

In 1907, however, Britain and Russia reached an agreement that divided Iran into spheres of influence, and Russia attempted to assert control over the capital at Tehran. This led to the suppression of the new Majlis by the Cossack Brigade, a Russian-trained force first created in 1878 and loyal to the monarchy. In July, 1908 a counterattack by tribal and other revolutionary forces restored the Majlis, forced Mohammed Ali Shah to flee, and installed his son Ahmed Mizra as shah. The new central government, however, was too weak to avoid further fighting, and Iran became the center of a Russian-British-German-U.S. struggle for influence.

In 1911 Russia introduced troops into Iran to ensure control by the monarchy and kept its forces in Iran until the Communists deposed the czars in 1917. Russian forces then gradually withdrew. The new Communist regime in the Soviet Union agreed to a treaty in 1921 that gave up all of Russia's former privileges except the right to send in troops if the country should ever become a base for anti-Soviet activities.

Britain had introduced its own troops into Iran at the beginning of World War I, and Maj. Percy Sykes organized a 5,000 man force called the South Persian Rifles, which he recruited from the area around Bandar Abbas. Britain soon gained control over most of southern Iran, and when Russian troops began to leave the country after the Leninist coup in 1917, Britain attempted to assert control over Iran. It reached an agreement with Ahmed Shah in 1919 that placed British advisors in power in most key military and economic positions, made Britain the sole major arms supplier to Iran, and allowed Britain to dismiss the Cossack Brigade's Russian officers and most of its existing Persian officers. This agreement seemed to give Britain control over the one real military force in the country.

These British actions, however, left Soviet Communist forces occupying the Caspian portion of Iran and provoked a revolt on the part of Iran's secular leaders and Reza Khan, the new commander of the Cossack Brigade. On February 21, 1921, an Iranian journalist named Sayyid Zia al-Din Tbatabai and Reza Khan organized a bloodless coup. The Cossack Brigade marched on Tehran, and Tbatabai and Reza Khan seized power and abrogated all agreements with Britain.

Although the coup was originally led by a civilian, Reza Khan had sole control over the military. Tbatabai quickly found he had no real power. He fled Iran three months after the coup, and Reza Khan manipulated a series of Iranian cabinets to consolidate his power over the country. In October, 1923, the last Qajar shah, Ahmed Shah, bowed to the inevitable, appointed Reza Khan prime minister, and left Iran. Reza Khan then used Iran's growing oil wealth to further consolidate power. While Reza Khan showed some interest in a republican regime, Iran's religious leaders and conservatives opposed most efforts at reform. As a result, Reza Khan had the Majlis appoint him commander in chief for life of the armed forces in February, 1925. He then called a new Majlis. On October 31, 1925, the Qajar dynasty was formally declared to have ended, and on April 25, 1926, Reza Khan was declared shah and his family was given rights of succession.

Reza Shah proved able to suppress resistance by both republican reformers and the conservative clergy. He established tight control over all secular political activity and abolished the veil for women, ended religious control over civil law, and eliminated many of the privileges of the mullahs. He established universal conscription in 1926 and organized a 40,000 man army equipped with modern weapons and under his personal control. He also enforced his rule over all of Iran's classes. He deprived the aristocracy of its titles and power. He weakened the merchant and middle class with state monopolies and taxes, and he ruthlessly taxed the peasantry.

Reza Shah permitted four tightly controlled political parties to exist in

1927 but never allowed real political opposition. He also made the Communist Party illegal in 1931. This was partly a reaction to pressure from the Soviet Union. Although the USSR had evacuated northern Iran in 1921, it had done so only after trying to organize an independent Gilan republic. The treaty of friendship that the Soviet Union signed with Iran on February 21, 1921, gave it the right to intervene in the face of any foreign threat to the USSR based in Iran, and the Soviets took growing advantage of their control of most of Iran's trade, which moved north through the Caspian. This allowed them to force favorable fishery agreements on Iran and to pressure Iran into signing favorable naval, commercial, and customs agreements in 1927 and 1935.

Reza Shah turned to Germany as a counterbalance to Britain and the Soviet Union and shifted Iran's trade to Germany. He obtained German technical and economic advisors and even used German propagandists to help him popularize his rule. He declared neutrality on September 4, 1939, at the beginning of World War II. Tensions grew with Britain and the USSR, however, first because Britain prevented German equipment and trade from reaching Iran and then because Reza Shah prevented any shipment of Allied war supplies to the Soviet Union across Iran. On August 26, 1941, the Soviets and the British invaded Iran. The USSR moved substantial forces down from the north. Britain destroyed the Iranian navy at Khorramshar and sent in troops from Iraq and the Gulf. Reza Shah put up token resistance for three days and then abdicated in favor of his son, Mohammed Reza Pahlavi, on September 16, 1941. Iran was divided into British and Soviet zones of occupation.

This Anglo-Soviet cooperation lasted during World War II, but the USSR actively supported the Iranian Communist Party, or Tudeh, and tried to lay the groundwork for either Communist overthrow of the shah or the creation of an independent Marxist state in northern Iran. At the same time, the British occupation forces in the south seized food from Iran to send to the USSR, creating a state of near starvation in some areas and triggering riots in Tehran that had to be put down by machine gunning Iranian crowds. These British actions left a legacy of anti-Western resentment that was compounded when the Soviet Union, Britain, and the U.S. began a scramble for postwar oil concessions in 1944. The fall of Reza Shah had also allowed new political parties to surface that challenged the power of his son. These included the Tudeh and a strong nationalist movement under Mohammed Mossadeq.

British policy towards Iran shifted significantly once the Labour Party came to power and Britain faced the economic pressures of peace. British occupation forces left Iran in February, 1946. The USSR took a different stance. It attempted to create new Kurdish and Azerbaijani states in Iran, and Soviet troops remained in the north. This allowed the Tudeh Party to seize public buildings in northwest Iran with Soviet support in November, 1945, and Soviet troops halted Iranian forces when they attempted to regain control.

The Soviet-backed Democratic Party of Azerbaijan declared independence in December, 1945, and the Soviet Union supported Mustpha Barzani in declaring a separate Republic of Mahabad in the Kurdish areas in the northwest in January, 1946. Barzani's declaration of independence was unusual because he had previously operated in Iraq and had been expelled from Iraq in 1943. The USSR used its presence in Iran to provide Barzani with bases and arms and the money necessary to create a Democratic Party of Kurdistan in Iran.

These Soviet actions might have permanently split off the northern part of Iran, but Ahmed Qavam, a politician friendly to the Tudeh, was made prime minister. He negotiated a settlement with the Azerbaijanis that was acceptable to the USSR. The U.S. saw these Soviet actions as a serious threat to Iranian sovereignty and control of Gulf oil. It put pressure on the USSR to withdraw its troops and encouraged Iran to offer the Soviet Union important oil concessions for such a withdrawal. While the U.S. had never had more than a token military contingent in Iran, and had withdrawn it in 1945, the Soviet Union seems to have felt that consolidating its occupation of Eastern Europe and the Kuriles had higher priority. As a result, the USSR withdrew its forces from Iran on May 9, 1946.

Iran, however, was now a mix of feuding regional and ethnic factions. Key southern tribes strongly opposed the pro-Russian government in Tehran and the growing power of the Tudeh Party. At the same time, ethnic Arab protests took place in southwestern Iran. At this point, the Iranian army became a primary factor in Iranian politics and allied itself with the shah and other conservatives. In October, 1946 the shah ordered a restructuring of the cabinet that left Qavam in power but expelled all members of the Tudeh. Iran then claimed that the Azerbaijanis had violated their agreement with Iran and sent the Iranian army into the north, ending the Azerbaijani republic and Kurdish republic of Mahabad. In July, 1947 a new Majlis, with U.S. support, rejected the oil concessions offered to the USSR, and Mossadeq played a leading role in forcing Qavam from office for his prior concessions to the USSR.

The U.S. sent a military aid mission to the new pro-Western government in October, 1947. This was the start of a major U.S. military and economic aid effort. Although Britain retained its oil concessions in Iran, the U.S. replaced Britain as the key Western power in the country. These events left the shah dependent on Western support at a time when the rise of Arab nationalism was mirrored by secular and religious nationalism in Iran.

The British-owned Anglo-Iranian Oil Company became the target of this new Iranian nationalism, and this triggered a major internal crisis in April, 1951, when Mossadeq became prime minister. Mossadeq nationalized the oil company, gradually took most of the power away from his colleagues in the Majlis and from the shah, and attempted to purge the military forces of its pro-shah officers. The shah responded by trying to dismiss Mossadeq in August, 1953 and by making Gen. Fazullah Zahedi prime minister. This led to a political struggle in which Mossadeq initially kept power, and the shah left the country. Zahedi, however, was able to exploit the fact that Mossadeq's erratic authoritarianism had alienated virtually all of his political colleagues and rivals, and with British and U.S. aid, he used the armed forces to overthrow Mossadeq.

The shah returned to Iran after Zahedi's countercoup and used his control of the armed forces and internal security forces gradually to enforce the same kind of authoritarian rule that his father had once had. He manipulated the elections of 1954 and 1956 to take control of the Majlis. The Majlis became little more than a political tool for the shah, who reigned as a virtual autocrat. He instituted a series of reforms in a steadily accelerating effort to modernize the country and make it a major power, and he aligned himself firmly with the West. Iran joined the short lived Baghdad Pact on October 11, 1955, and developed growing military ties to the United States.

While some military officers did attempt to overthrow the shah in 1958, the coup had no real backing. The shah had nearly complete control over the military by the early 1960s and became more and more ambitious. He simultaneously sought to rush his nation forward toward full development, create massive modern military forces, and become the dominant power in the region. In 1963 he also began a process of land reform that he called the White Revolution and radically shifted the electoral laws, giving women the vote. While he faced opposition from conservatives and the clergy, he used his army and internal security forces to crush any organized protests.

Not all of the shah's ambitions were peaceful. He made a brief claim to Bahrain when Britain announced it was leaving the Gulf, although he never seriously tried to back this claim with force. He seized the islands of Greater and Lesser Tunbs and Abu Musa from Ras al-Khaimah on November 30, 1971. These islands gave Iran strategic positions in the lower Gulf, and the shah timed his seizure for maximum effect: It occurred just as British forces were leaving, but on the day before Ras al-Khaimah and the United Arab Emirates gained independence.

The shah helped drive the massive rise in oil prices that began in 1974 and gave him the revenues he needed for still more ambitious attempts to modernize Iran and build up its military forces. The shah also engaged in a long confrontation with Iraq over control of the Shatt al Arab. The shah demanded control over half of the channel, which had previously been under Iraqi control to the Iranian shoreline. Iran's forces and artillery sporadically attacked Iraq's positions on the border beginning in January, 1972. Iraq began to strike back in June, and border clashes continued through February, 1975. This fighting was particularly serious in February and March, 1974, when Iraqi forces attempted to seize the disputed border areas and Iranian forces counterattacked. A cease-fire was arranged on March 7, 1974—after quiet U.S. and Soviet intervention and diplomatic action by the UN.

The shah did more than use his own military forces to put pressure on Iraq. He provided increasing amounts of arms and money to Barzani's Kurdish forces. This was the same Barzani who had once attempted to seize Kurdish territory in Iran but who had been fighting Iraq since the 1960s. The shah's support helped persuade Barzani to reject an Iraqi ultimatum of March 11, 1974, that offered him limited self-rule and to go on fighting.

The increasingly bloody fighting between Iraq and the Kurds gave the shah greater leverage in his negotiations with Iraq. As a result, the Iraqi government was forced to concede to most of the shah's demands. It agreed to halt all fighting on the border in February, 1975 and on March 6, 1975, signed an agreement that became known as the Algiers accord. The shah had scored a major triumph and kept his side of the bargain. He promptly halted the flow of money and arms to Barzani, and the Kurdish movement soon collapsed. Barzani fled to Iran and was then sent into exile in the U.S., where he died.[11]

The shah seemed to dominate the Gulf. His navy was the largest in the region, and he controlled strategic islands near the Straits of Hormuz. He had defeated Iraq and had also successfully intervened in Oman, where the shah supported Sultan Qabus against the Dhofar rebels backed by the PDRY. He had the largest and most modern air force in the region and a modern army with the region's only major attack helicopter force, and he was courted by the U.S., Soviet Union, and Europe alike.

The shah, however, had growing domestic problems after 1976. He increasingly lost touch with Iran's lower and middle classes. His White Revolution, which was supposed to lead to massive land reform, did little more in many areas than take the land away from the landowners and seize it for the shah's Pahlavi Foundation. The government of Iran became increasingly corrupt, and Western profiteering became the rule rather than the exception. The shah alienated the Muslim clergy and did nothing to protect the lower classes when a drop in oil revenues created massive urban unemployment in the late 1970s. The result was a series of popular uprisings and riots, led by both the Muslim clergy and secular reformers. The most important figure in this uprising, however, became the Ayatollah Ruhollah Khomeini—a charismatic religious leader the shah had driven into exile.

It is uncertain whether the shah could have crushed the growing rebellion by using the armed forces. Many officers and other ranks came to support Khomeini and the revolution. The shah, however, was suffering from cancer and was slow to react and indecisive. He failed to take action, and this time there was no General Zahedi to save him. The shah fled the country on December 6, 1978.

Khomeini flew back from exile in France shortly after the shah left the country, and he received a triumphant popular welcome. He then proceeded to restructure Iran's political system and society around his concept of an Islamic state. After a popular referendum, Iran was proclaimed an Islamic republic in April, 1979. A series of civil and ethnic conflicts, struggles between religious and Marxist parties, and upheavals and purges in the armed forces followed that gradually gave Khomeini nearly total power over the state.

Khomeini's rise to power also led Iran into a major confrontation with the U.S. The shah entered the U.S. for treatment of his cancer on October 22, 1979. Iran's new leaders viewed this as a potential conspiracy between the U.S. and the shah and as a symbol of American treachery. On November 4, Iranian "students" seized the U.S. embassy compound in Tehran with the support of the Iranian government and took the U.S. diplomats in the embassy hostage. The Iranian government proved helpless to free the Americans without Khomeini's permission, and this led to a long hostage crisis during which the U.S. and other Western nations halted all arms transfers to Iran. It also led to an unsuccessful raid by U.S. special forces, who tried to recover the U.S. hostages on April 24, 1980. The crisis ended only after the U.S. presidential election in 1982. By this time the American diplomats had been captive for more than two years, and the crisis left a lasting bitterness on both sides.

During this same period, many of the shah's officers were forced out of the military, and Khomeini's supporters began to create a new military force called the Revolutionary Guards. This political turmoil weakened Iran's military forces at a time when Iran's new religious government faced a military challenge from its Kurds and hard-line Marxist revolutionaries like the People's Mujahideen. It also occurred at a point when Khomeini was calling for the overthrow of Iran's secular ruler, Saddam Hussein, and Iran was sending "missionaries" to persuade Iraq's Shi'ites to rise up against the Baath Party. Border clashes between Iran and Iraq occurred during much of 1980, and Saddam Hussein decided on war. Iraq repudiated the Algiers accord on September 17, 1980. It then invaded Iran. This invasion led to eight years of bloody war between the two countries.

Iran was the victor during much of the fighting. It drove Iraq out of southwestern Iran by July, 1982 and launched repeated offensives in Iraq, seizing the Faw Peninsula in 1987 and threatening the security of Basra. Iran, however, never developed a cohesive replacement for the shah's regular army, and the fervor of its Revolutionary Guards was not an adequate counter to Iraq's massive firepower and armor and its air superiority. Iraq had free access to Western and Soviet bloc arms, whereas Iran's militant Islamic ideology and actions during the U.S. embassy hostage crisis deprived it of access to most Western arms.

Although Iran dominated the fighting during 1987 and early 1988, it did so only by exhausting its forces, which suffered massive casualties. Iraq launched a series of major offensives in the spring of 1988, supported by vastly superior armor, virtual air supremacy, and the use of poison gas. By the time of the August, 1988 cease-fire, Iran had been decisively defeated on the battlefield, had lost more than 50% of its major army equipment, and was devastated by war and internal political extremism. Its economic development had virtually halted for nearly a decade, while its population had increased at a rate of over 3% per year.[12]

Iran Since the End of the Iran-Iraq War

Within a year, however, Iran's situation began to improve. Khomeini's death on June 3, 1989, brought the more pragmatic Ali Akbar Hashemi Rafsanjani to power. Although he was challenged by a number of radicals and extremists, Rafsanjani proved able to install his own cabinet on August 19, 1989. Rafsanjani purged such extremists as Interior Minister Ali Akbar Mohtashemi and Intelligence Minister Mohammed Reyshari. He also appointed a number of leading technocrats, although he retained hard-liners like Mohammed Khatani as minister of Islamic guidance and made Khomeini's personal representative to the Iranian Revolutionary Guard Corps (IRGC) the new minister of the interior.[13]

Khomeini's death also replaced his charismatic religious leadership with that of the far less powerful Ayatollah Ali Hoseni Khameni. While Khameni has sometimes echoed Khomeini's extremist rhetoric, he does not seem to have opposed Rafsanjani's growing efforts to deal with the political realities of international life and the economic realities of internal development. Iran abandoned many of Khomeini's dysfunctional attempts at Islamic socialism and shifted to a much more realistic emphasis on capitalism and private enterprise.[14]

The end of the Iran-Iraq War and Khomeini's death also gradually brought more stability to the armed forces, although the situation initially deteriorated after the August, 1988 cease-fire. Iran's Revolutionary Guards were purged. Mohsen Rezai, the IRGC commander since 1981, was removed from power—supposedly because of the IRGC's poor performance at Faw and for misuse of defense funds. Brig. Gen. Ismail Sohrabi was dismissed as chief of staff for the failure of Iranian forces to hold at Faw, a number of other regular army officers were dismissed or arrested, and some may have been executed.[15]

Khomeini had blocked Rafsanjani's efforts to merge the Revolutionary Guards with the regular army during June, 1988 until Khomeini died in June, 1989, and Khomeini put a hard-line mullah in a position where he had nearly equal authority to Rafsanjani and supervisory authority over the IRGC minister Ali Shamkhani and IRGC commander Mohsen Rezai. This reinforced the feuding between the regular forces and IRGC that had helped contribute to Iran's defeat.[16] Rafsanjani and Khameni, however, reached a working accord after Khomeini's death. Rafsanjani resigned as commander of the armed forces when he became president on September 2, 1989, and Khameni replaced him. Shamkhani was then moved from the role of IRCG minister to commander of the navy in October, 1989. Akbar Torkan, a close supporter of Rafsanjani, was appointed minister of defense and armed forces logistics and given a portfolio that combined supervision of the regular forces and IRGC.[17]

Pragmatic professionals were appointed to other senior positions. These included Brig. Gen. Hassan Firuzabadi as chief of staff of the armed forces general staff and Brig. Gen. Ali Shahbazi as chief of the army staff. Rafsanjani and Khameni also retained professionals like Brig. Gen. Mansur Sattari as air force commander and Brig. Gen. Hussein Hansani-Sadi as commander of armed forces ground forces. This gave the regular forces the most effective and stable command they had enjoyed since 1979.

While it is difficult to be sure of the loyalties involved, the high command of the IRGC was also extensively reorganized. Mohammed Baqr Zuiilqadr was made chief of staff of the IRGC Central Headquarters in 1989 and given special responsibility for enforcing discipline and requiring the IRGC to implement orders. Mustpha Uzadi was appointed head of the IRGC ground forces in 1989, Hussein Dehqan was appointed head of the IRGC air forces in

April, 1990, and Alireza Afshar was appointed commander of the Basij, or volunteer forces, in January, 1990.[18] These appointments seem to have brought more stable and compliant leadership to the IRGC, although Hussein Alai remained commander of the IRGC naval forces and Maj. Gen. Qassem Ali Zahirnezhad—a Khomeini loyalist—remained Khameni's chief military advisor and Iran's highest ranking army officer.[19]

Rafsanjani and Khameni seem to have cooperated in the selection of candidates for Iran's parliament in 1992, although Rafsanjani was clearly in charge. The ruling religious group in Iran is the Council of Guardians, and it is charged with reviewing all candidates for the Consultative Assembly. Some 3,240 potential candidates applied to the Council of Guardians to run for the 270 seats in the Consultative Assembly. Rafsanjani seems to have used his influence to weed out candidates he felt were radical or extremist as a means of consolidating his power over both the government and the military.

The election took place on April 10, 1992, with a second round in early May. It was the first election since Khomeini's death, and both rounds of voting gave a clear majority in the Consultative Assembly to supporters of Rafsanjani and those favoring more pragmatic economic policies. Hard-liners like Mehdi Karrubi and Mohtashemi lost power, and Rafsanjani was able to replace a large number of hard-line ideologues in the civil service with technocrats. Many experts felt that the victory would allow Rafsanjani to press on with the privatization plans and reductions in subsidies he had sought since 1989, although some believed Iran's hard-line bureaucrats might prove harder to reform than its Consultative Assembly.[20]

It is difficult to be certain of the relative position of Rafsanjani and Khameni after the election. Khameni retained nominal control over the armed forces. There were few signs of active feuding, however, and Khameni lacks the kind of prestige and charisma that allowed Khomeini to exploit the position of supreme religious leader to act as a virtual shah. The most Khameni has done so far is to become a voice of anti-Western orthodoxy without challenging Rafsanjani directly on any major issue.

The clergy has also allowed Rafsanjani to liberalize private economic activity and to allow exiles to return to their businesses as long as they do not challenge the clergy's new role in the economy. The main instruments of clerical power in the economy are the *bunyods*, or large religious foundations, formed to manage the property and assets confiscated from the Shah and his supporters after the revolution. This gives the clergy considerable wealth and economic leverage; the largest of these *bunyods*, the Foundation for the Deprived, had a budget of $10 billion in 1992.

This economic pragmatism is vital. The war with Iraq and Iran's population growth have left the Iranian economy extremely weak and heavily dependent on food imports. While the clergy has made some real progress in land reform, the slums surrounding Iran's cities are far poorer and more crowded than at the time the shah fell. Poverty helped lead to riots and the imposition of martial law in Arak, Shiraz, and Mashed in mid-1992. The government was forced to set up special anti-riot police forces, and Iran's chief justice, Mohammed Yazdi, threatened swift punishment and the use of firing squads. This did not stop new riots in Tabriz in July, when some 30,000 protesters reacted to the razing of 300 squatter dwellings.

Other aspects of the internal security situation are somewhat better. The importance of any remaining political splits between the regular army and the IRGC may also be exaggerated. It has been more than a decade since the fall of the shah, and most of Iran's current military manpower has no Western training or history of loyalty to the former monarchy. The Iranian high command has been chosen on the basis of loyalty to Rafsanjani, there is improved coordination between the various elements of the regular armored forces and the IRGC, and some experts believe that Rafsanjani may slowly cut the IRGC in size and turn it into a paramilitary internal security force.[21]

Iran's Activities Outside Iran

Iran was one of the few countries to benefit from the Gulf War. Iraq lost much of its weaponry while Iran's opposition to Iraq's invasion of Kuwait gave Iran new respectability. Iran also gained much better access to the world's arms market. Beginning in 1991, it was able to import first line tanks like the T-72 and aircraft like the MiG-29 and Su-24 from the Russian republic. While these imports were still small enough in 1992 to be classified as defensive, Iran also obtained long range surface-to-surface missiles from North Korea. It obtained equipment and supplies for its biological and chemical weapons efforts and got increased—if still limited—imports of high technology for its nuclear weapons program.

At the same time, Iran has not given up attempting to export Islamic fundamentalism. It has shifted away from highly public ideological pronouncements, but it has provided money and cadres throughout the Middle East and Central Asia.[22] While any talk of a "Caspian alliance" seems premature at best and only Azerbaijan has a Shi'ite majority, Iran did open embassies in Azerbaijan, Turkmenistan, and Tadzhikistan in 1991. It has tried to revive the long dormant Economic Development Council once formed by Iran, Turkey, and Pakistan in the mid-1960s. The Azerbaijan, Kirghiz, Tadzhik, Turkmen, and Uzbek republics joined the council in a summit meeting on February 17, 1992. Iran also announced at this meeting that it had signed a Caspian Sea cooperation pact with Azerbaijan, Russia, Kazakhstan, and Turkmenistan.

These Iranian efforts have led Turkey and Saudi Arabia to provide money and advisors to competing secular and Islamic elements. It is difficult, however, to tell whether Iran has real ambitions to dominate any of the republics or is simply seeking economic and cultural influence. Turkey joined with Iran to condemn Armenian attacks on the Azerbaijani enclave of Nagorno-Karabakh in May, 1992, and the Muslim republics are major potential markets for Iran, and non-Muslim republics like the Ukraine are equally important potential markets for Iranian gas and oil.[23]

Iran has largely abandoned active efforts to subvert its neighbors in the southern Gulf. It gave back to Kuwait the six Kuwaiti airliners that Iraq had seized and flown to Iran during the Gulf War in May, 1992, and Iran made concerted efforts to improve political and economic relations. Nevertheless, it has maintained at least low level contact with anti-regime Shi'ites in Bahrain, Kuwait, Qatar, Saudi Arabia's eastern province, and the UAE. It has provided support to Islamic fundamentalist movements outside the Gulf, including those in Algeria, Morocco, Tunisia, and Egypt. It has been particularly active in backing the fundamentalist FIS movement in Algeria, although the rise of Islamic fundamentalism in Algeria is certainly of native origin and has been sustained largely by decades of misrule by Algeria's military junta.

Iran has also become involved in a new dispute with the United Arab Emirates over the rights of Arabs living in Abu Musa. When the shah seized Abu Musa in 1971, he allowed 700 Arabs from the UAE to remain in the island and effectively split control of the island's population with the UAE. In April, 1992 Iran took control of the entire island, expelled about 100 foreign workers without Iranian visas, and expelled many of the Arab residents. Iran claimed that it had not received a fair share of the offshore oil production from the island, although the Iranian media soon began to refer to the entire island as Iranian territory and as part of Hormuzgan province.

During April 25–May 4, 1992, Iran staged the largest amphibious exercise it had conducted since the end of the Iran-Iraq War. This exercise took place at the Straits of Hormuz, at the same time that Iran was seizing control of Abu Musa. It lasted 11 days, practiced an effort to block the straits to an outside invader (the U.S.), covered an area of some 10,000 square miles of ocean, and involved 45 surface ships, 150 small craft, and an unknown number of Iranian air force aircraft.

The UAE reacted with a proposal by which it would solve the sovereignty problem by leasing the entire island to Iran and altering the share of oil. When this proposal failed, Iran and the UAE also became involved in a major diplomatic clash over the issue.

In September, 1992 the UAE took an increasingly hard line, and obtained support from the Gulf Cooperation Council (GCC) and the Arab League. Iran countered by charging that the GCC states and Arab League states had become U.S. plotters. Iran broke off talks on the issue on September 28, 1992, after the UAE chose to make it the subject of GCC and Arab League diplomacy and renewed its claims to the two Tunbs. Rafsanjani declared the issue a U.S. "conspiracy... to justify its illegitimate presence in the Gulf."[24]

Iran plays an active political role in nations like Lebanon and Sudan and has supported anti-Baathist Iraqi Kurds and anti-Baathist Iraqi Shi'ite forces in southern Iraq with money, arms, and training facilities in Iran. While Iran no longer maintains large Revolutionary Guard cadres in Lebanon and provides the Hizbollah and Party of God faction with fewer funds and arms, it still is a significant force in the Shi'ite politics of southern Lebanon and in the fighting among Shi'ite elements, the South Lebanon Army, and Israel. It also provides training, funds, and arms to a number of Palestinian extremist groups that attack Israel, and some reports indicate that it provided support for the May 17, 1992 bombing of the Israeli embassy in Buenos Aires.[25]

Iran plays a major role in supporting the Sudan's hard-line Islamic fundamentalist government, now led by Lt. Gen. Omar Hassab al-Bashir and religious leaders like Sheik Hassan al-Tourabi. It has encouraged steady increases in the application of Islamic law, and certain sources report that Iran shipped at least $17 million worth of arms to the Sudan in 1991, and continued to provide arms in 1992. Iranian support for religious extremism in the Sudan is contributing to the extension of the bloody civil war between the Sudan's Arab and non-Arab populations and is steadily reducing the tolerance for Christian and secular elements in the northern Sudan.

These sources also indicate that Iran has provided training and support to Nafei Ali Nafel, the head of the Sudan's intelligence service. There is almost certainly some truth in these reports. Ali Falahan, the head of Iran's secret services, and Mohsen Rezai, the head of its Revolutionary Guards, have visited the Sudan on several occasions. What are far more controversial are reports that Iran has sent 1,000 to 2,000 Revolutionary Guards to assist the Sudan's military forces.[26]

Iranian Military Expenditures and Conventional Arms Transfers

Iran's military expenditures and arms imports have played a critical role in shaping its military capabilities, but they have fluctuated sharply with time. Iran's high military expenditures and arms imports during the 1960s and 1970s made it the dominant military power in the Gulf. Iran was forced to reduce its expenditures in the late 1970s, however, when a reduction in oil prices triggered a major recession and Iran fell into economic turmoil following the fall of the shah. Iran lost its access to Western arms after 1979, following the U.S. embassy hostage crisis, and this created major problems in keeping Iran's existing military equipment operational.

The beginning of the Iran-Iraq War in 1980 led Iran to raise military expenditures and seek arms imports from other countries. Iran's economy never recovered from the shock of the revolution and the Iraqi invasion, however, and Iran was forced to buy most of its arms from the PRC, North Korea, the Soviet bloc, other developing countries, and the gray market. As a result, Iran could not compete with Iraq in military spending or arms imports during 1980–1988.

This situation eased after the end of the Iran-Iraq War in 1988 and because of Iran's support of the UN during the Gulf War. Iran's economy began to recover from both the Iran-Iraq War and mismanagement during the time of Khomeini. Its oil markets partially recovered, and it found a new source of advanced arms in the Russian republic and Eastern Europe, while continuing to expand its purchases from the PRC and North Korea.

It is impossible to describe these trends with any reliability because of the uncertainty of the data involved. ACDA sources indicate, however, that Iran decreased its annual military expenditures from $25,300 million in 1978 to $16,620 million in 1979 and $14,700 million in 1980. As a result of the Iran-Iraq War, it then spent $16,210 million in 1981, $18,260 million in 1982, $15,940 million in 1983, $22,240 million in 1984, and $24,770 million in 1985.[27]

The U.S. does not provide estimates of Iranian defense spending after

1985, but the IISS estimates that Iranian economic problems and defeat in 1988 reduced Iran's defense spending to $9,900 million in FY1987–88, $5,770 million in FY1989–90, $3,180 million in 1990, and $3,770 million in 1991.[28] These estimates, however, do not include procurement, and British government experts estimate that Iran actually spent $19,000 million on military forces in 1991 and planned to spend $14.5 billion in 1992. It seems likely that Iran will spend at least $8 billion to $10 billion annually on defense in 1992, 1993, and 1994.[29]

Any estimate of the burden military expenditures have placed on Iran's economy are even more uncertain than estimates of the size of these military expenditures, and Iranian official economic statistics have little reliability. Iran does, however, seem to have spent as much as 20% of its GDP on defense during the Iran-Iraq War and about 50% of its central government expenditures.[30]

During the 1980s, Iran never had enough hard currency and access to the world market to raise its arms imports to the levels it reached under the shah. It did, however, conduct a massive effort to buy arms once the Iran-Iraq War began, and this was reflected in its arms deliveries during 1982–1988. ACDA estimates that Iran imported $2,100 million worth of arms in 1978, $1,500 million in 1979, $420 million in 1980, $925 million in 1981, $1,600 million in 1982, $825 million in 1983, $2,700 million in 1984, $1,900 million in 1985, $2,600 million in 1986, $2,000 million in 1987, $2,300 million in 1988, and $1,300 million in 1989.[31]

During 1979–1983, Iran ordered $5.4 billion worth of arms compared to Iraqi orders of $17.6 billion. These figures indicate that Iraq imported more than three times as many arms as Iran, and yet they understate Iran's problems. Because Iran found it virtually impossible to obtain arms from its prior Western suppliers after 1979, it was forced to turn to other sources. As a result, it obtained only $1,300 million worth of arms from the U.S. during 1979–1983, almost all of these during 1979. It also only obtained $140 million worth of arms from the UK, $20 million from France, $5 million from West Germany, and $30 million from Italy. In contrast, during 1979–1983 Iran obtained $975 million worth of arms from the USSR, $230 million from the PRC, $40 million from Poland, $5 million from Romania, and $2,600 million from other nations.[32]

This shift towards new suppliers is also reflected in Iran's arms imports during the second half of the Iran-Iraq War. During 1974–1978, Iran ordered $10.5 billion worth of arms compared to Iraqi orders of $29.7 billion. Iran obtained only $10 million worth of arms from the U.S., although it did somewhat better with European suppliers, acquiring $100 million worth of arms from the UK, $100 million from France, $200 million from West Germany, and $30 million from Italy. Iran's relations with the USSR also deteriorated during this period, and Iran obtained only $5 million worth of arms from the USSR. Iran did much better, however, with the PRC and Eastern Europe. It obtained $2,500 million from the PRC, $70 million from Poland, $20 million from Czechoslovakia, and $800 million from Bulgaria. Iran's dependence on North Korea, Third World suppliers, and a wide variety of covert sources is illustrated by its acquisition of $6,705 million worth of arms from other nations.[33]

According to the most recent ACDA reports, Iran imported a total of $10,250 million worth of arms during 1985–1989, including $10 million from the U.S., $75 million from France, $100 million from the UK, $2,800 million from the PRC, $50 million from West Germany, $1,400 million from other Warsaw Pact countries, $3,345 million from other European countries, $40 million from other Middle Eastern countries, $2,000 million from other East Asian states, $210 million from Latin America, and $220 million from other countries in the world.[34] Such data do not include covert Israeli and U.S. arms deliveries during the early and mid-1980s. These deliveries were relatively small but helped Iran with critical parts for aircraft and surface-to-air missile systems, and in obtaining modern TOW anti-tank weapons.[35] At the same time, such purchases from the U.S. and Israel and various black market purchases from Western Europe did not prevent Iran from experiencing serious difficulties in importing new equipment, many critical spare parts, and sophisticated munitions.

These arms import problems also had a major impact on the outcome of the Iran-Iraq War. While Iran did find Chinese, North Korean, and East European substitutes for some of its land weapons, shortages in Western arms, parts, and munitions helped deprive Iran of much of its armor and naval and air power. Even worse, Iran lost most of its Soviet bloc and Asian arms in 1988. According to most estimates, Iran lost over 40% of its major army equipment during its final battles before the August, 1988 cease-fire.

This helps explain why Iran ordered $9.7 billion worth of new arms between 1988 and 1991—with $2.86 billion in 1990 and $1.9 billion in 1991— even though its GDP in 1992 was still only about half its 1978 and 1979 levels. It had become a massive food importer, and its industrial capacity had shrunk by as much as 60%.[36] The main sources of new orders were $4.8 billion from the USSR, $1.9 billion from the PRC, $0.2 billion from major West European countries, $1.2 billion from the rest of Europe, and $1.6 billion from other states. The CIA estimates that Iran is likely to import about $1.5 billion a year worth of arms through the year 2000.

Iran took delivery of $6.9 billion worth of arms during 1988–1991, with $1.4 billion worth of arms in 1990 and over $1.5 billion in 1991. Deliveries included $2.1 billion from the USSR, $2.0 billion from the PRC, $0.3 billion from West Europe, $1.0 billion from the rest of Europe, and $1.5 billion from other states.

These purchases reflected Iran's new access to arms from the Russian republic and East Europe and heavy dependence on the PRC. They are large enough so that Iran ranked third in new arms orders in the developing world during the period between the end of the Iran-Iraq War and the Gulf War, and fourth in deliveries.

Access to Russian supplies was particularly important because it gave Iran access to more advanced technology. Rafsanjani seems to have reached a $1.9 billion sales agreement with Russia during a June, 1989 trip to Moscow that traded the delivery of gas through the IGAT II pipeline for Soviet agreement to sell Iran 48 MiG-29 fighters, 100 T-72 tanks, and other equipment and services. Iran may also have made a $6 billion arms deal with Russia in July, 1991.

According to some Iranian Mujahideen reports, an agreement was signed in Moscow between Lt. Gen. Yevgeny Shaposhnikov and General Sattari, the head of the Iranian air force, for Iran to buy a T-72 assembly plant, 122mm and 130mm guns, 100 MiG-21 fighters, a MiG-29 assembly plant, 48 MiG-31 air defense fighters, 24 Su-24 strike fighters, and 2 IL-76s equipped as airborne warning aircraft.

It is difficult to determine whether Iranian arms import and force expansion plans are defensive, offensive, or part of a buildup that as yet has no clear strategic direction. Some sources reported in mid-1992 that Iran had a $10 billion arms plan to acquire new army, air defense, air, and naval equipment during 1990–1994. Other sources indicated that it had a plan that would increase its tank strength from 500 in 1990 to 1,400 in 1997, its combat aircraft strength from 275 to 350, its surface-to-air missile strength from 90 major launchers to 300, its surface-to-surface missile strength from 30 major launchers to 60, and its submarine strength from none to 3. Less reliable sources reported orders of 400 more Soviet T-72s and 500 BMP-2s in 1992 and orders of 170 North Korean Scud B and Scud Cs and PRC-made M-11 missiles in 1991. It was clear that Iran continued to make major purchases, but there were far more numbers and sources than facts.[37]

Iran is also rebuilding and expanding its defense industry, which the shah first began to expand in 1970.[38] It seems to be investing about $250 million a year in conventional arms and a larger amount in missiles and weapons of mass destruction.[39] According to Akbar Torkan, its minister of defense and armed forces logistics, it has merged its plans for the regular army and Revolutionary Guards into one system to make them more efficient, and it has tripled its output of arms since 1979.

Iran had at least 240 state owned arms plants in 1992, employed about 45,000 people, and planned to expand its operations to a level that would employ 60,000 people within five years. While Iran has sometimes exaggerated its domestic arms production capabilities, it has had Soviet, North Korean, PRC, Israeli, Pakistani, Argentine, Brazilian, Taiwanese, and German help in expanding its facilities. It can manufacture some aircraft and armored weapons parts, wheeled armored vehicles, artillery weapons and parts, artillery and small arms ammunition, rockets, small arms, and mortars. It is trying, with PRC assistance, to produce parts for its F-4s, F-5s, and F-14s.[40]

Iran's Demographics and Military Manpower

Iran's current military capabilities are heavily influenced by its demographics. Iran is by far the most heavily populated Gulf state, and this gives it a major potential advantage in building up its military forces. At the same time, this manpower base has deep ethnic divisions, and Iran's ability to transform it into military power is severely limited by economic problems and access to arms imports.

In 1991 Iran had a population of about 59.1 million, growing at a rate of

3.6%. This population was about 51% Persian, 25% Azerbaijani, 9% Kurd, 8% Gilaki and Mazandarani, 2% Lur, 1% Baloch, 1% Arab, and 3% other. Iran is about 95% Shi'ite Muslim, but has 4% Sunni Muslim and 1% Zoroastrian, Christian, Jewish, and Bahai.[41] It has a wide variety of linguistic groups. Only 58% of the population speaks some form of Persian, 26% speaks some form of Turkic, 9% Kurdish, and five other linguistic groups total about 7% of the population.

Iran is one of the few Middle Eastern states to promote birth control—reversing Khomeini's position on the issue. This program has had strong support from Rafsanjani, who doubled funding from $75 million to $150 million between 1991 and 1992. Partly because of these birth control efforts, the government estimates that its birthrate has dropped from 3.9% in 1985 to 2.7% in late 1991. This still, however, leaves it with a population of 59 million—with 20% under the age of 5 and 45% under the age of 15—and its oil income in constant dollars will be about the same in 1992 as it was in 1979. Further, even at this reduced rate it will have 87 million people by the year 2000—more than twice the 37 million people it had when the Shah fell.

Iran's total male manpower pool is about 12.75 million, counting the population between the ages of 15 and 49. The CIA estimates that 7.589 million males are fit for military service and that 576,000 reach military age each year.[42] The IISS estimates that there are 3.078 million males between the ages of 13 and 17, 2.659 million between the ages of 18 and 22, and 4.182 million between the ages of 23 and 32.[43]

Estimates differ sharply regarding Iran's total military manpower. The IISS has estimated that Iran has about 528,000 full time actives in its regular forces, plus 350,000 men in its reserves. It estimates that it has 170,000 men in its Revolutionary Guards (Pasdaran Inquilab), 150,000 in its Popular Mobilization Army (Basij), 45,000 in its gendarmerie, and around 12,000 men in an Iranian-trained and -funded Kurdish Democratic Party militia. This would give a total of 727,000 full time and part time soldiers—a small fraction of Iran's potential manpower strength.

One expert estimated in 1992 that Iran's regular active strength was only about 470,000 men but did not have estimates for the other portions of Iran's forces. Other sources indicate that the IRGC has a total of about 150,000–200,000 men and that the active strength of the Basij had declined sharply since the end of the Iran-Iraq War and is now under 30,000 men. In peacetime the Basij is used largely for civil projects or activities where the regime seeks to mobilize youth for a single task or propaganda purposes. There is also a small Qod (ex-service battalion) force within the IRGC that acts as an active commando or strike force and which is used in Lebanon, the Sudan, and unconventional warfare missions.

The Iranian Army

The Iranian land forces are in a considerable state of turmoil, and it is difficult to make anything approaching accurate estimates of its strength.[44] Before its defeats in 1988, Iran's regular army had around 300,000–350,000 active men, including 250,000 conscripts, and a paper pool of up to 350,000 reserves—organized into Qods. Estimates differ sharply as to the army's combat unit strength, but it seemed to have at least three and probably four major army headquarters along the front with Iraq. It had three to four mechanized "divisions" (each with a paper strength of three brigades of nine armored and eighteen mechanized battalions), seven infantry divisions, one to two independent airborne brigades, and one special forces division with three to four brigades. Many of these units were understrength in manpower and equipment, and Iran often tended to report brigades as if they were divisions.

The Revolutionary Guard Corps that first came into existence after the revolution had 300,000–350,000 men, organized into eleven regional commands. These forces had at least eight "divisions" and many independent regiments and brigades of very different composition. Some estimates combined these units into a total strength of twenty-one divisions. The IRGC was organized into border, infantry, armored, special forces, and paratroop units, and had its own engineering, artillery, and air defense support units.

The IRGC had priority over Iran's other forces and was getting the largest share of the new equipment Iran was obtaining from the PRC, North Korea, and the Third World. Regular army units tended to be starved for supplies unless they were actually committed to an offensive. They were being treated as a dwindling asset which must conserve irreplaceable skills and key equipment items, while the IRGC was treated as the forces of the future.

The IRGC was also supported by Basij volunteer units, organized into around 500 lightly equipped battalions. These battalions were supposed to have about 300–350 men but had a wide range of strengths. Estimates of the total size of the Basij forces differ sharply, but they seem to have an effective strength of around 130,000 and a mobilization pool in excess of 500,000.

Iran's land forces were much stronger in terms of manpower than equipment. Iran's isolation from the West had lasted for nearly a decade, and Iran's ground forces were an awkward mix of many different types and a total strength of around 1,000 Soviet-made T-54/55, 260 Chinese-made T-59s, some Soviet-made T-62s and T-72s, some British-made Chieftain Mark 3/5s, and some U.S.-made M-47s, M-48s, and M-60A1s. Iran had more operational PRC- and North Korean–made T-54, T-55, and T-59 tanks than Western ones.

Iran had roughly 500 operational BTR-50, BTR-60, and Urutu armored personnel carriers and around 250 M-113s which remained from the days of the shah. It had roughly 180 BMP-1 and 130 EE-9 Cascaval armored infantry fighting vehicles (AIFVs). It was heavily dependent on Soviet bloc, PRC, and North Korean artillery. It had between 750 and 1,500 major artillery weapons, 30 self-propelled M-107 175mm guns, M-101 105mm howitzers, 36 Oto Melara 105mm howitzers, M-109A1 155mm howitzers, M-110 203mm howitzers, Chinese-made Type-63 12 x 107mm multiple rocket launchers, and 65 Soviet-made BM-21 40 x 122mm multiple rocket launchers. It may also have had some 180mm SS-40 Astros weapons.

Its air defense weapons strength probably totaled around 1,500 ZU-23 23mm towed, ZSU-23-4 23mm self-propelled, 35mm towed, 37mm towed, and ZSU-57-2 57mm self-propelled anti-aircraft guns. While Iran was able to buy and manufacture enough parts to keep a few of its helicopters flying, most of its once massive force of over 700 helicopters—including its AH-1 Cobra attack, CH-47C heavy transport, and Bell 214A, AB-205A, and AB-206 light helicopters—were either nonoperational or only partly operational.

Iran's equipment problems grew far worse after Iran's defeats in spring and summer, 1988. These defeats were so severe that they led to the disintegration of some elements of the IRGC and even Iran's main regular army units. They also led to massive equipment losses. While exact numbers are in dispute, Iran clearly lost over half of its operational armor between February and July, 1988.

Iraq seems to have been broadly correct in claiming to have captured some 1,298 Iranian tanks and heavy armored fighting vehicles, 155 other armored fighting vehicles, 512 armored personnel carriers, large amounts of artillery, 6,196 mortars, 8,050 RPGs and recoilless rifles, 60,694 rifles, 322 pistols, 501 pieces of heavy engineering equipment, 6,156 pieces of communications gear, 16,863 items of chemical warfare defense equipment, and 24,257 caskets.[45] The disintegration of Iran's armed forces was obvious in that much of this captured equipment showed no sign of combat damage or wear: Much was abandoned in the field, either out of panic or because of supply problems.

After the August, 1988 cease-fire in the Iran-Iraq War, Iran had to rebuild its army from the ground up . This rebuilding started slowly. Iran imported only about $500 million worth of arms between August, 1988 and May, 1989. This compared with $1.4 billion worth of Iraqi arms imports during the same period. Iran imported only about 50 new armored weapons and a little over 200 major new artillery and anti-aircraft weapons during this time. Iraq imported over 300 armored weapons, more than 240 artillery and anti-aircraft weapons, more than 100 new surface-to-air missile systems, more than 50 helicopters, and more than 50 combat aircraft.

After 1989, however, Iran stepped up its arms imports and took full advantage of the fact that Iraq's invasion of Kuwait not only led to the eventual decimation of Iraqi forces but gave Iran a new respectability that eased its ability to order arms and add oil revenues. Iran purchased ammunition, armor, and artillery from the Soviet Union, North Korea, and the PRC. It made deals with Czechoslovakia and Romania to buy tanks and missiles, including 180 Czech T-54 and T-55 tanks. According to some reports, Iran was able to produce the small arms, mortars, and multiple rocket launchers it needed to replace its wartime losses. Czechoslovakia helped Iran to expand its ammunition production and to manufacture anti-tank and anti-air guided missiles. Iran also assembled SA-7s using parts covertly supplied through Poland by the USSR.[46]

During 1990–1992, Iran placed major new weapons orders to rebuild its forces. Reports differ as to whether Iran was acquiring 200 T-72s and a T-72 production plant from the USSR, or had ordered 1,500 T-72s from Czechoslovakia. There were also reports Iran planned to order 1,500 T-54s/T-55s and 300 T-72s from Poland. What was clear was that Iran was getting additional main battle tanks and other armored vehicles from some source and had found a supply of parts for its M-113 armored personnel carriers.[47]

Iran also got large deliveries of artillery from North Korea, China, Bulgaria, and the USSR. These included large numbers of 122mm weapons and M-46 130mm guns as well as large numbers of rocket launchers.[48] Most experts also agree with figures published by the director of the CIA, who estimated that Iran's arms imports were worth about \$2 billion a year in 1992.[49]

These deliveries gave Iran land forces with from 320,000 to 400,000 men in mid-1992. These forces remained divided between regular army forces, with around 200,000 to 240,000 men, and Iranian Revolutionary Guards and other paramilitary forces, with a total of about 100,000–130,000 men. Iran had an unknown number of Russian, Chinese, North Korean, and possibly some Syrian advisors.

The regular army received priority in terms of equipment and support after 1989 and was organized into a force of about twelve division equivalents, with around forty maneuver brigades. They included four armored, up to two mechanized divisions, five to seven infantry divisions, and one special forces division with four brigades. There were at least two other independent brigades.

While experts disagreed over the details, the regular army seemed to be trying to make its existing force strength effective rather than build up new units. It had learned from the Gulf War that a reliance on mass rather than quality was ineffective. It was seeking to give its existing unit strength substantially more armor and artillery and emphasize specialized independent brigades rather than infantry divisions.

Estimates of Iran's equipment holdings in 1992 are exceptionally uncertain, but those of the regular army are somewhat better known than those of the Revolutionary Guards. The regular army seemed to have 700–800 tanks. These main battle tanks consisted of about 300 remaining M-48s and M-60s, 150 Chieftains, 50–70 T-72s, and the rest were T-54s and T-55s. Iran also had 40–50 British supplied Scorpions, 40–50 BMPs, and some 700–750 M-113s, BTR-50s, BTR-60s, and BTR-152s.[50] Iran had an unknown number of British Chieftain bridging tanks.

As has been noted earlier, Iran was actively seeking to expand its tank strength and seems to have wanted at least 1,500 to 2,000 tanks by the year 2000. It was trying to modernize its other armored vehicle strength rather than expand it, with an emphasis on converting from armored personnel carriers to armored infantry fighting vehicles.

The army had 1,500–2,500 medium and heavy artillery weapons. These included some M-110 self-propelled and M-115 towed 203mm howitzers and M-107 self-propelled 175mm guns, 70–100 M-109 155mm self-propelled howitzers, and 100–130 M-110 towed 105mm howitzers surviving from the U.S. arms imported during the time of the shah. It also had 150–170 Austrian GHN-45 and French AMX towed 155mm gun/howitzers, Soviet 2S1 122mm self-propelled howitzers, Czech Type-83 towed 152mm gun/howitzers, Soviet M-1943 towed 152mm howitzers, North Korean and Soviet M-46 towed

130mm guns, PRC-made T-59 towed 130mm guns, PRC 122mm towed how-itzers, and other former Soviet bloc, PRC, and North Korean weapons. It had roughly 150–300 multiple rocket launchers, including PRC Type-63 107mm and Soviet BM-21 122mm towed weapons, and 1,500–2,000 mortars.

As was the case with its other armored vehicles, Iran seemed to be trying to modernize this artillery strength rather than expand it. It was also seeking more modern fire control and targeting systems.

The army still retained 100–110 AH-1J attack helicopters and 31 CH-47C, 100 Bell-214A, 20 AB-205A, and 50 AB-206 transport and support helicopters supplied by the U.S. and France. Operational readiness levels were low, perhaps only about 25% of inventory.

The army was badly understrength, and some combat and support units only had about 65–80% of the strength needed to fully man its forces. It was short of trained technicians, officers, and NCOs and was only beginning to rebuild the level of training and discipline it had when the shah fell. Logistics, combat engineering, and support capabilities were limited and dependent on reinforcement from the civil sector for any sustained operations. Iran was trying to import spare parts and to repair its older Western equipment but was having only limited success.

The land portion of the IRGC was organized into eleven regional commands. Most sources indicate that the IRGC forces were organized into twelve to fifteen "divisions," which had manning levels of less than regimental size, plus eighteen to twenty-three independent brigades. Some sources put the number of divisions at thirty, with four armored divisions, but this count seems to lump divisions and brigades together. There were also many small independent units or "brigades," including armored, infantry, special forces, paratroop, air defense, artillery, missile, engineer, and border defense units. The IRGC forces were largely infantry and were being converted to internal security forces and border guards—rather than expanded. The regular army was being converted to a heavier force with a conventional command structure. The army and IRGC forces both had missile and rocket forces as well as offensive and defensive chemical warfare capabilities.

The Iranian army and IRGC possessed numerous anti-tank weapons, including Dragon, TOW, and AT-3 ATGMs, 3.5" rockets, and PG-7s. It had about 1,500 air defense guns, large numbers of small surface-to-air missiles, and increasing numbers of the HN-5 light surface-to-air missiles.[51]

This mix of different forces and equipment has not made rebuilding Iran's land forces easy. There has been little standardization, limited to moderate standardization of ammunition, and a wide mix of support and service requirements. Iran's forces have nine types of tanks, seven types of anti-tank missiles, and a wide range of other equipment. Much of the army and IRGC equipment—particularly the more modern Western tanks and helicopters—is deadlined because of a lack of spares and maintenance skills. The Communist bloc equipment is often less sophisticated, and the army's overall mix of equipment involves so many different types and generations that it is difficult to support and maintain.

Iran has as yet done comparatively little to retrain its forces into land units that can conduct effective armored maneuvers or combined arms operations. Many of Iran's units no longer have the manpower and equipment to be employed in anything other than static defensive battles. The military organization Iran reports on paper has little to do with reality, its high command and logistic system is divided and ineffective, and many Iranian combat units have low overall manpower quality. It is unclear how easily Iran's units can be rebuilt, and whether Iran can ever recover the mix of nationalist and revolutionary fervor it had after Iraq first invaded Iran.

The Iranian Air Force

The current strength of the Iranian air force is equally difficult to estimate.[52] Iran had 85,000 men and 447 combat aircraft in its air force at the time the shah fell from power, but it steadily lost strength from 1980 to 1988. The air force suffered combat losses in the Iran-Iraq War. It was cut off from its U.S. suppliers and lost foreign technical support. It was purged of most of the pilots that served under the shah and of many other officers and technical personnel.

Iran did end the Iran-Iraq War with significant stocks of U.S.-made aircraft and excellent sheltered air bases at Bandar Abbas, Bushehr, Ghaleh-Marghi, Isfahan, Kharg Island, Khatami, Mehrabad, Shiraz, Tabriz, and Tehran. Only about 60 to 90 of its U.S.-made fighters, however, were operational. These were organized into four fighter–ground attack squadrons with 20–35 F-4Es, four fighter–ground attack squadrons with 20–45 F-5Es, one interceptor squadron with 10–12 F-14s, and one reconnaissance squadron with 5 F-5s and 3 RF-4Es.

Iran, probably, however, had 20 F-4s and 20–40 F-14s in storage that could not be repaired without access to Western parts and technical support. Even its "operational" aircraft were increasingly more awkward mixes of the original aircraft, parts cannibalized from other Iranian aircraft, and parts obtained on the fringes of the international arms market. Most could fly only limited numbers of sorties and have at least partially nonfunctional avionics. Most of Iran's more sophisticated AWG-9 and APQ-120 fire control radars are not operational. While Iran's F-4E forces improved in readiness because of deliveries of spare parts from various unidentified sources, none was fully operational in the sense of being able to conduct sustained operations with all systems fully effective and reliable. Iran's F-14As could not use their Phoenix missiles, and Iran could at most fire only limited numbers of the AGM-65 Mavericks that had once been its main air-to-surface guided weapons.

Many of Iran's U.S.-supplied radars and Improved Hawk missiles, and British-made Rapier squadrons and Tigercat launch units no longer functioned. Iran's ground based air defense was increasingly dependent on deliveries of Chinese-made CSA-1s, variants of the obsolete Soviet-made SA-2. Its only other air defense systems consisted of various versions of the SA-7 manportable short range missile and large numbers of AA guns and automatic weapons.

This situation improved significantly between 1988 and 1992. By 1992 the Iranian air force and air defense force built back to a total of around 25,000–35,000 men and some 200–230 combat aircraft—although it was critically short of pilots and technicians, less than 50% of the U.S.-supplied aircraft could be made operational, and Iran's F-14s still could not fire their AGM-54A Phoenix missiles.

The air force had about 12,000–16,000 men and 8–12 squadrons. The operational portion of its remaining U.S.-supplied inventory included 40–60 F-4D/E and 40–45 F-5E/F attack fighters, 60 F-14 air defense fighters, 5 RF-5 and 5–10 RF-4E reconnaissance fighters, 5 P-3F maritime reconnaissance aircraft, and large numbers of transports and helicopters. Many of these aircraft had only limited operational capability, few could support sustained sortie rates higher than one every three to four days, and the ability of the avionics on these aircraft to properly fire their air-to-air and air-to-surface missiles seemed uncertain.

Iran had also lost much of its air control and warning capability. Its radars and communications system had not been improved or properly maintained since the shah's fall, and it had lost much of its ability to train operators, technicians, and commanders to use its Western-supplied equipment effectively. It had only minimal capability to fight a large scale air war or maintain an effective air defense system.[53]

Iran, however, was getting deliveries of jet combat aircraft from other sources. It had imported 15–30 F-7M fighters from the PRC (out of a possible total order of 50–72). Some reports indicate Iran modified these fighters to use Western avionics at old Iranian Aircraft Industries facilities, and that the PRC sold Iran 2,500 PL-2 and PL-2A air-to-air missiles (Chinese copies of the Sidewinder) and PL-7 air-to-air missiles (Chinese copies of the Matra Magique R-550).

Iran obtained 10–15 F-5s from Vietnam, although the F-5s were likely to be used for spares to keep Iran's existing aircraft operational.[54] Most importantly, it had taken delivery on 30–40 MiG-29 aircraft from the USSR out of a possible total order of 40–50) and delivery on 18–36 Su-24s.[55] These deliveries not only gave Iran first line Soviet aircraft, they included the support equipment and training to allow it to rebuild its air force using Soviet equipment and maintain relatively high operational aircraft and training rates.

The MiG-29s were almost certainly late model MiG-29As or MiG-29Bs. These aircraft are designed for the forward area air superiority and escort mission, including deep penetration air-to-air combat. They also have an interesting mix of strengths and weaknesses. Their flight performance and flying qualities are excellent and roughly equivalent to that of the best Western fighters. They have a maximum takeoff weight of 39,000 pounds, a maximum afterburner thrust of 18,300 pounds, a flight envelope of 2.35 Mach at 36,000 feet, a thrust-to-weight ratio of 1:1+, a service ceiling of 56,000 feet, a maximum sustained load, or "G" factor, of 9, a maximum sea level climb rate of 65,000 feet per minute, a ferry range of 1,130 nautical miles, a takeoff run of 790 feet, and a landing run of 1,970 feet.[56]

The MiG-29's avionics and weapons are relatively modern. The MiG-29 has an advanced coherent pulse Doppler radar with look-down/shoot-down capabilities that can detect a fighter sized (2 square meter) target at a range of 130 kilometers (70 nautical miles), and track at 70 kilometers (38 nautical miles). It has a track while scan range of 80 kilometers (44 nautical miles) against a 5 square meter target and a target file capacity of 10. It is also designed to operate with the radar off or in the passive mode and using ground controlled intercept.[57]

The MiG-29 has an infrared search and track system collimated with a laser range finder, a helmet mounted sight, internal ECM, SPO-15 radar warning receiver, modern inertial navigation, and the modern Odds Rod IFF. The range of the infrared search and track system against an F-16 sized target is 15 kilometers (8.2 nautical miles). The maximum slant range of the laser is 14 kilometers (7.7 nautical miles), and its normal operating range is 8 kilometers (4.4 nautical miles). The MiG-29 can carry up to six air-to-air missiles, a 30mm gun, a wide mix of bombs, and 57mm, 84mm, and 240mm air-to-ground rockets. A typical air combat load would include 250 rounds of 30mm gun ammunition, 335 gallons of external fuel, 4 AA-8 Aphid infrared guided missiles, and 2 AA-10 Alamo radar guided medium range air-to-air missiles.

Even the improved MiG-29B, however, has a number of ergonomic problems. The cockpit frames and high cockpit sills limit visibility. The display is fussy and uses outdated dials and indicators similar to those of the F-4. There is only a medium angle heads-up display and only partial hands-on system control. The CRT display is dated, and the cockpit is cramped. Still, the helmet mounted sight allows the pilot to slave the Radar, IRST, and HUM together for intercepts and covert attacks using off-boresight cueing.[58]

As has been noted earlier, the Su-24 is a twin seat swing wing aircraft that is roughly equivalent in terms of weight to the F-111, although it has nearly twice the thrust loading, and about one-third more wing loading. The Su-24 can carry payloads of nearly 25,000 pounds and operate on missions with a 1,300 kilometer radius when carrying 6,600 pounds of fuel. With a more typical 8,818 pound (4,000 kilogram) combat load, it has a mission radius of about 790 kilometers in the LO-LO-LO profile and 1,600 kilometers in the LO-HI-LO profile. With extended range fuel tanks and airborne refueling, the Su-24 can reach virtually any target in Iraq and the southern Gulf.[59]

Although it is not clear what variant of the Su-24 has gone to Iran, it seems likely to be the Su-24D, which includes a sophisticated radar warning receiver, an improved electronic warfare suite, an improved terrain avoidance radar, satellite communications, and an aerial refueling probe; it can deliver electro-optical, laser, and radar guided bombs and missiles.[60] These can include up to three AS-7 Kerry radio command guided missile (5 kilometer range), one AS-9 Kyle anti-radiation missile with passive radar guidance and an active radar fuse (90 kilometer range), three AS-10 Karen passive laser guided missiles with an active laser fuse (10 kilometer range), three AS-11 Kilter anti-radiation missiles with passive radar guidance and an active radar fuse (50 kilometer range), three AS-12 Kegler anti-radiation missiles with passive radar guidance and an active radar fuse (35 kilometer range), three AS-13 Kingposts, and three AS-14 Kedge semi-active laser guided missiles with an active laser fuse (12 kilometer range). It can also carry demolition bombs, retarded bombs, cluster bombs, fuel air bombs, and chemical bombs.[61]

This transfer of Soviet aircraft had the added benefit of enabling the Iranian air force to use many of the Iraqi aircraft that fled to Iran during the Gulf War. There is some question about the exact number of aircraft involved, but Iraq officially claimed that they include 24 Mirage F-1s, 22 Su-24s, 40 Su-22s, 4 Su-20s, 7 Su-25s, 4 MiG-29s, 7 MiG-23Ls, 4 MiG-23BNs, 1 MiG-23UB, 2 B-747s, 1 B-707, 1 B-727, 2 B-737s, 14 IL-76s, 1 Adnan, 2 Dassault Falcon 20s, 3 Dassault Falcon 50s, 1 Lockheed Jetstar, 1 A-300, and 5 A-310s. The A-300 and A-310s were aircraft Iraq stole from Kuwait Airways, and Iran agreed to return these aircraft to Kuwait in July, 1992. That same month, however, Iran announced it would not return any of the Iraqi combat aircraft to Iraq. There were reports that Iran had already begun to fly Iraqi MiG-29s and would absorb the MiG-29s, Su-24s, and Su-20/Su-22s into its force structure.

Iran's overall force expansion goal was hard to determine, but Iran had little prospect of keeping its U.S.-supplied aircraft operational much beyond the year 2000. This meant it was hard pressed to convert to Soviet fighters fast enough to offset its losses of U.S. types, and Iran had found—as had Pakistan earlier—that the Chinese F-7M fighter was a low performance aircraft that was extremely difficult to overhaul.[62]

Iran's transport assets included one tanker/transport squadron with 4 B-707s, and 5 transport squadrons with 9 747Fs, 11 B-707s, 1 B-727, 20 C-130E/Hs, 3 Commander 690s, 9 F-27s, and 2 Falcon 20As. It had 2 AB-206A, 39 Bell 214C, and 5 CH-47 transport helicopters.

Iran's land based air defense forces included about 10,000–12,000 regulars and 10,000–12,000 IRGC personnel. It is not possible to distinguish between the major weapons holdings of the regular air force and IRGC, but their total holdings seem to have included 30 Improved Hawk fire units (90+ launchers), 30 Rapier fire units in five squadrons, 10–15 Tigercat fire units, 50–60 SA-2 and HQ-23 (CSA-1) launchers (PRC-made equivalents of the SA-2), 20–30 SA-6 launchers, a few RBS-70s, and 10–15 Soviet-made SA-5 launchers. They also included large numbers of manportable SA-7s, HN-5s, and possibly SA-14s, and around 2,000 anti-aircraft guns.[63]

Many of the Western-supplied SAMs in Iran's order of battle were not operational, and the Iranian air defense system consisted of crudely integrated radars and inadequate data processing systems and command and control links.[64]

There were reports, however, that Iran was importing three more batteries of SA-5 missiles from the USSR and that it was getting continued deliveries of the CSA-1 and new deliveries of Soviet or PRC radars. There were also reports from the People's Mujahideen that Iran was planning to buy the advanced SA-10 or SA-12 heavy surface-to-air missile/anti-tactical ballistic missile systems from Russia, and a next generation warning and command and control system. Such deliveries would allow Iran to rebuild its ground-based air defenses and early warning sensor system and provide a greatly improved command and control system for its air force.[65]

The Iranian Navy

The Iranian navy was by far the strongest navy in the Gulf at the time the shah fell.[66] It had a strength of over 20,000, a modern main naval headquarters at Bandar Abbas, and well equipped bases at Khorramshar, Bushehr, Bandar Abbas, Bandar Khomeini, and Bandar Lengh. Its strength included two U.S. Sumner-class and one British Battle-class destroyers; four Saam frigates, four ex-US PF-103 frigates, nine Kaman-class missile ships with Harpoon, seven large patrol craft, and large numbers of other patrol craft, mine vessels, and amphibious ships. It has six P-3F Orion maritime reconnaissance aircraft, six S-65A assault helicopters, twenty SH-3D ASW helicopters, six RH-53D mine sweeping helicopters, twenty-four support helicopters, and eleven transport aircraft.

The shah had four modified Spruance-class (Kooroush-class) destroyers with SM-1 Standard air defense missiles and modern ASW gear on order, plus three Tang-class submarines that were to be used to train the Iranian navy to use six Type-209 submarines that were to be ordered from Germany. Four additional Hengam-class LSTs and a large replenishment oiler were on order from Britain.

Once the Khomeini regime took power, however, it canceled the orders for the Spruance-class destroyers and Tang and T-209 submarines and two of the four LSTs. The Iranian navy also suffered serious damage to at least two of its destroyers during 1980–1986 because of the Iran-Iraq War, and many of its key combat weapons and sensors ceased to be operational because of a lack of Western resupply and technical support. Three of its Saam-class frigates seem to have had many of their weapons systems and sensors become nonoperational, and it lost one of its US PF-103 corvettes. It lost two Kaman-class patrol boats and two more were seriously damaged—two were evidently hit during Karballa 5. The Kaman-class ships seem to have had only a few operational Harpoon missiles. The navy lost two of its mine sweepers, and the only remaining mine vessel was in the Caspian. Its amphibious strength at the end of 1986 consisted of three marine battalions, four Hengam LSTs, four ex-Dutch LSMs, and six BH-7 Mark 4 Hovercraft. It had one oceangoing replenishment ship, one repair, and two fleet supply oilers.

Iran's naval encounters with the U.S. during 1987 and 1988 made this situation much worse. On September 21, 1987, the U.S. sank the *Iran Ajar* while it was laying mines in the Gulf. On October 8, 1987, the U.S. sank an IRGC Boghammar and several Boston Whalers. Then on April 18, 1988, the Iranian navy challenged the U.S. Navy while the U.S. was attacking several IRGC-occupied oil platforms in retaliation for the mining of the USS *Roberts*. The U.S. sank the Iranian guided missile frigate *Sahand* and the guided missile patrol boat *Joshan*, crippled another guided missile patrol boat, the *Sabalan*, and sank another Boghammar and damaged one more.

The Iranian navy also lost significant amounts of its trained maintenance personnel in various purges and upheavals during the revolution, and many of its key radar and electronic systems are either no longer operational or have severe reliability and endurance problems. This includes the Contraves Sea Hunter, SPG-34, and Mark 37, 51, and 61 fire control systems; the WM-28 tactical and fire control radars; the Plessey AWS 1 and SPS6 search radars; and SPS-37 air surveillance radars. Iran now has severe shortages in both anti-ship and anti-air missiles such as the RIM-66 Standard (anti-aircraft), Sea Cat (anti-aircraft), and RGM-84 Harpoon (anti-ship). All of the Western missiles in the navy's inventory have long exceeded their maximum reliable storage life, and Iran's stocks of Harpoons may be limited to seven missiles for its Kaman-class fast attack craft.[67]

As is the case with its ground and air forces, however, Iran has had time to rebuild some of its naval capabilities. In 1992 its regular navy, naval portion of the Revolutionary Guards, and marines totaled around 38,000 men— with about 18,000 regulars and 20,000 Iranian Naval Revolutionary Guard forces.

While much of the navy still had limited operational capability, its strength was already impressive by Gulf standards, and Iran was receiving significant logistic and technical support from Pakistan.[68] According to IISS and JCSS estimates, its operational inventory included 3 destroyers, 5 frigates, 29 patrol and coastal combatants, 3 mine warfare ships, 9 armed helicopters, and 10 amphibious ships and craft. Iran had enough amphibious lift to move about 800–900 troops and 25–30 tanks.[69]

Its strength still included two Sumner-class destroyers that displaced 3,200 tons and were armed with four paired elevating Standard SM-1MR surface-to-surface missile launchers, two twin 5" gun mounts, six Mark 32 torpedo tubes, and an Agusta AB 204AS helicopter. It also included a 3,400-ton Battle-class ship armed with four paired elevating Standard SM-1MR surface-to-surface missile launchers, two twin 5" gun mounts, a single Contraves RTN-10X Sea Hunter fire control radar, and a quadruple Sea Cat ship-to-air missile launcher. These ships had relatively modern air and sea search radars and some ESM and EW gear in the late 1970s but now have relatively obsolete on-board electronics.[70]

Iran also had three Vosper Mark 5 Saam-class frigates armed with one 5-missile Sea Killer surface-to-surface missile launcher and one Mark 8 4.5" gun mount each, and two U.S. PF-103 corvettes with two 3" guns. Its smaller ships included 10 Kaman-class (Combattante II) fast attack boats armed with Harpoon or C-802 missiles and one 76mm gun; nine large patrol craft and fast attack craft (three North Korean and six U.S.); two to three MSC 292/268 and one to two Cape-class mine sweepers; and twelve to fourteen BH-7 and SRN-6 Hovercraft. Many of Iran's smaller ships were modified during the Iran-Iraq War to mount extra small arms and/or the Chinese-made C-801 and C-802 anti-ship missiles.

Jane's indicated that Iran had considerable amphibious assets, including one Fogue-class LSL, four modern Hengam-class (Larak-class) amphibious support ships, five LSTs, three LCTs, more than twelve LCUs, and about fifty small patrol craft. This gave it the ability to deploy about 800 to 1,200 troops in an amphibious assault. It had one replenishment ship, two fleet supply ships, one repair ship, two water tankers, seven support ships, and twenty-six tugs, tenders, and utility craft. While any such estimates are uncertain and it is not possible to distinguish between the holdings of the navy and the IRGC, Iran also had forty-seven barges and service craft, two floating docks, about 100 coastal patrol craft, thirty-five Boghammar 41 foot craft, thirty-five Boston Whaler 22 foot craft, and large numbers of river craft.

Opinions differed as to how much of this force was operational. Iran was clearly able to operate some of its British-made Saam-class fast attack craft. Accordingly to some reports, it could also operate at least one destroyer, two frigates, six to ten fast attack craft (FAC), seven large patrol boats, forty coastal patrol boats, a maximum of fourteen Hovercraft, and fifty-seven amphibious assault ships, logistic ships, and small patrol boats. This still gives it a total force of more than eighty vessels.[71] It had significant stocks of U.S. Mark 65 and Soviet AMD 500, AMAG-1, and KRAB anti-ship mines and may have bought PRC-made versions of the Soviet mines. It had claimed to be making its own nonmagnetic acoustic free-floating and remote controlled mines.

The Iranian navy's air capability consisted of one or two operational P-3F Orion maritime patrol aircraft out of an original inventory of five. None of the surviving P-3Fs had operational radars, and their crews used binoculars. It also had up to twelve Sikorsky SH-3D ASW helicopters, two RH-53D mine laying helicopters, and seven Agusta-Bell AB-212 helicopters equipped with Italian-made Sea Killer missiles. It used Iranian Air Force AH-1J attack helicopters equipped with French AS-12 missiles in naval missions, and adapted Hercules C-130 and Fokker Friendship aircraft for mine laying and patrol missions.

Iran was also seeking new naval weapons to try to offset the weakness of its surface forces. It purchased two to three 27-ton midget submarines from North Korea in 1988, although it is unclear that it is able to operate them successfully.[72] U.S intelligence sources reported in 1992 that Iran planned to buy two to three Soviet Kilo-class submarines and several mini-submarines weighing roughly 400 tons, and planned to deploy them at its main naval base at Chah Bahar, beginning in late 1992. They also indicated that Iran sent crews for training at a Russian-controlled naval base in Latvia and that Iran purchased the submarines to acquire the ability to threaten tanker traffic in the Gulf and passing through the Straits of Hormuz.

Although some press reports surfaced that Russia had broken off the deal because of U.S. pressure and Iranian funding problems, two of the submarines seem to have been transferred to Iran by October, 1992.[73] The Kilos give Iran a way of operating in the Gulf and in the Gulf of Oman that reduces its vulnerability to air and surface attack, and the mini-submarines offer the ability to hide in the shallow depths and currents near the straits. Iran can improve its ability to target the submarines using its shore based radars and patrol aircraft.

Iran has definitely obtained 60–100 C-801 or YF-6 missiles from the PRC. These short range anti-ship missiles can be launched from the land, ships, and aircraft. They have a range of approximately 70 kilometers in the surface-to-surface mode and use J-Band active radar guidance. According to People's Mujahideen sources, Iran has also sought more advanced anti-ship missiles from North Korea and China, 8–12 missile patrol boats, and possibly frigates. There is no way to know how realistic these reports are or when such ships and missiles might be delivered. Iran will have to make some such order by the mid-1990s to keep up its present strength. Its older Western-supplied ships cannot be made fully modern and kept operational without a comprehensive refit, which could only be done in Western shipyards.

Iran's new Naval Guards force was supposedly merged with the regular navy when Admiral Shamkhani was made commander of both forces in 1989. However, in 1992 it still had 20,000 men, five island bases, a facility at Nowshahr Naval Academy on the Caspian Sea, fast patrol boats, and CSS-2 Silkworm anti-ship missiles. No accurate estimate of its naval strength exists, but it was equipped with at least thirty to forty Swedish-built fast interceptor craft, small launches equipped with anti-tank guided missiles, and at least thirty Zodiac rubber dinghies to carry out rocket, small arms, and recoilless rifle attacks.

The Swedish fast interceptor craft are built by Boghammar Marine and can reach speeds up to 69 knots; they have a range of up to 926 kilometers with a 1,000 pound equipment load. The Boghammars are equipped with heavy machine guns, grenade launchers, and 106mm recoilless rifles. The Swedish boats and Zodiacs are extremely difficult to detect by radar in anything but the calmest sea state. Based at a number of offshore islands and oil platforms, their key concentrations are at Al Farisiyah, Halul Island (an oil platform), Sirri, Abu Musa, and Larak. The naval IRGC also included naval artillery frogman and mine laying units. They had extensive stocks of scuba equipment and an underwater combat center at Bandar Abbas.[74]

The guards have operated Iran's PRC-supplied Silkworm surface-to-ship missiles since they were first delivered during the Iran-Iraq War. The Silkworm is designated the HY-2 or Sea Eagle 2 by the PRC. A copy of the Soviet CSS-N-2 Styx missile, it is made by the China Precision Machinery Import and Export Corporation. It has an 80–90 kilometer range and a 450 kilogram warhead. It climbs to 145 meters (600 feet) after launch and then drops to a cruise profile at 30 meters (100 feet). There are two variants. One uses radar active homing at ranges from the target of 8 kilometers (4.5 nautical miles). The other is set to use passive IR homing and a radar altimeter to keep it at a constant height over the water.[75] Iran fired at least eight Silkworms against targets in Kuwait during the Iran-Iraq War, three of which were hits.

In 1992 the naval branch of the IRGC had three to four operational land based anti-ship missile units with three to six Silkworm launchers each and a total of fifty to sixty missiles. At least some of these units were deployed near Iran's naval base at Chah Bahar, Bandar Abbas, and at Khuestak near the Straits of Hormuz to cover the entrance to the Gulf. They may also have formed a new unit using PRC-supplied C-801 anti-ship and ship-to-ship missiles.[76]

Paramilitary and Hostile Military Forces

The current state of Iran's paramilitary forces is difficult to determine. They have two main elements: the Basij and the gendarmerie. The Basij is a popular reserve force that is controlled by the Revolutionary Guards and consists largely of youths, men who have completed military service, and the elderly. During the Iran-Iraq War, the Basij was organized into poorly trained and equipped infantry units which were often used in Iran's human wave assaults.

Since the war, the Basij has been restructured into a pool that can be called up in wartime, and there are up to 500 battalions with about 300–350 men each that have three companies or four platoons. These units are equipped with small arms, when they are equipped at all, and can act as little more than a force to secure rear areas or deal with ethnic forces or popular riots. They do, however, act as a potential way of expanding the IRGC in terms of crisis and war and serve the political purpose of giving the regime a large loyal internal security force. There is also a large home guard which serves some of the purposes of the Basij but is a static militia force tied to local defense missions.

The gendarmerie is part of the Ministry of Interior and consists of about 45,000 men, including border guards, that are organized as a paramilitary police force with wheeled armored vehicles, light patrol aircraft (Cessna 185/310 and AB-205 and AB-206s), coastal patrol craft, and harbor patrol craft. It keeps order throughout the rural areas of Iran and deals with ethnic and tribal security problems. It has a regional and regimental organization but no real military training and equipment other than automatic weapons, mortars, and light anti-tank weapons. A new force of tribal guards is being formed which may either be part of the gendarmerie or the IRGC.

Iran's Kurds are divided into pro- and anti-regime elements. The Kurdish Democratic Party (KDP) is pro-regime and has a militia of about 12,000 men. The Kurdish Communist Party has small anti-regime cadres, and the Democratic Party of Iranian Kurdistan (DPIK) is an anti-regime movement with up to 10,000 part time irregulars. Iraq's persecution of its Kurds and the large number of Iraqi Kurds that are now refugees in Iran have boosted Kurdish support for the regime. Iran also seems to be training and arming Iraqi Kurdish refugees for possible use against Iraq.

The leading anti-regime force is the Iraqi-backed National Liberation Army (NLA), which is under the command of the People's Mujahideen of Iran and led by Massoud Rajavi and Mariam Rajavi. While the NLA has recently claimed to be Washington based, it has been Iraqi-funded, -trained, and -equipped ever since 1986. It owes many of its origins to the Marxist Mujahideen e-Khalq, which was originally an anti-shah underground force and which lost a struggle for power with Khomeini during the first few years of the Iranian revolution.

The NLA has often claimed to have larger forces, to have defeated Iranian forces in 1988, and to have captured substantial amounts of Iranian equipment. In fact, it seems to have suffered a major defeat the moment it advanced without Iraqi support and had to retreat back to Iraq after losing more than 1,000 troops and abandoning much of its equipment. It has since been reequipped by Iran and has limited amounts of armor.

It is difficult to separate the fiction in the NLA's claims from reality. Reports in 1992 that it built up its forces from 15,000 to 45,000 troops seem exaggerated. Its claims to be led by Mariam Rajavi and to have female generals and female troops seem little more than propaganda. Iran does feel the Mujahideen is serious enough, however, to have used its aircraft to attack its main camp about 65 miles northwest of Baghdad. Approximately 8–12 Iranian F-4s and F-5s attacked the camp on April 5, 1992. This marked the first Iranian attack on Iraqi territory since the cease-fire in the Iran-Iraq War in 1988.[77]

Iran and Weapons of Mass Destruction

Iran has long sought weapons of mass destruction and the means to deliver them, although its efforts cannot be compared to those of Iraq. Iran has lacked the resources to finance a massive worldwide purchasing effort, and its revolutionary turmoil has limited its access to foreign technology and has hindered the efficiency of its industrial base. Iran has, however, sought long range missiles, produced chemical weapons, developed biological weapons, and made efforts to acquire nuclear weapons.

Iran's Long Range Missile Programs

Iran relied on its air force under the shah and made no effort to acquire long range missiles until the beginning of the Iran-Iraq War. Iraq began to fire FROG-7s at Iranian positions during the first weeks of the Iran-Iraq conflict, however, and Iran responded by trying to develop and employ its own long range unguided rockets. This effort had made considerable progress by the mid-1980s. Iran claimed that it had over 100 factories manufacturing some sort of part or equipment for missiles and rockets, with major production facilities at Sirjan and Isfahan, facilities at Sharoud, a test monitor facility at Tabas, and a launch facility at Rafsanjan.

These Iranian claims are unquestionably exaggerated, but Iran did succeed in producing its own version of a Chinese Type-83 artillery rocket, which it called the Oghab. This rocket was manufactured at Semnan, about 185 kilometers east of Tehran, in a factory built with Chinese help. The rocket is fired from Mercedes-Benz LA911B trucks, with three rockets per truck. It also tried to develop an original design for a long range rocket, which it called the Iran-130.[78]

Iran used the Oghab in combat almost as soon as it entered production. It made about 325 Oghab rockets and is believed to have fired roughly 240–270 out of this total between 1985 and the cease-fire in the Iran-Iraq War. The Oghabs had a range of only 40 kilometers, however, and they lacked the range and accuracy to hit anything smaller than large targets like assembly areas and cities. The Oghabs also had only a 70–300 kilogram warhead, and their operational CEP proved to be in excess of 1,000 meters.[79] Further, Iran had no way to accurately target the Oghab. The most it could do was to launch the Oghabs at the Iraqi cities near the border. These targets included Basra, Abu al-Khasib, Al-Zubayr, Umm Qasr, Mandali, Khanaqin, and Banmil, but the Oghab had such a small warhead that even successful hits in urban areas did only minor damage. Such strikes had far less effect than artillery barrages.[80]

Iran failed to develop and produce its longer range Iran-130, or Nazeat, in any numbers before the end of the Iran-Iraq War. The full details of this system remain unclear, but it seems to have been an attempt to use commercially available components and a simple inertial guidance system to build a missile that could reach ranges of about 80 miles (130 kilometers). It is 355 mm in diameter, 5.9 meters long, weighs 950 kilograms, and has a 150 kilogram warhead. Its maximum range is 90 kilometers.[81]

In practice, this "guided missile" was little more than a solid fuel free rocket with a jury-rigged guidance system. It proved highly inaccurate and unreliable and reached a maximum range of only about 120 kilometers. Its payload seems to have been several hundred kilograms at most. Some Iran-130s were deployed to the regular IRGC, and the first such missiles were fired against Al-Amarah on March 19, 1988. Four more were fired against the city in April, but it is unclear that any of these strikes hit their targets or had any tactical effect.

Since the end of the Iran-Iraq War, Iran has exhibited another large rocket called the Shahin 2. It too, has a 355 mm diameter but is only 3.87 meters long and weighs only 580 kilograms. It evidently has two warheads: a 180 kilogram conventional warhead and another warhead that may either be chemical or use submunitions. Both the Nazeat and Shahin are now in service with the regular Iranian armed forces.

In contrast to its efforts with free rockets, Iranian attempts to use the Soviet-designed Scud B guided missile did have an impact on the war. The Scud B is a relatively old design that first became operational in 1967; it has a maximum range of 290–310 kilometers with its normal conventional payload and a maximum flight time of 325 seconds.[82] The missile is 11.25 meters long and 85 centimeters in diameter, weighs 6,300 kilograms, and has a warhead weighing about 1,000 kilograms, of which 800 kilograms are high explosive and 200 are the warhead structure and fusing system.[83] It has a single stage storable liquid rocket engine and is usually deployed on the MAZ-543 eight wheel transporter-erector-launcher. It has a strap-down inertial guidance using three gyros to correct its ballistic trajectory, and it uses internal graphite jet vane steering. It has a warhead that detaches from the missile body during the final fall towards target. This provides added stability and allows the warhead to hit at a velocity above Mach 1.5.[84]

Iran fired its first Scuds in March, 1985. It fired as many as 14 Scuds in 1985, 8 in 1986, 18 in 1987, and 77 in 1988. These missile attacks initially were more effective than those of Iraq. All of Iraq's major cities were comparatively close to its border with Iran, but Tehran and most of Iran's major cities that had not already been targets in the war were outside the range of Iraqi Scud attacks. Iran could never exploit its range advantage, however, because it lacked the number of missiles needed to sustain frequent attacks or deliver large amounts of high explosive at a given time, and Iraq had vastly superior air resources it could use as a substitute for or supplement to missile attacks. Further, most Iranian missiles struck outside Baghdad.[85] Even the missiles that did hit inside the city often hit in open spaces, and even direct hits on buildings rarely produced high casualties. Iran never hit any of its proclaimed major targets.

Like Iraq, Iran sought to improve the capabilities of its Scuds throughout most of the 1980s. Iran, however, had no real success in developing longer range missiles during the Iran-Iraq War, and its wartime claims to be manufacturing Scuds in Iran were false. Although Iran claimed during the course of 1985–1988 that it had over 100 factories manufacturing some sort of part or equipment for missiles and rockets, it failed to demonstrate any production capability at late as 1991.[86]

Iran's need to obtain longer range missiles explains why Iran continued to buy an estimated 200–300 Scud Bs from North Korea between 1987 and 1992. Israeli experts estimate Iran had 250–300 Scuds in mid-1992, with 15–30 launchers.

Iran did, however, go further. There are many reports that it has negotiated for the PRC's "M-9" and "M-11" group of missiles and is also seeking a new Chinese missile with a 1,000 kilometer range. Iran definitely bought a longer range North Korean system. A senior North Korean delegation traveled to Tehran to close the deal on November 29, 1990, and met with Mohsen Rezai, the commander of the IRGC. Iran either bought the missile then or placed its order shortly thereafter.

North Korea seems to have completed development of this improved Scud in 1987. It had a range of 500–600 kilometers, a payload of at least 500 kilograms, and relatively high accuracy and reliability. Various sources indicate that anywhere from 15 to several hundred of the missiles were delivered to Iran during 1991 and that Iran successfully tested one of the Scuds in May, 1991.

It is hard to be sure of all the facts surrounding these deliveries. Iran did fly in some of these missiles during 1990–1991 using its B-747s. It seems unlikely, however, that Iran had more than 20–30 North Korean missiles by mid-1992, and reports of holdings of several hundred may represent an acquisition goal for the late 1990s. Iran does seem to have fired at least one North Korean missile some 500 kilometers from a test site near Qom to a target area south of Shahroud.[87]

Iran also served as a transshipment point for North Korean missile deliveries during 1992. A North Korean vessel called the *Dae Hung Ho,* bringing missile parts for Syria, docked at Bandar Abbas in May, 1992. Iran then flew these parts to Syria. An Iranian ship coming from North Korea and a second North Korean ship followed, carrying missiles and machine tools for both Syria and Iran.

It seems likely that Iran and Syria are cooperating with North Korea in the development of missile production capabilities for the Scud C. At least 20 Scud Cs have gone to Syria from Iran as well as production equipment for the Syrian Scud C plants near Hamah and Aleppo. Some sources believe that

Iran and Syria plan to cooperate in acquiring and producing a longer range North Korean missile called the No-Dong 1, with a range of 1,000 kilometers. Libya may also be interested in the No-Dong 1.[88]

There are also strong indications that Iran has bought 150–200 PRC-made CSS-8 missiles, with ranges of approximately 150 kilometers. Further, it is virtually certain that Iran has had at least some Chinese aid for part of its nuclear weapons effort and is continuing to manufacture chemical weapons and develop biological weapons.

Iranian Chemical Weapons

Like Iraq, Iran signed the Geneva Protocols of 1925 prohibiting the use of poison gas, and both have signed the Biological Warfare Convention of 1972 banning the development, production, and deployment or stockpiling of biological weapons.[89] Nevertheless, Iran has actively sought weapons of mass destruction since the early 1970s and used poison gas during the Iran-Iraq War.

Iran became serious about chemical warfare much later than Iraq, but it is hardly surprising that Iraq's use of chemical weapons against Iran during the early 1980s led Iran to purchase massive stocks of chemical defense gear and develop its own chemical agents. The purchase of defense gear proved relatively easy, and Iran obtained large stocks of such gear after 1984. Iran also obtained large stocks of nonlethal CS gas, although it quickly found such gas had limited military impact—since it could only be used effectively in closed areas or very small open air areas.

Acquiring poisonous chemical agents proved more difficult. Iran did not have the capacity to manufacture poisonous chemical agents when Iraq launched its first chemical attacks during 1982–1983.[90] While Iran may have made limited use of chemical mortar and artillery rounds as early as 1985—and possibly as early as 1984—these rounds were almost certainly captured from Iran.[91]

As a result Iran had to begin a crash effort to create a domestic chemical weapons production capability in 1983–1984. It sought aid from European firms like Lurgi to produce large "pesticide" plants and began to try to obtain the needed feedstock from a wide range of sources, relying heavily on its embassy in Bonn to manage the necessary deals. While Lurgi did not provide the pesticide plant Iran sought, Iran did obtain substantial support from other European firms and feedstocks from a wide range of Western sources.

These included the purchase of 75 tons of thiodiglycol, a key precursor of mustard gas, from the U.S. firm of Alcolac International during 1987. Iran used the German firm of Colimex, the Greek firm of Cy Savas Oikonomidis, and the Singaporean firm of Hallet Enterprises as fronts for these purchases. Iran also bought 120 tons of sodium cyanide from Rotexchemie International in Germany.

Some reports indicate that Iran attempted to buy sarin nerve gas weapons in the U.S. and obtained South Korean support in building two chemical weapons plants which were sold under the cover of being pesticide plants.

Some sources indicate that Iran had a major chemical weapons plant in operation at Damghan by March, 1989 and that it may have begun to test fire Scuds with chemical warheads. Mujahideen sources also claim it set up a chemical bomb and warhead plant operated by the Zakaria Al-Razi chemical company near Mahshar in southern Iran.

Another Iranian poison gas plant seems to have been built at Qazvin, about 150 kilometers west of Tehran, with the aid of Bayer and Lurgi Metallurgie (a subsidiary of Hoechst). This plant is reported to have been completed between November, 1987 and January, 1988 and to have used technology and equipment supplied by BASF of Germany, an unidentified Yugoslav firm, and Ciba-Geigy of Switzerland. Purportedly a pesticide plant, its true purpose was poison gas production using phosphorous organic compounds. Efforts to allow it to produce V-agent nerve gases, possibly amiton, seem to have been blocked by U.S., British, and German efforts to stop John Brown Engineering and Lurgi from designing and building a precursor plant.[92]

Iran began to produce enough lethal agents to load its own weapons before these plants went into operation.[93] The director of the CIA and informed observers in the Gulf indicated that Iran could produce mustard gas and blood agents like hydrogen cyanide, phosgene gas, and chlorine gas by 1987.[94] These gas agents were loaded into bombs and artillery shells, and were used sporadically against Iraq in 1987 and 1988.[95]

Iran was beginning to produce significant amounts of mustard gas and nerve gas by the time of the August, 1988 cease-fire but never succeeded in using poison gas effectively during the war.[96] Iranian troops could not be trained and equipped to use chemical weapons effectively at a time when Iraqi forces had vastly superior experience and were scoring major victories along the entire front. It is interesting to note, however, that debates took place in the Iranian Majlis in late 1988 over the safety of IRGC gas plants located near Iranian towns, and that Rafsanjani described chemical and biological weapons as "poor man's atomic bombs [that] can easily be produced. We should at least consider them for our defense. Although the use of such weapons is inhuman, the war taught us that international laws are only scraps of paper."[97]

The exact status of Iran's current capabilities is unknown. It is clear, however, that Iran has established a significant chemical weapons production capability, including mustard gas, phosgene gas, and blood agents. Some sources claim Iran has nerve gases such as V-agents. Others indicate that Iran's nerve gas plants are not yet operational. If not, Syria and North Korea are possible sources of the needed feedstocks and any additional equipment. Virtually all sources agree that Iran is seeking to obtain and/or manufacture surface-to-surface missiles that could be used for both chemical and nuclear strikes.[98]

Western intelligence experts agree that Iran can already deliver fairly large amounts of chemical weapons using artillery and aircraft, and some say that Iraq acquired chemical warhead technology for its Scud Bs and longer range North Korean missiles from North Korea.

Iranian Biological Weapons

Experts also agree that there are strong indications that Iran is actively working on biological weapons. Rumors of such biological weapons activity surfaced as early as 1982, along with reports that Iran was working on the production of mycotoxins, a simple biological agent that requires limited laboratory facilities.[99] These rumors were confirmed by U.S. intelligence sources in August, 1989, when it became clear that Iran was trying to buy two new strains of fungus from Canada and the Netherlands.[100] German sources indicated that Iran had successfully purchased such cultures several years earlier.

The Imam Reza Medical Center at Mashed Medical Sciences University and the Iranian Research Organization for Science and Technology were identified as the end users for this purchasing effort, but it is likely that the true end user is an Iranian government agency specializing in biological warfare. It also seems likely that Iran has conducted extensive research on more lethal active agents like anthrax and on biotoxins. Little is known about the state of the Iranian effort, weaponization, and volume of production. Unclassified sources have identified a facility at Damghan as working on both biological and chemical weapons research and production, and Iran may be producing biological weapons at a pesticide facility near Tehran.[101]

Iranian Nuclear Weapons

Like other Middle Eastern proliferators, Iran has found it difficult to build nuclear weapons. Nevertheless, Iran has long been involved in trying to create a nuclear weapons program. Iran began its efforts while the shah was still in power and had excellent access to Western technology. As a result, Iran's initial efforts were far more ambitious than those of Iraq.

In the early 1970s, the shah acquired Iran's first nuclear reactor from the U.S. for the Amirabad Nuclear Research Center (now called the Amirabad Technical College) in Tehran. This 5 megawatt reactor was originally supplied by the U.S. and started up in 1967. It is regularly inspected by the IAEA, but it uses a core with 93% enriched uranium, which is suitable for some forms of nuclear weapon.

The shah established the Atomic Energy Organization of Iran in 1974 and rapidly began to negotiate for nuclear power plants. He concluded an extendable ten year nuclear fuel contract with the U.S. in 1974, with Germany in 1976, and with France in 1977. In 1975 he purchased a 10% share in a Eurodif uranium enrichment plant being built at Tricastin in France that was part of a French, Belgian, Spanish, and Italian consortium. Under the agreement the shah signed, Iran was to have full access to the enrichment technology Eurodif developed, and he agreed to buy a quota of enriched uranium from the new plant.[102]

The shah sought more than weapons. He wanted to develop a nuclear power capability to reduce Iran's internal demand for oil, expand Iran's industrial infrastructure, and protect Iran's industrial growth once it depleted its oil reserves. This led the shah to create an extremely ambitious plan calling for a network of twenty-three power reactors throughout Iran that was to be operating by the mid-1990s and for the purchase of nuclear power plants from Germany and France. By the time the shah fell in January, 1979, he was attempting to purchase a total of twelve nuclear power plants from the FRG, France, and the U.S. Two 1,300 megawatt German plants at Bushehr were already 60% and 75% completed, and site preparation work had begun on the first of two 935 megawatt French plants at Darkhouin that were to be supplied by Framatome.[103] Thousands of Iranians were training in nuclear technology in France, the FRG, India, the UK, and the U.S.

Far less publicly, the shah began a nuclear weapons research program based at the Amirabad Research Center.[104] This research effort included studies of weapons designs, plutonium recovery from spent reactor fuel, and a laser enrichment program which began in 1975 and led to a complex and illegal effort to obtain laser separation technology from the U.S. This latter effort continued from 1976 until the shah's ouster, and four lasers operating in the critical 16 micron band were shipped to Iran in October, 1978.[105] At the same time, Iran worked on ways to obtain plutonium. It created a secret reprocessing research effort to use enriched uranium and set up a small nuclear weapons design team.[106]

In 1976 Iran signed a secret contract to buy $700 million worth of yellow cake from South Africa, and seems to have reached an agreement to buy up to 1,000 metric tons a year.[107] It is unclear how much of this ore South Africa shipped before it agreed to adopt IAEA export restrictions in 1984, and whether South Africa really honors such export restrictions even now. Some sources indicate that South Africa still made major deliveries as late as 1988–1989.[108] Iran also tried to purchase 26.2 kilograms of highly enriched uranium; the application to the U.S. for this purchase was still pending when the shah fell.

The new Khomeini government let much of the shah's nuclear power program collapse during 1979 and 1980, although it kept the core nuclear research effort going. The Khomeini government began to revive the nuclear program in 1981, however, after Iraq had invaded Iran's territory. The government provided new funds to the research teams operating the U.S.-supplied reactor at the Amirabad Center, although it continued to operate the reactor under IAEA safeguards. At least one senior official of the new government, Mohammed Behesti, stated to senior officials managing the nuclear research effort in 1981 that the mandate of Iran's nuclear program was now to develop a nuclear weapon. Khameni implied the same thing in a speech to the Atomic Energy Organization in 1987, and some experts maintain that the IRGC moved a great deal of the experts and equipment at the Amirabad Center to a new nuclear weapons research facility near Isfahan in the mid-1980s.[109]

Iran also seems to have revitalized its laser isotope separation program in 1983 and held several conferences on the subject, including an international conference in September, 1987. In 1984 it opened a new nuclear research center in Isfahan, located about 4 kilometers outside the city and between the villages of Shahrida and Fulashans. This facility was built on a scale far beyond the needs of peaceful research, and Iran sought French and Pakistani help for a new research reactor for this center. The Khomeini government may also have obtained several thousand pounds of uranium dioxide from Argentina by purchasing it through Algeria. Uranium dioxide is considerably more refined than yellow cake and much easier to use in irradiating material in a reactor to produce plutonium.[110]

Unlike many Iranian facilities, the center at Isfahan was not declared to the IAEA until 1992, when the agency was allowed to make a cursory inspection. While Iran could not get a reactor from France or Pakistan, it had more success with China, buying a subcritical research reactor from the PRC in 1985 and a Calutron in 1987. This Calutron was only a 1 milliamp machine, versus the 600 milliamp machines Iraq used in its weapons enrichment efforts; it was so small that it was suitable only for research purposes—specifically, to test insulators and liners and to produce stable isotopes of zinc for pharmaceutical purposes.

Iran also began to recruit nuclear scientists and tried to renew its power reactor program as a way of getting enriched material. In 1984 the Khomeini government began to restart work at the Bushehr reactor complex, although the FRG officially refused to support the rebuilding effort until the war ended. Iran got around this refusal by obtaining Argentine support in completing the Bushehr 1 reactor, which was 75% finished. On November 6, 1985, the international edition of *Kayhan* ran a government ad asking Iranian nuclear scientists to return home, all expenses paid, to attend a conference on nuclear research at Bushehr that was scheduled for March 14–19, 1986. Reports surfaced in April, 1987 that the Argentine nuclear power agency had signed an agreement with Iran.[111] This agency works closely with West Germany's Kraftwerke Union, which had the original contract for the reactor. The Spanish firm Impresarios Agupados may also have been part of the consortium.[112]

These Iranian efforts suffered major setbacks during the Iran-Iraq War when Iraq repeatedly bombed Iran's reactor projects at Bushehr. Iraqi bombings occurred on March 24, 1984; February 12, 1985; March 4, 1985; July 12, 1986; November 17, 1987; November 19, 1987; and July 19, 1988. The 1987 and 1988 raids may have been a response to Iran's transferral of IAEA-safeguarded material to the area in February, 1987.[113] At least some foreign technicians died during these bombings, and work on the reactors was often suspended. While the German Kraftwerke Union officially pulled out of the Bushehr project in September, 1980, it or a proxy firm seems to have been working on the reactor when Iraqi aircraft bombed it on November 17, 1987. Several Kraftwerke technicians were injured and one was killed.[114]

Since 1987 the course of the Iranian program has become harder to trace, and it has been the source of many unconfirmed rumors—many inspired by the Iraqi-financed Iranian People's Mujahideen. U.S. experts believe that Iran has such a program but that it is not nearly as advanced as Iraq's program was before the Gulf War. The International Atomic Energy Agency has also inspected many facilities that the People's Mujahideen rumored to be the site of Iran's nuclear weapons efforts in February, 1992. The IAEA conducted merely a "familiarization tour" and may have been led to a decoy site when it thought it was investigating a facility called Maallem Kelayah. Nevertheless, the IAEA did not find any of the supposed evidence.

Part of the reason the Iranian program is difficult to analyze is that since Iraq destroyed its nearly completed reactors near Bushehr, Iran has attempted to build its program slowly by concentrating on research. This is a much less visible approach than the effort Iraq made, leaping forward by massive investments.

Even so, Iran has not always been successful. For example, Argentina agreed to train Iranian technicians at its José Balaseiro Nuclear Institute and sold Iran $5.5 million worth of uranium for its small Amirabad reactor in May, 1987. A team from the Argentine nuclear power agency visited Iran in late 1987 and early 1988 and seems to have agreed to sell Iran the technology necessary to operate its reactor with 20% enriched uranium as a substitute for the highly enriched core provided by the U.S., and possibly uranium enrichment and plutonium reprocessing technology as well.[115] Changes in Argentina's government, however, made it much less willing to support proliferation. The Argentine government announced in February, 1992 that it was canceling an $18 million nuclear technology sale to Iran because it had not signed a nuclear safeguards arrangement. Argentine press sources suggested that Argentina was simply reacting to U.S. pressure.[116]

Iran has had equal problems in restarting its reactor program. It does seem to have had some success in getting German help in rebuilding one of its reactors near Bushehr after the cease-fire in the Iran-Iraq War.[117] It has not, however, found a source of new major reactors, although it has certainly tried. In February, 1990 a Spanish paper reported that Associated Enterprises of Spain was negotiating to complete the two nuclear power plants at Bushehr. Another Spanish firm called ENUSA (National Uranium Enterprises) was to provide the fuel, and Kraftwerke would also be involved. Later reports indicated that a ten man delegation from Iran's Ministry of Industry was in Madrid negotiating with the director of Associated Enterprises, Adolfo García Rodriguez.[118]

These reports were followed in March, 1990 by reports that the USSR had provided an initial agreement to work on two 440 megawatt nuclear power plants in Iran, and that this might include both a new power plant and completion of the two main power reactors at Bushehr.[119] The same month, reports surfaced that South Korea was exploring the possibility of participating in rebuilding the facilities at Bushehr and that the Korea Power Engineering Company had sent a survey team to Iran to look at the project.[120]

Iran has also sought nuclear reactors from India. In 1992 Iran and India were said to be negotiating the sale of a 10 megawatt research reactor. While such a reactor is comparatively small, it can still produce enough plutonium or enriched uranium to produce the fissile material for about one bomb a year if it is run twenty-four hours a day. India seems to have offered a 5 megawatt reactor for research purposes, but Iran apparently pressed hard for a larger 10 megawatt reactor. These same sources indicated that Iran was seeking a 220 megawatt power reactor. According to some sources, India was finally persuaded to sell Iran the 10 megawatt reactor and even signed an agreement on November 11, 1991, but delayed or halted the deal after intervention by the U.S.[121]

Given that none of these reports of new reactor programs has yet been followed by major construction activity and that Iran's only significant reactor is the small 5 megawatt research reactor that the U.S. supplied it in 1967, it is unlikely that Iran will have nuclear weapons before the late 1990s.[122] The U.S. reactor is under IAEA inspection, as the reactor at Bushehr will be, even if it comes on line early enough to be a potential source of weapons grade material.

Iran has, however, engaged in activities which may give it more of the resources it needs. Iran has found sources of raw material. While it has never been able to use the shah's 10% investment in Eurodif to obtain enriched material, there are significant uranium deposits (at least 5,000 tons) in the Shaghand region of Iran's Yazd province.[123] There are also reports that Iran has a uranium processing or enrichment facility at Pilcaniyeu. Iran announced plans to set up a yellow cake plant in Yazd province in 1987, and this facility was under construction by 1989.[124] It may have opened a new uranium ore processing plant close to its Shaghand uranium mine in March, 1990, and it seems to have extended its search for uranium ore into three new areas.[125]

Iran has also found sources of nuclear technology. On February 7, 1990, the speaker of the Majlis publicly toured the Iranian Atomic Energy Organization and opened the Jabir Ibn al-Hayyan Laboratory to train Iranian nuclear technicians.[126] Reports surfaced later that Iran had at least 200 scientists and a work force of about 2,000 conducting nuclear research.

Pakistan signed a nuclear cooperation agreement with Iran in 1987. Specialists from Iran's Atomic Energy Organization began to train in Pakistan, and Abdelkadr Khan, who has directed much of Pakistan's effort to develop nuclear weapons material, visited Tehran and Bushehr in February, 1986 and January, 1987. There are some reports that Pakistan is aiding Iran in developing plutonium extraction and other weapons technologies. There are also reports that Iran may have obtained nuclear weapons materials and technology from India, North Korea, and the PRC.[127] However, Pakistan denied it was giving Iran assistance in creating a nuclear center at Kazmin in November, 1990. It also indicated in 1992 that it had denied an Iranian request to provide nuclear weapons technology, and U.S. experts indicated that this denial was probably correct.[128]

Iran also strengthened its research ties to the PRC, although their military significance has sometimes been exaggerated. The two countries signed a broad nuclear research cooperation agreement in 1990. On January 21, 1991, Torkan, Iran's minister of defense and armed forces logistics, signed an agreement with Gen. Jiang Xua, the deputy director of China's Commission on Science, Technology, and Industry for National Defense, to build a small 27 kilowatt research reactor at Iran's nuclear weapons research facility at Isfahan. This reactor was to be built by the China Nuclear Energy Industry Corporation, and major construction was under way by September, 1991. The reactor was large enough to be useful for weapons design purposes but was far too small to produce enough fissile materials for a bomb. Unconfirmed reports also surfaced in September, 1992, that the PRC had sold Iran at 300 megawatt power reactor.[129]

There is no evidence that Iran has major facilities to enrich uranium or design and produce weapons. The People's Mujahideen reported that Iran has a number of major nuclear weapons facilities, including a weapons site called Maallem Kelayah, near Qazvin on the Caspian. This facility is said to be an IRGC facility that was established in 1987 and in which Iran has since invested $300 million. This site was supposed to house the 10 megawatt reactor Iran tried to buy from India. There is a debate over the supposed visit the IAEA made to this facility in February, 1992. According to some sources, the IAEA team was taken to a resort with a similar name.

The People's Mujahideen has also claimed that Iran is seeking to obtain two 450 megawatt reactors for a large site at Gorgan on the Caspian, which will be installed under the direction of Russian physicists. It has claimed that the PRC has provided uranium enrichment equipment and technicians for the site at Darkhouin, where Iran once planned to build a French reactor; that a nuclear reactor is being constructed at Karaj; and that another nuclear weapons facility exists in the south central part of Iran near the Iraqi border. The Mujahideen has also claimed that the ammonia and urea plant that the British firm of MW Kellog is building at Bojnurd, in Khorassan province near the border with Turkistan, may be adapted to produce heavy water.

It has also listed Amir Kabar Technical University, the Atomic Energy Organization of Iran, Dor Argham Ltd., the Education and Research Institute, GAM Iranian Communications, Ghods Research Center, Iran Argham Co., Iran Electronic Industries, Iranian Research Organization, Ministry of Sepah, Research and Development Group, Sezemane Sanaye Defa, the Sharif University of Technology, Taradis Iran Computer Company, and Zakaria Razi Chemical Company as fronts for the Iranian nuclear weapons effort. It has also inspired or encouraged reports that Iran has bought nuclear warheads from Kazakhstan.[130]

The IAEA, however, conducted a limited inspection of six of these sites for the first time in February, 1992. It found no sign of weapons activity at any of these sites. Even if one ignores the debate over the site at Maallem Kelayah, the IAEA confirmed that the Calutron at Isfahan was far too small for weapons purposes, and it found only minor uranium exploration efforts at Shaghand.[131] Similarly, reports that Iran has hired large numbers of former Soviet scientists, bought weapons grade material from the former Soviet Union, or even bought nuclear armed missiles from Kazakhstan during 1992 all proved exaggerated or incorrect.[132]

In spite of these developments, it seems clear that Iran is willing to allocate major resources to continuing its nuclear weapons efforts, as well as continue its efforts to improve its chemical weapons and develop biological weapons. Robert Gates, the director of Central Intelligence, testified to Congress in February, 1992 that Iran was "building up its special weapons capability as part of a massive . . . effort to develop its military and defense capability."[133] Further, Iran's difficulties in nuclear proliferation may well lead it to accelerate its production of chemical and biological weapons and to develop and produce more lethal systems.

Strategic Interests and Arms Control

Regardless of the Arab proverb, the enemy of our enemy is not necessarily our friend. While Iran's rhetoric has moderated since the Gulf War, some of its actions have not. It has encouraged Shi'ite extremist groups to launch attacks against the SLA in southern Lebanon and to attempt to penetrate into Israel. In fact, Iran has become a pillar of the hard-line rejectionist effort that denies Israel's right to exist. Iran has strongly supported Islamic hard-liners in the civil war in the Sudan and has become politically active in seeking support in the Soviet Islamic republics: Kazakhstan, Kirghizia, Turkmenistan, Tadzhikistan, Uzbekistan, and Azerbaijan. While most of these republics are Sunni and are expanding their ties with Turkey and Saudi Arabia, Azerbaijan is largely Shi'ite and shares linguistic roots with Iran.

It is difficult, however, to describe Iran's military buildup as aggressive. Iran still faces a major threat from Iraq. Iraq still deploys a large part of its forces along the Iranian border, and the cease-fire in the Iran-Iraq War has several major unresolved issues—including war reparation damages and prisoners of war.[134] Iran could scarcely be expected to accept the force levels it had at the end of the Iran-Iraq War. Its active tank forces had been cut from 1,735 to 600, and it had lost nearly 1,000 other armored vehicles during the last six months of the war and nearly half of its artillery. It had only 160 aircraft, and many were not operational.

Iran's government has also become more pragmatic, if not inherently more moderate, under Rafsanjani. Iran has made several peacemaking attempts in Armenia and Azerbaijan, as well as encouraged Islamic extremism. It has greatly improved its relations with the southern Gulf states and its economic ties with Western Europe. It imported some $527 million worth of goods from the U.S. in 1991, a ninefold increase over 1989, although the U.S. continued to list Iran as a terrorist nation, and most of the candidates in Iran's 1992 elections continued to denounce the U.S.[135]

Nevertheless, Iran remains a threat to the security of its neighbors and moderate and secular states throughout the Middle East. There is no reason not to attempt to build closer political and economic relations, but any arms transfer policy must reflect that Iran has played a destablizing role in the Gulf ever since the fall of the shah. There is no reason for outside nations to support its military buildup and acquisition of weapons of mass destruction.

Iraq

	Manpower (1,000s)	Tanks	Aircraft	Defense Spending ($ millions)	Arms Imports ($ millions)	Arms Exports ($ millions)
1967	90	400–535	215	421	90	4
1973	105	990	224	1,180	628	0
1982	230	5,500	330	25,070	7,100	—
1988	900	5,500	513	16,500	4,600	80
1991	1,033	2,000–2,300	330–360	8,610	—	—

In order to understand Iraq's situation, it is necessary to understand its strategic position as well as its history.[136] Iraq is a nation of about 434,000 square kilometers, or about twice the size of Idaho. Its strategic position at the western end of the Gulf and in the northern tier places it close to the Soviet Union and gives it boundaries that span the distance between Southwest Asia and the Middle East. Iraq has a 1,448 kilometer land boundary with Iran, a 331 kilometer border with Turkey, a 605 kilometer border with Syria, a 134 kilometer border with Jordan, a 495 kilometer border with Saudi Arabia, a 191 kilometer border along the Saudi-Iraqi neutral zone, and a 240 kilometer border with Kuwait.[137]

Iraq's access to the Gulf consists of a 58 kilometer coastline on relatively shallow Gulf waters. Its only major port on the Gulf is Basra, which can be reached only via the Shatt al Arab. Its only naval base is Umm Qasr, which must be reached by a channel shared with Kuwait and dominated by the Kuwaiti Islands of Warbah and Bubiyan.[138]

In 1991 Iraq had a population of about 19.5 million, growing at a rate of 3.9%. This population is about 75–80% Arab, with 15–20% Kurdish, and 5% Turkic, Assyrian, and other. Iraq was deeply divided along religious lines. The CIA estimated that the population was 97% Muslim and 3% Christian and other, but divided between 60–65% Shi'ite and 32–37% Sunni.[139] Other sources indicate it was closer to 50–55% Shi'ite if Turkic and Kurds Sunnis are included. The total male manpower pool is about 4,300,000, counting the population from 15 to 49. The CIA estimates that 4,270,000 males are fit for military service, and that 228,000 reach military age each year.[140] The IISS estimates that there are 1,170,000 males between the ages of 13 and 17, 945,400 between the ages of 18 and 22, and 1,408,700 between the ages of 23 and 32.[141]

Iraq is one of the major oil states in the world, although it has far smaller reserves than Saudi Arabia. It had produced about 22.4 billion barrels of oil by the end of 1990 and had a high reserve-to-production ratio of 132:1.[142] As of January 1, 1992, it had estimated proved oil reserves of up to 100 billion barrels and gas reserves of 95,000 billion cubic feet. It had about 13% of the world's total oil reserves and produced at a rate of about 2.1 million barrels per day before the Gulf War.[143] It also had a share of the Saudi-Iraqi neutral zone, which had another 5 billion barrels of proven reserves and 1,000 billion cubic feet of gas.[144] Iraq has about 42.8 cubic kilometers of internal renewable water resources, which is high for a Middle Eastern country and which amounts to about 4,575 cubic meters per person, more than twice the total for a citizen of the U.S.[145]

Iraq's tragedy is that it has been blessed with immense oil wealth and other natural assets and one of the best educated populations in the Middle East, and cursed with some of the worst governments. Iraq's oil exports have varied sharply with world oil prices and Iraq's wars, but they brought in annual revenues of $6.8 billion to $26.0 billion during the 1980s.[146] Unlike many Gulf states, Iraq also has a relatively well developed manufacturing sector that accounted for over 10% of the GDP even during 1987–1988, the worst year of the Iran-Iraq War. About 12% of its land is arable, of which 4% is irrigated. Another 9% is suitable for grazing, and 3% is forest. While Iraq is a major food importer, this is largely because of government mismanagement. The Tigris and Euphrates rivers permit a major increase in production, and agriculture already employs 30% of the labor force, although it accounts for only 11% of the GNP.[147]

The Evolution of the Middle East's Most Militaristic State

While Iraq occupies a region that has played a critical role in history, the borders of the modern state are more an accident than an inheritance. The territory now included in Iraq came under Ottoman rule in 1638, but Iraq never existed as a nation-state within its present boundaries before Turkish occupation, and the area around Baghdad had never recovered from Tamerlane's sack of Baghdad in 1401 and decimation of the region's entire population. The Turks never treated the region as an entity, organizing it into three or four provinces, or *vilayets*, of the Ottoman Empire centered at Baghdad, Mosul, and Basra. Even when the Turks actually controlled the *vilayets* from Istanbul, they never attempted to impose direct rule over all the feuding ethnic and tribal groups that made up the territories now occupied by Iraq but focused on the control of urban areas and key lines of communication.

British interest in the region grew out of its interest in the security of the Gulf and approaches to India, and rivalry with Germany over influence in the Ottoman Empire. During World War I, Britain treated Iraq as a sideshow necessary to protect its oil interests in Iran (where oil was found in 1912) and occupied Basra and southern Iraq virtually without resistance in 1915. It was at this point that Britain dredged the Shatt al Arab to allow large vessels to move to Basra for the first time, turning it into a meaningful port. British forces suffered some reversals during 1916 but took Baghdad in March, 1917 and Mosul in October. By 1918 Britain held all of modern Iraq.

On April 25, 1920, Britain was awarded Iraq as a Class A mandate by the League of Nations and installed Sir Percy Cox as chief political officer who delegated actual control to his deputy, Col. Arnold Talbot Wilson. At the time, Iraq was in near chaos, with widespread civil warfare and tribal anarchy in the Shi'ite holy cities of An Najaf and Karbala. This anarchy turned to rebellion when it became known that Iraq was to be a mandate, rather than an independent part of the Arab world, and Britain brought in troops and the RAF to establish control.

The cost of the revolt in lives and economic destruction led Britain to abandon the idea of maintaining direct control over the country, and Britain rigged a one-question plebiscite as an excuse for placing Iraq under a pro-British king. The king Britain chose was a foreigner: Amir Faisal ibn Hussein, who came from the Hashemite dynasty which then ruled the Hijaz in what is now Saudi Arabia. Britain chose him because it owed the Hashemites a debt for their role in the Arab revolt that had helped exhaust Turkish military power during World War I but Faisal also had the support of much of Iraq's Sunni and Shi'ite leadership. Faisal was crowned on August 23, 1921, and Britain secured his rule by leaving RAF detachments in the country.

The king also had the support of many of the Arab officers who had served in the Ottoman Empire and had joined the Young Turks and then the Arab revolt.[148] These officers also supported him because Turkey put active pressure on the new state to return the *vilayet* of Mosul and because Iraq faced rebellion from many of the Kurds and Assyrians that had been included in its territory without any consultation or real opportunity to vote in the British plebiscite. In another key development, the Anglo-Persian Oil Company found oil near Basra in 1923, and the Turkish Oil Company (a British firm) found major oil reserves in the north in 1927.

The strongest of the Arab officers around the king was Nuri al-Said, who became the first chief of staff of the Iraqi army and acted as the most powerful figure in Iraq during much of the 1920s. He made a consistent effort to expand Iraq's military forces, and by the time the British mandate terminated in 1932, the army was the strongest force in Iraqi society. He also secured a new treaty with Britain that gave Iraq full control over its foreign affairs. This treaty was signed on June 30, 1930, and went into force on October 13, 1932.[149]

Faisal died in London on September 8, 1933, while Iraq was in the midst of an Assyrian rebellion. He was replaced by his twenty-one-year-old son Ghazi. The result was a weak central government that steadily lost power to the military. In 1936 Gen. Baqr Sidqi carried out a short lived military-reformist coup. Sidqi was assassinated in 1937, and six more coups took place by 1941. The country remained under military rule, and the military became increasingly anti-British in reaction to events in Palestine. While Iraq did break its diplomatic ties with Nazi Germany in 1939, many of the military resented this, which eventually led to a anti-British coup in 1941. When the Iraqi army besieged the British air base at Habbiniyah, the British responded by invading Iraq, and they occupied the country until 1945.

After 1945 Iraq remained under the rule of an uncertain and faltering pro-Western monarchy and figures like Nuri al-Said. The monarchy stayed in power largely because of Iraq's increasing oil wealth and British and U.S. support but had little political support from either Iraq's intelligentsia or most of its junior and middle ranking military officers. Both supporters of Nasser and the Baath Party became more influential, and Iraqi nationalism increasingly became directed against the monarchy. These pressures reached their culmination on July 14, 1958, when the leaders of Iraq's two armored brigades launched a coup that killed King Faisal II, the crown prince, and Prime Minister al-Said.

Iraq immediately broke with the West and turned to the Soviet Union for support and arms. The coup was followed, however, by a struggle for power between the two armored brigade commanders—the leftist nationalist Abdelkarim Kassem and an army officer, Col. Abdelsalem Mohammed Arif. Kassem won the struggle for power and proved to be extremely violent and authoritarian. He began a systematic effort to purge or execute any Baathist, Nasserite, or Communist rivals and created an increasingly more violent internal opposition. This led to a number of assassination attempts against Kassem, including one by a young Baathist militant called Saddam Hussein in October, 1959.

Kassem faced problems with his own military in March, 1959, when rebel military forces seized the town of Mosul. They did so with the support of Syria and Egypt, and Shammar tribesmen prepared to support them, but Syria was not willing to provide direct military support. As a result, Kassem was able to bring in loyal troops and use the air force to bomb rebel forces and villages and attack their bases in Syria. This ended the rebellion within the month, after killing large numbers of civilians.

It is ironic that Kassem had the support of Kurdish troops in suppressing the Mosul rebellion; they soon turned into an enemy. This was partly Kassem's fault. He had allowed Mustpha Barzani to return from exile in the USSR in 1958. While Barzani initially supported Kassem, he slowly built the Democratic Party of Kurdistan into an independent military force that ruthlessly crushed other Kurdish tribal opposition. During 1960 and 1961, he carved out a virtually independent enclave in northern Iraq, near the Turkish border, and this started a new war between the Kurds and Iraqis that lasted until 1970.

Kassem also contributed to regional tension. He laid claim to Kuwait when Britain granted it full independence in June, 1961. This forced Britain to rush troops and air units back to Kuwait, and Saudi Arabia also sent troops to support the new state. While Arab League forces replaced the British forces, Iraq and Kuwait continued their confrontation until 1963, when Iraq finally recognized Kuwait's independence.

This was partly the result of political changes in Iraq. On February 8, 1963, Arif succeeded in taking power back from Kassem. He led a coup in which Kassem and many of his supporters were shot. Arif then became "president," and a leading Baathist officer, Ahmed Hassan al-Baqr, became prime minister. They promptly organized a new series of purges and coups, killing thousands of Communists, supporters of Kassem, Kurds, and pro-Nasserites.

This change in political power led to a temporary accommodation between Syria and Iraq that led Syrian ground and air forces to cooperate in attacking Kurdish positions in Iraq, but near Syria, from June to November, 1963. Syrian forces also occupied secure areas, freeing Iraqi forces to conduct offensive operations.[150] The brief Syrian-Iraqi alliance had a major impact on the fighting with the Kurds and allowed the government to negotiate a cease-fire and autonomy agreement with Barzani in February, 1964.

A new source of conflict developed within Iraq, however, over whether Iraq should join the new United Arab Republic being formed by Egypt and Syria. Arif opposed such union, but the majority of the Baath Party supported it. As a result, Arif carried out a coup against the Baath on November 18, 1963, and set up a nonparty government. Arif then changed his position to oppose union with Egypt and had to put down a pro-Nasser coup in September, 1965.

As a result of this internal upheaval, Barzani was able to ignore the cease-fire agreement and to keep strengthening his enclave near Turkey. This led to steady fighting in the north and occasional incidents when Iraqi forces attacked Kurdish positions in Turkey and Iran. While Barzani reached a more favorable autonomy agreement with Arif in June, 1966, the Iraqi army rejected this agreement and forced the prime minister who had signed it to resign. The fighting continued until March, 1970, and Barzani emerged as a partial victor. Baghdad recognized local autonomy, but no firm agreement could be reached because the Iraqi government opposed giving the Kurds a fixed share of Iraq's oil revenues.

When Arif died in a helicopter crash in 1967, his brother, Maj. Gen. Abdelrahman Arif came to power. He survived another Nasserite coup in 1966 but was severely undermined by the poor performance of the Iraqi forces during the June War with Israel. He was overthrown by a bloodless coup on April 17, 1968, and a second coup established a Baath-dominated government on June 30, 1968.

This coup brought the mainstream of the Iraqi Baath Party and Ahmed Hassan al-Baqr back into power, governing through a small Revolutionary Command Council (RCC). The aftermath of this second coup, however, was anything but bloodless. The armed forces, civil service, and every element of Iraqi society went through new purges and trials, and there were thousands of additional executions. A number of show trials took place, including a spy trial after which eleven "spies"—including nine Jews—were publicly hanged. By 1970 much of the opposition to the Baath had been removed.

The government first attempted to deal with the Kurds by splitting the Kurdish movement, and it invited two of Barzani's rivals—Jalal Talabani and Ibrahim Ahmed—to Baghdad. When this failed to have any major impact on the Kurdish movement, the government offered a real autonomy agreement, one that allowed Barzani to keep his 15,000 troops. This agreement, however, was opposed by a number of senior Baath officials and led to new purges within the party.

Barzani then turned to the shah of Iran for military and financial support, building up his forces while awaiting the implementation of the autonomy agreement which was scheduled to take place on March 11, 1974. The shah supported the Kurds because Iraq had broken relations with Iran after the shah seized Abu Musa and the Tunbs in the Gulf, and because he was fighting a low level border war with Iraq. The shah encouraged Barzani to reject the autonomy agreement, which he did in early 1974. Barzani's forces, the Pesh Merga, then attacked Iraqi positions in the north.

The shah, however, cared nothing for the Kurds or Barzani—who had attempted to create an independent Kurdistan in Iran in 1946. The shah instead used the growing Kurdish threat to Baghdad to force Iraq into a favorable settlement of various border issues and joint control of the Shatt al Arab, and into halting any support for the shah's opponents. The moment Iraq signed the Algiers accord on March 6, 1975, the Shah cut off support to the Kurds—leaving them without arms and money to continue fighting.

This fighting did not prevent Iraq from indulging in aggressive adventures of its own. Iraq attempted to seize control of Kuwait once Britain withdrew from the Gulf in 1961. Although British and Arab League forces helped prevent an Iraqi invasion, Iraq then put pressure on Kuwait for the transfer of the islands of Bubiyan and Warbah in the Gulf and potentially oil rich areas near the unmarked Iraqi-Kuwaiti border. Minor border clashes occurred in 1963 and a more serious clash in 1967. On March 20, 1973, Iraqi forces seized the Kuwaiti border posts near Sametah, and Iraq made a serious covert effort to pressure Kuwait to cede or lease disputed Warbah and Bubiyan. Iraq withdrew only after mediation by Yasser Arafat and a substantial payment to Iraq.

During this same period, Saddam Hussein rose to power. Saddam not only gradually became more powerful than Arif, he proved himself to be a great deal more ruthless. He used force to dominate the elite of the Baath Party, much of which came from Tikrit, a small Sunni town about 100 miles north of Baghdad. Three different intraparty coup attempts were made to challenge Saddam's position by other Baath leaders and military officers in 1970, 1971, and 1973, and each time Saddam both won and imprisoned or executed his opposition. In May, 1978 he publicly executed twenty-one "Communists" for attempting to form cells within the army, and he more quietly purged and executed a number of other rivals. These struggles gave Saddam virtually unchallenged power, and he finally took the title of "president" on July 16, 1979—when Arif left office because of "illness."

Regardless of this bloodshed, the Baath made good use of some of Iraq's oil wealth between 1973 and 1979. Unlike many other oil states, Iraq channeled much of the money into economic development, improved housing and living standards, and better education and medical care.

The Impact of the Iran-Iraq War

The fall of the shah in late 1979, however, created a new set of problems for Iraq. While Saddam Hussein originally attempted to work out a modus vivendi with the Ayatollah Khomeini, he soon concluded that this was impossible. Khomeini called for the overthrow of the Baath Party, actively supported anti-Baath Shi'ite elements, and supported assassination attempts on Saddam and senior Baath officials. At the same time, the upheavals and purges in the Iranian military and Iran's break with the U.S. over the U.S. embassy hostage crisis seemed to offer Saddam a way of reversing the Algiers accords and even seizing part of Iran's oil rich south.

As a result, Saddam Hussein invaded Iran in September, 1980. A two corps force captured Iranian territory in the province of Khuzistan, which Iraq claimed was largely Arab and Arabic speaking. Iraq's goal was to seize the oil rich territory in southwest Iran either by creating an independent "Arabestan" or making the region part of Iraq. The province was only about 30% Arabic speaking, however, and more of its population proved loyal to a religious Iran than it did to a secular Iraq. In spite of Iraqi calls for an Arab uprising, only a small part of Iran's "Arabs" backed Iraq. At the same time, Iraq's forces proved to be slow moving and failed to take the major cities in the region before Iran could begin to organize its defenses. The Iraqi offensive stalled by early 1981, and Iraq became bogged down in urban and infantry warfare against a steadily better mobilized Iran.

The result was eight years of war. Iraq lost most of its initial conquests during late 1981 and early 1982. It never took Dezful or all of Abadan, and its forces gradually became restricted to positions along major lines of communication which Iran's forces could isolate and overrun. Although Iraq attempted a major counterattack in the spring of 1982, it could not seize more territory or inflict major casualties on Iran. Instead, it found its forces being split and isolated by Iranian infantry forces that could infiltrate around the Iraqi positions and that were willing to launch human wave attacks to overrun the Iraqi positions.

After several major defeats, Saddam Hussein tried to end the war by unilaterally withdrawing from Iran. Iran, however, did not accept an end to the war and invaded Iraq. From 1984 to 1987, Iran was on the offensive, and at some points in the fighting, it threatened to conquer Iraq. Iran was particularly successful in its offensives in 1986 and 1987. Iranian forces seized Iraq's Faw Peninsula and threatened Basra.

Iraq survived, but only because Khomeini had managed to alienate his neighbors, the West, and the Soviet bloc and had no major source of aid and advanced arms. Iran's forces remained politically divided between regular and revolutionary forces and could not obtain modern new weapons and aircraft or reliable sources of parts for the weapons and aircraft purchased before the fall of the shah. Iraq, in contrast, had access to modern Soviet and European arms and over $25 billion dollars in loans and aid from friendly Gulf states like Kuwait and Saudi Arabia. This allowed Iraq's central government expenditures to exceed its annual GNP throughout most of the Iran-Iraq War.[151]

By 1988 this advantage in money and arms allowed Iraq to reequip and retrain its military forces in spite of a constant series of Iranian offenses. At the same time, each Iranian offensive pitted badly equipped and partially trained Iranian forces against entrenched, well equipped, and increasingly better trained and organized Iraqi forces. Iran's revolutionary fervor sometimes produced important local victories, but it also produced a continuous stream of casualties and losses that politically and financially exhausted Iran.

By 1988 Iraq was able to train elite units in its Revolutionary Guards and regular army that were capable of counterattacking with the speed and effectiveness its forces had lacked when they first invaded Iran. Iraq then used its immense superiority in armor, artillery, air power, and poison gas to go on the counteroffensive. Beginning at Faw, Iraq fought four major battles during April to August, 1988. It retook Faw and then successfully attacked Iranian positions near Fish Lake opposite Basra and Salamjah and retook the territory Iran had conquered in the Majnoon marshes. A demoralized and poorly equipped and sustained Iranian army collapsed, and Iraq drove deep into the Iranian border area in the north and captured or destroyed nearly 66% of Iran's heavy armor and 50% of its armored personnel carriers and artillery. Iran recognized this defeat in agreeing to a cease-fire on August 20, 1988.[152]

Iraq emerged as the dominant military power in the Gulf after the Iran-Iraq War, but at a cost of over 100,000 lives, a total of 375,000 casualties, 60,000 prisoners of war, and an immense amount of national wealth.[153] Iraq had cut its rate of economic development and increase in per capita income by 70–80%. It was close to $100 billion in debt and in desperate need of money. It still needed a port on the Gulf that was secure from Iran, and it still had problems with its Kurds.

Iraq solved the Kurdish problem through a series of offensives, deportations, and massacres. Towards the end of the war, Iraq's forces already had attacked some Kurdish positions, using poison gas in a major attack on civilians near the Kurdish town of Halabjah on March 16, 1988. Immediately after the cease-fire in the Iran-Iraq War, it turned its military machine against several Kurdish areas, using armor, bombing, artillery, and poison gas. Some of these attacks were directed against Kurds who had fought on the side of Iran as virtual mercenaries and had done so until the final weeks of the Iran-Iraq War. Iraq also, however, deported or displaced hundreds of thousands of other Kurds in up to 4,000 villages, used gas on 40 to 70 other civilian targets, and may have killed 50,000 to 100,000 Kurdish civilians in the process of trying to create a secure buffer zone along the Iranian border.[154]

Saddam was less successful in dealing with his other problems. He continued to import massive amounts of arms and maintain large military forces, and he began to spend large amounts of money on civil development and reconstruction. He could not, however, find major new sources of revenues or loans and faced major problems in trying to repay his existing loans. According to many experts inside and outside Iraq, Saddam and his immediate coterie came to feel that he was the subject of a Western plot to limit his powers.[155]

As a result, Saddam Hussein provoked a crisis over the issue of oil quotas with Kuwait and the UAE in the spring and summer of 1990. Most Gulf and Western officials treated this crisis as an Iraqi effort to win loan forgiveness and financial concessions, but Saddam had decided on war. On July 17, he accused Kuwait and the UAE of "stabbing Iraq in the back." On July 18, Foreign Minister Tariq Aziz sent a letter to the Arab League that accused Kuwait of stealing Iraqi oil from the Rummaliah oil field located in both Iraq and Kuwait, building military installations, and refusing to cancel wartime loans that should have been aid. On July 19, Saddam Hussein was declared president for life by the Iraqi parliament.

While President Mubarak of Egypt and other Arab leaders sought to prevent the war by mediating the differences between Iraq and Kuwait, Iraq sent 30,000 troops to the Kuwaiti border on July 24. Although OPEC largely agreed to Iraq's demands on July 26–27, Iraq expanded its forces on the Kuwaiti border to 100,000 men on July 30, and talks between Iraq and Kuwait broke down on August 1. On August 2, 1990, Iraq invaded Kuwait and the Gulf War began.

Iraqi Military Expenditures and Conventional Arms Transfers

In order to understand the shifts in Iraq's military capabilities that resulted from the Gulf War, it is necessary to understand the scale of Iraqi defense expenditures and arms transfers before the conflict. Even by a conservative estimate, Iraq imported over $150 billion worth of arms and equipment to manufacture and deliver weapons of mass destruction between 1975 and 1991. It spent billions on fighting the Kurds during the early to mid-1970s. It spent several hundred billion more on the Iran-Iraq War, which Saddam Hussein started by invading Iran. It then lost as much as $100 billion by invading Kuwait—as the result both of attacks on its military equipment, infrastructure, and production facilities by the U.N. coalition and of lost economic opportunities.

Military expenditures and wartime losses drained Iraq's economy for nearly two decades. Iraq's oil wealth is relative. Measured in constant 1988 dollars, Iraq's GNP peaked in 1979 and 1980 at $118 billion and $120 billion, respectively. The Iran-Iraq War rapidly cut its GNP to $70.4 billion in 1981, and a combination of wartime damage and lower oil prices then cut it to levels of $70 billion throughout the rest of the 1980s. Iraq's GNP was $65.8 billion in 1988, about half of its GNP in 1980. Iraq kept its military expenditures as a percentage of GNP at around 30% from 1978 to 1984 by a combination of massive foreign borrowing and aid from southern Gulf states like Kuwait and Saudi Arabia. After 1984, however, Iraq exhausted its borrowing capability, and the Iran-Iraq War grew more threatening. As a result, military spending rose to 52% of the GNP in 1985 and stayed near 50% for the rest of the 1980s.[156]

By 1989, the year that lay between the Iran-Iraq War and Iraq's invasion of Kuwait, Iraq was experiencing a serious economic crisis. Experts disagree over the statistics involved but not over how serious the crisis was. According to the CIA, for example, Iraq's GNP was then $35 billion and its per capita income was only $1,940.[157] This level of per capita income is not unusual by Third World standards, but it was very low relative to Iraq's economy in 1979 and to the wealth of a far less developed Saudi Arabia—which had a GNP of $79 billion and a per capita income of $4,800.

There is no precise way to estimate Iraqi defense expenditures, since the nominal figures provided in Iraqi reports and foreign estimates seem to use very different definitions, and all seem to ignore loans, aid, and many expenditures on arms and weapons of mass destruction. ACDA estimates that Iraq spent $10,010 million on military forces in 1978, $11,350 million in 1979, $19,810 million in 1980, $24,610 million in 1981, $25,070 million in 1982,

$25,260 million in 1983, $25,940 million in 1984, and $18,970 million in 1985.[158]

The U.S. has not issued military spending estimates for the period after 1985, but the IISS estimates that Iraq spent $13,990 million in 1987, $12,870 million in 1988, and planned to spend $8.61 billion in 1990—before the Gulf War forced it to devote virtually its entire economy to the conflict.[159] While any accurate estimates are impossible, Iraq has probably spent over 40% of its GDP and 60% of its central government expenditures—including wartime losses—on defense in recent years.[160]

Iraq's arms imports were a massive burden, and there is no way to determine how many were included in the previous estimates of military spending. They were accelerated by both the arms race with Iran which began in the 1960s and the Iran-Iraq War during the period from 1980 to 1988. ACDA estimates that Iraq imported $2,400 million worth of arms in 1978, $3,200 million in 1979, $2,400 million in 1980, $4,200 million in 1981, $7,000 million in 1982, $6,800 million in 1983, $9,100 million in 1984, $4,600 million in 1985, $5,700 million in 1986, $5,400 million in 1987, $4,900 million in 1988, and $1,900 million in 1989.[161]

According to a conservative estimate, which ignores all expenditures on weapons of mass destruction and some deliveries of military related goods and services other than actual weapons, Iraq signed at least $30.5 billion worth of new arms agreements between 1983 and 1990.[162] This high volume of new agreements reflects Iraq's establishment of a broad network of suppliers during the 1980s. It shifted away from reliance on the Soviet bloc and bought an increasing number of weapons from Europe and the Third World.

During 1979–1983, the period that covers the fall of the shah of Iran and the first part of the Iran-Iraq War, Iraq took delivery on $17.6 billion worth of new arms, including $7.2 billion worth of arms from the USSR, $0.85 billion from Poland, $0.4 billion from Romania, $0.04 billion from Czechoslovakia, and $1.5 billion from the PRC. It obtained $3.8 billion from France, $0.41 billion from Italy, $0.28 billion from the UK, $0.14 billion from West Germany, and $3.0 billion from other countries.[163]

During the latter half of the Iran-Iraq War, 1984–1988, Iraq took delivery on $29.7 billion worth of new arms, including $15.4 billion worth of arms from the USSR, $0.75 billion from Poland, $0.65 billion from Bulgaria, $0.675 billion from Czechoslovakia, and $2.8 billion from the PRC. Iraq obtained $3.1 billion from France, $0.37 billion from Italy, $0.03 billion from the UK, $0.675 billion from West Germany, and $5.2 billion from other countries.[164] The U.S. did not transfer significant numbers of weapons to Iraq but did provide help during the Iran-Iraq War in the form of credits and loans that helped buy weapons; the U.S. also provided intelligence support.[165]

If one takes the period between 1988 and 1991—which covers the time from the end of the Iran-Iraq War in August, 1988 to the beginning of the embargo on arms shipments to Iraq in August, 1990—Iraq ordered only $3.1 billion worth of arms. Some $400 million were ordered from the USSR, $700 million from the PRC, $500 million from major West European states, $500 million from other European states, and $1.0 billion from other countries.

Iraq took delivery on $8.9 billion worth of arms during this period, including $4.1 billion worth of arms from the USSR, $1.0 billion from the PRC, $1.1 billion from major West European states, $1.7 billion from other European states, and $1.0 billion from other countries.[166] The difference between orders and deliveries reflects a cut in imports after the Iran-Iraq War, but Iraq was still making a massive effort at new orders when it invaded Kuwait. It was also shifting its orders away from lower technology Soviet, PRC, and Eastern European suppliers to higher technology Western European suppliers.

The resulting burden on Iraq's economy unquestionably helped lead to Iraq's invasion of Kuwait on August 1, 1990, and to the Gulf War. Iraq had an annual military budget of $12.9 billion in 1990. Iraq was spending an average of $721 per citizen on military forces, although it had an average per capita income of only $1,940. Iran lacked an effective air force and had lost so much of its land force equipment in the Iran-Iraq War that it could no longer challenge Iraq. In spite of the UN embargo beginning in August, 1990, Iraq took delivery on $1,435 million worth of arms and ordered $1,125 million more during 1990 alone. This level of expenditure raised Iraq's international debt to at least $40 billion—and some experts say in excess of $70 billion.[167] This was a debt burden that created the economic crisis that helped lead Iraq to invade Kuwait.[168]

From Iraq's Invasion to the Beginning of the Gulf War

These vast expenditures did not protect Iraq from the consequences of its invasion of Kuwait. Saddam Hussein fatally miscalculated the reaction of his neighbors, the United States, and the other nations of the world.

As was the case in the Iran-Iraq War, Iraq did enjoy some initial success. It conquered Kuwait in a matter of hours and rapidly moved Iraqi divisions to the Saudi border. It was poised to invade Saudi Arabia, and the Saudis had only one brigade between Iraq and control of the main Saudi oil fields and oil ports in the Gulf. Iraq, however, failed to intimidate Saudi Arabia. Although it supported Kuwait's government-in-exile, Saudi Arabia firmly resisted Iraqi pressure and rapidly gained the support of other Gulf states like Bahrain, Oman, Qatar, and the United Arab Emirates.

Saddam Hussein seems to have expected that the U.S. would protest his seizure of Kuwait but not take the large scale military action necessary to secure Saudi Arabia and actually liberate Kuwait. These expectations seem to have been based on an exaggerated view of Iraq's military capabilities after its "victory" in the Iran-Iraq War and his feeling that a U.S. that had withdrawn from Vietnam and Lebanon was too weak and indecisive to act. At the same time, he seems to have counted on the Soviet Union to give him at least tacit support in avoiding a war, and on the Arab world to protect him from outside intervention.

In fact, the U.S., the Soviet Union, most Arab nations, and the rest of the world reacted quickly and decisively. President Bush froze Iraqi assets within hours after the invasion, demanded Iraq's unconditional withdrawal from Kuwait on August 5, sent U.S. fighters and carrier forces to Saudi

Arabia on August 7, and put U.S. airborne and assault forces on alert. He notified Congress he was sending troops on August 9 and began a naval blockade on August 12.

The Soviet Union and most of the Arab world joined with the U.S. to condemn Iraq's actions, and the UN Security Council voted 13 to 2 to institute an economic boycott of Iraq on August 6 (Resolution 661) and a blockade of Iraq. While the Soviet Union did occasionally temporize and seek to head off a conflict during the months that followed, it never gave Iraq any tangible support for its position. In fact, the USSR put consistent pressure on Iraq to leave Kuwait.

All of the major states in the Arab world—including Egypt and Syria—strongly opposed Iraq, and many sent military forces to defend Saudi Arabia and liberate Kuwait. Only Jordan, Libya, the PLO, and Yemen gave Iraq support, and the Arab League voted against it. Iran steadily hardened its position against Iraq, and Europe and the developing world united against it from the start.

Equally important, this international unity in opposing aggression allowed the United Nations to take unprecedented action against Iraq. When Iraq began to take foreigners hostage on August 15, the UN Security Council voted unanimously to demand the release of all foreign nationals in Iraq and Kuwait (Resolution 664). On August 25, 1990, the Security Council voted 13 to 2 to authorize a naval and then an air blockade (Resolution 665). The Security Council showed a resolve and unity that eventually helped force Saddam to release all the foreign hostages he had taken after the UN first enforced its blockade.

During the months that followed, the UN voted for eleven more resolutions that put steadily growing pressure on Iraq. At the same time, U.S., British, French, Egyptian, and Syrian troops built up in large numbers, and Saudi Arabia redeployed its army and national guard forces into the area near Kuwait.

Iraq's response was to try to negotiate an end to the blockade, although Saddam threatened on September 23 to destroy the oil fields of the Middle East if Iraq was "strangled" by the UN blockade. It was at this time that the Kuwaiti government-in-exile announced that Iraq had mined Kuwait's oil fields with plastic explosives. Iraq also steadily built up its forces in the Kuwaiti theater of operations. On November 11, Iraq mobilized 60,000 reservists, called up 100,000 conscripts for its regular and people's army forces, and moved 6 to 7 more divisions to southern Iraq.

On November 29, the UN passed a resolution establishing a deadline that authorized the nations allied with Kuwait "to use all necessary means" if Iraq did not withdraw from Kuwait by January 15, 1991. As a result, Iraq came under steadily escalating pressure until the end of the United Nation's deadline. It suffered from the economic costs of the blockade, could not draw on most of Kuwait's assets, ceased to be able to export oil, and lost any significant source of arms imports.

Saddam Hussein refused to withdraw from Kuwait and sent still more troops to defend the Saudi-Kuwaiti border and Iraq's border with Saudi

Arabia. By some estimates, Iraq deployed about 545,000 men and 12 heavy and 31 light divisions in the Kuwaiti theater of operations by the time the UN deadline expired.[169]

Iraq could not, however, correct many of the major defects in its military forces. It carried out its military buildup without any clear doctrine for conducting land and air combat and without developing an air doctrine to deal with the massive Western advantage in air combat technology. It had a defense plan, but only a vague war plan. It did not unify its airborne and land based air defense forces. It did far too little to train its land forces for the combat to come, did not emphasize combined arms or combined operations tailored to the new threat it faced, left many training and technical decisions to individual units that could only be made at the command level, failed to deal with the UN coalition's advantages in desert warfare and night combat, and remained close to its defenses and did not aggressively patrol. In many ways, it simply repeated the actions that had won the Iran-Iraq War.

During this same period, the U.S. Congress voted to authorize President Bush to use force against Iraq on January 12, 1991. The U.S. also completed a military buildup that went from a few token air units in August to a land-sea-air force of 527,000 men and women. By mid-January, 1991, this force included over 110 naval vessels, 2,000 tanks, 2,200 armored personnel carriers, 1,800 fixed wing aircraft, and 1,700 helicopters. Other elements of the 31 nation UN coalition force included about 118,000 Saudi troops, 43,000 British troops with 170 tanks and 72 combat aircraft, 40,000 Egyptian troops with 2 armored divisions of 250 tanks, 16,000 French troops with tanks and combat aircraft, and 20,000 Syrian troops with 2 divisions, and troops and aircraft from Canada, Oman, Qatar, and the United Arab Emirates.

While it is difficult to make reliable comparisons of the force ratios involved, U.S. reports after the war indicate that the total UN coalition had well in excess of 600,000 ground troops to Iraq's maximum of 545,000 men. The UN coalition had 3,360 tanks to Iraq's 4,230; 3,633 artillery weapons to 3,110; 4,050 other armored vehicles to 2,870; 1,959 helicopters to 160; and some 2,700 aircraft to 770.

The Air Offensive in the Gulf War

The fighting began on January 17, 1991, when U.S.-led air units launched a devastating series of air attacks against Iraq's command and control facilities, communications systems, air bases, and land based air defenses. Allied air forces flew about 1,000 sorties during the first 14 hours. The UN attacks involved the first use of sea and air launched cruise missiles, including some 200 Tomahawks and F-117 stealth aircraft. The F-117s flew 31% of the attacks during the first day and attacked even heavily defended targets like downtown Baghdad with complete immunity.

Within days, the coalition air forces shattered Iraq's air warfare capabilities and left Iraq with no way to strike back except to launch its Al-Hussein and Al-Abbas missiles. Iraq began these missile strikes with attacks on Israel and Saudi Arabia on the second day of the war and persisted until the war ended in a cease-fire. Yet although Iraq launched 40 Scud variants against

Israel and 46 against Saudi Arabia, they never succeeded in doing major military damage. Equally important, they did not provoke Israel into retaliating, in part because the U.S. rushed Patriot air defense missiles to both Israel and Saudi Arabia.

The Arab members of the UN coalition remained united throughout the war. The only major impact of the Al-Hussein and Al-Hijarah strikes was to force the coalition air forces into a massive hide-and-seek game to try to kill Iraqi missile units. While the attacks on the Iraqi Scuds did divert sorties from other targets, they also broadened the damage to Iraqi targets outside the Kuwaiti theater of operations.

By the third day of the war, the coalition air strikes against Iraq's main air defenses and air units were so successful that their targets expanded to include more Iraqi strategic targets like electric power plants, key headquarters, civil and army communications, and Iraq's plants and facilities for the production of biological, chemical, and nuclear warfare.

Although Iraq had begun the war with some 770 combat aircraft, 24 main operating bases, 30 dispersal bases, and a massive network of surface-to-air missiles, the coalition's advantage in air command and control, training, technology, and weapons gave it decisive air superiority. Iraq was unable to win a single air-to-air engagement, losing 35 aircraft. By the sixth day of the air war, Iraq found itself virtually unable to use its air force or air defenses, and Iraqi aircraft began to flee to Iran—hoping that Iran would return the aircraft and pilots after the war. Iraq halted any significant effort to use its aircraft in combat after the fourteenth day of the air war, and Iraq's remaining air defenses proved vulnerable to electronic warfare and anti-radiation missiles throughout the rest of the war.

On the eighth day of the air war, the coalition air forces were able to shift from the mission of gaining air superiority over Iraq and Kuwait, disrupting Iraqi command and control, and destroying Iraq's weapons of mass destruction to a primary focus on destroying the Iraqi field army in the Kuwaiti theater of operations. This phase lasted for the next twenty-fix days. It involved massive strikes by unguided and precision weapons on land forces like the Republican Guards, key supply and communications facilities in the border area, artillery units, other tank forces, and Iraq's defensive barriers.

By January 17, coalition land forces were ready to redeploy from positions in Saudi Arabia near the Gulf coast and southeastern Kuwaiti-Saudi border to attack positions all along the border and far to the west along the Iraqi-Saudi border. These redeployments later allowed the coalition ground forces to drive deep into Iraq without the Iraqis' having any conclusive warning that they had moved.

U.S. Marine Expeditionary Forces—and Saudi, Syrian, and Egyptian forces moved north from the center of Kuwait's southern border towards Kuwait City. At the same time, French and U.S. forces in the 7th Corps drove far to the west, where they could launch an attack to cut off southern Iraq from Baghdad and drive around Kuwait to move against Basra from the west. British and U.S. Army forces in the 18th Corps drove to areas on the Saudi-Iraqi border just west of Kuwait. By the time they were complete, Gen.

Norman Schwartzkopf, the coalition commander, had positioned two full armored corps along the Iraqi border to the west of Kuwait without the Iraqis' detecting these movements. This achieved a degree of strategic surprise that was essential to what he later called his "Hail Mary play."

Iraq's only attempt at a counterattack on land occurred on January 29. A 1,500 man Iraqi battalion with about 70 tanks and 50 other armored vehicles attacked the undefended and evacuated Saudi border town of Khafji on the Gulf coast. Smaller Iraqi units crossed the Saudi-Kuwaiti border at two other locations. U.S. Marine forces and coalition air power soon engaged the Iraqi troops, and Saudi and Qatari troops counterattacked on January 30. Khafji was cleared of Iraqi troops on January 31, and Iraq lost 25–40 tanks and 15–20 armored personnel carriers. After the failure of this attack, Iraq remained relatively static and made little effort aggressively to patrol the border. In contrast, when Iraq attacked Khafji, the coalition had already flown more than 30,000 sorties, half of which were in combat. The allies had lost 19 aircraft and conducted their air offensive with nearly total air supremacy.

By February 6, coalition aircraft had flown some 50,000 sorties, about half of them attack sorties against Iraqi targets. The U.S. had also rushed in its last ground units, bringing their total manpower to 503,000, while other coalition land forces had reached 200,000. The coalition had already executed the most successful air offensive in history, but the air attacks did not continue without problems. On February 13, the coalition launched its most controversial attack strike of the war. F-117 stealth fighters bombed an underground shelter in Baghdad that UN commanders believed was a military command bunker but that Iraq was also using as a civilian air raid shelter. Between 200 and 400 Iraqi civilians were killed.

The bombing continued, however, and on February 22, President Bush gave Iraq an ultimatum stating that Iraq must withdraw from Kuwait by 8 P.M. the next day, withdraw from Kuwait City in forty-eight hours, withdraw from all of Kuwait in seven days, release all prisoners of war, remove all booby traps and provide maps of all minefields, and release all Kuwaitis and return all Kuwaiti property. Iraq refused to meet all of these conditions, although it agreed to begin a withdrawal if the UN would agree to end all sanctions and restrictions once that withdrawal was complete.

The Air-Land Battle Phase of the Gulf War

At 0400 hours on February 24, the UN coalition shifted from strategic bombing and preparatory air attacks to the use of a modified version of the "air-land battle" concept that the U.S. had developed to meet the Warsaw Pact's most modern forces in Europe. By this time, Iraqi ground forces had been hit by well in excess of 40,000 attack sorties. These air attacks continued throughout the land fighting.

The UN coalition land attack was a complex mix of thrusts that penetrated Iraqi defensive lines in and to the immediate west of Kuwait, sweeping armored movements from positions along the Iraqi-Saudi border beginning at positions to the west of Iraq's defensive lines and moving towards positions on the Gulf south of Basra, and a mix of armor and heliborne assault forces that leaped north to cut off communications from Baghdad to Basra.

A Saudi-Kuwaiti-GCC force thrust north through Iraqi lines into Kuwait along the Gulf coast. The 1st and 2nd U.S. Marine divisions, reinforced by a U.S. armored cavalry brigade, attacked north in the middle of the Kuwaiti border at the notch where the border is closest to Kuwait City. A Saudi-Egyptian task force attacked along the western part of the Kuwaiti-Saudi border, and U.S. and British forces penetrated northeast towards Iraq's Republican Guard divisions and positions in Iraq north of Kuwait. French forces and the U.S. 101st Airborne Division moved north to Nasseriyah on the Euphrates River, and the U.S. 24th Mechanized Division moved to the northeast to cut Iraq's lines of retreat towards Basra.

The UN coalition forces had excellent combined arms, combined operations, and offensive maneuver training backed by superb intelligence and logistics. In contrast, they attacked an Iraqi force which was equipped with modern weapons but had trained and organized to fight a relatively static trench war against an Iran that lacked significant air power. The coalition had other advantages. The land forces it sent into combat roughly equaled the weapons strength and manpower of the Iraqi forces but were mainly highly motivated professionals. The Iraqi forces were largely conscript forces, and their motivation had been severely weakened by having to invade a fellow Arab state, poor central organization, and relentless coalition bombing. In short, the land battle pitted the forces of the future against the forces of the past.

Iraq had deployed a large part of its forces to deal with an amphibious attack that never came and had made no real provision for the UN's massive flanking attack from the west. Its defensive positions had often been poorly organized, and the Iraqi troops had been demoralized or suffered from large scale desertions because of the preceding air bombardment. Throughout the land campaign, they suffered from a lack of leadership, coherent direction in conducting counterattacks and retreats, and a breakdown of resupply

The coalition took advantage of this situation by advancing far more quickly than Iraqi forces could retreat and regroup and exploiting its surprise attack from the west. It used rapidly moving round-the-clock armored and heliborne maneuvers, precisely targeted artillery fire, deceptions like the threat of an amphibious landing, effective use of air and attack helicopter support, and use of advanced land warfare technologies. These technologies ranged from thermal tank sights that could spot Iraqi targets long before they could see coalition armor to hand-held satellite navigation devices that allowed coalition forces to precisely locate themselves in the desert.

The devastating impact of the 100 hour air-land battle is indicated by the coalition forces' succeess in reaching every intermediate objective ahead of schedule and achieving a rate of advance so fast that many allied forces did not pause and regroup as had originally been planned. While a few of the Republic Guard and Iraqi armored and mechanized divisions fought well at the battalion level, the Iraqi army disintegrated, abandoning much of its equipment. Officers often fled before their men, and the retreat from positions in southern and central Kuwait and Kuwait City turned into a disorganized panic.

On February 27 the Iraqi collapse reached the point where President Bush announced that the UN coalition would suspend offensive operations at 0800 Kuwaiti time on February 28 if Iraq agreed to end all military action; comply with all UN resolutions; free all prisoners of war, Kuwaiti nationals, and third country nationals; release the remains of all UN forces killed in action; and reveal the locations of all land and sea mines in Kuwait. The fighting ended in a cease-fire on February 28, when Iraq's foreign minister, Tariq Aziz, announced that Iraq would comply with all twelve UN resolutions dealing with Iraq's invasion of Kuwait.

The scale of the Iraqi defeat is indicated by U.S. Department of Defense estimates issued just after the conclusion of the fighting that stated UN coalition forces had captured more than 50,000 prisoners of war, destroyed nearly 3,000 Iraqi tanks out of 4,030 in southern Iraq and Kuwait, destroyed about 1,000 of 2,870 other armored vehicles, and destroyed nearly 1,005 artillery weapons out of 3,110.[170] These estimates compare with coalition combat losses of 4 tanks, 9 other armored vehicles, and 1 artillery weapon. While such estimates later proved uncertain, they are valid as a broad indication of the scale of the Iraqi defeat at the time of the cease-fire.

Personnel losses were amazingly small compared to these equipment losses—and the U.S. Central Command (USCENTCOM) raised its estimate of Iraqi POWs to 80,000 and Iraqi losses to 3,300 tanks, 2,100 other armored vehicles, and 2,200 artillery pieces on March 3, 1991.[171] While the Defense Intelligence Agency (DIA) initially gave an estimate of Iraqi killed as high as 100,000, it now seems likely that the total was only about 25,000 to 55,000.[172] Total UN coalition losses are difficult to estimate because of the unwillingness of several Arab states to provide accurate figures, but on the U.S. side 147 were killed in action or died later from combat wounds, 121 died from nonhostile causes, 212 were wounded in action, and 44 were missing in action at the time the war ended. According to one estimate, Britain lost 16 killed, 31 wounded in action, and 12 missing. Egypt had 9 killed and 75 wounded. France lost 2 killed and 28 wounded. Italy lost 1 killed. Saudi Arabia lost 29 killed, 53 wounded in action, and 9 missing. Senegal had 8 wounded, and the UAE had 6 killed.[173]

When the air-land phase ended on February 28, the UN coalition had dropped a total of 88,500 tons of ordnance, 6,520 tons of which were precision guided weapons. It had killed 44 Iraqi aircraft in air-to-air combat, destroyed a total of 216 aircraft, and destroyed nearly 600 aircraft shelters and damaged 375 others. UN coalition air forces had also destroyed 54 bridges or made them inoperable.[174] Although coalition air forces had flown some 109,876 sorties by the end of the war, the coalition lost only 38 aircraft—the lowest loss rate of any air combat in history and less than the normal accident rate per sortie in combat training.

The only strategic damage Iraq was able to do Kuwait and the UN coalition in return was to set Kuwaiti oil wells on fire, beginning by using explosions to ignite 150 wells on February 2. By the time Iraq finished, 600 wells were burning. Although these fires were not fully extinguished until 1991, they did nothing to affect allied air and land operations or slow the pace of the war.

The war did end, however, under conditions that are likely to be debated for many years. The UN coalition forces halted without destroying the Iraqi ground forces still in the theater or weakening the ability of several of the Republican Guard units around Basra to put down the Shi'ite rebellion that followed. There were several political and military reasons for this. If the UN forces had pressed on, they would have greatly increased Iraqi casualties, most of whom would have been conscripts in regular forces, and the UN could not have destroyed the remaining Republican Guard forces in the region without moving into the populated area in and around Basra. This might have provoked a confrontation with Iran or involved the UN in the Shi'ite uprising that took place after the cease-fire and in a civil war. The UN land forces were approaching exhaustion after record rates of movement and would have taken a day or two to regroup. Flying conditions were affected by the worst weather in the Gulf's history, hampering the use of attack aircraft. There is no question, however, that UN restraint allowed something like 15–20% of the prewar equipment inventory of the Iraqi army and many Iraqi soldiers to survive.

After the cease-fire, many also argued that the UN should have exploited its victory to drive Saddam Hussein from power—even if this meant a much deeper involvement in the war and advancing to Baghdad. In view of the events that followed, there may be a strategic case for such a position. The UN mandate, however, did not extend to occupying and restructuring Iraq. Few, if any, of the Arab members of the UN coalition and few Arab and Third World supporters of UN action would have condoned such intervention. Such intervention risked partitioning Iraq into Kurdish, Sunni, and Shi'ite zones and could have embroiled the UN in a prolonged civil war in which it was far from clear that the regime or regimes that emerged from the fighting would be stable or decisively more legitimate and peaceful than the Baath regime governing Iraq. At the time, the U.S. and other leaders of the coalition concluded that fighting a war was one thing and remaking a nation was another.

Iraq's Situation After the Cease-Fire

On April 3, 1991, the UN Security Council passed Resolution 687 setting forth the final terms of a cease-fire. These terms required Iraq to (1) recognize the Kuwaiti-Iraqi border agreement of 1963; (2) accept a UN guarantee of the border; (3) allow the UN to establish a peace observer force in a zone along the Iraqi-Kuwaiti border 10 kilometers in Iraq and 5 kilometers in Kuwait; (4) reaffirm its commitment to the chemical warfare and nuclear nonproliferation treaties; (5) allow the UN to inspect the destruction of all biological, chemical, and nuclear weapons, ballistic missiles, and related facilities, equipment, and supplies; (6) accept liability for Kuwait's losses; (7) accept liability for all prewar debts; (8) return all Kuwaiti POWs; and (9) renounce terrorism. Iraq accepted these terms on April 4.

Sweeping as the UN victory was, it did not change the fundamental balance of power in the Gulf. It did liberate Kuwait, it did destroy much of Iraq's offensive military power, and it did deprive Iraq of much of its capability to build and deliver weapons of mass destruction. It did not wipe out Iraq's immense military machine, it did not destroy Saddam Hussein's control over Iraq, it did not bring a stable peace to the Gulf, and it did not create more liberal or democratic regimes throughout the Middle East.

The Arab portion of the coalition that defeated Iraq did not hold together for more than a few months or produce any decisive momentum towards a lasting peace in the Gulf or between the Arab states and Israel. In spite of some mutinies in the south, Saddam Hussein was able slowly to reestablish control over all of Iraq's forces within the first four weeks after the war. His liberalization measures after the war proved to be a political charade followed by new purges and repression.

Even before the UN voted on the final terms of the cease-fire agreement, Saddam began to act. On March 5, 1991, two days after the initial agreement to halt the fighting, Saddam appointed his cousin Ali Hassan al-Majid as minister of the interior. Majid had led the suppression of the Kurds in 1988, and his appointment was clearly designed to help Saddam take a harder line in suppressing Kurdish and Shi'ite uprisings.

On March 20, U.S. fighters shot down Iraqi fighters who were violating the cease-fire by attacking targets near the Kurdish town of Kirkuk. Saddam ruthlessly put down a Shi'ite uprising in the south centered in Basra and Karbala. He was equally ruthless in putting down the major Kurdish uprising in the north. In both cases, the small military forces that Shi'ite and Kurdish ethnic groups were able to muster proved no match for Iraq's main force combat units, in spite of the damage they had received during the war.

Saddam also began a complex political struggle with the UN over the issue of sanctions and humanitarian aid. He refused to agree on arrangements to allow Iraq to begin exporting oil in return for paying reparations to Kuwait, and he used some aid Iraq did receive to improve his political hold on the Iraqi people.[175] He used his control over the Iraqi government to force a level of austerity that allowed him to maintain his military machine and security apparatus and apparently drew on massive secret deposits that Iraq made overseas before the war to ensure that the military, Baath officials, and Sunni portions of Iraq maintained reasonable living standards.

Some of this political struggle was reflected in Saddam's shuffling of personnel and covert U.S. attempts to overthrow his regime. Right after the war, Saddam attempted to make his regime appear more democratic and talked of democratic reform and ethnic autonomy. On March 23, 1991, he announced that he was making Foreign Minister Saadoun Hammadi prime minister. Hammadi was a Shi'ite who had advocated a more liberal and democratic form of Baathism. Iraq tentatively accepted Kurdish autonomy on March 24 and announced on May 8, 1991, that the ruling Revolutionary Command Council of the Baath would be abolished and replaced with a more democratic government. It also declared an amnesty for deserters who were not officers.

These reforms, however, were little more than a smoke screen. The Baath leadership systematically purged the military, suppressed any real dissent, violated the civil rights of Iraqi citizens, and put military pressure on the Kurds and Shi'ites.

When the RCC finally announced the law allowing opposition parties on July, 4, 1991, it was amended to create vaguely defined security restrictions that allowed the government to ban virtually any party it wanted and explicitly forbade any ethnic or sectarian parties. By the time the law was passed on September 3, 1991, it had no real meaning. Further, Prime Minister Hammadi was removed from power on September 16 and replaced with another Shi'ite, Mohammed Hamaz Zubeidi, who seemed little more than a stooge. This reinforced the impression that the days of liberalization had vanished and the Baath had restored its control over most of Iraq.

On October 12, 1991, Saddam felt strong enough to announce at an Iraqi-organized "conference of Arab popular forces" that Iraq could withstand the UN sanctions for twenty years. On November 6, 1991, he also began to shake up the Iraqi government. While he appointed Hammadi to a symbolic advisory position, he reorganized the military and security services to include more men who owed him personal allegiance.

He purged the national assembly on December 10, 1991, and later that month dismissed the minister of health, AbdelSalem al-Said, making him the scapegoat for the deteriorating economic and public health conditions caused by the UN sanctions. On December 23, the Interior Ministry warned that an amnesty for turning in unlicensed firearms would last just ten more days. In January, in his newspaper, *Babil*, Saddam's elder son, Uday, called for the public execution of dissidents.

Saddam went through another cabinet purge on July 30, 1992. He made his foreign minister, Ahmed Hussein, the finance minister and promoted the deputy foreign minister, Mohammed Said Sahahf, to foreign minister. He dismissed the former finance minister, Majid Abd Jaafer, and made the head of the Iraqi Atomic Energy Organization, Humam Abdel Khaliq Abdel Ghafur, the minister of education. The reasons for these changes are unclear, but they seem to have been designed to tighten control over domestic affairs.

Iraqi officials increasingly attempted to manipulate world opinion by making grossly exaggerated claims that the UN sanctions were causing widespread hardship and loss of life. For example, on November 26, 1991, government spokesmen claimed the sanctions had caused 68,093 Iraqi deaths but by January 11, 1992, claimed that Iraq had rebuilt 75% of its power grid, 85% of its oil refining capability, and 99 of 123 damaged bridges.

It is clear that the UN sanctions succeeded in putting growing pressure on Saddam's regime. By November, 1991, many food prices had risen by several hundred percent over their prewar levels, Iraq's agricultural output had fallen by 70–75%, and its industrial output had fallen by 50%. While some smuggling took place, largely through Jordan and across the Turkish border, the Iraqi economy suffered badly from a lack of imports and export revenues from oil sales.

By spring, 1992 Saddam seems to have spent much of the money he held in secret foreign accounts, and food imports through Aqaba dropped from 550,000 tons in May, 1992 to 160,000 tons in June and 80,000 tons in July. The number of trucks crossing the Jordanian border dropped from 400 a day in late 1991 to fewer than 200 in June, 1992. The Iraqi dinar had to be devalued from 14 per dollar in July, 1992 to 24, and Saddam executed more than 40 merchants in an attempt both to limit profiteering and deflect the blame for price rises and food shortages away from his regime.

Before the war, Iraq's military machine had depended on $3–5 billion worth of annual arms imports, plus massive imports of equipment for weapons of mass destruction and the services of thousands of foreign technicians. The UN sanctions were almost completely successful in cutting off these military related imports, including spare parts, and Iraq was unable to replace its foreign technicians and military advisors. As a result, Iraqi readiness declined sharply after August, 1990 and the damage done during the Gulf War. While Iraq retained a large inventory of weapons after the fighting, more and more became inoperable as Iraq ceased to be able to repair them.

The U.S. was widely reported to have responded by making covert attempts to overthrow Saddam and the Baath by backing various democratic and religious opposition leaders outside Iraq and flooding Iraq with fake currency. The U.S. clearly did support Kurdish, Shi'ite, and Sunni efforts to create a united opposition, but the Iraqi government, not the U.S., seems to have been the source of the sudden increase in currency. The U.S. apparently rejected direct covert action against Saddam because of the risk of civil war while the opposition was still so weak.[176]

The Crisis with the Kurds

The UN and U.S. did not provide active military support for the Shi'ite or Kurdish uprisings that took place right after the war. They stood by, hoping on the one hand that the uprisings might lead the Iraqi military to overthrow Saddam Hussein and fearing on the other that Iraq would become divided into an Iranian-dominated Shi'ite enclave and Sunni and Kurdish areas. The UN tacitly allowed Iraqi troops and helicopters to operate against the various uprisings, although it did force Iraq to observe the terms of the cease-fire and to stop using its combat aircraft against the Kurds. U.S. F-15s shot down one Iraqi air force Su-22 on March 20 and another on March 22.

By limiting itself to attacks on Iraqi fixed wing fighters, the UN created a situation in which Iraqi forces were able to attack the Shi'ites and Kurds with little resistance. Iraqi forces retook Karbala in the south and Kirkuk in the north by March 28. They drove some 70,000 Shi'ites across the border into Iran, killed and imprisoned many others, and trapped still others in the extensive marsh areas in the south.[177]

In the north, Iraq surrounded cities like Irbil and Kirkuk with army units and then sent brigades to control all key routes and bridges. It used artillery, multiple rocket launchers, and armed helicopters against any pockets of resistance. The Kurdish guerrilla forces had only a negligible capability to resist. The long history of Iraqi attacks on Kurdish civilians led many Kurds to flee as the Iraqi troops advanced, and 1 to 1.5 million Kurdish refugees had moved near to or crossed the Turkish and Iranian borders.[178] This forced the U.S. and UN to intervene to protect the Kurds and prevent the establishment of refugee camps and enclaves along the border areas. On April 5, the UN passed Resolution 688 condemning and demanding an end to Iraqi repression of the Kurds.

By April 7, the U.S. had begun air drops of food. On April 8, Secretary of State Baker promised the Kurds food, shelter, and medicine, and President Bush established an airlift called Operation Provide Comfort. Repeated Iraqi attacks on the Kurds led the U.S. to declare on April 10, 1991, that Iraq would not be permitted to fly aircraft north of the 36th parallel. The UN also put heavy pressure on the Iraqi government to halt its attacks and U.S. and allied troops to move into northern Iraq to help set up refugee camps in the border area.

On April 18, 1991, Iraq signed an agreement that effectively created a UN-controlled and -demilitarized security zone for the Kurds in Iraq north of the 36th parallel. The agreement allowed the UN to station 500 security guards to protect relief operations and was to remain in force until December 31, 1991, with the possibility of renewal.

Iraq, however, immediately began to test the UN's resolve. Some 200 Iraqi policemen attacked Kurds in the town of Zakhu on April 21. Iraqi anti-aircraft artillery fired on U.S. reconnaissance jets patrolling northern Iraq on May 7. Iraqi troops fired on British troops in Dahuq on May 13, and fired on a U.S. Army helicopter on May 14. They clashed with Kurdish demonstrators on June 5, and on June 6 stole 7 tons of relief supplies intended for the Kurds.

When it became apparent that these tactics did little more than provoke the UN, Saddam entered into prolonged negotiations with the Kurds that allowed him to delay any real settlement until UN forces had left northern Iraq and until the long standing tensions between Turkey and the Kurds had largely shut off any support to the Kurds from the north. In early May the UN forces in Iraq reached a peak of about 15,000 men, including French, Dutch, Italian, British, and U.S. elements, but there was no political support for the kind of long term occupation that would have fully secured Kurdish autonomy. UN forces left Dahuq on June 15, and the number of troops in Iraq dropped to around 8,000. The UN force was cut to 5,100 on June 23. The UN withdrew all forces from Iraq on July 15, 1991, although it left a small brigade in southern Turkey.

Saddam then enforced a near economic boycott on the Kurds in an effort to push them into a political settlement. He insisted that the Baghdad government keep control of Kirkuk and all of Iraq's oil revenues, and Iraqi forces began to shell and attack rebellious towns beginning in the summer of 1991. By that time, more extreme Kurdish groups like the Marxist Partiya Kartkeen Kurdistan (PKK) were actively training new anti-Iraqi troops and had about 2,000–4,000 men in the field and 5,000–10,000 irregulars.[179]

Iraq began providing money and arms to rebellious Kurdish groups in Turkey in the summer of 1991. This contributed to Turkey's unwillingness to allow UN forces to remain on its soil, and the rest left when the UN agreement with Turkey that allowed it to station troops on Turkish soil expired on September 30, 1991. Turkish military forces had already begun to conduct sporadic raids against Kurdish rebel groups in Iraq and Turkey, and they continued to do so in the months that followed. On November 18, 1991, Iraqi troops attacked Kurdish positions near Irbil. Iraq seems to have massed a force of 18,000 men during this attack in positions where they could have entered and seized the city, but it did not act because of its fear of reprisals by the UN.

On November 25, after some political resistance, Iraq allowed a six-month extension of the humanitarian relief agreement affecting aid to the Kurds. Iraq also agreed to lift its economic blockade, although it did not really do so. This Iraqi pressure on the Kurds led the U.S. to seek Turkish agreement to extend the allied relief effort based in Turkey for six months, and Turkey complied on January 3, 1992. This allowed the U.S. to keep about 1,800 military personnel in Turkey and gave basing for British, French, and U.S. aircraft to provide security for the Kurds.

Iraq did not send troops into the Kurdish safety zone, and Baghdad continued to negotiate with the two mainstream Kurdish political groups led by Barzani and Talabani. Saddam Hussein did, however, put growing pressure on the Kurds. Iraqi aircraft appeared over Kurdish territory in violation of the terms of the Gulf War cease-fire, Iraqi forces sporadically shelled Kurdish areas, and Iraqi troops effectively sealed off many Kurdish areas from Turkish or UN support.[180] Saddam enforced a partial embargo over shipments going to Kurdish territory and redeployed his army to positions from which it could quickly invade unoccupied Kurdish territory around Irbil, Chamcharmal, Kifri, and Suleimaniya.

On January 15, these Iraqi actions led the Kurds to suspend autonomy talks with the Iraqi government, and the Kurdish leaders announced they would hold elections for a unified Kurdish leadership by April 3. These elections were held in mid-May, 1992 but did not produce a conclusive result, ending instead in charges of corruption and the use of force.

The resulting deadlock between Talabani's Patriotic Union of Kurdistan and Barzani's Kurdish Democratic Party led both parties to agree to set up a joint "government" with its capital at Irbil. They agreed to create a 105 man assembly, which met for the first time on July 4, 1992. The assembly had fifty delegates each for the Barzani and Talabani factions and five seats for Kurdish Christians. The Iraqi government called the new government "illegal" and labeled its fifteen ministers "bandits."

By August, 1992, most foreign relief workers had been forced to leave the country, and only 326 of 500 UN security personnel remained to police the Kurdish security zone. Nearly 4 million Kurds in northern Iraq lived in an uneasy state of near autonomy. Iraqi aircraft stayed south of the 36th parallel, but nearly 100,000 Iraqi troops were deployed on the 180 mile border of the Kurdish occupied area, and minor clashes and artillery exchanges were common.

The Kurds had adequate food and had begun to recover from fighting with the Iraqi government that had destroyed nearly 2,000 of the 4,000 Kurdish towns and villages in the region since 1970. At the same time, they had little support from Iran and extremely uneasy relations with Turkey— which feared increased efforts at separatism by Turkish Kurds.

The Kurdish region had lost much of its economic and transportation infrastructure during the fighting after the Gulf War. It also had limited self-defense capability. While the Kurds claimed to have mobilized a force of up to 50,000 men, they had no real combat formations and were hard put to deploy organized combat units with more than a few hundred men. The Kurdish groups were often good guerrilla fighters but had few heavy weapons and little capability for regular war. Limited German arms shipments did little to guarantee that Iraq would not reassert its control the moment UN pressure weakened, or would not repeat a process of purges, forced relocation, and executions that had cost up to 300,000 lives since the early 1970s.[181]

Iraq's Crisis with Its Shi'ites

The situation was no more stable in the south. Iraq's Shi'ites launched major uprisings in much of southern Iraq during the days after Iraq's defeat. They briefly held many of the major cities in the south, including Karbala, Al Hillah, Al Kut, and Al-Amarah. There was bitter fighting in the area around Basra and Al-Zubayr, and Iran allowed the Badr Brigade, a 5,000–7,000 man force of exiled Iraqi Shi'ites under the leadership of Mohammed Baqr Hakim, to enter Iraq and support the Shi'ites.

The Shi'ites were deeply divided, however, and did not unite against Saddam Hussein's forces. The limited number of regular Iraqi units that went over to the Shi'ite side could not sustain themselves or act as an organized combat force, the Badr Brigade took heavy casualties and had to withdraw, and the anti-regime Shi'ites never succeeded in creating a separate enclave, Hostile Shi'ites fled into Iran and hid in the nearly 6,000 square miles of marshes formed at the mouth of the Tigris-Euphrates and east of Amarah, Nasseriyah, and Basra. This created the nucleus for a Shi'ite resistance and gradually led to guerrilla warfare in the marsh areas.

The UN did attempt to provide humanitarian relief for the refugees, but the situation was different from the Kurdish crisis in the north. There was never a separate enclave, and Iraqi troops and security forces, as well as Shi'ites loyal to Saddam, were always mixed with the general Shi'ite population. The UN did set up a humanitarian relief center in the marsh area in July, 1991, but the Iraqi government organized protest riots and made effective operation impossible. On July 14, it told the UN personnel manning the center to leave, cutting the Shi'ites off from any aid.

This situation grew steadily worse during the fall and winter of 1991 and 1992. Once the central government recovered full control over the rest of the populated areas in the south, the Iraqi government began a campaign to root out these Shi'ites. In April, 1992, 36,000–40,000 Iraqi troops were sent into the area, and Iraqi forces built roads and fire bases in the swamps. They began to selectively drain marshes thought to have deserters and Shi'ite rebels and began to fight their way through an area with thousands of small islets, 10 foot reeds, and date palm thickets.

The Iraqi forces were hunting some 10,000–20,000 deserters and Shi'ites in the marshes, but these were so poorly organized that only 3,000–6,000 could be classified as guerrillas. The Shi'ites were equipped only with small arms and flat bottom boats, although they had some Iranian and Iraqi exile support, including some from the Badr Brigade. Thousands of Shi'ite civilians had also fled into the marshes and become the target of Iraqi operations.

This fighting continued throughout the spring and summer, and on April 5, 1992, Iraq and Iran had their first significant military exchange since the Iran-Iraq War. Iraq had been providing money and arms to the Mujahideen-e-Khalq, a radical Marxist Iranian opposition movement which had military camps and forces in Iraq. The Mujahideen launched several small raids on Iran, and Iran sent twelve F-4 and F-5 fighters to attack the Asraf camp about 60 miles northeast of Baghdad. The aircraft attacked in six waves, dropping cluster bombs, firing rockets, and strafing. One Iranian F-4 was lost to anti-aircraft fire during the attack. Iraq responded by scrambling ten of its fighters for the first time since the Gulf War, in violation of UN Resolutions 686 and 687.

In June the Iraqi minister of defense, Maj. Gen. Hassan al-Majid took over direction of the fighting, and it appeared that Iraq had moved additional elements of its 3rd and 4th corps above Basra and east of Amarah. Reports indicated that by August, 1992, the government had deployed five to six divisions against the Shi'ites, including Republican Guard units, and was using artillery, attack helicopters, and fixed wing fighters. Saddam Hussein's son Qusai and his half brother Wathban al-Ibrahimi were also said to play a role in overseeing the security operations in the south.

At the same time, other security measures were taken in the south. Curfews were enforced in most areas, Shi'ite religious schools and printing houses were closed, and some Shi'ite assemblies were forbidden. Government arrests reportedly reduced the clergy in the Shi'ite holy city of Najif from 8,000 before the Iran-Iraq War to less than 800 by the end of 1991 and had driven most of the members of key opposition groups like Al-Dawa al-Islamiya (Islamic Call) and the Supreme Islamic Revolution in Iraq (SIRI) out of the country. The government began relocating the marsh Arabs (Madan) and expanding its plans to drain the marshes. It seems to have begun work on a 350 mile canal to divert water out of the area.

Iraqi government attacks on the Shi'ites became so intense that on August 11, 1992, Britain, France, and the U.S. issued a formal warning to Iraq to cease violating Security Council Resolution 688, which called for an end to all internal repression in the country.[182]

The Struggle to Eliminate Iraq's Weapons of Mass Destruction

These struggles with the Kurds and Shi'ites were accompanied by another duel between Saddam Hussein and the UN coalition. While Iraq accepted the terms of the UN Security Council resolution on March 3, 1991, and announced that it had voided the annexation of Kuwait on March 5, Saddam began to try to undercut the sanctions limiting his internal control over Iraq almost immediately after Iraq signed the April cease-fire. The result was a constant test of wills and a series of incidents in which Iraq challenged the UN to the point where the U.S. and other coalition nations would retaliate with force.

Iraq was particularly aggressive in resisting the UN effort to ensure the elimination of Iraq's weapons of mass destruction. Iraqi forces were detected salvaging equipment for missiles and weapons of mass destruction and cleaning up suspect sites on April 5.

The Iraqi government lied to the UN in its first declaration of its holdings of weapons of mass destruction on April 18, 1991. It claimed it only had 52 Scud missiles and modified Scud missiles, 10,000 chemical warheads, 1,500 chemical bombs and shells, and 1,000 tons of mustard and nerve gas after the war—although the UN later found it had far more missiles and at least 46,000 surviving chemical weapons. Iraq lied about its nuclear weapons effort in its April 29, 1991, declaration to the IAEA.

Iraq denied IAEA teams access to a facility where it was loading equipment onto trucks on June 25, and it fired warning shots at UN inspectors on June 28. Under pressure from the UN, it disclosed a major secret nuclear research project on July 8, 1991, but denied this was part of a nuclear weapons program. One day later, UN inspectors found evidence to the contrary in another facility.

Iraq destroyed or hid records, denied the UN access or timely access to facilities, and dispersed and hid every weapon and piece of equipment it had any hope of concealing. Iraq was found to be burying nuclear equipment on July 10. It gave the UN a formal pledge that it had disclosed all of its nuclear facilities on July 18 but then released new data that it had limited amounts of enriched plutonium on August 5 and admitted to the possession of 17.6 pounds of irradiated uranium on August 8. It finally admitted to a biological weapons development effort at Salman Pak on August 15. Four days later it admitted it was developing the super guns whose existence it had earlier denied.

On September 9 it attempted to deny UN inspectors the right to use German helicopters and the following day was discovered to have welded together parts of Scud launchers it had claimed to have destroyed. That same month it resorted to detaining 44 UN inspectors who had discovered Iraqi nuclear weapons plans in a site in Baghdad and complied with inspection only after a U.S. threat to use force. The inspectors found evidence of a systematic Iraqi coverup of its nuclear program and indications Iraq had explored yet another uranium enrichment technique.

On November 11 the UN Security Council reacted by passing UN Resolution 715, which called for aggressive inspections and dismantling of Iraq's industrial facilities that could be used to produce weapons of mass destruction. The seventh UN inspection mission was not impeded during its efforts later that month, but Iraq failed to meet a deadline requiring it to provide a list of all plants and equipment that could be used to manufacture weapons of mass destruction, and the UN announced on November 23 that a new mission was going to Iraq to search for previously undisclosed missile sites and sites for the production of biological weapons.

There were reports in January, 1992 that Iraq had secretly shipped nuclear materials to Algeria. These reports could not be confirmed, but on January 12, UN inspectors raided Iraqi facilities to try to find centrifuge manufacturing components. The inspectors did not find the equipment, but Iraq admitted to having bought it and claimed to have destroyed the material after the cease-fire.

On January 25 the secretary general addressed the UN on Iraq's record of compliance with the terms of the cease-fire, and his report contained several additional examples of noncompliance. On February 2, reports surfaced that Iraq had begun to take its MiG-23 fighters out of their protective revetments and was flying limited missions. On February 28 Iraq again refused to comply with a UN deadline—this time for the destruction of missile production facilities. The UN team sent to carry out the destruction left Iraq without succeeding. The UN issued a deadline for compliance of March 9. Iraq ignored the date, and Prime Minister John Major of Britain warned that the UN might have to use force.

The U.S. sent the carrier *America* and several escort ships into the Gulf on March 13, and the following day U.S. officials issued background briefs that the U.S. might have to use force. On March 17 Iraqi foreign minister Aziz agreed to a new plan to destroy Iraqi facilities. A 35 man UN team went to Baghdad to carry out the destruction of the facilities, but IAEA representatives then charged that Iraq was failing to comply in disclosing the details of its nuclear program and demanded that Iraq allow the destruction of the technical core of its Al Atheer nuclear weapons facility.

A new element of tension was added to the Iraqi-UN relationship in May, 1992, when the details of UN efforts to remap the Iraqi-Kuwaiti border became public. UN experts working with the British data on the original 1932 demarcation found that Iraqi officials had moved their border posts 4,290 feet south of the proper line in 1943 and that the border was in fact just south of Umm Qasr. This gave Kuwait a considerable amount of territory along one of Iraq's key channels to the Gulf and most of the territory occupied by the Iraqi naval base at Umm Qasr.

Iraq responded by claiming that it had never approved the 1932 demarcation worked out by the British, and senior Iraqi officials like Saddam Hussein made statements that came close to renewing Iraq's claim to Kuwait. In July Saddam's half-brother Barzan Tikriti went further, calling for the unification of Kuwait and Iraq, and on August 2—the anniversary of Iraq's invasion of Kuwait in 1990—Radio Baghdad demanded "the return of Kuwait, a usurped territory."

By July, 1992, the UN and Iraq were again poised on the edge of military confrontation. Iraq had flown more than 150 military aircraft sorties since April. A total of five Iraqi divisions and 50,000 men were deployed in the marshes, supported by SU-25 attack fighters and armed PC-7 trainers. Up to half of Iraq's thirty remaining regular army divisions were positioned to attack the Kurds in the north. These developments led the U.S. to seek UN permission to use force in Iraq. At the same time, the U.S. deployed a Patriot missile battalion to Kuwait, and U.S. Marines conducted a joint exercise with Kuwaiti forces along the Kuwaiti coast.

This crisis over the Iraqi threat to the Shi'ites was soon joined by another crisis over the UN inspection effort. On July 5, Iraq denied the UN inspectors access to a Ministry of Agriculture building that was suspected of housing records and possibly equipment relating to Iraq's development of chemical, biological, and nuclear weapons. Iraq did not allow the inspection until three weeks later—and only after the U.S., Britain, and France threatened force, the U.S. sent 2,400 more troops to Kuwait for training exercises, and the UN brokered a compromise that removed all U.S. members from the inspection team.

The moment this crisis eased, Iraq demanded that the UN not enter any of its ministries because this was a violation of Iraqi sovereignty. It also stepped up pressure on the Shi'ites in the south. This again brought the UN to the brink of using military force. By this time, the U.S. had sent a major planning mission to Saudi Arabia; deployed F-117A stealth fighters, F-15E, and F-4G Wild Weasel aircraft to Saudi Arabia; increased the readiness of its carrier task force and amphibious assault ships in the Gulf; developed new targeting options for its cruise missiles; readied B-52s for deployment to Diego Garcia; and had 5,200 U.S troops exercising in Kuwait.

The No-Fly Zone in the South

The combination of Iraqi pressure on the Kurds, pressure on the Shi'ites, and resistance to UN efforts to destroy Iraq's weapons of mass destruction pushed the UN towards issuing a new set of ultimatums. In fact, Iraq's resistance to UN inspections might well have triggered a UN ultimatum on August 17 if an erroneous report in the *New York Times* had not embarrassed the UN. The report indicated that the Bush administration was going to attack immediately and was only acting to improve its standing in the polls.

Two days later, the UN took another approach. At the urging of the U.S., Britain, and France, it announced a "no-fly zone" that prohibited Iraqi fighters from flying south of the 32nd parallel. This zone was designed to protect the Shi'ites as well as demonstrate the UN's resolve in ensuring the elimination of Iraq's weapons of mass destruction and in protecting the Kurds. It went into effect on August 27 and covered Iraq south of Najaf. It included many southern cites—such as Al-Amarah, Samawah, Nasseriyah, Basra, and Umm Qasr—as well as the marshes.

Iraq responded by rejecting the UN's right to enforce the zone, and expelling some UN aid personnel, but it pulled its aircraft back to bases north of the 32nd parallel. About 40 Iraqi helicopters and thirty fighters, including Su-25s, had been deployed in the south.

Iraq had little choice. The U.S. began enforcement of the no-fly zone with both land and sea based aircraft and the support of Saudi refueling aircraft, AWACS, and air defense fighters. It had eighteen ships in the Gulf, led by the carrier *Independence* with sixty combat aircraft, including twenty-four F-14As and twenty-four F/A-18s. The U.S. force also included three cruisers, two frigates, one amphibious assault ship, and three auxilliary ships. It had a command ship and two destroyers in port in Dhahran and a frigate in port in Dubai. In addition, it had two destroyers, a frigate, and an auxilliary ship in the Red Sea.

The USAF deployed at least twenty-six F-15s in Saudi Arabia, plus EF-111 and RC-135 electronic warfare aircraft, tanker aircraft, and E-3A AWACS. Britain deployed six Tornado fighters, and France was in the process of deploying ten Mirage fighters. The U.S. also deployed Patriot batteries to Kuwait and Bahrain and manned six Patriot batteries in Saudi Arabia to deal with the risk of Scud missile attacks and mass air raids.

The total U.S. forces in the Gulf had reached 24,500 men, including 5,981 ground forces, 4,250 air force personnel, and 14,089 naval personnel. In addition, the U.S. deployed 78 aircraft in the north, including 52 fighters, to protect the Kurds and enforce the no-fly zone north of the 36th parallel.

At the same time, the UN could not dismiss the fact that Iraq could still use its ground forces to suppress the Shi'ites in the south and was deployed to attack the Kurds in the north.

In the north, Iraq had 7–8 divisions, and 70,000–85,000 troops from its 4th Corps and 3rd Corps and Republican Guards spread out through the Kurdish areas from Karbala and Al Kut in the north to Nasseriyah and Zubayr in the south. Iraqi forces were regularly shelling Kurdish positions near the border of the Turkish security zone. Iraq had some 16–18 divisions and 145,000–170,000 troops from its 1st Corps and 5th Corps and Republican Guards spread out along the southern edge of the Kurdish security zone from Dahuk through Al Kuwayr, Irbil, and Kifri to Khanaqin.

In the south, Iraq had eight to ten more divisions, with at least 60,000 men and Iraqi forces, including armored and mechanized units and elements of the Republican Guards. This was more than adequate to deal with 8,000–20,000 Shi'ite deserters and rebels and the thousands of dissident civilians in the swamps.

The new no-fly zone struck a blow against Saddam Hussein's regime in terms of prestige and military pressure and sent a clear signal that the UN would continue the embargo and destruction of Iraq's weapons of mass destruction. At the same time, the situation was at best unstable.

The no-fly zone was also a signal that UN military action might take place at any time, and confrontation could escalate into at least limited war. No-fly zones could not by themselves protect either the Kurds in the north or the Shi'ites in the south. At the same time, they effectively divided Iraq into three parts. This presented the risk that Iraq might break up into Kurdish and Shi'ite mini-states or see Saddam Hussein launch a major civil war.

The unity of the UN coalition also eroded during this crisis. Egypt, Syria, and most other Arab members of the coalition did not support the new UN action because of their fear that it might cause the breakup of Iraq. Kuwait openly supported the UN, but the other Gulf states were silent. Saudi Arabia provided full military cooperation but kept a low political profile. Bahrain provided support to the U.S. but refused to let Britain base Tornado fighters on the island. Turkey continued to allow the U.S. to enforce the no-fly zone in the north but did not permit U.S. forces stationed in Turkey to help enforce the new no-fly zone in the south. Turkey was now fighting a low level civil war with its own Kurds, and it was clear that it increasingly feared that the Kurdish enclave in Iraq threatened Turkey's security.

Finally, it was far from clear that the new UN effort would overthrow Saddam Hussein or force a long term change in the behavior of his regime. Saddam still had tight control over massive military and internal security forces. His control over Iraq's resources allowed him to manipulate the economy to protect the Baath and military from the effects of the UN embargo. The only predictable aspect of the situation in the northern Gulf was that it was likely to prolong confrontation and present a constant risk of at least limited war.[183]

The Impact of the Gulf War on Iraqi Military Forces and the Iraqi Army

The postwar political situation in Iraq was shaped as much by Saddam Hussein's continued military power as by any other factor. This power existed because Iraq had spent so much on military forces before the Gulf War that even its catastrophic losses during the conflict could not destroy the Iraqi military machine. When Iraq invaded Kuwait on August 2, 1990, the Iraqi army was the fourth largest army in the world. Its active regular strength had increased from 180,000 men in early 1980, before the start of the Iran-Iraq War, to over 800,000 men in early 1990—before Saddam Hussein took his decision to invade Kuwait. Its forces had the potential to mobilize as many as 2 million men, or roughly 75% of all Iraqi men between 18 and 34. The Iraqi army's tank strength had risen from 2,700 to at least 5,700 weapons between 1980 and 1990, and its total tube artillery strength had risen from 2,300 weapons to 3,700.[184]

By the time Iraq had invaded Kuwait, its army had mobilized to as many as 955,000 men (including 480,000 reserves). These were organized into 7 to 8 corps and about 60 to 66 division equivalents.[185] While estimates differ sharply as to the exact division strength involved, they seem to have included 7 armored and mechanized divisions, 8 Republican Guard divisions, 40 infantry divisions, 20 special forces and commando brigades, and 2 surface-to-surface missile brigades with at least 50 FROG-7 launchers, up to several hundred Scud and improved Scud launchers, and at least 1,200 Scud and Scud variant missiles. This would have given the Iraqi army a total mobilized strength of about 230 brigade equivalents, with up to 50 armored and mechanized brigade equivalents.

The Republican Guards were Iraq's most effective force. Iraq had recognized the need for elite forces once Iran had invaded Iraqi territory, and it had expanded a guard force originally designed to protect the capital and the president. The Republican Guards received special equipment and training during the war and played a major role in defending Basra in 1987 and 1988. As a result of their success, they had grown to eight divisions by the end of the Iran-Iraq War, plus a large number of independent infantry and artillery brigades.

By August, 1990, the Republican Guards totaled nearly 20% of the Iraqi army. In peacetime they reported to the State Special Security Apparatus rather than the Ministry of Defense, although they were subordinated to military headquarters for specific military operations. They had special training in offensive and maneuver warfare, chemical warfare, and counterattacks and were equipped with T-72 main battle tanks, BMP armored fighting vehicles, French GCT self-propelled howitzers, and Austrian GHN-45 towed howitzers, the most modern weapons in the Iraqi army. Republican Guard battalions had nine more tanks than regular army battalions, and the Republican Guard's support, armored recovery, and engineering equipment was superior to that of other Iraqi army forces.[186]

The rest of the Iraqi army totaled more than fifty divisions by mid-1990. Its basic operational level was the corps, which normally consisted of several divisions and large numbers of support units. Divisions usually consisted of three brigades. The bulk of the regular army divisions were infantry forces equipped with 1960s vintage Soviet- and PRC-made equipment, but there were several high quality armored and mechanized divisions. The armored divisions had two armored brigades and one mechanized brigade. The mechanized divisions had two mechanized brigades and one armored brigade. Infantry divisions had three infantry brigades and one tank battalion. Iraqi divisions generally had four artillery battalions and sometimes more. Most brigades had four battalions. The armored brigades had three armored and one mechanized battalion. The mechanized brigades had three mechanized and one tank battalion.[187]

There was also a Popular Army, which had been created in 1971 as a Baath Party militia. It was a highly political force designed to counter any threat from the regular forces, and it had poor training and equipment before the Iran-Iraq War. In spite of several efforts to improve it during the early 1980s, it consistently performed poorly during the Iran-Iraq War even when Popular Army units were finally integrated into regular army formations. By mid-1990 the Popular Army had been reduced to 250,000 from a wartime high of 650,000 and was no longer integrated into the regular army. It included only Baath Party members and was used for rear area and internal security purposes.[188]

The Iraqi army as a whole was extremely well equipped by Third World standards. It had at least 5,700 tanks, and many experts believe the figure was closer to 6,700.[189] Up to 1,500 of its tanks were T-72s, 1,500 were T-62s, 2,000 to 3,000 were Soviet bloc–supplied T-54 and T-55s, up to 1,500 were PRC- and North Korean–supplied T-59s and M-77s, and about 150 were captured Iranian Chieftain, M-47, and M-60 tanks—although many of these Western-made tanks were being transferred to Jordan.

Iraq had recently begun to upgrade some of its T-55s with the T-72 125mm gun and loading system, side skirts, new passive night vision equipment, and four forward firing smoke dispensers on either side of the turret. One version of this new tank, the T-72M1 (Assad Babyl), had a raised turret roof and cupola; another had few turret modifications; and some T-55s were modernized only with new night vision systems and appliqué multilayer passive armor on the glacis, hull sides, and turret front and rear. It is unclear how much of the new two piece 125mm ammunition any of these modified T-55s could carry or how quickly these conversions were introduced into Iraqi forces.[190] These were also some T-54s and T-55s converted to carry Soviet 160mm mortars with a range of 8 kilometers, and a few T-54s which had the turrets replaced with a hydraulically elevated mast with an armored observation cabin on top. This cabin could be raised to a maximum height of 25 meters and was used for reconnaissance and targeting.

In addition to its 5,700 main battle tanks, Iraq had more than 3,000 heavy tank transporters. It also had at least 3,500 to 4,000 other armored vehicles. An IISS estimate indicates a strength of 100 PT-76 light tanks and 2,500 armored reconnaissance vehicles, including 1,300 BDRM-2s; 300 AML-60, AML-90, ERC-90 Sagaie, MOWAG, and Rolands; 600 EE-9 Cascavals; and 300 EEF-3 Jararacaras. It also had 1,500 BMP-1 and BMP-2 armored infantry fighting vehicles and 6,000 armored personnel carriers, including BTR-50s, BTR-60s, BTR-152s, OT-62s, OT-64s, 1,500 MTLBs, 1,000 YW-531s, M-113s, Panhard M-3s, and EE-11 Urutus.

The Iraqi army had large numbers of anti-tank weapons, including AT-3 Saggers, AT-4 Spigots, SS-11s, Milans, and HOTs. Many were advanced third generation systems mounted on armored vehicles like the BDRM-2 and 100 VC-TH. Iraq also had the anti-tank guns mentioned earlier and a wide variety of anti-tank rocket launchers, including 73mm, 82mm, and 107mm weapons.

Iraq had one of the most formidable artillery forces in the world. Its major tube artillery included 3,000 to 5,000 towed and 500 self-propelled weapons. The towed weapons included a wide mix of Western and Soviet bloc types, ranging from 105mm to 155mm. Key types included 100 D-30 and 400 M-1939 122mm weapons, M-46 and T-59-1 130mm weapons, and 100 G-5, 200 GHN-45, and some M-114 155mm weapons. Its self-propelled artillery weapons included 2S1 122mm weapons, 2S3 152mm weapons, and 85 AUF-1 (GCT) and some captured M-109A1/A2 155mm weapons. It also had well over 200 multiple rocket launchers, including types from 107mm to 300mm. Its more modern multiple rocket launchers included 60 127mm Astros II, Astros SS-30s, and Astros SS-60s. In addition, it had large numbers of towed 85mm and 100mm anti-tank guns and 81mm, 120mm, 160mm, and 240mm mortars.

Iraq had developed a locally produced version of the Yugoslav D-30 122mm towed howitzer which it called the Saddam. It had also developed two new 6 x 6 wheeled self-propelled artillery weapons, the 155mm Majnoon and 210mm Al-Faw. The Majnoon weighs 43 tons and is fitted with a 8.06 meter barrel that can fire a 45.5 kilogram full-bore base-bleed projectile up to 38 kilometers, with a maximum rate of fire of four rounds per minute and a sustained rate of fire of one. The Al-Faw weighs 48 tons and is fitted with a 11.13 meter barrel that can fire a 109.4 kilogram full-bore base-bleed projectile up to 57.3 kilometers, with a maximum rate of fire of four rounds per minute and a sustained rate of fire of one. Iraq claimed these weapons have a maximum road speed of 90 kilometers per hour and a cross-country speed of

60–70 kilometers per hour. These weapons were still in the prototype stage at the beginning of the Gulf War.

Iraq also developed a new four barrel 120mm mortar mounted on a Soviet MTLB armored vehicle similar to the Austrian Noricum. It is unclear how many were actually deployed at the time of the war, but it is unlikely that they were deployed in significant strength. Iraq did, however, have the capacity to manufacture and deploy large numbers of multiple rocket launchers. These included copies of the PRC 12 round 107mm weapon, the Egyptian 122mm 30 round Saqr 36, a locally designed 30mm rocket system, and a truck fitted with 35 rounds of 81mm rockets.

Iraq also has extensive surface-to-surface rocket missile forces. These included a minimum of 24–30 foreign supplied FROG launchers and 100–150 Scud launchers. Iraq had developed its own cluster munition warhead version of the FROG, called the Laith 90, with its range increased from 70 to 90 kilometers. It had also developed the Ababeel 100 artillery rocket system using a 400 mm diameter rocket mounted in a four launcher canister on a truck, which it claimed had either 300 anti-tank fragmentation bomblets or 25 anti-tank minelets and had a range of 100 kilometers. In addition, it had several locally produced multiple rocket launcher systems. These include a copy of the Yugoslav 12 round 262mm multiple rocket launcher, with a maximum range of 50 kilometers, and a family of shorter range systems called the Sajeel, which were copies of the Brazilian Astros II SS-30, SS-40, and SS 60. These had ranges of 30–60 kilometers, and some had rockets with anti-armor, anti-personnel bomblets. There were large numbers of experimental systems, including one called the Baqr, which used a Soviet SA-3 missile converted to the ground-to-ground role. No estimate exists of how many of these Iraqi-produced rocket systems were operational and deployed, but most seem to have been in the prototype stage.[191]

The army had 489 helicopters, of which 189 were armed. The armed types included 56 Bo-105s with AS-11s and HOT; 40 Mi-24s; 30 SA-316s with AS-12s; 13 SA-321s, some armed with Exocets; and 20 SA-342s armed with machine guns and cannon. The other helicopters included 15 heavy transports, 225 medium transports, and 124 light helicopters.

Iraq had a separate air defense command that cooperated with the air force as part of an integrated air defense system. It also, however, had many lighter air defense weapons that were deployed with army units at the corps level or lower. These included some 7,000 anti-aircraft guns, with a number of ZSU-23-4 radar guided self-propelled weapons and numerous heavy AA guns ranging from 85mm to 130mm. Iraq also had some 15,000 mobile and manportable SA-7, SA-8, SA-9, SA-13, SA-14, and SA-16 weapons and roughly 100 Roland fire units on self-propelled armored vehicles.[192]

The Iraqi Army During the Gulf War

Postwar estimates of the forces Iraq deployed into the Kuwaiti theater during the Gulf War have become increasingly controversial as more data become available. The Department of Defense estimates that by the time the air portion of the Gulf War began, the total deployed strength of the entire

Iraqi army was 1.2 million men, 69–71 division equivalents, 5,800 tanks, 5,100 armored personnel carriers, and 3,850 artillery pieces. The forces in northern Iraq and Kurdistan included 2 corps with 17–18 infantry divisions and 6 forces commands. The forces in western Iraq included 2 armored regiments and 1–2 infantry divisions. The forces in central Iraq included 1 corps and 3 infantry divisions, and the forces in Baghdad included 2–4 Republican Guard brigades and 1 mechanized division in the process of formation.

Estimates differ as to how many forces Iraq actually deployed into the Kuwaiti theater of operations during the months between its August 2, 1990, invasion of Kuwait and the beginning of the Gulf War. One Department of Defense after-action estimate indicates that they included 5 corps with 35–36 divisions, of which 11 were armored and mechanized divisions, 25–26 were infantry divisions, and 1 was a special forces division. Eight more division equivalents were nearby or in the Kuwaiti theater as independent elements, bringing some estimates of the total forces to 43 divisions. If all of these forces had been properly manned and equipped, there would have been a total of 500,000–540,000 troops in the Kuwaiti theater—with about 50% in Kuwait. Iraqi forces would have included 140,000 Republican Guards, 4,200–4,500 tanks, 2,880 armored personnel carriers, 3,100 artillery pieces, SA-2 and SA-3 launchers, and a large number of shorter range missiles and AA weapons.[193]

Another detailed estimate of the deployment of Iraqi army forces in Kuwait is shown in Table 6.4, which indicates that virtually all sources agree that Iraqi units differed sharply in quality. As can be seen from this table, only about half the army units deployed to the Kuwaiti theater represented first line divisions, and some of these were infantry units. Only about 10–12 divisions were truly top quality forces by Iraqi standards.[194]

Once again, even the most authoritative Department of Defense estimates are contradictory, but they indicate that Iraq's forces were organized into a force of four infantry divisions and one mechanized division deployed along Kuwait's coast. The front line infantry divisions along the main defense line west from the coast on the Kuwaiti-Saudi border were organized into the 7th Corps, with the 52nd Armored Division in reserve. The other front line infantry divisions to the east of Wadi al-Batin were organized into the 4th Corps, with the 6th armored and 1st mechanized divisions in reserve. The operational reserve in the eastern part of the Kuwaiti theater was called the 2 Armored Corps and had the 51st Mechanized Division and the 17th Armored Division. It was both a counterattack and blocking force with the additional mission of countering any air or amphibious landings. A theater reserve of at least six Republican Guard divisions was positioned along the Iraqi-Kuwaiti border. The key elements of this force included the Tawakalna Mechanized Division, the Medina Armored Division, and the Hammurabi Armored Division. The Adnan and Nebuchadnezzar infantry divisions were kept back to defend the approaches to Basra.[195]

This force was deployed in at least two defensive belts, with a few triangular fortifications along the Saudi-Iraqi border. The defensive belts con-

TABLE 6.4 Iraqi Army Deployments in the Kuwaiti Theater of Operations

Function of Force	Division Strength			
	Armored	Mechanized	Infantry	Total
Forward Barrier Defense: Light screening force to defend border area. Moderate to low quality forces designed to absorb shock of offensive. They lacked mobility and were designed to delay the UN forces by taking high losses. They were, however, backed with heavy firepower in support and had good light weaponry, Including AA guns and anti-tank weapons.	0	0	8–11	8–11
Forward Reserve: Higher quality forces that were supposed to rush to halt an allied penetration, stiffening the forward defenses and ideally arriving before the allies could penetrate the forward defenses. Some were heavily equipped with armor and artillery.	2	2	4	8
Coastal Defense Force: Screening forces. They were supposed to hold against the initial phase of an amphibious assault or heliborne assault and secure Kuwait City. The Iraqi 3rd Corps headquarters was near Al Jahra, at the end of the bay of Kuwait.				
Regular Army Heavy Reserve: Critical force in trying to contain major breakthroughs or even in launching counterattacks. It covered attacks on the border, penetrations or flanking moves around Kuwait, and amphibious/air assaults.	3 1/3	1	0	4 1/3
Republican Guards Reserve: This force acted as both the ultimate mobile heavy reserve and as elite infantry defending the approaches to Basra and Umm Qasr.	2	1–2	2	5–6
Regular Army Infantry Reserve: Infantry divisions needed to screen the northwestern approach to Basra and Shuaiba, Basra, and the territory just north of Basra.	0	0	3	3
Total	7 1/3	4–5	21–25	33–36 1/3

SOURCE: Adapted from U.S. Department of Defense press brief, January, 1991.

sisted of minefields and oil-filled fire trenches, covered with interlocking fields of fire from armor, artillery, and automatic weapons. The Republican Guards and regular army mechanized and tank forces provided strong mobile reserves and counterattack capabilities. Strong defenses also existed along the seacoast, with naval and land mines and fortified high rise apartment buildings. Iraq also constructed a major new road network, with buried command posts and communications lines. Individual weapons were revetted, and there were anti-tank ditches and berms. All of these forces were trained for chemical warfare.

These estimates of the size of Iraq's forces, however, disguise a number of major problems that contributed to its rapid defeat. Iraq in many ways repeated the defenses that had won the Iran-Iraq War, although the Iranians had virtually no functioning air power and very limited armored maneuver capability. The Iraqi army was still an infantry force in many ways and was composed largely of poorly trained conscripts. Iraqi commanders rarely showed initiative, and all of the Iraqi services had a rigid top-down command and control system. Most Iraqi infantry units were trained only for static defense along a continuous line, were manned with low grade conscripts and officers, and had limited skill in maneuver. Emphasis was placed on holding a continuous front, and there was limited ability to withdraw, cross-reinforce, and reconcentrate, except in selected Republican Guard and regular army units.

Maintenance was poor and completion of defense lines erratic. Many forces were exposed by the open desert terrain, and the sand blew off many minefields. Little effort was made to keep positions, alternative positions, and ditches from filling with sand. While there was a total of 30 days of ammunition in theater and 3 days within each combat unit, food deliveries were poor and many desertions took place. Rather than the 540,000 men required, Iraq may have been down to total manning levels well below 430,000–480,000 men when the war began.[196]

The quality of the Iraqi force was very uneven, and the Iraqi high command failed to appraise Iraq's weaknesses correctly or to understand the range of technologies and capabilities the coalition forces possessed. Combined arms capabilities were weak, and artillery lacked mobility and the ability to switch fires rapidly as well as beyond visual range targeting capabilities. The air force had limited ability to support combined operations, and Iraq had no space assets and could not fly reconnaissance missions because of the strength of allied air power. Iraq's land and air communications were overcentralized and insecure, and its land forces depended on land links, radio systems, and centralized nodes that the coalition could jam, decrypt, or destroy.

The Iraqi forces lacked sophisticated night vision devices, fire control computers, and the thermal sights that allowed UN forces to engage at very long ranges and target beyond visual range. They had poor counterbattery targeting and fire control systems. The logistics system was overextended, slow reacting, and complex, and only limited emphasis was placed on battlefield recovery and repair.

These limitations in Iraq's forces proved to be as important as the well publicized successes of the UN coalition in using air power, high technology, deception, and armored maneuver. It is not surprising, therefore, that the Iraqi army suffered major losses during the Gulf War, although experts differ sharply about how many Iraqis died during the Gulf War, how much equipment and munitions were destroyed or lost, and how many combat units lost cohesion or combat effectiveness. Table 6.5 shows the Department of Defense estimate of losses issued at the end of the war.[197]

Seen in terms of damage to major formations, the Department of Defense

TABLE 6.5 U.S. Estimates of Iraqi Losses as of February 24, 1991

Category of Loss	Total in Kuwaiti Theater of Operations	Estimated Losses as of February 24, 1991	Losses as Percentage of Total
Ground forces in the theater			
Personnel	540,000	30,000–60,000	6–12
Main battle tanks	4,280	1,772	41
Other armored fighting vehicles	2,800	948	34
Artillery	3,110	1,474	47
Total Iraqi ground forces			
Personnel	1,000,000	40,000–70,000	NA
Main battle tanks	5,800	1,772	31
Armored personnel carriers	5,100	948	19
Artillery	3,850	1,474	38
Total air forces			
Active combat aircraft	750	324	43
Aircraft shelters	594	375	63
Major surface-to-air missiles	?	?	60
Major radars	?	?	50
Other major military facilities			
Major command and control sites	?	?	50
Major facilities for missiles and weapons of mass destruction	32–33	32–33	100

Source: Adapted from data in Department of Defense, *The Conduct of the Persian Gulf War: Final Report*, Washington, Department of Defense, April, 1992, pp. 104—113, 202—206, 353.

estimated after the war that ten Iraqi infantry divisions, one armored division, and one mechanized division had been reduced to from zero to 25% of their combat strength. Six more infantry, two mechanized, and four armored divisions had been reduced to 25–50% of their combat strength. Six infantry, two mechanized, and one armored division had been reduced to 50–75% of their combat strength, and five infantry divisions, one special forces division, one mechanized, and two armored divisions retained 75–100% of their combat strength.[198]

Another estimate, provided by the House Armed Services Committee, is shown in Table 6.6. This estimate reflects an independent effort to judge Iraqi army strength and losses during the course of the Gulf War. Highly impressionistic, the House estimate was made as part of a political effort to argue for reduced defense budgets, but it has the merit that it does not rely on manpower strength estimates based on multiplying the theoretical manpower and equipment holdings of typical Iraqi units times the number of units in place, the method used by the U.S. Defense Intelligence Agency before the war, or unverifiable estimates of Iraqi losses by the UN coalition. The truth probably lies somewhere between the data shown in Table 6.6 and

TABLE 6.6 Iraqi Army Strength and Losses During the Gulf War

Estimated Strength	Description of Iraqi Force
Prewar strength	
547,000 TO&E strength	Estimate of total manpower based on table of organization for 42 divisions
186,000 understrength	Estimate of number of men missing from the table of organization, estimated strength based on an average of 34% understrength manning obtained from estimates by captured Iraqi officers who reported their units ranged from zero to 66% understrength.
361,000 net total	Actual manning of Iraq forces at the time the land war began.
Changes during the conflict	
153,000 deserted	Deserted during the air war and air-land battle. An average derived from interviews with senior Iraqi POWs, who reported 20–50% of their deployed strength deserted—an average of 42% for all the units covered.
Losses during the air war	
17,000 injured during the air war	Based on POW estimates which indicated that their units suffered 2–16% injuries.
9,000 killed during the air war	Based on POW estimates with senior officers. The range among units was 1–6% of the troops deployed, with an average of 2.5%.
Losses after the conflict	
63,000 captured	The only number that can be firmly verified.
120,000 escaped or killed during the air-land battle	The number remaining if all the other figures in the House Armed Services Committee estimate are accurate. An the end of the fighting, one intelligence estimate based on aerial reconnaissance of the fleeing Iraqi troops placed the number of escapees at 100,000. Such numbers, however, are only a rough estimate.

SOURCE: Adapted by the author from Les Aspin and William Dickinson, "Defense for a New Era," House Armed Services Committee, April, 1992, pp. 29–33.

the estimates given earlier, but there is no way to establish the facts at this point.

The Iraqi Army After the Gulf War

If these figures are correct and air losses outside the Kuwaiti theater are taken into account, Iraq's army may have emerged from the Gulf War with as few as 25–33% of its prewar division strength, about 20% of its heavy armored and mechanized brigade strength, and 20–25% of its total manpower. It may have lost about 50% of its total operational tank strength, 40% of its other armored vehicles, and 50% of its artillery—although these figures include some recoverable equipment inside Iraq or equipment that could be repaired.

The Iraqi army was also in a state of political upheaval. Some elements had joined the Shi'ite and Kurdish rebels that attempted to seize power in the south and north right after the war, and other commanders and units either wavered in their loyalty or hesitated in obeying Saddam Hussein's orders. Many Iraqi troops also became disaffected.[200]

None of the forces that challenged Saddam, however, were strong enough to confront the regular military units that remained loyal or to cope with Iraq's vast security apparatus. During the course of 1991 and 1992, Saddam's forces smashed the Shi'ite uprising in the south. They quickly defeated a Kurdish uprising that threatened to seize control of the north and Mosul in the first weeks after the cease-fire, and left the Kurds isolated in a UN-secured enclave. Saddam then methodically purged the military, the security services, and his government and reorganized his forces.

Iraq's military buildup before the Gulf War had also been so great that by September, 1992—after a little over a year of recovery—Iraq's military forces were estimated to retain 500,000 to 650,000 men. The Iraqi army had from 300,000 to 400,000 men, or about 40% of its prewar strength. These forces were often manned by poorly trained and motivated conscripts who had been drafted after the Gulf War or who had been defeated in that conflict. They were stiffened, however, by Republican Guard forces and a ruthless mix of internal security forces.

The army was reported to be organized into five main corps, with a 4th Border Guard force along the Syrian border, a 5th Border Guard force along the border with Saudi Arabia, and a 3rd Screening Force along the western border of Kuwait. The Iraqi army had a total of twenty-four to thirty divisions. These included an uncertain mix of armored, mechanized, and infantry divisions. According to British and Israeli sources, there were three regular armored divisions, three regular mechanized divisions, and fifteen to seventeen regular infantry divisions. The Republican Guards had three armored divisions, one mechanized division, three to four infantry divisions, and a special forces unit.

This estimate of total strength would give the Iraqi army a numerical strength of about twenty-eight to thirty-three division equivalents versus the more than fifty-four division equivalents before the Gulf War. However, such figures ignore that Iraqi divisions after the war had far less manpower and equipment strength and combat capability than the divisions before the war. It is also impossible to take account of some fifteen to twenty special forces and commando units that existed before the war but whose postwar status is unknown, and the impact of Iraq's demobilization of many reserve units.[201]

What is clear is that Iraq was also able recover much of the equipment that it initially abandoned or which had fallen into hostile use in Iraq, and the moment the UN forces left, Iraq conducted a massive scavenging hunt in the Iraqi territory the UN had occupied. Iraq also sent infiltrators into Kuwait in an effort to regain equipment, spare parts, and munitions.[202]

Iraq restored some kind of higher army command structure, although it may have purged as many as 1,500 senior officers and shot others and went through a long series of major command shake-ups. It also seems to have had to radically restructure its prewar corps organization. Its 5th Corps remained in the north around Mosul and the areas near the Turkish border, and its 1st Corps covered the Iranian border north of Baghdad, but its others seem to have been mixed throughout central, eastern, and southern Iraq.[203]

This force structure is continuing to change as Iraq rebuilds and reorganizes its forces. Iraq cannot, however, recover its force strength beyond the limits imposed by its equipment losses until major new sources of arms become available. Current estimates indicate that these equipment losses place severe limits on every major aspect of land force capability. Rough estimates of the desired table of organization and equipment for Iraqi divisions are shown in Table 6.7, but few units actually approached this strength before the war, and most are now far below this level of manpower and equipment.

In August 1992 the Iraqi army's major holdings seemed to include only 2,100–3,000 tanks, or less than half the 6,700 tanks it had before the war. These tanks were largely T-54s, T-55s, M-77s, T-62s, and T-72s, and with about 400–600 T-59s and T-60s. It also had about 300–500 M-48s, M-60s, and Chieftains captured from Iran. Iraq had lost about two-thirds of its prewar T-72 strength and only had about 570–670 T-72s left, plus about 100 T-62s According to some estimates, only about 2,000–2,300 of these tanks were operational.

Iraq's surviving strength of other armored vehicles was a subject of intense debate, but one estimate indicated that it included 1,500 armored reconnaissance vehicles (BDRM-2, EE-3, EE-9, AML-60, AML-90) versus 2,500 before the war; 900 BMP-1 and BMP-2 other armored fighting vehicles versus 2,000 before the war; and 2,000 APCs (BTR-50, BTR-60, BTR-152, OT-62, OT-64, MTLB, YW-531, M-113, M-3, EE-11) versus 7,100 before the war. Other estimates indicate Iraq may have had some 2,800–3,100 other armored vehicles versus 5,100 before the war. Many of these vehicles had limited operational capability.[204]

Iraq's surviving artillery included about 900–1,000 towed artillery weapons (105mm, 122mm, 130mm, and 155mm), 250–300 self-propelled artillery weapons (2S1 122mm, 2S3 152mm, M-109A/1/A2 and GCT AUF-1 155mm),

TABLE 6.7 Iraqi Division Organization

Type	Regular Army			Republican Guard		
	Armored	Mech.	Infantry	Armored	Mech.	Infantry
Personnel	12,100	12,200	14,100	13,800	13,800	14,300
Tanks	245	175	78	308	220	44
OAFVs	472	544	6	538	622	6
Artillery	114	114	78	144	138	18
Air defense guns	90	90	54	90	90	54
SAMs	50	50	0	50	50	0

Source: Department of Defense Public Affairs press briefing handout, September, 1990.

200–250 multiple rocket launchers, and 4,000–5,000 mortars. This compares with 3,000–5,000 towed weapons and 500 self-propelled weapons before the war. As is often the case in such estimates, the data on multiple rocket launchers are too contradictory to make any estimate of wartime losses possible, although many such weapons were destroyed or abandoned.[205]

The Iraqi army lost large numbers of anti-tank weapons during the fighting, many of which were recovered intact by the UN coalition forces. Nevertheless, Iraq still has substantial anti-tank warfare capability. Its guided weapons include an unknown number of Milans and HOT launchers on VC-TH armored vehicles, and over 2,000 85mm and 100mm anti-tank guns and heavy recoilless rifles.

There are definitional problems in counting Iraq's surviving anti-aircraft guns because some estimates include machine guns and others only heavier weapons. Prewar estimates put the total number of weapons including machine guns at around 7,000 and the number of heavier weapons at 4,000. Postwar estimates do not break out these totals and include SA-7, SA-8, SA-9, SA-13, SA-14, and SA-16 weapons and Roland fire units on self-propelled armored vehicles. According to such estimates, Iraq seemed to have about 3,200 air defense guns and thousands of small surface-to-air missiles in 1992—or 50–66% of its prewar strength.

Helicopter estimates are equally uncertain. The army aviation force seems to retain as many as 120 of the 159 armed helicopters that Iraq possessed before the war. These include 20 Bo-105 attack helicopters with SS-11 and HOT missiles, 30 Mi-24s, SA-3126s with AS-12s, 5 SA-321s with Exocet, and 40 SA-342s. No reliable estimate exists of the number of surviving heavy, medium, and light transports and utility helicopters.

Iraq's surviving inventory of army equipment, however, is much more impressive than its military capabilities. Although Iraq built up significant war fighting capabilities during the Iran-Iraq War, its forces had many defects even before they suffered major losses during the fighting in 1991. Like many other Middle East armies, Iraq armed with little regard to standardization and ease of supply, training, and maintenance. The army was dependent on a wide mix of equipment supplied by the former Soviet bloc, France and Italy, other European states, and Third World countries. Much of Iraq's equipment was deadlined or had limited operational equipment because of a lack of spares and ammunition.

The Gulf War made this situation far worse. Iraq has been cut off from major arms imports and foreign technical support since August, 1990. Its army needed at least $1 billion a year worth of arms imports before it suffered the losses of the Gulf War, and it was organized to deal with attrition through resupply of new equipment rather than by repairing damaged or worn equipment. Iraq not only faces wartime losses but a steady decline in operational equipment strength and equipment sustainability and reparability.

Much of the Iraqi army's equipment is deadlined or only partially operational. Spare parts are critically short for even minor combat repairs, and sustainability is very low. These problems are increased by the breakdown of much of the Iraqi army logistic and supply system and by the maldeployment of a great deal of equipment and stocks, and Iraq is constrained by a very short supply of some critical munitions. This prevents Iraq from conducting effective combined arms warfare.

The effectiveness of the army has also been severely degraded by the shattering of many of Iraq's best armored and mechanized units, including its heavy Republican Guard units. Many officers and technicians were lost in the fighting, and the Iraqi forces have been subject to recurrent purges and upheavals ever since the end of the conflict. There has been no large scale training since early 1990, and many units are filled in with a mix of experienced troops and low grade conscripts and reservists. At least half of the Iraqi order of battle consists of hollow forces that will take years to rebuild to the level of capability they had before the fighting.

Iraqi Elite Land Units After the War

The Republican Guards make a particularly interesting case study in the changes in Iraq's forces since the Gulf War. There is a tendency in some commentaries on Iraq to treat the Republican Guards as being all of Iraq's elite forces, although many regular army armored and mechanized units were as well equipped and trained and played at least as important a role in combat during the Iran-Iraq War. Nevertheless, the Republican Guard Forces Command (RGFC, or Al Faris Forces Command) has been a mainstay of Iraqi military capability and of critical importance in securing Saddam Hussein and the Baath's control over Iraq.

Before the war, the Republican Guards had a total of roughly 12 division equivalents and 150,000 men. It is important to note that these divisions were not standardized and that many were infantry units tailored more for peacetime control of Iraq than combat power. The term "division" was also misleading. Even by Iraqi standards, a division slice required about 20,000 men to produce a field deployable division with a combat strength of 10,000 men. This would have required a Republican Guard force of at least 240,000 men, indicating that many guard divisions were little more than reinforced brigades. Further, one armored division could have up to twice the heavy armor of another, and training and readiness standards varied sharply by brigade or regiment.

Estimates indicate the Gulf War left Iraq's elite Republican Guards with about seven division equivalents. These include three armored (Al Nida, Al Hammurabi, Al Medina), one mechanized (Al Abid), and three to four infantry division (Al Adnan, Al Nebuchadnezzar, Al Baghdad, and possibly one unidentified) equivalents. Two special forces brigades seem to have survived from the prewar special forces division, and up to four independent infantry formations—nominally of brigade strength.[206] According to U.S. and Israeli experts, the surviving Republican Guards force had a total of between 60,000 and 80,000 men, and twenty-six to thirty brigade equivalents (six to eight armored, three to four mechanized, and the rest infantry).[207] This means that even the reduced Republican Guard force consists of units with 65–75% of the manning needed for its combat units and about half the total manpower needed to deploy and sustain a force of seven full divisions.[208]

This force has been created by deactivating up to five Republican Guard divisions that existed before the war, and probably a number of additional formations. Many of the divisions were concentrated around Baghdad in August, 1992, although at least one division was located in the north near the Kurdish security zone, one division was located in the south to control Karbala and Al Kut, and another division was deployed to control Al Amarah and help support operations against the Shi'ite rebels.

The equipment holdings of the surviving units are almost impossible to estimate but seem to be about 66–75% of what they were before the war. A very rough estimate of the total equipment holdings of the Republican Guards would be around 650–800 tanks (at least 550 T-72s), 800–1,100 other armored vehicles (about 50% BMP 1/2 and 25% MT-LB), and 350–500 artillery weapons. Given probable operational readiness, a force whose organizational strength exceeded seven divisions only had total equipment holdings equivalent to those of two U.S. armored divisions. While the Republican Guards were training again, their training and command and control do not function effectively above the battalion level, and they would need several years to fully reorganize and train for full divisional or corps level combat.[209]

The trust the regime placed in the Republican Guards is also somewhat unclear. There are reports that a heavy new layering of Saddam Hussein loyalists was promoted to senior positions after the war and that guard deployments around Baghdad were structured to prevent any one unit from acting against the regime. Iraq also retained at least two Presidential Guard infantry brigades and a Presidential Guard armored unit deployed in Baghdad as part of a force of around 8,000–14,000 men.[210] These Presidential Guards were equipped with T-62 and T-72 tanks and modern infantry fighting vehicles.

The exact relationship the Presidential Guards have with the Republican Guards is unclear, but they seemed to be directly under Saddam Hussein's control. It is also clear that Saddam Hussein sees the control of these forces— as well as control of his military intelligence department—as absolutely critical to his survival. He has changed the line of authority over the Republican Guards, Presidential Guards, and military intelligence department several times since the Gulf War. Each time, he has either replaced a nonrelative with a relative or has appointed a new (and presumably more loyal) relative.

For example, Saddam conducted at least six major shake-ups of his military command structure between November, 1990, and August, 1992—four of which were completed before June, 1991. Saddam replaced his minister of defense, Lt. Gen. Saadi Tuma Abbas (a professional solider and hero of the Iran-Iraq War) with his son-in-law, Hussein Kamil al-Majid, on April 6, 1991. He did this following the regrouping of his forces after Iraq's defeat in the Gulf War, and his intention clearly was to provide greater political control over the military. In late June, he replaced Lt. Gen. Hussein Rachid, who had been military chief of staff since November with Lt. Gen. Iyad Futiyeh al-Rawi, the loyalist commander of the Republican Guards. He also removed Maj. Gen. Wafiq Jassim Sammair as head of military intelligence and seems to have purged its command to put in more loyal officers.

It is obvious, however, that such actions did not always give Saddam added power. In November, 1991, he replaced Hussein Kamel, minister of defense, with another paternal cousin, Ali Hassan al-Majid. Reports differ over whether Hussein Kamel was removed because of his youth and inexperience in rebuilding the military (he was 37 and had no real military experience) or because of tensions within Saddam's coterie.

In any case, the new appointment put Majid, who had played a ruthless role in crushing the Kurdish uprising after the Gulf War, in charge of the Ministry of Defense, the Presidential and Republican Guards, and military intelligence. Hussein then named a maternal half-brother, Wathban Ibrahim Hassan, the new minister of interior and head of the civil security forces. Wathban had previously been removed from the regime when his brother (another half-brother of Saddam), Barzan al-Tikriti, was purged as intelligence chief in 1988. He also brought back Gen. Sabr al-Douri, a close associate and former head of military intelligence, to be head of the secret police, or Mukhabarat.[211]

In April, 1992 Saddam Hussein rotated many of his key commanders to forestall any risk of a coup. Rachid, a hero of the Iran-Iraq War, was made commander of the Republican Guards. Kamel Yassin, a member of the Baath ruling council and Saddam's brother-in-law and cousin, was made head of security in the military, and his brother, Irshid Yassin, remained head of Saddam's personal security force. Rawi, another hero of the Iran-Iraq War and a key Hussein loyalist, was made chief of staff.

On June 29, Ahmed Chalabi, a Shi'ite leader who was a member of the anti-Baath Iraqi National Conference, told reporters of a coup attempt within the military. Initial reports claimed that a mechanized brigade of the Republican Guard under the command of Brig. Sabri Mahmoud in Taji, an industrial area northwest of Baghdad, was preparing an assault on Saddam Hussein's headquarters in Baghdad when the coup was detected and halted by Iranian security forces. Other reports talked of fighting between the military security forces in Baghdad and Kirkuk during June 30 to July 2, and U.S. intelligence received one report of such a coup attempt.

There was no confirmation of these reports, however, and some U.S. experts concluded that they were spawned by the command upheavals following a new large scale purge of up to 135 military officers. Other experts indicated that Saddam called a large meeting of his loyal officers together, charged the U.S. and Jordan with supporting a military coup against him, and then used this as a rationale for his purge. These latter accounts are supported by the timing of reports of the coup attempt, which came after rumors of meetings between Jordanian and CIA officials at which King Hussein had agreed to allow the CIA to station in Jordan agents who were attempting to overthrow Saddam. While the details of such arrangements are impossible to confirm, King Hussein issued a denial of any Jordanian complicity in a plot against Saddam. Further, Jordan did begin to enforce sanctions on transshipments of goods and oil to Iraq, although it refused to allow UN inspectors into Aqaba.[212]

The Iraqi Air Force Before the Gulf War

The active strength of the Iraqi air force at the time the war began is a subject of considerable debate, and U.S. government sources reported a much larger inventory of combat aircraft during the war than most unofficial sources had reported before it. According to a U.S. Air Force estimate, Iraq had the sixth largest air force in the world by the summer of 1990. Precise estimates of its prewar strength are difficult to make because of the number of aircraft in delivery, in storage, and in training and conversion units. Most estimates indicate that it had 700 to 770 fighter, bomber, and armed trainer aircraft, supported by 200 other transport and special purpose aircraft, including an Iraqi-built airborne early warning aircraft derived from the Soviet IL-76 transports.[213]

Iraq's combat aircraft included French Mirage F-1 fighters, the export version of the Soviet MiG-29 Fulcrum interceptor and air superiority fighter, the MiG-27 Flogger strike fighter, the MiG-25 Foxbat interceptor, the MiG-23 Flogger fighter bomber, the MiG-21 Fishbed fighter, the Sukhoi Su-25 Frogfoot ground attack airplane, the Sukhoi Su-24 Fencer long range strike aircraft, Tupolev Tu-16 Badger and Tu-22 Blinder bombers, and the Su-7, Su-20, and Su-22 Fitter family of attack fighters. Iraq also had PRC-made H-6 and J-7 aircraft and Czech L-39 armed trainers.[214]

In view of the scale of Iraq's defeat during the Gulf War, it is important to note that it had three of the most sophisticated combat aircraft in the world. These included the MiG-29, Su-24, and Mirage F-1, whose performance has been discussed in earlier chapters. The 65 French-made Mirage F-1s were the elite section of the Iraqi air force and carried a wide range of the latest French and Soviet guided missiles and munitions as well as laser guided air-to-surface weapons. Their pilots were French trained and had more air-to-air combat training than the pilots flying Soviet-made aircraft.

Iraq was also improving its ability to use its new Soviet fighters. It had exercised and trained its MiG-29 units to operate with its Aidan airborne warning aircraft. Its Su-24s were Su-24Ds, with a sophisticated radar warning receiver, an improved electronic warfare suite, an improved terrain avoidance radar, satellite communications, and an aerial refueling probe; they can deliver electro-optical, laser, and radar guided bombs and missiles.[215] Unlike many strike/attack aircraft the USSR delivered to the Third World, the Su-24Ds could carry the latest Soviet munitions and payloads of nearly 25,000 pounds, and they could operate on missions with a 1,300 kilometer radius when carrying 6,600 pounds of fuel. With a more typical 8,818 pound (4,000 kilogram) combat load, it has a mission radius of about 790 kilometers in the LO-LO-LO profile and 1,600 kilometers in the LO-HI-LO profile.[216]

The Iraqi Mirage F-1s included Mirage F-1EQs which could carry Exocets and other advanced French air-to-ground missiles and could be refueled in flight. The F-1EQ5s carried a Thompson CSF Atlas laser designator pod which could designate targets at ranges of up to 10 kilometers. Modified to carry the Soviet AS-14 Kedge air-to-ground missile, which has a maximum range of 12 kilometers and uses semi-active laser guidance with an active laser fuse, they could also deliver the Aerospatiale AS-30L laser guided bomb which can glide to ranges of 12–15 kilometers. Iraq had fitted French airborne refueling probes to its MiG-23 Flogger Hs as well.[217]

It is difficult to estimate total Iraqi manning and equipment strength by type. The Iraqi air force seems to have had a strength of roughly 40,000 men in mid-1990, including some 10,000 air defense personnel. Many estimates of Iraq's strength before the war seem to undercount deliveries after 1987. The working estimate shown in Table 6.8 may be more accurate, although only 750 fixed wing aircraft seem to have been confirmed as operational in any kind of combat status.[218]

Estimates of Iraq's offensive air strength differ sharply by source, but the Iraqi air force seems to have had two bomber squadrons with 7–12 Tu-22 Blinders and 8–14 Tu-16 Badgers (including 4 PRC-made B/H-6Ds). It had roughly 22 fighter ground attack squadrons: one with 16–48 Su-24s, five with 70–90 MiG-23BM/Ns (24 Flogger E and 50 Flogger F), four with 23–34 Mirage F-1EQ-200s with Exocet and 35 Mirage F-1EQ5s and EQ6s, four with

TABLE 6.8 Iraq's Air Order of Battle Before the Gulf War

105	F-6s, Xian F-7s and unidentified types of MiG-21
65	MiG-21PFM Fishbed F
30	MiG-21MF Fishbed J
20	MiG-21UTI Mongol
40	MiG-23BN Flogger E
22	MiG-25 Foxbat A/E
38	MiG-29 Fulcrum B
10	MiG-29U Fulcrum C
40	Su-25 Frogfoot
150	Su-7/20/22 Fitter A/C/D/J/H
48	Su-24 Fencer E
50	MiG-23BN Flogger F
8	Tu-22 Blinder A
14	Tu-16/B6D Badger
65	Mirage F-1EQ/EQ4-200/EQ5-200/EQ6-200
30	MiG-17 Fresco
34	Hunters (up for sale for several years)
30	MiG-19/F-6 Farmer
8	MiG-15R Foxbat B
807	Total resources

Iraqi air force helicopter inventory

60	Hughes-300/530 combat helicopters in 1983
26	Hughes-530 combat helicopters in late 1985
40	Mi-8 Hip assault transports
40	Mi-24 Hind gunships

SOURCES: Adapted from Dick Palowski, *Changes in Threat Air Combat Doctrine and Force Structure*, 24th Edition, Fort Worth, General Dynamics DWIC-91, February, 1992, p. II-361; Department of Defense, *Conduct of the Persian Gulf War: Final Report*, Washington, Department of Defense, April, 1992, pp. 10–12, and IISS, *Military Balance.*

40–60 Su-25A/Bs, four with 70 Su-20/Su-22s, two with 30 Su-7s, and two with 30 J-6s. According to some reports, it also had up to 40 MiG-27 Flogger Js.[219]

These Iraqi attack forces had considerable combat experience but an uncertain mix of capabilities. The bomber units lacked the electronic warfare and low altitude penetration capability to survive against Western air forces. The Su-24 units were just entering service and did not have the experience and advanced training to be fully effective. The Mirage units were relatively well trained but had no experience in operating against strong air defenses. They lacked the extremely sophisticated electronic warfare equipment necessary to challenge the UN coalition's advanced defenses, although Iraq did succeed in some of its jamming efforts. The MiG-23s had uncertain readiness and training, and some had relatively poor attack avionics. The Su-25s were A-10-like close air support fighters that could not survive without air superiority. The J-6s were little more than glorified trainers, and the Su-7, Su-20, Su-22 force had very mixed training standards, and only part of this force was really combat effective.

The Iraqi air force had 13–17 interceptor squadrons with 22–25 MiG-25A/Es, 30 Mirage F-1EQs, 35 MiG-29s, 40 J-7s, and 190 MiG-21s.[220] It had at least 290 air defense capable aircraft. These air defense units often had lower training and readiness than the attack units, but the newer aircraft had readiness rates of around 80%.[221] They had little experience from the Iran-Iraq War because Iran rarely challenged Iraqi air defenses after the first years of the war. Training standards were very mixed, although they were relatively high for the Mirage F-1 units. Iraq was attempting to improve its fighter performance by establishing training links to Jordan. This allowed some Iraqi pilots to fly missions near the Israeli border as well as cooperate in limited reconnaissance missions.[222]

Although some had good infrared countermeasures, many of the aircraft had limited radar and electronic warfare capabilities and were extremely vulnerable to allied jamming and the superior radars and missiles on aircraft like the F-15. Most of the air defense fighters except the Mirage F-1s were highly dependent on data from ground controlled intercept stations to locate an attacking aircraft, and these stations were put out of action during the first days of the war. Further, while Iraq did conduct good training for some of its air units by Third World standards, it had nothing approaching the kind of computerized air combat training available to NATO forces.

Iraq had one reconnaissance squadron with five MiG-21s and seven to eight MiG-25s, two types of Soviet-made remotely piloted vehicles, and at least developmental versions of two Iraqi-built RPVs called the Al Yamamah-A, a multimission RPV carrying daylight and infrared cameras, and Scarab-3, a modification of the British TTL-3 Banshee target drone.

These reconnaissance assets were largely useless against the UN coalition. They were far too limited in scale to cover the rapidly changing coalition forces, could not penetrate its defended air space, and were tied to a slow and cumbersome photo processing system that not only took far too long to process reconnaissance information but generally had major problems routing information to the proper user even during periods when the Iraqi command and control system was fully intact. As a result, Iraqi forces were blind in comparison with the highly sophisticated mix of airborne and space reconnaissance systems available to the UN coalition.

Iraq had recognized many of these defects during the Iran-Iraq War and was trying to correct them when the Gulf War began. One example of such efforts was the IL-76 Candid that Iraq modified to act as an Aidan AEW aircraft. The first such aircraft, called the Baghdad 1, had its rear cargo ramp replaced by a GRC radome with an Iraqi-modified version of the French Thompson CSF Tiger surveillance radar. The radome had a 9 meter (30 foot) diameter dome that rose about 13 meters (43 feet) above the fuselage and the Candid. The rotating mechanism and radar were integrated into the aircraft in Iraq.

The radar's signal processing was modified to remove ground clutter. Electronic support measures were also installed, along with an improved radio navigation system. Iraq claimed the radar could track targets out to 350 kilometers and had a real-time down link using direct data transfer or voice. Coverage was said to exceed 180 degrees. This system is believed to have been used in the last stages of the Iran-Iraq War, and an improved version called the Baghdad 2 was in development, with direct fighter air control capabilities. It is important to note, however, that it had far less coverage and electronic warfare capabilities than the E-3A AWACS flown by the UN coalition and no real chance of survival against a Western-type air force.[223]

The Iraqi air force was seeking major changes in its combat air strength, although its future structure was uncertain. Iraq recognized the superiority of Western fighters during the Iran-Iraq War and planned to buy the Mirage 2000 as a follow-on to its Mirage F-1s. At one point, it announced an intention to buy 54 Mirage 2000 fighter bombers equipped with Matra ECM pods, with an option to buy 12 more. Baghdad also discussed plans to build a coproduction facility in Iraq, and eventually buy over 100 Mirage 2000 aircraft.

Iraq had trouble financing its purchases from France, however, because of its failure to meet the payment schedule on an existing arms debt that may have reached $6 billion. Iraq also seems to have developed reservations about the Mirage 2000's performance after talking to Jordanian experts about possible problems in the aircraft's radar and air combat avionics.[224] As a result, Iraq was examining the purchase of additional MiG-29s, Su-24s, and advanced Soviet attack aircraft like the MiG-27.

Iraq was considering orders of Alphajet trainers assembled in Egypt and had about 80 Brazilian EMB-212 Tucano trainers. It was looking into coproduction of the Tucano in Iraq—and had ordered Astros II multiple rocket launchers, Piranha air-to-air missiles, SS-30 and SS-60 rockets, and APCs—but it had the same financing problems with these orders that it had with France. It owed Brazil at least $120 million for past purchases when the war began.[225]

Acquiring the Mirage 2000s might have made a difference if Iraq had several years to absorb the new aircraft, but Iraq emphasized procurement efforts over readiness and sustainability. Iraq's constant purchases of new aircraft and munitions forced it to retrain and reorganize its forces, ensuring that many units were always in the process of conversion to new aircraft, tactics, and munitions. The constant turbulence in air units meant limited time to train as units, and the expansion of the force meant shortages of skilled pilots and ground crews and a massive problem in trying to support so many different types and models of aircraft. Something like one-third of Iraq's total air combat strength was not really operational, and at least another third had relatively low operational standards and very poor sustainability. Further, the use of so many aircraft types presented serious problems in redeploying from base to base, since no base could effectively support more than a few types of aircraft.

Unlike many Middle Eastern air forces, that of Iraq was able to obtain a wide range of modern air ordnance from the Soviet bloc and West. Its air-to-air missile inventory included Soviet-made AA-2s, AA-6s, AA-7s, and AA-8s. Its French-made inventory included R-530s and R-550 Magiques. Iraqi inventories of air-to-surface missiles included French-made AS-30 laser guided bombs, Soviet-made X29L laser guided missiles modified to extend their range to 12–15 kilometers, Thompson CSF Atlas laser designators, Armatts, AM-39 Exocets, up to three types of cluster bombs, and electro-optical guided missiles. It included AS-4 Kitchen and AS-5 Kelt long range air-to-ship missiles, AS-14 Kedge air-to-ground missiles, and possibly an air launched version of the PRC-made C-801. Iraq had large stocks of napalm, binary chemical bombs, bomblet dispensers and possibly some fuel air explosive (FAE) weapons. Iraq exhibited 9,000 kilogram bombs for its Tu-16s, with up to 8,800 pounds worth of TNT. These have impact, proximity, and air burst fuses and were developed for attacks on rear echelon forces.[226]

All of these munitions, however, depended for their effectiveness on Iraq's ability to compete in air combat and electronic warfare and to penetrate enemy defenses without encountering effective land based air defenses. In practice, the combination of the E-3A and F-15 gave the UN coalition a decisive advantage in command and control, radar range and target characterization, and beyond visual range combat.

As has been discussed earlier, the Iraqi army air corps added at least 160 combat helicopters to Iraq's air strength, including 40–45 Mi-24 Hind with AT-2 Swatter, 20–50 SA-342 Gazelle (some with HOT), 56 Bo-105 with SS-11 and HOT, 30 SA-316B Alouette III with AS-12, and 10–13 SA-321 Super Frelons. Some of the Super Frelons were equipped with AM-38 Exocet and some with AS-12 missiles. As was the case with Iraq's fighters, however, helicopter training was mixed in quality. Many units acquired reasonable proficiency in attack missions during the Iran-Iraq War, but comparatively few learned to fly the complex attack and exit maneuvers or nap of the earth low altitude flight techniques necessary to survive against a sophisticated enemy. Like the Iraqi air force, the helicopter pilots also had no experience in flying against a force equipped with advanced look-down radars and electronic warfare assets, and they were often relatively easy to target.

Iraq's air base and logistic system was excellent by regional standards. It operated from 24 main operating bases and 30 dispersal bases. The main operating bases were well designed and built to withstand conventional attack. Iraq could shelter nearly all its aircraft. Many bases had multiple taxiways with multiple runways. New underground shelters based on Warsaw Pact models had been built by Yugoslav contractors at the main operating bases near Basra, Kirkuk, Mosul, Rashid, H-3, Shaiba, Habbiniyah, and other bases, and they were believed to be capable of withstanding air bursts from nuclear attacks. Iraq had structured its highway system to provide dispersal bases, deployed runway repair kits, and provided large numbers of surface-to-air missiles and anti-aircraft guns to defend each base.[227] The critical weaknesses in the basing system were (1) that it depended on the survival of the Iraqi command, control, and warning system to use the sheltered aircraft; (2) that it needed effective surviving air defenses to cover the bases against sustained attack; and (3) the shelters proved vulnerable to the earth penetrating weapons that the U.S. deployed in the final weeks before the air war.

Iraq's land based air defenses had been extensively reorganized after Israel's Osiraq raid in 1981. A network of radars, surface-to-air missiles, and anti-aircraft guns surrounds strategic and industrial areas, particularly near Baghdad. A French-supplied C^3 system called the KARI was completed in 1986–1987 but was never really tested during the Iran-Iraq War. Under this system, the national air defense operations center (ADOC) in Baghdad controlled Iraq's air defenses. The ADOC maintained the overall air picture and established priorities for air defense engagements. There were sector operations centers (SOCs) subordinate to the ADOC, each controlling air defense operations in a specific geographic area. The ADOC and SOCs had large numbers of weapons systems and extensive C^3I assets. Although the system was French-supplied, Iraq patterned its overall air defense network and operations on Soviet models, creating a strongly internetted, redundant, and layered air defense system that included a wide variety of radars, hardened and buried command and control sites, interceptors, surface-to-air missiles, and anti-aircraft artillery.[228]

According to one U.S. estimate, Iraq had a total of 16,000 radar guided and heat seeking surface-to-air missiles, including the lighter army systems described earlier and SA-2s, SA-3s, and SA-6s. The heavier surface-to-air defense missiles were operated by an air defense force organized into air defense units which were part of the army but tied operationally to the air force. They had approximately 20–30 operational SA-2 batteries with 160 launch units, 25–50 SA-3 batteries with 140 launch units, and 36–55 SA-6 batteries with well over 100 fire units. Iraq claimed to have modified the SA-2 missile to use an infrared terminal seeker to supplement the normal radio command guidance system, but it is unclear that such systems were actually deployed.

Iraq's lighter surface-to-air defenses included 20 SA-8 batteries with 30–40 fire units, 60–100 SA-9 fire units, some SA-13s, and 50–66 Rolands.[229] To put this air defense strength into perspective, Baghdad had more dense air defenses at the start of the Gulf War than any city in Eastern Europe, and more than seven times the total SAM launcher strength deployed in Hanoi during the height of the Vietnam War.

The U.S. Department of Defense released a highly detailed postwar estimate of Iraq's land based air defense at the time the Gulf War began that credited Iraq with 3,679 major missiles, not including 6,500 SA-7s, 400 SA-9s, 192 SA-13s, and 288 SA-14s. It indicated that Iraq had 972 anti-aircraft artillery sites, 2,404 fixed anti-aircraft guns, and 6,100 mobile AA guns. These deployments still reflect the basic concentrations of Iraq's surviving air defense weapons. The details by region are shown in Table 6.9.

Many of the surface-to-air missile and command and control units in the Iraqi system, however, had low operational readiness and proficiency. Electronic warfare capability was good by Third World standards but scarcely competitive with U.S. capability. Training failed to deal with saturation and advanced countermeasure attacks and was not realistic in dealing with more conventional penetrations by advanced attack aircraft, and the overall sensor/battle management system remained poor. This was demonstrated all too clearly when Iraqi guns and missiles shot down an Egyptian Alphajet flying to an arms show in Baghdad in April, 1989, although it flew along a preannounced flight corridor at the scheduled time.[230] Iraq still could not keep its land based air control and warning and C³I systems operational twenty-four hours a day.

Iraq's transport aircraft included 2 squadrons with 10 AN-12s, 6 AN-24s, 2 AN-26s, 19 IL-76s, 19 IL-14s, and 1 DH Heron. Iraq has been using the IL-76 as a tanker since 1985 and has modified some of its MiG-23BNs for airborne refueling by using the same system as on its Mirage F-1EQs.[231] The Iraqi air force had large reserves of training aircraft, including MiG-15s, MiG-21s, MiG-23Us, 2 Tu-22s, 16 Mirage F-1BQs, 50 PC-7s, and 21 EMB-312s.

TABLE 6.9 Deployment of Iraq's Air Defense Weapons Before the Gulf War

Type	Mosul/Kirkuk	Baghdad	H-2/H-3	Tallil/Jailbah	Basra	Total
Missiles	122	552	90	10	118	892
AAA sites	39	380	138	73	167	455
Guns	110	1,267	281	180	442	2,280
SA-2	1	10	1	1	2	15
SA-3	12	16	0	0	0	28
SA-6	0	8	6	0	8	22
SA-8	1	15	0	0	0	16
Roland	2	9	6	2	5	24
ZSU-23/4	0	8	0	0	5	13
S-60	8	10	3	2	14	37

Source: Department of Defense, *Conduct of the Persian Gulf War: Final Report*, Washington, Department of Defense, April, 1992, p. 241.

The Iraqi Air Force During the Gulf War

Estimates of Iraqi losses during the Gulf War remain somewhat uncertain, and many reports of the details of the air war are contradictory. It became brutally clear during the first hours of the war, however, that the UN coalition could successfully penetrate even the most heavily defended Iraqi targets with stealth and advanced air defense countermeasures and could destroy critical links in the Iraqi command and control system. Within a matter of days, it became equally clear that UN coalition air combat systems could absolutely dominate Iraqi air space and that the coalition had the attack assets necessary to destroy Iraqi aircraft in their shelters.[232]

Iraq's air force could not begin to operate effectively in an environment where it had no real combat experience in operating its air defense command and control system, wretched command leadership, and poor prewar training and operational readiness standards. Further, it immediately lost protection from Iraq's surface based air defenses and the support of the major radars and command and control facilities used to manage the air battle and control combat from the ground. Within hours of the first day of combat, however, the sector operations centers no longer could operate together and began to lose capability. Most hardened SOCs and intercept operations centers (IOCs) were destroyed or neutralized during the first few days. Iraqi radar activity had average 1,700 emitters during the period before the war. By January 20 it was down to fewer than 200 emitters, and by January 21 it was down to 100 emitters, where it remained for the rest of the war. Iraq's early warning radars were so badly damaged during the first few days that it had to rely on the uncoordinated medium range radars of its surface-to-air missiles.[233]

Individual Iraqi fighters often showed considerable courage in attempting to close their attacks, but they were outranged by the radars of the E-3A AWACS and F-15s. Even the best Iraqi aircraft lacked radars, air-to-air weapons, and electronic warfare assets that could compete with the mix of assets in coalition forces, and Iraq's lack of air-to-air combat training and experience quickly became apparent. At the same time, Iraq had lost all reconnaissance capability and quickly learned it could not risk flying attack aircraft into defended areas to attack even large fixed area targets.

Iraq's loss of radars, command and control facilities, and vulnerability to airborne anti-radiation missiles also shattered its ground defenses. AA guns and surface-to-air missiles fired vast numbers of rounds without really having a target and often after the attacking aircraft had left. At the same time, Iraqi AA and surface-to-air missile units became more and more reluctant to turn on their radars—often firing uselessly without any real guidance.

The result was an air campaign that decisively defeated Iraq by the third day of the war. Iraqi air units had the potential ability to fly 200–300 combat sorties per day on a sustained basis. They flew an average of 55 combat patrol and training sorties per day and an average of 40 support sorties during the two weeks before the beginning of the Gulf War on January 16,

1991. The coalition air attacks prevented Iraqi aircraft from coming close to even their training and prewar patrol levels.

On the first night of the war, the Iraqi air force flew about 25 combat and 90 support sorties. The second day it flew about 25 combat sorties and 20 support sorties. The third day it reached its peak of 55 combat sorties and 5 support sorties and sustained about 30 combat and 40 support sorties per day during the rest of the week. However, Iraq lost 14 fighters to F-15s during this period and quickly found that its air combat and support sorties had a negligible impact on allied operations.[234]

On January 23, the seventh day of the war, the coalition shifted to attacking Iraqi aircraft in their shelters. By this time, the Iraqi air defense system had virtually collapsed. On January 25 the coalition successfully attacked Iraq's hardened Yugoslav shelters. As a result, on January 27 Iraq began to fly many of its top combat aircraft to Iran and to disperse other types outside air bases on roads and in towns near the bases. The coalition then shifted to flying "barrier" patrols over Iraq to prevent air activity, and Iraq virtually halted all air activity. It flew no fixed wing aircraft sorties from the fifteenth to the eighteenth day of the war. It did start flying 10–15 combat sorties a day during the four days thereafter, when the UN temporarily halted its barrier patrols, but flew no sorties between the twenty-sixth and thirty-eighth day of the war. It flew fewer than 10 sorties on the day the land war began and no sorties for the rest of the war.[235]

The critical importance of superior aircraft radars and beyond visual range kill capability is illustrated by the fact that all fixed wing air combat kills in the war were made by the F-15, the most advanced U.S. fighter. Most kills were made by the AIM-7 radar guided missile, and no air-to-air combat kills against fixed wing aircraft were made in dogfights using cannon. The Department of Defense credits five MiG-29 kills to AIM-7s, six Mirage F-1 kills to AIM-7s and two Mirage F-1 kills to AIM-9s, two MiG-25 kills to AIM-7s, six MiG-23 kills to AIM-7s and two to ASIM-9s, two MiG-25 kills to AIM-9s, three Su-7/Su-17 kills to AIM-7s, one MiG-21 to Aim-7s and three to Aim-9s, one IL-76 to AIM-7s, two helicopters to AIM-7s, one helicopter to AIM-9s, and two helicopters to guns.[236]

By the end of the Gulf War, the Department of Defense estimated that 324 of Iraq's original force of 750 active combat aircraft were destroyed, captured, or relocated out of Iraq. A total of 44 Iraqi aircraft of all types had been killed in air-to-air combat, 113 to 120 Iraqi aircraft had fled to Iran, and another 170 to 200 were destroyed on the ground. If one includes only combat aircraft, a total of 33 Iraqi aircraft had been killed in air-to-air combat, 109 Iraqi aircraft had fled to Iran, and another 151 were destroyed on the ground.[237]

Many of Iraq's best fighters, including many of its MiG-29s, Su-24 strike fighters, and Mirage F-1EQ5s fled to Iran. The Mirages included many, if not most, of Iraq's air refuelable fighters. According to U.S. Air Force estimates, the coalition also destroyed 375 of the 594 hardened shelters on Iraqi air bases.[238] Total Iraqi air combat losses totaled 40 aircraft, including 5 MiG-29s, 8 Mirage F-1s, 4 MiG-21s, 7 MiG-23s, 2 MiG-25s, 2 Su-25s, 6 Su-7/20/22s, and 6 helicopters. Iraq also lost many of its air defense and other radars, about one-third of its SA-2s and SA-6s, some of its SA-3s, and large numbers of its mobile SA-8, SA-9, and SA-13 systems. It lost more than half of its major command and control centers, and large numbers of anti-aircraft guns.[239]

The Iraqi Air Force After the Gulf War

In late 1992 the Iraqi air force still had at least 30,000 men, including some 7,000–15,000 air defense personnel.[240] It also had approximately 330–370 combat aircraft, less the Iraqi aircraft still in Iran, although many of the aircraft in Iraq were damaged or not operational.[241] One estimate included 6–7 HD-6, Tu-16, and Tu-22 bombers. They included 130 J-6, MiG-23BN, MiG-27, Mirage F-1EQ5, Su-7, Su-20, and Su-25 attack fighters; 120 J-7, MiG-21, MiG-25, Mirage F1-EQ, and MiG-29 air defense fighters; MiG-21 and MiG-25 reconnaissance fighters; 15 old Hawker Hunters; a surviving IL-76 Adnan AEW aircraft; 2 IL-76 tankers; and large numbers of transports and helicopters. Total surviving inventory estimates by aircraft varied sharply by source but included about 30 Mirage F-1s, 15 MiG-29s, 60 MiG-23s, 15 MiG-25s, 130–150 MiG-21s, and 60 Su-17s, Su-20s, and Su-22s. Iraq still had comparatively large numbers of remotely piloted vehicles as well.[242]

The air force also retained 20–25 Improved Hawk launchers seized from Kuwait, 110–160 SA-2 launchers, 90–100 SA-3 launchers, 100–125 SA-6s, 20–35 SA-8s, 30–45 SA-9s, some SA-13s, and around 55–65 Crotale/Roland surface-to-air missile units. Iraq also had numerous manportable SA-7s and SA-14s, and some SA-16s. Some radars and limited elements of its C^3I system were operating, but most of its surface-to-air missile units, radars, automated data processing and transfer system, and central command and communications facilities had not been operational since early in the Gulf War, and there was no way to determine their true operational strength. It is impossible to tell how many of Iraq's underground command and personnel shelters survived the war, but it seems likely that about half survived the coalition bombing campaign.

More generally, the Iraqi air force had only been able to conduct limited combat aircraft operations since the UN cease-fire in February, 1991, and its training and readiness had unquestionably deteriorated with time. It had growing shortages of spare parts and had no access to the Soviet and French technical support it had relied on before the war. The Iranian government announced in late July, 1992 that it would expropriate the 132 Iraq combat aircraft that had taken refuge in Iran during the war—aircraft worth roughly $1.2 billion.[243]

The Iraqi air force was still large enough to retain considerable combat capability and flew some fighter and attack helicopter sorties against Shi'ites in southern Iraq in June and July, 1992. It was clear by August, 1992, however, that the Iraqi air force was operating at considerably less than half its prewar ability to generate and sustain combat sorties, had lost much of its sensor and command and control capabilities, and was losing more and more of its effectiveness with time. It was also clear that Iraq could not rebuild its air force to anything approaching its prewar strength without massive foreign assistance.

The Iraqi Navy

Iraq's navy has never been strong or effective. It played only a negligible role in the Iran-Iraq War, where Iran dominated the Gulf until the Western intervention to protect tanker traffic in 1987. While the Iraqi navy did operate in the northern Gulf, it acquired little wartime experience. Iraq's smaller ships occasionally attacked Iran's Khor Musa convoys and mined some of the Iranian waters in the upper Gulf. Most of Iraq's warships, however, were trapped in port by Iran's air and naval forces during 1980–1987 and by Iran's mining and blocking of the Shatt al Arab.

Ironically, Iraq had allowed its navy to run down before the Iran-Iraq War because it was awaiting the arrival of frigates and corvettes which were under construction in Italy. At the start of the war, it had only one training frigate, eight fast attack craft armed with Styx SSM, four FAC armed with torpedoes, three large and eight coastal patrol boats, two Polnocny-class landing craft, and some inshore patrol vessels. Iraq seems to have lost three missile FAC, two torpedo FAC, its two Polnocny landing craft, five patrol boats, and many small craft in the fighting.

This situation might have been different if the Iraqi navy had been able to obtain more of the twelve warships it had ordered from Italy. These included four Lupo-class vessels, six corvettes, and two support vessels. During the war, however, the Italian government ordered an embargo on arms shipments. As a result, Iraq received only two Assad-class (Esmeralda-class) corvettes and the supply ship *Agnadeen*. The rest of the ships were held at La Spezia.

After the Iran-Iraq War, Iraq could not finance delivery of the rest of the vessels. Iraq was able to pay only about 600 billion lira ($441 million) out of the total cost of 3.6 trillion lira. This meant that it was still negotiating to obtain the rest of the ships when the Gulf War began. The key combat ships awaiting delivery included the four Lupo-class 2,525-ton frigates—each of which has eight Otomat 2 ship-to-ship missile launchers (160 kilometer range), one Oto Melara 127mm gun, six 324mm torpedo tubes, one Albatross/Aspide surface-to-air missile launcher with eight missiles, and one Agusta AB-212ASW helicopter. There were also four Assad-class 685-ton ships with six Otomat 2 missile launchers, one four cell Albatross surface-to-air missile launcher, and one Oto Melara 76mm gun.[244]

At the beginning of the Gulf War, Iraq's only major combat ships consisted of the two Assad-class corvettes that Italy had delivered in 1986. These ships had two Otomat 2 launchers with two missiles each and an Agusta AB-212ASW helicopter instead of six Otomats. These Assad-class vessels had not been fully equipped with weapons and put through sea trials. Iraq's only other frigate, an obsolete Yugoslav 1,850-ton training ship, with 57mm and 40mm guns and four empty Exocet launchers, was laid up in port.

Iraq's smaller warships consisted of six Osa II and two Osa I guided missile fast attack craft with four Styx missiles. While the Styx missiles had maximum ranges of 46 or 95 kilometers, the Osas had very limited long range target acquisition capability and were highly vulnerable to countermeasures.[245] Iraq also had four old P-6 fast attack craft which may not have been operable. It had three large SO-1 patrol craft, five Zhuk coastal patrol craft, two Soviet T-43 and three Yevgenya-class oceangoing mine sweepers, three Polnocny-class LSMs and three LSTs.

Iraq also had thousands of mines. These included several types of naval mines, and it was building its own Sigeel 400 mine: an air droppable nonmagnetic bottom mine detonated by an acoustic sensor, with 400 kilograms of explosive. Iraq was developing a family of eight nonmagnetic bottom mines.[246] Iraq also had one modern support ship held in Italy, two old Poluchat-class torpedo support ships, one tanker, and one small support ship.

The Iraqi navy was also expanding its helicopter strength. It had about six of the thirteen Aerospatiale SA-321s with Exocet it ordered before and during the Iran-Iraq War. In addition, Iraq was buying six Aerospatiale AS-332F Super Pumas, fitted with Varan search and fire control radars and Exocets, and six SA-365Ns, which use Agrion chin mounted radars and are armed with four AS-15T air-to-ship missiles each. The AS-15Ts have a range of up to 15 kilometers and are a much cheaper way to attack small ships than the Exocet.[247]

It is hardly surprising, therefore, that Iraq's navy was then virtually destroyed as an operational force during the Gulf War. It now has a paper strength of around 2,500 men with the Yugoslav training frigate, one Osa-class missile boat, one replenishment tanker, and three 5,800-ton transport ships.[248] These ships survived only because they were not committed to combat. Iraq lost many of its patrol and coastal combatants during the war, and the Iraqi navy has little real operational capability. Italy has turned the four Lupo-class ships over to its own navy, and the final disposition of the remaining four Assad-class ships is uncertain.[249]

Iraq does, however, retain some of its land based Silkworm missile systems, which have ranges of up to 100 kilometers, and large numbers of mines. On February 25, 1991, Iraq fired two Silkworm missiles against UN coalition ships during the Gulf War. One failed and crashed into the sea; the other was destroyed by British Aerospace Sea Darts fired by the HMS *Gloucester*. Iraq may also have some Faw 70, Faw 150, and Faw 200 missiles, which it claims are Iraqi-made versions of the Soviet SSC-3 Styx.[250]

Iraq and Weapons of Mass Destruction

No country in the Middle East, and perhaps in the developing world, has spent so much to acquire weapons of mass destruction as has Iraq. While there is no way of precisely costing Iraq's effort to acquire long range missiles and biological, chemical, and nuclear weapons, few outside experts think that Iraq has spent less than $10 billion dollars. The U.S. government has released a list of 52 businesses and 32 front organizations that Iraq used to buy the materials and technology it needed for such weapons.[251]

The sheer scale of this effort did not become clear until after the Gulf War.

Under the terms of the cease-fire in the Gulf War, Iraq committed itself to allowing the UN-inspected destruction of its biological, chemical, and nuclear weapons facilities and its long range missiles. On April 3, 1991, the UN created a special commission to prepare a plan for the destruction and removal of Iraq's biological, chemical, and nuclear weapons materials and facilities. This commission authorized the International Atomic Energy Agency to carry out part of this task and created a force of UN inspectors to perform the rest.

From the data allied intelligence efforts uncovered during the Gulf War and the postwar UN inspection effort, it became apparent that Iraq had far more missiles and launchers than experts had suspected before the war, that it had taken routes to acquiring nuclear material unknown to Western intelligence, and that it had far larger numbers of missile, biological, chemical, and nuclear facilities than previously thought.

At the same time, Iraq continued to make every effort to conceal these facilities from the UN inspectors that were supposed to supervise them as part of the terms of the 1991 cease-fire. In late 1991 Iraq had declared seven missile facilities, no biological and nuclear weapons facilities, and eleven chemical weapons facilities. UN experts privately estimated that Iraq had fifty-two missile storage, assembly, and maintenance facilities; thirteen facilities associated with biological weapons; forty-eight facilities associated with chemical weapons; and 20 facilities associated with nuclear weapons. Even these totals may well have been an undercount.

The evidence on Iraq's weapons of mass destruction is, therefore, uncertain and in a state of constant flux. Nevertheless, the data already available provide an impressive lesson in how dangerous proliferation can be in today's world and what a Third World dictator can accomplish when he has virtually unrestricted access to his nation's resources.

Iraq's Missile Weapons and the Development of the Al-Hussein

Iraq started the use of surface-to-surface missiles and rockets in the Iran-Iraq War by firing FROG-7s at Iranian positions during the first weeks of the conflict. Iraq soon found, however, that these rockets had little military effect. They did not carry an effective conventional warhead, and Iraq lacked any means of effective beyond visual range targeting. Proof of these shortcomings occurred early in the war when Iraq fired four FROG-7 surface-to-surface rockets in an attempt to disorganize some of the staging areas of the Iranian army near Dezful and Ahwaz. The rockets exploded without producing any significant casualties.

The reasons the FROGs proved ineffective are easy to understand and illustrate why the proliferation of long range guided missiles is being given so high a priority relative to unguided rockets. The FROG-7, which is also called the R65A or Luna, is an obsolete system. While it does have a warhead with up to 455 kilograms of high explosive, it was designed primarily to use nuclear warheads and is too inaccurate for use as a conventional weapon.[252]

As already mentioned, however, Iraq is thought to have produced its own cluster munition warhead version of the FROG, the Laith 90, with a range of

90 kilometers. It also claimed to have an Ababeel 100 artillery rocket system using a 400mm rocket mounted in a four launcher canister on a truck, which Iraq said had either 300 anti-tank fragmentation bomblets or 25 anti-tank minelets and had a range of 100 kilometers. These systems were not used during the Gulf War, and no estimate exists of how many of these systems were operational and deployed. Most experts believe they were still in the prototype stage when the Gulf War began.[253]

Iraq made more effective use of the Scud in the Iran-Iraq War, largely against Iranian population centers to the rear of the battlefield.[254] Iraq initially used the unmodified Scud B, with a range of 280 kilometers, a CEP of 900 meters, and a 1,000 kilogram warhead.[255] Iraq first acquired these missiles in 1975 and used them against Iran as early as October, 1980. Typical targets included cities nearer the border like Dezful, Ahwaz, Khorramabad, and Borujerd (190 kilometers from the Iran-Iraq border). Iraq could not attack key targets like the Iranian capital of Tehran with the Scud B, however, because Tehran was about 510 kilometers from the Iraqi border—about 220 kilometers beyond the range of the Scud B.[256]

From 1982 onwards Iraq tried to acquire the longer range missiles it needed to attack targets deep in Iran. There is still considerable uncertainty as to exactly how Iraq got the technology to modify its Scuds. Various sources have claimed Iraq received Chinese, Egyptian, French, German, and/or Soviet help. All of these claims may be true, and other nations seem to be involved.

In any case, these efforts first paid off in August, 1987, when Iraq announced it had tested a new missile called the Al-Hussein. The U.S. officially indicates that this missile had a range of about 375–400 miles (650 kilometers) and a CEP of 3,000 meters.[257] One Israeli source estimates that it has a maximum range of 600 kilometers, a warhead weight of 300 kilograms, a flight time of 420 seconds, and a CEP of around 1,700–2,300 meters.[258] Other experts indicate it has a range of 375 miles and a warhead weight of only 250 pounds.[259]

This meant that Al-Hussein gave Iraq Scuds that could reach Tehran and Qom from positions south of Baghdad, and Iraq soon began to use them. Iraq fired an average of nearly three Scuds a day, and some estimates indicate that it fired over 160 missiles at Tehran between February 29 and April 18, 1988.[260]

There is still some controversy over the way in which Iraq extended the range of the system. It could have modified a standard Scud by cutting its warhead payload from around 800 kilograms to around 200–250 kilograms, altering it to burn all its propellant at the cost of reliability, or doing both.[261] The last explanation seems most likely. Iraq could also have got higher payloads of up to 500 kilograms by using strap-on boosters— since there are unconfirmed reports of weld marks and other alterations on fragments of the Scuds recovered in Iran—but most experts now discount this possibility.

The improved Iraqi Scuds may have had refire times of 60 minutes versus 160 minutes for the earlier model. The precise range capabilities of Al-

Hussein could not be determined as a result of the attacks made during either the Iran-Iraq or Gulf wars because the Iraqis regularly moved the missile launch sites during this phase of their attack.[262]

The Al-Hijarah and Iraq's Missile Developments
After the Iran-Iraq War

After the August, 1988 cease-fire, Iraq went on to develop more advanced missiles. On April 25, 1988, Iraq tested a longer range missile which was initially called the Al-Abbas but was later renamed the Al-Hijarah, or Stones, after the stones used by the Palestinian children and teenagers in the *intifada*. This new missile reached a target area about 750 kilometers from the launch site.

The Al-Hijarah underwent further development during 1988 and 1989 and matured into a system with a range of 700–900 kilometers, a 100–300 kilogram payload, and a flight time of 540 seconds, and it seems to have an operational CEP at a maximum range of 2,500–3,000 meters.[263] This maximum range was not tested during the Gulf War, and some experts suggest the missile's range may be well below 800 kilometers and the payload below 200 kilograms. The Al-Hijarah's CEP seems to have been around 3,000 meters.[264] The Al-Hijarah missile was a still further modification of the Scud with additional fuel capacity rather than an original design. This accounts for the fact that it proved to be unstable during the Gulf War, often breaking up upon reentry.

Iraq also quietly tested and deployed chemical warheads for both its regular and longer range Scuds.[265] The timing of Iraq's chemical warhead tests is uncertain, but UN inspection efforts later showed that Iraq had binary chemical warheads for all three of its Scud variants at the time of the Gulf War.[266] It is doubtful that these warheads were particularly reliable or effective, but they could still have been used as terror weapons.

These developments were possible because Iraq invested up to $3 billion on missile and other advanced weapons facilities between 1980 and 1990. The agency managing this massive missile research and development establishment seems to have been the State Organization for Technical Industries—Saad General Establishment, although some sources report it was managed by the office of Lt. Gen. Amer Hammoudi al-Saadi, the first deputy minister of industry and military industrialization and head of Iraq's Military Production Authority. Some sources refer to this as Project 395, but so many designations have been applied to various Iraqi facilities and activities that there is no way to be sure of the program's title.[267]

The details of the various programs under the Military Production Authority are also far from clear, but one key missile development facility, with tunnels and rocket motor test ramps, was located at Al Kindi near Mosul in northern Iraq and nicknamed Saad 16. Iraq also built a chemical and fuel facility called DO-1, or Project 96, at Al-Hillah, about 17 kilometers south of Baghdad, and an engineering workshop and Scud assembly plant called DO-2, or Project 124, near Falluja.[268] The scale of Iraq's efforts at Al-Hillah is evident from an explosion at the Al-Hillah missile facility on August 17,

1989, which killed up to 700 people but did not produce a prolonged halt in work at the site.[269]

There was also a major space research center at Al-Anbar in the desert near Karbala.[270] There was a rocket test range called DO-3 near Karbala, and several experts maintain that Iraq had at least three to four additional major fuel production, missile production, and testing facilities.[271] These included two facilities west of Rutbah, one near Mosul, and one near Mahmudiya.[272]

These facilities did far more than work on modified versions of the Scud. Iraq established research links with Argentina and Egypt and joined them in a project known as Badar 2000. This project was supposed to turn a large Argentine weather rocket called the Condor, which Argentina had developed in the late 1970s, into a two stage, solid fuel long range missile. While Egypt and Argentina seem to have canceled their work on the Condor project after considerable pressure from the U.S., Iraq obtained a great deal of technology from Argentina and the various European firms as a result of the project.[273]

Iraq continued the Condor project in Iraq, where it was managed largely by Iraqis but with a wide range of foreign experts and some technical workers hired in Pakistan. Despite the rivalry between Argentina and Brazil, Iraq also hired a twenty-three man missile technology development team from Brazil. This team was led by retired Maj. Brig. Hugo de Olivera Piva, the ex-director of Brazil's Aerospace Technology Center. Piva headed the effort to convert Brazil's Sonda IV space rocket into a missile large enough to carry a nuclear warhead.[274]

Iraq bought still further aid from the PRC and Europe. The details of Iraqi relations with the PRC are unclear, but they seem to have involved extensive cooperation in further modification of the Scud and aid in completing a Scud production facility. Some of the key Europeans involved included former MBB employees, a German construction firm called Zublin, a Swiss firm called Consen, and Austrian firms such as Consultico, Feneberg GmbH, and the Austrian subsidiaries of the British firms BBC Brown Boveri and Bacon.

Consen, a consortium staffed by former MBB employees, was particularly important. According to various reports, it procured technology for Iraq's Technical Corps for Special Projects between 1987 and 1989 and acted as a prime contractor for both Iraq's Saad 16 facility and Project 395—which some reports indicate included the Project 73 missile workshops near Falluja, the Project 1157 missile test area near Karbala, and the Project 96 rocket propellant production facility near Mahmudiya.[275] Consen acted as the prime contractor for more than $400 million worth of projects under the direction of the Technical Corps for Special Projects and State Organization for Technical Industries. Consen was closed down in early 1989 but was replaced by a Swiss firm called Vufvaltun und Financierung AG.[276]

The Technical Corps for Special Projects, yet another front for Iraqi proliferation efforts, was headed by Gen. Hussein Kamil. According to some reports, it was able to purchase missile related technology from twenty-two different European and U.S. companies. Iraq has helped finance these various efforts to buy missile technology in the West—as well as other military technology and technology for weapons of mass destruction—by using the Atlanta branch of Italy's Banca Nazional del Lavoro to launder some 2,500 letters of credit worth nearly $3 billion.[277]

Throughout the period between the cease-fire in the Iran-Iraq War and the Gulf War, Iraq continued to develop its missile research facilities at its Saad 16 research complex south of Baghdad (where some reports indicate it carried out much of its work on the Condor II) and at Al-Anbar, 80 kilometers west of Baghdad.[278] It explored further cooperation in missile design with both Brazilian and French aerospace officials, and some French aerospace officials seem to have visited secret Iraqi missile research facilities. Another firm reported to have become involved in the Iraqi missile research effort is Matrix-Churchill of the UK. Iraq also established new cover companies to manage this technology transfer effort, including Techcorp, the Technology and Development Corporation, and NASR State Enterprise for Mechanical Industries.[279]

This vast network of facilities and foreign supply and advisory efforts began to pay off about nine months before the Gulf War. On December 5, 1989, Iraq tested a new long range booster, which reached a range close to 1,500 nautical miles.[280] This three stage system was called the Al-Abid, and it seems to have been a 48 ton missile that used a cluster of five Scud boosters in its primary stage. The other two stages may not have been activated during the test. Nevertheless, the test showed Iraq would eventually be capable of launching a satellite into orbit or firing much longer range missiles. Reports had previously surfaced that Iraq's scientific research center and Brazil's space agency had been discussing Brazilian supply of a surveillance satellite. Such a satellite could have critical value in providing Iraq with the long range targeting data it needs and the ability to improve its operational accuracy by allowing it to locate the precise point its missiles actually hit.[281]

On December 14, 1989—virtually at the same time the Western members of the Missile Technology Control Regime (MTCR) were holding a meeting in London—Iraq announced it had developed a new missile called the Tamuz 1, and claimed it had tested the missile twice and that the launches had reached ranges of up to 1,500 kilometers.[282] The Tamuz was probably only on the drawing board rather than a real system. It seems to have been designed as a three stage, liquid fueled, 48 ton missile similar to the Al-Abid booster system—with five Al-Abbas boosters in the first stage, one in the second stage, and a third stage with a 750 kilogram payload.[283]

Some experts believed the Tamuz could have a range of roughly 2,000 kilometers once it was deployed with its completed guidance package, but others suggested a range of 1,250 kilometers was more likely once a military payload was added. Such a missile would be very complex, involve a great deal of launch preparation and launch time, and require large fixed facilities. It would, however, be the first Iraqi missile with the range payload to deliver a large nuclear weapon, or large chemical or biological weapons payload, against any target in Israel and Iran from launch sites deep in Iraq.

While any such performance estimates are highly controversial, one expert gave a comparison of the performance characteristics of Iraq's existing missiles and the Tamuz, as shown in Table 6.10.[284]

The second new missile seemed to be a solid fuel missile with roughly the same or somewhat shorter range. Iraq did not describe the details of this system, but it seemed to be a distinct new missile that was being developed in addition to the work on the Condor project. Ranges of 1,000 to 2,000 kilometers have been claimed for these missiles.[285] It became clear from UN inspections after the Gulf War that Iraq had been actively working on nuclear warhead designs for its missiles.[286]

Iraq likewise improved its missile deployment capabilities. It had both Soviet-made transporter-erector-launchers for its regular and improved Scuds and large numbers of Iraqi-made launchers. It also set up pre-surveyed sites and some sites with fixed launchers. In February, 1990, U.S. intelligence detected Iraqi construction of five fixed missile launcher complexes in western Iraq. These complexes included 28 operational launchers, and even the 600 kilometer range Al-Hussein could reach the Israeli cities of Tel Aviv and Haifa and Israel's nuclear facility in Dimona from these launchers. They also could reach targets throughout Syria and in much of Turkey.

Iraq's "Super Guns"

Finally, Iraq was experimenting with the use of advanced "gun" systems to launch its missiles at the time the Gulf War began, although these systems were still in the early developmental stage. This Iraqi effort became public on April 10, 1990, when British customs officials at Teeside seized eight steel tubes bound for Iraq. These tubes were part of a giant "cannon" that could hurl projectiles hundreds of miles. They also were part of a series of shipments. Britain later disclosed that forty-four such tubes had already been

TABLE 6.10 Comparative Performance of Iraqi Surface-to-Surface Missile Systems

	Normal Scud B	Al-Hussein	Al-Hijarah	Tamuz
Date first appeared		August 3, 1987	March 18, 1988	December 7, 1989
Number of stages	1	1	2	3
Diameter	0.884 m	0.884 m	0.884 m	
Length	11.7 m	12.55 m	13 m	
Weight	6,300 kg	7,340 kg	34,500 kg	
Range	280 km	600 km	750 km	1,200–1,500 km
Chemical warhead	985 kg total	190 kg total	220 kg	
	555 kg agent	107 kg agent		
CEP	900 m	3,000 m	3,000 m	
Flight time	6.0–6.5 min	8.0–9.0 min	10–12 min	
Flight Mach	4.0	4.0	4.0	
Fuse	variable proximity	variable proximity	variable proximity	

SOURCES: Department of Defense, *Conduct of the Persian Gulf War: Final Report*, Washington, Department of Defense, April, 1992, pp. 16–18; working paper by Dick Palwoski.

sent to Iraq, and that devices that could serve as the breach for such a "gun" had been intercepted in Turkey.[287]

UN inspection teams later found that Iraq already had a 356mm meter gun for trial purposes and that the tubes were to been used in two 1,000mm prototype guns. The 356mm experimental gun had been operational for several years, tested seven times, and then had evidently not been used for about a year before the Gulf War. It was built into the slope of a mountain at Jabal Hamrayn, about 200 kilometers north of Baghdad. The British firm of Walter Sommers had supplied the steel tubing for the 356mm gun during mid-1988 through early 1989. It was hardly a highly lethal long range weapon. It fired a projectile of 75 kilograms (165 pounds) but carried only 15 kilograms (30 pounds) of high explosive. Its total range was about 150–180 kilometers (93–120 miles), and Israel was some 825 kilometers (550 miles) away.[288]

Neither of the 1,000mm guns was assembled, and only one had sufficient components to indicate it would be operational in the near future. The parts for this gun were stored at Iskabdariyah. According to some reports, it was supposed to be about 131 feet (40 meters) long, with a 39" breech, and weigh up to 402 tons.[289] The steel tubes, what seems to have been a recoil mechanism, and a frame for swinging the tube up to 60 meters, were all to be made by Walter Sommers and Sheffield Forgemasters in the UK.[290] Iraq also ordered large amounts of propellants to be used for the gun from a firm in Belgium. This came to light when the British firm Astra bought the Belgian company of PRB and found the order on its books.[291]

These "super guns" had been designed by Gerald Bull, a Canadian ballistics expert who was murdered outside his home in Brussels on March 22, 1990. Several explanations have been advanced regarding the purpose of Bull's 1,000mm super guns, ranging from a satellite launcher to a system designed to attack Iran and Israel at long distances. Bull's primary interest was in space, and he headed a firm called Space Research Corporation headquartered in Brussels.[292] While experts disagreed over the exact technology and performance of the weapon, most estimated that it was an extension of work that Bull had done earlier for the U.S. and Canada in what was called Project Harp.[293]

Data released by the UN inspection teams indicated that each gun was to be in 26 sections and about 160 meters long (the length of 1.5 football fields). It was to fire a 1,000 kilogram (2,200 pound) projectile with 408 kilograms (898 pounds) of high explosive or payload.[294] Some experts estimate that it would have had a range of up to 1,000 miles, others that it was designed to put payloads of 300 to 500 pounds into orbit.[295]

According to some sources, the 1,000mm gun was designed to fire fin stabilized rockets and possibly to employ traveling charge technology. This technology burns solid fuel at the base of a rocket as the rocket moves up the barrel. The rocket gases prevent a vacuum from forming at the base of the projectile and slowing it down. The barrel is flanged rather than rifled, and a tight seal between the projectile and the barrel is far less critical than in a normal artillery projectile. The rocket may also use a second motor to provide additional power after the projectile leaves the barrel.[296]

Iraq's Missile Activity During the Gulf War

While there is still no way to tell exactly how many missiles Iraq had in inventory at the beginning of the Gulf War, it almost certainly had over 1,000 Scuds of all types, and at least several hundred extended range Al-Hussein and Al-Abbas missiles. Although it is difficult to determine the precise point at which Iraq decided to go to war, it also expanded its missile deployments to cover its western as well as its eastern borders.

In March, 1990, Iraq deployed from twelve to eighteen fixed Al-Abbas missile launchers at three fixed sites in southern, western, and northern Iraq. The northern and southern sites gave Iraq the ability to strike deeper into Iran, but the western and southern sites gave Iraq the ability to strike at other targets and provided coverage of targets in Israel, Syria, and Turkey.[297] The site nearest to Israel was near the H-2 airfield in western Iraq, on the road between Iraq and Jordan, and had six launchers oriented towards targets in Israel or Syria. In addition, Iraq had nine prepared launch sites for Scud missiles with sixty-two launch positions, although several normally did not have launchers deployed.[298]

In April, 1990 information surfaced that Iraq was setting up a new missile test range in Mauritania in West Africa that gave Iraq the ability to test missiles in excess of 1,000 miles—trials that were impossible in Iraq without crossing international borders. Finally, in July, 1990 it became apparent that Iraq had quietly sought to buy titanium furnaces from the U.S. These furnaces can be used to manufacture a number of lightweight titanium missile parts, including advanced nose cone designs for warheads.[299]

The Condor, Tamuz, and any other new missiles were still in the development stage when the Gulf War took place. However, on October 9, 1990, Saddam Hussein announced that Iraq had developed yet another new missile that could hit Israel. The timing of this announcement was suspicious. It came in the midst of a growing confrontation between Iraq and the nations supporting the UN blockade and military coalition that came as a reaction to Iraq's invasion of Kuwait. It also came the day after a major clash between Israelis and Palestinians at the Temple Mount in Jerusalem that Saddam Hussein was trying to exploit to weaken Arab support for the UN.[300]

In any case, Iraq's efforts to use its existing missiles were serious enough. In some ways, Iraq's fixed Scud sites became more "deception targets" than actual launch sites.[301] Between its invasion of Kuwait in August, 1990 and the start of the Gulf War, Iraq created a wide range of presurveyed and fixed missile sites to try to counter the buildup of forces supporting the UN. While many experts believed that Iraq still only had 36 Scud B launchers at the time the war began, they ignored the new transporter-erector-launcher called the Al-Walid that Iraq exhibited at the Baghdad International Arms Exhibition in 1989. Iraq modified over 100 additional vehicles to act as TELs and continued to build fixed launch sites until the Gulf War started.[302]

Iraq also sharply reduced its dependence on fixed sites and sites that allied intelligence had detected before the actual fighting in the Gulf War began. Iraq presurveyed and set up a large number of sites in the launch areas that could be used to fire on Israel and Saudi Arabia in the months before combat began. This allowed it to scatter its missile units over a wide territory and to hide many with camouflage, in civil buildings, or in other places of concealment. Its new TELs and support vehicles were difficult to distinguish from commercial vehicles without extensive reconnaissance, and they usually moved at night. Iraq also deployed its missiles and equipment shortly before a firing to minimize their vulnerability by making targeting far more difficult.

The range of equipment Iraq deployed with its missile units during the Gulf War is uncertain. Iraq is known to have used the Soviet End Tray meteorological radar associated with the FROG-7 and Scud B in some of its missile deployments and the UAZ-452T support vehicles. It is not known how effective any of this support equipment was at the ranges of the Al-Hussein and Al-Hijarah. Iraq did, however, develop relatively simple truck mounted launchers to supplement its sophisticated and expensive Soviet TELs. This gave it far more missile launchers than the UN coalition estimated at the start of the Gulf War and made wartime targeting and enforcement of the postwar cease-fire extremely difficult.[303]

Iraq may have had as many as 225 of these cheaper launchers by the time the Gulf War took place, in addition to the 36 Soviet-style TELs.[304] It took advantage of these launchers throughout the course of the Gulf War, and its surface-to-surface missile campaign was perhaps its only "success" of the war. The total pattern of launches is shown in Table 6.11. The first Scud strike came late in the afternoon of January 17, in the form of two Scuds aimed at Israel. The first strike on Saudi Arabia took place on January 18. These systems might have caused large scale panic if it had not been for the Patriot air defense system. A Patriot hit the second round of Scuds aimed at Dhahran at 17,000 feet, and the U.S. provided aid to Israel in readying its Patriot missile systems, rushing 32 missiles to Israel in 17 hours.

The Patriot system, however, was only a point defense anti-tactical ballistic missile system and could not provide anything approaching a leak proof defense system. It also could not prevent missile debris and warheads from falling on populated areas. As a result, the UN coalition was forced into a massive Scud hunt that consumed some 2,493 sorties. The coalition had to

TABLE 6.11 Iraqi Surface-to-Surface Missile Launches During the Gulf War

Result Total	Target			
	Israel	Saudi Arabia	Bahrain	
Total fired	40	48	3	91
Missed country	1	3	2	6
Missed target area	15	11	1	27
Intercepted by Patriot	34	11	0	45
Hit target	0	13	0	13
Debris hit	7	7	0	14

Source: Office of the Secretary of Defense, Public Affairs, March, 1991.

create two "Scud boxes" to cover the areas launching missiles against Israel and Saudi Arabia. Both the U.S. and UK deployed special operations forces to help find the missiles, and the U.S. used F-15Es, with Lantirn directed by JSTARS to target and kill missiles, and F-16C/Ds and A-10s to patrol roads and key launch areas. It also used B-52s and F-117As to hit storage and production facilities.

This effort never succeeded in halting the Iraqi Scud launches, although it certainly affected launch rates, accuracy, and reliability. With over 1,000 missiles—and some estimates go up to 2,000—there was no way to locate and destroy all the missiles. The Iraqis were able to hide Scud TELs in towns and beneath underpasses. They also adopted "scoot and shoot" tactics that made it very difficult to detect and kill missiles when they were ready to launch. As a result, Iraq was able to launch its peak firing rate of 10 missiles as late as the tenth day of the war and launched its last missiles on February 25. It also scored its only major strike against U.S. forces when a chance hit near Dhahran killed 28 U.S. soldiers and wounded 97 others. The U.S. was still striking at Iraqi Scud forces when the war ended on February 27.[305]

Iraq did not use missiles with chemical weapons during the Gulf War, and the damage done by its missile strikes was relatively limited—although one missile did kill a large number of U.S. combat troops and the attack on Israel damaged several urban areas. It is unclear whether this failure to use chemical weapons came about because of Iraq's fear of retaliation or because Iraq's Al-Hussein and Al-Hijarah missiles lacked the range payload and reliability to carry more than a token chemical warhead.

UN inspectors did confirm that Iraq had chemical warheads for its missiles, although the inspectors also concluded that the warheads were very crude. Soviet technicians who inspected the Iraqi missiles considered much of the basic missile work to be crude as well, and that explained the breakup of many Iraqi modified Scuds during their approach towards targets in Israel. Inspectors found, too, that the chemical warheads were imbalanced and would have made these problems far worse—potentially making the warheads burn up or depriving them of much of their effectiveness.[306]

Iraq's Missile Activity After the Gulf War

There is no way to tell how much of Iraq's missile activity survived the Gulf War, and there are radically different estimates of how much of its equipment it dispersed before the UN coalition attacks or recovered and hid after the war. Iraq initially declared that it had 52 ballistic missiles, 38 launchers, 30 chemical filled warheads, and 23 conventionally armed warheads at five sites. It eventually admitted that it had 9 more missiles at one of the sites.[307]

According to the ongoing work of the UN, at least 17 facilities have been identified since the war as being areas where the Iraqi government conducted research, production, testing, and repair of ballistic missiles, launchers, and rocket fuel.[308] By February, 1992, the UN had destroyed all the stocks that Iraq had declared and a substantial amount of additional equipment. The items destroyed included 62 missiles, 11 missile decoys, dozens of fixed and mobile launchers, 8 missile transporters, and 146 missile storage units.[309] The UN also found the 30 chemical warheads for Iraq's Scud missiles stored in the Dujael area, some 18 miles away from the position Iraq had declared. Sixteen used a unitary nerve gas warhead and 14 were binary.[310]

It was clear, however, that Iraq might have concealed a large number of missiles and Iraqi-made launchers, as well as much of the manufacturing equipment, parts, and test equipment that it had purchased before the war. Some estimates indicated that Iraq had imported a total of 800 Scuds to launch or modify before the war, and that well over 100 missiles might still be left. In fact, in testimony before Congress in January, 1992, the director of the CIA estimated that the total might be "hundreds."[311] While there is no way to know what number is correct, Iraq had established underground missile storage sites before the war and seemed to be building new sites after the cease-fire. Some Iraqi stocks of concealed missiles seem likely.[312] Further, Iraq continued to defy UN orders to destroy the equipment the UN did discover, and in February began to deploy the special fuel trucks used to launch Scud missiles in areas outside Baghdad.[313]

Iraqi Chemical Weapons Programs

Iraq is a signatory to the Geneva Protocols of 1925 prohibiting the use of poison gas and the Biological Warfare Convention of 1972 banning the development, production, and deployment or stockpiling of biological weapons. This did not, however, prevent it from producing and using chemical weapons in the Iran-Iraq War. Chemical weapons offered Iraq a highly lethal form of warfare that was well within its technical and manufacturing capability.

A great deal of information has become public since the Gulf War, in spite of the covert nature of Iraq's efforts, but there is no way to be certain of what Iraq has successfully been able to conceal. The uncertainties regarding Iraq's acquisition of chemical weapons are particularly striking during the period before the mid-1970s. Iraq seems to have been actively interested in chemical weapons since the 1960s, but it is impossible to date the point at which it began to seek such weapons or establish technical capabilities to produce and use them. According to some U.S. experts, Iraq first sought chemical weapons from Egypt and the USSR following Egypt's use of chemical weapons in the Yemens. Some Israeli experts believe that Iraq first acquired small amounts of chemical weapons from the USSR in the 1970s, and that Iraq may have had assistance from Egypt in developing production and storage techniques in the period before the Camp David accords.[314] Iraqi forces do seem to have had limited chemical warfare training based on Soviet doctrine by the early 1970s and may well have had some training support from Soviet and Egyptian officers.[315]

It seems likely that Iraq first decided to create laboratory scale facilities to produce chemical weapons around the time of the October War in 1973. This was a period when there were numerous reports that Egyptian and Israeli forces were equipped with chemical weapons, and Iraq faced a growing threat from the military buildup in Iran and from its Kurdish rebels.[316] There also are reports that Iraq may have used poison gas shells or bombs against its Kurdish rebels during its campaigns of 1973–1975.[317] These reports cannot be confirmed, but many Western experts agree that Iraq weaponized mustard gas for use by mortars and artillery by the late 1970s and had mustard gas shells for at least 120mm mortars and 130mm artillery.[318]

Iraq initially turned to U.S. and British firms for help in setting up insecticide and fertilizer plants. When this failed, Iraq turned to firms from West Germany, Switzerland, France, the Netherlands, Belgium, and Italy, and obtained most of the components it needed.[319] Iraq obtained a special "pesticide" plant and three other small pilot facilities from Pilot Plant, a unit of Karl Kolb—a major West German laboratory equipment supplier. The Kolb-supplied plant had some of the special equipment necessary to make sarin nerve gas but not special pumps.[320] Iraq also purchased technical assistance from a West German firm called Fritz Werner.[321] It received heavy duty pumps and chemicals from Water Engineering Trading GmbH of Hamburg, which sold some $11 million worth of equipment and tons of chemicals, including trichloride, a nerve gas precursor; Iraq also obtained equipment from Quast, which provided reactor vessels, centrifuges, and piping line with Hastalloy.[322]

It is unclear how successful Iraq's efforts were when the Iran-Iraq War began. Iraq was probably producing some mustard gas at Samara and was constructing two small pilot plants with a planned capacity of around 30–50 tons per year to produce nerve gas at Samara.[323] These two plants were designed to produce only small amounts of nerve agents and had to use specialized feedstocks that were difficult to come by. Iraq may, however, have had enough nonlethal CS gas or some form of blister agents to have used them in the attack on Susangerd in November, 1980; attacks on Dezful and other areas in mid-1981; in defending against the Iranian attacks on Dezful and Sush in late March, 1982; and in the battles to defend Basra and Mandali in the fall and winter of 1982. Iraq may also have used mustard gas during some of these battles.[324]

By 1983 Iraqi production of mustard gas was sufficient for Iraq to begin to deliver small amounts of gas with artillery, fighters, and Mi-8 helicopters. It is unclear exactly when Iraq developed bombs using chemical agents, but Iraq seems to have used 250 kilogram bombs it bought from Spain, dropped by Fitter aircraft. The gas in these bombs was exceptionally pure, and this indicates that Iraq was still producing batches under laboratory conditions rather than mass producing mustard gas in tons. This mustard gas seems to have been produced at the Iraqi chemical weapons facility at Samara.[325]

Mustard gas offered Iraq significant military advantages—advantages which apply to any future uses of this gas. Mustard gas is a blistering agent which is 10 to 100 times less lethal than the simpler nerve agents in terms of direct exposure and slow to act on those who are exposed. Lethality, however, is not the only issue in measuring the effectiveness of chemical weapons. Mustard gas is easier to produce, handle, and deliver. It attacks the lungs, eyes, and skin, and gas masks alone are not sufficient protection.

Mustard gas can also be more effective than many nerve gases for several important tactical purposes, particularly against infantry or exposed humans in other target areas. It persists for several days to several weeks, and its wounds are slow to heal. Limited exposures to mustard gas can blind or blister for periods of 4 to 6 weeks. Casualties consume large amounts of medical services and support. These properties of mustard gas gave it considerable effectiveness against Iranian infantry, which often spent considerable time in static exposed locations and had relatively poor medical facilities.

In order to obtain the massive amounts of mustard gas it needed for larger scale operations, Iraq made major new efforts to acquire technology and feedstock overseas. For example, to obtain 500 metric tons of a chemical called thiodiglycol,[326] the Iraqi State Ministry of Pesticide Production turned to a unit of Phillips Petroleum Company in Tessenderloo, Belgium.[327]

Other firms that gave Iraq more direct support in building its first mustard gas production facility seem to have included Montedison of Italy, Melchemie of the Netherlands, and Atomchem of France, with engineering support from Technipetrol of Italy. These and other firms are reported to have helped Iraq build a mustard gas plant at Akashat, about 16 kilometers from Rutbah and 370 kilometers from Baghdad.[328]

These problems in obtaining feedstocks abroad led Iraq to increase its efforts to build the facilities it needed to manufacture ethylene oxide and other chemicals to make thiodiglycol and produce mustard gas and to eliminate its dependence on outside sources. Iraq had already begun to build up ethylene production facilities in the late 1970s. These were located at Petrochemical Complex No. 1 near Basra. Basra, however, was within range of Iranian artillery fire at the start of the war and soon came under fire again in the early 1980s. As a result, the Basra facility may not have begun large scale production until 1987 or 1988. This may explain why Iraq began construction of a new Petrochemical Complex No. 2 ethylene plant near Musayyib in 1988, with a target date of 1991 for actual operations.[329]

While the resulting history of Iraq's ethylene production is uncertain, the Basra plant was designed with a capacity to produce 410,000 tons of ethylene products a year and the Musayyib facility to produce 420,000 tons of ethylene and 67,000 tons of ethylene oxide.[330] Iraq completed construction of the special refinery and other facilities necessary to make thiodiglycol. As a result, Iraq's industrial complex at Falluja, northwest of Baghdad, seems to have been able to make thiodiglycol, and possibly some precursors for nerve gas, before the August, 1988 cease-fire.[331]

Iraq also acquired the equipment and feedstock to make nerve gas and set up a precursor plant at Habbiniyah.[332] Iraq's initial goal was to produce nonpersistent nerve gas, consisting of G-agents like tabun (GA) and sarin (GB). These agents are extremely lethal and act almost instantly when the skin, eyes, and wet tissues of their victims are exposed. Nerve gases are difficult to detect, and troops require excellent protection and an antidote in order to prevent high casualties.

The G-agents persist for only a few minutes to a few days and allow an attacker relatively rapid tactical movement into exposed areas. In contrast, persistent agents may remain lethal for several days to several weeks. Friendly troops can operate in exposed areas only if they have full protection and can occupy the area for only a limited amount of time. This is why persistent agents are much better suited to fixed targets like air bases and logistic centers or in defensive operations where they can be used against the rear areas of the enemy with only limited risk to friendly troops.[333]

U.S. customs stopped another State Ministry of Pesticide Production order for 74 barrels of potassium fluoride, another precursor of sarin nerve gas, in February, 1984. The order was placed by Al-Haddad Enterprises, owned by Sahib al-Haddad, a naturalized Iraqi citizen. The shipment was not then illegal because the chemical was not yet controlled, and there is no clear way of determining how many other shipments occurred in the U.S. or other countries. However, at least one Dutch firm—Melchemie Holland—has since been convicted of export violations for selling phosphorous oxychloride, another precursor of nerve gas. Iraqi agents also bought large amounts of equipment from a West German firm in Dreireich that it seems to have claimed would be used to make organophosphate fertilizer but which could help in the manufacture of nerve gas.[334]

A major new Iraqi research center for chemical weapons was set up at Salman Pak, 56 kilometers south of Baghdad. This facility has since expanded for work on biological and other advanced weapons. According to some reports, it has experimented with cyanide, hydrogen cyanide, cyanogen chloride, and Lewisite gases as well as the nerve, mustard, and CS gases that Iraq came to use extensively in the Iran-Iraq War.[335]

Iraq created a major production center for mustard gas and tabun and sarin nerve agents at Samara. The Samara complex occupied 26 square kilometers in an area about 100 kilometers north of Baghdad and was constructed with numerous heavily sheltered facilities defended by troops and SA-2 missiles. The complex became the largest single Iraqi production facility for mustard gas. Production seems to have begun in 1983 and climbed steadily to the point where Iraq could produce large quantities of mustard gas in 1985. The initial output of mustard gas seems to have been about 60 tons per year, and Iraq was able to use the gas to fill bombs, artillery shells, and rockets—including 250 kilogram bombs based on Spanish designs. These Iraqi weapons at first were filled with mustard gas so pure that it seems to have been produced in laboratory scale facilities, but later batches contained the impurities associated with large scale production.[336]

West German firms and technicians helped Iraq to set up these pilot plants at Samara, which eventually expanded to a total production capacity of 48 tons per year. West German equipment for the nerve gas plants at Samara—and evidently for the nerve gas at other plants—as well as large amounts of chemicals were purchased through firms in West Germany, Austria, and Italy. Production of large quantities of tabun began in 1984, and production of sarin began in 1985 or 1986. Samara did not reach full capacity production of either mustard or nerve gases, however, until the late 1980s.[337] The Samara complex also housed one of the "insecticide plants" obtained earlier from the West, and this complex now serves as the nucleus for new facilities to produce large amounts of the feedstock to manufacture nerve gas without depending on imports of specialized chemicals. Iraq also may have established another plant near Karbala to produce nerve gas. According to some reports, this plant may be the facility developing nerve gas warheads for Iraq's long range missiles.[338]

Further, Iraq began a major effort to produce the precursor chemicals or feedstocks necessary to manufacture nerve gas without dependence on outside sources. Iraq was able to take advantage of its phosphate mines at Akashat and was already developing a phosphate industry centered at Akashat and Al Qaim. The powdered detergent and fertilizer plants it had set up to use its phosphate ore could be adapted to make some of the necessary feedstocks. As a result, Iraq expanded its facility at Rutbah, just south of Akashat. This facility now seems to produce nerve agents using acids and other chemical components, and it may have become the Iraqi facility which is most free of dependence on chemical imports of any kind. Iraq also established a complex called Project 9320 in the area which has three factories to produce secondary chemicals to aid in the manufacture of nerve gas. This complex was built largely by West German firms and technicians and has large underground storage tanks. Additional facilities seem to be under construction to transform basic phosphorous into precursor chemicals for the manufacture of nerve gas.[339]

Iraq set up a gas warfare complex at Falluja. Some reports credit the Falluja facility with having three plants capable of producing 1,000 tons per month of sarin and large amounts of persistent VX nerve gas by the late 1980s.[340] V-agents like VX retain their lethal effect for periods of several days to several weeks. They are slightly slower to kill than G-agents, but they kill far more quickly than mustard gas.[341] These reports also indicate that Falluja is the main center of Iraqi loading of artillery shells and rockets with nerve gas.[342] West German and Austrian firms gave Iraq the capabilities it needed to experiment with hydrogen cyanide, cyanogen chloride, and Lewisite as well.[343]

As UN inspectors found after the Gulf War, Iraq set up a plant to arm chemical weapons at Al-Muthana. This seems to have been the only place that Iraq actually armed rockets, shells, bombs, and warheads with chemical agents. When UN inspectors examined the facility after the war, it still had 225 tons of nerve agent and 280 tons of mustard gas.[344]

Iraq expanded from production levels of about 10 tons a month of all types of gases by late 1985 to a capacity of over 50 tons per month by late 1986.[345] In late 1987 Iraq could produce over 60 tons of mustard gas a month and 4 tons each of tabun and sarin.[346] In early 1988 Iraq could produce over 70 tons of mustard gas a month and 6 tons each of tabun and sarin.[347] It may have had the technical capability to produce soman, a choking agent like phosgene, blood agents like hydrogen cyanide and cyanogen cyanide, vesicants like Lewisite, and agents like Adamsite and chloropicrin.[348]

These production efforts expanded steadily from the August, 1988 cease-fire in the Iran-Iraq War to the beginning of the Gulf War. Iraq continued to import additional precursors from nations like the United Kingdom and to produce large amounts of mustard and nerve gas weapons until its operations were halted by coalition bombing.[349] It had at least ten major storage bunkers for chemical weapons scattered throughout Iraq when the bombing began. Iraq was able to produce up to 3,500 tons of mustard gas and 2,000 tons of sarin and tabun a year by 1990, or more than 20 times the amount it could produce in 1985. It had a major plant producing tabun near Samara, and three facilities producing sarin near Falluja.[350]

It was also producing persistent agents VX and VR-55, and its plant at Falluja was being expanded to a capacity of 2,000 tons per month. This production would have given Iraq enough chemical agents to arm 250,000–500,000 tube and rocket artillery rounds each year, as well as smaller numbers of bombs.[351]

Iraq made it clear during early 1990 that it had binary chemical weapons—a technology it seems to have acquired in 1984 or 1985 and used in at least crude form in most of the weapons it deployed during the latter half of the Iran-Iraq War. Further, reports surfaced that Iraq might also be able to manufacture blood agents like cyanide and "dusty" mustard gas.[352] Blood agents rapidly defeat most military gas masks. "Dusty" mustard gas is a powder form which is very persistent and can coat particles only several microns in size, so small that they may be able to penetrate protective clothing and filters.

Iraq also experimented with "double channel" or "cocktail" chemical weapons that mix several chemical agents together to provide different kinds of lethality and/or defeat different forms of protection. Some sources indicate that Iraq used "cocktails" of cyanogen with mustard gas and tabun in Kurdistan. Saddam Hussein stated on April 2, 1990, that Iraq had had "double-combined chemical" weapons since the last year of the war.[353] Iraq does, however, seem to have had some significant problems in keeping its agents pure and in developing corrosion proof materials. The UN inspection teams charged with destroying Iraq's chemical weapons after the war found that nearly 25% of them leaked, although it was often impossible to distinguish among problems with the chemical agents, problems with the weapons design, and problems because of wartime damage or rapid postwar movement and inadequate storage.[354]

By the time the Gulf War began, Iraqi doctrine called for the regular training of all combined arms elements in chemical warfare. Iraqi field forces were equipped with numerous dual capable delivery systems and sophisticated chemical protection, reconnaissance, and decontamination gear. Delivery systems included rifle grenades, 81mm mortars; 152mm, 130mm, and 122mm artillery rounds; bombs; bomblets; 90mm air-to-ground rockets; 216 kilogram FROG and 555 kilogram Scud warheads; and possibly land mines and cruise missiles.[355]

UN inspections after the war determined that most of the chemical rounds for these weapons were not binary. They used a tube or canister of a single chemical agent in a plastic tube surrounded by a burster explosive like

TNT. This weapons design made it difficult to store the rounds since Iraq's chemical agents were often impure or corrosive and the quality control of many rounds was poor. It helps to explain both the leaks found in Iraqi rounds after the war and reports that Iraqi rounds armed in the summer of 1990 had begun to leak by the time the war began.[356]

While regular army and air force units fired the weapons that actually delivered the chemical, special chemical troops integrated throughout all of the branches of the Iraqi armed forces were responsible for the care, buildup, and delivery of chemical weapons. They had a status approaching that of a separate combat arm and included units and sub-units responsible for chemical defense, radiation and chemical reconnaissance, the operation of smoke and flame generators, the identification of chemical targets and meteorological analysis, and decontamination. Each corps had a chemical battalion, each independent brigade or division had a chemical company, regiments had chemical platoons, and chemical sections were assigned to battalions or platoons with weapons capable of delivering chemical warheads. As many as 50% of Iraq's combat aircraft and artillery weapons could deliver chemical rounds.[357]

Once it invaded Kuwait, Iraq quickly resorted to threats to use chemical weapons in dealing with the Western and Arab reaction to its invasion of Kuwait and buildup on the Saudi border. It conspicuously loaded its aircraft with chemical weapons before removing the weapons and placing them in storage. It dispersed chemical weapons in a wide range of areas, and on August 20, 1990, Hussein gave a speech stating that foreign hostages would be dispersed to military and key civil locations throughout Iraq, including Iraq's major chemical weapons production facilities.

By November, 1990 Iraq had built up large dispersed and sheltered stocks of chemical weapons in its territory outside the Kuwaiti theater of operations. It deployed a wide range of delivery systems to its forces supporting the invasion of Kuwait, deployed protection and decontamination gear, and built decontamination trenches in the forward and rear areas. As has been noted earlier, however, Iraq never used chemical weapons during the Gulf War. This may have been the result of many factors: Iraqi fear of coalition or Israeli retaliation with nuclear or chemical weapons, the shattering impact of coalition bombing and its loss of effective command and control and distribution capability, or the rapid understanding that the coalition could expand its conventional strategic bombing campaign to devastating levels.

There is no question, however, that Iraq had ample stocks of chemical weapons and that it equipped its units with chemical protection and decontamination gear, and with the operational instructions for using chemical weapons.[358] Iraq's possible range of agents is shown in Table 6.12. Iraq initially declared to the UN that it had 355 tons of mustard gas and nerve agents, 650 tons of intermediate chemicals, 6,920 chemical filled rocket warheads, 1,376 aerial bombs, and 105 artillery shells, virtually all at Samara.[359] As of February, 1992 the UN had found at least 46,000 chemical weapons versus the 10,000 to 11,000 that Iraq had initially declared and 3,000 tons of raw materials for chemical weapons versus the 650 tons that Iraq had origi-

TABLE 6.12 Probable Iraqi Chemical Agents

Type of Agent	Delivery Method	Symptoms	Effects	Rate of Action
Confirmed				
Blistering: Mustard (possibly dusty mustard)	Missile, artillery, bomb, aerial spray, land mine	No early symptoms for mustard types; searing of eyes, stinging of skin	Blisters skin, destroys respiratory tract, causes temporary blindness	Minutes
Nerve: Sarin (GB), tabun (GB), VK/VX?	Missile, artillery, bomb, aerial spray, land mine	Difficulty breathing, drooling, nausea, vomiting, convulsions	Incapacitates or kills when delivered in high concentrations	Seconds
Suspected in at least limited amounts				
Blood: Cyanide	Missile, artillery, bomb	Convulsions and coma	Incapacitates or kills when delivered in high concentrations	Minutes
Possible at experimental level				
Choking: Phosgene	Missile, artillery, bomb	Coughing, choking, nausea, headache	Damages and floods lungs	Hours

Sources: James Blackwell, *Thunder in the Desert*, New York, Bantam, 1990, p. 35; Dick Palowski, *Changes in Threat Air Combat Doctrine and Force Structure*, 24th Edition, Fort Worth, General Dynamics DWIC-91, February, 1992, pp. II-336 to II-338; Department of Defense, *Conduct of the Persian Gulf War: Final Report*, Washington, Department of Defense, April, 1992, pp. 16–18.

nally claimed. UN and U.S. sources were estimating that Iraq might have 54,000 to 79,000 more rounds than it declared.[360]

The 46,000 rounds the UN was able to inspect and start destroying included 20,000 mortar rounds of nonlethal CS gas, plus 26,000 rounds filled with nerve agent or mustard gas. The lethal rounds included large numbers of 122mm and 155mm artillery shells, 250 kilogram and other bombs, and 30 Scud missile warheads. Iraq had ample time to disperse many of its chemical weapons, precursors, and production systems before the Gulf War began, and it continued to hide and disperse them after it signed a cease-fire.[361]

While UN inspectors discovered a great deal of Iraq's chemical weapons and production equipment, including some concealed in a milk plant near Mosul, most experts believed as of 1992 that Iraq retained significant stocks of weapons. Robert Gates, the director of CIA, testified to Congress in 1992 that much of Iraq's "hard to get production equipment" for chemical weapons had been "hidden" before the allied bombing attacks. He also estimated that "if UN sanctions are relaxed, we believe Iraq could produce modest quantities of chemical agents almost immediately, but it would take a year or more to recover the chemical weapons capability it previously enjoyed."[362]

Iraqi Biological Weapons

The history of Iraq's efforts to develop biological weapons is less clear than that of its efforts to develop chemical weapons. This illustrates a key problem in tracking the proliferation of weapons of mass destruction in the Middle East. Biological weapons are an effective and relatively cheap way of acquiring weapons of mass destruction. At the same time, efforts to develop such weapons can be extremely difficult to detect and actual production can be concealed far more easily than can the facilities to produce chemical and nuclear weapons.

There have been some highly controversial charges that Iraq has used mycotoxins against its Kurdish population since early in the Iran-Iraq War, but these charges have not been confirmed.[363] Most of the examples and symptoms cited in these charges can also be more easily explained because of the sanitary and health conditions affecting the population in the area. The use of mycotoxins, or "yellow rain," weapons cannot be ruled out, but reports that the Iraqi secret service used biological agents or toxins to poison the food in Kurdish refugee camps in mid-1989, producing 700 dead and 4,000 casualties, seem dubious.[364]

Virtually all Western experts agree, however, that Iraq began working on biological weapons in the 1970s and was producing biological weapons at four different facilities when the Gulf War began.[365] U.S. government sources have since listed anthrax and botulinum toxin as being among the weapons Iraq was producing.[366] While these are not exotic biological agents, botulinum toxin is about 3 million times more potent than a nerve agent like sarin. A Scud missile warhead capable of optimal distribution of its full payload of botulinum could contaminate an area of 3,700 square kilometers, or sixteen times the theoretical area that could be covered with the same payload of sarin. It is also important to note that by the time any symptoms appear, treatment for botulinum has little chance of success. Rapid field detection methods do not exist for biological agents, but botulinum can debilitate in a few hours and kill in as little as twelve. In contrast, anthrax can cover an even larger area. It is less lethal and takes two to four days to kill, but it is also much more persistent.[367]

Iraq has strongly denied developing such weapons as well as reports that it has used them against the Kurds.[368] Nevertheless, there are strong indications that Iraq not only produced agents like botulin and anthrax but conducted research into typhoid, cholera, tularemia, and equine encephalitis.[369]

After the Gulf War, it became clear that Iraq's main sites of research were the Biological Research Center of the Scientific Research Council in Baghdad and the Nuclear Research Institute of the Atomic Energy Commission in Tuwaitha, which housed one of the leading biological research laboratories in Iraq. Salman Pak seems to have been involved in the development and production of biological weapons as well as chemical weapons. Work was also done by the Genetic Engineering and Biotechnology Research Center established shortly after the Iran-Iraq War. Iraq was one of the first nations to ratify a UN agreement setting up international centers for such research in Trieste and New Delhi.[370]

Iraq seems to have established tight censorship over these facilities. There was a sharp increase in the number of Iraqi papers on biological research between 1979 and 1981, then a sharp decrease between 1981 and 1985 and another rise in production. This timing coincides with some of the impacts of the Iran-Iraq War, but Iraq seems to have prevented any unclassified publications on anthrax and botulinum neurotoxins throughout this period. A postwar study found one Iraqi article on each area during the entire period from 1969 to 1991, although anthrax is a potential health hazard in Iraq. Similarly, no Iraqi research was published on tularemia and West Nile fever, although Iraq acquired the cultures for these diseases as well as seventeen shipments of cultures of various toxins and bacteria from the American Type Culture Collection during the period between 1985 and 1991.[371]

Some of Iraq's biological warfare facilities were colocated with industrial plants. The Iraqi Ministry of Industry and Military Industrialization created a State Enterprise for Drug Industries at Samara which consolidated plants originally built with Soviet assistance but which later benefited from East German and West German support. It also established a research laboratory for the State Enterprise for Drug Industries which was located in close proximity to the Iraqi State Ministry of Pesticide Production.[372]

Another dubious aspect of Iraqi activity is the Al-Kindi Company for Serum and Vaccine Production, a major French-designed factory for manufacturing the vaccine for hoof and mouth disease at Doura, near Baghdad. Some reports indicate the factory can make up to 12 million doses per year and has a research effort designed to allow it to manufacture up to 15 different vaccines. The Arab Company for Antibiotic Industries in Baghdad is an Iraqi-Jordanian-Saudi government owned firm that is building a factory capable of making 200 tons of penicillin a year. This project received extensive support from a West German firm called V-Konsult Ingenieur.[373]

There are also reports that Iraq acquired mobile toxicological laboratories from West German companies. These laboratories are theoretically for "agricultural chemistry," but the West German firms involved in supplying them include Karl Kolb, a company that actively helped Iraq acquire chemical weapons.[374] Further, the West German firms of Josef Kuhn and Plato-Kühn seem to have sold Iraq 2.7 grams of mycotoxins called T-2 and HT-2 that it acquired from the parent U.S. company, Sigma Chemie.[375] The State Department has charged that these are the same toxins used by Vietnam in Cambodia and the USSR in Afghanistan.

A wide number of companies may have deliberately or inadvertently helped Iraq in its biological weapons efforts. Sigma Chemie is also reported to have transferred precursor viruses for biological weapons, and Iraq seems to have obtained the strains for a number of viruses that can be used for biological warfare from centers in the U.S. under the guise of requesting them for medical research. Other firms seem to include Swatek and Cerny (Austria; sanitary equipment), Labsco GmbH (Germany, biological equipment), Rhein-Bayern Vehicle Construction (Germany; mobile toxicological laboratory), Anton Eyerle (Germany; mobile toxicological laboratory), and Iveco Magrius Deutz (Germany; vehicles for mobile laboratories).[376]

There is no reliable way to determine all the biological weapons Iraq was developing before the Gulf War, although the head of the British government's Defense Arms Control Unit, Peter Verker, has stated that "biological research activities for military purposes had been undertaken at Salman Pak since 1986, and included research into some of the most effective biological agents—the organisms which cause gas gangrene (clostridium perfringens), anthrax (Bacillus anthracis), and botulism (Clostridium botulinum)."[377]

UN inspection teams have also found brucellosis and tularemia.[378] Other biological weapons might include equine encephalitis and possibly cholera and typhoid. What is obvious is that Iraq had both production facilities at Salman Pak and at least some stockpiles of toxins and probably of stable weapons like anthrax. It is also clear that Iraq had at least three to six other biological warfare sites and probably a number of other storage facilities.

Many of these facilities had not been inspected by the UN in the early spring of 1992, and it seems likely that Iraq still had stocks of some biological weapons. Further, having the technology, it could rapidly set up covert production centers at university research centers, medical goods and drug production plants, or virtually any other facility where it could maintain a secure biological research and production activity. Robert Gates, director of the CIA, responded to questions about Iraq's biological weapons effort in January, 1992 by stating that "the biological weapons program was also damaged, but critical equipment for it, too, was hidden during the war." Iraq could produce biological agents "in a matter of weeks."[379]

Iraqi Nuclear Weapons Efforts

Iraq denied that it was seeking nuclear weapons from the time this was first suspected in the 1970s until an admission was forced upon it by UN inspectors in 1991. Long before this admission, however, there was overwhelming evidence that Iraq had sought specialized expertise and technology which had only limited secondary applications and in ways which could only be explained by a covert nuclear weapons program.[380]

Iraq's major nuclear research efforts began in 1959, when it ordered a small research reactor from the Soviet Union. This 5 megawatt light-water reactor, called the IRT-2000, used highly enriched uranium and went on line in 1968. It was later used to test the production of plutonium from spent reactor fuel, although no confirmed reports exist regarding these tests until 1988.[381]

Iraq's next major reactor acquisition effort was the purchase of the Isis or Tamuz 2 reactor from France in 1976. This small 800 kilowatt light-water reactor using highly enriched uranium went on line in 1980. During this period, Iraq established a significant nuclear research effort and set up a laboratory scale uranium purification plant at Tuwaitha with Italian support. Iraq is known to have tried unsuccessfully to purchase bulk depleted uranium and reactor fuel pins from the U.S. and Canada.[382]

The key step Iraq took in developing a nuclear weapon during the late 1970s and early 1980s was the purchase of the Osiraq (Tamuz 1) light-water reactor from France in 1976, which originally was designed to use 158 pounds (78 kilograms) of highly enriched uranium. This amount would have been sufficient to manufacture up to three nuclear weapons.[383] Iraq also obtained Italian assistance in developing fuel fabrication capability and in obtaining a plutonium reprocessing technology with a capacity of up to 8 kilograms per year. This equipment included three radiologically shielded "hot cells," which could extract plutonium from uranium irradiated in a reactor, and related equipment suitable for producing plutonium.[384] The hot cells were particularly important to a nuclear weapons effort because the 40 megawatt Osiraq reactor was unusually large for research purposes and could be used to irradiate uranium in hot cells to produce plutonium.

Experts still disagree over the extent to which the Osiraq reactor complex was designed for nuclear weapons purposes, but it now seems clear that Iraq was interested in nuclear weapons and not in nuclear power. While Iraq claimed that the reactor was purely for research purposes, its covert efforts to acquire plutonium hot cells and reprocessing capability make these claims extremely unlikely. So does Iraq's insistence during this period on obtaining 158 pounds of highly enriched uranium from France—although France eventually reacted to international pressure by limiting its supply to Iraq to 55 pounds at any one time.[385]

Further, Iraq bought large amounts of natural uranium from Brazil, Portugal, Niger, and Italy in 1980 and 1981 that it could not process into reactor fuel but could process into uranium to irradiate into plutonium.[386] (Plutonium can be produced by exposing uranium to neutrons within a reactor and then chemically separating out the uranium.) Iraq also placed an order in early 1980 for 25,000 pounds of depleted uranium fuel pins from a West German firm called NUKEM. The pins were sized for irradiation in the Osiraq reactor and had no other real purpose than to produce about 10 to 12 kilograms of weapons grade plutonium. By 1990 Iraq had at least 332,000 kilograms of yellow cake, 116,000 kilograms of UO_2, 2,577 kilograms of UCl_4, 0.465 kilograms of UF_6, 1,850 kilograms of ADU, 2,050 kilograms of UO_3, 310 kilograms of UF_4, and 2,255 kilograms of UO_4.[387]

Iraq could count on being able to use the irradiation approach to proliferation because of the limits to international inspection before the Gulf War. Although the Osiraq reactor was under IAEA inspection authority and French technicians were working at the site, Iraq seems to have followed roughly the same approach to disguising its nuclear weapons efforts that Sweden had used in the early 1960s. The fuel cells at the Osiraq reactor were subject to inspection only after Iraq declared that material was present. The IAEA had no right to inspect the cells on an ongoing basis or to investigate the fabrication of the material being inspected. According to one Israeli source, the reactor also had a covert chamber for irradiating uranium which allowed it to produce significant amounts of plutonium—enough to produce one to two bombs over a period of two to three years. This allowed Iraq to "comply" with the IAEA while developing an ability to handle plutonium technology and stockpiling material for weapons purposes.[388]

This mix of factors that led Israel to a series of efforts to halt or destroy the reactor. Israeli agents almost certainly planted a bomb in April, 1979 that destroyed the reactor's first set of core structures while they were still awaiting shipment to Iraq in Seine-sur-Mer, France. Israeli agents also seem to have assassinated Yahya el-Meshad, an Egyptian physicist working for Iraq, and to have bombed several of the French and Italian companies working on the project.[389] Finally, on June 7, 1981, Israel launched the highly publicized air raid that destroyed the reactor before it could become operational.

At the time when Israel attacked and destroyed the reactor, Iraq was negotiating to buy a heavy-water power reactor from Italy and a sizable reprocessing facility whose purpose was almost certainly plutonium production. This series of deals seems to have halted, however, after it became clear that Israel would take military action to prevent it from going forward.[390]

While France initially agreed to rebuild the Osiraq reactor, it failed to do so because of a mix of U.S. and other international pressures, the Iran-Iraq War, and Iraqi payment problems.[391] This forced Iraq to find other ways to produce its fissionable material. Iraq continued to give the search for a replacement for Osiraq very high priority, but it also started a major uranium enrichment effort and tried to develop a capability to process plutonium.

Iraq used nuclear power as its cover in attempting to obtain new nuclear reactors. In 1984—in the midst of the Iran-Iraq War, while unable to export its oil and while nearly bankrupt—Iraq announced it was seeking to provide 10% of its power needs with nuclear power and had contracted with the Soviet Union in 1984 to build a 440 megawatt plant at a cost of $2 billion. The plant was supposed to be built by the Soviet Atomnergo group, but even before Iraq's invasion of Kuwait, there was no sign that Iraq would get the USSR to start construction or that the Soviet Union would build a new reactor Iraq could integrate into a weapons development cycle.

In March, 1989 Saddam Hussein declared that Saudi Arabia had agreed to finance the rebuilding of the reactor during a visit of King Fahd to Baghdad.[392] This announcement, however, was not confirmed by Saudi Arabia and still left the issue of who would actually rebuild the reactor unclear. No progress was made between March, 1989 and the virtual severing of Saudi-Iraqi relations following Iraq's invasion of Kuwait in August, 1990. Iraq also sought Latin American support in building an uncontrolled reactor somewhere in northern Iraq but seems to have had equally little success.

Iraq was far more successful in obtaining support to find other ways of acquiring fissile materials and in getting nuclear weapons technology. Reports of Iraqi cooperation with other proliferating nations during this period are uncertain, but it seems likely that such cooperation took place. Iraq cooperated with Brazil in some aspects of missile research during this period, and Brazil is actively involved in manufacturing centrifuges and has used many of the same suppliers for its centrifuge development effort as has Iraq. Brazil sold Iraq substantial amounts of uranium and had a research cooperation agreement with Iraq that lasted at least to 1989. Argentina sold Iraq uranium and missile technology and may have cooperated with Iraq on some aspects of fissile material manufacture.

While Pakistan has closer ties to Iran than to Iraq, Iraq has had a nuclear research cooperation agreement with Pakistan and Egypt since 1985. At least some Pakistani scientists associated with Pakistan's centrifuge plant at Kahuta, near Islamabad, seem to have visited Iraq. Iraq was also the leading member of the Arab Atomic Energy Commission, which was established in December, 1988 and includes Jordan, Kuwait, Lebanon, Libya, Palestine, Saudi Arabia, Syria, and Tunisia.[393]

Iraq's Nuclear Efforts After 1988

It is certain that Iraq spent up to $10 billion during the 1980s to acquire Calutron and centrifuge enrichment facilities, on other methods of enrichment, and on acquiring virtually all of the technology and equipment to use fissile material in a nuclear weapon.[394] At the time the Gulf War began, Iraq had over 5,000 workers involved in its nuclear weapons effort and the following major facilities:[395]

- *Abu Ghraib:* Military base and fuel rod storage.
- *Abu Sukhayr:* Exploratory mine located about 25 kilometers southwest of Najar. Production from September, 1988 to end of 1990, when the mine was flooded. Uranium in ore ranged from 80 to 800 ppm.
- *Akashat:* Phosphate and open faced uranium mine. Uranium extraction.
- *Amil:* Liquid nitrogen for Calutron program.
- *Amir:* Calutron component manufacturing of magnet cores, return irons, ion sources, collector parts.
- *Ameen:* Calutron component manufacturing—prototype components.
- *Atheer:* Nuclear weapons design and testing of high explosives. Hydrodynamic studies. Large cold isostatic press for shaping explosive charges by Asea Brown Boveri. High temperature vacuum induction furnaces by Arthur Pfeiffer Vakuum Technik. Planned casting and machining of fissile material, machining of uranium plates, and assembly of explosive structure and core of nuclear weapons. Plasma coating molds and mold fabrication. Design of regular implosion type nuclear weapon.[396]
- *Badr:* Centrifuge component manufacturing. Civil contracting for Al-Furat project.
- *Daura (SEHEE):* Calutron component manufacturing —vacuum chamber parts. Civil contracting for Furat project.
- *Fao:* Civil contracting for Furat project.
- *Falluja:* Military base and equipment storage.
- *Furat:* Centrifuge research. Two centrifuge manufacturing sites. Maraging centrifuge facility. Had begun with a Beams type and was capable of making the more advanced Zippe type by mid-1987. Iraq initially claimed it was capable of producing up to 200 centrifuges a year. The manufacturing equipment intended for installation indicates that the true figure was 2,000.
- *IRT-5000:* Po-210 production.
- *Jezira:* Uranium processing; UCl_4 production. Calutron and centrifuge production.

- *Al Hadre:* High explosives research and hydrodynamic studies.
- *Hatteen:* High explosives research; main explosive structure research.
- *Musayyib:* Materials research and high explosive test site. Test range for shaped charges. Power plant. Nuclear weapons laboratories.
- *Mosul:* UCl₄ production.
- *Nafad:* Calutron component storage.
- *Nasser Works:* Centrifuge component manufacturing and machining.
- *Al Qaa Qaa:* Development of nonnuclear components and explosives for nuclear weapons. HMX production and casting for weapon, pressing and machining, main explosive structure of weapon, explosive lens building, and lens assembly. Detonator research. Exploding bridge wire detonators. Research facility for Ministry of Industry and Military Industrialization.
- *Al Qaim:* Superphosphated fertilizer plant, uranium extraction plant, and yellow cake production.
- *Al Radwan:* Centrifuge component manufacturing—magnet cores, return irons, ion sources, collector parts.
- *Al Rashidiya:* Maraging centrifuge facility.
- *Saddam Works:* Calutron component manufacturing and centrifuge machining.
- *Salladine:* Calutron component manufacturing—electrical control panels.
- *Ash Shakyli:* Warehouse storing centrifuge components.
- *Sharqat:* About 250 kilometers north of Baghdad. Work started in 1988. Three groups of facilities. Uranium enrichment for Calutron. An Iraqi duplicate of Tarmiyah, with 600mm and 1,200mm Calutrons, but not yet operational.
- *Suwayra:* Nuclear equipment.
- *Tarmiya:* Calutron research. Main production site for uranium enrichment; eight working 1,200mm Calutrons; seventeen 1,200mm improved Calutrons being installed. Building for twenty 600mm Calutrons under construction. Capacity of ninety 600mm and 1,200mm Calutrons. This could have produced 15 kilograms of 93% enriched uranium per year and more of less enriched uranium. (This complex was built by the Yugoslav Federal Directorate of Supply and Procurement and equipped by the Yugoslav firm of EMO Electrical Engineering).[397] Also a computer facility.
- *Technical University of Baghdad:* Streak video cameras and related equipment suitable for weaponization work by Hamamatsu.[398]
- *Tikrit:* Storage of yellow cake.
- *Tuwaitha:* A major research and production center. Site of damaged Tamuz 1 and Tamuz 2 reactors, and IRT-5000 reactor (heavily damaged in war). Nuclear physics labs. Main computer facility with IBM-370 mainframe and many IBM PS/2s. Uranium research and development. UCl₄ and UF₆ production. Calutron and centrifuge tests, plutonium separation, and chemical separation; five working Calutrons. Gaseous diffusion research. Po-210 extraction and neutron initiator research and design. UF₄ production. Metal reduction, casting, and machining. Research on implosion nuclear weapon. Firing system research and design.
- *Zaafariniya:* Al Dijla and Al Rabiya sites fabricated Calutron components.
- *Walid:* Centrifuge factory.

Most of these facilities were not declared to the IAEA and were not subject to its inspection, and many became known only after the UN inspections began, following the Gulf War. While Iraq relied on dispersal and secrecy to protect some of these facilities, it also established massive surface-to-air missile defenses at major facilities like Tuwaitha.[399] These defenses were combined with hardened shelters at locations like Tuwaitha and Al Atheer, and Iraq had at least one underground facility in a mountain near Irbil.[400]

Iraq's critical problem was to obtain fissile material. In the late 1980s, Iraq had a total of just 27.5 pounds (11.3 kilograms) of French-supplied 93% enriched uranium for the Tamuz 1 reactor destroyed by Israel, and 22.3 kilograms of Russian-supplied uranium with levels of enrichment varying from 36% to 80% for its Russian IRT-5000 research reactor.[401] Only the French material could be used in a bomb. Using this limited amount of material to build even a single weapon required the use of very complex implosion technology. Enriched uranium cannot be used in the simpler weapon designs made possible by using plutonium or mixes of uranium and plutonium. Iraq would have had no surplus material to test its weapon design.[402]

As a result, Iraq simultaneously pursued several approaches to getting the weapons grade material it needed. Iraq turned to the international black market in arms for fissile material but made little progress. For example, Iraqi officers failed in 1984 to purchase some 33.9 kilograms (74.6 pounds) of plutonium from Italian arms smugglers in what seems to have been little more than a confidence scheme.[403]

The UN special commission did find after the Gulf War that Iraq had managed to extract a little over 5 grams of weapons grade plutonium from reactor fuel that was subject to IAEA inspection. Later examination indicated that the plutonium came from two sources. First, 2.26 grams of plutonium had been at a small laboratory at the Tuwaitha Nuclear Research Center. This had evidently been separated between 1982 and 1988 after the IAEA exempted five fuel elements from inspection which contained 10% enriched uranium for the Soviet IRT-5000 research reactor. Such an IAEA exemption is normal for small amounts of material used for research purposes. The second batch of 3 grams was also separated at Tuwaitha. This time, however, Iraq used natural uranium that it had separated at Al Qaim in northern Iraq. Iraq inserted about 11 kilograms of this processed uranium into its research reactor. Iraq had sent another 8 kilograms to Tuwaitha by the start of the war, but this had not been processed by the time the UN inspected the facility.

This plutonium enrichment activity demonstrates Iraq's interest in nuclear weapons, but it must be kept in careful perspective. If Iraq had used its laboratory in this way round the clock for a year, it would have obtained only 100 grams of plutonium. It takes approximately 8 to 10 kilograms to make a nuclear weapon, and there is no evidence that Iraq had a secret reactor or large scale facility for plutonium production.[404]

Iraq also turned to cascade technology but had little success. It studied gaseous diffusion from 1982 to 1987 but concluded that it required a more advanced industrial infrastructure than Iraq had available and abandoned it for centrifuge and Calutron technology.[405] Iraq actively sought centrifuge technology from the U.S., Europe, and the PRC, and this led to a number of incidents over attempts to smuggle equipment to Iraq. The U.S. blocked an attempt to acquire the specialized pumps needed for cascade facilities in February, 1989 as well as other Iraqi attempts to smuggle centrifuge technology from the U.S. to Iraq in 1988 and 1989.

Nevertheless, Iraq made significant progress towards creating a centrifuge enrichment capability and meeting a long term goal of 10,000 operating centrifuges.[406] Iraq had a Beams type centrifuge by mid-1987 and a more advanced Zippe type by mid-1988. The UN special commission discovered that Iraq purchased centrifuge technology and equipment from thirteen different German companies and found a plant at Furat that the Iraqis claimed was capable of producing up to 200 centrifuges a year that had escaped the UN bombing.[407]

Iraq seems to have had the designs for an early URENCO G1 centrifuge (possibly obtained through Interatom, a wholly owned subsidiary of Siemens), some of the designs for the URENCO G2 and G3 centrifuges, and a 1988 centrifuge design by MAN Technologies of Munich.[408] It acquired the specialized drill presses and rolling machines or lathes for manufacturing enrichment centrifuges from H&H Metallform Maschinenbau of Drensteinfurt in West Germany during 1987–1988.[409] It acquired machinery to manufacture end caps and flow-forming machines to make the thin and precisely machined rotors for centrifuges out of maraging steel tubes from H&H and other German companies and Schaublin in Switzerland. It acquired 240,000 ferrite magnet spacers, 300 tons of special aluminum alloy for vacuum housings, and 84 tons of special aluminum alloy for molecular pumps. In 1989 Iraq acquired at least 100 tons of maraging steel 350, a high nickel content steel whose primary use is in uranium centrifuges. Some of this steel seems to have come from Export Union Düsseldorf, although not enough was found to provide for a major centrifuge manufacturing effort. Some experts believe Iraq's rotors were also still of low grade at the time of UN inspection.[410]

Iraq obtained samarium cobalt magnets (used to hold the centrifuge in place during high speed rotation) from West Germany and the PRC. It attempted to buy the specialized vacuum pumps used to circulate uranium hexafluoride gas through gas centrifuges from CVC products of Rochester, New York. When this failed, it seems to have acquired them in Europe.[411]

Iraq set up a hydrogen fluoride plant at Al Qaim in a facility plant used for phosphate production. (Hydrogen fluoride is needed to produce uranium fluoride gas.)[412] Iraq made enough progress to set up a maraging centrifuge facility at Furat, and another at Al Rashidiya. The West German investigation of the actions of H&H and technicians associated with MAN indicated that this manufacturer played a major role in setting up a nuclear materials research and centrifuge manufacturing plant at Tuwaitha and that research and development work on centrifuges was taking place at the Saad 16 center near Mosul. It also indicated that a former MAN employee, Bruno

Stemmler, played a critical role in making Iraq's centrifuge design function.[413]

A number of other firms played a deliberate or inadvertent role in helping Iraq to acquire centrifuge capability. These include a number of Austrian, German, and Swiss firms, and one U.S. firm. UN reports have named Acomel (high frequency converters for operating centrifuges), Degussa (large oxidation furnaces), Du Pont (Krytox nuclear grade fluorinated vacuum pump oil), Leybold Heraeus (electron beam welder), Neue Magdelburger Werkzeugmaschinenfabrik (large centrifuge machines), Dr. Reutlinger & Söhne (horizontal and vertical balancing machines), and NUPRO, VAT, and Balzer (different types of bellows valves).[414]

Iraq planned to have a 100 machine cascade in operation by 1993 and a 500 machine cascade in operation by 1996. It would probably have had at least 2,000 machines on line by the late 1990s. Under optimal conditions, a line or cascade of 2,000 centrifuges can produce 40 to 50 pounds of highly enriched uranium a year, or about enough to produce one bomb.

The centrifuge, however, is a difficult path to enrichment, and few developing countries are likely to get anything approaching this level of output.[415] The UN special commission found serious problems in the quality of Iraq's centrifuge technology and production equipment. Pakistan seems to have taken nine years to build a centrifuge enrichment facility but still only seems to have about 1,000 out of 14,000 centrifuges running at its plant at any one time. Brazil took ten years to get a small plant running at Aramar, with only 50–75 centrifuges, although it was well on its way to operating a full scale 2,000–3,000 centrifuge plant by 1990.[416]

As for other methods of enrichment, Iraq showed no interest in laser isotope separation, limited interest in chemical and jet nozzle separation, and a major interest in Calutron enrichment. Iraq tried both Japanese and French techniques for chemical separation which rely on catalysts to speed up the exchanges between U-235 and U-238. It abandoned the Japanese technique but continued working on the French technique in order to obtain a relatively cheap and efficient method of low level enrichment. It seems to have made limited progress in jet nozzle technology and abandoned it.[417]

Iraq's efforts to use Calutrons was somewhat more successful and was discovered only after the Gulf War. The Iraqi effort to keep these facilities was so covert that it led a number of experts to speculate that Iraq had taken advantage of deception techniques to hide its activities from U.S. satellites; it had learned such techniques from the Soviets after the Israeli attack on Osiraq and from studying U.S. satellite photos of Iran that the U.S. had supplied to Iraq during the Iran-Iraq War.[418]

Iraq's major Calutron facilities have been listed earlier, but the UN has not fully disclosed what it has discovered about the Iraqi Calutron effort or the names of its foreign suppliers. It is clear, however, that Iraq set up electromagnetic isotope separation (EMIS) facilities at Al Dijla, Tarmiya, Al Rabiya, Al Hamath, and in the Zaafariniya section of Baghdad.[419] After the Gulf War, the UN special commission found these involved the production of massive equipment assemblies that included at least thirty 12 foot disks weighing 60 tons. These were supplied by a number of Austrian and German firms, including Voest-Alpine of Austria. They also included the Federal Directorate of Supply and Procurement in Yugoslavia.[420]

While several Calutrons were built, their importance was sometimes exaggerated in the press. Iraqi plans seem to have called for seventy alpha and twenty beta Calutrons to have become operational during August, 1989–December, 1992, but only eight alpha Calutrons were installed by the end of 1989. Iraq was just beginning to install another seventeen alpha machines when the UN attacked in 1990, and it is unlikely that Iraq could have had enough machines operational to produce one nuclear weapon a year before 1994 at the earliest. The machines that were installed do not appear to have been functioning with high reliability, at a significant scale, or with the output required to support a major weapons effort. They could, however, have been more effective as a way of preparing material for further enrichment by centrifuges. The UN special commission noted that the Calutrons could be used for high capacity–low enrichment operation and the centrifuges for low capacity–high enrichment.[421]

Iraq seems to have produced only grams of enriched uranium and milligrams of 40–45% enriched uranium in the facility at Tuwaitha, which was constructed in 1985–1986. Iraq did not begin operating the Calutrons at Tarmiya until February, 1990 and produced a total of 500 grams of 4% enriched uranium with some at a high of 10%. The facility at Tarmiya was still in the test bed stage, and each Calutron had four ion sources and a design beam current of 145 milliamps of uranium ions. Iraq was experiencing problems in keeping all the ion sources operating at once and in maintaining stable beams but had evidently solved all the development problems except the ion source.[422]

When the war began it was installing a circular system, or racetrack, of seventeen Calutrons to produce low enriched uranium, with the goal of installing up to seventy low enrichment units and twenty high enrichment units. None of the high enrichment Calutrons was installed or operating, but UN officials speculated that they might eventually have produced 12–90 kilograms of uranium a year with an enrichment level of at least 90%. This, however, required all four beams in each machine to operate at 145 milliamps and all machines to operate an average 55% of the time. An output of 8–9 kilograms would have been more likely.

As this enrichment effort moved forward, Iraq steadily expanded what it later admitted was its nuclear weapons design facility at Atheer.[423] The UN identified several firms as providing equipment or technical data for the Atheer facility. They include Asea Brown Boveri of Switzerland (large cold isostatic press), Arthur Pfeiffer Vakuum Technik (very high temperature furnaces), and Hamamatsu of Japan (high speed video cameras).[424]

Atheer was involved in research relating to the production of plutonium, polonium 210, natural uranium metal, enriched uranium metal, and yellow cerium sulfide. It worked on detonation and neutronic tests, nuclear initiation, and flash X-rays. It also worked on firing systems, control, and guidance. Projects included explosive lens testing and analysis, natural uranium reflector design, polonium-beryllium initiators, hardened iron tampers, synchronization and timing systems, pulse power equipment, charging power equipment, junction switches, capacitors, and related measurements.[425] The UN found some 40,000 pages of documents relating to the Iraqi nuclear weapons design effort and sophisticated one and two dimensional computer codes tailored to nuclear weapons design.[426]

Work by the UN inspection teams found that Iraq had concluded that gun type devices need more material, although they were simpler and had fewer calculation requirements. This led Iraq to concentrate on an intermediary implosion type device and to focus on a yield of 20 kilotons—similar to the nominal yield of the weapon dropped on Nagasaki. Iraq had performed 20 detonation experiments relating to such designs by May 31, 1990, the last date referred to in UN-held Iraqi reports.[427] It is important to note that few records have yet been discovered for the period after May, 1990.

Because Iraq calculated that minor shifts in design could produce a yield as low as 1 kiloton, and lacked predetermined values for several critical calculations, it was using one dimensional integrated codes for much of its design work. It conducted weaponization studies, hydrodynamic calculations, exploding wire studies, initial initiator studies, flash X-ray studies, energy source studies, neptunium and U-233 experiments, and Li-6 experiments. The bulk of this calculation work seems to have been done at Tuwaitha using an IBM 370 mainframe and smaller IBM PS/2 computers, although the hydrostatic calculations were performed on an NEC mainframe computer.[428]

Iraq also purchased components for the high melting point explosive (HMX) and rapid detonation explosive (RDX) needed to compress fissile material into critical mass.[429] It obtained polonium 210 from Bismuth and completed 20 tests of a polonium-beryllium initiator.[430] Iraq obtained X-ray crystal measurement, mass spectrometers, and beryllium. It bought some $96 million worth of computers from the U.S. between 1984 and 1990, about $26 million of which went to Iraqi military facilities, and large amounts of optical fiber.[431] Further, the UN special commission reported that Iraq was producing, or had obtained, up to 220 pounds of lithium 6 a year. Lithium 6 can be used both in thermonuclear weapons and to enhance the yield of fission weapons. The UN concluded from Iraqi records that Iraq was using lithium to work on a boosted weapon.[432]

The exact level of Iraq's success in warhead design at the time the Gulf War began is still a matter of some debate. The report of IAEA director Hans Blix to the UN Security Council on the results of the sixth IAEA inspection of Iraq makes it clear, however, that Iraq had made substantial progress:

> The key result of the sixth inspection is the uncovering of documents that show conclusively that Iraq was very well advanced in a program to develop an implosion-type nuclear weapon and that links existed to a surface-to-surface missile project. Indeed, so advanced has this program been deemed to be that the time needed to reach bomb-making capacity seems to have been determined by the time necessary for the enrichment facilities, rather than the weapons design activities. ... The sixth report also

uncovered evidence of broad based Iraqi international procurement efforts in violation
of laws of States from which the export originated. However, much, if not most of the
procurement of which evidence will be available, will be found to pertain to equipment
and material not subject to export controls elsewhere.[433]

This statement and evidence discovered by the UN inspection teams leaves little doubt that Iraq had most of the technical capability to make an implosion type fission weapon. In fact, the U.S. seems to have helped Iraqis in developing some of the explosion technology involved by inviting them to a conference in Portland, Oregon, on denotation techniques.[434]

There is less certainty, however, that Iraq could have deployed a weapon without testing. Iraq might not have found predictability of yield to be critical. Even a partial success, or "fizzle," that produced a 5–6 kiloton yield is still an extremely effective weapon. An outright failure to explode, however, could cost Iraq roughly $100 to $200 million per weapon until it developed a major fissile material production capability and would represent a significant portion of Iraq's total stockpile.

Further, Iraq faced the risk that a nuclear weapon susceptible to shock, accidental triggering, or partial detonation from causes ranging from static electricity to misuse of safety interlocks could do devastating damage to Iraqi territory. There are some indications that the bomb Iraq designed crammed so much high explosive into a narrow area that it was highly sensitive to shock and accidental detonation.[435]

Iraq also faced the challenge of mating a nuclear weapon to a delivery system. It had to develop the technology necessary to carry bombs on airplanes in ways that ensure safety and proper release, develop accurate delivery methods, and fuse the bombs to provide reliable control over the height of burst.[436] It had to develop similar technology for missiles, as well as missiles that are so reliable that there is almost a zero chance of the loss of one of Iraq's limited number of warheads. The warhead performance of Iraq's longer range missiles was extremely unreliable at the time of the Gulf War and presented a risk of missing a target by several kilometers and of misses that could detonate at virtually any point within their maximum range if the missile malfunctions.

Iraq's effort in March, 1990 to smuggle from the U.S. high speed, high voltage capacitors suitable for use in nuclear weapons provides a good example of some of the other problems Iraq faced in moving from the possession of most of the technology it needs to all of the technology it needs for nuclear weapons. On March 28, 1990, five people were arrested in London's Heathrow Airport after an 18 month sting operation in which U.S. and British officials tracked Iraq's purchasing efforts to buy military capacitors. These efforts were made by the London-based firms called Euromac and Atlas Equipment, which were fronts for an Iraqi purchasing mission involving the efforts of at least three members of Iraq's Al Qaa Qaa military research and development establishment.[437] Euromac had previously been involved in smuggling cluster bomb parts out of Italy, and some of the Iraqi government personnel involved had ties to the facilities at Tuwaitha and

Iraq's Saad 16 military facility near Mosul, which are key centers for such nuclear weapons research.[438]

It is not absolutely certain that Iraq wanted the capacitors for nuclear weapons. They do have a number of other potential military applications, such as triggering the high explosive charges in a gas cannon. The capacitors are co-axial, high voltage, low inductance devices that have exceptional resistance to humidity, vibration, and shock. Nevertheless, they are identical to the devices used in U.S. nuclear weapons, and they are perfectly suited to deliver the instant burst of electricity, or triggering charge, necessary to detonate all of the high explosive hemispheres surrounding nuclear material in order to ensure that it is compressed into critical mass with optimum efficiency.[439]

Finally, Iraq faced the problem of nuclear weapons security. The seizure of a nuclear weapon could give any political faction a dominant role in a coup attempt or struggle for power. In the case of a revolution or ideological struggle, it could easily threaten the existence of the regime or lead to the use of a weapon that could trigger a major war. Creating effective security systems and devices, however, is not easy. Security devices that are internal in the weapon are probably the only way of ensuring a reasonable degree of central government control, but effective designs must be built into every aspect of the weapons design and can interfere with weapons function. Less stringent protection systems can be bypassed in relatively short periods of time or by disassembling one weapon to learn how to bypass the security systems on the others.

As for the future, UN coalition attacks destroyed many of Iraq's nuclear facilities during the Gulf War, and UN inspection teams found and destroyed many others.[440] The IAEA has removed the enriched material from the two small research reactors still operating at Tuwaitha, and the UN bombing and special commission efforts have destroyed facilities for plutonium production, uranium production, hexafluoride conversion, and uranium mining and milling.[441]

The UN bombing and postwar inspection and dismantling effort cannot, however, deny Iraq the advantages of the technology it has acquired from two decades of nuclear weapons development efforts. As CIA director Gates noted in testimony before Congress, "Iraq will remain a primary proliferation threat at least as long as Saddam Hussein remains in power. . . . The cadre of scientists and engineers trained for these programs will be able to reconstitute any dormant program quickly."[442] Nevertheless, the UN effort does confront Iraq with a massive problem in investment and in reacquiring the complex mix of equipment and facilities it had before the Gulf War.

If the UN sanctions are fully enforced, it will probably be at least five to eight years before Iraq's nuclear efforts can recover once the UN inspection effort ends. It could well be many years longer before Iraq can build up substantial nuclear forces. This would not, however, prevent Iraq from creating the kind of "nuclear ambiguity" that is already present in India and Pakistan. Iraq may well have a credible enough potential to possess a bomb to influence the regional balances years before it has an effective device. On the one hand this will increase its political and strategic leverage. On the other hand such ambiguity could make Iraq a high priority target and lead to preemptive attacks by a state like Israel.

Strategic Interests and Arms Control

Prophecy is a dangerous game at any time and is virtually impossible in the case of Iraq. There is no way to predict how long Saddam Hussein and the Baath regime will last or whether any successor government will ultimately prove less authoritarian or aggressive. The future unity and resolve of the UN coalition is somewhat uncertain, and there are limits to how long and how thoroughly the current embargo can be applied.

There is a very real risk that Kurdish and Shi'ite separatism could provoke some form of civil war. Turkey's confrontation with its own Kurds and Iran's support of Iraqi Shi'ites are other major wild cards in the game. Turkey may well reach the point where it fears Kurdish separatism more than Iraq. While Iraq's Shi'ites are Arabs, are often Iraqi nationalists, and have somewhat different religious practices from Iran's Shi'ites, it is possible that Iran may be able to either acquire part of Iraq's territory or create a significant pro-Iranian Shi'ite resistance in Iraq.

Even if Iraq does not force another military confrontation with the UN— and this seemed as likely as not in the fall of 1992—the one outcome of the current crisis that does seem nearly certain is that Iraq will remain a major threat to regional peace. Iraq not only retains a significant capability to build weapons of mass destruction, its overall mix of conventional forces is still formidable by regional standards. Iraq's forces are large enough to pose a major threat to Kuwait and Saudi Arabia if they could not obtain U.S. aid. It has enough conventional forces to enable Iraq to defend against any attack by Iran, and its forces should be fully capable of dealing with any of the various Kurdish or Shi'ite militias that are internal threats to Saddam Hussein's power as well as suppressing Iraq's Kurdish and Shi'ite regions by force.

Iraq has, however, lost much of its prewar offensive capability. It also will find it almost impossible to make use of its present forces in any sustained conflict without major resupply of munitions and spare parts, and its forces will steadily deteriorate with time. Iraq's concept of readiness and sustainability has been to import virtually all of its needs. It has never developed the kind of internal maintenance and logistic systems necessary to keep its equipment operational, and throughout the Iran-Iraq War it depended on emergency shipments of parts, arms, and munitions to make up for the weaknesses in its forces.

Iraq's domestic arms industry was also crippled in the Gulf War and was never capable of producing significant amounts of modern heavy military equipment before the war. As a result, not only is Iraq currently limited in military power, the UN embargo ensures that it will slowly and steadily decline to a restricted defensive capability. This could be threatening to regional stability if Iran achieves the major arms orders it is seeking and gains a decisive edge over Iraq.

There is every reason to deny Iraq arms orders, as well as any technology and dual use technology it can use for weapons of mass destruction. Iraq was dependent on some $3–5 billion of annual arms imports in the period before the Gulf War. Effective sanctions will steadily undercut Iraq's ability to threaten its own people, as well as its neighbors, and the authoritarianism of Saddam Hussein's regime. Iraq has played the role of an aggressor or destabilizing state for virtually its entire postcolonial existence. It retains enough military capability in spite of the Gulf War to threaten its southern neighbors if they do not receive outside support, and it has the technical skills and at least some of the equipment to manufacture and deliver weapons of mass destruction. No case can be made for even limited arms transfers unless a more democratic, stable, and ethnically balanced government comes to power in the future.

Dealing with the Strategic Challenge from Iran and Iraq

Neither arms transfers nor arms control alone can bring stability to the Gulf. The only effective solution is to target arms control against Iran and Iraq while supporting selective arms transfers to build up the defense capabilities of Bahrain, Kuwait, Oman, Qatar, Saudi Arabia, and the UAE. Arms sales to both Iran and Iraq must be restricted as much as possible, with special attention to weapons of mass destruction, missiles and long range strike aircraft, heavy armor, and amphibious and heliborne lift. At the same time, selective arms transfers are needed to build up the capability of the southern Gulf states to forge an effective deterrent to low and mid intensity attacks and permit rapid reinforcement from the West. The forces and facilities of the southern Gulf states also need to be structured to allow rapid deployment of U.S. air power and heavy divisions. Providing the equivalent of forward air bases and prepositioned army equipment is the only way in which external reinforcements can offset the mid and long term threat of significant Iranian and Iraqi attacks on the southern Gulf.

The worst possible path that outside nations could follow would be to treat Iran or Iraq as open markets for arms, or to return to the Cold War struggle for influence in the northern Gulf. The U.S. and the heirs of the Soviet Union need to recognize that their past efforts to make either Iran or Iraq into allies or strategic pillars have been dismal failures. The U.S. never benefited from its military support of Iran and indeed was forced to intervene against Iran during 1987–1988. The Soviet Union never obtained any meaningful form of strategic advantage or support from its arms transfers to Iraq.

Unfortunately, the history of the arms race in the Gulf is essentially the history of outside rivalry, a failure to limit arms transfers to Iran and Iraq, and a failure to establish a viable deterrent in the southern Gulf. In spite of decades of continuing war and crisis in the region, the defeat of Iran in the Iran-Iraq War, and the defeat of Iraq in the Gulf War, it is far from clear that the pattern that has shaped these conflicts and crises will change.

Notes

1. See Robert Gates, "Statement of the Director of Central Intelligence Before the U.S. House of Representatives Armed Services Committee Defense Policy Panel," March 27, 1992.

2. The military manpower, force strength, and equipment estimates in this section are made by the author using a wide range of sources, including computerized data bases, interviews, and press clipping services. Most are impossible to reference in ways of use to the reader. The force strength statistics are generally taken from the latest edition of International Institute for Strategic Studies, *Military Balance* (IISS, London), in this case the 1991–1992 edition.

Extensive use has also been made of the annual editions of the Jaffee Center for Strategic Studies, *The Military Balance in the Middle East* (JCSS, Tel Aviv), especially the 1990–1991 edition and working materials from the coming edition. Material has also been drawn from computer print outs from NEXIS, the United States Naval Institute data base, and from the DMS/FI Market Intelligence Reports data base. Other sources include *Military Technology*, "World Defense Almanac for 1991–1992," published in 1992; Foreign Affairs Division, "Middle East Arms Control and Related Issues," Washington, Congressional Research Service, 91-384F, May 1, 1991; and *Middle East Economic Digest*, "MEED Special Report: Defense," Volume 35, December 13, 1991.

Weapons data are taken from many sources, including computerized material available in NEXIS and various editions of *Jane's Fighting Ships* (Jane's Publishing); *Jane's Naval Weapons Systems* (Jane's Publishing); *Jane's Armour and Artillery* (Jane's Publishing); *Jane's Infantry Weapons* (Jane's Publishing); *Jane's Military Vehicles and Logistics* (Jane's Publishing); *Jane's Land-Based Air Defence* (Jane's Publishing); *Jane's All the World's Aircraft* (Jane's Publishing); *Jane's Battlefield Surveillance Systems* (Jane's Publishing); *Jane's Radar and Electronic Warfare Systems* (Jane's Publishing), *Jane's C^3I Systems* (Jane's Publishing); *Jane's Air-Launched Weapons Systems* (Jane's Publishing); *Jane's Defence Appointments & Procurement Handbook (Middle East Edition)* (Jane's Publishing); *Tanks of the World* (Bernard and Grafe); *Weyer's Warships* (Bernard and Grafe); and *Warplanes of the World* (Bernard and Grafe).

Other military background, effectiveness, strength, organizational, and history data are taken from Anthony H. Cordesman, *The Gulf and the Search for Strategic Stability*, Boulder, Westview, 1984, *The Gulf and the West*, Boulder, Westview, 1988; and *Weapons of Mass Destruction in the Middle East*, London, Brassey's/RUSI, 1991; Anthony H. Cordesman and Abraham Wagner, *The Lessons of Modern War*, Volume 2, Boulder, Westview, 1990; Department of Defense, *Conduct of the Persian Gulf War: Final Report*, Department of Defense, April, 1992, pp. 10–12; the relevant country or war sections of Herbert K. Tillema, *International Conflict Since 1945*, Boulder, Westview, 1991; Department of Defense and Department of State, *Congressional Presentation for Security Assistance Programs, Fiscal Year 1993*, Washington, Department of State, 1992; various annual editions of John Laffin's *The World in Conflict* or *War Annual*, London, Brassey's; and John Keegan, *World Armies*, London, Macmillan, 1983.

3. Many of these borders are in dispute, particularly the boundaries with Afghanistan and Pakistan. Iran seemed close to an agreement with Iraq in the spring of 1991, but the agreement was not committed to writing before the invasion of Kuwait led to a breakdown of negotiations. Iran also occupies three islands claimed by the UAE: Jazireh Greater Tunb, Lesser Tunb, and Abu Musa.

4. CIA, *World Factbook, 1991*, pp. 146–147.

5. *Petroleum Economist*; Petroleum Finance Company; and Congressional Quarterly, *The Middle East*, 7th Edition, Washington, Congressional Quarterly, 1990, p. 195.

6. *Oil and Gas Journal*, September 23, 1991, p. 62.

7. Congressional Quarterly, *The Middle East*, 7th Edition, Washington, Congressional Quarterly, 1990, p. 195.

8. *OJJ Special, Oil and Gas Journal*, December 30, 1991, pp. 43–49. Other estimates indicate that Iran has only 63 billion barrels of proven reserves and 52 billion barrels of probable reserves. See Joseph P. Riva, Jr., of the Congressional Research Service, writing in *Oil and Gas Journal*, September 23, 1991, p. 62.

9. This, however, only amounts to about 1,362 cubic meters per person, less than half the total for a citizen of the U.S. *Los Angeles Times*, January 28, 1992, p. C-1.

10. Some estimates put Iran's 1991 oil revenues at about $15 billion and its domestic spending needs at $15 billion. Economist Intelligence Unit, *Country Report on Iran, 1991*; *New York Times*, February 11, 1992, p. A-11; *Defense News*, March 2, 1992, pp. 3 and 29; *Washington Post*, September 10, 1991, p. A-21; February 2, 1992, p. A-1; *Wall Street Journal*, September 16, 1991, p. A-1; *Washington Times*, April 29, 1989, p. A-9; *Jane's Defence Weekly*, June 17, 1989, pp. 1254–1255; *Los Angeles Times*, January 13, 1992, p. A9.

11. The CIA had helped provide training to Barzani's forces with the support and financing of the shah.

12. For a detailed history of these events, and analysis of the fighting, see Anthony H. Cordesman and Abraham Wagner, *The Lessons of Modern War*, Volume 2, Boulder, Westview, 1990.

13. *Washington Post*, August 20, 1989, p. A-1.

14. *Defense News*, March 2, 1992, pp. 3 and 29; *Washington Post*, September 10, 1991, p. A-21; *Wall Street Journal*, September 16, 1991, p. A-1; *Washington Times*, April 29, 1989, p. A-9; *Jane's Defence Weekly*, June 17, 1989, pp. 1254–1255; *Los Angeles Times*, January 13, 1992, p. A9.

15. These purges continued in March and April of 1989. *Washington Times*, April 20, 1989, p. A-2.

16. *Jane's Defence Weekly*, June 30, 1990, pp. 1301–1302.

17. *New York Times*, September 3, 1989, p. A-4; *Washington Post*, September 3, 1989, p. A-25.

18. Afshar was deputy chief of staff at the armed forces headquarters when Rafsanjani had command over the military.

19. *Jane's Defence Weekly*, June 30, 1990, pp. 1301–1302; March 18, 1989, p. 428; *Baltimore Sun*, February 28, 1989, p. 2A; *Washington Times*, March 23, 1989, p. A-7; April 20, 1989, p. A-2.

20. *New York Times*, March 24, 1992, p. A-8; May 10, 1992, p. A-15; *Washington Post*, April 14, 1992, p. A-16; April 18, 1992, pp. A-14, A-20; *Washington Times*, April 15, 1992, p. A-1; May 18, 1992, p. E-4; *Wall Street Journal*, April 16, 1992, p. A-18.

21. *Jane's Defence Weekly*, March 18, 1989, p. 428; *Baltimore Sun*, February 28, 1989, p. 2A; *Washington Times*, March 23, 1989, p. A-7; May 26, 1992, p. A-2; June 9, 1992, p. A-2; June 16, 1992, p. A-2; July 8, 1992, p. A-7; *The Estimate*, October 13–16, 1989, p. 1; *Washington Post*, April 28, 1992, p. A-1; July 16, 1992, p. A-18; *Wall Street Journal*, May 5, 1992, p. A-1.

22. *Washington Times*, December 17, 1991, p. F-4; November 20, 1991, p. A-7.

23. *Defense News*, March 2, 1992, pp. 3 and 29; *Washington Post*, March 2, 1991, p. A-17; May 20, 1992, p. A-25; May 27, 1992, p. A-19; *Washington Times*, February 28, 1992, p. F-1; *New York Times*, February 22, 1992, p. A-4.

24. *Washington Post*, April 17, 1992, p. A-18, September 25, 1992, p. 31; September 29, 1992, p. A-15; *New York Times*, April 16, 1992; September 17, 1992, p. A-12; *Armed Forces Journal*, July, 1992, p. 23.

25. *Washington Post*, March 2, 1991, p. A-17; *Washington Times*, February 28, 1992, p. F-1; May 8, 1992, p. 9; *Security Intelligence Report*, November 4, 1991, p. 4; *Economist*, November 16, 1991, p. 51; UPI, January 14, 1992; Paul Wilkinson, "Terrorism, Iran, and the Gulf Region," *Jane's Intelligence Review*, May, 1992, pp. 222–224.

26. *New York Times*, December 31, 1991, p. A-7; *Washington Post*, March 2, 1991, p. A-17; *Washington Times*, February 28, 1992, p. F-1; *Philadelphia Inquirer*, January 16, 1992; *Newsweek*, February 24, 1992, p. 32.

27. Arms Control and Disarmament Agency (ACDA), *World Military Expenditures and Arms Transfers, 1989*, Washington, GPO, 1990, p. 60.

28. IISS, *Military Balance*, 1990–1991 and 1991–1992 editions.

29. British sources quoted in *Jane's Defence Weekly*, February 1, 1992, p. 158. *The Egyptian Gazette* projected expenditures of $5 billion per year in 1992, 1993, and 1994 in its January 29, 1992, issue. The Jaffee Center estimated expenditures of $8.5 billion in 1989 and $8.6 billion in 1990. Andrew Duncan of the IISS estimated expenditures of $10 billion annually in 1992, 1993, and 1994 in *Defense News*, January 27, 1992.

30. Author's guesstimate. Iran claimed in February, 1992 that it was spending only 1.3% of its GNP on defense. *Washington Times*, February 20, 1992, p. A-9.

31. Arms Control and Disarmament Agency (ACDA), *World Military Expenditures and Arms Transfers, 1990*, Washington, GPO, 1990, Table II.

32. Arms Control and Disarmament Agency (ACDA), *World Military Expenditures and Arms Transfers, 1985*, Washington, GPO, 1985, p. 134.

33. Arms Control and Disarmament Agency (ACDA), *World Military Expenditures and Arms Transfers, 1989*, Washington, GPO, 1990, p. 117.

34. Arms Control and Disarmament Agency (ACDA), *World Military Expenditures and Arms Transfers, 1990*, Washington, GPO, 1990, pp. 133–134.

35. *New York Times*, December 8, 1991, p. 1; Richard M. Preece, *Arms Shipments to Iran*, Congressional Research Service IB87022, October 26, 1988.

36. This total compares with a total of $8.9 billion in new orders during 1983–1986—the height of the Iran-Iraq War.

37. Richard F. Grimmett, *Conventional Arms Transfers to the Third World, 1984–1991*, Washington, Congressional Research Service, CRS-9 1-577F, July 20, 1992, pp. CRS-53 and CRS-66; Robert Gates, "Statement of the Director of Central Intelligence Before the U.S. House of Representatives Armed Services Committee Defense Policy Panel," March 27, 1992; *Washington Times*, June 4, 1992, p. G-3; *New York Times*, August 8, 1992, p. 2; *Sunday Times* (London), May 31, 1992, pp. 22–23.

38. Iran has long been making light arms and ammunition. The shah set up the Import Substitute Industrialization (ISI) program in 1970 with the goal of making Iran self-sufficient in arms.

39. *Jane's Defence Weekly*, June 30, 1989, pp. 1299–1301.

40. Northrop helped Iran set up Iran Aircraft Industries in 1970, but this virtually ceased operation in 1979. *Jane's Defence Weekly*, February 4, 1989, pp. 163 and 167; February 11, 1989, p. 219; November 19, 1988, pp. 1252–1253; June 30, 1989, pp. 1299–1301; February 11, 1992, p. 159.

41. Based on CIA estimates. Sources disagree sharply on the exact percentages involved.

42. *Washington Post*, May 8, 1992, p. A-17; CIA, *World Factbaook, 1991*.

43. IISS, *Military Balance, 1991–1992*. While Iran occasionally shows women in military roles for propaganda purposes, it does not employ them in any meaningful military roles.

44. In addition to the general sources on Iranian force strength referenced at the beginning of this section, this analysis draws on the *Washington Times*, May 2, 1989, p. A-9; June 23, 1989, p. A-9; March 1, 1992, p. B-3; March 22, 1989, p. A-8; January 17, 1992, p. A-1; February 20, 1992, p. 9; *Armed Forces Journal*, March, 1992, pp. 26–27; *Defense Electronics*, March, 1992, p. 16; *Inside the Air Force*, February 28, 1992, p. 1; *Jane's Defence Weekly*, November 19, 1988, pp. 1252–1253; June 3, 1988, p. 1057; February 11, 1989, p. 219; June 30, 1990, pp. 1299–1302; February 11, 1992, pp. 158–159; *Armed Forces* (UK), May, 1989, pp. 206–209; *Washington Post*, June 23, 1989, p. A-1; August 18, 1989, p. A-25; August 20, 1989, p. A-1; September 3, 1989, p. A-25; February 1, 1992, p. A-1; February 2, 1992, p. A-1; February 5, 1992, p. A-19; *New York Times*, September 3, 1989, p. A-4; *The Estimate*, October 13–26, 1989, p. 1; *Christian Science Monitor*, February 6, 1992, p. 19; *Philadelphia Inquirer*, February 6, 1992, p. A-6; *Los Angeles Times*, January 7, 1992, p. A-1; *Baltimore Sun*, January 25, 1992, p. 4A;

Defense News, January 27, 1922, p. 45; February 17, 1992, p. 1; *Chicago Tribune,* January 19, 1992, p. 1.

45. The author visited this display in August after a substantial amount of the equipment had been moved to Jordan and to other areas. Even then, there were immense stocks of heavy weapons, almost all of which had been abandoned without any combat damage. It should be noted, however, that Iraq made claims about capturing tanks that seem to have included all light tanks and BMP-1s.

46. *Washington Times,* March 9, 1989, p. A-1, and March 22, 1989, p. A-8; May 2, 1989, p. A-9; June 23, 1989, p. A-9; *Washington Post,* June 23, 1989, p. A-1; *Los Angeles Times,* February 14, 1989, p. 5; *Jane's Defence Weekly,* February 4, 1989, pp. 163 and 167; February 11, 1992, p. 159.

47. Reports differed sharply. One indicated that the Soviet Union was selling T-72s for as little as $50,000 each, while another indicated that it was selling Iran a T-72 production plant for $9 billion. Yet Marshal Yevgeny Shaposhnikov, the senior military officer in the CIS, stated that it had curbed all sales to Iran on February 1, 1992. *Washington Post,* February 1, 1992, p. A-1; February 2, 1992, p. A-19; *Los Angeles Times,* January 7, 1992, p. A-7.

48. *Jane's Defence Weekly,* February 4, 1989, pp. 163 and 167; February 11, 1992, p. 159; *Washington Times,* June 23, 1989, p. A-9.

49. *Washington Post,* March 28, 1992, p. A-1.

50. Based on estimates by an Israeli civilian expert.

51. Adapted from interviews with U.S., British, and Israeli experts and Iranian exiles and the IISS, Annapolis, and JCSS data bases, and the *Washington Times,* January 16, 1992, p. G-4; *Washington Post,* February 1, 1992, p. A1; February 2, 1992, pp. A1 and A25; February 5, p. A-19; *Financial Times,* February 6, 1992, p. 4; *Christian Science Monitor,* February 6, 1992, p. 19; *Defense News,* February 17, 1992, p. 1.

52. In addition to the general sources on Iranian force strength referenced at the beginning of this section, this analysis draws on the *Washington Times,* May 2, 1989, p. A-9; June 23, 1989, p. A-9; March 1, 1992, p. B-3; March 22, 1989, p. A-8; January 17, 1992, p. A-1; February 20, 1992, p. 9; *Armed Forces Journal,* March, 1992, pp. 26–27; *Defense Electronics,* March, 1992, p. 16; *Inside the Air Force,* February 28, 1992, p. 1; *Jane's Defence Weekly,* November 19, 1988, pp. 1252–1253; June 3, 1988, p. 1057; February 11, 1989, p. 219; June 30, 1990, pp. 1299–1302; February 11, 1992, pp. 158–159; *Armed Forces* (UK), May, 1989, pp. 206–209; *Washington Post,* June 23, 1989, p. A-1; August 18, 1989, p. A-25; August 20, 1989, p. A-1; September 3, 1989, p. A-25; February 1, 1992, p. A-1; February 2, 1992, p. A-1; February 5, 1992, p. A-19; *New York Times,* September 3, 1989, p. A-4; *The Estimate,* October 13–26, 1989, p. 1; *Christian Science Monitor,* February 6, 1992, p. 19; *Philadelphia Inquirer,* February 6, 1992, p. A-6; *Los Angeles Times,* January 7, 1992, p. A-1; *Baltimore Sun,* January 25, 1992, p. 4A; *Defense News,* January 27, 1922, p. 45; February 17, 1992, p. 1; *Chicago Tribune,* January 19, 1992, p. 1.

53. Based on interviews with British, Israeli, and U.S. experts. Reports of MiG-31s do not seem to be correct. Adapted from the IISS, Annapolis, and JCSS data bases, and the *Washington Times,* January 16, 1992, p. G-4; *Washington Post,* February 1, 1992, p. A1; February 2, 1992, pp. A1 and A25; February 5, 1992, p. A-19; *Financial Times,* February 6, 1992, p. 4; *Christian Science Monitor,* February 6, 1992, p. 19; *Defense News,* February 17, 1992, p. 1.

54. Based on interviews with British, Israeli, and U.S. experts. *Washington Times,* January 16, 1992, p. G-4; *Washington Post,* February 1, 1992, p. A1; February 2, 1992, pp. A1 and A25; February 5, 1992, p. A-19; *Financial Times,* February 6, 1992, p. 4; *Christian Science Monitor,* February 6, 1992, p. 19; *Defense News,* February 17, 1992, p. 1.

55. *Washington Times,* January 16, 1992, p. G-4; *Washington Post,* February 1, 1992, p. A1; February 2, 1992, pp. A1 and A25; February 5, 1992, p. A-19; *Financial Times,* February 6, 1992, p. 4; *Christian Science Monitor,* February 6, 1992, p. 19; *Defense News,* February 17, 1992, p. 1; *Jane's Defence Weekly,* February 1, 1992, p. 159.

56. Dick Palowski, *Changes in Threat Air Combat Doctrine and Force Structure*, 24th Edition, General Dynamics DWIC-91, Fort Worth Division, February, 1992, pp. I-85 to I–117.

57. Dick Palowski, *Changes in Threat Air Combat Doctrine and Force Structure*, 24th Edition, General Dynamics DWIC-91, Fort Worth Division, February, 1992, pp. I-85 to I–117.

58. Dick Palowski, *Changes in Threat Air Combat Doctrine and Force Structure*, 24th Edition, General Dynamics DWIC-91, Fort Worth Division, February, 1992, pp. I-85 to I–117.

59. *Aviation Week and Space Technology*, April 10, 1989, pp. 19–20; *New York Times*, April 5, 1989, and September 7, 1989; *Washington Times*, January 16, 1989; *FBIS/NES*, April 10, 1989.

60. The Su-24 has a wing area of 575 square feet, an empty weight of 41,845 pounds, carries 3,385 gallons or 22,000 pounds of fuel, has a takeoff weight of 871,570 pounds with bombs and two external fuel tanks, carries 2,800 gallons or 18,200 pounds of external fuel, has a combat thrust-to-weight ratio of 1.02, a combat wing loading of 96 pounds per square foot, and a maximum load factor of 7.5G. *Jane's Soviet Intelligence Review*, July, 1990, pp. 298–300; *Jane's Defence Weekly*, June 25, 1985, pp. 1226–1227; and Dick Palowski, *Changes in Threat Air Combat Doctrine and Force Structure*, 24th Edition, General Dynamics DWIC-91, Fort Worth Division, February, 1992, pp. I-65 and I-110 to I–117.

61. Dick Palowski, *Changes in Threat Air Combat Doctrine and Force Structure*, 24th Edition, General Dynamics DWIC-91, Fort Worth Division, February, 1992, pp. I-65 and I-110 to I–117.

62. USAF briefing, September, 1981. One B-727 and 2 B-767ERs are unaccounted for.

63. *Washington Times*, January 16, 1992, p. G-4; *Washington Post*, February 1, 1992, p. A1; February 2, 1992, pp. A1 and A25; February 5, 1992, p. A-19; *Financial Times*, February 6, 1992, p. 4; *Christian Science Monitor*, February 6, 1992, p. 19; *Defense News*, February 17, 1992, p. 1.

64. Adapted from the IISS, Annapolis, and JCSS data bases, and the *Washington Times*, January 16, 1992, p. G-4; *Washington Post*, February 1, 1992, p. A1; February 2, 1992, pp. A1 and A25; February 5, 1992, p. A-19; *Financial Times*, February 6, 1992, p. 4; *Christian Science Monitor*, February 6, 1992, p. 19; *Defense News*, February 17, 1992, p. 1.

65. Based on interviews with British, U.S., and Israel experts. *Washington Times*, January 16, 1992, p. G-4; *Washington Post*, February 1, 1992, p. A1; February 2, 1992, pp. A1 and A25; February 5, 1992, p. A-19; *Financial Times*, February 6, 1992, p. 4; *Christian Science Monitor*, February 6, 1992, p. 19; *Defense News*, February 17, 1992, p. 1.

66. In addition to the general sources on Iranian force strength referenced at the beginning of this section, this analysis draws on John Jordan, "The Iranian Navy," *Jane's Intelligence Review*, May, 1992, pp. 213–216; the *Washington Times*, May 2, 1989, p. A-9; June 23, 1989, p. A-9; March 1, 1992, p. B-3; March 22, 1989, p. A-8; January 17, 1992, p. A-1; February 20, 1992, p. 9; *Armed Forces Journal*, March, 1992, pp. 26–27; *Defense Electronics*, March, 1992, p. 16; *Inside the Air Force*, February 28, 1992, p. 1; *Jane's Defence Weekly*, November 19, 1988, pp. 1252–1253; June 3, 1988, p. 1057; February 11, 1989, p. 219; June 30, 1990, pp. 1299–1302; February 11, 1992, pp. 158–159; *Armed Forces* (UK), May, 1989, pp. 206–209; *Washington Post*, June 23, 1989, p. A-1; August 18, 1989, p. A-25; August 20, 1989, p. A-1; September 3, 1989, p. A-25; February 1, 1992, p. A-1; February 2, 1992, p. A-1; February 5, 1992, p. A-19; *New York Times*, September 3, 1989, p. A-4; *The Estimate*, October 13-26, 1989, p. 1; *Christian Science Monitor*, February 6, 1992, p. 19; *Philadelphia Inquirer*, February 6, 1992, p. A-6; *Los Angeles Times*, January 7, 1992, p. A-1; *Baltimore Sun*, January 25, 1992, p. 4A; *Defense News*, January 27, 1922, p. 45; February 17, 1992, p. 1; *Chicago Tribune*, January 19, 1992, p. 1.

67. Larry Dickerson, "Iranian Power Projection in the Persian Gulf," *World Weapons Review*, August 12, 1987, p. 7.

68. FBIS-NES-89-144, July 28, 1989, p. 51; FBIS-NES-89-191, October 4, 1989, p. 66; FBIS-NES-89-206, October 26, 1989, p. 66; FBIS-NES-89-214, November 7, 1989, p. 73; *International Defense Review*, June, 1990, pp. 51–52.

69. Adapted from the IISS, Annapolis, and JCSS data bases, and the *Washington Times*, January 16, 1992, p. G-4; *Washington Post*, February 1, 1992, p. A1; February 2, 1992, pp. A1 and A25; February 5, 1992, p. A-19; *Financial Times*, February 6, 1992, p. 4; *Christian Science Monitor*, February 6, 1992, p. 19; *Defense News*, February 17, 1992, p. 1.

70. *Jane's Fighting Ships, 1991–1992*, pp. 285–291.

71. Adapted from the IISS, Annapolis, and JCSS data bases, and the *Washington Times*, January 16, 1992, p. G-4; *Washington Post*, February 1, 1992, p. A1; February 2, 1992, pp. A1 and A25; February 5, 1992, p. A-19; *Financial Times*, February 6, 1992, p. 4; *Christian Science Monitor*, February 6, 1992, p. 19; *Defense News*, February 17, 1992, p. 1.

72. The submarines lay mines, have a five man crew, and have a speed of 6 knots. Iran claims to have made one of the submarines. The first underwent trials in 1987. The second was delivered in 1988. These ships are difficult to use in mine laying and often require frogmen to place the mines. It is not surprising if Iran abandoned them as lacking effectiveness once the Iran-Iraq War was over. *Jane's Fighting Ships, 1991–1992*, p. 286.

73. *Washington Times*, January 16, 1992, p. G-4; *Washington Post*, February 1, 1992, p. A1; February 2, 1992, pp. A1 and A25; February 5, 1992, p. A-19; September 26, 1992, p. A-15; *Financial Times*, February 6, 1992, p. 4; *Christian Science Monitor*, February 6, 1992, p. 19; *Defense News*, February 17, 1992, p. 1.

74. These assessments are based on various editions of IISS, *Military Balance*; Jaffee Center, *Middle East Military Balance*, and *Jane's Defence Weekly*, July 11, 1987, p. 15.

75. *Jane's Defence Weekly*, June 6, 1987, p. 1113; Dick Palowski, *Changes in Threat Air Combat Doctrine and Force Structure*, 24th Edition, Fort Worth, General Dynamics DWIC-91, February, 1992.

76. *Washington Times*, March 9, 1989, p. A-1; *Los Angeles Times*, February 14, 1989, p. 5.

77. *Armed Forces Journal*, March, 1992, pp. 26–28; *Washington Times*, January 16, 1992, p. G-4; April 6, 1992, p. 8; *Washington Post*, April 8, 1992, p. A-19.

78. The following details of the Iranian missile program are taken from W. Seth Carus and Joseph S. Bermudez, "Iran's Growing Missile Forces," *Jane's Defence Weekly*, July 23, 1988, pp. 126–131.

79. Iran publicly displayed the Oghab at a military show in Libreville in 1989. *Jane's Defence Weekly*, February 11, 1989, p. 219; Lora Lumpe, Lisbeth Gronlund, and David C. Wright, "Third World Missiles Fall Short," *Bulletin of the Atomic Scientists*, March, 1992, pp. 30–36.

80. *Jane's Defence Weekly*, June 20, 1987, p. 1289; Lora Lumpe, Lisbeth Gronlund, and David C. Wright, "Third World Missiles Fall Short," *Bulletin of the Atomic Scientists*, March, 1992, pp. 30–36.

81. Some estimates indicate a range of up to 200 kilometers. For background on the system, see *Financial Times*, June 8, 1988, p. 20, and *The Middle East*, April 1988, pp. 1 and 18.

82. The reader should be aware that all such performance data are nominal and that various sources report significant differences in given performance characteristics.

83. CRS Report for Congress, *Missile Proliferation: Survey of Emerging Missile Forces*, Congressional Research Service, Report 88-642F, February 9, 1989, pp. 52–53.

84. Edward L. Korb, editor, *The World's Missile Systems*, 7th Edition, General Dynamics, Pomona Division, April, 1982, pp. 223–226.

85. Iran had to target an inherently inaccurate missile without the kind of maps, satellite aids, and other targeting systems to correct for the fact the world is not perfectly round and the inevitable bias errors in the missile's guidance systems. Beyond visual range targeting in excess of 200 miles is a major problem for nations without extensive test ranges and satellite or other advanced intelligence systems.

86. The following details of the Iranian missile program are taken from W. Seth Carus and Joseph S. Bermudez, "Iran's Growing Missile Forces," *Jane's Defence Weekly*, July 23, 1988, pp. 126–131.

87. *Baltimore Sun*, March 9, 1989; *New York Times*, March 12, 1992, p. A-12; March 18, 1992, p. A-12; *Washington Post*, February 2, 1992, p. A-1; Lora Lumpe, Lisbeth Gronlund, and David C. Wright, "Third World Missiles Fall Short," *Bulletin of the Atomic Scientists*, March, 1992, pp. 30–36; "North Korea Coners ME Missile Market," *Mednews*, Vol. 5, 16, May 18, 1992, pp. 1–5; *Newsweek*, June 22, 1992, pp. 42–44.

88. Iran allowed a North Korean freighter, the *Dae Hung Ho*, to dock at Bandar Abbas and then transshipped the missiles to Syria by air. Syria is reported to have allowed Iran to deliver arms to the Hizbollah Party of God faction in Lebanon in return. *Defense News*, October 16, 1989, p. 60; *Washington Times*, June 18, 1990, p. A1; March 10, 1992, p. A-3; Lora Lumpe, Lisbeth Gronlund, and David C. Wright, "Third World Missiles Fall Short," *Bulletin of the Atomic Scientists*, March, 1992, pp. 30–36; *Mednews*, Vol. 5, 16, May 18, 1992, pp. 1–5; *Newsweek*, June 22, 1992, pp. 42–44; Washington Times, May 24, 1991, p. 5.

89. General references for this section include "Chemical and Biological Warfare," hearing before the Committee on Foreign Relations, U.S. Senate, 91st Congress, April 30, 1969; Department of Political and Security Council Affairs, *Chemical and Bacteriological (Biological) Weapons and the Effects of Their Possible Use*, Report of the Secretary General, United Nations, New York, 1969; unpublished testimony of W. Seth Carus before the Committee on Governmental Affairs, U.S. Senate, February 9, 1989; W. Seth Carus, "Chemical Weapons in the Middle East," *Policy Focus*, Number 9, Washington Institute for Near East Policy, December, 1988; unpublished testimony of David Goldberg, Foreign Science and Technology Center, U.S. Army Intelligence Agency, before the Committee on Governmental Affairs, U.S. Senate, February 9, 1989; unpublished testimony of Barry J. Erlick, senior biological warfare analyst, U.S. Army, before the Committee on Governmental Affairs, U.S. Senate, February 9, 1989; unpublished testimony of Robert Mullen Cook-Deegan, Physicians for Human Rights, before the Committee on Governmental Affairs, U.S. Senate, February 9, 1989; Elisa D. Harris, "Chemical Weapons Proliferation in the Developing World," RUSI and Brassey's *Defense Yearbook, 1989*, London, 1988, pp. 67–88; and "Winds of Death: Iraq's Use of Poison Gas Against Its Kurdish Population," Report of a Medical Mission to Turkish Kurdistan by Physicians for Human Rights, February, 1989.

90. *Washington Times*, October 29, 1986, p. 9-A.

91. *Washington Times*, October 29, 1986, p. 9-A.

92. Iran was caught trying to buy 430 drums of thiodiglycol feedstock in April, 1988 from a U.S. firm called Alcolac. *Baltimore Sun*, February 11, 1988, p. 6; Kenneth R. Timmerman, *Weapons of Mass Destruction: The Cases of Iran, Syria, and Libya*, Simon Wiesenthal Center, Los Angeles, August, 1992, pp. 28–45.

93. While rumors surfaced in November, 1986 that Iran had bought nerve gas bombs and warheads from Libya—which had obtained such weapons from the USSR— these reports were almost certainly false. Iran does not seem to have used nerve gas at any time during the conflict.

94. Unpublished "Statement of the Honorable William H. Webster, Director, Central Intelligence Agency, Before the Committee on Governmental Affairs, Hearings on Global Spread of Chemical and Biological Weapons," February 9, 1989.

95. Unpublished "Statement of the Honorable William H. Webster, Director, Central Intelligence Agency, Before the Committee on Governmental Affairs, Hearings on Global Spread of Chemical and Biological Weapons," February 9, 1989.

96. Unpublished "Statement of the Honorable William H. Webster, Director, Central Intelligence Agency, Before the Committee on Governmental Affairs, Hearings on Global Spread of Chemical and Biological Weapons," February 9, 1989.

97. IRNA (English), October 19, 1988, as reported in FBIS, *Near East and South Asia*, October 19, 1988, pp. 55–56.

98. Working papers by Leonard Spector; *Observer*, June 12, 1988; *U.S. News and World Report*, February 12, 1990; *FBIS-NES*, March 23, 1990, p. 57; *Defense and Foreign Affairs*,

November 20, 1989, p. 2; *New York Times,* July 1, 1989; May 9, 1989; June 27, 1989; *Financial Times,* February 6, 1992, p. 3.

99. Such reports begin in the SIPRI Yearbooks in 1982 and occur sporadically through the 1988 edition.

100. *New York Times,* August 13, 1989, p. 11.

101. James Smith, "Biological Weapons Developments," *Jane's Intelligence Review,* November, 1991, pp. 483–487; *New York Times,* August 13, 1989, p. 11; Kenneth R. Timmerman, *Weapons of Mass Destruction: The Cases of Iran, Syria, and Libya,* Simon Wiesenthal Center, Los Angeles, August, 1992, pp. 28–45.

102. Working papers by Leonard Spector; Daniel Poneman, *Nuclear Power in the Developing World,* London, Allen and Unwin, 1982, Chapter 5; "Iran's Nuclear Weapons Program," *Mednews,* Vol. 5, 17/18, June 8, 1992, pp. 1–7.

103. Some reports indicate that one reactor at Bushehr was 80% complete.

104. Much of this analysis is based on research by Leonard Spector of the Carnegie Endowment.

105. The lasers were exported by a firm headed by Jeffery Earkens, who had worked on classified laser enrichment technology. They seem to have been filled with gases that did not produce the optimal wave length for nuclear enrichment but could be refilled with the gases necessary to produce the required wave length.

106. *Los Angeles Times,* August 22, 1979; Leonard Spector, *Going Nuclear,* Cambridge, Ballinger, 1987, pp. 47–53; Shyam Bhatia, *Nuclear Rivals in the Middle East,* London, Routledge, 1988, p. 85; JPRS-NTD, December 23, 1989.

107. *Observer,* May 17, 1987.

108. Yellow cake is not subject to IAEA inspection. Kenneth R. Timmerman, *Weapons of Mass Destruction: The Cases of Iran, Syria, and Libya,* Simon Wiesenthal Center, Los Angeles, August, 1992, pp. 28–45.

109. Working papers by Leonard Spector, and *Washington Post,* April 12, 1987.

110. Uranium dioxide is normally subject to IAEA safeguards and inspection, but Argentine compliance is uncertain. Argentina sold at least 3 metric tons to Algeria in January, 1986. *Nucleonics Week,* May 7, 1987, p. 6.

111. Argentina has not ratified the nuclear nonproliferation treaty, but Iran is an NPT signatory, and Argentina has agreed to IAEA safeguards. It is unclear what impact the Argentinean agreement with Iran will have on Iran's nuclear weapons program. As has been discussed earlier, agreement to IAEA safeguards and inspection does not preclude the development of a nuclear weapon.

112. *Washington Times,* April 22, 1987, p. 6; *Economist,* "Foreign Report," April 2, 1987, p. 7; "Iran's Nuclear Weapons Program," *Mednews,* Vol. 5,17/18, June 8, 1992, pp. 1–7.

113. Many of the details on these aspects of the Iranian effort are drawn from working papers provided by Leonard Spector of the Carnegie Endowment, and Warren Donnelly of the Congressional Research Service. Also see *Nucleonics Week,* November 19, 1987, p. 1; November 26, 1987, p. 5; March 3, 1988, p. 7; July 28, 1988, p. 15.

114. *Nucleonics Week,* November 19, 1987, p. 1; November 26, 1987, p. 5.

115. The U.S. had supplied 11 pounds of 93% enriched uranium in the mid-1970s, but this was largely depleted and could not keep the reactor running continuously. Based upon work by Leonard Spector; *Nucleonics Week,* May 14 ,1989, p. 2; *Observer,* March 6, 1988.

116. Reuters, February 7, 1992, AM Cycle, and *Rio Negro,* February 7, 1992.

117. The German firm may be Siemens or one of its subsidiaries, like KWU of Brazil. Agence France Presse, February 12, 1992; *Los Angeles Times,* January 27, 1991, p. 1; Agence France Presse, December 2, 1991.

118. *Nuclear Engineering International,* March, 1990, p. 3.

119. Tehran Domestic Service, March 7, 1990; *Nuclear News,* April, 1990, p. 19; *Nuclear Engineering International,* May, 1990, p. 7.

120. *Korea Times,* March 2, 1990.

121. *Washington Post,* November 15, 1991, p. A-33; Agence France Presse, November 20, 1991; AP AM Cycle, November 15, 1991; "Iran's Nuclear Weapons Program," *Mednews,* Vol. 5, 17/18, June 8, 1992, pp. 1–7.

122. *Nuclear Fuel,* November 25, 1991, p. 8.

123. The agreements made under the shah have given Iran about 250–300 metric tons of uranium enriched to 3%. During 1980–1990, Iran refused to accept the material or pay for it. When Iran did ask for the material in 1991, France used the fact that Iran's option to obtain enriched material for its investment had expired to deny Iran shipment of the material guaranteed under the original terms of the Iranian investment. *Washington Times,* November 15, 1991, p. F-4; David Albright and Mark Hibbs, "Spotlight Shifts to Iran," *Bulletin of the Atomic Scientists,* March, 1992, pp. 9–12.

124. *Washington Post,* April 12, 1987, p. D-1; James Bruce, "Iraq and Iran: Running the Nuclear Technology Race," *Jane's Defence Weekly,* December 5, 1988, p. 1307; working papers by Leonard Spector; JPRS-TND, October 6, 1989, p. 19.

125. *El Independiente* (Madrid), February 5 and 6, 1990; *FBIS-Middle East,* December 1, 1988.

126. *El Independiente* (Madrid), February 5 and 6, 1990; *FBIS-Middle East,* December 1, 1988.

127. Working papers by Leonard Spector; *Observer,* June 12, 1988; *U.S. News and World Report,* February 12, 1990; *FBIS-NES,* March 23, 1990, p. 57; *FBIS-EAS,* December 9, 1989; December 11, 1989; *Defense and Foreign Affairs,* November 20, 1989, p. 2; *New York Times,* May 8, 1989; June 27, 1989.

128. *FBIS-Near East,* December 1, 1988, and April 4, 1989; David Albright and Mark Hibbs, "Spotlight Shifts to Iran," *Bulletin of the Atomic Scientists,* March, 1992, pp. 9–12.

129. *Washington Times,* November 6, 1991, p. F-4; November 1, 1991, p. 7; *Los_Angeles Times,* October 31, 1991, p. B-4; March 17, 1992, p. 1; David Albright and Mark Hibbs, "Spotlight Shifts to Iran," *Bulletin of the Atomic Scientists,* March, 1992, pp. 9–12; *Washington Post,* October 31, 1991, p. 1; January 12, 1992, p. C-7; February 2, 1992, p. A-1, September 12, 1992, p. A-13; "Iran's Nuclear Weapons Program," *Mednews,* Vol. 5, 17/18, June 8, 1992, pp. 1–7; *New York Times,* September 11, 1992, p. A-6..

130. *Washington Times,* November 15, 1991, p. F-4; *Washington Post,* February 7, 1992, p. A-18; February 15, 1992, p. A-29; AP PM Cycle, February 6, 1992; "Iran's Nuclear Weapons Program," *Mednews,* Vol. 5, 17/18, June 8, 1992, pp. 1–7

131. *Washington Post,* February 15, 1992, pp. A-29–A-30; *Los Angeles Times,* March 17, 1992, p. 1; AP, AM Cycle, February 12, 1992; Agence France Presse, February 12, 1992.

132. Although the possibility is a real one. *Financial Times,* January 30, 1992, p. 4; Agence France Presse, January 26, 1992; *Sunday Times,* January 26, 1992.

133. *Los Angeles Times,* March 17, 1992, p. 1.

134. Estimates differ sharply over the prisoner of war issue. Iraq seems to have over 15,000 Iranian POWs, and Iran seems to hold over 30,000 Iraqis.

135. *New York Times,* March 22, 1992, p. A-9; April 10, 1992, p. A-3; *Washington Post,* April 10, 1992, p. A-46; April 16, 1992, p. 40.

136. The military manpower, force strength, and equipment estimates in this section are made by the author using a wide range of sources, including computerized data bases, interviews, and press clipping services. Most are impossible to reference in ways of use to the reader. The force strength statistics are generally taken from the latest edition of International Institute for Strategic Studies, *Military Balance* (IISS, London), in this case the 1991–1992 edition.

Extensive use has also been made of the annual editions of the Jaffee Center for Strategic Studies, *The Military Balance in the Middle East* (JCSS, Tel Aviv), especially the 1990–1991 edition and working materials from the coming edition. Material has also been drawn from computer print outs from NEXIS, the United States Naval Institute data base, and from the DMS/FI Market Intelligence Reports data base. Other sources include *Military Technology*, "World Defense Almanac for 1991–1992," published in 1992; Foreign Affairs Division, "Middle East Arms Control and Related Issues," Washington, Congressional Research Service, 91-384F, May 1, 1991; and *Middle East Economic Digest*, "MEED Special Report: Defense," Volume 35, December 13, 1991.

Weapons data are taken from many sources, including computerized material available in NEXIS, and various editions of *Jane's Fighting Ships* (Jane's Publishing); *Jane's Naval Weapons Systems* (Jane's Publishing); *Jane's Armour and Artillery* (Jane's Publishing); *Jane's Infantry Weapons* (Jane's Publishing); *Jane's Military Vehicles and Logistics* (Jane's Publishing); *Jane's Land-Based Air Defence* (Jane's Publishing); *Jane's All the World's Aircraft* (Jane's Publishing); *Jane's Battlefield Surveillance Systems* (Jane's Publishing); *Jane's Radar and Electronic Warfare Systems* (Jane's Publishing), *Jane's C³I Systems* (Jane's Publishing); *Jane's Air-Launched Weapons Systems* (Jane's Publishing); *Jane's Defence Appointments & Procurement Handbook (Middle East Edition)* (Jane's Publishing); *Tanks of the World* (Bernard and Grafe); *Weyer's Warships* (Bernard and Grafe); and *Warplanes of the World* (Bernard and Grafe).

Other military background, effectiveness, strength, organizational, and history data are taken from Anthony H. Cordesman, *The Gulf and the Search for Strategic Stability*, Boulder, Westview, 1984, *The Gulf and the West*, Boulder, Westview, 1988, and *Weapons of Mass Destruction in the Middle East*, London, Brassey's/RUSI, 1991; Anthony H. Cordesman and Abraham Wagner, *The Lessons of Modern War*, Volume 2, Boulder, Westview, 1990; Department of Defense, *Conduct of the Persian Gulf War: Final Report*, Department of Defense, April, 1992, pp. 10–12; Norman Friedman, *Desert Victory*, Annapolis, Naval Institute Press, 1991; Bruce W. Watson, *Military Lessons of the Gulf War*, London, Greenhill, 1991; James F. Dunnigham and Austin Bay, *From Shield to Storm*, New York, Morrow; Roy Braybrook, *Air Power: The Coalition and Iraqi Air Forces*, London, Osprey, 1991; James Blackwell, *Thunder in the Desert*, New York, Bantam, 1990; the relevant country or war sections of Herbert K. Tillema, *International Conflict Since 1945*, Boulder, Westview, 1991; Department of Defense and Department of State, *Congressional Presentation for Security Assistance Programs, Fiscal Year 1993*, Washington, Department of State, 1992; various annual editions of John Laffin's *The World in Conflict* or *War Annual*, London, Brassey's; and John Keegan, *World Armies*, London, Macmillan, 1983.

137. Many of these borders are in dispute. Agreements were signed with Saudi Arabia in December, 1981, and Iraq seemed close to an agreement with Iran in the spring of 1991, but the Saudi agreement has never been ratified, and the agreement with Iran was not committed to writing before the invasion of Kuwait led to a breakdown of negotiations.

138. CIA, *World Factbook, 1991*, pp. 148–149.

139. Based on CIA estimates. Sources disagree sharply on the exact percentages involved.

140. CIA, *World Factbook, 1991*.

141. IISS, *Military Balance, 1991–1992*.

142. *Oil and Gas Journal*, September 23, 1991, p. 62.

143. *OJJ Special, Oil and Gas Journal*, December 30, 1991, pp. 43–49. Other estimates indicate that Iran has 100 billion barrels of proven reserves and 45 billion barrels of probable reserves. See Joseph P. Riva, Jr., of the Congressional Research Service, writing in the *Oil and Gas Journal*, September 23, 1991, p. 62.

144. *OJJ Special, Oil and Gas Journal*, December 30, 1991, pp. 43–49.

145. *Los Angeles Times*, January 28, 1992, p. C-1.

146. *Petroleum Economist*; Petroleum Finance Company; and Congressional Quarterly, *The Middle East*, 7th Edition, Washington, Congressional Quarterly, 1990, p. 195.

147. CIA, *World Factbook, 1991*, pp. 148–149.

148. Turkey recruited Sunni Arabs only until 1906.

149. Britain retained air bases at Habbiniyah and Shuaiba, the right to consult in foreign affairs, and free passage of troops through the country.

150. Herbert K. Tillema in *International Conflict Since 1945*, Boulder, Westview, 1991, p. 148.

151. Based on various World Bank working papers and editions of CIA, *World Factbook*, most notably the 1991 edition, pp. 148–149.

152. For a detailed history of these events and analysis of the fighting, see Anthony H. Cordesman and Abraham Wagner, *The Lessons of Modern War*, Volume 2, Boulder, Westview, 1990; Anthony H. Cordesman, *The Gulf and The West*, Boulder, Westview, 1988; and *The Iran-Iraq War and Western Security*, London, Jane's, 1987; and Department of Defense, *Conduct of the Persian Gulf War: Final Report*, Department of Defense, April, 1992, pp. 10–12.

153. Department of Defense, *Conduct of the Persian Gulf War: Final Report*, Department of Defense, April, 1992, pp. 10–12.

154. Some estimates of the Kurdish dead go as high as 300,000 but seem to be exaggerated. See Staff Report, "Kurdistan in the Time of Saddam Hussein," Committee on Foreign Relations of the U.S. Senate, S. Prt. 102-56, November, 1991. *Philadelphia Inquirer*, February 14 ,1992, p. A-23; *Washington Post*, February 22, 1992, p. 1; *Jane's Defence Weekly*, August 12, 1989, p. 249; *Toronto Star*, April 6, 1992, p. 11.

155. The author spent several hours listening to this conspiracy theory being expounded by senior Baath and Iraqi government officials in late 1989.

156. Arms Control and Disarmament Agency (ACDA), *World Military Expenditures and Arms Transfers, 1989*, Washington, GPO, 1990, p. 51.

157. CIA, *World Factbook, 1991*, pp. 148–149.

158. Arms Control and Disarmament Agency (ACDA), *World Military Expenditures and Arms Transfers, 1989*, Washington, GPO, 1990, Table I.

159. IISS, *Military Balance*, 1990–1991 and 1991–1992 editions.

160. Estimate based on recent reporting and Arms Control and Disarmament Agency (ACDA), *World Military Expenditures and Arms Transfers, 1989*, Washington, GPO, 1990, Table I.

161. Arms Control and Disarmament Agency (ACDA), *World Military Expenditures and Arms Transfers, 1990*, Washington, GPO, 1990, Table II.

162. Richard F. Grimmett, *Conventional Arms Transfers to the Third World, 1983–1990*, Washington, Congressional Research Service, CRS-9 1-578F, August 2, 1991, p. CRS-54.

163. Arms Control and Disarmament Agency (ACDA), *World Military Expenditures and Arms Transfers, 1985*, Washington, GPO, 1985, p. 134.

164. Arms Control and Disarmament Agency (ACDA), *World Military Expenditures and Arms Transfers, 1989*, Washington, GPO, 1990, p. 117.

165. *Los Angeles Times*, February 24, 1992, p. A-1.

166. Richard F. Grimmett, *Conventional Arms Transfers to the Third World, 1984–1991*, Washington, Congressional Research Service, CRS-92-577F, July 20, 1991, pp. CRS-58 and CRS-70; Kenneth Katzman, "Iraq's Campaign to Acquire and Develop High Technology," Congressional Research Service, CRS-92-611F, August 3, 1991. U.S. reporting on this subject is inconsistent. Arms Control and Disarmament Agency (ACDA), *World Military Expenditures and Arms Transfers, 1990*, Washington, GPO, 1990, p. 133 indicates that Iraq imported a total of $22,750 million worth of arms during 1985–1989, including $13,000 million from the Soviet Union, $1,700 million from France, $20 million from the UK, $1,600 million from the PRC, $90 million from West Germany, $2,900 million from other Warsaw Pact countries, $1,500 million from other European countries, $420 million from other Middle Eastern countries, $20 million from other East Asian states, $1,300 million from Latin America, and $200 million from other countries in the world.

167. U.S. Air Force, "Reaching Globally, Reaching Powerfully: The United States Air

Force in the Gulf War," Washington, Department of the Air Force, September, 1991, pp. 3–4

168. Richard F. Grimmett, *Conventional Arms Transfers to the Third World, 1983–1990*, Washington, Congressional Research Service, CRS-9 1-578F, August 2, 1991.

169. As will be explained in the following, such estimates are very uncertain. This estimate is taken from U.S. Air Force, "Reaching Globally, Reaching Powerfully: The United States Air Force in the Gulf War," Washington, Department of the Air Force, September, 1991, pp. 4–5.

170. Department of Defense press release, February 28, 1991. USCENTCOM raised the number of Iraqi POWs to 80,000 and Iraqi losses to 3,300 tanks, 2,100 other armored vehicles, and 2,200 artillery pieces in a press release made on March 3, 1991.

171. USCENTCOM press release of March 3, 1991. The U.S. lost 182 killed to all causes during the war from January 16 to March 1, 1991. Department of Defense press release, March 3, 1991.

172. The U.S. Defense Intelligence Agency (DIA) estimated on June 4, 1991, that 100,000 Iraqi soldiers died, 300,000 were wounded, 150,000 deserted, and 60,000 were taken prisoner of war. DIA noted, however, that these estimates could be 50% or more in error (Department of Defense press release, June 6, 1991.) Later studies have steadily reduced the number of killed and wounded and increased the number of deserted. These estimates do not include losses in the Shi'ite and Kurdish uprisings that followed the cease-fire.

173. Reuters, March 4, 1991.

174. Estimates differ by source even within the United States government and are discussed in more detail shortly. This estimate is taken from U.S. Air Force, "Reaching Globally, Reaching Powerfully: The United States Air Force in the Gulf War," Washington, Department of the Air Force, September, 1991; and Dick Palowski, *Changes in Threat Air Combat Doctrine and Force Structure*, 24th Edition, Fort Worth, General Dynamics DWIC-91, February, 1992, pp. 11-374 to 11-378.

175. *Economist*, August 23, 1991, p. 36; *New York Times*, June 3, 1991; June 11, 1991, p. A-10; November 3, 1991, p. 4; *Washington Post*, July 19, 191, p. A-16.

176. U.S. Congress, House Committee on Foreign Affairs, Subcommittee on Europe and the Middle East, Hearing on UN role in the Persian Gulf and Iraqi Compliance with UN resolutions, October 21, 1991; Kenneth Katzman, "Iraq's Post-War Compliance Record: A Chronology," Congressional Research Service, 92-320-F, March 31, 1992; *Economist*, August 23, 1991, p. 36; *Guardian*, August 11, 1991, p. 13; *Washington Post*, October 22, 1991, p. A-17; December 10, 1991, p. A-31; February 24, 1992, p. A-11; June 18, 1992, p. A-26; July 20, 1992, p. A-3; July 22, 1992, p. A-21; June 20, 1992, p. A-13; July 27, 1992, p. A-14; August 7, 1992, p. A-16; *Los Angeles Times*, May 31, 1992, p. A-1; *New York Times*, May 27, 1992, p. A-1; June 2, 1992, p. A-3; June 16, 1992, p. A-3; June 19, 1992, p. A-19; July 28, 1992, p. A-8; August 5, 1992, p. A-8; *Baltimore Sun*, October 25, 1991, p. 4a; January 16, 1992, p. 7a; *Philadelphia Inquirer*, July 27, 1991, p. 4A; *Washington Times*, February 26, 1992, p. A-1.

177. Shi'ites and Iraqi deserters fled into the Huwaizah marshes which begin south of Amara between the Tigris and the border with Iran, and the other marsh areas along the Euphrates east of Nasseriyah, and extend down past the junction of the two rivers to Basra. *New York Times*, March 15, 1991, p. 1.

178. A maximum of 400,000 moved into Turkey and 300,000 moved near to the Turkish border, 800,000 moved into Iran, and 700,000 moved near to the Iranian border. These estimates are high, and the true number may have only been 50–66% as large.

179. *Economist*, August 23, 1991, p. 36; *Washington Times*, October 8, 1991, p. 7; October 11, 1991, p. A-9; November, 18, 1991, p. A-7; *New York Times*, November 6, 1991, p. 16; November 15, 1991, p. A-9; *Washington Post*, July 20, 1991, p. A-14; July 22, 1991, p. A-18; September 10, 1991, p. A-24; *International Defense Review*, 7/1991, pp. 703–704.

180. *Economist*, August 23, 1991, p. 36; *Guardian*, January 14, 1992, p. 8; *New York Times*, October 9, 1991, p. A-6; October 20, 1991, p. A-1; October 27, 1991, p. A-3; August 12, 1992,

p. A-1; *Baltimore Sun*, January 16, 1992, p. 7A; October 28, 1991, p. A-2; *Washington Post*, October 12, 1991, p. A-20; October 26, 1991, p. A-15; May 19, 1992, p. A-12; May 21, 1992, p. A-44; May 23, 1992, p. A-20. For a discussion of some of the history and activities involved, see Ofra Bengio, "Baghdad Between Sh'ia and Kurds," *Policy Focus*, No. 18, Washington, Washington Institute for Near East Policy, February, 1992; *Turkish Times*, June 15, 1992, p. 1; *Christian Science Monitor*, June 10, 1992, p. 1.

181. Iraqi troops had occupied Kirkuk. *New York Times*, March 12, 1992, p. A-10; March 31, 1992, p. A-1; *Washington Post*, April 4, 1992, p. 19; *Philadelphia Inquirer*, April 5, 1992, p. 3.

182. Anti-Baath groups claimed up to 10,000 armed rebels and 100,000 civilians were present in the marshes, but these estimates seem sharply exaggerated. *Washington Post*, April 30, 1992, p. A-37; July 2, 1992, p. A-32; July 24, 1992, p. A-32; August 12, 1992, p. A-23; August 17, 1992, p. A-1; *New York Times*, August 12, 1992, p. A-6; *Washington Times*, August 9, 1992, p. A-10; *Economist*, August 8, 1992, p. 36; *Jane's Defence Weekly*, June 6, 1992, p. 967; *U.S. News and World Report*, May 25, 1992, p. 53.

183. *Washington Post*, April 8, 1992, p. A-19; May 5, 1992, p. A-19; July 16, 1992, p. A-14; July 18, 1992, p. A-1; July 22, 1992, p. A-1; July 28, 1992, p. A-1; July 31, 1991, p. A-20; August 2, 1992, p. A-8; August 4, 1992, p. 14; August 6, 1992, p. A-25; August 10, 1992, p. A-11; August 17, 1992, p. A-1; August 18, 1992, pp. A-1 and A-16; August 19, 1992, p. A-19; *New York Times*, July 16, 1992, p. A-7; July 20, 1992, p. A-3; July 23, 1992, pp. A-1 and A-6; July 25, 1992, p. A-1; July 28, 1992, p. A-7; August 15, 1992, p. A-1; August 17, 1992, p. A-1; August 18, 1992, pp. A-1 and A-6; August 19, 1992, p. A-1; *Aviation Week*, August 10, 1992, p. 23; *U.S. News and World Report*, August 10, 1992, p. 20; *Philadelphia Inquirer*, July 27, 1992, p. 1; August 1, 1992, p. 1; *Washington Times*, April 6, 1992, p. A-8; July 6, 1992, p. A-2; August 3, 1992, p. A-1; August 16, 1992, p. A-7; August 18, 1992, p. A-1; August 19, 1992, p. A-3; *Baltimore Sun*, June 2, 1992, p. 4a; August 3, 1992, p. 3a; *Independent* (UK), July 31, 1992, p. 10; *Los Angeles Times*, July 26, 1992, p. A-1; July 30, 1992, p. 2; August 3, 1992, p. 1; August 18, 1992, p. C-2; August 19, 1992, p. 3; *Atlanta Constitution*, July 30, 1992, p. 8. Many of the details of Iraqi noncompliance with the portions of the UN resolution dealing with the Kurds, Shi'ites, and weapons of mass destruction are taken from Kenneth Katzman, "Iraq's Post-War Compliance Record: A Chronology," Congressional Research Service, 92-320-F, March 31, 1992.

184. U.S. Air Force, "Reaching Globally, Reaching Powerfully: The United States Air Force in the Gulf War," Washington, Department of the Air Force, September, 1991, pp. 4–5.

185. Office of the Secretary of Defense, *Conduct of the Persian Gulf Conflict: An Interim Report*, Washington, Department of Defense, August, 1991, pp. 2–4. Some estimates show seven corps.

186. Department of Defense, *Conduct of the Persian Gulf War: Final Report*, Department of Defense, April, 1992, pp. 10–12.

187. Department of Defense, *Conduct of the Persian Gulf War: Final Report*, Department of Defense, April, 1992, pp. 10–12.

188. Department of Defense, *Conduct of the Persian Gulf War: Final Report*, Department of Defense, April, 1992, pp. 10–12.

189. The higher estimate may well be correct but probably includes armor in storage. Many estimates of Iraqi equipment are based on its strength at the end of the Iran-Iraq War. Iraq took delivery on major amounts of arms from August, 1989 to August, 1990.

190. *Jane's Defence Weekly*, May 13, 1989, p. 836.

191. *London Financial Times*, July 26, 1989, p. 20; *Jane's Defence Weekly*, May 13, 1989, p. 837; April 22, 1989, p. 687; August 12, 1989, p. 255; September 30, 1989, p. 674; *Defense News*, May 8, 1989, p. 6; *International Defense Review*, 6/1989, pp. 835–841.

192. *London Financial Times*, April 29, 1989, p. 11; July 26, 1989, p. 20; *Jane's Defence Weekly*, May 13, 1989, p. 837; April 22, 1989, p. 687; August 12, 1989, p. 255; September 30,

1989, p. 674; *Defense News*, May 8, 1989, p. 6; *International Defense Review*, 6/1989, pp. 835–841.

193. It should be noted that there are sharp internal contradictions in the document from which this estimate is drawn. See Department of Defense, *The Conduct of the Persian Gulf War: Final Report*, Washington, Department of Defense, April, 1992, pp. 93–95, 104–113.

194. Data provided to the author by OSD Public Affairs and adapted from Department of Defense, *The Conduct of the Persian Gulf War: Final Report*, Washington, Department of Defense, April, 1992, pp. 93–95, 104.

195. Department of Defense, *The Conduct of the Persian Gulf War: Final Report*, Washington, Department of Defense, April, 1992, pp. 93–95, 104–113, 355, 401. Note that this report is often self-contradictory.

196. Department of Defense, *The Conduct of the Persian Gulf War: Final Report*, Washington, Department of Defense, April, 1992, pp. 104–113, 353.

197. Based on Department of Defense briefing to the media, February 23, 1991; Department of Defense, *The Conduct of the Persian Gulf War: Final Report*, Washington, Department of Defense, April, 1992, pp. 104–113, 353; and background interviews. Note that these are historical estimates made during the war by USCENTCOM. The cumulative rise in Iraqi losses estimated over time is as follows:

	Tanks	APCs	Artillery
Total in KTO	4,280	2,880	3,100
22 Jan	14	0	77
27 Jan	65	50	281
1 Feb	476	243	356
6 Feb	728	552	535
11 Feb	862	692	771
21 Feb	1,439	879	1,271
23 Feb	1,688	929	1,452
24 Feb	1,772	948	1,474

198. Department of Defense, *The Conduct of the Persian Gulf War: Final Report*, Washington, Department of Defense, April, 1992, p. 355.

199. Based on Les Aspin and William Dickinson, "Defense for a New Era," House Armed Services Committee, April, 1992, pp. 29–33; *Washington Post*, April 24, 1992, p. A-25; *New York Times*, April 24, 1992, p. A-6.

200. *Washington Post*, November 7, 1991, p. A-46; November 14, 1991, p. A-47; *Wall Street Journal*, November 11, 1991, p. A-10; *Jane's Defence Weekly*, November 16, 1991, p. 926; July 13, 1991, p. 61; *The Estimate*, November 22-December 5, 1991, p. 1; *New York Times*, November 7, 1991, p. 3; *Los Angeles Times*, November 14, 1991, p. 4; Michael Eisenstadt, "Recent Changes in Saddam's Inner Circle: Cracks in the Wall?" *Policywatch*, Number 22, November 22, 1991, pp. 1–2; *Baltimore Sun*, June 21, 1991, p. 7.

201. In addition to the sources listed at the start of the Iraq section, see Kenneth Katzman, "Iraq: Future Policy Options," Congressional Research Service, CRS 91-596F, December 12, 1991, pp. 23–30; FBIS, October 13, 1991; *Washington Times*, August 2, 1991, p. B-5; *London Financial Times*, October 4, 1991, p. 4; AP AM cycle, June 12, 1991; *New York Times*, March 25, 1991, p. A-1; March 12, 1992, p. A-10; *Washington Post*, January 7, 1992, p. A-8; March 13, 1992, p. A-19; August 6, 1992, p. A-39; *Jane's Defence Weekly*, August 8, 1992, p. 8; *Los Angeles Times*, August 18, 1992, p. C-2; *MedNews* Special Briefing, August, 1992, *RUSI Working Note*, August, 1992.

202. *New York Times*, August 8, 1991, p. A-12.

203. *Washington Post*, July 16, 1991, p. 14; November 7, 1991, p. A-46; November 14,

1991, p. A-47; *Wall Street Journal,* November 11, 1991, p. A-10; *Jane's Defence Weekly,* November 16, 1991, p. 926; July 13, 1991, p. 61; *The Estimate,* November 22-December 5, 1991, p. 1; *New York Times,* November 7, 1991, p. 3; *Los Angeles Times,* November 14, 1991, p. 4; Michael Eisenstadt, "Recent Changes in Saddam's Inner Circle: Cracks in the Wall?" *Policywatch,* Number 22, November 22, 1991, pp. 1–2; *Baltimore Sun,* June 21, 1991, p. 7; *Daily Telegraph,* July 11, 1991, p. 9; *London Times,* October 4, 1991, p. 12; Washington Times, September 4, 1991, p. A7.

204. More generic estimates gave Iraq only about 2,000–2,300 other armored vehicles. Interviews in London, December, 1991 and in Switzerland and Israel, January, 1992; *Jane's Defence Weekly,* February 22, 1992, p. 284; *Jerusalem Post,* January 25, 1992, p. 9; *Washington Times,* January 20, 1992, p. 10; January 17, 1992, p. A-1; *Wall Street Journal,* November 11, 1991, p. A-10; *Jane's Defence Weekly,* November 16, 1991, p. 926; February 22, 1992, p. 284; *The Estimate,* November 22-December 5, 1991, p. 1; Michael Eisenstadt, "Recent Changes in Saddam's Inner Circle: Cracks in the Wall?" *Policywatch,* Number 22, November 22, 1991, pp. 1–2; *Defense News,* February 24, 1992, p. 1; *Washington Post,* November 7, 1991, p. A-46; March 13, 1992, p. A-19; August 6, 1992, p. A-39; *Jane's Defence Weekly,* August 8, 1992, p. 8.

205. These and other army strength estimates are based upon interviews in London, December, 1991 and in Switzerland and Israel, January, 1992; *Jane's Defence Weekly,* February 22, 1992, p. 284; *Jerusalem Post,* January 25, 1992, p. 9; *New York Times,* March 12, 1992, p. A-10; *Washington Times,* January 20, 1992, p. 10; *Washington Post,* November 7, 1991, p. A-46; November 14, 1991, p. A-47; March 13, 1992, p. A-19; *Wall Street Journal,* November 11, 1991, p. A-10; *Jane's Defence Weekly,* November 16, 1991, p. 926; February 22, 1992, p. 284; *The Estimate,* November 22-December 5, 1991, p. 1; Michael Eisenstadt, "Recent Changes in Saddam's Inner Circle: Cracks in the Wall?" *Policywatch,* Number 22, November 22, 1991, pp. 1–2; *Defense News,* February 24, 1992, p. 1.

206. See the detailed history of the attack on Republican Guard units and the resulting losses by name in Department of Defense, *The Conduct of the Persian Gulf War: Final Report,* Washington, Department of Defense, April, 1992, pp. 93–95, 104–113, 355, 401.

207. Based on interviews during December, 1991, March, 1992, and September, 1992, and adapted to use the data in maps in Department of Defense, *The Conduct of the Persian Gulf War: Final Report,* Washington, Department of Defense, April, 1992, p. 355. Many of data regarding Iraqi force changes are taken from a single foreign source and must be regarded as exceptionally uncertain. The reader should also be aware that the Iraqi army was in a constant state of flux and that any estimates were difficult even for those with access to official data.

208. Interviews in Israel, January, 1992; *Jane's Defence Weekly,* February 22, 1992, p. 284; *Jerusalem Post,* January 25, 1992, p. 9; *Washington Times,* January 20, 1992, p. 10.

209. Interviews in Israel, January, 1992; *Jane's Defence Weekly,* February 22, 1992, p. 284; *Jerusalem Post,* January 25, 1992, p. 9; *Washington Times,* January 20, 1992, p. 10.

210. Interviews in London, December, 1991 and in Switzerland and Israel, January, 1992; *Jane's Defence Weekly,* February 22, 1992, p. 284; *Jerusalem Post,* January 25, 1992, p. 9; *Washington Times,* January 20, 1992, p. 10; *Washington Post,* November 7, 1991, p. A-46; November 14, 1991, p. A-47; *Wall Street Journal,* November 11, 1991, p. A-10; *Jane's Defence Weekly,* November 16, 1991, p. 926; February 22, 1992, p. 284; *The Estimate,* November 22-December 5, 1991, p. 1; Michael Eisenstadt, "Recent Changes in Saddam's Inner Circle: Cracks in the Wall?" *Policywatch,* Number 22, November 22, 1991, pp. 1–2; *Defense News,* February 24, 1992, p. 1.

211. Experts differ sharply on this detail. See *Washington Post,* September 14, 1991, p. A-31; November 7, 1991, p. A-46; November 14, 1991, p. A-47; December 14, 1991, p. A-15; *Wall Street Journal,* November 11, 1991, p. A-10; December 26, 1991, p. A-10; *Jane's Defence Weekly,* November 16, 1991, p. 926, July 13, 1991, p. 61; *The Estimate,* November 22-December 5, 1991, p. 1; *Washington Times,* November 26, 1991, p. A7; *New York Times,* November 7,

1991, p. 3; *Los Angeles Times*, November 14, 1991, p. 4; Michael Eisenstadt, "Recent Changes in Saddam's Inner Circle: Cracks in the Wall?" *Policywatch*, Number 22, November 22, 1991, pp. 1–2; *Baltimore Sun*, June 21, 1991, p. 7.

212. *Washington Post*, April 15, 1992, p. A-32; July 3, p. A-1; July 4, 1992, p. A-14; July 10, 1992, p. A-14; *New York Times*, July 4, 1992, p. A-4; July 6, 1992, p. A-6; July 7, 1992, p. A-3; July 10, 1992, p. A-3 .

213. U.S. Air Force, "Reaching Globally, Reaching Powerfully: The United States Air Force in the Gulf War," Washington, Department of the Air Force, September, 1991, pp. 4–5; *London Financial Times*, April 29, 1989, p. 11; July 26, 1989, p. 20; *Jane's Defence Weekly*, May 13, 1989, p. 837; April 22, 1989, p. 687; August 12, 1989, p. 255; September 30, 1989, p. 674; *Defense News*, May 8, 1989, p. 6; *International Defense Review*, 6/1989, pp. 835–841.

214. U.S. Air Force, "Reaching Globally, Reaching Powerfully: The United States Air Force in the Gulf War," Washington, Department of the Air Force, September, 1991, pp. 4–5.

215. The Su-24 has a wing area of 575 square feet, an empty weight of 41,845 pounds, carries 3,385 gallons or 22,000 pounds of fuel, has a takeoff weight of 871,570 pounds with bombs and two external fuel tanks, carries 2,800 gallons or 18,200 pounds of external fuel, has a combat thrust-to-weight ratio of 1.02, a combat wing loading of 96 pounds per square foot, and a maximum load factor of 7.5G. *Jane's Soviet Intelligence Review*, July, 1990, pp. 298–300; *Jane's Defence Weekly*, June 25, 1985, pp. 1226–1227; and Dick Palowski, *Changes in Threat Air Combat Doctrine and Force Structure*, 24th Edition, General Dynamics DWIC-91, Fort Worth Division, February, 1992, pp. I-65 and I-110 to I-117.

216. *Aviation Week and Space Technology*, April 10, 1989; pp. 19–20; *New York Times*, April 5, 1989; September 7, 1989; *Washington Times*, January 16, 1989; *FBIS/NES*, April 10, 1989.

217. *Jane's Defence Weekly*, July 8, 1989. Dick Palowski, *Changes in Threat Air Combat Doctrine and Force Structure*, 24th Edition, Fort Worth, General Dynamics DWIC-91, February, 1992, p. II-358. Palowski indicates that Mirage F-1s were utilized in both the interceptor and attack roles. Iraq placed its first order for 30 multirole F-EQs and 6 dual-seat F-1BQ with Magic AIMs in 1977, and the aircraft began delivery in January, 1981. They initially were deployed to Qayyarah air base, where a substantial French training and support organization was maintained. In late 1979, an additional order was placed for 24, and 29 more were ordered in 1982 that included 23 newly configured F-1EQ4-200s and 6 F-1BQ-200s with a fixed-probe air refueling system.

The Mirage F-1 is an "almost" all-weather (pulse radar) single seat interceptor with a short duration Mach 2.0 capability. The Cyrano IV radar has a 25 NM acquisition capability against bomber sized targets and around 15 NM capability against fighters. The Cyrano IV has a down look track capability utilizing a fixed echo elimination scheme, but it will not support Super 530 Radar Missile requirements. The Iraqi F-1s are configured primarily with Magic One, R550 IR Missiles and Super 530 of both the IR and SA type. Aircraft performance and handling is similar to a hard wing F-4. Some of the final delivered Mirage F-1s were fitted with the Agave radar optimized for anti-ship operations with Exocet. The Agave is not compatible with air-to-air radar missiles.

Iraq ordered 20 F-1EQ5-200s and 4 F-BQ5-200s, with Agave anti-ship radars replacing the Cyrano IV radars, and these were delivered by October, 1984. Up until that time, 5 Super Etendards were loaned to the Iraqi air force. By mid-1983 some 6 F-1s were lost in combat as well as 79 Soviet aircraft of various types. Another 24 F-1E/BQ6-200 Exocet capable aircraft were ordered in September, 1985, bringing the total F-1 fleet to 113 machines. The first of this last batch arrived in 1987. A further 12–16 order was put in for attrition aircraft in 1988. Towards the end of 1983, France delivered to Iraq 5 Super Etendards which were utilized as Exocet platforms for several years, then returned to the French when Mirage F-1s were received in their place.

The Iraqi Mirage F-1s were delivered with a full complement of French weapons:

- Super 530 SA & IR AIMs
- R550 IR AIM
- Aerospatiale AS-30L ASM
- Thompson-Brandt 68/100mm rockets
- Matra ARMAT ARM missile
- Exocets
- South African "cluster" bombs
- Matra conventional "slick" and "retarded" bombs

Mirage F-1s with Exocets operated long range missions that required airborne refueling with converted AN-12 "CUBs" using French buddy stores with drogues. There are probably several air refueling candidates for the Iraqi air force, including IL-76 conversions as demonstrated by the Soviets.

218. The extraordinary range of different estimates of Iraqi strength is illustrated in Norman Friedman, *Desert Victory*, Annapolis, Naval Institute Press, 1991, p. 308; Bruce W. Watson, *Military Lessons of the Gulf War*, London, Greenhill, 1991, pp. 61–81; James F. Dunnigham and Austin Bay, *From Shield to Storm*, New York, Morrow, p. 323; Roy Braybrook, *Air Power: The Coalition and Iraqi Air Forces*, London, Osprey, 1991, p. 7.

219. The high end of the range seems more correct and is based on Dick Palowski, *Changes in Threat Air Combat Doctrine and Force Structure*, 24th Edition, Fort Worth, General Dynamics DWIC-91, February, 1992, p. II-361. Some estimates of the Mirage strength go as high as 70 aircraft but seem to include aircraft in the air defense role. These same estimates show 60 Su-20s in the FGA units, and 40 F-6s and 40 Su-7s in other combat units.

220. Many of the MiG-21s were not operational. Iraq had up to 40 MiG-19s in quasi-operational status and possibly some F-6s.

221. Dick Palowski, *Changes in Threat Air Combat Doctrine and Force Structure*, 24th Edition, Fort Worth, General Dynamics DWIC-91, February, 1992, p. II-361.

222. *Jane's Defence Weekly*, March 3, 1990, p. 386.

223. *Jane's Defence Weekly*, May 13, 1989, p. 836 and October 7, 1989, p. 693; *Air International*, March, 1991, p. 118; Dick Palowski, *Changes in Threat Air Combat Doctrine and Force Structure*, 24th Edition, Fort Worth, General Dynamics DWIC-91, February, 1992, pp. II-354 to II-355. Some estimates imply the second aircraft was fully operational, but this is uncertain.

224. *Defense Electronics*, February, 1989, p. 10; *United States News and World Report*, April 10, 1989, p. 18.

225. *Jane's Defence Weekly*, April 22, 1989, pp. 697–698; August 5, 1989, p. 196; September 30, 1989, p. 674; February 10, 1990, p. 267; *International Defense Review*, 6/1989, pp. 835–841.

226. *Defense News*, May 8, 1989, p. 6. According to work by Dick Palowski, Iraq also has a supply of the AS-9 Kyle anti-radar missile, which is a scaled down derivative of the AS-4 Kitchen. It is believed that it has at least three interchangeable passive radar homing heads for each of the three main "ground and ship threat emitter" frequency bands. It is expected that the Iraqis have modified it to engage the Western Hawk and Patriot systems. The missile must be built up before each flight, specifically targeting the seeker to the specific threat system that is to be engaged. It is a bit smaller than the Kitchen, at 6.0 m long, 0.5 m in diameter, and having a 2.0 m wing span. The ARM version of the MiG-21 sized Kitchen utilizes a 1,000 kg HE warhead. The scaled Kyle has a launch weight of around 750 kg and utilizes a considerably smaller 250 kg warhead. It has two delta wings a mid body with a clipped delta vertical tail and horizontal tail planes. There is a folded lower vertical fin. It utilizes a liquid fueled rocket which requires fairly substantial ground support in preparation. It is employed as a "high flier," similar in profile to the Kitchen. It will go up to a Mach 2.0 cruise altitude of around 70,000 ft for a range of around 90 km and eventually high dive down in a steep 80 degree dive on the target. The Kyle has been replaced in the Soviet air force by several other missiles such as the AS-11 Kilter, AS-12 Kegler, and other

more modern systems. It is not believed that Iraq has any of these more advanced versions. See Duncan Lennox's assessment in the October 1989 *Jane's Soviet Intelligence Review*, p. 442.

227. Department of Defense, *Conduct of the Persian Gulf War: Final Report*, Department of Defense, April, 1992, pp. 13–15; Dick Palowski, *Changes in Threat Air Combat Doctrine and Force Structure*, 24th Edition, Fort Worth, General Dynamics DWIC-91, February, 1992, p. II-361.

228. Department of Defense, *Conduct of the Persian Gulf War: Final Report*, Department of Defense, April, 1992, pp. 13–15.

229. These estimates were projected by different sources and the launcher or fire unit counts seem to be either rounded or based on standard Soviet battery holdings. According to Palowski, Iraq had the following radar order of battle:

Early Warning & Surveillance

• Spoon Rest D/ P-12M	USSR(147–161 MHz)
• Flat Face A/ P-15	USSR(800–900 MHz)
• Squat Eye/ P-15M	USSR(800–900 MHz)
• Bar Lock/ P-35/37	USSR(2,695–3,125 MHz)
• Tall King/ P-14	USSR(160–180 MHz)
• TRS-2215 (mobile)	FR (E/F)
• TRS-2230	FR (E/F)
• AN/TPS-32 (3D)	US (2905–3080)
• AWACS (IL-76)	FR

Surface-to-Air Missile Systems

• SA-2	Fansong/Guideline
• SA-3	Low Blow/Goa
• SA-5	Square Pair/Gammon
• SA-6	Straight Flush/Gainful
• SA-7	Grail (IR hand held)
• SA-8	Land Roll/Gecko
• SA-9	Gaskin (IR vehicle mounted)
• SA-13	Gopher (IR vehicle mounted)
• SA-14	Gremlin (IR Hand Held)
• SA-15	Track with tube launched missiles (not confirmed)
• SA-16	(not confirmed)
• SA-19	Mounted on 2S6 Gun-Track (not confirmed)
• Roland	
• Hawk	
• Aspedite	

London Financial Times, April 29, 1989, p. 11; July 26, 1989, p. 20; *Jane's Defence Weekly*, May 13, 1989, p. 837; April 22, 1989, p. 687; August 12, 1989, p. 255; September 30, 1989, p. 674; *Defense News*, May 8, 1989, p. 6; *International Defense Review*, 6/1989, pp. 835–841.

230. The Iraqis were on alert after reports that Israel might attack Iraqi chemical and nuclear facilities. *Washington Post*, April 29, 1989, p. 16.

231. *Defense News*, May 8, 1989, p. 6.

232. This analysis of the air war relies heavily on the U.S. Air Force analysis in "Reaching Globally, Reaching Powerfully: The United States Air Force in the Gulf War," Washington, Department of the Air Force, September, 1991, pp. 32–34.

233. Department of Defense, *Conduct of the Persian Gulf War: Final Report*, Department of Defense, April, 1992, pp. 201–203.

234. Department of Defense, *Conduct of the Persian Gulf War: Final Report*, Department of Defense, April, 1992, pp. 202–206.

235. Department of Defense, *Conduct of the Persian Gulf War: Final Report*, Department of Defense, April, 1992, p. 204.

236. Department of Defense, *Conduct of the Persian Gulf War: Final Report*, Department of Defense, April, 1992, pp. 13–15 and 216. Palowski estimates Iraqi air-to-air combat losses and causes as follows:

> 5 MiG-29 Fulcrums:
>   3 AIM-7 Kills
>   2 Maneuvering Suicides
> 9 F-1 Mirages
>   6 AIM-7 Kills
>   2 AIM-9 Kills
>   1 Maneuvering Suicide
> 4 MiG-21/F-7 Fish beds:
>   3 AIM-9 Kills
>   1 AIM-7 Kill
> 8 MiG-23 Floggers:
>   6 AIM-7 Kills
>   2 AIM-9 Kills
> 2 MiG-25 Foxbats:
>   2 AIM-7 Kills
> 6 Su-7/17/22:
>   3 AIM-7 Kills
>   2 AIM-9 Kills
>   1 Mk-83 Bomb
> 2 Su-25 Frogfoot:
>   2 AIM-9 Kills
> 1 IL-76 Candid transport
>   20mm Gun (under debate as an AIM-7 Kill)
> 1 PC-9 Trainer
>   pilot bailout
> 6 Helicopters
>   2 AIM-7 Kills
>   1 AIM-9 Kill
>   2 Gun Kills
>   1 LGB
>
> 23 AIM-7 Kills
> 12 AIM-9 Kills
> 02 30mm Gun Kills
> 01 20mm Gun Kill
> 03 Maneuvering Suicides
> 01 Bailout
> 02 Air-to-Ground Ordnance (1 Walleye pending)
>
> Total 44

237. Department of Defense, *Conduct of the Persian Gulf War: Final Report*, Department of Defense, April, 1992, pp. 13–15, 202–206, and 216.

238. U.S. Air Force, "Reaching Globally, Reaching Powerfully: The United States Air Force in the Gulf War," Washington, Department of the Air Force, September, 1991, pp. 32–34; Department of Defense, *Conduct of the Persian Gulf War: Final Report*, Department of Defense, April, 1992, p. 204. Dick Palowski puts losses at 44 aircraft, including 6 MiG-29s,

11 Mirage F-1s, 4 MiG-21s, 8 MiG-23s, 2 MiG-25s, 2 Su-25s, 7 Su-7/20/22s, and 7 helicopters. Palowski, op cit., p. II-376.

239. While many sources provided a great deal of data on the causes of individual loses, much of these data conflict. F-15s seem to have shot down 35 aircraft, A-10s shot down 2, F-18s shot down 2, and F-14s may have shot down 1.

240. These and other air strength estimates are based upon interviews in London, December, 1991 and in Switzerland and Israel, January, 1992; *Jane's Defence Weekly*, February 22, 1992, p. 284; *Jerusalem Post*, January 25, 1992, p. 9; *Washington Times*, January 20, 1992, p. 10; *Washington Post*, November 7, 1991, p. A-46; November 14, 1991, p. A-47; *Wall Street Journal*, November 11, 1991, p. A-10; *Jane's Defence Weekly*, November 16, 1991, p. 926; February 22, 1992, p. 284; *The Estimate*, November 22-December 5, 1991, p. 1; Michael Eisenstadt, "Recent Changes in Saddam's Inner Circle: Cracks in the Wall?" *Policywatch*, Number 22, November 22, 1991, pp. 1-2; *Defense News*, February 24, 1992, p. 1.

241. The Department of Defense has stated that 137 Iraqi aircraft are in Iran. *Jane's Defence Weekly*, April 27, 1991, p. 684, provided the following list of Iraqi aircraft in Iran:

From the Iraqi Air Force		*From Kuwait Airlines (Total = 14)*	
24	Mirage F-1		
24	Su-24 Fencer	2	Boeing 767-200
40	Su-22 Fitter H	1	Airbus A300C4-600
04	Su-20 Fitter C	5	A310-200s
07	Su-25 Frogfoot	2	Boeing 767-200ER
04	MiG-23 Flogger F	2	Gulfstream IIIs
04	MiG-29 Fulcrum	2	BAe 125s
04	MiG-23ML Flogger G		
01	MiG-23U Flogger C		
02	Boeing 747s		
01	Boeing 707		
02	Boeing 737s		
01	Boeing 737 ?		
05	Airbus 310s		
01	Airbus 300		
15	IL-76s		
02	Mystere Falcon 20		
03	Falcon 50s		
01	Lockheed Jetstar		

Total 148

242. In addition to the sources listed at the start of the Iraq section, see Kenneth Katzman, "Iraq: Future Policy Options," Congressional Research Service, CRS 91-596F, December 12, 1991, pp. 23–30; FBIS, October 13, 1991; *Washington Times*, August 2, 1991, p. B-5; *London Financial Times*, October 4, 1991, p. 4; AP AM cycle, June 12, 1991; *New York Times*, March 25, 1991, p. A-1.

243. The SAM launcher estimates are based on discussions with an Israeli expert and are highly uncertain. Iran's decision was reported in the *New York Times*, July 31, 1992, p. 6.

244. *Jane's Defence Weekly*, February 11, 1989, p. 205; May 29, 1989, p. 1002; *Jane's Fighting Ships, 1991–1992*, pp. 292–293.

245. Department of Defense, *Conduct of the Persian Gulf War: Final Report*, Department of Defense, April, 1992, pp. 13–15.

246. *Defense News*, May 8, 1989, p. 6; Department of Defense, *Conduct of the Persian Gulf War: Final Report*, Department of Defense, April, 1992, pp. 13–15.

247. *Defense News*, May 8, 1989, p. 6.

248. *Jane's Fighting Ships, 1991–1992*, pp. 292–293.

249. *Military Technology*, 2/92, pp. 97–98.

250. These and other army strength estimates are based upon interviews in London, December, 1991 and in Switzerland and Israel, January, 1992; *Jane's Defence Weekly*, February 22, 1992, p. 284; *Jerusalem Post*, January 25, 1992, p. 9; *Washington Times*, January 20, 1992, p. 10; *Washington Post*, November 7, 1991, p. A-46; November 14, 1991, p. A-47; *Wall Street Journal*, November 11, 1991, p. A-10; *Jane's Defence Weekly*, November 16, 1991, p. 926; February 22, 1992, p. 284; *The Estimate*, November 22-December 5, 1991, p. 1; Michael Eisenstadt, "Recent Changes in Saddam's Inner Circle: Cracks in the Wall?" *Policywatch*, Number 22, November 22, 1991, pp. 1–2; *Defense News*, February 24, 1992, p. 1.

251. U.S. *Federal Register*, Volume 56, Number 64, p. 13584; *London Financial Times*, April 2, 1991, p. 1; *London Times*, April 3, 1991, p. 2; Kenneth Katzman, "Iraq's Campaign to Acquire and Develop High Technology," Congressional Research Service, CRS-92-611F, August 3, 1991.

252. The Iraqi-held version of the FROG-7 is a free rocket with a range of 11–70 kilometers, a CEP of 0.5–0.7 kilometers, and a 550 kilogram warhead. The FROG-7 has a single stage solid propellant rocket motor, and the main nozzle is surrounded by a ring of much smaller nozzles. This variant of the FROG was first exhibited in 1967. It is 9.0 meters long, 61 centimeters in diameter, and weighs 5,727 kilograms. The FROG-7 is normally mounted upon, and launched from, a wheeled erector launcher called the ZIL-135. While the FROG-7 is superior to early FROGs in reliability and accuracy, there is no guidance system other than a spin-stabilized ballistic trajectory. If any trajectory correction is made after launch, it will begin during boost. After boost, the trajectory is ballistic, and at long ranges the missile can strike up to 2 kilometers from its intended target. Iraq's Scud holdings included a wide range of types. *The World's Missile Systems*, 7th Edition, General Dynamics, Pomona Division, April, 1982, pp. 65–66.

253. *London Financial Times*, July 26, 1989, p. 20; *Jane's Defence Weekly*, May 13, 1989, p. 837; April 22, 1989, p. 687; August 12, 1989, p. 255; September 30, 1989, p. 674; *Defense News*, May 8, 1989, p. 6; *International Defense Review*, 6/1989, pp. 835–841.

254. "U.S. Reasserts Aim to Keep Oil Flowing From Persian Gulf," *Washington Times*, February 22, 1984, p. A-1.

255. Department of Defense, *Conduct of the Persian Gulf War: Final Report*, Department of Defense, April, 1992, pp. 13–15.

256. "Iraqis Fire Missiles on Iranian Cities," *Chicago Tribune*, February 25, 1984, p. 20; *Washington Post*, May 11, 1988, p. A-1.

257. *New York Times*, May 1, 1988, p. 1; *Los Angeles Times*, May 21, 1988, p. 18; *Washington Post*, May 11, 1988, p. A-1.

258. In spite of the knowledge gained during the Gulf War, sources still differ on other aspects of the performance of this system. According to some reports, the improved Iraqi Scuds have a CEP of 1,300 meters versus 1,000 meters for the Scud B, and carry only 600 kilograms versus 1,000 kilograms for the Scud B. According to other reports, Iraq has obtained Scud Ds from the USSR, although this seems unlikely. The Scud Ds are substantially more accurate than the Scud C, and can use minelet and submunition payloads, but there is no evidence the USSR has sold such systems to Third World states. Some reports indicate that Iraq has Soviet-made Scud C missiles with strap-on boosters. This seems doubtful because the missiles Iran recovered did not have such boosters, only a smaller warhead. David C. Isby, *Weapons and Tactics of the Soviet Army*, Fully Revised Edition, London, Jane's, 1988, pp. 296–301.

259. Working paper issued by the Israeli embassy in Washington, April, 1990. No author, title, or publisher listed. Also see Duncan Lennox, "Iraq-Ballistic Missiles," *Current News, Supplement*, Department of Defense, October 11, 1990, pp. B-4 to B-6; *Washington Post*, October 10, 1990, p. 19; Dick Palowski, *Changes in Threat Air Combat Doctrine and Force*

Structure, 24th Edition, Fort Worth, General Dynamics DWIC-91, February, 1992, pp. II-330 to II-331; *San Diego Navy Dispatch*, September 8, 1990, p. 26; *DAH-90*, December 1989, p. 30.

260. Hussein is the name of a grandson of Mohammed and the son of Ali. Ali was martyred in An Najaf and Hussein in Karbala, both in Iraq. *Washington Post*, May 11, 1988, p. A-1; Department of Defense, *Conduct of the Persian Gulf War: Final Report*, Department of Defense, April, 1992, pp. 13–15. Work done by Dick Palowski of General Dynamics describes the systems as follows:

Alert State and Deployment

State	Warhead	Missile	TEL
6	in storage	in storage	available
5	in storage	sys/comp cks	available
4	attached	fueled	available
3	attached	put on TEL	move to site
2	attached	erected	set up
1	fused	launched	crew dispersed

All of the Scuds are liquid fueled, and it takes a trained team around one hour to fuel and position the missile TEL. It would take another hour to reload the launcher and an additional hour to prepare it for launching, not counting driving time to and from the reload site. A chemical warhead would also be "filled" with the VX agent. These warheads utilize premixed agents that require crews in chemical warfare protective gear to fill them. The binary forms are not considered feasible for rocket employment at this time.

The Al-Hussein utilizes a reduced payload package (985 to 190 kg) to effect a 100% growth in range to 600 km (328 NM). The warhead inventory comprises nuclear, high explosive, ICM bomblets, chemical (985 kg with 555 kg active VX), or fuel-air explosive (FAE).

Iraq's 48 ton, three stage, Tamuz 1 heavy duty rocket is supposed to have put up a satellite, and its Abbas two stage 2,000 km (1,100 NM) SSM has been test fired. These advanced rockets could place Iraq into the ICBM club of the superpowers. Another rocket project, the Condor 2, was being done with the cooperation of Egypt and Argentina. Fortunately, it has been plagued with technical problems.

261. The USSR claimed that none of the Scuds it sold to Iraq had the range to reach Tehran. Iran claims to have recovered parts showing the Scuds used in the attacks were of recent Soviet manufacture. Some sources claim that Egypt, Italy, France, the FRG, PRC, and/or USSR helped the Iraqis add boosters or modify the missiles to use more of their fuel and/or a smaller warhead.

262. Baghdad has 23% of Iraq's population and is only 80 miles from the border. Tehran is about 290 miles from the front lines.

263. FBIS, *Middle East*, April 25, 1988, p. 1; Duncan Lennox, "Iraq-Ballistic Missiles," *Current News, Supplement*, Department of Defense, October 11, 1990, pp. B-4 to B-6.

264. Department of Defense, *Conduct of the Persian Gulf War: Final Report*, Department of Defense, April, 1992, pp. 16–18; *Defense and Foreign Affairs Weekly*, May 8-14, 1989, pp. 3 and 6. Iraq's minister of industry and military industrialization, Hussein Kamil, has denied Iraq is cooperating in missile development with any foreign country. *Jane's Defence Weekly*, May 13, 1989, p. 843.

265. *New York Times*, November 12, 1991, p. A-3; Department of Defense, *Conduct of the Persian Gulf War: Final Report*, Department of Defense, April, 1992, pp. 16–18.

266. Department of Defense, *Conduct of the Persian Gulf War: Final Report*, Department of Defense, April, 1992, pp. 16–18; *New York Times*, September 7, 1989, p. A-9; *New York Times*, March 30, 1990, p. 6; April 3, 1990, p. 1; November 12, 1991, p. A-3; *Christian Science Monitor*, January 23, 1992, p. 1; *Atlanta Constitution*, January 16, 1992, p. 1.

267. Kenneth R. Timmerman, *The Poison Gas Connection*, Los Angeles, Simon Wiesenthal Center, 1990, pp. 10–12 and 21–22.

268. *Flight International*, May 13, 1989, pp. 20–21, and work by Dick Palowski, provide a view of the DOT program that may be summarized as follows: European countries helped Iraq set up a series of rocket and chemical development, testing, and production projects. The scheme was always linked to the cooperative Condor 2 program with Argentina and Egypt. The Condor 2 was supposed to create a two staged, 1,000 km range (500 kg payload) growth derivative from the Argentine Condor 1 "weather rocket" developed with the help of MBB from Germany in the late 1970s. The central role of the Condor 2 project was played by a group of small Swiss companies, headed by Zug-based Consen, staffed by former MBB engineers. In 1984 Egypt contracted the Ifat Company, which also involved Argentina.

Iraq approached a Vienna-based consultancy, Consultco, with a project for Iraq alone, which became the DOT Program. A consortium was built with Zublin from Germany, two Austrian firms, and several other electrical firms. Money was generously received, and the work progressed. Thousands of Pakistani workers were recruited, and the Feneberg construction firm built the complexes. DOT incorporated three major tasks that Feneberg completed by March, 1989: DO-1; near Hilla, 50 km south of Baghdad, chemical rocket fuels development; DO-2; a collection of engineering workshops near the city of Falluja, adjacent to the Yugoslavian-built artillery and ammunition factory called SAAD 5; DO-3; a rocket testing range some 95 km south of Baghdad near Karbala.

269. The report also said that the fire took a week to fully extinguish and that up to one-third of the main complex had been destroyed, but this is not confirmed. *New York Times*, September 7, 1989, p. A-9; *Independent*, September 6, 1989.

270. *Washington Post*, May 3, 1989, p. A-19; Kenneth R. Timmerman, *The Poison Gas Connection*, Los Angeles, Simon Wiesenthal Center, 1990, pp. 21–22.

271. Task Force on Terrorism and Unconventional Warfare, *Chemical Weapons in the Third World: 2. Iraq's Expanding Chemical Arsenal*, House Republican Research Committee, U.S. House of Representatives, May 29, 1990, p. 11.

272. *Aviation Week and Space Technology*, August 27, 1990, p. 17, and Dick Palowski, *Changes in Threat Air Combat Doctrine and Force Structure*, 24th Edition, Fort Worth, General Dynamics DWIC-91, February, 1992, pp. II-323.

273. For a good summary report, see *Jane's Defence Weekly*, February 17, 1990, p. 295. Also see *Financial Times*, November 21, 1989, p. 1; *Washington Post*, September 20, 1989.

274. *Flight International*, May 13, 1989, p. 20; *Wall Street Journal*, August 30, 1990.

275. Michael Eisenstadt, "The Sword of the Arabs: Iraq's Strategic Weapons," Washington, Washington Institute for Near East Policy, Policy Paper 21, September, 1990, p. 22.

276. Michael Eisenstadt, "The Sword of the Arabs: Iraq's Strategic Weapons," Washington, Washington Institute for Near East Policy, Policy Paper 21, September, 1990, pp. 22–23.

277. Ruchita Vora, "Iraq Joins the Missile Club: Impact and Implications," *Strategic Analysis*, April, 1990, p. 59; *Flight International*, May 13, 1989, p. 20.

278. *Jane's Defence Weekly*, December 23, 1989, pp. 1371–1372.

279. *Jane's Defence Weekly*, December 23, 1989, pp. 1371–1372.

280. Some sources indicate that the booster is called the Al-Abbid, or Worshipper.

281. *The Middle East*, November, 1989, p. 19.

282. Department of Defense, *Conduct of the Persian Gulf War: Final Report*, Department of Defense, April, 1992, pp. 16–18; *New York Times*, September 7, 1989, p. A-9.

283. Duncan Lennox, "Iraq-Ballistic Missiles," *Current News, Supplement*, Department of Defense, October 11, 1990, pp. B-4 to B-6.

284. Working paper by Dick Palowski.

285. *New York Times*, December 5, 1989; *Washington Post*, December 9, 1989; *Aviation Week*, December 11, 1989, p. 31; *Defense Daily*, December 12, 1989, p. 381; *Financial Times*,

December 20, 1989; FBIS-WES, December 8, 1989, p. 23; *Jane's Defence Weekly*, December 23, 1989, pp. 1371–1372.

286. Reuters, October 4, 1991, AM Cycle.

287. Considerable debate has taken place since the war as to whether British officials knew about the gun much earlier and could have prevented deliveries of equipment to Iraq. *Washington Post*, January 16, 1992, p. 11; *London Financial Times*, January 22, 1992, p. 6.

288. The gun was aimed in the general direction of Israel. *Jane's Defence Weekly*, April 24, 1990; November 24, 1990; September 14, 1991, pp. 458–459; *Defense News*, November 11, 1991, p. 4; *U.S. News and World Report*, November 25, 1991, p. 36; Department of Defense, *Conduct of the Persian Gulf War: Final Report*, Department of Defense, April, 1992, pp. 16–18; *New York Times*, September 7, 1989, p. A-9.

289. Some sources estimate a barrel length of 153–160 meters. *Nature*, April 26, 1990, p. 811; *International Defense Review*, 5/1990, p. 481; *Financial Times*, April 18, 1990, p. 22; May 2, 1990, p. 18; *The Middle East*, March, 1990, pp. 17–18.

290. Space Research Corporation had also done extensive work for Israel. Other firms involved may have included Societa delle Funcine, Firpas, and Italian Technology Innovation of Italy; Amalgamated Trading Industries of Belgium; Advanced Technology Institute of Athens; PRB of Belgium; and Astra Defense Systems of the UK. It is uncertain how many of these firms were knowingly involved, if they were involved at all. *Jane's Defence Weekly*, April 28, 1990, pp. 770–771; *Washington Post*, April 19, 1990, p. A-37; *London Sunday Times*, April 22, 1990, p. 1.

291. *London Financial Times*, February 20, 1992, p. 8, February 28, 1992, p. 6. A U.S. firm called Kennametal of Pittsburgh has been accused of selling equipment that might have been used in the super gun effort, but the evidence is ambiguous. *Philadelphia Inquirer*, February 18, 1992, p. 1; *Wall Street Journal*, January 31, 1992, p. 3.

292. *Jane's Defence Weekly*, April 28, 1990, pp. 770–771; *Washington Post*, April 19, 1990, p. A-37; *London Sunday Times*, April 22, 1990, p. 1.

293. Project Harp had tested a gun based on combining two 16" guns bored out to a caliber of 16.69 inches with a total caliber length of L/86. This project demonstrated that such a device could launch 185 pound payloads up to altitudes of 118 miles (200 kilometers). Bull had claimed that such a device using a solid propellant rocket could deliver a 272 kilogram payload to ranges of 1,150 miles (1,852 kilometers), and 90 kilograms to 2,000 miles (3,200) kilometers. In addition to helping Israel develop 175mm gun rounds that reached ranges of 40 kilometers, Bull and SRC had previously helped Iraq develop its own Majnoon 155mm and Al Faw 210mm artillery weapons. *Jane's Defence Weekly*, April 28, 1990, pp. 770–771; June 2, 1990, p. 1063; *Washington Post*, April 19, 1990, p. A-37; *Economist*, May 5, 1990, p. 99; *Aviation Week*, May 7, 1990, p. 88; *Nature*, April 26, 1990, p. 811.

294. *Jane's Defence Weekly*, September 14, 1991, pp. 458–459; *Defense News*, November 11, 1991, p. 4; *Philadelphia Inquirer*, October 9, 1991, p. 12.

295. *Philadelphia Inquirer*, October 9, 1991, p. 12; *U.S. News and World Report*, November 25, 1991, p. 36.

296. Some experts seriously doubt whether the device would have worked. Bull, however, had an exceptional track record as a scientist. These are five types of super guns, in addition to the use of weapons for launching rocket assisted projectiles. These include the concentric charge cannon, gas cannon, the ram cannon, the coil gun, and the electromagnetic rail gun. (Only the concentric charge and gas cannons seem to fit the components being delivered to Iraq.)

A concentric charge cannon fits concentric charges of high explosive at regular intervals throughout the barrel of the gun. The intermediate propellant charges go off at regular intervals behind the projectile, building up a growing wave of gas behind it. This requires critical timing and may explain why Iraq attempted to smuggle in detonating capacitors from the U.S. earlier in April, 1990, although these also have application to nuclear weapons.

A gas cannon uses the explosion or compression of a secondary gas like hydrogen to amplify the force of an initial explosion. A normal cannon can accelerate projectiles only to about 3,500 kilometers per second; a gas cannon may be able to accelerate them to 5,000 to 6,000 kilometers per second.

A ram cannon uses a barrel filled with inflammable gases. The passage of a projectile through the barrel causes the gas to ignite behind it and push it even faster because of the constantly expanding explosive wave behind it.

A coil gun is an electromagnetic weapon with a series of current bearing loops. The current in each loop creates an electromagnetic field that passes through the center of the loop. If a smaller coil is then put at the center of the loop, on the axis, the magnetic field will induce a current in it which will induce a second magnetic field. This field will act in the opposite direction. The gun's magnetic field then throws the smaller coil along the access of the loops.

A rail gun puts its payload across two parallel rails. A current passes up one rail through the payload and down the other. This creates a magnetic field that moves the projectile along the tracks.

Technical sources include *International Defense Review*, No. 5, 1990, p. 481; *Financial Times*, April 18, 1990, p. 22; May 2, 1990, p. 18; *The Middle East*, March, 1990, pp. 17–18; *Nature*, Vol. 344, April 26, 1990; *Jane's Defence Review*, April 28, 1990, pp. 770–771; *Economist*, May 5, 1990, p. 99; *Fort Worth Star-Telegram*, April 24, 1990, p. 19; *Aviation Week*, May 7, 1990, p. 88; *Washington Post*, April 19, 1990, p. A-37.

297. *Washington Times*, March 29, 1990, pp. A-1 and A-8; April 29, 1990; *Washington Post*, April 30, 1990; *Jane's Defence Weekly*, October 29, 1988, p. 1045; *New York Times*, March 30, 1990, p. A-6.

298. U.S. Navy working paper, August, 1990. The sites wcre Wadi al Jabaryah, Luadl or Ratqa, H-2, Wadi Amil, Ishuayb al Awaj, Qasr Amij East, Qasr Amij West, Wadi Hawran, and Zawr Hawran.

299. *New York Times*, April 24, 1990, p. 13; *Washington Times*, May 30, 1990; July 10, 1990.

300. *Washington Post*, October 10, 1990, p. 19; *Financial Times* (London), October 10, 1990, p. 7.

301. See the deliberate furor Saddam Hussein created over the fixed sites in March, 1990. *New York Times*, March 30, 1990, p. 6.

302. Duncan Lennox, "Iraq-Ballistic Missiles," *Current News, Supplement*, Department of Defense, October 11, 1990, pp. B-4 to B-6.

303. Dick Palowski, *Changes in Threat Air Combat Doctrine and Force Structure*, 24th Edition, Fort Worth, General Dynamics DWIC-91, February, 1992, p. II-332; *UK Recognition Journal*, October, 1988, p. 312.

304. Some reports indicate that the U.S. firm of Terex in Bridgeport, Connecticut, assisted Iraq in making these units. *New York Times*, January 26, 1992, p. A-12.

305. These statistics are taken from a U.S. Department of Defense background briefing dated March, 1991.

306. *New York Times*, November 12, 1991, p. A-3; *Christian Science Monitor*, January 23, 1992, p. 1.

307. *Washington Post*, July 26, 1991, p. A-1; Rolf Ekrus, "Unearthing Iraq's Arsenal," *Arms Control Today*, April, 1992, pp. 6–9.

308. The UN refused to name the facilities at the time of this declaration because it feared this would allow Iraq to move some of the equipment and missiles in them. *Washington Post*, February 14, 1992, p. A-33.

309. *Washington Post*, February 14, 1992, p. A-33; January 15, 1992, p. A-18.

310. *Christian Science Monitor*, January 23, 1992, p. 1.

311. *Atlanta Constitution*, January 16, 1992, p. 1.

312. *Washington Post,* January 15, 1992, p. A-18; *Washington Times,* September 12, 1991, p. A8; March 5, 1992, p. 1. *U.S. News and World Report,* February 10, 1992, p. 22, published an article claiming that Iraq might have an underground factory and some 800 missiles. Gen. Colin Powell later indicated that he had seen no evidence of any underground facility and that Iraq's maximum holding might be about 250 missiles. *Albany Times Union,* February 5, 1992, p. 7.

313. *New York Times,* February 28, 1992, p. 28; *Washington Times,* February 11, 1992, p. 1.

314. Based upon discussions with Israeli sources in January, 1989.

315. The author visited the area several times during this period. Reports of such use were provided by both Iranian and Israeli officials and confirmed by a British expert. Also see W. A. Terrill, *Strategic Review,* Spring, 1986; D. Wood, *Jane's Defence Weekly,* March 31, 1984; Task Force on Terrorism and Unconventional Warfare, *Chemical Weapons in the Third World: 2. Iraq's Expanding Chemical Arsenal,* House Republican Research Committee, U.S. House of Representatives, May 29, 1990, p. 7.

316. Peter Dunn, "The Chemical War: Journey to Iran," *NBC Defense & Technology International,* pp. 28–37, and "Iran Keeps Chemical Options Open," pp. 12–14.

317. See W. A. Terrill, *Strategic Review,* Spring, 1986; D. Wood, *Jane's Defence Weekly,* March 31, 1984; Task Force on Terrorism and Unconventional Warfare, *Chemical Weapons in the Third World: 2. Iraq's Expanding Chemical Arsenal,* House Republican Research Committee, U.S. House of Representatives, May 29, 1990, p. 7.

318. Mustard "gas" is actually an oily liquid. It can be manufactured by three relatively simple processes: reacting vinyl chloride (which can be made from ethylene or acetylene) and hydrogen sulfide; reacting ethylene and sulfur monochloride; or reacting thiodiglycol with hydrogen chloride after making the thiodiglycol from ethylene or ethylene oxide and hydrogen sulfide. Sulfur and ethylene are produced by many refineries, and hydrogen chloride or chlorine gas can be made from salt, sea water, or petroleum brines. The manufacturing problem is not producing limited amounts but producing tons. For a good discussion of the early Iraqi effort to acquire chemical weapons, see David Ignatius, "Iraq's 13-year Search for Deadly Chemicals," *Washington Post,* Outlook section, September 25, 1988.

319. Based on work by Leonard Spector of the Carnegie Endowment for International Peace, and other working material.

320. *Christian Science Monitor,* December 12, 1988; BBC Panorama, 1986. The Iraqis had a natural reason to turn to Germany. Many Iraqis studied in Germany, and one, Amer Hammoudi al-Saadi, later became first deputy minister of industry and military industrialization in charge of Iraq's strategic weapons effort and military production authority.

321. *Christian Science Monitor,* April 13, 1988, p. 32.

322. There is no way to trace all the firms and countries involved, although a list is provided in the text. By October, 1990, 59 West German firms were under investigation by the West German government for arms sales to the Middle East. A classified report by Economics Minister Helmut Haussman has not been fully released but evidently found that 25 German firms had directly contributed to the sale of technology to produce poison gas. According to German government sources, at least five German companies played a critical role in building Iraq's chemical weapons production plants (Walter Engineering Trading of Hamburg; Karl Kolb of Dreireich bei Offenbach; Pilot Plant of Dreireich; Prussag of Hannover; and Heberger Bau of Schifferstadt bei Ludwigshafen; eight German firms helped build the Saad 16 research and development center for chemical, biological, and nuclear weapons near Mosul; at least five German companies helped Iraq modernize and extend the range of its Scuds and equip them with advanced warheads; and three German companies supplied Iraq with critical parts to build gas centrifuges (*Baltimore Sun,* October 14, 1990, p. 4). A report by Kenneth R. Timmerman of the Simon Wiesenthal Center of Los Angeles, *The Poison Gas Connection,* issued in late 1990, found that 29 German firms had played a critical role in helping Iraq to proliferate.

A working paper issued in September, 1990 by the Republican Staff of the Senate Foreign Relations Committee put this issue into a broader perspective. It found that a total of 87 German firms had helped Iraq with its proliferation and military production efforts, versus 18 for Austria, 17 for France, 16 for the United States, 15 for the United Kingdom, 12 for Spain, 12 for Switzerland, 10 for Italy, 8 for Belgium, 6 for India, 4 for Brazil, 3 for Argentina, 3 for the Netherlands, 2 for Japan, and 1 each for Chile, Greece, Poland, Kuwait, and Sweden. This same Senate working paper named 60 West German firms as contributing in some way to Iraq's development of chemical, biological, and nuclear weapons or long range missile developments. In addition, the Senate working paper named 3 Argentine firms, 12 Austrian firms, 6 Belgian firms, 4 Brazilian firms, 1 Egyptian firm, 13 French firms, 1 Greek firm, 6 Indian firms, 9 Italian firms, 1 Japanese firm, 1 Kuwaiti firm, 2 Dutch firms, 8 Spanish firms, 1 Swedish firm, 12 Swiss firms, 7 British firms, and 13 U.S. firms as having contributed at least some equipment and technology to Iraq's efforts at proliferation. Later reporting indicated U.S. firms unwittingly sold precursors to Iraq through a Dutch agent, Frans Van Anraat, using the firm Alcolac as a cover. Alcolac had sold some 528 tons of thiodiglycol to Iraq, but this seems to have been used up before the Gulf War (*Baltimore Sun*, June 28, 1991, p. D1).

323. This is a small amount. About 15–20 tons of a nerve agent like tabun are needed to cover a single square kilometer.

324. Iran claimed Iraq used nerve and phosgene gas delivered by FROG-7s and BM-21s and produced hundreds of killed and thousands of wounded as early as the Iraqi attack on Dezful in mid-1981. These reports do not seem true. Claims of the use of mycotoxins seem to reflect the results of poor sanitation conditions in the Iranian forces. Col., H.N., Commander of the IDF NBC Center, *Maarakhot*, No. 296, February, 1983; Task Force on Terrorism and Unconventional Warfare, *Chemical Weapons in the Third World: 2. Iraq's Expanding Chemical Arsenal*, House Republican Research Committee, U.S. House of Representatives, May 29, 1990, p. 7; Edgar O'Ballance, *The Gulf War*, London, Brassey's Defense Publishers, 1988, p. 77; Anthony H. Cordesman, and Abraham Wagner, *The Lessons of Modern War*, Volume 2, Boulder, Westview, 1990, pp. 122–123.

325. W. Seth Carus, *The Genie Unleashed: Iraq's Chemical and Biological Weapons Production*, Washington, Washington Institute Policy Papers, No. 14, 1989, p. 11.

326. John J. Fialka, "Fighting Dirty," *Wall Street Journal*, September 16, 1988, p. 1; *New York Times*, January 31, 1989, p. A-3; *Washington Post*, January 31, 1989, pp. A-1 and A-10. There are several ways of manufacturing mustard gas, but the use of thiodiglycol as a precursor is most common. Thiodiglycol has a number of commercial uses, including the manufacture of dyes and inks. When it is mixed with hydrochloric acid, it produces mustard gas. Thiodiglycol can be manufactured, however, using a reaction of ethylene oxide with hydrogen sulfide. These are relatively common industrial chemicals, and hydrogen sulfide can be obtained by removing it from sour natural gas or petroleum. Iraq mines sulfur and has a limited industrial capability to process sulfur.

327. Phillips has since claimed that it did not react to the first order for thiodiglycol because such orders were routine, and the Iraqi order because it was placed by KBS Holland B.V., a Dutch trading firm. It was only after the trading firm began to ship its initial order in July, 1983 that Phillips learned that the actual customer was in Iraq, and even then it paid little attention because it was said to be a large "agricultural" organization. In early 1984, when the State Ministry of Pesticide Production placed a second order for 500 tons, Phillips grew suspicious and canceled the order. Phillips then notified the Belgian government, which reacted by canceling Phillips's license to produce the chemical. A number of experts disagree, however, and feel that only limited amounts could have credibly been assumed to be used in printing, textiles, and automotive manufacturing. Iraq may also have obtained another 500 metric tons from other sources. This cannot be confirmed, but an American company called Alcolac was convicted of shipping thiodiglycol to both Iraq and Iran in 1987 and 1988. John J. Fialka, "Fighting Dirty," *Wall Street Journal*, September 16,

1988, p. 1; *New York Times,* January 31, 1989, p. A-3; *Washington Post,* January 31, 1989, p. A-1. Also see W. Seth Carus, *The Genie Unleashed: Iraq's Chemical and Biological Weapons Production,* Washington, Washington Institute Policy Papers, No. 14, 1989, p. 14. It takes roughly 1 metric ton of thiodiglycol to produce 1 ton of mustard gas.

328. Kenneth R. Timmerman, *The Poison Gas Connection,* Los Angeles, Simon Wiesenthal Center, 1990, pp. 9–10.

329. Task Force on Terrorism and Unconventional Warfare, *Chemical Weapons in the Third World: 2. Iraq's Expanding Chemical Arsenal,* House Republican Research Committee, U.S. House of Representatives, May 29, 1990, p. 8; Anthony H. Cordesman and Abraham Wagner, *The Lessons of Modern War,* Volume 2, Boulder, Westview, 1990, pp. 510–512; W. Seth Carus, *The Genie Unleashed: Iraq's Chemical and Biological Weapons Production,* Washington, Washington Institute Policy Papers, No. 14, 1989, pp. 11–17.

330. It takes 0.45 tons of ethylene oxide to make 1.0 tons of thiodiglycol. Carus, p. 15.

331. Task Force on Terrorism and Unconventional Warfare, *Chemical Weapons in the Third World: 2. Iraq's Expanding Chemical Arsenal,* House Republican Research Committee, U.S. House of Representatives, May 29, 1990, p. 8; Anthony H. Cordesman and Abraham Wagner, *The Lessons of Modern War,* Volume 2, Boulder, Westview, 1990, pp. 510–512; W. Seth Carus, *The Genie Unleashed: Iraq's Chemical and Biological Weapons Production,* Washington, Washington Institute Policy Papers, No. 14, 1989, pp. 11–17.

332. Nerve gases are more complex to manufacture than mustard gas. There are more ways to manufacture nerve gases, and many types of chemicals can be used, but sales of most of these chemicals—such as pinacolyl alcohol, potassium fluoride, phosphorous oxychloride, phosphorous trichloride, and trimethyl phosphite—are easy to track, and many have only limited commercial applications.

333. The persistence of chemical agents is dependent on wind and temperature and their dispersion as liquids or aerosols. Gases tend to disperse quickly in very hot weather and to persist far longer in cold weather. It is important to note that gases that may disperse in minutes under some conditions take days to disperse under others, and that persistent gases that last days or weeks in hot weather can last up to three times longer in cold weather.

334. Carus, p. 11.

335. *Jane's Defence Weekly,* January 9, 1988, p. 3; February 27, 1988, p. 336.

336. Unpublished "Statement of the Honorable William H. Webster, director, Central Intelligence Agency, before the Committee on Governmental Affairs, Hearings on Global Spread of Chemical and Biological Weapons," February 9, 1989; Task Force on Terrorism and Unconventional Warfare, *Chemical Weapons in the Third World: 2. Iraq's Expanding Chemical Arsenal,* House Republican Research Committee, U.S. House of Representatives, May 29, 1990, p. 8; Anthony H. Cordesman, and Abraham Wagner, *The Lessons of Modern War,* Volume 2, Boulder, Westview, 1990; W. Seth Carus, *The Genie Unleashed: Iraq's Chemical and Biological Weapons Production,* Washington, Washington Institute Policy Papers, No. 14, 1989; *New York Times,* March 27, 1984; *Wall Street Journal,* October 29, 1991, p. 24.

337. At least four batches of chemicals were bought in the United Kingdom. *London Financial Times,* November 5, 1991, p. 9. For general sources for this analysis, see unpublished "Statement of the Honorable William H. Webster, Director, Central Intelligence Agency, Before the Committee on Governmental Affairs, Hearings on Global Spread of Chemical and Biological Weapons," February 9, 1989; Task Force on Terrorism and Unconventional Warfare, *Chemical Weapons in the Third World: 2. Iraq's Expanding Chemical Arsenal,* House Republican Research Committee, U.S. House of Representatives, May 29, 1990, p. 8; Anthony H. Cordesman and Abraham Wagner, *The Lessons of Modern War,* Volume 2, Boulder, Westview, 1990; W. Seth Carus, *The Genie Unleashed: Iraq's Chemical and Biological Weapons Production,* Washington, Washington Institute Policy Papers, No. 14, 1989.

338. Task Force on Terrorism and Unconventional Warfare, *Chemical Weapons in the Third World: 2. Iraq's Expanding Chemical Arsenal,* House Republican Research Committee,

U.S. House of Representatives, May 29, 1990, p. 8; Anthony H. Cordesman, and Abraham Wagner, *The Lessons of Modern War*, Volume 2, Boulder, Westview, 1990, pp. 510–512; W. Seth Carus, *The Genie Unleashed: Iraq's Chemical and Biological Weapons Production*, Washington, Washington Institute Policy Papers, No. 14, 1989, pp. 11–17.

339. Task Force on Terrorism and Unconventional Warfare, *Chemical Weapons in the Third World: 2. Iraq's Expanding Chemical Arsenal*, House Republican Research Committee, U.S. House of Representatives, May 29, 1990, pp. 9–10.

340. Some of these reports may be exaggerated. There is no question that Falluja has large scale facilities, but some of these facilities seem to produce nothing but the precursor chemicals for sarin like phosphorous oxychloride and phosphorous trichloride. Falluja may be concentrating on the production of precursors. For a more pessimistic view, see Task Force on Terrorism and Unconventional Warfare, *Chemical Weapons in the Third World: 2. Iraq's Expanding Chemical Arsenal*, House Republican Research Committee, U.S. House of Representatives, May 29, 1990, p. 8.

341. W. Seth Carus, "Chemical Weapons in the Middle East," *Policy Focus*, Number 9, Washington Institute for Near East Policy, December, 1988, p. 4; "Iraq's Scare Tactic," *Newsweek*, August 2, 1982; *Washington Post*, April 5, 1988, p. A-1.

342. Peter Dunn, "The Chemical War: Journey to Iran," *NBC Defense & Technology International*, pp. 28–37; W. Seth Carus, *The Genie Unleashed: Iraq's Chemical and Biological Weapons Production*, Washington, Washington Institute Policy Papers, No. 14, 1989, pp. 22–23; *Foreign Report*, March 31, 1988, p. 12; and "Iran Keeps Chemical Options Open," pp. 12–14; *Jane's Defence Weekly*, January 9, 1988, p. 3; February 27, 1988, p. 336. The Austrian firms seem to have included Neuberger Holz und Kunststoffindustrie and Lenhardt Metallbau und Dachdecker. Five West German firms seem to have been involved, including WTB (Walter Thosti Boswau), Infraplan, and Karl Kolb.

343. Peter Dunn, "The Chemical War: Journey to Iran," *NBC Defense & Technology International*, pp. 28–37; W. Seth Carus, *The Genie Unleashed: Iraq's Chemical and Biological Weapons Production*, Washington, Washington Institute Policy Papers, No. 14, 1989, pp. 22–23; *Foreign Report*, March 31, 1988, p. 12; and "Iran Keeps Chemical Options Open," pp. 12–14; *Jane's Defence Weekly*, January 9, 1988, p. 3; February 27, 1988, p. 336.

344. *Christian Science Monitor*, January 23, 1992, p. 1.

345. "Iraq's Scare Tactic," *Newsweek*, August 2, 1982; *Washington Post*, April 5, 1988, p. A-1.

346. "Iraq's Scare Tactic," *Newsweek*, August 2, 1982; *Washington Post*, April 5, 1988, p. A-1; W. Seth Carus, *The Genie Unleashed: Iraq's Chemical and Biological Weapons Production*, Washington, Washington Institute Policy Papers, No. 14, 1989, pp. 7–9; Task Force on Terrorism and Unconventional Warfare, *Chemical Weapons in the Third World: 2. Iraq's Expanding Chemical Arsenal*, House Republican Research Committee, U.S. House of Representatives, May 29, 1990, p. 9.

347. "Iraq's Scare Tactic," *Newsweek*, August 2, 1982; *Washington Post*, April 5, 1988, p. A-1; W. Seth Carus, *The Genie Unleashed: Iraq's Chemical and Biological Weapons Production*, Washington, Washington Institute Policy Papers, No. 14, 1989, pp. 7–9.

348. Dick Palowski, *Changes in Threat Air Combat Doctrine and Force Structure*, 24th Edition, Fort Worth, General Dynamics DWIC-91, February, 1992, p. II-325.

349. It later became clear that Iraq had imported large amounts of thiodiglycol (whose main civil use is keeping the ink running in ballpoint pens) and thionyl chloride from Britain. *Independent*, July 28, 1991, p. 2; Peter Dunn, "The Chemical War: Journey to Iran," *NBC Defense & Technology International*, pp. 28–37; and "Iran Keeps Chemical Options Open," pp. 12–14.

350. W. Seth Carus, *The Genie Unleashed: Iraq's Chemical and Biological Weapons Production*, Washington, Washington Institute Policy Papers, No. 14, 1989, p. 22; Dick Palowski, *Changes in Threat Air Combat Doctrine and Force Structure*, 24th Edition, Fort Worth, General Dynamics DWIC-91, February, 1992, p. II-375.

351. The priority Iraq gave to chemical and biological weapons is illustrated by the fact that Hussein Kamil—Saddam Hussein's son-in-law and cousin—headed the Ministry of Industry and Military Industrialization during most of this period. This ministry is the branch of the Iraqi government responsible for the production of chemical and biological weapons. Michael Eisenstadt, "The Sword of the Arabs: Iraq's Strategic Weapons," Washington, Washington Institute for Near East Policy, Policy Paper 21, September, 1990, p. 7. W. Seth Carus, "Chemical Weapons in the Middle East," *Policy Focus*, Number 9, Washington Institute for Near East Policy, December, 1988, p. 4; "Iraq's Scare Tactic," *Newsweek*, August 2, 1982; *Washington Post*, April 5, 1988, p. A-1; Dick Palowski, *Changes in Threat Air Combat Doctrine and Force Structure*, 24th Edition, Fort Worth, General Dynamics DWIC-91, February, 1992, pp. II-325 and II-334; *Jane's Soviet Intelligence Review*, June, 1989, p. 256; *Foreign Report*, March 31, 1988, p. 1.

352. *New York Times*, April 3, 1990, p. 1.

353. *Jane's Defence Weekly*, January 9, 1988, and January 28, 1989; *Der Spiegel*, January 23, 1989; Task Force on Terrorism and Unconventional Warfare, *Chemical Weapons in the Third World: 2. Iraq's Expanding Chemical Arsenal*, House Republican Research Committee, U.S. House of Representatives, May 29, 1990, p. 10; Baghdad Domestic Service, April 2, 1990.

354. *Baltimore Sun*, November 3, 1991, p. 16A; *New York Times*, November 12, 1991, p. A-3; *Jane's Defence Weekly*, December 14, 1991, pp. 1144–1145; AP, December 12, 1991, PM cycle.

355. Michael Eisenstadt, "The Sword of the Arabs: Iraq's Strategic Weapons," Washington, Washington Institute for Near East Policy, Policy Paper 21, September, 1990, p. 7. W. Seth Carus, "Chemical Weapons in the Middle East," *Policy Focus*, Number 9, Washington Institute for Near East Policy, December, 1988, p. 4; "Iraq's Scare Tactic," *Newsweek*, August 2, 1982; *Washington Post*, April 5, 1988, p. A-1; Dick Palowski, *Changes in Threat Air Combat Doctrine and Force Structure*, 24th Edition, Fort Worth, General Dynamics DWIC-91, February, 1992, pp. II-325 and II-334; *Jane's Soviet Intelligence Review*, June, 1989, p. 256; *Foreign Report*, March 31, 1988, p. 1; *New York Times*, November 12, 1991.

356. *New York Times*, November 12, 1991; *London Times*, March 4, 1992, p. 10; *Christian Science Monitor*, January 23, 1992, p. 1.

357. Dick Palowski, *Changes in Threat Air Combat Doctrine and Force Structure*, 24th Edition, Fort Worth, General Dynamics DWIC-91, February, 1992, pp. II-326 to II-327.

358. The author visited many Iraqi positions with senior Saudi officers the week after the war. At several field headquarters positions, we found orders and instructions for the use of chemical weapons.

359. *Washington Post*, July 26, 1991, p. A-1.

360. *New York Times*, July 31, 1991, p. A-1; November 12, 1991, p. A-3; *Christian Science Monitor*, January 23, 1992, p. 1; AP, December 12, 1991, PM cycle.

361. *New York Times*, November 12, 1991, p. A3; *Christian Science Monitor*, January 23, 1992, p. 1; *Jane's Defence Weekly*, December 14, 1991, pp. 1144–1145; AP, December 12, 1991, PM cycle.

362. Department of Defense, *Conduct of the Persian Gulf War: Final Report*, Department of Defense, April, 1992, pp. 16–18; Rolf Ekrus, "Unearthing Iraq's Arsenal," *Arms Control Today*, April 1992, pp. 6–9; *Christian Science Monitor*, January 23, 1992, p. 1; *Atlanta Constitution*, January 16, 1992, p. 1; *Jane's Defence Weekly*, December 14, 1991, pp. 1144–1145; AP, December 12, 1991, PM cycle. The UN found nearly 100 metalworking machines for chemical weapons at the plant during a raid on November 20, 1991.

363. Many sources classify mycotoxins as chemical poisons. Unfortunately, mycotoxins have become one of those weapons that are popular with journalists or propagandists seeking to sensationalize a given conflict, and countries are often accused of using mycotoxins in cases where ambiguous symptoms are present. Iran has also been accused of producing and using mycotoxins.

364. Task Force on Terrorism and Unconventional Warfare, *Chemical Weapons in the*

Third World: 2. Iraq's Expanding Chemical Arsenal, House Republican Research Committee, U.S. House of Representatives, May 29, 1990, p. 12; *Wiener Zeitung*, June 25, 1989.

365. Department of Defense, *Conduct of the Persian Gulf War: Final Report*, Department of Defense, April, 1992, pp. 16–19.

366. For sample reporting, see Department of Defense, *Conduct of the Persian Gulf War: Final Report*, Department of Defense, April, 1992, pp. 16–18; *Washington Post*, January 26, 1989, p. A-16; *New York Times*, January 18, 1989, p. A-7; Reuters, January 17, 1989. A West German official, Friedhelm Ost, stated in early 1989 that Iraq was developing biological weapons research and might already have started the production of biological agents. The U.S. director of Central Intelligence, Judge Webster, publicly announced in October, 1990 that Iraq was producing biological weapons. *Washington Times*, January 27, 1989, p. 2; *Wall Street Journal*, January 23, 1989, p. A-11.

367. Department of Defense, *Conduct of the Persian Gulf War: Final Report*, Department of Defense, April, 1992, pp. 16–18.

368. W. Seth Carus, *The Genie Unleashed: Iraq's Chemical and Biological Weapons Production*, Washington, Washington Institute Policy Papers, No. 14, 1989, pp. 29–35.

369. *Washington Times*, January 19, 1989, p. A-8.

370. *Baltimore Sun*, August 19, 1990, p. 5-E; government of Canada, "Collateral Analysis and Verification of Biological and Toxin Research in Iraq," October, 1991.

371. Government of Canada, "Collateral Analysis and Verification of Biological and Toxin Research in Iraq," October, 1991.

372. Government of Canada, "Collateral Analysis and Verification of Biological and Toxin Research in Iraq," October, 1991.

373. *Middle East Economic Digest*, June 27, 1987, p. 16; August 29, 1987, p. 10; June 10, 1988, p. 9; June 24, 1988, p. 9; October 14, 1988, p. 20; February 10, 1989, p. 15; W. Seth Carus, *The Genie Unleashed: Iraq's Chemical and Biological Weapons Production*, Washington, Washington Institute Policy Papers, No. 14, 1989, pp. 33–35.

374. FBIS, *Daily Report, Western Europe*, January 23, 1989, p. 11; January 25, 1989, p. 8; and February 6, 1989, p. 9; *Der Spiegel*, January 23, 1989, pp. 16–27.

375. FBIS, *Daily Report, Western Europe*, January 30, 1989, pp. 9–10; *Wall Street Journal*, February 1, 1989, p. A-11.

376. Listed in Senate Foreign Relations Committee, Republican Staff, "Weapons Sales to Iraq," Working Paper, October 17, 1990.

377. *Jane's Defence Weekly*, September 14, 1991, p. 471.

378. *Jane's Defence Weekly*, September 14, 1991, p. 471.

379. *Atlanta Constitution*, January 16, 1992, p. 1.

380. Saddam Hussein repeated this denial on July 10, 1990. He stated that "we do not have nuclear weapons." He also went on to say, however, that "we would see no problem in a Western nation helping us to develop nuclear arms to help compensate for those owned by Israel." French TF1 Television network release, July 9, 1990; *Washington Times*, July 19, 1990, p. 2.

381. Based on work by Leonard Spector, and Atomic Energy Commission of Iraq, *Annual Report for 1988*, Baghdad, Iraq Atomic Energy Commission, 1989, p. 94.

382. Leonard S. Spector, *The Undeclared Bomb*, New York, Ballinger, 1988; Leonard S. Spector and Jacqueline R. Smith, *Nuclear Exports: The Challenge of Control*, Carnegie Endowment for Peace, Washington, April, 1990, pp. 21–26; *New York Times*, March 18, 1980; *Energy Daily*, October 2, 1980; and Michael Brenner, "Iran as a Nuclear Power in the Middle East," SAI, December 14, 1989, Appendix B.

383. The IAEA estimates that it takes 55 pounds (25 kilograms) of highly enriched uranium to make a nuclear weapon.

384. See Leonard S. Spector, *The Undeclared Bomb*, New York, Ballinger, 1988; Leonard S. Spector and Jacqueline R. Smith, *Nuclear Exports: The Challenge of Control*, Carnegie Endowment for Peace, Washington, April, 1990, pp. 21–26; Jed Snyder, "The Non-Proliferation

Regime: Managing the Impending Crisis," *Journal of Strategic Studies*, December, 1985, p. 11; Shyam Bhatia, *Nuclear Rivals in the Middle East*, London, Routledge, 1988, p. 85.

385. Half of the 55 pounds would have been in the core of Osiraq and unusable for weapons purposes, and the rest would have been irradiated in the nearby Isis reactor, both of which would have been subject to IAEA inspection. Based on work by Leonard Spector.

386. United Nations Security Council, *Report on the Eighth IAEA Inspection in Iraq Under Security Council Resolution 687*, November 11–18, 1991, New York, United Nations, S/23283 (English), pp. 21–23 and Annex 2.

387. Leonard Spector, *The New Nuclear Nations*, New York, Vintage, 1985, pp. 165–166; *Energy Daily*, October 2, 1980, p. 1.

388. For an excellent history of Iraq's nuclear weapons effort prior to 1983, see Jed C. Snyder, "The Road to Osirak: Baghdad's Quest for the Bomb," *Middle East Journal*, No. 37, Autumn, 1983, pp. 565–594. Also see Leonard Spector, *The New Nuclear Nations*, New York, Vintage, 1985, pp. 65–67.

389. Leonard Spector, *Proliferation Today*, New York, Vintage, 1984, pp. 175–178.

390. Shyam Bhatia, *Nuclear Rivals in the Middle East*, London, Routledge, 1988, p. 85.

391. See Andrew T. Parasiliti, "Iraq, Nuclear Weapons, and the Middle East," Middle East Institute, December 14, 1989, p. 3.

392. *Washington Post*, March 31, 1989, p. A-32.

393. Working papers by Leonard Spector; *Journal do Brazil*, May 22, 1988; William H. Webster, director of Central Intelligence, "Testimony Before the Committee on Governmental Affairs," U.S. Senate, May 18, 1989; *Washington Post*, September 29, 1989; *Mideast Markets*, June 12, 1989, p. 10; September 18, 1989, p. 11; October 16, 1989; *Financial Times Mid-East Market*, December 12, 1989; *Arms Control Today*, April, 1990, p. 27; *The Middle East*, May, 1990, pp. 11–14; *Nucleonics Week*, May 29, 1986, p. 6; *Defense News*, May 8, 1989; *Nuclear Engineering International*, December, 1988, p. 5.

394. The $10 billion figure is a UN staff estimate. See *New York Times*, October 14, 1991, p. A-6.

395. *Washington Post*, October 13, 1991, p. A-1; *Newsweek*, October 7, 1991, pp. 28–33; *U.S. News and World Report*, November 25, 1991, pp. 34–40; *Chicago Tribune*, October 6, 1991, p. I-28; United Nations Security Council, *Report on the First and Second IAEA Inspections in Iraq Under Security Council Resolution 687*, July 15, 1991, New York, United Nations, S/22788 (English); *Report on the Third IAEA Inspection in Iraq Under Security Council Resolution 687*, July 25, 1991, New York, United Nations, S/23283 (English); *Report on the Fourth IAEA Inspection in Iraq Under Security Council Resolution 687*, August 28, 1991, New York, United Nations, S/22986 (English); *Report on the Fifth IAEA Inspection in Iraq Under Security Council Resolution 687*, October 4, 1991, New York, United Nations, S/23112 (English); *Report on the Sixth IAEA Inspection in Iraq Under Security Council Resolution 687*, October 6, 1991, New York, United Nations, S/23122 (English); *Report on the Seventh IAEA Inspection in Iraq Under Security Council Resolution 687*, November 14, 1991, New York, United Nations, S/232215 (English); *Report on the Eighth IAEA Inspection in Iraq Under Security Council Resolution 687*, November 11-18, 1991, New York, United Nations, S/23283 (English); *Report on the Ninth IAEA Inspection in Iraq Under Security Council Resolution 687*, January 30, 1992, New York, United Nations, S/23505 (English).

396. United Nations Security Council, *Report on the Eighth IAEA Inspection in Iraq Under Security Council Resolution 687*, November 11-18, 1991, New York, United Nations, S/23283 (English), p. 14.

397. *U.S. News and World Report*, November 25, 1991, p. 36.

398. United Nations Security Council, *Report on the Eighth IAEA Inspection in Iraq Under Security Council Resolution 687*, November 11-18, 1991, New York, United Nations, S/23283 (English), p. 14.

399. James Bruce, "Iraq and Iran: Running the Nuclear Technology Race," *Jane's Defence Weekly*, December 5, 1988, p. 1307; *New York Times*, July 10, 1991.

400. *Washington Times*, August 29, 1990, p. 8; *South*, July, 1987, pp. 99–100; *Stern*, April 6, 1989, pp. 214–217; *Der Spiegel*, December 18-25, 1989, pp. 93–94; Michael Eisenstadt, "The Sword of the Arabs: Iraq's Strategic Weapons," Washington, Washington Institute for Near East Policy, Policy Paper 21, September, 1990, pp. 11–13.

401. *Nuclear Fuel*, August 5, 1991, Vol. 16, No. 16, p. 14.

402. It takes 15 to 25 kilograms to make one relatively simple nuclear weapon. More advanced weapons take substantially less. The IAEA did, however, certify on May 7, 1990, that all such material was still accounted for. IAEA Office, United Nations, New York, New York.

403. Leonard S. Spector, *The New Nuclear Nations*, New York, Vintage, 1985, pp. 44–54; FBIS, DR:NESA, Vol. 89, No. 66, April 7, 1989, p. 21; *Defense and Foreign Affairs Weekly*, Vol. 15, No. 15, April 17-23, 1989, p. 3.

404. *New York Times*, February 13, 1992, p. A-16; Zachary S. Davis and Warren H. Donnelly, "Iraq and Nuclear Weapons," Congressional Research Service, IB90113, February 13, 1992, p. 3; David Albright and Mark Hibbs, "News That the Front Page Missed," *Bulletin of the Atomic Scientists*, October, 1991, pp. 7–9.

405. Andrew T. Parasiliti, "Iraq, Nuclear Weapons, and the Middle East," The Middle East Institute, December 14, 1989, pp. 4–5; *Mideast Markets*, Vol. 16, No. 8, April 17, 1989, p. 15; and Vol. 16, No. 9, May 1, 1989, p. 12; *Washington Post*, March 31, 1989, p. A-1; *Report on the Seventh IAEA Inspection in Iraq Under Security Council Resolution 687*, November 14, 1991, New York, United Nations, S/23215 (English), p. 3.

406. *U.S. News and World Report*, Vol. 112, January 20, 1992, p. 45; *London Financial Times*, January 15, 1992, p. 1.

407. Maximum ultimate design capability was 2,000 centrifuges per year. *Washington Post*, May 5, 1989; *Rochester Democrat and Chronicle*, March 28, 1989; *New York Times*, January 15, 1992; David Albright and Mark Hibbs, "News That the Front Page Missed," *Bulletin of the Atomic Scientists*, October, 1991, pp. 7–9; *Report on the Seventh IAEA Inspection in Iraq Under Security Council Resolution 687*, November 14, 1991, New York, United Nations, S/ 232215 (English), p. 19; David Albright and Mark Hibbs, "Iraq's Shop-Till-You Drop Nuclear Program," *Bulletin of the Atomic Scientists*, April, 1992, pp. 27–37.

408. Gary Milhollin, "Building Saddam Hussein's Bomb," *New York Times*, March 8, 1992, pp. 30–31.

409. H&H was headed by Walter Busse, a former employee of MAN Technologies, which had built the uranium centrifuge assembly plant at Gronau in West Germany for URENCO. *Washington Post*, June 4, 1989; *Der Spiegel*, December 18, 1989; *FBIS-Western Europe*, December 20, 1989; *Nucleonics Week*, May 4, 1987, p. 1; *Wall Street Journal*, October 29, 1991, p. 24.

410. *Wall Street Journal*, October 7, 1991, p. A-10.

411. Michael Eisenstadt, "The Sword of the Arabs: Iraq's Strategic Weapons," Washington, Washington Institute for Near East Policy, Policy Paper 21, September, 1990, pp. 11–13; *Rochester Democrat and Chronicle*, March 28, 1988, pp. 1A and 10A; *Washington Post*, May 5, 1989, p. A-24.

412. *The Middle East*, May, 1990, pp. 11–14.

413. H&H seems to have provided machinery for the production of gas ultracentrifuges. *Washington Post*, June 4, 1989; *Los Angeles Times*, December 12, 1991, A-9; AP, December 11, 1991, AM cycle. Other firms named at this time included Schenk Werkzeug and Maschinenbau. *Der Spiegel*, December 18, 1989; *FBIS-Western Europe*, December 20, 1989; *Nucleonics Week*, May 4, 1987, p. 1; Gary Milhollin, "Building Saddam Hussein's Bomb," *New York Times*, March 8, 1992, pp. 30–31.

414. United Nations Security Council, *Report on the Eighth IAEA Inspection in Iraq Under Security Council Resolution 687*, November 11-18, 1991, New York, United Nations, S/23283 (English), p. 13. Press sources have named Neue Magdeburger Werkzeugmaschinenfabrik,

Schenk Werkzeug und Maschinenbau, Maschinenbau und Technikhandel, Dieburg, Rittal-Werk Rudolf Loh, Schmiedemeccanica (precision gear forgings), and Vakuum Apparat Technik. AP, December 11, 1991, AM Cycle; *Washington Post*, October 16, 1991, p. A-1. *Los Angeles Times*, December 15, 1991, p. A-9. The Senate Foreign Relations Committee has also named Fried, Krupp GmbH, Carl Zeiss, and MAN Aktiengesellschaft. *Washington Post*, October 18, 1991, p. A-3.

415. *New York Times*, January 15, 1992, p. A-1.
416. Michael Eisenstadt, "The Sword of the Arabs: Iraq's Strategic Weapons," Washington, Washington Institute for Near East Policy, Policy Paper 21, September, 1990, p. 15.
417. *Washington Post*, October 5, 1991, p. A-1; *Wall Street Journal*, October 29, 1991, p. 24.
418. *Washington Post*, November 2, 1991, p. C-1.
419. *New York Times*, January 15, 1992, p. A-1; *U.S. News and World Report*, January 20, 1992, p. 45; *Star Tribune*, November 22, 1991, p. 22A; *Christian Science Monitor*, October 23, 1991, p. 9.
420. *U.S. News and World Report*, November 25, 1991, p. 36; January 20, 1992, p. 45; United Nations Security Council, *Report on the Eighth IAEA Inspection in Iraq Under Security Council Resolution 687*, November 11–18, 1991, New York, United Nations, S/23283 (English); David Albright and Mark Hibbs, "Iraq's Shop-Till-You Drop Nuclear Program," *Bulletin of the Atomic Scientists*, April, 1992, pp. 27–37.
421. Zachary S. Davis and Warren H. Donnelly, "Iraq and Nuclear Weapons," Congressional Research Service, IB90113, February 13, 1992, p. 3; David Albright and Mark Hibbs, "Iraq and the Bomb: Were They Even Close?" *Bulletin of Atomic Scientists*, March, 1991, pp. 16–25; David Albright and Mark Hibbs, "It's All Over at Al Atheer," *Bulletin of Atomic Scientists*, June, 1992, pp. 8–10; "U.S. Experts Divided on Whether Iraqi Calutrons Procure U-235," *Nuclear Fuel*, June 24, 1991, pp. 3–4.
422. This analysis draws heavily on David Albright and Mark Hibbs, "Iraq and the Bomb: Were They Even Close?" *Bulletin of Atomic Scientists*, March, 1991, pp. 16–25; "U.S. Experts Divided on Whether Iraqi Calutrons Procure U-235," *Nuclear Fuel*, June 24, 1991, pp. 3–4.
423. Iraq made this admission to the UN on October 21, 1991. *New York Times*, October 14, 1991, p. A6; October 20, 1991, IV-5; United Nations Security Council, *Report on the Eighth IAEA Inspection in Iraq Under Security Council Resolution 687*, November 11–18, 1991, New York, United Nations, S/23283 (English), p. 9.
424. *Los Angeles Times*, December 12, 1991, p. A-9.
425. A full description of activities is not included because of their value in nuclear weapons design. United Nations Security Council, *Report on the Sixth IAEA Inspection in Iraq Under Security Council Resolution 687*, October 8, 1991, New York, United Nations, S/23122 (English).
426. *Washington Post*, October 5, 1991, p. A-1.
427. Gary Milhollin, "Building Saddam Hussein's Bomb," *New York Times*, March 8, 1992, pp. 30–31.
428. United Nations Security Council, *Report on the Eighth IAEA Inspection in Iraq Under Security Council Resolution 687*, November 11–18, 1991, New York, United Nations, S/23283 (English), pp. 14–15, 29; Gary Milhollin, "Building Saddam Hussein's Bomb," *New York Times*, March 8, 1992, pp. 30–31; *Report on the Seventh IAEA Inspection in Iraq Under Security Council Resolution 687*, November 14, 1991, New York, United Nations, S/232215 (English), p. 30.
429. *The Middle East*, May, 1990, pp. 11–14.
430. *U.S. News and World Report*, November 25, 1991, p. 36; United Nations Security Council, *Report on the Eighth IAEA Inspection in Iraq Under Security Council Resolution 687*, November 11–18, 1991, New York, United Nations, S/23283 (English), p. 29.
431. *U.S. News and World Report*, November 25, 1991, p. 36. This same article named a

number of possible U.S. suppliers, including Honeywell (computers), Canberra Industries (computer equipment to measure neutrons and for design specifications), Carl Zeiss (computer equipment to process photographic data), Databit (computer data transmission and circuit switches), Forney International (computer equipment for power stations), Hewlett-Packard (optical fiber cables, computers, frequency synthesizers, precision electronic and photo equipment), Perkin-Elmer (computers, precision electronic and photo equipment), Sackman Associates (computers, electronic assemblies, and photo equipment), and Westinghouse Electric (computer hardware and software for the Iraqi electric system). Many of these supplies almost certainly had little or nothing to do with the Iraqi nuclear effort.

432. Zachary S. Davis and Warren H. Donnelly, "Iraq and Nuclear Weapons," Congressional Research Service, IB90113, February 13, 1992, p. 4; *Washington Post*, October 9, 1991, p. A-17.

433. Report to the UN Security Council on October 8, 1991; *USA Today*, October 10, 1991, p. 6.

434. Gary Milhollin, "Building Saddam Hussein's Bomb," *New York Times*, March 8, 1992, pp. 30–31.

435. Gary Milhollin, "Building Saddam Hussein's Bomb," *New York Times*, March 8, 1992, pp. 30–31.

436. The problem of height of burst is critical because it determines the fallout effects of a weapon and the relative importance of blast, radiation, and thermal energy affecting a given target. Fusing is not necessarily different from the fusing needed for ordinary bombs, but the fusing on ordinary bombs often fails to function properly.

437. For general discussion, see *Wall Street Journal*, March 30, 1990, p. A-18; April 4, 1990, p. A-24; *The Middle East*, May, 1990, pp. 11–14; *Newsweek*, April 9, 1990, pp. 26–28; *Time*, June 11, 1990, p. 34.

438. The sting operation is a good example of what happens when a company that is concerned with proliferation takes immediate action to contact the officials in the country involved. A U.S. company called CSI Technologies of San Marcos, California, immediately contacted U.S. customs officials when it was contacted by Euromac, the Iraqi front organization, located in Thames Ditton, near London. U.S. officials contacted British officials, and they worked together to set up a series of meetings, some of which were televised, and to make the intercept and arrests at Heathrow Airport. Euromac was registered as a "general grocers and provision merchant." It is unclear that the Iraqis fully understood what they were ordering. Maxwell Laboratories of San Diego had been delivering other types of capacitors to Iraq, including 518 slow speed capacitors. Iraq then ordered 185 high speed capacitors. Maxwell Laboratories notified customs, and halted the shipment at customs' request. The new type of capacitor, however, was still unsuitable for nuclear weapons. Andrew T. Parasiliti, "Iraq, Nuclear Weapons, and the Middle East," The Middle East Institute, December 14, 1989, pp. 4–5; *Mideast Markets*, Vol. 16, No. 8, April 17, 1989, p. 15, and Vol. 16, No. 9, May 1, 1989, p. 12; *Washington Post*, March 31, 1989, p. A-1; *Los Angeles Times*, March 30, 1990; *Washington Post*, March 31, 1990, p. 2.

439. The core of a nuclear bomb consists of fissile material, a layer of outer explosives, and a firing circuit connected to all parts of the high explosive cover to detonate all of it at exactly the same moment and achieve maximum compression at the precise instant high energy neutrons are being injected into the compressed fissile core. *Washington Times*, March 28, 29, and 30, 1990; *Washington Post*, March 28, 29, and 30, 1990; *New York Times*, March 28, 29, and 30, 1990.

440. *Nucleonics Week*, January 24, 1991.

441. Zachary S. Davis and Warren H. Donnelly, "Iraq and Nuclear Weapons," Congressional Research Service, IB90113, February 13, 1992, p. 6.

442. *The Atlanta Constitution*, January 16, 1992; Rolf Ekrus, "Unearthing Iraq's Arsenal," *Arms Control Today*, April, 1992, pp. 6–9.

7

Trends in the Military Balance and Arms Sales in the Southern Gulf States

There are six southern Gulf states: Bahrain, Kuwait, Oman, Qatar, Saudi Arabia, and the UAE. Although these states differ in many ways, they all face a similar set of challenges in shaping their strategic position and military forces. They must try to develop enough deterrent and war fighting capability to check the threat from Iraq and Iran. They must resist hostile ideological and political challenges to conservative regimes. They must provide internal security and defend against other southern Gulf states in petty quarrels over border areas and islands.

At the same time, they must be prepared to deal with threats from outside the Gulf. A united Yemen poses the same low level threat to Saudi Arabia and Oman that the YAR and PDRY did before their unification. The Arab-Israeli conflict provides some risk of being dragged into a new war in the Levant, and the rise of Islamic fundamentalism in Iran and the Horn of Africa has replaced Arab socialism as an outside force for political instability.

While superpower rivalry has largely ceased to influence the Gulf, the end of the Cold War scarcely means freedom from intervention by East and West. Eastern Europe and the former Soviet republics are a source of cheap arms imports and uncertain alignments, and rise of the Islamic republics in the CIS creates the risk of new shifts in the balance of power in the northern Gulf. The West continues to be concerned with the security of its oil imports, with trade, and with its own arms sales. The southern Gulf states are both dependent on U.S. and other Western power projection capabilities for security against Iran and Iraq, and threatened by some aspects of that dependence.

Military Forces, Strategic Needs, and Vulnerabilities

The key statistical details of the military forces of the southern Gulf states, along with those for the states that are the most probable threats, are sum-

553

554

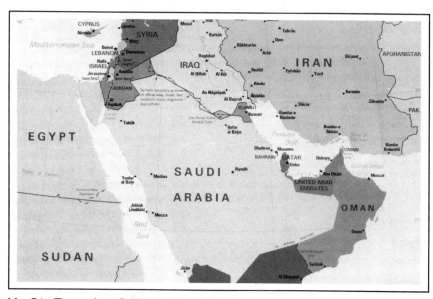

Map 7.1   The southern Gulf states. Source: U.S. Government

TABLE 7.1 The Size and Military Capabilities of the Southern Gulf States in 1992

	Size (sq. km.)	Population (millions)	GDP ($ billions)	Defense ($ billions)	Active Military Manpower	Tanks	Combat Aircraft	Major Combat Ships
Bahrain	620	540	4.0	.25	7,450	81	24	6
Kuwait	17,820	2,204	26.0	5.0	10,500	200	50	3
Oman	212,460	1,534	9.0	1.2	30,400	72	57	4
Qatar	11,000	518	7.0	0.6	7,500	24	18	3
Saudi Arabia	2,149,690	17,869	86.0	18.0	111,000	700	253	17
UAE	83,600	2,389	28.0	4.0	44,000	131	100	8
Subtotal	2,475,190	25,054	160.0	29.05	210,850	1,208	502	41
Iran	1,648,000	59,050	80.0	10.0	530,000	1,000	130	18
Iraq	434,920	19,524	35.0	6.0	400,000	2,300	300	11
Subtotal	2,082,920	78,574	115.0	16.0	930,000	3,300	430	29
Total Gulf	4,558,110	103,628	275.0	45.0	940,850	3,508	932	71
Yemen	527,970	10,062	6.0	1.0	65,000	1,275	101	8

Sources: Author's estimate adapted from IISS, *Military Balance, 1991–1992*; JCSS, *Middle East Military Balance, 1990–1991*; CIA, *The World Factbook, 1991*, Washington, GPO, 1991. Population figures are actual from July, 1991. Other estimates are for mid-1992. The data shown are taken from single sources for comparability purposes and often differ from the author's estimates for individual countries in the text.

marized in Table 7.1. It is clear from these statistics that the southern Gulf states have enough collective resources to provide a major regional deterrent and considerable self-defense capability.[1] Unfortunately, resources are important only to the point they have been transformed into military capability, and each of the forces listed in Table 7.1 has major limitations.

The southern Gulf states all have relatively small manpower pools to draw on for the space they must defend. They suffer from major diseconomies of scale. In many cases, the southern Gulf states have bought weapons for their prestige rather than their deterrent or combat capabilities. Most of the military forces in the smaller southern Gulf states have inadequate warning sensors and weak command and control systems. Most armies lack modern communications, battle management, and target acquisition systems. There is little heliborne or amphibious capability to move troops rapidly. There are limited AEW and AC&W assets. Most southern Gulf ships have inadequate air and missile defenses. The smaller navies have no mine warfare capability, and all forces have poor ability to conduct combined arms and combined operations. There are few modern reconnaissance and intelligence assets. The various states and military services differ sharply in sheltering and passive defense capability.

These problems are compounded by lack of standardization and poor interoperability. While they are gradually improving in individual military capability, many are still showpiece forces which cannot operate effectively except in carefully planned exercises. They have few native combat troops and have whole foreign manned combat units with little loyalty to the nation or regime.

Some of the southern Gulf states listed in Table 7.1 may spend a great deal on defense, but all face special problems in building up an adequate deterrent or defense capability. Saudi Arabia is the largest southern Gulf state in terms of both geography and military forces and is the key to any successful effort at regional cooperation in defense. Saudi Arabia has a low ratio of forces to the space which must be covered by its critical defensive areas. It cannot create an effective defense without its neighbors.

The smaller states spread along the coast of the southern Gulf. If any of these states fell into hostile hands, it would be a major strategic springboard for intervention by Iran or Iraq or a constant threat to the internal security of its neighbors. A hostile air force or navy based in the southern Gulf could also make it far more difficult for other Arab states or the U.S. to project power into the region.

Kuwait shares a common border with Iraq and is only a short distance from Iran. No foreseeable mix of Kuwaiti, other southern Gulf, other Arab, and/or U.S forces can offer Kuwait full security against another round of surprise Iraqi attacks or surprise Iranian air, amphibious, and missile attacks. Kuwait's small territory and population keep it militarily vulnerable while it has massive oil and gas resources to protect.

Bahrain, Qatar, UAE, and Oman do not share a common border with Iran or Iraq, but because they lack strategic depth and adequate air and coastal defense capabilities, all are vulnerable to Iraqi and Iranian attacks. Bahrain is small, relatively poor, and ethnically divided. Qatar is also small and lacks a sufficiently large native population to develop effective armed forces. The UAE shares the demographic and geographic problems of its smaller littoral neighbors and is further weakened by tensions among its individual sheikdoms. Oman must defend the Straits of Hormuz against any challenge by Iran and a long border with Yemen.

The Gulf Cooperation Council and Efforts at Collective Security

If military considerations were the only major factor driving national decisionmaking, these problems would make the southern Gulf states band together to create an effective structure for collective defense. While Saudi Arabia is the largest southern Gulf state, it is no more capable of defending itself without help from its neighbors and outside powers than is Bahrain or Qatar. The military balance in the Gulf region is clearly a function of how well the southern Gulf states work together to develop the following capabilities:

- Forces strong enough to provide direct defense against low to medium intensity threats and deter higher level threats by raising the threshold of risk to any attacker and/or inflicting retaliatory damage.

- Strong air and naval defenses along the Gulf Coast and opposite Yemen.
- Sufficient close air support and interdiction capability to compensate for weak land forces.
- Sufficient naval and naval air capability both to protect the coast and exposed oil and desalinization facilities against even the first wave of air and naval attack and to help defend shipping of all kinds.
- Enough land forces to allow an emphasis on air and naval forces to be effective.
- Air and missile strike capabilities adequate to inflict enough damage on enemy cities, oil facilities, and shipping to deter long range air and missile strikes through the threat of retaliation.
- A suitable mix of active and passive defenses and strike capabilities to a level adequate to deter missile attacks.
- Tactical mobility and lift for all forces capable of rapid cross-reinforcement of each country by some mix of other states.
- Sufficient sustaining capability to allow prolonged engagement with well supplied threat forces without becoming politically dependent on outside nations.
- Advanced and centralized sensor and C^3I systems to maximize the capability of high technology weapons systems and to serve as a partial substitute for insufficient unit strength, problems in force quality at the unit level, lack of command experience, and lack of experience in combined arms and combined operations.
- High technology advanced weapons systems to help compensate for inadequate unit strength and to maximize the effectiveness and value per dollar of key force elements.
- Large and survivable basing, support, and infrastructure facilities to enhance survivability, tactical mobility, and cross-reinforcement capability and to use passive defense as a substitute for mass and active defense.
- Advanced training and support facilities and sufficient foreign technicians and civilians to make maximum use of native military manpower and reduce technology transfer problems.
- Credible over-the-horizon reinforcement capability as a means of meeting high level or high lethality threats such as an all-out attack by a northern Gulf state, failure of a key force element, defense against new high technology threats, and defense against attacks on multiple fronts.
- Over-the-horizon reinforcement capability from the West or other Arab states to deal with major threats from Iran or Iraq.

The southern Gulf states made a beginning towards developing such capabilities when they set up the Gulf Cooperation Council in February, 1981. The creation of the GCC came largely as a result of the Iran-Iraq War and a long standing fear of both Iran and Iraq. It marked an important step towards effective military cooperation. All six southern Gulf states became members, and all pledged to move towards cooperation in both military affairs and internal security.

The GCC has since made progress in the form of common staff talks and limited numbers of common military exercises. It set up a token rapid deployment force in Hafr al-Batin and made efforts to develop common procurement policies.[2] It improved cooperation in intelligence and internal security after the uprising at the Grand Mosque in Saudi Arabia in 1979 and the coup attempt in Bahrain in 1981. Some aspects of this cooperation continued to improve during the Iran-Iraq War, as the southern Gulf states reacted to pro-Iranian bombings and assassination attempts in Kuwait and Saudi Arabia, and during the Gulf War, as they reacted to the threat of Iraqi attacks and terrorism.

While the GCC could not play a major military role during the Gulf War, it did play an important symbolic one. All of the GCC states cooperated with the UN coalition. Bahrain, Saudi Arabia, Oman, and the UAE provided massive aid in the form of basing, fuel, and aid in kind. All of the GCC states sent at least token forces to join the Arab land forces that fought in operation Desert Storm, and all made major efforts to improve both their own defenses and their cooperation.

Nevertheless, the southern Gulf states made little progress towards effective military cooperation during the Iran-Iraq War and the beginning of the Gulf War. Oman and Saudi Arabia proved to be rivals that could not agree on the shape joint forces should take. They have never set up an effective aid system to help their poorer members like Bahrain and Oman, and only Saudi Arabia ever provided its share of a $1.8 billion aid pledge to Bahrain.[3]

Before the Gulf War, Oman provided only grudging and cosmetic support for Saudi Arabia's call for the creation of a Gulf defense force at Al-Batin. This refusal came partly because the proposed force was to be under Saudi command and partly because the force was primarily oriented towards the defense of Kuwait. Oman and Kuwait also disagreed over other issues. Kuwait pressed for freer movement of Gulf labor than Oman preferred and refused to sign intelligence agreements that would provide more data on the movement of politically sensitive individuals.

Bahrain and Qatar indulged in petty border skirmishes. The different sheikdoms of the UAE divided against each other over their relations with other members of the GCC and over their relations with Iran, Iraq, and the West. For example, Abu Dhabi and Dubai refused to fully cooperate during the initial Peninsular Shield exercises, even though both are part of the UAE.

Oman proposed during the Gulf War that the southern Gulf states cooperate to create a 100,000 man GCC force, but it found itself virtually isolated within the GCC. Saudi Arabia pressed for a far less ambitious plan to upgrade the Peninsular Defense Force that had existed before the war but also received little real support. The resulting disputes among the GCC states have blocked substantive steps to create more integrated or interoperable forces.

While the GCC nations did appear to commit themselves to collective security arrangements involving Egypt and Syria when they met in Damascus in March, 1991, their Damascus Declaration soon turned out to be meaningless. Saudi Arabia and Kuwait quickly decided not to station large Egyptian or Syrian forces on their soil and cut back on payments and subsidies.

The most that could be agreed to was the idea of Egyptian and Syrian rapid return forces.

In spite of all the risks exposed by the Gulf War, the GCC still tends to substitute rhetoric for military cooperation and serious planning. Discussions of military standardization, common support facilities, and common military production facilities lead to far more words and studies than actions. The various member states still suffer from long standing border disputes and rivalries, and substantive cooperation tends to fade the moment that member states no longer face a common threat from Iran or Iraq.

Saudi Arabia

	Manpower (1,000s)	Tanks	Aircraft	Defense Spending ($ millions)	Arms Imports ($ millions)	Arms Exports ($ millions)
1967	50	24	40	1,270	47	—
1973	75	85	70	1,880	84	2
1982	80	450	191	22,040	3,200	—
1988	84	550	179	13,560	3,000	5
1991	112	700	250	31,860	—	—

Modern Saudi Arabia owes its existence to one of the few Arab military geniuses of the colonial period: Aziz ibn-Saud.[4] The Saud family had conquered much of Arabia once before, in alliance with Mohammed ibn-Abd al-Wahhab, who was the leader of a puritanical Islamic reform movement, but it had been driven from power by internal struggles and the Turks. It was living in virtual exile and obscurity when Ibn-Saud and a small group of followers seized Riyadh, the former Saud seat of power, from the Shammer tribes in 1902.

Ibn-Saud rapidly built up a confederation of tribes that gave him control over most of the Najd in eastern Arabia by 1906, and he forged the tribes of the area into a military brotherhood called the Ikhwan by creating military villages where he provided homes, mosques, funds, and weapons. By 1913 ibn-Saud's forces were challenging the Turks, and the start of World War I created a situation which soon led Britain to provide ibn-Saud with money and weapons. He used these resources to attack both the Turks and the rival Rachid dynasty, driving the Rachid dynasty out of power in 1921. By 1922 ibn-Saud had control over most of Arabia except the southern region of the Hijaz, with the holy cities of Mecca and Medina.

Ibn-Saud conquered the Hijaz between 1924 and 1925 and became a major regional military power that threatened Kuwait, Iraq, Oman, Yemen, and Jordan. By this time, however, the Ikhwan had become an internal threat to his rule, and ibn-Saud realized that any further military action might both deprive him of control over the territory he had conquered and lead to British intervention. As a result, he founded a small regular army and forged an alliance with many of the tribal leaders in the areas he had conquered. He acquired British machine guns, armored cars, and light artillery as well as support from the RAF. In January, 1930, he fought a major battle with the Ikhwan and brought them decisively under control. This victory effectively ended the period of Saudi conquests, except for a border war with Yemen during 1931–1934.

The depression of the 1930s threatened ibn-Saud's ability to fund his troops and supporters, but the discovery of oil in 1933 gave him the funds gradually to forge the tribal areas into a country. It also introduced U.S. influence into the region for the first time, which was reinforced by the establishment of military ties between the U.S. and Saudi Arabia during World War II. This led to the creation of a U.S. military training mission in 1952.

The period from the 1950s through the mid-1960s involved a long series of complex struggles among Saudi Arabia, its neighbors, and other elements of the Arab world. The rise of Nasser threatened the Saud family's control of the military forces and the country and led to deep divisions within the royal family.

When Ibn-Saud died in 1953, he was succeeded by his son Saud, who proved to be a weak and incompetent ruler, who provoked a number of quarrels with his neighbors, and who was unable to deal with the political threat of Nasser and other Arab socialist movements. Saudi Arabia became involved in a dispute over the Burami Oasis with Oman and the UAE during 1952–1955 and in an effort to seize control of part of western Oman during 1957–1959.

At the same time, Saudi Arabia was affected by the growing radicalism of Nasser's Egypt and the rebellion against Britain in the Aden protectorate between 1953 and 1959. It also became involved in a major civil war on its southern border in North Yemen between 1962 and 1967. North Yemen was ruled by a royal family that combined the role of ruler with that of imam of North Yemen's religious sect. The Imam Ahmed died in September, 1962, and his son al-Badr claimed the throne. On September 26, Nasser backed Col. Abdellah al-Salleh in a socialist coup against al-Badr. Threatened by the prospect of another socialist regime on Saudi Arabia's border, King Saud provided support for the imam. While none of these involvements confronted Saudi Arabia with direct external threats, they did lead to major efforts by Nasser and others to stimulate internal unrest and several coup attempts.

At the same time, King Saud could not manage the nation's finances, control the younger princes, or secure the loyalty of the armed forces. In 1964 the royal family combined to force Saud from power and brought Faisal, another of ibn-Saud's many sons, to power. Faisal proved to be an extremely shrewd and competent ruler. He strengthened Saudi aid to the royalists in Yemen and used Egypt's growing financial problems and military confrontation with Israel to reach an agreement that led Egyptian troops to withdraw from Yemen in 1967.

Faisal also took the decisions that created the modern Saudi armed forces. Two incidents drove Saudi Arabia to try to create an effective air force and army. The first occurred along the border with North Yemen (the YAR) in

November, 1969. Although Egypt had left North Yemen in 1967, the republican forces resisted and then drove back al-Badr's forces. Saudi Arabia supported him in counterattacking. Yemen then sent aircraft to attack the Saudi border area around Najran. These air raids continued until al-Badr's forces collapsed in late 1970. The second occurred on November 26, 1969, when South Yemen (the PDRY) attacked and captured Al-Wadiah, a Saudi border oasis, in an effort to halt Saudi support for anti-Marxist rebels in the border area. Saudi forces counterattacked, but the key to recovering the oasis was a series of air strikes on the PDRY. This demonstration of the practical realities of modern air power was a key factor in shaping Saudi perceptions.[5]

King Faisal was a critical force in triggering the Arab oil embargo after the October, 1973 conflict between the Arabs and Israel, and he then led the country in using its massive new oil wealth to modernize both the state and the military forces. By the time he was assassinated in March, 1975 and was replaced by King Khalid, Saudi Arabia was not only relatively stable but wealthy, and was taking the first steps to create a modern army and air force.

Between 1975 and 1990, Saudi Arabia emerged as a major world financial and oil power and as a significant political power in the Arab world. The royal family also established a relatively stable government and easily managed the transition in power when Khalid died in 1982 and was replaced by King Fahd. During the late 1970s and 1980s, Saudi Arabia played a major role in subsidizing conservative and moderate regimes throughout the Arab world, checking the influence of Khomeini in Bahrain and the southern Gulf, aiding Iraq in its war with Iran, and containing Marxist radicalism in the PDRY. Saudi Arabia has also gradually moderated its stance towards Israel.

Saudi Strengths and Vulnerabilities

Today Saudi Arabia has become the key to any attempt to create strategic stability in the Gulf. As it demonstrated during the Iran-Iraq War and Gulf War, Saudi Arabia can cooperate closely with the U.S. and the West in checking aggression from Iraq or Iran. This cooperation is shaped by more than immediate political considerations. As a conservative monarchy that lacks the population and skills to create military forces large enough to defend its territory or regional position, it is dependent on the power projection capabilities of the U.S. as the ultimate guarantee of its security.

At the same time, Saudi Arabia is highly vulnerable. While Saudi Arabia is large enough to develop significant defense and deterrent capabilities by southern Gulf standards, it faces serious problems in defending a large territory with potential threats on all its borders. Saudi Arabia's oil wealth also makes it the natural target of radical political movements and ambitious states throughout the Middle East. Saudi Arabia has extremely large oil reserves, by far the largest of any country in the world. It had produced about 62.4 billion barrels of oil by the end of 1990 and had a high reserve-to-production ratio of 112:1.[6] As of January 1, 1992, it had estimated proved oil reserves of up to 257 billion barrels, with probable additional reserves of 42 billion barrels, and gas reserves of 184,000 billion cubic feet. It had about 33%

of the world's total oil reserves and produced at a rate of about 6.3–8.2 million barrels per day during 1990 and 1991.[7] It also had a share of the Saudi-Iraqi neutral zone, which had another 5 billion barrels of proven reserves and 1,000 billion cubic feet of gas.[8]

Saudi Arabia's forces face a formidable problem in defending a large nation. Saudi Arabia has a land area of about 2,150,000 square kilometers, roughly one-fourth the size of the U.S. It has a 222 kilometer border with Kuwait, a 448 kilometer boundary with Iraq, a 198 kilometer boundary along the Iraqi-Saudi neutral zone, a 742 kilometer border with Jordan, a 1,458 kilometer border with Yemen, a 676 kilometer border with Oman, a 586 kilometer border with the UAE, and a 40 kilometer border with Qatar. A causeway connects Saudi Arabia with Bahrain. In addition, Saudi Arabia has a total of 2,510 kilometers of coastline on the Gulf and Red Sea, opposite to Iran, Egypt, the Sudan, Ethiopia, and Djibouti.[9] Saudi Arabia has only about 2.33 cubic kilometers of internal renewable water resources, which is very low, amounting to about 321 cubic meters per person, less than one-seventh the total for a citizen of the U.S.[10]

This mix of boundaries and coastlines explains both Saudi Arabia's importance in defending the southern Gulf and many of its defense problems. It is within easy air strike range of Iraq and amphibious and air range of Iran. It has had a long series of border problems and clashes with Yemen and risks being dragged into the Arab-Israeli conflict to the west. Its borders themselves are a source of potential tension. Saudi Arabia has no defined border with Yemen or the UAE, has only recently reached a border settlement with Oman, has not ratified its border agreements with Iraq, and disputes ownership of Qaruh and Umm al-Maradim islands with Kuwait. It also disputes its border with Qatar, and had a minor clash on September 30, 1992. This clash took place at a small outpost at Khofuous, about 80 miles southeast of Doha. Two Qataris were killed and a third taken prisoner.

Unlike the other southern Gulf states, Saudi Arabia must secure its borders against threats from the Yemens, the Red Sea, and the Levant as well as the Gulf. This mix of threats on its borders has also forced Saudi Arabia to disperse its military resources to forward bases throughout the country, and this has left it with limited forces on any given front.

Air power is Saudi Arabia's only means of compensating for the weakness and dispersal of its land and naval forces. Saudi Arabia can only use air power in such a role, however, if (1) its limited first line fighter strength has the range and refueling capability to mass quickly; (2) its air units can maintain a decisive technical and performance edge over threat forces; (3) it can provide sufficient air defense capability to provide air cover for Saudi ground forces, naval forces, and key targets; (4) it can provide sufficient dual capability in the attack mission to offset its limited ground strength and give it time to reinforce its army units; and (5) its air units are cumulatively strong enough to provide at least limited coverage of the northern Gulf or Red Sea front while facing an active threat on the other front.

Saudi Arabia is not without its internal problems. Saudi society as a whole is still divided into regional and tribal groups. Radical social changes have urbanized much of Saudi Arabia and produced considerable stress within Saudi society. This has led to the rise of Islamic fundamentalism, which challenges the process of secular development, and the ruling Saud-Wahhabi elite. These same changes have led to a demand for secular reform and the liberalization of Wahhabi restraints on commerce, the role of women, and social custom by a large number of businesspeople and secular educated professionals.[11]

This division reached major proportions before the Gulf War but became much more serious during and after the conflict. During 1990–1992, Islamic fundamentalists began to demand a return to superorthodoxy. At the same time, secular reformers have petitioned the king, and Saudi women even made a brief protest for women's rights by driving their own cars. While the king attempted to defuse this situation by compromising with both sides and forming an appointed council of advisors, or Majlis, the net result was a steady—if covert—rise in anti-Saud and anti-Wahhabi political action by Saudi Arabia's Islamic fundamentalists.

The challenge of Islamic fundamentalism within Saudi Arabia also led to growing concern within the government over Islamic extremism overseas. Although Saudi Arabia once tended to finance Islamic fundamentalist movements in Afghanistan, the Sudan, Ethiopia, Algeria, and many other areas with little concern for their exact character, the Saudi government became far more selective and more careful about distinguishing between religious fundamentalism and religious extremism. For example, Saudi Arabia is actively competing with Iran for influence over the rising religious institutions of the former Soviet Islamic republics.

While the Saud family still seems to be in secure control of the country and generally relies on co-opting its opposition rather than repressing it, the threat of Arab socialism has been replaced by the threat of Islamic fundamentalism. This helps explain why King Fahd reorganized his cabinet on August 5, 1991, and why he announced a series of reforms on November 17, 1991. These reforms included the formation of a council of Saudi citizens, the introduction of a written body of laws, and increased autonomy for the provinces. King Fahd announced these reforms over the state broadcasting network in his first major address since airing his response to Iraq's invasion of Kuwait.

King Fahd's announcement of a Majlis was at least partly a reaction to demands from both fundamentalists and secular reformers for greater participation in the government. It was followed by further speeches not only by the king but by senior religious figures like Sheik Abdel Aziz ibn-Baz, who denounced religious extremism, and by senior political figures like Prince Turki Faisal, who gave a rare speech in a mosque refuting some of the charges against the royal family.

The king announced on March 2, 1992, that the Majlis would have sixty-one members; that it would include the king, who would act as prime minister; that it would have a four year term of office; and that it would have limited powers, including the right to examine plans for economic and social development, question cabinet members, examine annual plans submitted by each ministry, and propose new laws or amendments. The king stated that similar ten man councils would be set up in each of the fourteen provinces and that the governors would have added power and autonomy. He issued a long list of laws setting forth in writing the basic rules of the government, the first codification of such laws since the founding of the kingdom sixty years earlier. These laws included provisions that made the king the commander in chief of the armed forces; called for power to pass to the most qualified member of the royal family rather than according to the order of succession; established an independent judiciary; guaranteed the privacy of the home, mail, and phone; and prohibited arbitrary arrest.

King Fahd announced the members of the new Majlis on September 23, 1992, the sixtieth anniversary of the founding of the monarchy. He appointed Mohammed bin Ibrahim bin Jubair as speaker. At the same time, the king stated that, "The democratic systems prevailing in the world are systems which, in their structure, do not suit this region and our people. . . . The system of free elections is not part of Islamic theology."[12]

It is unclear that the creation of a purely advisory Majlis, and written code of law, is enough to meet any group's expectations. There are roughly 62 princes who hold senior civil and military positions in the government, and this causes a substantial amount of jealousy. Religious fundamentalists like Sheik Haffan al-Safar have already rejected the king's reforms, as have Saudi moderates. More mainstream religious leaders like Sheik ibn-Baz—a venerated blind leader who has also publicly condemned Islamic fundamentalist cassettes—have opposed some of the government's efforts to suppress political opposition by the clergy, and 100 leading clerics signed a petition which, among other things, called for the punishment of all who gained wealth through illegal means, "whoever they are and without any exception of rank." The religious pressures that led to the fundamentalist uprising in the Grand Mosque on November 20, 1979, are still very real, as are the tensions between Shi'ites in the eastern province, the conservative Wahhabis in the Najd, and the Shafii Sunnis in the Hijaz.[13]

The strains of massive social change and urbanization, resulting from Saudi Arabia's oil wealth and growing exposure to the outside world, present a continuing challenge of another kind. Saudi Arabia maintains a high level of spending that has produced steady budget deficits and leads to yet more urbanization and unplanned social change.

The Saudi economy and Saudi political stability suffer from a failure to clearly demarcate the powers and rights of members of the royal family, who often abuse their political power to dominate major military and civil deals and developments. The Saud family is now also burdened with some 7,000 princes, many of whom demand special privileges and use their influence to violate Saudi law.[14] The ruling family is dominated by the Sudairi branch, whose leaders include the king; the minister of defense, Prince Sultan; the head of military intelligence, Prince Turki; and Prince Naif. They are balanced by Crown Prince and Deputy Prime Minister Abdellah and a number of other princes, including Prince Saud al-Faisal, the foreign minister and son of King Faisal.

These problems also extend to the command level, where the divisions among members of the royal family often prevent the selection of effective commanders or effective unity of command. One of Saudi Arabia's most brilliant officers, Prince Fahd ibn-Abdellah, was shunted aside because of a glass ceiling placed on the promotion of junior princes and his status as part of a secondary branch of the royal family. The de facto commander in chief of Saudi forces during the Gulf War, Prince Khalid ibn-Sultan, was forced to resign in September, 1991, when he asked to be promoted to the post of military chief of staff—a position effectively left vacant for several years because of the illness of the officer who formally held the title. Other senior Saudi officers unrelated to the royal family have been denied promotion because of a wide range of internal political disputes.[15]

There is still a heritage of regional tension between the followers of ibn-Saud in the Najd and the north and the citizens of the Hijaz around Mecca and Medina.[16] This tension is compounded by their adherence to different branches of Sunni law and tribal resentments and feuds dating back to the rise of ibn-Saud. More seriously, part of the population of the oil rich eastern province, probably at least 40%, is Shi'ite.[17] The regime has done a reasonably good job of providing a mix of personal incentives and internal security controls and has recently limited the abuse of police power, particularly the sudden search of Shi'ite homes. Nevertheless, there have been recurrent incidents of sabotage of oil facilities, and there are cells of radical Shi'ites in the eastern province who have obtained some support from Iran. The Shi'ite population is too small to succeed in any kind of uprising or separatism, but it does present a significant source of social tension in the world's most important oil producing area.

Saudi Defense Expenditures

Saudi Arabia has slowly built up modern military forces since the 1970s by what can only be called brute force methods. Beginning without anything approaching the modern infrastructure and educated populations of the Maghreb, Levant, or northern Gulf, Saudi Arabia has spent several hundred billion dollars to create a modern system of bases, the ability to train and support soldiers capable of operating modern military equipment, and a pool of equipment modern enough to give it a potential edge over Iran and Iraq.

This effort has been fueled by its petroleum sector. Saudi Arabia's oil reserves have given it immense oil wealth, although this wealth has varied sharply with oil prices and market conditions. Saudi oil revenues reached a peak of $133 billion a year in 1981, dropped to $46 billion in 1983, and averaged around $19 billion to $25 billion in 1984–1988.[18] Its oil revenues have risen since that time to $28.3 billion in 1989, or about 85% of all exports. Sharper rises occurred in 1990 and 1991 because of the Gulf War, but accurate figures are not yet available. Such shifts are critical to the Saudi economy and the expansion of Saudi military forces. The petroleum sector accounts for about 70% of all budget revenues and 33% of the Saudi GDP. Industrial production, much of it petroleum oriented, accounts for 37% of the GDP. Agriculture accounts for 10% of the GDP, but only because of wasteful government subsidies and the waste of irreplaceable fossil well water.[19]

Saudi Arabia's military development has, however, been an incredibly costly process. It has had the highest ratio of expenditures to active men in uniform of any country in the developing world for more than a quarter century. It also spent an average of 20% of its GNP on military forces during the 1980s, sums amounting to $14–24 billion, although its full time active manpower ranged from only 79,000 to 84,000. Most of these expenditures— probably on the order of 60–65%—have been on infrastructure, foreign services and maintenance, and basic manpower training. Saudi Arabia has had to convert a nomadic society into one capable of operating modern armor, ships, and aircraft, and has been able to do this only by creating entire military cities, new ports, and major road networks. No nation in military history has had to take a more brute force approach to creating the capability to use modern military technology.

Saudi Arabia has also experienced major swings in defense spending, many driven by its dependence on oil revenues. These problems became particularly acute at the end of the 1980s, when its oil revenues dropped to about one-fifth of their 1981 level of $133 billion and Saudi financial reserves dropped to as little as one-third their 1981 level of $190 billion. Saudi Arabia had to cut its original FY1986, FY1987, FY1988, FY1989, and FY1990 budget estimates and accept annual deficits ranging from $10 billion to $20 billion.[20] For example, its FY1988 budget was projected to be 141.2 billion riyals ($37.7 billion), down some 17% from the 1987 level of 170 billion riyals. Oil revenues were unofficially projected at 65.2 billion riyals. The 1988 deficit was projected to be 35.9 billion riyals ($9.57 billion) versus deficits of about 50 billion riyals in the previous four years. Saudi Arabia sought to reduce the deficit through utility surcharges, 12–20% import duties, hospital charges, airline fare increases, and local borrowing in the form of some $8 billion in bonds.[21]

The Gulf War made this situation much worse. Although Saudi oil revenues rose, the kingdom had to spend up to $55 billion on the costs of the crisis, ranging from payments to members of the UN coalition to expenses for the Saudi military and refugee housing. The 1991 budget deficit reached a record $21 billion, and the current account deficit rose to $24 billion. Saudi Arabia was forced to adopt a working budget for 1991 because it could not keep track of its expenditures and to raise its estimated 1992 budget by 27% over the 1990 budget to allow for unanticipated costs. It also had to borrow some $7 billion, $4.5 billion from internationally syndicated loans and $2.5 billion from local banks. This need to borrow while paying interest created new tensions with Saudi Arabia's Islamic fundamentalists—who believe that interest is forbidden by the Quran. While Saudi Arabia is attempting to reduce its borrowing in 1992, it will still run a major deficit, marking ten straight years of deficit spending. It also will still have a current account deficit of at least $1 billion, and debt servicing will rise to 10% of the Saudi budget.[22]

The potential offset to this financial situation is a massive Saudi investment in increasing oil production to a sustainable 10 million barrels a day and the enormous boost in the kingdom's share of the oil market during the Gulf War—rising from 5.4 million barrels a day before the war to 8.5 after the conflict. Saudi Arabia also probably still retains around $50 billion in the Saudi Arabian Monetary Authority (SAMA) and government entity foreign investments, and $20 billion in foreign assets controlled by public bodies.[23]

Precise estimates of Saudi military spending are impossible to make. Saudi Arabia does not report many of its costs in its budget documents and often adjusts its flow of defense expenditures without reporting them. One gets very different figures if one uses Saudi and outside sources, and the problem is compounded by the near impossibility of making accurate estimates of expenditures in constant riyals and constant dollars and riyal to dollar conversions.

If one looks at recent Saudi figures, the FY1986 Saudi defense budget was planned to be 64.6 billion riyals ($17.7 billion), or 32% of the total budget.[24] The oil revenue deficit then led to minor cuts and spending of about 64.09 billion riyals ($17.3 billion). The FY1987 defense budget was about 60.7 billion riyals, or $15.78 billion. The FY1988 defense budget, which includes the national guard and the Interior Ministry and its police forces, was originally planned to be about 50.8 billion riyals, or $13.21 billion. This was a cut of 9.9 billion riyals ($2.57 billion) from FY1988.[25] The 1987 budget seems, however, to have risen to 60.8 billion riyals, or $16.23 billion. Recent Saudi figures have varied sharply, but the FY1988 defense budget seems to have been 50.8 billion riyals ($13.6 billion), and the FY1989 defense budget 55.0 billion riyals ($14.69 billion).

The FY1990 budget was apparently 51.9 billion riyals ($18.86 billion), but expenditures may have been 119.216 billion riyals ($31.86 billion) if one includes $18 billion in Gulf War contributions to the U.S. and UK. The FY1991 defense budget seems to have reached 100.4 billion riyals ($26.8 billion), including $13.73 billion in contributions to the U.S., France, Britain, Kuwait, and other members of the UN coalition.[26] The FY1992 budget is projected at 54.3 billion riyals.[27] These figures do not include Saudi military aid to other Arab states, which seems to have peaked in FY1985, when a combination of aid to Iraq and Syria may have driven foreign aid expenditures to over $5 billion.[28]

U.S. estimates of Saudi military spending are different. If one uses ACDA and CIA sources, Saudi defense expenditures were $9.6 billion in 1978, $12.4 billion in 1979, $15.0 billion in 1980, $18.4 billion in 1981, $22.0 billion in 1982, $24.8 billion in 1983, $20.4 billion in 1984, $21.3 billion in 1985, $17.3 billion in 1986, $16.2 billion in 1987, $13.6 billion in 1988, $14.7 billion in 1989, and $13.9 billion in 1990 (less expenses for the Gulf War).[29]

While these debates over Saudi spending levels would normally be of only secondary interest, they provide one of the few broad indicators of overall military effort in the southern Gulf. Further, as a rough rule of thumb, in the 1990s Saudi Arabia must spend about $13 billion a year (in

1992 dollars) simply to maintain its present force readiness, and considerably more for major force expansion and improvement.

Saudi Arms Imports

Saudi Arabia has long had high levels of arms imports, although the cost estimates of such transfers are highly misleading relative to those of most other Middle East countries because they include such a large portion of construction and goods and services, which are called arms imports because they are funded as part of the U.S. foreign military sales program and other foreign sales programs. No other country in the developing world has paid so much to receive so few arms per dollar.

ACDA estimates that Saudi Arabia imported $1,500 million worth of arms in 1978, $1,200 million in 1979, $1,600 million in 1980, $2,700 million in 1981, $2,800 million in 1982, $3,800 million in 1983, $3,300 million in 1984, $3,800 million in 1985, $5,500 million in 1986, $7,000 million in 1987, $2,700 million in 1988, and $4,200 million in 1989.[30]

The ACDA estimates also show that Saudi Arabia gets most of its arms from three nations: the U.S., France, and Britain. According to ACDA, Saudi Arabia took delivery on $12.125 billion worth of arms during 1979–1983. This included $5.1 billion worth of arms from the U.S., $2.5 billion from France, $1.9 billion from the UK, $525 million from West Germany, $200 million from Italy, and $1,900 million from other countries.[31] It took delivery on $19.530 billion worth of arms during 1984–1988. This included $5.8 billion worth of arms from the U.S., $7.5 billion from France, $2.5 billion from the PRC, $2.1 billion from the UK, $30 million from Italy, and $1,600 million from other countries.[32]

According to ACDA's new methods of reporting, Saudi Arabia imported a total of $23,040 million worth of arms during 1985–1989, including $5,000 million from the U.S., $7,000 million from France, $7,700 million from the UK, $2,500 million from the PRC, $40 million from West Germany, $250 million from other European countries, $140 million from other East Asian states, $390 million from Latin America, and $20 million from other countries in the world.[33]

Other sources indicate that Saudi Arabia took delivery on $48.1 billion worth of arms during 1983–1989 and purchased 14.1% of all Third World arms sales agreements during 1982–1989.[34] If one looks at total transfers to the developing world, Saudi Arabia was the largest arms importer during 1984–1987 ($27.5 billion) and the largest during 1988–1991 ($26.8 billion). It must be stressed, however, that the figures for Saudi Arabia include substantial amounts of services, and the value of actual weapons transfers is around half the total reported.

During 1990 Saudi Arabia took delivery on $6,749 million worth of arms and ordered $18,649 million more. It took delivery on $7.1 billion worth of arms in 1991 and ordered $7.8 billion more. Its major source of deliveries was the UK, and its major source of new imports was the U.S. It ranked as the largest Third World state in terms of both deliveries and new agreements.[35] In this case, however, large amounts of the transfers consisted of in-kind support and arms transferred to the UN coalition during operation Desert Storm.

These dollar figures conceal major qualitative changes in Saudi arms imports since the mid-1980s, which have been further accelerated since the Gulf War. Until the mid-1980s, Saudi Arabia concentrated upon building up its military infrastructure and basic military capabilities. Since the mid-1980s, its imports have shifted to include a steadily increasing number of first line weapons systems. If Saudi Arabia imported relatively few arms per arms import dollar in the past and concentrated on building the foundation for modern forces, it now often buys more arms than it can readily absorb—using new arms deliveries to try to force the pace of military expansion even if this means considerable turbulence, shortages in skilled personnel, and overall undermanning in Saudi forces.

Many of Saudi Arabia's most advanced weapons systems have come from the United States, although Britain, France, and many other countries have been major suppliers. Saudi Arabia has shown that it will change suppliers if it is denied the weapons it wants. At the same time, it has shifted suppliers to suit its political goals or to offer major importing nations a partial offset for their expenditures on Saudi oil. There has also been a continuing tension over arms sales between Saudi Arabia and the United States. On the one hand, Saudi Arabia is dependent on U.S. support and power projection forces in any major emergency, and military relations are generally close. On the other hand, it feels U.S. arms sales and advisory services are often limited or denied because of U.S. ties to Israel, and many in the royal family and Saudi society resent the denial of arms sales and continuing pro-Israeli posturing and attacks by members of the U.S. Congress.

Saudi Military Manpower

The key military problem Saudi Arabia has faced since it decided to create modern military forces in the 1960s, and will continue to face until well after the year 2000, is manpower. Saudi Arabia has never had a proper census and has constantly attempted to exaggerate its total population because it feels this has strategic and political value in dealing with the rest of the Arab world. The latest CIA estimate is 17.9 million, which many experts believe may be 5–6 million too high. Saudi Arabia privately estimates about 8.5 million Saudis and 2.5 million foreigners. The IISS, for example, estimates the total population at 10.6 million.[36] The birthrate is estimated to be 3.7%. The population is about 90% Arab and 10% Afro-Asian. Virtually all Afro-Asians are foreign workers whose residence is dependent on work permits. The country is theoretically 100% Muslim, predominately Sunni and of the Wahhabi sect, although about 6–8% may be Shi'ite—largely in the eastern provinces.[37]

The labor force is estimated to be about 4.2 million, of which roughly 60% is foreign. About 33% of the labor force is native citizens working for the government, 28% is native in the industry and petroleum sector, 22% is native working in services, and 16% is native working in agriculture. The CIA estimates that about 6.7 million males in the work force between the ages of 15 and 49 are fit for military service, but many are foreign workers. It estimates that about 165,000 men a year reach age 17, when they become eligible for military service.[38] The IISS estimates there are 585,000 males between the ages of 13 and 17, 473,400 between the ages of 18 and 22, and 841,400 between the ages of 23 and 32.[39]

While Saudi Arabia exaggerates its population and military manpower for political purposes, it seems fairly clear that Saudi Arabia now has a total native population of only 7–9 million and only about 76,500–95,000 full time uniformed actives in its armed forces, plus 35,000–50,000 more full time actives in its paramilitary royal guards and national guard. Even if one includes part time manning and other paramilitary forces, this still raises the total national guard to a maximum of 55,000–70,000 men and adds a diverse mix of some 5,000–10,000 men in the customs, frontier, intelligence, and royal guards forces that have little value outside internal security missions.

This Saudi manpower situation compares with an Iranian population of roughly 60 million and peak military manning levels of over 1 million men, with an Iraqi population of roughly 20 million and peak military manning levels of nearly 1 million men, with a Syrian population of about 13 million and 400,000 men under arms, and with a total population in Yemen of about 9–11 million, with 63,000 under arms.[40] Equally important, Saudi military manpower is severely limited by continuing tribal and regional rivalries. Saudi Arabia is very cautious about recruiting from the regions (like the Hijaz) that opposed the Saudi conquest in the 1920s and 1930s or rival tribes like the Bani Sadr.

Saudi Arabia's regular military forces now comprise about 76,500 men. By Western standards, it would take about 100,000–150,000 men to adequately man the kingdom's current force structure. Even a full scale draft would probably fail to give the country the manpower to meet its limited force expansion plans. Over the years, Saudi Arabia has tried to compensate for these problems by

- A heavy dependence on foreign support and technicians (now over 14,000 personnel);
- Using small elements of foreign forces in key specialty and technical areas—such as combat engineers—to fill in the gaps in Saudi land forces. It formerly had some 10,000 Pakistani forces to fill out one brigade (the 12th Armored Brigade) at Tabuk. These Pakistanis have not been replaced, although possible contingency arrangements may exist with Egypt.[41]
- Use of French and British internal security experts;
- Selective undermanning while it builds its training and manpower base;
- Concentrating on building a fully effective air force as a first line deterrent and defense; and
- A de facto reliance on over-the-horizon reinforcement by the U.S., France, Egypt, Syria, or some other power to deal with high level or enduring conflicts.

These are all intelligent methods of reducing the Saudi manpower problem, but they still leave many gaps and weaknesses in Saudi forces. The limitations in Saudi military manpower are also forced on Saudi planners by Saudi demographics, by civil competition for skilled manpower—which still makes it extremely hard to retain army personnel in spite of the contraction of the Saudi economy—and by the need to maintain a national guard with up to 35,000 full time actives for internal political and security reasons.[42]

Some of these manpower constraints, however, will change significantly during the next decade. Saudi Arabia's high population growth rate will sharply increase the number of eligible men, and military service is becoming more popular. It pays about twice as much for new entrants as comparable civilian jobs, and the expectations of young Saudis are much more modest than they were in the 1970s and 1980s. The Gulf War marked a watershed in this respect. Saudi Arabia called for volunteers for the first time, expecting some 25,000 at most. It got 200,000 to 250,000. This showed that Saudi Arabia probably could expand its manpower significantly in future years.

Nevertheless, there is no way that Saudi Arabia can hope to compete with most of its larger neighbors in sheer manpower or land forces. While Saudi officials have talked about conscription for more than a decade, Saudi Arabia's religious establishment opposes this as a violation of Islamic law, and any full scale program would have unacceptable political and economic costs. Although Saudi Arabia's total population is uncertain, it is reasonably clear that the kingdom now has a maximum of about 1.8 million males eligible for military service. Only 90,000 new males fit for military service reach draft age every year, and it is unlikely that this number will climb above 180,000 before the year 2000.[43]

Saudi Arabia can only hope to reach and maintain a technical edge over regional threats by concentrating on the modernization and Saudization of its combat arms while continuing to rely on foreign support. The kingdom must allocate virtually all of its increasing output of skilled military manpower to operational forces and command roles, and it cannot hope to replace Western technical support. It has learned from the Gulf War, however, that it may be able to organize its land units to accept volunteers into support units with functions similar to their civil jobs and shift regular military personnel to combat functions. This is now being studied as a possible alternative to conscription.[44] If conscription is adopted, it is more likely to be a selective effort that will provide a limited increase in active manning levels rather than a broad popular draft that results in a major increase in Saudi total manning.

Equally significant, the kingdom has already drawn on most of the tribal and regional groupings it can count upon for political support. The rise of Islamic fundamentalism among the poorer and more tribal Saudis coupled with long standing hostility among a number of tribes in the Hijaz places additional serious limits on the Saudi recruiting base and the groups it can conscript.

It is very difficult to make any estimate of the degree to which Saudi

Arabia currently offsets its manpower shortages by the use of foreign troops and advisors. Further, the separation between formal military advisors and Western contractors is often more a matter of clothing than function. There are significant numbers of U.S., British, and French military advisors and at least several thousand Western contract personnel, many handling critical service and support functions for Saudi Arabia's most modern weapons. There are small cadres from Brazil and other arms sellers and at least several hundred PRC personnel servicing and operating Saudi Arabia's CSS-2 long range surface-to-surface missiles. There no longer seem to be whole Pakistani formations in Saudi Arabia, but there may still be over 1,000 Pakistani troops, some operating at the battalion level in the army.[45]

The Saudi Army

Saudi Arabia's manpower problems are most severe in the case of its army. The Saudi army had a total of just 38,000–43,000 men in late 1988, with another 56,000 full and part time troops in the national guard. In spite of crash efforts to build up the army's manpower during the Gulf War, efforts which sometimes raised combat unit manning by as much as 20%, the army's force structure was still undermanned by about 20–35%, and many individual units had worse manning levels.

In 1992 the army seemed to have expanded to around 60,000–70,000 men, although some Saudi claims put this manpower substantially higher. This expansion, however, has had mixed success. Saudi Arabia still cannot man its present strength of two armored, four mechanized, one infantry, and one airborne brigade and one royal guard regiment. It is experiencing serious difficulties in forming three independent artillery brigades and creating an aviation command. Even if it could fully man these forces, Saudi Arabia would have forces equivalent to little more than two divisions at a time when Iraq and Iran can both mobilize more than ten times this strength.

The army has significant problems in recruiting and training skilled technicians and NCOs. Yet even by Gulf standards, its existing force structure and equipment pool require a minimum of 90,000–110,000 men. While the Saudi army may be able to recruit these numbers, in the near term it will do so only at the cost of manpower quality. It will be hard pressed to build up to more than 100,000 men fully trained and combat capable before the late 1990s. In the interim, it will experience serious turbulence and manpower allocation problems and limited ability to sustain casualties. It will also be heavily dependent on contractor support for many service support, maintenance, and logistics functions.

This raises serious doubts about the kind of force expansion that is currently being debated in Saudi Arabia. Some reports indicate that a secret Saudi-U.S. joint security review called the Malcor Report was carried out after the Gulf War in August, 1991. Some sources indicate the plan called for a three corps Saudi force of seven divisions by the year 2000. Other reports indicate that it called for a nine division force of 90,000 men and the overall force expansion shown in Table 7.2.[46]

TABLE 7.2 Possible Saudi Force Expansion Plans for the Year 2000

	Mid-1991	On Order	Total by 1995	Goal for the Year 2000
M-1A2 Tanks	0	465	465	700
M-2 Bradley AFVs	0	200	200	550
Tornado Jets	72	48	120	?
F-15 Jets	60	38	98	132
Hawk Jets	29	60	89	?
Black Hawk Helicopters	12	88	100	?
Patriot Batteries	8	14	22	26
Modern Mine Vessels	4	1	5	11

SOURCE: Adapted from a working paper by Ted Atkenson of the CSIS.

It seems likely that Saudi goals are more modest. According to Saudi sources in late 1992, the government would like to create at least one more armored and mechanized brigade by the mid-1990s and expand to a total of five divisions by the year 2000. This change would involve a conversion from a brigade-oriented command structure to a division-oriented structure. It would provide three divisions in the north to defend Saudi Arabia's Gulf Coast and the border with Iraq, another division near al-Kharj or the capital, and a fifth division in the south.

These five divisions would be relatively light, and total combat unit manning would expand from a present total of about 37,500 to around 70,000. These also would depend on additional manpower or "fillers" from the National Guard and temporary duty civilians in their support forces. Such an approach is considerably more realistic than the Malcor plan but would still present a real challenge in terms of available manpower

Regardless of what estimate of Saudi plans or goals is correct, any real-world expansion of Saudi forces will still leave Saudi Arabia unable to defend its territory from an all-out attack by Iraq. It will also leave Saudi Arabia with major problems in concentrating its forces to aid Kuwait or deal with any sudden Iranian thrust across the Gulf to achieve a limited objective like the seizure of Bahrain. Further, the threat from the northern Gulf is only part of the threat Saudi Arabia faces. The Saudi army must defend a territory roughly the size of the U.S. east of the Mississippi. It must provide forces to defend its western border area, to deal with a continuing low level border conflict with Yemen, and to establish at least some defense along its Red Sea coast.

As a result, the Saudi army is normally scattered over much of the kingdom. It has brigade sized casernes at Khamis Mushayt and Shahrurah in the southeast, a garrison at Najran and Jubayl in the south, and brigade sized forces at King Khalid City in the north, Tabuk in the west, and Dammam in the east. The GCC Peninsular Shield Force is located at King Khalid City, which is near the border with Kuwait and Iraq. These deployments are partly a matter of internal security. Saudi forces are usually kept far away from key cities and political centers of power, primarily because the Saudi army cannot leave any of its border areas undefended.

These manpower and expansion problems are compounded by the Saudi army's need to operate a complex mix of different equipment from many different nations. The diversification of Saudi Arabia's sources of army equipment has greatly complicated its life-cycle costs and training and support burden. These problems have been further aggravated by Saudi Arabia's tendency to make purchases from its major oil customers that do not serve the army's needs and by the kingdom's inability to obtain a consistent supply of equipment from the U.S. because of U.S. domestic politics.

Much of the equipment the Saudi army has purchased has required modification or changes to its original technical and logistic support plan before it could be operated in large numbers, and some items still present major servicing problems. These problems have then been compounded by the need to support so many different types of equipment in distant border areas, by the erratic quality of contractor support, and by an overly ambitious effort to create a modern logistical system that has lacked proper Saudi and U.S. advisory management.

These problems are reflected in the equipment holdings and modernization plans of the Saudi army. Saudi Arabia had about 830 main battle tanks in late 1992. These tanks included 120 U.S.-made M-60A1s, 400 M-60A3s, and 300–310 French-made AMX-30s. Part of this tank force meets Saudi needs. Saudi Arabia found the M-60A3 to be a significant advance over the M-60A1 during the Gulf War, and all of Saudi Arabia's M-60A1s will be converted to the M-60A3. The M-60A3s have thermal sights, modern fire control computers, laser range finders, and engine and air intake improvements, although they do present some operational problems—the crew compartment cannot be cooled effectively and the M-60s can develop internal temperatures of well over 120°F. Much of this tank force is also relatively new. Saudi Arabia bought 150 M-60A3s, along with 15,000 depleted uranium 105mm anti-tank rounds, as part of an emergency order in August, 1990.[47]

The M-60A3 is capable of engaging any tank currently deployed in the region, although it lacks a decisive technical superiority over the T-72 and the other first line tanks in potential threat forces. It is likely to remain in the Saudi force structure through the year 2000. Saudi Arabia's inventory of French AMX-30s is a different story. The AMX-30 lacks the armor, firepower, and operational availability to be kept in service against threats armed with T-62s, T-72s, and other modern tanks like the T-80, M-60, Khalid, Merkava, Chieftain, and Challenger. While the adoption of newer anti-armor round technology has made up for the lack of penetrating power in the Obus G rounds that France originally sold the Saudi army, the AMX-30's fire control and range finding capability is inadequate to help Saudi tank crews make up for their lack of experience, and the AMX-30 lacks the power, cooling, and filtration for desert combat. Saudi Arabia has needed to phase the AMX-30s out of its force structure for nearly half a decade but is unlikely to do so before the late 1990s.

Saudi Arabia has long recognized the need for more modern tanks and sought improved armor beginning in the mid-1980s. Its goal was to develop a force using the M-1 tank. This offered not only one of the world's most effective weapons systems but one that could be fully supported and upgraded over time by the U.S. Army and that would improve U.S. Army rapid deployment capabilities. Saudi Arabia faced major uncertainties, however, over whether the U.S. Congress would permit such sales. As a result, it examined alternatives—including Brazilian, British, French, and German tanks. It announced in February, 1988 that it had short-listed the M-1A1 and EE-T1 Osoro for some form of coproduction in a purchase that might involve some 315 vehicles and a $1 billion contract. One issue delaying a decision to buy the M-1 was whether the U.S. was willing to sell the M-1A2 version of the M-1, with a 120mm gun. Another was that the Brazilian Osoro existed only in prototype form, and production could not begin until 1990 at the earliest.

The kingdom eventually decided to buy 315 M-1A2s in September, 1989, although the details of sale took roughly a year to complete and some debate over the sale still existed in May, 1992 because the U.S. Army had cut back on its own orders of the M-1A2.[48] The reasons for the Saudi decision, as well as the complexity and sophistication of modern tanks, become clear from an examination of the M-1A2's performance characteristics. The Saudis bought a version of the 68.5-ton M-1 with a 120mm gun, advanced armor, and thermal sights. The M-1A2 has line-of-sight gun stabilization which provides full shoot-on-the-move capability. A digital ballistic computer provides quick aiming correction based on automatic and manual inputs such as wind velocity, vehicle cant, and gun tube deflection. A laser range finder provides target data for the ballistic computer. The thermal imaging sight improves target acquisition during both day and night at ranges in excess of 3,000 meters.

A 1,500 horsepower engine, automatic transmission, and two final drives give the M-1A2 a top speed of 43 mph on hard surface roads. An advanced torsion bar and long stroke rotary shock absorber suspension give it cross-country speeds of up to 33 mph. Crew survivability is enhanced by the compartmented storage of fuel and ammunition and an automatic fire extinguisher system. The tank has a comparatively low profile and noise signature and has external smoke generators and grenade launchers for rapid concealment. Other key features of all M-1 tanks include:[49]

- Appliqué armor added to protect it against future Soviet-made weapons systems, and potential upgradability to active armor.
- A commander's independent thermal viewer to allow him to acquire targets in the dark or haze while the gunner is engaging other targets and to hand off such targets independently to the gunner.
- An improved commander's weapon station with excellent visibility and ballistic protection, an enlarged hatch, and protection against directed energy weapons.
- Precise position navigation and use of the satellite global positioning system (GPS).

- A carbon dioxide laser range finder that allows all-weather target engagement, reduces the risk of blinding friendly forces, and allows rapid enough calculation to engage helicopters.
- A systems integration package of features to reduce workload and crew fatigue.

Saudi Arabia also planned to buy modifications of the M-1A2 to tailor it to desert warfare. These included use of a Jaguar radio instead of a single channel ground/air system to improve inter-tank communication, a driver's thermal viewer to improve visibility through smoke and dust, a 2 kilowatt external auxiliary power unit, countermine equipment, hardware and software capable of displaying English and Arabic text, and Arabic labels.

This first M-1A2 sale was part of a $3.1 billion package that included 30 M-88A1 tank recovery vehicles, 175 M-998 utility trucks, 224 heavy tactical trucks, 29 heavy equipment transporters, 268 5-ton trucks, spares and support equipment, logistics support, ammunition, facilities design and construction, training aids and devices, and U.S. military training services.[50] Congress approved the sale after it became clear that Israel did not view it as a threat.[51]

Saudi Arabia made further M-1A2 tank purchases after Iraq's invasion of Kuwait. On September 27, 1990, it bought an armored vehicle package that included 150 M-1A2 tanks, 200 Bradley fight vehicles, 207 M-113 armored personnel carriers, 50 M-548 cargo carriers, 17 M-88A1 recovery vehicles, and 43 M-578 recovery vehicles. This order brought the total number of M-1A2s on order to 465 tanks, with delivery to begin in April, 1993 and take place over a three year period.[52]

Saudi Arabia reaffirmed its commitment to this sale in late July, 1992. Senior Saudi sources also indicated in September, 1992 that the Saudi Army would go ahead and buy enough M-1A2s to reach the total of 700. They indicated that Saudi Arabia planned to cap its total tank force at 1,200 tanks, with 700 M-1A2s and the rest M-60A3s.

Both Britain and France, however, continued to compete for the sale of the remaining 235 tanks. There is still a debate over exactly how many M-1A2s Saudi Arabia will buy, whether it needs and can afford a second type of modern tank, and whether it will buy surplus tanks that will provide de facto prepositioning for U.S. forces. Saudi Arabia is considering an order for 235 more M-1A2s, but a number of Saudi and outside experts wonder whether Saudi Arabia can absorb this many tanks, since it would bring Saudi armor to a total strength of 650 M-1A2s, 520 M-60A3s, and whatever portion of its AMX-30s it kept in service.[53]

At the same time, the Saudi army is concerned about relying on the M-1A2 because the cancellation of tank orders for the U.S. Army makes it uncertain whether the U.S. will be able to provide the infrastructure and modernization support Saudi Arabia needs.[54] All of these issues are likely to be solved in a traditional Saudi manner: obliquely, slowly, and with shifting compromises that suit as many different positions as possible.

The other armored fighting vehicles in the Saudi army offer no such prospect for standardization or orderly modernization. They present a nightmare both for the Saudi army and for the military analyst. Saudi Arabia has bought an extremely wide variety of types and sub-types. Many are highly specialized, and many seem to represent political efforts to allow given foreign suppliers some share of the Saudi market, regardless of military need. Further, it is not possible to separate some purchases for the army from purchases for the national guard, frontier force, and other paramilitary forces. The end result is that no data base seems accurate, although it is clear that the Saudi army has so many different types of other armored vehicles that this has become a major training, maintenance, logistic, maneuver, and readiness problem.

As a rough estimate, the Saudi army's holdings in 1992 included 230–240 AML-60 and AML-90 reconnaissance vehicles and 430–550 AMX-10P and 250 VAB/VCI mechanized infantry combat vehicles, command vehicles, and special purpose vehicles. It had 950–1,000 M-113, M-113A1, and other U.S. armored personnel carriers. It also had 30 EE-11 Brazilian Urutu, 110 German UR-416, and 120 Spanish BMR-600 and 40 Panhard M-3/VTT armored personnel carriers. Saudi Arabia has 150–200 additional armored mortar carriers, including M-106A1 and M-125s, large numbers of French- and U.S.-made armored recovery vehicles, armored bridging units, and large numbers of special purpose armored vehicles.[55]

Saudi Arabia also had 200 Bradley M-2A2 armored fighting vehicles entering service as a result of orders it had placed in 1988, plus 200 more M-2A2s, 207 M-113 armored personnel carriers, 50 M-548 cargo carriers, 17 M-88A1 recovery vehicles, and 43 M-578 recovery vehicles in the process of delivery as the result of its orders during the Gulf War.[56] The purchase of the M-2 is important both because Saudi Arabia's buy of the M-1A2 and M-2 provides a high degree of standardization and common support with U.S. Army power projection forces, and because the M-2A2's speed, protection, and firepower allow it to outmatch the Soviet armored fighting vehicles in most potential threat armies, many of which have better protection and firepower than various armored vehicles already in service with Saudi forces. The M-2A2 is also heavily armed and equipped with TOW-2 missiles and 25mm cannon, and it is air conditioned, which provides both protection against gas warfare and allows extended operation at desert heats.

Saudi Arabia may eventually order over 550 M-2A2s, and Saudi sources indicated in September, 1992 that Saudi Arabia might buy 700 M-2A2s and then standardize the M-113A1 for the rest of Saudi Arabia's armored fighting vehicles. Like the M-1A2 buy, such standardization would both improve Saudi army capabilities and provide a high degree of interoperability and standardization with U.S. Army forces.

The purchase of the M-2A2 will not, however, reduce Saudi Arabia's problems in training or solve all of its problems in supporting so many types of vehicles which are dependent for parts and technical support on many different countries. Saudi Arabia also scarcely reached a firm decision on its future purchases. It has 36 German Fuchsia chemical defense vehicles and additional French armored vehicles on order and is examining possible purchases of other armored vehicles from Brazil, Britain, and the FRG.[57]

The Saudi army had an excellent mix of small arms, light weaponry, and anti-tank weapons in 1992. These included TOW, HOT, and Dragon anti-tank guided missiles. Some 200 TOW launchers were mounted on VCC-1 armored fighting vehicles, 300 were mounted on M-113A1s or other U.S.-supplied armored vehicles, and 200 were mounted on VCC-1 armored vehicles. It had 90 HOT launchers mounted on AMX-10P armored fighting vehicles.

There were large numbers of TOW crew portable and Dragon manportable anti-tank guided weapons systems. It also had 450 Carl Gustav rocket launchers, M-72 LAW, and 75mm, 84mm, 90mm, and 106mm rocket launchers and recoilless rifles. Saudi Arabia ordered 4,460 TOW-2 missiles in April, 1987 and 150 more TOW IIA missile launchers with night vision sights and support equipment on September 27, 1990.[58] It will be well equipped with missiles that can kill T-72A, T-72M1, and other modern tanks. The Saudi army ordered French Apilas anti-tank weapons in 1991.

Proficiency in using these anti-tank weapons is uncertain. The level of crew and operator training is reasonable but often seems to lack consistency and realism. The units equipped with anti-tank weapons in armored vehicles seem to lack maneuver and combined arms training. Crews and men using older weapons are often less ready than those with the latest weapons, and units often lack aggressiveness in employing anti-tank weapons in exercises.

By 1992 the Saudi army had acquired large numbers of modern artillery weapons, including 60 Astros II multiple rocket launchers and 110–120 M-109A1/A2 and 65 GCT 155mm self-propelled howitzers. It also had 24 Model 56 and 90 M-101/M-102 105mm towed howitzers and 50–70 FH-70 and 90 M-198 155mm towed howitzers, plus some older towed weapons in storage. It had very large numbers of mortars, including over 400 120mm and 4.2" weapons, over 1,000 81mm weapons, and numerous light 60mm weapons.[59]

The Saudi army had more Astros II and M-198s on order and was steadily acquiring better mobile fire control and ammunition supply equipment. Most importantly, it ordered 9 MLRS, including vehicle mounted rocket launchers, 2,880 tactical rockets, 50 practice rockets, 9 MV-755A2 command post carriers, training and training equipment, and 20 AN/VRC-46 radio sets on September 27, 1990. The MLRS rocket uses a highly sophisticated warhead mixing anti-armor and anti-personnel bomblets. Each MLRS launcher is capable of inflicting more destruction on an area target or large maneuver target than a battalion of regular tube artillery or multiple rocket launchers and can do so at ranges in excess of 40 kilometers.[60]

The Saudi army, however, had only limited ability to use artillery in maneuver and combined arms warfare, to target effectively in counter-battery fire or at targets beyond visual range, and to shift and concentrate fires. Saudi Arabia has ordered new target acquisition radars—such as the AN/PPS-15A, MSTAR, or Rasit 3190B—to replace 1960 vintage systems and is steadily improving its counterbattery radars and fire control systems.[61]

Nevertheless, it seems likely that Saudi army artillery capabilities will suffer from manpower quality and some mobility and support problems well into the late 1990s.

It is not easy to separate the Saudi army's air defense assets from those in the air defense force, and sources disagree over which force operates given systems. The Saudi army seems to have had 18 anti-aircraft artillery batteries in 1992. It was equipped with Crotale radar guided missiles on tracked armored vehicles, over 300 Stingers, and 570 obsolete Redeye manportable surface-to-air missiles. Saudi Arabia had bought 50 Stinger launchers and 200 Stinger missiles on an emergency basis in August, 1990 and had additional Crotales and 700 launchers and 2,300 missiles for the French Mistral missile system on order.[62]

It also is not possible to separate the army's air defense gun holdings from those of the air defense force and national guard, but the army seems to have had 10 M-42 40mm, 50–60 AMX-30SA 30mm self-propelled, and 50–60 Vulcan M-163 anti-aircraft guns. It also seems to have had an unknown number of Bofors L-60/L-70 40mm and Oerlikon 35mm, and possibly 15 M-117 90mm, towed anti-aircraft guns.

While this is a stronger mix of air defense assets than is possessed by many Arab armies, training and readiness levels are moderate to low. It is also a relatively limited air defense capability to deal with any major threat from the north. The air defense corps is not a force that can easily support the army in mobile operations, and Saudi land forces will be heavily dependent on air power for air defense.

The Saudi army's search for helicopter forces raises different issues. Much of the Saudi army is now deployed nearly 600 miles from the kingdom's main oil facilities in the eastern province, although a brigade has deployed to the new King Fahd military city in the eastern province, and the combat elements of a brigade deployed to the new army base at King Khalid City near Hafr al-Batin in 1984. For the near future, the Saudi army will still be dispersed so that much of its strength will be deployed near Saudi Arabia's borders with the angles located at Tabuk, Hafr al-Batin, and Shahrurah–Khamis Mushayt.

Helicopters offer a limited solution to this problem. They can both provide rapid concentration of force and allow Saudi Arabia to make up for its lack of experience in large scale maneuver. In the mid-1980s, the Saudi army studied plans for developing a helicopter force using a total of 60–100 U.S. AH-64 attack, Black Hawk utility and support, and Chinook CH-47 transport helicopters by the mid-1990s. Growing political problems in obtaining weapons from the U.S. led Saudi Arabia to turn to Britain, however, and to purchase of 88 Black Hawk helicopters through Westland. Roughly 80 of these Westlands are to be attack helicopters with TOW-2. The rest were to be configured for SAR missions. This order, however, was divided into batches of 40 and 48 aircraft, and Saudi interest in other systems has raised questions about whether the army will buy the second batch of 48.[63]

In 1992 the Saudi army still had only 12 UN-60 Black Hawk troop transport helicopters, 8 UH-60 medical evacuation helicopters, 15 Bell 406 Helicopters, and 6 SA-365N medical evacuation helicopters. It also continued to experience serious support problems from some of its foreign contractors.[64] Saudi Arabia did, however, order 12 AH-64 Apache attack helicopters, 155 Hellfire missiles, 24 spare Hellfire launchers, 6 spare engines, and associated equipment from the U.S. in September, 1990. It then expressed an interest in buying 36 more AH-64s, for a total of 48 and was examining the purchase of more attack and support helicopters from the U.S., Italy, France, and a Franco-German consortium. In June, 1992 it bought 362 more Hellfire missiles, 3,500 Hydra-70 rockets, and 40 HMMWV vehicles and U.S. support services for its Apaches. It also bought 8 S-70 Sikorsky medevac helicopters.[65]

This purchase of advanced attack helicopters is a potential force multiplier for the Saudi army and would give it increased interoperability with the U.S. Army. At the same time, it raises the question of whether the Saudi army can provide the proper support. Modern combat helicopters require almost as much support as a light jet combat aircraft, and the AH-64 is so sophisticated that it requires support closer to that of a modern jet fighter. The U.S. Army is probably the only force that could support such Saudi purchases with the mix of conversion, training, and service capabilities the Saudis need to create an effective force. Even the purchase of the much simpler Westlands creates doubts about whether Saudi Arabia will get the support it needs to operate weapons systems that require training and service roughly equivalent to that necessary to operate a modern fighter aircraft.

Saudi logistic and support vehicles and equipment are good, as are Saudi facilities. The Saudi army is one of the few forces in the developing world which is organized to provide as much sustainability as maneuver and firepower. As has been noted earlier, Saudi Arabia has made major purchases of support equipment along with the purchase of its M-1A2s and M-2A2s. It is improving its field support vehicle strength and ordered 10,000 support vehicles from the U.S., including 1,200 high mobility multipurpose wheeled vehicles (HMMWVs).

In summary, there is no doubt that Saudi Arabia can expand its army. This expansion, however, will proceed far more slowly in reality than it may appear to do on paper, and it is uncertain that the army will have the manpower to operate its new major equipment orders as they are delivered. The Saudi army will also face continuing problems in concentrating the combat ready forces it does have. Without considerable strategic warning, it will not be able to concentrate significant forces on a given front unless it can move forces from another major military city and all the way across Saudi Arabia. This would take a minimum of a week to ten days. Even then, Saudi Arabia will lack the massive armored forces of its stronger neighbors.

Training has been a problem in the past and will continue to be one. U.S. advisors helped bring Saudi forces up to a level of readiness during the Gulf War that they had never before experienced and gave them their first real experience with large scale unit and combined arms training. Many Saudi officers at all levels absorbed this training very quickly, and the Saudi army did well during operation Desert Storm—very well if its low prewar readiness is considered. Many of the Saudi army's training plans since the war, however, have not been executed, and maneuver training has been poor to mediocre. Combined arms training and maneuver training has been particularly weak, and promotion at senior command levels remains political. Professionalism, not politicization, is the key to the successful expansion of the Saudi army, as well as any other military force.

The Saudi National Guard

Saudi Arabia must divide its manpower between the army and the national guard. The national guard is the successor of the Ikhwan and its successor, the White Army. It is a tribal force forged out of those elements loyal to the Saud family. It is also seen as a counterweight to any threat from the regular military forces and is used within the royal family to balance Sudairi control over the regular armed forces. The national guard is under the command of Prince Abdellah, who is descended from ibn-Saud and is currently the crown prince.

Although the national guard's future structure will depend upon the complex politics within the Saudi royal family, the Saudi national guard seems likely to remain a lightly armed internal security force whose main mission is internal security and ensuring the loyalty of Saudi Arabia's traditional tribes.[66] Estimates of active manning in the national guard differ sharply. The most recent IISS estimate is 35,000 actives and 20,000 tribal levies. A more realistic estimate may be 25,000–30,000 full time actives, 15,000 semi-active reserves, and 15,000 tribal levies. In any case, about 20–30% of the kingdom's active trained military manpower will be used in what is still largely a paramilitary force.

This use of manpower may be justified, given Saudi Arabia's needs and the fact that much of this manpower probably cannot be retrained to use heavy equipment. The national guard showed its potential value when it dealt with the Shi'ite uprising in the eastern province and siege of the Grand Mosque in Mecca in 1979 and put down the Iranian riots in Mecca in 1987. It also helped secure the eastern province during the Iran-Iraq War and Gulf War and fought reasonably well during the battle of Khafji. Nevertheless, the fuard is heavily dependent on outside contractors for service support, maintenance, and logistics. It also requires the support of the Saudi army and air force, or another country, for any operation involving significant armor, maneuver operations, firepower, or sustainability in combat and is not an effective deterrent or defense against outside invasion.

The national guard is being organized into modern military formations and rapidly expanded and is in a considerable state of turbulence. Even so, it has had some notable successes relative to its past status as a tribal force. It began to hold significant training exercises for its first 6,500 man mechanized brigade, the Imam Mohammed ibn-Saud Brigade, during the early 1980s. It has established a brigade sized presence, and a limited oil field security force in the eastern province. The Mohammed ibn-Saud brigade held its first major exercise in the desert about 250 miles west of Riyadh in early 1983. Units moved from as far away as the eastern province, and the key mechanized elements performed relatively well. While the guard experienced problems in translating tribal into regular military discipline and the force was well below its authorized manning level, its set-piece maneuvers were relatively successful.

The national guard formally inaugurated its second mechanized "brigade" in a ceremony on March 14, 1985. This new unit, called the King Abd al-Aziz Brigade, was formed after another relatively successful round of set-piece exercises (called Al-Areen) near Bisha. Prince Abdellah then spoke of expanding the guard to 35,000 men, and succeeded in building up a force of three mechanized "brigades" by 1989. The guard was used to help secure the eastern province during the Iran-Iraq War and was given special training and additional manning during the Gulf War. While the Guard was unable to deal with the initial Iraqi assault on Khafji and required extensive U.S. air and artillery support to retake the city, it did fight reasonably well during the rest of the battle.

In 1992 the national guard was organized into two mechanized brigades with four battalions each. It also had five infantry brigades (which included substantial part time elements), what seemed to be a special forces unit, a ceremonial cavalry squadron, an engineer battalion, and a special security battalion. Much of the national guard also remained a tribal force. These forces were grouped and deployed in five to seven regions, covering every critical urban and populated area in the country.

The manning of its combat forces drew upon the 25,000–35,000 men in its *firqa* (full time tribal) forces. The training of even these regular forces is erratic and varies by commander and unit. The 20,000–35,000 men in its *liwa* (part time irregular tribal levy) units often have very little training. Many of its "troops" were actually retired military, descendants of the troops that fought with King Abd al-Aziz, or the sons or relatives of tribal leaders.

These tribal forces are useful in securing Saudi Arabia's key facilities in a way that limits the ability of the army to conduct a coup, and its leaders are carefully chosen for their loyalty to the regime. It uses rival factions to counterbalance any attempt to seize control of the guard, and the guard provides a means through which the royal family allocates funds to tribal and Bedouin leaders. The guard helps key princes maintain close relations with the tribes in each region. It has not evolved into a force that can deal with urban disorder, oil field security problems, or border security problems, although it can do a good job of dealing with ethnic and tribal divisions.

This makes the guard politically vital to ensuring the integration of Saudi Arabia's tribes into its society, but it does not mean the guard can adequately defend against any well trained or sophisticated threat. The guard's mechanized brigades are emerging as relatively high quality forces by Saudi standards, but they lack firepower, heavy armor, air defense, and maneuver capability to take on mechanized infantry or armored forces. Its overall force structure and equipment lack the air mobility, specialized units, logistics, and maintenance capabilities to deal with a northern Gulf opponent, and its leadership is far better trained for paramilitary operations than real combat.

The guard is now equipped with about 1,012 V-150 Commando wheeled armored fighting vehicles which have a number of different configurations, including anti-tank guided missile carriers, cannon turrets, and main guns. These include roughly 100 V-150s configured as AIFVs (70 with 90mm guns), 100 armored command vehicles, 70–80 812mm mortar carriers, 50 armored recovery vehicles, 30 special purpose vehicles, and 350 configured as APCs. The guard has 40 M-102 105mm towed artillery weapons, 20–30 M-198 155mm howitzers, and 81mm mortars. It has large numbers of TOW anti-tank guided missiles, rocket launchers, and recoilless rifles, a limited number of helicopters, and 30 M-40 Vulcan 20mm anti-aircraft guns. At least 100 TOW fire units are mounted on V-150s.[67]

It is not yet clear how the national guard will modernize in the future. It will eventually have to replace its V-150s with systems with more armor, cross-country capability, and figure power, and its lack of technical sophistication gives it a strong incentive to standardize on a single new family of vehicles. The guard does have additional M-198 howitzers and HMMWV light transport vehicles. As for a replacement for the V-150, there are reports that the guard has 400–450 different versions of the Pirhana light armored vehicle (LAV) on order.[68] There are also reports the Saudi national guard plans to buy 1,117 LAV-25s from General Motors of Canada through the U.S. Army Tank Automotive Command (TACOM). This order would include ten different types of LAV-25s, including anti-tank, recovery, mortar, command, APC, ammunition carrier, ambulance, engineer, and assault gun. Some 325 would be armed with two man turrets with the 25mm McDonnell Douglas chain gun and thermal sights.[69]

The guard can continue to expand at a gradual rate, but it is likely to experience serious problems with any sudden major expansion of its forces. Prince Abdellah has evidently asked the guard's foreign advisors to study an expansion up to 80,000–100,000 regulars by the mid- to late 1990s. This would provide a force with 2 to 3 more mechanized brigades, 2 to 4 more infantry brigades, and a new mix of battalion sized formations for its part time forces.

This expansion may well not be possible, given the manpower available from loyal tribes and groups. It would also mean sharper competition for manpower from the regular army. Further, it would require the national guard to stay a relatively lightly armored force. While Prince Abdellah may have entertained ideas of buying heavy armor for the Guard in the 1980s, it will have trouble absorbing all the light armor it now has on order.

The Saudi Navy

The Saudi navy had an active strength of only 6,000 men in the mid-1980s but now seems to have about 9,500–10,200 men. In 1992 it had a strength of eight frigates, twelve patrol and coastal combatants, nine mine warfare ships, twelve amphibious craft, and seven support vessels. It also included a small 1,500 man marine force organized into an infantry regiment with two battalions and equipped with 140 BMR-60Ps. Saudi Arabia currently plans to slowly expand its Marine forces to 2,400 men.

The Saudi navy has completed the construction of two major, fully modern naval bases at Jiddah and Jubayl. Its deployments are divided into a western fleet with its main facilities at Jiddah and an eastern fleet with its main facilities at al Qatif/Jubayl. The navy also has facilities at Ras Tanura, Dammam, Yanbu, Ras al-Ghar, and Ras al-Mishab.[70] The Saudi navy has taken delivery on all the major frigates and support craft it ordered in the 1980s plus 24 missile equipped helicopters.[71] It has been seeking to expand its manpower from 7,800 to 10,000 men and has been examining the possible purchase of mine vessels and mine hunting helicopters, submarines, and ASW aircraft.

The major deliveries under the U.S. phase of the Saudi naval expansion effort have been completed for several years. The U.S. delivered nine 478-ton patrol gunboat guided missile (PGG) craft, armed with two twin Harpoon missile launchers, one 76mm gun, and light anti-aircraft (AA) weapons. It delivered four larger patrol-chaser guided missile (PCG) craft which the Saudis class as frigates.[72] These four 1,039-ton vessels have two quad Harpoon missile launchers, one 76mm gun, Vulcan and 20mm guns, and six 324mm torpedo tubes.

The U.S. delivered four MSC-322 class coastal mine sweepers, two large harbor tugs, two utility landing craft, and four LCM-6, four LCU-1610, and four LCM landing craft. Other U.S. deliveries included Harpoon missiles, Mark 46 torpedoes, and ammunition for the Saudi navy's 76mm guns and other weapons. The kingdom also took delivery on three Dammam-class torpedo boats from the FRG, with four 533mm torpedo tubes each.

In the early 1980s Saudi Arabia turned to France as the major source of its naval ships and weapons because of dissatisfaction with the U.S. Navy advisory effort and because it felt French ships were better suited to its mission requirements. The Saudi Navy signed its first major contract with France in 1980 in an effort to accelerate its modernization, obtain better support, and obtain more advanced ships than it could get from the U.S. It signed a modernization package costing $3.4 billion and then signed another contract that effectively made the French the primary source of support and modernization for future Saudi orders. This follow-on French program, which began in 1982, is called Sawari (Mast) I. It has reached a minimum value of 14 billion French francs, or $1.9 billion, and may have escalated in cost to $3.2 billion.

France delivered the four missile equipped 2,000-ton frigates by August, 1986. These are 2,870-ton vessels when fully loaded. They have eight Otomat 2 missile launchers, eight Crotale surface-to-air missile launchers, one 100mm gun, four twin Breda 35mm guns, four 533mm torpedo tubes, and one SA-365F helicopter.[73] France has also delivered two modified Durance-class fuel supply/replenishment vessels (Boraida-class), Otomat missiles for the frigates, twenty-four SA-365F Dauphin 2 helicopters (twenty missile equipped and four SAR-equipped), AS-15 missiles for the helicopters, and additional training services. The Otomat is the longest range anti-ship missile in Gulf service, with a range of 160 kilometers. Saudi crews trained in France to operate the vessels and helicopters.

The Saudi navy then considered plans for the new Sawari II program, which could cost an additional $1.6–2.12 billion. Prince Sultan first met with France's President François Mitterrand and Defense Minister Charles Hernu to discuss this program in May, 1983. The program would have provided at least two more 2,000-ton frigates and possibly 4,000-ton frigates as well. It also included buying some mine sweeping helicopters and maritime patrol aircraft as the first step in the procurement of much larger forces, including lift and troop-carrying helicopters, surveillance and intelligence equipment, and special warfare equipment.

While Saudi Arabia ordered twelve Super Pumas and twelve more patrol boats from France, it did not place major additional orders until 1990. It did not agree to the Sawari II program because of funding problems and because the Saudis experienced growing problems with their French ships that were more severe than their earlier problems with U.S. vessels. These maintenance and support problems were so serious in the late 1980s that Saudi Arabia even approached the U.S. to provide support for the French vessels.

Saudi Arabia signed a new support agreement with France in 1989, however, and during the Gulf War Saudi Arabia decided to order three F-3000 frigates, with delivery in 1997. These improved Lafayette-class frigates will be 3,700 tons fully loaded. They will have eight Exocet launchers, sixteen Aster 15 or one octuple Crotale surface-to-air missile launcher, one 100mm gun, two twin 30mm guns, four 324 mm torpedo launchers, and one SA-365F helicopter. The Saudi navy also ordered six additional Super Pumas and decided to raise its order for French patrol boats to twenty ships.[74]

Saudi Arabia's other plans to expand its naval forces now seem to center on its mine warfare units. It has four obsolete U.S. MSC-322 mine vessels (Addriyah-class) and one modern British Sandown-class MCC (Al Jawf–class). Saudi Arabia agreed to lease two Hunt-class mine vessels from Britain in July, 1988 and placed an order for six to eight Vosper Sandown-class mine countermeasure vessels (MCMVs), training by the Royal Navy, and new port facilities for mine warfare vessels from Ballast Nedam, as part of its $18 billion Al-Yamamah 2 program. Three of these orders have been funded, including the ship already delivered.[75] The Saudi navy may still be considering purchase of French-built Tripartite mine hunters, but the order for the Sandowns set an interesting precedent for standardization and interoperability, since Kuwait, Bahrain, Oman, Qatar, and the UAE are also actively examining orders of the Sandown or Tripartite mine warfare vessels.[76]

Saudi Arabia has deferred plans to buy coastal submarines. Nevertheless, it has sought to buy six to eight submarines and has discussed program costs of up to $1.5–3 billion. Saudi navy representatives visited several European manufacturers in 1986 and 1987, including the builders of the Walrus-class boats in the Netherlands, Vickers Type-2400 in the UK, and ILK 209/2000 and Kockums 471 in West Germany.

Saudi Arabia also considered an order for two AMD-BA Atlantique 2 (ANG) maritime patrol aircraft, and the order of two more Atlantique 2, Fokker F-27 Maritime Enforcers, or Lockheed P-3 Orions as part of a GCC maritime surveillance force. The AMD-BA Atlantique 2 (ANG) maritime patrol aircraft, however, proved to be too expensive. The other aircraft were considered largely as a supplement to the Saudi E-3As and to provide coverage for the rest of the southern Gulf. They depended on GCC cooperation and funding, and this has not been forthcoming.[77]

Saudi Arabia has a valid need for both modern mine warfare and MPA aircraft, but the requirement for submarines is dubious at best. There is no immediate submarine threat, and it is unclear how the Saudis could make cost-effective use of submarines as a strike force or retaliatory threat, given the size of their air force.

Saudi naval facilities are excellent. The Saudi navy's bases are exceptionally capable and well stocked. The main bases will eventually have up to five years of stocks on hand and will have initial deliveries of two years' worth of inventory. The Jubayl base is now the second largest naval base in the Gulf and stretches nearly 8 miles along the coast. It already has its own desalinization facility and is designed to be expandable up to 100% above its present capacity.

The Saudi navy is procuring an automated logistic system similar to that in the other services and with extensive modern command and control facilities. This system became operational, along with hardened command centers at Riyadh, Jubayl, and Jiddah, by the end of 1985. The navy was supposed to acquire automated data links to the E-3A and the ability to obtain data from the E-3A AWACS as it operated in the ocean surveillance mode by the late 1980s, but its C^3I system was not capable of supporting effective combat operations when the Gulf War began. Saudi Arabia purchased a $307 million upgrade of its C^3I system on September 27, 1990.[78] Other U.S.-designed facilities include a meteorology laboratory, a Harpoon missile and Mark 46 torpedo maintenance facility, an advanced technical training school, and a royal naval academy.

The Saudi navy is a relatively powerful force by regional standards, largely in terms of equipment. Its readiness is improving and has been helped by crash training efforts during operation Earnest Will (1987–1989) and during the Gulf War. However, its current equipment mix requires a force of close to 15,000 men. The navy is badly undermanned, and training standards are low. It is almost completely dependent on foreign maintenance and logistic support and contractors and is having problems operating its new French frigates, although it has gradually become fairly effective in operating its U.S.-supplied vessels. Even with automation and foreign support, the Saudi navy will not be able to operate much of its equipment effectively before the mid-1990s.

While the Saudi navy has made significant progress in recent years, it faces a decade of expansion before it can become a true two sea force capable of covering both Saudi Arabia's Gulf and Red Sea coasts. Even then, it will depend heavily on air support and will be dependent on reinforcement by USCENTCOM and the British, French, and/or U.S. navies.

The Saudi Air Force

Saudi Arabia has given its highest priority to the expansion of its air force, the only service that can cover Saudi Arabia's 2.3 million square kilometers of territory. It represents the investment most capable of cross-reinforcement of the other services. It also has the most impact in terms of regional prestige and the most credibility in terms of being able to support other GCC states or to operate with USCENTCOM forces in a major crisis.

In 1992 the RSAF had 17,000–18,000 men and fifteen combat squadrons with about 250 combat aircraft. These included six fighter–ground attack squadrons with 3/52 F-5Es and 3/45 Tornado IDS. They included five interceptor squadrons with F-15C/Ds and Tornado ADVs. The three large F-15C/Ds squadrons had seventy-two F-15Cs and twenty-one F-15Ds and put some of the F-15Ds in each squadron to perform both training and operational missions. The RSAF also had a reconnaissance squadron with ten RF-5Es, an airborne early warning squadron with five E-3As, and two multipurpose squadrons with twenty-one F-5Fs and fourteen F-5Bs. These latter two squadrons have both a training and combat mission.

The five E-3A AWACS aircraft have been steadily upgraded to replace their main computer memories and substitute semiconductors and bubble memories for their magnetic drums, tripling their memory capacity. Major radar system improvements had been made to improve data handling, sensitivity, provide real-time data to each console, and provide the same range coverage against smaller cross-section targets. Electronic support measures were installed in the aircraft for passive detection, location, and identification of electronic emitters; the software is updated beyond bloc 30/35, infrared countermeasures have been added to the engines, they have global positioning systems, and there are five additional operator consoles.[79]

The air force was equipped with modern munitions, including AIM-9L and AIM-9P infrared guided missiles, AIM-7F Sparrow and Skyflash radar guided missiles, and AGM-65 Maverick air-to-surface missiles. It had Rockeye, Sea Eagle, and Alarm air-to-ground weapons. Saudi Arabia had also bought MQM-74C Chukar II and Banshee remotely piloted vehicles for reconnaissance and target acquisition.

The support units in the air force included a tanker squadron with eight KE-3As and seven KC-130Hs, and three transport squadrons with seven C-130Es, thirty-four C-130Hs, five L-100-30HSs (hospital aircraft), and thirty-five C-212As. There were two helicopter squadrons with thirteen AB-206Bs, eight AB-205s, twenty-seven AB-212s, and seven KV-107s. There were thirty Hawk jet and 30 BAC-167 turboprop training aircraft capable of performing COIN and light attack functions with machine guns, cannons, and rockets. There was also a royal flight with four BAe-125s, four CN-235s, two Learjet 35s, two C-140s, six VC-130Hs, one Cessna 310, and two Gulfstream III fixed wing aircraft, and three AS-61 and AB-212 helicopters.

The Saudi air force is backed by excellent foreign support. During the 1970s and early 1980s, Saudi Arabia was able to draw on U.S. Air Force and contractor support to create some of the most modern air facilities in the world. No U.S. or NATO base has sheltering or hardening equal to the Saudi bases at Dhahran and Khamis Mushayt, and similar facilities will be built at all of Saudi Arabia's main operating bases. Saudi Arabia now performs most of the support and service for its Lockheed C-130s, and its F-5E/F units have also reached proficiency levels approaching those of many Western squadrons.

Saudi Arabia has also done a good job of operating today's most advanced fighters. The first of its 60 F-15C/Ds were operational in Dhahran by early 1983. A second squadron was formed at Taif by the end of 1983, and a third became operational at Khamis Mushayt in July, 1984. By late 1984 and early 1985, the Saudi air force was conducting major joint exercises in both the Gulf and Red Sea areas and conducting red-blue or aggressor exercises similar to those employed by the U.S. Air Force. Saudi Arabia has maintained these proficiency levels ever since and begun joint exercises with other members of the GCC. It has begun to provide crews for its five E-3As and operated these aircraft with great success in 1987 and 1988. Saudi aircraft attrition levels are significantly higher than those of the U.S., but overall training levels are good.

While Saudi Arabia has lacked some of the C^3I/BM systems, advanced avionics and electronics, munitions, and attack capabilities the USAF uses to achieve its high proficiency levels, it has also demonstrated a high level of squadron readiness, has begun to perform much of its own major support on the F-5, and provides Saudi support of the F-15 at its bases in Dhahran and Khamis Mushayt. Saudi Arabia has excellent stocks of air munitions and spares. For example, it ordered 101 shipsets of F-15 conformal fuel tanks, 909 AIM-7F, AIM-9P/L, 100 Harpoon ASM, and 1,600 Maverick missiles, JP-233 and BL 755 bombs and munitions before Iraq's invasion of Kuwait. It ordered large numbers of additional AIM-9Ls and AIM-7Fs in August, 1990, and ordered 2,000 Mark 84 2,000 pound bombs, 2,100 CBU-87 cluster munitions, 770 AIM-7Fs, and components for laser guided bombs in July, 1991. While there is no way to estimate Saudi stocks, they are almost certainly large enough to support both its air force and a major reinforcing deployment by the U.S. Air Force for a mid-intensity conflict.[80]

The Royal Saudi Air Force, however, has been in a period of constant transition for most of its existence, and this rate of transition has increased since the late 1980s. After trying for nearly five years to buy more F-15s and acquire an advanced attack mission capability from the U.S., the Saudis turned to Britain. In July, 1985 President Reagan sent King Fahd a letter stating that he could not obtain congressional approval of the sales Saudi Arabia sought. As a result, the Saudi air force initiated talks with Britain that led to an agreement in September, 1985 that Britain would provide a total of 60 Tornado ADV air defense fighters, 60 Tornado IDS/GR1 attack strikefighters, light attack aircraft, trainers, helicopters, munitions, and British support services.

That same month, Saudi Arabia signed a series of memorandums of understanding (MOUs) with Britain which gave Saudi Arabia the option of turning each MOU into an individual contract. These MOUs were called the al-Yamamah agreement. Saudi Arabia's first major actual contract under the MOUs cost $8 billion, but the total value grew to a total of $29 billion by 1992—including training, support, construction, and naval vessels. It was worth roughly $4 billion a year to Britain by the early 1990s. Saudi Arabia agreed to pay for al-Yamamah by bartering oil—which gave it guaranteed markets and allowed it to bypass some of the constraints imposed by OPEC quotas.

The first phase of the al-Yamamah program called for the purchase of 24 Tornado ADV air defense fighters; 48 Tornado IDS/GR1 ground attack fighters; 30 BAe Hawk 65 trainers; 30 Pilatus PC-9 trainers; and two Gulfstream aircraft, air weaponry, and ground support and training services.

The Tornado ADV did not prove to be a successful air defense fighter for either the British Royal Air Force or Saudi Arabia. It turned out to be underpowered. While its limited dogfight performance might not have been important in areas where long range missile combat is critical, the short distances and reaction times characteristic of many potential threats to Saudi Arabia required dogfight superiority. The radar warning receiver was not fully effective, and the Tornado's radar and air defense avionics experienced development and performance problems as did efforts to fully integrate and qualify advanced air-to-air missiles with the aircraft.

While some problems are not unusual in a new variant of aircraft, those in the case of the Tornado ADV were severe enough to prompt the RAF to talk about converting its air defense Tornadoes to reconnaissance, strike, or electronic warfare missions the moment it could obtain some form of Eurofighter. The RSAF's experience with the first eight Tornado ADVs was so negative that in 1989 it halted deliveries at 12 aircraft. The RSAF converted its order for the remaining 12 ADVs to IDVs, and it sought to convert the 12 Tornado ADVs it did receive to reconnaissance or strike attack aircraft.[81]

These problems did not prevent additional Saudi orders. In July, 1988 Saudi Arabia signed a letter of intent for a second phase of al-Yamamah. According to Saudi sources, the second phase included 48 more Tornado strike attack fighters. According to various British sources, it included 24 IDS and 24 ADV aircraft, or 36 IDS and 12 ADV aircraft. All sources agree that it included 60 Hawk 100/200 trainer fighters, Vosper Thorneycroft mine countermeasure vessels, C³I systems, and additional weapons, spares, ground support, and training. The Hawks included aircraft configured as the Hawk 200 single seat attack fighter. The Hawk 200 has combat radars, unlike the trainer, and was ordered with Sea Eagle anti-ship missiles.

The new series of MOUs also included 88 Sikorsky Black Hawk helicopters which Saudi Arabia ordered through Westland. The RSAF had already ordered 12 Black Hawks through the U.S., but these were transport versions of the aircraft and it feared that the U.S. Congress would not sell armed or attack versions. Accordingly, it ordered the 88 Black Hawks from Britain because it could get them with TOW air-to-surface missiles and also ordered 12 TOW conversion kits for the Black Hawks it had ordered from the U.S.

The total value of the MOUs that made up the second phase of al-Yamamah was approximately $18 billion, and the deal also included light transport aircraft (12 BAe 125s and 4 BAe 146s), and two major military cities and air bases for the new Tornado forces, complete with British support.[82] The new British-built military cities and air bases were to be located at Taiba (about 290 kilometers southwest of Tabuk) and at Al-Sulayyil (on the edge of the vast desert, or Empty Quarter that separates the rest of Saudi Arabia from Oman and Yemen). The air bases were to be equipped with at least 25 hardened multiple aircraft shelters. Saudi Arabia believed that its existing bases were adequate in the eastern province and near the PDRY but were not suited for a force of nearly 400 combat aircraft. This brought the potential total value of the two phases of al-Yamamah to $60 billion, projected over a fifteen year life for the programs.[83]

There were good reasons for the Saudi purchase of the first phase of the al-Yamamah package. Saudi Arabia's 12 BAC-167 trainers were only armed with 7.62mm machine guns. They no longer could be used in anything other than light support functions. It had bought its obsolete Lightning fighters from the UK under pressure from former Secretary of Defense Robert S. McNamara, the U.S. effectively forcing Saudi Arabia to buy the Lightning as part of a then covert three cornered deal in which the Lightning sale to Saudi Arabia was designed to allow the UK to buy the F-111 from the U.S.[84] Even when it was first delivered, the Lightning never had the range, dual capability, avionics, and performance Saudi Arabia needed.

Saudi Arabia made other aircraft purchases as a result of the Gulf War. It purchased 24 additional F-15C/Ds from USAF stocks, 8 C-130Hs, and 2 C-130H-30 aircraft and large numbers of AIM-9Ls and AIM-7Fs from the U.S. in late August, 1990. It also bought the Falcon Eye electronic warfare aircraft, although it knew that this lacked the sophistication and capability of U.S. and Israeli ELINT aircraft.[85]

Nevertheless, Saudi Arabia still faces significant problems in shaping its modernization plans for the 1990s. Saudi Arabia clearly needs more modern aircraft. Its F-5E-IIs and F-5Fs are relatively advanced models of the F-5E/F, equipped with an inertial navigation system (INS), refueling probes, and the ability to fire Mavericks (the F-5F can also fire laser guided bombs). The oldest of these F-5 aircraft, however, are nearing the end of their useful life, and the F-5 production line has long been closed.

The F-5Es are not cost-effective to upgrade and they require more than twice as much Saudi and foreign technical support manpower per plane as an F-15. The F-5E/Fs are also too short ranged and limited in avionics and payload to adequately cope with the kind of advanced threat aircraft being introduced into the region, or to deploy from one Saudi air base in support of another. They need to be phased into a training and light support role and to be phased out by the late 1990s. In fact, 20–30% of Saudi Arabia's F-5 strength is already devoted to full time training missions.

Saudi Arabia's 93 F-15C/Ds present different problems. They should have adequate performance to fill the first line air defense role until well after the year 2000, and they showed during the Gulf War that they could do an excellent job in air-to-air combat against the most advanced aircraft in service in potential threat nations. The Saudi F-15C/D, however, is configured as a one mission aircraft. Although the U.S. Air Force recommended that the Saudi air force be given a dual-capable advanced fighter back in 1977 when it conducted the original studies that led to the U.S. sale of the F-15, the U.S. never sold Saudi Arabia the bomb racks and attack systems necessary to make the F-15C/D effective in the air-to-ground role. As a result, a key part of Saudi Arabia's total first line fighter strength has been unable to perform effective attack missions or provide attack support to Saudi land and naval forces.

The Gulf War showed that the Tornado has given the Saudi air force a more modern strike attack aircraft, and Saudi Arabia now plans to contract for the 48 IDS/GR1 attack versions of Tornado that were part of the MOUs signed under the second phase of al-Yamamah. This will bring the total Tornado buy up to 120 strike attack aircraft. The Tornado proved during Desert Storm that it could be an effective strike fighter once it was equipped with new FLIR and laser designator pods, and it delivered over 1,000 laser guided bombs and ALARM missiles. It will meet Saudi Arabia's need for a long range deterrent to Iraq and Iran. However, the Tornado lacks the flexibility, maneuverability, and avionics to fly demanding missions using precision guided munitions against advanced air defenses. It does not meet all of Saudi Arabia's needs for a first line strike aircraft.

Saudi Arabia's solution to this complex mix of modernization problems has been to request the sale of 72 more F-15s. This includes 24 aircraft designed for air combat and 48 aircraft which are dual-capable in both the air defense and strike attack missions. All have been designated as the F-15XP, although they involve two types of aircraft. The proposed sale involves about $5 billion worth of aircraft and up to $4 billion worth of other arms and supplies—including $800 million worth of construction. These include 24 spare engines, 48 targeting and navigation pods, 900 AGM-65D/G Maverick air-to-surface missiles, 600 CBU-87 bombs, 700 GBU-10/12 bombs, and special mission planning systems.[86]

The 24 air defense versions of the F-15XP are air defense aircraft based on the F-15E air frame. They cannot use navigation and targeting pods or laser illuminators, and can drop only general purpose bombs. Their radars will be better than those on the F-15C/D, with a resolution of 60 feet at 20 nautical miles versus resolution of 530 feet in the F-15C/D. They will use the same AIM-7F and AIM-7M radar guided air-to-air missiles used by existing Saudi F-15C/Ds and the AIM-9S, which is the export version of the radar guided AIM-9M air-to-air missiles. They will have the technical capability to use advanced medium range air-to-air missile (AMRAAM), but the transfer of this missile has not been approved. Added to Saudi Arabia's existing 93 F-15C/Ds, they will give Saudi Arabia a total of 120 advanced air defense aircraft that can be used in attack roles.

The 48 strike attack variants of the F-15E Strike Eagle have also been designated as the F-15XP. They will differ from the U.S. Air Force version of the F-15E in several important ways. They will use the AAQ-20 Pathfinder navigation pods, the AAQ-20 Sharpshooter targeting pods, and a laser illuminator. The Pathfinder pods will have a terrain following radar but will have reduced ECCM capabilities that will allow them to be tracked by U.S. types of fighters. The Sharpshooter pods for the F-15XP will have only limited versus full cluster bomb delivery capability. They will deliver the A/B version of the electro-optical Maverick and the D/G version of the IR Maverick but will not have a missile boresight correlator, will only have a single fire rather than multiple fire capability for Maverick, and will not be equipped to deliver the HARM anti-radiation missile.

The F-15XP will not be supplied with conformal fuel tanks of the kind supplied on the F-15E, thereby depriving it of two extra tangential stores stations for carrying extra munitions and of some of its ability to carry precision guided weapons. This will not affect Saudi Arabia in launching defensive missions against Iran and Iraq, but will force it to trade range for payload in any missions flown against Israel.

The F-15XP will have a de-tuned version of the APG-70 radar on the 15E, which cannot use the AMRAAM. The radar on the F-15XP will have only 60% of the bandwidth of the regular APG-70 and only 16 channels rather than the regular 32. It will not have a computerized mapping capability, and will have only a resolution of 60 feet at 15 nautical miles versus 8.5 feet at 20 nautical miles in the F-15E.

The F-15XP will have altered software for the AWG-27 armament control system. It will lack a data transfer module, and its ASW-51 auto flight control will not include the terrain following mode. It will use a commercial grade secure voice and global positioning system navigation system.

Most importantly, its electronic warfare suite will be missionized only for use against non-U.S. aircraft and threats in the Gulf and Red Sea area. This means substantial modifications to the ALQ-135 internal countermeasures set, the ALR-56C radar warning receiver, the ALE-45 countermeasures dispenser, and MX-9287 interference blanker set. The ALQ-135 will not have the capability to jam friendly aircraft by type, and the radar warning receiver will also not identify these aircraft by type.

These modifications will have no impact on Saudi capability to deal with any threat aircraft in Iran and Iraq, but they effectively preclude effective penetration into Israel's air space because Israeli fighters, surface-to-air defenses, and electronic warfare assets all use U.S. or Israeli designed systems, and none of the electronic warfare assets on the XP will be tuned to counter such systems.[87] The one issue that has not been decided is the engine on the XP. The F-15E is now powered by the Pratt and Whitney F-100-229 engine, but can be powered by the GE F-110. The two companies will compete for the sale of the 168 engines involved in the sale.

The F-15XP sale request now seems likely to win the approval of Congress. President Bush announced that he would send the sale forward for congressional review on September 14, 1992, and did so only after congressional leaders assured him that they had the votes to ensure that Congress would not block the sale. Israel's new Labor government has indicated that it does not pose the same objections to the sale as did the Likud. The improvement in U.S.-Israeli relations since the election of a Labor government has led the Bush administration to push for provision of $10 billion worth of loan guarantees to Israel, and Congress seems likely to support the sale on the ground that it does not pose a major threat to Israel and offers the U.S. major revenues and increased jobs in the midst of a serious recession.

Saudi Arabia has consistently lived up to its agreements regarding the transfer and use of technology ever since the sale of F-15s were agreed to in 1978. The F-15XP sale does, however, raise legitimate concerns about the impact on the security of Israel of U.S. arms sales to friendly states like Saudi Arabia and Egypt. These issues can be resolved in three basic ways: first, by tailoring the sales to provide the capabilities that friendly Arab states need while limiting their ability to threaten Israel; second, by ensuring that Israel retains its military "edge" in other ways; and third, by ensuring that Israel receives the aid it needs to maintain a strong overall force posture.

The importance of the technical differences between the F-15E and the F-15XP have already been described. It is important to point out, however, that the potential risk of the aircraft being used in an attack on Israel, or being used by an unfriendly regime in the event of some unforeseen coup, is also limited by the conditions of the sale. Saudi Arabia cannot man or support depot level maintenance for either the overall aircraft or the APG-70 radar.

Saudi Arabia must rely on U.S. technicians and technical support to keep the aircraft operating well beyond the year 2005. As Iran showed during the first weeks of the Iran-Iraq War, even a relatively sophisticated air force can lose much of its operational strength in a few days if it no longer has sophisticated technical support, and the only aircraft Iran had with sophisticated avionics was the F-14—which could not use its Phoenix missiles by the time the Iran-Iraq War started.[88]

The RSAF will not receive the aircraft until 1995–1997, and it will then receive the aircraft at the rate of one squadron a year. Another year will be required to fully absorb the aircraft into its force structure. This timing not only ensures that Israeli modernization can compensate in part for the sale, but that Saudi Arabia will be phasing out its F-5EIIs relatively early in the operational life of the F-15XP—limiting a potential threat to Israel. By 1999, all of Saudi Arabia's F-5s will be over twenty years old, and its initial F-15C/ Ds will be twelve to eighteen years old.

Equally important, the sophistication of the F-15XP and of modern combat aircraft and munitions limits the risk of technology transfer. The performance of the F-15XP is determined largely by the software its computer and other avionics use to recognize threats, launch air combat and attack munitions, counter enemy sensors and weapons, and navigate to target. No nation other than the U.S. can alter the software on the F-15XP.

Saudi Arabia will have no software optimized to attack U.S. or Israeli air and air defense systems, and the existing software cannot be modernized to deal with any changes in existing systems, operate a single new weapon, or deal with a single new threat without U.S. approval. It also cannot be upgraded as part of the U.S. Air Force multi-stage improvement programs (MSIPs) planned for the F-15E without U.S. approval. Given the probable 20 year operating life of the F-15XP (1995–2015), this is a critical constraint on Saudi use of the F-15XP for missions against Israel or U.S. forces but one that in no way restricts its value for any of the purposes for which Saudi Arabia needs the aircraft.

The issue of ensuring that Israel retains its military edge in other ways requires a clear U.S. commitment to provide Israel with enough technology superior to that of any potential Arab threat as to offset the impact of U.S. arms transfers. The exact extent to which the U.S. provides this level of technology transfer will always be the subject of intense debate between the U.S. and Israel, with Israel asking for more than the U.S. will readily provide.

In practice President Bush and Secretary Cheney made a commitment to provide such technology at the time they announced the sale of the F-15XP. Meeting this commitment will be simplified by the fact that Israel's edge is no longer determined by "platforms"—the airframe of an aircraft or the body of a tank—but rather by the complex mix of electronics and munitions associated with that platform. This edge also will be determined by Israel's vastly superior experience.

On September 24, 1992, more than thirty senators—led by Senators John McCain of Arizona and Joseph Lieberman of Connecticut—wrote President Bush, calling for a program that included: (1) providing $10 billion in loan guarantees; (2) maintaining the existing level of military and economic aid to Israel in constant dollars on a long term basis; (3) providing long term military and economic aid to Egypt to ensure the safety of the Camp David accords; (4) giving Israel the same technology sharing arrangements as our NATO allies; (5) establishing cooperation in civil space activities; (6) improving cooperation in intelligence; (7) improving other aspects of military cooperation; and (8) promptly implementing prior agreements to preposition $300 million worth of equipment in Israel and to provide Israel with $700 million worth of military equipment made surplus by the end of the Cold War.

Two days later, the Bush administration made it clear that Israel would continue to be given an edge in terms of electronic warfare, munitions types and warheads, software, satellite intelligence, and a wide range of other capabilities. It also agreed that the U.S. would soon preposition $300 million worth of U.S. munitions and equipment in Israel and transfer the $700 million worth of surplus military stocks that the U.S. no longer needed for NATO, which includes additional Apache AH-64 attack helicopters and Black Hawk special mission helicopters as well as other systems.

As part of this effort, the U.S. and Israel established special working groups on prepositioning, the transfer of stocks of surplus U.S. military equipment, intelligence-sharing, the expansion of high technology military cooperation, and the development of a global protection system against missile attacks through a combination of intelligence sharing, ground and space based early warning systems, and use of the THAAD or Arrow to intercept theater range missiles.[89]

The Bush administration agreed to provide Israel with $10 billion in loan guarantees before the F-15 sale to Saudi Arabia, and Congress approved them on October 1, 1992. Israel seems willing to respond by accelerating economic reform and limiting further investment in settlements to security settlements. The U.S. and Israel are also discussing whether the U.S. should make a long term commitment to Israel to continue to provide $1.8 billion in annual aid. It is clear that there is firm bipartisan U.S. commitment to provide Israel with both the technology and aid necessary to offset any increased risk from U.S. arms transfers to Saudi Arabia and the southern Gulf states.

It is also clear that the sale of F-15XPs to Saudi Arabia would provide major strategic benefits for both the Royal Saudi Air Force and the U.S. The U.S. and Royal Saudi Air Forces have already proven they can cooperate closely. They worked together during the Iran-Iraq War before the U.S. reflagging operation and then during operation Earnest Will. They fought together during the war with Iraq, and they are now cooperating in Operation Southern Watch in enforcing the no fly zone over southern Iraq.

Saudi Arabia will complete transfer and absorption of the aircraft into its force structure during 1995–1999. The first full squadron of F-15XPs should become fully operational in mid-1996, the second in 1997, and the third in 1998.

By this time, the F-15XP will still be the most advanced strike-fighter in the world, with the exception of the F-15E. It will give Saudi Arabia a decisive edge over Iraq and Iran well beyond the year 2000. It will fully meet Saudi Arabia's desire for an F-15E–like aircraft that can attack deep into Iraqi or Iranian territory, defend itself in air-to-air combat, and launch air-to-ground ordnance from outside the range of short range air defense missiles. It can also be rapidly upgraded in an emergency if Iran or Iraq should acquire new types of fighters with unforeseen capabilities.

At the same time, Saudi operation of the F-15XP will ensure interoperability between the U.S. and Saudi air forces. It means that Saudi Arabia will buy additional service and training facilities, munitions, spare parts, and specialized electronics facilities that can support both Saudi and U.S. F-15 strike attack aircraft as well as Saudi and U.S. F-15 air defense fighters. Such facilities and munitions stocks will vastly improve U.S. rapid deployment capabilities in the Gulf. They will give the U.S. the ability to deploy well over 72 F-15E attack aircraft in a matter of days and then operate them in sustained high sortie rates against well equipped Iraqi or Iranian forces.

The F-15XP buy will also mean interoperability at every level of operations, from the individual pilot level to the kind of large scale command and control and battle management that the U.S. and Saudi Arabia employed against Iraq in the Gulf War. It would also mean strengthening not only the deterrent value of Saudi forces but the combined deterrent value of Saudi forces and U.S. reinforcements.

Important as the F-15XP sale is to the future of the RSAF, Saudi Arabia does not plan to reduce the purchases made under the second phase of al-Yamamah if the U.S. does sell the F-15s. In April, 1992 Britain announced that Saudi Arabia had agreed to a financing package for the $2.7 billion sale and indicated that the deal would again be financed "off-budget" by shifting oil revenue directly to a London account.

The purchase of the additional aircraft was also made more feasible by not turning other MOUs into firm contracts. On August 24, 1992, Saudi Arabia cut the number of new air bases it would buy from two to one. This was possible because during the Gulf War Saudi Arabia found that its existing facilities could sustain the buildup of some 500,000 foreign troops and that there was substantial over-capacity. The decision saved Saudi Arabia from $15.6 to $19.5 billion and gave Saudi Arabia money it could use to complete the buy of 48 Tornado IDS/GR1s.

Saudi Arabia does, however, face significant funding problems because of the Gulf War, and its existing orders may strain its resources. The contract is also structured so that Saudi Arabia can delay or cancel the purchase of individual elements.[90] If the F-15XP sale should fail for any reason, Saudi Arabia would also gain an incentive to wait for a Eurofighter rather than buy air defense variants of the Tornado.

The final major uncertainty in Saudi air force modernization is the replacement of the F-5EII. Saudi Arabia has talked about buying Hawks, F-16s, and F-18s as direct replacements for 95 of its F-5s. However, it has concluded that the buy of 72 F-15XP aircraft and of 48 more Tornado IDS/GR1s plus additional Hawks should allow it to phase out its F-5s without a major new buy of additional aircraft.

Cost is part of the reason for this decision, but Saudi Arabia also found that major diseconomies of scale arise in trying to make a limited buy of a new advanced fighter like the F-16 or F-18. It takes about 50% to 100% more Saudi and foreign manpower to support a new type as it does to add an additional F-15 or Tornado, and it creates major problems in terms of additional facilities and maintenance stockpiles.[91]

The Saudi air force faces further challenges that go far beyond selecting new aircraft. It is still largely a defensive air force, as became clear during operation Desert Storm. The Saudi air force flew some 6,800 sorties during the Gulf War (January 17, 1991 to February 28, 1991) and some 2,000 sorties over the Kuwaiti theater of operations and Iraq. These sorties were primarily offensive and defensive counterair, although the Saudi air force flew interdiction, airlift, and AWACS sorties.

Saudi F-15C pilots performed well in the air defense missions. They also did well in air-to-air combat during the brief period when Iraq actively engaged in such combat, and one Saudi pilot scored a double kill. Saudi Arabia was the only southern Gulf country with a modern concept of air defense operations. It built on previous experience in working with the USAF. During the Iran-Iraq War, it developed a patrol line called the Fahd Line near the center of the Gulf, a scramble line where aircraft on alert took off the moment an intruder came close, and inner defense lines covered by its Improved Hawk missiles. This system was modified during the Gulf War initially to cover both the north and south because of the possible risk of hostile air attacks from Yemen and the Sudan. During the rest of the war, Saudi Arabia steadily refined its system, working with the U.S. Air Force and other UN coalition forces to develop a layered system of land and airborne sensors and defense lines that could cover threats from Iraq as well as Iran.

At the same time, the Saudi air force showed that it had some serious weaknesses. It could not plan or control its own operations on a large scale. It had no force-on-force doctrine or ability to operate beyond the squadron level. The war revealed language, communications, interservice cooperation, and mission planning problems. Coordination problems often emerged between the Saudi air force and the Ministry of Defense. The air force also lacked the pilot numbers to operate its aircraft properly, and some Saudi Tornadoes were flown by British pilots. Added foreign technicians had to be brought in to maintain reasonable sortie rates with the F-15s and Tornadoes, and the war showed the air force will be dependent on such technicians for at least the next decade.

The Saudi Air Force initially had problems in finding the manpower to operate its AWACS and could not easily integrate AWACS data into its command operations center in Riyadh and SOCs throughout the kingdom. It operates these centers, although the air defense force has responsibility for some functions and the radars and equipment at surface-to-air missile sites.

Saudi Arabia learned a great deal from the Gulf War, however, and received accelerated training assistance from the U.S. As a result, it is considering buying four additional AWACS aircraft. These aircraft would allow Saudi Arabia to support continuous air defense and maritime surveillance coverage over both coasts. They also would greatly ease U.S. deployment problems in reinforcing Saudi Arabia or its smaller southern Gulf neighbors. The U.S. and Saudi Arabia have found that flying a full air defense and air control and warning screen against a northern Gulf state like Iraq or Iran can require up to four simultaneous orbits by AWACS aircraft, or 9–12 aircraft. Saudi Arabia can only fly two orbits with its current total of five E-3As.

The Saudi AWACS also badly need the passive ELINT systems being fitted to U.S. AWACS. These electronic intelligence systems, called the AN/AYR-1, provide the ability to detect, locate, and identify the radar emissions of ships, aircraft, and ground systems—often indicating their precise type and location. They also need the upgraded CC-2E central computer, GPS navigation system, and Class 2H version of the secure joint tactical information distribution system (JTIDS). This Block 30/35 upgrade will only be available for U.S. aircraft during 1995–1999, however, and it is unclear whether it will be provided to Saudi Arabia.

The Saudi air force did not do well in electronic warfare and reconnaissance missions. The Saudi RF-5 force proved largely useless in seeking out targets and rapidly processing information, and Saudi Arabia was almost completely dependent on the U.S. for reconnaissance and intelligence. While the Saudi air force could fly against fixed, lightly defended interdiction targets, it could do so only with foreign planning and support. It proved to have little operational flexibility in adapting from range training to actual close air support missions, and communication between the Saudi air force and army was so poor that it presented major problems.

These weaknesses are not unusual in even the best air forces in the developing world, and the Saudi air force is by far the most effective air force in the southern Gulf and one of the most effective air forces in the Arab world. At the same time, the deficiencies it revealed during operation Desert Storm indicate that Saudi Arabia would have major problems in defending against Iraq or Iran unless it had extensive foreign support. It will be a minimum of ten years before the air force can bring its offensive capabilities up to the level of its defensive capabilities. It will need at least a decade more of U.S. and British assistance to become an effective air force capable of force-on-force operations and combined operations.

The Saudi Air Defense Forces

The creation of a separate Saudi air defense corps to provide fixed and mobile land based air defense of key targets throughout the kingdom was intended to shape a more professional service and to reduce the manpower quality and leadership problems that emerged when these air defense forces were subordinated to the army.

In 1992 this 4,000 man force had some 33 surface-to-air missile batteries: 17 batteries with 96–128 Improved Hawk fire units, 9–10 batteries with 40–50 Crotale fire units, 15 batteries with 50–60 Shahine fire units, and some AMX-30SA 30mm self-propelled guns.[92] The Shahine units are static units for the defense of air bases and key targets. All of the Shahine systems are to be upgraded as the result of an agreement with France signed in 1991. These units provided close-in defense capability for virtually all of Saudi Arabia's major cities, ports, oil facilities, and military bases. The air defense corps also has 93 M-163 Vulcan 20mm anti-aircraft guns, 128 35mm AA guns, and 150 L/70 40mm guns (most in storage).[93]

Saudi Arabia is also taking delivery on 6 Patriot fire units or batteries, 384 Patriot long range air defense missiles, 6 AN/MPQ-53 radar sets, 6 engagement control stations, and 48 launcher stations. These systems are currently manned by U.S forces and not only will greatly improve its low to high level air defense capability, they will provide substantial defense against medium range and theater ballistic missiles. Saudi Arabia had purchased these units in autumn 1990 as part of its Gulf War arms package. It indicated in 1991 that it wanted to buy 14 more Patriot fire units (with 64 Patriot long range air defense missiles, 1 AN/MPQ-53 radar set, 1 engagement control station, and 8 launcher stations each) to defend all its cities, military bases, and major oil facilities. While Saudi Arabia and the U.S. Army had not completed full planning for such a system, preliminary studies indicated that it might require a total of 26 fire units.[94]

The Saudi Patriot units were to be upgraded to the PAC-3 version of the Patriot with far better software, radar processing capabilities, longer range missiles, better guidance systems, and more lethal warheads. Unlike the PAC-1 and PAC-2 systems used during the Gulf War, these Patriots are specifically designed to kill missiles at comparatively long ranges and to fully discriminate between warheads and decoys and parts of the missile body.[95]

Saudi Arabia has steadily reorganized much of its ground based air defense and made significant further improvements during the Gulf War, but the corps has been slow to acquire the quality of manpower it needs. It also has lacked the systems integration, battle management systems, and C³I software and integration it needs for effective operation.

Unfortunately, U.S. contractors' efforts to improve the integration of the Saudis' Improved Hawks, Shahines (Improved Crotalè), anti-aircraft guns, and land based radars and C³I systems have failed, as have the initial efforts to integrate many of these systems into a modern air defense system as part of the Peace Shield program.

The Saudi air defense network was first developed in the 1960s and used U.S. and British radars. Saudi Arabia then added a number of bits and pieces. It bought a Thomson CSF air command and control system and four Westinghouse AN/TPS-43 three dimensional radars in 1980. It then ordered AN/TPS-43G radars in 1981 to modernize its system as part of the Peace Pulse program, and it updated its system to provide command and data links to its E-3A AWACS. This left Saudi Arabia with major communications and C³I integration problems which it attempted to solve by giving major contracts to Boeing and Litton.[96]

The Litton system involved a $1.7 billion effort to provide C³I, sensors, and communications systems; handle the interface between missiles and other air defense systems; build sites; and train personnel. Key elements involved 17 major communications links installed in S-280C militarized transportable shelters and included both line-of-sight and tropospheric scatter links of 72 channel capacity. The field phase involved 34 low level and 34 high level shelters. While there is some dispute as to responsibility, the system was only partially operational when the contract was due to be completed. It still seems to be experiencing operational problems, although some may be the result of a lack of trained Saudi personnel.[97]

The Peace Shield program was a far more ambitious $8.5 billion effort to give Saudi Arabia a system of 17 AN/FPS-117(V)3 long range three-dimensional radar systems fully netted with its AN-TPS-43 and AN-TPS-72 short and medium range radars. It was to have (1) a central command operations center (COC) at Riyadh; (2) five sector command centers (SCCs) at Dhahran, Taif, Tabuk, Khamis Mushayt, and Al-Kharj to cover the country; and (3) additional sector operations centers at each major air base. It was to use a tropospheric scattering and microwave communications system to integrate Saudi Arabia's surface-to-air missile defenses, some anti-aircraft gun units, its radars, its E-3A AWACS aircraft and fighters, and six major regional underground operating centers and numerous smaller sites—all of which were to be managed by a command center in Riyadh.

The software and systems integration efforts required to make Peace Shield effective were years behind schedule at the time of the Gulf War, however, and the U.S. Air Force Electronic Systems Division issued a show cause notice and then terminated Boeing's work on the program in January, 1991. Saudi Arabia had to begin again with a new contractor, shifting from Boeing to Hughes in July, 1991 at a cost of $837 million.[98]

The Peace Shield system is to be revised to use Hughes AMD-44 workstations, Hughes HDP-6200 large screen displays, a modern data processing architecture, and far more advanced software. It will evidently adapt the concept of layered defense that Saudi Arabia developed during the Iran-Iraq War. There will be a patrol line like the Fahd Line near the center of the Gulf or covering the forward area on other borders, a scramble line, and inner defense lines covered by its Improved Hawk missiles.

Saudi Arabia also purchased a third C^3I/BM integration and system in March, 1989 called Falcon Eye. A tactical radar system which involves the supply of Westinghouse AN/TPS-70 radars with related computers, software, communications systems, and systems integration, it is to be managed by Ferranti. Falcon Eye is supposed to integrate data from ground rangers and the E-3A force and be down linked to the 12 Skyguard/Gun King batteries in the air defense corps. It is also supposed to be compatible with Peace Pulse and Peace Shield. The first phase of the system was supposed to become fully operational in 1992.

The success of the Peace Shield and Falcon Eye systems will be critical to determining how well the corps can absorb the Patriot missile units Saudi Arabia is buying. It will not be operational until February, 1996, however, versus the original date of 1993. Like all of Saudi Arabia's sophisticated air systems, it will also be heavily dependent on U.S. technical assistance (and de facto assistance in operating the weapons) until well after the year 2000.[99]

More generally, the question arises whether the existence of a separate air defense corps is the right long term solution to Saudi Arabia's military needs. The existence of a separate Saudi air defense corps does help reduce the chances of any kind of coup attempt by creating a separate check on air force operations, but its ability to fight in defensive positions against superior forces will depend heavily on the quality of its air cover, the ability of the Saudi air force to link its operations with those of the army, and its ability to provide close air and interdiction support. In the long run, integrating smaller and mobile systems into the army, and the larger missiles and C^3I system into the air force, might be more successful.[100]

Further, Saudi Arabia clearly needs to integrate its system with that of Kuwait and Bahrain. This is crucial to both Saudi Arabia's future security and the ability of the West to reinforce Bahrain and Kuwait effectively because of their small size and air space. Kuwait is particularly vulnerable because it shares a common border with Iraq and proximity to Iran and desperately requires a survivable air defense and land and maritime surveillance system. No Kuwaiti-based system can provide such characteristics unless it is integrated into a Saudi system, preferably with close links to Bahrain, Qatar, and the UAE.

Saudi Paramilitary Forces

Saudi Arabia has several important paramilitary forces in addition to its national guard. This reflects a system of layered forces designed to protect the regime. The regular army provides external security but is kept away from urban areas. The national guard provides security from loyal tribes and groups under a different chain of command. There is a separate 15,000 man frontier force, and the Ministry of Interior and other groups provide internal security at the political and intelligence levels.

The frontier force covers land and sea borders. It performs a host of patrol and surveillance missions, is equipped with four wheel drive vehicles and automatic weapons, and can act as a light defensive screen. About 4,500 men in the frontier force are assigned to a coast guard. It is equipped with four inshore medium patrol craft, 30 light inshore patrol boats, 16 Hovercraft, the royal yacht, and about 400 small boats. The frontier force has done much of the fighting with Yemen in recent years and has taken some significant casualties.

Saudi Arabia is considering building a border surveillance system that would use patrol aircraft, remotely piloted vehicles, and early warning systems to detect intruders and border crossings. There would be a 12 kilometer deep security zone around all 6,500 kilometers of the land and sea borders, with a mix of acoustic, seismic, radar, magnetic, and infrared sensors to detect movements of men and vehicles in the border area. It would be supported by small manned patrol aircraft and unmanned remotely piloted vehicles where there might be some threat from the intruder. Thompson CSF completed a $5 million feasibility study for this system in early 1990, and a consortium led by E Systems and one led by Thompson CSF submitted bids to Saudi Arabia in May, 1991. The estimated cost of the system is around $3 billion, and it would take several years to complete.[101]

There is a special security force with 500 men and UR-416 APCs. Little is known about this force, which seems to be designed to deal with terrorism and hijacking. A large special investigations force is something like the British Criminal Investigation Department but with political as well as criminal justice functions. There is also a royal intelligence office, with some security and anti-terrorism functions, under Prince Turki Faisal. Finally, Saudi Arabia has a large gendarmerie, or national police force, with more than 15,000 men.

It is impossible for an outsider to appraise the effectiveness of these forces or even identify their precise functions. It should be noted, however, that Saudi Arabia is not a particularly repressive society and tolerates a great deal of highly vocal dissent. It shows no tolerance for organized violence.

Saudi Missile Capabilities and Weapons of Mass Destruction

The most controversial development in Saudi forces is the purchase of Chinese CSS-2 (DF-3) long range surface-to-surface missiles, which are deployed as part of the air defense force. The Saudis have bought a package of 20–50 missiles and support at a cost of about $3–3.5 billion, although most estimates put the number at 20–24 missiles and 10–12 launchers.[102]

The CSS-2 missiles are mobile, although they were initially deployed to fixed sites. They are currently deployed in two battalions. One is located at the Al-Sulayyil Oasis, roughly 475 kilometers south to southwest of Riyadh. Al-Sulayyil is also to be the site of one of Saudi Arabia's new air bases for its Tornado fighter bombers. A second battalion is located at Al-Juaifer near the Al-Kharj air base south of Riyadh. Another site or training facility seems to exist in southwestern Saudi Arabia at a place called Al-Liddam.

Commercial satellite photos of the site at Al-Sulayyil show a headquarters and transportation complex with 60 buildings or tents, a transportation center, a command and control complex with roughly 40 buildings and tents, a secure area, a construction area, a bunker which may be a fixed launcher site, other launch areas with bunkers for missile storage, an additional launch area, and three 150 meter long white buildings that may be missile assembly facilities.[103]

The Saudis evidently cannot fire the missiles without Chinese technical support, and Chinese technicians are deploying and operating the missiles under Saudi supervision. Ballast Nedam, a subsidiary of British Aerospace, has recently extended the runway at the Al-Sulayyil air base to 3,000 meters. There are some signs that Saudi Arabia may be deploying surface-to-air missiles to defend the facility.[104]

None of the Saudi missiles is now armed with weapons of mass destruction. Saudi Arabia is a signatory to the NPT, and Saudi Arabia and the government of the PRC have assured U.S. officials that the missiles will remain conventional. The Saudi government has provided a written statement that "nuclear and chemical warheads would not be obtained or used with the missiles." U.S. experts believe that Saudi Arabia has kept its word, although the Saudis have refused a U.S. request to inspect the missile sites in Saudi Arabia.[105]

However, there are good reasons to question the value of such missiles as long as they only have conventional warheads.[106] The CSS-2s deployed in the PRC are all nuclear armed missiles, which can carry 1–3 megaton warheads. They have a maximum range of about 2,200 miles (3,500 kilometers), an inertial guidance system, and a single stage refrigerated liquid fuel rocket motor. The version of the CSS-2 that the PRC has sold to Saudi Arabia is heavily modified and has a special large conventional warhead, weighing up to 3,500–4,000 pounds. This added warhead weight cuts the maximum range of the missile to anywhere from 1,550 nautical miles (2,400 kilometers) to 1,950 nautical miles (3,100 kilometers).

A conventional warhead of this size is more effective than the warhead on a Scud but is scarcely a weapon of mass destruction or even an effective conventional weapon. Assuming an optimal ratio of high explosive (HE) to total weight, the warhead of the CSS-2 could destroy buildings out to a radius of 200–250 feet, seriously damage buildings out to a radius of 300–350 feet, and kill or injure people with projectiles to a distance of up to 1,000 feet.[107] This is substantially less destructive power than would result from a single sortie by a modern strike fighter.

The CSS-2 has other limitations. It is an obsolete missile first designed in 1971. While an improved version has deployed, most experts still estimate that the missile has a CEP of nearly 2–4 kilometers and lacks the accuracy to hit anything other than large area targets like cities or industrial facilities. Even then, each missile would still only have the effective lethality of a single 2,000 pound bomb. It requires large amounts of technical support and ground equipment and takes hours to make ready for firing.[108]

The Saudi purchase of the CSS-2 raises serious issues on several grounds:

- A very costly weapons system is being procured in very small numbers with very low lethality.

- As now configured, the missile system may do more to provoke attack or escalation than to deter attack or provide retaliatory capability;
- Saudi acquisition of chemical or nuclear warheads would nevertheless radically improve the value of the system as a deterrent or retaliatory weapon.

The result is a destabilizing situation in which Saudi motives are unclear and will remain so in spite of any inspection agreements and other countries have an added incentive to join the missile arms race, acquire weapons of mass destruction, or preempt in a conflict. While the Saudi purchase may be a logical reaction to such problems as Israeli nuclear capabilities, the search for prestige, the Iran-Iraq missile war, and a desire to assert Saudi independence from the U.S., the net result may well do Saudi Arabia more harm than good.[109]

Strategic Interests and Arms Control

Saudi Arabia is not strong enough to serve as a proxy for Western military forces or as a pillar of Western security. It has many of the vulnerabilities of its smaller neighbors, and it can only achieve security through a combination of cooperative defense efforts with its neighbors and the West. At the same time, Saudi Arabia has the wealth and the population to act as the core of the GCC's efforts to build regional security. Further, it is large and strong enough so that Western military forces can remain over the horizon in many contingencies, and limited amounts of Western reinforcement should be adequate in most contingencies.

Unfortunately, Saudi Arabia currently lacks a viable plan to develop its own forces and any clear plans for cooperation either with its Gulf neighbors or the United States. The failure of the Damascus Declaration to produce any Egyptian or Syrian forces in the Gulf means that it would take weeks, and perhaps months, for combat capable Arab forces from outside the Gulf to deploy for war against a threat like Iraq. Similarly, the GCC's failure to agree on any specific plans for cooperation, interoperability, and integration has left Saudi Arabia without militarily effective allies in the Gulf.

The problems are equally serious in the case of Saudi cooperation with the West. Saudi Arabia did reach a tentative agreement for common training with U.S. forces in September, 1991. For reasons that will be discussed shortly, however, it rejected U.S. proposals to preposition two division sets of ground combat equipment in Saudi Arabia, although the U.S. could have left such equipment there when U.S. forces completed their withdrawal from the Gulf at the end of 1991.[110] This was an understandable reaction to the U.S. failure to guarantee Saudi Arabia arms and training to expand its own forces, to U.S. demands for a status of forces agreement ceding some aspects of Saudi sovereignty, and to pressure from Islamic fundamentalists to avoid any outside deployment on Saudi soil. It did, however, place serious limits on U.S. reinforcement capabilities.

Saudi Arabia has, however, tentatively agreed to expand the 15 year old military training mission treaty it signed in 1977. The U.S. has proposed arrangements under this treaty that would store up to 200 M-1A2s and 200 M-2s in the kingdom, plus spare parts and enough Air Force equipment to support 5 to 6 fighter wings. This would only be one-third of the amount of prepositioned equipment that the U.S. originally proposed, and the arrangement is evidently dependent on Saudi views after the U.S. presidential election and talks with the new administration. It would, though, allow the U.S. to deploy a sustainable heavy division to Saudi Arabia in less than 30 days.[111]

The uncertainties in U.S.-Saudi strategic cooperation are further illustrated by the Saudi request that the U.S. halt deployment of aircraft to Saudi Arabia from the U.S. in September, 1991, when it seemed that the U.S. might have to use force to make Iraq comply with all the terms of its cease-fire agreement with the UN. However, Saudi Arabia changed this position in August, 1992, when the U.S., UK, and France established a "no-fly" zone over Iraq. Saudi Arabia not only allowed U.S. aircraft to operate but provided refueling tankers, combat air defense patrols, and support from Saudi AWACS. This support was critical to the U.S., Britain, and France since it allowed them to establish the no-fly zone with fewer than 150 aircraft. They would have had to provide roughly 100 more aircraft without Saudi support.[112]

At the other end of the issue, the West has not shown that it can provide Saudi Arabia with the right arms transfers, training, and support effort. The U.S. still experiences major problems because of domestic political debates over the impact of such arms transfers on the security of Israel, and European suppliers often profiteer rather than ensure suitable packages of training and support. If Saudi Arabia has been slow to lay the foundation for effective efforts at common defense, so has the West.

Further, the West has often been slow to understand the Saudi emphasis on informal cooperation and low profile activities. Saudi internal and external stability depends on keeping strategic cooperation as quiet as possible, while the U.S. has been particularly insistent on formal and public arrangements. This U.S. insistence hurt both the U.S. and Saudi Arabia after the Gulf War. Saudi Arabia offered to allow U.S. Army prepositioning of major armor, artillery, and other equipment in Saudi warehouses at Saudi cost and under joint U.S.-Saudi Guard. The U.S. insisted on a formal status of forces agreement, flying the U.S. flag, total U.S. control of the facility, and large numbers of U.S. personnel. It also presented the U.S. plan complete with long computer lists of additional equipment.

The Saudis rejected the U.S. plan both because of the way in which it was presented and because the U.S. insistence on an overt basing facility openly violated the royal family's pledge to the Islamic clergy not to grant bases or formally base non-Muslim forces in the kingdom. It also meant a nearly certain crisis with hard-line Islamic fundamentalists.

Saudi Arabia prefers to use a similar degree of indirection in modernizing, in supporting the Arab-Israeli peace process, and in limiting the influence of Arab and Islamic radicals. The West and Israel prefer formal and visible arrangements. Israel has often made the mistake of treating Saudi Arabia and other moderate and conservative Arab states as enemies and insisting on formal arrangements as signs of progress. It is important that both the West and Israel understand that Saudi Arabia must preserve its Islamic character, avoid provoking Arabic radicals, and minimize the risk of confrontation with Iran, Iraq, and Syria. Informal success is always preferable to formal failure, but this is a lesson that the U.S. and Israel find very difficult to learn.

Similar problems emerge out of Western efforts to pressure Saudi Arabia and the other Gulf states towards Western-style democracy, legal systems, and secular approaches to social change. The Saudi royal family, like every royal family in the southern Gulf, could do more to move towards representative institutions, improve civil rights, and establish a rule of law. The West needs to understand, however, that the Saudi royal family and most Gulf royal families can only advance change as fast as their societies accept it. In Saudi Arabia, for example, there is already a major fundamentalist reaction to the existing rate of change, and accelerating change or any kind of elections would lead to conservative reaction, not progress.

Similarly, the West must be very careful to distinguish between the hopes and desires of Western-educated Gulf professionals and reality. In the case of Saudi Arabia, there are many instances of corruption and the abuse of civil law within the royal family. However, the history of the Saudi professional and middle class—particularly the Hijazi, who are often critics of the royal family—is scarcely better. The same is equally true of the clergy, in part because of the archaic methods of religious funding and taxation still used throughout much of Islam. Demanding change is very different from the ability to achieve real progress.

These problems will not prevent Saudi Arabia from slowly improving its military capabilities, but they do mean that any major progress in collective or cooperative defense efforts will be slow and as dependent on changes in Western attitudes as on changes in the attitudes of Saudi Arabia. Equally important, a continuing Saudi failure to reach any agreement with the U.S. to preposition equipment and munitions on Saudi soil or to buy equipment U.S. forces could use in an emergency would prevent Saudi Arabia and Kuwait from ensuring that U.S. land forces could deploy to the northern Gulf in time to defend either country against an invasion by Iraq. Similarly, the current limits on U.S. and Saudi cooperation seriously inhibit the ability to create effective air and maritime reinforcement capabilities to deal with a threat from either Iran or Iraq.

Kuwait

	Manpower (1,000s)	Tanks	Aircraft	Defense Spending ($ millions)	Arms Imports ($ millions)	Arms Exports ($ millions)
1967	8			192	3	—
1973	14	100	34	334	4	—
1982	13	275	36	1,179	110	—
1988	15	275	36	1,340	190	—
1991	8	250	42	13,100	—	—

Kuwait has some of the richest oil resources in the world.[113] It produced a total of about 27 billion barrels of oil by the end of 1990 and had an extremely high reserve-to-production ratio of 194:1.[114] As of January 1, 1992, it had estimated proved oil reserves of up to 97 billion barrels, with probable reserves of at least 4 billion more and gas reserves of 48,000 billion cubic feet. It had about 12% of the world's total oil reserves and produced at a rate of about 1.01 million barrels per day during 1990, before the Iraqi invasion.[115] In contrast to oil, Kuwait has only about 0.01 cubic kilometers of internal renewable water resources, which is extremely low, amounting to about 10 cubic meters per person, one of the lowest levels of any nation in the world.[116]

Kuwait began its history in the early 1700s as a small fishing village at the western end of the Gulf, when a number of families from the Anayza tribe in Saudi Arabia emigrated into the area. The original settlers appointed a member of the Sabah family as sheik in 1756, and it has been ruled by the family ever since. Kuwait did come under limited Ottoman rule and paid tribute to the Ottoman Empire. The sheik of Kuwait accepted the title of provincial governor from the Ottomans in 1871, but Kuwait retained a high degree of independence until it came under British protection in 1881. Kuwait successfully sought full British protection in 1899, when the Ottoman Empire attempted to assert control over Kuwait. This led to an agreement that Kuwait would not permit any other government to send agents or representatives, and Britain appointed a political agent in 1904. Britain negotiated a treaty regularizing this relationship with Turkey in 1913, but the treaty was never ratified because of World War I.

Kuwait remained little more than a village until the end of the 1920s. It kept its independence during the period of Saud conquest because of British diplomatic action. In 1922 Sir Percy Cox, the British agent, called together the representatives of Kuwait, its newly formed League of Nations mandate called Iraq, and Saudi Arabia (then the Sultanate of Najd) in negotiations that led to the Treaty of Muhammara (May 1, 1922) and the Protocol of Uqayr (December 2, 1922). These agreements laid the boundaries of modern Kuwait, although Kuwait lost a significant amount of territory occupied by pro-Kuwaiti Bedouin to Saudi Arabia.

At the time of these negotiations, Kuwait lacked water and significant port facilities, and its economy was tied to fishing and pearling. Kuwait's economy was devastated when Japan introduced cultured pearls, and Kuwait might have disappeared as a significant political and economic entity except for the discovery of oil in the 1930s. Oil revitalized the Kuwaiti economy and started its gradual transformation into one of the world's wealthiest city-states. It raised Kuwait's population from around 75,000 in the late 1930s to over two million when the Gulf War began.

Kuwait's history was relatively peaceful between the discovery of oil and the time it achieved independence from Britain in 1961. Saudi Arabia did not press any of its claims to disputed territory and offshore drilling areas. Iraq recognized Kuwait's independence in 1932 and did not challenge Kuwait's sovereignty while the Iraqi monarchy remained tied to British support and influence.

The Iraqi monarchy fell in 1958, however, and Britain withdrew from the Gulf in 1961. Kuwait became fully independent on June 19, 1961. Only a week after the withdrawal of British forces, Iraq made claims to Kuwait which were based on tenuous rights as the inheritor of the Ottoman Empire. Iraq moved troops towards the border. It halted only when Britain rushed troops back into the country and when it became obvious the Arab League was prepared to challenge its claims.

This Iraqi pressure and fear of Arab socialism helped lead the Sabah family to issue Kuwait's first constitution in November, 1962, establishing the emir as a hereditary monarch, an emir's council, and a popular national assembly, with the electorate limited to the descendants of Kuwait's population in 1920. The national assembly was allowed to operate from 1963 to 1976 and again from 1981 to 1986. The Sabah family suppressed the assembly in 1976 because of growing political radicalism and pressure from Saudi Arabia, which opposed any popularly elected forum at that time. It suppressed the assembly in 1986 because of its growing desire for increased power, debates over stock market fraud and corruption involving the royal family, and conflicts that threatened to increase tension with Kuwait's neighbors.

Kuwait also adopted a policy of negotiating with any power that threatened it and of attempting to use its oil wealth to compensate for its military weakness. It gave money to the PLO and aid to other Arab states. It provided funds to Syria and Iraq, supported Arab trade and oil embargoes, and terminated its treaty with Britain in 1971 in an effort to show it no longer had colonial ties. It bought military equipment from the U.S. and Europe but established relations with the Soviet Union in 1963 and eventually bought Soviet arms in an effort to minimize the risk of hostile Soviet pressure. Over the years, this policy of buying off the threat became the foundation of Kuwait's security.

These policies helped Kuwait reach a border agreement with Iraq in 1963 and get the votes it needed to join the UN. Nevertheless, Iraq continued to make sporadic claims to Kuwait and never formally abandoned its claims to the Kuwaiti islands of Bubiyan and Warhab on the northeastern edge of the Kuwaiti-Iraqi border. They control the channel to Iraq's only direct access to the Gulf and its naval base at Umm Qasr and are near its oil loading terminal in the Gulf off Faw.

Iraq again threatened Kuwait in 1965, 1967, and 1972. It occupied Kuwait's border post at Sametah on March 20, 1973, in a further effort to put pressure on Kuwait to cede it control of the islands in the Gulf. This led to the deployment of Saudi troops to the border. Iraq withdrew in early April, but only after mediation by Yasser Arafat and a substantial Kuwaiti bribe to Iraq. Iraq then attempted to lease Warhab and half of Bubiyan in 1975 for a period of 99 years. According to some reports, Iraq briefly sent troops into Kuwait again in 1976 and withdrew only after another Kuwaiti payment.[117]

This situation did not change in the 1980s. Although Kuwait was a critical source of financial aid to Iraq during the Iran-Iraq War, Iraq again sought to lease Bubiyan and Warhab in 1980 and provoked another border incident in 1983. When Kuwait refused to lease the two islands, Iraq sent a token force across the border. This Iraqi pressure led to a sudden visit to Baghdad by Kuwait's prime minister, Saad Sabah, on November 10–13, 1984. Once again, Iraq was bought off by a substantial payment, although Iraq did establish a Hovercraft base across the river from Warhab.[118]

Control of the two islands had become steadily more important to Iraq because it was clear that it was never likely to secure its access to the Gulf through the Shatt al Arab, which it shared with Iran. Further, the Shatt al Arab had suffered from 10 years of silting and mining during the Iran-Iraq War. As a result, Iraq had steadily expanded the city of Basra to the south, the town of Al-Bayer just southwest of Basra, and its naval base at Umm Qasr. It had moved south into territory that probably belonged to Kuwait near Umm Qasr and the border town of Safwan, and had expanded a canal called the Shatt al Basra from Umm Qasr to a position midway between Basra and Al-Zubayr. This made the Khor Abd Allah, the channel from the Gulf to Umm Qasr to the north of Bubiyan and Warhab, steadily more important.[119]

Kuwait also had some minor border problems with Saudi Arabia after independence. In 1966 Kuwait and Saudi Arabia negotiated an end to the neutral zone that had originally been established between them to give nomadic tribes freer access to grazing rights. In August, 1976 Saudi Arabia successfully pressured Kuwait to dissolve its popular assembly, and Saudi Arabia dealt with a dispute over offshore drilling rights by sending troops to occupy the two islands of Umm al-Maradim and Gharo in June, 1977.

In spite of its past difficulties, Kuwait was one of Iraq's most important allies during the Iran-Iraq War. It supplied Iraq with at least $13.2 billion in grants and loans and with up to $22 billion in overall assistance, although Iraq put new pressure on Kuwait to lease Warhab and Bubiyan in 1980.[120] This Kuwaiti support for Iraq created problems between Kuwait and Iran. Iran conducted several overflights and air strikes on Kuwait to try to intimidate it into reducing its support for Iraq. While Kuwait's Shi'ites had been reasonably well integrated into Kuwaiti society and provided a number of its native technocrats, some fraction of the Shi'ite population did side with Iran during the Iran-Iraq War.

These problems grew more severe after 1982, as Iran drove Iraq out of Iran and counterattacked into Iraq, and as Iraq became more dependent on Kuwaiti financial aid and the transshipment of goods from Kuwait. On December 12, 1983, Shi'ites bombed the French and U.S. embassies; 17 Shi'ites were later convicted of the bombing. In May, 1985, pro-Iranian Shi'ites attempted to assassinate the emir of Kuwait, and Iran's conquest of Faw in 1986 brought it within striking distance of Kuwait. Pro-Iranian Shi'ites bombed Kuwait's oil facilities in June, 1986, and in January, April, May, and June, 1987.

These threats to Kuwait were a key factor that led it to seek U.S. and Soviet assistance in reflagging its tankers. Although Kuwait joined the GCC when it was formed in May, 1981, this did little to improve its security. While the GCC created the Peninsular Shield Force in the mid-1980s that was supposed to have 10,000 men, the reality was little more than a reinforced Saudi brigade based at Hafr al-Batin with no real mobility and sustainability. As a result, when Iran began to strike at Kuwaiti and southern Gulf tankers—in an effort to compensate for Arab support of Iraq and Iraq's strikes on Iran's oil facilities and tanker traffic—Kuwait was forced to turn to the West.

It played upon U.S. fears of Soviet influence in the Gulf and an Iranian victory in the Gulf War to obtain U.S. agreement to reflag Kuwaiti tankers with the U.S. flag and provide U.S. Navy escorts. This reflagging led to U.S. military confrontations with Iran during 1987 and 1988 and played a significant role in Iran's eventual defeat.

As has been discussed in the previous chapter, however, Kuwait earned little gratitude from Iraq. Iraq had emerged from the Iran-Iraq War as a kind of victor, but it had won because of some $37 billion in loans from Kuwait and its other Arab neighbors and massive loans from the West and other countries. By late 1989 Iraq desperately needed to reschedule these loans. The required principal and interest on the non-Arab debt alone would have consumed half of Iraq's $13 billion in annual oil revenues. At the same time, Iraq had a military budget of $12.9 billion in 1990, or approximately $700 per citizen in a country with a per capita income of $1,950.[121]

Iraq demanded forgiveness of its Arab loans during 1988 and 1989 and called for new grant aid as the sole defender of the Arab cause against Persia. It made new requests to lease Warhab and parts of Bubiyan in 1989 and rejected the attempts of Kuwait's emir to reach a general border settlement when he visited Iraq in September, 1989.[122] By mid-1990, when Iraq's cash reserves were equal to a mere three months of imports and inflation was running at 40%, Iraq decided on war. Saddam Hussein accused Kuwait of "stabbing Iraq in the back," and Iraqi foreign minister Tariq Aziz claimed that Kuwait had "implemented a plot to escalate the pace of gradual systematic advance toward Iraqi territory. The Kuwait government set up military establishments, police posts, oil installations, and farms on Iraqi territory."[123] Iraq claimed that Kuwait and the UAE were conspiring to keep oil prices low and were violating their oil quotas, and that Kuwait was stealing oil from the Rummaliah oil field, whose southern tip enters Kuwaiti territory. The end result was Iraq's invasion of Kuwait on August 2, 1990, and the Gulf War.

Kuwait's military role in the Gulf War will be summarized shortly, but the liberation of Kuwait has scarcely created a lasting basis for its security. The war has almost certainly left a legacy of lasting Iraqi irredentism. The efforts to demarcate the Kuwaiti-Iraqi border may also lead to moving it north. There is no firm historical record of the border marking points, which consisted of a long vanished border and a field of date palms at Safwan that Iraqi farmers steadily expanded south after the marking of the border in 1923. If the border is corrected to go back to the original line, this would secure Kuwait's control over the Ratga oil field on its northern border, but it would also give Kuwait control over more of the Rummaliah oil field and threaten Iraqi access to the port facilities at Umm Qasr.[124]

The tensions between Kuwait and Iran have eased since the 1988 cease-fire in the Iran-Iraq War, and relations have improved because of Iran's tacit support of Kuwait in the Gulf War. There is still, however, tension between Kuwait's dominant Sunnis and its Shi'ites. There is a festering debate over the sentencing and treatment of Shi'ites arrested for bombing incidents, there has been continuing discrimination against Shi'ites without good political connections, and the ruling Sabah family has allowed the political police, internal security forces, and royal intelligence to investigate and arrest individual Shi'ites.

Kuwait has ruthlessly driven many of its nearly 400,000 prewar Palestinian and Jordanian workers out of the country because of the support the PLO and Jordan gave to Iraq during the Gulf War. Since the Gulf War others have been arrested and executed by the Kuwaiti government with little real evidence, or tortured or killed by Kuwaiti vigilantes who had at least the initial tolerance of the government. Only about 7,000 had work permits in May, 1992. Kuwait's treatment of these workers may someday lead to Jordanian or PLO reprisals.[125]

The ruling Sabah family also faces serious questions about its leadership from many native Kuwaiti Sunnis. The royal family did nothing to prepare the country for war, and key members showed little leadership during the initial fighting once Iraq invaded. Most of the leadership during the war came from the professional military and foreign advisors and from a resistance movement that organized largely on its own. The emir, Sheik Jaber al-Ahmed, showed no leadership after the war, returning only slowly and putting the repair of his palace before the needs of the people. He also gave little recognition to the Kuwaiti resistance, treating it more as a threat to the regime than an aid to the country. Kuwait has drawn down heavily on its Fund for the Future, which totaled up to $100 billion before the war, and the regime has less political ability to use money to co-opt its opposition.

Kuwait has obligated up to $65 billion since the Gulf War—nearly 65% of its invested assets overseas before the war. It has obligated some $20 billion for repairs and modernization of its oil facilities and $20 billion more to repay bad loans—most stemming from the collapse of Kuwait's fraudulent stock market and owed to or by families fully able to pay their debts. Kuwait has also made massive arms purchases. As a result, its current budget will have a deficit of $18 billion out of total spending of $21 billion, and the country has borrowed $5.5 billion from international banks.

Such borrowing may be practical, given that Kuwait will earn at least $3 billion from oil in 1992 and normally has revenues of $10 billion; it is often more economic to borrow than liquidate investments. Kuwait also must restructure much of its infrastructure and housing if it wants to keep the population close to its present 1.2 million (700,000 Kuwaitis) rather than rise back to the 2.5 million level it had before the Gulf War. Nevertheless, the Kuwaiti royal family has almost certainly spent far beyond Kuwait's immediate requirements or ability to absorb what it has purchased.[126]

As for other threats, Syria has occasionally backed anti-Iraqi groups operating in Kuwait and has sometimes made demands for aid that have been tantamount to blackmail. Some local sources claim that both Syria and Iraq sought aid during the 1980s by threats against members of the royal family.

On the positive side, Kuwait was able to restore much of its economic activity and most urban services by mid-1991. In spite of apocalyptic predictions, the 732 oil well fires Iraq set during its withdrawal did not produce fatal environmental problems, and all were put out by the end of October, 1991. Kuwait was able to begin oil exports and had set a goal of 1 million barrels per day by mid-1992. By fall 1992, the emir had lifted censorship and ended most of the serious abuses of Kuwait's legal system. He had restored most civil rights and made heavily qualified promises of increased democracy.

Kuwait was scarcely, however, a unified nation and lacked popular leadership. In June, 1992 the speaker of the national council criticized the U.S. ambassador for "talking about democracy" and "encouraging the local opposition." The emir blocked plans to organize seminars on elections although the last assembly had been dismissed in 1986, and elections were scheduled for October, 1992. The voting population was still limited to men of 21 years or older who could trace their or their forebears' Kuwaiti residence back to 1920. This represented only 81,400 males out of a total population of 600,000, or 13.5%.

The government's actions did little to ensure support for the regime. In late May, 1992 Kuwaiti businessmen elected the board of the Chamber of Commerce and Industry. Some 11,500 businessmen voted, and 23 of 24 seats went to candidates opposing the current government.

When elections for the 50 man national assembly took place on October 6, 1992, they were fought over the issues of power sharing, the fiscal accountability of the Sabah family, and whether an open investigation should be made into the events leading to Kuwait's unpreparedness on August 2, 1990. The voters chose between 278 candidates, most of whom ran as independents. The results scarcely created a radical assembly, but it was clear that a large majority seriously questioned the conduct of the royal family and that even Kuwait's carefully selected sample of voters favored increased democracy.

Nine of the 50 new members were Islamists, 7 were associated with Islam, 17 had served in the National Assembly which had been suspended by the emir in 1986, and 9 had served in the National Council, a surrogate legislature elected in 1990 by the emir. A total of 35 were Islamists, traditional politicians, and secular liberals who had called for a parliament that could put stronger checks and balances on the government.[127]

Kuwait's Military Vulnerability

Kuwait is one of the most strategically exposed states in the world, and Iraq's invasion of Kuwait was a brutal demonstration of that fact. The bulk of Kuwait's military forces disintegrated during the first hours of Iraq's invasion on August 2, 1990. Kuwait was completely unprepared for the invasion, although several Kuwaiti commanders had pressed to put its forces on the alert and move them into defensive positions. As a result, much of Kuwait's military equipment was captured and much of the rest lost or destroyed. Only some of its aircraft, a few vessels, and a limited amount of land equipment escaped to Saudi Arabia.

Even if Kuwait's forces had been prepared, they were far too weak to have withstood Iraq and defend a geographic position as vulnerable as Kuwait. Its total territory is only about 17,800 square kilometers, or roughly the size of New Jersey. Kuwait has a 240 kilometer long border with Iraq and a 222 kilometer border with Saudi Arabia. Kuwait's terrain consists largely of slightly undulating desert plains and has few defensive barriers. The only significant elevation in the country is the Al-Mutla Ridge, just north of the city of Al-Jahra, and the pass through this ridge from the north into Kuwait City is the only real defensive position against Iraq. The gorge of Al-Batin (Hafr al-Batin) forms a limited barrier to the west. The one defensive line north of the Bay of Kuwait provides a slight advantage to the defender, and the road net between Kuwait City and Basra in Iraq allows rapid movement of troops.

Kuwait's one real chance to defend is to be fully deployed along these defensive positions before Iraqi forces attack. Kuwait lacks the numbers ever to win a meeting engagement, and the terrain favors the attacker. The desert in northern Kuwait permits relatively easy movement by armor, and there are a number of highways and road links that fill the area. Kuwait has some 3,000 kilometers of roads, 2,500 kilometers of which are paved. Kuwait is also highly vulnerable to air assault, with seven airfields, four of which are paved and have runways 2,400–3,439 meters long. There are many areas in Kuwait where paved roads allow rapid movement by armor; all of Kuwait can be quickly crossed by helicopter, and the 499 kilometer coastline has many areas where amphibious craft can land.

Kuwait faces equally serious problems in defending Bubiyan and Warhab. These low lying sand islands with large amounts of salt marsh have no particular resources, but they control the channel to Umm Qasr, Iraq's only naval base with direct access to the Gulf.

Kuwaiti Defense Spending and Arms Imports
Before the Gulf War

During the 1980s, Kuwait attempted to deal with this mix of vulnerabilities by relatively high levels of military spending. It spent over $1 billion annually on defense beginning in the early 1980s, with levels of around $1.5 billion during 1983–1985—when it felt most threatened by Iran. ACDA estimates that Kuwait spent $766 million on defense in 1979, $892 million in 1980, $858 million in 1981, $1,120 million in 1982, $1,399 million in 1983, $1,430 million in 1984, $1,525 million in 1985, $1,300 million in 1986, $1,263 million in 1987, $1,273 million in 1988, and $1,964 million in 1989.[128] This averaged around 5–6% of its GDP on defense and 12–14% of its central government expenditures.

ACDA estimates that Kuwait imported $60 million worth of arms in 1979, $40 million in 1980, $120 million in 1981, $110 million in 1982, $140 million in 1983, $600 million in 1984, $350 million in 1985, $140 million in 1986, $160 million in 1987, $210 million in 1988, and $490 million in 1989.[129]

Kuwait's total arms imports during 1981–1985, totaling $1,005 million, reflect its policy of buying from many different sources in an effort to obtain broad diplomatic and political support. Roughly $90 million came from the USSR, $230 million came from the U.S., $360 million from France, $20 million from the UK, $210 million from the FRG, $80 million from Italy, and $15 million from other states.[130] Its total arms imports during 1984–1988 were $1,325 million, with $180 million coming from the USSR, $210 million from the U.S., $525 million from France, $110 million from the UK, $150 million from the FRG, and $150 million from other states.[131] Kuwait imported a total of $1,345 million worth of arms during 1985–1989, $180 million worth from the Soviet Union, $150 million from the U.S., $450 million from France, $110 million from the UK, $5 million from other Warsaw Pact countries, $20 million from other European countries, and $430 million from other Middle Eastern countries.[132]

Kuwait's Military Forces Before the Gulf War

At the time Iraq invaded, Kuwait's military forces had a paper strength of around 20,000 men. These included large numbers of what were little more than Bedouin mercenaries, and Kuwait was heavily dependent on foreign personnel for its technical support, service and logistic support, maintenance, and training. These included British, Jordanian, Pakistani, Egyptian, and French personnel and were often of mediocre quality. When they were competent, they were generally ignored whenever their advice required any change in Kuwaiti bureaucratic procedures.

There were U.S., British, and French military and contractor support missions for virtually all of Kuwait's more advanced and Western-supplied military equipment. It did, however, have some well trained officers, some of whom attended Sandhurst. Other officers and some NCOs and technicians had trained in the U.S., Pakistan, and Jordan. The officer corps and NCOs were relatively loyal and were recruited from the ruling family and loyal tribes. Unfortunately, recruitment and promotion were dominated by favoritism rather than performance.

Kuwait also was unable to recruit its other ranks from its own citizens. Its population before the Iraqi invasion was only about 2.2 million, and less than 30% of this was native Kuwaiti. Other Arabs, including Palestinians, totaled 39%. The rest included 9% South Asians, 4% Iranian, and 20.1% other. Only about 19,500 males reached military age in 1990, and the total male work force from ages 15 to 49—including expatriates—was a mere 442,000.[133]

While Kuwait did try to get its citizens to join the armed forces and offered good pay and privileges, few volunteered in a country that offered so many more rewarding alternatives. A draft was little more successful. In theory, Kuwait has a draft requiring two years of service, except for university students, who only had to serve one year. There were so many exemptions, however, that the draft existed largely on paper. As a result, most of the "Kuwaitis" in the military forces in 1990 were from tribal groups and were not really citizens. These Bedouin were raised as tribal levies, had no reason to be loyal to the Kuwaiti government, were poorly treated and paid, and often deserted.

Kuwait's total army manpower was only about 16,000 men when the Gulf War began in the middle of 1990. While Kuwait's order of battle had two armored brigades, one mechanized brigade, and an artillery brigade with a self-propelled artillery regiment and one surface-to-surface missile battalion, this order of battle was little more than a hollow shell. Its total army manpower was equivalent to only two Western brigade slices, and all of its forces were seriously undermanned.

Kuwait had very limited ability to effectively employ its strength of 275 main battle tanks (of which 165 were first-line Chieftains, 70 were low quality Vickers Mark 1s, and 40 were obsolete Centurions) in anything other than a set-piece defense. Even its Chieftain tanks were underpowered and experienced continuing overheating and maintenance problems.[134] Kuwait had ordered the Yugoslav M-84, an inferior and poorly assembled version of the early Soviet T-72, as a replacement tank, but these were not in service. Kuwait's reasons for purchasing this system are unclear.

Kuwait had more capability to use its lighter armor but only in set-piece defensive maneuvers. This armor included 50 BMP-2 and 100 AT-105 Saxon and Saladin armored fighting vehicles, 100 Saracen and 200 M-113 APCs, and 90 Ferret armored cars. It had British Scorpions and Soviet BMP-2 armored fighting vehicles on order.[135]

Kuwait had bought a wide range of anti-tank weapons, including the AT-4, BGM-71A Improved TOW, HOT, M-47 Dragon, and Vigilant, and it has 56 M-901 ITV armored TOW carriers. It has 4,000 Improved TOW missiles on order. This was a good mix of anti-tank weapons but training and support effort was uncertain.

The artillery strength of the Kuwaiti army included 36 M-109A2 self-propelled and 40 AMX Mark F-3 towed 155mm howitzers and approximately 16 old M-101 towed 105mm howitzers, but it had no combat training in using such artillery beyond set-piece and firing range exercises. Kuwait's surface-to-surface missile battalion had 12 FROG-7 launchers, but these had little more than symbolic importance.

Kuwait was gradually developing improved army land based air defenses, although it had too many diverse types and poor training in operating them. Kuwait had Soviet-supplied SA-7s, SA-6s, and ZSU 23-4s and two batteries of SA-8s. The U.S. had refused to sell it the Stinger, but Kuwait had more SA-7s, Egyptian Saqr Eyes, and gun missile defense systems on order. There were reports of additional orders for SA-6s and SA-8s and for Crotale or Sea Wolf light surface-to-air missile systems, although Britain was then reluctant to sell Kuwait a key system in service in the British navy because it feared losing details of the technology to the USSR.[136]

In terms of basing, the Kuwaiti army had a massive $100 million military complex about 20 miles from Kuwait City. These facilities, however, owed more to political convenience, and an effort to maintain high living standards than to military effectiveness. They were vulnerable to air attack and overcentralized both the deployment of Kuwait's forces and their support functions in fixed locations.

Kuwait's army had poor overall training, little coordination or effective command above the brigade level, and a maintenance and logistic system that was a bureaucratic nightmare in which paperwork had complete priority over military effectiveness. Further, Kuwait lacked the ability to deploy and sustain its forces in the field without foreign civilian support. Kuwait had concluded an agreement with Turkey to provide for more advanced training, but this came too late to affect its military proficiency.[137]

Kuwait was just beginning to create a real navy when Iraq invaded. It had created a 2,100 man naval force to replace its coast guard, but this force was completely dependent on foreign contractors for training, maintenance, logistics, and often actual operations. It was based at Qalayah and Shuwaikh and had recently acquired $29 million worth of new naval facilities. There were major civil ship repair facilities at Kuwait City's Shuwaikh harbor, including a 190 meter floating dock with a 35,000 DWT repair capability.[138]

The core of the Kuwaiti navy consisted of eight Lurssen guided missile patrol boats. Two of these boats were FPB-57s and six were TNC-45s. They had 76mm Oto Melara guns, twin 40mm guns, and four Exocet MM-40 missile launchers each. It should be noted that these patrol boats had some important limitations common to virtually all GCC naval vessels. They lacked air defense capability, and while their voice communications were good, they could not be integrated into a data link exchange network. Crewing them also required nearly 60% of Kuwait's native naval manning.[139]

Kuwait received five 55 meter South Korean missile patrol boats beginning in August, 1987, and these were based in Kuwait's offshore islands. They had anti-ship missiles, helicopter pads, and a Hovercraft docking facility. The ships were not fully combat ready, but they did increase Kuwait's shallow water defense capability. Kuwait also had forty-seven 11–24 meter patrol craft; four modern British Cheverton LCTs, three LCUs, and three LSUs; four tugs, six launches; and some light coastal vessels and support craft. The Kuwaiti air force provided additional support in the form of Super Puma helicopters equipped with Exocet.

Finally, Kuwait had six SRN-6 Hovercraft, Exocet-capable SA 365N Dauphin II helicopters, twenty Magnum Sedan patrol boats, two Italian 18.4 meter patrol boats, two 20 meter Italian patrol boats, and more South Korean patrol boats on order. It was negotiating with the Netherlands to buy two Alkmaar-class mine hunters, and the Dutch parliament had approved the loan of two such vessels until new production was available.

While this naval strength was reasonable for a small navy, it also required a manpower base of 5,000–8,000 men in uniform, or three to four times the manpower Kuwait actually possessed. Kuwait got around some of these requirements by being heavily dependent on foreign technicians, but overall readiness was poor.

Kuwait's 2,200 man air force was slowly improving in effectiveness, and it had roughly 70 combat aircraft and 18 armed helicopters. It had good basing facilities at Kuwait International Airport, Ahmed al-Jaber Air Base, and Ali al-Salem Air Base. Housing and other facilities were good.

Its combat strength included thirty A-4KU/TA-4KU attack fighters, some of which were being placed into storage to await the delivery of new F-18 multirole fighters Kuwait had ordered from the U.S.[140] The A-4s were adequate attack aircraft but had no air combat radars. They could only be used in dogfights where ground based radars or Kuwait's Mirage F-1s guided them to a target. This made them hopelessly inferior to Iraq's modern fighters in air-to-air combat capability.

The air force had an active operational strength of twenty-four new Mirage F-1BK/CK fighters and twelve Mark 64 Hawk COIN/trainer aircraft. Kuwait's air weapons inventory included AIM-9 Sidewinders, Matra Super R-530, and R-550 Magique air-to-air missiles—with AS-11 and AS-12 air-to-surface missiles and twelve AM-39 air-to-ship missiles on order. Kuwait had also ordered the French SA-365N maritime attack system.

The Mirage F-1 aircraft had proved hard to maintain, however, and Kuwait had lost several of the aircraft to accidents. Because the radar of the Mirage F-1 was unreliable and its 55 kilometer air intercept range proved too short to meet Kuwait's operational needs, Kuwait was forced to use its A-4 attack aircraft in the combat air patrol role when it needed to create an air defense screen. Further, Kuwait was so short of air force personnel that it contracted for Pakistani service and support crews.[141]

Kuwaiti training was adequate for interdiction and close air support missions against targets that lacked good ground based air defenses but was not suited for attacks on Iraqi forces. Kuwaiti pilots also had relatively limited air-to-air combat training and were severely hampered by an inadequate air command and control system and air warning and surveillance coverage. Little effort was made to develop a force that could maintain a high alert status or work with the army in effective combined operations. The Mirage F-1s did, however, maintain a limited alert status during the Iran-Iraq War.

Kuwait had ordered 40 U.S. F/A-18 fighters in July, 1985 at a cost of $1.9 billion. This sale also included 120 AIM-9 Sidewinder air-to-air missiles, 200 AIM-4 Sparrows, 40 AGM-84 Harpoon anti-ship missiles, and 300 Maverick AGM-65G anti-ship/anti–hard point missiles. Its U.S. approval, however, came only after a bitter fight between the Reagan administration and Congress. The sale came so close to collapse that the USSR offered Kuwait the MiG-29, and in order for the administration to win approval of the sale, Kuwait had to give up its effort to order 200 IR Maverick AGM-65D anti-tank missiles. Kuwait also had to agree to base the F/A-18s only in Kuwait, not to acquire a refueling capability, and to exchange one A-4KU for every F/A-18 delivered to Kuwait.

This left Kuwait with very limited—if not token—levels of munitions stocks for its new aircraft and without an advanced anti-tank weapon for the F/A-18. Further, the F/A-18s were not to begin delivery until January, 1992, and Kuwait would not receive its active strength of twenty-eight fighters and eight fighter trainers until June, 1993. Its remaining four attrition aircraft would not be delivered until after 1994. Had this schedule been followed, it would have meant major turbulence and transition problems for at least half a decade. Its chief virtue was that it promised to give Kuwait an advanced air defense/air attack fighter and advanced munitions and support facilities standardized with those used by the U.S. Navy and U.S. Marines, which could significantly improve U.S. over-the-horizon reinforcement capability.[142]

The Kuwaiti air force had nine transport aircraft, including one B-707-200, six C-130-30s, and two DC-9s.[143] The air force operated forty-six helicopters; these included twenty-three to thirty SA-342K Gazelle attack helicopters, twenty-three of these equipped with HOT. They also included five to six AS-332 Super Pumas equipped with Exocet and ten to twelve SA-330 Pumas. It had six AS-332F Super Pumas on order. The helicopter crews had moderate training and good foreign maintenance support.

Kuwait had a French-designed semi-automated air defense, control, and warning system, but it had only limited radar coverage of Iraq, Iran, and the Gulf. It also had limited readiness and operational reliability, and Kuwait does not seem to have been able to take advantage of many of the computerized features of the system because of software and training problems. The Kuwaiti air force did benefit from data exchanges with the E-3As flying in Saudi Arabia, but the quality of the data links was uncertain. This system did not allow either Kuwaiti fighters or its surface-to-air missiles to react quickly and effectively enough to deal with Iranian or Iraqi intruders into Kuwait's air space.

In August 1990, Kuwait's air force had five batteries of Improved Hawk surface-to-air missiles with twenty-four twin launcher fire units, twelve SA-8 surface-to-air missile launcher units, and an unknown number of SA-7 and SA-14 manportable surface-to-air missiles. It also had 20mm and 35mm anti-aircraft guns and may have had two Shahine batteries on order. Kuwait had serious problems in absorbing its more sophisticated surface-to-air missiles. This became clear in 1987, when efforts were made to resite the missiles to defend against attacks by Iran's Silkworm missiles. It is unclear how many IHawk units were really combat ready when Iraq invaded. The U.S. refusal to sell Kuwait Stinger missiles in June, 1984 had led Kuwait to delay the purchase of Hawk systems and to respond by buying some $327 million worth of light Soviet arms—none of which could be netted into an effective air defense system.

Finally, Kuwait had separate national guards, palace guards, and border guards equipped with a total of twenty V-150 and sixty-two V-300 Commando armored personnel carriers. The national guards were intended for civil control and had little military capability. The Ministry of the Interior ran special political and anti-terrorist police forces and was responsible for internal intelligence and security. These security and intelligence forces had a poor reputation before Iraq's invasion, and their actions after Kuwait's liberation indicate that this reputation was justified.

Kuwait's Military Forces During the Gulf War

The main factors that led to Iraq's invasion have already been described. It is important to note, however, that Iraq's hostility went beyond Kuwait. In April, 1990 Saddam Hussein claimed a new regional role in leading the area, and he demanded that the U.S. withdraw from the Gulf. On July 1, 1990, he announced that Iraq had binary weapons—"a deterrent sufficient to confront the Israeli nuclear weapon"—and he began a series of speeches threatening all of the southern Gulf states for failing to recognize Iraq as the only nation that had defended them against the Persian threat. On July 17, he accused both Kuwait and the UAE of working with the U.S. to cheat on oil production quotas.

Egypt, Jordan, Saudi Arabia, and the Arab League all made negotiating efforts, but the Iraqi representative walked out of a final meeting in Jiddah, Saudi Arabia, on August 1, 1990, in spite of substantial concessions by Kuwait. He claimed that Kuwait had refused to negotiate over Iraqi claims to Warhab and Bubiyan, was stealing oil from Iraq's Rummaliah oil field, and had refused to negotiate over forgiveness of Iraq's debt to Kuwait. In retrospect, Iraq never seems to have negotiated seriously.

Republican Guard divisions moved south from positions around Baghdad shortly before Saddam Hussein's speech on July 17. A Republican Guard armored division had moved into the Kuwaiti border area by July 21, and some 3,000 military vehicles were on the roads south from Baghdad to the Kuwaiti border. By August 1, there were eight Republican Guard divisions (two armored, one mechanized, one special forces, and four infantry) between Basra and the Kuwaiti border. Some units had moved as far as 700 kilometers from their normal peacetime locations. There was a total strike force of 140,000 troops and more than 1,500 tanks and armored combat vehicles, plus artillery, support, and logistics.[144]

Iraq invaded Kuwait at 0100 Kuwaiti time on August 2, 1990. Three Republican Guard divisions attacked across the Kuwaiti frontier. A mechanized infantry and an armored division led the main attack along an axis from Safwan to Abdally, driving south towards the Al-Jahra pass. Another armored division supported attack further to the west. At 0130, an Iraqi special forces task group attacked Kuwait City in a heliborne assault against key government facilities. Other Iraqi special forces units made an amphibious assault on the emir's palace and other critical locations. The emir escaped to Saudi Arabia, but his brother was killed when Iraqi forces attacked the Dasman Palace.

The three attacking armored and mechanized divisions, supported by Iraqi fighters, quickly linked up at Al-Jahra. The two divisions supporting the main attack continued east to Kuwait City, where they joined up with the heliborne and amphibious special forces units at 0530—a little more than four hours after the invasion began. They had secured the city by 1900 that evening. The remaining Iraqi armored division moved south from Al-Jahra to blocking positions along the main routes into Kuwait from Saudi Arabia. By late on the evening of August 2, Iraqi tanks were moving into Kuwait's ports.

Kuwait's forces were never really given a test. Kuwait's government mobilized after Saddam Hussein's threats on July 17 but reduced the alert levels to 25% a week later and did not bring its forces to combat readiness because of its conviction that its confrontation with Iraq could be solved through peaceful means and fear of provoking Iraq. The key ministers in charge of Kuwait's defense and internal security did nothing to prepare Kuwait's forces for war or to lead them once the war had begun. A number of senior commanders fled south rather than try to rally their troops.[145]

As a result, the most the air force could do was fly a few sorties and flee to Saudi Arabia. The Kuwaiti forces, however, lacked leadership and not courage. Scattered elements of the palace guards and army defended some key buildings for a few hours and tried to recapture the palace. Elements of the Kuwaiti 35th Armored Brigade engaged the advancing Republican Guard forces, and some minor elements of the land forces attempted to defend the southern part of the country. Much of the army, navy, and air defense forces had no choice other than to surrender, however, and much of their equipment was captured intact. Iraqi forces were able to secure the country down to the Kuwaiti-Saudi border by the end of August 3.

On August 4, Iraq began a full scale movement of its forces to establish defensive positions. Additional Republican Guard infantry divisions that had deployed to the border in late July moved into Kuwait, occupied Kuwait City, and secured the routes of communication to Iraq. Other divisions moved south towards Saudi Arabia. By August 6, there were eleven Iraqi divisions in Kuwait, and on August 8 Saddam Hussein announced that Kuwait was the "nineteenth province—an eternal part of Iraq."

Iraq's subsequent brutality and looting of the country created a major resistance element in Kuwait, led largely by Kuwaiti citizens but also involving many Palestinians and non-Kuwaiti Bedouins. Kuwait also created new volunteer liberation forces in Saudi Arabia. On paper, these forces built up to a strength of 11,000–14,000 men by the time of Kuwait's liberation in late February, 1991. In practice, these forces had only limited combat training and could do little more during the battle to liberate Kuwait than perform defensive and internal security roles. Their main contribution to the Arab part of the UN coalition was symbolism—demonstrating that Kuwait was playing a role in its own liberation. In many ways, the various freedom fighters that stayed behind in Kuwait and organized themselves played a far more serious role in tying down Iraqi forces and helping to liberate the country.

When the liberation finally came, Iraq set 732 of Kuwait's 858 operating oil wells on fire.[146] Kuwait's economy had ceased to exist, it had no utilities and urban services, and most of its infrastructure needed repair. Although a number of these problems had developed months before the war, Kuwait's government was unprepared to deal with many aspects of the problems it faced. It took nearly six months to organize itself in Kuwait, largely ignored the freedom fighters that had helped liberate the country, and allowed massive purges of Palestinians and anyone else suspected of aiding Iraq. The results were deeply divisive and did nothing to unite the country around the search for effective defense.

Kuwait's Defense Debates Following the Gulf War

Since its liberation, Kuwait has had to drastically rethink virtually every aspect of its defense plans and force structure. On the one hand, it is brutally clear that Kuwait cannot rely on a combination of diplomatic maneuvering, "aid" to potential threats, and a limited deterrent force for its security. On the other hand, it is equally clear that Kuwait faces the following major strategic problems:

- Its goal of creating a roughly 30,000 man force will not allow it to defend against an Iraqi or Iranian attack but is still too high to be practical. Further, its refusal to offer full citizenship to the children of immigrants, regardless of background and loyalty, deprives it of a critical source of manpower.
- It is acting on the conviction that its military forces must be purged of any elements that are not fully loyal to Kuwait. This had led Kuwait, rightly or wrongly, to reject about half of its pre-invasion manpower.
- The country has no strategic depth and will remain highly vulnerable to Iraq and Iran as long as these nations have major military forces.
- Saudi Arabia and the other GCC states cannot provide the mix of land and air strength necessary to halt an Iraqi attack before it seizes Kuwait or provide the kind of air and missile defense screen necessary to defend Kuwait against Iran.
- Egypt and Syria are unlikely to provide an adequate Arab military force under financial and political conditions that Kuwait finds acceptable and may be unable to project effective military power this far from their home bases.
- The U.S. cannot project land power rapidly enough to move armored and mechanized forces large enough to defeat an Iraqi attack without either a month of strategic warning or a combination of prepositioned equipment, forward deployment force elements, and constant training. At the same time, the effective use of U.S. air power requires access to both Saudi and Kuwaiti bases, prepositioned munitions, and a fully modern and interoperable combination of sheltered air bases, surface-to-air defenses, and C^3I systems.

The full nature of Kuwait's solution to those problems is unclear at this time. It is awaiting the completion of U.S., British, and Kuwaiti studies of its future force requirements. At the same time, it is trying to pursue a combination of restructuring Kuwaiti forces, encouraging U.S. prepositioning, seeking to strengthen its military ties to Saudi Arabia, and negotiating with Egypt. The success of these efforts is as unpredictable as the rate at which Iran and Iraq will rearm. Kuwait has, however, begun actively to rebuild its forces.

While it is impossible clearly to distinguish Kuwait's defense spending from its aid to the nations in the UN coalition that liberated it, it spent at least $1.5 billion in rebuilding its forces in Saudi Arabia after its territory was occupied by Iraq, and some $5 billion in 1991. Some reports talk about future spending levels as high as $9 billion a year, but this raises serious questions about financing. As has been touched upon earlier, Kuwait spent more than $10 billion on war-related expenses. While its assets ranged from $80–100 billion before the war, some estimates put its assets at around $30–50 billion after the conflict, and Kuwait has obligations to pay for oil field repairs and modernization and pay off bad debts from its stock market scandal of several years earlier. The emirate incurred a massive budget deficit in 1991 and 1992 and borrowed $5.5 billion in a syndicated loan from commercial banks.[147]

Kuwait has experienced major problems with manpower. It has driven out some 300,000 Palestinians, and while they never played a direct role in Kuwait's military forces, they did staff some of the Ministry of Defense's technical and support function, including some aspects of contracting and procurement. Kuwait has also purged its army of some 10,000 Bedouin who were not Kuwaiti citizens but who generally fought well against the Iraqis or in the resistance. Its remaining eligible male population is only about 160,000, and it recruited only 1,000 citizens into the armed forces in 1991— partly because of its failure to integrate the resistance into the armed forces and the royal family's failure to provide convincing new leadership for the armed forces.[148]

This has given Kuwait new forces of between 8,200 and 9,200 men, or about half the manpower it had before the Iraqi invasion. This manpower seems to be largely Kuwaiti and to include large numbers of personnel recruited for the liberation of Kuwait after August, 1990. Most of this manpower seems to be composed of actual citizens, although Kuwait has had to bring back some of the Bedouin it fired from the armed forces, and there is no sign of a draft. Kuwait is heavily dependent on foreign personnel for its technical support, service and logistic support, maintenance, and training. U.S., British, and French military and contractor support missions have returned to Kuwait.[149]

There are serious morale and leadership problems among Kuwait's officers and enlisted men. Rightly or wrongly, many feel that their senior commanders were often promoted purely for family and political reasons and deserted in the face of the enemy when Iraq attacked. Many feel the royal family deliberately ignored those who fought in the resistance and allowed postwar contracts to be awarded out of favoritism and corruption. They also question the government's efforts to study what went wrong and learn from the lessons of the war.

These feelings have gone beyond silent resentment. In April, 1991 a group of senior officers sent the emir a letter calling for the investigation and dismissal of Defense Minster Sheik Nawaf al-Ahmed al-Sabah for failing to mobilize, for pulling forces back from the border shortly before the invasion, for ordering the Kuwaiti tanks in the border area not to fire on the advancing Iraqi troops, and for fleeing the country without giving orders to Kuwait's forces once the war had begun. They also called for the investigation of Interior Minister Sheik Salem Sabah al-Salem for taking no action to provide suitable warning and internal security measures. The emir dealt with this situation by making al-Sabah minister of social affairs and labor, but he also made al-Salem the new minister of defense.[150]

In January, 1992 the government faced a revolt by junior and mid-grade officers. They demanded the resignation of up to 100 military officers and defense personnel, including 20 generals and a number of members of the royal family. Some 14 officers were retired, but this did not satisfy military or public opinion. While the new minister of defense, al-Salem, has gradually improved relations with some of the military, the royal family will have to do much to rebuild the respect and loyalty of the armed forces.[151]

Kuwait also faces major uncertainties as to whether it will ever recover the equipment that Iraq seized and took back to Iraq. The Kuwaiti minister of defense stated in 1992 that Iraq would not give back the equipment and that Kuwait would not take back equipment in the condition that it would be in after Iraqi use. He accused Jordan of working with Iraq to ensure that Iraq can use the IHawks it took from Kuwait, and indicated that Kuwait would requip Kuwait's forces on the basis of British, Kuwaiti, and U.S. studies of Kuwaiti security needs.[152]

At virtually the same time, however, the Kuwaiti deputy chief of staff, Brig. Gen. Jaber al-Sabah stated that Iraq had agreed to return all captured equipment by summer 1992 and that this included 200 Chieftain tanks, many Soviet BMP-2 armored fighting vehicles, and hundreds of trucks. At the same time, however, he indicated that Iraq was actively testing its captured IHawks, that some of the A-4s Iraq had captured had been so damaged that they had to be flown back to Kuwait in slings, that six Mirage F-1s had been declared missing or destroyed, that four Hawk trainers were returned in bad condition, that a returned C-130 had been seriously damaged, and that the patrol boats Iraq returned to Kuwait had been damaged so severely that they had to be returned by land.[153]

Kuwait's Military Forces After the Gulf War

Kuwait's army manpower totaled about 8,500 regulars in mid-1992. It was loosely organized into two mechanized armored brigades and a special forces battalion, with three infantry brigades forming, although the best brigade had only 1,000–1,500 men and its actual manpower was equivalent to less than one Western brigade slice. Most of Kuwait's units have only one-fourth their prewar strength.[154]

Its armor consisted of about 18 surviving Chieftains and roughly 90 Yugoslav M-84 equivalents of the T-72, out of some 110 on order. The M-84 tanks were not fully equivalent to the T-72 and had mediocre armor and relatively unsophisticated fire control and sighting systems.

Kuwait is discussing the purchase of U.S. M-1A2 or British Challenger 2 main battle tanks as a substitute and matching U.S. M-2 or British Warrior armored fighting vehicles to modernize its forces. It needs at least 200 new tanks and AFVs and may buy more as a form of prepositioning for British or U.S. reinforcements. There were reports in late September 1992 that Kuwait might buy as many as 760 tanks and 644 armored infantry carrying vehicles.

Kuwait held trials to choose these new tanks in August and September of 1992. The U.S. M-1A2 seemed to have the advantage, with a top speed of 65 km/h versus 50 for the Challenger 2, superior braking, three hits out of three at 2,000 meters versus one out of three, ten hits versus eight at 4,000 meters, six hits firing on a slope versus two, and four hunter killer hits in 32 seconds out of four fired versus three hits out of four in 66 seconds. Similarly, the M-2 Bradley outscored the Warrior with a 90% hit-on-the-move score versus 16% for the Warrior, and three TOW hits out of three firings versus one for the Warrior. Some reports indicated, however, that Kuwait might make a political decision to buy land equipment from the UK, naval equipment from France, and air equipment from the U.S. in an effort to ensure multiple sources of reinforcements.[155]

Other armor included 40–50 BMP-2s, 10–15 BDRMs, some Ferret and Saladin armored fighting vehicles, about 45–50 M-113s, 35–45 Fahd APCs, some armored mortar carriers, and roughly 20 special purpose and armored engineering vehicles. It was discussing orders of British GKN warriors and other armored vehicles and had ordered up to 700 unarmored Humvee troop carriers and support vehicles. Kuwait's surviving anti-tank weapons and new orders included TOW and HOT anti-tank guided weapons and at least 200 Carl Gustav 84mm rocket launchers.[156]

The artillery strength of the Kuwaiti army included several M-109A2 self-propelled 155mm howitzers; M-56 and M-101 towed 105mm howitzers; some 122mm, 130mm, and 152mm weapons that seem to have been captured from Iraq; and a few multiple rocket launchers. It was discussing an order of 18 GIAT 155mm artillery weapons from France and 78 155mm artillery weapons from ARMSCOR in South Africa.[157] Surviving army land based air defenses included SA-7s, SA-14s, ZSU-23-4s, and some 14.5mm and 20mm light anti-aircraft guns.

In spite of U.S. and Saudi training during the war with Iraq, Kuwait's restructured land forces have substantially less military capability than before the war, particularly in any form of maneuver, independent artillery action, or use of armor. The army still depends on foreign civilian support to sustain its forces in the field.

Kuwait faces equal problems in restructuring its navy and air force. In terms of basing, the Kuwaiti army must rebuild its military complexes at virtually every level, although many buildings were intact. This involves at least $275 million in damage for all eleven of Kuwait's military bases.[158]

The Kuwaiti navy had only about 300 men in its naval forces in mid-1992 based at Adami and Shuwaikh. It was not able to use most of its base at Qalayah near Mina Sud, although some reconstruction was under way. It lost most of its twenty-three ships and its main force of eight missile patrol boats, and its only major surviving naval craft consist of one FPB-57 and one TNC-45 missile patrol boat. These each have one 76mm Oto Melara gun, twin 40mm guns, and four Exocet MM-40 missile launchers (two twin launchers).[159]

Kuwait will have to completely rebuild its naval base, 100 kilometers south of Kuwait City. The Kuwaiti navy has, however, been reequipped with seventeen small patrol boats from Britain's Cougar Marine. These boats replace those destroyed during the war, and some of the boats were used by Kuwait's forces during the liberation of Kuwait. The seventeen boats include three catamarans, three 33' ultra-fast patrol boats, three 35' ultra-fast patrol boats, four 38' ultra-fast patrol boats, and four small ultra-fast patrol boats. The five South Korean Seagull-class patrol boats Kuwait had ordered in 1986 were seized by Iraq and were destroyed during the war, but Kuwait still has to take delivery on five more ordered in 1988. The coast guard also has two Australian 30 meter patrol boats on order.[160]

Kuwait's air force consisted of about 200 regulars and 800 support personnel, or half its prewar strength. Its two main bases at Ali al-Salem (Al-Jahra) north of Kuwait City and Ahmed al-Jaber (Al-Ahmadi) south of Kuwait City suffered serious damage. Its forces were operating out of Kuwait City airport, although the U.S. Corps of Engineers was rushing repairs on both bases and hoped to have the base at Ali al-Salem completed in time to base Kuwait's new F/A-18s by late 1992.[161]

It had roughly 20 A-4KU/TA-4KU attack fighters out of a prewar total of 30, 15 Mirage F-1BK/CK fighters out of a prewar total of 23, and 6 surviving armed Hawk trainers. Many of these surviving aircraft had only limited operational capability, although Kuwait retained a stock of Matra 530 and 550 missiles.[162]

Kuwait was, however, taking delivery of its first F/A-18C/Ds. Its order of 32 U.S. F/A-18C and 8 F/A-18D fighters, AIM-9 Sidewinder air-to-air missiles, AIM-4 Sparrows, AGM-84 Harpoon anti-ship missiles, and Maverick AGM-65G anti-ship/anti–hard point missiles has become critical to rebuilding an effective air force. Kuwait had taken delivery of 12 F/A-18C/Ds by June, 1992 and was discussing the order of up to 35 more of these aircraft with the U.S., as well as plans to refurbish 15 of its Mirage F-1s with France. It had also ordered 12 Tucano T Mark trainers and was considering the purchase of British Hawk trainer fighters.[163]

Many of Kuwait's other aircraft were destroyed or seized during the war. The air force did, however, retain 12 SA-342K Gazelle attack helicopters equipped with HOT anti-tank guided missiles and 5–6 AS-332 Super Pumas and 6 SA-330 Pumas. It also had some C-130 transport aircraft. Kuwait was also planning to expand its attack helicopter force through the purchase of 20 AH-64 Apache attack helicopters. The Apache will present problems because it requires roughly the same training and support effort as a modern fighter aircraft. It does, however, offer a number of unique advantages to a nation like Kuwait. It is a highly lethal day-night all-weather tank killer that can quickly reach any position in Kuwait and can evade or survive many of the mobile short range air defenses in Iraqi and Iranian forces. Its Hellfire missiles can be used against landing and small craft as well, and it can perform an armed reconnaissance mission, which the Gazelle cannot. In a country as small as Kuwait, it can be based out of major airfields, which reduces the support problem, and Kuwait's purchase of the AH-64 improves its ability to support and interoperate with a key weapon in U.S. power projection forces.[164]

Kuwait's land based air defense system was virtually destroyed during the war, along with most of its radars and light air defense batteries. Its four batteries of Improved Hawk surface-to-air missiles were transferred to Iraq, with little immediate prospect of their recovery. As a result, Kuwait was in the process of rebuilding its air defenses from the ground up. It had placed a $2.5 billion order with the U.S. for six Improved Hawk batteries, six Patriot fire units, and 450 Patriot and 342 IHawk guided missiles. Egypt has also indicated that Kuwait may order two battalions' worth of the Amoun defense system. This would include eight modified four round Sparrow surface-to-air missile launchers, Oerlikon-Contraves twin 35mm towed anti-aircraft guns, four modified Skyguard fire control systems, and two longer range radars—possibly the AN-TPS-63.[165]

It is not clear what degree of integration Kuwait will achieve with Saudi Arabia and Bahrain, but such movement will determine Kuwait's future security and the ability of the West to reinforce Kuwait, with its limited air space, common border with Iraq, and proximity to Iran. No Kuwaiti-based system can provide survivable air defense and land and maritime surveillance unless it is integrated into a Saudi system, preferably one closely tied to Bahrain, Qatar, and the UAE.

Kuwait is also considering building a security fence similar to the one under study by Saudi Arabia. This fence would consist of IR sensors, pressure sensors, electrified wires, trenches, barbed wire, and electronic sensors. The Ministry of Interior would operate the fence, and it would cover the entire 198 kilometer (124 mile) border with Iraq. Contending companies have proposed different approaches to such a system. Thomson-CSF and Thorn favor infrared sensors. Racal Comsec and Hughes favor terrestrial sensors and pressure cable sensors, and some experts favor tethered aerostats carrying radars. Western advisors, however, have cautioned that such a fence could be a waste of money. While the sensors might have some value, the fence would have little use as a barrier and could be highly manpower intensive.[166]

Strategic Interests and Arms Control

There are many reasons to criticize the leadership that the Kuwaiti royal family has shown since the war. The Kuwaiti government has done many things well, but it has wasted money in many areas while failing to spending them in others, and its policy toward its Palestinians and other immigrants has been far more vindictive than sensible. Its citizenship policies seem likely to contribute to further internal security problems and limit its military manpower. Kuwait is also the one southern Gulf country that could easily move toward more democratic reform, and the failure of the royal family to lead reform is also likely to create future internal security problems. It is unfortunate that a nation that has both outstanding younger members of its royal family and outstanding technocrats is being led by an older generation of the Sabah family, ministers, and civil servants who fall far short of the leadership qualities the nation needs.

Nevertheless, the West has no choice other than to provide Kuwait with arms and support. Kuwait has no immediate prospect of being able to defend its own territory. It requires substantial additional arms imports if it is to create a limited regional deterrent or to acquire the levels of munitions, weapons, and military facilities to allow either an Arab or U.S. force to come to its aid. Without access to such arms imports, Kuwait will be hopelessly weak. Further, Kuwait has no foreseeable chance of reducing its dependence on foreign technicians or support during the next decade. It will be unable to use its arms against any nation without supplier assistance, although Iran and Iraq could operate many Kuwaiti weapons systems if these were seized in a future invasion.

The Gulf Cooperation Council offers no near or midterm prospect of supplying the kind of reinforcements that could defend Kuwait's northern border. While outside Arab forces could help secure Kuwait, Egypt is the only nation that could provide sustainable and combat effective forces, and it is not structured to provide this kind of power projection force. Even if Kuwait and Egypt reached a political and financial agreement, Egypt lacks anything approaching the high technology power projection capabilities of the United States.

Kuwait has shown that it is willing to make major investments in its own defense. In late August, 1992 Kuwait announced that it would spend a total of 3.5 billion Kuwaiti dinars ($12 billion) on modernization efforts and advanced weapons over the next twelve years. The Higher Defense Council was authorized to spend these funds beginning in FY1992–93. It also indicated that it had spent 6.2 billion Kuwaiti dinars in FY1990–91 and might spend 4 billion dinars in FY1991–92. These sums evidently did not include nonrecurrent war costs of 4.5 billion dinars in FY1991–92, and 2.1 billion dinars in FY1992–93.[167]

Kuwait will require the support of U.S. and other Western forces in any serious crisis with Iraq and Iran until well after the year 2000. This explains why Kuwait signed a 10 year joint defense agreement with the U.S. in September, 1991. The agreement allowed the U.S. to preposition stocks and equipment on Kuwaiti soil and gave the U.S. access to its ports and airfields in an emergency. It called for Kuwait to pay the U.S. $215 million for prepositioning aid and support, including $50 million in 1992. Prepositioning was to include the equipment for three armored companies and three mechanized companies, including 58 M-1A2 tanks, M-2s, artillery, and other equipment, plus the construction of some $125 million in storage and reception facilities.

The agreement also provided for joint training. U.S. and Kuwaiti forces had completed two joint exercises by May, 1992: One involved 2,300 Marines and the other 1,000 special forces. Kuwait reached a similar agreement with Britain in February, 1992 and conducted its first joint exercise with British forces in May. It is likely to sign a similar agreement with France.

The importance of such strategic cooperation became all too clear in August and September of 1992. The confrontation between Iraq and the UN over the elimination of weapons of mass destruction and Iraq's treatment of its Shi'ites and Kurds forced the U.S. to transform U.S. Army, Marine Corps, and Navy exercises into a demonstration that the U.S. could protect Kuwait against any military adventures by Iraq. The U.S. rushed Patriot batteries to both Kuwait and Bahrain, conducting a test prepositioning exercise called Native Fury 92, and an amphibious reinforcement exercise called Eager Mace 92. It deployed 1,900 Marines and 2,400 soldiers, including two armored and two mechanized companies.[168]

The practical problem with such agreements is that Kuwait has virtually no strategic depth, and Iraq and Iran can threaten access to Kuwait in a crisis. Further, Iraq will soon recover sufficient military capability to overrun Kuwait and equipment prepositioned in Kuwait. Effective security arrangements in the upper Gulf require similar Western agreements with Saudi Arabia, which has so far refused to sign them.

Bahrain

	Manpower (1,000s)	Tanks	Aircraft	Defense Spending ($ millions)	Arms Imports ($ millions)	Arms Exports ($ millions)
1967	2	—	—	—	—	—
1973	2	—	—	5	—	—
1982	2	—	—	281	5	—
1988	5	54	12	187	30	—
1991	7	80	24	201	—	—

Bahrain is one of the smallest countries in the Middle East, with a total land area of 620 square kilometers—roughly the size of the greater metropolitan area of Washington, D.C. The main island has a coastline of 161 kilometers and is connected by a causeway with Saudi Arabia. It is within a short flying time from Iraq and is very vulnerable to any naval or air attack from Iran.

Bahrain has long disputed the control of islands and reefs between Bahrain and Qatar. There have been several armed incidents when the two countries have deployed troops or contested control of the sixteen Hawar Islands (where Bahrain quietly maintains military forces) and reef or shoal of Fasht-e-Dibal. The most serious incident between the two countries occurred in 1985–1986. Bahrain built a coast guard station on the Fasht-e-Dibal in 1985, attempting to assert sovereignty over the area. On April 26, 1986, Qatari troops landed by helicopter and arrested the Bahraini forces on the shoal. Qatar occupied the site for over a month, until Bahrain agreed to destroy the facilities it had built.[169]

Bahrain's total population is only 537,000, and only a little over 60% of that population is native Bahraini. This mix of size and population does not allow Bahrain to develop significant military forces.

Bahrain is a monarchy ruled by the Khalifa family, which has been in power for most of the period since 1783, although the Iranian Safavid dynasty sometimes dominated the country from 1602 to 1782. It became one of the British trucial states in 1861, as part of Britain's effort to secure the approaches to India and as part of Kuwait's own effort to secure its position against the Ottomans and Iranians. It signed treaties expanding Britain's role in 1880 and 1892. Oil was first discovered in Bahrain in 1932, and this early oil wealth has made it one of the most sophisticated states in the southern Gulf.

Once Britain decided to leave the Gulf in January, 1968, it joined Bahrain to a federation that included Qatar and the seven sheikdoms that later became the United Arab Emirates. While this federation was established in July, 1968, both Bahrain and Qatar were then far more developed states than the emirates that became part of the UAE and had little reason to stay in a federation that promised to create as many political and economic problems as it would solve. As a result, Bahrain chose full independence in 1971, when Britain left the Gulf.

Ever since, Bahrain has been allied with Saudi Arabia and the United States. The U.S. naval task force in the Gulf has both shielded Bahrain and benefited from the use of Bahrain's port and airfield. Bahrain provided the U.S. with extensive support and naval and air facilities during its intervention in the Gulf in 1987–1988, when the U.S. checked Iranian efforts to interfere with Kuwaiti and Saudi shipping. It provided equally strong support in 1990–1991 during the Gulf War and signed a formal security agreement with the U.S. in 1991.

Bahrain is deeply divided in ethnic and religious terms. The ruling Khalifa family is Sunni, although 70% of Bahrain's totally Islamic population is Shi'ite. Bahrain is also divided along national and ethnic lines. About 63% is Bahraini, 13% Asian, 10% other Arab, 8% Iranian, and 6% a mix of other groups.[170] The result is a society where the native Shi'ites rule and prosper through discrimination and subordination of the Shi'ites and non-Arabs.

These divisions have created a number of political and security problems. The large number of Shi'ites and Iranians led the shah of Iran to make a claim to Bahrain in 1970, although he desisted in this claim after Britain refused to acknowledge it. It also helped lead to the breakup of Bahrain's constituent assembly. Created in 1972, this assembly broke up in 1975 in large part because of left wing political pressure led by Shi'ite politicians. There is considerable evidence that Iran sponsored a coup attempt in Bahrain in 1981 after Khomeini came to power. This coup attempt or uprising was broken up before any fighting began but has left an increased heritage of friction between the ruling family and many younger Shi'ites.[171]

The Khalifa regime has made efforts to improve social services, but it still tends to be discriminatory in dealing with the nation's Shi'ite majority and has not extended equal privileges to its large "foreign" population—a problem which is of considerable importance in a nation where less than 12% of the people can trace their roots back to families that were living in Bahrain in 1921.[172]

The current ruler, Sheik Isa ibn-Salman al-Khalifa, does hold frequent meetings of his Majlis and has made some statements that promise additional democracy. Bahrain does, however, have strict censorship and limits activities of trade unions. Its criminal justice system is administered primarily to ensure internal security, as the government's favoritism and corruption have created growing hostility among younger Shi'ites, leading to several sabotage attempts.

The royal family is able to move freely with only moderate security measures, but two new arms caches were discovered in 1984, and as many as 30 people may have been arrested. A new and relatively well organized opposition movement called the Islamic Front began to form cells in the Shi'ite villages in 1986 and had organized some cells to conduct guerrilla and sabotage operations in 1987. This led to 60–100 arrests in 1988. While only about 10% of Bahrain's Shi'ites currently seem to sympathize actively with the more open and radical opposition to the emir, this is at least partly the result of constant efforts by Bahrain's British-led security services, bribes and cooption of opposition elements, and the surveillance imposed by a large network of informers.

Bahrain is still an oil power, but a small one by Gulf standards as its reserves are declining. As of January 1, 1992, it had estimated proved oil reserves of up to 83,490 million barrels and gas reserves of 48,000 billion cubic feet. It had far less than 1% of the world's total oil reserves and produced at a rate of only about 38,000 barrels per day during 1990 and 1991.[173] Even this production was made possible only by a huge workover of its oil field and gas injection and could be sustained for a maximum of just 30 years. Bahrain is already making full use of its gas reserves, and more than 80% of the oil that flows through its refinery now comes from Saudi Arabia.[174]

Bahrain is not a wealthy state by southern Gulf standards. Although 85% of its export receipts, 60% of its government revenues, and 20% of its GDP come from petroleum products and processing, it is heavily dependent on a refinery using Saudi oil and an aluminum smelter built largely with Saudi aid to support much of its economy. It has long had budget deficits which have been offset by Saudi aid and has no practical way to expand its aluminum production (which accounts for another 10% of its GDP). Its GDP is around $3.5 billion. Its Sunnis generally have substantially higher incomes than its Shi'ites.[175]

Bahrain experienced a sharp contraction of its offshore banking operations as a result of recent wars and the oil glut that began in the mid-1980s. This has cut per capita income from $10,000 in 1985 to around $7,000 in 1992.[176] It has also created an unusual amount of unemployment among the native labor forces, particularly among young Shi'ites. Saudi Arabia does, however, seem likely to continue to subsidize Bahrain's 250,000 barrel per day BAPCO refinery by providing 70% of its oil. Bahrain has developed a considerable tourist industry because of its liberal social policies, however, and is diversifying into industries using its still extensive gas feedstock.

Bahrain's Military Manpower, Military Expenditures, and Arms Imports

Bahrain's total male manpower pool is about 188,000, counting the population from 15 to 49. The CIA estimates that 104,000 males are fit for military service, but this includes a large number of foreigners, and only 42% of the labor force is Bahraini.[177] The IISS estimates that there are 22,100 males between the ages of 13 and 17, 20,400 between the ages of 18 and 22, and 45,800 between the ages of 23 and 32.[178] Military service is not a popular career, and few native Shi'ites are allowed into the armed forces, but at least half of Bahrain's officers, NCOs, and technicians are native. Bahrain is, however, heavily dependent on foreign contract personnel for support.

Bahrain's military expenditures have always been low by Gulf standards.[179] ACDA estimates that Bahrain spent $108 million on military forces in 1978, $143 million in 1979, $157 million in 1980, $215 million in 1981, $281 million in 1982, $166 million in 1983, $148 million in 1984, $151 million in 1985, $161 million in 1986, $160 million in 1987, $187 million in 1988, and $196 million in 1989.[180] Bahrain spends about 4–8% of its GDP and 10–20% of its central government expenditures on defense. These expenditures rose by a limited amount in 1990 and 1991 because there was little Bahrain could do to expand its forces to respond to the Gulf War. The IISS estimates that Bahrain's military expenditures were $183 million in 1989, $201.9 million in 1990, and $193.9 million in 1991. Bahrain did, however, lose nearly $2 billion because of the collapse of trade and tourism and spent over $50 million beyond its defense budget to help UN coalition forces.[181]

Bahrain has also spent comparatively little on arms. ACDA estimates that Bahrain imported $20 million worth of arms in 1979, $40 million in 1980, $40 million in 1981, $5 million in 1982, $30 million in 1983, $40 million in 1984, $10 million in 1985, $50 million in 1986, $370 million in 1987, $30 million in 1988, and $50 million in 1989.[182] It also estimates that Bahrain took delivery on $120 million worth of arms during 1979–1983. This included $10 million worth of arms from the U.S., $40 million from France, $40 million from West Germany, $10 million from Italy, and $20 million from other countries.[183] Bahrain took delivery on $505 million worth of arms during 1984–1988. This included $250 million worth of arms from the U.S., $60 million from France, $2.5 million from the PRC, $5 million from the UK, $180 million from the FRG, and $5 million from other countries.[184] ACDA's 1992 tallies show that Bahrain imported a total of $515 million worth of arms during 1985–1989, with $260 million from the U.S., $50 million from France, $5 million from the UK, and $200 million from Germany.[185]

The Bahraini Army

In 1992 Bahrain's military forces totaled a maximum of about 7,450 men, including a number of Pakistanis, Jordanians, and Sudanese. Its army had 6,000 men, organized into a tank battalion, two infantry battalions, a special forces battalion, an armored car squadron, two field artillery batteries, and two mortar batteries. A small company or battalion sized element is deployed to King Khalid City as part of the GCC's Peninsular Shield Force. Bahrain's tank and infantry battalions are the size of regiments in several other Arab countries and total 1,000 to 1,500 men.

The army mixes U.S. and French equipment and has been expanding relatively rapidly for such a small force. It has 81 M-60A3 tanks and 22 AML-90 armored infantry fighting vehicles.[186] Its other armored vehicles include

10 AT-105 Saxon and 111 Panhard AML-M-3/VTT APCs and 20 Ferret, Shoreland, and Saladin armored cars in its security forces. It has 8 105mm and 22 M-198 155mm towed artillery weapons. It also has 10 120mm mortars, limited numbers of 81mm mortars, 15 BGM-71A TOW and TOW-2 anti-tank guided weapons, 26 106–120mm recoilless rifles, and large numbers of LAWs and other rocket launchers.

The army operates Bahrain's air defenses, which include approximately 10 Crotale launchers, 40 RBS-70 surface-to-air missile fire units, and 20 manportable Stinger surface-to-air missile launchers. Bahrain also has 10–15 radar guided 35mm Oerlikon air defense guns and 10–15 obsolete unguided 40mm anti-aircraft guns.[187]

The army is all volunteer, relatively well paid, has good privileges and housing, and is manned with Sunnis and carefully screened foreigners. Nevertheless, it has many qualitative problems. It has suffered from the loss of a number of Jordanian officers and personnel that served in the army as a result of Jordan's support of Iraq during the Gulf War.[188] Many of its combat elements are still transitioning into full combat capability and are dependent on foreign advisors.

The army has not been able fully to absorb the new equipment Bahrain ordered as a result of the Iran-Iraq and Gulf wars and has a number of training, maintenance, support, and logistic problems. It is heavily dependent on foreign technicians and often lacks the expertise to properly manage and coordinate their efforts. Training and proficiency levels are inadequate if the army has to go into combat against a foreign force. The army is also poorly equipped for point defense of its own forces and Bahraini territory. The army is, however, probably effective to suppress any uprising or coup by any radical element in the nation's Shi'ite majority.

Bahrain faces serious problems in covering all of its territory with its small land forces and limited firepower. Bahrain consists of a total of thirty-three islands, and it has a very poor ratio of firepower to manpower. It is seeking to obtain the U.S. multiple launch rocket system as a force multiplier and has ordered nine fire units.[189] The MLRS offers about sixteen times as much firepower as a 155mm gun and has the range to cover most of Bahrain. It would also provide Bahrain with considerable firepower in any confrontation with Qatar over the Fasht-e-Dibal and Hawar Islands.[190]

Bahrain also badly needs a medium surface-to-air missile system that is linked to an effective command and control system and sensor net. The Improved Hawk would provide such a capability, but it would have to be linked to a forward deployed radar system and the Saudi air defense system to be fully effective. Bahrain cannot provide sufficient warning against an Iraqi or Iranian air attack without the support of Saudi or U.S. AWACS or U.S. ships and maritime patrol aircraft.[191]

The Bahraini Navy

Bahrain is slowly building up its naval forces. Its navy, part of the Ministry of Interior, had 300 men in early 1988 and was equipped with two 632-ton Lurssen 62-001 63 meter missile corvettes. These were armed with two twin MM-40 Exocet missile launchers, dual purpose Oto Melara 76mm guns, two twin Breda 40mm guns, and two triple 234mm torpedo tubes and carried a SA-365F helicopter. Bahrain had two Lurssen TNC(FPB)-45 missile fast patrol boats with four single cell MM-40 Exocets. Bahrain also had two Lurssen FPB-38 gunboats with two 40mm twin Bofors and twenty-two other small patrol boats ranging from 11 to 15.3 meters.[192]

Since that time, Bahrain has built its navy up to the point where it had roughly 650–1,000 men in 1992. It still had two Lurssen 62-001 63 meter missile corvettes, but it now had four 259-ton Lurssen TNC(FPB)-45 missile fast patrol boats. These were armed with four single cell MM-40 Exocets, a 76mm gun, and two twin Breda 40mm guns. Bahrain also had two Lurssen 38 fast attack craft armed with twin Breda 40mm guns and mine launchers, a 420-ton LCU support ship, two amphibious craft, eleven small and coastal patrol craft, seven small craft, one Hovercraft, and one tug. Four more U.S. landing craft are on order.[193]

While the navy has some good native personnel, it is dependent on foreign advisors and it will take Bahrain some time before it can effectively man and operate its ships. Bahrain's small navy will also remain dependent on expatriate support to maintain and operate some of its more advanced sensors, weapons systems, and communications gear.

Bahrain is, however, getting considerable support from the U.S. Middle East force, which uses the island's harbor and wharfage facilities. The U.S. Navy has long had close relations with Bahrain's navy, and these relations have become even closer as a result of the U.S. buildup in the Gulf in 1987–1988 and the Gulf War. Bahrain's naval base at Jufair is also well equipped, and it has excellent commercial shipbuilding and repair capabilities.

Bahrain has a separate 180 man coast guard, also under the Ministry of Interior. It is equipped with six coastal patrol craft, ten motorized dhows, three landing craft, and one Hovercraft. This force has a large number of British advisors and seems to be effective, but it is more a police and customs force than a military force.

The Bahraini Air Force

Bahrain's air force acquired its first modern combat aircraft—four F-5Es and two F-5Fs—in 1986. In 1992 it had an 800 man force with twenty-four combat aircraft and twelve armed helicopters. Its main combat aircraft still consisted of eight F-5Es and four F-5Fs.[194] It was, however, deploying eight F-16Cs and four F-16Ds that it had purchased in 1990. Bahrain also had twelve AB-212 helicopters, eight of which are armed with SS-12 missiles, machine guns, and rockets, and four armed Bo-105 helicopters. Three of the unarmed AB-212s are equipped with Bendix 1400 long range maritime radars. Most of these aircraft are based at Sheik Isa Air Base, a large, modern air base on the main island.

The operation of Bahrain's combat aircraft is dependent on foreign technical support, but Bahrain's air force has trained some good native pilots. It also has done a reasonably good job of structuring its arms orders. When Bahrain ordered its F-16s from the U.S. in January, 1987 and June, 1988, it did so as part of a $400 million arms package that included a total of 16 F-16C/D fighters, Sidewinder air-to-air missiles, AGM-65 Maverick air-to-surface missiles, AN/A LE-40 chaff dispensers, and spares, support, and training. It also bought AN/ALQ-131 electronic countermeasure pods.[195]

Bahrain has since ordered eight Apache AH-64 attack helicopters and is discussing orders of the Patriot with the U.S. and Saudi Arabia. Like the MLRS, the AH-64s furnish the kind of long range strike system that gives Bahrain the ability rapidly to defend all the coasts on its main island as well as its smaller islands. The U.S. deployed a Patriot battery to Bahrain in August, 1992 because of rising tension with Iraq, and this provided Bahrain's first real air defense system as well as protection against missile attacks. The Patriot may be technically and financially ambitious for Bahrain, but permanent siting of such a unit would greatly extend the lethality and area coverage of its air defenses and provide a limited ballistic missile defense capability.[196]

Its latest orders will give Bahrain a total of twelve F-5s, sixteen F-16s, eight AH-64s, Improved Hawk missiles, and possibly Patriots. Bahrain's air force should be able to complete the transition to the F-16 and A-64 by the mid-1990s. It will, however, remain dependent on foreign maintenance and technical support through at least the year 2000.

Bahrain's command and control system has been improved by the creation of a modern underground operations center at Sheik Isa Air Base, and Bahrain now seems to have secure digital, voice, and Teletype links to Saudi Arabia and to U.S. ships. Yet, Bahrain still seems to do a mediocre job in using these links internally and in cooperating on air and maritime traffic data with Saudi Arabia and the other GCC states. Bahrain has Cossor SSR and Plessey Watchman air traffic control radars or is acquiring them.

Bahrain will have adequate warning of an Iranian or Iraqi attack, however, only if it receives information from an airborne warning and air control platform like the U.S. or Saudi AWACS and if it is fully integrated into Saudi Arabia's air defense system. There are tentative plans to provide for such integration as part of the Saudi Yamamah 2 program. Both Hughes and Ferranti have made proposals that would provide a major improvement in regional air defense capability and U.S. air reinforcement capability, particularly if the Saudi-Bahraini system were integrated with that of Kuwait and the UAE.

Bahrain's Internal Security Forces

Bahrain's British- and Pakistani-led internal security forces include a 9,000 man police force called the Public Security Force, which is larger than the army and part of the Ministry of Interior. It is well armed with light weaponry and has two Hughes 500, two Bell 412, and one Bell 205 helicopters. There seems to be some rivalry between the army and police. The police, however, seem to be the dominant internal security force and are supported by elite security, counter-terrorist, and intelligence units. These forces are virtually all Sunni or foreign.

All of Bahrain's military and paramilitary services are under the direct leadership of the royal family, and all have good pay and privileges. The army and police are likely to side with the royal family and with any Saudi forces that come to its aid in coup attempt or civil crisis.

In broad terms, Bahrain has significantly improved its internal security efforts since a Shi'ite-Iranian coup attempt in December, 1981. It has quietly consulted with Britain and the United States regarding both internal security assistance and defense against Iran and discussed contingency plans for Saudi military assistance. Bahrain has also improved its treatment of its Shi'ite majority, its controls over foreign labor, and its surveillance of the relatively limited elements of the Popular Front for the Liberation of Oman (PFLOAG) in the country.

None of the current internal or external pressures on Bahrain seems immediately threatening, but it is uncertain how long it can go on without an improvement in the treatment of the Shi'ites, better sharing of wealth, and some broadening of power. Saudi Arabia is now providing Bahrain with the economic support it needs, but it cannot provide it with political cohesion.

Bahrain and Qatar's ongoing rivalry over the Hawar Islands and the coral reef of Fasht-e-Dibal is also a general warning regarding the ability to develop collective security arrangements with the other GCC states. The most serious clash took place between Bahrain and Qatar on April 26, 1986, when Qatari helicopters fired on construction crews working on Fasht-e-Dibal and Qatari forces landed and seized thirty Bahraini workers. Bahrain claimed these work crews were building a GCC facility to monitor tanker traffic, and Qatar claimed it was a Bahraini coast guard base.[197] Both nations then called military alerts and deployed troops. Bahrain reinforced Hawar, and Qatar reinforced Fasht-e-Dibal. The countercharges included claims that Qatar might seek Iranian aid.[198] While GCC attempts at mediation finally succeeded and a GCC observation team was sent to end the disagreement, this did not prevent another round of accusations and tension in the immediate aftermath of the Gulf War. Bahrain and Qatar were still arguing over the issue in mid-1992.

Strategic Interests and Arms Control

Like those of most of the smaller Gulf states, Bahrain's forces are too small to provide security against a threat from Iran and Iraq and do not pose a serious danger to any other state. Bahrain does, however, play an important strategic role because it allows the U.S. use of its airfields and ports and permits the U.S. to maintain a small headquarters and some prepositioned stocks. Bahrain strongly supported the U.S. during operation Earnest Will in 1987–1988 and supported the UN coalition in 1990 and 1991.

Bahrain signed a ten year security agreement with the U.S. in October, 1991. Bahrain, like Kuwait, is dependent on the U.S. as the only state large enough to provide the naval and other power projection forces capable of defending it against a threat from Iran or Iraq. The agreement calls for more joint exercises, U.S. access to Bahrain's ports and airfields, and prepositioning of an undefined amount of U.S. equipment, probably at Manama. This is one of the few formal agreements to increase cooperation between the U.S. and a southern Gulf state to emerge after the Gulf War; strengthening Bahrain remains a Western strategic priority.[199]

The major uncertainty Bahrain faces is internal reform, which is easier to call for than to implement. Unless Bahrain receives significant external economic aid, it will find it very difficult to co-opt its Shi'ite majority into a stable representative government. What seems to be needed is slow reform, with a steady increase in the number of Shi'ite officials and a reduction in corruption, nepotism, and favoritism. Some members of Bahrain's ruling family favor such reforms, as do many of its technocrats and military. The question is whether the changes will actually take place.

Qatar

	Manpower (1,000s)	Tanks	Aircraft	Defense Spending ($ millions)	Arms Imports ($ millions)	Arms Exports ($ millions)
1967	1	—	—	—	—	—
1973	3	—	4	78	—	—
1982	6	24	9	948	270	—
1988	7	24	13	1,800	30	—
1991	8	30	20	1,900	—	—

Qatar is a small peninsular nation that occupies a strategic position in the central portion of the southern Gulf but is shielded from most threats from the northern Gulf by Saudi Arabia and Bahrain.[200] It has an area of 11,000 square kilometers and a 563 kilometer coastline. Its borders with the UAE and Bahrain are in dispute, but it has only 60 kilometers of land boundaries: 40 kilometers with Saudi Arabia and 20 kilometers with the UAE.

Qatar survives on oil and gas revenues and has relatively high revenues per capita. Its total national per capita income is about $12,500 per year, and it has the largest ratio of Rolls Royces to total population of any nation in the world. Qatar has limited total oil reserves. It had produced about 4.4 billion barrels of oil by the end of 1990 and had a moderate reserve-to-production ratio of 19:1.[201] As of January 1, 1992, it had estimated proved oil reserves of 2.6 billion barrels, and total reserves of 3.7 to 4.0 billion barrels. It produced oil at a rate of 140,000 to 400,000 million barrels per day during 1990 and 1991. Qatar's North Dome or North Field also, however, has gas reserves in excess of 380 trillion cubic feet, with produceable reserves of about 162,000 billion cubic feet. This makes Qatar the fourth or fifth largest nation in the world in terms of total gas reserves.[202]

Qatar was the last small Gulf state to come under British protection and did not join the trucial states until 1916—after repudiating Ottoman sovereignty during World War I. Oil was first discovered in Qatar in 1949. When

Britain decided to pull out of the Gulf in January, 1968, it attempted to make Qatar part of a federation that included Bahrain and the seven sheikdoms that later became the UAE. Like Bahrain, Qatar chose independence in 1971.

Qatar has since been a monarchy ruled by the Thani family, which dominates most of the cabinet. The Thani family has been divided by internal quarrels in the past, however, and the current sheik, Khalifa ibn-Hamad al-Thani, deposed his relative Ahmed ibn-Ali al-Thani in a family coup in 1972. While the sheik has now ruled for twenty years and his son, Sheik Hamad ibn-Khalifa al-Thani, is now both the heir apparent and the defense minister, this does not necessarily assure the succession or internal stability. There is no organized internal opposition, and Qatar has an appointed Majlis, or assembly, but the Thani family, a tribal group with over 2,000 members, dominates the government and has long taken a large share of the country's wealth. Its refusal to distribute the nation's wealth and continuing squabbles among the royal family have led to at least some disaffection among young Qataris.

As has been noted earlier, Qatar has a long standing dispute with Bahrain over control of the Hawar Islands and Fasht-e-Dibal off of Qatar's northwest coast, which demarcate the border between Bahrain and Qatar. The dispute is sometimes said to involve offshore oil rights but seems to be more a feud between rival royal families than one involving serious economic issues. Qatar has generally been more moderate on the issue than Bahrain and has quietly tolerated a Bahraini military presence on the Hawar Islands.

Qatar provided the UN coalition with strong support during the Gulf War and has recently improved its relations with the United States. It has, however, seen the U.S. presence in Bahrain as a potential aid to Bahrain's desire for full control of the Hawars and Fasht-e-Dibal. As a result, Qatar has been cautious about its relations with the West and has also sometimes distanced itself from the U.S. to reduce the risk of problems with its large expatriate population.

Qatar has also been careful to avoid tying its security too closely to Saudi Arabia, and Qatari forces had a petty border clash with Saudi Arabia on September 30, 1992. The clash took place at a small outpost at Khofuous, about 80 miles southeast of Doha, and two Qataris were killed and a third taken prisoner.

Qatar has been relatively aggressive in improving its relations with Iran. It has tentatively agreed to obtain fresh water from Iran's Karun River by financing a $13 billion pipeline under the Gulf and has discussed joint oil and gas projects with the Iranian government. Qatar did, however, support the UAE against Iran from April to September, 1992 when Iran seized full control of Abu Musa and expelled the UAE from the southern half.[203]

Qatari Military Manpower, Military Expenditures, and Arms Transfers

Qatar has never maintained large military forces and lacks the manpower to do so. Its total population is 518,479 with a growth rate of 5.3%. Nearly half the population, and over 85% of its 104,000 man work force, are non-Qatari.

While Qatar is 95% Muslim, it is divided into 40% Arab, 18% Pakistani, 18% Indian, 10% Iranian, and 14% other ethnic groups. Qatar is a comparatively wealthy state even by Gulf standards. Its GNP is $6.6 billion.[204]

Qatar has, however, attempted to improve its military forces since the start of the Iran-Iraq War in 1980. Qatar's military manpower slowly increased from 5,000 in the early 1980s to 6,000 in 1985 and 7,500 in 1992. There are obvious reasons for this small force. Even if one ignores that 85% of the work force is foreign, the total male manpower pool is only about 235,000, counting the population from 15 to 49. The CIA estimates that 126,000 males are fit for military service and that 4,242 reach military age each year. The IISS estimates that there are 17,400 males between the ages of 13 and 17, 17,800 between the ages of 18 and 22, and 45,640 between the ages of 23 and 32.

Qatar increased its annual military expenditures from around $260 million in 1978 and $475 million in 1979 to $604–$780 million annually in 1982 through 1985. Reporting of the Qatari defense budget has been erratic. ACDA does not report expenditures after 1985. The IISS reports that Qatar spent $154.2 million in 1987 and $1.44 billion in 1991.[205] Qatar seems to have spent about 10% of its GDP and 20% of its central government expenditures on defense in recent years.[206]

Qatar's arms imports have varied sharply by year. They totaled $20 million in 1978, $20 million in 1979, $90 million in 1980, $270 million in 1981, $240 million in 1983, $210 million in 1984, were negligible in 1985, $80 million in 1986, were negligible in 1987, $30 million in 1988, and were again negligible in 1989.[207]

The bulk of Qatar's arms have come from France. Qatar imported a total of $765 million worth of arms during 1979–1983, with $10 million from the U.S., $440 million from France, $310 million from the UK, and $5 million from other countries.[208] Qatar imported a total of $360 million worth of arms during 1984–1988, with $10 million from the U.S., $300 million from France, $20 million from the UK, and $30 million from other countries.[209] According to ACDA in 1992, Qatar imported a total of $160 million worth of arms during 1985–1989, worth $10 million from the U.S., $100 million from France, $20 million from the UK, and $30 million from Latin America.[210]

The Qatari Army

The Qatari armed forces are commanded by members of the royal family, and Maj. Gen. Hamad ibn-Khalifa al-Thani combines the jobs of heir apparent, minister of defense, and commander in chief. Two other members of the Thani family serve as commander of the air force and chief of the royal family. Officers and enlisted men are recruited from members of the royal family and the leading desert tribes. In the past Qatar has drawn heavily on nomadic tribes which cross the Qatari-Saudi border, but it has been forced to increase its intake of urbanized Arabs. Pay and privileges are good, and there have been no visible signs of disaffection within the military.

Qatar's main military problem is manpower. Qatar's military forces total about 11,000 men, including some paramilitary forces. It lacks the native manpower to field significant military forces. While it has tried to recruit citizens and Bedouin, it is still dependent on foreign Arab and Pakistani recruits to fill out its combat units. It also seems to have British, Egyptian, French, Jordanian, and Pakistani "advisors" who play an active military role. Qatar has, however, created a growing pool of native personnel, who train in Britain, France, Jordan, Pakistan, and Saudi Arabia. An increasing number of young Qataris have joined the armed forces in recent years, and a steadily rising number of competent young native officers are being trained.

The Qatari army has a nominal strength of 7,000 to 8,000 men, and its order of battle includes an armored battalion, an infantry brigade of three mechanized infantry battalions, a royal guard regiment, one artillery battery, a special forces battalion, a field artillery regiment, and one Rapier surface-to-air missile battery. These are extremely small combat units by Western standards, since the total manpower in the Qatari army is too small to fill out even one Western regimental formation plus support. The royal guard and special forces units do, however, seem to be well trained as security and guard forces. The army is largely French-equipped and British- and Jordanian-trained. It played a creditable role in the battle of Khafji during the war to liberate Kuwait.

The army is still lightly equipped. In 1992 it had 24 AMX-30 tanks and a diverse mix of other armored fighting vehicles, including 40 AMX-10P/PCs, 30 AMX-VTTs, 180 VAB/VTTs, 40 EE-9 Cascavals, and 8 V-150 Mark 3 commando armored combat vehicles, plus 8 Saladin, 12 Ferrets, and 25 Saracen armored cars. The Ferrets are in storage, and additional AMX-10Ps were on order. Its anti-tank weapon defenses consisted of 25 HOT and 25 Milan anti-tank guided missile launchers and 40–50 106mm recoilless rifles. It also had an unknown number of light anti-tank rocket launchers.

Its artillery strength was very limited. It had 18 AMX Mark F-3 155mm self-propelled artillery weapons and 8 obsolete 25 pound (87mm) howitzers. The army also has limited numbers of mortars. Qatar did, however, order additional self-propelled howitzers in 1991. It also had 5 Astros II and 10 BM-21 122mm multiple rocket launchers, 15–20 120mm mortars, and 10 81mm mortars.[211]

Qatar's forces had only limited ability to use this armor and artillery. Some mechanized infantry battalions were reasonably effective, but most forces could at best conduct limited defensive operations. The army has limited maneuver training and only token tank warfare capability and cannot use its artillery effectively in combined arms, counterbattery fire, or beyond visual range targeting.

The army had 12 Rapier and 5 Roland fire units as short range air defense systems and Blowpipe and SA-7 manportable air defense missile systems. This gave it a limited capability to cover one point target or provide a loose defense screen over a wider area. Qatar bought at least 12 Stinger units stolen from the Afghan rebels. The U.S. refused to support these systems and demanded their return. It is unclear, however, that Qatar has the powerpacks to keep the Stingers operational.[212] Mistral air defense systems are on order, but these may not significantly improve Qatar's capabilities.

The army can probably deal with a threat from Bahrain but has little maneuver, combined arms, or combined operations capability. It should be adequate for internal security purposes, and its main function seems to be border patrol, defense of the territory disputed with Bahrain, and defense of the capital, oil, and desalinization facilities. The army has no real capability to operate at any distance from its peacetime casernes without foreign logistics, service support, and combat support.

The Qatari Navy

Qatar's navy has an authorized strength of about 1,200–1,500 men, many of whom are expatriates.[213] It has French and Pakistani advisors. Its main combat ships consist of three Combattante III 395-ton missile fast patrol boats made in the early 1980s. These are equipped with eight Exocet missiles, one 76mm Oto Melara gun, two Breda 40mm guns, and four twin 35mm guns. It also has six Vosper-Thorneycroft 33.5 meter patrol boats armed with four twin 35mm guns made in the mid-1970s. These ships are operated with a reasonable degree of professionalism by largely expatriate crews. They are adequate for local missions but lack effective air defense and sensors for surveillance and target acquisition.

Its other ships consist of six Damen Polycat 14.5 meter patrol boats (which may be operated by the marine police). The marine police also operate two 14.5 meter patrol boats, two 13.5 meter patrol boats, twenty-five Spear-class patrol boats, two Fairey Marine Interceptor-class rescue and assault boats, and five P-1200 patrol boats. There are two tugs.

Qatar ordered four Vita-class 350–400-ton fast attack boats from Vosper-Thorneycroft in June, 1992. These are 56 meter vessels equipped with a Thomson-CSF sensor and command suite, the NCS TACTICOS fully distributed combat management system, MM-40 Exocet ship-to-ship missiles, an Oto Melara 76mm gun, and the Signal Goalkeeper 30mm close-in defense system. They are to be delivered in 1996–1998.

Qatar has a small coastal defense force. It has a number of land based batteries, each of which has three MM-40 Exocet launchers with four missiles each. Its main base is near Doha, but it is building a naval base at Halul Island. Qatar is too small to play more than the most limited coastal defense role.

Training and operating standards are mediocre to poor, and the Qatari navy is still in the process of creating a modern force capable of more than short operations. Almost all maintenance and logistic support is done on a contract basis and seems to be adequate only for peacetime purposes.

The Qatari Air Force

Qatar's air force has only a little over 800 men and is based at the military airfield at Doha. Many of its pilots and officers are from Qatar, but it is heavily dependent on French and other foreign support of training, maintenance, logistics, and many C³I functions. It has 18 combat aircraft and 20 armed helicopters, including 6 Alphajets, 12 Mirage F-1E/Ds, and 20 armed SA-342s (12 armed with HOT and 8 with Exocet).[214] Qatar has AM-39 air-to-ship missiles for its Mirages, and they are equipped with R-530F Super and

R-550 Magic II missiles. Only Qatar's Mirages are really combat capable, and it has had serious maintenance and advanced training problems with all its combat aircraft. Qatar has 12 Westland Commando Mark 2 helicopters. It also has 4 transport aircraft and 2 SA-341G liaison helicopters.

Qatar has Plessey land based warning and surveillance radars and an underground command center at Doha airfield. This command center is similar in some ways to the one in Bahrain and the ones in Saudi Arabia, but it is unclear what kind of data links it has to other countries. Like Bahrain, it would need assistance from a Saudi or U.S. AWACS to provide adequate warning of an Iranian or Iraqi attack and would benefit greatly from integration into the Saudi air defense system. The air force has shelters for its Mirage fighters, and facilities and stocks are good. It trains with Saudi Arabia and has had French and British advisors.

The Qatari air force has 6–9 Roland surface-to-air missile launchers, 10–12 Rapiers, SA-7s, and some U.S. Stingers it bought from a source that stole them from the Afghan freedom fighters.[215] Unless these Stinger systems have been serviced, they are no longer operational. Qatar is studying the improvement of its air defense system. It has considered an order of Hawk MIM-23B surface-to-air missiles and 2 Shahine batteries, but it is unclear what it will purchase. Qatar has also negotiated to buy a squadron of modern fighters like the F-16 or Mirage 2000, but funding is now uncertain. Given probable delivery schedules, Qatar will lack modern land or air based air defense systems through the year 2000 and will have to rely on Saudi Arabia for most of its air and naval defense.

Qatari Paramilitary Forces

Qatar has a large 5,000–6,500 man police force with some paramilitary elements. They are organized along British lines, with special internal security forces. This force is equipped with three Lynx, two SA-342, and two Gazelle helicopters. It includes a large number of expatriates, including Egyptians, who seem to be carefully chosen to ensure their loyalty. There are special elements that deal with the control of foreign workers, immigration, intelligence, palace security, and surveillance operations. Like Bahrain, Qatar often uses informers rather than active repression.

Qatar has not experienced major internal security problems in recent years. The royal family has slightly improved the sharing of its oil wealth, and while Qatar has some Islamic fundamentalist elements, its society is gradually becoming more modernized without becoming radicalized. The Thani family has done a relatively good job of maintaining living standards and private sector opportunities in spite of declining oil revenues, and its recent cuts in government budgets and development activity have so far been healthy.

While there were rumors of a Libyan and Iranian Shi'ite-backed coup attempt in September, 1983, these reports have never been confirmed. What seems to be more serious are continuing rumors of feuding within the ruling family. There is a long standing dispute because the current ruler, Sheik Khalifa ibn-Hamad al-Thani, named his son heir in 1977, rather than his younger brother, Sheik Suhaim. This produced sporadic tension until Suhaim's death from a heart attack in 1985. Suhaim provided arms to some of the more distant members of the royal family and sought Saudi support for his claims with at least limited success. This has led to some tension between Qatar and Saudi Arabia.

These rivalries surfaced again during Qatar's 1986 border confrontation with Bahrain. There were rumors that Sheik Nasr ibn-Hamad, another younger brother of the ruler, had been shot in a family quarrel. The information minister, Isa Ghanim al-Kawari, issued a public denial of reports that he himself had been shot. It is obvious that some tensions still remain within the royal family over the control of key ministries, if not the succession.

Qatar's internal security problems with Shi'ite minorities and foreign workers seem limited. Although the nation is about 15% Shi'ite, there have been few signs of support for Khomeini. The fact that 90% of Qatar's labor force is expatriate and over 60% of its total population is expatriate has not presented serious problems except for workers who stay or come without work permits. There are few reports of troubles between Qatar and its comparatively large population of expatriate Iranians. Qatar has, however, greatly strengthened its security controls—particularly of Iranians and Shi'ites.

Strategic Interests and Arms Control

Qatar's forces currently pose a threat to no one, with the possible exception of Bahrain in the pointless feud over the Hawar Islands. While Qatar cannot absorb large arms transfers, its support of the UN coalition in the Gulf War and of Saudi forces in the battle of Khafji shows that its forces can fight. Qatar can play a useful—if somewhat symbolic—role in southern Gulf efforts to create an effective regional force if it and its neighbors are willing to embark on a serious effort at cooperation.

Like Bahrain and Kuwait, Qatar signed a security agreement with the U.S. in June, 1992 that provided for enhanced cooperation in deploying U.S. air reinforcements. It represented a significant advance in U.S.-Qatari relations, building on their cooperation during the Gulf War and showing that Qatar is willing to risk Iranian displeasure to improve its security position. Qatar still, however, faces the problem of internal reform and particularly of reaching some long term decision as to how it will deal with its massive dependence on foreign labor.

UAE

	Manpower (1,000s)	Tanks	Aircraft	Defense Spending ($ millions)	Arms Imports ($ millions)	Arms Exports ($ millions)
1967	4	—	—	—	—	—
1973	11	—	12	61	14	—
1982	44	118	52	1,980	50	—
1988	43	136	65	1,587	60	—
1991	48	130	100	2,590	—	—

The United Arab Emirates dominates the southern Gulf east of Bahrain and Qatar and reaches the Indian Ocean by dividing the main territory of Oman from its enclave on the Indian Ocean.[216] Its strategic importance lies in both its location and its possession of around 5% of the world's oil reserves. The effective defense of the Gulf against Iran, and of the flow of oil through the Gulf, requires both the support of the UAE and its defense.

The UAE, a moderate sized state by southern Gulf standards, is roughly the size of Maine. It has a land area of about 83,600 square kilometers. Virtually all of its population of 2.4 million is concentrated along its 1,448 kilometer coastline on the Gulf. Its land boundaries, however, total 1,016 kilometers—20 kilometers with Qatar, 586 kilometers with Saudi Arabia, and 410 kilometers with Oman. (These figures are approximate.) The border with Qatar is in dispute and the boundaries with Oman and Saudi Arabia are undefined.

The UAE still claims three islands that the shah of Iran seized from it on the day British forces evacuated the Gulf. These islands are strategically located in the lower Gulf and near the Straits of Hormuz and include Abu Musa, Tonb-e Bozorg (Greater Tunb), and Tonb-e Kuchek (Lesser Tunb). Iran, however, took total control of Abu Musa in the summer of 1992. Iran did so largely because it claimed it was not receiving a full share of the oil revenues from offshore facilities around the island, and it expelled 100 workers that had UAE, rather than Iranian, visas. Iran broke off talks on September 28, 1992, after the UAE made the issue the subject of GCC and Arab League diplomacy and renewed its claims to the two Tunbs.

The UAE has relatively large cumulative oil resources, but these are divided by sheikdom. It produced about 12.6 billion barrels of oil by the end of 1990 and had a moderate reserve-to-production ratio of 75:1.[217] As of January 1, 1992, Abu Dhabi had estimated proved oil reserves of up to 92.2 billion barrels and gas reserves of 182,800 billion cubic feet. Dubai had estimated proved oil reserves of up to 4 billion barrels and gas reserves of 4,600 billion cubic feet. Ras al-Khaimah had estimated proved oil reserves of up to 0.4 billion barrels and gas reserves of 1,200 billion cubic feet, and Sharjah had estimated proved oil reserves of up to 1.5 billion barrels and gas reserves of 10,700 billion cubic feet. If these claims were correct, the UAE as a whole had about 13% of the world's total oil reserves.[218]

The UAE situation in regard to water is radically different. The UAE has only about 0.42 cubic kilometers of internal renewable water resources, which is very low. It provides about 429 cubic meters per person per year, less than one-sixth the total for a citizen of the U.S.[219]

The Uncertain Union of Arab Emirates

The UAE was formed on December 2, 1971, out of seven small sheikdoms—Abu Dhabi, Dubai, Sharjah, Fujairah, Umm al-Quwain, Ajman, and Ras al-Khaimah. It is a federation governed by a supreme council of rulers, a prime minister, and a council of ministers. The federation has specific powers delegated by the ruling sheiks of each state, who make up the supreme council of rulers. All other powers are reserved to the sheiks. The chief of state is Sheik Zaid ibn-Sultan al-Nahyan, the ruler of Abu Dhabi. The vice-president is Sheik Maktum ibn-Rachid al-Maktum, the ruler of Dubai.

The sheikdoms that make up the UAE were part of the British trucial states, which were bound by a series of treaties signed in 1820, 1861, 1880, and 1892. The treaties did little to affect the domestic relations of each sheikdom but gave Britain responsibility for their foreign relations and defense, prohibited them from conducting their own foreign relations, and placed British advisors at each court. Britain signed these treaties to secure the western approaches to India; to limit Turkish, Iranian, and other European expansion in the Gulf; and to halt piracy in the region. The treaties offered the sheiks of the southern Gulf protection against their more powerful neighbors, a limited amount of security from each other, subsidies, and more stable trade.

The sheikdoms continued to be rivals in spite of the creation of treaties, and each had a long history of border feuds and struggles for power within its ruling royal family. Three of the states, however, emerged as more important than the others. Abu Dhabi became a major oil producer after 1959, Dubai became the commercial capital and found oil reserves of its own, and Sharjah was the center of British military operations in the trucial states and had a small British-trained military force called the Trucial Oman Scouts.[220]

Abu Dhabi experienced serious problems with Saudi Arabia in the early 1950s in a dispute that is still well remembered in the UAE, Oman, and Saudi Arabia. Abu Dhabi and Saudi Arabia's borders had never been demarcated and were tied as much to tribal and water rights as to geographic contiguity. The key part of the undemarcated area was the Burami Oasis, which was an important agricultural area, source of water, and a potential oil field. In 1952, Saudi troops occupied the Burami Oasis with the aid of Bedouin forces. Abu Dhabi asked for the aid of Oman, and Oman deployed troops near the area. Saudi Arabia, Oman, and Abu Dhabi agreed to keep their forces in place on October 26, 1952. They agreed to formal arbitration in 1954. Saudi Arabia and Oman then withdrew their forces, leaving small police units in the area. Saudi Arabia, however, became actively involved in supporting a revolt in Oman in which Imam Ghalib ibn-Ali attempted to seize power from the sultan. The Saudis used the Burami Oasis to move arms and money to the imam, and Britain became involved as the protector of Abu Dhabi and de facto protector of Oman. On October 26, 1956, the British-trained and -commanded Trucial Oman Scouts and the personal guard of the sultan of Oman occupied the Burami Oasis after a brief round of fighting.

The rights and wrongs of this issue are as unclear as those of most of the minor tribal squabbles in the Gulf, and Abu Dhabi has since cooperated closely with Saudi Arabia in many areas. Nevertheless, the Burami Oasis dispute still makes the UAE and Oman cautious about Saudi Arabia's emergence as a military power and potential dominator of the GCC.

Abu Dhabi, Dubai, Sharjah, Fujairah, Umm al-Quwain, Ajman, and Ras al-Khaimah were too small and fragile to seek independence upon Britain's departure from the Gulf. They were vulnerable to the threat posed by the

Baath, and various Marxist movements, and to claims by Iran and Saudi Arabia. Ras al-Khaimah did try to stand on its own initially, in part because of a long standing rivalry with a branch of the royal family in Sharjah. However, Ras al-Khaimah came into conflict with Iran, which claimed the Greater and Lesser Tunb Islands and the island of Abu Musa in the Gulf, seizing them on November, 30 1971—shortly after British forces left the Gulf. Several Iranian soldiers and four Ras al-Khaimah policemen died in the fighting during Iran's seizure of Greater Tunb Island.[221] In addition, a shift in the royal family in Sharjah brought a group more acceptable to Ras al-Khaimah to power. As a result, Ras al-Khaimah joined the federation that became the United Arab Emirates in 1972, although the regional ambitions of its sheik, Saqr ibn-Mohammed al-Qasimi, proved to be a source of continuing problems and led to considerable tension with Oman.

The history of the UAE since 1971 has not been peaceful. It has involved tension with Iran, and Abu Dhabi resolved a long standing struggle with Saudi Arabia over control of the Burami Oasis as late as 1974. Its history often consisted of continuing rivalry among its member states and sometimes rivalry within the ruling family of a given sheikdom. The often bloody feuds between and within sheikdoms may, however, have become largely a thing of the past.

The only near coup since the formation of the UAE occurred on June 17, 1987, when the sheik of Sharjah, Sultan ibn-Mohammed al-Qasimi, was deposed by his brother Abd al-Aziz Mohammed al-Qasimi. The coup took place while the sheik was in Britain and immediately raised the issue of the legitimacy of all rulers in the UAE. At the same time, Abu Dhabi backed Abd al-Aziz Mohammed al-Qasimi, and Dubai backed Sultan al-Qasimi, and a real threat developed that Abu Dhabi and the troops of Sharjah might support Abd al-Aziz Mohammed al-Qasimi, while Dubai sent forces to aid the sultan. The supreme council of rulers eventually resolved this issue by persuading the two brothers to accept a compromise whereby Sultan ibn-Mohammed al-Qasimi returned to power but Abd al-Aziz Mohammed al-Qasimi became crown prince and head of a ruling council. This compromise proved unstable, and factions in Sharjah sometimes still divide their loyalty and take sides in alignment with Abu Dhabi and Dubai.

Tensions continue between Abu Dhabi and Dubai. Abu Dhabi and Ajman tend to be allied and support the other Arab Gulf states, while Dubai often cooperates with Sharjah and Umm al-Quwain, and all have close relations with Iran. Fujairah divides the north of Oman from the south and has a special interest in relations with Oman. Ras al-Khaimah often pursues an independent course. This independence reached its height in 1977, when the ruling sheik attempted to seize part of Oman's territory and offshore oil fields. His troops were more than half Omani, however, and exhibited considerable independence of their own. They refused to attack Oman, and the sheik was forced to back down. It also led the UAE suddenly to raise military pay by 50%.

Abu Dhabi has clearly emerged as the largest and most powerful member of the UAE because of its large oil reserves, and Sheik Zaid has emerged as its de facto leader. The UAE has also steadily expanded its federal institutions with the aid of an increasingly stronger group of technocrats. Nevertheless, this has not prevented a long series of struggles for prestige among Abu Dhabi, Dubai, and the other sheikdoms. In spite of an agreement to integrate their military forces in May, 1976, Abu Dhabi and Dubai have continued to build up military forces they have never fully integrated. This is partly the fault of Sheik Zaid of Abu Dhabi. He appointed his son as commander of the UAE armed forces in 1978, without consulting Sheik Rachid of Dubai. As a result, Sheik Rachid effectively ended the integration agreement and created his own central military region command. He set up his own armored, special forces, and air units and bought his own air defense weapons.

Umm al-Quwain, Fujairah, Ras al-Khaimah, and Sharjah all have their own national guard forces. Because Sharjah also has a limited amount of oil production and Ras al-Khaimah began to produce oil in 1977, these sheikdoms maintain police units, intelligence branches, security forces, and military forces of their own.

Under the federation charter, each emirate is supposed to contribute 50% of its oil related income to help finance the national budget. The practice has been very uneven, and each sheikdom still controls most of its own budget. Similar differences affect foreign policy and regional security: Ras al-Khaimah still pursues a low level border dispute with Oman, although it does so against the opposition of the other sheiks in the UAE, and it has exhibited some separatist ambitions towards creating a Qasimi state that would include Sharjah. Similarly, Abu Dhabi backed Iraq solidly during the Iran-Iraq War and strongly supported efforts to build up the GCC, while Dubai and Sharjah tilted more towards Iran.

This helps explain why the UAE found it difficult to cooperate collectively with any of the GCC efforts to integrate southern Gulf defenses during the 1980s, although Abu Dhabi generally supported such moves. Further, Abu Dhabi has aligned itself more closely with Saudi Arabia and the West ever since Iran used its F-4s to attack the main pumping and loading facilities in the Al-Bakush offshore oil field in November, 1986. This attack seems to have come because Iraqi air strikes had damaged the Iranian facilities that drew oil from the same field being operated by Abu Dhabi, and Abu Dhabi kept producing from the common reservoir in spite of Iranian protests.

This Iranian attack led Abu Dhabi to turn to the U.S. and the West for aid in improving its air and naval defenses.[222] Iran responded by using its Revolutionary Guards to plant mines in the waters near the UAE's offshore fields and bombing one of Sharjah's facilities in 1988. This led to increasing cooperation between the UAE and U.S. during operation Earnest Will in 1987 and 1988 and laid the groundwork for even closer cooperation when the Gulf War began.

The UAE strongly backed the UN coalition during the Gulf War. It provided troops, but its most important contribution was extensive financial aid, basing rights, and aid in kind. This support for the UN reflected the sheikdoms' shared perception of Iraq as a common threat, Saddam Hussein having vigorously denounced UAE oil production policy in exactly the same way he denounced that of Kuwait during the months before Iraq's August, 1990 invasion.

UAE Military Spending and Arms Imports

The UAE is relatively wealthy, although this wealth is heavily dependent on oil prices, the UAE tends to spend all it earns, and it has often experienced a budget deficit.[223] The UAE has collectively spent a great deal on defense, increasing its annual military expenditures from around $822 million in 1978 to $1,900–2,100 million during 1981–1985. Defense spending dropped to around $1.6 billion during 1986–1990 but climbed in 1991 as the UAE reacted to Iraq's invasion of Kuwait, probably exceeding $2 billion.[224]

Individual annual defense expenditures totaled $1,197 million in 1979, $1,724 million in 1980, $1,980 million in 1982, $1,973 million in 1983, $1,932 million in 1984, $1901 million in 1985, $1,580 million in 1986, $1,590 million in 1987, $1,587 million in 1988, and $1,471 million in 1989.[225] The UAE has spent about 6–7% of its GDP and 36–51% of its central government expenditures on defense during the last decade.[226]

Like Saudi Arabia and Kuwait, the UAE faces significant near term funding problems because of the costs of the Gulf War. It had a budget deficit of $311 million in 1991, and this will increase to $1.14 billion in 1992, as the UAE pays off the costs of its support for the UN coalition. This has forced it to trim a number of civil expenses and limit military spending as well.[227]

The UAE's arms imports were relatively moderate through 1990, ranging from $60 million to $270 million annually through 1990. The UAE did, however, start a major arms import program shortly before the Gulf War: It imported about $850 million worth of arms during 1989 and $850 million more during 1990 and early 1991; its major supplier was France. ACDA estimates that the UAE imported $150 million worth of arms in 1979, $170 million in 1980, $240 million in 1981, $50 million in 1982, $40 million in 1983, $190 million in 1984, $190 million in 1985, $150 million in 1986, $230 million in 1987, $60 million in 1988, and $850 million worth in 1989.[228]

The UAE's total arms imports during 1979–1983 amounted to $620 million, with most of its arms coming from France and other European states. Roughly $20 million came from the U.S., $350 million from France, $90 million from the UK, $110 million from the FRG, $30 million from Italy, and $20 million from other states.[229] Its arms imports during 1984–1988 totaled $620 million and showed a shift towards U.S. weapons. Some $20 million came from the USSR, $350 million came from the U.S., $180 million from the UK, $70 million from the FRG, and $30 million from other states.[230]

ACDA changed its way of reporting arms sales by source in 1992. According to this reporting, the UAE imported a total of $1,495 million worth of arms during 1985–1989, $20 million worth from the Soviet Union, $340 million from the U.S., $725 million from France, $40 million from the UK, $280 million from other European countries, $80 million from other East Asian states, and $10 million from Latin America.[231]

UAE Military Manpower

Driven largely by oil income and an influx of foreign workers, the population of the UAE has risen from 150,000 in 1972 and 750,000 in 1982 to 2.4 million in 1991. It is now heavily concentrated in the major port cities of each sheikdom and is only about 19% native Emirian and 23% other Arab. Less than 20% of the population—virtually all of it Arab Muslim—holds citizenship. South Asians (largely workers and shopkeepers) make up 50% of the population and outnumber the total Arab population. The remaining 8% is largely Western and East Asian. About 80% of the population is nominally Sunni Muslim (a government figure which ignores the actual faith of many South Asians), and about 16% is Shi'ite. About 516,000 males between 15 and 49 are estimated to be fit for military service, but fewer than 20% of them are citizens.[232]

The UAE slowly expanded its total military forces from 25,000 men in the early 1980s to 44,000 in 1985, and its manpower has remained relatively constant since that date. The UAE is the only southern Gulf army to have trained women for combat. During the buildup following Iraq's invasion of Kuwait, Sheik Zaid sent 74 women for training by U.S. Army female personnel in the U.S. This training, however, was largely a token gesture.[233]

The UAE has found it very difficult to expand its forces. It has been able to train an increasing number of good native officers, and it is far less dependent on Pakistani and other expatriate officers and men than it was in the past. Nevertheless, its current military forces are more than half expatriate—including many Omanis. Its problems in force expansion include continuing feuds among its sheikdoms, limited total manpower, and dependence on foreign laborers.

The total male manpower pool is about 94,000, counting the population from 15 to 49. So much of this population is foreign, however, that the CIA cannot estimate how many males reach military age each year. The IISS estimates that there are 69,700 males between the ages of 13 and 17, 55,600 between the ages of 18 and 22, and 158,400 between the ages of 23 and 32.[234] There is no way to test the accuracy of these estimates, but the native manpower available for military service is clearly severely limited.

The UAE's Military Forces

Much of the UAE's defense and arms effort has been wasted in the past or spent on internal rivalry.[235] The sheikdoms that make up the UAE are deeply divided, and many of its 43,000 man military forces remain under the de facto command of individual sheiks. While arms purchases were supposed to be centralized after 1976, this simply was not the case. Dubai, for example, bought Italian-made tanks to have a supply of arms that Abu Dhabi could not influence. Even the command structure is uncertain. As a result of the power struggles between Abu Dhabi and Dubai, the responsibility for command, personnel, logistics, support matters, and procurement seems to vary according to the nature of internal politics and external crises. Abu Dhabi's forces are the only elements of the UAE armed forces that regularly participate in GCC exercises, although Dubai has sometimes contributed to such exercises.

The UAE has talked about conscription but has not implemented it and lacks the population and political consensus to do so. As a result, the UAE is still heavily dependent on foreign manpower from Jordan, Oman, the Sudan, and Pakistan at every level from mid-level officer down. There are also some British and Pakistani contract pilots and contract British officers. The UAE's forces have suffered in recent years, however, from friction between native UAE and Omani personnel. The UAE also seems to have dismissed some of its Jordanian and Sudanese personnel as a result of the Gulf War, although the number of Jordanians was reduced even before Jordan aligned itself with Iraq in 1990. As a result, the UAE may now have more manpower problems than it did in 1989.

The UAE Army

The UAE army has a nominal force strength of 40,000 men, including large numbers of Jordanians and Pakistanis. Its order of battle includes one armored brigade, one mechanized brigade, and three infantry brigades, including a royal guard brigade. In practice, these units are organized into formations controlled by Abu Dhabi, Dubai, and Sharjah—often without any standardization of equipment, training, or personnel career structures. Abu Dhabi has the western command with 22,000 men, one armored brigade, one mechanized brigade, and the royal guard brigade. Dubai has the central military region with 5,000 men and one brigade. Ras al-Khaimah has the northern military district with 1,700 men, and one brigade. Sharjah has its own regimental or brigade sized unit. Each military district is under the command of a son of the ruling sheik of the individual sheikdom involved, and the smaller sheikdoms have their independent guard forces and commands. Abu Dhabi contributes elements of its mechanized brigade to the Peninsular Defense Force at King Khalid City in Saudi Arabia.

This structure has severely inhibited the training and organization of UAE forces. The UAE has some good units at the battalion level but cannot operate defensively or offensively as a coherent force—particularly at any distance from its normal peacetime bases and casernes. Armored operations, air defense operations, maneuver warfare, combined arms, and combined operations are all critical weaknesses, and the UAE could not operate effectively at the brigade level. This situation is, however, gradually improving, largely as the result of declining rivalry among the sheikdoms and an understanding that more professionalism is vital if the army is to have any real value as either a deterrent or operational force.

Equipment is a problem for a number of reasons, primarily standardization, interoperability, and obsolescence. The UAE's heavy armor now consists of 131 main battle tanks, divided into 95 AMX-30 and 36 OF-40 Lions.[236] The AMX-30s are in two battalions in Abu Dhabi, and sources disagree as to whether there are 64 AMX-30s plus 4 recovery vehicles or all 95 AMX-30s plus 6 recovery vehicles in active service. In any case, the AMX-30s are lightly armored, lack modern firepower systems, and are obsolete. For several years, Abu Dhabi has been examining the option of joining Saudi Arabia in accepting a West German proposal to up-engine the AMX-30 and install a new fire control and make other improvements.

The OF-40s, Italian versions of the German Leopard, are virtually part of a different force. Dubai took delivery on the first 18 Oto Melara OF-40s in 1981, and then on 18 more plus 3 armored recovery vehicles. It has converted all of its OF-40s to the improved Mark 2 version, but its tank force has never had more than minimal effectiveness.[237]

The UAE needs new tanks if it is to develop the kind of strength that could deal with a threat from either Iraq or Iran. Abu Dhabi has been examining possible replacements in combination with Saudi Arabia since the late 1980s. Candidates include the AMX-40, EE-T1 with either a 105mm or 120mm gun, the Challenger, the M-1A1/2, and possibly the T-72. The UAE came close to signing an order for 337 M-1A1 tanks, 160–164 Bradley M-2 fighting vehicles, and 800–900 high mobility multipurpose wheeled vehicles in 1991, but it delayed the order pending further trials of the M-1, Challenger, and Leclerc in Kuwait and because of financing problems and uncertainty regarding congressional approval of the sale. It is now seriously considering a buy of 360 Leclerc tanks.[238]

The UAE's armor includes about 770 other fighting vehicles, among them 86 Scorpion light tanks, 90 AML-90 and VBC-40s in the armored reconnaissance role, and 20 AMX-10P infantry fighting vehicles. The UAE also has a wide range of APCs, including 96 Engessa EE-11 Urutus (some with TOW), 200 M-3 AML/VTTs, 90 VCRs, and 20VAB/VBCs. The UAE also has 60 armored recovery vehicles, including EE-9s and AMX-30s. It has over 100 armored cars—many in storage. These include AML-60s, 20 Ferrets, 70 Saladins, Saracens, and Shoreland Mark 2s.

This is far too wide a range of types and seller countries to allow easy standardization of maintenance and training, and some of these types are obsolete. To add to this confusion, various sources reported during 1991 and 1992 that the UAE had 160–164 Bradley M-2 fighting vehicles, 100 M-113A2s, Egyptian Fahd and Vickers Valkyr APCs, and 800–900 M-998 Hummer light reconnaissance vehicles on order. There is no way to evaluate the accuracy of such rumors, but it seems likely that there were no M-113A2s on order and that the Brazilian sale never went beyond sending armored vehicles to the UAE for evaluation purposes.

Further, in May, 1992, the UAE took a step that indicated it would follow a very different course. It took delivery on 50 Soviet BMP-2s and ordered 400 more. This gave it both the ability to standardize on a new combat vehicle and an excellent bargain. According to some reports, the UAE paid just $23,000 per vehicle, which compares with nearly $1 million for the Bradley. This raises some question as to whether the UAE would also buy Soviet tanks, but the chief of the UAE general staff, Gen. Sheik Mohammed ibn-Zayed, indicated that the UAE was still interested in Western tanks and had recently requested price and availability information on the purchase of 390 U.S. M-1A2 tanks.[239]

Although the UAE has improved its artillery strength in recent years, its forces still have serious limitations. The UAE army has 20 155mm AMX Mark F-3 self-propelled howitzers, 24 M-46 130mm towed guns, 72 105mm towed howitzers, 36 M-56 105mm pack howitzers, 20–24 120mm mortars, and 80 81mm mortars. The UAE has also acquired 18 LAU-97 70mm and 24–40 FIROS-25 122mm multiple rocket launchers.

The UAE can use this mix of artillery in set-piece firing exercises, at least by Gulf state standards, but even then it has problems in target acquisition and maneuver. The UAE needs to replace most of its towed weapons with self-propelled weapons to conduct armored and combined arms operations. It also lacks artillery sensors and fire control aids.

The UAE has an adequate number of anti-tank guided weapons launchers, including 15 BGM-71A Improved TOW launchers (some on EE-11s), 35 HOT launchers (some on armored vehicles), 65–70 Milans on EE-11s and 120 manportable Milan launchers, and an unknown number of obsolete Vigilant launchers. Its other anti-tank weapons include 106mm recoilless rifles and 84mm Carl Gustav M-2 recoilless rifles.

The UAE's short range air defenses include 9 Crotale launchers, 12 Rapier fire units, 18 Blowpipe fire units, and 12 RBS-70 fire units. There are 48 M-3 VDA self-propelled twin 30mm guns, 12 GCF-BM2 self-propelled twin 20mm guns, and a mix of roughly 100 14.5mm, 20mm, 30mm, and 35mm towed guns. The missiles and self-propelled guns are all adequate weapons systems, and the UAE has done relatively well in operating the Crotale. Nevertheless, the UAE has too many types of anti-tank and light air defense weapons, too few of any given system, and poor overall training.

In broad terms, the portion of the army under the command of Abu Dhabi and Dubai has steadily improved over time. It is, however, undertrained in every aspect of maneuver, combined arms, and combined operations warfare. There is no effective unit of command or combat training above the brigade level. Logistics, maintenance, service support, and combat support vary by sheikdom. While Abu Dhabi's forces are superior to the rest, all of the UAE's forces are organized to be heavily dependent on operating near their peacetime casernes and facilities.

The UAE Air Force

Like Saudi Arabia's, the UAE's air force is its most prestigious service. It now has 2,500 men, including the air defense forces and police air wing. The ground based air defense forces were shifted from army to air force command in 1988. Once again, Dubai has a separate force element, which includes about 700 men of this total. This is a very low overall manning level for an air force with 100 combat aircraft, 32 transport aircraft, and 19 armed helicopters, but overall proficiency levels are low—particularly in conducting realistic air strike and close air support missions. The UAE is heavily dependent on foreign pilots and technical support for all operations.

The UAE now has 28 Mirage 2000s and 14 Mirage IIIEADs in fighter–ground attack roles, and 15 Hawk MK-63s in attack/training missions. It has one squadron of 10 Mirage 5 ADs in air defense missions. The Hawk is a relatively simple aircraft to operate and maintain, and British experts indicate that the UAE is able to keep it at reasonable levels of effectiveness. In contrast, they indicate the Mirage-equipped forces have relatively low operational availability and limited combat training. They have evidently been overhauled and modified by Pakistan, but the Mirage IIIEADs are difficult to maintain and may present continuing operational problems. The UAE seems to have ordered additional Mirage 2000s after the Gulf War.

The UAE air force is having trouble absorbing its new Mirage 2000s. This, however, is only partly the fault of the UAE. Abu Dhabi refused to take delivery on the first 18 of the 36 Mirage 2000s for its air defense forces in early 1987 because they were not equipped to a special standard as specified. The UAE's dispute with France over the aircraft began in March, 1986. In spite of an agreement by Dassault-Breuget to modify the aircraft, the Mirage 2000s Dassault proposed to deliver did not have the quality of avionics that the UAE expected, could not fire special laser guided ordnance being developed by ISC-Ferranti, could not fire the same U.S. ordnance as other Gulf aircraft, and did not have fully compatible communications, IFF, and data links.

Dassault sought to deliver the aircraft first and then modify them. It had some justification in making this request because much of the problem with ISC-Ferranti may have been the fault of that contractor.[240] The UAE finally agreed to accept the aircraft in November, 1987, but only if Dassault later completed the necessary changes and paid penalties. This agreement was reached only after the UAE foreign minister visited Paris and threatened the French prime minister and minister of foreign affairs with excluding Dassault from the UAE market.[241] According to some sources, this experience, and the success of the Saudi and U.S. F-15s during the Gulf War have led the UAE to consider ordering F-15s from the U.S.

There are three Mirage 5RADs in the reconnaissance role, and some sources indicate there are eight more Mirage 2000 RADs. Four CASA C-212s are employed in an electronic warfare role but are of uncertain effectiveness. The UAE has actively investigated ordering C-130s equipped for electronic warfare, E-2C Hawkeye for the AWACS and maritime surveillance role, and two BN-Defender AEW aircraft. Its advanced air ordnance includes R-550 Magique air-to-air missiles, and AS-11, AS-12, and AM-39 Exocet air-to-ground missiles. It has some Beech MQM-107A RPVs, which it uses as target drones.

There are seven Hawk Mark 61s, two MB-339s, two Mirage IIIs, and eight Mirage 2000s in training units that can be used in light combat missions. Twelve more Hawks are on order.[242] There are also six to eight MB-326K and five MB-339A light attack aircraft operating in the COIN and training role, and twenty-one PC-7 trainers. Major weaponry includes the R-550 Magic AAM and HOT, AM-39 Exocet, AS-15TT, AS-12, and AS-11 ASMs.

The UAE has twelve SA-342K Gazelle attack helicopters with HOT ATGMS, and 7 SA-316/319 Alouette III with AS-11/12 air-to-surface missiles. Two AS-332Ks are armed for the anti-ship role. The UAE has also ordered twenty AH-63 Apache attack helicopters. These aircraft will present roughly the same advantages to the UAE that they do to Bahrain. They furnish the kind of long range strike system that will allow the UAE the ability to defend all its coastline and territory quickly and to conduct all-weather and night armed reconnaissance to deal with any amphibious landing. They also can be used to reinforce Saudi Arabia, Bahrain, or Kuwait.[243]

Overall pilot training is good, but the UAE is only slowly evolving away from an air force with limited training in day combat and with little central direction and overall organization. It is dependent on foreign technical personnel for the operation of virtually all its aircraft, and Saudi and British pilots indicate that it does very little realistic air-to-air combat training, would have serious problems in low altitude air defense and attack missions, has no real experience in combined operations, and needs to improve its munitions and ground-based intercept training.

Reports differ as to the UAE air force's transport force. It may include two L-100-30, four C-130Hs, one HS-125, one Falcon 20, five BN-2 Islanders, one G-222, five DHC-5Ds, and two Cessna 182s. Its transport helicopters seem to include two AB-205/Bell 205, six Bell 206A/L, four Bell 214, eight AS-332, one AS-350, and eleven SA-330 Pumas. There are three Bo-105 helicopters in the SAR role. Some reports indicate that the UAE has thirty A-129 Mangustas and Lynx helicopters on order.

The air force's main air bases at Abu Dhabi and Jebel Ali (Dubai) are sheltered and have light anti-aircraft defenses. It also has military fields at Batin in Abu Dhabi, Dubai, Fujairah, Ras al-Khaimah, and Sharjah. Abu Dhabi is creating a major modern air base at Suwaihan.

The UAE air force merged with the air defense force in January, 1988. This merger occurred because of growing coordination problems between the fighter force and land based air defenses.[244] The decision placed both commands under the former chief of the air force, Colonel al-Nahyan, and the head of the air defense force became deputy commander. He described the merger as leading to "faster decision making and closer cooperation . . . better performance in the use of weapons, and also flexibility in relaying orders from headquarters and carrying them out."[245]

The UAE is making progress along these lines. It has deployed an air defense brigade with three battalions. These are armed with the twelve Rapier and nine Crotale fire units, twelve RBS-70 light surface-to-air missiles listed earlier, SA-14s, light unguided anti-aircraft guns, and Skyguard radar guided twin Oerlikon 35mm anti-aircraft guns. The UAE has also formed five MIM-23B Improved Hawk batteries with 42 launchers (342 missiles).[246] It will take at least three years, however, to make these ground based air defense units fully manned and effective forces.

The UAE air force has Marconi, AN/TSQ-73, and AN-TPS-70 warning radars. It is supposed to acquire a greatly improved automated air defense command and control system along with its Improved Hawks, but its overall command and control and air control and warning capabilities are questionable. Some of the systems integration was evidently supposed to be carried out by ISC and Ferranti as part of a project called GMX or Al-Hakim. Ferranti's performance has evidently been questionable, and part of the contract may have been fraudulent.[247] It still seems to need effective battle management and warning capability, effective secure voice and data links to the Saudi air force, and a compatible IFF system. Like the other small Gulf states, it would also benefit greatly from full integration into the Saudi air defense system.

The UAE Navy

The UAE's small 1,800 man navy is largely a coastal defense force operated by Abu Dhabi. It is heavily dependent on foreign personnel and has poor to mediocre training, operating, and maintenance standards. It is not capable of independent operations except against another small southern Gulf state.

The UAE's major combat ships include two 630-ton German Type-62 Lurssen corvettes, each with two twin MM-40 Exocet launchers, Crotale anti-air missiles, one 76mm gun, and one Alouette helicopter. There are two recently delivered 260-ton Lurssen 45 meter fast attack craft, with four Exocet and one Mistral launcher each and one 76mm gun, and six Lurssen TNC-45 guided missile patrol boats, each with two twin MM-40 Exocet launchers, one 76mm gun, and two twin Breda 40mm guns. There are also six Vosper-Thorneycroft 33.5 meter patrol boats with twin 30mm guns. Abu Dhabi has ordered two Lurssen 62 meter patrol boats with Exocet, 76mm guns, and Goalkeeper close-in defense systems. If all these ships can be properly manned, the UAE will acquire a significant coastal defense capability.

The rest of the navy consists of three Keith Nelson 17 meter patrol boats, two Cheverton tenders, four landing craft, and one tug. A small coast guard, which is part of the Ministry of Interior, operates thirty-nine coastal patrol boats, and two Crestitalia 30 meter diver support vessels.

The navy conducts little realistic exercise training, although its proficiency has improved significantly since the late 1980s. It also remains highly dependent on foreign personnel and advisors and is scattered in a number of duplicative bases at Ajman, Mina Zaid, and Dalma (Abu Dhabi); Mina Rashid and Mina Jebel Ali (Dubai); Mina Saqr (Ras al-Khaimah); Fujairah; and Mina Khalid and Mina Khor Fakkan (Sharjah). A naval facility is under construction at Al-Qaffay Island, but reports that the UAE would create a major naval base at Taweela have not been confirmed.

Paramilitary and Security Forces

Like the other southern Gulf states, the UAE has large paramilitary police forces and security and intelligence units organized along British lines. In Abu Dhabi's case, these are controlled by the Ministry of Interior, but each sheikdom seems to have forces of its own. Abu Dhabi and Dubai seem to have competing intelligence and security units. There is also a small coast guard and border security force. None of these forces seems to be particularly repressive, although the UAE obviously exerts careful control over foreign laborers, maintains surveillance on its armed forces and particularly on foreign soldiers, and must be concerned with Iranian and Iraqi infiltration.

Strategic Interests and Arms Control

Regardless of the internal tensions in the UAE, there is no reason to assume that it will not remain a moderate state and friendly to the West. The UAE clearly needs to improve many of its forces for defensive purposes and if it is to play any role in collective security in the southern Gulf. Creating an effective air defense, maritime defense, and surveillance system in the UAE is also critical for regional defense and if the West ever has to project power in the face of a hostile Iran or rearmed Iraq. It would also contribute a great deal to regional security if the UAE's next generation of arms and munitions were standardized or interoperable with the equipment in USCENTCOM forces.

The main issue affecting future arms sales to the UAE is whether they can help lead to the creation of an effective deterrent, suitable defensive capabilities, and improved capacity to accept friendly power projection forces, or will become bogged down in the rivalry among sheikdoms. There is no simple answer to this question, and the best solution might well be for the UAE to develop a cohesive force improvement plan. There does seem to be significantly less political instability in the UAE than there was in the mid-1980s, although rivalry certainly continues.

The UAE's most progressive leader, Sheik al-Nahyan of Abu Dhabi, still has no clear successor, although Khalifa, the crown prince and deputy supreme commander of the armed forces, seems to be emerging as a possible candidate. The continued rivalry between Abu Dhabi and Dubai is particularly disturbing.

Dubai and Sharjah might also provide Iran with tacit support at some point in the future if a low level crisis arose between Iran and some other southern Gulf state, although Iran's seizure of all of Abu Musa from the UAE during April to October, 1992 seems to have made the more pro-Iranian members of the UAE more cautious about Iran's long term intentions. The UAE showed considerable unity in taking a hard line towards Iran in negotiating GCC and Arab League protests of Iran's decision to expel the UAE from Abu Musa and in demanding that Iran also return the Tunb islands.

Oman

	Manpower (1,000s)	Tanks	Aircraft	Defense Spending ($ millions)	Arms Imports ($ millions)	Arms Exports ($ millions)
1967	3	—	—	—	—	—
1973	8	—	12	287	13	—
1982	15	18	37	1,512	130	—
1988	27	39	63	1,371	30	—
1991	30	80	60	1,390	—	—

Oman is one of the larger southern Gulf states, with a total territory of 212,460 square kilometers, slightly smaller than the state of Kansas. Like most Gulf states, Oman has disputed borders. It still has not established an agreed demarcation of its 288 kilometer border area with Yemen—an area which may have oil—although it is actively negotiating a settlement and may complete one before the end of 1992. There is still some residual tension with Saudi Arabia over their 676 kilometer border and ownership of Western Oman, although both countries reached a demarcation agreement on May 21, 1992. Oman's 410 kilometer border with the UAE is not demarcated. Oman has a 1,700 kilometer coastline and faces threats to its position as the southern gate to the Gulf from Iran. The Musandam Peninsula at the entrance to the Gulf is a territorial enclave separated from the rest of Oman by the UAE. Roughly 17% of the world's oil production transited through the entrance to the Gulf in 1990.

Oman is a small oil power. It had produced of total of about 3.3 billion barrels of oil by the end of 1990 and had a moderate reserve-to-production ratio of 18:1.[249] As of September 1, 1992, Oman had estimated proved oil reserves of up to 4.55 billion barrels, with probable additional reserves of 2 billion barrels and gas reserves of 17 trillion cubic feet. These estimates do not include up to 30 billion barrels of heavy crude, which may eventually be produceable. Oman had about 0.5% of the world's total oil reserves; it produced at a rate of about 0.64 to 0.73 million barrels per day during 1990 and 1991 and planned to increase production to 0.775 million barrels per day in 1992. At this rate of production, it will have 20–25 years of reserves.[250] Oil provided 49% of Oman's GDP in 1990, and 80% of its government revenues; its only other major export is fish. All of Oman's oil is blended and is exported through Muscat, going largely to Asian markets. Oman has one 80,000 barrel per day refinery.[251]

Although Oman receives rain from the Indian Ocean monsoons, 70% of its annual rainfall of 100 mm evaporates without affecting the soil. Oman has only about 0.43 cubic kilometers of internal renewable water resources, which is very low, amounting to about 561 cubic meters per person, less than one-fifth the total for a citizen of the U.S. Its agriculture is marginal, and Oman has long drawn down on its fossil water by overpumping its aquifers. Oman has tried to solve this shortage with retention dams that will force the water into the soil and by repairing the 1,000 year old Persian system of underground aqueducts that once provided water in Oman's interior. Water, however, is likely to be a growing problem, and Oman is too poor to rely on increased food imports or provide alternative jobs.[252]

The Development of Oman's Military Forces

Oman was once one of the great sea powers of the Arab world and ruled an empire that included an enclave in India, Zanzibar, and Mombassa in East Africa. This empire broke up in 1856, however, and Oman's trade declined to the point where it became little more than a backward British protectorate. This sharply undercut the powers of the sultans, and they gradually lost control over both part of western Oman and the Dhofar region in the south.

Much of the territory of Oman came under tribal control from 1920 to 1957. This loss of control led to sporadic rebellions, the Burami Oasis dispute discussed in the analysis of the UAE, a Saudi effort to seize control of western Oman in the 1950s, and a much more serious Marxist attempt to seize control of the southern province of Dhofar.

The most important tribal struggle shaping modern Oman was the "imamate opposition," which began in the last century and involved differences over both religion and the Sultan's political authority. These tensions reached the level of open rebellion when Ghalib ibn-Ali became imam of Oman's Ibadhi sect in 1954.[253] Ibn-Ali proved to be extremely ambitious, and rejected the sultan's attempt to exert control over western Oman. He instead turned to the Arab League, applying for recognition as a separate country. Saudi Arabia backed him with money and arms and seems to have sought to use the rebellion to annex both the Burami Oasis and part of western Oman.

The Omanis, helped by the British, responded by sending the British-led Trucial Oman Scouts to drive the Saudis out of the oasis in November, 1955 and by deploying British troops to Nizwa and other towns and villages near Oman's border with Saudi Arabia. Ibn-Ali was forced to resign as imam, but his brother Talib fled to Saudi Arabia and organized tribal forces with Saudi support. Talib invaded Oman in early 1957, and his brother again proclaimed himself imam in June, 1957.

The British used the Trucial Oman Scouts and British troops from Aden to drive ibn-Ali's forces into the Jebel Akhdar Mountains in July; Britain then had the RAF bomb the rebels while it helped to train and equip the sultan's forces. When the sultan's forces failed, in part because of poor leadership and the sultan's alienation of the tribes in the area, Britain sent troops back and attacked the imam's positions in the Jebel Akhdar in August, 1957. British troops and the RAF continued to aid the sultan's forces until the imam's forces finally collapsed in early 1959, in part because of payments to his soldiers to desert him.

The Dhofar rebellion is a different and much grimmer story. Dhofar had long been under Omani control and had been annexed to Oman in 1879 but had a different dialect and tribal character. The sultans made no attempt to develop it or share any of Oman's revenues. This led to low level rebellion beginning in 1963, and the rebels increasingly drew on radicals and Marxists outside Dhofar for ideology, funds, and military support. By 1965 the Dhofar rebels controlled much of the countryside, and in June, 1965, they began to attack government strong points and installations.

The Dhofar rebellion became a major military problem in 1967, after Britain evacuated Aden. A new Marxist radical state called the People's Democratic Republic of Yemen emerged from the fighting. This state quickly began to provide arms and support to the Dhofar rebels, who were initially divided into the Dhofar Liberation Front (DLF), and the National Democratic Front for the Liberation of the Occupied Arabian Gulf, and the Popular Front for the Liberation of Oman (PFLO).

On June 11, 1970, the Dhofar rebels started a new offensive in the south and soon came to control virtually all of southern Oman except its main port city of Salalah. This led the British to aid the sultan's son, Qabus, to carry out a coup on July 23, 1970. Unlike his father, the Sandhurst-trained Qabus proved to be an effective and modern leader. He granted the Dhofari a considerable degree of autonomy and rapidly Omanized the armed forces. He offered the rebels amnesty, and a significant number of DLF and PFLO rebels joined him. The remaining rebels combined to form a splinter group of the Popular Front for the Liberation of Oman (PFLOAG) in February, 1972.

With British aid, Sultan Qabus created a mix of highly effective light infantry forces and recruited tribal militias from the Dhofar region. Sultan Qabus also made effective use of British advisors and troops, including elements of the Special Air Service (SAS). He went on the counteroffensive and began to attack PFLOAG positions in the PDRY with artillery and air power. He also sent Omani and SAS commando teams into the border area and Hauf to attack Dhofar rebel artillery positions and sanctuaries.

In December, 1973 the sultan obtained further aid from the shah of Iran, who sent an entire brigade of troops to Oman in 1973. At the same time, an increasing number of Dhofar rebels joined the sultan, as Marxist extremists came to dominate the PFLO and alienated the people with experiments such as the collectivization of children. By 1974 Oman was able to secure defensive positions called the Hornbeam line, about 50 miles from the border with the PDRY.

In 1975 the sultan obtained further support from Jordan and began to sweep the last areas near the border. Sources differ over the nature of Omani attacks on the PDRY. According to some sources, Iranian aircraft and Omani ships attacked the town of Hauf in the PDRY on October 17, 1975, and the PFLOAG withdrew from its last positions in Oman. According to others, the British Special Air Services (SAS) attacked Hauf on several occasions to pressure the PDRY to halt its support for the rebels. In any case, the sultan declared the end of the rebellion December 11, 1975. By 1975 Oman had secured positions called the Damavand line about 25 miles from the border. This effectively ended the rebellion, and Jordanian troops left Oman. Iran removed most of its forces in January, 1977—although some Iranian troops remained in the area until 1979—and most British troops left in March. By this time several thousand people, including many women and children, had died in the fighting.

Sultan Qabus has not only secured the country in the years that have followed the end of the Dhofar rebellion, he has done a great deal to develop it and has created a broadly based political leadership including several ministers who were once Dhofar rebels. While Oman is a relatively poor country, limited oil resources were discovered in 1967. It has used these resources wisely, with some of the best development planning of any Gulf state, and the people now have far higher living standards than in the mid-1970s.

The sultan has also steadily liberalized Oman, although Oman still has censorship, strict immigration controls, and active internal security forces. In 1981 the sultan created the State Consultative Council, Oman's first attempt at moving towards popular rule. The Council had fifty-five appointed members and met three times a year. While it had no formal power to veto the sultan's actions or legislation, debate was relatively free and often vigorous.

In 1991 the sultan announced that he would create a popular assembly. Its full powers are unclear, but it is expected to have at least some power to review legislation, include a broader representation of the population, and exclude government officials. The chamber included eleven government officials of under secretary rank who sat in their official capacity. The assembly will be structured to give additional representation to rural areas. Its members will be chosen by Oman's governors rather than the sultan and approved by the deputy prime minister after the sultan's endorsement. The new Majlis will also be empowered to call ministers to account and regularly to review legislation.[254]

If there is any major remaining internal security problem, it may be the succession. The sultan has no wife and is not expected to have an heir. One possible alternative is Said Fahr ibn-Mahmoud, the sultan's uncle and minister of defense. Another possible relative is Said Haitham ibn-Tarek, the cousin of the sultan, son of a former prime minister, and an under secretary in the foreign office. No formal steps have been taken, however, to deal with this issue.

The Dhofar rebels and internal security have not been Oman's only problems. When Abu Dhabi reached an agreement with Saudi Arabia over the Burami Oasis dispute in 1975, Abu Dhabi mistakenly ceded territory that belonged to Oman. While Saudi Arabia returned some of this territory in 1977, it has sporadically indicated that it still claims part of Oman. In 1977 the shah asserted joint control over the Straits of Hormuz. This arrangement effectively ended with his fall, although Iranian ships did attempt to enter Omani waters during the Iran-Iraq War.

Sheik Saqr of Ras al-Khaimah attempted to take control of part of Oman in 1977 and tried to place drilling rigs in Omani waters. Oman used military force to take back its territory. Oman reached a border settlement with Ras al-Khaimah but only after Zaid, the most powerful ruler in the UAE, strongly backed Sultan Qabus against Sheik Saqr.[255] Oman has also faced a military challenge from the PDRY over the control of potential oil fields in their undemarcated border area. This has not led to fighting as serious as the border clashes between Saudi Arabia and Yemen. In October, 1987, however, battalion or company sized forces fought in the area, and Oman launched air strikes against PDRY forces. The president of the PDRY visited Oman to try to defuse the situation in 1988. Even so, there have been further clashes, although it is unclear these have gone beyond exchanges of fire between small patrols.

Omani Military Expenditures and Arms Imports

Omani military expenditures have fluctuated with oil prices, but Oman has consistently tried to fund a transition from largely infantry forces to a more modern combined arms army during the last decade. Oman increased its annual military expenditures from around $700 million in 1979 to $1,059 million in 1980, $1,357 million in 1981, $1,512 million in 1982, $1,744 million in 1983, $1,894 million in 1984, and $1,937 million in 1985. Problems in oil revenues and diminishing tension in the Iran-Iraq War led it to spend $1,731 million in 1986, $1,518 million in 1987, $1,350 million in 1988, and $1,552 million in 1989.[256] Oman spent $1.39 billion in 1990 and $1.44 billion in 1991; it spent $1,513–$2,111 million in 1982 through 1985.[257] It spent $1.56 billion on defense in 1986, $1.51 billion in 1987, and $1.385 billion in 1988—over 20% of its GDP in recent years and 38–49% of its central government expenditures.[258] The other GCC states pledged to provide Oman with $1.8 billion in aid over twelve years in September, 1983, but it is unclear how much of this aid has been delivered.

Oman's recent arms imports have varied sharply by year. Its arms imports have never exceeded $350 million per year, a peak reached in 1983—when the Iran-Iraq War seemed most likely to threaten Oman in the form of Iranian pressure or attacks on the Musandam Peninsula and Goat Island in the Straits of Hormuz. ACDA estimates that Oman imported $30 million worth of arms in 1979, $100 million in 1980, $60 million in 1981, $130 million in 1982, $350 million in 1983, $310 million in 1984, $140 million in 1985, $110 million in 1986, $110 million in 1987, $30 million in 1988, and $60 million in 1989.[259]

While small by Gulf standards, these expenditures have presented financing problems because Oman's oil wealth and economy have not developed rapidly in recent years, and oil accounts for 40% of Oman's GDP and 80% of its government expenditures. Oman's GDP is currently around $8.5 billion, and its per capita income is now about $6,400, roughly 75% in real terms of what is was in the mid-1980s.[260]

The bulk of Oman's arms have come from the UK. Oman imported a total of $565 million worth of arms during 1979–1983, with $80 million from the U.S., $20 million from France, $430 million from the UK, $10 million from Italy, $5 million from the PRC, and $20 million from other countries.[261] Oman imported a total of $670 million worth of arms during 1984–1988, with $30 million from the U.S., $20 million from France, $330 million from the UK, $280 million from the FRG, and $10 million from other countries.[262]

In 1992 ACDA reported that the UAE imported a total of $445 million worth of arms during 1985–1989, with $30 million from the U.S., $200 million from the UK, $210 million from West Germany, and $5 million from other European countries.[263]

Omani Military Manpower and Readiness

Oman's military manpower has slowly increased from 15,000 in the early 1980s to 25,000 in 1985, 25,500 in 1988, and 30,400 in 1992. This minimal rate of increase reflects Oman's limited manpower base. Its total population is around 2.0 million, with a growth rate of about 3.5%. It is largely Arab, with some small Baluchi, Zanzibari Arabs, and South Asian elements. The population is largely Islamic and about 75% of the Ibadhi sect. The remainder includes Sunnis, some Shi'ites, and Hindus.[264]

The total male manpower pool is about 348,849, counting the population from 15 to 49. The CIA estimates that 197,870 males are fit for military service, and that 20,715 reach military age each year. The IISS estimates that there are 83,900 males between the ages of 13 and 17, 69,600 between the ages of 18 and 22, and 125,320 between the ages of 23 and 32. Given this manpower pool, a relatively undeveloped economy, and Oman's need to choose military manpower from groups loyal to the sultan, it is not surprising that Oman has kept its regular military forces relatively limited.

Further, manpower is now Oman's greatest military strength. Its troops are among the best trained and motivated troops in the southern Gulf, and Oman has a good cadre of Omani officers and NCOs and excellent British advisors. The sultan appointed an Omani officer to the post of commander of the army for the first time in 1984.[265] Oman again strengthened the role of Omanis in top leadership positions and throughout the officer corps in 1988 and 1990.

Oman will eventually convert the rest of its officer corps to native personnel but still has nearly 500 British officers and NCOs seconded to the Omani armed forces. It also has limited number of personnel from Jordan and Egypt, and large numbers of Pakistani Baluchis. Oman has established both specialized secondary schools to train its military intake and a central training center near Muscat. It also trains officer and technical personnel in Britain, the FRG, France, Jordan, and Saudi Arabia.

Unlike other members of the GCC, Oman has openly conducted military exercises with outside powers, including Britain, Egypt, France, and the U.S. While Oman established relations with the USSR in late September, 1985, Oman has long provided the U.S. with critical contingency and prepositioning facilities. These include airfields and prepositioned equipment at Masirah Island and airfield facilities at the international airport at Seeb, at Hasb, and at Thamrait in southern Oman, plus additional storage and naval facilities at Masirah and Ghanam.[266] The U.S. Army Corps of Engineers also upgraded the old 2,000 foot direct runway at Khasab with a 6,500 foot surface air base. These facilities played an important role during the U.S. buildup for Desert Storm.

British forces also make frequent use of Omani facilities, have an intelligence post near Muscat, and use the Omani base at Goat Island in the Straits of Hormuz and a new intelligence post at Qabal in the Musandam Peninsula for a variety of reconnaissance functions. Both U.S. and British forces made use of Omani facilities during the Western intervention in the Gulf in 1987–1988 and again during the Gulf War in 1990–1991.

The base at Goat Island and other facilities in the Musandam Peninsula are particularly important because they guard the Straits of Hormuz and are only 26 miles from Iran. More than 50 large ships, 60% of them tankers, passed through these waters every day during 1986 and 1987. The Musandam Peninsula is a small enclave with a population of about 12,000 separated from the rest of Oman by a 40 mile strip of the UAE. Since 1976 Oman has been developing the peninsula with the help of a U.S. firm called Tetra Tech International. It has spent nearly $5,000 per person in recent years to develop the region.[267]

Oman has conducted some impressive public military exercises since 1985. Its March, 1985 exercise, codename Thunder, involved roughly 10,000 men. It was the largest and most effective exercise that any GCC state had conducted, and Oman played an important role in GCC exercises ever since. Oman also exercises regularly with British forces. Refueled British RAF Tornadoes have flown nonstop to air bases in Oman, and in December, 1986 Oman held a joint exercise with Britain called Swiftsword. It involved over 5,000 British service men, including a 400 man landing by British marines, air drops, and air reinforcements. Some 5,000 Omani troops acted the role of defenders, while another 2,000 played the role of an anonymous enemy that looked very much like Iran.[268]

The Omani Army

Oman's force structure is significantly different from that of most other Gulf states and has less heavy and high technology equipment—although the Omani army is steadily expanding its armor and artillery strength. At the end of 1991, the Omani army had about 20,000 highly trained regulars. Omani soldiers and army officers are respected throughout the Gulf, and Omanis often form an important portion of the total military manpower of other GCC states, especially those of the UAE.

The Omani army is organized into a division with two brigade headquarters, one armored regiment with a tank squadron, one armored reconnaissance regiment with three armored car squadrons, five Omani and three Baluchi infantry regiments, an airborne regiment, one infantry reconnaissance regiment with three reconnaissance companies, and two independent reconnaissance companies. Its major support elements include two artillery regiments, an air defense battery, and a field engineer regiment with three squadrons.

There are several independent land force units: a royal household force with 4,000 men—including a royal guard brigade of 3,000 men, a 500 man special force regiment, a 150 man royal yacht squadron with a 3,800-ton yacht, and a 250 man royal flight—and the Musandam security force with an independent rifle company.[269]

Oman deploys some of its forces on the Saudi and UAE borders and in the Musandam Peninsula. It keeps at least a full brigade deployed along the mountainous border area with Yemen, however, and this is Oman's most effective force. The brigade has at least some British officers or advisors and operates from fire bases and strong points along the border. It also has reserve ground forces and supplies in Thamrait and Salalah and considerable helicopter support. Oman has another brigade in the north. The royal guard protects the sultan in Muscat. The road net and military communications system throughout Oman are surprisingly modern, and Omani infantry forces have considerable mobility.

The Omani army is still very lightly equipped. It has 33 Chieftain, 43 M-60A3, and 6 M-60A1 tanks, although it may have bought 40 more M-60A3s from surplus U.S. stocks during 1991.[270] Its other major armored vehicles include 37 Scorpion and 6 Sultan armored fighting vehicles, 4 VAB/VCI armored infantry fighting vehicles, 6 VAB/VCI armored personnel carriers, 40 Saladin armored cars, and 8 other armored vehicles. It has 8 TOW-II and

10 TOW launchers mounted on light vehicles, additional crew portable TOW launchers, and 50 Milan anti-tank guided weapons. It also has 10 106mm recoilless rifles and large numbers of 84mm Carl Gustav rocket launchers. Additional light anti-tank weapons are on order from Britain. Armored warfare training is almost solely in the mechanized infantry role; there is only token armored maneuver and tank warfare training.

The army relies on towed artillery weapons. They include 40 ROF light 105mm howitzers, 12 M-1946 and 22 Type 59-1 130mm guns, 36 D-30 122mm howitzers, 12 FH-70 155mm howitzers, and 25–30 70mm multiple rocket launchers. It also has 12 M-109A2 self-propelled artillery weapons, and 90–100 81mm and 15–20 120mm mortars. It has no sophisticated artillery targeting and fire control systems.

Oman has very few light air defense weapons. They include several 20mm unguided air defense guns (2 on VABs), 4 ZU-23-2 23mm guns, and 12 Bofors L/60 40mm guns. It also has 24 Blowpipe launchers, 28 RBS-70 fire units, and SA-7 light surface-to-air missiles.

The Omani army has proved to be effective in securing its border areas with Yemen and is highly effective in defending rough terrain. It has good basic training and does well in infantry and mountain combat. It is not, however, able to conduct more than token armored or artillery operations and is dependent on operating from nearby bases. Its regiments are also closer to battalions than actual regiments, and the army would need about 10,000 more men to fill its current order of battle out to the strength necessary to absorb substantial additional amounts of armor and artillery. Such manning is made difficult by both a lack of funds and the tribal character of the manpower, which still creates problems in terms of unit-to-unit and officer-to-enlisted relations. Nevertheless, Oman may pursue a plan to expand its army by 25% by the year 2000 and to at least double its present strength in armor.

The Omani Navy

Oman's navy must defend a 2,900 kilometer coastline, including the main shipping routes through the Straits of Hormuz. Oman has, however, built its navy up from 2,000 men in the mid-1980s to 3,400 in 1992, it has a long seafaring tradition, and it has had the services of excellent British advisors and officers. Oman is slowly converting to all-Omani naval forces, but the growth of the navy's size and technical sophistication has meant that this process has taken longer than Oman originally planned. Oman's navy personnel are gaining technical expertise, but they are still dependent on British support.

The Omani navy is headquartered at Seeb. It has four major combat ships, gunboats, eight patrol boats, and seven amphibious vessels and landing craft. It has a ship maintenance and repair facility at Muscat and naval bases at Ghanam Island, Mina Raysut near Salalah, Al-Masnaa al-Wudam Alwa (the main base), Alwi, Khasab, and Muscat. The new naval base at Al-Masnaa al-Wudam was begun in 1977 and opened in mid-1988.

Oman's principal ships consist of four 394-ton Province-class fast attack boats, armed with one 76mm Oto Melara L/62 gun, twin 40mm Breda Compact mountings, and six to eight MM-40 Exocet missiles. Three of the ships have 2 x 4 Exocet missiles each, and one has 2 x 3. They were handed over to Oman in 1982–1988. The radar and fire control system includes a Racal-Decca TM1226C surveillance radar and Phillips 307 director.

Additional Exocet missiles are on order from France, and Oman ordered two 1,400-ton, 83 meter missile corvettes from Vosper-Thorneycroft in late 1991. These ships will be armed with a 76mm gun, two 20mm guns, two nine barrel chaff/IR decoy launchers, and Exocet missiles. They will have modern radars, surveillance, and fire control systems and will be fitted with an octuple Crotale ship-to-air missile launcher to act as a close-in defense system. There will also be provisions for a 16 cell vertical-launch Seawolf missile system. No sonar or underwater defense systems are currently scheduled to be fitted, but they can be added at any time in the next two years.[271]

Oman has four 153-ton Brooke Marine (Al-Wafji) 37.5 meter fast patrol boats, at least two of which are now armed with Exocet. These ships were delivered in 1977, however, and none has adequate air defense or a sophisticated modern sensor package. The Omani navy also has four 61-ton (Seeb) 25 meter patrol boats armed with Oerlikon 20mm guns, and eleven 8–13 meter patrol boats.

Oman has one of the few GCC navies equipped for amphibious operations. It has one 2,500-ton and one 2,000-ton landing ship logistic (LSL), a 900-ton training ship with a helideck which is a converted royal yacht, three 230-ton LCMs, and two 130-ton LCUs in service. The LSLs have good command and control facilities, a helipad, and the ability to carry two landing craft each with 200–240 men and seven to eight tanks. They are well suited for missions like seizing an oil platform or small island. Oman's auxiliary craft include the royal yacht, a 5,186-ton support ship, a 1,380-ton coastal freighter, and a survey craft. The royal Oman police have thirteen small coastal patrol craft, three logistics support craft, and five inshore patrol craft.

The main limitations to the Omani navy are its lack of capital ships that could directly challenge Iranian ships, a lack of air defense capability, a lack of mine warfare capability, and a lack of maritime surveillance capability, although it has several transports it uses for visual airborne surveillance. Like ASW, however, these are missions which the Omani navy can probably safely leave to the U.S. and UK until it is ready for more sophisticated and more expensive missions.

Both British and U.S. ships and maritime patrol aircraft routinely support Oman in patrolling the approaches to the Straits of Hormuz, and the U.S. can rapidly supplement Omani forces with over-the-horizon reinforcements. The modernization of Omani forces should allow them to deal with low level contingencies and create some deterrent capability against medium level conflicts even without U.S. reinforcements.

The Omani Air Force

The Omani air force has about 3,000 men. Oman has experienced problems in getting the skilled manpower it needs for its air force and still has only about 70% of its minimum requirement for pilots, but it is gradually building up a cadre of native pilots. It also has a technical school and is trying to improve the technical base of its air force manpower. Its combat and technical training is still limited, however, and although the Omani air force is very small for a nation the size of Oman, it is still heavily dependent on foreign support and technicians.

Oman currently has 57 combat aircraft and no armed helicopters. The combat aircraft include 2 attack squadrons with 22 Jaguar S(0), Mark 1/2s, and T-2s based at Masirah Island. The Jaguars are good attack aircraft but have only limited visual air-to-air combat capability using guns and AIM-9-P4 infrared missiles.[272] Other combat aircraft include a fighter–ground attack squadron with 16 Hawker Hunter FGA-6/FR-10/T-67 light attack/trainers based at Thamrait. There is a COIN/training squadron with 12 BAC-167 Mark 82 Strikemasters and 7 BN-2 Defenders. Oman's air ordnance is relatively unsophisticated and includes R-550 Magique and AIM-9P air-to-air missiles and BL-755 cluster bombs. Some 300 more AIM-9Ps are on order.

Oman sought to buy up to two squadrons of F-16 or Tornado fighters during the mid-1980s and planned to expand Thamrait air base into a fully modern facility to base them. In 1985 Britain offered preferential terms for a Tornado sale, and Oman ordered eight Tornadoes as part of a $340 million arms package.[273] Oman ran into funding problems, however, and lacked the skilled manpower to operate such a force. As a result, it ordered two AS-202-18 trainers and sixteen Hawk trainers from the UK in 1990 at a cost of £150 million. The sixteen Hawks will include a mix of series 20 fighter/air defense aircraft and series 100 two-seat fighter trainers. Delivery will take place in 1993 and allow Oman to retire its aging Hunters to a training role.[274]

Oman's air defenses have undergone two major phases of improvement. The first during the early 1970s and the second in 1985. The first provided a mobile British Aerospace system that integrated warning and command and control radars with Oman's Jaguars, Hunters, and BAC-176 Strikemaster aircraft and with 28 Rapier fire units. Marconi provided early warning radars and communications systems. In 1985 Marconi received a contract to expand and improve the system. It provided two long range Martello third dimensional radars, with associated display and handling systems. These are now operational and are linked to two improved SOCs, one improved control and reporting center (CRC), and one new CRC. The CRCs in Muscat and the border with Yemen are linked by tropospheric scatter communications systems. Oman has other air defense system improvements and C^3 equipment from France.[275]

Oman does not have any major surface-to-air missile systems in service or on order. The air force does, however, have two air defense squadrons, equipped with 28 Rapier surface-to-air missile fire units and Blindfire radars. These deploy around Oman's air bases and have moderate readiness. Oman shelters its main air bases at Masirah and Thamrait, which have been greatly improved with U.S. aid. It has additional military airfields and strips at Khasab on the Musandam Peninsula, collocated at the modern international airport at Seeb near Muscat, Nizwa, and Salalah.

Oman has three transport squadrons, one with three BAC-111 and two with three C-130H Hercules, one Mystere-Falcon 20, seven Britten-Norman BN-2 Defender/Islanders, and fifteen Short Skyvan 3M STOL aircraft. Oman has found the Skyvans to have great value in mountain and desert operations. The Omani air force helicopter force includes three AB-206 Jet Rangers, twenty AB-205s, and three AB-212B/Bell 212s. The royal flight has two Gulfstreams, one DC-8, one B-747SP, two AS-202-18 Bravos, and two AS-332 and four SA-330 helicopters.

In broad terms, the Omani air force has evolved in an environment where the emphasis has been on close air support and interdiction missions in support of its ground forces. It has received moderate to good training in visual range air-to-air combat, but it is still dogfight oriented in air-to-air combat at a time when potential enemies like Iran are beginning to emphasize the use of radar vectoring, advanced look-down/shoot-down radars, and long range missile combat. Maintenance and logistics seem to be good, but Oman has no modern radar or infrared reconnaissance assets and would need foreign assistance to conduct any significant form of electronic warfare.

Omani Paramilitary Forces

Oman has 3,500 men in its tribal forces, most of very low capability, and approximately 7,000–9,000 men in police, coast guard, and border forces. The latter units are reasonably effective and operate some light aircraft, helicopters, and patrol boats. The police coast guard has 400 men and 15 AT-105 armored personnel carriers, 11 coastal and 3 inshore patrol craft, 13 support craft, and 28 speed boats. The air wing of the police has 1 B-727, 2 Learjets, 2 Do-228-100s, two Merlin IVAs, 3 DHC-5 Buffalos, 6 Bell 214s, and 1 Hughes 369. There is a small 85 man security force on the Musandam Peninsula called the Shikuk Tribal Militia.

Strategic Interests and Arms Control

In spite of past tensions with tribal groups in western Oman and a Marxist-sponsored rebellion in the Dhofar region in the south in the 1960s and 1970s, Oman no longer faces major internal security problems. It is one of the best managed states in the Near East and Southwest Asia. While its population is becoming increasingly politicized and somewhat less tolerant of Britain's role in Oman's government, the sultan has co-opted a large number of former rebels, modernized his government, and increased the rate of Omanization to the point where British contract personnel play a far more limited role. Oman's five year plans have been relatively successful, in spite of the country's limited oil revenues. This has helped to offset the constant up and down cycles in its oil revenues, which have provided nearly 80% of government revenues.

Oman has consistently supported the West in ensuring the security of the Gulf and access to its oil exports. While it has placed some limits on U.S. access to facilities and exercises, it has done so only out of political necessity.

The Omanis argue, with much justification, that they have provided considerably more support than they have received in return in the form of arms transfers and aid. While Oman does not need major shipments of arms, it is clearly one of the few Gulf nations that is underarmed for its own defense. It needs to modernize and improve the equipment of all of its military services. An arms embargo would leave it too weak and too dependent on aging or obsolete equipment.

Oman has also argued for a 100,000–200,000 man joint Gulf Cooperation Council force, with the chairmanship rotating among the six members. This degree of integration is politically premature and has revived some of the rivalry between Saudi Arabia (which sees itself as the natural leader of the GCC) and Oman (which is pressing for equality among each state). At the same time, integrated forces along the lines of NATO are the only way that the small Gulf states can achieve any overall military effectiveness.[276]

The Southern Gulf States:
The Problem May Be the Solution

The southern Gulf states face several major security problems. The first is cooperation. If Bahrain, Kuwait, Oman, Qatar, Saudi Arabia, and the UAE are ever to create an effective regional deterrent and minimize the need for U.S. and other power projection forces in an emergency, they must make significant further progress in each of the following areas:

- Creating an effective planning system for collective defense, and truly standardized and/or interoperable forces.
- Integrating C^3I and sensor nets for air and naval combat.
- Creating joint air defense and air attack capabilities.
- Establishing effective cross-reinforcement and tactical mobility capabilities.
- Setting up joint training, support, and infrastructure facilities.
- Creating joint air and naval strike forces.
- Deploying joint land defenses of the Yemeni border and of the Kuwaiti–northwestern Saudi borders.
- Preparing for outside or over-the-horizon reinforcement.

It will be years—if ever—before the southern Gulf states cooperate effectively in these areas, and this leads to the second major problem affecting the military balance in the Gulf. The Gulf states must rely on Western power projection capabilities as the only substitute for strong collective defense, and they are so valuable strategically that the West must defend them. Yet it is difficult for the southern Gulf states to cooperate with the West. They must deal with the rise of Islamic fundamentalism, ongoing cuts in Western power projection forces, vestigial fears of any form of Western presence or prepositioning, the difficulties created by U.S. ties to Israel, and the problems the U.S. has in acting as a reliable advisor and source of arms in the face of U.S. domestic political opposition to any arms sale that might threaten Israel.

Preparing for outside or over-the-horizon reinforcement is critical in any scenario involving a major Iraqi or Iranian threat. So far, however, only Bahrain, Kuwait, and Oman have signed agreements that would speed the deployment of U.S., British, and other Western forces. While useful, such arrangements lack strategic depth. Saudi cooperation is needed to preposition U.S. Army armor and other divisional equipment to allow the rapid buildup of armored forces. Large stocks of munitions and spares are needed to support U.S. Air Force units. The UAE and Oman need to make their air units, air defense units, naval forces, AC&W and C^{3}I facilities interoperable with U.S. forces to allow effective naval and air operations.

The third problem that both the southern Gulf states and the West face is that improved defense cooperation and improved Western power projection capability require a careful and well thought out approach to arms sales and arms control. At present, however, West and East are rushing in to compete for sales that offer little prospect of integrated or interoperable defense efforts. Arms control efforts focus on all arms transfers to the entire region, when they should focus on regionwide efforts to shut down the flow of all weapons of mass destruction and target efforts to restrict the flow of conventional arms to prevent transfers to Iran, Iraq, and the unstable regimes in the Red Sea area.

While there are many ways that these problems could be solved that would meet the needs of the individual southern Gulf states, secure their collective interests, and improve Western power projection, the real-world reaction to these problems may well be that the southern Gulf states and the West continue to live with them. Frustrating as this nonsolution will be—and has already been—there seems to be no practical alternative to a series of unstable and informal alliances. Security is too important to each southern Gulf state. Oil is too important to the West. Arms sales are too important to whichever nation wants to sell. The future of the southern Gulf may get worse; there is little realistic prospect that it can get better.

Notes

1. It is important that the reader understand that there is no consistency in the statistical data provided on the Middle East. The author has used a wide range of sources throughout this book and has often had to make his own estimates. The data on the GCC countries are, however, particularly uncertain, and the author has often had to change sources to get consistent or comparable data on a given point. This leads to the use of contradictory data for the same measurement, often because of differences in definition or time of estimate, but sometimes simply because accurate data are not available. The reader should be aware that such statistical information is better than no information but must be regarded as approximate and should be checked with at least three to four different sources before being used for specialized analytic purposes.

2. While this force is sometimes referred to as having 12,000 men, reliable Gulf sources indicate that it has always been well under 10,000.

3. *Defense News*, March 30, 1992, wire service release.

4. The military manpower, force strength, and equipment estimates in this section are made by the author using a wide range of sources, including computerized data bases,

interviews, and press clipping services. Most are impossible to reference in ways of use to the reader. The force strength statistics are generally taken from interviews and from the sources reference for each paragraph. They also draw heavily on his *The Gulf and the Search for Strategic Stability* (Boulder, Westview, 1984) and *The Gulf and the West* (Boulder, Westview, 1988).

Extensive use has also been made of the annual editions of the International Institute for Strategic Studies *Military Balance* (IISS, London), in this case the 1991–1992 edition, and of the Jaffee Center for Strategic Studies, *The Military Balance in the Middle East* (JCSS, Tel Aviv), especially the 1990–1991 edition and working materials from the coming edition. Material has also been drawn from computer print outs from NEXIS, the United States Naval Institute data base, and from the DMS/FI Market Intelligence Reports data base. Other sources include *Military Technology*, "World Defense Almanac for 1991–1992," published in 1992; Foreign Affairs Division, "Middle East Arms Control and Related Issues," Washington, Congressional Research Service, 91-384F, May 1, 1991; Anthony R. Tucker, "Saudi Arabia's Military Build-Up," *Armed Forces*, February, 1989, pp. 62–66; Jacob Goldberg, "The Saudi Military Build-up: Strategy and Risks," *Middle East Review*, Spring, 1989, pp. 3–12; and *Middle East Economic Digest*, "MEED Special Report: Defense," Volume 35, December 13, 1991.

Weapons data are taken from many sources, including computerized material available in NEXIS, and various editions of *Jane's Fighting Ships* (Jane's Publishing); *Jane's Naval Weapons Systems* (Jane's Publishing); *Jane's Armour and Artillery* (Jane's Publishing); *Jane's Infantry Weapons* (Jane's Publishing); *Jane's Military Vehicles and Logistics* (Jane's Publishing); *Jane's Land-Based Air Defence* (Jane's Publishing); *Jane's All the World's Aircraft* (Jane's Publishing); *Jane's Battlefield Surveillance Systems* (Jane's Publishing); *Jane's Radar and Electronic Warfare Systems* (Jane's Publishing), *Jane's C^{3}I Systems* (Jane's Publishing); *Jane's Air-Launched Weapons Systems* (Jane's Publishing); *Jane's Defence Appointments & Procurement Handbook (Middle East Edition)* (Jane's Publishing); *Tanks of the World* (Bernard and Grafe); *Weyer's Warships* (Bernard and Grafe); and *Warplanes of the World* (Bernard and Grafe).

Other military background, effectiveness, strength, organizational, and history data are taken from Anthony H. Cordesman, *The Gulf and the Search for Strategic Stability*, Boulder, Westview, 1984; *The Gulf and the West*, Boulder, Westview, 1988, and *Weapons of Mass Destruction in the Middle East*, London, Brassey's/RUSI, 1991; Anthony H. Cordesman and Abraham Wagner, *The Lessons of Modern War*, Volume II, Boulder, Westview, 1989; the relevant country or war sections of Herbert K. Tillema, *International Conflict Since 1945*, Boulder, Westview, 1991; Department of Defense, *Conduct of the Persian Gulf War; Final Report to Congress*, Washington, Department of Defense, April, 1992; Department of Defense and Department of State, *Congressional Presentation for Security Assistance Programs, Fiscal Year 1993*, Washington, Department of State, 1992; various annual editions of John Laffin's *The World in Conflict* or *War Annual*, London, Brassey's; and John Keegan, *World Armies*, London, Macmillan, 1983.

5. Ironically, the experience was reversed in March, 1973. The PDRY air force strafed the Saudi garrison at Al-Wadiah in an effort to persuade Saudi Arabia to end its support for anti-PDRY rebels.

6. *Oil and Gas Journal*, September 23, 1991, p. 62.

7. *OJJ Special, Oil and Gas Journal*, December 30, 1991, pp. 43–49; other estimates indicate 260 billion barrels of proven reserves and 42 billion barrels of probable reserves. See Joseph P. Riva, Jr., of the Congressional Research Service, writing in the *Oil and Gas Journal*, September 23, 1991, p. 62. These estimates have become increasingly more political in recent years as each major producer in the Gulf has tried to exaggerate its reserves and relative importance.

8. *OJJ Special, Oil and Gas Journal*, December 30, 1991, pp. 43–49.

9. CIA, *World Factbook, 1991*, pp. 273–274.

10. *Los Angeles Times*, January 28, 1992, p. C-1.

11. The author has encountered many of these attitudes during his visits to Saudi Arabia. For typical U.S. reporting, see the *Baltimore Sun*, July 28, 1991, p. 11-A; *Security Intelligence*, February 10, 1992, p. 8; *New York Times*, January 30, 1992, p. 3, March 1, 1992, p. 8.

12. *New York Times*, August 6, 1991, p. A-5; November 18, 1991, p. A-3; December 31, 1991, p. A-1; *Washington Post*, December 31, 1991, p. A-10; March 2, 1992, p. A-1; March 6, 1992, p. A-16; September 18, 1992, p. A-31; *Boston Globe*, September 18, 1992, p. 6; *Chicago Tribune*, September 18, 1992, p. I-4.

13. *Christian Science Monitor*, March 16, 1992, p. 19; Dilip Hero, "Saudi Reforms: Too Little and 32 Years Late," *The Nation*, April 13, 1992, pp. 486–487; *Newsweek*, March 16, 1992, p. 45; *New York Times*, December 31, 1991, p. A-1; January 1, 1992, p. 3; February 25, 1992, p. A-6; March 2, 1992, p. A-1; March 9, 1992, pp. A1 and A7; March 30, 1992, p. A-6; Fred Halliday, "Facelift for a Tribal Dictatorship," *Guardian Weekly*, March 15, 1992; *Manchester Guardian Weekly*, March 8, 1992, p. 10; *Economist*, March 7, 1992, pp. 42–43; *Washington Post*, December 31, 1992, p. A-10; March 6, 1992, p. A16; *Financial Times*, March 3, 1992, p. 4; *Boston Globe*, September 18, 1992, p. 6.

14. Estimates range from 2,000 to 7,000 princes. The higher figure represents many sons with little or no influence who are descended from collateral branches of the family. The 2,000 figure is a rough estimate of the number who have any real influence. The main power is concentrated in first and second generation sons descended directly from Abdel Aziz.

15. This dismissal was partly the result of the fact that Khalid had used U.S. Green Berets during the buildup for Desert Storm to help reorganize Saudi forces and remove some of their bureaucratic rigidities. This caused considerable resentment and made Khalid's promotion more difficult, although it significantly improved Saudi performance during the Gulf War. *New York Times*, October 15, 1991, p. 1; *Washington Post*, March 15, 1992, p. A-35.

16. The reader should be aware that this often leads to exaggerated reports of tension and corruption. Anyone who has lived in Saudi Arabia becomes aware that royal family rumors, and rumors of internal conflicts, are almost a national sport. The Hijazi are masters of this sport, although sometimes surpassed by whatever businessman has just suffered in a   deal   with one of the princes. It is far harder for a Westerner to understand the pressures building up within the Islamic fundamentalists, but the movement does affect a significant number of Saudi youths and often has intense support at the university level. Cassettes are circulated nationally, and many very well educated Saudis support fundamentalism, as well as many traditionalists.

17. Figures referring to 60–70% Shi'ite do not seem to be correct.

18. Congressional Quarterly, *The Middle East*, 7th Edition, Washington, Congressional Quarterly, 1990, p. 117.

19. CIA, *World Factbook, 1991*, pp. 273–274.

20. The FY1988 budget was planned to have a $10 billion deficit, with $8 billion in foreign borrowing. It involved the first foreign borrowing in 25 years and the first increase in taxes in eight years—all on foreign businesses. The actual budget reached a $15–17 billion deficit by the year's end, with some $10 billion in financing. *Economist*, January 16, 1988, p. 59; *Defense News*, January 18, 1988, p. 4.

21. An effort to impose taxes of up to 30% on foreigners was withdrawn shortly after it was proposed. Nearly two-thirds of the bonds were bought by the Saudi Arabian government. *Wall Street Journal*, December 31, 1987, p. 4; January 5, 1988, p. 21; January 6, 1988, p.

12; January 7, 1988, p. 16; January 12, 1988, p. 2; *Washington Post,* December 31, 1987, p. E-3; January 12, 1988, p. C-3; *Economist,* January 16–22, 1988, p. 59; *New York Times,* January 6, 1988, p. A-1; *Chicago Tribune,* January 27, 1988, pp. 3–7.

22. *Middle East Economic Digest,* January 17, 1992, pp. 4–5; March 20, 1992, pp. 10–16.

23. *Middle East Economic Digest,* January 17, 1992, pp. 4–5; March 20, 1992, pp. 10–16.

24. Saudi Arabia shifted its fiscal year to a calendar year in 1988.

25. *Defense News,* January 18, 1988, p. 4.

26. Based on estimates by the International Institute for Strategic Studies.

27. *Middle East Economic Digest,* January 17, 1992, pp. 4–5.

28. Data are based on excerpts of the Saudi national budgets and reporting by the IISS. CIA, ACDA, SIPRI, and other estimates often differ significantly. The reader should also be aware that many major arms transactions in all Middle East countries are handled privately by their defense ministers, often on a multiyear basis. Many of these transactions are not reported to or through the central bank. Saudi Arabia, like other oil exporting states, complicates this situation further by using oil barter arrangements, offset arrangements, and constantly renegotiating major arms deals while deliveries are in progress. The data published in the IISS *Military Balance, 1987–1988,* indicate that the total manpower fit for service could be about 50–70% of the CIA estimate. (See p. 110.)

29. The reader should be aware that there is little historical consistency in ACDA or CIA estimates of Saudi defense spending, and estimates are constantly revised by billions of dollars for relatively long periods of time. While ACDA provides an estimate of spending in constant dollars, an examination of the conversion method quickly reveals that it is little more than a guesstimate. See Arms Control and Disarmament Agency (ACDA), *World Military Expenditures and Arms Transfers, 1989,* Washington, GPO, 1990, Table I; Arms Control and Disarmament Agency (ACDA), *World Military Expenditures and Arms Transfers, 1990,* Washington, GPO, 1990, Table II; and Saudi Arabia section in the CIA, *World Factbook, 1991.*

30. Arms Control and Disarmament Agency (ACDA), *World Military Expenditures and Arms Transfers, 1989,* Washington, GPO, 1990, Table II.

31. Arms Control and Disarmament Agency (ACDA), *World Military Expenditures and Arms Transfers, 1985,* Washington, GPO, 1985, pp. 133–134.

32. Arms Control and Disarmament Agency (ACDA), *World Military Expenditures and Arms Transfers, 1989,* Washington, GPO, 1990, pp. 117–118.

33. Arms Control and Disarmament Agency (ACDA), *World Military Expenditures and Arms Transfers, 1990,* Washington, GPO, 1990, pp. 133–134.

34. See "High Costs of the Persian Gulf War," Arms Control and Disarmament Agency (ACDA), *World Military Expenditures and Arms Transfers, 1987,* Washington, GPO, 1988, pp. 21–23, and Richard F. Grimmett, *Trends in Conventional Arms Transfers to the Third World by Major Supplier, 1982–1989,* Congressional Research Service, Library of Congress, Washington, 90-298F, June 19, 1990.

35. Richard F. Grimmett, *Conventional Arms Transfers to the Third World, 1983–1990,* Washington, Congressional Research Service, CRS-91-578F, August 2, 1991, p. 69; and *Conventional Arms Transfers to the Third World, 1984–1991,* Washington, Congressional Research Service, CRS-92-577F, July 20, 1991, p. 60, 67.

36. IISS, *Military Balance, 1991–1992,* p. 117.

37. Adapted largely from the CIA, *World Factbook, 1991,* pp. 273–274. The Saudi census claimed a population of 7 million in 1977.

38. CIA, *World Factbook, 1991,* pp. 273–274.

39. IISS, *Military Balance, 1991–1992,* p. 117.

40. Unless otherwise specified, the military data quoted here are taken from the relevant country sections of the IISS, *Military Balance, 1987–1988;* CIA, *The World Factbook, 1986;* and

Ze'ev Eytan, *The Middle East Military Balance, 1986,* Jaffee Center for Strategic Studies, Tel Aviv University, Tel Aviv, 1987.

41. These Pakistani forces left the kingdom in 1988 and 1989.

42. Estimates of active manning in the national guard differ sharply. The most recent IISS estimate is 35,000 actives, and 20,000 tribal levies. The author's estimate is 15,000 full time actives, 15,000 semi-active reserves, and 15,000 tribal levies.

43. These figures are the author's estimate. The CIA estimates a total manpower pool of 6,663,217 military age males between 15 and 49, and 3,724,610 fit for military service. It estimates 165,167 reach age 17 annually. CIA, *The World Factbook, 1991,* pp. 273–274. The IISS estimates a total population of 10,600,000, with 473,000 males between the ages of 17 and 22, and 841,000 between the ages of 23 and 32. The IISS estimates are based on British figures which seem far less politicized than the CIA data, which seem to be deliberately adjusted to please Saudi Arabia.

44. *Jane's Defence Weekly,* May 15, 1985; *New York Times,* April 28, 1985.

45. The data available to the author were so much in conflict that it proved impossible to provide even a useful range.

46. Maj. Gen. Dennis Malcor was sent to Saudi Arabia to survey its military requirements after the Gulf War. *Washington Post,* March 15, 1992, p. A-35; *New York Times,* October 15, 1991, p. A-1; *Jane's Defence Weekly,* December 14, 1991, p. 1175.

47. Richard F. Grimmett, "Arms Sales to Saudi Arabia," Congressional Research Service, IB91007, August 28, 1991, p. 4.

48. *Inside the Army,* April 6, 1992, p. 1; *Inside the Pentagon,* April 9, 1992, p. 2.

49. Department of Defense, "Sale of Abrams Tanks to Saudi Arabia," Background Information, November 1, 1989.

50. Department of Defense fax, July 18, 1990; *Defense Week,* March 12, 1990. p. 3.

51. *Defense News,* November 13, 1989, p. 3; March 12, 1990, p. 3; *Washington Post,* October 12, 1989, p. A-9; October 16, 1989, p. A-17; Department of Defense Background Paper, November 1, 1989; *Insight,* September 25, 1989, p. 34; *Philadelphia Inquirer,* September 30, 1989, p. 5-A; *New York Times,* September 28, 1989, p. A-1.

52. *Jane's Defence Weekly,* February 6, 1988, p. 191; March 7, 1992; Richard F. Grimmett, "Arms Sales to Saudi Arabia," Congressional Research Service, IB91007, August 28, 1991, p. 4; *Defense Daily,* February 14, 1992, p. 251; *Defense News,* March 30, 1992, p. 6.

53. *Defense News,* March 30, 1992, p. 6; *Defense Daily,* February 14, 1992, p. 251; *Jane's Defence Weekly,* February 6, 1988, p. 191; March 7, 1992; *Inside the Army,* April 6, 1992, p. 1; *Inside the Pentagon,* April 9, 1992, p. 2.

54. *Jane's Defence Weekly,* February 6, 1988, p. 191; March 7, 1992; *Defense Daily,* February 14, 1992, p. 251; *Defense News,* March 30, 1992, p. 6.

55. IISS, *Military Balance,* DMS computer data base, interviews in Saudi Arabia in February, 1991, discussions with Saudi experts in December, 1990, and *Defense News,* February 22, 1988, p. 3. These figures are based largely on Saudi data obtained in March, 1991 and differ significantly from IISS and most Western data bases.

56. The first 200 M-2s were produced at a rate of 2 in FY89, 98 in FY90, and 100 in FY91. *Jane's Defence Weekly,* September 9, 1989, p. 452; *Wall Street Journal,* June 2, 1988, p. 56; *Aviation Week,* June 17, 1991, p. 129.

57. DMS computer data base, interviews in Saudi Arabia in February, 1991, discussions with Saudi experts in December, 1990, and *Defense News,* February 22, 1988, p. 3.

58. Richard F. Grimmett, "Arms Sales to Saudi Arabia," Congressional Research Service, IB91007, August 28, 1991, p. 4.

59. *Aviation Week,* June 17, 1991, p. 129; Richard F. Grimmett, "Arms Sales to Saudi Arabia," Congressional Research Service, IB91007, August 28, 1991, p. 4; IISS and JCSS military balances; DMS computer data base, interviews in Saudi Arabia in February, 1991,

discussions with Saudi experts in December, 1990, and *Defense News*, February 22, 1988, p. 3.

60. Richard F. Grimmett, "Arms Sales to Saudi Arabia," Congressional Research Service, IB91007, August 28, 1991, p. 4.

61. *Jane's Defence Weekly*, March 11, 1989, p. 393.

62. Richard F. Grimmett, "Arms Sales to Saudi Arabia," Congressional Research Service, IB91007, August 28, 1991, p. 4; *Jane's Defence Weekly*, December 17, 1988, p. 1546; June 25, 1989, p. 1296.

63. *Aviation Week*, April 2, 1990, p. 44; *Jane's Defence Weekly*, November 16, 1991, p. 927; *Wall Street Journal*, October 7, 1991, p. 16.

64. *Jane's Defence Weekly*, July 22, 1989, p. 105.

65. *Jane's Defence Weekly*, December 14, 1991, p. 1175; June 13, 1992, p. 1013; Richard F. Grimmett, "Arms Sales to Saudi Arabia," Congressional Research Service, IB91007, August 28, 1991, p. 4.

66. For an interesting Israeli view of the role of the national guard in the mid-1980s, see Mordechai Abir, "Saudi Security and Military Endeavor," *Jerusalem Quarterly*, No. 33, Fall, 1984, pp. 79–94.

67. Author's estimate based on interviews in Saudi Arabia; "Saudi National Guard Fact Sheet," DSAA I-01514, June 5, 1990; FMC data; DMS computer print outs; and the IISS and JCSS military balances.

68. Some reports indicate long range plans to buy 1,200 to 2,100 Piranhas.

69. *Jane's Defence Weekly*, March 7, 1992, p. 388.

70. Historical sources for the analysis of the Saudi navy include James Bruce and Paul Bear, "Latest Arab Force Levels Operating in the Gulf," *Jane's Defence Weekly*, December 12, 1987, pp. 1360–1361; and various editions of the "Middle Eastern, North African, and South Asian Navies," sections of the March issue of *Proceedings*.

71. These include 20 AS-365N Dauphin helicopters with AS-15TT air-to-surface missiles, and 4 search and rescue versions of the same helicopter.

72. They are Tacoma-class ASUWs, with 2x4 Harpoon launchers, and 2x3 ASTT (Mark 46 lightweight torpedo launchers).

73. These are French F-2000 class vessels with 4x533mm and 2x406mm ASTT torpedo launchers, one Dauphin helicopter, one 100mm gun, and 8 Otomat 2 missile launchers.

74. *London Financial Times*, June 13, 1989, p. B-5; *Wall Street Journal*, June 7, 1988, p. 31; *Jane's Defence Weekly*, December 17, 1988, p. 1546; June 25, 1989, p. 1296; *International Defense Review*, 7/1989, p. 884.

75. The Sandown-class ships are 500-ton mine hunters with glass reinforced plastic hulls, Type 2903 Variable Depth Sonar, remote control mine disposal systems, and Plessey NAUTIS-M command, control, and navigation systems. *Defense News*, March 20, 1989, p. 24; April 24, 1989, p. 28; *Jane's Defence Weekly*, October 26, 1991, p. 770.

76. *Jane's Defence Weekly*, July 16, 1987, p. 58.

77. *Jane's Defence Weekly*, December 12, 1987, pp. 1360–1361.

78. Richard F. Grimmett, "Arms Sales to Saudi Arabia," Congressional Research Service, IB91007, August 28, 1991, p. 4.

79. Fax from Department of Defense, OSD/LA, January 11, 1987; *Baltimore Sun*, September 26, 1989, p. E-9; *Jane's Defence Weekly*, October 7, 1989, p. 744.

80. *Washington Post*, July 30, 1991, p. A-12; Richard F. Grimmett, "Arms Sales to Saudi Arabia," Congressional Research Service, IB91007, August 28, 1991, p. 4.

81. *Jane's Defence Weekly*, March 28, 1992, pp. 533–535.

82. *Jane's Defence Weekly*, July 9, 1988, p. 23; July 16, 1988, p. 59; July 23, 1988, pp. 111 and 122–123; March 28, 1992, pp. 533–535; *Newsweek*, July 25, 1988, p. 47; *New York Times*, July 11, 1988, p. 1, and July 12, 1988, p. 3.

83. *Jane's Defence Weekly*, July 9, 1988, p. 23; July 16, 1988, p. 59; and July 23, 1988, pp. 111

and 122–123; June 15, 1991, p. 998; October 26, 1991, p. 770; March 28, 1992, pp. 533–535; *Newsweek*, July 25, 1988, p. 47; *New York Times*, July 11, 1988, p. 1, and July 12, 1988, p. 3.

84. See the author's, *The Gulf and the Search for Strategic Stability*, pp. 122–126.

85. Richard F. Grimmett, "Arms Sales to Saudi Arabia," Congressional Research Service, IB91007, August 28, 1991, p. 3.

86. *Aviation Week*, September 21, 1992, p. 26; *New York Times*, September 12, 1992, p. A-1, September 15, 1992, p. A-1.

87. Comparisons based on data provided by McDonnell Douglas in May, 1992. *Business Week*, March 16, 1992, p. 37; *Defense Daily*, January 28, 1992, p. 133; *London Financial Times*, November 6, 1991, p. 1; January 21, 1992, p. 28; *Washington Post*, November 6, 1991, p. C-1; January 24, 1992, p. 7; September 3, 1992, p. A-39; *Jane's Defence Weekly*, October 26, 1991, p. 770; January 25, 1992, p. 102; *Guardian*, November 7, 1991, p. 11; *Wall Street Journal*, November 6, 1991, p. 3; *Aerospace Daily*, October 28, 1991, p. 152; November 8, 1991, p. 221; November 14, 1991, p. 247; *Defense News*, February 24, 1991, p. 3; December 23, 1991, p. 1.

88. There are unconfirmed reports that air force officers loyal to the shah ensured that the F-14s were not fully operational.

89. *Aviation Week*, September 21, 1992, p. 26; *New York Times*, September 12, 1992, p. A-1; September 15, 1992, p. A-1; *Washington Post*, September 27, 1992, p. A-16.

90. The deal would be in addition to the $3.5 billion Yamamah 1 sale and bring total related sales to around $10 billion. *Jane's Defence Weekly*, April 11, 1992, p. 597; *Flight International*, April 21, 1992, p. 21; *Defense News*, August 31, 1992, p. 40.

91. *Signal*, August, 1991, p. 116; *Aviation Week*, December 5, 1988, p. 23; *Aerospace Daily*, October 28, 1991, p. 152.

92. The Hawks are MIM-23Bs.

93. IISS, *Military Balance, 1991–1992*, p. 118.

94. Richard F. Grimmett, "Arms Sales to Saudi Arabia," Congressional Research Service, IB91007, August 28, 1991, p. 3; *Defense News*, September 23, 1991, pp. 1 and 36; *Washington Post*, November 12, 1991, p. C-1; *New York Times*, November 9, 1991, p. 3; *Jane's Defence Weekly*, October 19, 1991, p. 699; *Washington Times*, October 24, 1991, p. A-4; *Defense Daily*, November 8, 1991, p. 223; November 11, 1991, p. A-14.

95. Raytheon background brief, February, 1992; *Defense News*, September 23, 1991, pp. 1 and 36.

96. *Flight International*, July 23, 1991, p. 18; *Jane's Defence Weekly*, July 15, 1989, p. 57.

97. *Flight International*, July 23, 1991, p. 18; *Jane's Defence Weekly*, July 15, 1989, p. 57.

98. *Jane's Defence Weekly*, July 15, 1989, p. 57; January 19, 1991; July 20, 1991, p. 97; *London Financial Times*, July 5, 1991; p. 5; *Flight International*, July 23, 1991, p. 18.

99. *Jane's Defence Weekly*, January 19, 1991; July 20, 1991, p. 97; *London Financial Times*, July 5, 1991, p. 5; *Flight International*, July 23, 1991, p. 18.

100. The Saudi air defense corps renewed its contract for technical assistance support from Raytheon for its IHawk surface-to-air missiles in May, 1986. This contract has been running since 1976 and was renewed for three years at a cost of $518 million. *Jane's Defence Weekly*, June 7, 1986, p. 1019.

101. *Defense News*, November 11, 1991, p. 36.

102. *Defense News*, April 8, 1991, p. 1; *Defense and Foreign Affairs Weekly*, November 28, 1988, p. 1; *Washington Post*, September 20, 1988, p. A-8; *Jane's Defence Weekly*, October 1, 1988, pp. 744–755.

103. *Jane's Defence Weekly*, October 1, 1988, pp. 744–755.

104. *Jane's Defence Weekly*, October 1, 1990, pp. 744–746.

105. *Washington Times*, October 4, 1988, p. A-2; *Christian Science Monitor*, October 8, 1988, p. 2.

106. Shuey, Lenhart, Snyder, Donnelly, Mielke, and Moteff, *Missile Proliferation: Survey*

of Emerging Missile Forces, Washington, D.C., Congressional Research Service, Report 88-642F, February 9, 1989, pp. 64–65.

107. The warhead could also be enhanced with submunitions, a proximity fuse to detonate before impact to give an optimum burst pattern and widen the area covered by shrapnel, and a time delay fuse to allow the warhead to fully penetrate a building before exploding. Shuey, Lenhart, Snyder, Donnelly, Mielke, and Moteff, *Missile Proliferation: Survey of Emerging Missile Forces,* Washington, D.C., Congressional Research Service, Report 88-642F, 1989, pp. 23–24.

108. U.S. experts have never monitored a test of the conventional version of the missile. CEP stands for circular error probable, and is an indication of a missile's accuracy. The figure represents the radius of a circle in which half the warheads are expected to fall. It should be noted, however, that the theoretical figures applies only to missiles that operate perfectly up to the point which the missile has left the launcher and at least its first booster and guidance system are operating perfectly. Operational CEPs can only be guesstimated but will be much lower. Missiles generally do not have fail-safe warheads. A substantial number will have partial failures and deliver their warhead far from their intended targets. *Jane's Defence Weekly,* October 1, 1990, pp. 744–746; Fred Donovan, "Mideast Missile Flexing," *Arms Control Today,* May, 1990, p. 31; Shuey, Lenhart, Snyder, Donnelly, Mielke, and Moteff, *Missile Proliferation: Survey of Emerging Missile Forces,* Washington, D.C., Congressional Research Service, Report 88-642F, February 9, 1989.

109. *Wall Street Journal,* April 4, 1988, p. 13; *Arms Control Today,* May, 1988, p. 24; *New York Times,* April 26, 1988, p. A-10; *Los Angeles Times,* May 4, 1988, p. I-7; *Washington Times,* May 4, 1988, p. 8; *Washington Post,* March, 1988, p. 1.

110. At one point, the U.S. seems to have considered a plan to preposition enough equipment for an entire corps of three divisions and 150,000 men. *New York Times,* October 15, 1992, p. A-1.

111. *Jane's Defence Weekly,* September 14, 1991, p. 452; November 2, 1991, p. 793; January 25, 1992, p. 107; April 4, 1992, p. 549; *New York Times,* October 13, 1991, p. A-1; *Los Angeles Times,* August 5, 1991, p. 4; October 22, 1991, A-3; *Washington Post,* October 20, 1991, p. 1; March 17, 1992, p. 35; May 31, 1992, p. A-10.

112. It should be noted that the U.S. already had 300 combat aircraft in Saudi Arabia and 150 on two carriers, and that Saudi Arabia objected to additional deployments, not to cooperation with the U.S. *New York Times,* September 25, 1991, p. A-14; September 27, 1991, p. A-1; September 30 ,1991, p. A-5.

113. The military manpower, force strength, and equipment estimates in this section are made by the author using a wide range of sources, including computerized data bases, interviews, and press clipping services. Most are impossible to reference in ways of use to the reader. The force strength statistics are generally taken from interviews and from the sources reference for each paragraph. The data for the pre–Gulf War estimates also draw heavily on his *The Gulf and the Search for Strategic Stability* (Boulder, Westview, 1984) and *The Gulf and the West* (Boulder, Westview, 1988).

Extensive use has also been made of the annual editions of the International Institute for Strategic Studies, *Military Balance* (IISS, London), in this case the 1991–1992 edition, and of the Jaffee Center for Strategic Studies, *The Military Balance in the Middle East* (JCSS, Tel Aviv), especially the 1990–1991 edition and working materials from the coming edition. Material has also been drawn from computer print outs from NEXIS, the United States Naval Institute data base, and from the DMS/FI Market Intelligence Reports data base. Other sources include *Jane's Defence Weekly,* December 14, 1991, p. 1174; March 28, 1992, pp. 528–531; *New York Times,* January 14, 1992, p. 4; *London Financial Times,* July 8, 1991, p. 3; January 7, 1992, p. 4; *Defense News,* February 10, 1992, p. 38; Theodore Craig, "Kuwait: Background, Restoration, and Questions for the United States," Congressional Research

Service, 91-288F, May 21, 1992; Department of Defense, *Conduct of the Persian Gulf War; Final Report to Congress*, Washington, Department of Defense, April, 1992, pp. 2–10; *Military Technology*, "World Defense Almanac for 1991–1992," published in 1992; Foreign Affairs Division, "Middle East Arms Control and Related Issues," Washington, Congressional Research Service, 91-384F, May 1, 1991; and *Middle East Economic Digest*, "MEED Special Report: Defense," Volume 35, December 13, 1991.

Weapons data are taken from many sources, including computerized material available in NEXIS, and various editions of *Jane's Fighting Ships* (Jane's Publishing); *Jane's Naval Weapons Systems* (Jane's Publishing); *Jane's Armour and Artillery* (Jane's Publishing); *Jane's Infantry Weapons* (Jane's Publishing); *Jane's Military Vehicles and Logistics* (Jane's Publishing); *Jane's Land-Based Air Defence* (Jane's Publishing); *Jane's All the World's Aircraft* (Jane's Publishing); *Jane's Battlefield Surveillance Systems* (Jane's Publishing); *Jane's Radar and Electronic Warfare Systems* (Jane's Publishing), *Jane's C^3I Systems* (Jane's Publishing); *Jane's Air-Launched Weapons Systems* (Jane's Publishing); *Jane's Defence Appointments & Procurement Handbook (Middle East Edition)* (Jane's Publishing); *Tanks of the World* (Bernard and Grafe); *Weyer's Warships* (Bernard and Grafe); and *Warplanes of the World* (Bernard and Grafe).

Other military background, effectiveness, strength, organizational, and history data are taken from Anthony H. Cordesman, *The Gulf and the Search for Strategic Stability*, Boulder, Westview, 1984; *The Gulf and the West*, Boulder, Westview, 1988; and *Weapons of Mass Destruction in the Middle East*, London, Brassey's/RUSI, 1991; Anthony H. Cordesman and Abraham Wagner, *The Lessons of Modern War*, Volume II, Boulder, Westview, 1989; the relevant country or war sections of Herbert K. Tillema, *International Conflict Since 1945*, Boulder, Westview, 1991; Department of Defense and Department of State, *Congressional Presentation for Security Assistance Programs, Fiscal Year 1993*, Washington, Department of State, 1992; various annual editions of John Laffin's *The World in Conflict* or *War Annual*, London, Brassey's; and John Keegan, *World Armies*, London, Macmillan, 1983.

114. *Oil and Gas Journal*, September 23, 1991, p. 62.

115. *OJJ Special, Oil and Gas Journal*, December 30, 1991, pp. 43–49; other estimates indicate 97 billion barrels of proven reserves and 4 billion barrels of probable reserves. See Joseph P. Riva, Jr., of the Congressional Research Service, writing in the *Oil and Gas Journal*, September 23, 1991, p. 62. These estimates have become increasingly more political in recent years as each major producer in the Gulf has tried to exaggerate its reserves and relative importance.

116. *Los Angeles Times*, January 28, 1992, p. C-1.

117. Alfred B. Prados, "Iraq and Kuwait: Conflicting Historical Claims," Congressional Research Service, 91-34F, January 11, 1991, p. 4.

118. *Washington Post*, December 19, 1987, p. A-27.

119. Department of Defense, *Conduct of the Persian Gulf War; Final Report to Congress*, Washington, Department of Defense, April, 1992, pp. 6–7.

120. *American Arab Affairs*, Fall, 1989, p. 30; *Los Angeles Times*, December 2, 1990, pp. M-4 and M-8; Theodore Craig, "Kuwait: Background, Restoration, and Questions for the United States," Congressional Research Service, 91-288F, May 21, 1992, p. 9.

121. Department of Defense, *Conduct of the Persian Gulf War; Final Report to Congress*, Washington, Department of Defense, April, 1992, pp. 3–4.

122. Alfred B. Prados, "Iraq and Kuwait: Conflicting Historical Claims," Congressional Research Service, 91-34F, January 11, 1991, p. 4.

123. FBIS NES-90-138, July 18, 1990, p. 21; Theodore Craig, "Kuwait: Background, Restoration, and Questions for the United States," Congressional Research Service, 91-288F, May 21, 1992, p. 8; Department of Defense, *Conduct of the Persian Gulf War; Final Report to Congress*, Washington, Department of Defense, April, 1992, pp. 2–10.

124. The border was laid out relatively quickly by a single British agent, Maj. John More,

and no follow-up effort was made to create a formal survey or border markings. *Economist,* February 29, 1992, p. 45; *Philadelphia Inquirer,* February 20, 1992, p. A-16; *Wall Street Journal,* December 5, 1991, p. A-1.

125. *London Financial Times,* February 26, 1992, pp. III-1 to III-3; *The Sunday Times,* January 19, 1992, p. 1; *Time,* August 5, 1991, p. 32; *Washington Times,* May 27 ,1992, p. A-7.

126. *London Financial Times,* February 26, 1992, pp. III-1 to III-3; *The Sunday Times,* January 19, 1992, p. 1; *Time,* August 5, 1991, p. 32; *New York Times,* May 4, 1992, p. A-1; *Christian Science Monitor,* May 29, 1992, p. 8.

127. *Chicago Tribune,* November 3, 1991, p. I-14; *Washington Post,* November 7, 1991, p. 1; June 5, 1992, p. A-1; June 6, 1992, p. A-17; October 3, 1992, pp. A-13–14; October 6, 1992, p. A-18; October 7, 1992, p. A-27; *Wall Street Journal,* October 24, 1991, p. A-2; Joseph P. Riva, "Kuwaiti Oil Well Fires Updated," Congressional Research Service, 91-313, June 26, 1991; *Washington Times,* May 28, 1992, p. A-7.

128. Arms Control and Disarmament Agency (ACDA), *World Military Expenditures and Arms Transfers, 1990,* Washington, GPO, 1990, Table I.

129. Arms Control and Disarmament Agency (ACDA), *World Military Expenditures and Arms Transfers, 1990,* Washington, GPO, 1990, Table II.

130. Arms Control and Disarmament Agency, *World Military Expenditures, 1986,* Washington, GPO, 1987.

131. Arms Control and Disarmament Agency, *World Military Expenditures, 1989,* Washington, GPO, 1990, p. 117.

132. Arms Control and Disarmament Agency (ACDA), *World Military Expenditures and Arms Transfers, 1990,* Washington, GPO, 1990, pp. 133–134.

133. CIA, *World Factbook, 1991,* pp. 173–174.

134. Kuwait is considering up-engining the tanks with new British or German engines. *Jane's Defence Weekly,* February 28, 1987, p. 323.

135. *Washington Times,* July 14, 1988, p. 2.

136. *Jane's Defence Weekly,* January 30, 1987, p. 151.

137. *Jane's Defence Weekly,* February 28, 1987, p. 314, and March 7, 1987, p. 359.

138. I am indebted to Lt. Com. Jerry Ferguson, one of my students at Georgetown University, for much of the research, and many of the insights, on Gulf naval and air forces presented in this chapter.

139. The 76mm and 40mm guns can provide some air defense but with little lethality. The TNC-45s have very complicated electronics, virtually all of which are maintained by foreign technicians. The voice network system used by the TNC-45 is so slow that it is virtually hopeless for air defense operations and generally creates confusion and increases delay and vulnerability if any attempt is made to use it.

140. Aircraft actually in storage included 12 Lightnings, 4 Hunters, and 9 BAC-167 Strikemasters.

141. The A-4s lack an air intercept radar and can only engage in visual combat using guns or Sidewinder missiles.

142. *Defense News,* August 8, 1988, p. 7; *Jane's Defence Weekly,* August 13, 1988, p. 246; *Washington Times,* July 25, 1988, p. 1; *Newsweek,* August 25, 1988, p. 47.

143. Sources differ. The JCSS is shown. The IISS says 2 DC-9, 4 L-100-30.

144. The history of Iraq's invasion is adapted from Department of Defense, *Conduct of the Persian Gulf War; Final Report to Congress,* Washington, Department of Defense, April, 1992, pp. 2–10.

145. *New York Times,* January 14, 1992, p. 4.

146. Kuwait has a total of about 1,386 wells, including shut-ins. *Chicago Tribune,* November 3, 1991, p. I-14; Joseph P. Riva, "Kuwaiti Oil Well Fires Updated," Congressional Research Service, 91-313, June 26, 1991.

147. *London Financial Times*, January 7, 1992, p. 4; *New York Times*, May 4, 1992, p. A-1; *Christian Science Monitor*, May 29, 1992, p. 8.

148. *Jane's Defence Weekly*, March 28, 1992, p. 531.

149. Estimates of Kuwait's restructured forces are based on material provided by the Kuwaiti embassy, the Jaffee Center, the Congressional Research Service, and the IISS, *Military Balance, 1991–1992*, pp. 110–111; *New York Times*, January 14, 1992, p. 4; *London Financial Times*, February 26, 1992, p. III-1.

150. *New York Times*, May 24, 1991, p. 8; *London Financial Times*, June 21, 1992, p. 18.

151. *New York Times*, January 14, 1992, p. 4; *London Financial Times*, July 8, 1991, p. 3; February 26, 1992, p. III-1; *Jane's Defence Weekly*, December 14, 1991, p. 1174.

152. *Defense News*, February 10, 1992, p. 38.

153. *Defense News*, February 24, 1992, pp. 1 and 82.

154. *Jane's Defence Weekly*, December 14, 1991, p. 1174; *London Financial Times*, November 18, 1991, p. 4.

155. *Jane's Defence Weekly*, March 28, 1992, p. 531; May 23, 1992, p. 878; May 30, 1992, p. 911; August 15, 1992, p. 5; September 5, 1992, p. 5; *London Financial Times*, July 8, 1991, p. 3; *Defense Week*, August 24, 1992, p. 1; *Defense News*, September 28, 1992, p. 18.

156. *Jane's Defence Weekly*, February 8, 1992, p. 187; February 22, 1992, p. 274; *Defense News*, November 18, 1991, p. 37; *London Financial Times*, February 16, 1992, p. 4.

157. *Jane's Defence Weekly*, March 28, 1992, pp. 530–531.

158. *Defense News*, November 18, 1991, p. 37; November 25, 1991, p. 22.

159. *Jane's Defence Weekly*, February 22, 1992, p. 274; *Defense News*, November 18, 1991, p. 37; November 25, 1991, p. 22.

160. *International Defense Review*, 10/1991, p. 1152.

161. Full repairs will not be completed until 1994. *Defense News*, November 18, 1991, p. 37.

162. *Jane's Defence Weekly*, December 14, 1991, p. 1174; *Defense News*, November 18, 1991, p. 37.

163. The F/A-18s are the first delivered with the new F-404-GE-402 17,754 lb. thrust engines. *St. Louis Post Dispatch*, October 9, 1991, p. B-1; *Aviation Week*, February 3, 1992, p. 63; *Jane's Defence Weekly*, October 26, 1991, p. 753; February 22, 1992, p. 274; March 28, 1992, p. 531; May 23, 1992, p. 879.

164. *Jane's Defence Weekly*, March 28, 1992, p. 530.

165. The Amoun is a modification of the Contraves-Raytheon system and has improved missile guidance and tracking, ground clutter rejection, and computer hardware and software. *Washington Post*, March 12, 1992, p. A-23; *Jane's Defence Weekly*, December 14, 1991, p. 1174; February 29, 1992, p. 341; March 21, 1992; March 28, 1992, p. 531; *Defense News*, November 18, 1991, p. 3.

166. *Defense News*, March 2, 1992, p. 1; *Armed Forces Journal*, July, 1992, p. 29.

167. *London Financial Times*, August 24, 1992, p. 3.

168. *Jane's Defence Weekly*, February 22, 1992, p. 274; March 7, 1992, p. 375; August 1, 1992, p. A-10; August 4, 1992, p. A-14; August 8, 1992, p. 6; August 15, 1992, p. A-15; *Defense News*, September 9, 1991, p. 1; November 18, 1991, p. 3; February 17, 1992, p. 3; June 15, 1992, p. 26; *Stars and Stripes*, March 3, 1992, p. 8; *London Financial Times*, July 8, 1991, p. 3; *Washington Post*, August 28, 1991, p. A-7; September 6, 1991, p. A-24; August 15, 1992, p. A-15; *Washington Times*, December 6, 1991, p. A-2; August 5, 1992, p. A-1; *Aviation Week*, September 9, 1991, p. 21.

169. Herbert K. Tillema, *International Conflict Since 1945*, Boulder, Westview, 1991, p. 156.

170. All demographic statistics used for Bahrain and the rest of the GCC states are based on CIA estimates in the relevant country sections of *The World Factbook, 1991*, Washington, GPO, 1991, p. 23.

171. The coup involved arms shipped from Iran to Bahrain, the use of the Iranian embassy to support the coup attempt, and the training of Bahraini citizens in Iran. While some expatriates were arrested, the core force in the coup was some 73 Bahraini youths, all Shi'ite.

172. This definition of residency was the criterion for being able to vote for Bahrain's parliament before it was dissolved in 1976. Only 3% of the male population qualified.

173. *OJJ Special, Oil and Gas Journal*, December 30, 1991, pp. 43–49; other estimates indicate 260 billion barrels of proven reserves and 42 billion barrels of probable reserves. See Joseph P. Riva, Jr., of the Congressional Research Service, writing in the *Oil and Gas Journal*, September 23, 1991, p. 62. These estimates have become increasingly more political in recent years as each major producer in the Gulf has tried to exaggerate its reserves and relative importance.

174. *Middle East Economic Review*, November 22, 1991, pp. 13–16.

175. CIA, *World Factbook, 1991*, and *Middle East Economic Review*, November 22, 1991, pp. 13–16.

176. *Defense News*, March 16, 1992, p. 16.

177. CIA, *World Factbook, 1991*.

178. IISS, *Military Balance, 1991–1992*. While Iran occasionally shows women in military roles for propaganda purposes, it does not employ them in any meaningful military roles.

179. Bahraini defense expenditure was officially set at 50.7 million dinars ($135 million) in 1986, 53.9 billion dinars ($143 million) in 1987, and 62 billion dinars in 1988 ($165 million). It seems to have risen to an average of around $200 million annually in 1987 if one includes Saudi aid. Estimates based on Bahraini data and reporting in Jane's *Defence Weekly*, March 15, 1986, p. 452.

180. Arms Control and Disarmament Agency (ACDA), *World Military Expenditures and Arms Transfers, 1990*, Washington, GPO, 1990, Table I.

181. *Middle East Economic Digest*, November 22, 1991, pp. 13–16.

182. Arms Control and Disarmament Agency (ACDA), *World Military Expenditures and Arms Transfers, 1990*, Washington, GPO, 1990, Table II.

183. Arms Control and Disarmament Agency (ACDA), *World Military Expenditures and Arms Transfers, 1985*, Washington, GPO, 1985, pp. 133–134.

184. Arms Control and Disarmament Agency (ACDA), *World Military Expenditures and Arms Transfers, 1989*, Washington, GPO, 1990, pp. 117–118.

185. Arms Control and Disarmament Agency (ACDA), *World Military Expenditures and Arms Transfers, 1990*, Washington, GPO, 1992, pp. 133–134.

186. *Defense News*, March 16, 1992, p. 6.

187. One Bahraini source claims 40 Crotale launchers. This estimate seems to be too high.

188. There were unconfirmed reports in 1989 that Bahrain was also recruiting Sudanese. If so, some of these may also have left Bahrain's armed forces.

189. *Defense News*, March 16, 1992, p. 6.

190. *Defense News*, February 2, 1987, p. 15; March 30, 1992, p. 22.

191. *Washington Post*, December 2, 1987, p. A-25, and December 18, 1987, p. A-25; *Defense Electronics*, February, 1988, p. 11.

192. *Jane's Defence Weekly*, February 13, 1988, p. 247.

193. *Defense News*, March 16, 1992, p. 16.

194. At a cost of $114 million and as part of a package including 60 AIM-9-P3 missiles. DMS Intelligence data base.

195. These orders were purchased with the help of Saudi and UAE aid. *Jane's Defence Weekly*, February 7, 1987; *New York Times*, January 28, 1987, p. 2; *Washington Post*, January 21, 1987, p. A-15; *Defense News*, February 2, 1987, p. 15; March 30, 1992, p. 22.

196. *Jane's Defence Weekly*, March 28, 1992, p. 530.

197. *Defense and Foreign Affairs Weekly*, May 26-June 1, 1986, p. 4.

198. *Jane's Defence Weekly*, June 14, 1986, p. 1087, and *Defense and Foreign Affairs Weekly*, May 26, 1986, p. 4.

199. *Jane's Defence Weekly*, November 9, 1991, p. 869; *Washington Post*, October 28, 1991, p. 5-A.

200. The military manpower, force strength, and equipment estimates in this section are made by the author using a wide range of sources, including computerized data bases, interviews, and press clipping services. Most are impossible to reference in ways of use to the reader. The force strength statistics are generally taken from interviews and from the sources reference for each paragraph. They also draw heavily on his *The Gulf and the Search for Strategic Stability* (Boulder, Westview, 1984) and *The Gulf and the West* (Boulder, Westview, 1988).

Extensive use has also been made of the annual editions of the International Institute for Strategic Studies, *Military Balance* (IISS, London), in this case the 1991–1992 edition, and of the Jaffee Center for Strategic Studies, *The Military Balance in the Middle East* (JCSS, Tel Aviv), especially the 1990–1991 edition and working materials from the coming edition. Material has also been drawn from computer print outs from NEXIS, the United States Naval Institute data base, and from the DMS/FI Market Intelligence Reports data base. Other sources include *Military Technology*, "World Defense Almanac for 1991–1992," published in 1992; Foreign Affairs Division, "Middle East Arms Control and Related Issues," Washington, Congressional Research Service, 91-384F, May 1, 1991; and *Middle East Economic Digest*, "MEED Special Report: Defense," Volume 35, December 13, 1991.

Weapons data are taken from many sources, including computerized material available in NEXIS, and various editions of *Jane's Fighting Ships* (Jane's Publishing); *Jane's Naval Weapons Systems* (Jane's Publishing); *Jane's Armour and Artillery* (Jane's Publishing); *Jane's Infantry Weapons* (Jane's Publishing); *Jane's Military Vehicles and Logistics* (Jane's Publishing); *Jane's Land-Based Air Defence* (Jane's Publishing); *Jane's All the World's Aircraft* (Jane's Publishing); *Jane's Battlefield Surveillance Systems* (Jane's Publishing); *Jane's Radar and Electronic Warfare Systems* (Jane's Publishing), *Jane's C^3I Systems* (Jane's Publishing); *Jane's Air-Launched Weapons Systems* (Jane's Publishing); *Jane's Defence Appointments & Procurement Handbook (Middle East Edition)* (Jane's Publishing); *Tanks of the World* (Bernard and Grafe); *Weyer's Warships* (Bernard and Grafe); and *Warplanes of the World* (Bernard and Grafe).

Other military background, effectiveness, strength, organizational, and history data are taken from Anthony H. Cordesman, *The Gulf and the Search for Strategic Stability*, Boulder, Westview, 1984; *The Gulf and the West*, Boulder, Westview, 1988; and *Weapons of Mass Destruction in the Middle East*, London, Brassey's/RUSI, 1991; Anthony H. Cordesman and Abraham Wagner, *The Lessons of Modern War*, Volume II, Boulder, Westview, 1989; the relevant country or war sections of Herbert K. Tillema, *International Conflict Since 1945*, Boulder, Westview, 1991; Department of Defense and Department of State, *Congressional Presentation for Security Assistance Programs, Fiscal Year 1993*, Washington, Department of State, 1992; various annual editions of John Laffin's *The World in Conflict* or *War Annual*, London, Brassey's; and John Keegan, *World Armies*, London, Macmillan, 1983.

201. *Oil and Gas Journal*, September 23, 1991, p. 62.

202. *OJJ Special, Oil and Gas Journal*, December 30, 1991, pp. 43–49; other estimates indicate 2 billion barrels of proven reserves and 2 billion barrels of probable reserves. See Joseph P. Riva, Jr., of the Congressional Research Service, writing in the *Oil and Gas Journal*, September 23, 1991, p. 62, and his "Persian Gulf Oil: Its Critical Importance to World Oil Supplies," Congressional Research Service 91-220 SPR, March 5, 1991. Estimates of oil reserves have become increasingly more political in recent years as each major producer in the Gulf has tried to exaggerate its reserves and relative importance. Gas estimates are based upon *The Middle East*, May, 1991, p. 33.

203. *Le Monde,* January 29, 1992, p. 16; Middle East News Network, January 6, 1992; *Washington Post,* October 1, 1992, p. A-19; *Washington Tiimes,* October 1, 1992, p. A-7.

204. IISS, *Military Balance, 1991–1992;* Arms Control and Disarmament Agency (ACDA), *World Military Expenditures and Arms Transfers, 1989,* Washington, GPO, 1990, pp. 62, 104, and 117; CIA, *World Factbook, 1991,* pp. 258–259.

205. IISS, *Military Balance,* 1990–1991 and 1991–1992 editions.

206. Arms Control and Disarmament Agency (ACDA), *World Military Expenditures and Arms Transfers, 1989,* Washington, GPO, 1990, p. 60.

207. Arms Control and Disarmament Agency (ACDA), *World Military Expenditures and Arms Transfers, 1990,* Washington, GPO, 1990, Table II.

208. Arms Control and Disarmament Agency (ACDA), *World Military Expenditures and Arms Transfers, 1985,* Washington, GPO, 1985, p. 134.

209. Arms Control and Disarmament Agency (ACDA), *World Military Expenditures and Arms Transfers, 1989,* Washington, GPO, 1990, p. 134.

210. Arms Control and Disarmament Agency (ACDA), *World Military Expenditures and Arms Transfers, 1990,* Washington, GPO, 1990, pp. 133–134.

211. These numbers are very uncertain. They are based on interviews and have been rounded to the nearest 5.

212. *Los Angeles Times,* April 1, 1988, p. B-4.

213. Some estimates put actual manning as low as 700.

214. Three Hunter FGA-78/T-79s and one T-79 seem to be in storage.

215. The U.S. demanded their return and was refused.

216. The military manpower, force strength, and equipment estimates in this section are made by the author using a wide range of sources, including computerized data bases, interviews, and press clipping services. Most are impossible to reference in ways of use to the reader. The force strength statistics are generally taken from interviews and from the sources reference for each paragraph. They also draw heavily on his *The Gulf and the Search for Strategic Stability* (Boulder, Westview, 1984) and *The Gulf and the West* (Boulder, Westview, 1988).

Extensive use has also been made of the annual editions of the International Institute for Strategic Studies, *Military Balance* (IISS, London), in this case the 1991–1992 edition, and of the Jaffee Center for Strategic Studies, *The Military Balance in the Middle East* (JCSS, Tel Aviv), especially the 1990–1991 edition and working materials from the coming edition. Material has also been drawn from computer print outs from NEXIS, the United States Naval Institute data base, and from the DMS/FI Market Intelligence Reports data base. Other sources include *Military Technology,* "World Defense Almanac for 1991–1992," published in 1992; Foreign Affairs Division, "Middle East Arms Control and Related Issues," Washington, Congressional Research Service, 91-384F, May 1, 1991; and *Middle East Economic Digest,* "MEED Special Report: Defense," Volume 35, December 13, 1991.

Weapons data are taken from many sources, including computerized material available in NEXIS, and various editions of *Jane's Fighting Ships* (Jane's Publishing); *Jane's Naval Weapons Systems* (Jane's Publishing); *Jane's Armour and Artillery* (Jane's Publishing); *Jane's Infantry Weapons* (Jane's Publishing); *Jane's Military Vehicles and Logistics* (Jane's Publishing); *Jane's Land-Based Air Defence* (Jane's Publishing); *Jane's All the World's Aircraft* (Jane's Publishing); *Jane's Battlefield Surveillance Systems* (Jane's Publishing); *Jane's Radar and Electronic Warfare Systems* (Jane's Publishing), *Jane's C^3I Systems* (Jane's Publishing); *Jane's Air-Launched Weapons Systems* (Jane's Publishing); *Jane's Defence Appointments & Procurement Handbook (Middle East Edition)* (Jane's Publishing); *Tanks of the World* (Bernard and Grafe); *Weyer's Warships* (Bernard and Grafe); and *Warplanes of the World* (Bernard and Grafe).

Other military background, effectiveness, strength, organizational, and history data are taken from Anthony H. Cordesman, *The Gulf and the Search for Strategic Stability,* Boulder,

Westview, 1984; *The Gulf and the West*, Boulder, Wesiview, 1988; and *Weapons of Mass Destruction in the Middle East*, London, Brassey's/RUSI, 1991; Anthony H. Cordesman and Abraham Wagner, *The Lessons of Modern War*, Volume II, Boulder, Westview, 1989; the relevant country or war sections of Herbert K. Tillema, *International Conflict Since 1945*, Boulder, Westview, 1991; Department of Defense and Department of State, *Congressional Presentation for Security Assistance Programs, Fiscal Year 1993*, Washington, Department of State, 1992; various annual editions of John Laffin's *The World in Conflict* or *War Annual*, London, Brassey's; and John Keegan, *World Armies*, London, Macmillan, 1983.

217. *Oil and Gas Journal*, September 23, 1991, p. 62.

218. *OJJ Special, Oil and Gas Journal*, December 30, 1991, pp. 43–49; other estimates indicate that the UAE as a whole has 56.2 billion barrels of proven reserves and 49 billion barrels of probable reserves. See Joseph P. Riva, Jr., of the Congressional Research Service, writing in the *Oil and Gas Journal*, September 23, 1991, p. 62. These estimates have become increasingly more political in recent years as each major producer in the Gulf has tried to exaggerate its reserves and relative importance. *Washington Post*, September 25, 1992, p. A-31; September 29, 1992, p. A-15; *Christian Science Monitor*, September 18, 1992, p. 6; *New York Times*, September 13, 1992, p. A-22; September 17, 1992, p. A-19.

219. *Los Angeles Times*, January 28, 1992, p. C-1.

220. Formed in 1966, when Britain began its withdrawal from Aden. The main British military base was at Bahrain.

221. Herbert K. Tillema in *International Conflict Since 1945*, Boulder, Westview, 1991, p. 149.

222. For more details, see the author's *The Gulf and the West* and *Lessons of Modern War*, Volume II.

223. *Wall Street Journal*, December 22, 1987, p. 16.

224. Estimates for 1978–1988 are based on ACDA data. Estimates for 1989–1991 are based on IISS and CIA data.

225. Arms Control and Disarmament Agency, *World Military Expenditures, 1990*, Washington, GPO, 1990, Table I.

226. Arms Control and Disarmament Agency, *World Military Expenditures, 1990*, Washington, GPO, 1990, Table I.

227. *The Middle East*, February, 1992, pp. 19–20.

228. Arms Control and Disarmament Agency, *World Military Expenditures and Arms Transfers, 1990*, Washington, GPO, 1990, Table II.

229. Arms Control and Disarmament Agency, *World Military Expenditures, 1986*, Washington, GPO, 1987.

230. Arms Control and Disarmament Agency, *World Military Expenditures, 1986*, Washington, GPO, 1987.

231. Arms Control and Disarmament Agency, *World Military Expenditures and Arms Transfers, 1990*, Washington, GPO, 1990, pp. 133–134.

232. CIA, *World Factbook, 1991*, pp. 320–321.

233. *Wall Street Journal*, August 8, 1991, p. A-1.

234. CIA, *World Factbook, 1991*, pp. 320–321.

235. The force strength data in this section are adapted from interviews and various editions of the IISS, *Military Balance*, and the JCSS, *Middle East Military Balance*.

236. The Italian-made OF-40s are the only tanks operational in the world in this configuration.

237. France demonstrated the AMX-40 in trials in both Qatar and the UAE. *Jane's Defence Weekly*, June 6, 1987, p. 1092.

238. *Defense News*, April 22, 1991, p. 1; September 16, 1991, p. 1; December 9, 1991, p. 1.

239. These reports are dubious. Brazilian firms often leak false orders while trying to

win new business. The EDT-FILA is a three radar system with a scanning area of 2–25 kilometers. *Defense News*, April 22, 1991, p. 1; December 9, 1991, p. A-1; May 25, 1991, p. 1.

240. *Financial Times*, December 21, 1991, p. 1; *Washington Times*, December 25, 1989, p. A-2.

241. *Defense News*, January 5, 1987, p. 19; *Jane's Defence Weekly*, October 17, 1987; December 5, 1987, p. 1302.

242. According to some reports, 3 Alphajet attack aircraft and 10 aging Hunter FGA-76/T-77s are in storage.

243. *Jane's Defence Weekly*, June 15, 1991, p. 1001.

244. *Jane's Defence Weekly*, February 20, 1988, p. 301.

245. The deputy commander was not named because of UAE security policies. *Jane's Defence Weekly*, February 20, 1988, p. 301.

246. The U.S. temporarily delayed the sale of a $170 million upgrade package for the IHawks in June, 1987, because of the coup attempt in Sharjah.

247. *Financial Times*, December 21, 1991, p. 1.

248. The military manpower, force strength, and equipment estimates in this section are made by the author using a wide range of sources, including computerized data bases, interviews, and press clipping services. Most are impossible to reference in ways of use to the reader. The force strength statistics are generally taken from interviews and from the sources reference for each paragraph. They also draw heavily on his *The Gulf and the Search for Strategic Stability* (Boulder, Westview, 1984) and *The Gulf and the West* (Boulder, Westview, 1988).

Extensive use has also been made of the annual editions of the International Institute for Strategic Studies, *Military Balance* (IISS, London), in this case the 1991–1992 edition, and of the Jaffee Center for Strategic Studies, *The Military Balance in the Middle East* (JCSS, Tel Aviv), especially the 1990–1991 edition and working materials from the coming edition. Material has also been drawn from computer print outs from NEXIS, the United States Naval Institute data base, and from the DMS/FI Market Intelligence Reports data base. Other sources include *Military Technology*, "World Defense Almanac for 1991–1992," published in 1992; Foreign Affairs Division, "Middle East Arms Control and Related Issues," Washington, Congressional Research Service, 91-384F, May 1, 1991; and *Middle East Economic Digest*, "MEED Special Report: Defense," Volume 35, December 13, 1991.

Weapons data are taken from many sources, including computerized material available in NEXIS, and various editions of *Jane's Fighting Ships* (Jane's Publishing); *Jane's Naval Weapons Systems* (Jane's Publishing); *Jane's Armour and Artillery* (Jane's Publishing); *Jane's Infantry Weapons* (Jane's Publishing); *Jane's Military Vehicles and Logistics* (Jane's Publishing); *Jane's Land-Based Air Defence* (Jane's Publishing); *Jane's All the World's Aircraft* (Jane's Publishing); *Jane's Battlefield Surveillance Systems* (Jane's Publishing); *Jane's Radar and Electronic Warfare Systems* (Jane's Publishing), *Jane's C³I Systems* (Jane's Publishing); *Jane's Air-Launched Weapons Systems* (Jane's Publishing); *Jane's Defence Appointments & Procurement Handbook (Middle East Edition)* (Jane's Publishing); *Tanks of the World* (Bernard and Grafe); *Weyer's Warships* (Bernard and Grafe); and *Warplanes of the World* (Bernard and Grafe).

Other military background, effectiveness, strength, organizational, and history data are taken from Maj. Gen. Edward Fursdon, "Oman's 20th National Day Anniversary," *Navy International*, January, 1991, pp. 20–21; "Oman: A Financial Times Survey," *Financial Times*, November 21, 1991; Anthony H. Cordesman, *The Gulf and the Search for Strategic Stability*, Boulder, Westview, 1984; *The Gulf and the West*, Boulder, Westview, 1988; and *Weapons of Mass Destruction in the Middle East*, London, Brassey's/RUSI, 1991; Anthony H. Cordesman and Abraham Wagner, *The Lessons of Modern War*, Volume II Boulder, Westview, 1989; the relevant country or war sections of Herbert K. Tillema, *International Conflict Since 1945*, Boulder, Westview, 1991; Department of Defense and Department of State, *Congressional*

Presentation for Security Assistance Programs, Fiscal Year 1993, Washington, Department of State, 1992; various annual editions of John Laffin's *The World in Conflict* or *War Annual*, London, Brassey's; and John Keegan, *World Armies*, London, Macmillan, 1983.

249. *Oil and Gas Journal*, September 23, 1991, p. 62.

250. *OJJ Special, Oil and Gas Journal*, December 30, 1991, pp. 43–49; other estimates indicate 4.3 billion barrels of proven reserves and 2 billion barrels of probable reserves. See Joseph P. Riva, Jr., of the Congressional Research Service, writing in the *Oil and Gas Journal*, September 23, 1991, p. 62. These estimates have become increasingly more political in recent years as each major producer in the Gulf has tried to exaggerate its reserves and relative importance.

251. Mark Nicholson, "A Tough Hurdle," *Oman: A Financial Times Survey*, November 20, 1991, pp. I–IV.

252. *Los Angeles Times*, January 28, 1992, p. C-1; *Oman: A Financial Times Survey*, November 20, 1991, pp. I–IV.

253. The Ibadhis are relatively liberal and tolerant. They make up about 75% of Oman's native population. CIA, *World Factbook, 1991*, pp. 236–237.

254. *Oman: A Financial Times Survey*, November 20, 1991, pp. I–IV.

255. Sheik Saqr made several attempts to take territory from his neighbors and was anything but a popular ruler.

256. Arms Control and Disarmament Agency (ACDA), *World Military Expenditures and Arms Transfers, 1990*, Washington, GPO, 1990, Table I.

257. IISS, *Military Balance*, 1990–1991 and 1991–1992 editions.

258. Arms Control and Disarmament Agency (ACDA), *World Military Expenditures and Arms Transfers, 1989*, Washington, GPO, 1990, p. 60.

259. Arms Control and Disarmament Agency (ACDA), *World Military Expenditures and Arms Transfers, 1990*, Washington, GPO, 1990, Table II.

260. Arms Control and Disarmament Agency (ACDA), *World Military Expenditures and Arms Transfers, 1989*, Washington, GPO, 1990, p. 102; CIA, *World Factbook, 1991*, pp. 341–342.

261. Arms Control and Disarmament Agency (ACDA), *World Military Expenditures and Arms Transfers, 1985*, Washington, GPO, 1985, p. 134.

262. Arms Control and Disarmament Agency (ACDA), *World Military Expenditures and Arms Transfers, 1989*, Washington, GPO, 1990, p. 134.

263. Arms Control and Disarmament Agency (ACDA), *World Military Expenditures and Arms Transfers, 1990*, Washington, GPO, 1990, pp. 133–134.

264. CIA, *World Factbook, 1991*, pp. 236–237.

265. The army commander, Maj. Gen. Naseeb bin Haman bin Sultan Ruwaihi, was qualified for the post. It is important to note, however, that he was appointed at the end of 1984 when Gen. Sir Timothy Creasy was replaced as chief of defense staff by Lt. Gen. John Watts. There are rumors this replacement occurred partly because of his insistence on an exemplary jail sentence for Robin Walsh, a British MOD official accused of misappropriating $8,700 in MOD funds. Walsh died in an Omani jail in October, 1984. This was followed by broader accusations that up to $74 million annually was being wrongly appropriated by the Ministry of Defense, and that both British and Omani officials knew of the problem. *EIU Regional Review*, pp. 186–187.

266. The U.S. has spent over $300 million on upgrading these facilities. *Washington Post*, July 19, 1985, p. A-29.

267. There are two major radars at Goat Island. It is garrisoned by 250 Omani soldiers and marines and 10 Britons. *New York Times*, December 22, 1986, p. A18; *Defense News*, December 1, 1986, p. 6; *Washington Post*, March 24, 1986, p. A-13; *Christian Science Monitor*, October 30, 1979; *Time*, December 2, 1985, p. 58.

268. Richard Green, editor, *Middle East Review, 1986*, London, Middle East Review Com-

pany, 1986, pp. 167–168; *New York Times*, December 22, 1986, p. A18; *Defense News*, December 1, 1986, p. 6; *Jane's Defence Weekly*, November 22, 1986, and December 6, 1986; *Chicago Tribune*, November 18, 1985, p. I-12.

269. IISS, *Military Balance,*1991–1992, p. 116.

270. *Oman: A Financial Times Survey*, November 20, 1991, pp. I–IV.

271. *Jane's Defence Weekly*, September 7, 1991, p. 387; February 22, 1992, p. 273; May 23, 1992, p. 881.

272. Oman bought some 300 AIM-9P4s in late October, 1985. *Baltimore Sun*, October 11, 1985, p. 9A; *Oman: A Financial Times Survey*, November 20, 1991, pp. I–IV.

273. Economist Intelligence Unit, *EIU Regional Review: The Middle East and North Africa, 1986*, Economist Publications, New York, 1986, p. 193.

274. *Oman: A Financial Times Survey*, November 20, 1991, pp. I–IV.

275. *Washington Times*, May 9, 1985, p. 7.

276. *Defense News*, December 9, 1991, p. 42.

8

Trends in the Military Balance and Arms Sales in the Red Sea and the Horn

While the Gulf is of critical importance in terms of oil supplies, the Red Sea can be bypassed by sailing around the Cape. Nevertheless, the Red Sea is of potential strategic importance. Over 325 million tons of cargo, or roughly 10% of the world's commercial shipping, passes through the Suez Canal and Bab el Mandeb each year. This is roughly 45–50 ships a day and over 18,000 ships a year. It is also approximately one-third more cargo than passes through the Panama Canal.

Yemen poses a potential threat to both Saudi Arabia and Oman. The other Red Sea states—Ethiopia, Djibouti, Somalia, and the Sudan—can serve as bases for naval and air forces that can attack ships moving through the Red Sea and the Gulf of Yemen. They also can serve as air bases for powers hostile to Egypt, Israel, and Saudi Arabia. Although none of these states currently poses a major threat to its neighbors, several are highly unstable, and the Red Sea region offers little prospect of near term stability.

The Military Trends in the Red Sea Area

The overall military efforts of the states in the Red Sea area are summarized in Table 8.1. No Red Sea state has particularly strong military forces by Middle East standards, but these forces are the product of long and enduring conflicts. Ethiopia, Somalia, the Sudan, and Yemen have made the Red Sea area a region of civil wars. While these civil wars have received less public attention than those in other parts of the Middle East, they have cost hundreds of thousands of lives and created far higher casualties and human suffering than the struggles in Middle Eastern nations that have far higher levels of military forces, technology, and arms imports.

At the same time, there have been many border clashes, minor wars, and tensions among states. The two Yemens fought and feuded virtually from

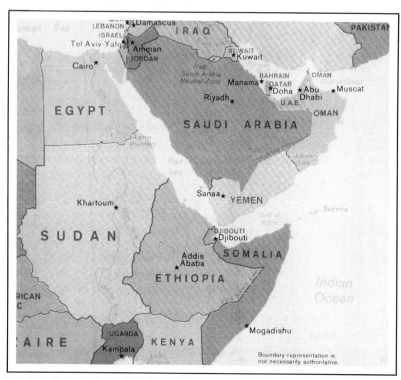

Map 8.1   The Red Sea and the Horn. Source: U.S. Government

TABLE 8.1 Comparative Military Effort of Red Sea and Key African States Affecting Red Sea Security

	Defense Expenditure in 1991 ($ millions)	Arms Imports 1985–1989 ($ millions)	Military Manpower	Battle Tanks	Combat Aircraft	Major Combat Ships
Saudi Arabia	26,810	23,040	76,500	700	253	20
Oman	1,440	445	30,400	82	57	12
Republic of Yemen	1,060	3,000	65,000	1,275	101	27
Sudan	650	330	71,500	230	51	2
Ethiopia	400	3,805	125,000	300	68	18
Somalia	22	160	65,000	293	63	6
Egypt	5,900	5,800	420,000	3,190	495	60
Libya	1,100	5,080	85,000	2,150	409	54
Israel	6,390	6,100	141,000	4,488	591	68
Djibouti	38	?	3,400	(45)	0	0
Chad	60	210	17,200	(63)	4	0
Central African Republic	20	?	6,500	4(14)	0	0
Zaire	65	170	50,700	80	28	2
Uganda	75	195	70,000	12(30)	19	0
Kenya	225	80	23,600	76	28	7

Note: Military data shown often differ from those in the text, which is adapted to include information from other sources. Figures in parentheses indicate country has somewhat similar equipment in form of lighter AFVs or armed training aircraft. Figures shown generally include total equipment inventory rather than strength that can be operationally deployed.

Sources: Adapted from the IISS, *Military Balance, 1991/1992*; ACDA computer data base for *World Arms Transfers and Military Expenditures, 1990*.

the day of their independence to the day of their merger. The former PDRY backed the Dhofar rebels in a war in Oman. Border tensions between the Yemens and Saudi Arabia have led to several major clashes, and Ethiopia, the Sudan, and Somalia have all been involved in border wars. This situation does not seem likely to change in the future; new civil wars and border wars are almost certain to occur.

The trends in Red Sea forces shown in Table 8.2 also reflect the impact of a long series of military confrontations and civil wars. At the same time, it is apparent from these trends that the Red Sea states are the "poor relations" of the Middle East. In spite of long and bloody civil wars, Ethiopia is the only Red Sea state to have received the kind of massive arms transfers common elsewhere in the Middle East, and none of the Red Sea states has been able to spend anything like the money per man in service as have the Gulf states or Levant. All of the Red Sea countries are exceptionally poor, and military forces and arms imports have had a powerful impact in consuming funds needed for economic development and sheer survival.

TABLE 8.2 Trends in Forces in the Red Sea Area (in current $ millions)

Military Expenditures

	1979	1980	1981	1982	1983	1984	1985	1986	1987	1988	1989	1990	1991
North Yemen[a]	320	278	393	537	551	434	379	368	379	641	618	1000	1006
South Yemen[a]	87	101	135	156	171	197	198	211	207	217	36	26	36
Djibouti													
Sudan	279	302	317	442	230	236	220	201	313	286	339	320	340
Ethiopia	254	321	331	357	363	389	382	388	432	440	763	536	500
Somalia	38	23	30	31	31	25	39	31	60	60	39	19	21
Total	978	1025	1206	1523	1346	1281	1218	1199	1391	1644	1795	1901	1903

Arms Imports

	1972	1974	1976	1978	1980	1982	1984	1986	1988	1990	1992	1994
North Yemen[a]	10	10	20	110	575	420	80	280	430	400	400	400
South Yemen[a]	20	40	40	350	700	250	330	110	380			
Sudan	20	30	50	120	100	240	110	50	90	70	80	90
Ethiopia	10	10	50	1500	725	575	1200	330	700	840	570	470
Somalia	20	90	100	240	200	130	90	20	30	70	60	60
Total	80	180	260	2320	2300	1615	1810	790	1630	1380	1110	1020

Arms Imports by Supplier During 1985–1989

	Total	USSR	U.S.	France	UK	PRC	FRG	Other Warsaw Pact	Other Europe	Middle East	Other East Asia	Latin America	Others
North Yemen[a]	1765	1600	20	0	0	0	5	40	0	40	20	0	40
South Yemen[a]	1400	1400	0	0	0	0	0	0	0	0	0	0	0
Sudan	330	0	100	0	0	50	0	20	20	70	0	0	70
Ethiopia	3805	3600	0	0	0	20	0	60	10	0	110	0	5
Somalia	160	0	5	0	0	0	30	0	0	150	0	0	0
Total	7460	6600	125	0	0	70	35	120	30	260	130	0	115

Military Manpower

	1967	1973	1975	1977	1979	1981	1983	1985	1987	1989	1991
North Yemen[a]	10	31	42	40	36	30	22	28	43	62	65
South Yemen[a]	10	12	19	20	20	23	25	27	40	88	
Sudan	20	35	50	50	65	87	86	65	59	65	72
Ethiopia	45	50	144	228	250	240	240	240	300	250	65
Djibouti	1	2	2	2	3	3	3	3	4	5	3
Somalia	16	25	30	53	54	54	48	43	50	47	8
Total	102	155	287	393	428	487	424	406	486	517	426

Major Military Equipment

Main Battle Tanks

	1973	1979	1982	1984	1988	1990	1992
North Yemen[a]	30	232	714	664	664	715	1270
South Yemen[a]	50	260	470	450	480	480	—
Djibouti	0	0	0	0	0	0	20
Ethiopia	50	624	790	1020	750	1300	300
Sudan	130	150	190	173	175	215	215
Somalia	150	80	140	240	293	290	270
Total	410	1346	2304	2447	2362	3000	2075

Combat Aircraft

	1973	1979	1982	1984	1988	1990	1992
North Yemen[a]	28	11	75	76	83	87	100
South Yemen[a]	20	109	114	103	114	94	—
Djibouti	0	0	0	0	0	0	4
Ethiopia	37	100	113	160	143	120	68
Sudan	50	36	30	34	45	53	50
Somalia	100	25	55	64	63	56	50
Total	235	281	387	437	448	410	272

[a]North Yemen and South Yemen merged into a single country in 1990.
Sources: Adapted from various editions of the IISS, Military Balance, and ACDA, World Military Expenditures and Arms Transfers.

Yemen

	Manpower (1,000s)	Tanks	Aircraft	Defense Spending ($ millions)	Arms Imports ($ millions)	Arms Exports ($ millions)
1967						
YAR	10	12	6	7	10	—
PDRY	10	10	3	26	2	—
1973						
YAR	31	30	28	24	3	—
PDRY	12	50	28	31	42	—
1982						
YAR	22	714	75	435	420	—
PDRY	25	470	114	162	303	—
1988						
YAR	62	715	83	280	400	—
PDRY	88	480	114	380	380	—
1991	65	1,270	100	1,000	—	—

Yemen was unified on May 22, 1990, and is now a country of some 527,970 square kilometers, about twice the size of Wyoming.[1] It shares a 1,458 kilometer border with Saudi Arabia and a 288 kilometer border with Oman. It has a 1,906 kilometer coastline on the Red Sea and controls the Bab el Mandeb, the eastern exit to the Red Sea, and the strategic island of Socotra in the Gulf of Aden. Both its border with Saudi Arabia and the administrative line with Oman are disputed.

The population of Yemen is about 10.1 million, with a growth rate of about 3.2%. It is about 90% Arab and 10% Afro-Arab, with a few Indians and Somalis. The north is a mix of Sunni and Shi'ite Muslim, and many key tribal leaders are Shi'ites of the Zaidi sect, which dominates the government. The current president of Yemen, Ali Salleh, is a Zaidi. The south is largely Sunni Muslim, with some Christians and Hindus. More than half of all the inhabitants of Yemen, including most of the south, are Sunnis of the Shafii sect.[2]

Military Developments in Yemen

Yemen was formed out of North and South Yemen, and the two Yemens took very different routes to unification. North Yemen was loosely governed by the Turkish empire after 1517, although the imams of the Zaidi sect controlled the country and had considerable authority. North Yemen received full independence from the Turkish empire in 1918, as a result of World War I.

In contrast, Britain seized the port of Aden and the surrounding Aden protectorate (a group of quasi-independent sheikdoms) to secure the routes to India and create a coaling station in the early nineteenth century, and it ruled the area from India until the late 1800s. In spite of claims to the region by North Yemen, neither the people of Aden nor those of the various tribal protectorates showed much interest in nationalism until the 1930s, and even then, such nationalism had its origins in the politics of Hindus and Muslims that Britain brought over as workers from India.

North Yemen was governed after World War I by an imam from the Hamid al-Din family, which in 1891 had succeeded in making the imamate of the leading Zaidi sect hereditary rather than elected. In the period after 1918, the Imam Yahya sought to establish central state control over the tribes in North Yemen and expand his territory. He was checked by Saudi forces in 1934, however, and lost the territory of the Asir to Saudi Arabia. The Imam Yahya was forced to sign a treaty with Saudi Arabia in 1936 that recognized Saudi control over the Asir but left several other border issues unsettled.

The imam was not a popular leader and never fully succeeded in controlling the two main tribal groups in North Yemen: the Zaidi and Shafii. He was assassinated during a military coup attempt in February, 1948. Although Abdellah al-Wazir briefly seized power, Yahya's sons successfully fought a short civil war against al-Wazir, and the Imam Yahya was succeeded by his son Ahmed.

Ahmed was an erratic leader prone to violence and mood swings, and he became addicted to morphine. He did attempt some reforms: He tried to establish a modern nontribal army and joined North Yemen to the UAR in March, 1958, but he ultimately succeeded in doing little more than creating an increasingly politicized and pro-Nasser palace guard. He also alienated key tribes like the Hashid by executing their leaders. When Ahmed died in September, 1962, his son Mohammed al-Badr claimed the imamate. Eight days later, however, Col. Abdellah al-Salleh, the head of the imam's personal guard, seized power and proclaimed the creation of the Yemen Arab Republic. The imam's son fled the capital and raised many of the Zaidi tribes in his support. Al-Salleh organized his own forces, obtained the support of key Shafii tribes as well as a few Zaidi groups, and turned to Egypt for money and arms.

From 1962 to 1967, a bloody tribal civil war took place in which Imam al-Badr's forces were backed by Saudi Arabia, Jordan, and the conservative tribes, and the socialist government formed by al-Salleh was backed by Nasser and Egyptian troops. This led to a number of incidents on the Saudi border, and the Egyptian air force bombed targets in Saudi Arabia on several occasions between November, 1962 and May, 1967. By the time the Six Days' War began between Israel and the Arabs, some 20,000 Yemenis had died, some killed by the Egyptian use of poison gas. Egypt had taken serious casualties, and the cost of the war had led it to a gradual reduction of its forces in Yemen.

The crisis before and after the 1967 war made Nasser desperate for money. In August, 1967 Saudi Arabia agreed to provide aid in return for the exile of al-Salleh and the removal of Egyptian troops. Egypt agreed to refuse support of al-Salleh and withdrew all of its forces by October 16, 1967.

The imam's forces besieged Sanaa but divided into squabbling groups before they could seize the capital. Al-Salleh's forces then gradually drove the imam's forces back towards the Saudi border. They were driven out of their last stronghold in Sada and failed to recapture the town with Saudi aid. Although the YAR's air force bombed targets near the Saudi town of Najran, the Saudis eventually worked out an agreement between the rebels and al-

Salleh that effectively recognized the YAR in return for the creation of a consultative council that brought together most of the feuding tribes. This brought an end to the imamate and the monarchy.

The Struggle for Independence in South Yemen

Unlike the north, the south had to fight for independence. This fight began in December, 1947 in a series of riots and attacks on the Yemeni Jews. While this revolt was not directed against the British, it showed Marxist and Arab nationalist forces that they could exert power against the British. North Yemen also began to provide arms and money to anti-British factions, and fighting started among various tribal groups in 1952. The RAF replied with air raids in May, 1953, and Britain had to commit troops in June, 1955. After about four years of confused tribal fighting and occasional clashes with forces of North Yemen, the British pacified most of the tribal areas.

By 1960, tribal levies did most of the fighting on the British side, but Britain's military victories did little to halt the rise of nationalism and Marxism in Aden, and the various sheiks who rule in the tribal protectorates remained isolated and became increasingly ineffective in controlling their territories. The fighting resumed in 1961 and took on a new character after al-Salleh seized power in North Yemen. Britain backed the forces of the imam, and al-Salleh and Egypt began to provide arms and money to a pro-Nasser group called the National Front for the Liberation of South Yemen.

The British tribal forces and the RAF were able to contain the radical opposition groups during 1962. In January, 1963, however, Britain made the mistake of combining the tribal protectorates and Aden colony into the South Arabian Federation. The federation was unpopular in both Aden and the protectorates and started a new uprising in which Marxists played an increasingly important part. Between April, 1964 and October, 1965, the fighting reached the point where it became clear that Britain could not reexert control without deploying major forces. At the same time, Britain was involved in a major effort to reduce its military commitments east of Suez. Britain announced its intention to withdraw in February, 1966, and the war then became a struggle between the Front for the Liberation of Occupied South Yemen (FLOSY) and the far more radical National Liberation Front (NLF).

Britain attempted to back some of the traditional tribal leaders in preserving the South Arabian Federation and carried out another offensive in 1966. This offensive achieved little, however, and Britain withdrew to camps near the city of Aden in June, 1967, preparing to give up the colony. This left FLOSY and the NLF to fight for control of Aden and the surrounding tribal areas, and the NLF emerged the decisive victor. Britain left Aden and the South Arabian Federation on November 29, 1967, and the NLF proclaimed the creation of the People's Democratic Republic of Yemen the next day.

Some 300,000 members of the Front for the Liberation of Occupied South Yemen fled to the YAR, where they became a key source of friction between the two countries for the next two decades. While both the YAR and PDRY were led by regimes which had come to power proclaiming the need for a unified Yemen, these regimes were sharply divided in character and leadership, and the rhetoric of unity disguised a reality of bitter military rivalry.

Although the two countries began what became an intermittent series of unification talks in November, 1970, the YAR and PDRY disputed many parts of their border, including the control of Karaman Island. The FLOSY forces that the NLF had driven out of the PDRY showed no interest in the unity talks and launched a series of raids from their bases in the YAR into the PDRY. In October, 1971 the PDRY retaliated by attacking FLOSY positions in the YAR. This produced a series of pendular battles on each side of the border. YAR units crossed into the PDRY in September, 1972. The PDRY invaded the YAR's border regions in October. Kuwait and the Arab League persuaded both countries to accept a cease-fire in November, 1972, and the YAR and PDRY jointly declared that they would begin new unity talks.

This pattern of rhetoric, conflict, and rhetoric went on for well over a decade. The YAR and the PDRY continued to feud and fight minor border wars. At the same time, their governments were destabilized by a long series of tribal rivalries, coup attempts, successful coups, assassinations, and other internal divisions. The PDRY was generally the aggressor and attempted to force "unification" with the YAR on several occasions. The PDRY also had serious military clashes with Saudi Arabia and unsuccessfully backed the Dhofar rebels in Oman from 1967 to 1975.[3]

The Rise of Ali Abdellah Salleh in North Yemen

It was a successful assassination attempt that brought Salleh to power in the YAR. On June 24, 1978, the PDRY ambassador met with President Ahmed al-Ghasmi of the YAR to discuss unification. The ambassador of the PDRY was supposed to be carrying a private message from the president of the PDRY, but the sealed case that held this "message" actually contained a bomb that killed them both

It is still impossible to determine exactly what role Salleh played in the assassination of one of his predecessors, President Ibrahim Hamdi, or whether he gave the PDRY any encouragement in killing al-Ghasmi. It is equally impossible to determine what role Saudi subsidies played in destabilizing the political situation in the YAR. In any case, Salleh's rise to power created a "president" who not only managed to survive but who eventually became the president of a united Yemen. While Salleh was never able to unite all of the YAR's tribes or extend government control into all the rural areas, he did obtain the support of the powerful Hashid and Bakil tribes in the north and brought a degree of order that the YAR had not experienced since the fall of the imams.

The PDRY did not enjoy such stability. From 1969 on, bitter rivalries took place among various factions in the NLF, which resulted in a victory of hardline leftists. During 1970 all officers and political figures with any ties to the British or sheiks in the region were purged, and this was followed with what became a series of tribal purges as the leftist government attempted to create completely loyal rural areas. The net result, however, was Marxist tribalism, where ideology combined with tribal ties to fuel the conflicts among leftist leaders.

It is impossible to summarize all the complex shifts that took place in the PDRY's relations with Oman, the Dhofar rebels, Saudi Arabia, and the YAR during this period, but the result was constant intrigue and violence. It was also a complex rivalry among three of the PDRY's leaders: Salem Rubayya Ali, Abdelfattah Ismail, and Ali Nasr Mohammed. This rivalry played itself out over nearly twenty years, although Rubayya Ali was executed in 1978, after Ismail took power in a coup following the assassination of President al-Ghasmi of the YAR.

The assassination and the resulting changes in leadership in both countries helped trigger another round of fighting between the YAR and PDRY. Ismail supported a Marxist opposition group in the YAR called the National Democratic Front (NDF) and provided it with arms and training areas in the PDRY. In February, 1979, NDF forces invaded the YAR and seized positions near Ibb and Taiz. Regular YAR army forces then counterattacked and moved against NDF positions in the PDRY. The PDRY sent its own army into the YAR. Both countries seemed poised on the edge of a major war until Syria and Iraq helped mediate a cease-fire on March 19, 1979, with the aid of money from Kuwait and Saudi Arabia. In what had virtually become a tradition, presidents Salleh and Ismail then declared their intention to seek unification.

Civil War in the PDRY

While little real progress took place towards unification, the PDRY did seem to become more stable when an increasingly extreme Ismail was forced into exile in April, 1980. Ali Nasr Mohammed became president and proved to be far more pragmatic than Ismail. Unfortunately, this very pragmatism became a problem. It improved the PDRY's relations with its neighbors and its economy, but it also alienated extreme leftists in the leadership, like Vice-President Ali Antar. Even though Mohammed coordinated virtually all of his decisions with Moscow, Ismail was allowed to remain in exile in the USSR and to keep in touch with his supporters in the PDRY. From 1983 onwards, these hard-liners conspired to bring Ismail back and to overthrow Mohammed.[4]

The hard-liners succeeded in engineering the return of Ismail in February, 1985, and he became secretary of the ruling party. Other power struggles expanded the politburo from 13 to 16 members and the central committee from 47 to 77. On January 13, 1986, the struggles between the Ismail and Mohammed factions led to civil war, and intensive street fighting began throughout Aden. Various elements of the armed forces took different sides, but the navy backed Ismail and started firing into the city. This allowed the pro-Ismail forces gradually to win the fighting. Aden suffered major damage, as many as 10,000 civilians were killed, and 4,500 foreigners had to be evacuated, although the damage to civilians was brought under partial control when the Soviet advisors operating the munitions depots refused to provide either side with added weapons and munitions.[5]

Once the Ismail faction clearly came to dominate the fighting, Mohammed flew to Ethiopia and asked Mengistu to rush in added arms and possibly troops. Mengistu did not give him this support, and Mohammed was forced to return to the PDRY without the help he needed. Although he attempted to rally his supporters in the south and the east, he was unsuccessful and had to flee to the YAR. Only then did Ismail's supporters announce that Ismail had died during the fighting. It is not clear exactly how Ismail died, but news of his death was evidently kept secret to prevent riots by his supporters.

The Soviet Union then intervened by forcing the surviving factions to accept a moderate named Haydar Abu Baqr al-Attas as president. Attas was one of the few leaders of the PDRY who had not taken sides between the Mohammed and Ismail factions. He also had relatively good relations with some of the leaders in Kuwait and Saudi Arabia and seems to have been a sincere supporter of unification.

Attas faced major problems. By the time he took power, the PDRY's economy was devastated and it had suffered a total of 13,000–17,000 dead— including both military and civilians—and up to 65,000 people had fled to the YAR.[6] At the same time, Gorbachev was ending the kind of expansionism that had provided the PDRY with so much aid in the past. Although the PDRY provided the USSR with operating areas for its IL-38 May naval reconnaissance aircraft, secure operating facilities, and areas for its naval infantry to carry out landing exercises on the island of Socotra, the USSR refused to provide the massive additional economic aid that the PDRY needed to rebuild its military forces and economy. Gorbachev concluded that the PDRY had become more of a strategic liability than a strategic asset, and he gradually phased out the USSR's military presence.

These Soviet actions helped lead to the breakdown of Marxist authoritarianism in the PDRY and to the collapse of its economy. Industry and trade virtually halted, and farmers refused to send food to Aden and other cities at the government's prices.[7] These changes, however, helped create a political climate in which the long series of efforts to establish a united Yemen took on new meaning. Unification negotiations that had previously done little more than lead to new conflicts took on a different character, and the leadership elites of the YAR and PDRY gradually agreed on plans to merge the two countries. After at least three centuries of separation and a quarter century of tension and conflict, the Republic of Yemen came into existence on May 22, 1990.

The Unification of Yemen

The agreement that led to unification worked surprisingly well, and Yemen held its first real popular election a year later. A two day referendum was held on May 15–16, 1991, to vote on the 128 article constitution that had been approved by the new unity government. Approximately 1.36 million voted out of roughly 4 million eligible voters, and more than 1 million people approved the new constitution. It was a striking step forward in political development, although scarcely one without problems.

The first of these problems was deciding on the political power to be given to each of the existing regimes and the shape of the interim government. The leaders of the People's Democratic Republic of Yemen and the Yemen Arab Republic agreed to full popular elections in November, 1992. In doing so, they agreed to a fundamental change in the leadership of the country after the elections which strongly favored the north. The YAR had had a total population of 9 million, plus up to 2 million expatriates, versus a maximum of 2 million in the PDRY. The YAR also had military forces that had not suffered from the shock of civil war and had most of the new country's oil reserves.

At the same time, the interim government reflected a careful balancing act between north and south. Salleh became the first president, while the former secretary general of the PDRY's Socialist Party, Ali Salem al-Baidh, became vice-president. The ruling presidential council had three northerners and three southerners, and the cabinet had twenty ministers from the north and nineteen from the south. The new parliament had 301 seats, 159 of which were filled with members from the YAR's *shura*, 111 from the PDRY's supreme people's council, and 32 from other political parties.

The second problem was the rise of new political parties. Salleh's People's General Conference (PGC) became the largest political party after unification and continued to reflect many of the religious and tribal factions in the former YAR. Almost immediately, however, new parties arose in the north which mirrored tribal divisions or favored a more Islamic structure of government.

The PDRY's Communist Party was renamed the Yemen Socialist Party (YSP) but could not shake off its history. It gained little support in the north and suffered from internal rivalries that had grown out of the civil war and tensions with former PDRY exiles. A number of leading YSP members were attacked or assassinated during 1991 and 1992.

Almost immediately after unification, new parties emerged that opposed both the PGC and YSP and rejected the new constitution because it called *shari'a* (Islamic law) the "main" rather than "sole" source of law. The Al-Islah, a religious party opposed to Yemen's secular constitution, seemed to become the second largest party in the country. Its leader, Abdellah ibn-Hussein Ahmar, was not an extreme fundamentalist but did call for a conversion of the legal system to Islamic law. Another major Islamic party emerged in the south, the League of the Sons of Yemen led by Abdelrahman al-Jifri. It considered the constitutional referendum illegal and called for immediate popular elections. Similar opposition emerged from powerful tribal leaders.

By September, 1992, there were at least seventeen political parties contending for power—most far more Islamic than either of the two parties that had formed the interim government. This posed the risk that Yemen's experiment in democracy would lead to the same secular-Islamic split that was affecting many other nascent democracies in the Arab world. Some experts also believed that Al-Islah was heavily financed by Saudis who were attempting to revive the power of conservative northern tribal leaders.

The third problem was that unification at the top of the political structure still left considerable uncertainty as to the direction the new country would take. While a unified military command was created, the country initially kept two currencies, airlines, and sets of military forces. There were further divisions in custom and legal practice. Northerners, who showed no reluctance to use narcotics like *qat*, opposed the existence of a brewery in the south. Former exiles from the PDRY promptly began to sue for recovery of land and property that had been seized by the PDRY. Laws in the PDRY that had protected the right of women to equal employment, equal treatment during divorce, and choice of a husband were quietly rescinded, while some question arose over the legal rights of women to inherit and control property.[8]

There were, however, advances as well as problems. Unification led to political liberalization and reform. The collapse of Marxism in the PDRY led to the disbandment of much of the secret police and to a less corrupt legal system and more rights for women. President Salleh retained his internal security system and Iraqi security advisors, but the north also liberalized after unification. Open political debate took place and involved only sporadic violence. Some 50 newspapers and publications appeared reflecting every possible range of opinion. While civil rights and the rule of law scarcely improved to Western standards, they became better than at any time since independence.[9]

The political uncertainties the new republic faced were compounded by external events which offset any initial benefit that unification might have had in solving the two countries' economic problems. Unification created a united Yemen with a GNP of around $5.3 billion but with a per capita income of only $545. The PDRY's economy was in ruins, and the YAR's economy had grown by an average of just 2–3% since the mid-1970s. As a result, economic growth had fallen far below the population growth, which was well in excess of 3%.[10] A steady drop in living standards had taken place, and Yemen had the highest rate of debt per capita in the Middle East—offset only by Yemen's reliance on a parallel economy and remittances from foreign labor.

Yemen's only real hope of economic development was oil. Oil had been discovered in the Marib/Al-Jawf basin in 1984, and exports had begun in 1987. As of January 1, 1992, Yemen had estimated proved oil reserves of 4 billion barrels and gas reserves of 7,000 billion cubic feet. Although no significant production took place during the 1980s, Yemen produced at a rate of about 190,000 to 200,000 million barrels per day during 1990 and 1991 and earned some $900 million in oil revenues between mid-1990 and the end of 1991. More importantly, Yemen's exports had the potential to grow to 600,000 to 800,000 million barrels a day by the mid- to late 1990s.[11]

This dependence on oil, however, created new problems. The PDRY's and YAR's search for oil led to clashes with Saudi Arabia and Oman over drilling rights in the border area during the late 1980s, and these clashes continued after unification. Fighting sometimes became serious along the Saudi-Yemeni border and led to casualties in the Saudi frontier force on several occasions. There were reports that Saudi Arabia had taken several Yemenis prisoner in 1987 and that fighting had taken place near Ifrine in northern Hadramhaut province in June, 1989.

This fighting reduced outside Arab aid to Yemen, and tensions increased sharply in 1990. Yemen accused Saudi Arabia of paying Yemeni tribes to disrupt Yemen's unification in May, 1990, and Yemen supported Iraq when it invaded Kuwait in August, 1990. Salleh seems to have seen Iraq as a potential counterbalance to Saudi Arabia and had relatively close ties to Iraq when the Gulf War began. He was using Iraqi security advisors, had received some military aid from Iraq, and had joined with Iraq, Egypt, and Jordan in forming the Arab Cooperation Council in 1990.

Saudi Arabia and Kuwait quickly retaliated, ceasing all aid to Yemen, and U.S. aid was cut from $42 million in FY1990 to less than $4 million in FY1991 and $6 million in FY1992. Saudi journalists accused Yemen of plotting with Iraq in September, 1990, and Riyadh Television Service allowed individuals identified as Yemeni tribal sheiks to broadcast an attack that included the remark, "We also condemn the Yemeni authority of the Sanhani ignoramus Ali Abdellah Salleh, that parasitical and ignorant leader." Saudi Arabia announced the deployment of Saudi troops near the border in October, 1990.

Yemen responded by demanding that the 1936 treaty be redrawn to rectify the borders and halt Saudi control of Yemeni lands outside Taif. In November, Salleh announced over the Sanaa Domestic Service that Yemen's unification "is the sign of a pan-Arab awakening embodying the dreams of the Arab masses in a borderless great Arab homeland, a unified nation." This reference to a borderless nation seemed to be a direct reference to the rationale Saddam Hussein had used for annexing Kuwait.[12]

Saudi Arabia expelled many of its Yemeni workers. Up to 800,000—about half the total number of expatriates—were forced to leave the southern Gulf countries during and after the Gulf War. This deprived Yemen of up to $350 million per month in worker remittances and raised unemployment to at least 27% by mid-1991 and to as high as 40% by fall, 1992. Yemen could meet only about 20% of its foreign debt commitments during 1990 and 1991 on a foreign debt that totaled some $7.8 billion—about 66% of which was owed to Eastern European countries.

The resulting economic impacts were particularly serious in the south, which had no previous experience in controlling a market economy. Food prices in the south rose by 150% to 400%. They also severely limited what Yemen could do to absorb or aid refugees from Somalia, which began to experience a massive famine by mid-1992.

While Yemen submitted a bill to the UN for $1.6 billion for its share of the damages caused by the Gulf War, it obtained no support from its Arab neighbors and faced a future in which many of its workers might not be allowed to return to Saudi Arabia or the other southern Gulf countries. Yemen also faced new problems on its border. Saudi troops occupied the Al-Baqah border post in Yemen in April, 1991. While Salleh asked President Mubarak to intercede with Saudi Arabia in October, 1991, this had little effect. Saudi Arabia responded by reviving claims based on disputes as to where the former Turkish border had run between the 17th and 18th parallels, and which included about 25% of the territory of the former PDRY.

Saudi Arabia stepped up its efforts to influence the Yemeni elections. It encouraged Yemenis in the area to acquire Saudi passports, and in May, 1992 it sent letters to the six leading oil companies in Yemen claiming that 12 of the 20 concessions Yemen had granted to foreign oil firms were in Saudi territory, warning the oil companies that they were working in disputed territory, and stating that Saudi Arabia intended to reassert its rights. This Saudi warning did not affect the operations of Hunt Oil, which was pumping all of the 180,000 barrels per day being produced in the Marib area. It did, however, affect the exploratory operations of British Petroleum, Phillips, ELF-Acquitaine, and Atlantic Richfield.

While Saudi Arabia agreed to border talks with Yemen in September, 1992—after intervention by Oman and the U.S.—it was far from clear that such talks could resolve the situation either quickly or on a lasting basis.[13]

Military Expenditures and Arms Transfers

The military expenditures and arms transfers of the YAR and PDRY serve as little more than a memorial to violence and waste. Both states spent far more of their limited resources on military expenditures and arms transfers than their economies and peoples could afford.

The YAR generally won the race to build up the largest forces. It was an Arab socialist state but also the more conservative and pro-Western of the two Yemens. It quickly learned to play East off against West and to exploit the PDRY's radicalism in seeking aid from the Arab world. As a result, it, benefited from Saudi aid and some Western aid and arms sales, although it got most of its weapons and military aid from the USSR.

ACDA estimates that the YAR's military budget was $107 million in 1978, $320 million in 1979, $278 million in 1980, $393 million in 1981, $537 million in 1982, $551 million in 1983, $434 million in 1984, $379 million in 1985, $368 million in 1986, $379 million in 1987, $641 million in 1988, and $618 million in 1989.[14] This estimate could put the YAR's military spending at anywhere from 7 to 13% of the GNP and 22 to 39% of central government expenditures.

The IISS puts the YAR's military spending at $713.35 million in 1986, $745.5 million in 1987, and $762.8 million in 1988. These expenditure levels are about one-eighth those of Israel during the same period, and one fifth those of Syria. The IISS estimates that Jordan spent $467 million in 1989, $571 million in 1990 and $587 million in 1992.[15]

As for arms imports, ACDA estimates that the YAR imported $110 million worth of arms in 1978, $480 million in 1979, $575 million in 1980, $1,000 million in 1981, $420 million in 1982, $490 million in 1983, $80 million in 1984, $230 million in 1985, $280 million in 1986, $400 million in 1987, $430 million in 1988, and $420 million in 1989.[16]

These arms imports came principally from the former Soviet Union. ACDA estimates that the YAR's arms imports during 1979–1983 totaled $2,355 million, with $1,200 million from the USSR, $200 million from the

U.S., $30 million from France, $10 million from West Germany, $5 million from Italy, $250 million from Romania, $10 million from Poland, and $65 million from other countries.[17] During 1984–1988, the YAR got $1,420 million worth of arms imports, with $1,300 million from the USSR, $30 million from the U.S., $5 million from the UK, and $90 million from other countries.[18]

ACDA changed its way of reporting arms sales by source in 1992. This new style of reporting does not, however, indicate any reduction in dependence on the USSR. North Yemen imported a total of $1,765 million worth of arms during 1985–1989, with a total of $1,600 million from the Soviet Union, $20 million from the U.S., $5 million from West Germany, $40 million from other Warsaw Pact countries, $40 million from other Middle Eastern countries, $20 million from other East Asian states, and $40 million from other developing countries.[19]

The regime in the PDRY was so extreme that few nations would deal with it, and virtually all of its military aid and arms sales came from the Soviet bloc. ACDA estimates that the PDRY's military budget was $97 million in 1978, $87 million in 1979, $101 million in 1980, $135 million in 1981, $156 million in 1982, $171 million in 1983, $197 million in 1984, $198 million in 1985, $211 million in 1986, $207 million in 1987, and $217 million in 1988.[20] The PDRY's military spending seems to have been equivalent to about 14–21% of its GNP and at 22–37% of central government expenditures, but the USSR may have offset many of the operating costs of PDRY military forces.

The PDRY's arms imports fluctuated from year to year, depending on Soviet policy. They ranged from a peak of $775 million in 1983 to levels of around $300 million annually during the late 1980s. ACDA estimates that the PDRY imported $350 million worth of arms in 1978, $500 million in 1979, $700 million in 1980. $500 million in 1981, $250 million in 1982, $775 million in 1983, $330 million in 1984, $390 million in 1985, $110 million in 1986, $300 million in 1987, $380 million in 1988, and $230 million in 1989.[21]

The uncertainty in some ACDA estimates is indicated by its report that the PDRY took delivery on $1,510 million worth of arms during 1979–1983. This included $1,500 million worth of arms from the Soviet Union and $10 million from other countries.[22] ACDA also estimates, however, that the PDRY took delivery on $1,510 million worth of arms during 1984–1988 and that this total included $1,500 million worth of arms from the Soviet Union and $10 million from other countries.[23] ACDA changed its way of reporting arms sales by source in 1992. This indicates that the PDRY imported a total of $1,400 million worth of arms during 1985–1989, with all $1,400 million coming from the Soviet Union.[24]

The Military Forces of Yemen

Most of these military expenditures and arms imports have been wasted.[25] The PDRY never organized effective regular military forces, and its political struggles made most of its senior commanders more interested in politics than military leadership. The PDRY often got more arms than it could effectively operate and lost much of its military equipment during its civil war. The YAR did somewhat better but never could fully absorb the equipment it got from the Soviet bloc. The YAR never got enough equipment, training, and support from the West to develop modern forces.

Nevertheless, the military buildup in both countries left a unified Yemen with major military assets to draw upon. It also seems to have been able to spend about $1,000 million on military forces in 1990 and $1,060 million in 1991.[26] As a result, some estimates indicate that Yemen now has a total military force of some 105,000 men. There is considerable doubt, however, as to how many of these forces should be counted as full time actives. The IISS counts only 65,000 full time actives with a total of 45,000 conscripts; another 40,000 men are estimated to be part time or in reserve forces.

Depending on the source, Yemen's regular army has 65,000 to over 80,000 men, including part time manpower. It is organized into 34 main maneuver brigades, with a total of nine armored brigades, nineteen infantry brigades, five mechanized brigades, two airborne and commando brigades, five militia brigades, seven artillery brigades, and two surface-to-surface missile brigades.

The Yemeni Army and Paramilitary Forces

The army is equipped with around 1,275 main battle tanks, including 725 T-55s and T-54s, 250 T-62s, 50 M-60A1s, and 250 T-34s. It has around 300 BMP and BMP-1 armored infantry fighting vehicles and 335 armored reconnaissance vehicles—including 125 AML-90s, 60 AML-245s, and 150 BDRM-2s. The army has 690 armored personnel carriers, including 90 M-113s and 600 older Soviet BTR-50s, BTR-60s, and BTR-152s. Many of these armored vehicles are deadlined or have limited operational capability. Yemen conducts almost no armored maneuver training and has limited ability to use its armor even in defensive roles. It has more armored vehicles than crews to operate them.

Yemen is equipped with anti-tank weapons and crew served weapons it can use somewhat more effectively. These include 12 TOW and 24 Dragon fire units and large numbers of AT-3 Sagger anti-tank guided weapons. They include 40 T-12 100mm anti-tank guns, 75mm and 82mm recoilless rifles, LAW and other rocket launchers, and 460 mortars.

Yemen has no self-propelled artillery weapons and relies on some 400–550 towed artillery weapons, ranging from 85mm to 155mm. Many are obsolete, and there are at least six different calibers and nine different types—including 100 D-44 85mm weapons; 35 M-101A1 105mm weapons; 30 M-1931 and M-1937, 150 D-30, and 980 M-1939 122mm weapons; 90 M-46 130mm guns, 40 D-20 152mm weapons, and 12 M-114 155mm weapons. Yemen has 20 SU-85 85mm and 70 SU-100 100mm assault guns. These armored self-propelled systems are obsolete and increasingly difficult to maintain.

Yemen also has large numbers of towed and self-propelled multiple rocket launchers, including 290 BM-21 122mm weapons, 50 BM-13 140mm weapons, and 35 BM-24 240mm weapons. It has 250 81mm, 110 82mm and 120mm, and 100 160mm mortars. Yemen's total mix of towed artillery and multiple rocket launchers gives it considerable firepower, but it lacks anything approaching effective training, and modern targeting, counterbattery, fire control, and command and control equipment. Its wide mix of types also makes effective supply and maintenance difficult. Yemen has 12 FROG-7, 6 Scud B, and 17 SS-21 surface-to-surface missile launchers. Its missile strength and the operational status of these missile systems are unclear.

Yemen has a paramilitary central security organization with up to 20,000 men and a force of tribal levies with up to 20,000 men. The true strength of these two forces is unknown, however, and the figure of 20,000 men is probably both exaggerated and counts a large number of part time or reserve forces.

The Yemeni Air Force

The strength and readiness of the Yemeni air force is uncertain, although it seems to have about 2,500–3,500 men, 100–160 combat aircraft, and 20 armed helicopters. It evidently has four fighter–ground attack squadrons, with 1/11 F-5Es and 3/37 Su-20s and Su-22s. The F-5Es have limited operational readiness, and the attack capability and training of the S-20/22 forces is limited.

The Yemeni air force has 4 fighter squadrons with 47 MiG-21s, some MiG-17s, and some MiG-15 trainers. Some of these units are reasonably effective in day intercept roles, but overall capability is poor. There are 20 Mi-24 and Mi-35 armed helicopters. Their combat readiness is unknown. Yemen also has 27 transport aircraft—including 3 An-12s, 1 An-24, 10 An-26s, 1 C-130Hs, 4 C-47s, 3 Twin Otters, 2 F-27s, and 2 Skyvan 3Ms. It has nearly 50 transport helicopters—including 5 AB-212s, 2 AB-214s, and 40 Mi-8s.

Yemen does not have a modern or well organized air defense system. It does, however, have some radar and inter-site communications capability and numerous Soviet-supplied surface-to-air missile batteries: While estimates of the strength of these forces differ sharply, they seem to include 80–100 SA-2 launchers, 20–25 SA-3 launchers, and 30–35 SA-6 launchers.[27] Yemen also has numerous anti-aircraft guns, including 52 20mm M-176s, 20 M-163 self-propelled Vulcans, 200 ZU-23 and ZSU-23-4 22mm weapons, 200 37mm M-1939s, and 120 57mm S-60s.[28]

The Yemeni Navy

The Yemeni navy is adequate only for inshore and coastal patrol missions. It has roughly 1,500–2,000 men with main bases at Aden and Hodeida and facilities at Al-Muka, the Perim islands, Al-Mukalla, and Socotra. It has twenty-five to twenty-seven combatants. These include two 580-ton Tarantul I–class corvettes with one 76mm gun, two twin SSN-2C Styx anti-ship missile launchers with 45 NM range, one quad SA-N-5 surface-to-air missile launcher, and ASW rocket launchers.[29] It also has six 245-ton Osa-II guided missile patrol boats with four SSN-2Bs and two twin 30mm guns.

In addition, Yemen has eight coastal patrol boats, nineteen inshore patrol boats, one Natya-class 790-ton oceangoing mine sweeper, and six Yevgenya-class 90-ton inshore mine sweepers. Many of these ships have inexperienced crews or limited operational availability, and while Yemen can lay mines, it would have serious problems in trying to sweep anything other than large magnetic mines.

Yemen does have relatively large amphibious lift capabilities: It has one 3,900-ton Ropucha-class LST capable of carrying 200 men and nine tanks, two Polnocny-class 800-ton LSMs capable of carrying 100 troops and six tanks, two 145-ton LCUs, and two 70-ton LCVPs. It does not, however, seem to have practiced any significant amphibious landings or to have conducted amphibious exercises. These ships seem to be used largely for transport purposes. It also has one support ship, two small harbor tankers, and three coastal patrol craft and one tug in its customs service.

Strategic Interests and Arms Control

The creation of united Yemen has ended much of the internal strife in the Yemens and reduced the border conflicts fomented by the Marxist tribalist government of the PDRY. The new government, however, owes its roots to two militaristic regimes and continues to deploy and arm much larger military forces than its economy can really permit. It has not ended chronic mismanagement of the economy, dealt with the fact that drugs are the key crop in much of the country, or attempted to check a population growth rate substantially higher than the economy can sustain without far more attention to agricultural development. Smuggling and the drug trade consume nearly 20% of the GDP and have created a parallel economy within Yemen.[30]

Further, Yemen must now live with the fact that it provided Iraq with political support after its invasion of Kuwait. It is unlikely that either Saudi Arabia or Kuwait will re-admit Yemeni workers in the same numbers and with the same preferential treatment they were offered in the past or provide any significant economic aid.[31]

Future border tensions and clashes with Saudi Arabia seem likely. Salleh formed an interagency committee to try to reach a border settlement with both Saudi Arabia and Oman. He succeeded in reaching a settlement with Oman in 1992, but the situation is very different in the case of Saudi Arabia. Saudi-Yemeni relations have deteriorated steadily since the Gulf War.[32] It is also impossible to rule out a secular-Islamic conflict, at least at a political level, and there is at least some possibility that unification will fail. Regardless of the very real progress that Yemen has made during the last two years, serious tribal, religious, and ideological rivalries can divide the country— particularly if its economic problems continue or grow worse.

Although Yemen badly needs economic aid and development, there is little reason to encourage arms transfers of any kind to Yemen. Yemen already has the forces it needs for defense—particularly since the only threat is largely over border areas where Yemen has provoked most of the conflict. The past arms import levels of North Yemen and South Yemen totaled nearly $1 billion annually in two of the poorest nations on earth and helped make a major contribution to the nation's lack of growth and development. Yemen does need economic aid, although it is unclear that its present government is capable of honestly or effectively using most aid unless it is tied to specific projects. It does not need arms.

Sudan

	Manpower (1,000s)	Tanks	Aircraft	Defense Spending ($ millions)	Arms Imports ($ millions)	Arms Exports ($ millions)
1967	20	37	19	44	3	—
1973	35	130	50	95	6	—
1982	86	190	30	270	240	—
1988	65	175	45	175	60	—
1991	72	215	50	320	—	—

The Sudan is one of the largest nations in Africa.[33] It has a total area of 2,505,810 square kilometers, about one quarter the size of the U.S. Its strategic importance lies largely in its control of much of the water flow of the Nile, its 853 kilometer coastline on the Red Sea, and its boundaries with many other nations in Africa. It has a 1,165 kilometer boundary with the Central African Republic, a 1,360 kilometer boundary with Chad, a 1,273 kilometer boundary with Egypt, a 2,221 kilometer boundary with Ethiopia, a 232 kilometer boundary with Kenya, a 383 kilometer boundary with Libya, a 483 kilometer boundary with Uganda, and a 628 kilometer boundary with Zaire.

The Sudan had a population in late 1991 of about 27.2 million with a growth rate of about 3.0%. It is deeply divided along ethnic lines. About 52% of the population is black, 39% Arab, 6% Beja, 2% foreign, and 1% is other. The Arabs in the north are nearly all Sunni Muslims, as are many blacks, making the nation about 70% Muslim. About 20% of the population is animist and 5% is Christian, virtually all blacks in the south. This has led to bitter divisions between Arab and non-Arab, Muslim and non-Muslim, and divided the north from the south.[34]

Military Developments in the Sudan

Britain forced unity on the northern and southern Sudan after 1899, although it continued to have to send troops into the south as late as 1928. This forced unification has been a problem ever since. When Britain permitted limited local rule in 1955, a number of the southern black military units in the Equatoria Corps opposed unification, which meant domination by the Arabs in the north. Mutinies took place in the cities of Nazra and Juba, and black troops killed their Arab officers. Khartoum sent troops and put the uprisings down by force, but the black survivors of the mutiny created guerrilla forces that eventually banded together in a movement called the Anya-Nya, or Land Freedom Army.[35]

The Sudan was given full independence in 1956, but this independence revealed another major problem in the Sudan. The Sudan was poorly governed when it gained independence and has never had effective leadership to this day. Chronic misgovernment wasted the Sudan's immense economic opportunities and helped cause a series of full scale civil wars between the largely Arab-Islamic north and tribal Christian-animist south. The result has been more than fourteen years of intermittent civil war, the destruction of the economy of much of the south, and the death of as many as 1 million people.

In the period immediately after independence, black elements that formed the Anya-Nya movement gradually developed irregular forces, and sporadic raids and fighting occurred in the south. This fighting became more intense in 1958, when northern military leaders under Gen. Ibrahim Abboud seized control over the government in Khartoum. The military attempted to control the south through severe repression of black opposition, and Anya-Nya gained in power and evolved into a movement called the Sudan African National Union (SANU) in 1963, under the leadership of Emilio Tafeng. SANU set up base camps in Uganda and Zaire, and this provoked Khartoum to send more troops into the south and raid the SANU camps near Abo in Zaire in May, 1964. The result was a civil war that continued until 1972.

Abboud's military rule lasted until December, 1964, when he was replaced by a civilian government under Sadiq al-Mahdi. Mahdi proved to be too weak to govern, however, and a period of instability followed in which various Marxist elements gained increasing power. The only benefit of the new civilian government was that it attempted to negotiate a peace settlement with the black leaders in the south, and it began negotiations with SANU in Khartoum in March, 1965, with Egyptian and Ugandan observers.

These negotiations failed, and the Egyptian and Sudanese governments seem to have bribed and pressured Milton Obote, the leader of Uganda, into suppressing the rebel camps in Uganda. Sudanese forces also crossed into Uganda in October and November, 1966 and attacked the SANU/Anya-Nya bases. They repeated these attacks in 1968, and while Uganda protested the 1968 invasion, it settled for a cash payment.

The Anya-Nya lacked effective military leadership and support until 1969, when Joseph Lagu emerged as a relatively strong leader and Israel began to provide arms, money, and training support to put pressure on Egypt and the Sudan. Obote's fall from power and replacement by Idi Amin added a new dimension to the situation, and fighting continued along the Sudanese-Ugandan border throughout 1969–1972.

The government in the Sudan changed again, however, and the new government became more willing to negotiate. Col. Gaafar Mohammed Nimeiri seized power in 1969. He originally used Marxist and socialist rhetoric and aligned himself with Egypt, Libya, and the USSR. He also ruthlessly suppressed any Islamic opposition and in 1970 put down a Mahdist rebellion of the Antar sect with unusual violence even for the Sudan.

Nimeiri's position shifted in 1971, however, when a Communist coup captured him but made the mistake of trying to use him as a figurehead. Nimeiri outmaneuvered the Communists and reasserted control. He then broadened his political base in the north and began negotiations with the south. These negotiations brought an end to the civil war in March, 1972.

Ethiopia negotiated a cease-fire between Nimeiri and what was now called the Southern Sudanese Liberation Movement, ending black military resistance by granting the south a considerable degree of autonomy.

Unfortunately, Nimeiri proved no better than his predecessors at managing the Sudan's economy, and it degenerated steadily under his rule. The state attempted to manage crop prices in ways that often fixed the sale price lower than the costs of production. Similar state controls over virtually every aspect of the economy reduced a state that was once supposed to be the bread basket of the Arab world to an economic basket case instead.

Nimeiri also could not maintain a stable political balance in a region where Libya and Ethiopia were becoming increasingly radicalized. In 1975 and 1976, he faced a new challenge from Qadhafi when Libya backed Mahdist supporters in a pro-Islamic coup. Nimeiri was able to maintain control of Khartoum in 1976 because the Egyptian air force intervened on his behalf and Egypt rushed in military supplies; the fighting left over 1,000 dead.

Nimeiri then became involved in the complex Arab political maneuvering over Sadat's peace initiative and a low level border struggle with Ethiopia. While the struggle with Ethiopia was brought to a temporary halt in 1979, Nimeiri's other political problems became more complex. A series of coups in the semi-autonomous south left him uncertain as to whether the south would remain stable. At the same time, Qadhafi poured money into Mahdist training camps. This left Nimeiri with both a rising threat from Islamic fundamentalism and worsening economic problems.

Nimeiri responded by refusing to support the Camp David accords, allowing more Islamic elements into his government, and making a deal with Qadhafi. At the same time, he accepted Saudi aid that was tied to his willingness to support an Islamic form of government. The result, however, was that Nimeiri had to enforce a harsh interpretation of Islamic law over the entire country that drove much of the south into open rebellion.

In 1983 a young officer in the Sudanese army named John Garang—who had a degree in agricultural economics from the University of Iowa and had attended the infantry school at Fort Benning, Georgia—formed a new Sudanese People's Liberation Army (SPLA) out of the anti-government elements that had supported the black Sudanese cause between 1955 and 1972. Garang proved to be a competent military leader, and the SPLA soon evolved into a force capable of fighting a sustained civil war. Its military forces were called the Anyana (literally, "venom" of the viper).[36]

Post-Nimeiri Political Developments in the Sudan

Nimeiri's polices failed to keep him in power. In April, 1985 he was overthrown by a military coup led by Gen. Abdelrahman Swar al-Dahab. After a year of control by a transitional military council, the country held popular elections in April, 1986 that made Sadiq al-Mahdi premier of a coalition government. Although al-Mahdi was now the head of the Umma, the Sudan's largest political party, he turned out to be a weak leader and went through three coalition governments and a number of transitional governments in three years. He was a dismal administrator in a nation where poor administration was the normal standard, did little to reduce the tensions between the Arab north and Christian and animist south, and did nothing to end the abuses of Islamic law that Nimeiri instituted as part of his last bid to retain power.

Equally important, al-Mahdi did nothing to create a stable peace with the south and would not obtain agreement on a peace settlement supported by his main coalition partners, the Democratic Unionist Party, because of opposition by the fundamentalist National Islamic Front. He also did little to organize effectively to deal with a famine that began in the south in 1988 and eventually killed nearly 250,000 people.[37]

Al-Mahdi's failure to negotiate effectively with Garang and his tolerance of massacres of the Dinka and Nuer tribes in the south by government armed tribes like the Rizeigat led to growing tension with the army. Although al-Mahdi finally agreed to the peace settlement the army demanded and tried to get $250 million worth of arms from Libya to please the armed forces, these efforts came too late to save him and prevent Garang from going on a full scale offensive.[38]

In June, 1989 al-Mahdi was overthrown by a military junta led by Lt. Gen. Omar Hassab al-Bashir, who had been an associate of General Dahab when the latter overthrew Numeiri. Bashir initially appeared to have an interest in pragmatism and in a peace settlement with the south, but the new junta had an unstable and increasingly extreme Islamic fundamentalist character and did little to try to bring peace or economic recovery.[39]

In spite of Egyptian and Saudi efforts at moderation, the junta was increasingly influenced by Hassan al-Tourabi, an extreme authoritarian Islamic fundamentalist who headed an international movement called the International Muslim Brotherhood and was firmly committed to eliminating the opposition in the south.[40] The Sudan converted its legal system to a fundamentalist interpretation of *shari'a* on November 15, 1991, and proceeded to enforce this interpretation with considerable extremism and little attention to human rights. The government steadily reduced its tolerance for Christian and secular elements in northern Sudan. Further, it attempted to add a new layer of laws and regulations relating to Islamic economics over the Sudan's crippling mix of state controls that had evolved out of "Arab socialism."[41]

As a result, the civil war in the Sudan became more serious. Arab tribes attacked black Sudanese tribes in the border areas between Arab and black, creating a new theater of civil war.[42] The SPLA initially was more successful than the government, however, and the SPLA scored major new gains during the rainy seasons from 1988 to 1990 (May–October). It expanded its operations northward, besieged Juba, and seized the Sudanese army outpost at Jaku along the Sudanese-Ethiopian border. In 1990 the SPLA was able to hold positions near Kumuk and Gizen and control over 100 outposts and villages in the southern Sudan. The SPLA was also able to obtain better access to arms, although starvation and disease increased the number of civilian casualties among the black population it depended on for support.

In 1990, however, the situation began to change. Three factors favored the government. The first was the fall of President Mengistu of Ethiopia, which deprived Garang of his strongest backer, much of his arms and supplies, and a sanctuary and communications base. The second was Iranian military aid to the government in Khartoum, and the third was a major split within the SPLA.

In August, 1991, the SPLA divided into two main camps. One was led by Garang, who was a member of the Dinka tribe and continued to advocate a unified, secular Sudan. The other faction was led by Reik Machar and was formed by SPLA officers in the Nasir who were members of the Nuer tribe. This new group became the so-called Black Faction of the SPLA, which advocated complete independence. Reik accused Garang of being a dictator and leading a rule of terror within the party. Reik and other Nasir officers set up their own SPLA camps and on occasion allied themselves with Khartoum in fighting Garang. The Black Faction was sometimes joined by the Anya-Nya II, which was a smaller faction that split off of the SPLA and which developed ties to Khartoum.

Garang might have been able put down the rebellion within the SPLA if the Black Faction had not turned to Khartoum. Only a critical airlift of arms from Khartoum to Leer saved Reik from Garang's forces in November, 1991. The arms shipment gave Reik the time he needed to rebuild his forces, however, and then to go on the offensive. The Black Faction advanced through the Dinka area of Bor and Kongor; the fighting killed thousands of Dinka civilians.

The divisions in the SPLA gave the government forces time to reorganize, and Iranian aid gave them superiority in firepower. They broke the SPLA siege and went on the offensive. By mid-April, 1992, government forces had scored major gains in the south. They had seized enough territory so that the SPLA could no longer maintain secure areas, and the UN had to cease all humanitarian aid for the roughly 1.5 million refugees in what had been SPLA-controlled territory. Government forces then seized Shambe (about 662 miles south of Khartoum), which the SPLA had used as a central supply point and to intercept river traffic between government held strong points and towns. By May, government forces were attacking Ngangala, only 60 miles from the main SPLA headquarters in Torit.

Government forces still sometimes took heavy losses, but their offensive did not halt with the start of the rainy season in May, and Iran increased its arms shipments. Some estimates indicate that the Khartoum government received several hundred tons of ammunition, up to 50,000 Heckler and Koch G3 automatic rifles, artillery, and five dismantled PRC-made F-6 fighters. In mid-May, Garang had to move part of his headquarters out of Torit to Kajo Kaji, some 75 miles away. This centered SPLA operations close to the west bank of the Nile on the border with Uganda. It also seriously undercut Garang's potential negotiating leverage with Khartoum.

While Saudi Arabia provided Garang with limited aid, government forces took Kapeota in late May and Torit on July 14, 1992. This seizure of Torit drove much of Garang's force into the bush. It marked a possible turning point in a war that had now lasted nine years, cost at least 500,000 lives, and created over 1 million refugees.

Yet Garang's force retreated largely intact, and government forces had won similar victories in the past. While Garang had definitely lost much of the south, he was also strong enough to besiege Juba in late August, 1992 and to force the UN to cut off aid flights to that city. Khartoum continued to take thousands of casualties and broadened the draft law to raise its total regular forces in the south from 80,000–100,000 to 120,000–140,000.

The prospects for any kind of peace were also limited by Khartoum's failure to help reconciliation with the south. Both the army and the government's militia—the 6,000 to 8,000 man Popular Defense Force—were guilty of widespread abuses of southern Sudanese. The government drove some 500,000 Christian and animist refugees from the south out of the slums of Khartoum into poorly organized camps in the desert that offered only an uncertain hope of survival. Islamic law was enforced with growing ruthlessness. Schools, law enforcement, and civil service offices were purged of non-Muslims, and many Christian churches were closed. The government mandated Islamic dress in the north, and the south was left with a devastated economy that the government did little to aid.

The UN estimated by the fall of 1992 that some 7.6 million people needed drought and famine aid, but the government was so poor that it had to remove most of its subsidies on food and fuel. Even in the north, the power grid, irrigation systems, and public transport often broke down. The north-south rail system could carry only 10% of the volume it had carried in 1989. The government also lacked the funds to make payment on the Sudan's foreign debt or to curb inflation in a country that had already experienced 120% inflation since the start of the year.[43]

Sudanese Military Relations with Iran and Other Islamic States

These pressures inevitably led the Sudan to seek foreign military support. Bashir first turned to Iraq for aid and arms—opposing the UN coalition effort in 1990 and 1991—and then turned to aid from Iran once Saddam Hussein was defeated. The details of the Sudan's relations with Iraq are controversial. There are unconfirmed reports that Iraq sent 2,000–7,000 troops and artillery to aid the Sudan to help defend Juba in the southern Sudan in 1990, provided the Sudan with surface-to-air missile launchers, and deployed Mirage F-1 aircraft to the Sudanese base at Wadi Sayyidana north of Khartoum.[44]

In any case, the Sudan's alignment with Iraq ended when Iraq suffered a shattering defeat at the hands of the UN coalition. In spite of official Sudanese denials, the Sudan then allied itself with Iran. While estimates differ, Iran seems to have shipped some $20–40 million worth of arms to the Sudan in 1991. In addition to the arms shipments described earlier, Iran may have sent up to 90 PRC-made tanks, artillery, small arms, 1,000 RPGs, ammunition, spare parts, and possibly anti-ship missiles.

Iran provided training and aid to Nafei Ali Nafel, the head of the Sudan's intelligence service. Ali Falahan, the head of Iran's secret services, and Mohsen Rezai, the head of its Revolutionary Guards, visited the Sudan on several occasions, and a major delegation headed by President Rafsanjani visited the Sudan on December 17, 1991. These visits were followed by unconfirmed reports that Iran sent 1,000 to 2,000 Revolutionary Guards to assist the Sudan's military forces in 1991 and that it seems to be providing aid to the Sudan in transforming its militia into a Revolutionary Guard type force.

The Sudan also strengthened its ties to Islamic fundamentalists in Algeria, Egypt, Jordan, Dubai, Morocco, and Tunisia. This led a number of experts to believe that Iran is working with the Sudan in operating training camps and bases for Islamic extremist groups from many Middle Eastern countries. According to some reports, there were up to thirty Iranian-Sudanese military training and Islamic education camps in the Sudan by 1992. This Iranian-Sudanese cooperation with such movements is difficult to document but seems to include Palestinian extremist groups like the Abu Nidal organization, Popular Liberation Front for the Liberation of Palestine, Islamic Jihad for the Liberation of Palestine, and Lebanese Hizbollah.[45] As a result, fundamentalism in the Sudan seems to have reached a level too extreme for Qadhafi. He cut back on cooperation with the Sudan in various training camps and international efforts and withdrew some officers and troops from the Sudan because of his fear of Islamic subversion.[46]

Military Expenditures and Arms Transfers

The impact of civil war and misgovernment on the Sudan is especially tragic because it is one of the world's poorest countries, with a per capita income of about $330. Civil war and chronic mismanagement of the economy have led to a steadily declining GDP, where the true scope of the decline is almost impossible to measure because of the lack of adequate statistics and the failure to cost the catastrophic degeneration of much of the nation's infrastructure. Although 80% of the population is in agriculture, it produces only 35% of the GDP, and output is extremely uncertain because of poor local management, lack of investment, chronic water problems, and government interference.[47]

In spite of these problems, military forces have consumed at least 15% of the GDP, and probably 20–25% if all paramilitary and factional forces could be counted. The Sudan's formal defense budgets ranged from $130 million to $270 million annually during the 1980s but have never reflected the true cost of its arms imports or its civil wars. ACDA estimates that the Sudan's military budget was $156 million in 1978, $279 million in 1979, $302 million in 1980, $317 million in 1981, $442 million in 1982, $230 million in 1983, $236 million in 1984, $220 million in 1985, $201 million in 1986, $313 million in 1987, $286 million in 1988, and $339 million in 1989.[48] The IISS puts the Sudan's military spending at $460–570 million in 1989 and $320 million in 1990.[49]

The Sudan's arms imports have fluctuated from year to year, ranging from a peak of $240 million in 1982 to levels of around $40 million to $60 million annually during the late 1980s. ACDA estimates that the Sudan imported $120 million worth of arms in 1978, $100 million in 1979, $100 million in 1980, $150 million in 1981, $240 million in 1982, $100 million in 1983, $110 million in 1984, $40 million in 1985, $50 million in 1986, $80 million in 1987, $90 million in 1988, and $80 million in 1989.[50]

The Sudan has increasingly turned to the Third World for arms as its government has shifted to Islamic extremism. During 1979–1983, its arms imports totaled $640 million, of which $110 million came from the U.S., $10 million each from France and the UK, $270 million from West Germany, $10 million from Italy, $70 million from the PRC, $60 million from Poland, and $100 million from a variety of other countries.[51] During 1984–1988, when Nimeiri had begun his shift towards Islamic fundamentalism, the Sudan got only $350 million worth of arms imports, with $120 million from the U.S., $30 million from France, $30 million from the PRC, $10 million from the UK, and $160 million from other countries.[52]

The data involved, however, are contradictory. ACDA changed its way of reporting arms sales by source in 1992. According to this new style of reporting, the Sudan imported a total of $330 million worth of arms during 1985–1989, with a total of $100 million from the U.S., $50 million from the PRC, $20 million from other Warsaw Pact countries, $20 million from other European countries, $70 million from other Middle Eastern countries, and $70 million from other developing countries.[53] These data are not compatible with the early ACDA reporting which covers virtually the same period.

The Sudan's Military Forces

The Sudan has enough total manpower to support massive military forces. The CIA estimated that there were 6,177,000 males in the age group from 15 to 49 in 1991, 3,792,000 males fit for military service, and 307,000 males reaching military age every year.[54] The IISS estimated in late 1991 that there were a total of about 1,507,000 men and 1,426,000 women in the age group from 13 to 17 years, 1,253,000 men and 1,186,000 women in the age group from 18 to 22 years, and 1,900,000 men and 1,834,000 women in the age group from 23 to 32 years.[55]

The Sudan's civil war, collapsing economy, and reduced military expenditures and arms transfers place severe limits on the Sudan's military forces, however, and these problems are compounded by purges, political divisions, and corruption within the military forces. The Arab or Khartoum government military forces in the north have approximately 140,000 to 180,000 men, with about 70,000 trained regulars. They also include a 500 man national guard, a 2,500 man border guard (with 10 battalions), and a popular defense force with 15,000–20,000 men.

The army is organized into six regional commands or infantry divisions, with one armored division headquarters, one airborne division, one republican guard brigade, two armored brigades, one mechanized infantry brigade, seventeen infantry brigades, one paratroop brigade, one reconnaissance brigade, and one air assault brigade. Major support forces include three artillery regiments and one engineer division.

The army does have substantial equipment holdings—including 230 main battle tanks with 200 T-54/T-55s, 20 M-60A3s, and 10 Type-59s. Its other armored vehicles include 70 Type-62 light tanks and 6 AML-60, 15 Saladin, 50 Ferret, and 30 BDRM 1/2 armored reconnaissance vehicles. It has a wide assortment of 286 APCs, including 40 BTR-50 and BTR-152s, 30 OT-62/OT-64s, 36 M-113s, 80 V-100s and V-150s, and 100 Walids. Sudanese forces, however, have little functional training in armored warfare and can only conduct light mechanized infantry or largely static defensive operations. Overall maintenance and training standards are bad.

The Sudan has roughly 150 artillery weapons. Its towed artillery includes 18 M-101 and 6 Model 56 105mm weapons; 4 D-74, 24 M-198, and 42 Type 54/D-30 122mm weapons; 27 M-46 and Type-59-1 130mm weapons; 4 D-20 152mm weapons, and 12 M-114A1 155mm weapons. It has 6 AMX Mark 3 155mm self-propelled weapons and 4 BM-21 122mm rocket launchers. It has large numbers of 81mm mortars and at least 36 M-43 and M-49 120mm mortars. It also has 18 M-1942 76mm and 20 M-1944 100mm anti-tank guns. The Sudan can employ this artillery in static fire but has little capability to switch fires, manage mobile operations or combined arms, or effectively target its weapons.

The Sudan lacks modern anti-tank weapons. It relies on anti-tank guns and has only 4 obsolete Swingfire launchers. It does, however, have large numbers of rocket launchers and some M-40A1 106mm recoilless rifles. It has large numbers of towed unguided anti-aircraft guns, ranging from 20 to 100mm, and some self-propelled M-163 20mm weapons. It has little training and organization to use these weapons effectively. Its only mobile surface-to-air missiles consist of SA-7s and some aging Redeyes. Overall readiness standards are poor, and 33–50% of the equipment in the Arab forces has at best limited operational capability.

The air force has about 6,000 men, including the air defense force. It has fifty-one combat aircraft and two armed aircraft. It is organized into fighter–ground attack units with seven F-5Es, two F-5Fs, ten J-5s, and nine J-6s. Its fighter forces have eight MiG-21s, three MiG-23s, and six J-6s; its COIN forces have three BAC-167s and three Jet Provost Mark 55s, two C-212s in a reconnaissance role, and two Mi-24 attack helicopters. Training and readiness standards are poor, and many of the aircraft are not combat effective. It also has a significant number of training aircraft and fairly large numbers of transport aircraft. Its fixed wing transport assets include five AN-24s, five C-130Hs, four C-212s, two DHC-5Ds, six EMB-110Ps, one F-27, and two Falcon 20/50s. Its transport helicopters include eleven AB-412s, fifteen IAR/SA-330s, four Mi-4s, and fourteen Mi-8s.

The small Sudanese navy was established in 1962 and operates in both the Red Sea and the Nile. It has about 500 men and bases at Port Sudan on the Red Sea and Khartoum on the Nile. Most of its older ships have had to be withdrawn from service, and it has very poor ability to maintain and operate its remaining vessels. It now has two ex-Iranian 130-ton Kadir coastal patrol craft armed with one 20mm Oerlikon gun each, four Yugoslav 20-ton Type-15 inshore patrol craft armed with one 20mm Oerlikon gun, and four ex-Iranian 10-ton gunboats armed with 12.7mm machine guns that it uses for river warfare. It also has two 410-ton Yugoslav DTM-221 utility landing craft and two CASA C-212 maritime aircraft with search radars. It is unclear that these aircraft are fully operational.[56]

The SPLA in the south had about 55,000 men before it divided into warring factions in 1991. The current manpower and equipment holdings of the SPLA are difficult to estimate. They seem to consist largely of small arms, although some armor, artillery, and gunboats have been captured from the Arab forces. The SPLA also has large numbers of mortars, rocket launchers, automatic weapons, light anti-aircraft guns, and SA-7 surface-to-air missiles. It is unclear whether the SPLA still has effective bases in Ethiopia or how much support it is getting from other African countries.

Strategic Interests and Arms Control

The end of the Cold War leaves East and West with no reason to encourage arms transfers to any faction in the Sudan, and every reason to use political and economic pressure to halt military aid from Iran, Saudi Arabia, and other Islamic states. The issue in the Sudan is not Islam but extremism and racism. It is unclear that the Sudan's government can use economic aid without a massive shift in policy, although aid can be helpful on a purely humanitarian basis. As for peacemaking efforts, they now seem likely to fail unless they are based on permanent partition of the country.

Ethiopia

	Manpower (1,000s)	Tanks	Aircraft	Defense Spending ($ millions)	Arms Imports ($ millions)	Arms Exports ($ millions)
1967	45	20	11	29	13	—
1973	50	50	50	62	13	—
1982	240	790	30	358	575	—
1988	250	750	45	440	725	—
1991	65	300	50	536	—	—

Ethiopia occupies an important strategic position in the Horn of Africa.[57] It is a large country of about 1,221,900 square kilometers, or slightly less than twice the size of the state of Texas. Its strategic importance consists largely of its 1,094 kilometer coastline on the Red Sea. It also has 5,141 kilometers in land boundaries. These boundaries include a 459 kilometer border with Djibouti, a 861 kilometer border with Kenya, a 1,600 kilometer border with Somalia, and a 2,221 kilometer border with the Sudan. The border with Somalia is disputed, particularly control of the Ogaden region, which is largely Somali. Ethiopia has also had border disputes with Egypt and Kenya and may not have totally given up a claim to Djibouti.[58]

Ethiopia is one of the poorest countries in Africa and is deeply divided along ethnic and religious lines. It had a total population in mid-1991 of about 53,191,000, with a growth rate of 3.1% The population was about 40% Oromo, 32% Amhara and Tigrean, 9% Sidamo, 6% Shankella, 6% Somali, 4%

Afar, 2% Gurage, and 1% other. It was about 40–45% Muslim, 35–40% Ethiopian Orthodox, 15–20% animist, and 5% other. It is linguistically divided into Amharic, Tigrinya, Orominga, Guaranginga, Somali, Arabic, and English.[59]

Ethiopia's Military Development

Modern Ethiopia emerged from a series of conquests by Ethiopian emperors during the period from 1855 and 1913, and from the Emperor Menelik's victory against Italy at the battle of Adowa in 1896, one of the first major defeats of a colonial army. Haile Selassie became regent in 1916. He took Ethiopia's first steps to create modern military forces a year later, when he created the imperial bodyguard and began to send young officers to Western military schools like St. Cyr. He imported foreign military officers to train his army after he became emperor in 1930 and set up a military academy at Holeta in 1934.

Ethiopia was far from ready to defend itself against a full scale Western incursion, however, and Mussolini's invasion in October, 1935 pitted an Italian army with modern armor and poison gas against Ethiopian forces still equipped largely with small arms. After Mussolini's victory, Haile Selassie was forced into exile and did not return until Britain liberated Ethiopia in 1941.

The course of this liberation changed the map of Africa and led to many of modern Ethiopia's internal problems. The British seized all of Italy's colonies in Africa, and Emperor Selassie's political maneuvering eventually led to the inclusion of a largely Muslim Eritrea and Tigre into Ethiopia. Both had previously sought full independence, and fighting against unification with Italy had begun in Eritrea during 1949–1950.[60] When Britain arranged for the transfer of Eritrea to Ethiopia, this created popular resentment which eventually led to the formation of the Eritrean Liberation Front and the Ethiopian People's Liberation Front in 1958 and finally to a rebellion against Ethiopian rule.

Somewhat similar problems occurred in the Ogaden region. Britain, France, and Italy had divided the Somali tribal territory in the Horn of Africa in the nineteenth century, and Italy seized the tribal area of the Haud and Ogaden and made them part of the colony of Italian East Africa. After World War II, Britain transferred these areas to Ethiopia when it granted British and Italian Somalia independence in June, 1961. It did so although the Ogaden was ethnically Somali and the population of the Ogaden almost certainly favored unification with Somalia. As result, unification led to an immediate tribal revolt which Ethiopia crushed with troops.

Somalia responded by providing the Somali nationalists in the Ogaden with arms, bases, and training. This led to new fighting in 1963, after Ethiopia attempted to tax the Somali herdspeople in the area. In June Somali nationalists in the Nassir Allah movement started to attack Ethiopian government installations in the Ogaden. Somali troops joined the guerrillas in November, and both countries moved troops to their border. Ethiopia conducted air strikes on Nassir Allah bases in Somalia in January, 1964, and scattered border fighting went on until the Sudan mediated a cease-fire on March 30, 1964.

During this period, Ethiopia's military forces dominated the region. They were not strong by Middle East standards, but they were comparatively well organized and equipped by the standards of the Horn of Africa. Britain trained and organized these forces from 1941 to 1951, creating a force of ten infantry battalions, an armored car regiment, and an artillery regiment. In 1951 the U.S. replaced Britain and began to provide aid under the Truman Doctrine. In 1953 the U.S. deployed a military advisory group that remained in Ethiopia until 1977.

The U.S. and Britain were not Ethiopia's only advisors. Swedes helped set up the Ethiopian air force and Norwegians the navy. Indian officers staffed the military academy that was set up at Harar in 1958 and run according to the model of Sandhurst. The U.S. was, however, the largest single supplier of advice and arms and obtained use of a large communications station at Kagnew in return.

This foreign support did not ensure the loyalty of Ethiopia's troops to the emperor. While they fought in Korea and served with UN forces in the Congo in the early 1960s, they became increasingly politicized while remaining divided along ethnic and tribal lines. In 1960 the 6,000 man imperial bodyguard and 26,000 man army became heavily involved in a coup attempt against the emperor and were extensively purged. Plots and coup attempts continued from 1960 to 1974, and a number of senior and junior officers were executed. This situation was made worse by gross corruption within the emperor's court and senior command and by poor wages and living conditions for junior officers and NCOs.

Further, the armed forces reacted to a growing rebellion in Eritrea and Tigre which increasingly exposed the emperor's lack of leadership and ability to appoint effective commanders. The new fighting was largely the emperor's fault. When Eritrea had been joined to Ethiopia in 1952, this was supposed to be part of a federation agreement that gave it considerable autonomy. Eritrean nationalists had formed an Eritrean Democratic Front (EDF) in 1955 with a Muslim and tribal base.

The EDF might have remained a largely political movement, but Haile Selassie unilaterally abrogated the autonomy agreement in 1962, and declared Eritrea to be a province. As a result, the EDF was renamed the Eritrean Liberation Front (ELF) and shifted to armed resistance. This fighting increased steadily as the ELF got support from Egypt, Cuba, and the PRC. By 1967 the ELF was strong enough to directly attack Ethiopian regular forces. This led Ethiopia to attack the tribal and other population groups supporting the ELF and drive many into the Sudan. Ethiopia then raided across the border, and minor clashes took place between Ethiopian and Sudanese troops from March, 1967 to March, 1968.

This fighting intensified again in 1970, when elements that formed the Marxist Popular Liberation Front (PLF) broke with the ELF, and the Ethiopian army was confronted with two groups fighting for Ethiopian independence. Both movements established training areas and supply centers in the

Sudan, and the Eritrean movement acquired a steadily larger number of trained guerrillas. Emperor Selassie showed no ability to deal with these threats and blocked virtually every other type of reform. He tried to preserve a feudal system that made no real allowance for economic or land reform.

In 1974 a group of young officers reacted to the emperor's failures by starting an uprising in Borena that triggered a creeping coup. The military forces divided over what should be done, and an armed forces coordinating committee was set up to try to resolve the differences within the army. This coordinating committee gradually came under radical control, and the military finally seized power by setting up a provisional military administrative council, or Derg. Senior ministers were removed from office and the emperor was deposed in September. In November the more radical elements included in the coordinating committee launched a coup within the military and executed some sixty top ministers and generals.

The Rise of Mengistu

This coup brought Brig. Gene. Tefri Bante, the head of Derg, to power. He in turn was assassinated in a February, 1977 coup launched by Lt. Col. Mengistu Haile-Mariam. Although the nature of the new Mengistu regime was initially uncertain and its leadership was divided, the Derg became steadily more extreme. Mengistu was a radical Marxist who was fully capable of consolidating power into his own hands, he eliminated twelve of the fifteen men who originally joined him in organizing the coup against Bante. In 1978 Mengistu systematically executed virtually any political, military, or civil leader who appeared to oppose him. This Derg terror continued until 1987. It alienated the Ethiopian Christian population (35–40%) and undercut the army, while solidifying the Muslim population (40–45%) in opposition to the government.

These shifts in Ethiopia's leadership triggered a complex shift in relations in the Horn of Africa during 1974–1979. The U.S., which had been Ethiopia's largest military supplier, ceased all aid, and its advisors left the country. This isolated Ethiopia and left it in desperate need of outside aid. After the Derg came to power, Somalia began to organize the Ogaden rebels into an actual army. They were trained and equipped as Somali troops, wearing Somali uniforms without the normal badges and insignia. These guerrilla forces invaded Ethiopia in June, 1977. When their offensive stalled in July, Somalia launched a full scale invasion. Ethiopia retaliated with air raids into Somali territory, but the Ethiopian army performed extremely poorly. By October Somalia had conquered most of the Ogaden.

Mengistu responded by appealing to the Soviet Union for aid. While the USSR was then Somalia's main source of military support, it decided Ethiopia was the greater prize and rushed in military equipment—including large numbers of T-54s, some 600 other armored vehicles, 400 artillery pieces, and BM-21 multiple rocket launchers—and deployed some 17,000 Cuban troops and tank crews from the PDRY. By March, 1978 the USSR had built up a greatly expanded Ethiopian army of some 40,000 regulars and 80,000 irregulars, and this force drove the Somali army back across its borders. Cuban troops then took up defensive positions on the Somali border, which they maintained until October, 1979.

Somalia broke with the Soviet Union in November, 1979 and turned to the U.S. for aid. It also continued its support for the Ogaden rebels, Somali troops assisting them in new raids on Ethiopia in 1980. Ethiopia replied with scattered air raids. After a year of confused fighting, Ethiopian troops invaded the Balemballe area in Somalia in June, 1982. They also raided Lalwale in Somalia in 1984. By this time, the Ethiopians had a huge advantage. Ongoing arms deliveries had led to the creation of a huge Soviet-supplied and Cuban-supported Ethiopian army, but the U.S. never attempted to arm or supply Somalia to carry on its war. As a result, Ethiopia continued to win its military battles.

Ethiopia also helped arm rivals to Somalia's dictator, Mohammed Siad Barre, and helped create the rebel movements like the Somali National Movement and Somali Salvation Democratic Front that eventually drove Barre from power. Ethiopia did, however, reach an accommodation with Somalia in 1978, after a new round of fighting in the Todghere region in February, 1987. By this time both Barre and Mengistu faced sufficient internal problems at home so they were willing to sign an agreement on April 3, 1988, that demilitarized their border and allowed them to resume diplomatic relations.[61]

Part of the reason that Ethiopia signed the agreement was its growing internal problems. Mengistu's efforts to back Marxist movements in neighboring states led to an increasing confrontation with the Sudan after 1974, and the Sudan responded by providing additional arms to ELF and PLF—now referred to as the (Islamic) Eritrean People's Liberation Front (EPLF). At the same time, a new armed liberation movement had emerged in Tigre, the coastal province just to the east of Eritrea, called the Tigre People's Liberation Front (TPLF). By February, 1976, the fighting with this movement had escalated to a new civil war.

Ethiopia responded with air strikes on the rebel bases in the Sudan. Rather than intimidate Nimeiri, however, these raids provoked him. Nimeiri shifted from covert support of the rebels to a formal recognition of Eritrean independence in January, 1977. This led to at least one border clash between Ethiopian and Sudanese troops in April, 1977 and more intense fighting in Eritrea and Tigre. The fighting produced serious casualties on both sides, and the impact on the civilian population was made worse after 1984 by recurrent famine.

These civil wars not only led to further Soviet arms deliveries, they led to the sustained deployment of Cuban troops. Roughly 12,000 to 18,000 Cuban forces were deployed during the period between 1977 and 1984–1986. The Cubans refused direct support for Ethiopia against the EPLF and TPLF, but their presence greatly aided the Ethiopian government by reducing the need to deploy troops against Somalia. Cuba also deployed up to 9,000 troops to help the Derg secure control of the region around the capital of Addis Ababa. At the same time, Ethiopia increasingly became involved in backing groups that opposed Nimeiri, and it provided money and arms to the Sudan People's Liberation Movement, a Marxist group in the Sudan.

Thanks to the steady flow of Soviet aid, Ethiopia became one of the largest military powers in the Red Sea area. The Mengistu government received more than $6 billion in Soviet bloc arms between 1977 and 1990 and signed agreements for $1 billion more. It also received Israeli military assistance after 1988, largely as part of an Israeli effort to block the successful emergence of new Arab mini-states on the coast of the Red Sea.

The extent of Soviet involvement in Ethiopia during the 1980s is indicated by the major arms deliveries to the port of Assab. To help Ethiopia in its 1985 campaign against the Eritrean rebels, the Soviets sent T-55 tanks, APCs and AFVs, and more MiG-23 fighter bombers. Direct Soviet logistic and advisory support was the only reason that Ethiopia was able to deploy some 50,000 troops in less than three weeks in August, 1985 and could capture the key town of Barentu even though it was the rainy season.[62] Soviet advisors also helped Ethiopia carry out air raids on Eritrean camps in the Sudan in August, 1987.

Military Expenditures and Arms Transfers

A review of Ethiopian military expenditures and arms transfers helps put the scale of this Soviet effort into perspective. Ethiopia's annual defense budgets are hard to analyze because most estimates ignore arms transfers and only deal with national expenditures. It is clear, however, that military expenditures rose from $120 million in 1978 to around $400–$430 million annually in 1987 and 1988.

ACDA estimates that Ethiopia's military budget was $120 million in 1978, $254 million in 1979, $321 million in 1980, $331 million in 1981, $357 million in 1982, $363 million in 1983, $389 million in 1984, $382 million in 1985, $388 million in 1986, $432 million in 1987, $512 million in 1988, and $763 million in 1989.[63] This would put Ethiopia's military spending at about 8–10% of the GNP and at 23–38% of central government expenditures. The IISS estimates that Ethiopia spent $472 million in 1989 and $536 million in 1990.[64] The Soviet Union subsidized a large part of these military expenditures.

The Soviet Union provided massive arms transfers, which surged whenever Ethiopia got into military trouble. ACDA estimates that Ethiopia imported $1,500 million worth of arms in 1978, $330 million in 1979, $775 million in 1980, $430 million in 1981, $575 million in 1982, $975 million in 1983, $1,200 million in 1984, $775 million in 1985, $330 million in 1986, $1,000 million in 1987, $700 million in 1988, and $900 million in 1989.[65]

Ethiopia's total arms imports during 1979–1983 reached $1.9 billion, of which virtually all came from the Soviet Union. ACDA estimates that $1.8 billion came from the USSR, $20 million came from Italy, $10 million came from Czechoslovakia, and $60 million came from a variety of other countries.[66] Similarly, the Soviet military aid effort to Ethiopia provided $3.9 billion worth of arms during 1984–1988, out of total imports of $4.1 billion. The rest consisted of $20 million from the PRC, $30 million from Italy, $20 million from Czechoslovakia and $130 million from other countries.[67] By its new method of reporting, the ACDA showed that Ethiopia imported a total of $3,805 million worth of arms during 1985–1989, with a total of $3,600 million from the Soviet Union, $20 million from the PRC, $60 million from other Warsaw Pact countries, $10 million from other European countries, $110 million from other East Asian states, and $5 million from other developing countries.[68]

The Soviet Union did get some things in return. Ethiopia provided the only Soviet naval base in the Red Sea, on the island of Dahlak. The USSR deployed a 8,500-ton floating dry dock, floating piers, helipads, fuel and water storage, a submarine tender, and other repair ships. Soviet-guided missile cruisers and nuclear submarines occasionally called at Dahlak for service, and Soviet IL-38 May aircraft operated from Dahlak until they were destroyed by Eritrean rebels in May, 1984. These facilities, however, were scarcely worth the steadily rising price of Soviet aid to Ethiopia.[69]

The Collapse of the Mengistu Regime

The massive Soviet military aid effort also could not save the Mengistu regime. A combination of the political and economic backlash from prolonged civil wars, economic mismanagement, famine, ideological extremism, and the actions of a ruthless police state steadily undercut Mengistu and the Derg. This was made worse by human suffering. Partly because of actions by the government, at least 300,000 people died of famine in 1984–1985, and at least again that many died during 1987–1990. The rains failed totally in 1989 and came too late in 1990.

In spite of President Mengistu's belated efforts to declare Ethiopia a democratic republic in September, 1987 and to offer limited autonomy to various rebel groups, the EPLF and TPLF continued to fight Ethiopian forces and inflicted major defeats. In March, 1988 the EPLF broke through the government lines south of Nafka and crushed the Ethiopian garrison at Afbet. Ethiopia lost thousands of soldiers, and the EPLF captured large amounts of weapons and supplies. In January, 1989 the TPLF captured virtually all of Tigre province.

While the EPLF continued to seek independence, the TPLF sought power over the rest of Ethiopia. It expanded its ties to other tribal and ethnic groups, particularly the Ethiopian People's Democratic Front, and renamed itself the Ethiopian People's Revolutionary Democratic Front (EPRDF). It later included the Ethiopian People's Revolutionary Party (EPRP) and Ethiopian People's Democratic Movement (EPDM), a largely Amhara splinter group of the EPRP. The TPLF also improved its cooperation with the EPLF and the largely Muslim Oromos in the Oromo Liberation Front (OLF).[70]

These changes in the rebel forces steadily improved their military effectiveness and produced increasingly higher casualties among Mengistu's forces. They also isolated the Mengistu government, whose main support came from the Christian Amharas, who were only 25% of the population. Mengistu was forced to take unpopular measures like the conscription of 13 to 14 year olds. At the same time, Mengistu's problems were made worse by famine and near famine in much of the country.

The steady degeneration of the situation helped lead to a major coup attempt against the regime in May, 1989 while Mengistu was in Berlin. It involved Gen. Tesfaye Gebre Kidan, a former minister of defense; Col. Tesfaye Wold Selassie, the interior affairs minister; the commander of the air force; commander in chief of the army; the commander of the country's largest army units; and thousands of troops. The coup attempt failed, however, because the minister of defense remained loyal to Mengistu and was able to rally superior forces, and the rebels were never able to take key strong points like the main radio station and airport. As a result, most of the coup's leaders were shot.

Mengistu again tried to obtain popular support by taking a more moderate stance, but he did so far too late to have any hope of compromise with the rebel factions or of uniting the armed forces.[71] Mengistu faced another critical problem. The USSR began slowly to phase out aid to Ethiopia in the late 1980s, as Gorbachev's reforms made it less and less willing to indulge in pointless ideological adventures in the Third World. Coupled to the final withdrawal of Cuban troops, this left Mengistu dependent on forces that lost the willingness and capability to fight. While Israel attempted to replace Soviet and Cuban aid to both free the Ethiopian Jews and limit Arab influence in the Red Sea, there was little Israel could do.[72]

The Fall of Mengistu

Mengistu did launch a counterattack against the EPRDF in early 1990, but the attack failed and its net effect was simply to weaken the military forces opposing the EPLF. In February, 1990 the EPLF captured the port of Massawa and surrounded some 120,000 government troops in Asmera. The EPLF and EPRDF then regrouped. In February, 1991 the EPRDF launched a major offensive and captured the provinces of Gondar and Gojjam, giving it control over much of Ethiopia's grain supply. It then advanced deep into Wollo and Shoa provinces.

These offensives virtually isolated the Mengistu government from most of the provinces outside the capital by May, 1991, and it was forced to pull its remaining troops back to the capital. While the U.S. tried to mediate an orderly transfer of power from Mengistu to the EPRDF and other opposition parties, Mengistu gradually lost control over his armed forces and fled to Zimbabwe. The EPLF seized the remaining forces of the government's 2nd Army in Eritrea and took control of the provincial capital of Asmera.

As a result, the remnants of the Mengistu regime under caretaker president Tesfaye Gebre Kidan collapsed on May 28, 1991, and the EPRDF took control in the capital of Addis Ababa. One day later, Issaias Afwerki, the secretary general of the EPLF, announced the formation of a provisional government in Eritrea with the goal of setting up a referendum that would eventually lead to an independent country of Eritrea. The majority of the Ethiopian navy fled to Saudi Arabia with the collapse of the regime, although three Osa-class missile patrol boats were sunk. Part of the air force and several army helicopters fled to Djibouti.

Ethiopia After Mengistu

After Mengistu's fall, the Ethiopian People's Revolutionary Democratic Front allowed the Eritrean People's Liberation Front under Afwerki to form an interim government in Eritrea and constructed its own government in Ethiopia.[73] The EPRDF showed unusual wisdom in creating this new system, it brought some twenty different factions into a national unity government in early July, 1991.

While the leader of the EPRDF, Meles Zenawi, became president, he did not rule by force but attempted conciliation. The EPRDF also gave the predominantly Muslim Oromos in the Oromo Liberation Front four cabinet posts and twelve seats in the council of representatives to try to reduce Muslim separatism. This was an unusual sharing of power, although the EPRDF kept the offices of prime minister, minister of defense, and minister of foreign affairs and thirty-two seats in the council of representatives. During its first year, the new government seemed committed to making good on its promises of democratic elections in 1993, trying to unite the country, and economic reform.

In 1992, however, the capital still had to be patrolled by troops from the EPRDF, and serious ethnic divisions existed within all of Ethiopia's fourteen provinces. The largely muslim Tigrean leaders of the EPRDF dominated the government. They were distrusted by the Amharan Christians in the capital.

More serious divisions emerged between the EPRDF and the Oromos. Clashes took place between EPRDF and Oromo forces in the OLF in 1992 which had to be resolved by a formal cease-fire to allow the smooth flow of aid. Some Oromos supported the creation of a separate Oromo state, and this raised serious issues for the future because the Oromos made up 40–50% of the population. Unity talks have had little success, and the OLF does not recognize the Oromo People's Democratic Organization (OPDO), the Oromo part of the EPRDF, as having any real legitimacy.

These problems became even more serious when the transitional government held elections in June, 1992. The elections attempted to create a common political structure for some eighty tribes in thirty political parties, contending for power in fourteen different provinces. The OLF and a number of other parties claimed that the EPRDF was rigging the election, and Nadhi Gammada, the political head of the OLF, accused the EPRDF of being a new colonizer. The OLF boycotted the elections when they were held on June 21, 1992, and sent its 15,000 man militia out of the encampment areas assigned as part of the peace accord and into the country.

The outside observers invited by the government differed sharply over the handling of the election and the validity of Oromo charges that its candidates had been arrested and their offices had been shut down. There was no question, however, that the election led to new clashes between OLF and EPRDF forces, and new fighting erupted in the south.

By mid-July, at least ten parties from the south had formed a Democratic Alliance of Southern Peoples. The alliance called for the annulment of the elections and threatened that its ten members of the eighty-seven member council of representatives would renounce their seats. They accused the EPRDF of pulling its troops out of their encampment areas and claimed that unfair elections were held in the Afar and Somali areas as well as in the Oromo region. On July 27 the government announced the creation of a board to correct election errors, but the future of Ethiopia's government was far from clear.

The new government faced a number of additional challenges. Besides the OLF and at least three other Oromo liberation movements, there were seven or more opposition parties to the EDRDF and a total of twenty-nine other liberation movements. The government had to repatriate some 200,000 Ethiopian refugees from Djibouti, Kenya, Somalia, and the Sudan. It had to repatriate the former soldiers of the Mengistu regime, demilitarize the various armed forces in the country, and repair an economy and infrastructure devastated by war and famine. While Ethiopia's economy grew by 3.8% during 1986–1990 as a result of Mengistu's gradual move away from Marxism, this growth did little to offset a long prior period of negative growth and the shattering cost of the war that followed.

The debates following the election also did little to resolve the future of the Amharas, who now faced an end to Christian domination of the country. Although they still made up about 25% of the population, they now had to live in a nation that was ruled by Muslims, surrounded by states in which there is a rising tide of Islamic fundamentalism.

Ethiopia also faced the question of its future relations with the EPLF and other Eritrean liberation movements. The Eritrean People's Liberation Front had been fighting since 1961 and seemed committed to seeking full independence when an agreed referendum takes place in 1993. Eritrean independence, however, could cut Addis Ababa and the rest of Ethiopia off from its ports at Massawa and Assab on the Red Sea and leave Tigre without any port of its own. Assab handled 70% of Ethiopia's trade before the war. Many of Ethiopia's non-Eritrean leaders oppose such independence and might consider force to prevent it. At the same time, the new government that came to power in May, 1991 included twenty-four different groups from Ethiopia's many nationalities and did not seem capable of coherent military action.[74]

Ethiopian Military Forces

Like the Sudan, Ethiopia has immense manpower resources to draw upon, but civil war, economic problems, and ethnic divisions limited the growth of its military forces long before the fall of the Mengistu regime. The CIA estimated in late 1991 that there were 11,718,000 males in the age group from 15 to 49, 6,072,000 males fit for military service, and 609,000 males reaching the military age of 18 annually.[75] The IISS estimated in late 1991 that there were a total of about 2,887,000 males and 2,799,000 females in the age group from 13 to 17 years, 2,446,000 men and 2,389,000 women in the age group from 18 to 22 years, and 3,778,000 men and 3,696,000 women in the age group from 23 to 32 years.[76]

At their peak, Ethiopian forces totaled about 319,000 men. It is almost impossible to estimate the present military strength of the key factions in Ethiopia, although the EPRDF seems to have about 65,000 men—some 55,000 of whom are part of the Tigre Liberation Army. The remainder belong to the Oromo People's Democratic Army and smaller groups. The EPLF seems to have another 60,000 men. Some elements of the former Ethiopian forces are still intact.

The total inventory of military equipment in Ethiopia before the collapse included at least 1,300 T-54, T-55, and T-62 tanks; 250 BMP-1 and BDRM armored fighting vehicles; 1,100 armored personnel carriers; 700 towed artillery weapons; 6 self-propelled artillery weapons; large numbers of multiple rocket launchers; and massive amounts of small arms and squad served weapons like recoilless rifles and anti-tank launchers. The navy had 2 frigates, 20 patrol craft and light combatants, and 5 amphibious vessels. The air force had 78 MiG-21MFs, 37 MiG-23BNs, and 20 armed helicopters.[77]

Estimates differ sharply on the equipment that survived the last year of the war. In 1992 Ethiopia seemed to have 300 T-34s, T-54s, T-55s, T-62s, and M-47s. It also seemed to have 350 other armored vehicles, including BDRMs, BMPs, BTR-60s, BTR-152s, and M-113s. There were probably over 400 towed artillery weapons, but any such number is speculative. These weapons included D-44 85mm weapons, D-30 122mm weapons, M-46 130mm weapons, BM-21 multiple rocket launchers, and large numbers of 81mm, 82mm, and 120mm mortars.

There were numerous AT-3 Saggers anti-tank guided weapons and 82mm and 107mm recoilless rifles. There were over 300 anti-aircraft guns, ranging from 23mm to 100mm and including some radar guided self-propelled ZSU-23-4 23mm weapons. The army also retained control over Ethiopia's 20 SA-2 and 30 SA-3 launchers, which generally were not affected by the fighting, and substantial numbers of SA-7s and SA-9s.

The navy had 3,500–4,000 men before Mengistu's fall. It had two 1,180-ton Petya II–class frigates armed with four 76mm guns and ten 406mm torpedo tubes. Its smaller combat ships included two 250-ton Turya-class hydrofoils armed with two 57mm guns and four 533mm torpedoes; four 245-ton Osa II–class guided missile patrol boats armed with Styx missiles; two 200-ton Soviet MOL-class fast attack torpedo boats; three 118-ton Swift large patrol craft; and four 50-ton Zhuk-class coastal patrol craft. Its support ships included a 2,800-ton training ship with one 127mm gun; two 800-ton Polnocny B-class LTCs, one 670-ton French Edic-class LTC, two 995-ton Chamo-class LCLS, four Soviet T 4–class LCVPs, a coastal tanker, and four 11.5-ton coastal patrol craft.

Many of these ships fled to Yemen and Saudi Arabia or were scuttled after Mengistu lost power. Many of the ships that did not escape were not operational. The navy bases at Massawa and Assab suffered substantial damage during the fall of the ports in the spring of 1991.

Like the navy, the air force broke up during the collapse of the Mengistu regime, and only about 50% of its aircraft were operational before the rebels triumphed in their spring offensive. In 1992 there were about 68 fighter aircraft left in the country, including 50 MiG-21MFs and 18 MiG-23BNs. There were also some 18 Mi-24 attack helicopters. Fixed wing transport assets seemed to include 6 An-12s, 2 DH-6s, 2 L-100-300s, 3 U-17s, and 1 Yak-40; rotary wing aircraft included 1 IAR-330, 30 Mi-8s, 3 UH-1s, and 2 Mi-14s. There is no firm report on how many are operational.[78]

Strategic Interests and Arms Control

It is unclear whether the situation in Ethiopia will degenerate into yet another civil war.[79] What is clear is that the end of the Cold War has ended any need for the U.S. or any other outside states to build a major military relationship with Ethiopia, and no case can be made for further major arms transfers.

The last thing Ethiopia needs is more killing. If current developments in Ethiopia do anything, they create a good case for U.S. and Western aid and support for democracy and economic reform. Even before the collapse of the central government in 1991, the nation's GNP was only about $6.6 billion for a population of 53 million. Per capita income was only about $130. The economic situation has deteriorated ever since, and there is certain to be a recurrent risk of famine unless Ethiopia can shift from civil strife to meeting its people's needs.[80]

Djibouti

	Manpower (1,000s)	Tanks	Aircraft	Defense Spending ($ millions)	Arms Imports ($ millions)	Arms Exports ($ millions)
1967	—	—	—	—	—	—
1973	—	—	—	—	—	—
1982	4	0	0	—	—	—
1988	4	0	0	26	—	—
1991	3	0	0	29	—	—

Djibouti is a small former French colony located on the southern coast of the Red Sea.[81] It has a territory of about 22,000 square kilometers, a little smaller than the state of Massachusetts. It has a 314 kilometer coastline on the Red Sea, a 459 kilometer border with Ethiopia, and a 58 kilometer border with Somalia. Both Ethiopia and Somalia have occasionally claimed part of Djibouti's territory.

Djibouti's security and politics are complicated by its demographics, Although France once called Djibouti the French Territory of the Afars and the Issas, it has always had a Somali majority. The French favored the Afars during the 1960s and 1970s, and this led to considerable tension between the two ethnic groups. Splits in the Afar elite brought the Issas to power in 1977, however, and they were able to create a single party state with an Issa (Somali) president and an Afar (Ethiopian) prime minister in 1979. Ever since, there have been opposition political parties in exile and Afar political movements designed to restore Afar control of the country or to expand Afar power.

Military Developments in Djibouti

Djibouti only exists because France sought the territory during 1897 in order to gain a port at the entrance to the Red Sea that would rival Britain's control of Aden. It has acquired new strategic significance, however, because it is the main French port and military base in the Gulf area and because it is the port for the only rail link to Ethiopia's capital of Addis Ababa.

Djibouti was one of the last colonies in Africa. It was granted local self-government in 1956, but a popular referendum indicated that the majority of the population wanted to remain a part of French territory in 1958. This led to problems with Somalia, when it became independent in 1960. Somalia claimed that French Somalia should become part of Somalia, although the French argued that Djibouti had an Afar majority. These tensions led to Somali riots against de Gaulle when he visited Djibouti in August, 1967, although another plebiscite indicated that the majority of the population still wanted to stay part of French territory.

From 1967 to 1976, France and the Afars took one side while Somalia and the Issas took another. French troops and police had to be used in 1970 and 1971 to suppress Issa-sponsored incidents, and civil violence became common after 1972. In February, 1976, Somalis that were part of a movement called the Front for the Liberation of the Somali Coast seized a school bus and took it to the border post near Loyoda. French troops clashed with Somali police when they attempted to prevent the French from recovering the bus.

In spite of these tensions, France gradually mediated an independence agreement that granted added rights to the Issas. As a result, Djibouti was given full independence in June, 1977, after elections supervised by French troops. The elections reversed the previous pattern of power. The country came under the control of the Rassemblement Populaire pour le Progrès, an Issa-dominated group that established a single party political system. This led to new violence in December when the Afars protested the rights given to the Issas. The leaders of the new state then realized they could remain independent only with French military aid, and France has played a key role in ensuring Djibouti's stability and security ever since.

Djibouti not only was too small to defend itself, it was extremely poor in resources. It had virtually no arable land, and only 9% of its land could be used for grazing. This made its economic survival dependent on its status as a free trade area and on the profits from French use of its facilities. As a result, it continued to support a 1977 treaty that allowed French military forces to remain on its soil, and it often aligned itself with the West.

In spite of the French presence, recurrent low level clashes took place between Issas and Afars after 1977. The government arrested a number of Afars in January, 1991 for what it charged was an attack on a military barracks; those arrested included Ali Aref Bourhan, a major opposition leader. These government actions led to Afar attacks on the northern towns of Obock and Tadjourah in November, 1991 involving thousands of Afars and led by the Front for the Restoration of Unity and Democracy (FRUD), an Afar group with ties to Ethiopia. The FRUD attacks caught the government of Hassan Gouled Aptidon by surprise, and it demanded French intervention under the 1977 military agreement.

France initially argued that the matter was an internal affair and did not merit French intervention. The guerrilla war between Afars and Issas became so serious by January, 1992, however, that France offered to send troops to secure the Ethiopian-Djibouti forces. Djibouti then insisted on a French-Djibouti force, which France rejected. When internal violence increased in February, though, France sent troops into threatened areas and assumed a peacekeeping role.

The cause of the fighting is somewhat unclear. The Aptidon government has charged that the Afars are supported by pro-Mengistu Afars in Ethiopia. Ethiopian and Eritrean forces have been deployed to the border area to check Afar separatism, however, and the head of the Afar movement in the Zenawi government of Ethiopia is Ali Mira, who returned from exile as a strong opponent of the pro-Mengistu factions of Ethiopia's Afars. There is little evidence of any Ethiopian military support for Djibouti's Afars.

French experts assert that the FRUD movement is largely native Afar and a natural reaction to the rigidity of Aptidon and the Issas in rejecting political reform and a proper sharing of power. Other experts disagree, saying that while FRUD may lack active support from Ethiopia, it does consist of pro-Mengistu Afars now living in Djibouti. They also estimate that the FRUD can now mobilize more than 3,000 armed men.[82]

The political situation has also been affected by problems in the economy. Djibouti has suffered in recent years from a decline in the use of its facilities resulting from the civil war in Ethiopia and a massive influx of refugees. In 1991 it had 40% unemployment, a declining growth rate, a GDP of only $340 million per year, and a per capita income of $1,030. Its total foreign debt was about $355 million, more than its annual GDP. Even so, Djibouti's citizens have an income six to eight times that of their neighbors in Ethiopia and Somalia. [83]

Some shifts in power seem inevitable. President Aptidon is expected to retire when his second term is over in 1993, and he seems to have selected Ismail Omar Guelleh, his nephew, as his successor. Guelleh, an Issa of the Mamassen clan, seems to have the backing of the army and the security forces. He is not, however, popular with the French. As a result, Ismail Gueddi, the president's chief of staff, is also a possible candidate, as are Mohammed Djama Elabe, Prime Minister Barkat Gourad Hamadou (an Afar), and a number of other figures.

There is also at least some chance that Ali Aref, the main Afar leader during the 1960s and 1970s, could reemerge as a major political figure. While Aref's dictatorial conduct led to splits between the Afars that brought the present Issa-led government to power, and Aref has since been accused of supporting assassination attempts against government leaders, it is possible that some Afar leader like Aref could gain significant support.

Any election, however, assumes that a relative peace exists between Afars and Issas and that a one party state can adapt enough to give both ethnic groups a reasonable share of power. In spite of the FRUD insurrection,

Aptidon has indicated that this may be possible. Although Djibouti became a one party government in 1981, there has been considerable pressure to restore a multiparty system now that it is no longer threatened by the conflicts in Ethiopia and Somalia. Aptidon agreed to allow multiparty elections in June, 1992, and they may be held in September. The question is whether they will help end the civil war, or simply become part of the growing clashes between Afars and Issas.

Djibouti's Military Forces

The U.S. government does not publish detailed statistics on Djibouti's defense expenditures and arms transfers. According to the IISS, Djibouti spent about $29 million on defense in 1986, $34 million in 1987, $26 million in 1988, and $26 million in 1989.[84] The CIA estimates that Djibouti spent about $29 million annually on defense in recent years.[85]

Djibouti has limited military manpower. The CIA estimated in 1991 that there were 89,500 males in the age group from 15 to 49 and 52,000 males fit for military service.[86] The IISS estimated in late 1991 that there were a total of about 22,900 men and 22,400 women in the age group from 13 to 17 years, 18,900 men and 18,800 women in the age group from 18 to 22 years, and 29,100 men and 28,800 women in the age group from 23 to 32 years.[87]

Given its poverty and limited manpower base, it is not surprising that Djibouti's armed forces total only 3,400 men, including 600 in the gendarmerie. Its army has only 2,600 men, organized into north and south commands. Its combat units include an infantry battalion with mortar and anti-tank platoons, an armored squadron, a border commando company, and an airborne company. There is one support battalion.

The army has no tanks. Its other armor includes 45 armored reconnaissance vehicles, with ten BDRM-2s, four AML-60s, sixteen AML-90s, and fifteen M-11 VBLs, and ten BTR-60 APCs. Its artillery includes six M-56 105mm pack howitzers, twenty 81mm mortars, and four 120mm mortars. Djibouti has no modern anti-tank weapons but has eighteen 106mm M-40A1 recoilless rifles, six 120mm rocket launchers, and seventy 73mm, 89mm, and LRAC rocket launchers. The army's only other equipment includes five M-693 23mm self-propelled anti-aircraft guns, two ZU-23s, and an unknown number of 40mm L/70 anti-aircraft guns.

Djibouti's navy consists of about eighty men with eight light patrol boats. These include one 30-ton Tecimar-class coastal patrol craft with 12.7mm machine guns and two 35-ton Plascoa-class coastal patrol craft armed with one GIAT 20mm gun and one 12.7mm machine gun. It also has three Sea Riders, which are rigid inflatable craft.[88]

Djibouti's air force has eighty men and no combat aircraft or helicopters. Its only operational aircraft are six transport aircraft (two C-212s, two N-2501s, one Cessna U206G, and one Socata 235GT) and six transport helicopters (three AS-355s, two SE-3130s, and one SA-330). It does, however, have eighteen aircraft and helicopters that defected from Ethiopia, including some MiG-23s, AN-12s, Mi-8s, and Mi-24s.

Strategic Interests and Arms Control

Djibouti supported the U.S. and the UN during the Gulf War and allowed U.S. aircraft and ships to use its facilities. It has played a moderate role in the Horn and, for all its internal problems, is one of the more stable states in the region.

Djibouti relies on the French fleet, the French air force, and the deployment of French troops for its security. France normally keeps 4,000 men deployed in Djibouti, with one Foreign Legion regiment, one regular infantry regiment, and one fighter–ground attack squadron. It is uncertain how long France will maintain these forces, but Djibouti has no foreseeable hope of defending itself against either Ethiopia or Somalia. It also has considerable strategic importance as a staging point for any French forces helping to defend the Gulf and to any power seeking a port to control the eastern entrance to the Red Sea.

Maintaining as much stability in Djibouti as ethnic conflict permits is in the interests of both the West and the region. This can best be accomplished through foreign aid and by encouraging France to maintain its role in Djibouti, the Red Sea area, and the Indian Ocean. Any effort to build up Djibouti's military forces would do little more than encourage civil war and could not give Djibouti any real capability to defend itself against an unstable Ethiopia or Somalia.

Somalia

	Manpower (1,000s)	Tanks	Aircraft	Defense Spending ($ millions)	Arms Imports ($ millions)	Arms Exports ($ millions)
1967	16	18	12	8	—	—
1973	25	150	100	19	39	—
1982	54	140	55	50	130	—
1988	47	290	63	60	30	—
1991	8	270	50	19	—	—

Somalia is a nation of 673,660 square kilometers, slightly smaller than Texas.[89] It has a 58 kilometer border with Djibouti, a 1,600 kilometer border with Ethiopia, a 682 kilometer border with Kenya, and a 3,025 kilometer coastline on the Gulf of Aden and the Red Sea. Somalia disputed all of these borders when it won independence and still does. It claims the Ogaden province in Ethiopia and much of its southern border area, has made tentative claims to Djibouti, and claims ethnic Somali territory in Kenya.[90]

Somali Military Developments

Somalia achieved independence in 1960 and was created out of parts of the former British and Italian colonies in northwest Africa. Although the result was a nation formed largely out of Somali-speaking tribes, there was no real sense of national consciousness. The tribes were divided into six clans and often contested for power. The leading four clans were all Sameli and included the Dir in the northwest, the Isaq in the north, the Darod in the central west, and Hawiye on the coast. The two lesser Sab clans include the Rahanwin and Digil.

In 1960 Somalia was ruled by the Hawiye and Darod clans, but an increasing number of Dir and Isaq clansmen came into government and the military forces after independence, and two key elements of the Darod clan (the Marehan and Mijerteyn) had long standing feuds that divided the clan. These shifts in the power of the various clans led to a long period of political unrest, culminating in the assassination of President Shirmake in 1969. They also contributed to a pattern of government based on nepotism and corruption that did little to aid the country's development.

In October, 1969 the army carried out a coup which brought Siad Barre to power as a military dictator, governing through a supreme revolutionary council. Barre saw scientific socialism as a means of unifying the clans and declared Somalia a socialist state in 1970. Barre also played East off against West. He allowed the USSR to set up air and maritime facilities which included airfields at Uanle Uen, Hargeisa, and Galcao; a radar base at Agfoi; and maritime bases at Bir Kao and on several islands. In 1974 Somalia signed a treaty of friendship and cooperation with the USSR, giving Barre access to large amounts of Soviet and Cuban weapons.

Ironically, Barre initially attempted to destroy the power of the clans as part of his socialist ethic, and he used the military to conduct several education campaigns to reduce corruption and nepotism. As time went on, however, Barre began to exploit nepotism and clan allegiances as a way of obtaining personal control over the country and the SRC. He increasingly relied on his own Marehan clan, a sub-clan of the Darod family, and members of the Ogaden and Dulbahante, also sub-clans of the Darod.

Once he consolidated power, Barre attempted to use Somalia's new Soviet bloc equipment to conquer the Ogaden in 1977 and 1978 with a Somali-trained, -equipped, and -supplied West Somali Liberation Front in the north and an Abo Liberation Front in the south. Both fronts were little more than extensions of the Somali army. He had great initial success, reaching the gates of Harar.

As has been discussed earlier, however, the Soviet Union chose to shift its alliances to the Marxist Mengistu government in Ethiopia. The USSR not only left Somalia and cut off military supplies, it provided Ethiopia with Cuban troops and pilots and massive supplies of new weapons and equipment. By March, 1978 this allowed Ethiopia to shatter the Somali forces and drive them out of the Ogaden.

Ethiopia also actively subverted the various Somali clans, triggering at least one coup attempt in 1978. Ethiopia helped found the Somali Salvation Democratic Front (SSDF) by providing money to members of the Majerteen clan. Officers of the Majerteen clan then attempted to assassinate Barre. Barre replied by ruthlessly killing their leaders and then helped fund rival factions. The subsequent feuding caused the collapse of the SSDF in the mid-1980s.

Military Expenditures and Arms Transfers

The Soviet shift to Ethiopia forced Barre to turn to the U.S. and the West for military support and aid, although he never received anything approaching the level of aid he sought. Somalia's annual defense budgets slowly rose from $14 million in 1973 to around $38 million in 1979 and then dropped below $40 million annually during the rest of the 1980s. ACDA indicates they reached $58 million in 1978, $38 million in 1979, $23 million in 1980, $30 million in 1981, $31 million in 1982, $31 million in 1983, $25 million in 1984, and $31 million in 1986.[91] The IISS has issued defense spending estimates of $83 million in 1986, $46 million in 1988, and $18.05 million in 1989.[92]

Somalia's arms imports fluctuated from year to year, and reporting on them is exceptionally uncertain. ACDA indicates they often exceeded defense expenditures and reached $240 million in 1978, $130 million in 1979, $200 million in 1980, $60 million in 1981, $130 million in 1982, $70 million in 1983, $90 million in 1984, $60 million in 1985, $20 million in 1986, $20 million in 1987, $30 million in 1988, and $30 million in 1989.[93]

Somalia got little from the U.S. during the early 1980s. Its arms imports during 1979–1983 totaled $580 million, of which $30 million came from the USSR, $5 million each from France and the UK, $410 million from Italy, $50 million from the PRC, $10 million from Poland, and $70 million from a variety of other countries.[94] This situation changed during the mid-1980s, although Somalia never got large amounts of arms from the U.S. by Middle East standards. During 1984–1988, Somalis got only $200 million worth of imports, with $60 million from the U.S., $10 million each from France and the PRC, $20 million from Italy, and $100 million from other countries.[95]

ACDA's new style of reporting indicated that Somalia imported a total of $160 million worth of arms during 1985–1989, with a total of $50 million from the U.S., $10 million from France, $5 million from the PRC, $10 million from other Warsaw Pact countries, $20 million from other European countries, $10 million from other Middle Eastern countries, $5 million from other East Asian states, and $50 million from other developing countries.[96]

Somali Military Forces and the Impact of Civil War

None of these arms transfers dealt with the main problem Somalia faced, which was tribalism. From 1969 onwards, Barre used his control of the tribes in the south to suppress the Isaq clan in the north: While the Darods make up about 25% of the population, the Isaqs make up another 20% of the nation's population and are a very powerful clan. They formed their own Somali National Movement (SMN) in 1981 centered in the cities of Berbera, Borana, Burao, and Hargeisa.

Barre's repressive efforts did as much to divide the country and create clan and tribal opposition as they did to solve his immediate military problems. He also progressively favored his own Marehan sub-clan in appointments and in dealing with the country's series of economic crises. This increasingly left him dependent on the Marehan, with lesser support from the

Dulbahante sub-clan. It also left him vulnerable to pressure from Ethiopia, which provided money to any clan or movement that would challenge Barre.

Barre attempted to deal with this situation by ending his conflict with Ethiopia. An agreement to restore relations between Ethiopia and Somalia was signed on April 15, 1988, and appeared to offer both Mengistu and Barre a way of eliminating a costly and pointless border war. However, the SNM rejected the agreement and launched an attack on the Barre government.

In late May, 1988, SNM guerrillas attacked government officials in Hargeisa and Burao in the north. The Somali army then launched savage attacks on these cities and their civilian populations during the rest of 1988 and 1989 in the area of Hargeisa, Berbera, and Burao; thousands of Somalis were killed, and some 350,000 Isaqs fled to Ethiopia.[97] At the same time, Barre launched a crackdown in the south that alienated many of the southern clans. He also split with the Ogadeni sub-clan of his Darod clan because it objected to the peace agreement with Ethiopia. In 1989 he fired his Ogadeni minister of defense, and this led to the first open split within his army. In late 1989 Omar Jess and about 200 Ogadeni soliders deserted from the Somali army.

Instead of reducing his opposition, Barre managed simply to alienate many of his former supporters. In 1989 at least nine anti-Barre clan movements were established, and two new anti-Barre military groups were formed: the United Somali Congress (USC), a predominately Hawiye group, and the Somali Patriotic Movement (SPM), formed largely from tribes in the Ogaden.[98]

By this time, Barre was also in his eighties, and the nation's economy had virtually collapsed. He could not unite enough tribal groups in his support to maintain effective military forces. His efforts to assert control did little more than lead to a broader civil war, with some elements of the southern clans attacking Barre, along with elements of the Ogadenis who had fled Ethiopia after their defeat fighting for Barre. As a result, Barre's control over the country weakened steadily in 1989 and 1990.

The rebel United Somali Congress began to infiltrate Mogadishu in late 1990, preparing for an effort to seize the city. Barre countered by a house-to-house search in December, 1990, but this triggered the USC coup rather than prevented it. The Barre forces then seem to have panicked, although they were larger and better equipped than the USC, and reacted to uprisings and incidents throughout the city by going into a state of near collapse. As a result, the USC drove Barre and his Somali Revolutionary Socialist Party regime out of power. After four weeks of bloody fighting which killed at least several thousand civilians, Barre and his advisors fled to his clan stronghold in the south. This left the USC in charge of the capital and allowed the SMN to seize complete control in the north.[99]

While relations between the various anti-Barre groups had been relatively smooth until Barre's departure, the USC declared itself the government on January 27, 1991, without consulting any of the other anti-Barre groups. It announced that its head, Ali Mahdi Mohammed, was president. The SNM reacted in May, 1991 by declaring that northern Somalia was an independent country and seceded. At the same time, the USC alienated many of the clans in the south, which retreated to their own territorial strongholds. The Somali Patriotic Movement formed its own enclave, and the USC itself divided between the supporters of Ali Mahdi and the head of the USC's military forces and its chairman, Gen. Mohammed Farah Aideed. While both Mahdi and Aideed were Hawiyes, they belonged to different sub-clans (Mahdi is an Abgal and Aideed a Habra Gadir) and split their clan as well as the USC.

In spite of repeated efforts to reconcile the factions within the USC, Somalia deteriorated into a state of constant low level civil war. The Aideed faction gained control of Kismayu and became one of the strongest factions in Mogadishu, while Mahdi became dependent on militia groups. At least six major armed factions emerged, including that of Barre, who operated out of his clan stronghold in southern Somalia near the Kenyan border.

By the fall of 1991, the Mahdi-Aideed rivalry within the USC led to constant fighting in the capital. At least several thousand more Somalians died before an attempt was made to form a unity government in October, 1991. This government was headed by a third leader, Prime Minister Omar Arteh Ghalib, and included 83 ministers and assistant ministers in an effort to include every faction. General Aideed rejected the unity government, however, and it failed to bring peace to the capital or the country.

Each faction continued to arm while the country's economy moved towards collapse, urban services broke down in Mogadishu, and food became scarce in many areas. The fighting between Mahdi and Aideed also grew more intense, and a February 14, 1992, cease-fire brokered by the UN did nothing more than lead Aideed to try to outmaneuver Mahdi by using the cease-fire to move his forces. Mogadishu became a battlefield for warring gangs using artillery, machine guns, and 106mm recoilless rifles. Peace efforts by neutral clans did little more than reduce the use of artillery, and any benefits from the reduction in fighting were outweighed by the already ruinous state of the capital and the widespread malnutrition and starvation. The situation in a would-be independent Somaliland in the north was little better. Berbera had lost much of its population, Hargeisa and Burao were in ruins, and SMN forces continued to clash with the USC.

The UN formed the Operation in Somalia (UNOSOM) in April, 1992 in an effort to halt the fighting and guard relief workers. It had a 50 man unarmed peace monitoring group and a 500 man armed force. The UN could not stop the bloodshed, however, and Aideed forced Barre into exile in Kenya in May. A combination of total economic collapse, civil disorder, and drought meant that about 4.5 million people out of Somalia's population of 6 million were living on the edge of starvation.

Repeated efforts to get Somalia's factions to allow the transit of outside aid failed during May to September, 1992. By the early summer, relief efforts were paralyzed by clan fighting and outright banditry. While the UN strengthened its forces, many Somalis fled the country and many died. The economic distribution system consisted of little other than looting and relief transfers, and many towns in the south starved to death. Guerrilla warfare prevented agricultural efforts even where there was water, and at least 25% of the nation's livestock perished between January and July.

The country's acting prime minister, Ghalib, requested a 10,000 man UN peacekeeping force, but the UN could only send 500 troops and step up the flow of supplies. Aideed opposed a UN peacekeeping effort, and without his support, there was little any outside force could do to bring real order. Accordingly, the U.S. arranged an airlift based in northern Kenya designed to fly in aid to individual cities and bypass armed areas and the chaos in the ports. This increased the flow of aid to the south and the center of the country, but Somalia showed no signs of order or recovery in September, 1992, and it was clear that even active outside military intervention could not prevent hundreds of thousands more deaths.[100]

Somalia's Military Forces Before Barre's Fall

Somalia's regular armed forces have been replaced with paramilitary forces loyal to Somalia's divided ethnic factions. Before the collapse of the Barre government, however, the Somali armed forces consisted of about 65,000 men, more than half of whom were extremely low quality conscripts.

The Somali army had a nominal strength of 60,000 men with 3 tank brigades, 44 mechanized and infantry brigades, 6 commando brigades, 3 field artillery brigades, 30 field artillery battalions, and 40 air defense battalions. Most of these "brigades" were about the size of reinforced battalions in other Middle East armies, and many were severely understrength. Training was very limited, and the officer corps was highly political, corrupt, and tribally aligned.

The army had an inventory of some 290 tanks, including 30 Centurions, 120 M-47s, 30 T-34s, and 110 T-54/T-55s.[101] Its other armored vehicles included 10 M-41 and 10 PT-76 light tanks, and 30 BDRM,-2, 15 AML-90, 10 Ferret, and 30 Saladin armored reconnaissance vehicles. It also had some 484 armored personnel carriers, including 64 BTR-40/50/60s, 100 BTR-152s, 310 Fiat 6614/6616s, and 10 Panhards. The army had very little armored warfare capability except in executing limited maneuvers using armor to support infantry operations. Its ability to conduct sustained operations with armored vehicles was very limited, and the mix of different types of vehicles from different supplier countries made these training, maintenance, and sustainability problems worse.

Somalia did have a comparatively large number of towed artillery weapons and substantial stocks of artillery munitions. It had approximately 300 weapons at the time of the collapse of the Barre government, with 23 M-1944 100mm, 100 M-56 105mm, 92 M-1938/D-30 122mm, and 18 M-198 155mm weapons. It also had 120 81mm, 200 M-41 82mm, and 50 M-1943 120mm mortars. Somalia had only minimal ability to maneuver its artillery, shift fires, carry out beyond visual range targeting, and conduct counterbattery operations. It could, however, conduct mass fire against area targets and attack targets that could be visually located.

The army's other weapons included TOW and 100 Milan anti-tank guided weapons, with at least 20 of the TOW launchers mounted on vehicles. It had 300 LRAC 89mm rocket launchers and 60 M-40A1 106mm recoilless rifles. Its air defense weaponry consisted of 20–50 SA-7 launchers, 50 ZU-32-2 and

4 ZSU-23-4 anti-aircraft guns, 160 M-1939/Type-63 37mm anti-aircraft guns, 20 S-60 57mm anti-aircraft guns, 24 KS-19 100mm anti-aircraft guns, and an unknown number of 20mm and 40mm anti-aircraft guns. The army had considerably better proficiency with these light weapons than with its heavy weapons and often used its anti-aircraft guns as area fire weapons against light vehicles and infantry.

The small Somali navy was based at Berbera, Mogadishu, and Kismayu. It had 2,000 men and 2 245-ton Soviet Osa II–class missile patrol boats with 4 SS-N-2 Styx missiles each, 4 200-ton Soviet Mol-class fast attack craft, and 1 Soviet 800-ton Polnocny class LCT, and 1 Soviet 70-ton LCM, and several patrol ships and coastal combatants.[102]

The 2,500 man air force had 56 combat aircraft, including 10 MiG-17 and 4 Hunter attack aircraft, 22 J-6 and 8 MiG-21 air defense fighters, 1 Hunter FR-76 reconnaissance aircraft, and 6 SF-260W COIN aircraft. The air force also operated Somalia's larger surface-to-air missile systems, including 42 SA-2 and 9 SA-3 launchers. Its fixed wing transport aircraft included 3 An-2s, 3 An-24s, 2 An-26s, 4 BN-2s, 1 C-212, and 1 G-222. Its helicopters included 6 Mi-4s, 2 Mi-8s, 1 Agusta Bell 204, and 4 Agusta Bell 212s. In practice, the air force had only about 30–40% of its aircraft operational—almost all severely limited by low training and maintenance standards. It had only minimal capability to operate Somalia's air defense warning system and surface-to-air missiles.[103]

Somalia also had an 8,000 man national police force, a 1,500 man border guard force, and a people's militia with a nominal strength of 20,000 men. These units had lost much of their strength long before the collapse of the Barre government.

Somalia's Military Forces After Barre's Fall

There is no way to know how many of these forces and weapons survive. The military equipment captured from the Barre government was divided among tribal factions, but much of it was rendered inoperable and much cannot be operated because of a lack of skills and spare parts. It is also impossible to track the various military factions from day to day. Immediately after the overthrow of Barre, the United Somali Congress had about 6,500 full time men under arms, divided between the Somali National Movement in the north and the various factions in the south. At least 30,000 men, however, were operating in part time forces or in support of the tribal factions.

The breakup of the anti-Barre factions soon after driving Barre out of the country led to a new civil war and fighting between the factions that used much of the equipment captured from the Barre government. Scattered artillery fire took place throughout the capital, indicating that many of the simpler army weapons had fallen into factional hands, but there were few reports of any use of armor. Light army weaponry was widely dispersed, falling into both factional hands and those of private citizens who bought or stole weapons to defend themselves.

Strategic Interests and Arms Control

Somalia has lost most of its strategic importance with the end of the Cold War and has degenerated into a state of civil war that needs every possible mediation and aid effort. As with the situation in the Sudan and Ethiopia, no case can be made for further arms transfers to Somalia. The present GDP is less than $1.7 billion and the per capita income under $210. There has been negative economic growth for at least four years, and the population growth rate is 3.3% in spite of famine and refugee deaths. Unfortunately, sufficient arms and ammunition exist to allow a Somali civil war to continue for some time even if no covert low level arms transfers occur to any of the factions involved.

The Problem of the Red Sea and the Horn

The Cold War, regional conflicts, and internal religious and ethnic conflicts have turned Somalia and the Sudan into living hells, threaten fragile and divided governments in Djibouti and Ethiopia, and raise serious questions about the long term stability of Yemen. We can only hope that the end of the Cold War will end the era in which outside powers ignored the cost that building up local military forces and making major arms transfers exerted in human suffering.

Ethiopia, Somalia, the Sudan, and Yemen will be far better off as abandoned pawns than as the focus of superpower strategic interests. While Djibouti does benefit from the presence of France, the problem persists whether France will push for a more stable and democratic government or allow tensions between Afars and Issas to fester because political pressure is strategically inconvenient.

What all five states have in common is that none needs more arms or military support. In each case local ethnic groups need to work out their own future, either as part of the same country or as new and divided nations. It must also be said, however, that each of these nations is largely a self-inflicted wound. East and West may have armed tribalism and religious hatred, but they did not create them. Further, political and economic reform must come from within, not be demanded in the form of aid. Unfortunately, the prospects of such reform are uncertain at best. Djibouti, Ethiopia, and Yemen all suffer from problems that their governments may or may not resolve. Somalia and the Sudan may well descend into near barbarism before civil war exhausts their leaders into something approaching common sense.

Notes

1. The military manpower, force strength, and equipment estimates in this section are made by the author using a wide range of sources, including computerized data bases, interviews, and press clipping services. Most are impossible to reference in ways of use to the reader. The force strength statistics are generally taken from the latest edition of the International Institute for Strategic Studies, *Military Balance* (IISS, London), in this case the 1991–1992 edition. Extensive use has also been made of the annual editions of the Jaffee

Center for Strategic Studies, *The Military Balance in the Middle East* (JCSS, Tel Aviv), especially the 1990–1991 edition and working materials from the coming edition. Material has also been drawn from computer print outs from NEXIS, the United States Naval Institute data base, and from the DMS/FI Market Intelligence Reports data base. Other sources include *Military Technology*, "World Defense Almanac for 1991–1992," published in 1992; country reports of the Economist Intelligence Unit (EIU); Foreign Affairs Division, "Middle East Arms Control and Related Issues," Washington, Congressional Research Service, 91-384F, May 1, 1991; and *Middle East Economic Digest*, "MEED Special Report: Defense," Volume 35, December 13, 1991.

Weapons data are taken from many sources, including computerized material available in NEXIS, and various editions of *Jane's Fighting Ships* (Jane's Publishing); *Jane's Naval Weapons Systems* (Jane's Publishing); *Jane's Armour and Artillery* (Jane's Publishing); *Jane's Infantry Weapons* (Jane's Publishing); *Jane's Military Vehicles and Logistics* (Jane's Publishing); *Jane's Land-Based Air Defence* (Jane's Publishing); *Jane's All the World's Aircraft* (Jane's Publishing); *Jane's Battlefield Surveillance Systems* (Jane's Publishing); *Jane's Radar and Electronic Warfare Systems* (Jane's Publishing), *Jane's C^{3}I Systems* (Jane's Publishing); *Jane's Air-Launched Weapons Systems* (Jane's Publishing); *Jane's Defence Appointments & Procurement Handbook (Middle East Edition)* (Jane's Publishing); *Tanks of the World* (Bernard and Grafe); *Weyer's Warships* (Bernard and Grafe); and *Warplanes of the World* (Bernard and Grafe).

Other military background, effectiveness, strength, organizational, and history data are taken from Mark N. Katz, "Yemeni Unity and Saudi Security," *Middle East Policy*, Vol. 1, No. 1, 1992, pp. 117–135; Lij Imru Zelleke, *The Horn of Africa, A Strategic Survey*, Washington, International Security Council, 1989; John Bennet, "The Military Balance and Internal Security in the Horn of Africa," student paper for NSS/Security Problems of the Middle East, Georgetown University, 1990; Norman Cigar, "Soviet–South Yemeni Relations: The Gorbachev Era," *Journal of South Asian and Middle Eastern Studies*, Summer, 1989, pp. 3–38; John Byington, "The Military Balance and Internal Security in the Horn of Africa," student paper for NSS/Security Problems of the Middle East, Georgetown University, 1990; Stephen Page, *The Soviet Union and the Yemens: Influence in Asymmetrical Relationships*, New York, Praeger, 1985; Richard F. Nyrop, *The Yemens: Country Studies*, Washington, Department of the Army, 1985; Kirk Campbell, "Yemen," Washington, Congressional Research Service, 91-540F, July 10, 1991; Mark Katz, "Camels and Commissars," *The National Interest*, Winter 1988/1989, No. 14, pp. 121–124; the relevant country or war sections of Herbert K. Tillema, *International Conflict Since 1945*, Boulder, Westview, 1991; Department of Defense and Department of State, *Congressional Presentation for Security Assistance Programs, Fiscal Year 1993*, Washington, Department of State, 1992; various annual editions of John Laffin's *The World in Conflict* or *War Annual*, London, Brassey's; and John Keegan, *World Armies*, London, Macmillan, 1983; Anthony H. Cordesman, "The Military Forces of the Yemens," *Armed Forces*, July, 1988, pp. 302–305; *The Gulf and the Search for Strategic Stability*, Boulder, Westview, 1984, and *The Gulf and the West*, Boulder, Westview, 1988.

2. CIA, *World Factbook, 1991*, pp. 341–342.

3. It is difficult to establish a fixed time period for the Dhofar rebellion. It can be argued that the rebellion began in 1964. It was in 1967, however, that large flows of arms began through the PDRY. These were first provided by the PRC and then by the USSR, most moving through a supply base in Hauf in Yemen.

4. Other hard-liners included Defense Minister Qassem, Deputy Prime Minister Ali Badeeb, Construction Minister Fadil Abdullah, and Local Government Minister Ali Al Beedh. For a detailed description of the war, see John Laffin, *The War Annual I*, London, Brassey's, 1986, pp. 143–147.

5. There were then about 2,000 Soviet advisors, as many as 10,000 Soviet military personnel, and 400 Cubans in the PDRY.

6. Some estimates put the dead as low as 5,000+. *Time,* January 9, 1989, pp. 35–36; Fred Halliday, "Moscow's Crisis Management, The Case of South Yemen," *Middle East Report,* #151, March-April 1988.

7. *New York Times,* October 20, 1989, p. A-5; November 23, 1991, p. A-2; *The Middle East,* April, 1989, pp. 18–19; *Time,* January 9, 1989, pp. 35–36; Kirk Campbell, "Yemen," Washington, Congressional Research Service, 91-540F, July 10, 1991.

8. Kirk Campbell, "Yemen," Washington, Congressional Research Service, 91-540F, July 10, 1991, pp. 3–4; *Christian Science Monitor,* May 21, 1992, p. 5; *Washington Post,* July 29, 1992, p. A-19; *Los Angeles Times,* June 1, 1992, p. A-2; *London Financial Times,* August 13, 1992, p. 4.

9. *Economist,* December 9, 1989, p. 42; March 3, 1990, p. 40; *Washington Times,* December 27, 1989, p. A-2; *Philadelphia Inquirer,* December 2, 1989, p. 14A; December 17, 1989, p. 26A; *The Middle East,* May, 1988, pp. 23–26; *The Middle East,* December, 1991, pp. 37–38.

10. CIA, *World Factbook, 1991,* pp. 341–342.

11. Yemen probably had additional proven reserves of 2 billion barrels in 1990. Its reserve-to-production ratio was 57:1. *OJJ Special, Oil and Gas Journal,* December 30, 1991, pp. 43–49; other estimates indicate it has 4 billion barrels of proven reserves and 2 billion barrels of probable reserves. See Joseph P. Riva, Jr., of the Congressional Research Service, writing in the *Oil and Gas Journal,* September 23, 1991, p. 62; *New York Times,* November 23, 1991, p. 2; Joseph P. Riva, "Persian Gulf Oil: Its Critical Importance to World Oil Supplies," Congressional Research Service 91-220 SPR, March 5, 1991, pp. 3–4; *The Middle East,* December, 1991, pp. 37–38; *New York Times,* June 7, 1992, p. A-7.

12. Taken from work by Jonathan S. Mark, a student at Georgetown.

13. Some estimates put the loss of remittances at a maximum of $800 million per year. Kirk Campbell, "Yemen," Washington, Congressional Research Service, 91-540F, July 10, 1991; *New York Times,* November 23, 1991, p. 2; *Middle East Report,* May-June, 1991, pp. 26–41; *Christian Science Monitor,* May 21, 1992, p. 5; Reuters, May 19, 1991, BC cycle; Agence France Presse, May 20, 1991; Xinhua General News Service, May 22, 1992, Item 0522206; *Boston Globe,* July 25, 1992, p. 2; Middle East News Network, August 19, 1992; *Washington Post,* July 29, 1992, p. A-19; July 12, 1992, p. A-20; *Los Angeles Times,* June 1, 1992, p. A-2; *London Financial Times,* August 13, 1992, p. 4; *Chicago Tribune,* July 12, 1992, p. I-15; *New York Times,* June 7, 1992, p. A-7; June 27, 1992, p. A-4; *Washington Times,* June 27, 1992, p. A-3.

14. Arms Control and Disarmament Agency (ACDA), *World Military Expenditures and Arms Transfers, 1990,* Washington, GPO, 1990, Table I.

15. IISS, *Military Balance, 1987–1988, 1988–1989, 1989–1990,* and *1991–1992.*

16. Arms Control and Disarmament Agency (ACDA), *World Military Expenditures and Arms Transfers, 1990,* Washington, GPO, 1990, Table II.

17. Arms Control and Disarmament Agency, *World Military Expenditures and Arms Transfers, 1985,* pp. 98, 134, 140, 146.

18. Arms Control and Disarmament Agency (ACDA), *World Military Expenditures and Arms Transfers, 1989,* Washington, GPO, 1990, p. 118; Arms Control and Disarmament Agency (ACDA), *World Military Expenditures and Arms Transfers, 1986,* Washington, GPO, 1987, p. 143.

19. Arms Control and Disarmament Agency (ACDA), *World Military Expenditures and Arms Transfers, 1990,* Washington, GPO, 1990, pp. 133–134.

20. It is almost impossible to estimate PDRY military expenditures with any accuracy after 1986. Arms Control and Disarmament Agency (ACDA), *World Military Expenditures and Arms Transfers, 1990,* Washington, GPO, 1990, Table I.

21. Arms Control and Disarmament Agency (ACDA), *World Military Expenditures and Arms Transfers, 1990,* Washington, GPO, 1990, Table II.

22. Arms Control and Disarmament Agency (ACDA), *World Military Expenditures and Arms Transfers, 1985,* Washington, GPO, 1985, pp. 133–134.

23. Arms Control and Disarmament Agency (ACDA), *World Military Expenditures and Arms Transfers, 1989*, Washington, GPO, 1990, pp. 117–118.

24. Arms Control and Disarmament Agency (ACDA), *World Military Expenditures and Arms Transfers, 1990*, Washington, GPO, 1990, pp. 133–134.

25. Unclassified sources differ sharply as to the current actively equipment holdings of the Yemeni armed forces, and interviews provided little additional data on Yemen's forces. The most reliable source seems to be the International Institute for Strategic Studies. The figures for army and air force equipment holdings are taken primarily from this source. The data for the navy are taken primarily from Jane's.

26. IISS, *Military Balance, 1991–1992*, pp. 123–124.

27. Egyptian estimate. It is not clear how much of this equipment is operational.

28. IISS estimate.

29. The Styx is a sea skimmer at the end of its run, with IR or active radar homing, a 513 kilogram warhead, and a speed of Mach 0.9.

30. *New York Times*, November 23, 1991, p. 2.

31. *New York Times*, November 23, 1991, p. 2; Kirk Campbell, "Yemen," Washington, Congressional Research Service, 91-540F, July 10, 1991.

32. BBC translation of Yemeni Republic Radio, Aden 1810, October 31, 1991; *Platt's Oilgram News*, October 15, 1991, p. 6.

33. The military manpower, force strength, and equipment estimates in this section are made by the author using a wide range of sources, including computerized data bases, interviews, and press clipping services. Most are impossible to reference in ways of use to the reader. The force strength statistics are generally taken from interviews and from the sources reference for each paragraph. They also draw heavily on his *The Gulf and the Search for Strategic Stability* (Boulder, Westview, 1984) and *The Gulf and the West* (Boulder, Westview, 1988).

Extensive use has also been made of the annual editions of the International Institute for Strategic Studies, *Military Balance* (IISS, London), in this case the 1991–1992 edition, and of the Jaffee Center for Strategic Studies, *The Military Balance in the Middle East* (JCSS, Tel Aviv), especially the 1990–1991 edition and working materials from the coming edition. Material has also been drawn from computer print outs from NEXIS, the United States Naval Institute data base, and from the DMS/FI Market Intelligence Reports data base. Other sources include *Military Technology*, "World Defense Almanac for 1991–1992," published in 1992; Foreign Affairs Division, "Middle East Arms Control and Related Issues," Washington, Congressional Research Service, 91-384F, May 1, 1991; and *Middle East Economic Digest*, "MEED Special Report: Defense," Volume 35, December 13, 1991.

Weapons data are taken from many sources, including computerized material available in NEXIS, and various editions of *Jane's Fighting Ships* (Jane's Publishing); *Jane's Naval Weapons Systems* (Jane's Publishing); *Jane's Armour and Artillery* (Jane's Publishing); *Jane's Infantry Weapons* (Jane's Publishing); *Jane's Military Vehicles and Logistics* (Jane's Publishing); *Jane's Land-Based Air Defence* (Jane's Publishing); *Jane's All the World's Aircraft* (Jane's Publishing); *Jane's Battlefield Surveillance Systems* (Jane's Publishing); *Jane's Radar and Electronic Warfare Systems* (Jane's Publishing), *Jane's C³I Systems* (Jane's Publishing); *Jane's Air-Launched Weapons Systems* (Jane's Publishing); *Jane's Defence Appointments & Procurement Handbook (Middle East Edition)* (Jane's Publishing); *Tanks of the World* (Bernard and Grafe); *Weyer's Warships* (Bernard and Grafe); and *Warplanes of the World* (Bernard and Grafe).

Other military background, effectiveness, strength, organizational, and history data are taken from Anthony H. Cordesman, *The Gulf and the Search for Strategic Stability*, Boulder, Westview, 1984, and *The Gulf and the West*, Boulder, Westview, 1988; "Sudan: The Longest War," *World & I*, October, 1989; Lij Imru Zelleke, *The Horn of Africa, A Strategic Survey*, Washington, International Security Council, 1989; the relevant country or war sections of Herbert K. Tillema, *International Conflict Since 1945*, Boulder, Westview, 1991; Department of Defense and Department of State, *Congressional Presentation for Security Assistance Programs, Fiscal Year 1993*, Washington, Department of State, 1992; various annual editions of John Laffin's *The World in Conflict* or *War Annual*, London, Brassey's; and John Keegan, *World Armies*, London, Macmillan, 1983.

34. CIA, *World Factbook, 1991*, pp. 293–294.

35. Herbert K. Tillema in *International Conflict Since 1945*, Boulder, Westview, 1991, pp. 104–105; *Baltimore Sun*, March 5, 1989, p. 14A.

36. *Insight*, April 17, 1989, p. 26.

37. Raymond W. Copson, "Sudan: Foreign Assistance Facts," Congressional Research Service IB-85065, February 18, 1992.

38. The southern region in the Sudan runs on an east-west line from areas north of Awil in the west to areas north of Malakal and Nasir in the east. World & I, "Sudan: The Longest War," *Washington Times*, October, 1989, p, 192; "Bitter Historical Split Blocks Solution to Festering Crisis," *Insight*, April 17, 1989, p. 26; *New York Times*, November 14, 1988, p. A-10; March 26, 1989, p. A-5; *Wall Street Journal*, April 11, 1989, p. A-19; *Washington Post*, March 4, 1989, p. A-18; March 13, 1989, p. A-29; *Los Angeles Times*, February 26, 1989, p. I-1.

39. The cabinet affairs minister, Col. Tayib Ibrahim Mohammed Khair, has emerged as Bashir's hatchet man in these purges and in many of the more violent efforts to suppress any opposition and the SPLA. *Christian Science Monitor*, August 18, 1989, p. 6; *Insight*, April 17, 1989, p. 26; *U.S. News and World Report*, July 24, 1989, pp. 32, 37; *Washington Post*, July 1, 1989, p. A-12; July 8, 1989, p. A-22.

40. Ironically, Tourabi is Mahdi's brother-in-law. Both are Western educated: Tourabi has law doctorates from the University of London and the Sudan; Mahdi is a graduate of Oxford. *Financial Times*, February 13, 1992, p. 4; *Washington Post*, March 21, 1992, p. A-20.

41. *The Middle East*, June, 1991, p. 24; *Wall Street Journal*, January 31, 1991, p. A-14; *Washington Post*, March 7, 1992, p. A-18.

42. *New York Times*, January 5, 1990, p. A-2; January 7, 1990, p. A-12.

43. *Economist*, April 25, 1992, p. 46; *Christian Science Monitor*, February 7, 1992, p. 7; May 8, 1992, p. 6; *Guardian Weekly*, September 15, 1991, p. 16; *New York Times*, April 15, 1992, p. A-3; June 1, 1992, p. A-6; June 3, 1992, p. A-4; June 8, 1992, p. A-8; *Washington Times*, April 16, 1992, p. A-2; May 25, 1992, p. A-2; May 29, 1992, p. A-2; July 15, 1992, p. A-11; July 19, 1992, p. C-3, August 29, 1992, p. A-2; *Philadelphia Inquirer*, August 31, 1992, p. A-10; *Baltimore Sun*, March 20, 1992, p. 5-A; *Jane's Defence Weekly*, May 9, 1992, p. 806.

44. Yossef Bodansky and Vaughn S. Forrest, "Iran's Shadow Over the Red Sea," House of Representatives, Task Force on Terrorism and Unconventional Warfare, February 3, 1992, p. 1.

45. *New York Times*, December 31, 1991, p. A-7; January 26, 1992, p. A-12; *Washington Post*, March 2, 1991, p. A-17, January 31, 1992, p. A-13; March 12, 1992, p. A-21; *Washington Times*, February 28, 1992, p. F-1; *Philadelphia Inquirer*, January 16, 1992; *Financial Times*, February 13, 1992; p. 4; Yossef Bodansky and Vaughn S. Forrest, "Iran's Shadow Over the Red Sea," House of Representatives, Task Force on Terrorism and Unconventional Warfare, February 3, 1992; *The Estimate*, April 10, 1992, p. 5; *Christian Science Monitor*, March 31, 1992, p. 5; *Washington Times*, March 6, 1992, p. A-10; *Washington Post*, March 12, 1992, p. A-21.

46. For a list of camps, locations, and specific movements using facilities in the Sudan, see Yossef Bodansky and Vaughn S. Forrest, "Iran's Shadow Over the Red Sea," House of Representatives, Task Force on Terrorism and Unconventional Warfare, February 3, 1992.

47. CIA, *World Factbook, 1991*, pp. 293–294.

48. Arms Control and Disarmament Agency (ACDA), *World Military Expenditures and Arms Transfers, 1990*, Washington, GPO, 1990, Table I.

49. IISS, *Military Balance, 1987–1988, 1988–1989, 1989–1990*, and *1991–1992*.

50. Arms Control and Disarmament Agency (ACDA), *World Military Expenditures and Arms Transfers, 1990*, Washington, GPO, 1990, Table II.

51. Arms Control and Disarmament Agency, *World Military Expenditures and Arms Transfers, 1985,* pp. 98, 131, 140, 146.

52. Arms Control and Disarmament Agency (ACDA), *World Military Expenditures and Arms Transfers, 1989,* Washington, GPO, 1990, p. 115; Arms Control and Disarmament Agency (ACDA), *World Military Expenditures and Arms Transfers, 1986,* Washington, GPO, 1987, p. 143. Some estimates put the value of Soviet arms transfers from 1977 to 1990 at roughly $11 billion.

53. Arms Control and Disarmament Agency (ACDA), *World Military Expenditures and Arms Transfers, 1990,* Washington, GPO, 1990, pp. 133–134.

54. CIA, *World Factbook, 1991,* pp. 200–201.

55. IISS, *Military Balance, 1991–1992.*

56. Estimate based primarily on *Jane's Fighting Ships, 1991–1992,* pp. 511–512.

57. The military manpower, force strength, and equipment estimates in this section are made by the author using a wide range of sources, including computerized data bases, interviews, and press clipping services. Most are impossible to reference in ways of use to the reader. The force strength statistics are generally taken from interviews and from the sources reference for each paragraph.

Extensive use has also been made of the annual editions of the International Institute for Strategic Studies, *Military Balance* (IISS, London), in this case the 1991–1992 edition, and of the Jaffee Center for Strategic Studies, *The Military Balance in the Middle East* (JCSS, Tel Aviv), especially the 1990–1991 edition and working materials from the coming edition. Material has also been drawn from computer print outs from NEXIS, the United States Naval Institute data base, and from the DMS/FI Market Intelligence Reports data base. Other sources include *Military Technology,* "World Defense Almanac for 1991–1992," published in 1992; Foreign Affairs Division, "Middle East Arms Control and Related Issues," Washington, Congressional Research Service, 91-384F, May 1, 1991; and *Middle East Economic Digest,* "MEED Special Report: Defense," Volume 35, December 13, 1991.

Weapons data are taken from many sources, including computerized material available in NEXIS, and various editions of *Jane's Fighting Ships* (Jane's Publishing); *Jane's Naval Weapons Systems* (Jane's Publishing); *Jane's Armour and Artillery* (Jane's Publishing); *Jane's Infantry Weapons* (Jane's Publishing); *Jane's Military Vehicles and Logistics* (Jane's Publishing); *Jane's Land-Based Air Defence* (Jane's Publishing); *Jane's All the World's Aircraft* (Jane's Publishing); *Jane's Battlefield Surveillance Systems* (Jane's Publishing); *Jane's Radar and Electronic Warfare Systems* (Jane's Publishing), *Jane's C³I Systems* (Jane's Publishing); *Jane's Air-Launched Weapons Systems* (Jane's Publishing); *Jane's Defence Appointments & Procurement Handbook (Middle East Edition)* (Jane's Publishing); *Tanks of the World* (Bernard and Grafe); *Weyer's Warships* (Bernard and Grafe); and *Warplanes of the World* (Bernard and Grafe).

Other military background, effectiveness, strength, organizational, and history data are taken from Theodore Dagne, "The Horn of Africa: A Trip Report," Congressional Research Service 91-823, November 15, 1991; Lij Imru Zelleke, *The Horn of Africa, A Strategic Survey,* Washington, International Security Council, 1989; Anthony R. Tucker, "Ethiopia's Intractable Wars," *Armed Forces,* July, 1989, pp. 321–325; Lt. Col. David R. Mets, "The Dilemmas of the Horn," *Proceedings of the Naval Institute,* April, 1985, pp. 49–57; Samuel Makinda, "Shifting Alliances in the Horn of Africa," *Survival,* January/February, 1985, pp. 11–19; Anthony H. Cordesman, *The Gulf and the Search for Strategic Stability,* Boulder, Westview, 1984; *The Gulf and the West,* Boulder, Westview, 1988; Anthony H. Cordesman and Abraham Wagner, *The Lessons of Modern War,* Volume II, Boulder, Westview, 1989; the relevant country or war sections of Herbert K. Tillema, *International Conflict Since 1945,* Boulder, Westview, 1991; Department of Defense and Department of State, *Congressional Presentation for Security Assistance Programs, Fiscal Year 1993,* Washington, Department of State, 1992; various annual editions of John Laffin's *The World in Conflict* or *War Annual,* London, Brassey's; and John Keegan, *World Armies,* London, Macmillan, 1983.

58. CIA, *World Factbook, 1991*, pp. 94–95.

59. CIA, *World Factbook, 1991*, pp. 94–95.

60. Ironically, Ethiopia funded many of the Eritrean nationalist groups at this time in an effort to prevent any reunion of Eritrea with Italy.

61. Herbert K. Tillema in *International Conflict Since 1945*, Boulder, Westview, 1991, p. 97.

62. *Soviet Military Power, 1986*, GPO, Washington, 1986, p. 134, and *Soviet Military Power, 1987*, pp. 134–135.

63. Arms Control and Disarmament Agency (ACDA), *World Military Expenditures and Arms Transfers, 1990*, Washington, GPO, 1990, Table I.

64. IISS, *Military Balance, 1987–1988, 1988–1989, 1989–1990*, and *1991–1992*.

65. Arms Control and Disarmament Agency (ACDA), *World Military Expenditures and Arms Transfers, 1990*, Washington, GPO, 1990, Table II.

66. Arms Control and Disarmament Agency, *World Military Expenditures and Arms Transfers, 1985*, pp. 98, 131, 140, 146.

67. Arms Control and Disarmament Agency (ACDA), *World Military Expenditures and Arms Transfers, 1989*, Washington, GPO, 1990, p. 115; Arms Control and Disarmament Agency (ACDA), *World Military Expenditures and Arms Transfers, 1986*, Washington, GPO, 1987, p. 143. Some estimates put the value of Soviet arms transfers from 1977 to 1990 at roughly $11 billion.

68. Arms Control and Disarmament Agency (ACDA), *World Military Expenditures and Arms Transfers, 1990*, Washington, GPO, 1990, pp. 133–134.

69. Department of Defense, *Soviet Military Power, 1985*, pp. 123–129; *Soviet Military Power, 1986*, GPO, Washington, 1986; *Soviet Military Power, 1987*, pp. 134–135.

70. Theodore S. Dagne, "Recent Political Developments in Ethiopia and Somalia," Congressional Research Service 91-452F, May 31, 1991, and "Ethiopia: New Thinking in U.S. Policy," Congressional Research Service 91-489F, June 18, 1991. For good discussions of Soviet and Ethiopian strategy in the Horn see Lt. Col. David R. Mets, "The Dilemmas of the Horn," *Proceedings of the Naval Institute*, April, 1985, pp. 49–57; and Samuel Makinda, "Shifting Alliances in the Horn of Africa," *Survival*, January/February, 1985, pp. 11–19.

71. *New York Times*, May 18, 1989, p. A-3; *Washington Post*, May 17, 1989, p. A-25; May 18, 1989, p. A-41; May 19, 1989, p. A-29; May 20, 1989, p. A-17.

72. Israel may well have provided Ethiopia with cluster bombs, as well as air force and army advisors. See Anthony R. Tucker, "Ethiopia's Intractable Wars," *Armed Forces*, July, 1989, pp. 321–325; Anthony R. Tucker, "Conflict in the Horn of Africa," *Jane's Defence Weekly*, December 17, 1988, p. 1557; *Economist*, February 24, 1990, pp. 40–41; *New York Times*, January 1, 1989, p. E-4; January 21, 1990, p. 1; February 14, 1990, p. A-15; *Miami Herald*, February 25, 1990, p. 17-A; *Washington Post*, September 9, 1989, p. A-11; November 7, 1989, p. A-21; February 10, 1990, p. A-17; *Washington Times*, October 12, 1989, p. 8; December 11, 1989, p. A-8; *Philadelphia Inquirer*, February 9, 1990, p. 13A; *Insight*, November 6, 1989, p. 34; Aradom Tedla, "Eritrea—Waiting for the World to Act," *The World and I*, March, 1989, pp. 130–139.

73. *Washington Post*, August 17, 1991, p. A-16.

74. *Time*, July 15, 1991, pp. 34–35; *Africa News*, December 23, 1991, pp. 18–19; July 6, 1992, p. 6; *Economist*, September 14, 1991, pp. 44–45; *Christian Science Monitor*, June 19, 1992, p. 2; June 26, 1992, p. 6; *Washington Times*, June 20, 1992, p. A-9; *Washington Post*, June 22, 1992, p. A-11; June 24, 1992, p. A-24; Agence France Presse, July 15, 1992; BBC, July 30, 1992, ME/1446/ii; Theodore S. Dagne, "Ethiopia: The Struggle for Unity and Democracy," Congressional Research Service 92-507F, June 20, 1992.

75. CIA, *The World Factbook, 1991*, pp. 200–201.

76. IISS, *Military Balance, 1991–1992*.

77. Based upon the IISS, *Military Balance, 1990–1991*.

78. Based upon the IISS, *Military Balance, 1991–1992*.

79. Much of the political analysis in this section is based on Theodore Dagne, "Ethiopia: War and Famine," Congressional Research Service IB90049, August 5, 1991; "Recent Political Developments in Ethiopia and Somalia," Congressional Research Service 91-452F, May 31, 1991; "Ethiopia: New Thinking in U.S. Policy," Congressional Research Service 91-489F, June 18, 1991; and "The Horn of Africa: A Trip Report," Congressional Research Service 91-823, November 15, 1991. Also see Jennifer Parmelee, "Battle Won, Eritrean Leader Looks Ahead to Life After Independence," *Washington Post*, August 17, 1991, p. A-16, "Ethiopia Plies Democracy, Contentiously," *Washington Post*, October 22, 1991, p. A-8; and "Ethiopia Begins the Road to Recovery," *Washington Post*, February 2, 1992; Herbert Lewis, "Beginning Again," *Africa Report*, September-October, 1991, pp. 59–67; and Jane Perlez, "A New Chance for a Fractured Land," *The New York Times*, September 22, 1991.

80. CIA, *World Factbook, 1991*, pp. 94–95.

81. The military manpower, force strength, and equipment estimates in this section are made by the author using a wide range of sources, including computerized data bases, interviews, and press clipping services. Most are impossible to reference in ways of use to the reader. The force strength statistics are generally taken from interviews and from the sources reference for each paragraph. They also draw heavily on his *The Gulf and the Search for Strategic Stability* (Boulder, Westview, 1984) and *The Gulf and the West* (Boulder, Westview, 1988).

Extensive use has also been made of the annual editions of the International Institute for Strategic Studies, *Military Balance* (IISS, London), in this case the 1991–1992 edition, and of the Jaffee Center for Strategic Studies, *The Military Balance in the Middle East* (JCSS, Tel Aviv), especially the 1990–1991 edition and working materials from the coming edition. Material has also been drawn from computer print outs from NEXIS, the United States Naval Institute data base, and from the DMS/FI Market Intelligence Reports data base. Other sources include *Military Technology*, "World Defense Almanac for 1991–1992," published in 1992; Foreign Affairs Division, "Middle East Arms Control and Related Issues," Washington, Congressional Research Service, 91-384F, May 1, 1991; and *Middle East Economic Digest*, "MEED Special Report: Defense," Volume 35, December 13, 1991.

Weapons data are taken from many sources, including computerized material available in NEXIS, and various editions of *Jane's Fighting Ships* (Jane's Publishing); *Jane's Naval Weapons Systems* (Jane's Publishing); *Jane's Armour and Artillery* (Jane's Publishing); *Jane's Infantry Weapons* (Jane's Publishing); *Jane's Military Vehicles and Logistics* (Jane's Publishing); *Jane's Land-Based Air Defence* (Jane's Publishing); *Jane's All the World's Aircraft* (Jane's Publishing); *Jane's Battlefield Surveillance Systems* (Jane's Publishing); *Jane's Radar and Electronic Warfare Systems* (Jane's Publishing), *Jane's C³I Systems* (Jane's Publishing); *Jane's Air-Launched Weapons Systems* (Jane's Publishing); *Jane's Defence Appointments & Procurement Handbook (Middle East Edition)* (Jane's Publishing); *Tanks of the World* (Bernard and Grafe); *Weyer's Warships* (Bernard and Grafe); and *Warplanes of the World* (Bernard and Grafe).

Other military background, effectiveness, strength, organizational, and history data are taken from Anthony H. Cordesman, *The Gulf and the Search for Strategic Stability*, Boulder, Westview, 1984; *The Gulf and the West*, Boulder, Westview, 1988; and *Weapons of Mass Destruction in the Middle East*, London, Brassey's/RUSI, 1991; Anthony H. Cordesman and Abraham Wagner, *The Lessons of Modern War*, Volume II, Boulder, Westview, 1989; Theodore Dagne, "The Horn of Africa: A Trip Report," Congressional Research Service 91-823, November 15, 1991; Lij Imru Zelleke, *The Horn of Africa, A Strategic Survey*, Washington, International Security Council, 1989; the relevant country or war sections of Herbert K. Tillema, *International Conflict Since 1945*, Boulder, Westview, 1991; Department of Defense and Department of State, *Congressional Presentation for Security Assistance Programs, Fiscal Year 1993*, Washington, Department of State, 1992; various annual editions of John Laffin's *The World in Conflict* or *War Annual*, London, Brassey's, and John Keegan, *World Armies*, London, Macmillan, 1983.

82. Theodore Dagne, "The Horn of Africa: A Trip Report," Congressional Research Service 91-823, November 15, 1991, pp. 25–28; "Djibouti: Political Unrest—Prospects for Reconciliation," Congressional Research Service 92-537F, June 30, 1992.

83. CIA, *World Factbook, 1991;* Department of Defense and Department of State, *Congressional Presentation for Security Assistance Programs, Fiscal Year 1993*, Washington, Department of State, 1992.

84. IISS, *Military Balance, 1988–1989* and *1991–1992,* sections on Djibouti.

85. CIA, *World Factbook, 1991*, pp. 83–84.

86. CIA, *World Factbook, 1991*, pp. 200-201.

87. IISS, *Military Balance, 1991–1992.*

88. Estimate based primarily on *Jane's Fighting Ships, 1991–1992*, p. 155.

89. The military manpower, force strength, and equipment estimates in this section are made by the author using a wide range of sources, including computerized data bases, interviews, and press clipping services. Most are impossible to reference in ways of use to the reader. The force strength statistics are generally taken from interviews and from the sources reference for each paragraph. They also draw heavily on his *The Gulf and the Search for Strategic Stability* (Boulder, Westview, 1984) and *The Gulf and the West* (Boulder, Westview, 1988).

Extensive use has also been made of the annual editions of the International Institute for Strategic Studies *Military Balance* (IISS, London), in this case the 1991–1992 edition, and of the Jaffee Center for Strategic Studies, *The Military Balance in the Middle East* (JCSS, Tel Aviv), especially the 1990–1991 edition and working materials from the coming edition. Material has also been drawn from computer print outs from NEXIS, the United States Naval Institute data base, and from the DMS/FI Market Intelligence Reports data base. Other sources include the *Military Technology*, "World Defense Almanac for 1991–1992," published in 1992; Foreign Affairs Division, "Middle East Arms Control and Related Issues," Washington, Congressional Research Service, 91-384F, May 1, 1991; and *Middle East Economic Digest*, "MEED Special Report: Defense," Volume 35, December 13, 1991.

Weapons data are taken from many sources, including computerized material available in NEXIS, and various editions of *Jane's Fighting Ships* (Jane's Publishing); *Jane's Naval Weapons Systems* (Jane's Publishing); *Jane's Armour and Artillery* (Jane's Publishing); *Jane's Infantry Weapons* (Jane's Publishing); *Jane's Military Vehicles and Logistics* (Jane's Publishing); *Jane's Land-Based Air Defence* (Jane's Publishing); *Jane's All the World's Aircraft* (Jane's Publishing); *Jane's Battlefield Surveillance Systems* (Jane's Publishing); *Jane's Radar and Electronic Warfare Systems* (Jane's Publishing), *Jane's C³I Systems* (Jane's Publishing); *Jane's Air-Launched Weapons Systems* (Jane's Publishing); *Jane's Defence Appointments & Procurement Handbook (Middle East Edition)* (Jane's Publishing); *Tanks of the World* (Bernard and Grafe); *Weyer's Warships* (Bernard and Grafe); and *Warplanes of the World* (Bernard and Grafe).

Other military background, effectiveness, strength, organizational, and history data are taken from Anthony H. Cordesman, *The Gulf and the Search for Strategic Stability*, Boulder, Westview, 1984; *The Gulf and the West*, Boulder, Westview, 1988; and *Weapons of Mass Destruction in the Middle East*, London, Brassey's/RUSI, 1991; Anthony H. Cordesman and Abraham Wagner, *The Lessons of Modern War*, Volume II, Boulder, Westview, 1989; Lij Imru Zelleke, *The Horn of Africa, A Strategic Survey*, Washington, International Security Council, 1989; Peter Biles, "Filling the Vacuum," *Africa Report*, Nov/Dec 1991, pp. 35–37; Theodore Dagne, "The Horn of Africa: A Trip Report," Congressional Research Service 91-823, November 15, 1991; Edmond J. Keller, "A New Direction for U.S.-Somalia Relations," *The World & I*, April, 1989, pp. 127–132; the relevant country or war sections of Herbert K. Tillema, *International Conflict Since 1945*, Boulder, Westview, 1991; Department of Defense and Department of State, *Congressional Presentation for Security Assistance Programs, Fiscal Year 1993*, Washington, Department of State, 1992; various annual editions of John Laffin's

The World in Conflict or *War Annual*, London, Brassey's; and John Keegan, *World Armies*, London, Macmillan, 1983.

90. Estimates differ, but Somalia today seems to be about 85% Somali, with the rest mainly Bantu. There were about 30,000 Arabs, 3,000 Europeans, and 800 Asians in 1991. Virtually all Somalis are Sunni. The total population is around 6,709,000, with a growth rate of 3.3%. The CIA estimated that there were 1,601,000 males between the ages of 15 and 49, and 903,000 fit for military service. The IISS estimated in late 1991 that there were a total of about 353,000 men and 335,000 women in the age group from 13 to 17 years, 285,000 men and 290,000 women in the age group from 18 to 22 years, and 438,000 men and 454,000 women in the age group from 23 to 32 years.

91. Arms Control and Disarmament Agency (ACDA), *World Military Expenditures and Arms Transfers, 1990*, Washington, GPO, 1990, Table I.

92. IISS, *Military Balance, 1991–1992*, p. 64.

93. Arms Control and Disarmament Agency (ACDA), *World Military Expenditures and Arms Transfers, 1990*, Washington, GPO, 1990, Table II. The IISS has issued defense spending estimates of $83 million in 1986, $46 million in 1988, and $18.05 million in 1989.

94. Arms Control and Disarmament Agency, *World Military Expenditures and Arms Transfers, 1985*, pp. 98, 131, 140, 146.

95. Arms Control and Disarmament Agency (ACDA), *World Military Expenditures and Arms Transfers, 1989*, Washington, GPO, 1990, p. 115; Arms Control and Disarmament Agency (ACDA), *World Military Expenditures and Arms Transfers, 1986*, Washington, GPO, 1987, p. 143. Some estimates put the value of Soviet arms transfers from 1977 to 1990 at roughly $11 billion.

96. Arms Control and Disarmament Agency (ACDA), *World Military Expenditures and Arms Transfers, 1990*, Washington, GPO, 1992, pp. 133–134.

97. *Manchester Guardian Weekly*, January 15, 1989, p. 10; *Washington Post*, September 10, 1989, p. A-28; General Accounting Office, "Somalia: Observations Regarding the Northern Conflict and Resulting Conditions," Washington, GAO/NSIAD-89-159, May, 1989; Kayode Soyinka, "The Collapse Born of Civil War," *World Press Review*, March, 1989, pp. 28–29; Bureau of Public Affairs, "The U.S. and Sudan: Peace and Relief," U.S. State Department, February, 1989; *U.S. News and World Report*, July 24, 1989, p. 32; *Washington Post*, February 19, 1990, p. A-21; *Christian Science Monitor*, October 23, 1989, p. A-15.

98. Somalian clans do not occupy single parts of the country. The Dir dominate the area in the northwest near Djibouti and some enclaves along the coast near Mogadishu; the Isaq dominate the area from Ethiopia north to the Gulf of Aden. The Darod occupy the area of the Horn extending southwest deep into Ethiopia and also occupy the south of the country extending into Kenya. The Hawiye occupy the area north of the capital about halfway to the Horn and to the west to areas near Ethiopia. There are numerous other clans.

99. *Financial Times*, April 15, 1991, p. 16; *Christian Science Monitor*, December 16, 1991, p. 8; *Washington Post*, November 22, 1991, p. A-36.

100. *Economist*, February 22, 1992, pp. 33–34; July 18, 1992, p. 41; August 1, 1992, p. 36; August 15, 1992, p. 32; *New York Times*, January 30, 1992, p. A-2; April 4, 1991, p. A-3; February 27, 1992, p. A-3; July 19, 1992, p. A-1; July 20, 1992, p. A-3; July 25, 1992, p. A-1; August 15, 1992, p. A-1; August 30, 1992, p. A-12; *Washington Post*, January 11, 1992, p. A-1; February 15, 1992, p. A-28; February 16, 1992, p. A-44; June 7, 1992, p. A-32; July 4, 1992, p. A-1; July 20, 1992, p. A-12; August 24, 1992, p. A-13; August 29, 1992, p. A-1; *Washington Times*, January 24, 1992, p. A-9; May 1, 1992, p. A-16; August 18, 1992, p. 9; Theodore S. Dagne, "Somalia: A Country at War—Prospects for Peace and Reconciliation," Congressional Research Service, CRS 92-522F, June 15, 1992.

101. Army equipment data are based on the author's estimate adapted from the IISS, *Military Balance, 1990–1991*, p. 117.

102. Estimate based primarily on *Jane's Fighting Ships, 1991–1992*, pp. 487–488.

103. Statistics are extrapolated from the IISS, *Military Balance, 1990–1991*, p. 117.

9

Strategic Interests, Arms Control, and Regional Stability: Conflict or Synergy?

From a broad perspective, political developments in the Middle East are not without hope. The Arab-Israeli peace talks may or may not produce tangible benefits over the next few years, but a dialogue and peace process have begun. The military tensions between Israel and Syria now seem more likely to produce deterrence than war, and the Palestinian uprising seems more likely to lead to confinable tensions and incidents than the kind of intense civil conflict that has taken place in Somalia and the Sudan.

The UN coalition's attack on Iraq has not removed that country's threat to peace, but it has destroyed most of Iraq's facilities to produce weapons of mass destruction and has demonstrated that aggression in the Gulf will be met with determination and force. While the tensions in North Africa continue, Libya does not pose a major military threat to its neighbors, and the peace negotiations between Morocco and the Polisario show at least faltering signs of promise.

The cease-fire in the Iran-Iraq War has held, with little sign of any immediate renewal of the conflict. The supposedly "unstable" southern Gulf states continue to enjoy considerable stability. Yemen is at relative peace, and the new regime governing a "united" Yemen seems more concerned with development and the rights of its citizens than any of the former governments of the PDRY and YAR. Ethiopia has at least some prospects for peace, although the civil war in Somalia has led to bloody fighting and widespread famine.

Yet any analysis of the Middle East that focuses solely on military developments and the arms race is necessarily bleak and pessimistic. The brief historical introductions to each country and the analysis of current patterns of military development are scarcely balanced histories, although they portray valid pictures of the Middle East to the extent that they communicate a very real tragedy. The military buildups and arms races in virtually every nation in the region have led to a vast waste of scarce manpower and financial resources, and frequent outbreaks of war have damaged or devastated every nation and people in the region.

No one can look at the complex patterns of struggle and conflict in the region and the patterns in military developments without concern and foreboding. There is a risk that far bloodier wars may occur than in the past. Further, it is painfully clear that even if such wars do not occur, the economic and social strains that military forces currently impose on Middle Eastern states will remain major barriers to development and civil welfare. Finally, the political and economic strains in the region are combining to push many nations towards at least the acquisition of a covert capability to proliferate the weapons of mass destruction.

The practical problem is how best to alter this situation. One answer is clearly peace negotiations and international pressure to resolve conflicts and disputes through peaceful and legal means. A second answer is arms control, and a third is to build up the forces of defensive states while weakening those of aggressor or destabilizing nations.

The previous country-by-country analysis has shown that none of these solutions is adequate in itself. Peace negotiations will not resolve many regional disputes with any stability or security and often will not even produce cosmetic settlements in the near term. There are still too many regional leaders and ethnic conflicts which cannot be contained by such means.

Arms control can play a major role in efforts to halt the military buildup in the region and in proliferation, but it can also be destabilizing if it attempts to treat all states as being equal and as having the same intentions and character. If arms control offers the prospect of workable treaties and verification methods, it also threatens to produce agreements that either have no real meaning or that bind those states whose regimes conform to international law while allowing other regimes to violate the letter and spirit of such agreements.

Building up the forces of the weaker or defensive states is only a partial solution, and then for a limited number of countries. Strength and deterrence are often little more than expensive illusions. Without peace negotiations or arms control, arms transfers and force expansion efforts—no matter how well intended or well targeted—will often fail to produce adequate local forces, will always fail to limit the regional arms race, and will inevitably lead to future wars.

What is required is a synergistic balance of all three efforts tailored to the specific needs and character of each sub-region and nation in the Middle East. Above all, such efforts must be sensitive to the very real differences among nations and must acknowledge that the struggle between Arab nations and Israel is only one part of the mosaic of tensions and conflicts; treating all Arab or Middle Eastern states alike is as meaningless as any other form of prejudice or racism. The Maghreb is not the Levant, the Levant is not the Gulf, and the Gulf is not the Horn. Tunisia is not Libya, Israel is not Syria, and Saudi Arabia is not Iraq. If there is any central message that emerges from the preceding analysis, it is that peace negotiations, arms control, and efforts to build up or maintain local military forces must be carefully targeted to achieve specific ends.

The Problem of Peace Negotiations

The preceding chapters have made it brutally clear that peace negotiations are not likely to end most of the rivalries and prospects for conflict in the region in the near future. Further, many arms races are likely to go on even when a peace is agreed to. No political agreement can eliminate the distrust, doubt, and fear of decades that shape much of the modern Middle East.

In some cases, it may be impossible to achieve meaningful negotiations for years. It others, negotiations may simply become a verbal form of conflict as countries struggle to win popular and world opinion. In many cases, the most that can be hoped for is a lack of active conflict while negotiations progress, steps towards confidence building measures, or agreement on a limited range of problems or areas of cooperation. Few peace processes are likely to be worse than no peace process, but they cannot be confused with an end to military confrontation or conflict.

Even when peace settlements are reached, they may do little to halt arms races or may simply alter them in character. No foreseeable Arab-Israeli peace settlement, for example, will leave the major actors secure enough to avoid further arms purchases and modernization. Trading territory for peace and limiting specific arms will also oblige Israel and any Arab states involved to restructure their forces, and often to make massive investments in new arms, facilities, and other military concerns.

It is also dangerously naive to assume that UN or international peace-keeping forces can provide security for many peace settlements in the region. Short of general disarmament, UN and other international forces will never be strong enough to do more than act as a buffer or mediator for nations that want to keep a peace. Only balanced military capabilities on both sides can firmly deter violations of a peace agreement and prevent nations from going to war. The same is true even of security guarantees by nations like the United States. The U.S. cannot hope to intervene quickly enough in many potential conflicts to alter the outcome and is extremely unlikely to deploy major land and air forces in the region to enforce a given peace.

Patience and professional diplomacy are the obvious keys to success, and success may often be possible. It is likely to take years to reach major agreements, however, and there are likely to be many setbacks. Negotiations will not be a substitute for arms control or arms transfers, and long after many peace settlements are reached, the nations involved will still be competing in military buildups that both keep the peace through deterrence and threaten it through military rivalry.

The Problem of Arms Control

Like peace negotiations, arms control requires informed subtlety rather than ideology or good intentions. There is no question that efforts need to be made to contain the arms race, but sweeping efforts to halt all arms transfers or apply regionwide solutions that do not take account of regional differences simply do not track with the realities in individual Middle Eastern states. States that drive the regional arms race—Iran, Iraq, Libya, and Syria—need one kind of treatment. States that are weak or require continuing arms transfers to maintain their security or move towards a peace settlement—Israel, Egypt, and Saudi Arabia and the other southern Gulf states—need quite another.

The complexity of the arms control problem in the region is also illustrated by several points that have surfaced in the preceding analysis:

- *There is no clear correlation between the volume of arms transfers and war, except when arms go to aggressor or destabilizing states.* If one looks at the historical pattern of arms transfers documented in the previous data, it is true that aggressor or destabilizing states are often major arms purchasers. So, however, are defensive states. In cases involving civil conflict—which have tended to be the bloodiest conflicts in the region—low to moderate levels of arms transfers have been more than adequate to sustain extremely high civilian and military casualties.

- *The arms race is driven largely by a few aggressive states.* Over the past forty years, a relative handful of states has driven the arms race to dangerous proportions. Since the Camp David accords, these nations have obviously included Iran, Iraq, Libya, and Syria. Other destabilizing or aggressor states (at least in terms of civil or local conflict) have included Ethiopia, Somalia, the Sudan, and Yemen. Algeria and Morocco have long remained on the edge of such a category, and Morocco has waged a sustained war. In contrast, three of the region's largest arms purchasers—Egypt, Israel, and Saudi Arabia—have been defensive states. At least since the mid-1970s, their arms purchases have contributed largely to regional stability. A number of other states are both militarily weak and threatened by their neighbors; these include Tunisia, Chad, Lebanon, Jordan, Kuwait, Bahrain, Qatar, the UAE, and Oman.

- *Technological sophistication does not tend to produce wars with the highest civilian and military casualties.* These come from relatively low technology civil wars. It is interesting to compare the Arab-Israeli wars after 1950, fought on military lines by well equipped professional armies, with the civil wars in the Horn of Africa, fought largely on ethnic lines with low technology land weaponry. The modern Arab-Israeli wars have tended to be short, intense, and relatively low in casualties. The civil wars in Ethiopia, Somalia, and the Sudan were extremely bloody. Similarly, even the intense and destructive war to liberate Kuwait, fought with free ranging air power, produced a decisive result and an end to the fight with far fewer casualties than the World War I–like war of attrition between an Iranian force with low technology and an Iraqi opponent with moderate technology.

- *Even a total end to arms shipments would not prevent further war in most parts of the Middle East.* The nations involved are already armed to the point where a halt to arms shipments might often encourage war by creating a "use or lose" response, or allowing nations who emphasize mass to overcome the qualitative advantage of their present opponents.

- *The key issue is not defensive versus offensive arms.* All arms transfers tend to be destabilizing when they go to states which are seeking to expand their regional power and influence. There is no meaningful distinction between offensive and defensive arms sold to aggressor or destabilizing states. These states are already so well armed that any improvement in defense frees offensive assets for offensive action. Similarly, states involved in civil conflicts can use virtually any form of arms against rival factions. Anti-aircraft guns are a classic example. While seemingly a defensive weapon, they make excellent weapons against personnel and light armored vehicles. Similarly, improved command, control, and communications systems have no offensive power in themselves but can vastly improve the offensive power of air and armored forces.

- *At the same time, weapons of mass destruction, surface-to-surface missiles, long range strike aircraft, and modern main battle tanks are more destabilizing than other weapons.* Controlling the type of arms transfers cannot prevent conflict, but some weapons unquestionably are worse than others. Aggressor states will find it far harder to threaten or attack their neighbors if they are denied modern armor, strike aircraft and long range missiles, or weapons of mass destruction. At the same time, armor is the best defense against armor. A purely defensive air force lacks the deterrent impact of an air force with strike capability and the ability to support counteroffensive operations. A nation that is militarily weak or lacks strategic depth can deter with weapons of mass destruction and long range missiles.

- *There is little prospect that an uncontrolled arms race will result in a stable balance of deterrence or terror.* With the exception of Israel, deterrence along East-West lines seems unlikely to enhance stability and the security of individual states in the Middle East. The history of Iraq—and the pattern of the arms buildup in Iran, Iraq, and Syria—offers little real prospect that such states would accept a stable balance of terror or that sheer strength could sustain the peace. Similar patterns emerge in Algeria, Morocco, Yemen, and the Horn. Many Middle Eastern regimes will take risks and will go to war.

- *Reducing conventional arms transfers or selectively controlling proliferation may have counterproductive results.* It is not possible to separate controls on one element of the arms race from the others. A given state's treatment of the five basic elements of the regional arms race—conventional arms, long range strike systems, nuclear weapons, chemical weapons, and biological weapons—will be dictated by how it perceives its own interests. If conventional weapons are controlled or its conventional forces are limited, it may well seek weapons of mass destruction. If nuclear weapons are too expensive, it may seek cheaper conventional weapons. If chemical weapons are controlled, it may turn to more covert and easier to acquire technology like biological weapons. If it is denied long range missiles, it may seek strike aircraft, and if both are denied, it may turn to the covert delivery of weapons of mass destruction. The arms race is fungible, and selective controls will tend to drive it along the path of least resistance.

- *Confidence building measures can be helpful but are not a solution.* Confidence building measures—like peace negotiations—are successful only to the extent that the nations involved want them to be successful. If nations are edging towards peace, or at least "correct relations," controls on exercises, scale and type of training, mobilization, force deployments, call-ups, and the many other confidence building measures that have been advocated over the years can be very useful. They not only can defuse the military situation, they build up dialogue and trust and lay the groundwork for more serious forms of arms control and negotiation. It is obvious, however, that confidence building measures will not limit states that are ready or nearly ready to go to war. Only major changes in force structure or disarmament can seriously affect many of the confrontations in the Middle East.

- *The future intentions and motivations of arms suppliers are extremely unclear.* With the end of the Cold War, East and West should be able to make a similar end to the rivalry to sell arms to given target states. This rivalry never produced either client states that served the seller's interest or any clear benefits in terms of broader strategic interests. In many ways, it also failed to produce any profits. Preferential Soviet bloc sales certainly cost the Soviet bloc more than they produced in barter and soft currency transfers. Western intervention in the Gulf in 1987–1991, along with the high cost of other interventions and swings in oil prices, almost certainly cost Western economies far more than the benefits of those arms sales that produced hard currency were worth. It is already clear, however, that East-West rivalry threatens to be replaced by a conflict between those sellers who are seeking to bring strategic stability and some degree of peace to the region and those who are primarily interested in hard currency and profits. Some "rogue merchants" have already emerged. North Korea is an example of such a state, and the PRC threatens to become one. The Soviet Union and East Europe could easily replace ideological sales with profit-oriented ones that will be equally damaging. Many Western and neutral governments seem unable to bring any coherence to their arms sales—often declaring one policy while playing complex power games with individual countries or turning a blind eye to the sales and operations of individual firms. Rhetoric to the contrary, most of the world's arms sellers have already rushed to seize the moral low ground of the arms trade.

The Problem of Military Buildups

Any examination of the military trends in the Middle East demonstrates that the current pattern of arms transfers and military buildups makes a new world disorder far more likely than a new world order. The region can only move towards peace if nations in the Middle East and supplier states outside it alike realize that every effort must be made to create a stable military balance of deterrence among rival states and to cut off arms to states torn apart by civil war.

The practical problem is to link arms transfers to peace negotiations and arms control efforts and to a deliberate policy of strengthening those states that are likely to keep the peace at the expense of those who are not. At the same time, it means selective transfers in other cases where given arms or technologies will reinforce deterrence even though it is impossible to name some states as aggressors and the others as defensive. This approach to arms transfers will also have to be coupled to Western or UN power projection capabilities, at least in the Gulf. No pattern of arms transfers to the southern Gulf states can guarantee their near and mid-term security as long as Iran and Iraq can rearm.

Unfortunately, the end of the Cold War has not yet created a climate in which Western nations can cooperate efficiently with each other, in which the East can easily give up the hard currency benefits of arms sales, or Third World arms suppliers have great incentive to show restraint. The current efforts to create a supplier dialogue are an important step forward, as are the increasing number of bilateral and multilateral talks on arms sales among various suppliers. Nevertheless, stability will often be possible only if major supplier states like the U.S. unilaterally take action to provide stabilizing arms transfers.

It is also not practical to try to link all or most arms transfers to goals like peace negotiations and arms control efforts. Such linkage is desirable and sometimes possible, but in case after case, insufficient progress will exist in the first two areas to allow such linkage to be effective. The possible exception lies in the transfer of weapons of mass destruction, major new delivery systems for such weapons, and the technology to manufacture such weapons and delivery systems. No real case can be made in the Middle East for encouraging further transfers of this kind. If there is an inequity in Israel's monopoly of nuclear weapons, it is counterbalanced in part by Libyan, Iranian, Iraqi, and Syrian possession of chemical and biological weapons or the necessary technology to manufacture them, and Israel may well need its nuclear deterrent as the ultimate security guarantee for trading territory for peace.

Equal care must be shown in trying to link every arms transfer to exaggerated views of the Arab threat to Israel or to goals such as introducing Western style democracy to the Middle East. No arms transfer to any part of the Middle East can be done as if that transfer could be totally isolated from the other rivalries and uncertainties in the region. At the same time, viewing nations like Saudi Arabia as a major threat to Israel makes no more sense than treating Israel as a major threat to Saudi Arabia. This is particularly true in an era when conventional arms transfers are often the alternative to efforts to build up forces with weapons of mass destruction, when most importing nations remain dependent on the supplier state for technical support and service, and when any limits on supply by one supplier state must be based on the probability of similar restraint by others.

The Rule of Law and the Illusion of Democracy

While this is not a book on the politics of the Middle East per se, the previous analysis should make it clear that Western style democracy is neither the answer to the problem of conflict in the Middle East nor a practical substitute for the rule of law and human rights. Most of the states in the Middle East have a long, long way to go before they can establish democratic and secular regimes, and much of the Islamic world may not follow this path in the near future.

The discussion of the internal security situation in many Middle Eastern states makes it clear that a sudden rush to democracy would simply give extremist or radical movements power or lead to a major new repression of human rights. Demanding that Middle Eastern states copy the methods of government that it has taken the West hundreds of years to evolve ignores the postwar history of the Middle East and the culture, political history, and internal tensions of most Middle Eastern states.

The rule of law is a different issue. Regimes can protect basic human rights and enforce a meaningful legal system without copying Western democracy and long before they can create stable parliamentary institutions. Virtually all Middle Eastern states have formally committed themselves to adhering to the rule of law, no matter how often they may ignore this commitment in practice, and there is no inherent reason that Islamic law should be lacking in mercy or regard for human rights.

The Question of Hope

In summary, there are no magic answers to the problems of the Middle East, and there is little prospect that any combination of peace negotiations, arms control, and regional security arrangements can prevent future conflicts. The specter of weapons of mass destruction is very real, and one that current arms control proposals may be able to weaken but can scarcely exorcise.

The key question for all Middle Eastern nations is whether they can eventually find the leadership to change this situation. This leadership cannot come from the outside, and it cannot be created by persuading blocs of Middle Eastern states to adhere to ambitious regional agreements. It can only come slowly, virtually one nation at a time. The key question for nations outside the Middle East is whether they can find the leadership to help the Middle East move methodically towards some degree of strategic stability or will continue to act on a basis of political and military opportunism. In both cases, sweeping rhetoric will not be a substitute for carefully reasoned realism.

Appendix:
Sources and Methods

Readers familiar with the problems of analyzing and quantifying the military balance in the Middle East will already be aware that many of the statements and statistics in this book are highly uncertain. There are few contemporary military analysts writing on many of the countries reported upon in this book. Middle Eastern governments go to great effort to conceal the nature of virtually every aspect of their national security activity, and it is important that the reader understand the sources and methods used by the author.

Sources

It was possible to visit Bahrain, Egypt, Iraq, Israel, Jordan, Kuwait, Saudi Arabia, Syria, and a number of other countries during the work on this book for in-depth interviews on both national and neighboring forces. Interviews also took place with a wide range of experts in the United States, United Kingdom, France, Switzerland, and Germany. Portions of the manuscript were circulated for informal review by attachés and diplomats in several of the countries covered in the book, and some chapters were modified extensively in response. No interviews or comments are referenced by source, however, unless those concerned specifically gave their permission, and no source is quoted by name. This is necessary to protect the individuals involved.

The historical data used are drawn from a wide range of sources but are confined largely to basic chronological data and do not seem worth referencing in detail, except as done in specific notes in given country chapters. The historical analysis draws heavily on the excellent summaries of individual conflicts provided by Herbert K. Tillema in *International Conflict Since 1945* (Boulder: Westview, 1991); work in various annual editions of John Laffin's *The World in Conflict* or *War Annual* (London: Brassey's) and in John Keegan's *World Armies* (London: Macmillan, 1983); the author's writings in books like *The Gulf and the Search for Strategic Stability* (Boulder: Westview, 1984) and *The Gulf and the West* (Boulder: Westview, 1988), and joint work by the author with Abraham Wagner in *The Lessons of Modern War*, Volume 1 (Boulder, Westview, 1990). For consistency's sake, the chronology normally conforms to that in Tillema's work. The reader should be aware that many dates vary according to source or are controversial.

The CIA *World Factbook* was chosen over other international data sources because it is generally the most reliable source, particularly in comparison with the poor quality and heavily politicized figures provided in many UN publications. The sources for data on arms control are explained in depth in Chapter 2, along with the reasons for choosing given sources.

The military manpower, force strength, and equipment estimates given throughout the book were made by the author using a wide range of sources, including computerized data bases, interviews, and press clipping services. Most are impossible to reference in any practical way. The force strength statistics are generally taken from the 1991–1992 edition of the International Institute for Strategic Studies, *Military Balance* (London: IISS). Extensive use has also been made of the annual editions of the Jaffee Center for Strategic Studies, *The Military Balance in the Middle East* (Tel Aviv: JCSS), especially the 1990–1991 edition and working materials from the coming edition. Specific references are given at the start of each country section and within the text when this seems useful. Most interviews are not referenced, except by country when this might be helpful and the individual involved permitted some form of attribution.

Material has also been drawn from computer print outs from the United States Naval Institute data base and from the DMS/FI Market Intelligence Reports data base. Other sources include the *Military Technology*, "World Defense Almanac for 1991–1992," published in 1992; computerized material available in NEXIS, and the latest annual editions of *Jane's Fighting Ships, Jane's Naval Weapons Systems, Jane's Armour and Artillery, Jane's Infantry Weapons, Jane's Military Vehicles and Logistics, Jane's Land-Based Air Defence, Jane's All the World's Aircraft, Jane's Battlefield Surveillance Systems, Jane's Radar and Electronic Warfare Systems, Jane's C3I Systems, Jane's Air-Launched Weapons Systems, Jane's Defence Appointments and Procurement Handbook (Middle East Edition)* (all Jane's Publishing), as well as *Tanks of the World, Weyer's Warships,* and *Warplanes of the World* (all three Bernard and Grafe).

Extensive use has also been made of media sources, including translations of radio broadcasts and news materials, articles, books, and similar materials. These are referenced in some cases, where computer print outs were available giving specific broadcast times and dates. Many transcribed broadcasts did not permit this kind of specific attribution.

Much of the analysis presented in this study is based on sources which are in conflict. While computer data bases allowed some cross-correlation and checking of media reporting, the reporting on factors like force strengths, unit types and identities, tactics, and conflict outcomes is often contradictory, and comparing and citing multiple sources is simply not practical.

Mapping and location names also presented a major problem. The author used U.S. Army and U.S. Air Force detailed maps, commercial maps, and in some cases commercial satellite photos. In many cases, however, the place names and terrain descriptions used in the combat reporting by both sides, and by independent observers, presented major contradictions that could not be resolved from available maps. This made it impossible to confirm the details of given battles and to provide meaningful maps of those battles. This was particularly true in the case of conflict in areas where the land is subject to seasonal or deliberate flooding and where major changes can take place in the size and nature of water barriers. Similarly, many battles in mountainous terrain involved the use of local names or approximate locations which make it difficult to trace the action.

Methods

This book is intended to summarize the military capabilities of individual countries within a broad regional and historical context. It is not intended as a general history of the region, and the reader should understand that military history is inherently conflict oriented and not a portrayal of the culture or social values of a society.

In many cases, figures and data were adjusted on a "best guess" basis. In others, the original data provided by a given source were used without adjustment, even though this leads to numerous conflicts in dates, place names, force strengths, and so on within the material presented, particularly between summary tables surveying a number of countries and the best estimates for a specific country in the text. The choice is one of presenting the actual data provided by a given source or trying to reconcile all figures, names, and similar material. It seemed best to provide contradictory estimates and give the reader some idea of the range of uncertainty involved.

The reader should be aware that the numbers used in this book are highly approximate and not revealed truth. Similarly, many of the value judgments regarding military effectiveness are made on the basis of U.S. military experience and standards. Although the author has lived in the Middle East and worked as a U.S. advisor to several Middle Eastern governments, he feels that any attempt to create some Middle Eastern standard of reference is likely to be far more arbitrary than basing such judgments on his own military background.

Finally, this book deliberately focuses on military capabilities and is only indirectly concerned with military politics. It tries to minimize any discussion of the internal political situations of given nations except as these are necessary to understand what is happening to the forces in a given country and when they can be based on a reasonable assurance that what is being reported is fact. The Middle East is filled with rumors about military politics, but such rumors rarely turn out to be true.

Security Problems of the Middle East and Southwest Asia: A Selected Annotated Bibliography

The detailed bibliography used for each section is described in the endnotes. The following references are useful as general backgound.

Abdel, Majid Farid, ed., *The Red Sea: Prospects for Stability*, London, Croom Helm, 1984, pp. 84–94. A useful collection of articles on the Red Sea with some data on military forces.

Abir, Mordechai, *Saudi Arabia in the Oil Era: Regime and Elites—Conflict and Collaboration*, Boulder, Westview, 1988. An interesting Israeli perspective on Saudi politics and internal security, supported by unusually detailed research into Saudi sources.

Adan, Avrahham (Bren), *On the Banks of the Suez*, San Francisco, Presidio, 1980. The best eyewitness account of the fighting in the Sinai in 1973 from an Israeli perspective.

Africa Watch Report, *Somalia: A Government at War with its Own People*, Washington, Africa Watch, 1990. A grim analysis of the human impact of the civil war in Somalia, circa 1988.

Akehurst, John, *We Won a War: The Campaign in Oman 1965–1975*, Salisbury, The Chantry, 1982. A very useful history of the fighting by one of the soldiers actually involved.

Akins, James E., et al., *Oil and Security in the Arabian Gulf*, New York, St. Martin's, 1981. A good description of regional and security issues in the Gulf from a U.S. and Saudi perspective.

Albrecht, Gerhard, *Weyer's Warships of the World*, Annapolis, Nautical & Aviation Publishing. A good summary reference on the size and structure of Middle Eastern fleets.

Aliboni, Roberto, *The Red Sea Region*, Syracuse, Syracuse University Press, 1985. Useful data on the military tensions in the Red Sea area.

Amnesty International publishes a wide range of publications citing the internal security problems and abuses of military and paramilitary forces in many countries in the Middle East.

Anthony, John Duke, *Goals in the Gulf: America's Interests and the Gulf Cooperation Council*, Washington, National Council on U.S.-Arab Relations, 1985. One of the best introductions to the role of the GCC in the military balance.

Arco series of illustrated guides, New York, Salamander Books, Arco. A useful series of guides for understanding the performance of key weapons systems used in the Middle East.

Arlinghaus, Bruce, *Arms for Africa*, Lexington, Mass., Lexington Books, 1983. A somewhat dated description of the flow of arms sales to North Africa.

Armed Forces (UK). Has ceased publication, but had interesting reporting on military developments in the region and on power projection capabilities.

Armed Forces Journal International. Limited coverage of region, but still has some good articles. Good coverage of U.S. power projection capabilities.

Arms Control and Disarmament Agency (ACDA), *World Military Expenditures and Arms*

Transfers, Washington, GPO. An annual, U.S. government document describing the trends in military expenditure and arms transfers in every country and region in the world, with summary data on manpower trends and weapons transfers by type.

Army, Department of, country studies. Individual volumes on each Middle Eastern country with good summary descriptions of their military forces and political-military history. Available from the Government Printing Office.

Asher, Jerry, and Eric Hammel, *Duel for the Golan*, New York, Morrow, 1987. A detailed account of Israeli-Syrian armored combat on the Golan in 1973. The best available description of this aspect of armored warfare in the Middle East.

Aspin, Les, and William Dickenson, *Defense for a New Era*, Washington, GPO, 1992. Some interesting data on the estimated impact of the Gulf War on Iraq.

Assiri, Abdul-Reda, *Kuwait's Foreign Policy*, Boulder, Westview, 1989. A Kuwaiti view of how Kuwait's policy allows it to survive in a threatened area and of its use of informal ties to the superpowers to balance regional powers.

Axelgard, Frederick W., *Iraq in Transition: A Political, Economic, and Strategic Perspective*, Boulder, Westview, 1986. Useful background on Iraq's strategic and military interests.

al-Azharly, M. S., ed., *The Iran-Iraq War: A Historical, Economic, and Political Analysis*, New York, St. Martin's, 1984. A useful, if dated, collection of essays on Gulf security.

Badeeb, Saeed M., *The Saudi-Egyptian Conflict over North Yemen*, Boulder, Westview, 1986. One of the few books that attempts to treat the war in depth and reasonably objectively from all sides.

Badri, Magdoub, and Zohdy, *The Ramadan War, 1973*, New York, Hippocrene, 1974. One of the few Arab views of combat against Israel in English.

Bailey, Clinton, *Jordan's Palestinian Challenge, 1948–1983*, Boulder, Westview, 1984. A dated but useful study of the importance of the Palestinian movement to Jordan's security and military behavior.

Baker, A. D., ed., *Combat Fleets of the World, Their Ships, Aircraft, and Armament*, Annapolis, Naval Institute Press. A good series on the size and structure of Middle Eastern fleets.

Barker, A. J., *Arab-Israeli Wars*, New York, Hippocrene, 1980. A good journeyman account of the wars without any major bias.

Bass, Gail, and Bonnie Jean Cordes, *Actions Against Non-Nuclear Energy Facilities: September 1981–September 1982*, Santa Monica, Calif., Rand, 1983. Useful technical data relating to weapons of mass destruction.

Bavly, Dan, and Eliahu Saltpeter, *Fire in Beirut*, New York, Syein and Day, 1984. An Israeli view of the events in the Lebanon war in 1982.

Be'eri, Eliezer, *Army Officers in Arab Politics and Society*, New York, Praeger, 1970. Still a classic study of the importance of human factors in Arab military forces.

Beit-Hallahmi, Benjamin, *The Israeli Connection: Who Arms Israel and Why*, New York, Pantheon, 1987. An analysis of U.S. arms transfers to Israel that traces Israel's role in quid pro quo arms operations like the Iran-Contra arms transfers and military ties to South Africa.

Ben Horin, Yoav, and Barry Posen, *Israel's Strategic Doctrine*, Santa Monica, Calif., Rand, 1981. A useful summary of Israeli strategic doctrine in the period just before the 1982 fighting.

Ben Porat, et al., *Kippur, Special Edition*, Tel Aviv, 1973. A good impression of Israeli views of the military balance and the impact of the Arab attack written immediately after the war.

Beres, Louis Rene, *Security or Armageddon*, Lexington, Mass., Lexington Books, 1986. An interesting set of different articles arguing for and against the existence of an Israeli nuclear deterrent.

Bidwell, Robert, *The Two Yemens*, Boulder, Longman/Westview, 1983. A good overview of the history of the Yemens ending in 1979. Good background on developments in both the YAR and PDRY at the end of the 1970s.

Bill, James A., *The Eagle and the Lion: The Tragedy of American-Iranian Relations*, New Haven, Yale University Press, 1988. A trenchant, if sometimes strident, critique of U.S. policy towards Iran. Many valid criticisms of the U.S. effort.

Blackwell, James, *Thunder in the Desert*, New York, Bantam, 1991. An excellent treatment of the land portion of the Gulf War.

Blechman, Barry M., and Stephan S. Kaplan, *Force Without War*, Washington, Brookings, 1978. A classic study of the problems the U.S. faces in using military power in the Middle East.

Brower, Kenneth S., "The Middle East Military Balance: Israel versus the Rest," *International Defense Review*, 7/1986, pp. 907–913. A summary view of the Arab-Israel balance written from an Israeli point of view.

Carus, W. Seth, "The Military Balance of Power in the Middle East," *Current History*, January, 1978. A good overview of the balance from a pro-Israeli perspective.

——, "The Genie Unleashed: Iraq's Chemical and Biological Weapons Production," Policy Papers No. 14, Washington, The Washington Institute for Near East Policy, 1989. An excellent treatment of Iraq's acquisition of weapons of mass destruction.

Carver, Michael, *War Since 1945*, London, Weidenfeld and Nicholson, 1980. A good summary overview of the trends in the regional military balance in terms of their impact on low intensity combat between 1945 and 1980.

Central Intelligence Agency, *Handbook of Economic Statistics*, Washington, GPO. An annual with good summary statistics on many aspects of the Middle East, including some summary data on U.S. and Soviet arms sales and military advisors.

——, *The World Factbook*, Washington, GPO. Probably the best overall statistical and base fact summary on the Middle East. Does, however, often include questionable or uncertain data.

Chubin, Shahram, ed., *Security in the Persian Gulf: The Role of Outside Powers*, and *Security in the Persian Gulf: Domestic Political Factors*, London, International Institute for Strategic Studies, 1981. Excellent perspective on the security situation in the Gulf before the Iraq-Iraq War.

Chubin, Shahram, and Charles Tripp, *Iran and Iraq at War*, Boulder, Westview, 1988. A solid description of the political and economic factors surrounding and shaping the war, with summary data on the military balance.

Clawson, Patrick, and Howard Rosen, *The Economic Consequences of Peace for Israel, the Palestinians, and Jordan*, Washington, The Washington Institute for Near East Policy, Policy Papers Number 25, 1991. One of the only serious economic studies of the burden of military spending on the economies of Israel, the occupied territories, and Jordan. Good treatments of the problems of water, labor, state interference in the economy, and operations for peace and economic interdependence.

Cobban, Helena, *The Superpowers and the Syrian-Israeli Conflict*, New York, Praeger, 1991. A solid analysis of the many U.S. and Soviet rivalries shaping Syria's military forces and security situation. Some analysis of the trends in the regional arms race.

Coffey, Joseph I., and Gianni Bonvicini, *The Atlantic Alliance and the Middle East*, London, Macmillan, 1989. A useful survey of Western power projection capabilities and the issues involved, but written before Western intervention in the Gulf in 1987 and 1988. Now useful largely for historical purposes.

Cooper, Mark N., *Transformation of Egypt*, Baltimore, Johns Hopkins University Press, 1982. Good historical background on the Egyptian politics behind the 1973 war, the transition from Nasser to Sadat, and the problems contributing to Sadat's assassination.

Cordesman, Anthony H., *The Gulf and the West*, Boulder, Westview, 1988. Updates *The Gulf and the Search for Strategic Stability* to cover the regional changes in the military balance and strategic situation in the Gulf between 1984 and 1987, the Iran-Iraq War, and the Western naval intervention in the Gulf.

————, *The Arab-Israeli Military Balance and the Art of Operations*, Washington, University Press of America–AEI, 1987. A description of the changes in the regional military balance between 1945 and 1987 and of the changes in Israeli and Arab tactics and forces during this period.

————, *The Iran-Iraq War and Western Security, 1984–1987*, London, Jane's, 1987. A detailed description of the military balance in the Gulf and the history of the Iran-Iraq War between 1983 and 1987.

————, *Western Strategic Relations with Saudi Arabia*, London, Croom Helm, 1986. A detailed description of the military balance in Southwest Asia written from a U.S. and Saudi perspective.

————, *Jordan and the Middle East Balance*, Washington, Middle East Institute, 1978 and 1985. The original edition and update provide a great deal of technical and historical data on the trends in the military balance.

————, *The Gulf and the Search for Strategic Stability*, Boulder, Westview, 1984. A detailed description of the military balance and strategic situation in the Gulf describing the history of the military forces and security situation in each country in the region, as well as the power projection capabilities and impact of the forces of outside states.

Cordesman, Anthony H., and Abraham R. Wagner, *The Lessons of Modern War*, Volume One: *The Arab-Israeli Conflicts*, Boulder, Westview, 1990. Detailed analysis of the military lessons of each Arab-Israeli conflict and of the changes in the military balance following the 1982 war.

————, *The Lessons of Modern War*, Volume Two: *The Iran-Iraq Conflict*, Boulder, Westview, 1990. Covers the entire history of the Iran-Iraq War from its beginnings in 1979 to the August, 1988 cease-fire.

————, *The Lessons of Modern War*, Volume Three: *The Afghan and Falklands Conflicts*, Boulder, Westview, 1990. Covers the Afghan war from its start in 1979 to the first year following Soviet withdrawal.

Cottam, Richard W., *Iran and the United States: A Cold War Case Study*, Pittsburgh, University of Pittsburgh Press, 1988. A liberal critique of U.S. policy arguing against U.S. efforts to use Third World countries as partners in joint security efforts.

Cottrell, Alvin J., and Robert J. Hanks, "The Strait of Hormuz: Strategic Chokepoint," in Cottrell and Hanks, *Sea Power and Strategy in the Indian Ocean*, Beverly Hills, Calif., Sage Publications, 1981. A useful description of the military situation in the Red Sea, Gulf, and Indian Ocean areas in the early 1980s.

Darwish, Adel, and Gregory Alexander, *Unholy Babylon: The Secret History of Saddam's War*, London, Victor Gollancz, 1991. An interesting analysis of the history of Saddam and the Baath and the events behind Iraq's invasion of Kuwait, but a great deal of the material has no stated source and seems dubious.

Dawisha, Adeed I., *Saudi Arabia's Search for Security*, Adelphi Paper No. 158, London, International Institute for Strategic Studies, Winter 1979-1980. Still a useful picture of Saudi security interests from a Saudi perspective.

Deeb, Mary-Jane, *Libya's Foreign Policy in North Africa*, Boulder, Westview, 1990. A description of Libya's foreign policy since 1969, tracing the reasons for Libya's military and foreign policy actions.

Department of Defense, *Conduct of the Persian Gulf War: Final Report to Congress*, Washington, Department of Defense, April, 1992. By far the most authoritative analysis to date of the Gulf War, flawed by some political editing at the command level and a failure to revise damage and threat estimates on the basis of postwar knowledge.

Department of State, *Congressional Presentation for Security Assistance Programs.* An annual document summarizing the details of U.S. military assistance to the Middle East.

Dougherty, James E., *The Horn of Africa: A Map of Political-Strategic Conflict,* Cambridge, Mass., Institute for Foreign Policy Analysis, 1982. A useful, if dated, description of the security and military issues in the Horn.

Dunn, Keith A., "Constraints on the U.S.S.R. in Southwest Asia: A Military Analysis," *Orbis,* 25, 3 (Fall 1981): 607–629. A good discussion of the practical constraints on Soviet military intervention in the Middle East.

Dunnigan, James F., and Austin Bay, *From Shield to Storm,* New York, Morrow, 1992. More a data dump than a book, but a great deal of useful information on the Gulf War.

Dupuy, Trevor N., *Elusive Victory: The Arab-Israeli Wars, 1947–1974,* New York, Harper & Row, 1978. The best single source of accurate detail on the course of the fighting between the Arabs and Israel from the war of independence through 1973.

———, and Paul Martell, *Flawed Victory,* Washington, Hero Books, 1985. A similarly excellent book on the 1982 fighting.

Economist. Not always reliable, but by far the best weekly news magazine covering the region.

Economist Intelligence Unit, *The Gulf War: A Survey of Political Issues and Economic Consequences,* London, Economist Publications, 1984. An erratic and largely economic treatment of the war and balance.

El-Edroos, S. A., *The Hashemite Arab Army, 1908–1979,* Amman, Publishing Committee, 1980. An excellent book on the Arab-Israeli conflicts from a Jordanian perspective. The best pro-Arab account of the fighting and the shifts in the balance.

Epstein, Joshua M., *Strategy and Force Planning: The Case of the Persian Gulf,* Washington, Brookings, 1987. A good discussion of the problems the U.S. and USSR would encounter in intervening in Iran.

Eshel, David, *Born in Battle,* Series Nos. 1, 3, 12, and 16, Tel Aviv, Eshel Dramit, 1978. An Israeli military publication with a great deal of data seen from an Israeli perspective. Key publications in the series include:

———, *Peace for Galilee,* Special edition of the Born in Battle Series, Tel Aviv, Eshel Dramit, 1982.

———, *The Israeli Air Force,* Tel Aviv, Eshel Dramit, 1980.

———, *The Israeli Commandos,* Tel Aviv, Eshel Dramit, 1979.

———, *The Lebanon War,* Tel Aviv, Eshel Dramit, 1982.

———, *The U.S. Rapid Deployment Forces,* New York, Arco Publishing, 1985.

———, *The Yom Kippur War,* Tel Aviv, Eshel Dramit, 1978.

———, *War of Desperation,* London, Osprey, 1985. Strongly pro-Israeli book on the impact of the 1973 and 1982 fighting on the balance with a great deal of useful data on the war.

Eveland, Wilbur Crane, *Ropes of Sand: America's Failure in the Middle East,* New York, Norton, 1980. A classic historical analysis of the problems in America's approach to security issues in the Middle East in the 1950s.

Feldman, Shai, *Israeli Nuclear Deterrence: A Strategy for the 1980s,* New York, Columbia University Press, 1982. The best explanation of the rationale for Israel's nuclear deterrent.

Fisk, Robert, *Pity the Nation: The Abduction of Lebanon,* New York, Atheneum, 1990. A unique book on the 1982 war in Lebanon which tells the story from the Lebanese side as seen by all of the major factions. Written from the viewpoint of a journalist working in Lebanon at the time.

Friedman, Norman, *Desert Victory: The War for Kuwait,* Annapolis, Naval Institute Press, 1991. A good but early description of the Gulf War focused on naval power.

Fromkin, David, *A Peace to End All Peace: The Fall of the Ottoman Empire and the Creation of the*

Modern Middle East, New York, Avon Books, 1989. A good treatment of the impact of the fall of the Ottoman Empire on both the Middle East and the origins of several key Middle Eastern military forces.

Fukuyama, Francis, *The Soviet Union and Iraq Since 1968*, Santa Monica, Rand, 1980. An excellent study of the problems the USSR had in trying to trade arms for influence in Iraq.

Gabriel, Richard A., *Operation Peace for Galilee*, New York, Hill and Norton, 1983.

————, *Fighting Armies: Antagonists in the Middle East, a Combat Assessment*, Westport, Greenwood Press, 1983. An interesting survey of the military capabilities of different states in the Middle East in the early 1980s.

GAO, "Somalia: Observations Regarding the Northern Conflict and Resulting Conditions," Washington, U.S. General Accounting Office, GAO/NSIAD-89-159, 1989. Good summary of the conditions leading to the civil war in Somalia.

Gerber, Haim, *Islam, Guerrilla War, and Revolution*, Boulder, Lynne Rienner, 1988. An interesting analysis of the impact of ideology on guerrilla war, with special attention to South Yemen and Algeria.

Golan, Galia, *The Soviet Union and the Israeli War in Lebanon*, Research Paper 46, Jerusalem, Soviet and East European Research Center, 1982. A good summary of the dynamics of Soviet influence on the Arab-Israeli military balance in time of crisis.

Goodman, Hirsch, and W. Seth Carus, *The Future Battlefield and the Arab-Israeli Conflict*, New Brunswick, Transaction Publishers, 1989 (Washington Institute for Middle East Policy). Interesting Israeli-U.S. study of the forces shaping the Arab-Israeli military balance, with a strong emphasis on technology.

Green, Stephen, *Taking Sides*, New York, Morrow, 1984. An analysis of the U.S. decision to provide military assistance to Israel that claims the U.S. intervened on Israel's side in the 1967 war.

Grimmett, Richard F., *Trends in Conventional Arms Transfers to the Third World by Major Supplier*, Washington, CRS Report. An excellent annual series on the total pattern of arms flows to the region.

Grossman, David, *Yellow Wind*, New York, Farrar, Straus, and Giroux, 1988. A highly personal series of insights into Israeli-Palestinian tensions just before the *intifada*.

Grummon, Stephen R., *The Iran-Iraq War: Islam Embattled*, Washington Paper 92, Center for Strategic and International Studies, New York, Praeger, 1982. A useful early treatment of the Iran-Iraq War.

Haddad, George M., *Revolutions and Military Rule in the Middle East*, New York, Robert Speller and Sons, 1973. A three volume and highly detailed history of the impact of military coups and Marxism on the Arab world and northern tier up to the early 1970s. Perhaps the only country-by-country survey dealing with all these issues in the period before the October War.

Haffa, Robert P., Jr., *The Half War: Planning U.S. Deployment Forces to Meet a Limited Contingency, 1960–1983*, Boulder, Westview, 1984. An excellent detailed description of the history of the rapid deployment force (RDF) and the rapid deployment joint task force (RDTJF) and the problems in U.S. power projection in the region.

Hagelin, Björn, *Neutrality and Foreign Military Sales*, Boulder, Westview, 1990. One of the few treatments of the role neutral states play in arms sales in the Middle East.

Hameed, Mazher, *Arabia Imperiled: The Security Imperatives of the Arab Gulf States*, Washington, Middle East Assessments Group, 1986. An excellent description of Gulf security issues from a Saudi-American perspective.

Handel, Michael I., *Israel's Political Military Doctrine*, Occasional Papers in International Affairs, No. 30, Cambridge, Harvard University Center for International Affairs, 1973.

Hanks, Robert, *The U.S. Military Presence in the Middle East: Problems and Prospects*, Cambridge, Mass., Institute for Foreign Policy Analysis, 1982. A good summary of the practical impact of the U.S. on the military balance in the Middle East.

Harkabi, Yehoshafat, "Reflections on National Defence Policy," *Jerusalem Quarterly*, No. 18 (Winter, 1981), pp. 121–140. An interesting and probing critique of the strategic impact of Israeli military supremacy written just before the 1982 war.

Heikel, Mohammed, *The Road to Ramadan*, New York, Quadrangle, 1975. A good pro-Arab and pro-Egyptian view of the reasons for the 1973 fighting.

Held, Colbert, *Middle East Patterns*, Boulder, Westview, 1989. An attempt to explain the dynamics of the Middle East, including recent conflicts, in terms of spatial analysis and geographic factors.

Henze, Paul B., "Arming the Horn," Working Paper No. 43, Washington, International Studies Program, Wilson Center, July, 1983. A good paper on the military problems in the Horn in the early 1980s.

———, *Ethiopia's Prospects for the 1990s*, Santa Monica, Rand, 1989. A short but useful summary of the economic disaster caused by the Mengistu regime in Ethiopia.

Hersh, Seymour M., *The Samson Option: Israel's Nuclear Arsenal and American Foreign Policy*, New York, Random House, 1991. A worst case analysis of both the size of the Israeli nuclear force and the risks it poses for the region and U.S. foreign policy.

Herzog, Chaim, *The Arab-Israeli Wars*, New York, Random House, 1982. A good history of the wars from an Israeli perspective, with good data on the balance but shallow and sometimes inaccurate in its description of the fighting in 1982.

Hickman, William F., *Ravaged and Reborn: The Iranian Army, 1982*. Staff paper, Washington, Brookings, 1982. A useful early treatment of the impact of the fall of the shah on the Gulf military balance.

Hodges, Tony, *Western Sahara: The Roots of a Desert War*, Westport, Hill & Company, 1983. Dated, but a very useful history of the origins of the conflict.

Horani, Albert, *A History of the Arab Peoples*, Cambridge, Belknap, 1991. An updated overview of the rise and development of Arab civilization and of the current impact of Islam and the concept of the Arab nation.

Hurewitz, J. C., *Middle East Politics: The Military Dimension*, New York, Praeger, 1969. A classic historical introduction to the military problems of the region.

International Defense Review. This bimonthly magazine has some good military articles on the region and interesting news items and arms transfer data.

International Institute for Strategic Studies, *The Military Balance*, London, various years. A key reference on the size and equipment of the military forces in each Middle Eastern country. Often has gaps and errors, but best unclassified publication around.

Isby, David C., *Weapons and Tactics of the Soviet Army*, Fully Revised Edition, London, Jane's, 1987. By far the best reference on the Soviet equipment and tactics going to the Middle East and excellent background on the Soviet experience in Afghanistan.

Jaffee Center for Strategic Studies, *The Middle East Military Balance*, Boulder, Westview. An excellent annual Israeli overview of the strength of forces in the Middle East with supporting essays and content. Authors vary from year to year.

———, *Israel's Options for Peace*, Report of a JCSS Study Group, Tel Aviv, Jaffee Center, 1989. A useful overview of Israeli views on the territory-for-peace issue with annexes on the military balance.

Jane's, *All the World's Aircraft*, London, various years.

———, *Armour and Artillery*, London, various years.

———, *Aviation Annual*, London, various years.

———, *Combat Support Equipment*, London, various years.

———, *Defence Review*, London, various years.

———, *Fighting Ships*, London, various years.

————, *Infantry Weapons*, London, various years.

————, *Israel's Armour*, Tel Aviv, Eshel Dramit, 1978.

————, *Military Annual*, London, various years.

————, *Military Communications*, London, various years.

————, *Naval Annual*, London, various years.

————, *Naval Review*, London, various years.

————, *Weapons Systems*, London, various years.

Jane's Defence Weekly. Detailed coverage of the Middle East is unusual, but has good one page summaries of military issues. Also has many good updates on arms transfers and military developments in the various miscellaneous news sections.

Johnson, Maxwell Orme, *The Military as an Instrument of U.S. Policy in Southwest Asia: The Rapid Deployment Joint Task Force, 1979–1982*, Boulder, Westview, 1983 . A good description of U.S. military capabilities in the Gulf.

Jones, Rodney W., *Nuclear Proliferation: Islam, the Bomb and South Asia*, Washington Paper No. 82, Center for Strategic and International Studies, Beverly Hills, Calif., Sage Publications, 1981. Still a good introduction to the impact of the proliferation of weapons of mass destruction on the region.

————, ed., *Small Nuclear Forces and U.S. Security Policy*, Lexington, Mass., Lexington Books, 1984. A good discussion of the impact of nuclear war in the Middle East.

Joyner, Christopher C., *The Persian Gulf War: Lessons for Strategy, Law, and Diplomacy*, New York, Greenwood, 1990. Some very good essays on the national diplomatic and military issues affecting the Iran-Iraq War.

Kaplan, Stephen S., *Diplomacy of Power*, Washington, Brookings, 1981. An excellent introduction to the history of Soviet power projection and military influence on the regional military balance.

Karsh, Efraim, *The Cautious Bear*, Boulder, Westview, 1985. A good description of Soviet military interventions and arms transfers.

————, *The Iran-Iraq War: The Military Implications*, London, IISS Adelphi Paper No. 220, 1987. A good summary history of the Iran-Iraq War through late 1986.

Keegan, John, *World Armies*, New York, Facts on File, 1979.

————, *World Armies*, 2nd ed., London, Macmillan, 1983. A classic reference on the history of each military force in the Middle East.

Kelly, J. B., *Arabia, the Gulf, and the West*, New York, Basic Books, 1980. A good study of many of the historical tensions and politics in the Arabian Peninsula, marred by anti-Saudi bias and nostalgia for the British Empire.

Kemp, Geoffrey, *The Control of the Middle East Arms Race*, Washington, Carnegie, 1991. Excellent review of the problems of Middle East arms control with unusual attention to the problem of preserving regional stability.

Khalidi, Rashid, *Under Siege*, New York, Columbia University Press, 1986. A good history of the 1982 fighting and its impact on the balance from a pro-Arab perspective.

Khalidi, Walid, *Conflict and Violence in Lebanon*, Cambridge, Harvard Center for International Affairs, 1984. A good history of the civil fighting in Lebanon and its impact on Lebanese military forces.

al-Khalil, Samir, *Republic of Fear*, New York, Pantheon Books, 1990. A detailed critique and history of the Iraqi Baathist Party and Saddam Hussein's rise to power.

Kidron, Michael, and Dan Smith, *The War Atlas*, New York, Simon and Schuster, 1983. A mildly useful overview of the patterns in world arms and arms sales.

Klieman, Aaron S., *Israel's Global Reach*, London, Pergamon-Brassey's, 1985. A useful discussion of the impact of Israel's arms sales and access to technology on the balance.

Kolleck, Teddy, *Jerusalem*, Washington, The Washington Institute for Near East Policy, Policy Papers 22, 1990. One of the best practical treatments of the security and political issues affecting Jerusalem.

Kostiner, Joseph, *South Yemen's Revolutionary Strategy, 1970–1985*, Boulder, Westview, 1989. A good study of the political forces that shaped South Yemen's conflicts with Oman and North Yemen. Slight Israeli bias.

Kronsky, Herbert, and Stephen Weissman, *The Islamic Bomb*, New York, Times Books, 1981. In spite of its title, a good history of both Arab and Israeli efforts to acquire nuclear weapons.

Laffin, John L., *The Dagger of Islam*, London, Sphere, 1979. A somewhat overblown but interesting study of the growth of Arab military forces.

————, *The War of Desperation, Lebanon 1982–1985*, London, Osprey, 1982. An interesting and strongly pro-Israeli account of the fighting in Lebanon.

————, *The War Annual*, London, Brassey's. An interesting annual attempt to summarize the state of all major military actions in the Third World.

Lambeth, Benjamin S., *Moscow's Lessons from the 1982 Lebanon Air War*, Santa Monica, Rand, 1984. A very useful study of the changing impact of air power on the Middle East balance.

Lee, David, *Flight from the Middle East*, London, HMSO Books, 1980. A key source on British military policy and action in the Gulf and Yemen between 1945 and 1972. One of the few books to report on developments from a military perspective.

Lefebvre, Jeffrey, *Arms for the Horn*, Pittsburgh, University of Pittsburgh Press, 1991. One of the few in-depth studies of the role of the superpowers and other arms suppliers in shaping the pattern of violence in the Horn.

Levite, Ariel, *Offense and Defense in Israeli Strategy*, Boulder, Westview, 1989. A summary of the evolution of Israeli strategy and its impact on IDF performance in combat.

Levran, Aharon, and Zeev Eytan, *The Middle East: Military Balance*, 1987–1988, Boulder, Westview, 1988. A good comparison of the military balance in the Middle East written from an Israeli viewpoint. Tends to somewhat exaggerate Arab capabilities.

Litwak, Robert, ed., *Security in the Persian Gulf: Sources of Inter-State Conflict*, London, International Institute for Strategic Studies, 1981. A good survey of the regional tensions in the Gulf just before the Iran-Iraq War.

Long, David E., *The United States and Saudi Arabia: Ambivalent Allies*, Boulder, Westview, 1985. An excellent treatment of the history of U.S.-Saudi military relations and their impact on the Gulf military balance.

Long, David E., and Bernard Reich, *The Government and Politics of the Middle East and North Africa*, Boulder, Westview, 1980. An excellent quick reference on the recent political history of all major Middle East states.

Luttwak, Edward, and Dan Horowitz, *The Israeli Army*, New York, Harper & Row, 1975. Still one of the best books ever written on the formation of the Israeli army and the reasons for its success.

McDonald, John, and Clyde Burleson, *Flight from Dhahran*, Englewood Cliffs, N.J., Prentice-Hall, 1981. A classic history of Britain's problems in its military intervention in the Gulf region.

McNaugher, Thomas L., *Arms and Oil: U.S. Military Security Policy Toward the Persian Gulf*, Washington, Brookings, 1985. An excellent treatment of regional military issues and their impact on U.S. military interests and capabilities.

Makinda, Samuel, "Shifting Alliances in the Horn of Africa," *Survival*, January/February, 1985, pp. 11–19. Good background on the military balance in the Horn.

Martin, Lenore G., *The Unstable Gulf: Threats from Within*, Lexington, Mass., D. C. Heath, 1984. A useful book on the internal politico-military trends in the Gulf region.

Maull, Hans, and Otto Pick, *The Gulf War*, London, Pinter, 1989. Some interesting essays speculating on the impact of the Gulf War but written nearly a year before the cease-fire.

Mets, David R., "The Dilemmas of the Horn," *Proceedings of the Naval Institute*, April, 1985, pp. 49–57. Good background on the military balance in the Horn.

The Middle East. Monthly British publication. Pro-Arab bias, but good reporting. Good new coverage of politico-military developments from a regional perspective.

Middle East Policy (formerly *Arab-American Affairs*). A quarterly with a slight Arab bias but generally good articles. Far more contemporary than many other periodicals in the field. Good book reviews and bibliography.

The Middle East Quarterly. Publication of the Middle East Institute. Poor coverage of politico-military developments, but still has interesting articles. Good book reviews.

Miller, Judith, and Laurie Mylroie, *Saddam Hussein and the Crisis in the Gulf*, New York, Times Books, 1990. An interesting study of the modern political history of Iraq and the internal developments that led Iraq into the Gulf War.

Mylroie, Laurie, *The Future of Iraq*, Washington, The Washington Institute for Near East Policy, Policy Papers 24, 1991. A critique of Saddam Hussein and the Baath written shortly after the Gulf War, arguing that the U.S. should have deposed Saddam Hussein.

Naff, Thomas, ed., *Gulf Security and the Iran Iraq War*, Washington, National Defense University Press, 1985. A useful collection of essays on the war.

Neff, Donald, *Warriors at Suez*, New York, Linden, 1981. The best book available on the 1965 war and its strategic and political dynamics.

———, *Warriors for Jerusalem*, New York, Linden, 1984. An excellent and objective description of the 1967 fighting between the Arabs and Israel.

———, *Warriors Against Israel*, Brattleboro, Amana, 1988. One of the best descriptions of the political and strategic context shaping the 1973 war.

Neuman, Stephanie, *Defense Planning in Less-Industrialized States*, Lexington, Mass., Lexington Books, 1984. Useful material on the organization of the defense activities in a number of Middle Eastern states.

Newell, Nancy Peabody, and Richard S. Newell, *The Struggle for Afghanistan*, Ithaca, Cornell University Press, 1981. An excellent early treatment of the impact of the fighting in Afghanistan.

Noyes, James H., *The Clouded Lens*, Stanford, Calif., Hoover Institution, 1982. A classic and still useful treatment of U.S. attempts to create proxy forces or "pillars" in the Gulf region.

O'Ballance, Edgar, *No Victor, No Vanquished*, San Rafael, Presidio, 1978. A Good tactical history of the 1973 war, with good maps and detail.

———, *The Gulf War*, London, Brassey's, 1988. An excellent tactical history of the war running through 1986.

———, *The Electronic War in the Middle East, 1968–1970*, Hamden, Conn., Archon, 1974. A pioneering study in the impact of technology on war in the Middle East which describes the history of the canal war between Israel and Egypt.

Pelletiere, Stephen C., and Douglas V. Johnson, *Lessons Learned: The Iran-Iraq War*, Carlisle Barracks, U.S. Army War College, 1991. One of the better military analyses of the war. Again, somewhat uncritical of Iraqi capabilities.

Pelletiere, Stephen C., Douglas V. Johnson, and Lief R. Rosenberger, *Iraqi Power and U.S. Security in the Middle East*, Carlisle Barracks, U.S. Army War College, 1990. A good analysis of the growth of Iraqi military power. Somewhat uncritical of Iraqi capabilities.

Peres, Shimon, *Military Aspects of the Arab-Israeli Conflict*, Tel Aviv, UPP, 1975. A collection of conference papers on the 1973 war. Some are still useful

Perlmutter, Amos, *Military and Politics in Israel, Nation Building and Role Expansion*, New York, Praeger, 1969.

———, *Politics and the Military in Israel, 1967–1977*, London, Cass, 1978.

———, "Begin's Rhetoric and Sharon's Tactics," *Foreign Affairs*, Fall, 1982. Useful insight into the role of military politics on the regional balance.

Perlmutter, Amos, Michael Handel, and Uri Bar-Joseph, *Two Minutes Over Baghdad*, London, Corgi, 1982. A good journalistic description of the Israeli raid on Osiraq from an Israeli perspective.

Peterson, Eric, *The Gulf Cooperation Council: Search for Unity in a Dynamic Region*, Boulder, Westview, 1988. One of the best overall surveys of the development and impact of the GCC.

Peterson, J. E., "Defending Arabia: Evolution of Responsibility," Orbis, 28, 2 (Fall, 1984), pp. 465–488.

———, *Oman in the Twentieth Century: Political Foundations of an Emerging State*, London, Croom Helm, 1978.

———, *Yemen: The Search for a Modern State*, Baltimore, Johns Hopkins University Press, 1982.

———, *Defending Arabia*, New York, St. Martin's, 1986. Good treatments of the security issues and their strategic impact in a number of key countries in Arabia.

———, *Saudi Arabia and the Gulf States*, Washington, The Middle East Institute and DIA Defense Academic Research Support Program, September, 1988. Good collection of essays on security issues relating to Saudi Arabia and its place in the Gulf and the Middle East.

Pierre, Andrew J., *The Global Politics of Arms Sales*, Princeton, N.J., Princeton University Press, 1982. A good discussion of the politics behind the flow of arms into the region.

Pipes, Daniel, *Damascus Courts the West: Syrian Politics, 1989–1991*, Washington, The Washington Institute for Near East Policy, Policy Papers 26, 1992. A good, if somewhat pro-Israeli, analysis of recent developments in Syrian national security policy.

Pry, Peter, *Israel's Nuclear Arsenal*, Boulder, Westview, 1984. Useful data on Israel's development of nuclear weapons.

Quandt, William B., *Saudi Arabia in the 1980s: Foreign Policy, Security and Oil*, Washington, Brookings, 1982. A useful analysis of Saudi Arabia's strategic value to the West.

———, *Camp David, Peacemaking and Politics*, Washington, Brookings, 1986. The best book treating the negotiating history and politics of the Camp David accords.

———, *The United States and Egypt*, Washington, Brookings, 1990. A good short overview of the changing nature of U.S. and Egyptian security relations.

Rabinovich, Itamar, *The War for Lebanon, 1970–1983*, Ithaca, Cornell University Press, 1984. An interesting but somewhat erratic treatment of the struggle for Lebanon from Black September to the 1982 war.

Randall, Jonathan C., *Going All the Way*, New York, Viking Press, 1983. A classic description of the practical problems that all sides faced in trying to use military force to achieve political objectives during the 1982 fighting.

Reich, Bernard, and Gershon R. Kieval, *Israeli National Security Policy: Political Actors and Perspectives*, New York, Macmillan, 1985. Some interesting essays on the political factors shaping Israeli security policy.

Roberts, Samuel, *Party and Policy in Israel*, Boulder, Westview, 1989. A good up-to-date analysis of the divisions between hawk and dove in Israeli politics.

Rubenstein, Alvin Z., *Red Star over the Nile*, Princeton, Princeton University Press, 1977. An excellent treatment of the problems the USSR and Egypt faced during their relationship from the time of Nasser to Sadat's expulsion of all Soviet military advisors.

———, *The Great Game: Rivalry in the Persian Gulf and South Asia*, New York, Praeger, 1983. A broad description of conflicting U.S. and Soviet strategic interests in the region.

———, *Soviet Policy Towards Turkey, Iran, and Afghanistan: The Dynamics of Influence*, New York, Praeger, 1982. A good summary of overall Soviet interests in the region ranging from Turkey to Afghanistan. Some useful military data.

Ruszkiewicz, John J., "A Case Study in the Yemen Arab Republic," *Armed Forces Journal*,

September, 1980, pp. 62–72. An interesting case study in the realities, and lack of them, involved in the conflict between the Yemens.

Safran, Nadav, *Israel: The Embattled Ally,* Cambridge, Belknap Press, 1982. A good discussion of the U.S.-Israeli relationship after 1967 and the problems Israel faced before the 1982 war. Pro-Israeli.

———, *From War to War,* New York, Pegasus, 1969. A good treatment of the impact of the military balance on the Arab-Israeli struggle from 1945 to 1967. Pro-Israeli.

———, *Saudi Arabia: The Ceaseless Quest for Security,* Cambridge, Belknap Press, 1985. Useful data on U.S. and Saudi military relations but written from an outsider's point of view and with too much faith in uncertain statistics.

Saivetz, Carol R., *The Soviet Union and the Gulf in the 1980s,* Boulder, Westview, 1989. One of the best contemporary works on the impact of the USSR on Gulf security.

Sandwick, John A., *The Gulf Cooperation Council: Moderation and Stability in an Interdependent World,* Boulder, Westview, 1987. Some excellent essays on the origins of the GCC and its initial efforts at military, economic, and political cooperation.

Sauldie, Madan, *Super Powers in the Horn of Africa,* New Delhi, Sterling Publishers, 1987. A good study of the impact of U.S. and Soviet policy on military developments in the Horn of Africa.

Schahgaldian, Nikola B., *The Iranian Military Under the Islamic Republic,* Santa Monica, Rand, 1987. A very good early study of the shifts in the Iranian military under Khomeini and during the Iran-Iraq War.

Schiff, Ze'ev, "Security for Peace: Israel's Minimal Security Requirements in Negotiations with the Palestinians," Washington, Policy Papers No. 15, The Washington Institute for Near East Policy, 1989. The best current analysis of the different options in terms of territory and military conditions for a peace settlement.

———, "The Israeli Defense Forces After Lebanon: Crisis, Change, and Uncertainty," *Middle East Insight,* 4, 3, 1985, pp. 15–23. Good analysis of the negative impact of the 1982 war on the IDF.

———, "The Green Light," *Foreign Policy,* Spring, 1983. Dubious argument that Haig gave Sharon a green light for the 1982 attack on Lebanon.

———, *A History of the Israeli Army,* New York, Macmillan, 1985. The best summary history of the development of Israeli military forces.

———, "The Palestinian Surprise," *Armed Forces Journal,* February, 1984.

Schiff, Ze'ev, and Ehud Ya'ari, *Israel's War in Lebanon,* New York, Simon and Schuster, 1984. An excellent study of the problems of the 1982 fighting and its aftermath from an Israeli perspective.

Schiff, Ze'ev, and Hirsch Goodman, "The Road to War: Ariel Sharon's Modern Day Putsch," *Spectrum,* April/May, 1984.

———, *Earthquake,* Jerusalem, 1973. One of the best books written right after the 1973 war.

Schmid, Alex P., *Soviet Military Interventions Since 1945,* New Brunswick, N.J., Transaction, 1985. Useful data on Soviet military interventions in the Middle East.

Sciolino, Elaine, *The Outlaw State, Saddam Hussein's Quest for Power and the Gulf Crisis,* New York, Wiley, 1991. One of the better researched and written analyses of the reasons for Saddam Hussein's invasion of Kuwait and the behavior of modern Iraq.

Seale, Patrick, *Asad: The Struggle for the Middle East,* Berkeley, University of California Press, 1988. The best book on Assad and modern Syria and its political role in the region.

Sella, Amon, *Soviet Political and Military Conduct in the Middle East,* London, Macmillan, 1981. A good summary view of Soviet intervention in the region from an Israeli perspective.

Shalev, Aryeh, *The West Bank: Line of Defense,* New York, Praeger, 1985. A somewhat exaggerated case for the importance of the West Bank as a defensive buffer zone.

El-Shazly, Saad, *The Crossing of Suez*, San Francisco, American Mideast Research, 1980. A very good picture of the 1973 fighting from an Egyptian perspective, written by a senior officer opposed to Sadat.

Shimshoni, Jonathan, *Israel and Conventional Deterrence*, Ithaca, Cornell University Press, 1988. An interesting scholarly treatment of deterrence theory using border warfare from 1953 to 1970 as a case study.

Shultz, Anne Tibbits, *Buying Security; Iran Under the Monarchy*, Boulder, Westview, 1989. A good history of the impact of Iran's arms purchases and their impact on the general mismanagement of the economy under the shah.

Sick, Gary G., *All Fall Down: America's Tragic Encounter with Iran*, New York, Random House, 1985. The best description of the collapse of the U.S. effort to use the shah as a military pillar in the Gulf.

Sicker, Martin, *Israel's Quest for Security*, New York, Praeger, 1989. Some useful insights into Israel's unique security requirements.

SIPRI, *World Armaments and Disarmaments: SIPRI Yearbook*, London, Taylor & Francis. An annual. Useful data on arms transfers and shifts in the regional balance of weapons of mass destruction.

Sirriyeh, Hussein, *Lebanon: Dimensions of Conflict*, London, Adelphi Paper 243, IISS, 1989. Good overview of the forces that have thrust Lebanon into conflict and kept it there.

Skogmo, Björn, *UNIFIL: International Peacekeeping in Lebanon, 1978–1988*, Boulder, Lynne Rienner, 1988. A grimly realistic picture of the political problems inherent in the UN peacekeeping effort in Lebanon.

Snyder, Jed C., and Samuel F. Wells, Jr., eds., *Defending the Fringe: NATO, the Mediterranean, and the Persian Gulf*, Boulder, Westview, 1987. A good collection of essays on the security problems in the area from the Mediterranean to the Gulf.

Spector, Leonard, *Going Nuclear*, Cambridge, Ballinger, 1987. Excellent overview of the regional and national trends in nuclear proliferation.

Stanley, Bruce E., *National Movements in Africa and the Middle East*, Boulder, Westview, 1990. Some useful articles on nationalism in Southwest Asia and North Africa.

Stookey, Robert W., *South Yemen: A Marxist Republic in Arabia*, Boulder, Westview, 1982. Useful data on the origins and initial history of the PDRY.

Susser, Asher, *In the Back Door: Jordan's Disengagement and the Middle East Peace Process*, Washington, The Washington Institute for Near East Policy, Policy Papers 19, 1990. Useful background and insights into the impact of the *intifada* on King Hussein's decision to remove Jordan from the peace process and the possible impact on regional security.

Tahir-Kheli, Sharin, and Shaheen Ayubi, *The Iran-Iraq War: New Weapons, Old Conflicts*, New York, Praeger, 1983. A good collection of essays written early in the war.

Talal, Hassan Bin, *Palestinian Self-Determination: A Study of the West Bank and Gaza Strip*, New York, Quartet, 1981. A short book by the crown prince of Jordan expressing Jordan's views on the peace process and Palestinian issues just before the 1982 war.

Tillema, Herbert K., *International Armed Conflict Since 1945: A Bibliographic Handbook of Wars and Military Interventions*, Boulder, Westview, 1991. An excellent bibliographic analysis and summary of recent wars and conflicts by region.

Timermann, Jacobo, *The Longest War*, New York, Knopf, 1982. An impassioned critique of Israel's military role written by an Israeli.

United Nations, *Handbook of International Trade and Statistics*, Geneva, United Nations Publications. An annual reporting data submitted by member countries. Little effort at comparability or verifying the quality of the data involved.

U.S. Congress, House of Representatives, Subcommittee on Energy and Power, Committee on Energy and Commerce, "U.S. Energy Outlook," 101st Congress, First Session, February 7, 1989, Serial No. 101-14. A good collection of testimony on future U.S. dependence on oil imports.

U.S. News and World Report, *Triumph Without Victory*, New York, Random House, 1992. An interesting investigative report on the Gulf War, with a great deal of technical data.

Urban, Mark, "Fire in Galilee," a three-part series in *Armed Forces*, March, April, and May 1986. Provides some good insights into the shifts in the Syrian-Israeli balance.

———, *War in Afghanistan*, New York, St. Martin's, 1988. One of the best military histories now available of the war in Afghanistan now available.

van Creveld, Martin, *Military Lessons of the Yom Kippur War: Historical Perspectives*, Washington Paper No. 24, Beverly Hills, Calif., Sage Publications, 1975. A good treatment of the impact of the 1973 war on Israeli thinking.

———, "Not Exactly a Triumph," *Jerusalem Post Magazine*, December 10, 1982.

Vatikiotis, J. P., *Politics and the Military in Jordan*, New York, Praeger, 1967. One of the few histories that traces the full history of the British military advisory effort in Jordan.

von Pikva, Otto, *Armies of the Middle East*, New York, Mayflower, 1979. One of the few really good comparative surveys of Middle Eastern military forces.

Wald, Emanuel, *The Wald Report: The Decline of Israeli National Security Since 1967*, Boulder, Westview, 1992. Perhaps the best revisionist critique of Israeli military forces ever written. Asserts a massive decline has taken place in Israeli forces and strategy since 1967. A strong pro-Sharon bias, leading to a very interesting alternative explanation of events during the 1982 war.

Waterbury, John, *The Egypt of Nasser and Sadat: The Political Economy of Two Regimes*, Princeton, Princeton University Press, 1983. Still relevant for its insights into the economic and political problems shaping the history of Egypt's armed forces and strategic position.

Watson, Bruce W., Bruce George, Peter Tsouras, and B. L. Cyr, *Military Lessons of the Gulf War*, London, Greenhill Books, 1991. An early, largely British, attempt to analyze the lessons of the Gulf War.

Wenner, Manfred W., *North Yemen: The Yemen Arab Republic After Twenty-Five Years*, Boulder, Lynne Rienner, 1990. Good background essays on the political and social forces that have shaped North Yemen's role in regional conflicts.

Whetten, Lawrence L., *The Canal War: Four Power Conflict in the Middle East*, Cambridge, MIT, 1974. The best description of the canal war and its impact on the military balance.

Woodward, Bob, *The Commanders*, New York, Simon and Schuster, 1991. The best book to date on the U.S. command decisions that shaped the history of the Gulf War.

Woodward, Peter, *Sudan, 1898–1989: The Unstable State*, Boulder, Lynne Rienner, 1990. An excellent summary of the historical and political forces shaping the long series of conflicts in the Sudan.

Wright, Robin, *In the Name of God: The Khomeini Decade*, New York, Touchstone, 1989. One of the few books to provide a clear picture of the values of the Iranian revolution from the Iranian side. Written by one of the few journalists actually to interview many of the key actors in Iran.

Yaacov, Bar Siman Tov, *The Israeli-Egyptian War of Attrition, 1969–1970*, New York, Columbia University Press, 1980. A good description of the canal war from an Israeli perspective.

Yaniv, Avner, *Deterrence Without the Bomb: The Politics of Israeli Strategy*, Lexington, Mass., Lexington Books, 1987. A good, but now dated, treatment of the evolution of Israeli strategy.

Yergin, Daniel, *The Prize*, New York, Simon and Schuster, 1991. By far the best history of the impact of oil on the West and the Middle East, and of the various oil crises that have affected the Middle East.

Yodfat, Aryeh Y., *The Soviet Union and the Arabian Peninsula: Soviet Policy Towards the Persian Gulf and Arabia*, New York, St. Martin's, 1983. A routine anti-Soviet work with useful detail.

Yohannes, Okbazghi, *Eritrea: A Pawn in World Politics*, Gainesville, University of Florida Press, 1991. An interesting treatment of the Eritrean issue, written from an Eritrean perspective.

Zabih, Sepehr, *The Iranian Military in Revolution and War*, London, Routledge, 1988. A very good treatment of the Iran-Iraq War, written from an Iranian perspective.

Zelniker, Shimshon, *The Superpowers and the Horn of Africa*, Tel Aviv, Center for Strategic Studies, Tel Aviv University, Paper No. 18, September, 1982. The U.S. and Soviet competition for the Horn from an Israeli perspective.

About the Book and Author

This comprehensive new analysis goes far beyond today's headlines and the basic facts and figures on the military forces in the region. Tracing the origin of the military forces in each Middle East country, Tony Cordesman discusses current security developments and provides a qualitative and quantitative analysis of the strength and effectiveness of every army, navy, air force, and air defense force in the region.

The author assesses current modernization and force expansion plans, force improvement priorities, and the ability of each force to absorb new military equipment. He also looks at each country's internal security situations, the role the military plays in its government, and internal tensions and civil wars. In addition to analyzing regular forces, Cordesman examines all of the paramilitary and rebel forces in the region.

Cordesman's detailed analysis provides fresh insights into several specific regional issues. In the Maghreb, he focuses on the war for control of the Western Sahara, the role of the military in Algeria's internal security, and Libya's impact on the political and military stability of the Middle East. He then analyzes Israel's new approach to force planning, the risks of an Israeli-Syrian conflict, Jordan's growing military and internal security problems, efforts to rebuild Lebanon's military forces, and military developments within the PLO. Turning to the Red Sea states, Cordesman discusses the military changes in Yemen since unification and the Gulf War; Yemen's confrontation with Saudi Arabia; the history of the civil wars in the Sudan, Ethiopia, and Somalia; and the risk that the Horn of Africa will suffer further from civil war in the future.

Special attention is given to Iran and Iraq. Cordesman examines Iran's new military buildup in light of the political changes since the death of Khomeini and the military changes since the Iran-Iraq War and the Gulf War. He offers the first comprehensive analysis of the impact of the Gulf War on Iraq's military forces and explains what Iraq is doing to rebuild its capabilities. The author also evaluates the forces of the southern Gulf states, tracing the problems created by their failure to develop effective regional cooperation and national force plans.

After the Storm is unique in combining the evaluation of conventional forces with assessments of developments in biological, chemical, and nuclear weapons. Cordesman provides technical descriptions of these weapons systems and documents their proliferation. Summary tables and charts present key statistics for the region, formatted in ways that allow quick country-to-country comparisons. The author closes with assessments of the prospects for arms control in each country, the impact of those nations' military status on Western strategic interests, and the need for Western military assistance and power projection.

Anthony H. Cordesman has served in senior positions in the office of the secretary of defense, NATO, and in Iran and other posts in the Middle East. He is currently adjunct professor of national security at Georgetown University, national security assistant to Senator John McCain, and a special consultant on military affairs for ABC News.

Index